The **Rough Guide** to

Scandinavia

written and researched by

**Phil Lee, Lone Mouritsen, Roger Edward Norum,
Jeroen van** [...]

D0774302

NEW YORK • LONDON • DELHI

www.roughguides.com

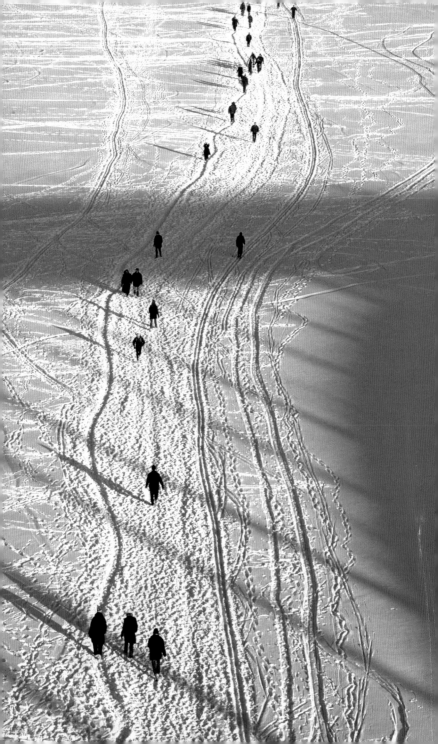

Contents

Scandinavian style
insert following p.264

The Great Outdoors
insert following p.568

◀◀ Oil-seed rape field, Sweden ◀ Walkers on frozen Lake Mälaren, Sweden

Introduction to

Scandinavia

Scandinavia – Denmark, Norway, Sweden and Finland –
conjures up resonant images: wild, untamed lands, fjords,
reindeer and the Midnight Sun; and wealthy, healthy, blue-
eyed blondes enjoying life in a benevolent welfare state.
The region does hold some of Europe's most unspoilt
terrain, and is certainly affluent by Western European
standards, with a high quality of life and little poverty. But
it's by no means paradise: there's a social conformity that
can be stifling, and the problems of other industrialized
countries – drug addiction, racism, street violence
– are beginning to make themselves felt. Nonetheless,
Scandinavia is an enthralling and rewarding region to
explore. The larger part of the population clusters in the
south, where there's all the culture, nightlife and action
you'd expect, but with the exception of Denmark, these
are large, often physically inhospitable countries. Rural
traditions remain strong, not least in the great tracts of
land above the Arctic Circle, where the Sámi peoples
survive as they have done for thousands of years – by
reindeer herding, hunting and fishing.

Historically, the Scandinavian countries have been
closely entwined, though in spite of this they
remain strikingly individual. Easy to reach and
the best known of the Scandinavian countries,
Denmark is the geographical and social bridge
between Europe and Scandinavia. The Danes are
much the most gregarious of the Nordic peoples,
something manifest in the region's most relaxed and appealing capital,
Copenhagen, and the decidedly more permissive attitude to alcohol.

With great mountains, a remote and bluff northern coast and the mighty
western fjords, **Norway**'s raw, often inaccessible landscapes can demand

4

▲ Briksdalsbreen glacier walk, Norway

long, hard travel. Even by Scandinavian standards the country is sparsely populated, and people live in small communities along a coastline which stretches from the lower reaches of the North Sea right up to the Russian border.

The most "Scandinavian" country in the world's eyes, **Sweden** is affluent and boasts a social system and a tradition of consensus politics that are considered an enlightened model – though both have been shaken in recent years, as political infighting has led to the fragmentation of old alliances. Travelling around is simple enough, although Sweden has Scandinavia's least varied landscape – away from the southern cities and coastal regions an almost unbroken swath of lakes, forests and hills, in which most Swedes have a second, peaceful, weekend home.

▶ Helsinki, Finland

5

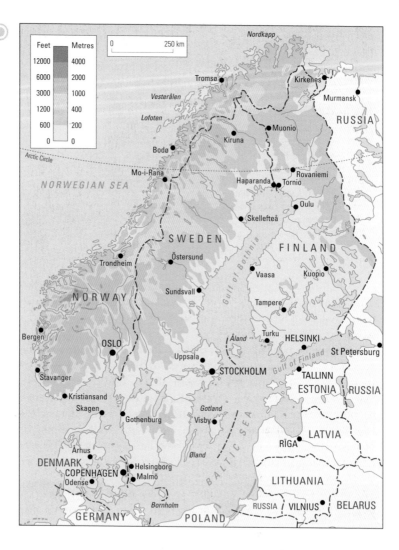

Perhaps the least known of the mainland Scandinavian countries, **Finland** was ruled for hundreds of years by the Swedes, and then the Russians – the country became independent only at the beginning of the twentieth century and has grown into a vibrant, confident nation. Its vast coniferous forests and great lake systems have produced a strong empathy between the Finns and the natural environment which is

Rural traditions remain strong, particularly in the great tracts of land above the Arctic Circle, where the Sámi peoples survive by reindeer herding, hunting and fishing

The Finnish sauna

One of the few Finnish words understood worldwide, sauna originated in the countryside. After toiling in the fields, workers would cleanse themselves by sweating profusely in a wooden hut heated by the steam generated by water thrown on hot stones. Today, saunas are an integral part of national culture and Finns of all ages can't get enough of them. A Finnish sauna is usually single-sex, nudity is pretty much compulsory and bathers must sit on sheets of paper or a board provided at the door to prevent sweat soaking into the benches. The end to a perfect sauna is a dip in a nearby lake, or, in winter, a refreshing roll in the snow.

hard to ignore. Also, though Finland is undeniably Scandinavian and looks to the West for its lifestyle, there are, historically and culturally, a number of similarities with Eastern Europe.

Travelling in Scandinavia is easy. Public transport is efficient and well coordinated, there is a minimum of border formalities between the countries and excellent connections between all the main towns and cities: indeed, it's perfectly feasible to visit several, if not all, of the mainland countries on one trip. From Western Europe it's simplest to enter Denmark, from where you can continue northwards into Norway (by boat) or Sweden (by boat or train), the two countries separated by a long north–south border. From Sweden's east coast there are ferries across to Finland, as well as a land border between the two in the far north.

As for **costs**, the Scandinavian countries are expensive by north European standards, but not excessively so. Their reputation for high prices is largely

▲ Traditional houses, Sweden

based on the cost of consumables – from books to meals and beer – rather than more substantial items, particularly accommodation, where first-rate budget opportunities are ubiquitous.

When to go

D eciding **when to go** isn't easy since, except for Denmark, Scandinavia experiences intense seasonal changes. The short summers (roughly mid-June to mid-August) can be as hot as in any southern European resort, with high temperatures regularly recorded in Denmark, southern Norway and Sweden, and the Baltic islands. Even the northern areas of each country are temperate, and the whole of the Norwegian west coast, for example, is warmed by the Gulf Stream. Rain, though,

Average maximum temperatures

	Jan	Feb	Mar	Apr	May	June	July	Aug	Sept	Oct	Nov	Dec
Denmark												
Copenhagen												
°F	36	36	41	51	61	67	71	70	64	54	45	40
°C	2	2	5	10	16	19	22	21	18	12	7	4
Norway												
Oslo												
°F	28	30	39	50	61	68	72	70	60	48	38	32
°C	-2	-1	4	10	16	20	22	21	16	9	3	0
Bergen												
°F	38	38	43	49	58	61	66	65	59	52	46	41
°C	3	3	6	9	14	16	19	19	15	11	8	5
Sweden												
Stockholm												
°F	30	30	37	47	58	67	71	68	60	49	40	35
°C	-1	-1	3	8	14	19	22	20	15	9	5	2
Gothenburg												
°F	34	34	39	49	60	66	70	68	61	51	43	38
°C	1	1	4	9	16	19	21	20	16	11	6	4
Finland												
Helsinki												
°F	26	25	32	44	56	66	71	68	59	47	37	31
°C	-3	-4	0	6	14	19	22	20	15	8	3	-1
Ivalo												
°F	24	24	31	45	58	67	72	69	57	45	35	29
°C	-5	-4	0	7	14	19	22	20	14	7	2	-2

Note that these are *average maximum temperatures*. The Gulf Stream can produce some very temperate year-round weather and, in summer, southern Scandinavia can be blisteringly hot. In winter, on the other hand, temperatures of -40°F are not unknown in the far north.

Sweden's fab four: ABBA

Having captured the world's attention by trouncing their Eurovision opponents with *Waterloo* in 1974, ABBA – lycra devotees Anni-Frid Lyngstad, Benny Andersson, Björn Ulvæus and Agnetha Fältskog – went on to become the biggest-selling group in the world, second only to Volvo as Sweden's largest export earner and topping the charts for a decade with hits such as *Mama Mia*, *Money Money Money* and *Dancing Queen* (the latter performed to celebrate the 1976 marriage of Sweden's King Carl Gustaf). Though the group split some twenty years ago following the divorces of the two band-member couples, ABBA's phenomenal kitsch appeal has endured, spawning a host of tribute bands and a successful musical, and ensuring that record sales remain remarkably healthy.

is regular and, in the far north of Norway especially – and to a lesser extent in Sweden and Finland – summer temperatures can plunge extremely low at night, so campers need decent equipment for extended spells of sleeping out. One bonus this far north, though not exactly a boon to sleep, is the almost constant daylight provided by the Midnight Sun.

The **summer** is celebrated everywhere with a host of outdoor events and festivities, and is the time when all the facilities for travellers (tourist offices, hotel and transport discounts, summer timetables) are functioning. However, it's also the most crowded time to visit, as the Scandinavians are all on holiday, too: go either side of summer (late May/ early June or September), when the weather is still reasonable, and you'll benefit from more peace and space. Autumn, especially, is a beautiful time to travel, with the trees and hillsides turning golden brown in a matter of days.

In **winter**, from November to around late May,

only Denmark retains a semblance of Western European weather, while the other countries suffer long, dark and extremely cold days. The cold may be severe, but it's crisp and sharp, never damp, and if you're well wrapped up the cities at least needn't be off limits – though, unless

▼ Reindeer, Finland

you're exceptionally hardy, the far north is best left to its own gloomy devices. You'll find broad climatic details in the introductions to each country; for mean temperatures all year round, check the **temperature chart** below.

What to take

t's as well to give some thought as to **what to take** – and worth packing that bit more to stave off hardship later. Expect occasional rain throughout the summer, and take a waterproof jacket as well as a spare sweater; a small, foldaway umbrella is useful, too. If camping, a warm sleeping bag and good walking shoes are vital (and useful, too, in sprawling cities

▲ Midnight sun, Norway

and the flat southern lands). Mosquitoes are a pest in summer, especially further north and in lake regions,

and some form of repellent is essential. For winter travel, take as many layers as you can pack. Gloves, a hat or scarf that covers your face, thick socks and thermal underwear are all obligatory.

► Bergen harbour, Norway

30

things not to miss

It's not possible to see everything Scandinavia has to offer in one trip, and we don't suggest you try. What follows is a selective taste of the region's highlights, from magnificent scenery and imposing castles to absorbing galleries and pristine medieval towns. They're arranged in five colour-coded categories, which you can browse through to find the very best things to see and experience. All highlights have a page reference to take you straight to the Guide, where you can find out more.

01 **Svalbard, Norway** Page **422** • Offering everything from glacier walks to snowmobile excursions, this archipelago in the Arctic Ocean is an impressively remote adventure tourism centre.

02 Vigelandsparken, Norway Page **272** • Whatever you do, don't miss this phantasmagorical open-air sculpture park.

03 Aurora borealis, Norway, Sweden and Finland see *Great Outdoors* colour section • When conditions are right, these amazing technicolour displays are an unforgettable sight.

04 Louisiana Museum of Modern Art, Denmark Page **129** • An outstanding collection housed in an equally arresting nineteenth-century villa overlooking the Øresund.

05 **Jotunheimen National Park, Norway** Page **291** • This craggy and severe mountain range is the most sumptuously beautiful example of Norway's wild mountain scenery.

06 Copenhagen's Nyhavn district, Denmark Page

109 • Best experienced at night, when the canalside restaurants and bars come into their own.

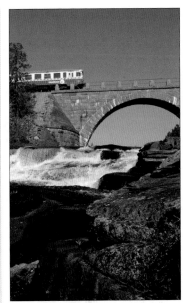

07 Inlandsbanan Railway, Sweden Page 619 • A chance to experience the raw beauty of virgin forests and crystal-clear mountain streams close up.

08 Vikingskipshuset, Norway Page 269 • An excellent place to view Viking longships at close hand.

09 Gamla Stan, Stockholm, Sweden Page **471** • This maze of medieval lanes and alleys form the heart of the Swedish capital.

10 Flåmsbana railway, Norway Page **339** • Zigzagging down a mountainside and inching through hairpin tunnels, this precipitous ride is a thrilling experience.

11 Husky safari, Finland
Page **790** • Sleigh through Lapland's silent snow-covered forests and across frozen lakes, and spend the night in a wilderness cabin.

12 Århus nightlife, Denmark Page **187** • With a host of excellent venues, Denmark's cultural capital is one of the best places in the country for a night out.

13 Icehotel, Sweden Page **639** • Experience a night in one of the most famous hotels in the world – at a chilly -5°C.

15 Danish pastry, Denmark

Page **74** • These ubiquitous buns are known as "Viennese bread" in their home territory – buy them fresh from bakeries in any town or city.

14 Stave churches, Norway
Page **296** • These elaborately carved churches are perhaps the most distinctive legacy of Norway's Viking era.

16 The Munch Museum, Norway
Page **274** • Huge collection of work from the country's finest artist, with several versions of *The Scream* alongside lesser-known paintings.

17 **Olavinlinna Castle, Finland** Page **750** • Perched atop an island, this is the best preserved medieval castle in Scandinavia.

18 **Sauna, Finland** see the *Great Outdoors* colour section • The traditional way to cleanse body and mind, saunas are best followed with an ice-cold dip in a lake or a roll in the snow.

19 **Tivoli Gardens midnight fireworks, Denmark** Page 115 • These glorious pyrotechnics are the time-honoured way to wind up a day in Copenhagen.

20 **Skåne, Sweden** Page 524 • The brilliantly hued southern countryside provides a wonderfully scenic backdrop for a gentle summertime drive.

22 Alta rock carvings, Norway
Page **409** • These prehistoric drawings provide an extraordinary reminder of north Norway's earliest peoples.

21 Whale-watching, Norway
Page **389** • Between late May and mid-September, safaris from remote Andenes can pretty much guarantee sightings.

23 Århus old town, Denmark
Page **179** • Holding several worthwhile churches and museums, the tight cluster of narrow medieval streets here is an atmospheric place for a wander.

24 **Grenen, Denmark** Page **204** • The meeting of the Skaggerak and Kattegat seas here makes suitably dramatic viewing.

25 **Kalmar Slott, Sweden** Page **560** • Beautifully remodelled into a Renaissance palace, this sensational twelfth-century stronghold lends a fairytale aspect to the Småland coast.

26 **Lofoten Islands, Norway** Page **391** • Huddled under a mighty and ravishingly beautiful mountain wall, the Lofotens' idyllic fishing villages are a highlight of any itinerary.

27 **Pickled herring, Denmark**
Page **71** • The ultimate Danish delicacies, best washed down with a cold beer.

28 **Santa Claus Village, Finland** Page **781** • Log cabins, reindeer and copious amounts of snow make this the place to meet Mr Claus.

29 Fürstenburg Galleries, Sweden Page **513** • These gloriously evocative paintings by Sweden's finest nineteenth-century artists are the highlight of Gothenburg Art Museum.

30 Skagen, Denmark Page **203** • Heather-topped sand dunes and yellow-painted houses play second fiddle to a slew of galleries displaying works from artists attracted here by the wonderful light.

Basics

Basics

Getting there

From the UK and Ireland, the most convenient way of getting to Scandinavia is by air – there's a good selection of flights and the cheapest fares are often less expensive than the long and arduous journey by train or coach. There are a few ferry services from Britain to Denmark, Norway and Sweden, though these can be pretty costly in high season and are really only worth considering if you're taking your car. From North America, a handful of airlines fly direct to the Scandinavian capitals, though it may be cheaper to route via London, picking up a budget flight onwards from there. There are no direct flights from Canada, Australia or New Zealand.

Though the waters have been muddied by the arrival of budget airlines, airfares still tend to depend on the **season**, with the highest from (roughly) early June to mid-September, when the weather is best; fares drop during the "shoulder" seasons – mid-September to early November and mid-April to early June – and you'll get the best prices during the low season, November through to April (excluding Christmas and New Year, when prices are hiked up and seats are at a premium). Bear in mind, though, that ticket prices from the UK are not subject to seasonal changes to the extent that they are in North America. Note also that flying on weekends is generally more expensive; price ranges quoted below assume midweek travel.

You can often cut costs by going through a **specialist flight agent** – either a consolidator, who buys up blocks of tickets from the airlines and sells them at a discount, or a **discount agent**, who in addition to dealing with discounted flights may also offer special student and youth fares and a range of other travel-related services such as insurance, rail passes, car rental, tours and the like. Bear in mind, though, that penalties for changing your plans on discounted tickets can be stiff. Some agents specialize in **charter flights**, which may be cheaper than scheduled services, but again departure dates are fixed and withdrawal penalties are high. Don't automatically assume that tickets purchased through a travel specialist will be cheapest – once you get a quote, check with the airlines and you may turn up an even better deal.

Students might be able to find cheaper flights through the major student travel agencies, such as Council Travel, STA Travel or, for Canadian students, Travel CUTS.

Booking flights online

Many airlines and discount travel websites offer you the opportunity to **book tickets online**, so cutting out the costs of agents and middlemen.

Online booking agents and general travel sites

Ⓦ **www.cheapflights.com** (UK, Ireland & US); Ⓦ **www.cheapflights.ca** (Canada); Ⓦ **www .cheapflights.com.au** (Australia). Comprehensive sites providing details of bargain flights to anywhere in the world, including Scandinavia.
Ⓦ **www.ebookers.com** (UK) Efficient, easy to use flight finder, with competitive fares.
Ⓦ **www.expedia.com** (US); Ⓦ **www.expedia .co.uk** (UK); Ⓦ **www.expedia.ca** (Canada). Discount airfares, all-airline search engine and daily deals.
Ⓦ **www.flynow.com** (UK) Simple to use independent travel site offering good-value fares.
Ⓦ **www.hotwire.com** (US). Last-minute savings of up to forty percent on regular published fares. Travellers must be at least 18 and there are no refunds, transfers or changes allowed. Log-in required. If you're looking for the cheapest possible scheduled flight, this is probably your best bet.
Ⓦ **www.kelkoo.co.uk** (UK) Useful price-comparison site, checking several sources of low-cost flights (and other goods & services) according to specific criteria.
Ⓦ **www.lastminute.com** (UK); Ⓦ **www .lastminute.com.au** (Australia). Good last-minute holiday package and flight-only deals.

ⓦ www.opodo.co.uk (UK) Popular and reliable source of low airfares. Owned by, and run in conjunction with, nine major European airlines.

ⓦ www.orbitz.com (US) Comprehensive travel resource, with the usual flight, car hire and hotel deals but also great follow-up customer service.

ⓦ www.qixo.com A comparison search that trawls through other ticket sites – including agencies and airlines – to find the best deals from any country.

ⓦ www.travelocity.com (US) and ⓦ www.travelocity.co.uk (UK) Destination guides, hot web fares and best deals for car hire, accommodation and lodging.

ⓦ www.zuji.com.au (Australia). Destination guides, hot fares and great deals for car rental, accommodation and lodging.

Flights from Britain

There's a good choice of direct flights **from London** to Copenhagen, Oslo, Stockholm and Helsinki, plus a scattering to the same four destinations from the UK's **regional airports**. Other cities and towns in Scandinavia are less well served, and although there are a handful of direct flights to the likes of Bergen and Stavanger, you'll probably end up flying to one of the four capital cities and catching a connecting flight from there, not necessarily for much more money. Scandinavian Airlines (SAS) is the main local carrier, but has recently come under intense pressure from several budget airlines, most notably Ryanair.

As for **ticket prices**, the intensity of the competition between the airlines means that there's a plethora of special deals. The best starting point is the **Internet**. Airline websites give up-to-the-minute information about timetables, fares and special offers, while online booking agents (see p.27) can cut costs, as can flight and travel agents (see p.29). As examples, Ryanair have charged as little as £20 (not including taxes)

for a return from London Stansted to Oslo (Torp), though £130 is the more usual price, while SAS currently charge around £100 for the return flight from Birmingham to Copenhagen.

Flight times are insignificant – it's just one hour from Aberdeen to Stavanger, about two hours fifteen minutes from London to Oslo. The only thing to watch is the **location of the airport** – Oslo (Torp), for example, is 110km from Oslo itself, and the same applies to Stockholm (Skavsta).

For air travel within Scandinavia, you might consider buying an **air pass**, usually sold only in conjunction with SAS tickets from Britain; for details, see the box below.

Airlines and flight routeings from Britain

bmi baby ☎0870/264 2229, ⓦ www.bmibaby.com. Aberdeen to Esbjerg; and Edinburgh and Glasgow to Copenhagen.

British Airways ☎0870/850 9850, ⓦ www.britishairways.com. London Heathrow to Copenhagen, Oslo, Stockholm and Helsinki; and Manchester to Oslo.

Finnair ☎0870/241 4411, ⓦ www.finnair.com. Birmingham to Helsinki; Edinburgh to Helsinki and Stockholm; Glasgow to Helsinki and Stockholm; London Heathrow to Helsinki and Stockholm; and Manchester to Helsinki and Stockholm.

KLM ☎0870/507 4074, ⓦ www.klm.com. Aberdeen, Birmingham International, Bristol, Cardiff, Durham Tees Valley, Edinburgh, Glasgow, Humberside, Leeds/Bradford, London City, London Heathrow, Manchester, Newcastle and Norwich direct to Amsterdam Schiphol, from where there are onward flights and connections to Bergen, Kristiansand, Oslo, Stavanger, Sandefjord, and Trondheim in Norway; Aalborg, Billund and Copenhagen in Denmark; Gothenburg and Stockholm Arlanda in Sweden; and Helsinki in Finland.

Maersk Air ☎020/7333 0066, ⓦ www.maersk-air.com. London Gatwick and Manchester to Copenhagen.

Air passes in Scandinavia

The SAS **Visit Scandinavia Air Pass** comes in the form of discount coupons for air travel within Norway, Sweden, Denmark and Finland. It can only be purchased in conjunction with an international flight on SAS in your home country. The coupons are valid for three months from arrival and cost £50–80 depending on the distance and route. The main advantage of the pass is that you're guaranteed a low fare. Although you may be able to get a cheaper flight once you're in Scandinavia, this can't be relied upon, and the £50–80 tariff is very reasonable.

Norwegian Air Shuttle ☎0047/21 49 00 15 (in Norway), ⊛www.norwegian.no. London Stansted to Bergen, Oslo and Trondheim.

Ryanair ☎0906/270 5656 (25p per minute), ⊛www.ryanair.com. Glasgow Prestwick to Gothenburg, Oslo Torp and Stockholm Skavsta; Liverpool to Oslo Torp; London Stansted to Århus, Esbjerg, Gothenburg, Haugesund, Malmo, Oslo Torp and Stockholm Skavsta; Luton to Esbjerg and Stockholm Vasteras; Newcastle to Oslo Torp.

SAS Scandinavian Airlines ☎0870/607 27727, ⊛www.scandinavian.net. Aberdeen to Stavanger; Birmingham to Copenhagen; Edinburgh to Copenhagen; Manchester to Bergen, Copenhagen, Oslo and Stockholm; Newcastle to Copenhagen; London Heathrow to Bergen, Copenhagen, Gothenburg, Oslo, Stavanger and Stockholm.

SN (Brussels Airlines) ☎0870/735 2345, ⊛www.flysn.com. Birmingham, Bristol, London Gatwick, London Heathrow, Manchester and Southampton to Brussels International, from where there are onward flights and connections to Aarhus, Billund and Copenhagen (Denmark); Oslo (Norway); Gothenburg and Stockholm (Sweden); and Helsinki (Finland).

Snowflake ☎0046/8797 4000, ⊛www .flysnowflake.com. Frequent flights from Aberdeen, Birmingham, London, Manchester and Newcastle to Copenhagen Kastrup and from Edinburgh, London and Manchester to Stockholm Arlanda. Part of the SAS group.

Sterling ☎0870/787 8038, ⊛www.sterlingticket .com. Frequent flights: Edinburgh, Manchester and London Gatwick to Copenhagen; plus Edinburgh to Oslo, Helsinki and Stockholm.

Discount flight and travel agents in Britain and Northern Ireland

Bridge the World ☎0870/814 4400, ⊛www .bridgetheworld.com. Specializing in round-the-world tickets, with good deals aimed at the backpacker market.

ebookers ☎0870/010 7000, ⊛www.ebookers .com. Low fares on an extensive selection of scheduled flights and package deals.

Flightcentre ☎0870/890 8099, ⊛www .flightcentre.co.uk. Rock-bottom fares.

Flights4Less ☎0871/222 3423, ⊛www .flights4less.co.uk. Good discount airfares. Part of Lastminute.com.

Holidays4Less ☎0871/222 3423, ⊛www .holidays4less.co.uk. Offshoot of Lastminute.com, offering discounted package deals.

North South Travel ☎01245/608 291, ⊛www .northsouthtravel.co.uk. Friendly, competitive travel agency, offering discounted fares. Profits are used to support projects in the developing world, especially the promotion of sustainable tourism.

Premier Travel ☎028/7126 3333, ⊛www .premiertravel.uk.com. Discount flight specialists.

Rosetta Travel ☎028/9064 4996, ⊛www .rosettatravel.com. Flight and holiday agent, specializing in deals direct from Belfast.

STA Travel ☎0870/160 0599, ⊛www.statravel .co.uk. Specialists in low-cost flights and tours for students and under-26s, though other customers welcome.

Top Deck ☎020/8879 6789, ⊛www.topdecktravel .co.uk. Long-established agent dealing in discount flights.

Trailfinders ☎0845/058 5858, ⊛www.trailfinders .co.uk. One of the UK's best-informed and most efficient agents for independent travellers.

Travel Care ☎0870/112 0085, ⊛www.travelcare .co.uk. Flights, holiday deals and city breaks around the world.

Packages and organized tours

Don't be put off by the idea of visiting Scandinavia on an **inclusive package**. In such an expensive part of Europe, it can be the cheapest way to do things, and may also be the only way to reach remote parts of the region at inhospitable times of year; if you just want to see one city and its environs, then **city break** packages often work out cheaper than arranging the same trip independently. Prices include return travel, usually by plane, and accommodation (with breakfast), with most operators offering a range from hostel to luxury-class hotel. As a broad guide, two-night hotel stays in one of the Scandinavian capital cities will cost £300 per person. If you stay for a week, rates per night fall considerably.

There are also an increasing number of operators offering **special-interest holidays** to Scandinavia, from camping tours to Arctic cruises. Prices for these are a good deal higher than those for city breaks, but are generally excellent value for money.

Tour operators in Britain

Anglers' World Holidays ☎01246/221 717, ⊛www.anglers-world.co.uk. Angling holidays in Norway.

Arctic Experience/Discover the World ☎01737/218 800, ⊛www.discover-the-world .co.uk. Specialist adventure tours including whale-watching in Norway, wildlife in Spitsbergen and dog-sledging in Lapland.

Ashley Jazz Tours ☎01886/888 335. Specializing in jazz tours, such as organized group trips to the Gothenburg Jazz Festival.

Crystal Holidays ☎0870/402 0291, ⓦwww .crystalholidays.co.uk. Country tours and Norwegian skiing holidays.

DA Study Tours ☎01383/882 200. Coach tours for culture vultures to Denmark, Norway and Sweden.

DFDS Seaways ☎0870 5333 000, ⓦwww .dfdsseaways.co.uk. This ferry company offers breaks in Norway and Sweden, including two nights on board ship and two or three nights at the destination; especially good deals out of season.

Emagine ☎0870/902 5399, ⓦwww.emagine -travel.co.uk. Tailor-made Finnish and Swedish holidays, Helsinki city breaks and cruises. Specialist in Lapland – and Santa Claus – trips.

Inntravel ☎01653/617 788, ⓦwww.inntravel .co.uk. Outdoor holidays in Norway including skiing, walking, dog-sledging, fjord cruises, and whale- and reindeer-watching.

Insight ☎01475/741 203, ⓦwww.insighttours .com. City tours and "Spectacular Scandinavia and its fjords" – a 15-day trip for £1450.

ScanMeridian ☎020/7431 5322, ⓦwww .scanmeridian.co.uk. Scandinavia specialists offering city breaks, fly-drive, cottage holidays, cruises and tailor-made trips.

Scantours ☎020/7839 2927, ⓦwww.scantoursuk .com. Huge range of packages and tailor-made holidays to every Scandinavian nook and cranny.

Specialised Tours ☎01342/712 785, ⓦwww .specialisedtours.com. Specialists in Scandinavia offering independent, tailor-made or group city breaks and holidays.

Taber Holidays ☎01274/594 656, ⓦwww .taberhols.co.uk. Scandinavian specialists with dozens of options, including self-catering holidays, fjord cruises, motoring tours and guided coach trips.

Flights from Ireland

From the Republic of Ireland, the prime supplier of direct flights to Scandinavia is SAS, who fly direct **from Dublin** to Oslo, Copenhagen and Stockholm; their main rival is the budget airline Ryanair, and the two compete with each in offering cheap deals and flights. **Fares** are very reasonable, with the cost of a return working out at €150–200 depending on seat availability. SAS passengers flying from Ireland can also purchase the Visit Scandinavia Air Pass (see box on p.28).

For airline routeings from Ireland, see below; for onward flights from the UK, see p.28.

Airlines and flight routeings from Ireland

Aer Lingus ☎0818/365 000, ⓦwww.aerlingus.ie. Dublin to Copenhagen.

bmi ☎01/407 3036, ⓦwww.flybmi.com. Belfast, Dublin and Cork to London Heathrow.

British Airways ☎1-890/626 747, ⓦwww .britishairways.com. Cork, Dublin and Shannon to London or Manchester.

Finnair ☎01/844 6565, ⓦwww.finnair.com. Dublin to Helsinki (summer only).

FlyNordic ☎0046/8528 06820 ⓦwww.flynordic .com. Frequent flights from Dublin to Stockholm.

Ryanair ☎1530/787 787 at 33c per minute, ⓦwww.ryanair.com. Shannon to Stockholm Skavsta; Cork, Derry, Dublin, Kerry, Knock and Shannon to London Stansted.

SAS Scandinavian Airlines ☎01/844 5440, ⓦwww.scandinavian.net. Dublin to Copenhagen, Oslo and Stockholm.

Snowflake ☎0046/8797 4000, ⓦwww .flysnowflake.com. Frequent flights from Dublin to Copenhagen Kastrup and Stockholm Arlanda.

Sterling ☎0870/787 8038 (in UK), ⓦwww .sterlingticket.com. Frequent flights from Dublin to Stockholm.

Discount flight and travel agents in Ireland

CIE Tours International ☎01/703 1888, ⓦwww.cietours.ie. General flight and tour agent.

ebookers ☎01/241 5689, ⓦwww.ebookers.ie. Low fares on an extensive selection of scheduled flights and package deals.

Go Holidays ☎01/874 4126, ⓦwww.goholidays .ie. City breaks and package tours.

Joe Walsh Tours ☎01/676 0991, ⓦwww .joewalshtours.ie. Long-established general budget fares and holidays agent.

Lee Travel ☎021/427 7111, ⓦwww.leetravel.ie. Flights and holidays worldwide.

Neenan Travel ☎01/607 9900, ⓦwww .neenantrav.ie. Specialists in city breaks.

Trailfinders ☎01/677 7888, ⓦwww.trailfinders .ie. One of the best-informed and most efficient agents for independent travellers; they produce a very useful quarterly magazine worth scrutinizing for round-the-world routes.

usit NOW Republic of Ireland ☎01/602 1600, Northern Ireland ☎028/9032 7111; ⓦwww .usitnow.ie. Student and youth specialists for flights and trains.

World Travel Centre ☎01/416 7007, ⊛www
.worldtravel.ie. Excellent fares to Europe and
worldwide.

Packages and organized tours

Not many operators run **package tours** to
Scandinavia from Ireland, although where
available these may be the cheapest way to
travel, and sometimes the only way to reach
remote parts of the region at inhospitable
times of year. Likewise, city-break packages
may well work out cheaper than arranging
the same trip independently. British operators are listed on p.29, some Irish options
are listed below.

Tour operators in Ireland
Crystal Holidays Dublin ☎01/433 1043, ⊛www
.crystalholidays.ie. City breaks and skiing holidays.
Go Holidays Dublin ☎01/874 4126, ⊛www
.goholidays.ie. Package tour specialists with one- or
two-centre city breaks to Copenhagen, Helsinki and
Stockholm.
Rosetta Travel Belfast ☎028/9064 4996,
⊛www.rosettatravel.com. Flight and holiday agent.

Flights from the US and Canada

From **North America**, Scandinavia is well
served by numerous American and European
airlines, though the vast majority of flights
involve **changing planes** in a European hub
city such as London or Paris (for onward
flights from the UK to Scandinavia, see
p.28); and if you don't live in a US hub city
you may well have to change planes more
than once. **Direct flights** are obviously preferable, and if you can be fairly flexible with
your departure dates you'll be able to take
advantage of the special promotional fares
offered regularly by the airlines concerned
– Continental, SAS and Finnair. However,
the difference in price between nonstop
and stopover flights is, in general terms at
least, surprisingly small. The **flying time** on
a direct, nonstop flight from the east coast
of North America to Scandinavia is eight or
nine hours.

    Fares from North America to Copenhagen,
Helsinki, Oslo and Stockholm are fairly similar, whichever carrier you choose, but it's
still worth shopping around for the fastest

routings and the best deals. If you're visiting more than one country, an **air pass**
(see p.28) might be another way of reducing costs. As sample summertime fares, an
economy return on Continental's nonstop
flight from New York to Oslo will cost in the
region of US$1800; a nonstop Finnair flight
from New York to Helsinki anywhere between
US$1200 and US$1700; and a Delta stopover return from New York to Stockholm
US$1500–1700. Finnair charge CDN$1200–
1300 for a direct Toronto–Helsinki return, and
SAS US$1500 for a return from Seattle to
Copenhagen. Special deals, flight agents (see
p.32) and online booking (see p.27) can often
halve these prices.

Airlines and flight routeings from North America

Air Canada ☎1-888/247-2262, ⊛www.aircanada
.ca. Daily from Toronto (with connections from
Vancouver) to Frankfurt, London and Zurich, from
where there are onward connections to major
Scandinavian cities.
Air France US ☎1-800/237-2747, ⊛www
.airfrance.com, Canada ☎1-800/667-2747,
⊛www.airfrance.ca. Daily flights from many North
American cities to Paris, from where there are
connecting flights to major Scandinavian cities.
American Airlines ☎1-800/433-7300, ⊛www
.aa.com. Daily flights from Chicago to Stockholm, via
London.
British Airways ☎1-800/AIRWAYS, ⊛www
.british-airways.com. Daily flights from 22 North
American cities to London Heathrow.
Continental Airlines domestic ☎1-800/523-
3273, international ☎1-800/231-0856, ⊛www
.continental.com. Daily flights between various major
North American and European cities, from where
there are connections to Scandinavia. Also direct daily
flights from New York to Oslo.
Delta Air Lines domestic ☎1-800/221-1212,
international ☎1-800/241-4141, ⊛www.delta.com.
Frequent flights from all the major North American
hub cities to London and Amsterdam, and onward
flights to Scandinavia
Finnair ☎1-800/950-5000, ⊛www.finnair.com.
Direct flights from New York and Toronto to Helsinki.
Icelandair ☎1-800/223-5500, ⊛www.icelandair
.com. Direct flights from New York, Baltimore,
Boston, Minneapolis, Orlando and San Francisco to
Reykjavik, from where there are onward connections
to Copenhagen, Oslo, Stockholm and Helsinki. Some
flights allow a three-night stopover in Reykjavik.

Lufthansa US ☎1-800/645-3880, Canada ☎1-800/563-5954, ☻www.lufthansa-usa.com. Daily flights from major North American cities to Frankfurt, from where there are onward flights to Scandinavia.
Northwest/KLM Airlines domestic ☎1-800/225-2525, international ☎1-800/447-4747, ☻www .nwa.com, ☻www.klm.com. Frequent flights from all the major North American hub cities, either direct or via Amsterdam, to all four Scandinavian capital cities.
SAS (Scandinavian Airlines) ☎1-800/221-2350, ☻www.scandinavian.net. Direct flights from Chicago, New York (Newark), Seattle and Washington DC to Copenhagen; also direct from New York (Newark) and Chicago to Stockholm. Onward flights from Copenhagen and Stockholm to a bevy of Scandinavian towns and cities.
Virgin Atlantic Airways ☎1-800/862-8621, ☻www.virgin-atlantic.com. Daily flights from various US cities to London, with onward connections to Scandinavia.

Discount flight and travel agents in North America

Educational Travel Center ☎1-800/747-5551 or 608/256-5551, ☻www.edtrav.com. Low-cost fares worldwide, student/youth discount offers, Eurail passes, car rental and tours.
Flightcentre US ☎1-866/WORLD-51, ☻www .flightcentre.us, Canada ☎1-888/WORLD-55, ☻www.flightcentre.ca. Rock-bottom fares from North America to all four Scandinavian capitals.
STA Travel US ☎1-800/329-9537, Canada ☎1-888/427-5639; ☻www.statravel.com. Worldwide specialists in independent travel; also student IDs, travel insurance, car rental, rail passes and more.
Student Flights ☎1-800/255-8000 or 480/951-1177, ☻www.isecard.com/studentflights. Student/ youth fares from North America to Scandinavia, plus student IDs and European rail and bus passes.
Travel Cuts US ☎1-800/592-CUTS, Canada ☎1-888/246-9762, ☻www.travelcuts.com. Popular, long-established student-travel organization, with worldwide offers.
Travelers Advantage ☎1-877/259-2691, ☻www .travelersadvantage.com. Discount travel club, with cashback deals and discounted car rental. Membership required ($1 for three months' trial).
Travelosophy US ☎1-800/332-2687, ☻www .itravelosophy.com. Good range of discounted and student fares.

Packages and organized tours

A substantial number of companies in North America operate **organized tours** around Scandinavia, ranging from city breaks to deluxe cruises or cycling holidays. Group tours can be very expensive, however, and sometimes don't include the airfare, so check what you're getting. If your visit is focused on cities, you could simply book a hotel-plus-flight package (which can work out cheaper than booking the two separately). Scanam and Passage Tours offer very reasonable weekend deals in the low season (see below). Tour reservations can often be made through your local travel agent.

Tour operators in North America

Abercrombie and Kent ☎1-800/554-7016, ☻www.abercrombiekent.com. Upmarket company offering tailor-made Scandinavian and Baltic coach tours and cruises.
Adventure Center ☎1-800/228 4747, ☻www .adventurecenter.com. Good range of treks in Swedish and Finnish Lapland, from four to fifteen days, mostly camping. Adventurous stuff.
Adventures Abroad ☎1-800/665-3998, ☻www .adventures-abroad.com. Specializing in small-group tours, and offering a variety of Scandinavian packages.
Backroads ☎1-800/462-2848, ☻www .backroads.com. Specializing in activity holidays, including a six-day cycle tour of Denmark and a six-day hiking tour of the Norwegian mountains, glaciers and fjords.
Borton Overseas ☎1-800/843-0602, ☻www .bortonoverseas.com. Adventure-vacation specialists, with a large selection of biking, hiking, rafting, birdwatching, dog-sledging and cross-country skiing tours, plus farm and cabin stays and city packages.
Brekke Tours – Spirit of Scandinavia ☎1-800/437-5302, ☻www.brekketours.com. A well-established company offering a host of sightseeing and cultural tours in Scandinavia.
Euro-Bike & Walking Tours ☎1-800/321-6060, ☻www.eurobike.com. Summer cycling and walking tours of Denmark.
Nordic Saga Tours ☎1-800/848 6449, ☻www .nordicsaga.com. Packages, flights and information on air passes within Scandinavia.
Norwegian Coastal Voyage Inc ☎1-800/323-7436, ☻www.coastalvoyage.com. A mixture of escorted and independent cruises along the Norwegian coastline, to Svalbard and on the Gota canal in Sweden.
Passage Tours ☎1-800/548-5960, ☻www .passagetours.com. Scandinavian specialist offering

tours like "The Northern Lights" and dog-sledging, whale-watching, ski packages and fjord excursions.

Picasso Travel ☎1-800/995-7997, ⊛www .nordiquetours.com. A wide range of Scandinavian packages including "Scandinavian capitals", Lapland and the Norwegian fjords.

Scanam World Tours ☎1-800/545-2204, ⊛www.scanamtours.com. Scandinavian specialist offering group and individual tours and cruises.

Scand-America Tours ☎1-800/886-8428, ⊛www.scandamerica.com. A wide variety of packages – everything from dog-sledging to garden tours – throughout Scandinavia.

Scantours ☎1-800/223-7226, ⊛www.scantours .com. Major Scandinavian holiday specialists offering vacation packages, hotel bookings and customized itineraries, including cruises and city sightseeing tours.

Vantage Deluxe World Travel ☎1-800/322-6677, ⊛www.vantagetravel.com. Deluxe group tours and cruises in Scandinavia.

Flights from Australia and New Zealand

There's no shortage of flights to Scandinavia **from Australia and New Zealand**, but all of them involve at least one stop. Singapore and Thai Airways offer two of the more direct routes out of Sydney (stopping in Singapore and Bangkok respectively). Otherwise, airlines flying out of Australia and New Zealand often use SAS and Finnair for connecting services on to Scandinavia: SAS fly from Tokyo, Singapore and Bangkok to Copenhagen, Finnair from Tokyo, Hong Kong, Bangkok and Singapore to Helsinki. One other option is to pick up a cheap ticket to London, and then continue your journey onto Scandinavia with one of the UK's no-frills budget airlines (see p.29). If you intend to take in a number of other European countries on your trip, it might be worth buying a Eurail or ScanRail pass before you go (see p.35); train passes are available from most travel agents, or from branches of CIT or Bentours (see p.35); an SAS air pass (see p.28) is another money-saving option.

Tickets purchased direct from the airlines tend to be expensive, with published fares to Europe ranging from A$2000/NZ$2200 in low season to A$3500/NZ$3800 in high season. Travel agents can offer better deals on **fares**, and have the latest information on special promotions, such as free stopovers en route and fly-drive-accommodation packages. Flight Centre and STA generally offer the best discounts, especially for students and those under 26.

For extended trips, visiting Scandinavia as part of a **round-the-world** (RTW) ticket can be good value. Fares are based either on the number of continents you visit, or the number of miles you travel, and tickets are usually cheapest through travel agents. The lowest-priced tickets usually involve three to four stopovers, with prices rising the further you travel or the more stops you add.

Airlines in and flight routings from Australia and New Zealand

Air New Zealand Australia ☎13 24 76, ⊛www .airnz.com.au, New Zealand ☎0800/737 000, ⊛www.airnz.co.nz. Frequent flights from Auckland to Singapore, Hong Kong and Taipei, from where partner airlines carry passengers to Frankfurt and Munich for onward flights to the capitals of Scandinavia. Also frequent flights from Auckland to Los Angeles and London.

British Airways Australia ☎1300/767 177, New Zealand ☎0800/274 847 or 09/356 8690; ⊛www .britishairways.com. Frequent one–stop flights to London (in conjunction with Qantas), from Adelaide, Auckland, Brisbane, Melbourne, Perth and Sydney, with onward flights to Scandinavia.

Cathay Pacific Australia ☎13 17 47, New Zealand ☎0508/800 454 or 09/379 0861; ⊛www .cathaypacific.com. Frequent flights from Perth, Adelaide, Melbourne, Sydney, Brisbane, Cairns and Auckland to Hong Kong, with onward connections to Amsterdam, London, Paris and Frankfurt, and partner airlines services on from London to Helsinki, Stockholm and Copenhagen.

Finnair Australia ☎02/9244 2299, ⊛www.finnair .com. Frequent flights to Helsinki from Singapore, Bangkok, Hong Kong, Peking, Shanghai, Tokyo and Osaka. Partner airline flights to these Asian airports from all major Australian and New Zealand airports.

Malaysia Airlines Australia ☎13 26 27, New Zealand ☎0800/777 747, ⊛www.malaysia-airlines .com. Frequent flights from Adelaide, Auckland, Brisbane, Melbourne, Perth and Sydney to Kuala Lumpur, with onward flights to a variety of European destinations, including Amsterdam, Frankfurt, London, Manchester and Stockholm.

Qantas Australia ☎13 13 13, New Zealand ☎0800/808 767 or 09/357 8900; ⊛www.qantas .com. Frequent one–stop flights, in conjunction with British Airways, from Adelaide, Auckland, Brisbane,

Melbourne, Perth and Sydney to London, for onward flights to Scandinavia.

SAS Scandinavian Airlines Australia ☎1300/727 707, ⊛www.scandinavian.net. Sydney to Copenhagen via Bangkok, Singapore or Tokyo; and Sydney to Helsinki, Oslo and Stockholm via Bangkok, Singapore or Tokyo and Copenhagen.

Singapore Airlines Australia ☎13 10 11, New Zealand ☎0800/808 909; ⊛www.singaporeair .com. Adelaide, Brisbane, Melbourne, Perth, Sydney and Auckland to Copenhagen and London, via Singapore.

Thai Airways Australia ☎1300/651 960, New Zealand ☎09/377 3886; ⊛www.thaiair.com. Brisbane, Melbourne, Perth, Sydney and Auckland to Stockholm and Copenhagen, via Bangkok.

Discount flight and travel agents in Australia and New Zealand

CIT Australia ☎02/9267 1255, ⊛www.cittravel .com.au. Europe-wide rail passes.

Flight Centre Australia ☎13 31 33, ⊛www .flightcentre.com.au; New Zealand ☎0800 243 544, ⊛www.flightcentre.co.nz. Rock-bottom fares worldwide.

Holiday Shoppe New Zealand ☎0800/808 480, ⊛www.holidayshoppe.co.nz. Great deals on flights, hotels and holidays.

OTC Australia ☎1300/855 118, ⊛www.otctravel .com.au. Deals on flights, hotels and holidays.

STA Travel Australia ☎1300/733 035, New Zealand ☎0508/782 872; ⊛www.statravel.com. Specialists in low-cost flights and holiday deals. Good discounts for students and under-26s. Great deals for students.

Trailfinders Australia ☎02/9247 7666, ⊛www .trailfinders.com.au. One of the best-informed and most efficient agents for independent travellers.

travel.com Australia ☎1300/130 482 or 02/9249 5444, ⊛www.travel.com.au; New Zealand ☎0800/468 332, ⊛www.travel.co.nz. Comprehensive online travel company, with discounted fares and good flight and hotel deals.

Packages and organized tours

There are very few **package holidays** to Scandinavia originating in Australia and New Zealand. Your best bet is probably Bentours, who can put together a package for you, and are about the only agents who offer skiing holidays. Alternatively, you can go with one of the UK agents (listed on p.29), which a greater choice of holidays and prices.

Tour operators in Australia and New Zealand

Adventures Abroad New Zealand ☎0800/800 434, ⊛www.adventures-abroad.com. Wide range of Scandinavian packages from one to three weeks.

Bentours Australia ☎02/9241 1353, ⊛www .bentours.com.au. Ferry, rail, bus and hotel passes and a host of scenic tours throughout Scandinavia including fjord-travel and cycling in Denmark.

Explore Holidays Australia ⊛www .exploreholidays.com.au. Stockholm mini-stays and 21-day adventure tours through central and northern Sweden and coastal Norway. Bookings through travel agents or STA travel (see above).

By rail from the UK

Taking a **train** can be a relaxing, if long-winded, way of getting from the UK to Scandinavia, though it is likely to work out much more expensive than flying, especially if you're over 26. A number of deals involving rail passes (see below) make it possible to cut costs, however, and there's the added advantage of being able to break your journey – travelling to Oslo from London, for instance, you could stop off at Brussels, Hamburg, Copenhagen and Gothenburg.

The largest UK company dealing with train travel within Europe is **Rail Europe** (see p.35). They sell all the rail passes available, and will through-ticket you from London Waterloo to Copenhagen on the fastest and most convenient routeing, normally via Brussels (on Eurostar) and Hamburg. To get the cheapest **fares** with Rail Europe, you'll need to book around fourteen days in advance, and include one Saturday night in your time away. With this type of ticket, the adult return fare from **London to Copenhagen** is currently £300–350, more if you have a sleeper berth, and the journey takes around twenty hours. Getting to Norway, Sweden or Finland by train from Britain involves first travelling to Copenhagen, as described above, and then taking one of the daily services onward at the cost of another £50 or so return.

Rail contacts

In the UK and Ireland

Eurostar ☎08705/186 186, ⊛www.eurostar.co.uk. Timetables and online booking for Eurostar trains.

Rail Europe UK ☏08708/371 371, ⊛www
.raileurope.co.uk. Pan-European train bookings,
including discounted rail fares for under-26s on a
variety of routes; also sells every sort of European
rail pass (though for Eurail consult ⊛www
.raileurope.com), and is an agent for Eurostar.

In North America
Eurorail International Canada ☏1-888/667-
9734, ⊛www.europrail.net. Eurail and many
individual country passes.
Rail Europe US ☏1-877/257-2887, Canada ☏1-
800/361-7245; ⊛www.raileurope.com/us. Official
North American Eurail agent; also sells multinational
passes and most single-country passes.
ScanTours US ☏1-800/223-7226 or 310/636-
4656, ⊛www.scantours.com. Eurail and many
other European country passes.

In Australia and New Zealand
CIT Australia ☏02/9267 1255, ⊛www.cittravel
.com.au. Europe-wide rail passes.
Bentours Australia ☏02/9241 1353, ⊛www
.bentours.com.au. Scandinavian rail and bus passes.
Rail Plus Australia ☏613/9642 8644, New
Zealand ☏649/377 5415; ⊛www.railplus.com.au.
Most European rail passes and tickets.
Trailfinders Australia ☏02/9247 7666, ⊛www
.trailfinders.com.au. All European rail passes.

Rail passes

Rail passes can reduce the cost of train
travel significantly, especially if you plan to
travel extensively around Scandinavia or visit
as part of a wider tour of Europe. There's
a huge array of passes available, covering
regions as well as individual countries. Some
have to be bought before leaving home,
while others can only be purchased in the
country itself. **Rail Europe** is the umbrella
company for all national and international
rail tickets, and its comprehensive website

(see p.36) is the most useful source of information on available passes; it also gives all
current prices. For details of rail passes for
use specifically within Scandinavia, such as
ScanRail, see "Getting Around", p.45; for
information on individual country passes see
the "Getting Around" section of the relevant
country.

Inter-Rail pass
If you have no clear itinerary, the **Inter-Rail
pass** (⊛ www.raileurope.co.uk/inter-rail)
might be your best bet. These are only available to European residents, and you will be
asked to provide proof of residency before
being allowed to purchase one. They come
in over-26 and (cheaper) under-26 versions,
and cover 29 European countries grouped
together in **zones**. These zones include **A**:
UK and the Republic of Ireland; **B**: Norway,
Sweden, Finland; **C**: Germany, Austria,
Switzerland, Denmark; and **E**: France,
Belgium, Netherlands, Luxembourg. The
passes are available for 16 days (one zone
only; £215), 22 days (two zones only; £295),
and one month (all zones; £405); those aged
12 to 26 years get a thirty percent discount
on the above prices. Inter-Rail passes do not
include travel between Britain and the continent, although holders are eligible for discounts cross-Channel ferries and Eurostar
trains.

Eurail Pass
The **Eurail pass** (only available to non-
Europeans) is not likely to pay for itself if
you're planning to stick to one Scandinavian
country. The pass, which must be purchased
before arrival in Europe, allows unlimited free
first-class train travel in seventeen European
countries, including all four covered in this

Useful timetable publications

The red-covered **Thomas Cook European Timetable** details schedules of over
50,000 trains in Europe, as well as timings of over 200 ferry routes and rail-connecting
bus services. It's updated and issued every month; main changes are in the June edition (published end of May), which has details of the summer European schedules,
and the October one (published end of September), which includes winter schedules;
some have advance summer/winter timings also. The book can be purchased online
at ⊛www.thomascookpublishing.com or from branches of Thomas Cook, and costs
£9.90–11. Their useful *Rail Map of Europe* can also be purchased online for £6.

book, and is available in increments of 15 days, 21 days, one month, two months and three months. If you're under 26, you can save money with a **Eurail pass Youth**, which is valid for second-class travel; the same applies if you're travelling with between one and four companions on a joint **Eurail pass Saver**; both of these are available in the same increments as the standard Eurail pass. You stand a better chance of getting your money's worth out of a **Eurail pass Flexi**, which is good for ten or fifteen days' first-class travel within a two-month period. This, too, comes in under-26/second-class (**Eurail pass Youth Flexi**) and group (**Eurail pass Saver Flexi**) versions. A standard Eurail pass currently **costs** US$588 for 15 days, US$762 for 21 days, US$946 for one month, US$1338 for two months and US$1654 three months.

Details of prices for all these passes can be found on ⓦwww.raileurope.com; they can be purchased from the agents listed below.

By coach from Britain

A **coach journey** to Scandinavia from Britain can be an endurance test, and with airfares falling so dramatically it can actually prove more expensive than flying. It's only worth taking the bus if time is no object and price all-important, or if you specifically do not want to fly.

The major UK operator of international coach routes is **Eurolines** (UK ☏0870/514 3219), whose tickets are bookable online at ⓦ www.nationalexpress.com, though most major travel agents will oblige too. Eurolines run eight services weekly to **Copenhagen** either via Brussels (20hr) or Amsterdam (26hr). From Copenhagen there are connections on to **Gothenburg** (five weekly; 25hr 45min), **Stockholm** (three weekly; 30hr 30min) and **Oslo** (five weekly; 30hr 35min). There are no through-ticketed coach arrangements between Britain and Finland. **Fares** to Danish destinations start at £120 return, though advance booking – seven days or more – can provide a substantial discount; there are also discounts for the over-60s and those under 26.

Another option is the **Eurolines Pass**, which offers unlimited coach travel throughout much of Europe, including Denmark, southern Norway and Sweden but excluding much of the rest of Norway and Finland.

The pass is valid either for fifteen days (£169 mid-Sept to late June, £235 late June to mid-Sept); thirty days (£230/£315) or forty days (£255/£355). Once again, seniors and the under-26s are entitled to discounts of around ten percent.

There are no through services from anywhere in Britain outside London, though **National Express** buses connect with Eurolines buses in London from all over the British Isles.

By car and ferry from Britain

Car ferries departing from Harwich and Newcastle link Britain with Denmark, Sweden and Norway. **Fares** aren't cheap – prices vary enormously according to the season, number of passengers and type of cabin accommodation – but discounts and special deals, such as DFDS Seaways' discounted midweek returns, can reduce costs greatly. Not surprisingly, fares are usually at their lowest during the winter months. As an example, DFDS Seaways charge from as little as £34 per person for a low-season midweek return from Harwich to Esbjerg in Denmark, plus £50 each way for a car; in summer fares per person begin at £49, plus £57 for the car; these fares include a berth in a sleeping cabin. DFDS prices from Newcastle to Kristiansand (Norway) and Gothenburg (Sweden) are comparable. Fjord Line sailings from Newcastle to Stavanger, Haugesund and Bergen (all in Norway) offer a minimum fare in winter of £90 return for one or two passengers and car (plus £10 extra for a cabin berth), rising to around £330 for the same deal in summer (plus £20 extra for a cabin berth). There is no difference in prices between the three ports.

Ferry companies and routeings to Scandinavia

DFDS Seaways ☏0870/252 0524, ⓦwww .dfdsseaways.co.uk. Harwich to Esbjerg (20hrs); Newcastle to Kristiansand (18hrs) and Gothenburg (26hrs). Also Copenhagen and Helsingborg to Oslo (16hrs/14hrs).
Fjord Line ☏0191/296 1313, ⓦwww.fjordline .com. Newcastle to Stavanger (20hrs), Haugesund (23hrs), and Bergen (27hrs). Also Hantsholm in

Denmark to Egersund (19hrs), Haugesund (25hrs) and Bergen (29hrs) in Norway.

Northlink Ferries ☎0845/600 0449, ⊛www .northlinkferries.co.uk. Aberdeen and usually Kirkwall (Orkneys) to Lerwick (Shetland) – for onward ferries with Smyril Line to Bergen. The Aberdeen to Lerwick ferry takes 14hrs.

Smyril Line UK ☎01595/690 845, ⊛www .smyril-line.com. Smyril ferries shuttle around the north Atlantic, linking Iceland, the Faroe Islands, Lerwick in the Shetlands, Bergen in Norway and Hantsholm in Denmark. See Northlink Ferries above for services to the Shetlands. Journey time from Lerwick to Bergen is 21hrs.

Red tape and visas

EU, US, Canadian, Australian and New Zealand citizens need only a valid passport to enter Denmark, Norway, Sweden and Finland for up to three months. All other nationals should consult the relevant embassy about visa requirements.

For **longer stays**, EU nationals can apply for a residence permit while in the country, which, if it's granted, may be valid for up to five years. Non-EU nationals can only apply for residence permits before leaving home, and must be able to prove they can support themselves without working. Contact the relevant embassy in your country of origin.

In spite of the lack of restrictions, **checks** are frequently made on travellers at the major points of entry. If you're young and are carrying a rucksack, be prepared to prove that you have enough money to support yourself during your stay. You may also be asked how long you intend to stay and why. **Border controls** between the Scandinavian countries are patchy – sometimes no-one seems very bothered, while at other times you might have your car searched and have to answer endless questions.

Scandinavian embassies and consulates

Australia

Denmark Consulates in Sydney ☎061/29247 2224, ⊛www.gksydney.um.dk/en; and Victoria ☎061/39866 1242.
Finland Embassy in Canberra ☎02/6273 3800. There are also consulates and honorary consulates in Adelaide, Brisbane, Cairns, Darwin, Hobart,

Melbourne, Perth, Sydney and Victoria; for contact details, go to ⊛www.finland.org.au/fi.
Norway Embassy in Canberra ☎02/6273 3444, ✉emb.canberra@mfa.no.
Sweden Embassy in Canberra ☎02/6270 2700, ✉sweden@iimetro.com.au.

Canada

Denmark Embassy in Ottawa ☎613/562-1811, ⊛www.ambottawa.um.dk. Consulate in Toronto ☎1–416/962 5661, ⊛www.tradecomm.com.
Finland Embassy in Ottawa ☎613/288-2233, ✉embassy@finland.ca). There are also consulates and honorary consulates in Calgary, Edmonton, Halifax, Montréal, Québec, Regina, Sault Ste Marie, Sudbury, Thunder Bay, Timmins, Toronto and Winnipeg; for contact details, go to ⊛www.finland .org.au/fi.
Norway Embassy in Ottawa ☎613/238-6571, ✉emb.ottawa@mfa.no. There are also consulates in Calgary, Edmonton, Halifax, Montréal, Québec, Regina, Saint John, St John's, Toronto, Vancouver, Ville de la Baie and Winnipeg; for contact details, go to ⊛www.emb-norway.ca.
Sweden Embassy in Ottawa ☎613/244-8200, ✉sweden@bellnet.ca.

New Zealand

Denmark Consulate in Wellington ☎04/471 0520, ⊛www.danishconsulatesnz.org.nz.
Finland See Australia.
Norway See Australia
Sweden See Australia.

Republic of Ireland

Denmark Embassy in Dublin ☎01/475 6404, 🌐www.ambdublin.um.dk.

Finland Embassy in Dublin ☎01/478 1344. There are also consulates and honorary consulates in Cork, Galway and Limerick; for contact details, go to 🌐www.finland.ie/en.

Norway Embassy in Dublin ☎01/662 1800, 📧emb.dublin@mfa.no.

Sweden Embassy in Dublin ☎01/671 5822, 📧ambassaden.dublin@foreign.ministry.se.

UK

Denmark Embassy in London ☎020/7333 0200, 🌐www.amblondon.um.dk/en.

Finland Embassy in London ☎020/7838 6200, 🌐www.finemb.org.uk/en. There are also consulates and honorary consulates in Aberdeen, Belfast, Birmingham, Bristol, Cardiff, Dover, Dundee, Edinburgh, Glasgow, Harwich, Hull and Immingham; for contact details, go to 🌐www.formin.finland .fi/doc/eng/embassies.

Norway Embassy in London ☎020/7591 5500, 📧emb.london@mfa.no. Consulate in Edinburgh ☎0131/226 5701, 📧cgedi@mfa.no.

Sweden Embassy in London ☎020/7917 6400, 📧ambassaden.london@foreign.ministry.se.

US

Denmark Embassy in Washington, DC ☎1-202/234-4300, 🌐www.denmarkemb .org. Consulates in Chicago ☎1-312/787-8780, 🌐www.consulatedk.org; and New York ☎1-212/223-4545, 🌐www.gknewyork .um.dk.

Finland Embassy in Washington, DC ☎202/298-5800, 🌐www.finland.org. There are also consulates and honorary consulates in Albuquerque, Anchorage, Atlanta, Baltimore, Birmingham, Boston, Chicago, Dallas, Denver, Detroit, Fitchburg, Hancock, Honolulu, Houston, Lake Worth, Los Angeles and New York; for contact details, go to 🌐www.finland.org.

Norway Embassy in Washington, DC ☎202/333-6000; Consulate General in New York ☎212/421-7333, 📧cg.newyork@mfa.no; other consulates in Houston, Minneapolis and San Francisco, contact the Washington embassy.

Sweden Embassy in Washington ☎202/467-2600, 📧ambassaden.washington@ foreign.ministry.se. There are also consulates in Los Angeles, New York and San Francisco; for contact details, go to 🌐www.swedenabroad .com.

Money and banks

Of the three Scandinavian countries in the European Union (EU) – Denmark, Finland and Sweden – only Finland has joined the single European currency and converted to the euro. As a result you'll need a mixture of currencies if you're visiting more than one of the Scandinavian countries.

Finland changed over to the **euro** (€) in 2002, but Denmark and Norway use **kroner**, Sweden **kronor** – abbreviated respectively as Dkr, Nkr and Skr, or as DKK, NOK and SEK. In this guide, we've abbreviated each as "kr", except where it's not clear as to which country's money we're referring, in which case we've prefixed it with an "S" (Swedish), "D" (Danish) or "N" (Norwegian). Though they share a broadly similar **exchange rate**, the currencies are not interchangeable. See the "Costs, money and banks" sections of the individual country "Basics" for exchange rates, further details of the denominations of each currency, and of average daily costs.

ATMS, debit and credit cards

Scandinavia heaves with **ATMs**, with a particular concentration in all four capital cities. Most ATMs give instructions in a variety of languages, and accept a host of **debit cards**, including all those carrying the

Cirrus/Maestro logo. If in doubt, check with your bank to find out if the card you wish to use will be accepted – and if you need a new (international) PIN. You'll rarely be charged a transaction fee as the banks make their profits from applying different exchange rates. **Credit cards** can be used in ATMs too, but in this case transactions are treated as loans, with interest accruing daily from the date of withdrawal. All major credit cards, including American Express, Visa and MasterCard, are widely accepted across Scandinavia.

Travellers' cheques

The main advantage of buying **travellers' cheques** is that they are a safe way of carrying funds. All well-known brands of travellers' cheque in all major currencies are accepted throughout in Scandinavia, with euro and US dollar cheques being the most common. The usual fee for their purchase is one or two percent of face value, though this fee is often waived if you buy the cheques through a bank where you have an account. It's useful to purchase a selection of denominations. When you **cash your cheques**, you'll find that almost all banks make a percentage charge per transaction on top of a basic minimum charge.

In the event that cheques are **lost or stolen**, the issuing company will expect you to report the loss immediately. Make sure to keep the purchase agreement, a record of cheque serial numbers and the issuing company's emergency contact numbers safe and separate from the cheques themselves. Most companies claim to replace lost or stolen cheques within 24 hours.

Exchanging Money

Exchanging money is easy but usually expensive. Banks have standard exchange rates, but commissions can vary enormously and it's always worth shopping around. Post offices often provide good exchange rates, too. **Banking hours** vary from country to country – check each country's "Basics" section under "Costs, money and banks". Outside those times, and especially in more remote areas, you'll often find that you can change money at hostels, hotels, campsites, tourist offices, airports and ferry terminals – though usually at worse rates than at the bank.

Wiring money

Having **money wired** from home using one of the companies listed below is never convenient or cheap, and should be considered as a last resort – indeed it can actually be cheaper to have **your own bank** send the money through. For the latter, you need to nominate a receiving bank in Scandinavia and confirm the arrangement with them before you set the wheels in motion back home. The sending bank's fees are geared to the amount being transferred and the urgency of the service you require – for example standard transfers, taking five working days, start at around £20/US$40 for the first £2,000/US$3780 or so.

Money-wiring companies

Travelers Express/MoneyGram ⓦ www .moneygram.com; US ☎ 1-800/444-3010; Canada ☎ 1-800/933-3278; UK, Ireland and New Zealand ☎ 00800/6663 9472; Australia ☎ 0011800/6663 9472.
Western Union ⓦ www.westernunion.com; US and Canada ☎ 1-800/CALL-CASH; Australia ☎ 1800/501 500; New Zealand ☎ 0800/005 253; Republic of Ireland ☎ 66/947 5603; UK ☎ 0800/833 833.

Mail and telecommunications

BASICS | Mail and telecommunications

Post office opening hours and more specific information on how to use the mail and telephone systems in each country is given under the respective "Communications" sections.

Email

One of the best ways to keep in touch while travelling is to sign up for a **free Internet email address** with providers such as YahooMail (🌐www.yahoo.com) or Hotmail (🌐www.hotmail.com), enabling you to pick up and send mail from anywhere with Internet access. In addition, 🌐www.kropla.com is a useful website giving details of how to plug your laptop in when abroad, as well as listing international phone codes and providing information about electrical systems in different countries.

Mail

You can have letters sent **poste restante** to any post office in Scandinavia by addressing them "Poste Restante", followed by the name of the town and country. When picking mail up you'll need to take your passport; make sure to check under middle names and initials, as letters can get misfiled.

Telephones

Telephone boxes are plentiful across the whole of Scandinavia, and almost always work; English instructions are normally posted inside. To make a **direct call** to Britain or North America, dial the international access and country code, wait for the tone, then dial the area code (omitting the first 0 if there is one) and then the subscriber number.

Mobile phones

Most of Scandinavia is on the **mobile phone network**, which means hikers, skiers, climbers and other outdoors enthusiasts can contact someone by phone almost no matter where they are – invaluable if things go wrong. The region's mobile network is on the **GSM** band common to the rest of Europe, Australia and New Zealand. This means that the vast majority of mobile phones from these countries will work here though, if you haven't used your mobile abroad before, you should check with your phone company:

Useful telephone numbers and codes

International calls
Phoning abroad from Scandinavia
To Australia: ☎0061 + area code minus zero + number.
To Canada: ☎001 + area code + number.
To the Republic of Ireland: ☎00353 + area code minus zero + number.
To New Zealand: ☎0064 + area code minus zero + number.
To the UK: ☎0044 + area code minus zero + number.
To the US: ☎001 + area code + number.

Phoning Scandinavia from abroad
Dial your country's international access code, then:
Denmark ☎45 + number
Finland ☎358 + area code (without the zero), then the number
Norway ☎47 + number
Sweden ☎46 + area code (without the zero), then the number

some mobiles are, for example, barred from international use. It's also a good idea to check **call charges** as costs can be excruciating – particularly irritating is the supplementary charge that you pay on incoming calls. However, purchasing a **local SIM card** in any of the Scandinavian countries will reduce call charges dramatically; for more on this, see the "Mail and communications" sections of individual country "Basics".

Things are more complicated (and expensive) for Canadians and Americans. The **North American mobile network** is not compatible with the GSM system, so you'll need a **tri-band phone** which is able to switch from one band to the other.

Finally, international **texting** (SMS) via the GSM band is – or can be – dead easy. Depending on the mobile, there's often no need to tap in international codes, you just send the message as you would back home. Again, your phone company will, if necessary, offer advice and details of charges.

Health

Under reciprocal health arrangements involving members of the European Union (EU), nationals of all EU countries are entitled to free or discounted medical treatment within the respective public health care systems of Finland, Denmark and Sweden. Norway is not in the EU, but it is in the EEA (European Economic Area), under the terms of which nationals of all EU countries are also entitled to free or discounted medical treatment.

Non-EU nationals have to pay for medical attention in full and should take out their own medical insurance to travel to Scandinavia. EU/EEA citizens may want to consider private health insurance too, as it will cover the cost of items not within the EU's scheme, such as dental treatment and repatriation on medical grounds. That said, most private insurance policies don't cover prescription charges – their "excesses" are usually greater than the cost of the medicines. The more worthwhile policies promise to sort matters out before you pay (rather than after) in the case of major expense; if you do have to pay upfront, get and keep the receipts. For more on insurance, see p.42.

Seeking medical treatment

Across Scandinavia, your local pharmacy, tourist office or hotel should be able to provide the address of an **English-speaking doctor** or **dentist**. If you're seeking treatment under EU/EEA **reciprocal public** health agreements, double-check that the doctor/ dentist is working within (and seeing you as) a patient of the relevant public healthcare system. This being the case, you'll receive free or reduced-cost/government-subsidised treatment just as the locals do; any fees must be paid upfront, or at least at the end of your treatment, and are non-refundable – a good reason to have a private insurance policy. Sometimes you will be asked to produce documentation to prove you are eligible for EU/EEA health care, sometimes no-one bothers, but technically at least you should have your passport and your **European Health Insurance Card** (**EHIC**) to hand. The EHIC, the successor to the old E111 form, is issued in Britain at post offices, or online at ⓦwww.dh.gov.uk; in Ireland from local Health Boards or online at ⓦwww.ehic.ie. Allow a couple of weeks for your application to be processed. If, on the other hand, you have a travel insurance policy covering medical expenses, you can seek treatment in either the public or private health sectors, the main issue being whether – at least in major cases – you have to pay the costs upfront and then wait for reimbursement or not.

At almost all of Scandinavia's hospitals and clinics, there will be someone who speaks English. For **medical emergencies**, call ☏112.

Insurance

Most people will want to take out some kind of travel insurance. A typical policy usually provides cover for loss of baggage, tickets and – up to a certain limit – cash or cheques, as well as cancellation or curtailment of your journey.

Before paying for a new policy, however, it's worth checking whether you are already covered. Some all-risks home insurance policies may cover your possessions when overseas, and many private medical schemes include cover when abroad. In Canada, provincial health plans usually provide partial cover for medical mishaps overseas, while holders of official student/teacher/youth cards in Canada and the US are entitled to meagre accident coverage and hospital in-patient benefits. Students will often find that their student health coverage extends during the vacations and for one term beyond the date of last enrolment.

After exhausting the possibilities above, you might want to contact a specialist travel insurance company, or consider the travel insurance deal we offer (see box below). Most travel insurance policies exclude so-called dangerous sports unless an extra premium is paid: in Scandinavia this can

mean **hiking**, **whitewater rafting**, **climbing** and **skiing**, though probably not kayaking. Check carefully that any insurance policy you are considering will cover all of the activities you'll be doing. Many policies can be chopped and changed to exclude coverage you don't need – for example, sickness and accident benefits can often be excluded or included at all. If you do take medical coverage, ascertain whether benefits will be paid as treatment proceeds or only after return home, and whether there is a 24-hour medical emergency number. When securing baggage cover, make sure that the per-article limit – typically under £500 – will cover your most valuable possession. If you need to make a **claim**, you should keep receipts for medicines and medical treatment, and in the event you have anything stolen, you must obtain an official statement from the local police.

Rough Guides travel insurance

Rough Guides has teamed up with Columbus Direct to offer **travel insurance** that can be tailored to suit your needs. Readers can choose from many different travel insurance products, including a low-cost **backpacker** option for long stays; a **short break** option for city getaways; a typical **holiday package** option; and many others. There are also annual **multi-trip** policies for those who travel regularly, with variable levels of cover available. Different sports and activities (trekking, skiing, etc) can be covered if required on most policies.

Rough Guides travel insurance is available to the residents of 36 different countries with different language options to choose from via our website – ⓦ www.roughguides insurance.com – where you can also purchase the insurance. Alternatively, UK residents can call ☏0800/083 9507; US citizens ☏1-800/749-4922; and Australians ☏1-300/669 999. All other nationalities should call ☏+44 870/890 2843.

Information and maps

Before you leave, it may be worth contacting national tourist boards for free maps, timetables, accommodation listings and brochures – though don't go mad, since much of what you'll need can easily be obtained once you arrive. There's also a wealth of information available online – we've included a selection of general sites below, but country-specific lists are given in the relevant "Basics" sections of the Guide.

Almost every Scandinavian town (and even some villages) has a **tourist office**, where you can pick up free town plans and information, brochures and other bumph. Many book private rooms (sometimes youth hostel beds), rent bikes, sell local discount cards and change money. During summer, they're open daily until late evening; out of high season, shop hours are more usual, and in winter they're sometimes closed at weekends. You'll find full details of individual offices throughout the Guide.

National tourist board offices

Australia

For all four countries, contact the appropriate embassy or consulate in Australia (see p.37), or check ⓦ www.scandinavia.com.au.

Britain

Denmark 55 Sloane St, London SW1X 9SY ☎020/7259 5959, ⓦwww.visitdenmark.com.
Finland 3rd floor, 30–35 Pall Mall, London SW1Y 5LP ☎020/7365 2512, ⓦ www.visitfinland.com.
Norway 5th floor, Charles House, 5 Lower Regent St, London SW1Y 4LR ☎0906/302 2003 (premium-rate line), ⓦwww.visitnorway.com. No walk-in service.
Sweden 5 Upper Montague St, London W1H 2AG ☎0800/3080 3080 (free), ⓦwww.visitsweden.com.

Canada

For all four countries, contact the appropriate embassy or consulate in Canada (see p.37), or check ⓦ www.goscandinavia.com.

Ireland

No tourist board offices, but the embassies or consulates in Ireland (see p.38) handle tourist information.

New Zealand

For all four countries, contact the appropriate embassy or consulate in New Zealand (see p.37).

USA

Denmark Danish Tourist Board, 655 Third Ave, 18th Floor, New York, NY 10017 ☎1-212/885-9700, ⓦwww.visitdenmark.com.
Finland Finnish Tourist Board, 655 Third Ave, New York, NY 10017 ☎1-800-FIN-INFO, ⓦwww .gofinland.org.
Norway Norwegian Tourist Board, 655 Third Ave, New York, NY 10022 ☎1-212/885-9700, ⓦwww .norway.org.
Sweden PO Box 4649, Grand Central Station, New York, NY10163–4649 ☎1-212/886-9700, ⓦwww .visitsweden.com.

Scandinavia online

ⓦ **www.goscandinavia.com** The official website of the Scandinavian Tourist Board in North America, offering a general introduction to Scandinavia, latest travel deals and links to tourist board sites of each country.
ⓦ **www.itv.se/boreale/Sámieng.htm** Comprehensive introduction to the Sámi people and their culture, with features on history, music, art and reindeer.
ⓦ **www.santaclausoffice.fi** Email Santa directly in his den in Finnish Lapland.
ⓦ **www.scandinavia.com.au** Excellent source of info with useful sections on current events and exhibitions, plus helpful advice on where to go for best flight deals. Australia-orientated, as you might expect from the domain name.

Maps

The **maps** in this book should be adequate for most purposes, but drivers, cyclists and hikers will require something more detailed. Tourist offices often give out reasonably useful local road maps and town plans, but anything more detailed will require a trip to a bookshop. For **Scandinavia** as a whole, Cappelen (✆ www.cappelen.no) produces a good-quality road map on a scale of 1:800,000, though this can be hard to get hold of outside the region, in which case plumb for the more readily available Freytag & Berndt version (✆ www.freytagberndt.com). For really detailed plans of the **capital cities**, it's Cappelen again – their 1:10,000 city map series is outstanding, as are their maps of all four Scandinavian countries: **Denmark** (1:300,000); **Norway** (1:325,000); **Sweden** (1:700,000); and **Finland** (1:800,000).

If you're **hiking**, you'll need something even more detailed – a scale of 1:50,000 is the minimum requirement, 1:25,000 even better. Across the whole of Scandinavia, you can expect that tourist offices and bookshops in all the larger towns and cities as well as all the popular hiking areas will sell a wide range of adequate to excellent hiking maps, covering either their locality or the country as a whole.

Map outlets

In the UK and Ireland
Blackwell's Map and Travel Shop ✆ maps .blackwell.co.uk/index.html. Branches all over the UK; check the website for details.
Easons Bookshop 40 Lower O'Connell St, Dublin 1 ☎ 01/858 3800, ✆ www.eason.ie. Branches all over Ireland; call or check the website for details.
John Smith & Son Glasgow Caledonian University Bookshop, 70 Cowcaddens Rd, Glasgow G4 0BA ☎ 0141/332 8173, ✆ www.johnsmith.co.uk. Call or check the website for details of other branches in Scotland and England.
The Map Shop 30a Belvoir St, Leicester LE1 6QH ☎ 0116/247 1400, ✆ www.mapshopleicester.co.uk.
Stanfords 12–14 Long Acre, London WC2E 9LP ☎ 020/7836 1321, ✆ www.stanfords.co.uk. Also at 39 Spring Gardens, Manchester ☎ 0161/831 0250; and 29 Corn St, Bristol ☎ 0117/929 9966.
The Travel Bookshop 13–15 Blenheim Crescent, London W11 2EE ☎ 020/7229 5260, ✆ www .thetravelbookshop.co.uk.

Traveller 55 Grey St, Newcastle-upon-Tyne NE1 6EF ☎ 0191/261 5622, ✆ www.newtraveller.com.

In the US and Canada
Book Passage 51 Tamal Vista Blvd, Corte Madera, CA 94925, and 1 Ferry Building #34, San Francisco, CA 94111☎ 1-800/999-7909 or ☎ 415/927-0960, ✆ www.bookpassage.com.
Complete Traveller Bookstore 199 Madison Ave, New York, NY ☎ 212/685-9007, ✆ www .completetravellerbooks.com.
Distant Lands 56 S Raymond Ave, Pasadena, CA 91105 ☎ 1-800/310-3220, ✆ www.distantlands .com.
Elliot Bay Book Company 101 S Main St, Seattle, WA 98104 ☎ 1-800/962-5311, ✆ www .elliotbaybook.com.
Globe Corner Bookstore 28 Church St, Cambridge, MA 02138 ☎ 1-800/358-6013, ✆ www.globecorner.com.
Longitude Books 115 W 30th St #1206, New York, NY 10001 ☎ 1-800/342-2164, ✆ www .longitudebooks.com.
Map Link 30 S La Patera Lane, Unit 5, Santa Barbara, CA 93117 ☎ 805/692-6777 or 1-800/962-1394, ✆ www.maplink.com.
Map Town 400 5 Ave SW #100, Calgary, AB T2P 0L6 ☎ 1-877/921-6277 or ☎ 403/266-2241, ✆ www.maptown.com.
Travel Bug Bookstore 3065 W Broadway, Vancouver, BC V6K 2G9 ☎ 604/737-1122, ✆ www .travelbugbooks.ca.
World of Maps 1235 Wellington St, Ottawa, ON K1Y 3A3 ☎ 1-800/214-8524 or ☎ 613/724-6776, ✆ www.worldofmaps.com.

In Australia and New Zealand
Mapland (Australia) 372 Little Bourke St, Melbourne ☎ 03/9670 4383, ✆ www.mapland .com.au.
Map Shop (Australia) 6–10 Peel St, Adelaide ☎ 08/8231 2033, ✆ www.mapshop.net.au.
Map World (Australia) 371 Pitt St, Sydney ☎ 02/9261 3601, ✆ www.mapworld.net.au. Also at 900 Hay St, Perth ☎ 08/9322 5733; Jolimont Centre, Canberra ☎ 02/6230 4097; and 1981 Logan Road, Brisbane ☎ 07/3349 6633.
Map World (New Zealand) 173 Gloucester St, Christchurch ☎ 0800/627 967, ✆ www.mapworld .co.nz.

Getting around

Public transport systems are excellent throughout Scandinavia. Denmark, Norway, Sweden and Finland all have a reasonably comprehensive rail network which runs as far north as it dares before plentiful buses take over. Fjords and inordinate amounts of water – lakes, rivers and open sea – make ferries a major form of transport, too.

For more detailed transport information, see each country's individual "Getting Around" section, and the "Travel Details" at the end of every chapter.

By rail

Travel by train in Scandinavia isn't cheap, but a number of **passes** can ease the burden. If you're travelling to and around the region by train, the InterRail and Eurail passes (see "Getting there", p.35) can cut costs. If you're planning to travel by train only within Scandinavia itself, it's well worth considering a **ScanRail pass** (ⓦ www.scanrail.com), which covers all four countries and is available to all, although you do have to buy it before you leave home (for details of outlets see p.34). The ScanRail pass is available for travel on any five days in a two-month period (adult £171/US$291); any ten days in two months (adult £229/US$390) and 21 consecutive days (adult £266/US$453). Over-60s get a discount of about twelve percent on the full price of the pass, children fifty percent and people under 26 and over 12 get thirty percent. There's also an eight-day **ScanRail Drive Pass**, which allows five days of train travel and two days of car rental, with the option of adding additional car days. Note that a small supplement is charged for certain inter-city express trains.

Another possibility is the **EuroDomino Pass**, though it's only available to those who have been resident in Europe for six months. Valid for between three and eight days, it offers unlimited train travel within any one of 28 European countries – including Sweden, Denmark, Finland and Norway – over a one-month period. Like the ScanRail pass, you must purchase it before you leave home, and you'll need to buy a separate pass for each country you travel in. Denmark is the cheapest of the Scandinavian countries, with three days' travel within a month costing £79 and eight days £154, both per adult in standard (or second) class. Norway is the most expensive, with three days costing £134, eight days £253. There are discounts of around 25 percent for those aged 12–26 and 15 percent for the over-60s. For details of outlets, see individual "Basics" sections.

By air

Internal **flights** can be a surprisingly good bargain in Scandinavia, particularly if you're heading for the far north. During July and the early part of August, the main carrier SAS often has cheap set-price tickets to anywhere in mainland Scandinavia plus other discounts for families and young people. Contact SAS offices in Denmark, Norway and Sweden for the latest deals – they're detailed under "Listings" in the accounts of the capital cities. Also, check out the **air passes** on offer before leaving home (see box on p.28).

By car

Car rental is pricey, although some tourist offices do arrange summer deals which can bring the cost down a little. On the whole, expect to pay upwards of £350/US$605 a week for a small car; see each country's "Getting Around" section for specific prices and details of rules of the road and documentation.

You may well find it cheaper, especially if you're travelling from North America, to arrange car hire before you go; airlines sometimes have special deals with rental companies if you book your flight and car through them. For addresses of car rental firms in Scandinavia, see the "Listings" sections of major cities.

Car rental agencies

In North America

Alamo US ☎1-800/462-5266, ⊛www.alamo.com.
Auto Europe US and Canada ☎1-888/223-5555, ⊛www.autoeurope.com.
Europcar US and Canada ☎1-877/940 6900, ⊛www.europcar.com.
Europe by Car US ☎1-800/223-1516, ⊛www.europebycar.com.
Hertz US ☎1-800/654-3131, Canada ☎1-800/263-0600; ⊛www.hertz.com.
National US and Canada ☎1-800/962-7070, ⊛www.nationalcar.com.

In Britain

Europcar ☎0870/607 5000, ⊛www.europcar.co.uk.
National ☎0870/536 5365, ⊛www.nationalcar.co.uk.
Hertz ☎0870/844 8844, ⊛www.hertz.co.uk.
Holiday Autos ☎0870/400 0099, ⊛www.holidayautos.co.uk.

In Ireland

Europcar Northern Ireland ☎028/9442 3444, Republic of Ireland ☎01/614 2888, ⊛www.europcar.ie.
Hertz Republic of Ireland ☎01/676 7476, ⊛www.hertz.ie.
Holiday Autos Republic of Ireland ☎01/872 9366, ⊛www.holidayautos.ie.
Thrifty Republic of Ireland ☎1800/515 800, ⊛www.thrifty.ie.

In Australia

Europcar ☎1300/131 390, ⊛www.deltaeuropcar.com.au.
Hertz ☎13 30 39 or 03/9698 2555, ⊛www.hertz.com.au.
Holiday Autos ☎1300/554 432, ⊛www.holidayautos.com.au.
National ☎13 10 45, ⊛www.nationalcar.com.au.
Thrifty ☎1300/367 227, ⊛www.thrifty.com.au.

In New Zealand

Hertz ☎0800/654 321, ⊛www.hertz.co.nz.
Holiday Autos ☎0800/144 040, ⊛www.holidayautos.co.nz.
National ☎0800/800 115 or 03/366 5574, ⊛www.nationalcar.co.nz.
Thrifty ☎09/309 0111, ⊛www.thrifty.co.nz.

Accommodation

Accommodation is almost certainly going to be your major daily expense in Scandinavia. If you plan ahead, however, there are a number of ways to avoid paying over the (already high) odds. Youth hostels, campsites and cabins are the obvious budget options, and not just for tourists – they're popular with Scandinavians, too. There's also a series of discount passes available, for use in hotel chains all over Scandinavia.

Hotels

Scandinavian **hotels** are hardly ever inexpensive, but there again they often compare favourably with equivalent accommodation in, say, London or New York. Lots of Scandinavian hotels, usually dependent on business travellers, drop their prices drastically at weekends and during the summer holiday period, so it's always worth enquiring at the tourist office about special local deals. The major cities also feature cheap "packages", usually involving a night's hotel accommodation and a free city discount card. More details, and a guide to prices, are given under each country's "Accommodation" section, as well as under the specific town and city accounts.

Some Scandinavia-wide hotel chains operate a discount or **hotel cheque system** which you can organize before you leave. You either purchase cheques in advance, redeemable against a night's accommodation in any hotel belonging to the particular chain, or you buy a **hotel pass**, which entitles you to a hefty discount on normal room rates. There are a bewildering number of schemes available, but most only operate from June to September and all offer basically the same deal: consult your travel agent or one of the national tourist boards for further details.

Hostels

Joining the **Hostelling International** (HI) association gives you access to what is sometimes the only budget accommodation available in a particular town or village. Non-members can use HI hostels but will pay slightly more – the difference may add up to a sizeable sum over a couple of weeks, considering the low cost of annual membership. You'll also need a **sheet sleeping bag**, the only kind allowed in HI hostels. They can either be rented at the hostels or bought at camping shops. If you're planning to cook for yourself using youth hostel kitchens, bear in mind that many don't provide pots, pans and utensils – take at least the basic equipment with you.

You can join Hostelling International either at home (for addresses, see below) or in Scandinavia itself (the addresses of the relevant national hostelling organizations are given in each country's "Accommodation" section). For a complete listing of Scandinavian hostels, consult the annually-produced *Hostelling International Guide*, available from hostel associations and online via their websites.

Youth hostel associations

In Australia
Australia Youth Hostels Association ☏ 02/9261 1111, ⓦ www.yha.com.au.

In Canada
Hostelling International Canada ☏ 1-800/663 5777 or 613/237 7884, ⓦ www.hihostels.ca.

In England and Wales
Youth Hostel Association (YHA) ☏ 0870/770 8868, ⓦ www.yha.org.uk.

In Ireland
Irish Youth Hostel Association ☏ 01/830 4555, ⓦ www.irelandyha.org.

In New Zealand
Youth Hostelling Association New Zealand ☏ 0800/278 299 or 03/379 9970, ⓦ www.yha.co.nz.

In Northern Ireland
Hostelling International Northern Ireland ☏ 028/9032 4733, ⓦ www.hini.org.uk.

In Scotland
Scottish Youth Hostel Association ☏ 0870/155 3255, ⓦ www.syha.org.uk.

In the US
Hostelling International-American Youth Hostels ☏ 301/495-1240, ⓦ www.hiayh.org.

Camping

Camping is hugely popular in Scandinavia. If you're planning to use your tent a lot, a **Scandinavian camping card** is, at just £7/$14, a good and inexpensive investment. The card, which you can buy at the first member site you visit, gives discounts at member sites and serves as useful identification – indeed it is obligatory on some sites. Many campsites will take it instead of making you surrender your passport during your stay, and it covers you for third-party insurance when camping.

Further details on camping are given in each country's "Accommodation" section, but one general point to note is that most campsites in Scandinavia have furnished **cabins**; if you intend to use these, take a sleeping bag as bedding is not usually provided.

Crime and personal safety

Scandinavia is one of the most peaceful corners of Europe. You will find that public places are generally well lit and secure, most people are genuinely friendly and helpful, and that street crime and hassle relatively rare.

It would be foolish, however, to assume that problems don't exist. Each of the capital cities has its share of **petty crime**, often committed by drug addicts after easy money. Keep tabs on your cash and passport (and don't leave anything visible in your car when you leave it) and you should have little reason to visit the **police**. If you do, you'll find them courteous, concerned, and, perhaps most importantly, usually able to speak English. If you have something stolen, make sure you get a **police report** – essential if you are to make an insurance claim.

As for **offences** you might commit, being **drunk** on the streets can get you arrested, and **drinking and driving** is treated especially rigorously. **Drug** offences, too, meet with the same harsh attitude that prevails throughout most of Europe.

Gay Scandinavia

For both gays and lesbians, Scandinavia comprises one of the most liberated and tolerant regions in Europe. Gays are rarely discriminated against in law, and the age of consent is almost uniformly the same as for heterosexuals – fifteen in Denmark and Sweden, sixteen in Finland and Norway. Nevertheless – and perhaps as a result of this very tolerance – there is not much of a scene outside the four capitals; the websites of the national associations are all a useful starting point for further information and listings.

Gay and lesbian organizations in Scandinavia

Denmark
The Danish Association for Gays and Lesbians (*Landsforeningen for bøsser og Lebiske*) has its headquarters in Copenhagen at Teglgårdsstræde 13. Their website (ⓦ www.lbl.dk), which is in Danish and English (click on "gay guide"), provides general information, but for details of the scene you'll need to go to an affiliated website, ⓦ www.gayguide.dk.

Finland
In English and Finnish, the website of SETA (ⓦ www.seta.fi), the Organization for Sexual Equality in Finland, at Hietalahdenkatu 2 B 16,

FI-001800 Helsinki, provides general background information and signposts other Finnish websites that focus on the scene.

Norway
Norway's strong and politically effective gay and lesbian organization, the LLH (*Landsforeningen for lesbisk og homofil frigjøring*), has a national HQ in Oslo at Kongensgate 12 (ⓣ 23 10 39 39). Their website, ⓦ www.llh.no, is Norwegian-only, but there are links to other affiliated sites giving details of gay and lesbian events.

Sweden
Riksförbundet för sexuelt likaberattigande, Sweden's national gay and lesbian organization, operate a

Swedish-only website (@www.rfsl.se), though many of the links (to Gay Pride etc) are self-explanatory. They can be contacted at Sveavägen 57–59, 10126 Stockholm (☎08/457 13 00).

Contacts for gay and lesbian travellers

In the UK

@**www.gaytravel.co.uk** Online gay and lesbian travel agent, offering good deals on all types of holiday. Also lists gay- and lesbian-friendly hotels around the world.
Dream Waves Holidays ☎0870/042 2475, @www.gayholidaysdirect.com. Specializes in exclusively gay holidays, including skiing trips.
Madison Travel ☎01273/202 532, @www.madisontravel.co.uk. Established travel agents specializing in packages to gay- and lesbian-friendly mainstream destinations, and also to gay/lesbian destinations.
Respect Holidays ☎0870/770 0169, @www.respect-holidays.co.uk. Offers exclusively gay packages to all popular European resorts.

In the US and Canada

Damron ☎1-800/462-6654 or 415/255-0404, @www.damron.com. Publisher of the *Men's*
Travel Guide, a pocket-sized yearbook full of listings of hotels, bars, clubs and resources for gay men; the *Women's Traveler*, which provides similar listings for lesbians; and *Damron Accommodations*, which provides detailed listings of over 1000 accommodations for gays and lesbians worldwide. All of these titles are offered at a discount on the website. No specific city guides – everything is incorporated in the yearbooks.
gaytravel.com ☎1-800/GAY-TRAVEL, @www.gaytravel.com. The premier site for trip planning, bookings, and general information about international gay and lesbian travel – including city breaks to Copenhagen and Stockholm.
International Gay & Lesbian Travel Association ☎1-800/448-8550 or 954/776-2626, @www.iglta.org. Trade group that can provide a list of gay- and lesbian-owned or -friendly travel agents, accommodation and other travel businesses.

In Australia and New Zealand

Gay and Lesbian Tourism Australia @www.galta.com.au. Directory and links for gay and lesbian travel worldwide.
Tearaway Travel ☎1800/664 440 or 03/9510 6644, @www.tearaway.com. Gay-specific business dealing with international and domestic travel.

Travellers with disabilities

As you might expect, the Scandinavians have adopted a progressive and thoughtful approach to the issues surrounding disability and, as a result, there are decent facilities for travellers with disabilities across the whole region. An increasing number of hotels, hostels and campsites are equipped for disabled visitors, and are credited as such in the tourist literature by means of the standard wheelchair-in-a-box icon. Furthermore, on most main routes the trains have special carriages with wheelchair space, hydraulic lifts and toilets for the disabled; domestic flights either cater for or provide assistance to disabled customers; and new ships on all ferry routes have lifts and cabins designed for disabled people.

In the cities and larger towns, many **restaurants** and most **museums** and public places are wheelchair-accessible, and although facilities are not so advanced in the countryside, things are improving rapidly. Drivers will find that most motorway **service stations** are wheelchair-accessible and that, if you have a UK-registered vehicle, the disabled **car parking badge** is honoured. Note also that several of the larger car rental companies have modified vehicles available. On a less positive note, city pavements can be uneven and difficult to negotiate and, inevitably, winter snow and ice can make things much, much worse.

Getting to Scandinavia should be relatively straightforward too. Most airlines and shipping companies provide assistance to disabled travellers, while some also have specific facilities, such as DFDS Scandinavian Seaways ferries' specially adapted cabins.

Planning a holiday

Contacts for travellers with disabilities

In Denmark

The Danish Council of Organizations of Disabled People (*De Samvirkende invalideorganisationer*) Bogensegade 8, Copenhagen ☎3526 7035, ⊛www .handicap.dk. National umbrella organization for a coalition of disability groups with offices all over Denmark – check the website for local contact details; the local offices act as referral agencies.
⊛**www.visitdenmark.com** The thorough and extensive "Accessible Denmark" section within the Danish tourist board website has features on everything from transportation to services and organizations. Supporting brochures too can be ordered online.

In Finland

The Finnish Association of People with Mobility Disabilities (*Invalidiliitto*) Kumpulantie 1A, 00520 Helsinki (☎09/613 191, ⊛www .invalidiliitto.fi. A useful starting point for travellers with mobility concerns.

In Norway

Norwegian Association of the Disabled (Norges Handikapforbund) Schweigaardsgt 12, Oslo ☎24 10 24 00, ⊛www.nhf.no; postal address Postboks 9217, Grønland, 0134 Oslo. This organization produces a wide range of useful information, from general guidance on accessibility across the whole of the country through to comments about the major hotel chains and transport. The website is particularly good, and has an English-language version.

In Sweden

The Federation of Disabled Persons (*De Handikappades Riksforbund*; DHR) Katrinebergsvägen 6, Box 47305, 100 74 Stockholm ☎86 85 80 00, ⊛www.dhr.se. An excellent source of information and advice; the website is in English and Swedish.

In the UK and Ireland

Access Travel 6 The Hillock, Astley, Lancashire M29 7GW ☎01942/888 844, ⊛www.access -travel.co.uk. Tour operator that can arrange flights,

transfer and accommodation. This is a small business, personally checking out places before recommending.
Holiday Care 2nd floor, Imperial Building, Victoria Rd, Horley, Surrey RH6 7PZ ☎0845/124 9971 or 0208/760 0072, ⊛www.holidaycare.org.uk. Provides free lists of accessible accommodation abroad – including Scandinavian destinations. Information on financial help for holidays available too.
Irish Wheelchair Association Blackheath Drive, Clontarf, Dublin 3 ☎01/818 6400, ⊛www.iwa .ie. Useful information on travelling abroad with a wheelchair.
Tripscope The Vasapll Centre, Gill Ave, Bristol BS16 2QQ ☎0845/758 5641 ⊛www.tripscope .org.uk. This registered charity provides a national telephone information service offering free advice on UK and international transport for those with a mobility problem.

In the US and Canada

Access-Able ⊛www.access-able.com. Online resource for travellers with disabilities.
Directions Unlimited 123 Green Lane, Bedford Hills, NY 10507 ☎1-800/533-5343 or 914/241-1700. Travel agency specializing in bookings for people with disabilities.
Mobility International USA 451 Broadway, Eugene, OR 97401 ☎541/343-1284, ⊛www .miusa.org. Information and referral services, access guides, tours and exchange programmes.
Society for the Advancement of Travelers with Handicaps 347 5th Ave, New York, NY 10016 ☎212/447-7284, ⊛www.sath.org. Non-profit educational organization that has actively represented travellers with disabilities since 1976. Annual membership $45; $30 for students and seniors.
Wheels Up! ☎1-888/38-WHEELS, ⊛www .wheelsup.com. Provides discounted airfare, tour and cruise prices for disabled travellers, and publishes a free monthly newsletter. Comprehensive website.

In Australia and New Zealand

ACROD (Australian Council for Rehabilitation of the Disabled) PO Box 60, Curtin ACT 2605; ☎02/6282 4333 (also TTY), ⊛www.acrod.org.au. Provides lists of travel agencies and tour operators for people with disabilities.
Disabled Persons Assembly 4/173–175 Victoria St, Wellington, New Zealand ☎04/801 9100 (also TTY), ⊛www.dpa.org.nz. Resource centre with lists of travel agencies and tour operators for people with disabilities.

Outdoor activities

Scandinavia is a wonderful place if you love the great outdoors, with marvellous hiking, fishing, climbing and skiing to name but four of the most popular pursuits. Even better, you won't find the countryside overcrowded – there's plenty of space to get away from it all, almost everywhere, from one end of the region to the other. As you might expect, any kind of hunting is forbidden without a permit, and freshwater fishing always requires a special licence as is often the case with sea fishing too. Local tourist offices can fill you in on all the rules and regulations.

Hiking

Scandinavia offers the ultimate in **hiking** experiences – a landscape of rugged mountains, icy glaciers and deep green fjords, much of it far from the nearest road. Many of the best hiking areas have been set aside as **national parks**, with information centres, lodges and huts dotted along well-marked trails. Huts are usually run by national or local hiking organizations, and you will have to become a member to be able to use them or else pay premium rates; joining is not expensive. Tourist offices in hiking areas supply maps and leaflets describing local routes, but serious hiking requires proper maps – see p.44 for map suppliers. Note also that in many areas, solo hiking is strongly inadvisable; always take local advice about local trail, camping rules and weather conditions.

As far as **equipment** goes, for day walking you'll need warm clothing and gloves, waterproofs, and sun and mosquito protection; on all but the easiest and shortest hikes, a compass is a good idea. For long-distance treks you'll also need a sleeping bag, medical kit and a torch, plus a pair of sturdy, comfortable boots. Note that Camping Gaz is only available from selected outlets in Scandinavia – details from national tourist boards – so take your own supply. For hiking campers, a plastic survival bag keeps you and your pack dry.

If you're planning to camp, you should be aware of some specific **ground rules**. The landscape is there for everyone's use and camping rough is legal much of the time – but the Scandinavians are concerned to protect the environment both from the damage

caused by excessive tourism and the potential disasters that can result from ignorance or thoughtlessness.

Don't **light fires** anywhere other than at designated spots – and even these shouldn't be used in times of drought. **Tents** may only be placed on marked sites or, on some hikes, in other designated areas. When camping, do not break tree branches or leave **rubbish**; and try not to disturb nesting **birds**, especially in the spring.

In the northern reaches of Scandinavia, be wary of frightening **reindeer herds**, since if they scatter it can mean several extra days' work for the herder; also, avoid tramping over moss-covered stretches of moorland – the reindeer's staple diet. **Picking flowers**, **berries and mushrooms** is also usually prohibited in the north. If you are going to pick and eat anything, however, it's a wise idea, post-Chernobyl, to check on the latest advice from the authorities – tourist offices should know the score.

Finally, a word of warning about **glaciers**. They may seem slow-moving and innocuous, but they aren't. Never climb a glacier without a guide, never walk under one and always heed the instructions at the site. Guided crossings can be terrific; local tourist offices and hiking organizations have details – see the relevant accounts in the Guide.

Cycling, rafting and canoeing

Several package tour operators (see p.29 and p.32) offer **cycling tours** within Scandinavia – Denmark in particular is ideal for a cycling holiday, given its largely flat landscape and excellent network of cycle lanes covering more than 10,000km, all of them marked on the detailed cycling maps available from local bookshops and tourist offices.

Scandinavia's rivers and coastline afford ample opportunity for **canoeing**, **rafting** and **sea-kayaking**. Norway holds some of the wildest rivers on the continent, while Sweden, in particular, is criss-crossed with canoeing routes which have numerous places to stop and camp along the way, and all grades of difficulty from gentle paddling along winding rivers to white-water thrills. Scores of companies offer guided excursions in all these outdoor pursuits – see the Guide for further details.

Winter sports

Aside from the cities, which maintain their usual roster of activities and attractions, though sometimes with reduced opening hours, the big incentive for coming to Scandinavia in winter is the range of **winter sports** available: skiing, snowboarding,

dog-sledding, tobogganing, ice-skating, ski-doo safaris and ice fishing, to name a few. All are easy to arrange after arrival – in the first instance, contact the local tourist office.

Skiing

Scandinavia is an excellent place to ski, though **skiing** packages here tend to be more expensive than other European destinations. Even if you can't afford a package it's always easy to arrange a few days' cross-country skiing wherever you are – there are even ski runs within the city boundaries of Oslo and Stockholm, and plenty of places to rent equipment. Norway is particularly well equipped for **cross-country skiing**, with a large network of special trails (many floodlit after dark) of varying lengths, which often have cabins along the route in which to overnight. Check out the tourist board websites for each country (see p.43) for more information and details on the various skiing associations, who will be able to recommend routes and destinations matched to your trip.

Books

Precious few travellers have written in English about the joys of journeying around Scandinavia, though you might always dig out a copy of an old Baedeker's Norway and Sweden, if only for the phrasebook, from which you can learn how to pronounce "We must rope ourselves together to cross this glacier." Neither has Scandinavian history been a major preoccupation – with the notable exception of the Vikings, who have attracted the attention of a veritable raft of historians and translators whose works have focused on the surviving Sagas, a rich body of work mostly written in Iceland in the ninth and tenth centuries. Scandinavian fiction is, however, an entirely different matter, with a flood of translations appearing on the market, a charge that has been led by the immaculate crime novels of the Swede Henning Mankell.

Of the **publishers**, Peter Owen (@ www .peterowen.com) produces fine new translations of modern Scandinavian novels, as does Norvik Press (@ www.llt.uea.ac.uk /norvik_press), who also maintain an excellent back catalogue of classic Scandinavian novels and plays and some Scandinavian literary criticism. Finally, *The Babel Guide to Scandinavian Fiction in Translation* by Paul Binding reviews books available in English by leading Scandinavian writers – both classic and modern – though it could do with being updated – it was published in 1999.

Most of the books listed below should be readily available, though some are currently **out of print** (denoted o/p) – even these, though, are often available via websites such as Amazon. Titles marked with the 🏃 symbol are particularly recommended. For books by specific Scandinavian authors or titles related to specific countries see the relevant "Books" section for each country (Denmark p.90, Norway p.241, Sweden p.455 & Finland p.677).

Travel and general

Jeremy Cherfas *The Hunting of Whale*. Subtitled "A tragedy that must end", this is a convincing condemnation of whaling and all those – like Norway – involved in it.

Christer Elfving & Petra de Hamer *New Scandinavian Cooking*. A cook's tour through Scandinavia's capital cities mixing history, culinary trends and tips on the hottest chefs and restaurants with delicious modern recipes.

Tony Griffiths *Scandinavia*. A wide-ranging look at the cultural, artistic and political developments and exchanges of the last two centuries that have helped shape the Scandinavian psyche.

Sven Lindqvist *Bench Press*. Delightful little book delving into the nature of weight training – and the Swedish/Scandinavian attitude to it. Wry and perceptive cultural commentary.

Christopher Moseley, ed. *From Baltic Shores*. Anthology of contemporary short stories from Denmark, Finland, Sweden, Estonia, Latvia and Lithuania. Winter and the harshness of the climate are a recurring theme.

Ben Nimmo *In Forkbeard's Wake: Coasting Around Scandinavia*. Light and lively account of the author's sailing trip around Scandinavia, brimming with sailing mishaps and encounters with Nordic types – divers, fishermen, archeologists and a drunk Swedish dentist. An all too rare modern travel book on the area.

🏃 **Christoph Ransmayr** *The Terrors of Ice and Darkness*. Clever mingling of fact and fiction as the book's main character follows the route of the 1873 Austro-Hungarian expedition to the Arctic. A story of obsession and, ultimately, madness.

Roger Took *Running with Reindeer*. A thoughtful account of Took's extended visit to – and explorations of – Russia's Kola Peninsula in the 1990s, with much to say about the Sámi and their current predicaments.

Mary Wollstonecraft *A Short Residence in Sweden, Norway and Denmark*. A curiously self-indulgent account of Wollstonecraft's three-month solo sojourn through southern Scandinavia in 1795.

General history

T.K. Derry *A History of Scandinavia*. Authoritative history from the Stone Age to the 1990s. Rather dense and scholarly, but one of the only recent works on the topic in paperback.

Tony Griffiths *Scandinavia: At War with Trolls – A Modern History from the Napoleonic Era to the Third Millennium*. Engaging title for an engaging, well written and well researched book covering its subject in a very manageable 320 pages. First published in 2004.

Knut Helle et al *The Cambridge History of Scandinavia*. Comprehensive history, from the Stone Age onwards in three whopping (and expensive) volumes. No stone is left unturned.

John van der Kiste *Northern Crowns: Kings of Modern Scandinavia*. All you ever wanted to know about the Scandinavian monarchies, from the nineteenth century to the present day.

Chris Mann *Hitler's Arctic War*. A new account of one of the most critical – yet often overlooked – campaigns of World War II, chronicling the German campaigns in the inhospitable landscape of the Arctic both on sea and land.

P.V. Glob *The Bog People*. A fascinating study of the various Iron Age bodies discovered fully preserved in northwestern European peat bogs, most of them in Denmark. Excellent, if ghoulish, photographs.

Geoffrey Parker *The Thirty Years' War*. First published in the 1980s, and subsequently reprinted on several occasions, this book provides the authoritative account of the pan-European war that so deeply affected Scandinavia in general and Sweden in particular. Superbly written and researched.

Alexander Rumble, ed *The Reign of Cnut*. The king of much of Scandinavia and England, Cnut was the dominant figure in northern Europe in the early eleventh century. This scholarly study examines the man and his milieu.

The Vikings and Norse mythology

Johannes Brøndsted *The Vikings* (o/p). Classic and immensely readable account of the Viking period,

with valuable sections on social and cultural life, art, religious beliefs and customs. Out of print, but still easy to get hold of.

H.R. Ellis Davidson *The Gods and Myths of Northern Europe*. A handy, first-rate companion to the sagas, this "who's who" of Norse mythology includes some useful reviews of the more obscure gods.

John Haywood *Encyclopaedia of the Viking Age*. Well-selected and well-written accounts of everything to do with the Vikings and their era – from Adam of Bremen to York.

Gwyn Jones *A History of the Vikings*. Superbly crafted, erudite account of the Vikings, with sections on every aspect of their history and culture. The same author also wrote *Scandinavian Legends and Folk Tales* (o/p), an excellent and enjoyable analysis of its subject.

F. Donald Logan *The Vikings in History*. Scholarly – and radical – re-examination of the Vikings' impact on medieval Europe, indispensable for the Vikingophile.

Andrew Orchard *Cassell's Dictionary of Norse Myth and Legend*. Thorough guide to the complete cast of Scandinavian gods, trolls, heroes and monsters, complete with the social and historical background to the myths and coverage of topics such as burial rites, sacrificial practices and runes.

Jane Smiley et al *The Sagas of the Icelanders*. Easy to read translations of all the main sagas – galloping tales of derring-do from medieval Iceland. The index makes it an excellent reference book too.

Snorri Sturluson *Egil's Saga*, *Laxdaela Saga*, *Njal's Saga*, and *King Harald's Saga*. Icelandic sagas, written in the early years of the thirteenth century, but relating tales of ninth- and tenth-century derring-do. There's clan warfare in the Laxdaela and Njal sagas, more bloodthirstiness in Egil's, and a bit more biography in King Harald's, penned to celebrate one of the last and most ferocious Viking chieftains – Harald Hardråda (see p.231).

Directory

Addresses In Scandinavia addresses are always written with the number after the street name. In multi-floored buildings, the ground floor is always counted as the first floor, the first the second and so on.

Alcohol Except in Denmark, alcohol is very expensive throughout Scandinavia.

Books You'll find English-language titles in almost every bookshop, though at about twice the price you'd pay at home.

Left luggage There are luggage lockers in most train stations, ferry terminals and long-distance bus stations.

Mosquitoes Don't forget the insect repellent if you are venturing into the great outdoors during the summer.

Newspapers You'll find most British newspapers (and the occasional *International Herald Tribune* and *USA Today*) on sale in every capital city and many of the region's larger towns.

Radio The BBC's World Service can be picked up right across Scandinavia. Frequencies and schedules are listed on the BBC website (@ www.bbc.co.uk/world-service). The same applies to Radio Canada (@ www.rcinet.ca) and Voice of America (@ www.voa.gov).

Time Denmark, Sweden and Norway are one hour ahead of the UK and six to nine hours ahead of the continental USA; Finland is two hours ahead of the UK and seven to ten hours ahead of the continental USA.

Guide

Guide

Denmark

Denmark highlights

* **Smørrebrød** Rye bread loaded with Danish delicacies, these traditional open sandwiches are out of this world. See p.74

* **Christiania** Declared a "free city" In 1971, quirky Christiania is a fascinating place for a wander. See p.114

* **Ny Carlsberg Glyptotek** This gallery of Greek, Roman and Egyptian art and artefacts boasts one of the biggest (and best) collections of Etruscan art outside Italy. See p.115

* **Louisiana Museum of Modern Art** A marvellous collection set in an unusual building overlooking a sculpture park and the waters of the Øresund. See p.129

* **Island-hopping, Funen** Quaint villages and beautiful sandy beaches are the main draws of southern Funen's archipelago. See p.149

* **Danish bakeries** Every town has a bakery, selling the fresh-baked bread that's the foundation of a good Danish breakfast and, of course, delicious pastries. See p.156

* **Hindsholm Peninsula** This remote and beautiful area is best explored by bike. See p.158

* **Moesgård Prehistoric Museum, Århus** Get the lowdown on Danish civilizations since the Stone Age. See p.185

* **Djursland beaches** The white-sand beaches around Ebeltoft, Grenå and Fjellerup are some of Denmark's finest. See p.190

△ caption caption

Introduction and Basics

Delicately balanced between Scandinavia proper and mainland Europe, Denmark is a difficult country to pin down. In many ways it shares the characteristics of both regions: it's an EU member, and has prices and drinking laws that are broadly in line with the rest of Europe. But Danish social policies and style of government are distinctly Scandinavian: social benefits and the standard of living are high, and its politics are very much that of the consensus.

It may seem hard to believe, but it wasn't so long ago that tiny Denmark ruled a good chunk of northern Europe. Since imperialist times, however, the country's energies have been turned inwards, towards the development of a well-organized but rarely over-bureaucratic society that does much to foster a pride in Danish arts and culture and uphold the freedoms of the individual. Indeed, once here, it becomes easy to share the Danes' puzzlement as to why other small, formerly Empire-owning nations haven't followed their example.

Where to go

While Denmark is the easiest Scandinavian country in which to travel – both in terms of cost and distance – the landscape itself is the region's least dramatic: largely green, flat, farmland punctuated by innumerable fairytale half-timbered villages, with surprisingly few urban settlements. Apart from a scattering of small islands, the country is made up of three main **landmasses** – the islands of Zealand and Funen and the peninsula of Jutland, which extends northwards from Germany.

The vast majority of visitors make for **Zealand** (Sjælland) and, more specifically, **Copenhagen**, the country's one truly large city and an atmospheric and exciting focal point. The compact capital has everything: a beautiful old centre, a good array of museums – both national collections and smaller oddball establishments – and a boisterous nightlife. But Copenhagen has

---

Denmark on the net

ⓦ **www.visitdenmark.com** Official Danish Tourist Board website, with links to all regional sites.

ⓦ **www.useit.dk** Loads of useful, practical info, from cheap accommodation to nightlife and events listings. Primarily aimed at budget travellers in the Copenhagen area.

ⓦ **www.woco.dk** The stylish site of the Wonderful Copenhagen office, packed with the latest in restaurants, bars, nightlife and events.

ⓦ **www.aok.dk** Extensive English-language site with the latest listings for Copenhagen.

ⓦ **www.rejseplanen.dk** Door-to-door public transport journey planner, in English as well as Danish.

ⓦ **www.net-bb.dk** Nationwide farm holiday and private accommodation booking.

ⓦ **www.dmol.dk** Museum website with virtual tours of the best places.

ⓦ **www.cphpost.dk** English-language online newspaper which, despite the name – *Copenhagen Post* – covers stories from all around the country. It also has an excellent listings section for the Copenhagen area.

ⓦ **www.lego.com** Lots of games, virtual plastic bricks and information about the original Legoland at Billund, Denmark.

ⓦ **www.strandguide.dk** Guide to Danish nudist beaches with maps and details of facilities.

little in common with the rest of Zealand, which is largely quiet and rural. Zealand's smaller neighbour, **Funen** (Fyn), has only one urban draw in **Odense**, and is otherwise sedate, renowned for the cuteness of its villages, the sandy beaches of its southern coast – a major holiday destination – and numerous explorable small islands.

Only **Jutland** (Jylland) is far enough away from Copenhagen to enjoy a truly individual flavour, as well as Denmark's most varied scenery, ranging from soft green hills to desolate heathlands and windswept coastline. In **Århus**, Jutland also has the most lively and enjoyable city outside the capital.

When to go

Copenhagen attracts visitors all year round, but the intake peaks during July and August – which means **May**, **early June** and **September** are probably the most pleasant times to be there, although there's plenty happening in the city throughout the year. Anywhere else is enjoyably crowd-free all year round except for **July**, the Danish vacation month, when the population heads en masse for the countryside and the coastal strips – though, even then, only the most popular areas are uncomfortably crowded. Many **outdoor events** – from big music festivals to the staging of Viking plays – take

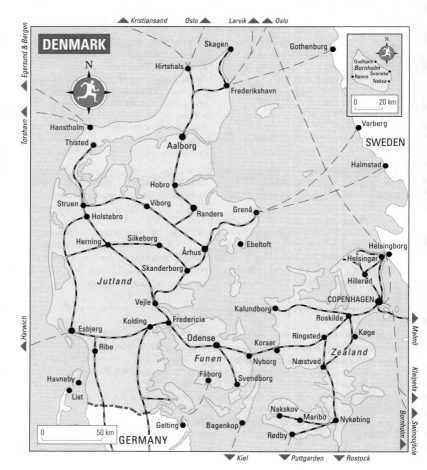

place between mid-June and mid-August, when all tourist facilities and transport services (including the more minor ferry links) are operating in full. In more isolated areas things begin to slacken off in September.

Denmark has the least extreme **climate** of the Scandinavian countries, but due to the proximity of the sea the weather can fluctuate rapidly. A wet day will as likely be followed by a sunny one and vice versa, and stiff breezes are common, especially along Jutland's west coast, where they can be particularly strong. **Summer** is on the whole sunny and clear: throughout July the temperature averages 20°C (68°F), often reaching 26°C (78°F). **Winter** conditions are cold but not severe: there's usually a snow covering from December to early February, and the temperature can at times drop as low as minus 15°C (5°F), but generally it hovers around or just below freezing point.

Getting there from the rest of Scandinavia

One look at a map will show you there'll be few problems **getting to Denmark** from the other Scandinavian countries. Links by **rail**, **sea** and **air** are fast and frequent all year round and, generally speaking, the journey to Denmark can be a rewarding part of your trip rather than a chore.

By train

Copenhagen is a major junction for **trains** between Europe and the rest of Scandinavia, and the new **Øresunds Link** – a part-tunnel, part-bridge connection between Copenhagen and Malmö in Sweden – has improved services immensely. Trains depart every twenty minutes and the journey from Malmö takes only 35 minutes. There are also several daily services to Copenhagen from the major Scandinavian cities – Stockholm, Gothenburg, Oslo, Bergen, Turku and Helsinki – and less frequent links (usually one a day in summer) with remoter spots in the far north, such as Narvik (in Norway) and Kiruna (in Sweden). InterRail, ScanRail and

Eurail **passes** are valid on all the international routes into Denmark (see Basics, p.35).

By bus

There are several direct **bus** links between the major Danish cities and the rest of Scandinavia, using either the Øresunds Link or the ferry routes outlined below. From Sweden to Copenhagen, there are usually two buses a day from Stockholm: one with Eurolines (www.eurolines.dk) and another with Swebus Express (www.swebusexpress .se). From Gothenburg there is one daily departure via Helsingborg with Säfflebussen (www.safflebussen.se), and another via Malmö with Swebus Express. The Gråhundsbus line (www.graahundbus.dk) connects Copenhagen with Malmö Airport as well as Malmö city. Eurolines, Säfflebus and Swebus Express all run daily departures from Oslo (Norway), though only Säfflebus goes via Gothenburg. **Fares** can vary enormously depending on the season and how far in advance tickets are booked. All companies have student/youth discounts.

By ferry

Since timetables and prices fluctuate constantly, ferry companies' websites or latest brochures are the best way to check precise details of the numerous **ferries** into Zealand and Jutland from Norway and Sweden; you can also contact any tourist office. There are sometimes reductions for railcard holders (see "Basics", p.35), and **fares** are usually a lot cheaper outside the peak period, roughly from the end of June to early August – though bear in mind that services are likely to be less frequent out of season, and possibly non-existent in winter. Even if you're heading for Copenhagen, don't disregard the possibility of a quicker, and cheaper, crossing into north Jutland – an interesting part of Denmark, with easy rail and bus links to the capital; or, from Sweden, reaching Denmark by way of the pretty island of Bornholm.

From Sweden

The cheapest route is the HH Ferries crossing **from Helsingborg** to Helsingør (www .hhferries.se; 20min; one-way tickets 22Skr for foot passengers, 300Skr for cars; both include extra fuel charges), which runs around the clock; you can walk, cycle or drive straight on board. Gothenburg–Copenhagen trains used to use this connection, but are now routed via the Øresunds Link **from Malmö** to Copenhagen, thus reducing the crossing time from fifty to thirty minutes. Two other operators make the same crossing – see the Helsingør section (p.129) for details.

Stena Line (⊛www.stenaline.se) has luxury boats sailing several times a day in summer **from Gothenburg** to Frederikshavn in Jutland (3hr 15min; one-way fares from 100Skr for foot passengers, or from 645Skr for cars; thirty percent discount for Eurail, ScanRail and InterRail pass holders). They also run a hydrofoil Express on the same route, which takes just two hours and costs, one-way, from 198Skr (cars from 945Skr). There's also a twice-daily Stena Line ferry (4hr) **from Varberg** to Grenå (for Århus) for a basic passenger fare that starts at 100Skr one-way (cars from 645Skr). All Stena Line car fares include five passengers. Cheapest departures are always the overnight journeys.

With time to spare, you could reach Denmark proper by way of **Bornholm**, a sizeable Danish island in the Baltic that's actually nearer to Sweden's south coast. Bornholm Ferries (⊛ www.bornholmferries .dk) run a twice-daily service between Ystad in Sweden and Rønne on Bornholm (express 1hr 20min; regular ferry 2hr 40min; from 204Skr). From Rønne, you can take the twice-daily (once in winter) Bornholm Ferries service to Køge, south of Copenhagen on the S-train network, but it's quicker to use the new bus route run by Bornholmerbussen (⊛ www.graahundbus.dk; 3hr; 200kr one-way) via Ystad, which uses the Øresunds Link and is cheaper, too.

From Norway

The only direct connection from Norway to Copenhagen is on the DFDS (⊛ www.dfds seaways.dk) crossing **from Oslo** (one-way fares from 688Nkr for foot passengers, 1230Nkr for cars), though you'll save a lot of money by taking one of the numerous routes to either Hansthom, Frederikshavn or Hirtshals in Jutland. From Oslo to Frederikshavn,

there are four to seven crossings a week with Stena (⊛www.stenaline.no; 8hr 30min; from 160–490Nkr one-way), and a similar number to Hirtshals with Color Line (⊛www.colorline .no; 8hr 30min; 190–460Nkr one-way). There are also connections **from Bergen via Haugesund and Egersund** to Hanstholm with Fjord Line (⊛ www.fjordline.com; one-way fares from Bergen 18hr, 200–540Nkr; from Haugesund 13hr 30min, 150–450Nkr; from Egersund: 8hr 30min, 100–360Nkr). Color Line also have services **from Bergen via Stavanger** to Hirsthals (from Bergen 16hr, 270Nkr–640Nkr; from Stavanger 11hr 15min, 190–460Nkr); **from Larvik** to Frederikshavn (6hr 15min; 190–460Nkr); and **from Kristiansand** to Hirtshals (4hr 30min; same fare). Any of these routes should be cheaper than the fare from Oslo – except perhaps on a summer weekend, when all the lines are at their most expensive.

By plane

SAS (⊛ www.scandinavian.net) operate around twenty direct **flights** daily into Copenhagen **from Oslo and Stockholm**, and eight daily from Helsinki; Finnair (⊛www .finnair.com) fly several times daily to Copenhagen from Helsinki. A number of discount airlines operate flights to Copenhagen from smaller airports and, increasingly, from larger cities, with varying degrees of affiliation with SAS. The Finnish SAS group airline **Blue 1** (⊛www.blue1.com) offer 1–3 daily flights from Helsinki, Oulu, Tampere, Turku and Vaasa. **Widerøe Flyveselskab** (⊛ www.wideroe.no) is the Norwegian equivalent, with two daily services from Trondheim. The independent budget airline **Norwegian Air Shuttle** (⊛www .norwegian.no) offer six daily flights from Oslo. **Fly Nordic** (⊛www.flynordic.com), a Swedish company, has low-cost flights from Gothenburg (1 daily) and Stockholm (4–5 daily), while the small Swedish **Skyways** (⊛ www .skyways.se) offer connections to Copenhagen from Karlstad (3–4 daily), Linköping (2–4 daily), Norrköping (1–3 daily) and Örebro (1–3 daily). Lastly, **Sterling Airlines** (⊛www.sterling .dk) offer 2–5 connections weekly from Gothenburg, 2–3 connections weekly from Oslo and 4–5 connections weekly from Stockholm. Check the websites for good deals, or contact a tourist office or travel agent to find out about special reduced-fare deals between the Scandinavian capitals – there are usually several each summer.

Copenhagen is very much the Danish hub of the SAS network (Århus is a poor second) and international arrivals often dovetail with domestic flights to other Danish cities, which cost little extra on top of the international fare; see p.68 for more details.

British Airways (🌐 www.britishairways .com) run three daily flights from Oslo, Stockholm and Gothenburg to Århus, and one daily flight from Gothenburg and Helsinki to Billund. Cimber Air has two daily connections from Stockholm and Oslo to Billund, while Danish Air Transport (🌐 www.dat.dk) connects Bergen and Stavanger with Billund and Esbjerg twice a week.

Fares for the services listed above vary enormously; one-way fares with budget airlines start at 200Dkr, while tickets with the larger national carriers are upwards of 1500Dkr. Under-26s can enjoy substantial discounts with the larger carriers, sometimes paying as little as 500Dkr. Again, check with a travel agent or visit the websites.

Costs, money and banks

Costs for virtually everything – eating, sleeping, travelling and entertainment – are **lower** in Denmark than in any other Scandinavian country.

If you come for just a few days, stay in youth hostels or on campsites and don't eat out, it's possible to survive on £25/US$44 a day. Otherwise, moving around the country, combining campsites or hostels with cheap hotel accommodation, visiting museums, eating in a restaurant each day as well as buying a few snacks and going for a drink in the evening, you can expect to spend a minimum of £30–40/US$53–70 per day.

Danish currency is the **krone** (plural kroner), made up of 100 øre, and comes in notes of 1000kr, 500kr, 200kr, 100kr and 50kr, and coins of 20kr, 10kr, 5kr, 2kr, 1kr, 50øre and 25øre.

At the time of writing, the **exchange rate** was 11.02kr to one pound sterling; 6.21kr

to one US dollar; 5.27kr to one Canadian dollar; 4.66kr to one Australian dollar; 4.35kr to one New Zealand dollar and 7.46kr to one euro.

Changing money

Banks are plentiful, and the easiest place to change travellers' cheques and foreign cash; there's a uniform commission of 30kr per transaction, so change as much as is feasible in one go. Forex exchange bureaux charge only 20kr to exchange cash and travellers' cheques but are much rarer. Most international airports, train stations and ferry ports have late-opening exchange facilities which charge a similar amount of commission. Alternatively, the red Kontanten **ATMs** are widespread and give cash advances on credit cards and, with your ATM card, will allow you to withdraw funds from your home account in local currency (check with your home bank); this can work out cheaper than changing cash or travellers' cheques.

Mail and communications

Like most other public bodies in the country, the Danish **post office** runs an exceedingly tight ship – within Denmark, anything you post is almost certain to arrive within two days. You can buy **stamps** from most newsagents, and from post offices, most of which are open Mon–Fri 9.30am–5pm, Sat 9.30am–1pm, with reduced hours in smaller communities. Mail under 50g costs 6.50kr to other parts of Europe, and 7.50kr to the rest of the world. **Poste restante** is available at any post office, and many hotels, youth hostels and campsites will hold mail ahead of your arrival.

Danish **public telephones** come in two forms. Coin-operated ones are white and require a minimum of 3kr for a local call (the machines irritatingly swallow one of the coins if the number is engaged), and

In an **emergency**, dial ☎ **112** from any phone box for a fast free connection to the emergency services.

5kr to go international; cards for the blue cardphones come in denominations of 30kr, 50kr and 100kr and work out a little cheaper – they're sold in newsagents and post offices. Most hotel rooms have a phone but it's much cheaper to make calls from the public phone at reception. Youth hostels and campsites generally have public phones; if not, the warden will probably let you use the house one for a payphone fee. You should be able to use your **mobile phone** in Denmark; for more on this, see "Basics", p.40. If you plan to make a lot of mobile calls while in Denmark, you might also invest in a Danish SIM card for use in your phone; these are available in all mobile phone shops. For 99kr, you'll get a Danish number plus about forty minutes of domestic calling time. The most commonly used network is TDC (the national landline network), but as coverage with Orange, Telia and others, they are just as good. Top-up cards can be bought in supermarkets, kiosks, and phone shops.

Calling Denmark from abroad, the **international code** is ☎ 45; codes for international calls from Denmark are given on p.40. To make a **collect international call**, dial ☎ 80 30 40 00 for the operator and ask to be connected to the operator in your own country, who will then put through the collect call – full instructions for this "Country Direct" system are displayed in phone booths, and you can dial ☎ 80 60 40 50 for free assistance. Be warned that **directory enquiries** (international ☎ 113, domestic ☎ 118) are expensive – the initial charge of 8kr per minute climbs ridiculously high whilst the operator puzzles out your request. Almost all operators speak English. To save money try a phone book (there should be one in all public phone booths), the national phone company's website, ⓦ www.teledanmark.dk, or the online (Danish-language) yellow pages, ⓦ www.degulesider.dk.

Internet access is available for free at most libraries and some tourist offices. Alternatively hotels, hostels and some sleep-ins will offer access for 20–30kr per hour, and Internet cafés can be found in most towns; we've detailed the most accessible in the Guide.

The media

For a country of its size, Denmark has an impressive number of newspapers and freesheets. By the lowest-common-denominator standards of the modern global media, the Danish press, with its predominantly serious and in-depth coverage of worthy issues, can't help but seem a little anachronistic.

If you can read Danish, your choices among the main daily **newspapers** (each costing 15–22kr) are *Politiken*, a reasonably impartial broadsheet with strong arts features; the conservative/centrist *Berlingske Tidende*; *Kristeligt Dagblad*, a Christian paper; *Jyllands-Posten*, a well-respected Jutland based right-wing paper; and *Information*, left-wing and intellectual. The weekly *Weekendavisen*, published on Thursdays, has excellent background features. The best sports coverage can be found in the two tabloids – *BT*, which has a conservative bias, and *Ekstra Bladet*. You'll find excellent **entertainment listings** in both *Jyllands-Posten* and *Politiken*, and every Thursday *Information* has a section devoted to listings, too. The free Danish **rock music** paper, the monthly *Gaffa*, lists most of the bigger shows, and innumerable similar regional papers do the same for their areas – find them in cafés, record shops and the like. The **English-language newspaper** *Copenhagen Post* covers domestic issues and has an in-depth listings section; it comes out every Friday and costs 15kr. **Overseas newspapers** are sold in all the main towns: most UK weekday titles cost 25–40kr and are available the day after publication from train stations and the bigger newsagents, which are also likely to stock recent issues of *USA Today*. There's also a very short News In English programme weekdays at 10.30am, 5.05pm and 10pm on Radio Denmark International (1062MHz).

After a slow start, **Danish television** has expanded rapidly. Ten years ago there was only one national station; today, there are four national and four cable channels. The four nationals are the non-commercial DR1 and DR2, and the commercial channels TV2 and TV2 Zulu – though, apart from the advertising, you'll probably struggle to spot the difference between them. The cable channels, some of which are shared with Sweden and Norway, are all commercial and prolific in American sitcoms and soaps (usually with Danish subtitles). If you're staying in a hotel, or a youth hostel with a TV room, you may also have the option of German and Swedish channels – plus a dozen cable and satellite stations.

Getting around

Despite being made up largely of islands, Denmark is a swift and easy country in which to travel. All types of **public transport** – trains, buses and the essential ferries – are punctual and efficient, and where you need to switch from one type to another, you'll find the timetables impressively well integrated.

And with Denmark being such a small country, you can get from one end to the other in half a day; even if, as is more likely, you're planning to see it all at leisure, you'll rarely need to do more than an hour's daily travelling. Besides being small, Denmark is also very flat, with scores of villages linked by country roads – ideal for effortless cycling.

Trains

Trains are easily the most efficient and convenient way to get about. Danske Statsbaner (DSB) – Danish State Railways – run an exhaustive and reliable network. InterRail, Eurail and ScanRail **passes** are valid on all routes except the few private lines that operate in some rural areas. There are just a few out-of-the-way regions that trains fail to penetrate, though these can be easily crossed by buses, which often run in conjunction with local train connections. Some of these buses are operated privately, but on those run by DSB, train passes are valid (for more on buses, see below).

Trains range from **inter-city expresses** (**IC Lyn**), with a buffet service, to smaller **local trains** (**regionaltog**). Departure times are listed on notices both on station concourses and the platforms (departures in yellow, arrivals in white), and announced over the loudspeaker. On the train, each station is usually called a few minutes before you arrive. Watch out for *stillekupé* – special

quiet compartments where children, pets and mobile phones are prohibited.

Tickets should be bought in advance from train stations, either from ticket booths or automated machines, which take all major credit cards but no cash. Trains don't require advance seat reservations (20kr), but then there's no guarantee that you'll get a seat. There's an extra charge of 40kr if you buy tickets on board. All trains have an inspector who checks tickets: he/she is almost certain to speak English and will normally be able to answer questions about routes and times. **Fares** are calculated on a zonal system. Copenhagen–Odense, for example, costs 230kr one-way, Copenhagen–Århus, 312kr. Both these fares include the cost of a seat reservation, and your train ticket will also get you around on the local buses (and S-trains in Copenhagen) in the departure and arrival town of your journey on the day the ticket is valid. The price of a return ticket is no cheaper than two one-ways. If you're between 16 and 25 and plan to do lots of train travel, it may be worthwhile buying a DSB Wildcard (175kr), which gives you a 25 percent discount on normal tickets and 50 percent **discount** if you avoid travelling on Friday or Sunday from 4am until 4am the next day. There are no student discounts, but people over 65 qualify for the same discounts as Wildcard holders. Travelling in a group of eight or more also entitles you to a 25–30 percent discount – get details from any Danish tourist office.

As for **timings**, DSB's Køreplan (30kr from any newsagent) details all DSB train, bus and ferry services inside (and long-distance routes outside) the country, including the local Copenhagen S-train system and all private services, and is a sound investment if you're planning to do a lot of travelling within the country. If you're not, smaller **timetables** detailing specific routes can be picked up for free at tourist offices and station ticket offices.

Buses

There are only a handful of **long-distance bus** services in Denmark. Abildskous Rutebiler (☎ 70 21 08 88, ⊛ www.abildskou. dk) run a swift service from **Copenhagen** to **Århus**, some via **Ebeltoft** (5–7 daily); to

Aalborg (2–5 daily); **Thisted** via **Viborg** and **Nykøbing Mors** (generally 2 daily); and **Silkeborg** (2 daily). One-way tickets to Ebeltoft, Arhus and Silkeborg cost 230kr (students pay 120kr at specified times) To Aalborg, Viborg, Nykøbing, Mors and Thisted, one-way tickets cost 240kr (students 140kr for travel at specified times).

Søndergaards Busser (☎ 70 10 00 33, ⓦ www.sondergaards-busser.dk) run a service between **Fjerritslev and Copenhagen** (2–4 daily), with stops in Løgstør, Hobro, Randers and Grenå; one-way tickets range from 240kr to 280kr (students get 100kr discount on certain less busy departures). Bornholmerbussen (☎ 44 68 44 00, ⓦ www .graahundbus.dk) run a service (3–5 daily; 200kr one-way) between Copenhagen and Bornholm, via the Øresunds Link and Ystad in Sweden. Bus fares represent quite a saving over full train fares but, while just as efficient, long-distance buses are much less comfortable than trains. However, buses really come into their own in the few areas where trains are scarce or connections complicated – much of Funen and northeast Jutland, for example – and if you're travelling from Esbjerg to Frederikshavn or Aalborg you save several hours, and a lot of timetable reading, by taking the bus. Around Jutland, the excellent government-run **X-busser** (☎ 98 90 09 00, ⓦ www.xbus .dk) are especially worth checking out, with a fast, efficient network that crisscrosses the peninsula: Esbjerg to Frederikshavn takes less than five hours. Buses are also often the best way of getting to smaller outlying towns; ask at the local tourist office or bus station for information.

Ferries

Ferries connect all the Danish islands, and vary in size and speed from the state-of-the-art catamaran linking Zealand and Jutland to raft-like affairs serving tiny, isolated settlements a few minutes off the (so-called) mainland. Where applicable, train and bus fares include the cost of ferry crossings (although you can also pay at the terminal and walk on), while the smaller ferries charge 25–75kr for foot passengers. Contact the nearest tourist office for full details.

Planes

Domestic flights are hardly essential in somewhere of Denmark's size, but can be handy if you're in a rush: from Copenhagen it's less than an hour's flying time to anywhere in the country. Three **airlines** operate domestic flights: SAS (☎ 60 72 77 27, ⓦ www.scandinavian.net), Cimber Air (☎ 74 42 22 23, ⓦ www.cimber.dk) and **Maersk Air** (ⓦ www.maersk-air.dk), now merged with Sterling Airways and also known as Sterling Airlines. **Fares** vary only slightly between the companies, although it can be worthwhile to check for special offers. The longer in advance you book, the cheaper the flight, and you can get good deals, such as 390kr one-way from Copenhagen to Rønne on Bornholm. Weekend tickets are generally cheaper than weekdays, from 592kr return between Copenhagen and Rønne if you book 21 days in advance; get details from an SAS desk or tourist office.

Driving and hitching

Given the excellent public transport system, the size of the country and the comparatively high price of petrol, **driving** isn't really economical unless you're in a group. **Car rental** is expensive, though it's worth checking the cut-price deals offered by some airlines. You'll need an international driving licence and must be aged at least 20 to take to the roads, although many firms won't rent vehicles to anyone under 25 – and some require you to be over 28. Costs start at around 2800kr a week for a small hatchback with unlimited mileage, Rent a Wreck (*Lej et lig*; ☎ 39 29 85 05, ⓦ www.lejetlig.dk) offers the best deal for limited mileage (100km per day) at 1750kr for a week – the cars aren't really wrecks, they're just not new. Danes drive on the right, and there's a speed limit in towns of 50kph, 80kph in open country and 110kph or 130kph on motorways. As in Sweden and Finland, headlights need to be used at all times. There are random breath tests for suspected drunken drivers, and the penalties are severe. When parked in a town, not on a meter, a parking-time disc must be displayed; get one from a tourist office, police station or bank. You set the time when you've parked on the hands of

Accommodation price codes

The hotels and guesthouses listed in the Denmark chapters of this Guide have been graded according to the following price bands, based on the cost of the **least expensive double room in summer**. Where weekend and summer rates are discounted, we've given two grades covering weekday and winter rates followed by weekend and summer rates (ie ❷/❸).

① Under 300kr
② 300–400kr
③ 400–500kr
④ 500–650kr

⑤ 650–900kr
⑥ 900–1300kr
⑦ Over 1300kr

---

the clock, then return before your allotted time (indicated by signs) is up. The national motoring organization, Forenede Danske Motorejere, operates a 24-hour **breakdown service** (℡45 88 00 25) for AA members; if you're not an AA member, Dansk Autohjælp (℡70 10 80 90) and Falck (℡70 10 20 30) can be summoned from call boxes by the road. A standard call-out fee will be charged – Dansk Autohjælp is the cheapest at 547kr per hour.

Hitching is illegal on motorways, but otherwise it's a fairly easy and reasonably safe way to get around; hitching isn't very common these days, though.

Cycling

Cycling is the ideal way to appreciate Denmark's pastoral (and mostly flat) landscape, as well as being a good method of getting around the towns. Traffic is sparse on most country roads and all large towns have cycle tracks – though watch out for sometimes less-than-careful drivers on main roads. Bikes can be **rented** at nearly all youth hostels and tourist offices, at most bike shops and at some train stations for around 50–75kr per day or 250kr per week; there's often a 200–500kr refundable deposit, too. For long-distance cycling, take the frequent westerly winds into account when **planning your route** – pedalling is easier facing east than west. The Danish cycling organization Dansk Cyklistforbund (℡33 32 31 21, ⓦwww.dcf.dk) offers cycling advice.

If the wind gets too strong, or your legs get too tired, you can take your bike on all types of public transport except city buses. On trains, you'll have to pay according to the zonal system used to calculate

passenger tickets – for example, 50kr to take your bike from Copenhagen to Århus, with 20kr on top if you want to reserve a place in advance. The brochure *Cyckle i Tog* (free from train stations) lists rates and rules in full. For a similar fee, long-distance buses have limited cycle space, while ferries let bikes on free or for a few kroner. Domestic flights charge around 200kr for airlifting your bike.

Accommodation

While less costly in Denmark than in other Nordic countries, **accommodation** is still going to be your major daily expense, and you should plan it carefully. **Hotels** are by no means off-limits if you seek out the better offers, and both **youth hostels**, **sleep-ins** and **campsites** are plentiful – and of a uniformly high standard. Coming to Denmark on a standard package trip (see Basics, p.29) is one way to stay in a **hotel** without spending a fortune. Another is simply to be selective. Most Danish hotel rooms include phone, TV and bathroom, for which you'll pay from around 700kr for a double (singles from around 450kr); going without the luxuries can result in big savings, and in most towns you'll find hotels offering rooms with access to a shared bathroom for as little as 500kr for a double (350kr a single). You'll find that rates may vary according to the season or day of the week, especially in the so-called "conference towns" where hotels are packed with business travellers during the week (Mon–Thurs) outside the summer season (roughly mid-June to mid-Aug). In these towns, rates are reduced significantly during summer and on weekends, and we've given two rates where this is the case (see box, p.69). In the rest of the country room rates tend to go up during the summer season and holidays.

Some **inns** (called *kro*) in country areas match basic hotel room prices – sometimes for rooms with full facilities. Other advantages of staying in a hotel or inn are the lack of a curfew (common in hostels in big cities) and the inclusion of an all-you-can-eat breakfast – so large you won't need to buy lunch.

Danish tourist offices overseas (see p.36) can provide a free list of hotels throughout the country, though much more accurate and extensive information can be found at local tourist offices and on tourist office websites. It's a good idea to **book in advance**, especially in peak season, which is most easily done via the tourist office or hotel website (listed in relevant places throughout the Guide chapters); booking directly on the net yourself can result in discounts of up to 35 percent.

Tourist offices can also supply details of **private rooms** in someone's home, vaguely akin to British-style bed and breakfasts (generally without the breakfast). These vary greatly, but reckon on paying 400–500kr for a double. Throughout the country, you'll come across places that call themselves **B&Bs**, though in reality no different to private rooms. There's a formal network of these B&Bs on Funen, and a useful annual catalogue details over one hundred rooms on the island. It's available from tourist offices and can also be accessed online at ⓦwww.bed-breakfast-fyn.dk. The countrywide B&B site ⓦwww.net-bb.dk is less user-friendly, but still worth checking out if you'd rather stay privately than in a hotel. Note that despite the name, breakfast isn't included in any B&B rates, and is only sometimes offered for an additional cost; there's often access to a kitchen, however.

Tourist offices can also supply details of **private rooms** in someone's home, vaguely akin to British-style bed-and-breakfasts (generally without breakfast). These vary greatly in price and standard, but reckon on paying 400–500kr for a double. Alternatively, staying on **farms** (*Bondegårdsferie*) is becoming increasingly popular in Denmark;

as well as your room, there's the opportunity to watch a farm at work. Information and catalogues can be obtained from Ferie på Landet, Ceresvej 2, 8410 Rønde (☏86 37 39 00, ⓦwww.bondegaardsferie.dk).

Youth hostels and sleep-ins

Youth hostels (*vandrerhjem*) are Denmark's cheapest option under a roof. Every town has one, they're much less pricey than hotels, and they have a high degree of comfort. Most offer a choice of various sizes of private room (we've given price codes for these in the Guide chapters), often with toilets and showers, and all have dormitory accommodation; nearly all have cooking facilities, too. **Rates** are around 110kr for a dormitory bed to 300–500kr for a private room. Other than those in major towns or ferry ports, it's rare for hostels to be full, but during the summer it's always wise to phone ahead to make a reservation, and to check on location – some hostels are several kilometres outside the town centre.

As with all Scandinavian hostels, sleeping bags are not allowed, so you need to bring either a sheet sleeping bag or rent hostel linen (40–50kr) – which can become expensive over a long stay. It's a good idea, too, to get an **HI card**, since without one you'll be hit with the cost of either an overnight card (35kr) or a year-long Danish membership card (160kr). If you're planning on doing a lot of hostelling, it's worth contacting Danhostel Danmarks Vandrerhjem, Vesterbrogade 39, DK-1620, Copenhagen V (☏33 31 36 12, ⓦwww.danhostel.dk) to get a copy of their free guide to Danish hostels, *Danmarks Vandrerhjem*, which is published in several languages including English, and for their informative hostel/campsite map of Denmark.

Sleep-ins are a similarly cheap option if you're on a budget but don't want to camp. Originally run by the local authorities, sleep-ins are now just a more traveller-oriented version of a hostel – privately run and generally always packed with young backpackers. Some open between May and August only, but most now open year-round. For bed and (shared) shower facilities, expect to pay around 100kr; bear in mind that you'll need your own sleeping bag, that only one night's stay is permitted in a few cases, and that there may be an age restriction (typically 16- to 24-year-olds only, although this may not be strictly enforced).

Camping

If you don't already have an International Camping Card from a camping organization in your own country, you'll need a Camping Card Scandinavia to **camp** in Denmark, which costs 80kr for both individuals and families, can be bought from any campsite and is valid on all official sites in Scandinavia until the end of the year in which it was bought. A Transit Pass can be used for a single overnight stay and costs 20kr per person. **Camping rough** without the landowner's permission is illegal and an on-the-spot fine may well be imposed. However, the Danish Forest and Nature Agency has initiated a two-year trial which allows free low-impact camping in some 200 designated woodland areas. The rules are strict: only one night at each site, only two tents per site, no open fires or camping stoves allowed and the site has to be left as you found it. Check ⓦ www.skovognatur.dk for information and a list of designated areas; local tourist offices should be able to advise if there are any nearby.

Campsites (*campingplads*) can be found virtually everywhere. All are open in June, July and August, many are open from April through to September, and a few operate all year round. There's a rigid **grading system**: one-star sites have toilets and at least one shower; two-stars also have basic cooking facilities and a food shop within 2km; three-stars include a laundry and a TV room; four-stars also have a shop; while five-stars include a cafeteria and other facilities such as a swimming pool. **Prices** vary only slightly from 55 to 65kr per person, though you may pay more at city sites or those in other particularly popular locations. Many campsites also have **cabin accommodation**, usually with cooking facilities, which at 2000–4000kr for a six-berth affair for a week may represent a saving for several people sharing, although on busy sites cabins are often booked up throughout the summer. Any Danish tourist office can give

you a free leaflet listing all the country's sites and the basic camping rules, or there's an official guide, *Camping Danmark*, available from kiosks, bookshops and tourist offices (95kr). For further information, contact the Campingrådet, Hesseløgade 16, DK-2100 København Ø (☏ 39 27 88 44, ⓦ www .campingraadet.dk).

Food and drink

Although good **food** can cost a lot, there are plenty of ways to eat affordably and healthily in Denmark, and with plenty of variety, too. Much the same applies to **drink**: the only Scandinavian country free of social drinking taboos, Denmark is an imbiber's delight – both for its huge choice of tipples, and for the number of places where they can be sampled. Traditional **Danish food** is centred on meat and fish: beef, veal, chicken and pork are frequent menu items – though rarely bacon, which is mainly exported – along with various forms of salmon, herring, eel, plaice and cod. Combinations of these are served with potatoes and another, usually boiled, vegetable. Ordinary **restaurant** meals can be expensive, especially in the evening, but there are other ways to eat Danish food that won't ruin your budget or your diet.

Breakfast

Breakfast (*morgenmad*) can be the tastiest and is certainly the healthiest (and most meat-free) Danish meal. Almost all hotels offer a sumptuous breakfast as a matter of course, as do youth hostels, though the latter don't include breakfast in their rates. You can often attack a buffet table laden with cereals, bread, cheese, boiled eggs, fruit juice, milk, coffee and tea for around 45kr. Breakfast elsewhere will be far less substantial: many cafés offer a very basic one for around 30kr, but you're well advised to go for **brunch** instead. Served until mid-afternoon, brunch is a filling option for late starters consisting of variations of international-style breakfasts (American, English etc) for 60–140kr depending on your craving. Later in the day, a tight budget may leave you dependent on self-catering.

Glossary of Danish food and drink terms

Basics

Brød	Bread
Bøfsandwich	Hamburger
Chokolade (varm)	Chocolate (hot)
Det kolde bord	Help-yourself cold buffet
Is	Ice cream
Kaffe (med fløde)	Coffee (with cream)
Letmælk	Semi-skimmed milk
Mælk	Milk
Kiks	Biscuits
Ostebord	Cheese board
Pølser	Frankfurters/ sausages
Sildebord	A selection of spiced and pickled herring
Skummetmælk	Skimmed milk
Smør	Butter
Smørrebrød	Open sandwiches
Sødmælk	Full-fat milk
Sukker	Sugar
Te	Tea
Wienerbrød	"Danish" pastry

Egg (æg) dishes

Kogt æg	Boiled egg
Omelet	Omelette
Røræg	Scrambled eggs
Spejlæg	Fried eggs

Fish (Fisk)

Ål	Eel
Forel	Trout
Gedde	Pike
Helleflynder	Halibut
Hummer	Lobster
Karpe	Carp
Klipfisk	Salt cod
Krabbe	Crab
Krebs	Crayfish
Laks	Salmon
Makrel	Mackerel
Rejer	Shrimp
Rogn	Roe
Rødspætte	Plaice
Røget Sild	Kipper
Sardiner	Sardines
Sild	Herring
Søtunge	Sole
Stør	Sturgeon
Store rejer	Prawns
Torsk	Cod

Meat (Kød)

And(ung)	Duck(ling)
Oksekød	Beef
Dyresteg	Venison
Fasan	Pheasant
Gås	Goose
Hare	Hare
Kalkun	Turkey
Kanin	Rabbit
Kylling	Chicken
Lam	Lamb
Lever	Liver
Rensdyr	Reindeer
Skinke	Ham
Svinekød	Pork

Vegetables (Grøntsager)

Artiskokker	Artichokes
Asparges	Asparagus
Blomkål	Cauliflower
Champignoner	Mushrooms
Grønne bønner	Runner beans
Gulerødder	Carrots
Brune bønner	Kidney beans
Hvidløg	Garlic
Julesalat	Chicory
Kartofler	Potatoes
Linser	Lentils
Løg	Onions
Majs	Sweetcorn
Majskolbe	Corn on the cob
Nudler	Noodles
Peberfrugt	Peppers
Persille	Parsley
Porrer	Leeks
Ris	Rice
Rødbeder	Beetroot
Rødkål	Red cabbage
Rosenkål	Brussels sprouts
Salat	Lettuce, salad
Salatagurk	Cucumber
Selleri	Celery

Lunch and snacks

You can track down an excellent-value **lunch** (*frokost*) simply by walking around and reading the signs chalked up outside any café, restaurant or *bodega* (a bar that also sells no-frills food). On these notices, put out between 11.30am and 2.30pm, you'll often see the word **tilbud**, which refers

Spinat	Spinach	*Rosiner*	Raisins
Turnips	Turnips	*Solbær*	Blackcurrants
		Stikkelsbær	Gooseberries
Fruit (Frugt)		*Svesker*	Prunes
Æbler	Apples	*Vindruer*	Grapes
Abrikoser	Apricots		
Ananas	Pineapple	**Drink (Drikke)**	
Appelsiner	Oranges	*Æblemost*	Apple juice
Bananer	Bananas	*Appelsinvand*	Orangeade
Blommer	Plums	*Citronvand*	Lemonade
Blåbær	Blueberries	*Eksport-Øl*	Export beer (very
Brombær	Blackberries		strong lager)
Citron	Lemon	*Fadøl*	Draught beer
Ferskner	Peaches	*Guldøl*	Strong beer
Grapefrugt	Grapefruit	*Husets vin*	House wine
Hindbær	Raspberries	*Hvidvin*	White wine
Jordbær	Strawberries	*Kærnemælk*	Buttermilk
Kirsebær	Cherries	*Mineralvand*	Soda water
Mandariner	Tangerines	*Øl*	Beer
Melon	Melon	*Rødvin*	Red wine
Pærer	Pears	*Tomatjuice*	Tomato juice
Rabarber	Rhubarb	*Vin*	Wine

Danish specialities

Æbleflæsk	Smoked bacon with onions and sautéed apple rings
Æggekage	Scrambled eggs with onions, chives, potatoes and bacon pieces
Boller i karry	Meatballs in curry sauce served with rice
Flæskesteg	A hunk of pork with crispy skin, served with red cabbage, potatoes and brown sauce
Frikadeller	Pork and beef meatballs
Grillstegt kylling	Grilled chicken
Hakkebøf	Thick minced-beef burgers fried with onions
Kalvebryst i frikasseé	Veal boiled with vegetables and served in a white sauce with peas and carrots
Kogt torsk	Poached cod in mustard sauce with boiled potatoes
Medisterpølse	A spiced pork sausage, usually served with boiled potatoes or stewed vegetables
Røget sild	Smoked herring on rye bread garnished with a raw egg yolk, radishes and chives
Sild i karry	Herring in curry sauce
Skidne æg	Poached or hard-boiled eggs in a cream sauce, spiced with fish mustard, served with rye bread and garnished with sliced bacon and chives
Skipper labskovs	Danish stew: small squares of beef boiled with potatoes, peppercorns and bay leaves
Stegt ål med stuvede kartofler	Fried eel with diced potatoes and white sauce

to the "special" priced dish, or **dagens ret**, meaning "dish of the day" – a plate of chilli con carne or lasagna for around 50kr, or a three-course set lunch for 80–120kr. Some restaurants offer a fixed-price (80–100kr) open buffet, where you can help yourself to as much as you like. A variation on this idea is the traditional Danish lunch, a choice of **smørrebrød**, or open sandwiches: slices of rye bread heaped with meat (commonly either ham, beef or liver pâté), fish (salmon, eel, caviar, cod roe, shrimp or herring) or cheese, and generously piled with assorted trimmings (mushrooms, cucumber, pickles or slices of lemon). A selection of three or four of these costs about 75kr. You can buy *smørrebrød* to go for 10–35kr from the special shops you'll see in every fairly sizeable town; one of them usually opens late, too, until 10pm. At cafés you'll always be able to find a bulky sandwich (30–50kr) or a filling portion of salad (usually served with fresh bread) for 50–70kr. Otherwise, the American **burger** franchises are as commonplace and as popular as you'd expect, as are **pizzerias**, which are dependable and affordable at any time of day, with many offering special deals such as all-you-can-eat salad with a basic pizza for about 50kr, or a more exotic dish or pizza topping for 50–70kr. **Shawarmas** (kebabs) and **China boxes** (your selection of Chinese dishes from a buffet served in a takeaway box) are also easy to find in most larger towns; both cost around 30kr. You can also get a very ordinary self-service meat, fish or omelette lunch in a **supermarket cafeteria** for 50–90kr.

Most Danes buy **snacks** from the very popular fast-food stands (*pølsevogn*) found on all main streets and at train stations. These serve various types of **sausage** (*pølser*) for 16–24kr: the hotdog with trimmings such as roasted onion, remoulade and pickled cucumber, the long thin wiener, the fatter frankfurter, or the franske hotdog, a sausage inside a cylindrical piece of bread. Alternatives include a **toasted ham and cheese sandwich** (*parisertoast*) for 12–15kr – vegetarians can ask for the ham to be left out – and **chips** (*pommes frites*), which come in big (*store*) and small (*lille*) forms. All of the above come with various types of ketchup and mustard to order.

If you just want a cup of **coffee** (all Italian or French versions are widely available, as is freshly made filter coffee) or **tea** (usually a fairly exotic teabag brew), drop into the nearest café, where either will cost 12–35kr. You help it down with a **Danish pastry** (*wienerbrød*), tastier and much less sweet than the imitations sold abroad under the same name.

Dinner

Dinner (*aftensmad*) in Denmark presents as much choice as lunch, but the cost can be a lot higher. Pizzerias and similar places keep their prices unchanged from lunchtime, and many youth hostels serve simple but filling evening meals for 50–75kr, though you have to order in advance. The most cost-effective dinners (70–90kr), however, are usually found in **ethnic restaurants** (most commonly Chinese or Middle Eastern, with a smaller number of Indian, Indonesian and Thai), which, besides à la carte dishes, often have a buffet table – ideal for gluttonous overindulgence – and you usually get soup and a dessert thrown in as well. The **Danish restaurants** that are promising for lunch often turn into expense-account affairs at night, offering an atmospheric, candle-lit setting for the slow devouring of immaculately prepared meat or fish; you'll be hard-pushed to spend less than 200kr per person.

Shops and markets

An especially tight budget may well leave you dependent on **shopping for food**. Brugsen, Føtex and Irma are the most commonly found **supermarkets** (usually open Mon–Fri 9am–5.30pm, later on Thurs & Fri, Sat 9am–5pm), and there's little difference in price between them. You'll also come across Aldi, Netto and Fakta, which are cheaper but more chaotic and with less choice. Smaller supermarkets may be open shorter hours, especially on Saturdays, when they tend to close at 1 or 2pm except on the first Saturday of the month. Late-night shopping is generally impossible, although in bigger towns, the DSB supermarket at the train station is likely to be open until midnight. The best spots for fresh fruit and veg are the Saturday and (sometimes) Wednesday **markets** held in most towns.

Drink

If you've arrived from near-teetotal Norway or Sweden, you're in for a shock. Not only is alcoholic **drink** entirely accepted in Denmark, it's quite common to see people strolling along the pedestrianized streets swigging from a bottle of beer, and although extreme drunkenness is frowned upon, alcohol is widely consumed throughout the day by most types of people.

Although you can buy booze more cheaply from supermarkets, the most sociable **places to drink** are pubs, bars and cafés, where the emphasis is on beer – although you can also get spirits and wine (or tea and coffee). There are also *bodegas* (see p.72), in which, as a very general rule, the mood tends to favour wines and spirits, and the customers are a bit older and more local than those found in cafés.

The cheapest type of beer is **bottled beer**, which costs 18–25kr for a third of a litre, and is less potent than so-called **gold beer** (*Guldøl* or *Elefantøl*), also in bottles and costing 20–30kr per bottle. **Draught beer** (*fadøl*) is more expensive, with a quarter of a litre costing 15–30kr, half a litre 30–45kr. It's a touch weaker than both types of bottled beer, but tastes fresher and is more popular. All Danish beer is lager-style, the most common brands being Carlsberg and Tuborg, and although a number of towns have their own locally brewed rivals, you'll need a finely tuned palate to spot much difference between them. One you will notice the taste of is Lys Pilsner, a very low-alcohol lager.

Most international **wines and spirits** are widely available, a shot of the hard stuff costing 15–35kr in a bar, a glass of wine upwards of 25kr. While in the country, you should investigate the many varieties of the schnapps-like **Akvavit**, which Danes consume as eagerly as beer, especially with meals; more than two or three turn most non-Danes pale. A tasty relative is the gloriously spicy and strong Gammel Dansk Bitter Dram – Akvavit-based but made with bitters, which tends to be drunk at breakfast time or as a pick-me-up during the day.

Directory

Emergencies ☎112. Ask for fire, police or ambulance.

Fishing Well stocked with bream, dace, roach, pike, trout, zander and much more, Denmark's lakes and rivers are a fishing enthusiast's dream. The only problem is bringing enough bait (more expensive than you might expect) to cope with the inevitably large catch. The time to come is in early or late summer, and the prime areas are in central Jutland, around Randers and Viborg, and slightly further north around Silkeborg and Skanderborg. For specialist angling trips, see the "Getting there" sections in "Basics", p.29.

Public holidays On the following days, all shops and banks are closed, while public transport and many museums run to Sunday schedules: January 1, Maundy Thursday, Good Friday, Easter Monday, Common Prayers Day (fourth Friday after Easter), Ascension Day (fortieth day after Easter), Whit Monday (eighth Monday after Easter), Labour Day (the afternoon of May 1 – unofficial, but observed by most work places), Constitution Day (June 5), Christmas Eve (afternoon only), Christmas Day and Boxing Day.

Sales tax A tax of 25 percent is added to almost everything you'll buy – but it's always included in the marked price.

Shops Opening hours are Mon–Thurs 10am–5.30pm, Fri 10am–6pm or 7pm, Sat 9am–1pm or 2pm, Sun closed. Supermarkets in larger towns open a bit later. On the first Saturday of the month shops stay open until 5pm.

Tipping Unless you need porters to help carry your luggage, you'll never be expected to tip – restaurant bills include a fifteen percent service charge.

History

Spending much time in Denmark soon makes you realize that its history is entirely disproportionate to its size. Nowadays a small – and often overlooked – nation, Denmark has nonetheless played an important role in key periods of European history, firstly as home-base of the Vikings, and later as a medieval superpower. Markers to the past, from prehistory to the wartime resistance movement, are never hard to find. Equally easy to spot are the benefits stemming from one of the earliest welfare state systems and some of western Europe's most liberal social policies.

Early settlements

Traces of human habitation, such as deer bones prized open for marrow, have been found in central Jutland and dated at 50,000 BC, but it's unlikely that any settlements of this time were permanent, as much of the land was still covered by ice. From 14,000 BC, tribes from more southerly parts of Europe arrived during the summer to hunt reindeer for their meat, and antlers which provided raw material for axes and other tools. The melting ice caused the shape of the land to change and the warmer climate enabled vast forests to grow in Jutland. From about 4000 BC, settlers with agricultural knowledge arrived: they lived in villages, grew wheat and barley and kept animals, and buried their dead in **dolmens** or megalithic graves.

The earliest metal and bronze finds are from 1800 BC, the result of trade with southern Europe. (The richness of some pieces indicates an awareness of the cultures of Crete and Mycenae.) By this time the country was widely cultivated and densely populated. Battles for control over individual areas saw the emergence of a ruling warrior class, and, around 500 AD, a tribe from Sweden calling themselves **Danes** migrated southwards and took control of what became known as **Danmark**.

The Viking era

Around 800 AD, under **King Godfred**, the Danish boundaries were marked out. However, following Charlemagne's conquest of the Saxons in Germany, the Franks began to threaten the Danes' territory, and they had to prepare an opposing force. The Danes built fast, seaworthy vessels and defeated Charlemagne easily. Then, with the Norwegians, they attacked Spanish ports and eventually invaded Britain. By 1033, the Danes controlled the whole of England and Normandy and dominated trade in the Baltic.

In Denmark itself, which then included much of what is now southern Sweden, the majority of people were farmers: the less wealthy paid taxes to the king and those who owned large tracts of land provided the monarch with military forces. In time, a **noble class** emerged, expecting and receiving privileges from the king in return for their support. Law-making was the responsibility of the *ting*, a type of council consisting of district noblemen. Above the district *ting* there was a provincial *ting*, charged with the election of the king. The successful candidate could be any member of the royal family, which led to a high level of feuding and bloodshed.

In 960, with the baptism of King **Harald** ("**Bluetooth**"), Denmark became officially Christian – principally, it's thought, to stave off imminent invasion by the German emperor. Nonetheless, Harald gave permission to a Frankish monk, **Ansgar**, to build the **first Danish church**, and Ansgar went on to take control of missionary activity throughout Scandinavia. Harald was succeeded by his son **Sweyn I** ("**Forkbeard**"). Though he was a pagan, Sweyn tolerated

Christianity, despite suspecting the missionaries of bringing a German influence to bear in Danish affairs. In 990 he joined with the Norwegians in attacking Britain, whose king was the well-named Ethelred "the Unready". Sweyn's son, **Knud I** ("**the Great**") – King Canute of England – married Ethelred's widow, took the British throne and soon controlled a sizeable empire around the North Sea – the zenith of Viking power.

The rise of the Church

During the eleventh and twelfth centuries, Denmark was weakened by violent **internal struggles**, not only between different would-be rulers but also among the Church, nobility and monarchy. Following the death of Sweyn II in 1074, two of his four sons, Knud and Harald, fought for the throne, with Harald (supported by the peasantry and the Church) emerging victorious. A mild and introspective individual, Harald was nonetheless a competent monarch, and introduced the first real Danish currency. He was constantly derided by Knud and his allies, however, and after his death in 1080 his brother became Knud II. He made generous donations to the Church, but his introduction of higher taxes and the absorption of all unclaimed land into the realm enraged the nobility. The farmers of north Jutland revolted in 1086, forcing Knud to flee to Odense, where he was slain on the high altar of Skt Alban's Kirke. The ten-year period of poor harvests that ensued was taken by many to be divine wrath, and there were reports of miracles occurring in Knud's tomb, leading to the murdered king's canonization in 1101.

The battles for power continued, and eventually, in 1131, a **civil war** broke out that was to simmer for two decades, with various claimants to the throne and their offspring slugging it out with the support of either the Church or nobility. During this time the power of the clergy escalated dramatically thanks to **Bishop Eskil**, who enjoyed a persuasive influence on the eventual successor, Erik III. Following Erik's

death in 1143, the disputes went on, leading to the division of the kingdom between two potential rulers, Sweyn and Knud. Sweyn's repeated acts of tyranny resulted in the death of Knud in Roskilde, but Knud's wounded aide, Valdemar, managed to escape and raise the Jutlanders in revolt at the **battle of Grathe Heath**, south of Viborg.

The Valdemar era

Valdemar I ("**the Great**") assumed the throne in 1157, strengthening the crown by ending the elective function of the *ting*, and shifting the power of choosing the monarch to the Church. Technically the *ting* still influenced the choice of king, but in practice hereditary succession became the rule.

After Bishop Eskil's retirement, **Absalon** became Archbishop of Denmark, erecting a fortress at the fishing village of **Havn** (later to become København – Copenhagen). Besides being a zealous churchman, Absalon possessed a sharp military mind and came to dominate Valdemar I and his successor, Knud IV. During this period, Denmark saw some of its best years, expanding to the south and east, and taking advantage of internal strife within Germany. In time, after Absalon's death and the succession of **Valdemar II**, Denmark controlled all trade along the south coast of the Baltic and in the North Sea east of the Ejder. Valdemar II was also responsible for subjugating Norway, and in 1219 he set out to conquer Estonia and take charge of Russian trade routes through the Gulf of Finland. According to Danish legend, the national flag, the Dannebrog, fell down from heaven during a battle in Estonia in 1219.

However, in 1223 Valdemar II was kidnapped by Count Henry of Schwerin (a Danish vassal) and forced to give up many Danish possessions. There was also a redrawing of the southern boundary of Jutland, which caused the Danish population of the region to be joined by a large number of Saxons from Holstein.

Within Denmark, the years of expansion had brought great prosperity. The rules of the *ting* were written down as the **Jutlandic Code**, thus unifying laws all over the country – an act which had the effect of concentrating powers of justice in the person of the monarch, rather than the *ting*. The increasingly affluent nobles, however, demanded greater rights if they were to be counted on to support the new king. The Church was envious of their growing power and much bickering ensued in the following years, resulting in the eventual installation of Valdemar II's son, Christoffer I, as monarch.

Christoffer died suddenly in Ribe when his only son Erik was two years old; Queen Margrethe took the role of regent until **Erik V** came of age. Erik's overbearing manner and penchant for German bodyguards annoyed the nobles, and they forced him to a meeting at Nyborg in 1282 where his powers were limited by a *håndfæstning*, or charter, that included an undertaking for annual consultation with a *Danehof*, or forum of nobles. In 1319 **Christoffer II** became king, after agreeing to an even sterner charter, which allowed for daily consultations with a *råd* – a council of nobles. In 1326, in lieu of a debt which Christoffer had no hope of repaying, **Count Gerd of Holstein** occupied a large portion of Jutland. Christoffer fled to Mecklenburg and Gerd installed the 12-year-old Valdemar, Duke of Schleswig, as a puppet king.

As they proceeded to divide the country among themselves, the Danish nobles became increasingly unpopular with both the Church and the peasantry. Christoffer attempted to take advantage of the internal discord to regain the crown in 1329 but was defeated in battle by Gerd. Under the peace terms, Gerd was given Jutland and Funen, while his cousin, Count Johan of Plön, was granted Zealand, Skåne, Lolland and Falster. In 1332 Skåne, the richest Danish province, inflicted a final insult on Christoffer when its inhabitants revolted against Johan and transferred their allegiance to the Swedish king, Magnus.

Gerd was murdered in 1340. The years of turmoil had taken their toll on all sections of Danish society: from Christoffer's death in 1332, the country had been without a monarch and it was felt that a re-establishment of the crown was essential to restoring stability. The throne was given to **Valdemar IV** and the monarchy strengthened by the taking back of former crown lands that had been given to nobles. Within twenty years Denmark had regained its former territory, with German forces driven back across the Ejder. The only loss was Estonia, a Danish possession since 1219, which was sold to the Order of Teutonic Knights.

In 1361, the buoyant king attacked and conquered Gotland, much to the annoyance of the Hanseatic League, a powerful Lübeck-based group of tradesmen who were using it as a Baltic trading base. A number of anti-Danish alliances sprang up and the country was slowly plundered until peace was agreed in 1370 under the **Treaty of Stralsund**. This guaranteed trade for the Hanseatic partners by granting them control of castles along the west coast of Skåne for fifteen years. It also laid down that the election of the Danish monarch had to be approved by the Hanseatic League – the peak of their power.

The Kalmar Union

Valdemar's daughter Margrethe forced the election of her 5-year-old son, Olav, as king in 1380, installing herself as regent. Following his untimely death after only a seven-year reign, Margrethe became Queen of Denmark and Norway, and later of Sweden as well – the first ruler of a united Scandinavia. In 1397, a formal document, the **Kalmar Union**, set out the rules of the union of the countries, which allowed for a Scandinavian federation sharing the same monarch and foreign policy, whilst each country had its own internal legislation. It became evident that Denmark was to be the dominant partner within the union when Margrethe placed Danish nobles in civic positions in Norway and Sweden but failed to reciprocate with Swedes and Norwegians in Denmark.

Erik VII ("**of Pomerania**") became king in 1396, and was determined to remove the Counts of Holstein who had taken possession of Schleswig in northern Germany. In 1413, he persuaded a meeting of the Danehof to declare the whole of Schleswig to be crown property, and three years later war broke out with the German-influenced nobility of the region. Unhappy with the Holstein privateers who were interfering with their trade, the Hanseatic League initially supported the king. But Erik also introduced important economic reforms within Denmark, ensuring that foreign goods reached Danish people through Danish merchants instead of coming directly from Hanseatic traders. This led to a war with the League, after which, in 1429, Erik imposed the **Sound Toll** (*Øresundstolden*) on shipping passing through the narrow strip of sea off the coast of Helsingør.

The conflicts with the Holsteiners and the Hanseatic League had, however, badly drained financial resources. Denmark still relied on hired armies to do its fighting, and the burden of taxation had caused widespread dissatisfaction, particularly in Sweden. With the Holstein forces gaining ground in Jutland, Erik fled to Gotland, and in 1439 Swedish and Danish nobles elected in his place **Christoffer III**, who acquiesced to the nobles' demands and ensured peace with the Hanseatic League by granting them exemption from the Sound Toll.

His sudden death in 1448 left – after internal struggle – **Christian I** to take the Danish throne. Following the death of his uncle and ally, the Count of Holstein, he united Schleswig and Holstein at Ribe in 1460 and became Count of Holstein and Duke of Schleswig. In Denmark itself he also instigated the *stændermøde*: a council of merchants, clergy, freehold peasants and nobility, forging a powerful position for the crown – a policy that was continued by his successor, Hans.

Hans died in 1513 and **Christian II** came to the throne, seeking to re-establish the power of the Kalmar Union and reduce the trading dominance of the Hanseatic League. He invaded Sweden in 1520 under the guise of protecting the Church, but soon crowned himself King of Sweden at a ceremony attended by the cream of the Swedish nobility, clergy and the merchant class – an amnesty being granted to those who had opposed him. It was, however, a trick. Once inside the castle, 82 of the "guests" were arrested on charges of heresy, sentenced to death, and executed – an event that became known as the **Stockholm Bloodbath**. This was supposed to subdue Swedish hostility to the Danish monarch but in fact had the opposite effect. Gustavus Vasa, previously one of six Swedish hostages held by Christian in Denmark, became the leader of a revolt that ended Christian's reign in Sweden and finished the Kalmar Union.

Internally, too, Christian faced a revolt, to which he responded with more brutality. At the end of 1522, a group of Jutish nobles banded together with the intention of overthrowing him, joining up with Duke Frederik of Holstein-Gottorp (heir to half of Schleswig-Holstein), who also regarded the Danish king with disfavour. The following January, the nobles renounced their royal oaths and, with the support of forces from Holstein, gained control of all of Jutland and Funen. As they prepared to invade Zealand, Christian fled to Holland, hoping to assemble an army and return. In his absence, Frederik of Holstein-Gottorp became **Frederik I**.

The Reformation

At the time of Frederik's acquisition of the crown there was a growing unease with the role of the Church in Denmark, especially with the power – and wealth – of the bishops. Frederik was a Catholic but refused to take sides in religious disputes and did nothing to prevent the destruction of churches, being well aware of the groundswell of peasant support for Lutheranism. Frederik I died in 1533 and the fate of the Reformation hinged on which of his two sons would succeed him. The elder and more obvious choice was Christian, but his open support for Lutheranism set the bishops and nobles against him. The younger son, Hans, was just 12 years old, but was favoured by the Church and the nobility. The civil war that ensued became known as the **Counts' War**, and ended in 1536 with Christian III on the throne and the establishment of the new Danish Lutheran Church, with a constitution placing the king at its head.

Danish–Swedish conflicts

New trading routes across the Atlantic had reduced the power of the Hanseatic League, and Christian's young and ambitious successor, **Frederik II**, saw this as a chance for expansion. Sweden, however, had its own expansionist designs, and the resulting **Seven Years' War** (1563–70) between the two countries caused widespread devastation and plunged the Danish economy into crisis.

The crisis turned out to be short-lived: price rises in the south of Europe led to increasing Danish affluence, reflected in the building of the elaborate castle of Kronborg in Helsingør. By the time **Christian IV** came to the throne in 1596, Denmark was a solvent and powerful nation. Christian's reign was to be characterized by bold new town layouts and great architectural works. Copenhagen became a major European capital, acquiring many of the buildings which still grace the city today, including Rosenborg, Børsen and Rundetårn.

To stem the rise of Swedish power after the Seven Years War, Christian IV took Denmark into the abortive **Thirty Years' War** in 1625, in which Danish defeat was total, and the king was widely condemned for his lack of foresight. The war led to increased taxes, inflation became rampant, and a number of merchants displayed their anger by petitioning the king over tax exemptions and other privileges enjoyed by nobles.

In 1657 Sweden occupied Jutland, and soon after marched across the frozen sea to Funen with the intention of continuing to Zealand. Hostilities ceased with the signing of the **Treaty of Roskilde**, under which Denmark finally lost all Swedish provinces. Sweden, however, was still suspicious of possible Danish involvement in Germany, and broke the terms of the treaty, commencing an advance through Zealand towards Copenhagen. The Dutch, to whom the Swedes had been allied, regarded this as a precursor to total Swedish control of commercial traffic through the Sound and sent a fleet to protect Copenhagen. This, plus a number of local uprisings within Denmark and attacks by Polish and Brandenburg forces on Sweden, halted the Swedes' advance and forced them to seek peace. The **Treaty of Copenhagen**, signed in 1660, acknowledged Swedish defeat but allowed the country to retain the Sound provinces acquired under the Treaty of Roskilde, so preventing either country from monopolizing trade through the Sound.

Absolute monarchy

In Denmark, the financial power of the nobles was fading as towns became established and the new merchant class grew. The advent of firearms caused the king to become less dependent on the foot soldiers provided by the nobles, and there was a general unease about the privileges – such as exemption from taxes – that the nobles continued to enjoy. Equally, few monarchs were content with their powers being limited by *håndfæstning*.

During the Swedish siege of Copenhagen, the king had promised special concessions to the city and its people, in the hope of encouraging them to withstand the assault. Among these was the right to determine their own rate of tax. A meeting of the city's burghers decided that everyone, including the nobility, should pay taxes; the nobles had little option but to submit. Sensing their power, the citizens went on to suggest that the crown become hereditary and end the *håndfæstning* system. Frederik III accepted and, with a full-scale ceremony in Copenhagen, was declared hereditary monarch. The task of writing a new constitution was left to the king, and its publication in 1665 revealed that he had made himself absolute monarch, bound only to uphold the Lutheran faith and ensure the unity of the kingdom. The king proceeded to rule, aided by a Privy Council in which seats were drawn mainly from the top posts within the civil service. The noble influence on royal decision-making had been drastically cut.

Christian V, king from 1670, instigated a broad system of royal honours, creating a new class of landowners who enjoyed exemptions from tax, and whose lack of concern for their tenants led Danish peasants into virtual serfdom. In 1699 **Frederik IV** set about creating a Danish militia to make the country less dependent on foreign mercenaries. While Sweden turned its allegiances towards Britain and Holland, Denmark re-established relations with the French, a situation which culminated in the **Great Northern War** (1709–20). One result of this was the emergence of Russia as a dominant force in the region, while Denmark emerged with a strong position in Schleswig, and Sweden's exemption from the Sound Toll was ended.

The two decades of peace that followed saw the arrival of **Pietism**, a form of Lutheranism which strove to renew the devotional ideal. Frederik embraced the doctrine towards the end of his life, and it was adopted in full by his son, **Christian VI**, who took the throne in 1730. He prohibited entertainment on Sunday, closed down the Royal Theatre, and made court life a sombre affair: attendance at church on Sundays became compulsory and confirmation obligatory.

The Enlightenment

Despite the beliefs of the monarch, Pietism was never widely popular, and by the 1740s its influence had waned considerably. The reign of **Frederik V**, from 1746, saw a great cultural awakening: grand buildings such as Amalienborg and Frederikskirke were erected in Copenhagen (though the latter's completion was delayed for twenty years), and there was a new flourishing of the arts. The king, perhaps as a reaction to the puritanism of his father, devoted himself to a life of pleasure and allowed control of the nation effectively to pass to the civil service. **Neutrality** was maintained and the economy benefited as a consequence.

In 1766, **Christian VII** took the crown. His mental state was unstable, his moods ranging from deep lethargy to rage and drunkenness. By 1771 he had become incapable of carrying out even the minimum of official duties. The king's council, filled by a fresh generation of ambitious young men, insisted that the king effect his own will – under guidance from them – and disregard the suggestions of his older advisers.

Decision-making became dominated by a German court physician, **Johann Friedrich Struensee**, who had accompanied the king on a tour of England and had gained much of the credit for the good behaviour of the unpredictable monarch. Struensee combined personal arrogance with a sympathy for many of the ideas then fashionable elsewhere in Europe; he spoke no Danish (German was the court language) and had no concern for Danish traditions. Through him a number of sweeping **reforms** were executed: the Privy Council was abolished, the Treasury became the supreme administrative organ, the death penalty was abolished, the moral code lost many of its legal sanctions, and the press was freed from censorship.

There was opposition from several quarters. Merchants complained about the freeing of trade, and the burghers of Copenhagen were unhappy about their city losing its autonomy. In addition, there were well-founded rumours about the relationship between Struensee and the queen. Since nothing was known outside the court of the king's mental state, it was assumed that the monarch was being held prisoner. Struensee was forced to reintroduce censorship of the press as their editorials began to mount attacks on him. The Royal Guards mutinied when their disbandment was ordered, while at the same time a coup was being plotted by Frederik V's second wife, Juliane Marie of Brunswick, and her son, Frederik. After a masked ball at the palace in 1772, Struensee was arrested and tried, and soon afterwards beheaded. The dazed king was paraded before his cheering subjects.

The court came under the control – in ascending order of influence – of Frederik, Juliane, and a minister, **Ove Høegh-Guldberg**. All those who had been appointed to office by Struensee were dismissed, and while Høegh-Guldberg eventually incurred the wrath of officials by operating in much the same arrogant fashion as Struensee had, he recognized – and exploited – the anti-German feelings that had been growing for some time. Danish became the language of command in the army and later the court language, and in 1776 it was declared that no foreigner should be given a position in royal office.

In the wider sphere, the country prospered through dealings in the Far East, and Copenhagen consolidated its role as the new centre of Baltic trade. The outbreak of the American War of Independence provided neutral Denmark with fresh commercial opportunities. In 1780 Denmark joined the **League of Armed Neutrality** with Russia, Prussia and Sweden, which had the effect of maintaining trading links across the Atlantic until the end of the war.

Faced with the subsequent conflict between Britain and revolutionary France, Denmark joined the second armed neutrality league with Russia and Sweden, until a British naval venture into the Baltic during 1801 obliged withdrawal. British fears that Denmark would join Napoleon's continental blockade resulted in a British attack led by Admiral Nelson, which destroyed the Danish fleet in Copenhagen. The pact between France and Russia left Denmark in a difficult situation. To oppose this alliance would leave them exposed to a French invasion of Jutland. To oppose the British and join with the French would adversely affect trade. As the Danes tried to stall for time, the British lost patience, occupying Zealand and commencing a three-day bombardment of Copenhagen. Sweden had aligned with the British and was demanding the ceding of Norway if Denmark were to be defeated – which, under the **Treaty of Kiel**, was exactly what happened.

The Age of Liberalism

The Napoleonic Wars destroyed Denmark's international prestige and left the country bankrupt, and the period up until 1830 was spent in recovery. Meanwhile, in the arts, a **national romantic movement** was gaining pace. The sculptor Thorvaldsen and the writer-philosopher Kierkegaard are perhaps the best-known figures to emerge from the era, but the most influential domestically was a theologian called **N.F.S. Grundtvig**, who, in 1810, developed a new form of Christianity – one that was free of dogma and drew on the virtues espoused by the heroes of Norse mythology. In 1825 he left the intellectual circles of Copenhagen and travelled the rural areas to guide a religious revival, eventually modifying his earlier ideas in favour of a new faith in the wisdom of "the people" – something that was to colour the future liberal movement.

On the political front, there was trouble brewing in Danish-speaking

Schleswig and German-speaking **Holstein**. The Treaty of Kiel had compelled Denmark to relinquish Holstein to the Confederation of German States – although, confusingly, the Danish king remained duke of the province. He promised to set up a consultative assembly for the region, while within Holstein a campaign sought to pressure the king into granting the duchy its own constitution. The campaign was suppressed, but the problems of the region were not resolved. Further demands called for a complete separation from Denmark, with the duchies being brought together as a single independent state. The establishment of consultative assemblies in both Holstein and Schleswig eventually came about in 1831, though they lacked any real political muscle.

Although absolutism had been far more benevolent towards the ordinary people in Denmark than elsewhere in Europe, interest was growing in the liberalism that was sweeping through the continent. In Copenhagen a group of scholars proffered the idea that Schleswig be brought closer to Danish affairs, and in pursuit of this they formed the Liberal Party and brought pressure to bear for a new liberal constitution. As the government wavered in its response, the liberal movement grew and its first newspaper, *Fædrelandet*, appeared in 1834.

In 1837, the crown agreed to the introduction of elected town councils and, four years later, to elected bodies in parishes and counties. Although the franchise was restricted, many small farmers gained political awareness through their participation in the local councils.

In 1839, **Christian VIII** came to the throne. As Crown Prince of Norway, Christian had approved a liberal constitution in that country, but surprised Danish liberals by not agreeing to a similar constitution at home. In 1848 he was succeeded by his son **Frederik VII**. Meanwhile, the liberals had organized themselves into the **National Liberal Party**, and the king signed a **new constitution** that made Denmark the most democratic country in Europe, guaranteeing freedom of speech, freedom of religious worship, and many civil liberties. Legislation was to be put in the hands of a **Rigsdag** (parliament), elected by popular vote and consisting of two chambers: the lower Folketing and upper Landsting. The king gave up the powers of an absolute monarch, but his signature was still required before bills approved by the Rigsdag could become law. And he could select his own ministers.

Within Schleswig-Holstein, however, there was little faith that the equality granted to them in the constitution would be upheld. A delegation from the duchies went to Copenhagen to call for Schleswig to be combined with Holstein within the German Confederation. A Danish compromise suggested a free constitution for Holstein with Schleswig remaining as part of Denmark, albeit with its own legislature and autonomy in its internal administration. The Schleswig-Holsteiners rejected this and formed a provisional government in Kiel.

The inevitable war that followed was to last for three years and, once Prussia's support was withdrawn, it ended in defeat for the duchies. The Danish prime minister, C.C. Hall, drew up a fresh constitution that excluded Holstein from Denmark. Despite widespread misgivings within the Rigsdag, the constitution was narrowly voted through. Frederik died before he could give the royal assent and it fell to **Christian IX** to put his name to the document that would almost certainly trigger another war.

It did, and under the peace terms Denmark ceded both Schleswig and Holstein to Germany, leaving the country smaller than it had been for centuries. The blame was laid firmly on the National Liberals, and the new government, appointed by the king and drawn from the country's affluent landowners, saw its initial task as replacing the constitution, drawn up to deal with the Schleswig-Holstein crisis, with one far less liberal in content. The election of 1866 resulted in a narrow majority in the Rigsdag favouring a new constitution. When this came to be implemented, it retained the procedure for election to the Folketing, but made the Landsting franchise dependent on land and money and allowed twelve of the 64 members to be selected by the king.

The landowners worked in limited cooperation with the National Liberals and the Centre Party (a less conservative version of the National Liberals). In opposition, a number of interests, encompassing everything from leftist radicals to followers of Grundtvig, were shortly combined into the **United Left**, which put forward the first political manifesto seen in Denmark. It called for equal taxation, universal suffrage in local elections, more freedom for the farmers, and contained a vague demand for closer links with the other Scandinavian countries. The United Left became the majority within the Folketing in 1872.

The ideas of **revolutionary socialism** had begun percolating through the country around 1871 via a series of pamphlets edited by Louis Pio, who attempted to organize a Danish Internationale. In April 1872, Pio led 1200 bricklayers into a strike, announcing a mass meeting on May 5. The government banned the meeting and had Pio arrested: he was sentenced to five years in prison and the Danish Internationale was banned. The workers, however, began forming trade unions and workers' associations.

The intellectual left also became active. A series of lectures delivered by Georg Brandes in Copenhagen cited Danish culture, in particular its literature, as dull and lifeless compared to that of other countries. He called for fresh works that questioned and examined society, instigating a bout of literary attacks on institutions such as marriage, chastity and the family. As a backlash, conservative groups in the

government formed themselves into the **United Right** under Prime Minister **J.B.S. Estrup**.

The left did their best to obstruct the government but gradually lost influence, while the strength of the right grew. In 1889, the left issued a manifesto calling for reductions in military expenditure, a declaration of neutrality, the provision of old-age pensions, sick pay, a limit to working hours, and votes for women. The elections of 1890 improved the left's position in the Folketing, and also saw the election of two **Social Democrats**. With this, the left moved further towards moderation and compromise with the right. The trade unions, whose membership escalated in proportion to the numbers employed in the new industries, grew in stature, and were united as the Association of Trade Unions in 1898. The Social Democratic Party grew stronger with the support of the industrial workers, although it had no direct connection with the trade unions.

Parliamentary democracy and World War I

By the end of the nineteenth century the power of the right was in severe decline. The elections of 1901, under the new conditions of a secret ballot, saw them reduced to the smallest group within the Folketing and heralded the beginning of **parliamentary democracy**.

The government of 1901 was the first real democratic administration, assembled with the intention of balancing differing political tendencies – and it brought in a number of reforms. Income tax was introduced on a sliding scale and free schooling beyond the primary level began. As years went by, Social Democrat support increased, while the left, such as it was, became increasingly conservative. In 1905 a breakaway group formed the **Radical Left** (*Det Radikale Venstre*), politically similar to the English Liberals, calling for the reduction of the armed forces to the status of coastal and border guards, greater social equality, and votes for women.

An alliance between the Radicals and Social Democrats enabled the two parties to gain a large majority in the Folketing in the election of 1913, and a year later conservative control of the Landsting was ended. Social advances were made, but further domestic progress was halted by international events as Europe prepared for war.

Denmark had enjoyed good trading relations with both Germany and Britain in the year preceding **World War I**, and was keen not to be seen to favour either side in the hostilities. On the announcement of the German mobilization, the now Radical-led cabinet, with the support of all the other parties, issued a **statement of neutrality** and was able to remain clear of direct involvement in the conflict.

At the conclusion of the war, attention was turned again towards Schleswig-Holstein, and under the **Treaty of Versailles** it was decided that Schleswig should be divided into two zones for a referendum. In the northern zone a return to unification with Denmark was favoured by a large percentage, while the southern zone elected to remain part of Germany. A new German–Danish border was drawn up just north of Flensburg.

High rates of unemployment and the success of the Russian Bolsheviks led to a series of strikes and demonstrations, the unrest coming to a head with the **Easter crisis** of 1920. During March of that year, a change in the electoral system towards greater proportional representation was agreed in the Folketing but the prime minister, **Carl Theodore Zahle**, whose Radicals stood to lose support through the change, refused to implement it. The king, Christian X, responded by dismissing him and asking **Otto Liebe** to form a caretaker government to oversee the changes. The royal intervention, while technically legal, incensed the Social Democrats and the trade unions, who were already facing a national lockout

by employers in response to demands for improved pay rates. Perceiving the threat of a right-wing coup, the unions began organizing a general strike to begin after the Easter holiday. There was a large republican demonstration outside Amalienborg.

On Easter Saturday, urgent negotiations between the king and the existing government concluded with an agreement that a mutually acceptable caretaker government would oversee the electoral change and a fresh election would immediately follow. Employers, fearful of the power the workers had shown, met many of the demands for higher wages.

The next government was dominated by the Radical Left. They fortified existing social policies, and increased state contributions to union unemployment funds. But a general economic depression continued, and there was widespread industrial unrest as the krone declined in value and living standards fell. A month-long **general strike** followed, and a workers' demonstration in Randers was subdued by the army.

Venstre and the Social Democrats jostled for position over the next decade, though under the new electoral system no one party could achieve enough power to undertake major reform. The economy did improve, however, and state influence spread further through Danish society than ever before. Enlightened reforms were put on the agenda, too, making a deliberately clean break with the moral standpoints of the past – notably on abortion and illegitimacy. Major public works were funded, such as the bridge between Funen and Jutland over the Lille Bælt, and the Stormstrømsbro, linking Zealand to Falster.

The Nazi occupation

While Denmark had little military significance for the Nazis, the sea off Norway was being used to transport iron ore from Sweden to Britain, and the fjords offered good shelter for a fleet engaged in a naval war in the Atlantic. To get to Norway, the Nazis planned an invasion of Denmark. At 4am on April 9, 1940, the German ambassador in Copenhagen informed Prime Minister Stauning that German troops were preparing to cross the Danish border and issued the ultimatum that unless Denmark agreed that the country could be used as a German military base – keeping control of its own affairs – Copenhagen would be bombed. To reject the demand was considered a postponement of the inevitable, and to save Danish bloodshed the government acquiesced at 6am. "They took us by telephone," said a Danish minister.

A national coalition government was formed which behaved according to protocol but gave no unnecessary concessions to the Germans. Censorship of the press and a ban on demonstrations were imposed, ostensibly intended to prevent the Nazis spreading propaganda. But these measures, like the swiftness of the initial agreement, were viewed by some Danes as capitulation and were to be a thorn in the side of the Social Democrats for years to come.

The government was reshuffled to include non-parliamentary experts, one of whom, **Erik Scavenius**, a former foreign minister, conceived an ill-fated plan to gain the confidence of the Germans. He issued a statement outlining the government's friendly attitude to the occupying power, and even praised the German military victory – which upset the Danish public and astonished the Germans, who asked whether Denmark would like to enter into commercial agreement immediately rather than wait until the end of the war. Scavenius was powerless to do anything other than agree, and a deal was signed within days. Under its terms, the krone was to be phased out and German currency made legal tender.

Public reaction was naturally hostile, and Scavenius was, not surprisingly, regarded as a traitor. Groups of Danes began a systematic display of antipathy to the Germans. Children

wore red, white and blue "RAF caps", Danish customers walked out of cafés when Germans entered, and the ban on demonstrations was flouted by groups who gathered to sing patriotic songs. On September 1, 1940, an estimated 739,000 Danes around the country gathered to sing the same song simultaneously. The king demonstrated his continued presence by riding on horseback each morning through Copenhagen.

Meanwhile, the Danish government continued its balancing act, knowing that failure to co-operate at least to some degree would lead to a complete Nazi takeover. It was with this in mind that Denmark signed the Anti-Comintern Pact making Communism illegal, but insisted on the insertion of a clause that allowed only Danish police to arrest Danish Communists.

Vilhelm Buhl, who was appointed prime minister on May 3, 1942, had been an outspoken opponent of the signing of the Anti-Comintern Pact and it was thought he might end the apparent appeasement. Instead, the tension between occupiers and occupied was to climax with Hitler's anger at the curt note received from Christian X in response to the Führer's birthday telegram. Although it was the king's standard reply, Hitler took the mere "thank you" as an insult and immediately replaced his functionaries in Denmark with hardliners who demanded a new pro-German government.

Scavenius took control and, in 1943, elections were called in an attempt to show that freedom of political expression could exist under German occupation. The government asked the public to demonstrate faith in national unity by voting for any one of the four parties in the coalition, and received overwhelming support in the largest ever turnout for a Danish election.

Awareness that German defeat was becoming inevitable stimulated a wave of strikes throughout the country. Berlin declared a state of emergency in Denmark, and demanded that the

Danish government comply – which it refused to do. Germany took over administration of the country, interning many politicians. The king was asked to appoint a cabinet from outside the Folketing, and Germans were free for the first time to round up Danish Jews. Resistance was organized under the leadership of the **Danish Freedom Council**. Sabotage was carefully co-ordinated, and an underground army, soon comprising over 43,000, prepared to assist in the Allied invasion. In June 1944, rising anti-Nazi violence led to a curfew being imposed in Copenhagen and assemblies of more than five people being banned, to which workers responded with a spontaneous general strike. German plans to starve the city had to be abandoned after five days.

The postwar period

After the German surrender in May 1945, a **liberation government** was created, composed equally of pre-war politicians and members of the Danish Freedom Council, with Vilhelm Buhl as prime minister. Its internal differences earned the administration the nickname "the debating club".

While the country had been spared the devastation seen elsewhere in Europe, it still found itself with massive economic problems and it soon became apparent that the liberation government could not function. In the ensuing election there was a swing to the Communists, and a minority Venstre government was formed. The immediate concern was to strengthen the economy, although the resurfacing of the southern Schleswig issue began to dominate the Rigsdag.

Domestic issues soon came to be overshadowed by the **international situation** as the Cold War began. Denmark had unreservedly joined the United Nations in 1945, and had joined the IMF and World Bank to gain financial help in restoring its economy. In 1947, Marshall Plan aid brought further assistance. As world power became polarized between East and West, the Danish government at first tried to remain impartial, but in 1947 agreed to join NATO – a total break with the established concept of Danish neutrality (though to this day, the Danes remain opposed to nuclear weapons).

The years after the war were marked by much political manoeuvring among the Radicals, Social Democrats and Conservatives, resulting in many hastily called elections and a number of ineffectual compromise coalitions distinguished mainly by the level of their infighting. Working-class support for the Social Democrats steadily eroded, and support for the Communists was largely transferred to the new, more revisionist, **Socialist People's Party**.

Social reforms, however, continued apace, not least in the 1960s, with the abandoning of all forms of censorship and the institution of free abortion on demand. Such measures are typical of more recent social policy, though Denmark's odd position between Scandinavia and the rest of mainland Europe still remains a niggling concern. A referendum held in 1972 to determine whether Denmark should join the EC resulted in a substantial majority in favour, making Denmark the first Scandinavian member of the community – Sweden, the second, didn't join until 1995 – though public enthusiasm remained lukewarm.

The 1970s and 1980s

Perhaps the biggest change in the 1970s was the foundation – and subsequent influence – of the new **Progress Party** (*Fremskridtspartiet*), headed by Mogens Glistrup, who claimed to have an income of over a million kroner but to be paying no income tax through manipulation of the tax laws. The Progress Party stood on a ticket of immigration curbs and drastic tax cuts, and Glistrup went on to compare tax avoidance with the sabotaging of Nazi railway lines during the war. He also announced that if elected he would replace the Danish defence force with an answering machine saying "we surrender" in Russian. He was eventually imprisoned after an investigation by the Danish tax office; released in 1985, he set himself up as a tax consultant.

The success of the Progress Party pointed to dissatisfaction with both the economy and the established parties' strategies for dealing with its problems. In September 1982, **Poul Schlüter** became the country's first Conservative prime minister of the twentieth century, leading the widest-ranging coalition yet seen – including Conservatives, the Venstre, Centre Democrats and Christian People's Party. In keeping with the prevailing political climate in the rest of Europe, the prescription for Denmark's economic malaise was seen to be spending cuts, not sparing the social services, and with an extension of taxation into areas such as pension funds. These policies continued until the snap election of 1987, which resulted in a significant swing to the left. Nevertheless, Schlüter was asked to form a new government, which he did in conjunction with the Progress Party in order to gain a single-seat working majority. A further election, in May 1988, largely served to affirm the new Schlüter-led government, if only, perhaps, because of the apparent lack of any workable alternative.

Into the new millennium

In January 1993 Schlüter's government was forced to resign over a political scandal (it was revealed that asylum had been denied to Sri Lankan Tamil refugees in the late 1980s and early 1990s, in contravention of Danish law). The Social Democrats, led by **Poul Nyrup Rasmussen**, took power in 1994 and formed a four-party coalition. For the first time in ten years Denmark was ruled by a majority government – a centre-left majority coalition which came under attack for its weak policies on tax reform, the welfare state and the thorny issue of **European union**.

Though traditionally a reluctant member of the EC, Denmark was carried into the European **Exchange Rate Mechanism** (or ERM, then viewed as the first step towards a single European currency) by Schlüter at the start of the 1990s, a move that transformed the Danish economy into one of the strongest in Europe and made its inflation rate the lowest of any EC member. The price for this, however, was soaring unemployment and further cuts in public spending.

The outcome of the **referendum on the Maastricht Treaty** (the blueprint for European political and monetary union) in June 1992, however, provided an unexpected upset to the Schlüter applecart. Despite calls for a "Yes" vote not only from the government but also from the opposition Social Democrats, over fifty percent of Danes rejected the treaty – severely embarrassing the prime minister and sending shivers down the spine of every western European government. The government and other pro-Europe parties didn't give up, however, but set to work on a revised version of the Maastricht Treaty, with the emphasis on protecting national interests – it included a pledge allowing the Danish people to reject citizenship of a united Europe.

A **second referendum** in May 1993 was a triumph for the government, with almost 57 percent of the Danish population voting in favour of the new Treaty. Anti-European feelings, already intense, reached boiling point, and the night after the referendum young left-wingers and anarchists came together in central Copenhagen to declare the area an "EU-free zone". The police moved in to break up the demonstration, battles with the demonstrators ensued, and for the first time ever the Danish police opened fire against a crowd of civilians. Fortunately nobody died, but the incident sparked off a major investigation into the actions of the police, and while Denmark avoided the risk of economic isolation in an increasingly integrated European community, doubts among the Danish people remain, along with a continuing dissatisfaction at the way the "Yes" vote was achieved.

Rasmussen and the Social Democrats retained the largest share of the vote in subsequent elections in 1998 and, as the new millennium dawned, the country was well placed for life in a new Europe. Danes were ranked at the top of the newly created "European Future Readiness Index", which measures social costs and problems such as environmental quality, healthcare costs, poverty and unemployment, while the organization Transparency International revealed that Denmark had been chosen as the world's **least corrupt nation**: of 99 countries surveyed, only Denmark received a perfect score on its "Anti-Corruption Index". All was not absolutely well, however. In 1999, crime and poverty in Copenhagen were becoming a serious worry for the first time in many years. Things came to a head during a November **riot** in the city when police used tear gas to quell more than one hundred protesters – the first such disturbance since the 1993 anti-Maastricht demonstrations. This time vandals wielded crowbars, bricks and bombs as they broke shop windows and set fires to protest about the extradition of a Danish hoodlum from Turkey. City officials were hoping dearly that it would not be the precursor of further violence.

Denmark today

In September 2000, the Danish people returned an unexpected "no" vote in the referendum held to decide if Denmark should finally enter the **Eurozone**. In spite of strong governmental support and many sound economic arguments for membership, 47 percent of the population voted against adopting the euro, leaving Denmark and the UK as the only two EU countries retaining a national currency. Support for the rejection came from the two political extremes, with the nationalist right wanting to retain "Danishness" in all its forms, and the extreme left seeking a less centralized government away from Brussels. Although financial doom was predicted as a consequence of the no vote, no major negative implications materialized and the Danish economy stayed solid.

In November 2001, the political tide changed further: Poul Nyrup Rasmussen and the centre-left coalition lost the election to a right-wing coalition led by **Anders Fogh Rasmussen**. This radical shift was widely regarded to have been a response to the global move to the political right which followed the September 11 attack in the US; a feeling of growing resentment against refugees and second-generation Danes (mainly from Turkey) had already been nurtured by the right-wing Pia Kærsgård, and after the World Trade Centre tragedy, people started listening. As well as taking a hostile position toward "foreigners", the new government marked itself as anti-environment (by way of massive scaling down of energy saving initiatives); anti-development (through cuts in overseas aid) and anti-culture (via the slashing of financial support to alternative types of entertainment). Fogh Rasmussen also upped the military budget and supported the invasion of Iraq, sending troops (and a much-ridiculed submarine) to the Gulf. Though significant anti-war demonstrations ensued, the election of February 2005 gave a second term to Fogh Rasmussen's conservative coalition, though the victory was seen more as a reaction against Social Democrat leader **Mogens Lykketoft**'s lack of charisma than a mark of support for Rasmussen's political platform. This failure to engage the electorate has left the average Dane feeling increasingly disconnected from politics.

On a lighter note, there was national joy in October 2005 when a new crown prince (and second in line to the throne) was born to Crown Prince Frederik and his Australian-born wife Mary. This served merely as a distraction, however, from more gloomy issues such as growing unease about the consequences of European expansion for the average Dane. This, combined with concerns about skyrocketing house prices, a general housing crisis and increasing taxes, has led to predictions of imminent economic downfall. Though the situation in Denmark appears relatively bright in the short term, the country's future prosperity seems increasingly fragile.

Books

Though there's not a huge amount of English-language books on Denmark, we've listed some of the best titles below. Those marked with a 🏃 represent essential reads.

History and philosophy

Inga Dahlsgård *Women in Denmark, Yesterday and Today* (o/p). A refreshing presentation of Danish history from the point of view of its women.

W. Glyn Jones *Denmark: A Modern History* (o/p). A valuable account of the twentieth century (up until 1984), with a commendable outline of pre-twentieth-century Danish history. Strong on politics, useful on social history and the arts, but disappointingly brief on recent grassroots movements.

🏃 **Søren Kierkegaard** *Either/Or.* Kierkegaard's most important work, packed with wry and wise musings on love, life and death in nineteenth-century Danish society; includes the (in)famous "Seducer's Diary".

🏃 **Roger Poole and Henrik Stangerup** (eds) *A Kierkegaard Reader* (o/p). By far the best and most accessible introduction to this notoriously difficult nineteenth-century Danish philosopher and writer, with a sparkling introductory essay.

Literature and biography

🏃 **Hans Christian Andersen** (ed. Naomi Lewis) *Hans Andersen's Fairy Tales.* Still the most internationally prominent figure of Danish literature, Andersen's fairy tales are so widely translated and read that the full clout of their allegorical content is often overlooked: interestingly, his first collection of such tales (published in 1835) was condemned for its "violence and questionable morals". *A Visit to Germany, Italy and Malta, 1840–1841* (o/p) is the most enduring of his travel works, while his autobiography, *The Fairy Tale of My Life*, is a fine alternative to the numerous sycophantic portraits which have appeared since.

Steen Steensen Blicher *Diary of a Parish Clerk; Twelve Stories.* Blicher was a keen observer of Jutish life, writing stark, realistic tales in local dialect and gathering a seminal collection of Jutish folk tales – published as *E. Bindstouw* in 1842.

Karen Blixen (Isak Dinesen) *Out of Africa; Letters from Africa; Seven Gothic Tales. Out of Africa*, the account of Blixen's attempts to run a coffee farm in Kenya after divorce from her husband, is a lyrical and moving tale. But it's in *Seven Gothic Tales* that Blixen's fiction was at its zenith: a flawlessly executed, weird, emotive work, full of twists in plot and strange, ambiguous characterization.

Tove Ditlevsen *Early Spring.* An autobiographical novel of growing up in the working-class Vesterbro district of Copenhagen during the 1930s. As an evocation of childhood and early adulthood, it's totally captivating.

Per Olov Enquist *The Visit of the Royal Physician.* Fascinating, witty and intriguing novel set in the Danish court in the 1760s: the king is a half-wit, the queen has a lover and the forces of the Enlightenment are arranged against the reactionaries. Great stuff.

Martin A. Hansen *The Liar.* An engaging novel, showing why Hansen was one of Denmark's most perceptive – and popular – authors during the postwar period. Set in the 1950s, the story examines the inner thoughts of a lonely schoolteacher living on a small Danish island.

Peter Høeg *Miss Smilla's Feeling for Snow.* A worldwide bestseller, this compelling thriller deals with Danish colonialism in Greenland and the issue of cultural identity.

Dea Trier Mørch *Winter's Child* (o/p). A wonderfully lucid sketch of modern Denmark as seen through the eyes of several women in the maternity ward of a Copenhagen hospital.

Evening Star, which deals with the effect of old age and death on a Danish family, is also worth getting hold of.

Judith Thurman *Isak Dinesen: The Life of Karen Blixen.* The most penetrating biography of Blixen, elucidating details of the farm period not found in the two "Africa" books.

Rose Tremain *Music and Silence.* Captivating historical novel that follows the lives of Christian IV, his consort, his English lutenist and their lovers. Life in the many castles around Denmark is brilliantly described, and the novel provides a fascinating insight into Danish aspirations and superstitions during the period.

A brief guide to Danish

In some ways, Danish is similar to German, but there are significant differences in pronunciation, Danes tending to swallow the ending of many words and leave certain letters silent. English is widely understood, as is German; young people, especially, often speak both fluently. And if you can speak Swedish or Norwegian then you should have little problem making yourself understood – all three languages share the same root.

In **pronunciation**, unfamiliar **vowels** include:

æ when long between air and tailor. When short like get. When next to r sounds more like hat.

å when long like saw, when short like on.

ø like fur but with the lips rounded.

e, when long, is similar to plate, when short somewhere between plate and hit; when unstressed it's as in above.

Consonants are pronounced as in English, except:

d at the end of a word after a vowel, or between a vowel and an unstressed e or i, like this. Sometimes silent at the end of a word.

g at the beginning of a word or syllable as in go. At the end of a word or long vowel, or before an unstressed e, usually like yet but sometimes like the Scottish loch. Sometimes mute after an a, e, or o.

hv like view.

hj like yet.

k as English except between vowels, when it's as in go.

p as English except between vowels, when it's as in bit.

r pronounced as in French from the back of the throat but often silent.

sj as in sheet.

t as English except between vowels, when it's as in do. Often mute when at the end of a word.

y between bee and pool.

Basics

Do you speak English?	**Taler De engelsk?**
Yes	**Ja**
No	**Nej**

I don't understand	**Jeg forstår det ikke**
I understand	**Jeg forstår**
Please	**Værså venlig**
Thank you	**Tak**
Excuse me	**Undskyld**
Good morning	**Godmorgen**
Good afternoon	**Goddag**
Goodnight	**Godnat**
Goodbye	**Farvel**
Yesterday	**I går**
Today	**I dag**
Tomorrow	**I morgen**
Day after tomorrow	**I overmorgen**
In the morning	**Om morgenen**
In the afternoon	**Om eftermiddagen**
In the evening	**Om aftenen**

Some signs

Entrance	**Indgang**
Exit	**Udgang**
Push/pull	**Skub/træk**
Danger	**Fare**
Gentlemen	**Herrer**
Ladies	**Damer**
Open	**Åben**
Closed	**Lukket**
Arrival	**Ankomst**
Departure	**Afgang**
Police	**Politi**
No smoking	**Rygning forbudt/ Ikke rygere**
No entry	**Ingen adgang**
No camping	**Campering forbudt**
No trespassing	**Adgang forbudt for uvedkommende**

Questions and directions

Where is?	**Hvor er?**
When?	**Hvornår?**

What?	Hvad?	13	**Tretten**
Why?	Hvorfor?	14	**Fjorten**
Who?	Hvem?	15	**Femten**
How much?	Hvor meget?	16	**Seksten**
How much does it cost?	Hvad koster det?	17	**Sytten**
		18	**Atten**
Here	Her	19	**Nitten**
There	Der	20	**Tyve**
Good/bad	God/dårlig	21	**Enogtyve**
Cheap/expensive	Billig/dyr	30	**Tredive**
Hot/cold	Varm/kold	40	**Fyrre**
Better/bigger/cheaper	Bedre/større/ billigere	50	**Halvtreds**
		60	**Tres**
Near/far	Nær/fjern	70	**Halvfjerds**
Left/right	Venstre/højre	80	**Firs**
Straight ahead	Ligeud	90	**Halvfems**
I'd like ...	Jeg vil gerne ha ...	100	**Hundrede**
Where is the youth	Hvor er	101	**Hundrede og et**
hostel?	vandrerhjemmet?	151	**Hundrede og enoghalvtreds**
Can we camp here?	Må vi campere her?		
It's too expensive	Det er for dyrt	200	**To hundrede**
Where are the toilets?	Hvor er toiletterne?	1000	**Tusind**
How far is it to ...?	Hvor langt er der til ...?		

Days and months

Monday	mandag
Tuesday	tirsdag
Wednesday	onsdag
Thursday	torsdag
Friday	fredag
Saturday	lørdag
Sunday	søndag
January	januar
February	februar
March	marts
April	april
May	maj
June	juni
July	juli
August	august
September	september
October	oktober
November	november
December	december
(Days and months are never capitalized)	

Where can I get a – train/bus/ferry to ...?	Hvor kan jeg tage toget/bussen/ færgen til ...?	
At what time does ...?	Hvornår går ...?	
Ticket	Billet	

Numbers

0	**Nul**
1	**En**
2	**To**
3	**Tre**
4	**Fire**
5	**Fem**
6	**Seks**
7	**Syv**
8	**Otte**
9	**Ni**
10	**Ti**
11	**Elleve**
12	**Tolv**

Glossary of Danish terms and words

Train station	**Banegård**	Old	**Gammel or Gamle**
Hill or ridge	**Bakke**	Sea	**Hav**
Cathedral	**Domkirke**	Harbour	**Havn**

Manor house	**Herregård**	Town hall	**Rådhus**
Railway	**Jernebane**	Wood or forest	**Skov**
Church	**Kirke**	Room	**Stue**
Cliff	**Klint**	Lake	**Sø**
Monastery	**Kloster**	Market square	**Torv**
Inn	**Kro**	Tower	**Tårn**
Square	**Plads**	Water	**Vand**
Coach station	**Rutebilstation**		

1.1

Zealand

As the largest of Denmark's islands and the home of its capital, Zealand (Sjælland) is the country's most important – and most visited – region. Though not an especially big city, Copenhagen dominates much of the island; the nearby towns, while far from being drab suburbia, tend inevitably to be dormitory territory. Only much further away, towards the west and south, does the pace become more provincial.

It would be perverse to come to Zealand and not visit **Copenhagen** – easily the most extrovert and cosmopolitan place in the country, and as lively by night as it is by day. But once there it's well worth making at least a brief journey into the country to see how different the rest of Denmark can be. Woods and expansive parklands appear almost as soon as you leave the city – and even if you don't like what you find, the swiftness of the metropolitan transport network, which covers almost half the island, means that you can be back in the capital in easy time for an evening drink.

North of Copenhagen, the coastal road passes the outstanding modern art museum of **Louisiana** and the absorbing Karen Blixen museum at **Rungsted** before reaching **Helsingør**, site of the renowned **Kronborg Slot** (better known as Elsinore Castle), an impressive fortification that nevertheless quite unfairly steals the spotlight from **Frederiksborg Slot**, an even more eye-catching castle in nearby **Hillerød**. West of Copenhagen and on the main route to Funen is **Roskilde**, a former capital with an extravagant cathedral that's still the last resting place for Danish monarchs, and with a gorgeous location on the Roskilde fjord – from where five Viking boats were salvaged that are now restored and displayed in a specially built museum. South of Copenhagen, at the end of the urban S-train system, is **Køge**, which – beyond the industrial sites that flank it – has a well-preserved medieval centre and long, sandy beaches lining its bay.

Further out from the sway of Copenhagen, central Zealand's towns are appreciably smaller, more scattered, and far less full of either commuters or day-trippers. **Ringsted**, plumb in the heart of the island, is another one-time capital, a fact recalled by the twelfth- and thirteenth-century royal tombs in its church. Further south, **Næstved**, surrounded by lush countryside, gives access to three smaller islands just off the coast: **Lolland**, **Falster** and **Møn**. Each of these is busy during the summer, but outside high season you'll find them green and peaceful, with Lolland offering a leisurely backdoor route, via Langeland, to Funen.

Not part of Zealand, but conveniently reached via Øresunds Link from Copenhagen, is the island of **Bornholm**. A huge slab of granite in the Baltic, it houses a few small fishing communities and has some fine beaches and an unusual history, making a stimulating detour if you're heading for Sweden – it's nearer Sweden than Denmark, with regular ferry connections to both countries.

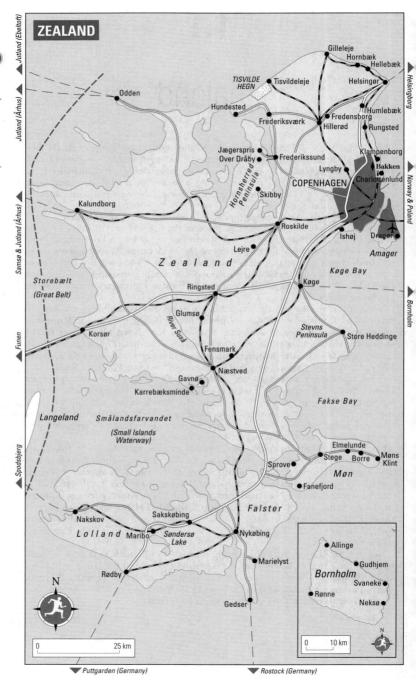

ZEALAND

Jutland (Ebeltoft)
Jutland (Århus)
Samsø & Jutland (Århus)
Funen
Spodsbjerg

Helsingborg
Norway & Poland
Bornholm

Gilleleje
Hornbæk
Hellebæk
TISVILDE HEGN
Tisvildeleje
Helsingør
Odden
Hundested
Humlebæk
Frederiksværk
Fredensborg
Rungsted
Hillerød
Jægerspris
Over Dråby
Frederikssund
Klampenborg
Hornsherred Peninsula
Lyngby
Bakken
COPENHAGEN
Charlottenlund
Kalundborg
Skibby
Roskilde
Ishøj
Drager
Lejre
Amager
Z e a l a n d
Køge Bay
Storebælt
(Great Belt)
Ringsted
Køge
Glumsø
River Suså
Stevns
Peninsula
Store Heddinge
Korsør
Fensmark
Næstved
Gavnø
Karrebæksminde
Fakse Bay
Langeland
Smålandsfarvandet
(Small Islands
Waterway)
Elmelunde
Møns
Klint
Sprove
Stege
Borre
Møn
Fanefjord
F a l s t e r
Nakskov
Sakskøbing
L o l l a n d   Maribo
Søndersø
Lake
Nykøbing
Marielyst
Rødby
Gedser

N
0   25 km

Bornholm
Allinge
Gudhjem
Svaneke
Rønne
Neksø
0   10 km
N

Puttgarden (Germany)
Rostock (Germany)

Copenhagen

As any Dane will tell you, **COPENHAGEN** is no introduction to Denmark; indeed, a greater contrast with the sleepy provincialism of the rest of the country would be hard to find. Despite that, the city completely dominates Denmark: it's the seat of all the nation's institutions – political, financial and artistic – and provides the driving force for the country's social reforms. Copenhagen is also Scandinavia's most affordable capital, and one of Europe's most user-friendly cities: small and welcoming, it's a place where people rather than cars set the pace, as evidenced by the multitude of pavement cafés and the number of thoroughfares that have been given over to pedestrians. In summer especially, there's a varied range of lively street entertainment, while at night the multitude of cosy bars, intimate clubs and live music venues could hardly be bettered. The history museums and galleries of Danish and international art, as well as a worthy batch of smaller collections, shouldn't be overlooked, either. If you're intent on heading north into Scandinavia's less populated (and pricier) reaches, you'd certainly be wise to spend a few days living it up in Copenhagen first.

There was no more than a tiny fishing settlement here until the twelfth century, when Bishop Absalon oversaw the building of a castle on the site of the present Christiansborg. The settlement's prosperity grew after Erik of Pomerania granted it special privileges and imposed the Sound Toll on vessels passing through the Øresund strait between Denmark and Sweden, which was then under Danish control. The revenue from the tolls enabled a self-confident trading centre to flourish. Following the demise of the Hanseatic ports, the city became the Baltic's principal harbour, earning the name København ("merchant's port"), and in 1443 it was made the Danish capital. A century later, Christian IV began the building programme that was the basis of the modern city: up went Rosenborg Slot, Børsen, Rundetårnet and the districts of Nyboder and Christianshavn, while in 1669 Frederik III graced the city with its first royal palace, Amalienborg, built for his queen, Sophie Amalie.

These structures still exist, like much of the Copenhagen from that time, and the taller of them remain the highest points in what is a refreshingly low skyline. This is an easy city to get around: you're unlikely to need to venture far from the central section, still largely hemmed in by the medieval ramparts (now a series of parks), which is where most of the activity and sights are contained.

Arrival, information and city transport

Whatever means you use to get to Copenhagen, you'll be within easy reach of the centre when you arrive. **Trains** pull into Central Station (*Hovedbanegården*), near Vesterbrogade, while **long-distance buses** from other parts of Denmark and abroad stop only a short bus or S-train ride from the centre: services from Århus, Aalborg and Fjerritslev stop at Valby S-train station, just west of the centre; buses from Bornholm at Central Station, and those from Gedser behind Central Station on Ingerslevsgade. Buses from elsewhere in Scandinavia stop at either Kvægtorvet or Ingerslevsgade, both behind Central Station. The direct bus from Sturup Airport in Malmö, Sweden (where many of the budget airlines operate to) also stops at Ingerslevsgade. **Ferries** from Bornholm dock at Køge Harbour, an S-train ride (line A and E) from the centre. Those from Norway and Poland dock at Dampfærgevej to the north of town; take bus #26 into the centre.

Modern **Kastrup Airport**, 8km southeast of the city on the eastern edge of the island of Amager, is the air hub of Scandinavia and your likely entry point if travelling by plane. Getting into Copenhagen from here couldn't be easier: one of the fastest airport-to-city train links (12min; 25.50kr) in Europe runs directly to Central Station six times an hour; there's one an hour (3min past the hour) from

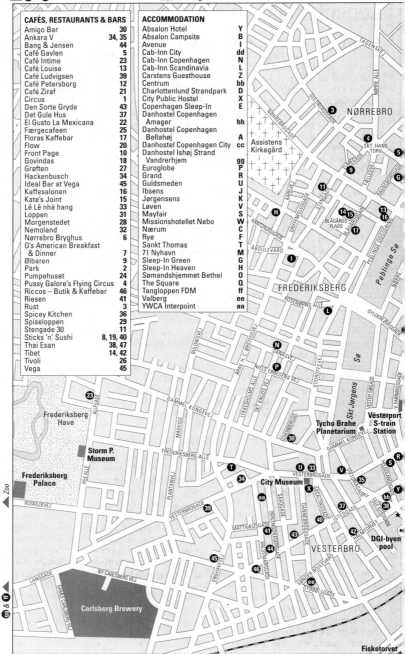

CAFÉS, RESTAURANTS & BARS

Amigo Bar	30
Ankara V	34, 35
Bang & Jensen	44
Café Gavlen	5
Café Intime	23
Café Louise	13
Café Ludvigsen	39
Café Petersborg	12
Café Ziraf	21
Circus	1
Den Sorte Gryde	43
Det Gule Hus	37
El Gusto La Mexicana	22
Færgecafeen	25
Floras Kaffebar	17
Flow	20
Front Page	10
Govindas	18
Grøften	27
Hackenbusch	34
Ideal Bar at Vega	45
Kaffesalonen	16
Kate's Joint	15
Lê Lê nhà hang	33
Loppen	31
Morgenstedet	28
Nemoland	32
Nørrebro Bryghus	6
O's American Breakfast & Dinner	7
Ølbaren	9
Park	2
Pumpehuset	24
Pussy Galore's Flying Circus	4
Riccos – Butik & Kaffebar	46
Riesen	41
Rust	3
Spicey Kitchen	36
Spiseloppen	29
Stengade 30	11
Sticks 'n' Sushi	8, 19, 40
Thai Esan	38, 47
Tibet	14, 42
Tivoli	26
Vega	45

ACCOMMODATION

Absalon Hotel	Y
Absalon Campsite	B
Avenue	I
Cab-Inn City	dd
Cab-Inn Copenhagen	N
Cab-Inn Scandinavia	L
Carstens Guesthouse	Z
Centrum	D
Charlottenlund Strandpark	X
City Public Hostel	E
Copenhagen Sleep-In	bb
Danhostel Copenhagen Amager	hh
Danhostel Copenhagen Bellahøj	A
Danhostel Copenhagen City	cc
Danhostel Ishøj Strand Vandrerhjem	gg
Euroglobe	P
Grand	R
Guldsmeden	U
Ibsens	J
Jørgensens	K
Løven	V
Mayfair	S
Missionshotellet Nebo	W
Nærum	C
Rye	F
Sankt Thomas	T
71 Nyhavn	M
Sleep-In Green	G
Sleep-In Heaven	H
Sømandshjemmet Bethel	O
The Square	Q
Tangloppen FDM	ff
Valberg	ee
YWCA Interpoint	aa

A & B

Grundtvigs Kirke

NØRREBRO

Assistens Kirkegård

SKT. HANS TORV

BLÅGÅRDS PLADS

Peblinge Sø

FREDERIKSBERG

Sø

Frederiksberg Have

Storm P. Museum

Frederiksberg Palace

Zoo

ROSKILDEVEJ

Carlsberg Brewery

NY CARLSBERG VEJ

Tycho Brahe Planetarium

Vesterport S-train Station

City Museum

VESTERBRO

DGI-byen pool

Fisketorvet

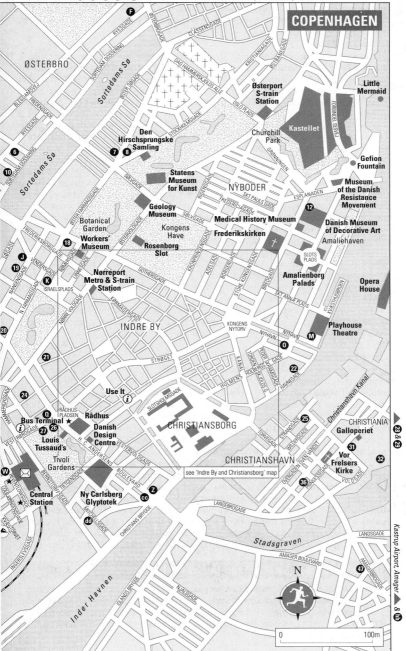

COPENHAGEN

ØSTERBRO

Sortedams Sø

Den Hirschsprungske Samling

Statens Museum for Kunst

NYBODER

Geology Museum

Botanical Garden

Kongens Have

Medical History Museum

Frederikskirken

Workers' Museum

Rosenborg Slot

Nørreport Metro & S-train Station

INDRE BY

STRØGET

KONGENS NYTORV

Use It

Rådhus

Danish Design Centre

CHRISTIANSBORG

Bus Terminal ★

Louis Tussaud's

Tivoli Gardens

Central Station ★

Ny Carlsberg Glyptotek

Østerport S-train Station

Churchill Park

Kastellet

Little Mermaid

Gefion Fountain

Museum of the Danish Resistance Movement

Danish Museum of Decorative Art

Amaliehaven

Amalienborg Palads

Opera House

Playhouse Theatre

NYHAVN

CHRISTIANSHAVN

Christianshavn Kanal

CHRISTIANIA

Galleriet

Vor Frelsers Kirke

see 'Indre By and Christiansborg' map

LANGEBROGADE

Stadsgraven

AMAGER BOULEVARD

Inder Havnen

N

Kastrup Airport, Amager ▲ & ⊞

0   100m

midnight to 5am. There's also a slower city bus (#250S; also 25.50kr) to Central Station and Rådhuspladsen, only really convenient if you want to get off on the way.

Information

Across the road from the Central Station at Vesterbrogade 4a Bernstorffsgade 1, the sparkling new Wonderful Copenhagen **tourist office** (May–June Mon–Sat 9am–6pm; July–Aug Mon–Sat 9am–8pm, Sun 10am–6pm; Sept–April Mon–Fri 9am–4pm, Sat 9am–2pm; ☎70 22 24 42, ⊛www.visitcopenhagen.com) offers maps, general information and accommodation reservations for hotels and hostels (booking fee 75kr). The office also provides countrywide information and distributes the free *Copenhagen This Week*, an up-to-date monthly news and listings magazine. Far better for youth and budget-oriented help, though, is the **Use-It** information centre (mid-June to mid-Sept daily 9am–7pm; rest of year Mon–Wed 11am–4pm, Thurs 11am–6pm, Fri 11am–2pm; ☎33 73 06 20, ⊛www.useit.dk), centrally placed in the Huset complex at Rådhusstræde 13. A wide range of help for travellers is available, including poste restante and free email services, accommodation booking (see p.102) and entertainment information, book exchange, luggage storage facilities and an extremely useful free magazine called *Playtime*. Finally, ⊛www.aok.dk has plenty of information on Copenhagen and Zealand, with particular emphasis on restaurants, music venues and events.

If you plan to visit many museums, either in Copenhagen or in nearby towns like Helsingør, Roskilde and Køge, you might want to buy a **Copenhagen Card**, which is valid for transport on the entire metropolitan system (which includes the towns mentioned above) and gives entry to most museums in the area. Obviously its worth will depend on your itinerary, but it can certainly save money if well used – especially since it also gets you twenty to fifty percent discounts on some car hire, ferry rides, and on guided bus and canal boat tours. Three-day (429kr) and 24-hour cards (199kr) are available from tourist offices, hotels and travel agents in the metropolitan region, and at train stations.

City transport

The best way to see most of Copenhagen is simply to **walk**: the inner city is compact and much of the central area pedestrianized. There is, however, an integrated zonal network of buses, electric **S-trains** (*S-tog*) and (since 2002) **Metro** trains covering Copenhagen and the surrounding areas, which run about every five to fifteen minutes between 5.30am and 12.30am, after which a night-bus (*Natbusserne*) system comes into operation – less frequent, but still with services once or twice an hour. S-train stations are marked by red hexagonal signs with a yellow "S" inside them, Metro stations with a large red "M", often on a round aluminium pillar – though both S-trains and Metros stop at some stations. Ten of the fourteen S-trains and Metros stop at the Central Station, and the four remaining lines run a circular route around the centre. Each line has a letter, from A to M (some letters are not used); lines running similar routes, but stopping at less stations, have a + symbol after the letter (eg H+); and each line is also colour-coded on route maps. It's essential to study a map before boarding a train or you could end up some way from your intended destination. Convenient stops include Nørreport, Christianshavn, Kongens Nytorv (the huge

Onward travel to Sweden and Norway – the Øresunds Link

Opened in July 2000, the **Øresunds Link** (see p.141) offers a quick tunnel and bridge connection between Copenhagen Central Station and Kastrup Airport, to Malmö and – via fast train – Stockholm, Gothenburg and Oslo. Using this link, the ride across the Øresund takes thirty minutes (around half an hour quicker than the old ferry–shuttle combination) and costs 71kr.

△ Bikes, Copenhagen

square/traffic circle beside Nyhavn canal) and Bella Centret − a five-minute walk from the *Copenhagen Hostel* on Amager.

So long as you avoid the rush hour (7–9am and 5–6pm), **buses** can be a swifter means of getting around once you get the hang of finding the stops − marked by yellow placards on signposts. The city's bus terminal is a black building adjacent to City Hall on the big open square called Rådhuspladsen, a block from both Central Station and Tivoli Gardens; you can pick up bus-route maps here, and get general information about the metropolitan transport system. **Night-bus** numbers always end with "N", and the stops are well marked by yellow signs on major routes into and out of the city. Another around-town option are the new city-run yellow **harbour buses**, which run along the harbourfront between Nordre Toldbod (near the Little Mermaid) and the Royal Library, and stop five times on the way (twice on the Christianshavn side).

You can use InterRail, ScanRail or Eurail cards on S-trains, but not on Metros, buses or harbour buses. The best ticket option after a **Copenhagen Card** (see p.100) or the **24-timer ticket** (100kr) − which covers the same transportation area but without admission to museums − is a two-zone (100kr) or three-zone (150kr) **klippekort**, which has ten stamps that you cancel individually according to the length of your journey; one stamp gives unlimited transfers within one hour in two or three zones respectively. Two simultaneous stamps are good for ninety minutes in four or six zones respectively, and three stamps allow two hours in six or nine zones respectively. Note that two or more people can use tickets from the same carnet simultaneously. For a single journey of less than an hour, use a **billet** (17kr), which is valid for unlimited transfers within two zones in that time. *Billets* can be bought on board buses or at train stations, while *klippekort* and 24-timers are only available at bus or train stations and HT Kortsalg kiosks; *klippekort* should be stamped when boarding the bus or via machines on train station platforms. Note that night-bus fares are double that of daytime rates (you'll have to buy twice the usual value in *billets*, and stamp *klippekort* twice). Except on buses, it's rare to be asked to show your ticket, but if you don't have one you face an instant fine of 500kr. Route maps can be picked up free at stations, and most free maps of the city include bus lines and a diagram of the Metro and S-train network.

The basic **taxi** fare within Copenhagen is generally a flat fare of 19kr (32kr if you book it in advance) plus 10kr per kilometre travelled (13kr after 4pm and 13kr at weekends) − only usually worthwhile if several people are sharing.

There's a taxi rank outside Central Station, or phone Taxamotor (☎38 10 10 10 for a cab, ☎35 39 35 35 for a minibus). Otherwise, just hail a cab in the street that's showing a green *Fri* sign on top. A fun alternative are the **cycle taxis** which you can hail just like regular taxis, or pick up at key transport points. Carrying a maximum of two people (or three kids), they charge an initial fare of 25kr, then 3kr for each additional minute.

Bikes can also be a good way to get around the city, and are handy for exploring the immediate countryside. The best places to rent them are Københavns Cyklebørs, Gothersgade 157 (☎33 14 07 17; ⊛www.cykelboersen.dk); Københavns Cykler, by the back (Istedgade) entrance to Central Station at Reventlowsgade 11 (☎33 33 86 13, ⊛www.copenhagen-bikes.dk); or Østerport Cykler (☎33 33 85 13), by Østerport Station at Oslo Plads 9. Bike rental normally costs 60–75kr per day or 270–340kr per week, plus a refundable 200–500kr deposit. Also bear in mind the free **City Bike scheme** (mid-April to early Nov; ⊛www.bycyklen.dk), whereby over 2000 free bikes (easily recognized by the advertisements painted onto their solid wheels) are scattered about the city at train stations and other busy locations; a refundable 20kr deposit unlocks one. The rules are simple: leave the bike in a rack when you've finished with it (you get your coin back automatically as you re-lock the bike), or just leave it out on a sidewalk, in which case someone else will happily return it and pocket the coin. Don't secure one with your own lock and don't take one outside the city limits (the old rampart lakes mark the border) or you risk a fine of up to 1000kr. If you want to cycle after dark, it's a good idea to get yourself some lights as you'll be fined if you're caught without. City Safari (☎33 23 94 90, ⊛www.citysafari.dk) offer two three-hour **guided bike tours** of the city: "Historic Copenhagen" at 1.30pm and "Copenhagen by Night" at 8pm, both for 259kr (including bike); book ahead.

Boat tours leave frequently from Gammel Strand and Nyhavn and sail around the canals and harbour. Cheapest is Netto-Bådene (☎32 54 41 02, ⊛www .havnerundfart.dk), which offers one-hour tours for 30kr that pass both Nyhavn and Christianshavn. DFDS Canal Tours (☎32 96 30 00, ⊛www.canal-tours .dk) have two fifty-minute options in very comfortable boats which go to either Nyhavn or Christianshavn; however, at 50kr, you'll get more for your money with Netto-Bådene. DFDS also run two **waterbuses**, one going east to the Trekroner fort/island, one going west to the new Fisketorvet shopping complex; both stop 12–15 times on the way. A two-day unlimited-use ticket costs 75kr, and a single trip 30kr. Finally, Kajak Ole (☎40 50 40 06, ⊛www.kajakole.dk) offer enjoyable guided **kayak tours** that depart from behind the new opera house (1.5hr 165kr; 2hr 185kr; 3hr 210kr).

Accommodation

Whether it's a hostel bed or a luxury hotel suite, **accommodation** isn't always easy to come by in Copenhagen, especially if you're arriving late in the day, or during July and August (the busiest time of year) when it's essential to book in advance, if only for the first night. If you arrive without a reservation or are trying to get a bed in the busy summer season, Wonderful Copenhagen's tourist information office (see p.100) will find you a hotel room, although queues for this service can be lengthy during high season, and it costs 75kr. You can also book in advance for free using their website (⊛www.bookcopenhagen.dk) or phone line (☎70 22 24 42). If you book in advance using an individual hotel's website, you can often get discounts of up to 35 percent. Alternatively Use-It (p.100) has a list of rooms available in the centre, from 300kr per double, and the very helpful staff may even call up and book for you without charging.

Note that we list a couple of gay- and lesbian-friendly accommodation options on p.126, and that all the places listed below are in the city centre unless otherwise stated, and are marked on the Copenhagen map (pp.98–99).

Hotels

You'll seldom find a grotty **hotel** in Copenhagen, though the cheaper ones often forgo the pleasures of private bathroom, phone and TV. Prices almost always include **breakfast** (unless otherwise stated, it's included in the rates for all places listed below). Most of the budget hotels are just west of the inner centre, around Istedgade – a slightly seedy (though rarely dangerous) area on the far side of the train station. This area is also home to a number of mid-range hotels, and there are further mid-price options around Nyhavn canal, on the other side of Indre By, and out towards the suburbs of Nørrebro and Frederiksberg.

Note that several of the places below offer discounts at the weekend; where this is the case, we've given two price codes, separated by a forward slash.

Absalon Helgolandsgade 15, Vesterbro ☎33 24 22 11, ⌨www.absalon-hotel.dk. Very large, quiet and relaxing family-run hotel near Central Station. Vast range of rooms to suit most budgets; those in the annex have sinks but share toilet and bath. ❹–❻

Avenue Åboulevard 29, Frederiksberg ☎35 37 31 11, ⌨www.avenuehotel.dk. Comfortable and welcoming place, on a main suburban boulevard but surprisingly close to downtown Copenhagen (take the Metro to Forum or bus #67, #68 or #69 from Central Station). Free parking. ❻

Cab-Inn City Mitchellsgade 14, Indre By ☎33 46 11 66; **Cab-Inn Copenhagen** Danasvej 32, Frederiksberg ☎33 21 04 00; and **Cab-Inn Scandinavia** Vodroffsvej 57, Frederiksberg ☎35 36 11 11; ⌨www.cab-inn.dk. Inspired by passenger cabins on the Oslo ferry, the small rooms, flip-up tables and tiny showers here may make you feel like a passenger on an overnight boat, but they're clean and safe, with pleasant staff and unbeatable prices. Breakfast (50kr) is not included. The two Frederiksberg branches are reached by bus #29 from Rådhuspladsen, and are within walking distance of Forum Metro Station. Cab-Inn City is a five-minute walk from Central Station. Cab-Inn Copenhagen is closed Nov–Feb. ❹

Centrum Helgolandsgade 14, Vesterbro ☎33 31 31 11, ⌨www.hotelcentrum.dk. Centrally located showpiece of contemporary Danish design, all whites, creams and wooden fittings. Guests get free access to the DGI-byen centre, where hotel are several pools and saunas. ❻

City Peder Skramsgade 24 Indre By ☎33 13 06 66, ⌨www.hotelcity.dk. Environmentally friendly Best Western chain-hotel serving lush organic breakfasts. Set in the central Nyhavn area, though you pay for the location. Bus #550S from Central Station or a short walk from Kongens Nytorv Metro. ❻

Euroglobe Niels Ebbesens Vej 22, Frederiksberg ☎33 79 79 54, ⌨www.hoteleuroglobe.dk. Occupying an old villa, this basic hotel offers exceptionally good value. The simple rooms share bathroom and kitchen facilities. Bus #29 from Rådhuspladsen. ❹

Grand Vesterbrogade 9A, Vesterbro ☎33 31 61 00, ⌨www.grandhotelcopenhagen.dk. Very popular with British travellers and businessmen, this stylish hotel is quite close to both the Tivoli Gardens and a row of British- and American-style pubs and restaurants. ❻

Guldsmeden Vesterbrogade 66, Vesterbro ☎33 25 15 00 ⌨www.hotelguldsmeden.dk. Close to the City Museum and the cafés on Vesterbro, the rooms at this charming small hotel are beautifully decorated in French colonial style. Bus #6A from Central Station. ❻

Ibsens Vendersgade, Indre By 23 ☎33 13 19 13, ⌨www.ibsenshotel.dk. Attractive rooms and a quiet yet central location near the city's picturesque lakes (bus #5A or #350S from Nørreport Station) make this place a winner. Bounteous Danish breakfast spread. ❻

Løven Vesterbrogade 30, Vesterbro ☎33 79 67 20, ⌨www.loeven.dk. Good-value – albeit slightly noisy – place two minutes' walk from Vesterport or Central Station. Rooms are basic; some have shared bath, others (245kr per person) sleep up to five people, and there's access to a guest kitchen. Breakfast (40kr) isn't included. ❸–❹

Mayfair Helgolandsgade 3, Vesterbro ☎33 31 48 01, ⌨www.themayfairhotel.dk. Part of the Comfort chain, offering Feng Shui harmonized "ye olde" English-style rooms with a colonial influence, with every modern convenience. Central location only ten minutes' walk from Central Station. ❻

Missionshotellet Nebo Istedgade 6, Vesterbro ☎33 21 12 17, ⌨www.nebo.dk. Small, clean, friendly and one of the best deals in this part of the city, though it's on one of the area's famously sleazy streets. Rooms with private bathroom cost a bit more, and parking is 25kr per day. ❹–❺

Rye Ryesgade 115, Østerbro ☎35 26 52 10, ⌨www.hotelrye.dk. Small hotel set in a former nursing home near Fælledparken and Parken stadium. The tastefully decorated rooms are spread over two floors and share bathroom facilities (they all come equipped with slippers and housecoat). Bus #14 from Rådhuspladsen or #15 from Central Station. **⑤**

Sankt Thomas Frederiksberg Allé 7, Frederiksberg ⑨33 21 64 64 795kr, ⓦwww.hotelsctthomas.dk. Friendly and excellent value, with a range of different rooms (some share toilets, others share all bathroom facilities), and free Internet access in the communal living room area. Bus #6A from Central Station and Rådhuspladsen. **④–⑤**

71 Nyhavn Nyhavn 71, Indre By ⑨33 43 62 00, ⓦwww.71nyhavnhotelcopenhagen.dk. Nineteenth-century warehouse right on the famous canals, which also houses one of the city's best restaurants. The 84 classy rooms come at a price and breakfast is not included. Bus #650S from Central Station or a five minute walk from Kongens Nytorv Metro station. **⑥**

The Square Rådhuspladsen 14 ⑨33 38 12 00, ⓦwww.thesquare.dk. Great new

addition to the city's hotels, slap-bang in the centre (hence no parking) and offering significant discounts during weekends. The smartly decorated, modern rooms have all the essential conveniences, including a well-stocked mini bar. **⑥**

Sømandshjemmet Bethel Nyhavn 22, Indre By ⑨33 13 03 70, ⓦwww.hotel-bethel.dk. Still aimed at professional sailors (visiting mariners get first priority), this central hotel is perfectly located for a night on the town. The bare and basic rooms are nothing to write home about, but you're paying for the location – the view from the rooms is fantastic. Bus #19 or Kongens Nytorv Metro Station. **⑤**

Valberg Sønder Boulevard 53, Vesterbro ⑨33 25 25 19, ⓦwww.valberg.dk. Occupying the fifth floor of a charming residential building at the quieter end of Vesterbro, the large apartment-like rooms have a kitchen, TV and bathroom with shower. Breakfast is delivered in a basket, and daily cleaning is included. Bus #10 from the Reventlowsgade exit of Central Station. **⑤**

Hostels and sleep-ins

Copenhagen has a great selection of **hostels** and **sleep-ins**, which are ideal for those on a budget – a dormitory bed costs 90–130kr. Space is only likely to be a problem in the peak summer months (June–August), when you should call ahead or turn up as early as possible on the day you want to stay. For the most up-to-date information, head for Use-It (see p.100).

If you're in Copenhagen for more than a couple of weeks, sub-letting a room in a **student hall** or **shared flat**, or renting a **private room** in someone's home (generally 150–200kr per person per day – ask at Use-It), can be a money-saving option. You can also arrange private rooms through the tourist office (see p.100) for a fee of 75kr, though you can only do so by visiting the office in person on the day itself. If you want to book a private room before you arrive, Bed & Breakfast in Denmark (⑨39 61 04 05, ⓦwww.bbdk.dk) can make advance arrangements for you, as well as book on the day. Their rooms cost between 300kr and 600kr for a double and breakfast is not included.

City Public Hostel Absalonsgade 8, Vesterbro ⑨33 31 20 70, ⓦwww.city-public-hostel.dk. Conveniently situated ten minutes' walk from Central Station between Vesterbrogade and Istedgade, with a noisy 68-bed dormitory on the lower floor, less crowded dorms of 6–20 beds on other levels, and a kitchen. Easygoing, and no curfew. Dorm beds are 130kr, bed linen is 35kr extra, and breakfast 25kr. Buses #6A and #26 stop close by. Open May to mid-Aug.

Copenhagen Sleep-In Blegdamsvej 132, Østerbro ⑨35 26 50 59, ⓦwww.sleep-in.dk. A vast hall divided into four- and six-bed compartments (dorm beds 110kr). Nice, if busy, atmosphere, with a young and friendly staff and sporadic free gigs by local bands; no curfew. If you don't have a sleeping bag you can rent sheets for 30kr (plus 40kr deposit). Bus #1A, #14, #15, #85N or #95N

from Rådhuspladsen or Central station. Open July & Aug.

Danhostel Copenhagen Amager Vejlands Allé 200, Amager ⑨32 52 29 08, ⓦwww.copenhagen-youthhostel.com. HI hostel with fairly frugal 2-bed (400kr per room) and 5-bed rooms, where dorms are 100kr. A ten-minute walk from Bella Center Metro, or take the E or A line S-train to Sjælør, then bus #4A: a 20–30min journey from the centre in total. It's a good twenty minutes' walk from the airport. Open 7am–1pm, check in 2–5pm, breakfast 40kr. Open mid-Jan to Nov.

Danhostel Copenhagen Danhostel Copenhagen Bellahøj Herbergvejen 8, Brønshøj ⑨38 28 97 15, ⓦwww.youth-hostel.dk. Located in a peaceful lakeside setting in a distant residential part of the city, this HI hostel is more homely than its rivals, offering cheap beds

(100kr) in large dorms (4–12 beds). Reception is open 24hr and there's no curfew, although there's a dormitory lockout from 10am–1pm. Breakfast is 45kr. Simple to reach, too: a 15min ride from the city centre on bus #2A, #11 or #13 (nightbus #82N). Open March to December.

Danhostel Copenhagen City H. C. Andersens Boulevard 50, Indre By ☎33.11.85.85, ⊛www .danhostel.dk. Brand new HI hostel in a multi-storey building overlooking the harbour and the green copper spires of the city. With 1020 beds (120kr) in four to eight-bed rooms, it prides itself on being the largest city hostel in Europe, A short walk from the Central Station or bus #5A. No curfew and open all year.

Danhostel Ishøj Strand Vandrerhjem Ishøj Strandvej 13, Ishøj ☎43 53 50 15, ⊛www .ishojstrand. A great HI hostel next to Køge beach park and the Arken modern art gallery, with a few two-person family rooms (❸) as well as dorm beds (118kr). Thirty minutes from the centre on A, A+ or E line S-trains, then bus #300S. Check in 2–6pm. Open all year.

Jørgensens Rømersgade 11, Indre By ☎33 13 81 86, ⊛www.hoteljoergensen.dk. A stone's throw from Nørreport station on Israels Plads, this was the city's first gay hotel in the 1980s and is now popular with both gay and straight travellers

(though there's an upper age limit of 35). Predominantly dormitory accommodation (6-, 9- and 12-bed rooms; beds 140kr), plus a few basic doubles (❹–❺), most with shared bathrooms. Breakfast included. Open all year.

Sleep-In Green Ravnsborggade 18, Nørrebro ☎35 37 77 77, ⊛www.sleep-in-green.dk. Eco-conscious hostel right in hip Nørrebro overlooking a pretty interior courtyard. Good all-volunteer staff and bright rooms with 8, 20 and 38 beds. Extra charges for bedding (30kr) and fabulous organic breakfast (40kr), and there's a noon–4pm lockout. Bus #5, #81N or #84N. 100kr. Open June–Oct.

Sleep-In Heaven 7th floor, Struenseegade 7, Nørrebro ☎35 35 46 48, ⊛www.sleepinheaven.com. Popular hostel outside the city centre with 4, 8 and 14 bed dorms, lockers, Internet access and a hotel bar plus courtyard; breakfast is 40kr. Buses #12, #69, or #92N. Open all year.

YWCA Interpoint Valdemarsgade 15, Vesterbro ☎33 31 15 74, ⊛www.ymca-interpoint.dk. Thirty-six cheap dorm beds (90kr) in 4-, 6- and 10-bed rooms; 12.30am curfew, and a 20kr charge for breakfast. Fifteen minutes' walk from Central Station, or bus #6A or #26. Reception open daily 8–11.30am, 3.30–6pm and 8pm–12.30am. Reservations must be taken before 9pm. Open July to mid-Aug.

Campsites

Only one of Copenhagen's various **campsites** is close to the city centre, but the others are fairly easily reached by public transport. There's little difference in price among them (60–75kr per person per night, plus up to 40kr per tent per night), nor in facilities: all have laundries, kitchen areas with cookers, also television rooms, playgrounds and the like.

If you arrive by campervan, there is an excellent option for a cheap central stay. For 35kr per vehicle per day and 75kr per person, *City Camp* (☎21 42 53 84, ⊛www.citycamp.dk), near the Fisketorvet shopping complex, offers safe parking and basic facilities such as showers and washing machines. Open June–Sept only.

Absalon Korsdalsvej 132, Rødovre ☎36 41 06 00, ⊛www.camping-absalon.dk. Occupying a large field next to a housing estate, about 9km to the southwest of the city. Take bus #1A to Avedøre Havnevej, from where it's a short walk (nightbus #93N). Reception open Mon, Thurs & Fri 9am–noon & 2–8pm; Tues, Wed, Sat & Sun 9am–noon & 2–6pm. Open all year.

Bellahøj Hvidkildevej Brønshøj ☎38 10 11 50. Near the *Bellahøj* youth hostel, this is Copenhagen's most central but least comfortable option, with long queues for the showers and cooking facilities. Bus #2A to Bellahøjvej (nightbus #82N). Open June–Aug.

Charlottenlund Strandpark Strandvejen 144B, Charlottenlund ☎39 62 36 88, ⊛www.camping copenhagen.dk. Beautifully situated at Charlottenlund

Fort and beach, 8km north of the city centre; take bus #14 (nightbus #85N). Check in noon–6pm. Open mid-May to mid-Sept.

Nærum Ravnebakken ☎45 80 19 57, ⊛www .camping-naerum.dk. Around 15km from the centre, but very pleasant: take bus #150S (nightbus #95N) from the Central Station or S-train line B to Jægersborg, then private train to Nærum. Open mid-March to mid-Sept.

Tangloppen FDM Ishøj Havn ☎43 54 07 67, ⊛www.fdm.dk/dinferie/fdmcamping/tangloppen. Some 17km south of the city centre, but close to some good and popular beaches. Take S-train A, A+ or E to Ishøj, then a two-minute walk or bus #128. Check-in after 3pm. Open May to mid-Sept.

The City

Exploring Copenhagen is supremely easy. Most of what you're likely to want to see can be found in the city's relatively small – and effortlessly walkable – centre, between the long inlet of the inner harbour (Inder Havnen) on the east and a semicircular series of lakes on the west. Within this area the divisions are well defined. **Indre By** forms the city's inner core, an intricate maze of streets, squares and alleys whose pleasure lies as much in its general daily bustle as in specific sights. The area **northeast of Indre By**, beyond the major thoroughfare of Gothersgade, is quite different, a boldly proportioned grid-pattern of streets and avenues built to accommodate the dwellings of the Danish nobility in the seventeenth century and reaching a pinnacle of affluence with the palaces of Amalienborg and Rosenborg.

CAFÉS, RESTAURANTS, BARS & CLUBS

Andy's Bar	4	Club Amigo	34	Jazzcup	2	O's American
Ankara	17	Cosy Bar	28	JazzHouse	21	Breakfast & Dinner 7
Atlas Bar	25	Den Grønne Kælder	5	JazzHuset Vognporten	44	Oscar 46
Bloomsday Bar	13	Domhuskælderen	38	Klaptræt	3	Pan Club 33
Bøf & Ost	20	Drop Inn	43	Konditoriet	23	Pasta Basta 22
Café Dan Turell	6	Els	8	Krasnapolsky	32	Peder Oxe 18
Café Ketchup	16	Gold Prag	39	L'Education Nationale	29	Ristorante Italiano 19
Café & Ølhalle 1892	1	Heaven	39	La Galette	37	RizRaz 10, 41
Café Sommersko	14	House of Souls	40	La Glace	27	Slotskælderen –
Can Can	45	Huset med det grønne træ	36	Masken	31	hos Gitte Kik 26
Cap Horn	11	Hviids Vinstue	15	Mojo	47	Thorvaldsens Hus 30
Charlie's Bar	12	Jailhouse CPH	24	Musen og Elefanten	42	Universitetscaféen 19
				Nyhavns Færgekro	9	Woodstock 35

The far end of this stretch is guarded, now as three hundred years ago, by the Kastellet, which lies within the fetching open spaces of Churchill Park.

Separated by a moat from Indre By, **Christiansborg** is the administrative centre for the whole country, housing the national parliament and government offices, as well as a number of museums and the ruins of Bishop Absalon's original castle. **Christianshavn**, facing Christiansborg across the inner harbour, provides further contrast, with its tightly proportioned and traditionally working-class streets and a pretty waterfront lined by Dutch-style dwellings. A few blocks to the east lies **Christiania**, the "free city" colonized by the young and homeless in the early 1970s, whose alternative society remains an enduring controversy in Danish life – and merits at least a quick look. **West of the city centre**, Vesterbrogade is the prime thoroughfare, beginning at the carefree delights of the Tivoli Gardens and running to the city fringes at Frederiksberg Have.

Indre By

The natural place from which to begin exploring Indre By (though not actually in it) is the buzzing open space of **Rådhuspladsen**. Here, the **Rådhus**, or City Hall (Mon–Fri 8am–5pm; guided tours in English Mon–Fri 3pm, Sat 10 & 11am; 30kr), has a spacious and elegant main hall that retains many of its original early twentieth-century features, not least the sculptured banisters heading up from the first floor; there's also a lift up to the **bell tower** (tours June–Sept Mon–Fri 10am, noon & 2pm, Sat noon; Oct–May Mon–Sat noon; 20kr), but the view over the city isn't particularly impressive. Note that the tower, but not the World Clock, is included in the Rådhus tour. More interesting is **Jens Olsen's World Clock** (Mon–Fri 10am–4pm, Sat 10am–1pm; 10kr), in a side room close to the entrance. What looks like a mass of inscrutable dials is an astronomical timepiece which took 27 years to perfect and contains a 570,000-year calendar plotting eclipses of the moon and sun, solar time, local time and various planetary orbits – all with incredible accuracy. At no. 57 Rådhuspladsen, and with an appeal of an entirely different kind, **Ripley's Believe It Or Not!** (June–Aug daily 9.30am–10.30pm; Sept–May Mon–Thurs & Sun 10am–6pm, Fri & Sat 10am–8pm; 80kr; ⍟www.topattractions .dk) is a collection of oddities based on the cartoons of American Robert L. Ripley – a life-size model of the world's tallest man and a bicycle made from matchsticks are just two of about hundreds of exhibits. Next door, also at no. 57 but to the right, **Hans Christian Andersen's Wonderful World** (same hours as Ripley's; 80kr, 128kr for a joint ticket with Ripley's, 210kr including Exploratorium and Guinness World Records Museum; ⍟www.topattractions.dk) opened in celebration of Hans Christian Andersen's two-hundredth anniversary in 2005. It offers a surprisingly engaging insight into his life in Copenhagen, and his many fairytales, but isn't nearly as in-depth as his museum in Odense (see p.153), his place of birth.

Along Strøget

Indre By proper begins with **Strøget** (literally "level measure"), also variously named Frederiksberggade, Nygade, Vimmelskaftet, Amagertorv and Østergade – which runs east–west across the district, lined by pricey stores and graceless fast-food dives. Very much the public face of Copenhagen, the strip is perfectly suited to ambling amongst the crowds of locals, tourists and street entertainers who parade along it. The most active part is usually around **Gammeltorv** and **Nytorv**, two adjacent squares ("old" and "new") flanking Strøget, where there's a hotdog stand and a couple of cafés, as well as stalls selling handmade jewellery and bric-a-brac. It was between these squares that the fifteenth-century Rådhus stood before it was destroyed by fire in 1795. A new Rådhus was erected on Nytorv a century later, and this is now the city's **Domhuset**, or Law Courts, marked by a suitably forbidding row of Neoclassical columns.

A few blocks east of here is the **Helligåndskirken** (daily noon–4pm), one of the oldest churches in the city, founded in the fourteenth century though largely rebuilt from 1728 onwards. While it's still in use as a place of worship, there are often art shows and other free exhibitions inside which provide a good excuse for a peek at the church's vaulted ceiling and slender granite columns. Just beyond, a path leads south off Strøget, through Højbro Plads and on to the grandiose (and now deconsecrated) **Skt Nikolaj Kirke** (daily noon–5pm; 20kr, free on Wed; ⊕www .nikolaj-ccac.dk); the building's upper floors are employed as one of Copenhagen's prime exhibition spaces for contemporary artists, while at ground level there's a pricey daytime café, packed with lunchers on business accounts.

The final section of Strøget is Østergade, where you'll find another international tourist pull, the **Guinness World Records Museum** (June–Aug daily 9.30am–10.30pm; Sept–May Mon–Thurs & Sun 10am–6pm, Fri & Sat 10am–8pm; 80kr, 119kr for a joint ticket with the Exploratorium, 210kr including Ripley's and H.C. Andersen's; ⊕www.topattractions.dk). It's much as you'd expect, with family-oriented exhibits on the world's tallest, fastest and smallest. Next door, along the same theme, **The Mystic Exploratorium** (June–Aug daily 9.30am–10.30pm; Sept–May Mon–Thurs & Sun 10am–6pm, Fri & Sat 10am–8pm; ⊕www.topattractions.dk; 60kr, or same joint tickets as Guinness museum) offers a surprisingly engaging chance to explore odd natural phenomena, such as how the weather works and how it can be manipulated (at least on a small scale). Beyond, Østergade flows past the swish and chic *Hotel d'Angleterre* into the biggest of the city squares, **Kongens Nytorv**. Built on what was the edge of the city in medieval times, the square has an equestrian statue of its creator, Christian V, in its centre and a couple of grandly ageing structures around two of its shallow angles. One of these, the **Kongelige Teater** or Royal Theatre, dates from 1874; the other, **Charlottenborg**, next door, was finished in 1683, at the same time as the square itself, for a son of Frederik III. It was later sold to Queen Charlotte Amalie, but since 1754 has been the home of the Royal Academy of Art, which uses some of the spacious rooms for eclectic art exhibitions (daily 10am–5pm, Thurs until 7pm; 30kr; ⊕www.charlottenborg-art.dk). Drop in, if only to glimpse the elegant interior.

The Latin Quarter and around

There's more interest among the tangle of buildings and streets **north of Strøget**. Crossing Gammeltorv and following Nørregade leads to the old university area, sometimes called the **Latin Quarter** – parts of it retain an academic function, which accounts for the book-carrying students milling around. The old university building is overlooked by Copenhagen's cathedral, **Vor Frue Kirke** (Mon–Thurs & Sat 8.30am–5pm, Fri 8.30–10.30am, Sun noon–3pm; free). Built on the site of a twelfth-century church, the present structure dates from 1829, when it was erected amidst the devastation caused by the British bombardment in 1807. The weighty figure of Christ behind the altar and the solemn statues of the apostles, some crafted by Bertel Thorvaldsen (for more on whom, see p.113), others by his pupils, merit a quick look. From the cathedral, dodge across Skindergade into **Gråbrødretorv**, a charming cobbled square filled with good cafés and restaurants and often crowded with buskers. The square dates back to 1238, when the city's first monastery was built here; today, it's a gathering place for locals in the know, who come in good weather to dine well or just enjoy a cool beer. Just northeast of here is the **Rundetårn** (June–Aug Mon–Sat 10am–8pm, Sun noon–8pm; Sept–May Mon–Sat 10am–5pm, Sun noon–5pm; 20kr; ⊕www.rundetaarn.dk), a round tower with a gradually ascending spiral ramp winding to its summit. It was built by Christian IV as an **observatory** – and perhaps also to provide a vantage point from which his subjects could admire his additions to the city. Today the best views are of the more immediate hive of medieval streets and the pedestrians filling them. Legend has it that Tsar Peter the Great sped to the top on horseback in 1715, pursued by the Tsarina in a six-horse carriage – a smoother technique than descending the cobbles on a skateboard, a short-lived fad in more recent times. If you're not quite up to trying that, look in on the contemporary **art gallery** part of the way up instead, which stages changing temporary exhibitions.

After leaving the Rundetårn, you could easily spend half an hour browsing the bookshops of Købmagergade, or visit the **Museum Erotica** (May–Sept daily 10am–11pm, Oct–April Sun–Thurs 11am–8pm, Fri & Sat 10am–10pm; 89kr; ⍟www.museumerotica.dk), which lurks along here at no. 24, a shrine to the erotic (and the just plain pornographic) through the ages. For something more traditional, head north along Købmagergade to the **Musical History Museum**, just off Kultorvet at Åbenrå 30 (May–Sept Mon–Wed & Fri–Sun 1–3.50pm; Oct–April Mon, Wed, Sat & Sun 1–3.50pm; 40kr; ⍟www.musikhistoriskmuseum.dk), where there's an impressive quantity of musical instruments and sound-producing devices spanning the globe and the last thousand years. Naturally the bulk come from Denmark (there are recordings to listen to), and there are some subtle insights into the social fabric of the nation to be gleaned from the yellowing photos of country dances and other get-togethers hung alongside the instruments.

Less musical sounds are provided by the cars hurtling along Nørre Voldgade, at the top of Kultorvet, which marks the edge of the pedestrianized streets of the old city. There are two reasons to queue up at the traffic lights and cross over: the first is the fruit-and-vegetable **market** – and Saturday flea market – on Israel Plads; the second is the **Workers' Museum** (*Arbejdermuseet*) at Rømersgade 22 (daily 10am–4pm; 50kr; ⍟www.arbejdermuseet.dk), an engrossing and thoughtful guide to working-class life in Copenhagen from the 1930s to the 1950s. Entering the museum, you walk down a reconstructed Copenhagen street – complete with passing tram and a shop window hawking the consumer durables of the day – and continue, via a backyard where washing hangs drying, through a printing works subsidized by the Marshall Plan and into a coffee shop, which sells an old-fashioned coffee-and-chicory blend by the cup. Elsewhere, mock-up house interiors contain family photos, newspapers and TVs showing newsreels of the time, while the permanent displays are backed up by some outstanding temporary exhibitions from labour movements around the world. There's a lunchtime restaurant in the basement serving good traditional Danish fare.

Gothersgade, the road marking the northern perimeter of Indre By, is home to the **Cinematek** (Tues–Fri 9.30am–10pm, Sat & Sun 12.30–10pm; ⍟www .cinemateket.dk), where there's a three-screen art-house cinema (tickets cost 50kr) and a *videotek* section where free films are shown.

North of Gothersgade

There's a profound change of mood **north of Gothersgade**. The congenial medieval alleyways of the old city give way to long, broad streets and a number of proud, aristocratic structures. There's a whole group of these in the **harbour area** near Nyhavn, although perhaps the most remarkable building of all is **Rosenborg Slot**, a short way to the west away from the harbour and close to several major **museums**.

From Nyhavn to Esplanaden

Running from Kongens Nytorv to the waterfront, its two sides divided by a slender canal, the wide but short street of **Nyhavn** is a former sailors' haunt that's now in the advanced stages of gentrification. One or two of the old tattoo shops remain, now looking decidedly artificial and increasingly outnumbered by small but expensive restaurants and cafés. The canalside is picturesque, though, with yachts moored on the water and well preserved eighteenth-century houses lining the street, three of which (numbers 18, 20 and 67) were lived in at various times by Hans Christian Andersen. Nyhavn is one of the city's most attractive places, with an astounding variety of restaurants crammed into the brightly painted townhouses alongside the canal. Fishing vessels, wooden pleasure craft and the city's canal tour boats fill the water with activity during the days, and a nightly ritual brings hundreds of young city residents to sit by the canal and drink "hand beers" bought at the nearest corner shop, facing off against the well-heeled tourists and locals dining at the extravagant restaurants and bars. The far end of Nyhavn was formerly the departure point for the boat to Rønne and, a block away at the end of Skt Annæ Plads, ferries for Oslo. Both have now been moved up to Nordhavnen, north of Østerport, and this area is now home to the state-of-the-art Playhouse theatre (ⓦwww.skuespilhus.dk), a design which sits happily with the new Opera House (see below) across the Inner Havnen on Holmen. The Playhouse is due to open in 2007; check the website for an update.

From Skt Annæ Plads, Amaliegade leads under a colonnade into the cobbled **Slots Plads**. The statue of Frederik V in its centre reputedly cost more than all four of the identical Rococo palaces that flank it – thanks to French sculptor Jacques Saly, who spent thirty years in Copenhagen at the court's expense creating it. Dating from the mid-eighteenth century, this quartet of imposing palaces provides a sudden burst of welcome symmetry into the city's generally haphazard layout. Two of them now serve as royal residences and there's a changing of the guard each day at noon when Queen Margarethe II is at home – generally attended by gangs of camera-toting observers.

Between the square and the harbour are the lavish modern gardens of **Amalie-haven**, giving views over to the grand Opera House building, while in the opposite direction, on Bredgade, looms the great dome of **Frederikskirken**, also known as the "Marmorkirken", or "Marble Church" (Mon, Tues & Thurs 10am–5pm; Wed 10am–6pm, Fri–Sun noon–5pm). Modelled on – and intended to rival – St Peter's in Rome, the church was begun in 1749, but because of its enormous cost lay unfinished until a century and a half later, when its most prominent feature (one of Europe's largest domes) was completed with Danish (rather than the more expensive Norwegian) marble. If you can time your visit to coincide with the **guided tour** (mid-June to Aug daily 1pm & 3pm; rest of the year Sat & Sun 1pm & 3pm; 20kr), the reward is the chance to climb first to the whispering gallery and then out onto the rim of the dome itself. From here there's a stunning, and usually blustery, view over the sharp geometry of Amalienborg and across the sea to the factories of Malmö in Sweden.

Over the road at Bredgade 62, the former Danish Surgical Academy now holds the **Medical History Museum** (guided tours only; in English mid-June to mid-Aug Sun 2pm; rest of the year in Danish only Wed–Fri 11am & 1pm, Sun 1pm; 30kr; ⓦwww.museion.ku.dk) – not a place to visit if you've spent the morning on a brewery binge, since the enthusiastically presented hour-long tour features aborted foetuses, straitjackets, syphilis treatments, amputated feet, eyeballs and a dissected head. Further along Bredgade at no. 68, the former Frederiksberg Hospital now houses the **Danish Museum of Decorative Art** (Tues & Thurs–Sun noon–4pm, Wed noon–6pm; 40kr; ⓦwww.kunstindustrimuseet.dk), a definite must if you have any interest in design. The exhibits trace the development of European – and particularly Danish – design, and examine the influence of Eastern styles on Western design. There's also an excellent café.

The Kastellet and around

A little way beyond the Museum of Decorative Art, Bredgade concludes at Esplanaden, facing the green space of **Churchill Park**. To the right, the German armoured car that was commandeered by Danes and used to bring news of the Nazi surrender marks the entrance to the **Museum of the Danish Resistance Movement** (*Frihedsmuseet*; May to mid-Sept Tues–Sat 10am–4pm, Sun 10am–5pm; mid-Sept to April Tues–Sat 11am–3pm, Sun 11am–4pm; 40kr, free Wed; ⓦwww .frihedsmuseet.dk). Initially, the Danes put up little resistance to the German invasion, but later the Nazis were given a systematically wretched time. The museum records the growth of the organized response and has a special section on the youths from Aalborg who formed themselves into the "Churchill Club". Feeling the adults weren't doing enough, this gang of 15-year-olds set about destroying German telegraph cables, blowing up cars and trains and stealing weapons. There's also a small but moving collection of artworks and handicrafts made by concentration camp inmates.

The road behind the museum crosses into the grounds of the **Kastellet** (daily 6am–sunset; free), a fortress built by Christian IV and expanded by his successors through the seventeenth century, after the loss of Danish possessions in Skåne had put the city within range of Swedish cannonballs. It's now occupied by the Danish army and its buildings are closed to the public. The tall arches and gateways, however, are an enjoyable setting for a stroll, as are the grassy slopes beside the moat. In a corner of the park, perched on some rocks just off the harbour bank – though you can't get there directly from the military compound, and must swing back to the road to find it – the **Little Mermaid** (*Den Lille Havfrue*) exerts an inexplicable magnetism on tourists. Since its unveiling in 1913, this bronze statue of a Hans Christian Andersen character, sculpted by Edvard Erichsen and paid for by the boss of the Carlsberg brewery, has become the best-known emblem of the city – a fact which has led to it being the victim of several subversive pranks: the original head disappeared in 1964, a cow's head was forced over the replacement in 1986, and more recently one of its arms was stolen. A hundred metres away is the far more spectacular **Gefion Fountain**, created by Anders Bundgaard and showing the goddess Gefion with her four sons, whom she's turned into oxen, having been promised in return as much land as she can plough in a single night. The legend goes that she ploughed a chunk of Sweden, then picked it up (creating Lake Vänern) and tossed it into the sea – where it became Zealand.

West from the harbour: Rosenborg Slot and the museums

Just southwest of the Kastellet lies **Nyboder**, a curious area of short, straight and narrow streets lined with rows of compact yellow dwellings. Although some of these are recently erected apartment blocks, the original houses, on which the newer constructions are modelled, were built by Christian IV to encourage his sailors to live in the city. The area at one time declined into a slum, but recent vigorous revamping has made it an increasingly sought-after district. The oldest (and prettiest) houses can be found along Skt Pauls Gade.

Across Sølvgade from Nyboder is the main entrance to **Rosenborg Slot** (June–Aug daily 10am–5pm; May & Sept daily 10am–4pm; Oct daily 11am–3pm; Nov–April Tues–Sun 11am–2pm; 65kr), a Dutch Renaissance palace and one of the most elegant buildings bequeathed by Christian IV to the city. Though intended as a country residence, Rosenborg served as the main domicile of Christian IV (he died here in 1648) and, until the end of the nineteenth century, the monarchs who succeeded him. It became a museum as early as 1830 and in the main building you can still see the rooms and furnishings used by the regal occupants. The highlights, though, are in the treasury downstairs, which displays the rich accessories worn by Christian IV (and his horse), the crown of absolute monarchs and the present crown jewels. Outside, the splendidly neat garden can be reached by leaving the palace itself and using the park's main entrance on the corner of Øster Voldgade and Sølvgade. On the west side of the Slot is Kongens Have, the city's oldest public park and a popular place for picnics, and, across Øster Voldgade, the **Botanical Garden** (*Botanisk Have*; April–Sept daily 8.30am–6pm; Oct–March Tues–Sun 8.30am–4pm; free; ＠www.botanic-garden.ku.dk), with its beautiful old Palm House.

Opposite Rosenborg Have, and marked by a few runic stones, is the **Geology Museum** (Tues–Sun 1–4pm; 25kr, free on Wed; ＠www.geologisk-museum.dk), which has a great meteorite section but is otherwise quite missable unless you're a mineral freak. More worthwhile is the neighbouring National Gallery, or **Statens Museum for Kunst**, Sølvegade 48–50 (Tues & Thurs–Sun 10am–5pm, Wed 10am–8pm; permanent collection 50kr or free on Wed, 70kr during special exhibitions; ＠www.smk.dk), a mammoth collection that's too large to take in on a short visit. While all the big cheeses have their patch – there are some minor Picassos and more major works by Matisse and Braque, Modigliani, Dürer and El Greco – it's the creations of Emil Nolde, with their bloated ravens, hunched figures and manic children, that best capture the mood of the place. In an effort to keep up with the times, the museum recently doubled in size, adding a new building for modern art (including contemporary Danish and other European work), which also has a restaurant and children's room, and affords good views of Kongens Have.

Art fans will find further rich pickings across the park behind the museum, in the fine **Den Hirschsprungske Samling** (Mon & Wed–Sun 11am–4pm; 35kr, free Wed; ⓦwww.hirschsprung.dk) on Stockholmsgade. Heinrich Hirschsprung was a late-nineteenth-century tobacco baron who sunk some of his profits into the patronage of emerging Danish artists, including the Skagen artists (see p.203). It was Hirschsprung's wish that on his death the collection – which also features Eckersburg, Købke and lesser names from the Danish mid-nineteenth-century Golden Age – would be given to the nation, but the government of the day vetoed the plan, and Hirschsprung set up his own gallery.

Christiansborg

Connected to Indre By by several short bridges, **Christiansborg** sits on the island of Slotsholmen. It's a mundane part of the city, but administratively – and historically – an important one. It was here, in the twelfth century, that Bishop Absalon built the castle that was the origin of the city, and the drab royal palace (completed in 1916) that occupies the site is nowadays given over primarily to government offices and the state parliament or **Folketinget** (guided tours in English: July–Sept daily 2pm; rest of the year Sun 2pm; free). Close to the bus stop on Christiansborg Slotsplads is the entrance to Christiansborg's main courtyard; in this passageway, you'll find the **Ruins under Christiansborg** (daily 9.30am–3.30pm, Oct–April closed Mon; 30kr), where a staircase leads down to the remains of Bishop Absalon's original castle. The first fortress suffered repeated mutilations by the Hanseatic League, and Erik of Pomerania had a replacement erected in 1390, into which he moved the royal court. This in turn was pulled down by Christian VI and another castle built between 1731 and 1745. The stone and brick walls that comprise the ruins, and the articles from the castles stored in an adjoining room, are surprisingly absorbing, the mood enhanced by the semi-darkness and lack of external noise. Turn left into the palace courtyard as you exit the ruins and you'll find the entrance to the **Royal Reception Rooms** (guided tours in English: May–Sept daily 11am, 1 & 3pm; Oct–April Tues–Sun 3pm; 60kr) on the right. They're used by the royal family to entertain important visitors, and it's worth popping in to peek at the richly decorated throne room, with delicate silk from Lyon covering the walls and a row of modern tapestries (made for the Queen's fiftieth birthday) depicting Denmark's colourful past.

There are a number of other less captivating museums in and around Christiansborg Slotsplads, to which the ticket office for the ruins can provide directions – the confusing array of buildings makes it easy to get lost. That said, you could probably sniff your way to the **Royal Stables** (May–Sept Fri–Sun 2–4pm; Oct–April Sat & Sun 2–4pm; 20kr), dating from 1745 and one of the few remaining parts of the original Baroque Christiansborg, lavishly decorated with pillars, vaulted ceilings and walls of Tuscan marble. Apparently not even the king's own chambers were this extravagant. Nearby, the **Theatre Museum** (Tues–Thurs 11am–3pm, Sat & Sun 1–4pm; 30kr) is housed in what was the eighteenth-century Court Theatre and displays original costumes, set-models and the old dressing rooms and boxes. Exiting the courtyard and walking through Tøjhusgade takes you to the **Armoury Museum** (*Tøjhusmuseet*; Tues–Sun noon–4pm, plus Mon in July; 40kr, free Wed; ⓦwww.thm.dk), an Eldorado for arms buffs where you can view weaponry from Christian IV's arsenal up until today, and a host of crests and coats of arms. A few strides further on, a small gateway leads into the gorgeous tree-lined grounds of the **Royal Library** – an excellent venue for a picnic. On the waterfront at Christians Brygge 8, the library's big black extension building (Mon–Sat 8am–11pm) includes spaces for temporary exhibits, a concert hall, conference rooms and restaurants. Finally, adjacent to Christiansborg Slotsplads sits the long, low form of the seventeenth-century **Børsen**, or Stock Exchange – with its spire of four entwined dragons' tails, it's one of the most distinctive buildings in the city and worth seeking out.

Around Christiansborg

On the far north side of Slotsholmen island is the palace chapel, **Christiansborg Slotskirke** (Sun noon–4pm, July daily noon–4pm; free), designed by prominent Golden Age architect C.F. Hansen and a beautiful example of Neoclassical architecture, with magnificent frieze by Bertel Thorvaldsen encircling the dome. In stark contrast to the elegant, light church, the bombastic and colourful **Thorvaldsen's Museum** next door (Tues–Sun 10am–5pm; 20kr, free Wed; ⊕www.thorvaldsens museum.dk) is home to an enormous collection of work and memorabilia of Denmark's most famous sculptor, and also houses the remains of the man himself. Despite negligible schooling, Bertel Thorvaldsen (1770–1844) drew his way into the Danish Academy of Fine Arts before moving onto Rome, where he perfected the heroic, classical figures for which he became famous. Nowadays he's not widely known outside Denmark, although in his day he enjoyed international renown and won commissions all over Europe.

Other than a selection of early works in the **basement**, the labels of the great, hulking statues read like a roll call of the famous and infamous: Vulcan, Adonis, John Russell, Gutenberg, Pius VII and Maximilian; while the **Christ Hall** contains the huge casts of the statues of Christ and Apostles which can be seen in Vor Frue Kirke (see p.108). A prolific and gifted sculptor, Thorvaldsen was something of a wit, too. Asked by the Swedish artist J.T. Sergel how he managed to make such beautiful figures, he held up the scraper with which he was working and replied, "With this".

There's another major collection a short walk west over the Slotsholmen moat: the **National Museum** (Tues–Sun 10am–5pm; 50kr, free Wed; ⊕www.natmus.dk) is really strongest (as you'd expect) on Danish history, and if you've any interest in the subject, you could easily spend a couple of hours here. A lot of the early stuff, ranging from prehistory to the Viking days, comes from Jutland – jewellery, bones and even bodies, all remarkably well preserved; much of it was only discovered after wartime fuel shortages led to large-scale digging of the Danish peat bogs. Informative explanatory texts help clarify the **Viking section**, whose best exhibits – apart from the familiar horned helmets – are the sacrificial gifts, among them the Sun Chariot, a model horse carrying a sun disc with adornments of gold and bronze. Further floors store a massive collection of almost anything and everything that featured in Christian-era Denmark up to the nineteenth century – finely engraved wooden altarpieces, furniture, clothing and more – as well as a good section on peasant life.

Christianshavn

From Christiansborg, the Knippels Bro bridge crosses the Inder Havnen to the island of Amager and into **Christianshavn**, built as an autonomous new town by Christian IV in the early sixteenth century to provide housing for workers in the shipbuilding industry. It was given features more common to Dutch port towns of the time, even down to a small canal (Wilders Christianshavn Kanal), and in parts the area is more redolent of Amsterdam than Copenhagen. Although its present inhabitants are fairly well-off – as evidenced by some immaculately preserved houses along Overgaden oven Vandet – Christianshavn still has the mood of a working-class quarter, with a group of secondhand shops along the district's main street, Torvegade.

Poking skywards through the trees near Torvegade is the blue-and-gold spire of **Vor Frelsers Kirke** (April–Aug Mon–Sat 11am–4.30pm, Sun noon–4.30pm; Sept–March Mon–Sat 11am–3.30pm, Sun noon–3.30pm; free; access to spire April–Oct only, 20kr), on the corner of Prinsessegade and Skt Annæ Gade. The **spire**, with its helter-skelter outside staircase, was added to the otherwise plain church in the mid-eighteenth century, instantly becoming one of the more recognizable features on the city's horizon. Climbing the spire (which you can do between April and October only) is fun, but not entirely without risk – though the rumour that its artchitect fell off it and died is, while plausible, untrue. To get to the spire, go through the church and up to a trap door which opens onto the platform where the external steps begin: there are four hundred of them, slanted and slippery (especially after rain) and gradually becoming smaller. The reward for reaching the top is a great view of Copenhagen and beyond.

Christiania

A few streets northeast of Vor Frelsers Kirke, **Christiania** occupies an area that was for centuries used as a barracks, before the soldiers moved out in 1971 and it was colonized by young and homeless people. It was declared a "**free city**" on September 24, 1971, with the aim of operating autonomously from Copenhagen, and its continued existence has fuelled one of the longest-running debates in Danish (and Scandinavian) society. One by-product of its idealism and the freedoms assumed by its residents (and, despite recent lapses, generally tolerated by successive governments and the police) was to make Christiania a refuge for petty criminals and shady individuals from all over the city. But the problems have inevitably been overplayed by Christiania's critics, and a surprising number of Danes – of all ages and from all walks of life – do support the place, not least because Christiania has performed usefully, and altruistically, when established bodies have been found wanting. An example has been in the weaning of heroin addicts off their habits (once, a 24-hour cordon was thrown around the area to prevent dealers reaching the addicts inside: reputedly the screams – of deprived junkies and suppliers being "dealt with" – could be heard all night). And Christiania residents have stepped in to provide free shelter and food for the homeless at Christmas when the city administration declined to do so.

The population of around one thousand is swelled in summer by the curious and the sympathetic, with many heading straight for the open hash market, known as Pusherstreet, where cannabis smoking was tolerated by the government until 2004, when a clampdown by the right-wing government saw raids designed to "normalize" things (ie stop trade), and resulted in so-called hash clubs popping up throughout the city. Since then, things have calmed down, and Pusherstreet remains open for business: Bob Marley and John Lennon blare out from the bars and the area is awash with psychedelic paintings. Residents ask people not to camp here, and tourists not to point cameras at the weirder-looking inhabitants. The craft shops and restaurants are fairly cheap, and nearly all are good, as are a couple of innovative music and performance art venues (see p.125). These, and the many imaginative dwellings, including some built on stilts in a small lake, make a visit worthwhile. Additionally, there are a number of alternative political and arts groups based in Christiania; for **information** on these – and on the district generally – call in to **Galopperiet** (Tues–Sun 2–7pm; Ⓦwww.gallopperiet.dk), to the right of the area's main entrance on Prinsessegade. Christiania can be quite confusing to navigate, so it's a good idea to go on one of the ninety-minute **guided tours** of the area, which are conducted by local residents (July–Aug daily 3pm, Sept–June Sat & Sun 3pm; 30kr; Ⓣ32 57 96 70; Ⓦwww.christiania.org); if you're in a group of four people or more, try to book at least one day in advance; otherwise, you can just turn up. Commencing with a short video presentation about Christiania's history, the tours are extremely informative, especially if you're interested in alternative ways of social organization.

Christiania is also the gateway to **Holmen**, once a forgotten naval station but now a complex of four art schools – the National School of Architecture, the National School of Theatre, the National Film School and the Rhythmical Music Conservatory – which the city plans to continue developing in coming years. Check the area for current developments – change is in the air and it's quickly becoming Europe's latest industrial zone to be taken over by artists and revellers.

Along Vesterbrogade

Hectic **Vesterbrogade** begins on the far side of Rådhuspladsen from Strøget, and its first attraction is Copenhagen's most famous after the Little Mermaid: the **Tivoli Gardens** (mid-April to mid-June & mid-Aug to late Sept Mon–Thurs & Sun 11am–11pm, Fri 11am–1am; Sat 11am–midnight, mid-June to mid-Aug Mon–Thurs & Sun 11am–midnight, Fri & Sat 11am–1am; mid-Nov to Dec daily 10am–11pm; 75kr; ⊛www.tivoli.dk). This park of many bland amusements, which first flung open its gates in 1843, was modelled on the Vauxhall Gardens in London, and in turn became the model for the Festival Gardens in London's Battersea Park. The name is now synonymous with Copenhagen at its most innocently pleasurable, and the opening of the gardens each April is taken to mark the beginning of summer. There are fountains, over 25 fairground rides (15, 30 or 45kr each, paid with 15kr tickets bought in books from two ticket outlets; these also sell 195kr passes which cover all the rides), and fireworks displays at midnight (Wed & Sat; between April and June call ☏33 75 10 01 for timings), as well as nightly entertainment in the central arena, encompassing everything from acrobats and jugglers to top rated international performers (look out for Friday Rock live music performances at 10pm). Naturally, it's overrated and overpriced, but an evening spent wandering among the revellers of all ages indulging in the mass consumption of ice cream is an experience worth having – once, at any rate. Close to the gardens' Vesterbrogade entrance, on the corner of Hans Christian Andersens Boulevard, is the predictable **Louis Tussaud's Wax Museum** (May–Sept 10am–11pm; rest of the year 10am–6pm; 80kr; ⊛www.tussaud.dk).

Behind the Tivoli, across Tietgensgade towards the harbour, is the dazzling **Ny Carlsberg Glyptotek**, Dantes Plads 7 (Tues–Sun 10am–4pm; 20kr, free Wed & Sun; ⊛www.glyptoteket.dk), opened in 1897 by brewer Carl Jacobsen as a venue for ordinary people to see classical art exhibited in classical style. Its centrepiece is the conservatory: "Being Danes," said Jacobsen, "we know more about flowers than art, and during the winter this greenery will make people pay a visit; and then, looking at the palms, they might find a moment for the statues." It's an idea that succeeded, and even now the gallery is well used – and not just by art lovers: there's a programme of classical music concerts every Sunday and some Wednesdays (call ☏33 41 81 41 for details), as well as a seasonal roster of other events, some free; pick up a schedule at the entrance.

As for the contents, this is by far Copenhagen's finest gallery, with a stirring array of Greek, Roman and Egyptian art and artefacts, as well as what is reckoned to be the biggest (and best) collection of Etruscan art outside Italy. There are excellent examples of nineteenth-century European art too, including a complete collection of Degas casts made from the fragile working sculptures he left at his death, Manet's *Absinthe Drinker*, and two small cases containing tiny caricatured heads by Honore Daumier. Easily missed, but actually the most startling room in the place, is an ante-chamber with just a few pieces – early works by Man Ray, some Chagall sketches and a Picasso pottery plate. There's also a French wing containing Impressionist art and work from Danish painting's so-called "Golden Age" (1800–50), plus a French-themed café on a balcony overlooking greenhouses of palm trees.

Finally, if you're at all interested in Denmark's world-class tradition of design, don't leave this area without at least looking in on the **Danish Design Centre**, 27–29 Hans Christian Andersens Boulevard (Mon, Tues, Thurs & Fri 10am–5pm, Wed

△ Arne Jacobsen's Egg Chair

10am–9pm, Sat & Sun 11am–4pm; 40kr; ⊛www.ddc.dk). The building, designed by Danish architect Henning Larsen, serves as an exhibit hall, research facility and showcase for all sorts of industrial design, from Bang & Olufsen stereo equipment to Børge Mogensen furniture.

Beyond the Tivoli Gardens

Just west of the train station, the streets between Vesterbrogade and **Istedgade** used to be Copenhagen's token red-light area, and the only part of the city where you might have felt unsafe. Over the years, though, the low rents attracted students and a large number of immigrant families, who are now, in turn, gradually being replaced by young middle-class families as the area undergoes the city's most extensive refurbishment programme. However, you can still walk along Istedgade and be likely to find rastas and Turks sipping tea from tulip glasses, plus a number of diverse (but well-priced) ethnic eateries.

At Vesterbrogade 59 is the **City Museum** (*Københavns Bymuseum*; Mon & Thurs–Sun 10am–4pm, Wed 10am–9pm; 20kr, free Fri; ⊛www.bymuseum.dk), which has reconstructed ramshackle house exteriors and tradesmen's signs from early Copenhagen. Looking at these, the impact of Christian IV becomes resoundingly apparent, and a large room details the form and cohesion that this monarch and amateur architect gave the city, even including a few of his own drawings. The rest of the city's history is told by paintings – far too many, in fact. Head upstairs for the room devoted to Søren Kierkegaard, much the most interesting part of the museum. It's filled with bits and bobs – furniture from his home, paintings of his girlfriend Regine Olsen, jewellery, books and manuscripts – that form an intriguing footnote to the life of this nineteenth-century Danish writer and philosopher (see below).

A few minutes to the north of Vesterbrogade, on the corner with Vester Søgade at Gammel Kongevej 10, is the **Tycho Brahe Planetarium** (Mon, Tues & Fri–Sun 10.30am–8.30pm, Wed & Thurs 9.30am–8.30pm; 25kr; ⍟www.tycho.dk); the biggest in Scandinavia, it's named after the world-famous Danish astronomer who invented instruments to accurately plot the sun, planets and stars for the first time. Apart from an astronomical- and space-related section, the in-house Omnimax Theatre, with a 1000-square-metre dome screen, is the best part of the Planetarium. Films (in 3D) are shown every hour on the hour, and cost a steep 90kr to watch (includes entrance ticket to Planetarium).

West to the Carlsberg Brewery and Frederiksberg Have

Way out west along Vesterbrogade (save your legs by taking bus #6A to Valby Langgade and crossing the street), down Gamle Carlsberg Vej, you'll find the **Carlsberg Brewery**'s Visitor Centre at no. 11 (Tues–Sun 10am–4pm; 40kr). Once you've made your way through the surprisingly absorbing centre, which depicts the history of Danish beer brewing and includes the new *Jacobsen Brewhouse* microbrewery, you get a free beer at the upstairs bar overlooking the copper brewing kettles. Inside the brewery proper, note the fine Elephant Gate that used to be the main entrance: four elephants carved in granite supporting the building.

Vesterbrogade finishes up opposite the **Frederiksberg Have**, which contains the Frederiksberg Palace, now used as a military academy and closed to the public. Throughout the eighteenth century, the city's top brass came here to mess about in boats along the network of canals that dissect the copious lime-tree groves, and its pleasant surrounds are now a popular weekend picnic spot for locals. While here, you might call in at the entertaining **Storm P. Museum** (May–Sept Tues–Sun 10am–4pm; Oct–April Wed, Sat & Sun 10am–4pm; 30kr), by the gate facing Frederiksberg Allé. It's packed with the satirical cartoons that made "Storm P." (Robert Storm Petersen) one of the most popular by-lines in Danish newspapers from the 1920s. Even if you don't understand the Danish captions, you'll gain an insight into the national sense of humour.

Beyond the Frederiksberg Palace, at Roskildevej 32 (buses #4A, #6A, #18 and #26), is Copenhagen's **Zoo** (April–May & Sept Mon–Fri 9am–5pm, Sat & Sun 9am–6pm; June–Aug daily 9am–6pm; Oct daily 9am–5pm; Nov–March daily 9am–4pm; 95kr; ⍟www.zoo.dk), which has the usual array of caged lions, elephants and monkeys, plus a special children's section.

Søren Kierkegaard

Søren Kierkegaard is inextricably linked with Copenhagen, yet his championing of individual will over social conventions and his rejection of materialism did little to endear him to his fellow Danes. Born in Copenhagen in 1813, Kierkegaard believed himself set on an "evil destiny" – partly the fault of his father, who is best remembered for having cursed God on a Jutland heath. Kierkegaard's first book, **Either/Or**, published in 1843, was inspired by his love affair with one **Regine Olsen**; she failed to understand it, however, and married someone else. Few other people understood *Either/Or*, in fact, and Kierkegaard, though devastated by the broken romance, came to revel in the enigma he had created, becoming a "walking mystery in the streets of Copenhagen" (he lived in a house on Nytorv). He was a prolific author, sometimes publishing two books on the same day and often writing under pseudonyms. His greatest philosophical works were written by 1846 and are often claimed to have laid the foundations of **existentialism**.

Out from the centre

Unlike many other major European cities, Copenhagen has only a few miles of drab housing estates on its periphery before the countryside begins. There are a number of things worth venturing out for, although none of them need keep you away from the main action for long.

Just northwest of the inner city, only fifteen minutes on foot from Indre By, is **Assistens Kirkegård**, a cemetery built to cope with the dead from the 1711–12 plague outbreak. More interestingly, it contains the graves of Hans Christian Andersen and Søren Kierkegaard – both well signposted, although not from the same entrance. If you get lost, look at the handy catalogue by the gate on Kapelvej. The cemetery is off Nørrebrogade in the district of Nørrebro: walk from the Nørreport station along Frederiksborggade and over the lake. Alternatively, buses #5A, and #350S run along the graveyard's edge. Further northwest is **Grundtvigs Kirke** (April–Oct Mon–Wed & Fri–Sat 9am–4pm, Thurs 9am–6pm, Sun noon–4pm; rest of the year Mon–Wed & Fri–Sat 9am–4pm, Thurs 9am–6pm, Sun noon–1pm), an astonishing yellow-brick creation whose gabled front resembles a massive church organ which rises upwards and completely dwarfs the row of terraced houses that share the street. Named after and dedicated to the founder of the Danish folk high schools, the church was designed by Jensens Klint and his son in 1913, but was not finished until 1926. From the city centre, it's a twenty-minute journey on buses #21 or #69. Get off in the small square of Bispetorv soon after passing the Bispebjerg Hospital; the church itself is in På Bjerget.

South of Copenhagen

If the weather's good, take a trip south to the **Amager beaches**, about half an hour away by Metro (get off at Lergravparken), from where it's a ten-minute walk. Less pretentious than the beaches to the north of the capital, Amager's beaches have both sandy and pebbly stretches, and shallow waters ideal for kids to paddle in. On the other side of the airport from the beaches (take bus #30, #31, #32 or #350S) lies **DRAGØR**, an atmospheric cobbled fishing village with a couple of good local history collections in the **Dragør Museum** by the harbour (May–Sept Tues–Sun noon–4pm; 20kr; ⊛www.dragoermuseum.dk; 20kr), and the **Amager Museum** (May–Sept Tues–Sun noon–4pm; Oct–April Wed & Sun noon–4pm; ⊛www.amager museet.dk; 30kr), a fifteen-minute walk away from Kirkevej (or take bus #30).

Further out from the city centre, on the road to Køge, the southern suburb of **Ishøj** is home to many ethnic communities, mainly from the Middle East, and an excellent museum of modern art, **Arken** (Tues & Thurs–Sun 10am–5pm, Wed 10am–9pm; 60kr; ⊛www.arken.dk). Looking very much like a ship, this sleek showcase rises from Ishøj beach and houses excellent temporary exhibitions, plus a glassed-in restaurant overlooking the bay that serves herring specialities for lunch. From central Copenhagen take the S-train line A or E to Ishøj station and then bus #128, a thirty-minute journey altogether.

North of Copenhagen

If you're tired of history, culture and the arts, you might fancy a trip to the **Experi-mentarium** (Mon, Wed, Thurs & Fri 9.30am–5pm, Tues 9.30am–9pm, Sat & Sun 11am–5pm; 115kr; ⊛www.experimentarium.dk), at the northern outskirts of Østerbro; take bus #1A, #14 or #21 northwards and get off at Tuborgvej. Located in a former beer-bottling hall, this workshop-cum-museum attempts to raise scientific awareness through some interesting and entertaining hands-on exhibits, such as a disco which beats to your biorhythms. There's a pavilion area for young children as well, with trick mirrors, a "Fairy-Tale Room", and the chance to build a house using "superlight" bricks. The constantly changing special exhibits are generally always well-made state-of-the-art affairs, and worth checking out.

Just outside the city limits, reached by S-train line C or bus #14 or #166, **CHARLOTTENLUND** has a lovely beach, good for sunbathing – as long as you can ignore the smoke-belching chimneys in the background. Its main attraction these days is the **Danish Aquarium** (daily: May to mid-Sept 10am–6pm; mid-Sept to Oct & Feb–April 10am–5pm; Nov–Jan 10am–4pm; 75kr; ✆www.danmarksak varium.dk), with its impressive collection of tropical fish, sharks, crocodiles and turtles. Nearby **Charlottenlund Fort**, these days housing a campsite (see p.105), has a few abandoned cannons and great views over the city and out to sea. If not camping, you're better off making for **Charlottenlund Slotshave**, a former manor house with a gorgeous park (open 24hr; free) perfect for strolling and picnicking.

If you're in the mood for an amusement park but can't face (or afford) Tivoli, venture out to **Bakken** (daily: July noon–midnight; late March to June & Aug varying hours between noon–midnight, call ✆39 63 35 44; free; tour passes to all 35 rides 119/239kr depending on time of year; ✆www.bakken.dk), close to the Klampenborg stop at the end of line C on the S-train network. Set in a corner of Kongens Dyrehave (the royal deer park), it's possibly more fun than its city counterpart – and certainly more down-to-earth – and besides the usual swings and roller-coasters offers easy walks through oak and beech woods. Strolling back towards Klampenborg along Christiansholmsvej, a left turn at the restaurant *Peter Lieps Hus* gives superb views over the Øresund.

Finally, half an hour's bus journey (#184) to the north is the village of **LYNGBY**, and its **Open-Air Museum** (*Frilandsmuseet*; late March to late Oct Tues–Sun 10am–5pm; 50kr, free Wed; ✆www.natmus.dk), set inside a large park and comprising restored seventeenth- to mid-nineteenth-century buildings, drawn from all over Denmark and its former territories. A walk through the park leads to the Sorgenfri Palace, one-time home of Frederik V (closed to the public). Take S-train line B to Sorgenfri.

Eating

Whether you want a quick coffee and pastry, or to sit down to a five-course gourmet dinner, you'll find more choice – and lower prices – in Copenhagen than in any other Scandinavian capital. Many of the city's innumerable **cafés** offer good-value, filling brunches, sandwiches and snacks, and double up in the evening as bars. There are also plenty of places selling shawarmas, kebabs, pizzas, pitta breads with falafel, china boxes and sushi, and as a general rule they get cheaper the further away from the centre you get. Most **restaurants** are open for lunch and dinner: prices tend to be higher in the evenings, but there are generally good-value deals at lunchtime, so those on a budget needn't deprive themselves of a blowout. Places in Indre By and Christiansborg are marked on the map on p.106; all others appear on the main Copenhagen map (p.99).

If you're stocking up for a **picnic** – or a trip to Sweden or Norway – take advantage of the numerous outlets selling *smørrebrød* (open sandwiches); Domhusets *Smørrebrød*, on Kattesundet 18, and Centrum *Smørrebrød*, Vesterbrogade 6c, are two of the most central. For more general food shopping, use one of the **supermarkets**: ISO at Vesterbrogade 23, Irma at Vesterbrogade 1 and Superbrugsen by Nørreport Station are all top-range. Netto and Fakta are by far the cheapest and more chaotic; you'll find Netto branches at Nørre Voldgade 94, Fiolstræde 9, Landemærket 11 and Kampmannsgade 1; and Fakta on Nørrebrogade 14–16 and on Borgergade 27.

Brunch and light snacks

Bang & Jensen Istedgade 130, Vesterbro. A popular café at the quieter end of Istedgade, with a renowned daily brunch (8am–4pm) from 75kr. There's also a breakfast buffet (8–11am) at 50kr, and sandwiches and light meals all day. Turns into a busy bar at night, especially when there's music on at nearby *Vega* (see p.126).

Café Gavlen Ryesgade 1, Nørrebro. Small, good-value café near the more pricey places on Sankt Hans Torv. Basic egg-and-bacon brunch for 40kr, three pieces of *smørrebrød* for 40kr, and a daily special for 55kr.

Café Ketchup Pilestræde 19, Indre By. Hugely trendy place with a glass-fronted café at front and an exceedingly posh and expensive restaurant out back. The café section is busy throughout the day, starting with brunch (11.30am–4pm) and onto sandwiches – try the Bali-style club sandwich – and light snacks. DJs play for a heaving crowd on Friday and Saturday nights. Closed Sun.

Café Sommersko Kronprinsensgade 6, Indre By. French-style café whose popularity hasn't declined one bit since it opened in the mid-1970s. Good both for its food and drinks – the filling Sunday brunch is especially recommended (95–100kr). Open until 4am during the weekends.

Den Sorte Gryde Istedgade 108, Vesterbro. Legendarily huge burgers (39kr for a 300g treat) but also good for traditional Danish fare. Try the *biksemad* (diced beef and potato served with pickled beetroot and a fried egg on top) for 52kr. Mostly take-away.

Det Gule Hus Istedgade 46, Vesterbro. Unmissable yellow villa offering great breakfast and brunch. Choose between pancakes (21kr), three types of brunch (one vegetarian, one decidedly carnivorous, and one French, all 69kr) or standard continental-type breakfast with fresh bread. Also lunch and dinner, including at least one veggie option, starting at 118kr.

Floras Kaffebar Blågårdsgade 27, Nørrebro. A temple to coffee serving more varieties than you can imagine, and with outdoor seating in summer. Cheapest main course (chilli con carne) is 69kr, plus homemade burgers, soups and cakes, served in an easygoing atmosphere. Come back at night

for cheaper-than-average beer and a game of backgammon.

Front Page Sortedams Dossering 21, Nørrebro. A beautiful spot overlooking one of Copenhagen's most picturesque lakes. Perfect for a quiet coffee and a sandwich, or a cool beer and some tapas.

Hackenbusch Vesterbrogade 124, Vesterbro. Colourful café-bar with an inventive blackboard menu. Dishes (always one vegetarian) from 88kr, and bargain burgers for 35kr on Tuesdays. Also breakfast and brunch.

Kaffesalonen Peblinge Dossering 6, Nørrebro. Super-hip former workers' caff with outdoor tables looking out onto a lake, and a popular waterside terrace on a floating dock in the summer, when it's perfect for an ice cream or a beer. Excellent brunch (78–98kr) and French-style cuisine such as lightly grilled tuna for lunch and dinner.

Klaptræet Kultorvet 11, Indre By. Popular, inexpensive refuelling spot for shoppers, serving coffee, huge sandwiches, chilli con carne, burgers, quiches and snacks.

Konditoriet Amagertorv 6, Indre By. Upstairs tea-room of the Royal Copenhagen porcelain and silverware shop, serving coffees, cocoa and fine Danish pastries, as well as finger sandwiches. Closed Sun.

La Galette Larsbjørnsstræde 9, Indre By. A bit difficult to find (you have to cross a courtyard to get to no.9) but worth it for the

△ Ice-cream and hotdog kiosk, Copenhagen

Late-night food

For late-night eating, as well as *Pasta Basta*, listed on p.123, and the late-opening cafés mentioned under "Nightlife", you might want to join the thespians munching fresh bread and rolls in *Herluf Trolle*, on Herluf Trolles Gade, just behind the Royal Theatre, which opens until 5am from Thursday till Saturday. Filling breakfasts can be had from 3am at *O's American Breakfast & Dinner* (see below).

authentic Breton pancakes (25–70kr), made with organic buckwheat and a whole array of fillings from smoked salmon to chocolate and chestnut mousse. Dinner only on Sun.

La Glace Skoubogade 29, Indre By. The place to go if you feel like spoiling yourself with something sweet – try the beautifully sculpted cream-heavy cakes and pots of real hot chocolate, or just a Danish and coffee. The cakes and traditions haven't changed much since this place opened in 1870, and for good reason.

O's American Breakfast & Dinner Øster Farimagsgade, Nyboder. American-style Southern cooking, with big breakfasts until late afternoon, then switches to Southern soul food and barbecue meals for dinner. There's another branch at Gothersgade 15, in Indre By nightlife area, where you can get breakfast from 3am during the weekend.

Park Østerbrogade 79, Østerbro. Beautifully decorated with crystal chandeliers and high stucco ceilings, *Park* is the perfect spot for a coffee, a burger (99kr) or light lunch (filling salads from 79kr) after a walk around Fælledparken.

Pussy Galore's Flying Circus Sankt Hans Torv 30, Nørrebro. Trendy café with outdoor seating on the square. Popular for brunch (8am–4pm; 85kr) and in the evenings, when beer and wine take priority.

Riccos – Butik & Kaffebar Istedgade 119, Vesterbro. With out a doubt the best coffee in town. The owner describes himself as a coffee nerd and if he's not working behind the counter, he's travelling the globe in search of the finest beans. Apart from coffee in various forms – hot as well as cold – there's also cakes and Italian ice cream.

Restaurants

Many of the city's **Danish restaurants** knock out affordable (around 80kr) and high-quality **lunches**, either from a set menu or from an open buffet. **Dinner** will always be more expensive, although Copenhagen's growing band of **ethnic restaurants** are making it increasingly affordable – many have adopted the Scandinavian open-table idea, offering all-you-can-eat meals from around 60kr, but don't plan a night's dancing after wading through one. These places are also usually the best bet for finding vegetarian food.

As a rule, Danes tend to finish dining early, if they dine out at all – most actually prefer eating at home. As a result, most restaurants in the city cater to tourists and stay open until 11pm or midnight. Roughly half the city's restaurants don't open at all on Sunday, and those that do keep shorter hours, usually opening for dinner only; we've specified closing days in the reviews below. Finally, Danes are keen on **reserving tables** in advance, and while you're unlikely to have to wait long for a place, it's still a good idea to ring ahead at the city's more popular spots. We've given telephone numbers for places where reservations are advisable.

Danish restaurants

Bøf & Ost Gråbrødretorv 13, Indre By ☎33 11 99 11. Set in a building which incorporates parts of a medieval monastery, *Bøf & Ost* ("steak and cheese") oozes history and offers a lunchtime buffet with ten different types of herring (98kr) as well as a metre-long list of *smørrebrød* toppings. The dinner menu is more in line with the name, with a selection of steaks (and fish) with cheesy sauces on offer.

Café Petersborg Bredgade 76, Nyboder ☎33 12 50 16. Served up in an appealing eighteenth-century building, the menu centres on traditional fare such as meatballs with red cabbage for 80kr, or old fashioned egg-cake (a type of scrambled eggs with bacon and chives served on rye bread) for 85kr, as well as lots of *smørrebrød* choices at lunchtime including a platter for 105kr. Open Mon–Fri

Café & Ølhalle 1892 Rømersgade 22, Nørreport ☎ 33 93 25 75. In the basement of the Workers' Museum (p.109), *Ølhalle* specializes in old-fashioned traditional Danish food that you won't find anywhere else. Try the *bidesild* (strong pickled herring) or *æbleflæsk* (stewed apple and pork), prepared just as they were 100 years ago. Lunchtime only, closed Mon.

Cap Horn Nyhavn 21, Indre By ☎ 33 12 85 04. One of the best spots to soak up Nyhavn's quayside atmosphere. Lunch options include herring galore and organic burgers; dinner is more elaborate (and pricey), but there's always a veggie dish (around 100kr) and a daily special for 130kr. Leave room for the creamy chocolate cake.

Domhuskælderen Nytorv 5, Indre By ☎ 33 14 84 55. Just off Strøget and busy with tourists and locals alike. The extensive lunch menu includes a range of different *smørrebrød* (from 50kr a piece). Dinner consists of more hearty pork, venison and guinea fowl dishes starting at 138kr.

Els Store Strandstræde 3, Indre By ☎ 33 14 13 41. Very plush, with a game-oriented menu and walls lined with elegant mid-nineteenth-century Danish art. A full five course dinner will set you back 485kr.

Færgecafeen Strandgade 50, Christianshavn ☎ 32 95 13 30. In a peaceful spot within the old ferry house, and offering outdoor canalside seating, a choice of *smørrebrød* for lunch and traditional steak, fish or casserole dishes for dinner. Closed Sun.

Grøften Tivoli Gardens, Vesterbro ☎ 33 12 11 25. *Grøften* continues to win admirers for its good traditional Danish food, served within the walls of the famous amusement park. The prawn sandwiches are locally famous, as is the *skibberlapskovs*, a traditional Danish stew; food is served as long as the gardens are open.

Huset med det grønne træ Gammeltorv 20, Indre By ☎ 33 12 87 86. Frequented largely by lawyers and solicitors from the law courts next door, the "House with the Green Tree" offers some of the finer Danish lunches in the downtown area, including delectable and consistently good *smørrebrød* and fourteen different types of schnapps. Lunch only. Closed Sun, and Sat April–Aug.

Nyhavns Færgekro Nyhavn 5, Indre By ☎ 33 15 15 88. Deservedly pricey traditional food – the scrumptious, fish-laden lunchtime buffet (89kr) is sublime. You can also try the upstairs à la carte restaurant with main courses such as entrecote or salmon steak from 165kr. Outdoor seating in summer.

Peder Oxe Gråbrødretorv 11, Indre By ☎ 33 11 00 77. Very popular steakhouse on a small square off Strøget. At lunchtime you can choose three pieces of heaped *smørrebrød* from a long, mouthwatering list of toppings (129kr) or try a ciabatta club sandwich for 98kr. Served in the evenings, their organic burgers (99kr) are superb, and the cellar holds some fine wines.

Slotskælderen – hos Gitte Kik Fortunstræde 4, Indre By ☎ 33 11 15 37. It may not look much from the outside but this is one of the best places in the country to sample *smørrebrød*; you simply pick your toppings from the heaped plates. A favourite politicians' hangout (parliament is across the canal). Lunchtime only. Closed Sun & Mon.

Spiseloppen Christiania ☎ 32 57 95 58. Since winning many culinary awards, *Spiseloppen* has hiked up its prices considerably (meals cost 140–200kr). That said, it's still good, and so are the portions; try roast New Zealand lamb or steamed cod in mustard sauce. Evenings only, closed Mon.

Thorvaldsens Hus Gammel Strand 34, Indre By ☎ 33 32 04 00. Across the canal from the Christiansborg Palace, and with outdoor seating in the summer, *Thorvaldsens* has grilled fish and a great selection of marinated and smoked herring on the lunchtime menu, and continues into the evening with fabulous gourmet cuisine such as lightly smoked mozzarella-stuffed duckling served with rhubarb chutney and parsley sauce, for a mere 189kr. Closed Mon.

Ethnic restaurants

Ankara Vesterbrogade 35, Vesterbro ☎ 33 31 92 33. Popular Turkish restaurant with an all-you-can-eat buffet costing 49kr at lunchtime, and 69kr in the evening. Belly dancing every Saturday.

Atlas Bar Larsbjørnsstræde 18, Indre By ☎ 33 15 03 52. Eco-conscious café-restaurant serving tasty Asian and South American dishes. The portions are enormous, with main courses starting at 95kr at lunchtime and 120kr in the evening. Closed Sun.

Circus Rosenvængets Allé 7, Østerbro ☎ 35 55 77 72. Trendy restaurant and café – keep an eye out for the murals from 1900, depicting a cow's journey from the field to the butchers' shop. Popular all day, and renowned for its weekend brunch, but especially busy during the evening for the French-, Spanish- and Italian-inspired main courses. If you're feeling flush try the delicious Italian sushi (175kr) made with cold risotto topped by truffles, swordfish, squid, figs and much more. Outdoor seating in summer.

El Gusto La Mexicana Havnegade 47, Christiansborg ☎ 33 11 32 16. Good-value, standard array of enchiladas, tostadas, burritos and chimichangas. The house speciality is fajitas filled with marinated chicken. Two courses for 209kr. Dinner only, and booking essential during weekends.

Gold Prag Gothersgade 39, Indre By ☎33 91 47 12. Authentic new Czech restaurant for the decidedly non-vegetarian – the huge portions of goulash and bread (75kr), washed down with mugs of Czech beer are heavenly. Open for dinner only, closed Sun.

House of Souls Vestergade 3, Indre By ☎33 91 11 81. Cajun/American restaurant in light, bright rooms with lots of New Orleans atmosphere. Try the seafood gumbo (82kr) or the jambalaya (155kr), a rice dish made with sausage, ham, shellfish and okra. Expect things to be spicy.

Kate's Joint Blågårdsgade 12, Nørrebro ☎35 37 44 96. Although unimpressive from the outside, this is a small, funky place serving quality dishes from around the globe. A few regulars include Jamaican jerk chicken and chicken tikka for 65kr, and there's always at least one vegetarian option.

L'Education Nationale Larsbjørnsstræde 12, Indre By ☎33 91 53 60. Authentic French cuisine – all ingredients, including the wine, are imported from France. Lunchtime favourites include croque monsieur and moules frite from 98kr, while dinner – try the hearty portions of cassoulet or the beef fillet – starts at 175kr. Closed Sun.

Lê Lê nhà hang Vesterbrogade 56, Vesterbro ☎33 22 71 35. Tiny, cheap-and-cheerful Vietnamese place serving quality Pho-rice noodle soup and fresh spring rolls for less than 75kr, and veggie dishes too. Dinner only, closed Tues.

Pasta Basta Valkendorfsgade 22, Indre By ☎33 11 21 31. An array of fish- and meat-based pasta dishes and pasta salads to which you can help yourself for 79kr. Open Fri & Sat until 5am, and until 3am during the rest of the week, this is a favourite first stop for late-night groovers and is wildly popular with locals anytime.

Ristorante Italiano Fiolstræde 2, Indre By ☎33 11 12 95. Hugely popular and sometimes boisterous pizza place frequented largely by students, and offering pizzas and pasta dishes for 59–118kr, as well as veal and steak mains.

Spicey Kitchen Torvegade 56, Christianshavn ☎32 95 28 29. Despite the name, this popular little restaurant serves lightly spiced Indian and Pakistani fare (with eight veggie options) for under 50kr per main course. Take-away also available.

Sticks 'n' Sushi Nansensgade 59, Nørreport ☎33 11 14 07. Copenhagen's first sushi restaurant, and still its best: the menu is extensive, with every ingredient explained, and the food of extremely high quality, while the decor is suitably minimalist. There's a take-away further down the road at no. 47, and more branches at Øster Farimagsgade 16 and Istedgade 62 which do both eat-in and take-away. Closed Sun.

Thai Esan Lille Istedgade 7, Vesterbro ☎33 24 98 54. Bargain Thai eating in this crammed but authentic restaurant, where main courses start at 74kr. There are two more branches, one around the corner at Halmtorvet 44 (also known as Ban Gaw 2) and on Amagerbrogade 16. Dinner only.

Tibet Blågårds Plads 10, Nørrebro ☎35 36 85 05. Unique and popular Tibetan restaurant with unusual dishes such as *momos* – steamed dumplings with either vegetable or meat fillings – and *thentuk*, thin rice noodles with lamb or beef. Closed Mon.

Vegetarian and organic

Den Grønne Kælder Pilestræde 48, Indre By ☎33 93 01 40. A simple tiled-floor vegetarian eatery offering very filling gourmet-style vegetarian meals and organic wines. Lunch starts at 65kr for a main course, and the scrumptious evening à la carte menu won't break the bank. Closed Sun.

Flow Gyldenløvesgade 10, Indre By. Organic vegetarian restaurant (with a take-away next door) serving Ayurveda-inspired meals that should make you feel more energetic, balanced and cheerful. The menu changes daily but can include dishes such as beetroot pie or cream-baked fennel, accompanied by homemade speltbread. Dinner only, and no alcohol or smoking.

Govindas Nørre Farimagsgade 82, Nørreport. Krishna-run restaurant producing good-value lacto-vegetarian Indian/Pakistani meals for 69kr. Smoke and alcohol free. Closed Sun.

Morgenstedet Langgade, Christiania. Tasty and mostly organic vegan and vegetarian salads, snacks and main meals at very affordable prices (meal of the day is 49kr). Smoking and alcohol prohibited. Closed Mon.

RizRaz Kompagnistræde 20, Indre By. Excellent-value Mediterranean food, with a vegetarian lunchtime buffet at 59kr, and an evening buffet at 69kr. Meat dishes have to be ordered separately. Popular with backpackers.

Drinking, nightlife and entertainment

An almost unchartable network of **cafés and bars** covers Copenhagen. You can get a **drink** – and usually a snack, too – in any of them, although some are especially noted for their congeniality and ambience, and it's these we've listed below.

Almost all the better cafés and bars are in – or close to – either Indre By, Vesterbro or the Nørrebro districts, and it's no hardship to sample several on the same night, though bear in mind that Fridays and Saturdays are very busy, and you'll probably need to queue before getting in anywhere. Most places open until midnight during the week and 2am during weekends; we've included opening hours for those that open later or close earlier.

With the plethora of late-opening cafés and bars, you'll never have to choose between going to a **club** and going to bed. If you do get a craving for a dancefloor fling, however, you'll find the discos, as most Danes call them, much like those in any major city, although they're generally more concerned with having a good time than defining the cutting edge of fashion. You'll be dancing alone if you turn up much before midnight; after that time, especially on Fridays and Saturdays, discos fill rapidly – and stay open until 5am. Another plus is that drink prices are seldom hiked up and admission is fairly cheap at 40–80kr. For full **listings** of events and all kinds of entertainment, check out the free monthly tourist magazine *Copenhagen This Week* (available from the tourist office), and keep an eye out for notices in Use-It (see p.100) and cafés all around the city.

The city also excels in **live music**. Major international names visit regularly, but it's with small-scale shows that Copenhagen really stands out. Minor gigs early in the week in cafés and bars are often free, making it a cheap and simple business to take in several places until you find something to your liking; later in the week there may be a modest cover charge. There are also a number of medium-sized halls that host the best of Danish and overseas rock, jazz, hip-hop and R&B acts. Things normally kick off around 10pm and, if not free, admission is 25–75kr. Throughout the summer, there are many **free concerts** in the city's parks, some featuring leading Danish bands. You can find out who's playing where by reading the latest copy of *Gaffa*, free from music and record shops, or by visiting ⓦwww.aok.dk, which is also good for general entertainment **information**.

New **film** releases, often in English with Danish subtitles, are shown all over the city; more esoteric fare is screened at Cinemateket on Gothersgade, Indre By (☎33 74 34 12, ⓦwww.dfi.dk), Husets Biograf in the Huset building at Magstræde 14, Indre By (☎33 32 40 77), Posthus Teateret nearby on Rådhusstræde 1 (☎33 11 66 11), or Vester Vov Vov, on Absalonsgade 5, Vesterbro (☎33 24 42 00, ⓦwww .vestervovvov.dk). Full listings are printed in all newspapers. For **kids' cinema**, both Palads by Vesterport station (☎70 13 12 11) and Cinemaxx on Fisketorvet in Vesterbro (☎70 10 12 02) have a special children's section, but films will more often than not be dubbed in Danish.

Note that all the places in Indre By appear on the Indre By map (p.106); all the others are marked on the main Copenhagen map (p.99).

Bars and cafés

Andy's Bar Gothersgade 33B, Indre By. Packed late-night bar (daily 11pm–6am) with a very jovial vibe – you'll end up leaving with lots of new friends, if only you could remember their names.

Bloomsday Bar Niels Hemmingsensgade 32, Indre By. Irish bar especially popular with Copenhagen's large Irish population, with a good selection of ales, lagers and cider, and a large-screen TV showing football and Irish music on Sunday afternoons.

Café Dan Turell Store Regnegade 3, Indre By . Something of an institution with the artier student crowd (it takes its name from a famous Danish writer) and a fine central place for a snack and a sociable tipple. Packed during weekends when

it's open until 2am; during the week it's open until midnight.

Café Louise Nørrebrogade 5, Nørrebro. Open until 9am during weekends and 7am during the week, this once traditional bar has become a legendary last stop after a night out. You have to ring a doorbell to get in, but sobriety is not a requirement of entry.

Café Ludvigsen Sundevedsgade 2, Vesterbro. The area's most popular pool bar, complete with jukebox and inexpensive beer as well as the requisite green baize. Crammed at weekends when it's open until 6am.

Charlie's Bar Pilestræde 33, Indre By. Award-winning Real Ale pub with an impressive array of draught beers and lagers, and even a Somerset cider, from 40kr a pint. Generally packed with beer enthusiasts.

Hviids Vinstue Kongens Nytorv 19, Indre By. Old-fashioned bar whose crowded rooms are patrolled by uniformed waiters. Outdoor seating in the summer.

Ideal Bar at Vega Engahavevej 40, Vesterbro. Part of the Vega music complex (see p.127) and known for its excellent cocktail bar and relaxed post-gig atmosphere, when the large leather sofas come in handy. Open Thurs–Sat from 7pm.

Krasnapolsky Vestergade 10, Indre By. The Danish avant-garde art hanging on the wall reflects the trendsetting reputation of this ultra-modern watering hole. Come here at least once, if only to drink at the very long bar. DJs Thurs–Sat, and tasty food, too.

Musen og Elefanten Vestergade 21, Indre By. Small cosy bar on two floors, serving Carlsberg's draught Elefant beer from a carved trunk.

Nemoland Christiania. Despite the government crackdown on Christiania, this is still one of the city's most popular open-air bars. In winter, the punters move indoors to the pool tables and backgammon boards.

Nørrebro Bryghus Ryesgade 3, Nørrebro. Immensely popular brewery pub with a range of home brews that sell out quicker than they can be bottled. Pricey restaurant, too.

Riesen Oehlenschlægersgade 36, Vesterbro. Small, crowded neighbourhood bar featuring Indie rock and affordable draught beer.

Universitetscaféen Fiolstræde 2, Nørreport (see Indre By map). A prime central location directly south of Nørreport Station. Open until 5am, and a good spot, early or late, for a leisurely beer. Outdoor seating during the summer and live blues or rock every Thursday.

Ølbaren Elmegade 2, Nørrebro. The name means "beer bar", and there's an incredible range from around the world, and a bartender that knows them all and can advise accordingly. Always packed. No smoking Mon & Sat.

Live music venues and clubs

Drop Inn Kompagnistræde 34, Indre By. Easygoing, unpretentious place near Huset with live blues or rock almost every night. Cheap beer (especially before 7pm) and late opening hours.

Jazzcup Gothersgade 107, Indre By ☏ 33 15 02 02. CD shop and café, with live jazz every Fri & Sat at 3.30pm and 2.30pm respectively. Some of the best local as well as international musicians from the world circuit play here.

JazzHouse Niels Hemmingsensgade 10, Indre By ☏ 33 15 26 00, ☏ www.jazzhouse.dk. Near

Amagertorv, this is the country's premier jazz venue, with regular performances from international names as well as Denmark's finest. Jazz here is defined in its broadest sense from world music to fusion, followed by a funky late night disco. Closed Sun & Mon.

JazzHuset Vognporten Rådhusstræde 13, Indre By ☏ 33 15 20 02. In the same building as Use-It (see p.100), with regular live bands: Monday is big-band night, Tuesday features jam sessions, and there's jazz on Fridays and Saturdays. Happy hour 8–9pm.

Loppen Bådsmandsstræde 43, Christiania ☏ 32 57 84 22, ☏ www.loppen.dk. On the edge of the "free city" and a suitably cool warehouse setting for both established and experimental Danish rock, jazz and performance artists, and quite a few British and American ones, too. There's a disco after the live act on Fri and Sat until 5am.

Mojo Løngangstræde 21, Indre By ☏ 33 11 64 53, ☏ www.mojo.dk. Cosy, low-key place that's renowned for its jazz and blues evenings – live music every night. Happy hour daily 8–10pm, and open till 5am every night.

Park Café Østerbrogade 79, Østerbro ☏ 35 42 62 48, ☏ www.park.dk. Plush high ceilinged café/bar in grand surroundings. There's a nightclub upstairs (Thurs–Sat until 5am), and a cocktail bar downstairs sometimes featuring mainstream pop/rock live music. Usually draws a fun, mixed crowd who spill out onto the rooftop terrace to cool off during summer. Fridays over 20s, Saturdays over 22s.

Pumpehuset Studiestræde 52, Indre By (see Copenhagen map) ☏ 33 93 19 60, ☏ www.pumpehuset.dk. Between Vesterport Station and Vor Frue Kirke, Copenhagen's former pumping station is now a live music venue offering a broad sweep of middle-strata rock, pop and funk from Denmark and around the world.

Rust Guldbergsgade 8, Nørrebro ☏ 35 24 52 00, ☏ www.rust.dk. Huge complex catering for all tastes: live indie-rock, pop and hip-hop acts on its main stage, and three dancefloors offering everything from breakbeat to Latin jazz. Open Wed–Sat 9pm–5am.

Stengade 30 Stengade 18, Nørrebro ☏ 35 36 09 38, ☏ www.stengade30.dk. Alternative-type place with a mixed bag of live music and club nights including regular hardcore metal, punk and indie sessions. Closed Mon, and open till 5am Thurs–Sat.

Stereo Bar Linnésgade 16, Nørreport (see Indre By map) ☏ 33 13 61 13. Once-trendy bar that's mellowed with age and is now the place for retro 1970s music, illuminated by lava lamps. There's a dancefloor in the basement playing mostly Latin, house, drum'n'bass and world music. Free entry. Open Wed–Sat 8pm–3am

Tivoli Vesterbrogade 3, Vesterbro ⓦ www.tivoli.dk. Surprisingly good, sometimes even groundbreaking, live outdoor rock-pop every Friday night at 10pm from April to September. Entry is free with general Tivoli admittance.

Vega Enghavevej 40, Vesterbro ⓣ 33 25 70 11, ⓦ www.vega.dk. Set in a former union hall, this large multi-levelled musical Mecca retains its 1950s and 1960s decor – zigzag tiles and

suchlike – while showcasing plenty of modern underground music. Two concert halls, Lille Vega and Store Vega, with international acts, a nightclub (Fri & Sat, free admission until 1am, over-20s only) and *Ideal Bar* (Wed–Sat). Invariably an excellent night out.

Woodstock Vestergade 12 ⓣ 33 11 20 71, Indre By. Pulls a large, fun-loving crowd eager to dance to anything with a beat – though the music is predominantly 1960s. Close to the Rådhus. Open till 5am Thurs–Sat.

Gay and lesbian Copenhagen

As you'd expect from the capital of a country with a very liberal attitude to homosexuality (the age of consent is 15, and gay marriages are legal as long as one of the partners is Danish), Copenhagen has a lively **gay scene**, which includes a good sprinkling of bars and clubs (one with a sauna), a bookshop and a few exclusively gay **accommodation options**, the latter all in Indre By: *Copenhagen Rainbow*, Frederiksberggade 25C (ⓣ33 14 10 20, ⓦwww.copenhagen-rainbow.dk; ⑤), *Hotel Windsor*, Frederiksborggade 30 (ⓣ33 11 08 30, ⓦwww.hotelwindsor.dk; ⑤) and *Carstens Guesthouse*, Christians Brygge 28, 5th floor (ⓣ40 50 91 07, ⓦwww .circuitq.dk; ④; see main Copenhagen map).

For **information**, visit ⓦwww.copenhagen-gay-life.dk, call the **gay switchboard** (ⓣ33 36 00 86) or contact the National Organization for Gay Men and Women (*Landsforeningen for Bøsser og Lesbiske*; ⓣ33 13 19 48, ⓦwww.lbl.dk), based at Teglgårdsstræde 13, where there's also a bookshop/café. Alternatively, check *Out & About* magazine – in Danish, but easily understood – which doesn't have listings but has ads announcing the latest happenings; or the monthly *Pan Magazine*, also in Danish. Both are free and available at most gay bars, where you should also be able to pick up a free English-language map of gay Copenhagen.

Unless otherwise stated, the places in Indre By appear on the map on p.106, and all the others on the main Copenhagen map, p.99.

Bars and clubs

Amigo Bar Schønbergsgade 4, Frederiksberg. Frequented by gay women and men of all ages; karaoke and snacks too.

Café Intime Allégade 25, Frederiksberg. Not the most interesting crowd, but a piano player every night and jazz on Sundays keeps things moving along.

Café Ziraf Sankt Peders Stræde 34, Indre By (see Copenhagen map). A popular lesbian hangout, this is a bright, friendly café serving delicious Italian fare and wines. Smoke-free on Wed.

Can Can Mikkel Bryggersgade 11, Indre By. A favourite late-night drinking spot for gay men, one block northwest of the Rådhus. Open until 5am Fri & Sat.

Club Amigo Studiestræde 31A, Indre By. One of several gay venues in Studiestræde, between Vesterport Station and Vor Frue Kirke, this enormous club offers, amongst other things, a bar, cinemas, sauna and solarium, pool room and video room. Gay men only.

Cosy Bar Studiestræde 24, Indre By. Frequented by men of all ages, this popular cruising venue gets busy late, and stays open right through until 8am.

Heaven Kompagnistræde 18, Indre By. ⓣ33 15 19 00. A daytime café downstairs which in the evening becomes a popular bar, mostly frequented by gay men, while upstairs holds a trendy restaurant (meals from 100kr) for which you should book tables in advance.

Jailhouse CPH Studiestræde 12, Indre By. Popular gay basement bar, designed as a jail with drinking "cells", handcuffs lying around and waiters dressed up in uniform. Upstairs there's a restaurant serving good-value traditional Danish food. Open Thurs–Sat.

Masken Studiestræde 33, Indre By. Great club-bar on two floors, often featuring drag shows and popular with a younger student crowd due to its affordable booze. Things don't pick up until 11pm and Fridays in particular are a bit cruisey.

Oscar Rådhuspladsen 77, Indre By. One of Copenhagen's coolest gay café-bars, with an excellent information point that's well stocked with maps and guides. In the evening, the clientele are mostly young and trendy.

Pan Club Knabrostræde 3, Indre By. Three-storey behemoth right in the centre of the city, just off Strøget, this is the unquestioned hub of the city's gay nightlife and is always buzzing.

Listings

Airlines British Airways, Rådhuspladsen 16 ☎70 12 80 22; Easyjet ☎70 12 43 21; Finnair, Nyropsgade 47 ☎33 36 45 45; SAS, Hammerichsgade 1–5 ☎70 10 30 00 (domestic reservations), ☎70 10 20 00 (overseas reservations).

Banks and exchange There's a Den Danske Bank at Kastrup Airport (daily 6am–8.30pm); Forex and X-Change at the Central Station (daily 7/8am–9pm) and Kontanten ATMs everywhere.

Bookshops Most of the city's bookshops are in the area around Fiolstræde and Købmagergade; all stock guidebooks and maps. The Book Trader, Skindergade 23 (www.booktrader.dk), has a varied selection of old and new books in English. For new books try GAD, at Vimmelskaftet 32 (on Strøget) and inside Central Station; Nordisk Korthandel, Studiestræde 26–30 (www.scan maps.dk); Arnold Busck, Købmagergade 49; and Boghallen, Rådhuspladsen 37.

Car parks Usually pay-and-display, with different rates depending on zone colour: in descending level of expense, zones are coloured red (20kr per hour), green (12kr) and blue (7kr). Downtown car parks are thin on the ground, but there's a handy one at the Statoil petrol station in Israel Plads (20kr per daytime hour during the week, 10kr per hour evenings and weekends) and another attached to the Q8 station near Vesterport Station at Nyropsgade 42.

Car rental Avis, Kampmannsgade 1 ☎70 24 77 07; Hertz, Ved Vesterport 3 ☎33 17 90 20; Europcar/InterRent, Gammel Kongevej 13 ☎33 55 99 00; Budget, Helgolandsgade 2 ☎33 55 70 00; Lej et Lig (Rent-a-Wreck), Strandlodsvej 17 ☎70 25 26 70.

Dentist Tandlægevagten, Oslo Plads 14 ☎35 38 02 51. Open for emergencies only, daily 8–9.30pm, Sat & Sun also 10am–noon. Turn up and be prepared to pay at least 200kr on the spot.

Doctors Call ☎33 15 46 00 Mon–Fri 8am–4pm or ☎70 13 00 41 evenings and weekends, and you'll be given the name of a doctor in your area. There's a consultation fee of 400–600kr, which must be paid in cash. For non-urgent treatment, get a list of doctors from the tourist office, Use-It, or a local health department (*Kommunens social og sundhedsforvaltning*).

Embassies Australia, Dampfærgevej 26 ☎70 26 36 76; Canada, Kristen Bernikowsgade 1 ☎33

48 32 00; Ireland, Østbanegade 21 ☎35 42 32 33; Netherlands, Toldbogade 33 ☎33 70 72 02; UK, Kastelsvej 40 ☎35 44 52 00; USA, Dag Hammerskjölds Allé 24 ☎35 55 31 44. Note that New Zealand uses the UK office.

Emergencies ☎112 for police or ambulance.

Hitching First check the car-share notices on Use-It notice boards. If they don't deliver anything, use the following routes (and remember you're not supposed to hitch on motorways). Heading south to Germany, take S-train line A or bus #10 or #650S to Ellebjerg station, which leaves you by the ring road, near the start of motorway E20. Going north to Helsingør and Sweden, take S-train line H or F to Ryparken (or bus #15, #150S or #184 to Hans Knudsen Plads) and hitch along Lyngbyvej (for the E4). West for Funen and Jutland, take S-train line B to Tåstrup, then walk along Køgevej and hitch from Roskildevej (A26).

Hospitals There are emergency departments at Bispebjerg Hospital, Bispebjerg Bakke 23 (☎35 31 35 31) and Frederiksberg Hospital, Nordre Fasanvej 57 (☎38 16 38 16); EU and Scandinavian nationals get free treatment, though others are unlikely to have to pay.

Internet access Free access is available at Use-It, Rådhusstræde 13, where you may have to wait, and at the city's libraries (but not the Royal Library) where you must call and book in advance. Most central are Hovedbiblioteket, Krystalgade 15–17 (☎33 73 60 60; Mon–Fri 10am–7pm, Sat 10am–2pm), Blågårds Bilbliotek, Blågårds Plads 5 (☎35 37 82 00; Mon–Thurs 10am–7pm, Fri 1–5pm, Sat 10am–2pm), Christianshavns Bibliotek, Dronningensgade 53 (☎32 54 64 78; Mon–Thurs 10am–7pm, Fri 10am–4pm, Sat 10am–2pm) and Østerbro Bibliotek, Dag hammarsjölds Allé 19 (☎35 38 16 48; Mon–Thurs 10am–7pm, Fri noon–5pm, Sat 10am–2pm). Internet cafés include Boomtown, Axeltorv 1–3 (daily 24hr; 30kr per hr); Nethouse, Amagerbrogade 44 (daily 24hr; 14kr per hr); Nethulen, Istedgade 114, Vesterbro (Mon–Fri 9.30am–11pm, Sat–Sun 4–11pm; 20kr per hr).

Late-opening shops The supermarket at Central Station is open daily from 8am until midnight.

Laundry Central laundries include Alaska Vask & Rens, Borgergade 2; Møntvask, Fælledvej 23; Møntvask, Valdemarsgade 38; and Møntvask,

Istedgade 45; and Vasketeria, Dronningensgade 42. A load costs about 30kr.

Left luggage The DSB Garderobe office (Mon–Sat 5.30–1am, Sun 6–1am) downstairs in Central Station stores luggage for 30–40kr per day per item, and there are also small and large lockers for 25–35kr per day. Luggage storage is free for a day at Use-It, Rådhusstræde 13.

Library Hovedbiblioteket, Krystalgade 15–17 (Mon–Fri 10am–7pm, Sat 10am–2pm), is the main city library, with mostly Danish books and magazines. Use it, Rådhusstræde 13, also has a very well-stocked reading room, with international magazines and newspapers.

Lost property The police department's lost property office is at Slotherrensvej 113, Vanløse ☎38 74 88 22. Otherwise, for things lost on a bus, call ☎36 13 14 15 (daily 7am–9.30pm); on trains, call the DSB office at Central Station ☎70 13 14 15 (daily 7am–10pm); on a plane, contact the airline or Kastrup Airport ☎32 31 23 70 (daily 6am–10.30pm).

Markets There's a good flea market at Israel Plads on Saturdays (mid-April to mid-Oct 9am–3pm; S-train or Metro to Nørreport Station or bus #5), and a popular antique market at Gammel Strand (May–Sept Fri 8am–5pm, Sat 9am–5pm). Try also the various summertime markets that pop up around Christiania, and the Saturday-morning markets behind Frederiksberg Rådhus (mid-April to mid-Oct 8am–2pm; bus #14 or #15), on Kongens Nytorv square (June to mid-Sept 10am–5pm) and along Assistens Kirkegårdens wall on Nørrebrogade (same hours; bus #5A).

Newspapers and news in English Overseas newspapers are sold at the stall in Rådhuspladsen and some newsagents along Strøget. There's also *Copenhagen Post* (✆www.cphpost.dk, comes out Fri; 15kr), a weekly English-language newspaper

with local news and listings. Radio Denmark (1062MHz in Copenhagen) broadcasts news in English Mon–Fri at 10.30am, 5.05pm and 10pm.

Pharmacy Steno Apotek, Vesterbrogade 6C and Sønderbro Apotek, Amagerbrogade 158, are both open 24 hours.

Post offices Main office at Fisketorvet (Mon–Fri 11am–6pm, Sat 10am–1pm); there's another at Central Station (Mon–Fri 8am–9pm, Sat & Sun 10am–4pm). Poste restante is available at Use-It, Rådhusstræde 13, 1466 Copenhagen K, or any named post office.

Swimming pools & saunas There are public pools and saunas at Angelgade 4, Vesterbro (☎33 22 05 00), Sanbjerggade 35, Nørrebro (☎35 85 19 55), Gunnar Nu Hansens Plads 3, Østerbro (☎35 26 45 36) and Helgesvej 29, Frederiksberg (☎38 14 04 00), and summer-only outdoor pools at Enghavevej 90, Vesterbro (☎33 21 49 00) and Borgmester Jensens Allé 50, Østerbro (☎35 39 08 04). All generally open Mon–Fri 8am–6.30pm, Sat 8am–2pm, and cost 22kr per person. The posh swim centre DGI-byen, at Tietgensgade 65 in Vesterbro (☎33 29 80 00), costs 49kr, and has pools of all shapes and sizes including one for diving, as well as jacuzzis and a massage and treatment clinic. The two new Harbour Pools in the Inner Havn are a fun alternative: Københavns Havnebad Copencabana at Fisketorvet (June–Aug 11am–7pm, Dybbelsbro S-train station), and Københavns Havnebad, Havnefronten Islandsbrygge, Amager (June–Aug 7am–7pm, Islands Brygge Metro stop or bus #33).

Travel agents Kilroy Travels, Skindergade 28 (☎33 11 00 44, ✆www.kilroytravels.com), can give advice on travelling around Denmark, the rest of Scandinavia and Europe. STA Travel, Fiolstræde 18 (☎33 14 15 01, ✆www.sta.com) offer youth and student tickets.

Around Zealand

It's easy to see more of Zealand by making day-trips out from the capital, although, depending on where you're heading next, it's often a better idea to pack your bags and leave Copenhagen altogether. Transport links are excellent throughout the region, making much of northern and central Zealand commuter territory for the capital; but that's hardly something you'd notice as you pass through dozens of tiny villages and large forests on the way to historic centres such as **Helsingør**, **Køge** and – an essential call if you're interested in Denmark's past – **Roskilde**. Except for the memorable vistas of the northern coast, and the explorable smaller **islands** off southern Zealand and **Bornholm** to the east, however, you'll find the soft green terrain varies little; and, unless you're a true nature lover, you'll soon want to push on (which is easily done) to the bigger cities in Funen and Jutland.

North Zealand

The **coast north of Copenhagen**, as far as Helsingør, rejoices under the tag of the "Danish Riviera", a label which neatly describes its line of tiny one-time fishing hamlets, now inhabited almost exclusively by the super-wealthy. It's best seen on the hour-long bus journey (#388) north to Helsingør from Klampenborg, itself the last stop on line B, C or F of the S-train system – the views of beckoning beaches are lovely. There's also a frequent 45-minute train service between Copenhagen and Helsingør; it's quicker than the bus, but you won't see much unless you break the journey, since views are obscured by trees almost the entire way. The north coast and the stretch of beaches between Helsingør and Gilleje is served by a network of private trains, on which the Copenhagen Card is valid, although InterRail, Eurail and ScanRail passes are not.

The Karen Blixen Museum, Humlebæk and Louisiana

There are two good reasons to get off the bus before Helsingør. The **Karen Blixen Museum** (May–Sept daily 10am–5pm; Oct–April Wed–Fri 1–4pm, Sat & Sun 11am–4pm; 40kr; ❀www.isak-dinesen.dk) is a fifteen-minute walk from Rungsted Kyst train station, on the *regionaltog* train line going north towards Helsingør; bus #388 stops just outside (and also at the station). The museum is housed in the family home of the writer who, while long a household name in Denmark for her short stories (often written under the pen name of Isak Dinesen) and outspoken opinions, enjoyed a resurgence of international popularity during the mid-1980s when the film *Out of Africa* – based on her 1937 autobiographical account of running a coffee plantation in Kenya – was released. After returning from Africa, Blixen lived here until her death in 1962, and much of the house is maintained as it was during her final years. Texts describing Blixen's eventful life (her father committed suicide and she married the twin brother of the man she loved, among other things) line the walls, while exhibits include a collection of first editions and the tiny typewriter she used in Africa. Even if you've never read a word of Blixen, it's hard not to be impressed by accounts of her spirit and strength, which shine through the museum. After seeing the house, make for the flower garden, where Blixen's simple grave lies beneath a protective beech tree.

In Humlebæk, the next community of any size, you'll find **Louisiana** (daily 10am–5pm, Wed until 10pm; 76kr; ❀www.louisiana.dk), a modern-art museum on the northern edge of the village at Gammel Strandvej 13, a short walk from the train station; bus #388 stops just outside. Even if you go nowhere else outside Copenhagen, it would be a shame to miss this: the setting alone is worth the journey, harmoniously combining art, architecture and landscape. The entrance is in a nineteenth-century villa, from which lead two carefully designed modern corridors containing the indoor collection, their windows giving views of the sculpture park and Øresund outside.

It seems churlish to mention individual items, but the museum's American section, in the south corridor, includes some devastating pieces by Edward Kienholz, Malcolm Morley's scintillatingly gross *Pacific Telephone Los Angeles Yellow Pages*, in which the telephone directory cover expands to monstrous proportions and coffee stains rib the city skyline like a weird metallic grid, and (in the reading room) Jim Dines' powerful series *The Desire*. You'll also find some of Giacometti's gangly figures haunting a room of their own off the north corridor, and an equally affecting handful of sculptures by Max Ernst squatting outside the windows and leering inwards. Except for some pieces by Per Kirkeby and paintings by various Danish luminaries of the CoBrA group, home-grown artists have a rather low profile, although their work is often featured in temporary exhibitions.

Helsingør

First impressions of **HELSINGØR** are none too enticing. The bus stops outside the noisy train station, outside which Havnepladsen is usually full of transit

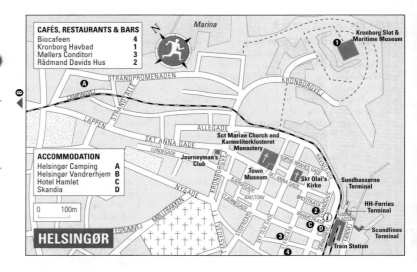

CAFÉS, RESTAURANTS & BARS
Biocafeen 4
Kronborg Havbad 1
Møllers Conditori 3
Rådmand Davids Hus 2

ACCOMMODATION
Helsingør Camping A
Helsingør Vandrerhjem B
Hotel Hamlet C
Skandia D

0 100m

HELSINGØR

passengers loitering around fast-food stalls before making for the ferry terminal, 100m distant. Away from the hustle, though, Helsingør is a quiet and likeable town. Strategically positioned on the four-kilometre strip of water linking the North Sea and the Baltic, the town's wealth was founded on the Sound Toll of 1429, which was levied on passing ships right up until the nineteenth century. Shipbuilding restored some of Helsingør's fortunes after the toll was abolished, but today it's once again the sliver of water between Denmark and Sweden, and the ferries across it to Helsingborg, which account for most of the town's livelihood.

The Town

Helsingør's main draw, on a sandy curl of land extending seawards like a raised fist, is **Kronborg Slot** (May–Sept daily 10.30am–5pm; April & Oct Tues–Sun 11am–4pm; Nov–March Tues–Sun 11am–3pm 50kr, joint ticket with Maritime Museum 75kr; ⊛www.kronborg.dk), famous principally as the setting – under the name of Elsinore Castle – for Shakespeare's *Hamlet*. Actually, the playwright never visited Helsingør, and his hero was based on one Amleth (or Amled), a tenth-century character lost in the mists of Danish mythology who certainly predated the castle – none of which has affected Kronborg's thriving trade in Hamlet souvenirs, nor the hundreds of requests asking for the whereabouts of "Hamlet's bedroom". The castle was awarded UNESCO World Heritage Site status in 2000 and, consequently, it has become markedly more visitor-friendly. **Guided tours** of the royal chambers take place daily at 2pm in English and well-informed attendants also hover in every room ready to answer questions.

Construction of the present castle, built on the site of Erik of Pomerania's fortress, was instigated during the sixteenth century by Frederik II. Frederik commissioned the Dutch architects Van Opbergen and Van Paaske, who took their ideas from the buildings of Antwerp. Various bits have been destroyed and rebuilt since, but it remains a grand affair, enhanced immeasurably by its setting, and with an interior (particularly the royal chapel) that is spectacularly ornate – appreciation, though, is hampered by the steady flow of tourists. Crowds are less of a problem in the labyrinthine **cellars** – the casemates – which can be seen on an English-language guided tour (daily noon and 1.30pm), which departs from the cellar entrance. The body of Holger Danske, a mythical hero from the legends of Charlemagne, is said to lie beneath the castle, ready to wake again when Denmark needs him, although the tacky Viking-style statue depicting the legend detracts somewhat from the cellars' authentic aura of decay. The castle also houses the surprisingly captivating national **Maritime Museum** (same hours; 40kr, joint ticket with the castle 75kr; @www .maritime-museum.dk), which, apart from a motley collection of model ships and nautical knick-knacks, contains relics from Denmark's colonial past in Greenland, India, the West Indies and west Africa, as well as, from 1852, the world's oldest surviving ship's biscuit.

Away from Kronborg and the harbour area, Helsingør has a well-preserved **medieval quarter**. **Stengade** is the main pedestrianized street, linked by Bjergegade to **Axeltorv**, the town's small market square and a good spot to linger over a beer – alternatively, stroll into nearby **Brostræde**, a narrow alleyway that's famous for *Brostræde Is*, which sells immense ice creams made with traditional ingredients. Near the corner of Stengade and Skt Anna Gade the **Skt Olai's Kirke** (Mon–Fri: May–Aug 10am–4pm; Sept–April 10am–2pm) contains a small but interesting exhibit on the building's history. Just beyond is the fifteenth-century **Sct Mariæ Church** (Mon–Sat 9am–noon, Thurs also 4–6pm) and, within the same walls, the fourteenth-century **Karmeliterklosteret Monastery** (mid-May to mid-Sept guided tours of both Mon–Fri at 2pm; 20kr) which originally served as a hospital, during which time it prided itself on its brain operations. The unnerving tools of this profession are still on show next door at the **Town Museum** (daily noon–4pm; 20kr), together with diagrams of the corrective insertions made into patients' heads. For something less disturbing, seek out the oddball **Journeymen's Club** (*Naverhulen*), tucked into a nearby courtyard at Skt Anna Gade 21 and cluttered with souvenirs of world travel, such as crab puppets and armadillo lampshades. Act interested and you might get a free guided tour; there are no set opening hours.

Practicalities

You can pick up a free map and get information on Helsingør from the **tourist office** (mid-June to mid-Aug Mon–Thurs 9am–5pm, Fri 9am–6pm, Sat 10am–3pm; rest of the year Mon–Fri 9am–4pm, Sat 10am–1pm; ☏49 21 13 33, @www .visithelsingor.dk), across Strandgade from the train station at Havnepladsen 3. Due to the high numbers of visiting tourists, the closest thing to a cheap **hotel** here is the *Skandia*, Bramstræde 1 (☏49 21 09 02, @www.hotel-skandia.dk; ❸), which is decent and clean; some rooms have a shared bath. If you can afford it, treat yourself to the "Hamlet" or "Ophelia" suites at the *Hotel Hamlet*, Bramstræde 5 (☏49 21 05 91;

Ferries to Sweden

Three **ferry lines** make the twenty-minute crossing from Helsingør to Helsingborg in Sweden. The main one, and probably the best option, is the **Scandlines** boat leaving every twenty minutes from 6am to 11.30pm and every thirty minutes at night from the main terminal by the train station (20kr one way, 36kr return; @www.scanlines.dk). The alternative options are **Sundbusserne**, which operates a small craft that only takes foot-passengers and is often heavily buffeted by the choppy waters. It runs every twenty minutes between 6.30am and 7.30pm (less frequent during weekends), and costs 21kr one way, 36kr for a return and 18kr for a Sunday day-return. HH Ferries offer the cheapest fares (17kr one way and 32kr return), but they dock a good walk from the centre of Helsingborg. Eurail and ScanRail passes are valid on Scandlines services, and InterRail and the Copenhagen Card holders get a fifty percent discount. It's perfectly feasible, and on a sunny day very enjoyable, to rent a **bike** at Kongevejen 17 (80kr a day) and cross to Helsingborg for a day's cycling along the Swedish coast. But take food and, especially, drink with you – both tend to be more expensive in Sweden than in Denmark, alcohol exorbitantly so.

www.hotelhamlet.dk; ⑥), a handsome white three-star with a fish and steak restaurant. There's also a **youth hostel** (☎49 21 16 40, www.helsingorhostel .dk; Feb–Nov; dorm beds 115kr) literally on the beach; it's a twenty-minute walk to the north along the coastal road (Nordre Strandvej), or take bus #340 from the station and get off just after the sports stadium. The *Helsingør Camping* **campsite**, at Standalleen 1 (☎49 21 58 56, www.helsingorcamping.dk), is closer to town and also by a beach, between the main road Lappen (which begins where Skt Annagade ends) and the sea.

For **eating**, the usual pizza and fast-food outlets are two-a-penny around Stengade. Worth seeking out is *Møllers Conditori*, Stengade 39, Denmark's oldest bakery, which has sizeable sandwiches and Danish pastries to follow. A little more expensively, there are fine Danish lunches in the small, atmospheric *Rådmand Davids Hus*, close to the train station at Standgade 70, and a good café, the *Kronborg Havbad*, right next to Kronborg Slot. Given the proximity of the capital, nightlife of note is a rare commodity, but for an evening drink, stroll the streets on either side of Stengade, where there are several decent bars including *Biocafeen*, Stengade 26, with live music in the evenings. Rowdier boozing goes on at the top end of Axeltorv, popular with Swedes taking advantage of Denmark's more liberal licensing laws.

Onwards from Helsingør: the North Zealand coast

Some of the best beaches in Zealand and several attractive fishing villages are within easy reach of Helsingør, either by bike, local bus or private train. No one particular place has the power to hold you for long, but the region as a whole is hard to beat for a few days' relaxation.

Hellebæk and Hornbæk

A string of fine beaches can be found simply by following Ndr. Strandvej from Helsingør towards the sleepy village of **HELLEBÆK**, some 5km north. At Hellebæk itself, part of the beach is a well-known, if unofficial, venue for nude bathing. Trains from Helsingør stop at Hellebæk and then continue for 7km to the moderately larger **HORNBÆK**, blessed with excellent beaches and fabulous views over the sea towards Kullen, the rocky promontory jutting out from the Swedish coast. Though fast becoming a playground for yacht-owners and their cronies, Hornbæk is a lovely spot to stay over. Staff at the **tourist office** (mid-June to Aug Mon 1–7pm, Tues & Thurs 1–5pm, Wed & Fri 10am–5pm, Sat 10am–2pm; rest of the year same hours, but closed Tues; ☎49 70 47 47, www.hornbaek.dk), in the library just off the main street, can find you private rooms from 420kr as well as pricier summer cottages, both with a 20kr booking fee. Or, from mid-June to mid-August, try the homely farmhouse pension *Ewaldsgården*, close by the train station at Johannes Ewalds Vej 5 (☎49 70 00 82, www.ewaldsgaarden.dk; ⑤), which has single, double and family rooms. Alternatively, a newly renovated former hospital around the corner at Sauntevej 18, *Hotel Bretagne* (☎49 70 16 66; ⑤–⑥) has charming rooms with a seaside feel; the more expensive ones are en suite. Just a few minutes' walk away at Planetvej 4, Hornbæk's **campsite** (☎49 70 02 23, www.camping-hornbaek.dk) is beautifully situated on the edge of a pine forest, and ten minutes' walk from the beach. For **food**, nothing beats the fresh fish from *Fiskehuset* on the harbour; there are a few tables outside, but their takeaway menu means you can eat gourmet fish anywhere along the beach.

Gilleleje and Tisvildeleje

From Hornbæk, trains continue fifteen minutes further along the coast to **GILLELEJE**, another appealing fishing village that does a roaring tourist trade. It's a good place for a short stopover, though unfortunately **accommodation** tends to be booked up far in advance; the only hotel in town is the prefab Swiss-chalet-style *Strand*, Vesterbrogade 4B (☎48 30 05 12, www.hotel-strand.dk; ⑤). Alternatively the **tourist office** on Gilleleje Hovedgade 6F (mid-June to Aug Mon–Sat

10am–6pm; May to mid-June Mon–Fri 10am–4pm, Sat 10am–1pm; rest of the year Mon–Fri 10am–4pm, Sat 9am–noon; ☎48 30 01 74, ✆www.gilleleje-turistbureau .dk) has a list of affordable **private rooms** from 325kr upwards, plus 25kr booking fee. A budget option is also the year-round **campsite**, just outside the village at Bregnerødvej 21 (☎49 71 97 55). If none of these appeal, the final option is to head west to the youth hostel in Tisvildeleje (see below).

While in Gilleleje, negotiate at least some of the footpath that runs along the top of the dunes, where, in 1835, **Søren Kierkegaard** took lengthy contemplative walks, later recalling: "I often stood there and reflected over my past life. The force of the sea and the struggle of the elements made me realize how unimportant I was." Ironically, so important would Kierkegaard become that a monument to him now stands on the path bearing his maxim: "Truth in life is to live for an idea." The tourist office has maps of the different routes he used to walk.

From Gilleleje, bus #363 largely follows the coast to the wilder **TISVILDELEJE** (a hour-long journey), where there are yet more beaches and Tisvilde Hegn (locally called simply "Hegn"), a forest of wind-tormented trees planted here during the eighteenth century to prevent sand drifts. The **youth hostel** at Bygmarken 30 (☎48 70 98 50, ✆www.helene.dk) is part of a holiday complex, the *Sankt Helene Centeret*, and has forty-odd family rooms with dorm beds (120kr) and some doubles (❸).

Inland from the coast: Hillerød and Frederiksborg Slot

It's hard to continue along the coast without first detouring **inland**, and in any case the effort is barely worthwhile. Trains from both Tisvildeleje and Gilleleje run to **HILLERØD**, in the heart of North Zealand, which – thanks to its magnificent castle – is the place to make for. Hillerød is forty minutes by S-train from Helsingør, and a similar distance from Copenhagen (last stop on line A and E). The town's main claim to fame is **Frederiksborg Slot** (daily: April–Oct 10am–5pm; Nov–March 11am–3pm; 60kr; ✆www.frederiksborgmuseet.dk), a castle which easily pushes the more famous Kronborg into second place and lies decorously across three small islands within an artificial lake. Buses #701 and #702 run from the train station to the castle, or it's a twenty-minute walk, following the signs (*Slottet*) through the town centre.

Frederiksborg Slot was the home of Frederik II and birthplace of his son Christian IV. At the turn of the seventeenth century, under the auspices of Christian, rebuilding began in an unorthodox Dutch Renaissance style. It's the unusual and prolific use of towers and spires, Gothic arches and flowery window ornamentation that still stands out, despite the changes wrought by fire and restoration.

You can see the exterior of the castle for free simply by walking through the main gates, across the seventeenth-century S-shaped bridge, and into the central courtyard. Since 1878, the interior has functioned as a **Museum of National History**, largely funded by the Carlsberg brewery magnate Carl Jacobsen in an attempt to create a Danish Versailles, and to heighten the nation's sense of history and cultural development. There's an illustrated guide to the castle and museum (60kr), but most of the sixty-odd rooms have detailed descriptions in English pasted on the walls. Many rooms are surprisingly free of furniture and household objects, and attention is drawn to the historical paintings and portrait – one of the finest collections in the country, a motley crew of flat-faced kings and thin consorts who between them ruled and misruled Denmark for centuries, giving way in later rooms to politicians, scientists and writers.

Two rooms deserve special mention. The **chapel**, where monarchs were crowned between 1671 and 1840, is exquisite, its vaults, pillars and arches gilded and embellished, and the contrasting black marble of the gallery riddled with gold lettering. The shields, in tiered rows around the chapel, are those of the knights of the Order of the Elephant, who sat with the king in the late seventeenth century. The **Great Hall**, above the chapel, is a reconstruction, but this doesn't detract from its beauty. It's bare but for the staggering wall and ceiling decorations: tapestries, wall reliefs, portraits and a glistening black-marble fireplace. In Christian IV's day the hall was a ballroom, and the polished floor still tempts you to some fancy footwork as you slide up and down its length.

Away from the often crowded interior, the **baroque gardens**, on the far side of the lake, are astonishingly intricate and have some photogenic views of the castle from their stepped terraces and are a good spot for a rest. The quickest way to them is through the narrow Mint Gate to the left of the main castle building, which adjoins a roofed-in bridge leading to the King's Wing. In summer you can also do a half-hour trip on the lake aboard the *M/F Frederiksborg* ferry, which leaves every half hour from outside the castle (mid-May to mid-Sept Mon–Sat 11am–5pm, Sun 1–5pm; 20kr).

Though Frederiksborg is the main reason to come to Hillerød, you could easily spend an absorbing half hour in the **Money Historical Museum** (Mon–Thurs 9.30am–4.30pm, Fri 9.30am–4pm; free) at Slotsgade 38. During the reigns of Frederik II and Christian IV all Danish coins were minted in Hillerød, and besides samples of these, the place displays currencies from all over the world.

If you do want to **stay**, the hostel section of the *Nordiske Lejerskole og Kursuscenter*, Lejerskolevej 4 (☎48 26 19 86, ⍟www.nordlejr.dk), has inexpensive private rooms (❷) with shared bathrooms as well as dorms (120kr). The only other budget option is the **campsite**, 1km from the centre by the agricultural showground at Blytækkervej 18 (☎48 26 48 54, ⍟www.publiccamp.dk/hilleroed; Easter to mid-Sept). The **tourist office**, Møllestræde 9 (Mon–Fri 9am–5pm; ☎48 24 26 26, ⍟www.hillerodturist.dk) can arrange **private rooms** for around 150kr per person (25kr booking fee). For **food**, the 𝕏 *Spisestedet Leonora*, in one of the castle's gatehouses, serves fantastic *smørrebrød* starting at 42kr a piece – one should suffice if you're not too famished. Otherwise the *Engelhardt's Café*, Slotsarkaderne 112, serves good-value sandwiches and light snacks.

Fredensborg Slot

Before leaving Hillerød altogether, it's worth taking a detour to the picturesque **Fredensborg Slot** (July daily 1–4.30pm; guided tours 40kr, joint ticket with the Reserved Garden 60kr). Take the train to Fredensborg (on the train line toward Helsingør), from where it's a short walk from the station. A residence of the Danish royalty, built by Frederik IV to commemorate the 1720 Peace Treaty with Sweden, the castle is only open in July when the Queen is staying at her other summer residence, Marselisborg in Århus (see p.185). During this period there are also guided tours of the so-called **Reserved Garden** next to the castle, where you'll find the Queen's veggie patch and herb garden, and a grand orangery opened in 1995 (same hours as the castle; 40kr, joint ticket with the castle 60kr). The rest of the garden is open for the remainder of the garden (daily dawn–dusk; free); stretching down to an expansive lake, its grand statue-lined alleyways are distinctly appealing for a wander.

West from Copenhagen: Roskilde and beyond

Between Copenhagen and the West Zealand coast, there's very little to see and explore other than the ancient former Danish capital of **ROSKILDE**, less than half an hour by train from the capital. There's been a community here since prehistoric times, and later the Roskilde fjord provided a route to the open sea that was used by the Vikings. But it was the arrival of Bishop Absalon in the twelfth century that made the place the base of the Danish church – and, as a consequence, the national capital for a while. Roskilde's importance waned after the Reformation, and it came to function mainly as a market for the neighbouring rural communities – much as it does today, as well as serving as dormitory territory for Copenhagen commuters. In high season, especially, it can be crammed with day-trippers seeking

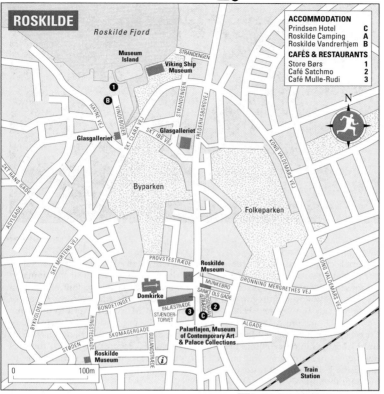

ROSKILDE

Roskilde Fjord

Museum Island

Viking Ship Museum

STRANDENGEN

N

HAVNE VEJ
VINDEBODER
SKT CLARA VEJ
SKT IBS VEJ
STRANDENGEN
FREDERIKSBORGVEJ
KONG VALDEMARS VEJ

Glasgalleriet
Glasgalleriet

SKT HANS GADE
ASTI GADE

Byparken

Folkeparken

SKT MORTENS VEJ

PROVSTESTRÆDE

Roskilde Museum

MUNKEBRO

DRONNING MERGRETHES VEJ

KONG VALDEMARS VEJ

BYKVÖLEN
RINGSTEDGADE
STÖDEN
SKOMAGERGADE
GULLANDSTRÆDE

BONDETINGET
Domkirke
PALÆSTRÆDE
STÆNDER-TORVET

SANKT OLS GADE
ROSSINGSTRÆDE

ALGADE

Palæfløjen, Museum of Contemporary Art & Palace Collections

Roskilde Museum

0   100m

Train Station

Roskilde Festival Site & Lejre

the dual blasts from the past supplied by its royal tombs and Viking boats, while the first week of each July sees a massive influx of visitors when it hosts the **Roskilde Festival** – northern Europe's biggest open-air rock event. Yet at any other time the ancient centre makes Roskilde one of Denmark's most appealing towns, and the surrounding countryside quiet and unspoilt.

The Town

The major pointer to the town's former status is the fabulous **Domkirke** (April–Sept Mon–Fri 9am–4.45pm, Sat 9am–noon, Sun 12.30–4.45pm; Oct–March Tues–Sat 10am–3.45pm, Sun 12.30–3.45pm; 25kr), founded by Bishop Absalon in 1170 on the site of a tenth-century church erected by Harald Bluetooth, and finished during the fourteenth century – although portions have been added right up to the twentieth. The result is a mishmash of architectural styles, though one that hangs together with surprising neatness. Every square inch seems adorned by some curious mark or etching, but it's the claustrophobic collection of coffins containing the regal remains of twenty-one kings and eighteen queens in four large **royal chapels** that really catches the eye. The most richly endowed chapel is that of Christian IV, a previously austere resting place jazzed-up – in typical early nineteenth-century Romantic style – with bronze statues, wall-length frescoes and vast paintings of scenes from his reign. A striking contrast is provided by the simple

△ Roskilde Domkirke

red-brick chapel just outside the cathedral, where Frederik IX was laid to rest in 1972. Try to get to the Domkirke just before the hour to see and hear the animated medieval **clock** above the main entrance: a model of St Jørgen gallops forward on his horse to wallop the dragon and the hour is marked by the creature's squeal of death. Upstairs in the Great Hall, a small **Cathedral Museum** (April to mid-June Mon–Fri 11am, 1pm & 2pm, Sat 10am, Sun 1pm & 2pm; mid-June to Sept Mon–Fri every 30min between 11.05am and 2.35pm, Sat every 30min between 9.05am and 11.35am, Sun every 30min between 1.05pm and 3.35pm; Oct–March Tues–Fri noon & 1pm, Sat noon, Sun 1pm & 2pm) provides an engrossing introduction to the Cathedral's colourful history. You'll need to get one of the staff to open up the museum for you.

From one end of the cathedral, a roofed passageway, the **Arch of Absalon** (not open to the public), feeds into the yellow **Bishop's Palace**. The incumbent bishop nowadays confines himself to one wing, while the others have been turned into showplaces for (predominantly) Danish art. The main building houses the **Museum of Contemporary Art** (*Museet for Samtidskunst*; Tues–Fri 11am–5pm, Sat & Sun noon–4pm; 30kr, Wed free), whose diverse temporary exhibitions reflect current trends. The theme continues in the west wing, where the **Palæfløjen** gallery (Tues–Sun noon–4pm; free), run by the local arts society, extends outdoors, turning up a collection of striking sculpture beneath the fruit trees of the bishop's garden. The less compelling **Palace Collections** (mid-May to mid-Sept daily 11am–4pm; rest of the year Sat noon–4pm; 25kr) are made up of paintings, furniture and other artefacts belonging to the wealthiest Roskilde families of the eighteenth and nineteenth centuries.

The **Roskilde Museum**, close to the cathedral at Sankt Ols Gade 18 (daily 11am–4pm; 25kr), is a little more enticing, with strong sections on medieval pottery and toys. Look out for the strange photos that satirist Gustav Wied (who lived in Roskilde for many years and whose rooms are reconstructed here) took of his family. The museum extends to Ringstedgade 6, a shop kitted out in early twentieth-century style, where locals dutifully turn up to buy traditional salted herring and sugar loaves.

More absorbing, and better known, is the **Viking Ship Museum** (daily 9am–5pm; ⓦwww.vikingeskibsmuseet.dk; May–Sept 75kr; rest of the year 45kr); it's set in the green surrounds of Strandengen on the banks of the fjord, fifteen minutes' walk north of the centre. This is one of Denmark's most interesting museums, with five excellent specimens of Viking shipbuilding given the space they deserve: there's a deep-sea trader, a merchant ship, a man-of-war, a ferry and a longship, each retrieved from the fjord where they had been sunk to block invading forces. Together, they give an impressive indication of the Vikings' nautical versatility, their skills in boat-building, and their far-ranging travels to places as various as Paris, Hamburg and North America. The material here tries hard to convince you that the Vikings sailed abroad not only to rape and pillage, but also to find places where they could quietly settle down and farm. Boat-building and sail-making demonstrations also take place outdoors all year, on the museum island – the Vikings' sails were spun from a special wool produced from wild Norwegian sheep. In the summer months, when the weather allows it, you can also experience the seaworthiness of the reconstructed ships moored on the fjord – you'll be handed an oar when you board and be expected to pull your weight as a crew member (50min; 50kr on top of the museum ticket). There's also a decent gift shop.

Whilst in town, take a moment to inspect the **Glasgalleriet**, Vindeboder 1 (Mon–Fri 10am–5.30pm, Sat & Sun noon–4.30pm; free; ⓦ www.glasgalleriet.dk), a good little glasswork gallery in the old Roskilde Gasworks building between the harbour and Byparken, the city's central park. This park, quiet and soothing and with views of the fjord, was once the stronghold of Viking power – a spot now marked by a hard-to-find plaque and a walking path to town, but nothing else.

Practicalities

Copenhagen is less than an hour's drive northeast of Roskilde, but if you're heading towards Funen or further south in Zealand it's easiest to **stay** here for the night. This is now a cheaper proposition than it once was, thanks to the classy wooden **youth hostel**, ⚓ *Roskilde Vandrerhjem*, ideally located on the harbour at Vindeboder 7 (☎46 35 21 84, ⓦ www.rova.dk; 120kr), which has dorms (120kr), double rooms (❸), a communal kitchen and a view of the water. If that's full, there's a **campsite** (☎46 75 79 96, ⓦ www.roskildecamping.dk; mid-March to mid-Sept) on the wooded edge of the fjord about 4km north of town – an appealing setting that means it gets very crowded at peak times; it's linked to the town centre by bus #603 towards Veddelev. There's also the pricey *Prindsen* hotel at Algade 13 (☎46 30 91 00, ⓦ www.prindsen.dk; ❻). For general information or to arrange a private room, call in at Roskilde's **tourist office** at Gullandstræde 15 (April–June Mon–Fri 9am–5pm, Sat 10am–1pm; July–Aug Mon–Fri 9am–6pm, Sat 10am–2pm; Sept–March Mon–Thurs 9am–5pm, Fri 9am–4pm, Sat 10am–1pm; ☎46 31 65 65, ⓦ www.visitroskilde.com).

Eating isn't a problem in Roskilde, with plenty of options. On the waterfront and across the docks from the museum at Havnevej 43 you'll find the fish restaurant

The Roskilde Festival

Held over four days and nights during the last weekend in June and the first weekend of July, the **Roskilde Festival** (ⓦ www.roskilde-festival.dk) has grown from humble beginnings into one of Europe's largest rock events, a weekend of live music that now attracts some 100,000 people annually. In the summer of 2000 the festival experienced its darkest moment when nine people died as a result of a crowd surge in front of the main stage. Since then, **safety** has been improved significantly and Roskilde is now deemed one of the world's safest festivals (pick up the leaflet about crowd safety at Use-It or from the festival organizers if you want to come prepared). There's a special free camping ground beside the festival site, to which shuttle buses run from the train station every ten minutes; tickets tend to sell out in advance so contact the tourist office or buy online if you want to make sure to get in.

Store Børs, which does home-smoked salmon for 78kr and fish lunches for 178kr. There are hordes of mainstream restaurants, cafés and pubs lining Skomagergade and Algade, just south of the Domkirke, and the maze of streets branching off it; try *Café Satchmo*, down the Rosenhave Stræde passageway, between the *Hotel Prindsen* and Bryggergården, for good *smørrebrød*.

Evening **entertainment** in Roskilde amounts to visiting the sprinkling of bars around the town centre (try such as *Café Mulle-Rudi*, Palæstræde 7), taking in the occasional free event in the town park, or a pleasant walk along the banks of the fjord. Serious revellers head for Copenhagen.

Lejre Historical-Archeological Centre and Ledreborg Slot

Some 8km west of Roskilde, Iron Age Denmark is kept alive and well at the **Lejre Historical-Archeological Centre**, by volunteer families who spend the summer living in a reconstructed Iron Age settlement, farming and carrying out domestic chores using implements – and wearing clothes – copied from those of the period. Modern-day visitors are welcome (mid-June to mid-Aug daily 10am–5pm; May to mid-June & mid-Aug to Sept Tues–Fri 10am–4pm, Sat & Sun 11am–5pm; 75kr/95kr depending on time of year; ⊕www.lejrecenter.dk), and can try their hand at grinding corn or paddling a dugout canoe. The serious scientific purpose is to gain an understanding of family life in Denmark 2500 years ago, but the centre can be a lot of fun to visit as a day-trip. To get here, take a local train from Roskilde to the village of Lejre; from Lejre station, bus #233 covers the 4km to the historical centre's entrance.

If you have time to spare on your way back, get off the bus a few stops before the train station at **Ledreborg Slot** (July–Aug daily 11am–5pm; June & Sept Sun 11am–5pm; 75kr) a beautiful eighteenth century castle with an imaginative French-style landscaped garden. The Holstein-Ledreborgs still live in the castle but in the summer it's open to the public and you can see the paintings, tapestries and furniture, and an interior left more or less as it was 250 years ago.

Beyond Roskilde: western Zealand

Beyond Roskilde, western Zealand is flat and bland. You might find yourself travelling through on the way to **Kalundborg**, from where ferries depart for Århus and the island of Samsø, or to **Korsør**, the other main town on the west coast, from where a bridge connects Zealand with Funen. Apart from these, the area's only real interest lies in the **Hornsherred Peninsula**, which divides the Roskilde fjord and Isefjord. There are long, quiet beaches along the peninsula's western coast, though the lack of a railway and the paucity of local buses means the region is best toured by bike – the Roskilde tourist office (see p.137) has maps of suggested routes. Make for the medieval frescoes in the eleventh-century churches at **Skibby** or **Over Dråby**, keep on northward for **Jægerspris** and its **castle** (50min guided tours only: mid-March to Oct Tues–Sun at 11am, noon, 1pm, 2pm & 3pm; 45kr), built during the fifteenth century as a royal hunting seat and last used by the eccentric Frederik VII, who lived here during the mid-1800s with his third wife, Grevinde Danner. She inherited the castle after the king's death and turned it into an institution for "poor and unfortunate girls". The most convenient place to stay in the area is the small *Lundebek – Kro og Kursuscenter* (⊕47 31 10 32, ⊕www.lundehuset .dk; closed Jan), which has singles, doubles (❷) and family rooms, as well as kitchen facilities. It's located at Skovnæsvej 2 near the Roskilde fjord bridge – the only bridge that crosses the fjord (as Route 53) from Frederikssund west to Jægerspris.

South from Copenhagen: Køge and around

Not too long ago, **KØGE** was best known for the pollution caused by the rubber factory and chemical works on its outskirts, and despite the town's fine sandy beaches, few ventured here to sample the waters of Køge Bay. In recent years, though, the place has been considerably cleaned up, while an extension of line E and A+ of the Copenhagen S-train network has linked the town to the capital, putting its evocatively preserved medieval centre and beaches within easy reach. It's also a good base for touring the **Stevns Peninsula**, which bulges into the sea just south of the town.

The town and beaches

Saturday is the best day to visit Køge: a variety of free entertainment sweeps through the main streets in the morning and from noon onwards the harbourside bars are at their liveliest. Walk from the **train station** along Jernbanegade and turn left into Nørregade for Torvet, which is the hub of the action. On a corner of the square is the **tourist office** (June–Aug Mon–Fri 9am–5pm, Sat 9am–2pm; Sept–May Mon–Fri 9am–5pm, Sat 10am–1pm; ☎56 67 60 01, ⓦwww.visitkoege .com), while nearby, at Nørregade 4, the **Køge Museum** (June–Aug Tues–Sun 11am–5pm, Sept–May Mon–Fri 1–5pm, Sat 11am–3pm, Sun 1–5pm; 30kr joint ticket with Køge Art Museum of Sketches) contains remnants from Køge's bloody past, not least the local executioner's sword. If the tales are to be believed, the beheading tool was wielded frequently on Torvet, a place which, perhaps not surprisingly, is also said to have been the scene of several incidents of witchcraft and haunting. On the site of what is today a clothes shop, the Devil is said to have appeared in the forms of a clergyman, a frog, a dog and a pig, to have thrown a boy from his bed out into the yard, and caused hands to swell – among other unwholesome occurrences.

Once its market stalls are cleared away, a suitably spooky stillness falls over Torvet and the narrow cobbled streets that run off it. One of these streets, Kirkestræde, is lined with sixteenth-century half-timbered houses and leads to **Skt Nikolai Kirke** (mid-June to Aug Mon–Fri 10am–4pm, Sun noon–4pm; Sept to mid-June Mon–Fri 10am–noon), where pirates captured in Køge Bay were hung from the **tower** – it's opened up every half an hour from July to mid-Aug Mon–Fri between 10am and 1.30pm (5kr). Along the nave, some of the carved angel faces on the pew ends lack noses, having been sliced off by drunken Swedish soldiers during the seventeenth century, while the font, an unattractive black-marble and pine item, replaces an earlier one defiled by a woman who performed "an unspeakable act" in it. On a more aesthetic level, the intriguing **Køge Art Museum of Sketches**, Nørregade 29 (Tues–Sun 10am–5pm; 30kr joint ticket with Køge Museum, free guided tour every Sun at 2pm; ⓦwww .skitsesamlingen.dk), focuses on the creative process from idea to finished work. Its collection includes drawings, sculptures and models made by important Danish artists of the twentieth century, plus temporary exhibitions of works in progress by both local and international artists. The highlight, on the third floor, is Bjørn Nørregård's colourful preparatory work for the Queen's tapestries on show at the Royal Reception Rooms in Copenhagen (see p.112).

The town's **beaches**, which draw many jaded Copenhageners on weekends, stretch along the bay to the north and south of the town. To take full advantage of the sands, **stay** at one of the two campsites beside the southerly beach: *Køge Sydstrand* (☎56 65 07 69, ⓦwww.publiccamp.dk/koge; April–Sept) is virtually on the sand, while *Vallø* (☎56 65 28 51, ⓦwww.dk-camp.dk/vallo) is across Strandvejen, close to a pine wood. Further away, 3km from the town centre along Vamdrupvej, is Køge's **youth hostel** (☎56 65 14 74, ⓦwww.danhostel.dk/koege; April to mid-Dec) with bunks (110kr) and some double rooms (❸). Take bus #210 from the train station and get off when the bus turns into Agerskovvej, from where it's a ten-minute walk. Staying in the town centre isn't expensive; head for the small and comfortable *Centralhotellet* (☎56 65 06 96; ❹), next door to the tourist office at Vestergade 3.

Around Køge: Stevns Peninsula

Stevns Peninsula, easily reached from Køge, is a fairly neglected part of Zealand, mainly because the coastline here is more rugged and less suited to swimming than that immediately around Køge or in north Zealand. The town of **STORE HEDDINGE**, where you'll find a curious octagonal limestone church, is the obvious starting point for explorations; you can get there on the private train line (InterRail, ScanRail and Eurail passes not valid) from Køge in half an hour. There's a simple **youth hostel** at Ved Munkevænget 1 (☎56 50 20 22, ⓦwww.danhostel.dk /store-heddinge; April–Sept), which has dorms (120kr) and exceptionally inexpensive doubles (❶). There are several **campsites** on the beaches to the south: the nearest to Køge is *Nordstevns*, Strandvejen 29 (☎56 67 70 03, ⓦwww.dk-camp.dk/nordstevns), in the woodlands around Strøby, accessible by the frequent bus #208 from Køge.

Central Zealand: Ringsted and around

Though now little more than a small farming town, **RINGSTED**'s central loca-tion made it one of the most important settlements in Zealand from the end of the Viking era until the Reformation. It was the burial place of medieval Danish mon-archs as well as being the site of a regional *ting*, the open-air court where prominent merchants and nobles made the administrative decisions for the province.

The three *ting* stones around which the nobles gathered remain in Ringsted's market square, but they're often concealed by the market itself, or the backsides of weary shoppers. It's the sturdy **Skt Bendts Kirke** (May to mid-Sept Mon–Fri 10am–noon & 1–5pm; mid-Sept to April Mon–Fri 1–3pm) that dominates the square, as it has done for over eight hundred years. Erected in 1170 under the direc-tion of Valdemar I, the church was the final resting place for all Danish monarchs until 1341. Many affluent Zealanders also had themselves buried here, presumably so that their souls could spend eternity in the very best company. Four thousand people are said to have been present for the church's consecration, and although these days it receives a mere trickle of visitors compared to those flocking to the royal tombs at Roskilde, it nevertheless represents a substantial chunk of Danish history. During the seventeenth century a number of the coffins were opened and the finds are collected in the **Museum Chapel** within the church. Besides the lead slab found inside Valdemar I's coffin, there are plaster casts of the skulls of Queen Bengård and Queen Sofia, a collection of coins found in the church and a replica of the Dagmar Cross, discovered when Queen Dagmar's tomb was opened in 1697 – the original is in the National Museum in Copenhagen.

Once you've seen the church you've more or less exhausted Ringsted. The town's only other noteworthy attraction is the **Ringsted Museum & Windmill** (Feb–Dec Tues–Thurs & Sun 11am–4pm; 25kr), on Køgevej, ten minutes' walk from the church. It's a surprisingly interesting introduction to the history of the local farming community, from the Danish land reform up until the present-day organic farming movement, and has an operating windmill from 1805 – you can buy freshly ground organic wheat flour, should you have the need.

Practicalities

For accommodation, Ringsted's **youth hostel** (☎57 61 15 26, ⓦwww.amtstue gaarden.dk) is handily situated across the road from the church – with no campsites nearby, this is the only budget option, and has doubles (❷) as well as dorms (118kr). Ringsted does have some pricey hotels, and the **tourist office** (mid-June to Aug Mon–Fri 10am–5pm, Sat 9am–2pm; Sept to mid-June Mon–Fri 10am–5pm, Sat 10am–1pm; ☎57 62 66 00, ⓦwww.met-2000.dk), a few doors along from the hostel toward Torvet, can advise on these as well as arranging private rooms (from 125kr per person). One decent hotel choice is the *Scandic* at Nørretorv 57 (☎57 61 93 00, ⓦwww.scandic-hotels.dk; ❻), which has comfortable rooms, a sauna, restaurant and children's playground.

Around Ringsted

Beyond Ringsted, the road and rail network out of Copenhagen splits into two: one line heads further south to the islands of Falster, Lolland and Møn (see p.142 and p.143) via Næstved, while the other heads westwards towards the multimillion-kroner combined **bridge and tunnel** that has carried road and rail traffic across the 18km-wide Store Bælt since it opened in 1998. There was a regular ferry between **KORSØR** on Zealand and Nyborg on Funen for more than two centuries, and archeological research on the mid-channel island of Sprogø suggests that Danes have been boating back and forth for many thousands of years. Up until recently there was no particular reason to stop in Korsør, but if you have any interest in grand engineering feats, a stop at the **Great Belt Bridge Centre** (daily 11am–5pm; free) is a definite must. Here you'll find robotic models, videos and interactive computer simulations detailing everything you could possibly want to know about the engineering expertise behind the project, which involved, amongst other things, the construction of what was briefly the world's longest suspension bridge. It's all described in an easily graspable way, and if you haven't already, you'll quickly grow to understand the construction's magnificence – the two bridge pylons, for example, are Denmark's highest points.

Another recently completed architectural feat covered by the centre, albeit with less enthusiasm, is the **Øresunds Link** – the 4km-long tunnel linking Kastrup on Amager with the artificial island of Peberholm, and from there a 7.8km-long bridge on to the Swedish coast, just outside Malmö. There's a miniature model of the Link as well as a couple of placards discussing its effect on the sea environment in Kattegat. You'll find the centre left of the bridge toll booths.

Southern Zealand and the islands

Southern Zealand is seriously rural, consisting almost solely of rich, rolling farmland and villages. South from Ringsted, most routes lead to **NÆSTVED**, by far the largest town in the region. Aside from a smartly restored medieval centre and a minor museum, however, Næstved has little to offer except its proximity to unspoilt countryside and the **River Suså**, whose lack of rapids and negligible current makes it a good base for novice **canoe trips** – although busy at weekends, it's free of crowds at other times. Canoes can be rented at Suså Kanoudlejning, Næsbyholm Allé 6, in nearby Glumsø (☎55 64 61 44, ✆www.kanoudlejning.dk), for 350kr a day. Off the river, time is best spent strolling amid the town's half-timbered buildings and visiting the **Næstved Museum** at Ringstedgade 4 (Tues–Sun 10am–4pm; 20kr; ✆www.naestved-museum.dk) for its jumble of (mainly religious) oddments and a fairly ordinary selection of historical arts and crafts from the town.

The local **tourist office** (July Mon–Fri 9am–6pm, Sat 9am–2pm; June & Aug Mon–Fri 9am–5pm, Sat 9am–2pm; Sept–May Mon–Fri 9am–4pm, Sat 9am–noon; ☎55 72 11 22, ✆www.visitnaestved.com) in the yellow house known as Det Gule Pakhus, Havnen 1, can fill you in on practical details and offer suggestions for **staying over** in Næstved. Alternatively, there are comfortable but pricey rooms at the charming *Vinhuset* (☎55 72 08 07, ✆www.hotel-vinhuset.dk; ❻), centrally located on the church square, Skt Peders Kirkeplads. Further from town but similarly priced is the nicely renovated *Menstrup Kro* (☎55 44 30 03, ✆www.menstrupkro.dk; ❺), which has a sauna, pool and tennis court. The only really cheap spot in town is the **youth hostel** at Præstøvej 65 (☎55 72 20 91, ✆www.danhostelnaestved.dk), which has dorm beds (120kr) and doubles (❷); from the train station (which is about 1km from the centre on Jernbanegade), turn left into Farimagsvej and left again along Præstøvej. The closest **campsite**, *De Hvide Svaner Camping* (✆www .dehvidesvaner.dk; ☎55 44 24 29; mid-June to mid-Oct), is on the coast by Karrebæksminde, 3km from a popular beach.

If you have the opportunity, take a trip to the island of **Gavnø**, a few miles south of Næstved at the mouth of the River Suså, to see its eponymous eighteenth-century

Rococo **palace** (daily: May 10am–5pm; June–Aug 10am–4pm; 57kr; ⊛www.gavnoe
.dk). The imposing structure itself is enhanced by a delightful tulip garden, which
attracts hordes of visitors when it's in bloom. Parts of the building are still occupied
by the descendants of the original owners, and there's a large collection of books and
paintings on display, as well as a butterfly house and a museum devoted to fire protection. The *Friheden* ferry (round-trip 75kr; ☎55 77 38 36; ⊛www.rundfart.dk) runs
about three times a day during the summer between Næstved, the palace, and Karrebæksminde. Also worth finding time for is the **Holmegaard Glassworks** (tours
Mon–Thurs 9.30–1.30pm, Fri 9.30–12.30pm, Sat & Sun 11am–2.30pm; free; ⊛www
.holmegaard.com), in the opposite direction at Fensmark, a fifteen minute journey by
bus #75 from Næstved. Tours allow you to witness professional glassblowers in their
metier as they create their famous designs. There's also a small museum and a shop.

Falster, Lolland and Møn

Off the south coast of Zealand lie three sizeable islands – **Falster**, **Lolland** and
Møn. All three are connected to the mainland by road, and Falster and Lolland
have rail links too, making them relatively easy to reach, but once there you'll need
your own transport to do any serious exploration outside the larger communities,
since local buses are rare; bikes can be rented from virtually all tourist offices and
campsites, however.

Falster

Falster is by far the least interesting of the trio. There are some pleasant woods on
the eastern side and some good, but very crowded, beaches, particularly around the
major resort of **MARIELYST** on the Baltic (eastern) coast. There's not much to
do in Marielyst except enjoy the beach and the bustling **nightlife**: bars, clubs and
cafés are plentiful. The two most affordable **hotels** are the *Marielyst Strand* (☎54 13
68 88, ⊛www.hotel-marielyst.dk; ❺) near the beach, and *Hotel Nørrevang* (☎54 13
62 62, ⊛www.norrevang.dk; ❺), close to the centre. You can also ask at the **tourist
office** at Marielyst Strandpark 3, just off Skovby Ringvej as you enter Marielyst
from Nykøbing (mid-June to Aug Mon–Sat 9am–4pm, Sun 10am–2pm; Sept to
mid-June Mon–Fri 9am–4pm, Sat 10am–2pm; ☎54 13 62 98, ⊛www.marielyst
.org), for a list of private rooms. Of the five **campsites** in the area, the best (both
close to the beach) are *Laxenborg Camping* (☎ & ⓕ54 13 62 89), Laksenborgvej 20,
and *Marielyst Camping* (☎54 13 53 07, ⊛www.marielyst-camping.dk), Marielyst
Strandvej 36.

The island's main town, **NYKØBING** – usually written Nykøbing F (for Falster)
– has a quaint medieval centre, and is of practical use for its **tourist office** at
Østergågade 7 (Mon–Thurs 10am–5pm, Fri 10am–6pm, Sat 10am–1pm; ☎54 85
13 03, ⊛www.tinf.dk), which handles enquiries on all three islands and can help
with private accommodation (around 200kr per person per night, plus a steep 60kr
booking fee). Nykøbing's main attraction is the **Medieval Centre** (May–Sept
daily 10am–4pm; 80kr; ⊛www.middelaldercentret.dk), an open-air experimental
museum set in a recreated village, which provides an insight into the hardship of
medieval life. If you're here with children, don't miss the **Folkepark Zoo** (daily:
May–Sept 9am–6pm; Oct–April 10am–4pm; 40kr), which offers the chance to
come face to face with a llama as well as some native Danish creatures. For hotel
accommodation, try the fancy *Falster* at Skovalleen (☎54 85 93 93, ⊛www.hotel
-falster.dk; ❺), or the cosier and slightly cheaper *Liselund* at Lundevej 22 (☎54 85
15 66; ⊛www.hotelliselund.dk; ❺), a ten-minute walk from the centre. There's also
the island's only **youth hostel** (☎54 85 66 99, ⊛www.danhostel.dk/nykoebing-
falster; closed mid-Dec to mid-Jan), about 2km from the Nykøbing train station
at Østre Allé 110, which has dorms (120kr) and doubles (❸), and an adjoining
campsite (☎54 85 45 45, ⊛www.fc-camp.dk; open all year).

If you're ultimately making for the port of **GEDSER**, to the south of Falster,
for the ferry to Rostock in Germany, don't bother getting off the train before the

ferry dock. Gedser itself doesn't have much to offer except for a decent beach to the east of town.

Lolland

Larger and less crowded than Falster, **Lolland** is otherwise much the same: wooded, with excellent beaches and lots of quiet, explorable corners. A private railway (InterRail, ScanRail and Eurail passes not valid) runs to Lolland from Nykøbing on Falster, taking in Sakskøbing, Maribo and finally Nakskov, at the western extremity of the island, near to where ferries cross to Langeland (alternatively, bus #800 goes straight from Nykøbing station onto the ferry, and continues on to Svenborg and Odense on Funen); there's also a DSB train from Nykøbing to Rødby on the south coast. Each town has a tourist office, youth hostel and campsite, but **MARIBO**, delectably positioned on the Søndersø lake, is the most scenic setting for a short stay. There's a **youth hostel** with dorms (100kr) and doubles (**②**) at Sdr Boulevard 82B (℡54 78 33 14, ⒲www.danhostel.dk/maribo); a **campsite** at Bangshavevej 25 (℡54 78 00 71, ⒲www.maribo-camping.dk; Easter to Oct), and a good-value two-star **hotel**, *Ebsens*, near the train station at Vestergade 32 (℡54 78 10 44, ℻54 75 60 44; **④/⑤**), which has a variety of rooms with both shared and en-suite bathrooms. The **tourist office** is easy to find in the old town hall on Torvet (Mon–Fri 10am–5pm, Sat 10am–1pm; ℡54 78 04 96, ⒲www.turistlolland.dk).

After the beaches, the island's top attraction is probably **Aalholm Slot** in the southeast and its **Automobile Museum** (June–Aug daily 10am–5pm; May & Sept to mid-Oct Sat & Sun 10am–4pm; 75kr; ⒲www.aalholm.dk), a magnificent twelfth-century castle which is sadly no longer open to the public. However, the museum in the grounds contains over two hundred antique cars, lovingly maintained by the castle's previous owner. Though Lolland is not the most obvious place to spot big game, you can see antelopes, zebra, giraffes and more at the drive-through **Knuthenborg Safari Park**, 7km north of Maribo (daily: July 9am–8pm, May–June & Aug–Sept 9am–6pm; 110kr; ⒲www.knuthenborg.dk). Lastly, for some of the region's most distinct cultural history, head for **Denmark's Sugar Museum**, at Løjtoftevej 22 in Nakskov on the west coast (Tues–Sun 1–4pm; 20kr). Most of Denmark's sugar beet is grown on Lolland – something you'll quickly notice when looking over the fields, and the museum's displays detail the history of the crop and of the Polish immigrants who came here to work in the fields and the processing plant.

Møn

Since it's not connected by train, **Møn** is the most difficult of the three islands to get to from Zealand, but it's well worth the effort of getting there: take bus #62 or #64 from Vordingborg (on the rail line from Copenhagen to Nykøbing). Møn is known for its white chalk cliffs, but what really sets it apart are the **Neolithic burial places** which litter the island by the score, and its unique whitewashed churches, many of which feature fourteenth-century frescoes depicting rural life – the work, apparently, of one peasant painter. The main town, **STEGE**, is, at least for those without their own transport, the most feasible base, since it's the hub of the island's minimal bus service and has a good if pricey **hotel**, the *Ellens Cabaret* (℡55 81 54 54; ℻55 81 58 91; **⑤**), at Langelinie 48 near the centre, and an inexpensive **campsite** on Falckvej 5 (℡55 81 84 04; May to mid-Sept). Of the six other campsites on the island, *Camping Møns Klint* at Klintvej 544 at **Møns Klint** (℡55 81 20 25, ⒲www.campingmoensklint.dk; April–Oct), to the east, is the best, while *Ulvshale Camping* (℡55 81 53 25, ⒲www.ulvscamp.dk; April–Oct) is right on the beach at the island's northernmost point. If you'd rather sleep in a bed, check out current options with the helpful Stege **tourist office**, by the bus station at Storegade 2 (mid-June to Aug Mon–Fri 9am–5pm, Sat 9am–6pm; Sept to mid-June Mon–Fri 10am–5pm, Sat 9am–noon; ℡55 86 04 10, ⒲www.visitmoen.com).

The best of the Neolithic barrows is **Kong Asker's Høj**, about 20km from Stege near **Sprove**, while the foremost frescoes can be admired at **ELMELUNDE** (daily: April–Sept 7am–5pm, Oct–March 8am–4pm; free), connected to Stege bus #52; and **FANEFJORD** (same hours as Elmelunde), reachable via bus #62 (get off at Store Damme, then walk); the latter also has a Neolithic barrow in its churchyard. As for the **cliffs** (*Møn Klint*), they're at the eastern end of the island and stretch for about eight kilometres. Bus #52 runs between the cliffs and Stege four to five times a day depending on the season. Fifteen minutes' walk from the cliffs, at Langeb-jergvej 1, is a basic **youth hostel** (☎55 81 20 30, ⍟www.danhostel.dk/moen; May to mid-Sept), which has dorms (105kr) and some private double rooms (●).

Bornholm

Much nearer to Sweden than Denmark, **Bornholm** was under Swedish rule for many years. After a long and bloody revolt, it was finally returned to Denmark in 1522 after the infamous Swedish governor according to legend was shot by a single silver bullet in the heart. Once an important Baltic trading post, its population now lives by fishing, farming and, increasingly, tourism. The coastline is blessed

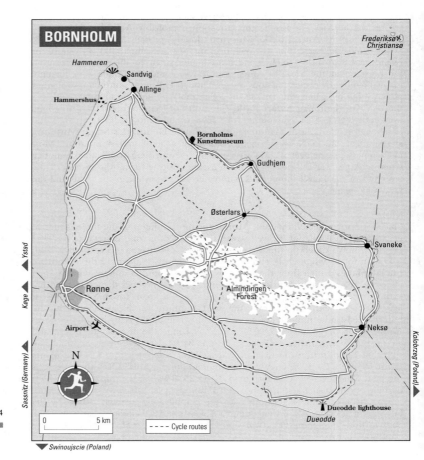

△ Smoked herring racks, Bornholm

with great beaches in the south and some invitingly rugged coastline and hilly landscapes to the north, while the island's centre is covered in woods with good walking and cycling possibilities. It's no wonder that Scandinavian, German and Polish holidaymakers fill the island each summer, especially now that the bridge-and-tunnel **Øresunds Link** between Copenhagen and Malmö makes travelling to Bornholm a lot quicker and easier than before. Buses now leave up to four times a day from Copenhagen, crossing over the Link to Malmö in Sweden and driving onto the ferry from Ystad to Rønne on Bornholm, a total journey time of three hours (visit ⦵www.graahundbus.dk for timetables and online bookings). Compared

.o six hours by direct ferry from Køge south of Copenhagen (see p.148) to Rønne – which used to be the quickest route (bar flying), and is still an option – this is a vast improvement. There's also a train link to Bornholm which catches the same Ystad–Rønne ferry as the bus, and takes just as long. All three travel options cost roughly the same. Bornholm is also quite feasible as a stopover if you're heading to Germany or Poland on one of several ferry crossings (see "Travel details", p.148).

To get the most out of Bornholm, you really need to travel around the whole coast – not difficult, since the island is only about 30km across from east to west – and spend at least three or four days doing it. **Getting around** is easy and best done by **bike**: the island is criss-crossed by some 235km of cycle tracks, of which a third follow the course of the old rail tracks. Bikes can be rented in the island's main town, Rønne, at Cykel-Centret, Søndergade 7 (℡56 95 06 05, ⓦwww .cykeludlejning-bornholm.dk) or Bornholm's Cykeludlejning, Nordre Kystvej 5 (℡56 95 13 59), as well as numerous other places around the island (ask at tourist offices); for maps, route suggestions and general inspiration visit ⓦbike.bornholm .info. If this seems too energetic, you can make use of the reliable **bus** services (all buses are equipped to carry bikes; information on ℡56 95 21 21, ⓦwww.bat.dk), but it's a good idea to check the timetable beforehand as some services are quite infrequent. **Accommodation** is straightforward, too: there's a youth hostel in each of the main settlements and campsites are sprinkled fairly liberally around the coast. Tourist offices can also help with private rooms. The peak weeks of the summer are very busy, and you should phone ahead to check there's space. But at any other time of year there'll be little difficulty. The **nightlife** on the island can also be surprisingly lively, although often limited to one spot in each town – invariably the café in the main square.

The island

Ferries from Copenhagen arrive in **RØNNE**, where the **tourist office** is right on the harbour at Ndr. Kystvej 3 (mid-June to mid-Aug daily 9am–5pm; early to mid-June & mid-Aug to late Aug Mon–Sat 9am–4pm; April–May & Sept–Oct Mon–Fri 9am–4pm, Sat 9am–noon; Nov–March Mon–Fri 9am–4pm; ℡56 95 95 00, ⓦwww.bornholminfo.dk). Staff can fill you in on accommodation and transport details, and give you a copy of *Bornholm Denne Uge*, the free weekly listings magazine – in Danish and German only, but still informative. If you've arrived on an overnight or early boat, the only place open for breakfast is the café at the ferry terminal. Otherwise, there are plenty of places to **eat** and stock up around the main town square, Store Torv.

The triangle between Store Torv and Lille Torv (literally, "large" and "small" squares) and the ferry terminal has the most charm, its streets lined with traditional wood-beamed townhouses painted in bright colours. Otherwise, Rønne lacks the character of many of the other island settlements. However, it's well worth taking in some detail on the island's turbulent history at the **Bornholms Museum**, Sct Mortensgade 29 (July & Aug daily 10am–5pm; April–June & Sept–Oct Mon–Sat 10am–5pm; Nov–March Mon–Sat 1–4pm; 35kr; ⓦwww.bornholmsmuseum.dk); look out for the large golden clothes pin found in a field early in 2002, which is one of Denmark's largest-ever archeological gold finds. If you do need to **stay over**, there are plenty of options: a youth hostel at Arsenalvej 12 (℡56 95 13 40, ⓦwww .danhostel-roenne.dk; June–Sept), which has some doubles (❷) as well as dorms (120kr); a campsite, *Galløkken Camping*, 1km from the ferry harbour at Strandvejen 4 (℡56 95 23 20, ⓦwww.gallokken.dk; mid-May to Aug); or the small *Sverres Hotel* at Skt Snellemark 2 (℡56 95 03 03, ⓦwww.sverres-hotel.dk; ❸) with a range of different rooms. Contact the tourist office for info on private rooms, which start at around 125kr per person per night.

If you're eager to get to the beach, head south to **DUEODDE**, where there's nothing but sand and a string of campsites. In summer Dueodde lighthouse is open to the public (May to mid-Oct 9am–dusk; 5kr), offering superb views. At the other corner of the eastern coast, surrounded by spectacular scenery of steep cliffs and affording great views, **SVANEKE** is a quiet place which until a few years ago was favoured by Danish retirees, but more recently experienced a massive influx of **craftsmen** – mostly potters and glass-blowers – whose workshops and fantastic exhibits have come to dominate the town scene. Svaneke won a Council of Europe prize for town preservation in the mid-1970s, and these days upmarket hotels and restaurants occupy some of the renovated old buildings. If you want to **stay**, first choice is the excellent *Siemsens Gaard*, Havnebryggen 9 (☎56 49 61 49, ⊛www .siemsens.dk; ❻), whose front rooms give great views. Otherwise, the youth hostel at Reberbanevej 9 (☎56 49 62 42, ⊛www.danhostel-svaneke.dk; April–Oct), near the Christiansø ferry landing, has doubles (❸) and dorms (120kr), and there are two campsites, both basic but beautifully situated near the cliffs; *Svaneke Familiecamping* (☎56 49 64 62, ⊛www.svaneke-camping.dk), Møllebakken 8, is slightly better equipped. The **tourist office** at Storegade 24 (June–Aug Mon–Fri 10am–5pm, Sat 9am–2pm; Sept–May Mon–Wed 10am–4pm, Thurs & Fri 11am–5pm; ☎56 49 70 79) should be able to help with any queries.

Halfway along the north coast, **GUDHJEM** is pretty too, its tiny streets winding their way around the foot of a hill. The town lends its name to a traditional open sandwich combination called *Sol over Gudhjem* ("sunrise over Gudhjem") – a slice of rye bread layered with smoked herring, raw egg yoke, chopped onion and capers, sold nationally in *smørrebrød* shops. If you want to taste it at source, head for the *Røgeri* (smokehouse) on Ejner Mikkelsensvej 13, near the harbour, where sandwiches cost 25kr. **Accommodation** in Gudhjem is plentiful. Most romantic is the pricey ⚓ *Jantzen's Hotel* (☎56 48 50 17, ⊛www.jantzenshotel .dk; ❻) close to the harbour at Brøddegade 33. Next door at no. 31, the cheaper *Therns Hotel* (☎56 48 50 99, ⊛www.therns-hotel.dk; ❺) is also nice; some rooms have shared bath. Best value, however, is the youth hostel at Ejner Mikkelsens Vej 14 (next door to the smokehouse) with comfortable three- and four-person rooms for 435kr and 470kr respectively. Buses run the 5km or so north to the **Bornholms Kunstmuseum** (May & Sept–Oct Tues–Sun 10am–5pm; June–Aug daily 10am–5pm; Nov–April Tues & Thurs 1–5pm, Sun 10am–5pm; 50kr; ⊛www.bornholms-kunstmuseum.dk), a gallery displaying works from the Bornholm School that thrived here in the first half of the twentieth century. Gudhjem is also a good jumping-off point for the six-kilometre trip inland to **ØSTERLARS**, site of the largest and most impressive of the island's fortified round churches, which date from the twelfth and thirteenth centuries. A similar distance further inland, right in the centre of the island, is Bornholm's largest (and Denmark's third largest) forest, **Almindingen**, criss-crossed by cycle paths, and boasting a lookout tower in the centre which affords fabulous views of the entire island. **SANDVIG**, on the island's northwest corner (12km from Gudhjem and reachable by bus #1 or #2 from Rønne and #7 or #9 from Gudhjem), is the start of another worthwhile walk, along **Hammeren**, the massive granite headland that juts out towards Sweden. Just south of Sandvig are the remains of the thirteenth-century **Hammershus**, not much in themselves but worth a visit for the views from the tall crag which the castle occupied, and noteworthy as northern Europe's largest castle ruin.

If Bornholm suddenly seems too big, and the weather's good, take one of the ferries (from Svaneke, Gudhjem or Allinge; check with ⊛www.christiansoefarten .dk or any tourist office for the latest details) to the tiny island of **Christiansø**, some 25km northeast of Bornholm – a speck in the Baltic that served as a naval base during the seventeenth century, and later as a prison; these days, the minuscule population prides itself on its spiced herring. From Christiansø there's a suspension bridge over to the island of **Frederiksø**, a breeding ground for eider ducks. If you want to savour the peace of these little islands, you can **stay** at the ⚓ *Gæstgiveriet* on Christiansø (☎56 46 20 15, ⊛www.christiansoekro.dk; ❺), one of the few lodgings in these parts, which also runs a campsite.

ravel details

Trains

Copenhagen to: Århus (38 daily; 3hr 16min); Esbjerg (9 daily; 3hr); Helsingør (every 20min; 45min); Næstved (2–3 hourly; 1hr); Nykøbing F (hourly; 1hr 40min); Odense (every 30min; 1hr 30min); Ringsted (3–4 hourly; 40min); Roskilde (every 5–10min; 25min); Rønne (3–5 daily via ferry from Ystad; 3hr).

Helsingør to: Gilleleje (2–3 hourly; 40min); Hellebæk (2–3 hourly; 10min); Hillerød (1–2 hourly; 32min); Hornbæk (2–3 hourly; 25min).

Køge to: Fakse (1–2 hourly; 34min); Store Heddinge (1–2 hourly; 30min).

Nykøbing F to: Maribo (1–2 hourly; 23min); Nakskov (1–2 hourly; 45min); Rødby (10 daily; 23min).

Roskilde to: Kalundborg (hourly, connects with ferry to Jutland; 1hr 10min).

Buses

Copenhagen to: Aalborg (3–5 daily; 4hr 45min direct, 5hr 10min via Ebeltoft); Århus (4–7 daily; 3hr direct, 4hr via Ebeltoft); Ebeltoft (2–3 daily; 3hr); Fjerritslev via Grenå, Randers, Hobro and Løgstør (2–5 daily; 6hr 15min), Rønne (3–5 daily; 3hr).

Nykøbing to: Odense via Svendborg (hourly; 3hr 40min).

Ferries

Allinge to: Christiansø (May–Sept Mon–Fri 1 daily; 1hr 10min).

Copenhagen to: Rønne (1 daily; 6hr).

Gudhjem to: Christiansø (July & Aug 3 daily; May–June & Sept 1 daily; Oct–April Mon–Fri 1 daily; 55min).

Kalundborg to: Århus (3–7 daily; 2hr 30min).

Odden to: Ebeltoft (7–15 daily; 45min); Århus (6–9 daily; 65min).

Svaneke to: Christiansø (May–Sept Mon–Fri 1 daily; 1hr 25min).

Tårs (Langeland) to: Spodsbjerg (10–33 daily; 45min).

International trains

Copenhagen to: Bergen (2–3 daily, change in Gothenburg and Oslo; 18hr 30min); Gothenburg (10 daily; 3hr 57min); Hamburg (4 daily; 4hr 30min); Helsinki (1–2 daily, change to ferry in Stockholm; 19hr 30min–22hr); Kiruna (1–2 daily, change in Stockholm; 22hr 30min–26hr 30min); Malmö (every 20min; 35min); Narvik (1–2 daily, change in Stockholm; 25hr 15min–29hr 15min); Oslo (3–4 daily, change in Gothenburg or Malmö; 8hr 20min); Stockholm (hourly, some change in Malmö; 5hr 20min); Turku (2–3 daily, change to ferry in Stockholm; 17hr 30min–21hr 15min).

International ferries and catamarans

Copenhagen to: Oslo, Norway (1 daily; 16hr); Swinoujscie, Poland (5–7 weekly; 9–11hr); Klaipeda, Lithuania (2–3 weekly; 16–18hr).

Gedser to: Rostock, Germany (9 daily in summer; rest of year 4 daily; 2hr).

Helsingør to: Helsingborg, Sweden (HH Ferries 31–49 daily; 20min; Sundbusserne 30–36 daily; 20min; Scandlines 60 daily in summer; 20min).

Neksø to: Kolobrzeg, Poland (catamaran 2–3 daily in summer; 2 hr).

Rødby to: Puttgarden, Germany (46 daily; 45min).

Rønne to: Sassnitz, Germany (1–2 daily in summer; rest of year 3 weekly; 3hr 30min); Swinoujscie, Poland (1 weekly; 5hr 15min); Ystad, Sweden (catamaran 2–5 daily; 1hr 20min; ferry 1–3 daily; 2hr 30min).

1.2

Funen

Known as "the garden of Denmark" for the lawn-like neatness of its fields and for the immense amount of fruit and vegetables that come from them, **Funen** (*Fyn*) is the smaller of the two main Danish islands, and one which many visitors pass quickly through on their way between Zealand and Jutland. The island's bucolic outlook and coastline draw many, but its attractions are mainly low-profile: grand castles and manor houses, the collections of the Funen painters and the birthplaces of writer Hans Christian Andersen and composer Carl Nielsen, who eulogized the distinctive sing-song Funen accent and claimed it inspired his music. Given its diminutive size, Funen is best explored by bicycle; otherwise, you'll be getting around on buses more often than trains, since the latter are relatively scarce.

Arriving from Zealand brings you through **Nyborg**, a town with a heavily restored twelfth-century castle, though there's little reason to linger long on the east coast and it's preferable to stay on the cross-country railway that continues to **Odense**, Denmark's third-largest city and an obvious base if you want to explore villages by day but would like some urban zip by night. Close by, the former fishing town of **Kerteminde** retains some faded charm, and is a good base for visiting both the Ladby Boat, an important Viking relic, and the isolated **Hindsholm Peninsula**. To the south, Funen's coastal life centres on maritime **Svendborg**, possibly the top scenic draw on Funen with its good beaches and fragmented archipelago of pretty **islands**. This is vacation territory for the most part, well served by ferries and connected by train with Odense via the island's only branch rail line.

East Funen

Travelling from Zealand to Funen takes you over the **Store Bælt** ("Great Belt"), the 18-kilometre road and rail link which connects the two islands, before bringing you to **Nyborg**, Funen's easternmost town and one that few visitors see more of than a train station.

Unless you're in a rush to reach Odense, spare a few hours for Nyborg's strollable old streets and thirteenth-century **castle**, for two hundred years the seat of Danish political power. Otherwise, apart from countless lookalike villages, there's not much in East Funen to detain you.

Nyborg

NYBORG is small and easily navigated and you'll have no trouble finding your way to **Nyborg Slot** (daily: July 10am–5pm; June & Aug 10am–4pm; April–May & Sept–Oct 10am–3pm; 30kr, for joint ticket with Mads Lerches Gård 45kr; Ⓦwww .museer-nyborg.dk), built around 1200 by Valdemar the Great as part of a chain of coastal fortresses to guard against Wend piracy. For more than two hundred years, the Danehof – a summertime national assembly involving king, clergy and nobility – met here (and in 1282 drew up the first Danish constitution), which effectively made Nyborg the Danish capital until 1443, when power moved to Copenhagen. The castle bears little evidence of those years, however. Many of the surrounding fortifications have been turned into ordinary homes and all that remains on view is

..arrow building holding the living quarters, its distinctive harlequin brickwork a result of 1920s restoration. Inside, low-beamed chambers lead into an expansive attic; the rooms themselves are much more evocative of the past than the odd table, chest, or suit of armour with which they are decorated. Most evocative is the **Danehof Hall**, where the assembly supposedly met and discussed the constitution. The unusual geometrical wall pattern was added in 1520. English-language **tours** (June–Aug Wed & Sat 2pm; rest of the year Sat 2pm; free) of the castle take you through all its nooks and crannies. For more local history, head down Slotsgade 11 to **Mads Lerches Gård** (same hours; 25kr, joint ticket with Nyborg Slot 45kr), a half-timbered merchant's house from the sixteenth century now housing the quaint town museum.

With the bright lights of Odense just 25km away to the west, there's little temptation to spend a night in Nyborg. If you decide to do so, though, there's the reasonably priced *Villa Gulle*, Østervoldgade 44 (☏65 30 11 88, ⊛www.villa-gulle .dk; ❹, en-suite ❺), and there's a beachside **campsite** (☏65 31 07 56, ⊛www .strandcamping.dk; April–Sept) at Hjejlevej 99. For further information, drop in to the **tourist office** at Torvet 9 (mid-June to mid-Aug Mon–Fri 9am–5pm, Sat 9.30am–2pm; rest of the year Mon–Fri 9am–4pm, Sat 9.30am–12.30pm; ☏65 31 02 80, ⊛www.nyborgturist.dk).

Odense and around

Funen's sole industrial centre and one of the oldest settlements in the country, **ODENSE** – named after Odin, chief of the Norse gods – gained prominence in the early nineteenth century when the opening of the Odense canal linked the city to the sea and made it the major transit point for the produce of the island's farms. Nowadays it's a pleasant provincial university town of museums and decent shopping, with a large manufacturing sector hugging the canal bank on the northern side of the city, well out of sight of the compact old centre. The **old town** houses some fine museums and – thanks to the resident students – a surprisingly vigorous nightlife. Odense is also known, throughout Denmark at least, as the birthplace of Hans Christian Andersen, and although it's all done quite discreetly, the fact is celebrated with souvenir shops and hotels catering for travellers lured by the prospect of a romantic Andersen experience – something they (almost inevitably) won't find. To the **north and south of town**, however, there are a few attractions of a rather different nature, from the reconstructed nineteenth-century buildings of Funen Village to the noel approach to the preshistoric era at the Iron Age Village.

Arrival, information and city transport

Long-distance **buses** terminate at the efficient **train station**, a ten-minute walk north of the city centre. In the centre, within the nineteenth-century Rådhus on Vestergade, you'll find the **tourist office** (mid-June to Aug Mon–Fri 9.30am–6pm, Sat & Sun 10am–3pm; rest of year Mon–Fri 9.30am–4.30pm, Sat 10am–1pm; ☏66 12 75 20, ⊛www.visitodense.com).

On Odense's **bus** system you pay 14kr as you enter to travel within the city limits: if you have to use more than one bus, ask the driver for a "change ticket" (*omstigning*) to use on the next bus. Better value if you're planning to see Odense's museums is the **Adventure Pass** (*Odense Eventyrpas*: one day for 120kr, two days 160kr), which gets you into most museums and gives you a discount where it doesn't, along with reductions on the *Odense Åfart* boat and admission to the zoo (see p.156); it allows unlimited travel on local buses. You can buy it from any tourist office as well as most train stations, youth hostels, campsites and hotels on Funen. If you can't face the buses, you can **rent a bike** at City Cykler, Vesterbro 27 (☏66 13 97 83, ⊛www.citycykler.dk; from 99kr per day, 500kr per week) or from Rolsted (☏66 17 77 36; 95kr per day, 500kr per week), next to the train station on Østre Stationsvej 33.

For **Internet** access, head for Game Play Net Café, Kongensgade 70 (daily noon–midnight; 25kr per hour) or Boomstown Netcafé, Pantheonsgade 4 (Mon–Thurs noon–1am, Fri noon–8am, Sat 11am–8am, Sun 11am–midnight; 25kr per hour). Free access is available at the large local library inside the train station, though you must book in advance on ☎65 51 43 01.

Accommodation

Thanks to Hans Christian Andersen, Odense has a plethora of pricey accommodation, although there are several affordable alternatives, including a number of central and affordable **B&Bs**, both quite close to the Andersen museums. There are also a couple of **hostels**, as well as a campsite in the city and another on the outskirts.

Hotels and B&Bs

Ansgar Østre Stationsvej 32 ☎66 11 96 93, ⓦwww.hotel-ansgar.dk. A short walk from the train station, this beautifully renovated hotel offers spacious, fully equipped rooms and a good restaurant. ⑤–⑥

Ansgarhus Motel Kirkegård Allé 19 ☎66 12 88 00, ⓦwww.ansgarhus.dk. One of Odense's cheaper options, conveniently located just outside the city centre – it's a fifteen-minute walk from the station via Jernbanegade, turning right down Vindersgade. Rooms are sparse but comfortable. ④

City Hotel Odense Hans Mules Gade 5 ☎66 12 12 58, ⓦwww.city-hotel-odense.dk. Bright and sparkling new upmarket option with a prominent yellow facade. Rooms are cosy with en-suite bathrooms. Just three minutes' walk from the train station: continue straight along Østre Stationsvej. ⑤

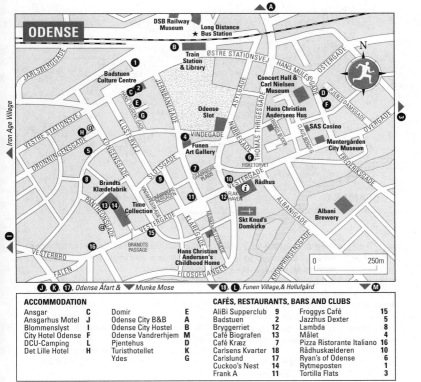

ACCOMMODATION

Ansgar	**C**	Domir	**E**
Ansgarhus Motel	**J**	Odense City B&B	**A**
Blommenslyst	**I**	Odense City Hostel	**B**
City Hotel Odense	**F**	Odense Vandrerhjem	**M**
DCU-Camping	**L**	Pjentehus	**D**
Det Lille Hotel	**H**	Turisthotellet	**K**
		Ydes	**G**

CAFÉS, RESTAURANTS, BARS AND CLUBS

AliBi Supperclub	**9**	Froggys Café	**15**
Badstuen	**2**	Jazzhus Dexter	**5**
Bryggerriet	**12**	Lambda	**8**
Café Biografen	**13**	Målet	**4**
Café Kræz	**7**	Pizza Ristorante Italiano	**16**
Carlsens Kvarter	**18**	Rådhuskælderen	**10**
Carlslund	**17**	Ryan's of Odense	**6**
Cuckoo's Nest	**14**	Rytmeposten	**1**
Frank A	**11**	Tortilla Flats	**3**

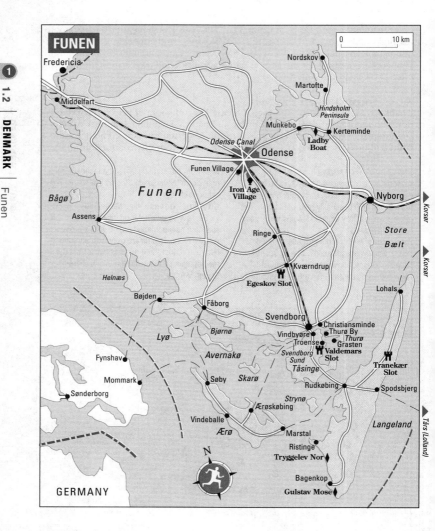

Det Lille Hotel Dronningensgade 5 ☎66 12 28 21, ⊛www.lillehotel.dk. Small hotel run by a friendly proprietor who has done plenty of travelling himself. Rooms are adequate with shared bathrooms. ❸

Domir Hans Tausens Gade 19 ☎66 12 14 27, ⊛www.domir.dk. Bright, welcoming and of a slightly higher standard than sister hotel *Ydes* further down the street. Rooms are pristine and all have private baths. ❹

Odense City B&B Billesgade 9 ☎66 13 00 74, ⊛www.odensecity-bedandbreakfast.dk. Good value, with smallish rooms and shared bathrooms; breakfast costs 40kr. Rooms are small and bathrooms shared. ❷

Pjentehus Pjentedamsgade 14 ☎66 12 15 55, ⊛www.pjentehus.dk. Located in the heart of Odense's cobbled section, this beautifully renovated old house has a garden that guests can use; rooms are adequate, if on the small side. Breakfast costs 40kr extra. ❷

Turisthotellet Gerthasminde 64 ☎66 11 26 92, ⊛www.turist-hotellet.dk. Cosy, Gothic-looking hotel – the small tower houses one of the rooms.

Other rooms aren't spacious, but the rates are reasonable. ❹

Ydes Hans Tausens Gade 11 ☏ 66 12 11 31, ⊚ www.ydes.dk. Cheaper and more basic than sister hotel *Domir* (see p.152); all rooms have private bathrooms. ❹

Hostels

Odense City Hostel Østre Stationsvej 31 ☏ 63 11 04 25, ⊚ www.cityhostel.dk. Next door to the train station, a friendly brightly decorated hostel with good doubles (❸) as well as dorms (120kr). **Odense Vandrerhjem** Kragsbjergvej 121 ☏ 66 13 04 25, ⊚ www.odense-danhostel.dk. Offers slightly cheaper rooms (❸) than its urban counterpart, and also much quieter. Dorm beds are 120kr. Located just outside town in a wood-beamed farmhouse; take bus #61 or #62 from the train station or cathedral south towards Tornbjerg or Fraugde and get out along Munkebjergvej at the junction with Vissenbjergvej. Open June–Sept.

Campsites

Blommenslyst Middelfartvej 494 ☏ 65 96 76 41, ⊚ www.blommenslyst-camping.dk. Facilities are pretty basic but the location, just next to a picturesque lake, is lovely. The site is about 10km from Odense; half-hourly buses #830, #831, #832 or #833 from the train station make the journey in twenty minutes.
DCU-Camping Odensevej 102 ☏ 66 11 47 02, ⊚ www.camping-odense.dk. The only campsite actually in Odense, near Funen Village, fully equipped with excellent cooking facilities. Take bus #21, #22 or #23 from the Rådhus or train station towards Højby.

The Town

Save for three outlying museums which are a bus ride away, Odense is easily explored on foot. There's a lot to be said for simply wandering around the compact **centre** with no particular destination in mind, but you shouldn't pass up the chance to visit the **Hans Christian Andersen** museums – very much what the town is known for – or fail to take in at least one of several absorbing **art collections**. Two other **museums** provide more offbeat fare: one celebrates composer Carl Nielsen – after Andersen, Odense's most famous son – and the other eulogizes Danish railways.

The Hans Christian Andersen museums and around

Odense's showpiece museum is the **Hans Christian Andersens Hus** (June–Aug daily 9am–6pm; Sept–May Tues–Sun 10am–4pm; 50kr; ⊚ www.odmus.dk), at Bangs Boder 29 in the house where the writer was born and which he described in *The Fairy Tale of My Life*. Oddly enough, Andersen was only really accepted in his own country towards the end of his life; his real admirers were abroad, which was perhaps why he travelled widely and left Odense at the first opportunity. He wrote novels and a few (best-forgotten) plays, but since his death it's his **fairy tales** that have gained most renown, partly autobiographical stories (not least *The Ugly Duckling*) that were influenced by *The Arabian Nights*, German folk stories, and the traditional Danish folk tales passed on by inmates of the Odense workhouse where his grandmother looked after the garden.

Few of the less-than-fairytale aspects of Andersen's life are touched upon in the museum, which was founded on the centenary of Andersen's birth when Odense first began to cash

△ Paper cutting by Hans Christian Andersen

in on its famous ex-citizen. The son of a hard-up cobbler, Andersen's first home was a single room that doubled as a workshop in what was then one of Odense's slum quarters. It was a rough upbringing: Hans's ill-tempered mother was fifteen years older than his father, whom she married when seven months pregnant with Hans (she also had an illegitimate daughter by another man); his grandfather was insane; and descriptions of his grandmother, often given charge of the young Hans, range from "mildly eccentric" to "a pathological liar".

There's a nagging falseness about some aspects of the collection, but as Andersen was a first-rate hoarder it's stuffed with intriguing items: bits of school reports, his certificate from Copenhagen University, early notes and manuscripts of his books, chunks of furniture, his umbrella, and paraphernalia from his travels, including the piece of rope he carried to facilitate escape from hotel rooms in the event of fire. A separate gallery contains a library of Andersen's works in seventy languages, and headphones for listening to some of his best-known tales as read by the likes of Sir Laurence Olivier. Nearby is a very mixed collection of illustrations and other art inspired by his writing.

The area around the museum, all half-timbered houses and spotlessly clean, car-free cobbled streets, lacks much character; indeed, if Andersen was around he'd hardly recognize the neighbourhood, which is now one of Odense's most expensive. For more realistic local history, head to the **Møntergården City Museum** (Tues–Sun 10am–4pm; free; ✆www.odmus.dk), a few streets away at Overgade 48–50, where there's an engrossing assemblage important archaeological pieces found on Funen, plus an immense coin collection – from as long ago and as far afield as England under Danelaw and Danish rule in Estonia.

There's more, but not much more, about Andersen at Munkemøllestræde 3–5, in the tiny **Hans Christian Andersen's Childhood Home** (June–Aug daily 10am–4pm; Sept–May Tues–Sun 11am–3pm; 10kr; ✆www.odmus.dk), the house where Andersen lived from 1807 to 1819 before moving to Copenhagen, where he spent the rest of his life. More interesting, though, is the nearby **Skt Knud's Domkirke** (April–Oct Mon–Sat 9am–5pm, Sun noon–5pm; Nov–March Mon–Sat 10am–4pm, Sun noon–5pm; ✆www.odense-domkirke.dk), whose crypt holds one of the most unusual and ancient finds Denmark has to offer: the **skeleton of Knud II**. Knud (aka Canute) was slain in 1086 – by Jutish farmers, angry at the taxes he'd imposed on them – in the original Skt Albani Kirke, the barest remains of which were found some years ago in the city park. The king was laid to rest in the original church in 1101, but the miraculous events of the following years (see "History", p.77) resulted in his canonization as Knud the Holy, and his remains were subsequently moved to the present Domkirke. Close to Knud's is another coffin, thought to hold the remains of his brother Benedict (though some claim them to be St Alban's, whose body was brought to Denmark by Knud), while displayed alongside is the fading, but impressive, Byzantine-style silk tapestry sent as a shroud by Knud's widow, Edele.

The cathedral itself is noteworthy, too. Mostly late thirteenth-century, it's the only example of pure Gothic church architecture in the country, set off by a finely detailed sixteenth-century wooden altarpiece that's rightly regarded as one of the greatest works of the Lübeck master-craftsman, Claus Berg.

Odense's art museums

The **Funen Art Gallery** (*Fyns Kunstmuseum*; Tues–Sun 10am–4pm; 30kr; ✆www.odmus.dk), a few minutes' walk from the cathedral at Jernbanegade 13, gives a good idea of the region's importance to Danish art during the late nineteenth century, when a number of Funen-based painters gave up creating portraits of the rich in favour of impressionistic landscapes and studies of the lives of the peasantry. The collection also contains some stirring works by many Nordic greats, among them Vilhelm Hammershøi, P.S. Krøyer, and Michael and Anne Ancher, but most striking of all is H.A. Brendekilde's enormously emotive *Udslidt* ("Worn Out"). The modern era isn't forgotten, with selections from Asger Jorn, Richard Mortensen and Egill Jacobsen, among many others, drawn from the museum's large collection.

For more modern art, walk along Vestergade and turn down Brandts Passage to reach **Brandts Klædefabrik** (⊛www.brandts.dk), a large former textile factory that's now given over to a number of cultural endeavours: three museums, a gallery, an art school, a music library and a cinema, along with cafés and restaurants. The **Art Exhibition Hall** here (*Kunsthallen*: July & Aug daily 10am–5pm; Sept–June Tues–Sun 10am–5pm; 30kr, combined ticket with the Photographic Art Museum and Danmarks Mediemuseum 50kr) is an increasingly prestigious spot for displays of work by high-flying new talent in art and design; close by are the varied displays of the **Museum of Photographic Art** (*Museet for Fotokunst*: same hours; 25kr, combined ticket 50kr), taken from the cream of modern (and some not so modern) art photography and almost always worth a look. There's also the more down-to-earth **Danmarks Mediemuseum** (same hours; ⊛www.mediemuseum.dk; 25kr, combined ticket 50kr), with its bulky machines and devices chronicling the development of printing, bookbinding and illustrating from the Middle Ages to the present. Further down Brandts Passage on the second floor of no. 29, the **Time Collection** (*Tidens Samling*; daily 10am–5pm; 30kr; ⊛www .tidenssamling.dk) gives an intimate insight into changing fashions and home interiors and clothing since the turn of the last century.

The Carl Nielsen and railway museums

The **Carl Nielsen Museum**, inside the concert hall at Claus Bergs Gade 11 (June–Aug Thurs & Fri 2–6pm, Sun noon–4pm; rest of the year Thurs & Fri 4–8pm, Sun noon–4pm; 25kr; ⊛www.odmus.dk), celebrates the life and work of Odense's second most famous son. Born in a village just outside Odense in 1865, Nielsen displayed prodigious musical gifts from an early age and joined the Odense military band as a cornet player when just 14 (wearing a specially shortened uniform). From there he went to study at the Copenhagen *conservatoire* and then on to gain worldwide acclaim as a composer, for his symphonies particularly, the musical cognoscenti in his own country regarding him as having salvaged Danish music from a period of decline. Despite his travels, and long period of residence in Copenhagen, Nielsen continually praised the inspirational qualities of Funen's nature and the island's tuneful dialect, even writing a somewhat sentimental essay romanticizing the landscape in which "even trees dream and talk in their sleep with a Funen lilt". If you've never heard of Nielsen, be assured that his music is nowhere near as half-baked as his prose: in the museum you can listen to some of his work on headphones, including excerpts from his major pieces and the polka he wrote when still a child. The actual **exhibits**, detailing Nielsen's life and achievements, are further enlivened by the accomplished sculptures of his wife, Anne Marie, many of them early studies for her equestrian statue of Christian IX that now stands outside the Royal Stables in Copenhagen.

The final museum in central Odense is hardly essential viewing unless you've been particularly impressed by the comfort and efficiency of modern Danish trains. The **DSB Railway Museum** (*Jernbanemuseum*; daily 10am–4pm; 48kr; ⊛www .jernbanemuseum.dk), immediately behind the station, houses some of the state railways' most treasured artefacts, which include royal and double-decker carriages and the reconstruction of an entire early twentieth-century station, as well as a feast of otherwise forgotten facts pertaining to the rise of Danish railways.

Around Odense

A couple of kilometres south of the city centre on Sejerskovvej, the open-air **Funen Village** museum (April–May & Sept–Oct Tues–Sun 10am–5pm; Nov–March Sun only 11am–3pm; 40kr; June–Aug 10am–7pm; 55kr; ⊛www.odmus .dk) comprises a reconstructed nineteenth-century country village which is lent an air of authenticity by its period gardens and wandering geese. From the farmhouse to the poorhouse, all the buildings are originals from other parts of Funen, their exteriors painstakingly reassembled and interiors carefully refurbished. In summer, the old trades are revived in the former workshops and crafthouses, and there are free shows at the open-air theatre. Though often crowded, the village is well worth a visit – look out, too, for the village-brewed beer, handed out free on special occasions. Bus #42 runs to the village from the city centre (get out at the Den Fynske Landsby sign), or do what the locals do and get on the *Odense Åfart* boat (ⓦwww.aafart.dk; 35kr single, 55kr return, 25 percent discount with an Adventure Pass), which runs along the canal from Munke Mose park in the city centre and terminates at Fruens Bøge, from where it's a short canalside walk to Funen Village. From May to mid-August, it sails daily on the hour from 10am to 5pm, and from mid-August to mid-September, daily at 11am, noon, 2 and 5pm. The *Odense Åfart* also stops at **Odense Zoo** (July daily 9am–7pm; May–June & Aug Mon–Fri 9am–6pm, Sat & Sun 9am–7pm; April & Sept–Oct Mon–Fri 9am–5pm, Sat & Sun 9am–6pm; Nov–March daily 9am–4pm; 100kr; ⓦwww.odensezoo.dk) on the way. A fifteen-minute bus ride south of the centre (bus #82 towards Neder Holluf), but worth a special detour, is **Hollufgård**, a sixteenth-century manor house (not open to the public), whose enjoyable landscaped **gardens** (daily dawn–dusk; free) are decorated with sculptures by students from the Danish Academy of Fine Arts.

Also easily reached from the town centre (bus #91 towards Allesø), the **Iron Age Village**, some 5km southeast at Store Klaus 40 (July to mid-Aug Mon–Fri & Sun 10am–4pm; mid-Aug to June Mon–Thurs 8.30am–3.30pm, Fri 8.30am–2pm; 25kr; ⓦwww.jernalderlandsbyen.dk), is one of many prehistoric collections in Denmark, but one that at least makes an effort to be different. There's a simulated TV news broadcast covering events in Bronze Age Denmark, alongside displays describing how ancient symbols are used in modern times.

Eating and drinking

Most of Odense's **restaurants** and **snack bars** are squeezed into the central part of town, which means there's a lot of competition and potentially some very good bargains during the day. Many of the places listed below are also good for a **drink** in the evenings. If the weather is right for outdoor eating, pick up a freshly made sandwich or pastry from the in-house bakery at 🍴 *Bakers Café*, across the road from the tourist office on Fisketorvet.

Badstuen Østre Stationsvej 26. A stone's throw from the station on the upper floor of the cultural centre, this inexpensive café offers some of the best meal deals in town. The dish of the day costs 35kr and is served promptly between 5.30pm and 6.30pm, while salads, open sandwiches and burgers go for 15kr throughout the day.

Bryggerriet Flakhaven 2. Close to the Rådhus and tourist office, this brewery-restaurant is a great place to ponder your day over a beer of the month (46kr a pint). Delightful meals include a herring *smørrebrød* platter for 78kr and spare ribs from 129kr. Outdoor seating in the summer.

Café Kræz Gråbrødre Plads 6. Just off Jernbanegade, serving tasty salads, sandwiches and soups, as well as pancakes with a beef or chicken filling (112kr). There's brunch (from 80kr) at weekends, outdoor seating and occasional live bands.

🏃 **Carlslund** Fruens Bøge Skov 7 ☏65 91 11 25, ⓦwww.restaurant-carlslund.dk. Near the Funen Village, this is a typical Danish restaurant which does delicious *smørrebrød* and is famous for its *æggekage* (literally "eggcake",

a sort of omelette with pork and chives) for 95kr. There's live jazz on summer Saturdays; check the website or call for info.

🏃 **Frank A** Jernbanegade 4. A short walk from the train station, offering good café fare and decent full meals: burgers, sandwiches and bagels from 69kr, and huge brunch daily from 10am (89kr). Outdoor seating during summer and busy most evenings for after-dinner drinking.

Froggys Café Vestergade 68. A pleasant spot for a quick café-style bite to eat during the day, or for more substantial evening meals such as butterfish in white wine sauce or hazelnut chicken. There's a DJ on weekend evenings until 5am, and a help-yourself brunch buffet on Sundays for 79kr.

Målet Jernbanegade 17. Reasonably priced Danish menu including fried plaice with rémoulade for 69kr; sports of any sort shown on a big screen.

Pizza Ristorante Italiano Vesterbro 9. Reliable pizzas and pasta at the best and oldest of the city's many pizzerias.

Tortilla Flats Frederiksgade 38. Mexican food at its best: tortillas, burritos and the whole enchilada.

Odense has a plethora of **late-opening cafés** that have usurped the role of night-clubs as evening hangouts. A good first stop is *Café Biografen* at Brandts Klædefabrik – enduringly fashionable and decorated with a dazzling display of movie posters; from there, move on to *Cuckoo's Nest* next door, which is one of the few spots with any life early in the week. For unpretentious drinking, *Carlsens Kvarter*, on the corner of Hunderupvej and Læssøgade, south of Hans Christian Andersen's Child-hood Home, is an inexpensive pub serving fruity Belgian beers and English ales, and occasionally hosting Danish folk music. *Ryan's of Odense* at Fisketorvet 12, just north of the Rådhus, is a true Irish pub, with live music on weekends.

If you're in the mood for a gamble, try your luck at the **casino** (daily 7pm–4am; 60kr; ⓦwww.casinoodense.dk) in the *SAS Hotel* on Claus Bergs Gade. For details on Odense's **gay and lesbian** scene, head for the Lambda organization's café at Vindegade 100 (Wed 8pm–midnight, Fri & Sat 10pm–2am; ☎40 89 62 49, ⓦwww.lambda.dk). Odense's **live music** scene is also worth investigating; pick up the leaflets spread out at most cafés, music shops and the tourist office for details of upcoming events. *Rytmeposten*, Østre Stationsvej 35 (☎66 13 60 20, ⓦwww.rytmeposten.dk), is Funen's prime live music venue, a converted post office where you'll often find heavy rock bands performing. Another busy spot is the radical cultural centre *Badstuen*, just opposite at Østre Stationsvej 26 (☎66 13 48 66, ⓦwww.badstuen.dk), which regularly hosts popular folk bands, while *Jazzhus Dexter*, Vindegade 65 (☎63 11 27 28, ⓦwww.dexter.dk), offers all types of **jazz**, from swing to fusion, four or five times a week until early morning. There's stand-up **comedy** at the *AliBi Supperclub*, Vintapperstræde 51 (☎66 14 82 99, ⓦwww.supperclub.dk), also featuring the hottest **club scene** during weekends. Otherwise, two or three times a week, there's easier rock for the over-25s at *Rådhuskælderen*, Vestergade 15–17 (☎66 12 58 08).

Kerteminde and around

A half-hour bus ride on bus #885 (40min with bus #890) northeast from Odense, past the huge cranes and construction platforms at Munkebo – until recently a tiny fishing hamlet but now the home of Denmark's biggest shipyard – lies **KER-TEMINDE**, itself a place with firm maritime links, originally in fishing and now increasingly in tourism. The town is a centre for sailing and holidaymaking, and can get oppressively busy during the peak weeks of the summer. At any other time of year, though, it makes for a well-spent day, split between the town itself and the Viking-era **Ladby Boat** just outside.

The heart of Kerteminde, around the fifteenth-century Skt Laurentius Kirke and along Langegade and Strandgade, is a neat and prettily preserved nucleus of shops and houses. By the harbour, across the road from the bus station on Margrethes Plads 1, **Fjord & Bæltcentret** (July to mid-Aug daily 10am–6pm; 85kr; mid-Feb to June & mid-Aug to Nov Mon–Fri 10am–4pm, Sat & Sun 10am–5pm; ⓦwww.fjord-baelt.dk), a state-of-the-art aquarium with a 50m-long underwater tunnel from where you can observe seals and porpoises in their natural sea environment, is worth a visit. On Strandgade itself, the **town museum** (*Farvergården*; Tues–Sun 10am–4pm; 25kr) has five reconstructed craft workshops and a collection of local fishing equipment. On a grander note, a ten-minute stroll north around the water-front brings you to the one-time house of the "birdman of Funen", the painter Johannes Larsen, on Møllebakken 14, which has been opened up as the **Johannes Larsen Museum** (June–Aug daily 10am–5pm; March–May, Sept & Oct Tues–Sun 10am–4pm; Nov–Feb Tues–Sun 11am–4pm; 60kr). During the late nineteenth century, Larsen produced etchings of rural landscapes and birdlife, going against the grain of prevailing art world trends in much the same way as the Skagen artists (see p.203). The house is kept as it was when Larsen lived there, with his furnishings and knick-knacks, many of his canvases and, in the dining room, his astonishing wall paintings. To the chagrin of the pious locals, the house became a haunt of the country's more bacchanalian artists and writers in its day, and the garden holds a sculpted female figure by frequent visitor Kai Nielsen. A story goes that during one particularly drunken party the piece was dropped and the legs broke off. Someone called the local *falck* (emergency services), but despite much inebriated pleading, the (sober) officer who rushed to the scene refused to take the sculpture to hospital.

Practicalities

Kerteminde's **tourist office**, around the corner from the Skt Laurentius Kirke (mid-June to Aug Mon–Sat 9am–5pm; Sept to mid-June Mon–Fri 9am–4pm, Sat 9.30am–12.30pm; ☎65 32 11 21, ⊛www.kerteminde-turist.dk), has details of Kerteminde's **accommodation** bargains. If you want to stay over at any other time, the only low-cost option is a dorm bed (120kr) at the youth hostel (☎65 32 39 29, ⊛www.danhostel.dk/kerteminde) at Skovvej 46, a ten-minute walk from the centre (cross the Kerteminde fjord by the road bridge, take the first major road left and then turn almost immediately right to reach it). There's also a **campsite**, *Kerteminde Camping* (☎65 32 19 71, ⊛www.dk-camp.dk/kertemindecamp; May to mid-Aug), not far from the Larsen museum at Hindsholmvej 80, the main road running along the seafront – a twenty-minute walk from the centre. If you want something more upmarket, try the three-star *Tørnøes Hotel*, Standgade 2 (☎65 32 16 05, ⊛www.tornoeshotel.dk; ◐).

Around Kerteminde: the Ladby Boat and Hindsholm Peninsula

About 4km southwest of Kerteminde in Ladby, along the banks of the fjord at Vikingvej 123, is the **Ladby Boat** (*Ladbyskibet*; June–Aug daily 10am–5pm; March–May & Sept–Oct Tues–Sun 10am–4pm; Nov–Feb Wed–Sun 11am–3pm; 25kr), a vessel dredged up from the fjord that was found to be the burial ship of a Viking chieftain. The 22-metre craft, along with the remains of the weapons, hunting dogs and horses that accompanied the deceased on his journey to Valhalla, is kept in a tiny purpose-built museum. It's an interesting find, but you'll need only half an hour for a close inspection. Blue Kerteminde town bus #482 runs to the museum several times a day from Monday to Friday, but it's more pleasant to rent a bike in town and cycle there.

△ Funen countryside

Cycling is also the best way to explore the **Hindsholm Peninsula**, north of Kerteminde, since it's quite small; if this seems too energetic, the tourist office should have the latest bus schedules. There's not actually much to see, save perhaps the ancient **underground burial chamber** (*Mårhøj Jættestue*) near Martofte, 10km due north of Kerteminde, which is open to the public (though the bodies, of course, are long gone). Outside high season, however, the area becomes an unparalleled spot to pitch a tent and revel in quiet seclusion. There are two **campsites** further into the peninsula: *Bøgebjerg Strand* (☎65 34 10 52, ⊛www.bogebjerg.dk; April to mid-Sept), on the shore opposite the island of Romsø; and, on the northernmost tip just past Nordskov at Fynshovedvej 748, *Fyns Hoved Camping* (☎65 34 10 14, ⊛www.dk-camp.dk/fynshoved).

Southern Funen and the islands

Southern Funen is noted above all for its many miles of sandy beaches, which are packed with tourists during the peak season. In July and August, the **islands** of the southern archipelago are more enticing: connected by an efficient network of ferries, they range from larger chunks of land such as Tåsinge, Langeland and Ærø – the latter two certainly worth a few nights' stay – to minute and sparsely populated places like Lyø or Avernakø, which are a pleasure to explore, if only for a few hours. From Odense, the simplest plan is to take a train to Svendborg, the main centre on the south coast, although you might also find the smaller Fåborg a good base; it's an hour's bus ride from Odense (#960, #961 or #962).

Svendborg

A favourite of the Danish yachting fraternity, with marinas clogging the coastline from here to Fåborg, 24km west, **SVENDBORG** exudes a certain gritty charm, with colourful houses lining cobbled lanes dipping down to the water. Svendborg is a pleasant place to plot your travels around the archipelago, and boasts some of the best nightlife in an otherwise very quiet region. While you're there, spend an hour or two meandering around the narrow backstreets, spattered with beautiful bronzes by one of Denmark's best-known sculptors, the locally born Kai Nielsen, and head down to the harbourfront to take in the bustling shipyard, packed with beautiful old wooden boats from all over Scandinavia and the Baltic.

Before heading off to the islands, a couple of historical collections might occupy a bit of your time. The **County Museum** (*Viebæltegård*; Tues–Sun 10am–4pm; 25kr; ☎62 21 02 61, ⊛www.svendborgmuseum.dk), located in the town's old poorhouse at Grubbemøllevej 13, has the usual regional collections as well as well-preserved finds from a Franciscan monastery, while on Fruenstræde 3, the beautiful **Anne Hvides Gård** (May–Aug Tues–Sun 10am–4pm; 25kr) is Svendborg's oldest secular building (dating from the sixteenth century), and now holds a museum displaying local artefacts alongside changing cultural exhibits. More entertaining is the **L. Lange & Co. Stove Museum** (10kr), Vestergade 45, an eccentric horde of cookers and burners produced by a well-known Svendborg-based firm from 1850 to 1984. It opens on request only; contact the County Museum. Lastly, the brand new **Naturama** (mid-June to mid-Aug Mon–Wed & Fri–Sun 10am–5pm, Thurs 10am–8pm; rest of the year closed Mon; 70kr; ⊛www.naturama.dk), Dronningemaen 30, offers a novel insight into the natural world. Spread over three floors of a circular building, displays follow the theme of water, land or air, using sound and light in a fancy way to make the stuffed animals look almost lifelike. Especially impressive are the five hundred birds dangling in the air on the top floor.

Practicalities

The Lange company's former foundry, next door to the Lange museum at Vestergade 45, is now the town's **youth hostel** (☎62 21 66 99, ⊛www.danhostel-svendborg.dk), which has dorms (120kr) and doubles (❷). Otherwise, there's the

The Helge steamer

Between early May and mid-September, the *Helge* steamer (built in 1924) leaves Svendborg three to five times daily for the island of **Tåsinge**, calling at Vindebyøre, Svendborg's extension just across the Svendborg Sund; zigzagging back to Christiansminde, a beach resort next to Svendborg's exclusive marina; then on to the thatched village of Troense, criss-crossed by quiet streets of carefully preserved houses; Grasten, on the small island of Thurø and a few minutes' walk from a beach campsite; and the seventeenth-century castle Valdemar's Slot. The return sailing time is two hours, and **tickets** (80kr round-trip from the harbour; information on ☏33 15 15 15) are good for one stop-off along the way, and are purchased on board.

The *Helge*'s last stop is the best: **Valdemar's Slot** (⊛www.valdemarsslot.dk), an imposing pile with Baroque interiors begun by Christian IV and continued by his son, Valdemar, who died before taking up residence. Filled with three centuries of furniture, paintings and tapestries, and a new section filled with hunting trophies and paraphernalia, the castle serves as a **museum** (July daily 10am–6pm; May–June & Aug daily 10am–5pm; Sept Tues–Sun 10am–5pm; Oct & April Sat & Sun 10am–5pm; 60kr). Outside, two separate wings hold a **yachting museum** (same hours; 40kr) with a number of finely crafted wooden yachts on display, and a **Toy Museum** (*Legetøjsmuseet*; same hours; 40kr), with a collection that should appeal to kids and adults alike. Note that a joint ticket for all three museums costs 120kr. While you're waiting for the *Helge* to carry you back to Svendborg, have a snack at the *Æblehaven Kiosk* just outside the castle, or go for a full-on meal at the exclusive *Restaurant Valdemars Slot* in the castle cellars. It's worth timing your trip to coincide with their lunch buffet (11.30am–2.30pm; 165kr) which excels in Funen delicacies. The restaurant's former tea pavilion, at the end of the courtyard, is no longer open, but the views out to the long, narrow island of Langeland from there are still great.

Should you want to stay over on Tåsinge, there are four **campsites** on the island; most convenient for the steamer and with access to a beautiful beach is *Vindebyøre Camping* (☏62 22 54 25, ⊛www.vindebyoere.dk). Tåsinge also houses a couple of **hotels**: the cosy, thatched *Det Lille* (☏62 22 53 41, ⊛www.detlillehotel.dk; ❹), offering rooms with shared facilities; or the grander *Troense* (☏62 22 54 12, ⊛www.hotel troense.dk; ❺) – both are in Troense.

pricey *Hotel Svendborg*, Centrumpladsen 1 (☏62 21 17 00, ⊛www.hotel-svendborg .dk; ❻), or, via a ten-minute bus ride along the coast (#202), the reasonably priced *Stella Maris Missionhotel* (☏62 21 38 91, ⊛www.stellamaris.dk; ❹, en-suite ❺), a grand white building overlooking the Svendborg sound with a range of different rooms. The **tourist office** (mid-June to Aug Mon–Fri 9.30am–6pm, Sat 9.30am–3pm; Sept to mid-June Mon–Fri 9.30am–5pm, Sat 9.30am–12.30pm; ☏62 21 09 80, ⊛www.visitsydfyn.dk), across the square from *Hotel Svendborg* at Centrumpladsen 4, deal with the entire southern Funen area and can provide details of accommodation, including numerous local **campsites**. They also stock the latest ferry timetables.

For **food**, don't miss the sublime meals at ⚓*Jette's Diner* on Kullinggade 1, and the traditional Danish sailors' fare on offer at *Restaurant Svendborgsund*, Havnepladsen 5 – try the *stegt flæsk* (fried pork and potatoes in creamy parsley sauce). The nightlife, such as it is, usually starts at café-bar *Under Uret*, Gerritsgade 50, and continues on to *Café Citronen*, Brogade 33, or *Standlyst*, Brogade 5, both of which have live music and all-night dancing at weekends.

Fåborg

An alternative base for the south coast, **FÅBORG** is a likeably small and sedate place, rarely as overwhelmed by holidaymakers as Svendborg and with equally good connections to the archipelago (ferries sail to Søby on Ærø, and to Bjørnø, Lyø and Avernakø). If you've an interest in Danish art, the town's other big attraction is the **Fåborg Museum** at Grønnegade 75 (April–Oct daily 10am–4pm; Nov–March Tues–Sun 11am–3pm; 40kr; ⊛www.faaborgmuseum.dk). Opened in 1910, the museum quickly became the major showcase for the **Funen artists**, particularly the work of Fritz Syberg and Peter Hansen, both of whom studied under the influential Kristian Zahrtmann in Copenhagen and typically filled their canvases with richly coloured depictions of Funen landscapes. Apart from the chance to admire the skills of the painters, the works demonstrate how little the Funen countryside has changed since they were painted the best part of a century ago.

Almost next door to the museum at Grønnegade 71–73 is one of the country's quaintest **youth hostels** (☎62 61 12 03, ⊛www.danhostel.dk/faaborg; April–Oct), with dorm beds (110kr) and eighteen inexpensive double rooms (❶). There's a **campsite** at Odensevej 140 (☎62 61 77 94), half a mile north of town, and a number of other camping areas on the beach as well. The bare-bones *Hotel Færgegården*, Christian den IX's Vej 31 (☎62 61 11 15, ⊛www.hotelfg.dk; ❺) by the harbour is the cheapest in town, while outside Fåborg, in the neighbouring village of Astrup, lies the simple *Hotel Mosegaard*, Nabgyden 31 (☎62 61 56 91, ⊛www.hotelmosegaard.dk; ❺). The **tourist office**, Banegårdspladsen 2A (May–Sept Mon–Sat 9am–5pm; Oct–April Mon–Sat 10am–5pm; ☎62 61 07 07, ⊛www.visitfaaborg.dk) can help with a list of inexpensive **private rooms** (❷, plus 25kr booking fee) and local travel information; they also sell DSB bus and train tickets.

For **food**, splash out and try the fish restaurant *Ved Brønden*, at Torvet 5, or the traditional Danish ⚒*Restaurant Tre Kroner*, Strandgade 1. Otherwise, there's a plethora of fast food places, and you can stock up on provisions at the Super Brugsen or Føtex markets, which are next to each other on Mellemgade near the bus station.

Around Fåborg: Egeskov Castle and the smaller islands

In Kværndrup, just twenty minutes from Fåborg by bus #920 (ten minutes by train from Svendborg, then short walk or ride on bus #920), is the Renaissance castle **Egeskov Slot** ("Oak-forest Castle"). You're allowed in (daily: May–June & Aug–Sept 10am–5pm; July 10am–5pm; 55kr; ⊛www.egeskov.dk), though it's really more impressive from the outside. To get to the castle you must first enter the beautifully manicured grounds (daily: May & Sept 10am–5pm; June & Aug 10am–6pm; July 10am–8pm; 90kr including eight museums), which makes the entry fee rather steep. The array of museums include one with displays on agriculture, horse-drawn vehicles and motorbikes; there's also a grocers' museum and, best of all, the **Egeskov Veteranmuseum**, which has some 300 antique cars. The stunning castle **gardens** include an intricate bamboo maze designed by Danish designer-cum-philosopher-cum-poet Peit Hein, as well as an award-winning rose garden and a romantic water garden surrounded by azaleas and rhododendrons. It's easy to spend an entire day lounging around here, but bear in mind that the grounds are packed with visitors during high season. If you want to stay overnight there's a free campsite (no facilities) next to the car park.

If you're looking for some quiet, it's easy enough to visit one of the three small islands of **Bjørnø**, **Lyø** and **Avernakø**. All are connected with Fåborg by small ferries (at least 5 daily; journey time 20–45min; information for Lyø and Avernakø on ☎62 61 23 07, ⊛www.oe-faergen.dk; and for Bjørnø ☎20 29 80 50, ⊛www.bjoernoe-faergen.dk). There's not much to do on the islands apart from walking in the beautiful countryside: rolling hills and fine sandy beaches abound. If you want to **stay** overnight, contact the tourist office in Fåborg (see above), which can arrange stays with local families for around 150kr per person per night.

Langeland

The largest of the southern islands, long, thin and fertile **Langeland** is just off the southeast coast of Funen, to which it's connected by road bridge (hence you don't need to catch a ferry to reach it). Frequent buses (#910) make the half-hour journey from Svendborg to **RUDKØBING**, the main town, from where there are ferry links to Marstal on Ærø; there's also a ferry to Tårs on Lolland (see p.143), leaving from Spodsbjerg, about 6km to the east. Rudkøbing itself doesn't have a lot to offer except for a laid-back atmosphere, a pleasant fishing harbour and the historical collection in the **Langelands Museum** at Jens Winthersvej 12 (Mon–Thurs 10am–4pm, Fri 10am–1pm; 25kr; ⊛www.langelandsmuseum.dk). The town's **tourist office**, at Torvet 5 (mid-June to Aug Mon–Fri 9am–5pm, Sat 9am–3pm; Sept to mid-June Mon–Fri 9.30am–4.30pm, Sat 9.30am–12.30pm; ☎62 51 35 05, ⊛www.langeland.dk), can provide advice on **accommodation** and has a long list of **private rooms** across the island starting at 125kr per person.

Alternatively, head for the low yellow **youth hostel** at Engdraget 11 (☎62 51 18 30, ⊛www.danhostel.dk/rudkobing), which has dorms (120kr) and doubles (**②**); or one of the island's nine **campsites**. Easiest to get to are *Færgegårdens Camping* at Spodsbjergvej 335 (☎62 50 11 36, ⊛www.spodsbjerg.dk), and *Billevænge Camping*, Spodsbjergvej 182 (☎62 50 10 06, ⊛www.billevaenge-camping.dk). However, if you have your own transport (the tourist office has a list of bicycle rental places starting at 40kr a day, and sells an excellent cycle map for 30kr), you can head out to one of the remoter sites such as the beachfront *Emmerbølle Strand Camping* (☎62 59 12 26, ⊛www.emmerbolle.dk), at Emmerbøllevej 24 near Tranekær (see below). **Hotel** choices include the budget *Spodsbjergvej Badehotel* at Spodsbjergvej 317 (☎ & ☎62 50 10 64; **③**), where all rooms share facilities; and the better-located if more expensive *Rudkøbing Skudehavn*, on the harbour at Havnegade 21 (☎62 51 46 00, ⊛www.sitecenter.dk/skudehavnen; **⑤**). If you plan on visiting on the last weekend in July, book accommodation early, as this is when the annual **Langelands Festival** takes place (⊛www.langelandsfestival.dk). Known as Denmark's largest garden party, this smallish music festival hosts mostly Danish bands alongside a few international acts – Runrig played in 2005.

North of Rudkøbing, Langeland consists mostly of farmland, sandy beaches and the occasional village, with just one sight to head for: the fairy-tale thirteenth-century **Tranekær Slot**, approximately 7km north of Rudkøbing and surrounded by the beautiful TICKON park (June to mid-Sept Mon–Fri 10am–5pm, Sun 1–5pm; 25kr), dotted with sculptures made by international artists from natural materials. There's a **museum** (same hours; 25kr) in the old water mill opposite the castle and park on the other side of the main road to Lohals, covering the history of Tranekær village and its castle. To find the island's best **beaches**, head 15km southwest of Rudkøbing to **Ristinge**, one of the loveliest in the country, or make for the southern coast, where there are also a couple of **bird sanctuaries**, Gulstav Mose and Tryggelev Nor. Local buses serve all the main sites on the island.

Ærø

For a more varied few days, take the ferry from Svendborg or Rudkøbing to **Ærø**, a pretty island just north of the German coast. Although getting here can require the better part of a day, it's worth the effort for the island's ancient burial sites, abundant stretches of sandy beach, traditional farms and, in the principal town of **Ærøskøbing**, a peach of a medieval merchants' town.

Ærøskøbing

When passing shipping brought prosperity to Ærø in the nineteenth century, the island historically split into three divisions: fisherfolk resided on the windy western tip at Søby; the wealthy shipping magnates and captains resided in Marstal, to the east; while the local middle classes collected in the town of **ÆRØSKØBING**. This is all beautifully described at **Ærø Museum** (mid-March to mid-Oct Mon–Fri 10am–4pm, Sat & Sun 11am–3pm; mid-Oct to mid-March Mon–Fri 10am–1pm; 20kr, joint ticket with the Bottle Ship Collection 50kr; ⊛ www.arremus.dk), Brogade **③**–**⑤**.

Ærøskøbing was awarded the European Nostra prize in 2003 as the best-preserved eighteenth century Danish town, and its narrow streets, lined with tidy houses, are made for wandering – look out for the oldest building, dating from 1645, at Søndergade 36. If it's raining, you could drop in to see the eye-catching **Bottle Ship Collection** (mid-June to July daily 10am–5pm; mid-March to mid-June & mid-July to mid-Oct daily 10am–4pm; mid-Oct to March Tues–Fri 1–3pm, Sat & Sun 10am–noon; ✆www.bottle-peter.dk; 25kr, joint ticket with Ærø Museum 50kr) at Smedegade 22, or **Hammerichs House** at Gyden 22 (mid-June to mid-Sept daily noon–4pm; 20kr), a riot of woodcarvings, furnishings and timepieces from bygone days.

Ærøskøbing's **tourist office** (mid-June to Aug Mon–Fri 9am–5pm, Sat 9am–2pm, Sun 9.30am–12.30pm; Sept–May Mon–Fri 9am–4pm, Sat 9am–12.30pm; ✆62 52 13 00, ✆www.arre.dk), on Vestergade 1, can give information on the island's burial places and other secluded spots. A local bus serves the island's main roads, but the best way to get around is by **bike**, though you'll need to pedal hard to get up some of the hills; the tourist office supplies free bike maps to help plan your route, and cycles can be rented for 50kr a day at Pilebækkens Cykler (✆62 52 11 10), Pillebækken 11, a BP gas station about 200m west of the main marketplace.

As for **accommodation**, there's the small *Det Lille Hotel* (✆62 52 23 00, ✆www.det-lille-hotel.dk; 4x), Smedegade 33, where all rooms share facilities. There's also a terrific youth hostel (✆62 52 10 44, ✆www.danhostel.dk/aeroeskoebing; April–Sept), with ocean views, friendly management and some doubles (①) as well as dorms (108kr); it's at Smedevejen 15, about 2km west of the ferry dock on the road to Marstal. Finally, *Ærøskøbing Camping* campsite, Sygehusvej 40B (✆62 52 18 54, ✆www.arrecamping.dk; May–Sept), is appealingly sited next to the beach. **Eating** options include *Det Lille Hotel's* good Danish restaurant at Smedegade 33, and the popular *Café Lille Claus*, a burger and fried-fish joint close by the ferry landing. There are fancier places along the main street, often stuffed with vacationing Germans. For provisions, there's a Netto supermarket in the town centre, and a good little bakery, *Ærøskøbing Bageri*, on Vestergade 62. When getting on or off the Svendborg ferry, be sure to look in on the smoked-fish place, *Ærøskøbing Røgeri*, facing the water at Havnen 15 – the fish is outstanding.

Nightlife is pretty much limited to a couple of bars: the *Strandskoven* by the water, and the *Arrebo Værtshus*, Vestergade 4, which sometimes hosts live music acts. Summertime brings the occasional open-air concert to the streets of town, too.

Marstal and beyond

If you're looking to escape the crowds, then **MARSTAL**, at the east end of the island and reached by bus from Ærøskøbing (or ferry from Rudkøbing in Langeland), is a good alternative base. Once there, don't miss the superb **Marstal Søfartsmuseum** (May & Sept daily 10am–4pm; June & Aug daily 9am–5pm; July daily 9am–8pm; Oct–April Tues–Fri 10am–4pm, Sat 11am–3pm; 40kr; ✆www.marstal-maritime-museum.dk), Prinsensgade 1, a collection of maritime paintings and ship models from Marstal's nineteenth-century golden age, when it was one of the busiest harbours in Denmark.

Most people staying here sleep on yachts or in holiday-home rentals, but there are a few budget options including the **youth hostel** at Færgestræde 29 (✆63 52 63 58, ✆www.danhostel.dk/marstal; April–Oct), which has dorms (100kr) and doubles (①), and is conveniently close to the town centre and the harbour. There's also a **campsite**, *Marstal Camping* (✆63 52 63 69, ✆www.aeroe.dk/marcamp; April–Oct), almost on the beach and with cabins, too. The reasonably priced, comfortable *Marstal* (✆62 53 13 52, ✆www.hotelmarstal.dk; ④), near the harbour at Dronningestræde 1A, is the nicest **hotel**; some rooms have shared bathrooms. For local information, contact the **tourist office** (mid-June to Aug Mon–Fri 9am–5pm, Sat 9am–2pm, Sun 9.30am–12.30pm; rest of year Mon–Fri 9am–4pm, Sat 9am–12.30pm; ✆62 52 21 00, ✆www.arre.dk) on Havnegade 5, near the youth hostel. **Bikes** can be rented at Nørremark Cykelforretning, Møllevejen 77 (☎62 53 14 77) for 50kr per day.

The **rest of the island** is speckled with fine inns (*kros*) and working farms such as *Graasten Farmhouse*, half way between Ærøskøbing and Marstal (☎62 52 24 25, ⓦwww.graastenfarmb-b.com; ➌), and the handsome *Vindeballe Kro* (☎62 52 16 13, 3x) at the centre of the island in Vindeballe, simple but with a good restaurant and bar downstairs.

Travel details

Trains

Odense to: Århus (2–3 hourly; 1hr 38min); Copenhagen (every 30min; 1hr 30min); Esbjerg (8 daily; 1hr 18min); Nyborg (every 30min; 14min); Svendborg (every 30min; 42min).

Buses

Kerteminde to: Nyborg (1–2 hourly; 35min).
Odense to: Fåborg (1–2 hourly; 50min–1hr 18min); Kerteminde (every 15min; 33min); Nyborg (every 30min; 54min); Svendborg (2–3 hourly; 1hr 20min).
Rudkøbing to: Lohals (26 daily; 36min); Spodsbjerg (9 daily; 10min); Svendborg (1–5 hourly; 25min).
Svendborg to: Fåborg (2–3 hourly; 43min); Rudkøbing (1–5 hourly; 25min); Nyborg (every 30min; 44min).

South coast ferries

Ferry connections are plentiful around the south coast archipelago and it's best to check the fine details locally. Some sailings continue all year, others only operate during the summer. One-way fares are 45–85kr per person. Frequencies given below are for weekdays; sailings are often reduced on weekends and public holidays.

Bøjden to: Fynshav (6–7 daily; 50min).
Søby to: Mommark (2–5 daily; 1hr).
Fåborg to: Lyø (2–4 daily via Avernakø; 1hr 10min); Søby (2–6 daily; 1hr).
Marstal to: Rudkøbing (3–6 daily; 1hr).
Spodsbjerg to: Tårs (10–22 daily; 45min).
Svendborg to: Ærøskøbing (3–6 daily; 1hr 15min); Drejø (4–5 daily via Skarø; 1hr 15min).

International trains

Odense to: Hamburg, changing in Kolding (1 daily; 3hr 44min).

1.3

Jutland

ong ago, the people of **Jutland** (*Jylland*), the Jutes – pronounced "yutes" – were quite a separate tribe from the more warlike Danes who occupied the eastern islands. In pagan times, the peninsula had its own rulers and wielded considerable power, and it was here that the legendary ninth-century monarch Harald Bluetooth began the process that turned the two tribes into a unified Christian nation. By the dawn of the Viking era, however, the Danes had spread west, absorbing the Jutes, and real power in Denmark gradually shifted towards Zealand.

This is where it has largely stayed, making unhurried lifestyles and rural calm (except for a couple of very likeable cities) the overriding impression of Jutland. This is a friendly land, populated by locals who seem to relish their position outside the national spotlight. Yet there's much to enjoy in the unspoilt towns and villages, and Jutland's comparatively large size and distance from Copenhagen make it perhaps the most distinctive and interesting area in the country.

There are also more regional variations in Jutland than you'll find elsewhere in Denmark. **South Jutland** is a territory long battled over by Denmark and Germany, though beyond the immaculately restored town of **Ribe** it holds little of abiding interest. Further north, **Esbjerg** gives easy access to the windswept beaches on the western coast as well as the hills, meadows and woodlands of eastern Jutland, and to some of the peninsula's better-known sights – from the old military stronghold of **Fredericia** and the ancient runic stones at **Jelling** to the modern bricks of **Legoland** at Billund.

Århus, halfway up the eastern coast, is Jutland's main urban centre and Denmark's second city and where, besides a wealth of history and cultural pursuits, you'll encounter the region's best nightlife. Just to the east, **Djursland** – the peninsula known as Denmark's nose – attracts thousands of visitors every year to its rolling hills and sandy beaches, the result of moraine formations after the last Ice Age. Århus is handy, too, for the optimistically titled **Lake District**, a small but appealing area between Skanderborg, Århus and Viborg. Further inland, the retreat of the ice sheets during the Ice Age left another terrain of sharp contrasts: stark heather-clad moors break suddenly into dense forests with swooping gorges and wide rivers – contrasts epitomized by the wild moorland at **Kongenshus** and the grassy vistas of **Hald Ege**. Ancient **Viborg** is a better base for seeing all this than dour **Randers**, and from here you can head north, either to the blustery beaches of **Limfjordslandet** or to old and vibrant **Aalborg**, which sits on the southern bank of the Limfjorden, a massive fjord that cuts through northern Jutland from Hals on the east coast to Thyborøn on the west coast, leaving the area north of the fjord separated from mainland Jutland.

North of the Limfjorden, you'll get a taste of Jutland at its most dramatic: a sandy semi-wilderness stretching north to **Skagen**, at the very tip of the peninsula. **Frederikshavn**, on the way, is the port for boats to Norway and Sweden, and is usually full of those countries' nationals stocking up with (what is for them) cheap liquor.

South Jutland

Best known as an entry and exit point (to the UK by sea and air, to Germany overland), more people pass through **south Jutland** than probably any other part

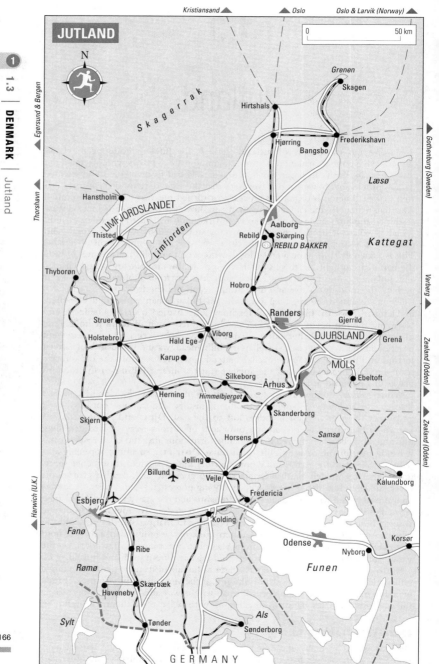

of the country. Though many head straight out for Copenhagen or the holiday areas of the west coast, it's becoming increasingly popular to linger a little. The engaging and well-preserved medieval town of **Ribe** is well worth a day's wander, while the beautiful coastline of sandy beaches and windswept dunes, backed up by some great seafood restaurants and a wonderful array of summer cottages, rightly attracts German tourists in their thousands. With the advent of **budget flights** to Esbjerg from the UK, south Jutland is also gaining something of a reputation as a weekend-break destination.

Esbjerg and around

South Jutland's only city is **ESBJERG** – and if this is your first view of the country, bear in mind it's an entirely untypical one. Esbjerg is a baby by Danish standards: purpose-built as a deep-water harbour during the nineteenth century, it went on to become one of the world's biggest fishing ports. Nowadays, it's used as a supply point for the North Sea oil industry and holds a large fish-oil factory, though it does maintain an air of its original Victorian-era charm, and handsome townhouses abound. Since both DFDS Seaways ferries and regular Ryanair and British Midland flights from the UK arrive here, you may find yourself staying for a few days. If you do, there are a few places worth a nose, most notably the **Esbjerg Performing Arts Centre** and the **Fisheries Museum**. The city also makes a great base from which to explore the surrounding area, particularly the superb beaches on the island of Fanø, a short ferry ride away.

Arrival, information and accommodation

The Esbjerg **tourist office**, at Skolegade 33 (mid-June to Aug Mon–Fri 9am–5pm, Sat 9.30am–2.30pm; Sept to mid-June Mon–Fri 10am–5pm, Sat 10am–1pm; ☏75 12 55 99, ⊛www.visitesbjerg.com), on a corner of the main square, Torvet, can give you all the practical information you might need, as well as leaflets describing a short self-guided walking tour of the city's early twentieth-century buildings, as well as three longer round-trip cycling routes around the area. The **passenger harbour** is a well-signposted fifteen-minute walk from the centre (bus #5), and trains depart to and from Copenhagen and Århus from the **train station** on Skolegade. Esbjerg **airport** is 9km south of the city centre. Buses (no number, marked "airport") leave every twenty minutes to and from the train station and cost 26kr one-way.

If you're staying, the tourist office can help in finding bed-and-breakfast-type **accommodation**; otherwise you'll find that the cheapest good hotel is the twin-towered *Cab-Inn*, Skolegade 14 (☏75 18 16 00, ⊛www.cabinn.com; ❹), renovated into a mixture of simple, inexpensive cabin-style rooms and more traditional hotel accommodation. Another low-price option is the basic *Park Hotel* at Torvegade 31 (☏75 12 08 68, ☏75 13 56 99; ❸), where all rooms share bathrooms, while the central *Ansgar*, Skolegade 36 (☏75 12 82 44, ⊛www.hotelansgar.dk; ❺), is a little more upmarket. The excellent *Britannia* on Torvet (☏75 13 01 11, ⊛www .britannia.dk; ❻) has furniture created by Danish design legend Arne Jacobsen in each room – stylish Swan chairs and sofas – as well as free parking and reductions of up to fifty percent on weekend packages. The *Danhostel Esbjerg* **youth hostel**, which has dorms (120kr) and some doubles (❸), is at Gammel Vardevej 80 (☏75 12 42 58, ⊛www.danhostel.dk/esbjerg; closed Dec & Jan), 25 minutes' walk north of the centre, or take a bus (#1, #4, #13, #40 or #41) from Skolegade. There's a well-equipped **campsite** with cabins, *Ådalens Camping*, at Gudenåvej 20 (☏75 15 88 22, ⊛www.adal.dk), 6km north of Esbjerg along the Sædding Strandvej coast road, and reached by bus #1 from Skolegade.

The City

The best place to get your bearings – and appreciate how small Esbjerg is – is from the top of the **Water Tower** (April–May & mid-Sept to Oct Sat & Sun 10am–4pm;

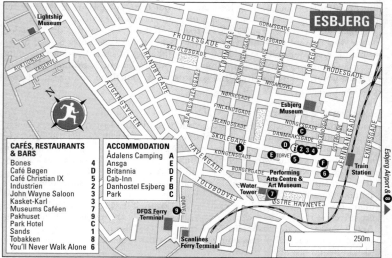

CAFÉS, RESTAURANTS
& BARS
Bones 4
Café Bøgen D
Café Christian IX 5
Industrien 2
John Wayne Saloon 3
Kasket-Karl 3
Museums Caféen 7
Pakhuset 9
Park Hotel C
Sands 1
Tobakken 8
You'll Never Walk Alone 6

ACCOMMODATION
Ådalens Camping A
Ansga E
Britannia D
Cab-Inn F
Danhostel Esjberg B
Park C

June to mid-Sept daily 10am–4pm; 15kr) at Havnegade 22, a short walk from the harbour towards the centre. There are sweeping views of the harbour and surrounding marshes, and on a good day you can see as far as Fanø. There's a small exhibit inside detailing the tower's history. Next door at Havnegade 18–20, the **Esbjerg Performing Arts Centre** (℡76 10 90 00, ⍟www.mhe.dk) houses various concert halls and exhibition areas, including the **Esbjerg Art Museum** (daily 10am–4pm; 40kr), a modest collection of contemporary pieces whose highlight is huge steel plates splattered in the blood of their creator, Danish *enfant terrible* Christian Lemmerz. The centre as a whole is one of Denmark's more groundbreaking cultural institutes and in recent times has exhibited – to much hand-wringing – Lemmerz's gory collection of dead pigs, and a forum on sex and pornography. The building itself is also something of an attraction, designed under the direction of Jørn Utzon, the architect responsible for the Sydney Opera House. A fascinating piece of modern architecture, it resembles a giant concrete tomb surrounded by massive white flowers. To get a sense of the city's newness drop into the **Esbjerg Museum** (June–Aug daily 10am–4pm; Sept–May Tues–Sun 10am–4pm; 30kr, free Wed; ⍟www.esbjergmuseum.dk) at Torvegade 45, where the meatiest of the few displays recalls the so-called "American period" of the 1890s, when Esbjerg's rapid

△ Man Meets the Sea

growth matched that of the US goldrush towns – albeit that the masses came here in search of herring rather than gold. The museum also houses an impressive collection of amber that includes some ancient jewellery.

If the Arts Centre has left you in the mood for more aesthetic appreciation, take a bus (#3 or #8 from the train station) out along the coastal road until you arrive at the four 9m-high ghostly figures known as the **Man Meets the Sea**. Put in place in 1995 by artist Sven Wiig Hansen, this bizarre piece of public art reflects on Esbjerg's relationship to the sea and provides an excellent photo opportunity. Just around the corner is the wonderful **Fisheries and Maritime Museum and Sealarium** on Tarphagevej (daily: July–Aug 10am–6pm; Sept–May 10am–5pm; 75kr; ⊛www.fimus.dk), where you can cast an eye over the old boats and other vestiges of the early Esbjerg fishing fleet. This is an excellent place to take the kids, not least because of the adjoining Sealarium, part of a seal research centre (feeding times 11am and 2.30pm). Some dark and spooky German wartime bunkers and an old working port – rebuilt brick by brick – make up the rest of this engaging museum.

With an hour to kill before your boat leaves, nip around the harbour to the **Lightship Museum** (May–Sept daily 10am–4pm; 20kr), which gives a vivid impression of the North Sea lightshipman's lot.

Eating, drinking and nightlife

Esbjerg's **eating** options are fairly limited if you're on a tight budget, though the usual run of hot-dog grills and bakeries is scattered throughout the city. In terms of **nightlife**, the city is geared to the thousands of sailors who pass through this busy port. There are a run of strip bars on Skolegade, but these can get quite rowdy and aren't recommended for the fainthearted. If you've just arrived from Britain and want to make a more gentle transition to Danish culture (and prices), sip a beer or two at one of the city's pubs, such as the English-style *You'll Never Walk Alone*, Kongensgade 10, or the equally sedate *Kasket-Karl*, Skolegade 17 – the latter shares premises with the livelier *John Wayne Saloon* dance club, which attracts a younger crowd. For live music check out what's on at *Tobakken*, the city's new concert venue at Gasværksvej 2 (☎75 18 00 00, ⊛www.tobakken.dk); or head for *Industrien*, Skolegade 27, which has DJs and live music as well as a bar and café; it's open till 5am from Thursday to Sunday.

Cafés and restaurants

Bones Skolegade 17. On the opposite corner to *Cab Inn*, this dependable chain offers decent value, with such offerings as mouthwatering barbecue ribs for 114kr, burgers for 105kr and steak with all the trimmings from 111kr.

Café Bøgen *Hotel Britannia*, Torvegade 14. Don't miss the Sunday Danish buffet lunch for 125kr; on sunny days there's a grill buffet on the terrace for 150kr.

Café Christian IX Torvet 17. Popular place on Esbjerg's main square, good for lunch or an early evening beer or coffee. There's sometimes live music at weekends.

Museums Caféen Performing Arts Centre, Havnegade 20. Excellent lunchtime herring platters

for 68kr and 98kr respectively for three and five types of herring. In the evening, a French-style three-course dinner menu for 278kr draws in a well-heeled crowd.

Pakhuset Dokvej 3. Set in Esbjerg's dock area, and offering well-prepared local-style fresh fish with all the trimmings for around 225kr (cheaper at lunchtime). Closed Sun & Mon.

Park Hotel Torvegade 31. This small, unpretentious hotel offers a good-value, tasty two-course lunch for 74kr.

Sands Skolegade 60 ⊛www.sands.dk. Excellent for traditional Danish food and service – try the daily special for 89kr, or the lunchtime *smørrebrød* platter for 109kr. Closed Sun.

Around Esbjerg: Fanø

From Esbjerg it's a straightforward ferry trip to **Fanø**, a long, flat island with superb beaches that draw German holidaymakers in droves during the summer. Scandlines ferries (℡33 15 15 15, ⊛www.scandlines.dk; 12min; 30kr return) run frequently between Esbjerg and the island's main village, **Nordby**, where the **tourist office** at the harbour (mid-June to Aug Mon–Fri 8.30am–6pm, Sat & Sun 9am–5pm; Sept to mid-June Mon–Fri 8.30am–5.30pm, Sat 9am–1pm, Sun 11am–1pm; ℡75 16 26 00, ⊛www.fanoeturistbureau.dk) can provide information on accommodation and the few sights (a couple of fairly ordinary local museums and a windmill). There are eight **campsites**, of which the best is *Feldberg Familie Camping* (℡75 16 36 80), almost on the beach.

Ribe

Just over half an hour by train south from Esbjerg lies the exquisitely preserved town of **RIBE**. In 856 Ansgar built one of the first Danish churches here as a base for his missionaries arriving from Germany; a hundred years later the town was a major staging post for pilgrims making their way south to Rome. Ribe's proximity to the sea allowed it to evolve into a significant trading port, but continued expansion was thwarted by the dual blows of the Reformation and the sanding-up of the harbour. Since then, not much appears to have changed. The surrounding marshlands, which have prevented the development of any large-scale industry, and a long-standing conservation programme have enabled Ribe to keep the appearance and size of medieval times, and its old town is a delight to wander in.

The Town

From Ribe's train station, Dagmarsgade cuts a straight path to Torvet and the **Domkirke** (May–June & mid-Aug to Sept Mon–Sat 10am–5pm, Sun noon–5pm; July to mid-Aug Mon–Sat 10am–5.30pm, Sun noon–5.30pm; Oct & April Mon–Sat 11am–4pm, Sun noon–4pm; Nov–March Mon–Sat 11am-3pm, Sun noon–3pm; 12kr), which towers above the town and dominates the wetlands for miles around. A sequel to Ansgar's original church, the cathedral was begun around 1150 using tufa – a suitably light material for the marshy base – brought, along with some of the Rhineland's architectural styles, by river from southern Germany.

Originally raised on a slight hill, the Domkirke is now a couple of metres below the surrounding streets, their level having risen due to the many centuries' worth of debris accumulated beneath them. The **interior** is not as spectacular as the cathedral's size and long history might suggest, having been stripped of much of its decoration by Hans Tausen, Bishop of Ribe, during the mid-sixteenth century. The thirteenth-century "Cat's Head Door" on the south side, a good example of the imported Romanesque design, is one of the few early decorative remains. More recent additions that catch the eye are the butcher's-slab altar and the colourful frescoes, mosaics and stained-glass windows by Carl-Henning Pedersen (a member of the CoBrA movement of mid-twentieth century artists from Copenhagen, Brussels and Amsterdam), added in the mid-1980s. After looking around, climb the 248 steps to peer out from the top of the red-brick **Citizens' Tower**, so named since it doesn't belong to the church but to the people whose taxes pay for its upkeep. The current tower's predecessor toppled into the nave on Christmas morning, 1283.

Heading away from the cathedral along Overdammen, you cross three streams, channelled at around 1250 to provide water for a mill. The houses on the right are the best of Ribe's many half-timbered structures. Turn left off Overdammen and walk along the riverside Skibbroen and you'll spot the **Flood Column** (*Stormflodssøjlen*), a stout wooden pole showing the levels of the numerous floods that plagued the town before protective dykes were built a century ago.

Continuing along Overdammen, Skt Nicolaj Gade cuts right to **Ribe Art Gallery** (July–Aug Tues–Sun 11am–5pm; Sept–June Tues–Sun 11am–4pm; 35kr), housing a reasonable display of works by Danish artists in a chronological progression that takes you from noble portraiture through pre-Raphaelite aestheticism to modern verism. On the first floor the highlight is *The Christening*, by Skagen painter Michael Ancher (see p.203). A handful of accomplished bronze sculptures is

The Nightwatchman of Ribe

At 10pm every evening between May and mid September – and also at 8pm from June to August – the **Nightwatchman of Ribe** emerges from the bar of the *Weis Stue* inn, Torvet 2 (see p.172), and makes his rounds. Before the advent of gas lighting, a nightwatchman would patrol every town in Denmark to help keep the sleeping populace safe from fire and flood. The last real nightwatchman of Ribe made his final tour in 1902, but thanks to the early development of tourism in the town, the custom had been reintroduced by 1932.

Dressed in a replica of the original uniform and carrying an original morning-star pike and lantern (the sharp tip doubling as a weapon), the watchman – a role filled for the last thirty years by octogenarian Aage Gran – walks the narrow alleys of Ribe singing songs written by Thomas Kingo (a local priest who lived in Ribe in the mid-eighteenth century), and talking about the town's history while stopping at points of interest. One song tells people to go to bed and to be careful with lighting fires – sensible advice when most of the town's dwellings are built from wood. It's obviously laid on for the tourists, but the tour is free and good fun.

supplemented by larger pieces on the back lawn, from where paths and footbridges lead back across the river to the town centre.

Ribe also has a couple of museums celebrating the town's Viking era. The **Museet Ribes Vikinger** (July–Aug daily 10am–6pm, Wed until 9pm; April–June, Sept–Oct daily 10am–4pm; Nov–March Tues–Sun 10am–4pm; 55kr; ⍟www.ribes vikinger.dk), opposite the train station, displays locally excavated remains, along with a full-size reconstructed Viking ship. If you've not had your fill, head for the **Ribe Viking Centre** (July–Aug daily 11am–5pm; May–June & Sept Mon–Fri 10am–3.30pm; 65kr; ⍟www.ribevikingecenter.dk), 3km south of the centre on Lystrupvej, which attempts to re-create the Viking lifestyle with costumed attendants demonstrating traditional Viking crafts.

That's more or less all there is to Ribe, save for the paltry remains of **Ribehus Slotsbanke**, a twenty-minute walk away on the northern side of the town. The twelfth-century castle that stood here was a popular haunt with Danish royalty for a couple of centuries but was already fairly dilapidated when it was demolished by Swedish bombardment in the mid-seventeenth century. The **statue** of Queen Dagmar, a recent addition to the site and standing in bewitching isolation, is the only visible reward for the trek out here.

Practicalities

Besides the usual services, the **tourist office** (June & Sept Mon–Fri 9am–5pm, Sat 10am–1pm; July–Aug Mon–Fri 9am–6pm, Sat 10am–5pm, Sun 10am–2pm; Oct–May Mon–Fri 9.30am–4.30pm, Sat 10am–1pm; ☏75 42 15 00, ⍟www .visitribe.dk), across the road to the rear of the cathedral, sells the *Town Walks in Old Ribe* leaflet, a useful aid to self-guided exploration (5kr).

If you intend to stick around for the nightwatchman's tour, you'll need to **stay overnight**. There's a good range of interesting and affordable accommodation, though in summer be sure to book ahead as everything gets packed. The tourist office publishes a list of private rooms that rent for about 200kr per person per night.

One reputable spot **to eat** is *Vægterkælderen*, close to the cathedral in the basement beneath the *Dagmar* hotel, serving two- (145kr) and three-course (175kr) lunches, and two-course dinners (195kr), mostly meaty Danish specialities and a couple of vegetarian dishes, plus heavily laden *smørrebrød* all day. *Restaurant Backhaus*, Grydergade 12, does good-value steaks and burgers; and there's excellent Danish fare at *Restaurant Sælhunden*, set in a wood-beamed listed building overlooking the harbour at Skibroen 13. Nearby *Kolvig Café and Restaurant* offers filling, reasonably-priced salads and sandwiches in a relaxed riverside setting. For coffee, try *Valdemar Sejr* next to the art gallery on Skt Nicolaj Gade, which is also a good spot for **drinks** and **music** in the evening. At night, *Vægterkælderen* (see p.171) has a lively bar, though the beer is cheaper (and the music louder) at the town's two discos, *Pepper's* and *Stenbohus*, which face each other just up the street; the latter has live blues, folk or rock acts at least once a week. If you're looking for atmosphere, hit the tiny but distinctive *Strygejernet* pub at Dagmarsgade 1, which serves light meals and snacks during the day and popular draught ales at night.

Accommodation

Dagmar Torvet ☏ 75 42 00 33, ⓦ www.hotel dagmar.dk. If you can afford it, try the beautifully restored Dagmar opposite the Domkirke, which dates from 1581 and claims to be the oldest hotel in Denmark; its gorgeous doubles come with period furniture and loads of character. ⑥

Den Gamle Arrest Torvet 11 ☏ 75 42 37 00, ⓦ www.dengamlearrest.dk. An intriguing option, originally built as a girls' boarding school and which later served as the town's jail. The double rooms are in the former cells, which these days lock from the inside. ④, en-suite ⑤

Fru Mathies Saltgade 15 ☏ 75 42 34 20, ⓦ www .frumathies.dk. A short walk from the centre across the river down Nederdammen, this bright yellow pub also has a few comfortable rooms, some of which share bathrooms. ④

Restaurant Backhaus Grydergade 12 ☏ 75 42 11 01, ⓦ www.backhaus-ribe.dk. A stone's throw from the domkirke, this popular restaurant (see p.170) also has a few simple rooms with shared facilities. ④

Ribe Camping ☏ 75 41 07 77, ⓦ www.ribe camping.dk. Some 2km distant along Farupvej (take bus #771), this pleasant campsite has cabins as well as pitches. Open April to Nov.

Ribe Danhostel Skt Pedersgade 16 ☏ 75 42 06 20, ⓦ www.danhostel.dk/ribe. An easy walk over the river from the town centre, and with some doubles (③) as well as dorms (120kr). Open May to mid-Sept.

Weis Stue Torvet 2 ☏ 75 42 07 00, ⓦ www.weis-stue.dk. With creaking floor-boards and wood-panelled walls, this wonderfully atmospheric place is where the Nightwatchman starts his tour (see p.171). Eight rooms, filled with antique crockery and furniture and all with shared toilet and bath. Advance booking is essential year-round. ④

Rømø and Tønder

From Skærbæk, a few kilometres south of Ribe by train, bus #29 heads across 12km of tidal flats to the island of **Rømø**. The actions of sea and wind have given the island a wild and unkempt appearance, as well as creating a wide beach along the eastern side and allowing wildlife to flourish all over. There's a good chance of seeing seals basking during the spring, while at the end of the summer many migratory wading birds can be found, dodging the island's plentiful sheep.

Rømø's **tourist office** on Havnebyvej 30 (July & Aug daily 9am–6pm; rest of the year 9am–5pm; ☏ 74 75 51 30, ⓦ www.romo.dk), just south of the causeway in the main village of **HAVNEBY**, can provide details on the island's bus service. There are several spots on Rømø **to stay**: ask at the tourist office for details of private rooms or summer cottages, for which you'll pay around 250kr per person per night. The best hotel on the island is the *Kommandørgården* (☏ 74 75 51 22, ⓦ www .kommandoergaarden.dk; ⑤), at Havnebyvej 21 in Østerby, a kilometre or so north of Havneby, which also has a **campsite** with four-person cabins. Of the two other camping options, best is *Lakolk Camping* (☏ 74 75 52 28, ⓦ www.lakolkcamping.dk; April to mid-Oct), on the island's windswept west coast at Kongsmark and reachable via bus #29. There's a **youth hostel** in Havneby itself at Lyngvejen 7 (☏ 74 75 51 88, ⓦ www.romo-vandrerhjem.dk; mid-March to mid-Nov), which has some doubles (③) as well as dorms (118kr).

Besides enjoying the sands, and the fact that Rømø is a noted **nude bathing** spot, it's possible to **cross the border to Germany** from here without returning to the Danish mainland by using the ferry that sails from Havneby to List, on the German island of Sylt (information on ☏ 73 75 53 03, ⓦ www.romo–sylt.dk; 50min).

Tønder

Back on the mainland, heading south from Skærbæk brings you to **TØNDER**, the chief settlement on the Danish side of the border with Germany. Founded in the thirteenth century, the town's cobbled streets still contain many ancient gabled buildings, and Tønder makes an attractive and low-key base for a day or two, especially if you're here around the end of August, when there's a terrific annual **jazz and folk festival**. In 2005, performers included Oysterband, Dougie Maclean, Hayseed Dixie and a host of other international acts, and there are always many free outdoor events, too. Contact the Tønder Festival office (℡74 72 46 10, ⊛www .tf.dk) for more details. Otherwise, the main sights in town are the arts and crafts displays at the **Tønder Museum** (June–Aug daily 10am–5pm; Sept–May Tues–Sun 10am–5pm; 40kr, includes entry to the Art Museum; ⊛www.tondermuseum.dk), in the gatehouse of the sixteenth-century castle, and the adjoining **South Jutland Art Museum** (same hours; 40kr, includes entry to the Tønder Museum; ⊛www .sonkunst.dk), with its changing exhibitions of twentieth-century North-European works. Danish Prince Joachim lives 4km to the west of Tønder in **Schackenborg Castle**, in the village of Møgeltønder (bus #606 outside school holidays) – there's no entry to the public, but the castle park is good for an hour's strolling and there's the possibility, if you're lucky, of a royal sighting.

First call for local information should be the **tourist office** on Torvet (July to mid-Aug Mon–Fri 10am–5pm, Sat 10am–2pm; mid-Aug to June Mon–Fri 9am–4pm, Sat 9am–noon; ℡74 72 12 20, ⊛www.visittonder.dk). There's a **youth hostel** 1km from the train station at Sønderport 4 (℡74 72 35 00, ⊛www.tonder -net.dk/danhostel; closed Christmas & Jan) with dorms (120kr) and doubles (❷); a **campsite** at Holmevej 2a (℡74 72 18 49, ⊛www.sydvest.dk; April–Sept); the comfortable *Hotel Tønderhus* at Jomfrustien 1, opposite the Tønder Museum (℡74 72 22 22, ⊛www.hoteltoenderhus.dk; ❻), and the somewhat cheaper, *Hostrup Hotel*, Søndergade 30 (℡74 72 21 29, ⊛www.hostrupshotel.dk; ❸) overlooking Vidå Lake.

Sønderborg

Despite lush green landscapes subsiding gently into a peaceful coastline, southern Jutland's eastern section holds comparatively few spots of interest and is best seen as part of a southerly route to Funen or Ærø (covered in the previous chapter). A lively provincial town in an area laden with campsites, **SØNDERBORG** straddles the once strategically important **Alssund**, a narrow but deep channel dividing the island of Als from the Jutland mainland. The campsites are evidence of the appeal of the region's sandy coastline, while the line of preserved earthworks on the mainland side of town is testament to Sønderborg's crucial place in Danish history. Beside them, and reachable by bus #1 from Sønderborg station, the **Battlefield Centre** (*Historiecenter Dybbøl Banke*; mid-April to Sept daily 10am–5pm; 45kr, mid-June to Mid-Aug 55kr; ⊛www.1864.dk), has multimedia displays that trace the details of the battle that took place here on April 18, 1864, when the Danes were defeated by the Prussians and medieval Sønderborg was all but destroyed. From then until 1918, when a plebiscite returned it to Denmark, northern Schleswig (in which Sønderborg stands) became part of Germany. A few kilometers away, south of Sønderborg on the main road, **Dybbøl Mill** (mid-April to Oct daily 10am–5pm; 25kr), where some of the most intense fighting took place, has been a national symbol for both Danes and Germans since 1864, and the story is recounted inside.

The bulk of the town lies across the Alssund, where your attention should focus on **Sønderborg Slot**, which may not be the grandest but is certainly one of Denmark's oldest castles, thought to have been started by Valdemar I in 1170 as a defence against the Wends. Inside, the **Museum of South Jutland** (May–Sept daily 10am–5pm; April Tues–Sun 10am–4pm; Oct–March Tues–Sun 1–4pm; 30kr; ⊛www.sonderborgslot.dk) comprises room after room of military mementoes. One of the more interesting sections tells of the four-day Als Republic of 1918, born as the German Reich's dissenting northern ports – Sønderborg, Bremen, Hamburg and Kiel – rebelled against the Kaiser and, in emulation of the then-recent Russian Revolution, raised a red banner over the town's barracks.

Practicalities

Trains go no further than the mainland section of the town, though long-distance **buses** continue across the Alssund, via a graceful modern road bridge, to Als and the bus station on Jernbanegade. Just downhill from the bus station, you'll find the **tourist office**, on Rådhustorvet 7 (mid-June to mid-Aug Mon–Fri 9.30am–6pm, Sat 9.30am–1pm; mid-Aug to mid-June Mon–Fri 9.30am–5pm, Sat 9.30am–1pm; ☎74 42 35 55, ⓦwww.visitsonderborg.com). Of the **hotels**, the *Arnkilhus*, Arnkilgade 13 (☎74 42 23 36, ⓦwww.arnkilhus.dk; ④) is best for price, though it's a short walk from the centre. The grandest place in town is undoubtedly the *Comwell*, Rosengade 2 (☎74 42 19 00, ⓦwww.comwell.com; ⑤) – look for big discounts on weekends. A good middle-ground option is the quirky *Hotel Sønderborg*, Kongevej 96 (☎74 42 34 33; ⑤) close to the centre yet near both beautiful woodlands and the coast. The shiny, modern **youth hostel** (☎74 42 31 12, ⓦwww .sonderborgdanhostel.dk; March–Oct), which has dorms (120kr) and some doubles (③), is a twenty-minute walk along Perlegade and Kærvej (bus #6), and is a little less centrally placed than the waterfront **campsite** on Ringgade 7 (☎74 42 41 89, ⓦwww.sonderborgcamping.dk; April–Sept).

The town's main shopping street, **Perlegade**, is close to the tourist office; past here, its name changes twice, first to Store Rådhusgade, then to Christian den Andens Gade. All along its length, though, the street takes on a Mediterranean air on warm evenings as smartly dressed Danes mill from bar to bar; locals often begin a weekend by shopping at the Perlegade end, then **eating** their way down to the other end of the street. There's a branch of the ubiquitous steakhouse chain, *Jensens Bøfhus*, at Perlegade 36; *Café Druen*, at Store Rådhusgade 1, has low-cost snacks, and next door there are good evening meals at English-style pub *Penny Lane* – both sometimes host live jazz and other music. Nearby on Brogade 2, *OX EN* offers sublime Argentinean steaks with all the trimmings from 149kr onwards, while the *Bella Italia*, on Lille Rådhusstræde 31, has filling Italian meals. By the harbour, on Søndre Havnegade 22, *Café au Lait* is good for drinks and light meals, as is the *Colosseum* next door. **Nightlife** is limited: along Store Rådhusgade, *Penny Lane* at no. 12 (with beers from all over the world), or *Café Druen* at no.1, are your best options. *Maybe Not Bob*, Rådhustorvet 5, is a slightly noisier place, popular with young locals.

Kolding

Even though it's handily placed on the main road and rail axes north of Tønder, **KOLDING** doesn't attract a lot of attention, and is even less of a draw these days now that the large new shopping mall on the outskirts has caused many of the quirky shops in the ancient centre to close. If you do find yourself here with time to spare, head a short way north from the centre to the Slotsø lake and the imaginatively renovated **castle of Koldinghus** (daily 10am–5pm; 60kr; ⓦwww.koldinghus.dk), a harmonious mix of ruined and modern structures housing sparsely furnished period rooms as well as changing design exhibitions and a good café. King Erik Kipling built a fortress here in 1268 to protect the Danish border against invasion from the German Duchy of Schleswig. In the fifteenth century, it was converted into a royal castle; in 1808, during the Napoleonic wars, Spanish troops stationed here stoked a fire so fierce (they weren't prepared for the cold Danish winters) that a chimney caught fire and the castle burnt down. It was since rebuilt but didn't regain its regional importance. Another worthwhile call in this direction, 3km beyond the lake (bus #4 from the train station), is the **Trapholt Art Museum** (daily 10am–5pm; 60kr; ⓦwww.trapholt.dk), its angular glass walls and shrill white interiors flooding the (mostly) modern art and design – including an interesting chair exhibition – with natural light.

The **tourist office** is at Akseltorv 8 (July to mid-Aug Mon–Fri 9.30am–7pm, Sat 9.30am–2.30pm; mid-Aug to June Mon–Fri 9.30am–5.30pm, Sat 9.30am–2pm; ☏76 33 21 00, ⊛www.visitkolding.dk). Predictably, the cheapest **accommodation** option is the youth hostel at Ørnsborgvej 10 (☏75 50 91 40, ⊛www.danhostel .dk/kolding; closed Dec & Jan), which has dorms (115kr) and a few doubles (❸). A more expensive option is the *Saxildhus Hotel* at Banegårdspladsen, opposite the train station (☏75 52 12 00, ⊛www.saxildhus.dk; ❺), but for atmosphere and tranquil scenery you can't beat the grand *Hotel Koldingfjord*, on the banks of Kolding Fjord at Fjordvej 154 (☏75 51 00 00, ⊛www.koldingfjord.dk: ❻; bus #4 from the train station). Built in 1911 as a Neoclassical palace, it has since seen incarnations as a school and a hospital, and its deluxe rooms afford stunning views of the fjord. The closest **campsite** is at Vonsildvej 19 (☏75 52 13 88, ⊛www.vonsild-camping .dk), 3km from the town centre via bus #3. There are several beachfront campsites further afield – contact the tourist office for details.

For an inexpensive place **to eat**, try the outstanding and generous portions of spare ribs at *Joe's Diner*, Låsbygade 27. For Italian, head for *Bella Italia*, Jernbanegade 40, and for huge sandwiches, try *Den Gyldne Ovn* at Bredgade 4. If you fancy a drink or a light meal, go to *Den Blå Café* on Lilletorv at Slotsgade 4, which has outdoor seating; for more excitement, head for *Knuds Garage*, Munkegade 5, a rock bar, or the *Pit Stop*, a live music venue and disco at Jernbanegade 54. For real ale, head to *You'll Never Walk Alone*, Klostergade 7A, where there's occasional live music.

Fredericia, Vejle and around

There's little that's unique about **east Jutland**, though its thick forests are a welcome change if you're coming directly from the windswept western side of the peninsula. As the main route between Funen and the big Jutland cities, it's a busy region with good transport links, but the area has only two sizeable towns: **Fredericia** is the more unusual, **Vejle** the more appealing – though neither justifies a lengthy stay.

Fredericia
FREDERICIA – junction of all the rail routes in east Jutland, and those connecting the peninsula with Funen – has one of the oddest histories (and layouts) in Denmark. It was founded in 1650 by Frederik III, who envisaged the town as a strategically placed reserve capital and a base from which to defend Jutland. Three nearby villages were demolished and their inhabitants forced to assist in the building of the new town – and afterwards they had no choice but to live in it. Military considerations required that Fredericia be built on a strict grid plan, with low buildings enclosed by high earthen ramparts, making it invisible to approaching armies. Even the town's later role as a railway hub hasn't destroyed its soldierly air, with memorials to victorious heroes and the only military tattoo in Denmark – an event that failed elsewhere in the country due to lack of interest.

The half-hour walk (or ten-minute ride on bus #2) from the **train station** along Vesterbrogade into the town centre takes you through the Danmarks Port, gateway to the most impressive section of the old ramparts. These stretch for 4km and rise 15m above the streets, and walking along the top gives a good view of the layout of the town. But it's the **Landsoldaten statue**, opposite Princes Port, that best exemplifies the local spirit. The bronze figure holds a rifle in its left hand, a sprig of leaves in the right, and its left foot rests on a captured cannon. The inscription on the statue reads "6 Juli 1849", the day the town's battalion made a momentous sortie against German troops in the first Schleswig war – an anniversary still celebrated as **Fredericia Day**. The downside of the battle was the five hundred Danes killed; they lie in a mass grave in the grounds of **Trinitatis Kirke** in Kongensgade.

Predictably, three hundred years of armed conflict form the core of the displays in the **Fredericia Museum** at Jernbanegade 10 (Tues–Sun noon–4pm; 20kr). There

FREDERICIA

ACCOMMODATION
Fredericia Vandrerhjem	B
Postgården	D
Sømandshjemmet	C
Trelde Næs	A

CAFÉS, RESTAURANTS & BARS
Bøf & Vino	2
Café Carlos	6
Café Filmer	4
Det Bruunske Pakhus	3
Jensens Bøfhus	1
Simon's Café	5

are also reconstructions of typical local house interiors from the seventeenth and eighteenth centuries, and a dreary selection of archeological finds only enlivened by a glittering cache of silverware in the crafts section.

Practicalities

Unless you want to laze around on Fredericia's fine **beaches**, which begin at the eastern end of the ramparts, there's little reason to hang around for very long. There are only two **hotels** in the centre: the good-value *Postgården* on Oldenborggade 4 (☎75 92 18 55, ⓦwww.postgaarden.dk; ❸, en-suite ❹), and the smaller, family-run *Sømandshjemmet* (☎75 92 01 99, ⓦwww.fsh.dk; ❺) on Gothersgade 40, both near the harbour and with restaurants. There's a modern **youth hostel**, *Fredericia Vandrerhjem*, west of the town at Vestre Ringvej 98 (☎75 92 12 87, ⓦwww.fredericia -danhostel.dk), with dorms (120kr) and plenty of doubles (❸); while the *Trelde Næs* **campsite** (☎75 95 71 83, ⓦwww.supercamp.dk; April–Oct) is beautifully situated on the Vejle fjord, though it's 15km north of town and adjacent to a public beach, so can get very crowded during fine weather and at holiday times. You can arrange private rooms with the centrally placed **tourist office**, Danmarksgade 2A (Mon–Fri 10am–5pm, Sat 10am–1pm; ☎75 92 13 77, ⓦwww.visitfredericia.com).

For **food**, *Simon's Café* on Axeltorv serves well prepared sandwiches, soups and salads, while *Café Carlos*, Sjællandsgade 56 (closed Mon), has good-value Spanish cuisine. There's also the predictable *Jensens Bøfhus* steakhouse, Danmarksgade 8; and *Bøf & Vino*, Danmarksgade 36, has a good selection of inexpensive Italian food. For **nightlife**, try the popular *Det Bruunske Pakhus* at Kirkestræde 3 (☎72 10 67 10, ⓦwww.bruunskepakhus.dk), which hosts a range of live bands every weekend from September till June; or *Café Filmer* at Jyllandsgade 20B, a café offering music, food and drinks.

Vejle

A twenty-minute train ride north of Fredericia, **VEJLE**, a compact harbour town on the mouth of the Vejle fjord, is home to the Tulip factory, from where 400 million sausages a year begin their journey to British breakfast tables. It's also the best base for exploring the contrasting pleasures of the Viking burial mounds at Jelling and – rather more famously – the Legoland complex at Billund, both within easy reach by bus or train.

The chief attraction in Vejle itself is **Skt Nicolai Kirke** (Mon–Fri 9am–5pm, Sat & Sun 9am–noon) in Kirke Torvet, in which a glass-topped coffin holds the peat-preserved body of a woman found in the Haraldskur bog in 1835. Originally the body was thought to be the corpse of a Viking queen, Gunhilde of Norway, but the claim was disputed and tests carried out in 1977 dated the body to around 490 BC – too old to be a Viking, but nonetheless still the best preserved "bog body" in the country. It's hidden away behind bars in the north transept, but if you want to have a look up close, the verger will let you in. Another macabre feature of the church, though you can't see it, are the 23 skulls hidden in sealed holes in the northern transept. Legend has it that they are the heads of thieves executed in 1630.

The **Museum of Art** at Flegborg 16 (Tues–Sun 11am–4pm; 50kr; ⓦ www.vejlekunst museum.dk) specializes in graphics and drawings (look out for the remarkable self-portrait by Rembrandt from 1563), has a collection of twentieth-century painting and sculpture, and often hosts innovative temporary exhibitions. Vejle Museum is slated to reopen in a new location in 2007; check at the tourist office for an update. Also operated by the museum, and a fabulous destination on a sunny day, is **Vejle Vindmølle** (May–Oct Tues–Sun 11am–4pm; free), a disused windmill which maintains its full complement of ropes, shafts and pinions, and displays a through-the-ages account of milling, from Neolithic blocks to modern roller mills. From the windmill, reached by climbing Kiddesvej (which leads off Søndergade), there are stupendous views across Vejle and its fjord. Wind power is dealt with in a completely different way at the new **Økolariet** interactive exhibition (Feb–Nov Sat–Thurs 11am–6pm; free; ⓦ www.okolariet.dk), next to the train station at Dæmningen 11. Set up at a state-of-the-art educational centre, it illustrates how human consumption affects the environment in various detrimental ways. The main themes are drinking water, waste, energy and home consumption; an intriguing history of the toilet is especially fascinating.

Practicalities

Across from the train station on Banegårdspladsen 6, the **tourist office** (mid-June to Aug Mon–Fri 9.30am–5.30pm, Sat 9.30am–1.30pm; Sept to mid-June Mon–Thurs 10am–5pm, Fri 10am–4.30pm, Sat 10am–noon; ☎75 82 19 55, ⓦ www.visitvejle .com) has a list of **accommodation** in private rooms for 175kr per person per night, but charges a steep 40kr booking fee. Otherwise, try for a room at the homely 〒 Park (☎75 82 24 66, ⓦ www.park-hotel.dk; ❺), Orla Lehmannsgade 5, or the pricier Torvehallerne, Kirketorvet 10–16 (☎79 42 79 10, ⓦ www.torvehallerne.com; ❻), which has a popular restaurant, a theatre and a restaurant in a greenery-filled conservatory amongst its attractions. Much less convenient, but with some doubles (❸) as well as dorms (115kr), is the **youth hostel** on Gammel Landevej (☎75 82 51 88, ⓦ www.vejle-danhostel.dk), a 5km journey on bus #2 from either the bus station on Nørretorv or the Vejle Trafikcentre outside the train station, opposite the tourist office. There's also a **campsite** at Helligkildevej 5 (☎75 82 33 35, ⓦ www.dk-camp .dk/vejlecamp), a few kilometres east and reachable on bus #10.

Central Vejle has plenty of inexpensive **places to eat**. In the Smitskegård court-yard, at Søndergade 14, Conrad Café serves substantial salads and smørrebrød through the afternoon, and drinks until midnight (sometimes with live music). Around the corner, the glass-walled Brasseriet at Hotel Torvehallerne has good, substantial meals (two courses for 159kr). For brunch (Fri–Sun), inexpensive salads, sandwiches and filling burgers, make for Caféen Vejle, inside the former prison at Klostergade 1, which is also a good place for a drink. Of the number of English-style **pubs** in town, most popular is the *Tartan* at Dæmningen 40.

Jelling and Legoland

A short hop northwest of Vejle, the village of **JELLING** is known to have been the site of pagan festivals and celebrations, and has two **burial mounds** thought to have contained King Gorm, Jutland's tenth-century ruler, and his queen, Thyra. The graves were found in the early twentieth century and, although only one coffin was actually recovered, there is evidence to suggest that the body of Gorm was removed by his son, Harald Bluetooth, and placed in the adjacent church – which Bluetooth himself built around 960 after his conversion to Christianity. In the grounds of the present church are two big **runic stones**, one erected by Gorm to the memory of Thyra, the other raised by Harald Bluetooth in honour of Gorm. The texts hewn into the granite record the era when Denmark began the transition to Christianity. Across the road from the stones on Gormsgade 23, the elegant new **Kongernes Jelling Exhibition Centre** (May to mid-June & Sept Tues–Sun 10am–4pm; mid-June to Aug daily 10am–5pm; Oct–April Tues–Sun 1–4pm; 40kr; ⓦwww .kongernesjelling.dk) provides a full breakdown of their history.

Train services from Vejle to Struer or Herning stop at Jelling: both run about once an hour on weekdays and less frequently at weekends; bus #211 runs hourly from Vejle bus station. There's also a **vintage train** between Vejle and Jelling, running every Sunday in July and on the first three Sundays in August (ⓣ75 58 60 60, ⓦwww.klk.dk). By **bike**, it's a scenic ride through the hamlet of Uhre and along the shores of Fårup Sø lake – you can rent a bike in Vejle from Buhl Jensen, Gormsgade 14–16 (ⓣ75 82 15 09; 75kr per day). If you want **to stay**, the *Jelling Kro*, Gormsgade 16 (ⓣ75 87 10 06, ⓦwww.jellingkro.dk; ❸), is pleasant and serves filling meals, or head for Jelling's **campsite** (ⓣ75 87 16 53, ⓦwww.jellingcamping. dk; April to mid-Sept), about 1km west of the church on Mølvangsvej.

Legoland Park

Twenty kilometres west of Vejle – to which it's linked by bus #244 – the village of **Billund** has been transformed into a major tourist centre, complete with international airport and rows of pricey hotels. It's all thanks to **Legoland Park** (April, May & Oct Mon–Fri 10am–6pm; June & mid-Aug to Sept daily 10am–8pm; July to mid-Aug daily 10am–9pm; Sat & Sun 10am–8pm; 185kr; ⓦwww.legoland.dk), a theme park celebrating the tiny plastic bricks that have filled many a Christmas stocking since a Danish carpenter, Ole Kirk Christiansen, started making wooden toys collectively named "Lego", from the Danish phrase *Leg Godt*, or "play well" (which also, by a happy coincidence, means "I study" and "I assemble" in Latin). In 1947, the Lego company began to manufacture its bricks in plastic, becoming the first company in Denmark to use the new plastic moulding-injection techniques – the Lego pieces (or "Automatic Binding Bricks", to be perfectly precise) we know today were first created in 1958. The park itself, featuring a cornucopia of elaborate model buildings, animals, planes and many other weird and wonderful things (such as Titania's Palace – home for the queen of the fairies), is aimed chiefly at kids, but anybody whose efforts at Lego construction have resulted in tears of frustration over missing corner bricks might like to discover what can be achieved when someone has 45 million pieces to play with.

If you want to stay, try the modern **youth hostel**, outside town at Ellehammers Allé (ⓣ75 33 27 77, ⓦwww.legoland-village.dk), which has no dorms, but a good supply of pricey double rooms (❺) and other family accommodation. Without a car, it's best to take a bus from the city centre to Legoland and walk the remaining 300m to the hostel. The other options in town are even more expensive, and can be laid out for you at Billund's **tourist office** (April, May & Oct Mon–Fri 10am–6pm, Sat & Sun 10am–8pm; June & mid-Aug to Sept daily 10am–8pm; July to mid-Aug daily 10am–9pm; ⓣ76 50 00 55, ⓦwww.visitbillund.dk), located by Legoland.

Horsens

Travelling north from Vejle, there's every chance you'll pass through **HORSENS**, a likeable though hardly exciting town whose Søndergade is claimed to be the widest main street in Denmark. Horsens was also the birthplace, in 1681, of **Vitus Bering**, who discovered what became known as the Bering Strait whilst on a mission on behalf of Peter the Great to find an Asian–American land bridge. A memorial to him stands in the park which also bears his name.

You can learn more about Vitus Bering at the **Horsens Museum** in Caroline Amalielunden park on Sundvej (July–Aug daily 10am–4pm; Sept–June Tues–Sun 11am–4pm; 30kr; ⊕www.horsensmuseum.dk); it also contains a run-of-the-mill collection of local knick-knacks. Around the corner on Carolinelundsvej 2 is the more enticing **Art Museum** (July & Aug Mon–Fri 10am–4pm, Sat & Sun 10am–5pm; Sept–June Tues–Fri 11am–4pm, Sat & Sun 11am–5pm; 30kr; ⊕www .horsenskunstmuseum.dk), specializes in art from the 1980s and 1990s and includes an outstanding collection of works by renowned Danish artist Zieler, as well as pieces by Bjørn Nørgaard, best known for the tapestries at the Royal Reception Room in Copenhagen (see p.139). There are also some Danish Golden Age masters and an honourable collection of works by local artists. However, if you only have time for one stop while in Horsens, head for the fascinating new **Industrimuseet** (July–Aug daily 10am–4pm; Sept–June Tues–Sun 11am–4pm; 40kr; ⊕www .industrimuseet.dk), set in the town's former electricity and gas works at Gasvej 17–19. The museum's aim is to give an insight into how industrialization took place in Denmark from 1860 up until today, and it does so very successfully. The extensive displays include a fully functioning printing press, a collection of the rare Danish Nimbus motorcycles (only 15000 were ever produced), six fully furnished workers' homes and a working telephone exchange. There's also a good café, *Gaslight*, which offers inexpensive menus from the 1950s, 1960s and 1970s.

There are plenty of **accommodation** options in Horsens, most expensively at the fancy peach-coloured *Jørgensens Hotel* (⊕75 62 16 00, ⊕www.jorgensens-hotel .dk; ❺/❻), housed in an eighteenth-century palace at Søndergade 17. Fifteen minutes' walk from the centre overlooking Horsens Fjord, the **youth hostel**, Flintebakken 150 (⊕75 61 67 77, ⊕www.danhostelhorsens.dk) has more afford-able dorms (120kr) and doubles (❸). Ask at the **tourist office**, Søndergade 26 (mid-June to Aug Mon–Fri 10am–5.30pm, Sat 10am–2pm; Sept to mid-June Mon–Fri 10am–4.30pm, Sat 10am–1pm; ⊕www.visithorsens.dk), for details of **private rooms** (from 260kr per double, plus a 40kr booking fee) and about walks in the area. Inexpensive **restaurants** include *Café Dolly*, Havne Allé 55, which does traditional Danish dishes such as fried pork and potatoes with parsley gravy. For a tasty burger head to *Mackie's*, at Graven 2 on the corner of Søndergade near the town's central pedestrian area. For Mexican, there's *Tequila Sunrise*, Smedegade 10, and there's also the usual *Jensens Bøfhus* at Åboulevarden 129 for steaks, with cheap afternoon specials on weekdays. During summer, local bars and cafés in the centre set chairs and tables outside for alfresco eating and drinking. The best include the *Corfitz* at Søndergade 23, an elegant place in the heart of town; the smaller *Koks*, Nørregade 10, which has occasional live bands; *Paddy's Irish Pub*, right in the centre at Torvet 2A; and *Club Etzo*, Graven 12, which has a disco and chill-out lounge.

Århus

Geographically at the heart of the country, and often regarded as Denmark's cul-tural capital, **ÅRHUS** typifies all that's good about Danish cities. It's small enough to get to know in a few hours, yet big and lively enough to have plenty to fill both days and nights, and the combination of laid-back atmosphere with a surpris-ing number of sights might keep you around longer than planned. Århus is also something of an architectural showcase, with several notable structures spanning a century of Danish and international design. A number of these buildings form the

ÅRHUS

ACCOMMODATION

Århus City Sleep-In	E
Århus Nord Camping	A
Århus Youth Hostel	B
Blommehaven	I
Cab-Inn Århus	D
Guldsmeden	C
Helnan Marselis	J
Ritz	G
Sportshotellet	H
Villa Provence	F

Labels on map: Natural History Museum, University, Steno Museum, Botanical Gardens, Den Gamle By, Vor Frue Kirke, Domkirke, Women's Museum, Viking Museum, ARoS, Concert Hall, Rådhus, Long-Distance Bus Station, Train Station, Bike Rental, Kalundborg & Odden Ferry Terminal

0 — 250m

H, I, J, 27, 28 Marselisborg Skov, Dyrehaven & Moesgård Prehistoric Museum ▼

CAFÉS, RESTAURANTS, BARS & CLUBS

Athena	12	Café Smagløs	9	Cross Café	17	Pinden	24
Billabong Bar	22	Café Svej	21	Dragen	18	Pinds Café	19
Bridgewater Pub	21	Carlton	10	Emmerys	4	Raadhus Kaféen	26
Broen	15	Casablanca	11	Fabrikken	2	Ris Ras Filliongongong	7
Bryggeriet	20	China Wok House	25	Gyngen	1	Seafood	28
Café Jorden	8	Cockney Pub	16	Hotel Royal	13	Twist & Shout	23
Café Kindrødt	5	Crêperiet	27	Karls Sandwichbar	3	Under Engle	6
						Under Masken	14

campus of Århus' university, whose students contribute to a nightlife that's on a par with that of Copenhagen.

Despite Viking-era origins, the city's present prosperity is due to its long, sheltered bay (on which a harbour was first constructed during the fifteenth century) and the more recent advent of railways, which made Århus a nationally important trade and transport centre. It's easily reached by train from all the country's bigger towns, is linked by sea with Zealand (a fast catamaran service linking Århus with Odden, and a slower ferry linking it with Kalundborg), and also has an international airport.

Arrival, information and city transport

Whichever form of public transport brings you to Århus, you'll be deposited within easy reach of the hotels and main points of interest. **Trains** and **buses** stop at their respective stations on Banegårdspladsen and Nybanegårdsgade, both on the southern edge of the city centre, from where it's a short walk to the **tourist office** on the first floor of the Rådhus (May to mid-June Mon–Fri 9.30am–5pm, Sat 10am–1pm; mid-June to Aug Mon–Fri 9.30am–6pm, Sat 9.30am–5pm, Sun 9.30am–1pm; Sept–April Mon–Fri 9.30am–4pm, Sat 10am–1pm; ☎87 31 50 10, ⊛www.visitaarhus.com). **Ferries** from Zealand dock just west of the centre at the end of Nørreport, a short distance from the heart of Old Århus. Buses from **Tirstrup Airport**, some 45km northeast of the city, arrive at (and leave from) the train station; the one-way fare for the fifty-minute journey is 80kr.

Getting around is best done on foot: the city centre is compact and you'll need to use **buses** only if you're venturing out to Moesgård Museum, the beaches or the woods on the city's outskirts. If you do, note that the transport system divides into four zones: one and two cover the whole central area; three and four reach into the countryside. The basic ticket is the so-called "**cash ticket**", which costs 17kr from the machine at the rear of the bus and is valid for any number of journeys for up to two hours from the time stamped on it. If you're around for several days and doing a lot of bus hopping (or using local trains, on which these tickets are also valid), you have three good options. An **Århus Pass** costs 97kr for 24 hours, 121kr for 48 hours and 171kr for an entire week, and covers unlimited travel and entrance to most museums, including ARoS Art Museum, as well as sightseeing tours (though you must book these at the tourist office first). There's also **multi-ride ticket** (*Klippekort*: 105kr), which is valid for ten trips within the immediate city area and can be used by more than one person at once; or a **24-hour ticket** (55kr), which covers public transport in all four zones and nothing else. These tickets can be bought at news-stands, campsites and shops displaying the "Århus Sporveje" sign. The driver won't check your ticket but a roving inspector might, and there's an instant fine of 500kr if you're caught travelling without one. You can get **bus information** at *Kommmune Information* in the Rådhus (Mon–Fri 10am–5.30pm; ☎89 40 10 10, lines open daily 4.30am–1am).

Cycling is another viable way to get around – as part of the very useful **citybike** scheme, there are 250 bikes distributed around the city, which you can use for free within the city limits by dropping a 20kr deposit into the slot on the bikes. If you're heading out of the city to Moesgård, for instance, the most central place to rent a bicycle is Cykelværkstedet Morten Mengel, Mejlgade 41 (☎86 19 29 27, ⊛www .mmcykler.dk), which charges 85kr for the first day, 50kr up to six following days, and 300kr for a full week.

Accommodation

Århus has some fairly reasonably priced hotel and hostel options, and the tourist office can help you find affordable **private rooms** (from 300kr a night). The Århus Bed & Breakfast network (☎86 27 51 30, ⊛www.aarhus-bed-and-breakfast .dk) can also help with rooms for 330kr a night, and self-contained apartments for 650kr a night.

Another option is to stay at a farmhouse some 15km west of the city, but you'll need your own transport to get there. The *Tarskov Mølle*, at Tarskovvej 1 in Harlev (☎86 94 25 44, ⊛www.tarskovmolle.dk; ❸), has its own water mill, forest and lake frontage. You could also try one of the inns surrounding Århus, such as *Malling Kro*, at Stationspladsen 2 in Malling, 12km south of Århus and half an hour by train towards Odder (☎86 93 10 25, ⊛www.mallingkro.dk; ❷, en-suite ❹); breakfast costs 50kr. The tourist office has a full list of inns in the Århus area.

Hotels and guesthouses
Cab-Inn Århus Kannikegade 14 ☎86 75 70 00, ⊛www.cabinn.com. Next to Århus Å River, the functional cabin-like rooms here (everything folds up and packs away) are very good value. Breakfast is 50kr. ❹

Guldsmeden Guldsmedegade 40 ☎86 13 45 56, ⊛www.hotelguldsmeden.dk. A small, homely hotel in the centre, ten minutes' walk from the station. Rooms are delicately decorated in French colonial style, and no two are the same; some have shared bath. Scrummy organic breakfast buffet included in the rates. Bus #1, #2, #6, #9 or #11. ❺, en-suite ❻

Helnan Marselis Strandvejen 25 ☎86 14 44 11, ⊛www.marselis.dk. Stunningly located hotel a few kilometres south of the centre right on the beach. All rooms overlook Århus Bay, and facilities include swimming pool, bar and restaurant, and Marselis woods are at the back door. Bus #6 or #19. ❺

Ritz Banegårdspladsen 12 ☎86 13 44 44, ⊛www.hotelritz.dk. As the name implies, this place, just next to the train station, is both pricey (though with discounts at weekends) and posh. Very elegant rooms with ornately carved furniture and plush bathrooms. ❻

Sportshotellet Stadion Allé 70 ☎86 14 30 00, ⊛www.atletion.dk. A functional hotel, part of the fancy sports stadium complex in the Marlisborg forest. The rooms are basic, with two single beds but all are en-suite, with a kitchenette on each floor. Take bus #19 from the station. Free parking. ❹

Villa Provence Fredens Torv 12 ☎86 18 24 00, ⊛www.villaprovence.dk. Classy new small hotel a stone's throw from the bus station. The range of rooms are all beautifully decorated in Provencal style, featuring old French-Belgian film posters. ❻

Sleep-ins and youth hostels
Århus City Sleep-In Havnegade 20 ☎86 19 20 55, ⊛www.citysleep-in.dk. Near both the city centre and harbour, offering dorm beds (110kr) and doubles (❷). Guests without their own sleeping bags have to rent sheets and blankets (45kr); other facilities include a games room, café and Internet access (20kr/hr). Bus #3 from the station, but you might as well walk. Open 24/7.

Århus Youth Hostel Marienlundsvej 10 ☎86 16 72 98, ⊛www.hostel-aarhus.dk. Much more peaceful than the central *Sleep-In*, this is 4km northeast of town in the middle of Risskov wood, close to the popular Den Permanente beach. As well as dorms (108kr), it has a hotel-style wing with double rooms (❸), too. Bus #1, #6 #8, #9, #16, #56 or #58.

Campsites
Århus Nord Randersvej 400, Lisbjerg ☎86 23 11 33, ⊛www.dk-camp.dk/aarhusnord. Some 8km north of the city centre and convenient for the E45 motorway, this campsite is only slightly cheaper than *Blommehaven*, and not nearly as well situated. Bus #117 or #118.

Blommehaven Ørneredevej 35, Højbjerg ☎86 27 02 07, ⊛www.blommehaven.dk. Overlooking the bay, with access to a beautiful beach, and about 4km south of the city centre. Bus #6 or #19. Open April–Aug.

The City
For reasons of simple chronology, Århus divides into two clearly defined parts: even combined, these fill a small and easily walkable area. The **old section**, close to the Domkirke, is a tight cluster of medieval streets with several interesting churches and a couple of museums, as well as the bulk of the city's nightlife. The (relatively) **new sections** of Århus form a collar around the old centre, inevitably with less character, but nonetheless holding plenty that's worth seeing, not least the city's major architectural works.

Old Århus
Søndergade is Århus's main street, a pedestrianized strip lined with shops and overpriced snack bars that leads from the train station (where it's initially called Ryesgade), through Skt Clemens Torv and across Århus Å River into the main town square, Bispetorvet. From here, the streets of the old centre form a web around the **Domkirke** (May–Sept Mon–Sat 9.30am–4pm; Oct–April Mon–Sat 10am–3pm). Take the trouble to push open the cathedral's sturdy doors, not just to appreciate

the soccer-pitch length – this is easily the longest church in Denmark – but to take in a couple of features that spruce up the plain Gothic interior, which is mostly a fifteenth-century rebuilding after the original twelfth-century structure was destroyed by fire. At the eastern end is one of few pre-Reformation survivors, a grand tripartite altarpiece by the noted Bernt Notke. Look also at the painted – as opposed to stained – glass window behind the altar, the work of Norwegian Emmanuel Vigeland (brother of Gustav); it's most effective when the sunlight falls directly on it.

From the time of the first settlement here, in the tenth century, the area around the cathedral has been at the core of Århus life. A number of Viking remains have been excavated on Skt Clemens Torv, across the road from the cathedral, and some of them are now displayed in the basement of the Nordea bank at Skt Clemens Torv 6 (entrance inside the bank on the left) as part of the **Viking Museum** (Mon–Fri 10am–4pm, Thurs until 5.30pm; free), which displays sections of the original ramparts and Viking tools alongside informative accounts of early Århus. Also close to the cathedral, in a former police station on Bispetorvet, the **Women's Museum** (*Kvindemuseet*; daily: June–Aug 10am–5pm; Sept–May Tues–Sun 10am–4pm; 30kr; ⓦ www.kvindemuseet.dk) is one of Denmark's most innovative, staging temporary exhibitions on aspects of women's lives past and present. After visiting the museums, venture into the narrow and enjoyable surrounding streets, lined by innumerable old and well-preserved buildings, many of which now house browsable antique shops or chic boutiques. The area is also home to some of the city's most enjoyable drinking spots (see p.187).

West along Vestergade from the Domkirke, the thirteenth-century **Vor Frue Kirke** (May–Aug Mon–Fri 10am–4pm, Sat 10am–2pm; Sept–April Mon–Fri 10am–2pm, Sat 10am–noon) is actually the site of three churches, the most notable of which is the eleventh-century **crypt church** (go in through the main church entrance and walk straight ahead), which was discovered, buried beneath several centuries' worth of rubbish, during restoration work on the main church in the 1950s. There's not exactly a lot to see, but the tiny, rough-stone building – resembling a hollowed-out cave – is strong on atmosphere, especially during the candle-lit Sunday services. Except for Claus Berg's fine altarpiece, there's not much to warrant a look in the main church. However, you can make your way (to the left of the entrance) through the cloister that remains from the pre-Reformation monastery – now an old folk's home – to see the medieval frescoes inside the third church, which depict local working people rather than the more commonly found biblical scenes.

Modern Århus

If you've visited the tourist office, you've already been inside the least interesting section of one of the modern city's major sights: the functional **Rådhus** on Rådhuspladsen, completed in 1941 and as capable of inciting high passions – for and against – today as it was when it opened. From the outside, it's easy to see why opinions should be so polarized: the coating of grey Norwegian marble lends a sickly pallor to the building. But on the inside (enter from Rådhuspladsen), the finer points of architects Arne Jacobsen and Erik Møller's vision make themselves apparent, amid the harmonious open-plan corridors and the extravagant quantities of glass. You're free to walk in and look for yourself, but it's worth taking one of the fascinating **guided tours** (in English, mid-June to early Sept Mon–Fri at 11am; 10kr). You can also tour the bell tower at noon and 2pm daily (same months; 5kr). Above the entrance hangs Hagedorn Olsen's huge mural, *A Human Society*, symbolically depicting the city emerging from the last war to face the future with optimism. In the council chamber, the lamps appear to hang suspended in mid-air (in fact they're held by almost invisible threads), and the shape of the council leader's chair is a distinctive curved form mirrored in numerous smaller features throughout the building, notably the ashtrays in the lifts – though many of these

△ Rådhus, Århus

have been pilfered by visitors. Perhaps most interesting of all, however, if only for the background story, are the walls of the small Civic Room, covered by intricate floral designs in which artist Albert Naur, working during the Nazi occupation, concealed various Allied insignia.

More recent examples of Århus's municipal architecture include the glass-fronted **Concert Hall** (*Musikhuset*; daily 11am–9pm; ⓦ www.musikhusetaarhus.dk), a short walk from the Rådhus along Vester Allé, which has been the city's main venue for opera and classical music since it opened in 1982. It's worth dropping into, if only for the small café where you might be entertained for free by a string quartet or a lone fiddler. A monthly list of forthcoming concerts and events is available from the box office or the tourist office.

Next door, the new art museum, **ARoS** (Tues–Sun 10am–5pm, Wed till 10pm; 70kr; ⓦ www.aros.dk), a remarkable building designed by the same architects as the Black Diamond extension to the Royal Library in Copenhagen (see p.113). Spread over seven floors, the collection gives a good overview of the main national trends, from late eighteenth-century formal portraits and landscapes by Jens Juel and finely etched scenes of domestic tension by Jørgen Sonne, through to more internationally renowned names, particularly Vilhelm Hammershoi, represented here by some of his moody interiors. There are lots of worthwhile modern pieces, too. Besides the radiant canvases of Asger Jorn and Richard Mortensen, don't miss Bjørn Nørgård's sculpted version of Christian IV's tomb: the original, in Roskilde Cathedral, is stacked with riches; this one features a coffee cup, an egg and a ball-point pen. Other highlights include the spookily lifelike five-metre-high sculpture, *Boy*, by Ron Mueck.

It's just a few minutes' walk from the Concert Hall and ARoS to Viborgvej and the city's best-known attraction, **Den Gamle By** ("The Old Town"; Jan 11am–3pm; 80kr; Feb, March, 10am–4pm; April–June & Sept–Nov 10am–5pm; July–Aug 9am–6pm; Dec 10am–7pm; ⓦ www.dengamleby.dk). An open-air museum of traditional Danish life, it consists of around seventy-five half-timbered townhouses (including a popular Mayor's House of 1597) from all over the country which have been moved here since the museum's inception in 1914. With many of the buildings used for their original purpose, the overall aim of the place is to give an impression of an old Danish market town, complete with bakers, craftsmen and the like. This is done very effectively, although sunny summer days bring big crowds, and the period flavour is strongest outside high season, when visitors are fewer.

A short walk from Den Gamle By, the **university campus** is a prime example of modern Danish architectural style. Sprawled across a hillside overlooking the city, the distinctive red-brick buildings, mostly designed by C.F. Møller and completed just after World War II, feature white-framed rectangular windows, and no decorative touches whatsoever. While on campus, there are two museums that might appeal: the **Natural History Museum** (July–Aug 10am–5pm; Sept–June 10am–4pm; 40kr; www.naturhistoriskmuseum.dk) has a large collection of stuffed birds and animals alongside some exhibits on Danish ecology, while the **Steno Museum** (Tues–Fri 9am–4pm, Sat & Sun 11am–4pm; 40kr; www.stenomuseet.dk) focuses on medical matters and also includes a small planetarium and a new herb garden. To get to the campus from the centre, take bus #2, #3, #11, #14, #54, #56 or #58.

Out from the centre

On Sundays Århus resembles a ghost town, with most locals spending the day in the parks, woodlands or beaches on the city's outskirts. If you're around on a Sunday – or, for that matter, any sunny day in the week – you could do much worse than join them. The closest beaches and woods are just **north of the city** at Risskov, near the youth hostel, easily reached on buses #6 or #16, or on any local trains headed for Grenå or Hornslets, some of which halt at the tiny Den Permanente train platform by the beach (but check before boarding, as not all trains stop here). Risskov's beach is narrow but scenic, with an old fashioned public bathhouse, and is clean enough for swimming, while the thick forest behind is criss-crossed with walking and cycling trails. There are a few ice-cream and hotdog stalls on the beach, but you might be better off taking your own picnic.

For a more varied day, head **south** through the thick Marselisborg Skov forest and on to the prehistoric museum at Moesgård. This is also ideal territory for cycling or hiking – see p.181 for details of bicycle rental. Contact the tourist office for suggestions about routes and maps.

Marselisborg Skov and Dyrehaven

The **Marselisborg Skov**, 4km south of the city centre, is a large park that contains the city's sports and horse-trotting stadiums and sees a regular procession of people exercising their dogs. It also holds the diminutive **Marselisborg Slot**, summer home of the Danish royals, whose landscaped grounds can be visited during daylight hours (free) when they're not in residence (usually at all times outside Easter, Christmas and late June to early Aug); if guards are posted by the gate, they're in and there's a changing of guards at noon. Further south, across Carl Nielsen Vej, the park turns into a dense forest, criss-crossed with footpaths but still easy to get lost in.

A simpler route to navigate, and one with better views, is along Strandvejen, which runs between the eastern side of the forest and the shore. Unbroken footpaths run along this part of the coast and there are many opportunities to scamper down to rarely crowded (though often pebbly) beaches. Also on this route, near the junction of Ørneredevej and Thorsmøllevej, is the **Dyrehaven**, or Deer Park – a protected section of the wood that's home to many deer. The animals can be seen (if you're lucky – they're not the most gregarious of creatures) from the marked paths running through the park from the gate on the main road.

Moesgård Prehistoric Museum

Occupying the buildings and grounds of an old manor house 10km south of Århus city centre, **Moesgård Prehistoric Museum** (April–Sept daily 10am–5pm; Oct–March Tues–Sun 10am–4pm; 45kr; www.moesmus.dk) traces the story of Danish civilizations from the Stone Age onwards with copious finds and easy-to-follow illustrations. It's the Iron Age which is most comprehensively covered and produces the most dramatic single exhibit: the **Grauballe Man**, the remains of a body, dated to 80 BC, which was discovered in a peat bog west of Århus in a state of such excellent preservation that it was even possible to discover what the deceased had eaten for breakfast (burnt porridge made from rye and barley) on the day of his death. Also remarkable is the extensive **Illerup Ådal** collection of weapons and military paraphernalia, dating from around 200 BC and recovered, in relatively good condition, from the Ådal bog. Only a roomful of imposing runic stones further on captures the imagination as powerfully. Bus #6 runs here direct from the city, while bus #19 takes a more scenic route along the edge of Århus Bay, leaving you with at least a 2km walk through woods to the museum.

Outside the museum, the **prehistoric trail** runs from the far corner of the courtyard to the sea and back again (follow the red dots), a distance of about 3km each way, heading past a scattering of reassembled prehistoric dwellings, monuments and burial places – a trail guide is available in English (10kr) and there's a map on the back of your entry ticket. On a fine day, the walk itself is as enjoyable as the actual sights, and you could easily linger for a picnic when you reach the coast, or stop for a coffee and a snack at the small but popular *Skovmøllen* restaurant en route. Bus #19 goes back to the city from a stop about a hundred metres back to the north of the trail's end at the beach.

Eating

Central Århus is loaded with **eating** possibilities and, while nothing is particularly cheap, a good and affordable bite can still be found in the right places. In general, it's wise to follow locals and students away from the heavily touristed Domkirke and Store Torv to streets such as Mejlgade, Nørre Allé, Vestergade or Skolegade – the latter has a number of unpretentious eateries – so unpretentious, in fact, that they often look closed when they're open. You'll find the best **lunch** bargains, for around 65kr, simply by cruising the cafés and restaurants of the old city and reading the notices chalked up outside them. If you're prepared to pay a bit more, Åboulevarden – the northern bank of a newly uncovered section of the Århus Å River – offers a string of trendy eating and drinking venues, and is a good place to head for **dinner**.

If money is tight, or you just want to stock up for a **picnic**, try the *Frokostspecialisten* outlet at Frederiks Allé 105. For more general food shopping, there's a branch of Brugsen on Søndergade, and a late-opening DSB **supermarket** (8am–midnight) at the train station. There are several other downtown supermarkets of varying quality – try the decent Super Brugsen at Nørre Allé, or the slightly less good Aldi across the way; at the former, local merchants peddle berries and beans fresh from the fields when in season.

Athena Store Torv 18. Good-value Greek restaurant – try the moussaka for 125kr – on the first floor overlooking the hustle and bustle of Store and Little Torv below. Dinner only.

Bryggeriet Sct Clemens Kannikegade 10–12. A popular brewery-cum-restaurant which does mouthwatering spare ribs for 125kr, best washed down with freshly tapped unfiltered beer; the steaks aren't bad, either. Lunch ranges from 65kr for dish of the day to a filling *smørrebrød* platter for 95kr. Closed Sun.

China Wok House Sønder Allé 9. As well as standard Chinese fare, this place also does an all-you-can-eat buffet (58kr at lunchtime, 109kr in the evening). Takeaway China boxes are sold from the front window.

Crêperiet Marselisborg Havnevej 24. Overlooking the harbour; try out the crêpes with twenty-four different fillings (75–112kr), the fish soups or onion consommé. Take bus #6 from the station.

Cross Café Åboulevarden 66. On the trendy bit of Åboulevarden, overlooking Århus Å river, and serving up generous brunch platters at 95kr as well as oversized salmon sandwiches.

Dragen Åboulevarden 64. For 108kr, you choose your ingredients from the wok buffet and have them stir-fried in front of you.

Emmerys Guldsmedegade 24–26. The city's oldest patisserie has now expanded its repertoire from wonderful freshly ground coffee and cakes to simple flavour-packet meals throughout the day. Fine wines and good beer as well. A three-course-meal will set you back less than 250kr.

Gyngen Mejlgade 53. Good-value, highly rated vegetarian meals served up within the Fronthuset culture centre; local bands sometimes play after dinner. Lunch only on Mon, and dinner only on Sun.

Karls Sandwichbar Klostergade 32. Undisputedly the best burgers in town. Huge and homemade, served with large portions of fries. Can't beat it.

Pinds Café Skolegade 11. Although it often looks deceptively shut, *Pinds* nonetheless opens long hours and does excellent *smørrebrød*, as well as inexpensive set lunches. Closed Sun and Mon.

🏃 Pinden Skolegade 29. The speciality here is *Stegt flæsk med persille sovs* (slices of fried pork with potatoes and parsley sauce). Six pieces of *flæsk* with potatoes go for 79kr, all-you-can-eat is 100kr.

Raadhuus Kaféen Sønder Allé 3. Near the tourist office, offering all-day Danish specials such as *frikadeller* (pork meatballs), gammon steak with asparagus, or *flæskeæggekage* (heavy-duty omelette with *flæsk*) for 75kr.

Seafood Marselisborg Havnevej 44. A great choice if you're prepared to splash out, with fantastic views of the Århus Bay area and a delectable range of seafood, from Brittany oysters to hake steamed in white wine. Main courses from 215kr.

Under Engle Mejlgade 28. Organic vegetarian restaurant that does a filling and healthy lunchtime menu for only 40kr and a two-course evening meal for 70kr. Bring your own wine.

Drinking and nightlife

Århus is the only place in Denmark with a **nightlife** scene to match that of Copenhagen, offering a diverse assortment of ways to be entertained, enlightened, or just inebriated, almost every night of the week. And while things sparkle socially all year round, if you visit during the **Århus Festival** (*Århus Festuge*), an orgy of arts events held annually over the first week in September (check what's on with the tourist office or visit ✪www.aarhusfestuge.dk), you'll find even more to occupy your time.

The city has a wonderful endowment of **cafés**, with many situated in the medieval streets close to the cathedral. There's little to choose between them – each pulls a lively, cosmopolitan crowd and the best plan is simply to wander around and try a few – but we've listed the most enduring options below. Between Thursday and Saturday, most cafés stay open until midnight (and some as late as 2am); we've specified these within the listings below.

Home to a music school that's produced some of the country's most successful performers, Århus boasts a music scene that's well known throughout Denmark – so if you're looking for **live music**, you won't have to look far. Basic details of all events are available from the tourist office, but a better source for rock music news is the Århus Billet Bureau, at Klostergade 20 (✆86 13 05 44, ✪www.aabb .dk), where you can pick up a variety of free local magazines and flyers advertising forthcoming gigs. Århus's **clubbing** scene is equally lively, with both *Voxhall* and *Train* (see p.188) staging club nights when they aren't hosting live bands, and plenty of more mainstream venues providing a less achingly cool place to dance. Early in the week, admission to any club is likely to be free; on Thursday, Friday or Saturday, you'll pay 40–60kr. Århus doesn't have the wide network of **gay clubs** you'll find in Copenhagen, though the long-established gay social centre *Pan Klubben*, south of the train station at Jægergårdsgade 42 (✆86 13 43 80, ✪www.panclub.dk), has a disco (Fri & Sat 10pm–6am). The second Friday of every month is lesbian-only night; otherwise there's a mixed crowd.

Cafés and bars

Billabong Bar Skolegade 26. The city's only Aussie bar, full of hardy outback types and serving local and foreign ales. Open daily till 2am.

The Bridgewater Pub Åboulevarden 22. On the banks of Arhus Å River, this English pub with real ales on tap is the place to go for your football fix, with three large screens and live NFL on Sundays. Open until 4am Fri & Sat.

Café Jorden Badstuegade 3. Popular café in the

medieval cathedral area, which serves quality brunch until mid-afternoon, and gets very lively at night when the drinkers arrive. Open until 2am daily.

Café Kindrødt Studsgade 8. Near the old quarter's better shopping streets and a great place to rest your feet or sample some of the good food during the day. Local revellers liven things up in the evenings. Open until 2am Thurs–Sat.

Café Smagløs Klostertorv 7. An old-timer of the café scene. Busy with lunchers during the day, and crowded with some of Århus's sizeable student population at night. Open until 3am Fri & Sat.

Café Svej Åboulevarden 22. Tucked in among the thick row of cafés and bars lining Århus Å River, with chairs spilling out onto the pavement, this is *the* place to be seen on sunny summer evenings.

Carlton Rosengade 23. In the centre of this quaint, café-heavy medieval quarter, and always buzzing at night. The food is slightly pricey, so most people only come to drink.

Casablanca Rosengade 12. A good place to start the evening, this is Århus's oldest café, with movie-themed decorations and live jazz on Wednesday evenings. Open until 2am Mon–Sat.

The Cockney Pub Maren Smeds Gyde 8. Popular real ale pub featuring haggis nights and whisky tasting sessions – and they pride themselves of making a proper cup of tea. Open until 2am Thurs–Sat.

Ris Ras Filliongongong Mejlgade 24. Named after a well-known Danish children's rhyme, this is another popular student hangout. *Ris Ras* excels in good beer and cigars, and there's an art gallery in the basement that's well worth checking out. Open until 2am daily.

Under Masken Bispegade 3. Cosy yet quirky bar, with masks from around the globe decorating the walls and a wide selection of foreign beers on sale. Open until 2am daily.

Clubs

Broen Nordhavnsgade 20 ☎86 13 14 29. This club on a boat moored in the harbour is divided into five separate sections with different decor and styles of music, from mainstream hip-hop to Frank Sinatra. Fri & Sat only.

Twist & Shout Frederiksgade 29 ☎86 18 08 55. Three storeys of different music styles: most of it's pretty mainstream, so no real surprises. A short walk from the town hall and tourist office. Closed Sun.

Fabrikken Klostergade 34 ☎86 76 06 76,

@www.chokoladefabikken.dk. The city's coolest club, playing the newest, hottest dance tunes. Massive discounts for students. Over 20s only. Fri & Sat 11pm–5am.

Hotel Royal Store Torv 4 ☎ 86 12 00 11. Glitzy hotel basement housing a combined casino/night-club that's liveliest early in the week. Smart dress code applies. Open daily until 4am.

Live music venues

Bent J Nørre Allé 66 ☎86 12 04 92, @www .jazzbarbentj.dk. By far the best jazz venue in town, this smoky, atmospheric pub has free jam sessions from 4pm on Fridays, and regular performances by bands (expect to pay 60–100kr). Closed Sun.

Fatter Eskild Skolegade 25 ☎86 19 44 11, @www.fattereskild.dk. Piano bar hosting Danish bar-bands and R&B acts five days a week. Open until 5am Fri & Sat, closed Sun & Mon.

Musikcafeen Mejlgade 53 ☎86 76 03 44, @www.musikcafeen.dk. On the first floor of the Fronthuset cultural centre, this is Århus's main venue for up-and-coming Danish and international bands, as well as live jazz, rock and the odd techno act. Entrance fee varies between 20kr and 150kr depending on who's playing. Closed Sun.

Musikhuset Thomas Jensens Allé ☎86 40 90 50, @www.musikhusetaarhus.dk. City-centre concert hall which plays host to classical music, opera and, occasionally, mainstream pop bands.

Train Toldbogade 6 ☎86 13 47 22, @www.train .dk. Attracting an older crowd and slightly more well-established bands than its rival *Voxhall* (see below). Gigs take place three or four nights a week; admission runs from 100kr to 350kr, with doors opening at 9pm and the main band starting a couple of hours later.

Voxhall Vester Allé 15 ☎87 30 97 97, @www .voxhall.dk. Århus's premier venue, hosting the cream of Danish and international independent acts from hip hop to world music. Tickets cost 50–200kr.

Listings

Airlines SAS (domestic and international) ☎70 10 20 00, @www.scandinavian.net; Maersk Air reservations ☎70 10 74 74, flight information ☎76 50 50 50, @www.maersk-air. com. Sun-Air reservations ☎75 33 16 11, information ☎76 50 01 00, @www.sun-air.dk and @www.ba.com.

Airport Tirstrup Airport (☎87 75 70 00; @www .aar.dk) is 45km east of the city. Buses for the airport leave from outside the train station; the fare is 80kr and the journey takes 50min.

Bookshops English Books and Secondhand Things, Frederiks Allé 53 (☎86 19 54 55, Mon–Fri 11.30am–5.30pm, Sat 11am–2pm), fully lives up to its name.

Bus enquiries Local buses ☎89 40 10 10; Abildskou's Århus–Copenhagen coach reservations ☎70 21 08 88, @www.abildskou.dk.

Car rental Avis, Spanien 63 ☎86 19 23 99, and Jens Baggesens Vej 27 ☎86 16 10 99 @www .avis.dk; Europcar, Sønder Allé 35 ☎89 33 11 11, @www.europcar.dk.

Doctor Between 4pm and 8pm, call ☎86 20 10 22. Outside these hours, contact the Kommunehospital (see Hospitals, below).

Ferries and catamarans Mols Linien to either Odden or Kalundborg on Zealand ☎70 10 14 18, ⊛www.mols-linien.dk.

Hospitals There are 24hr emergency departments at Århus Kommunehospital, Nørrebrogade 44 (☎87 31 50 50), and Århus Amtssygehus, Tage-Hansens Gade 2 (☎89 49 75 75).

Internet cafés Boomtown, Åboulevarden 21 (Mon–Thurs 10am–2am, Fri & Sat 10am–8am, gates shut at midnight, Sun 11am–midnight; 25kr per hr); Gate 58, Vestergade 58 daily 10am–midnight; 25kr per hr; Net House, Nørre Allé 66A daily noon–midnight; 25kr per hr).

Market There's a fruit, veg and flower market every Wed and Sat on Bispetorvet, beside the cathedral (early morning till noon), though the one on Sat mornings (until 2pm) along Ingerslevs Boulevard, south of the centre, is livelier.

Pharmacy Løve Apoteket, Store Torv 5 ☎86 12 00 22, is open 24 hours.

Police Århus Politisation, Ridderstræde 1 ☎87 31 14 48.

Post office Banegårdspladsen, by the train station (Mon–Fri 9.30am–6pm, Sat 10am–1pm).

Train enquiries ⊛www.dsb.dk has details of all services; you can also call ☎89 40 10 10 for info on regional services; ☎70 13 14 15 for inter-city services; and ☎70 13 14 16 for international trains.

Travel agents Kilroy Travels, Fredensgade 40 ☎70 15 40 15, ⊛www.kilroytravels.com.

Randers and Djursland

From rolling hills and lush valleys to sandy beaches, **Djursland**, the nose-shaped peninsula east of Århus, boasts some of the prettiest landscapes in Denmark – sufficient ingredients for a couple of days' pleasurable exploration. The southern coastal stretch, known as **Mols**, is especially delightful, its hills affording some superb views. Base yourself in the countryside close to Randers, and see the area by bike (see p.190 for details of rental outlets) or local buses.

Randers

A trading and manufacturing base since the thirteenth century, **RANDERS** is not a promising introduction to east Jutland. Its growth has continued apace over the years, leaving a tiny medieval centre miserably corralled by a bleak new industrial zone. The town's main historical sight is the house at **Storegade 13**, said to be the place where Danish nobleman Niels Ebbesen killed the German count, Gerd of Holstein, in 1340; a shutter on the upper storey is always left open to allow the count's ghost to escape lest the malevolent spirit should cause the building to burn down. However, Randers' biggest tourist attraction these days – one of the most popular in Jutland – is the **Randers Regnskov** (Randers Rainforest; mid-June to mid-Aug daily 10am–6pm; mid-Aug to mid-June Mon–Fri 10am–4pm, Sat & Sun 10am–5pm; 95kr; ⊛www.regnskoven.dk), a re-creation of tropical rainforests – African, Asian and South American – alongside the River Gudenå. Visitors wander through the dense, damp foliage, enclosed within three giant domes watching out for the birds, animals and amphibians, which include a number of rare turtles and a flying fox, not to mention a formidable assortment of vipers, boas, pythons, poison frogs and the like. The best part is undoubtedly the dark and spooky "night zoo", located in a dripping stone cave.

Otherwise, there are a couple of museums that are worth a visit, both in the Culture Centre near the bus station on Stenmannsgade 2. The grandly named **Museum of Danish Art** (Tues–Sun 11am–5pm; free; ⊛www.randerskunstmuseum.dk) on the second floor has a permanent collection of over 4000 pieces from the late eighteenth century up until today, mostly by Danish artists. You could easily kill a couple of hours here, if only for the wacky glass and mirror installation *Cosmic Space*, by the Faroese artist Trondur Patursson. The first floor holds the less captivating **Museum of Cultural History** (same hours; free; ⊛www.khm.dk) which provides a solid, if uninspiring, historical introduction to the region. A bit further down the road, at no. 9C, the **Elvis Unlimited Museum** (Mon–Fri

10am–5pm, Sat 10am–2pm; 30kr; ⊛www.elvispresley.dk) prides itself of being the only Elvis museum outside the US. An el Dorado for fans of the King, it has tons of paraphernalia on display, including his personal record collection, two of his guitars, some clothes and the Presley archives put together by the FBI.

Practicalities

The **bus station** is right in the centre at Dytmærsken 12, while the **train station** is ten minutes' walk out of town at Jernbanegade 29. First stop should be the **tourist office**, on the ring road leading to Randers Regnskov at Tørvebryggen 12 (mid-June to mid-Aug Mon–Fri 9.30am–5pm, Sat 10am–1pm; mid-Aug to mid-June Mon–Fri 9.30am–4pm, Sat 9am–1pm; ☎86 42 44 77, ⊛www.visitranders .com), from where you can get a list of private rooms which rent from 150kr per person per night – but be aware that some of them are a long way outside town. One of the best-value **hotels** is the *Gudenå*, Østervold 42 (☎86 40 44 11, ⊛www .hotel-gudenaa.dk; ❹/❺), in the former seaman's home overlooking the harbour. More upmarket are *Hotel Randers*, in the centre on Torvegade 11 (☎86 42 34 22, ⊛www.hotel-randers.dk; ❺/❻), and the *Scandic Hotel Kongens Ege* (☎86 43 03 00, ⊛www.scandic-hotels.com; ❹/❻), on Gammel Hadsundvej atop a wooded hill above the town, whose rooms give superb views over the city. Randers' status as "Conference City" means you'll pay a lot more for hotels during the week; the reviews above give the weekend rate followed by the weekday one. Randers' **youth hostel**, with dorms (120kr) and private rooms (❸), is only five minutes from the centre at Gethersvej 1 (☎86 42 50 44, ⊛www.danhostel.dk/randers; mid-Feb to Nov). The nearest **campsite**, with cabins and a swimming pool, is at Fladbro, 6km west of the town (☎86 42 93 61, ⊛www.fladbrocamping.dk): take bus #10 to the golf course, from where it's a ten-minute walk. Note that some #10 buses do go all the way to the campsite stop, so ask the driver.

Randers has plenty of relatively cheap **restaurants**: try the Greek dishes at *Hellas*, Vester Kirkestræde 3, or the filling lunchtime deals at ⽊ *Maren Knudsen Øl & Vinkælder* on Storegade. *Niels Ebbesens Spisehus*, in the historic setting of Storegade 13 (see p.189), offers the town's best *smørrebrød*: three slices at lunchtime for 70kr or a steak for 49kr, and tasty pork tenderloin with all the trimmings for 119kr on the dinner menu. As for **nightlife**, Storegade holds a good selection of bars where you can sample the local Thor beer; try the popular *Tante Olga*, Søndergade 6 (⊛www .tanteolga.dk), which has something going on every weekend (Thurs–Sat) – live blues and rock, or whisky tasting evenings. There's also the more peaceful *Café von Hatten*, Von Hattenstræde 7. In early August the town celebrates **Randers Ugen**, a week packed with all sorts of cultural events; the rest of the year, major rock concerts and theatre performances are put on regularly at Værket Musik & Teaterhus, a converted power station on Mariagervej (ticket office ☎86 43 29 00, ⊛www .vaerket.dk) – ask at the tourist office for details of what's on, or visit the website.

The best way to see the countryside around Randers is by **bike**. Schmidt Cykler, Kirkegade 7 (☎86 41 29 03), rents them for 50kr per day.

Djursland

East of Randers stretches the **Djursland peninsula**. With its hilly, wooded landscape, edged by some fine beaches, the southern area of **Mols** attracts huge numbers of tourists every year. **EBELTOFT** is the most popular destination, easily reached by regular bus from Århus, or by frequent ferry services from Odden in Zealand. A thriving market centre in medieval times, it was sacked by the invading Swedes in 1659 and has only emerged from economic decline thanks to tourism: try to arrive in early summer, before the cobbled streets are overrun by (mostly German) tourists shopping for souvenirs. The main sight in town is the **Fregatten Jylland** (daily: June–Aug 10am–7pm; Sept–Oct & April–May 10am–5pm; Nov–March 10am–4pm; 70kr; ⊛www.fregatten-jylland.dk), moored just behind the bus station. This beautifully restored nineteenth-century wooden frigate has lots of miniature famous sea battle scenarios on display downstairs in the galley. Nearby at Strandvejen 8, the **Glass Museum** (daily: July 10am–7pm Aug–June 10am–5pm; 40kr; ⓦ www.glasmuseet.dk) provides the chance to see local artisans demonstrating the fabulous art of glass blowing. Should you fancy staying in town, the best-value **hotel** is the small, no-frills *Ebeltoft* on Adelgade 44 (☎86 34 10 90; ❸), where rooms have shared facilities; or the *Ebeltoft Park Hotel*, on the beachfront at Vibæk Strandvej 4 (☎86 34 32 22, ⓦ www.ebeltoftparkhotel.dk; ❺); there's also a **youth hostel** at Søndergade 43 (☎86 34 20 53, ⓦ www.danhostel.dk/ebeltoft) with bunks (120kr) and doubles (❷). There are several **campsites** along the bay, the best being *Vibæk Camping* (☎86 34 12 14, ⓦ www.publiccamp.dk/vibaek), right on the beach a little way north of town.

△ Medieval buildings, Ebeltoft

At Jutland's easternmost point, **GRENÅ** grew up around its harbour in the nineteenth century, and it's still a relatively important port, with frequent ferry services to Varberg in Sweden. Though the town centre is pleasant enough, the main draw is the lush, wide and sandy beaches to the south. If you need **to stay** overnight, try for a room at the yellow *Hotel Grenaa Strand*, close to the harbour (☎86 32 68 14, ⓦ www.grenaastrand.dk; ❺); alternatively, there's a **youth hostel**, with bunks (120kr) and doubles (❸), at Ydesvej 4 (☎86 32 66 22, ⓦ www .danhostel.dk/grenaa; closed mid-Dec to mid-Jan). The best of the local **campsites** is *Grenå Strand Camping*, south of the harbour at Fulgsangvej 58 (☎86 32 17 18, ⓦ www.grenaastrandcamping.dk; April–Sept). Grenå is reachable by train from Århus (1hr 25min), while bus #214 runs hourly through the day from Randers bus station, the journey taking about ninety minutes.

If it's only beaches you're after, head 10km north of Grenå by local bus to **GJERRILD**, a small and quiet village with an inn, bakery, grocery and a small castle, Sostrup Slot, now a religious retreat run by Cistercian sisters. The beach here, **Nordstranden**, is one of the best in the country, far preferable to the pebbly offerings in the opposite direction. Budget accommodation alternatives are pretty much limited to Gjerrild's **youth hostel** (☎86 38 41 99, ⓦ www.danhostel.dk/gjerrild), with bunks (115kr) and doubles (❷), and an excellent **campsite** (☎86 38 42 00, ⓦ www.gnc.dk; April–Sept), 500m from the sands at Nordstranden.

The Lake District: Silkeborg, Viborg and around

Boundaried by a loose triangle formed by Skanderborg, Århus and Viborg, the grandly titled **Lake District** comprises several small lakes amid green, rolling woodlands which hold one of Denmark's highest points, the 147m Himmelbjerget.

If you've only seen Denmark's larger towns, this is a region well worth a couple of days' rural exploration, and there are innumerable campsites if you want to linger. The north–south rail route passes first through missable Skanderborg, but it's the Lake District's other main town, **Silkeborg**, spreading handsomely across several inlets, which serves as the area's lively centre. The region is easily accessed by train, although if coming from Århus you'll need to change at Langå to get straight into the lush patch around historic **Viborg**.

Silkeborg

SILKEBORG has little history of its own – it was still a small village in 1845 when the local river was harnessed to power a paper mill that brought a measure of growth and prosperity, something you can learn more about at the new **Paper Museum Bikuben**, Papirfabrikken 78 (May–Aug daily noon–5pm; 20kr; ⦿www .papirmuseet.dk) housed in the old paper mill. In 1938, the discovery of a well-preserved body of an Iron Age woman 15km west of Silkeborg added greatly to the appeal of the town's **Silkeborg Museum**, Hovedgårdsvej 7 (May to mid-Oct daily 10am–5pm; mid-Oct to April Sat & Sun noon–4pm; 40kr; ⦿www.silkeborg museum.dk). As preserved bodies go, however, the so-called **Elling Girl** has been overshadowed since 1952 by the discovery of the **Tollund Man**, a corpse of similar vintage also on display at the museum. Gruesome as it may sound, the man's head is in particularly good condition, with stubble still visible on the chin.

An equally worthwhile call is to see the excellent collection of abstract works by Asger Jorn and others in the **Museum of Art**, Gudenå 7 (April–Oct Tues–Sun 10am–5pm; Nov–March Tues–Fri noon–4pm, Sat & Sun 10am–5pm; 40kr; ⦿www .silkeborgkunstmuseum.dk). It was to Silkeborg that Jorn, Denmark's leading modern painter and founder member of the influential CoBrA (Copenhagen-Brussels-Amsterdam) group, came to recuperate from tuberculosis. From the 1950s until his death in 1973, Jorn donated an enormous amount of his own and other artists' work to the town, which displays them proudly in this purpose-built museum.

For something less cultural, the **Aqua** freshwater aquarium (mid-June to mid-Aug daily 10am–6pm; mid-Aug to mid-June Mon–Fri 10am–4pm, Sat & Sun 10am–5pm; 75kr; ⦿www.aqua-ferskvandsakvarium.dk), set in the beautiful old tuberculosis sanatorium at Vejlsøvej 55 on the southern edge of town, has a variety of freshwater fish alongside numerous water birds and mammals, including some cute otters. You can get here by taking the *Hjejle* steamer (4–6 trips daily; 110kr return), the world's oldest coal burning paddle steamer, from the Silkeborg Museum. After the aquarium, the steamer carries on along the Gudenåen river to the foot of **Himmelbjerget** ("Sky Mountain"), one of Denmark's tallest hills; from here the trek to the top takes about thirty minutes, and your reward is magnificent views of the surrounding area.

Practicalities

The helpful **tourist office**, by the harbour at Åhavevej 2A (April to mid-June and Sept–Oct Mon–Fri 9am–4pm, Sat 10am–1pm; mid-June to Aug Mon–Fri 9am–5pm, Sat & Sun 9am–2pm; Nov–March Mon–Fri 10am–3pm, Sat 10am–1pm; ⦿86 82 19 11, ⦿www.silkeborg.com), has a lengthy list of affordable private **accommodation** in what's a surprisingly expensive town; they charge a meagre 10kr booking fee per room. Hotel options include the old and atmospheric *Dania*, on Torvet (⦿86 82 01 11, ⦿www.hoteldania.dk; ⑥), a central hotel with en-suite rooms, offering reduced rates at weekends. There are many cheaper *kros* in the outlying countryside, such as *Signesminde Kro* at Viborgvej 145 (⦿86 85 54 43; ④), reached by bus #60 and town buses #31 and #32 from the railway station; and *Svostrup Kro* (⦿86 87 70 04, ⦿www.svostrup-kro.dk; ⑤), 8km distant off the road to Randers next to the Gudenå River. Budget accommodation is limited to the **youth hostel**, Åhavevej 55 (⦿86 82 36 42, ⦿www.danhostel.dk/silkeborg), which has dorms (120kr) and affordable triples and quads, though no doubles; and several

campsites: *Gudenåens Camping* (☎86 82 22 01, ⊛www.gudenaaenscamping.dk), to the south on Vejlsøvej, and *Silkeborg Sø Camping* (☎86 82 28 24, ⊛www.seacamp .dk), on the Århus road, are closest to town. To get to the former, walk about 2km from the main square down Christian VIII Vej and turn left onto Marienlundsvej; for the latter, begin at the square and head down Østergade, through two traffic lights to Århusbakken (also known as Århusvej). The tourist office organizes **canoe package trips** starting at 1150kr per canoe for three days, which include canoe and tent hire as well as campsite fees along the way. If you want to go it alone, many of the campsites rent out canoes, or try Sluskioskens Kanoudlejning (☎86 80 08 93; 300kr per day, 1650kr per week) at the harbour.

Viborg

For many years **VIBORG** was one of the most important communities in the country, at the junction of all the major roads across Jutland. From Knud in 1027 to Christian V in 1655, every Danish king was crowned here; Hans Tausen's Lutheran preaching began in Viborg in 1528, eight years before Denmark's official conversion from Catholicism; and until the early nineteenth century the town was the seat of a provincial assembly. As the national administrative axis shifted towards Zealand, however, Viborg's importance waned, and although it's still home to the high court of West Denmark, it's now primarily a market town.

Viborg is cut in half by a lake, which is spanned by the Randersvej bridge. Its centre is concentrated in a small area, though, and most parts of the old town are within a few minutes' walk of each other. The twin towers of the **Domkirke** (June–Aug Mon–Sat 10am–5pm, Sun noon–5pm; April, May & Sept Mon–Sat 11am–4pm, Sun noon–4pm; Oct–March Mon–Sat 11am–3pm, Sun noon–3pm) are the town's most visible feature and the most compelling reminder of its former glories. Begun by Bishop Eskil in 1130, the original cathedral was destroyed by fire in 1726 and rebuilt in the Baroque style by one Claus Stallknecht, though so badly that it had to be closed for two years and the work begun again. The interior is now dominated by the brilliant frescoes of Joakim Skovgaard, an artist commemorated by the **Skovgaard Museum** (daily: May–Sept 10am–12.30pm & 1.30–5pm; Oct–April 1.30–5pm; 20kr; ⊛www.skovgaardmuseet.dk) inside the former Rådhus across Gammel Torv from the cathedral – a neat building with which Claus Stallknecht made amends for his botched job of the cathedral. There's a good selection of Skovgaard's paintings on display – although they're a little anticlimactic after his splendid work in the cathedral – plus some works by other members of his family.

Two minutes' walk away on Store St Mikkelsgade, the late-Romanesque **Sortebrødre Kirke** is all that remains of the cloisters of the Dominican Black Friars, one of four monastic orders in Viborg abolished during the Reformation; you'll need to get the key from the sacristan office next door to get in. Inside the church, the sixteenth-century Belgian altarpiece is the star turn, with 89 gilded oak figures in high relief around the central Crucifixion scene.

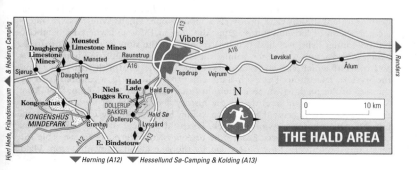

THE HALD AREA

For a broader perspective of Viborg's past, keep an hour spare for exploring the **District Museum** (*Stiftsmuseum*; mid-June to Aug daily 11am–5pm; Sept to mid-June Tues–Fri 1–4pm, Sat & Sun 11am–5pm; 25kr; ☻www.viborgstiftsmuseum .dk), on the northern side of Hjultorvet between Vestergade and Skt Hans Gade. The three well-stocked floors hold everything from prehistoric and archeological artefacts to clothes, furniture and household appliances.

Practicalities

Trains and **long-distance buses** arrive at their respective stations on Viborg's western side, roughly 1km from the centre. The **tourist office** is close to the cathedral, at Nytorv 9 (mid-May to mid-June Mon–Fri 9am–5pm, Sat 9.30am–12.30pm; mid-June to Aug Mon–Fri 9am–5pm, Sat 9am–2pm; Sept to mid-May Mon–Fri 9am–4pm, Sat 9.30am–12.30pm; ☎87 25 30 75, ☻www.visitviborg.dk). All Viborg's **hotels** are fairly pricey – best bets are the handsome *Palads*, Skt Mathias Gade 5 (☎86 62 37 00, ☻www.hotelpalads.dk; **⑤**); if a lake view appeals, try the even more expensive *Golf Hotel Viborg*, Randersvej 2 (☎86 61 02 22, ☻www.golf-hotel-viborg .dk; **⑤/⑥**). Also close to the lake, but on the opposite side to the town centre (a 2km walk or local bus #707), is the *Viborg Vandrerhjem* **youth hostel**, Vinkelvej 36 (☎86 67 17 81, ☻www.danhostel.dk/viborg), which has dorms (120kr) and some doubles (**②**); and the *Viborg Sø* **campsite** (☎86 67 13 11, ☻www.camping-viborg .dk). Contact the tourist office about private rooms in and around Viborg, which start at about 130kr per person.

During the day, you could do worse than pick up some *smørrebrød* (the best outlet is the Stjerneskuddet deli at Jernbanegade 14), and **eat** alfresco in one of the numerous parks or on the banks of the lake. Plenty of reasonably priced eating places can also be found along Skt Mathias Gade; try the popular *Jens Messing* at no. 48 (closed Sun), which offers simple meals starting at 55kr. *Café Morville*, Hjultorvet 2, is a fancy French/Italian inspired café-restaurant with DJ's enhancing the mood at night. Choices range between a cup of coffee or cool beer to mouthwatering steaks with new potatoes and veg (169kr). A little further out, *Medborgerhuset*, Vesterbrogade 13, serves a 45kr *dagens ret* (daily special, including a vegetarian option) from noon to 8pm on weekdays (Fri until 5pm), as well as *smørrebrød*, sandwiches and inexpensive coffee and cakes. The cellar restaurant ✻ *Brygger Bauers Grotter*, Skt Mathias Gade 61 (☎86 61 44 88, closed Sun), is a atmospheric spot for a candlelit dinner, although you'll find lower prices and a livelier atmosphere at the Mexican restaurant *Tortilla Flats* on Skt Mikkelsgade 2 (closed Mon). For quality steak, try the small and expensive *Den Gyldne Okse* (☎86 62 27 44) on Store Skt Peder Stræde 11, with meals from around 100kr.

Around Viborg

The area **around Viborg** is excellent for cycling, with plenty of pleasant spots within easy reach; there's also a decent local bus service. Leaving Viborg, heading south on Koldingvej and turning west towards Herning brings you to **Hald**, a beautiful area of soft hills and meadows on the shores of **Hald Sø**. For all its peace, though, the district's history is a violent one. This is where Niels Bugge led a rebellion of Jutland squires against the king in 1351, and where the Catholic bishop, Jorgen Friis, was besieged by Viborgers at the time of the Reformation. Much of the action took place around the manor houses that stood here, the sites and ruins of which can be reached by following the **footpath** that runs along the western lake shore. The path starts close to **Hald Lade**, a restored barn by the side of the road, where an exhibition (June–Aug daily noon–6pm; Sept–May Sat & Sun noon–6pm; free) details the history and geology of the area, and the more recent battle against the pollution killing Hald Sø. All the text is in Danish, but the many photos are worth a peek. This is also where the hilly lakeside area of **Dollerup Bakker** starts. From June to August rowing boats are available for rent from the historic *Niels Bugges Kro*, by the lakeside just downhill from Hald

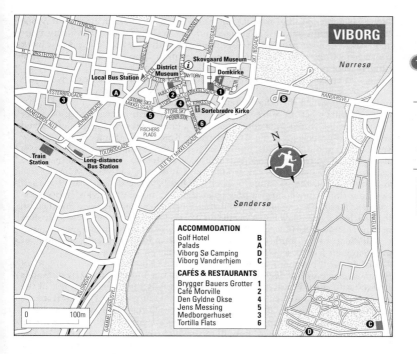

ACCOMMODATION

Golf Hotel	B
Palads	A
Viborg Sø Camping	D
Viborg Vandrerhjem	C

CAFÉS & RESTAURANTS

Brygger Bauers Grotter	1
Café Morville	2
Den Gyldne Okse	4
Jens Messing	5
Medborgerhuset	3
Tortilla Flats	6

Lade, which also does good meals and has four comfortable **rooms** (☎86 63 80 11, ⊛www.niels-bugges-kro.dk; ❺). Just to the south of here, a road leads from the village of Dollerup to **LYSGÅRD**, home to **E. Bindstouw** (June–Aug Tues–Sun 10am–5pm; 25kr), the old school house where **Steen Steensen Blicher** recorded his famous stories. Blicher would sit here in the evenings while poor locals wove socks beside the stove and told folk tales, which Blicher noted down for posterity. The small building still contains the fixtures and fittings of Blicher's time, including his writing board, stove, and even a few socks. To get here from Viborg, take the #54 bus from the local bus station.

West of Viborg

About 9km west of Viborg, beside the A16 between Mønsted and Raunstrup, the **Jutland Stone** marks the precise geographical centre of Jutland. There's not much to see, just a big inscribed rock and lots of cigarette ends. A few kilometres further, and markedly more interesting, are the **Mønsted Limestone Mines** (April–Oct daily 10am–5pm; 50kr; ⊛www.monsted-kalkgruber.dk), which wind underground for 60km. The mines stay at a constant temperature, regardless of external weather, and wandering around their cool, damp innards can be magically atmospheric, although a century ago conditions for the workers here were so horrific that when Frederik IV visited the place he was sufficiently appalled to bring about reforms – the mines were subsequently known as "Frederik's Quarries" or, more venom-ously, "The King's Graves". The site closes in winter, when the mines are taken over by an enormous colony of hibernating bats. Bus #28 from Viborg runs here.

A few kilometres further west near Daugbjerg (and also served by bus #28) is another set of **limestone mines** (daily: June 10am–4pm; July to mid-Aug 10am–6pm; mid-Aug to Oct & end March to May 11am–4pm; 45kr;

ⓦwww.daugbjerg-kalkgruber.dk), unlit and much narrower than those at Møn-sted, and therefore quite spooky. The entrance was found by chance fifty years ago and no one has yet charted the full extent of the passages; it's said that work began here at the time of Gorm, the tenth-century King of Jutland, and that the tunnels were used as hideouts by bandits.

A few kilometres south of Daugbjerg is **Kongenshus Mindepark** (early May to mid-Sept daily 10am–6pm; 12kr, 30kr for cars) – three thousand acres of protected moorland on which there have been attempts at agriculture since the mid-eight-eenth century, when an officer from Mecklenburg began keeping sheep here. For his troubles, the would-be shepherd received a grant from the king, Frederik V, and built the house that gives the park its name: Kongenshus (King's House). A few years later, a thousand or so German migrants (the so-called "potato Germans") also tried to cultivate the area, but to little avail. In the centre of the park is a memorial to the early pioneers; standing here, as the wind howls in your ears and you look around the stark and inhospitable heath, you can only marvel at their determination. Kongenshus has now opened up as a **hotel** (ⓣ97 54 81 25; ⓦwww .kongenshus.dk; ❸, en-suite ❹) and the delightful restaurant does fine Danish food such as a *smørrebrød* lunch platter for 135kr. There are also several **campsites** nearby: *Hessellund Sø-Camping* (ⓣ97 10 16 04, ⓦwww.hessellund-camping.dk; April to mid-Sept) to the south near Karup, and *Haderup* (ⓣ97 45 21 88; mid-May to mid-Sept), off Jens Jensenvej to the west, are the closest and best.

Further west beyond Daugbjerg, and about 30km from Viborg, is one of the most successful of Denmark's heritage tourism projects, the **Hjerl Hedes Frilandsmuseum** (April–Oct daily 10am–5pm; July 80kr, Aug 70kr, rest of the year 50kr; ⓦwww.hjerlhede.dk). This open-air museum attempts to re-create the development of a local village from the years 1500 to 1900, with examples of a forge, an inn, a school, mills, a vicarage, a dairy, a grocer's shop and farms, all relocated from their original sites around Jutland. By far the best time to come is during summer (mid-June to mid-Aug), when the place is brought to life by a hundred or so men, women and children dressed in traditional costumes, who provide demonstrations of the old crafts and farming methods. To get here from Viborg, take the train to Vinderup (5–10 daily; 35min), from where it's an eight-kilometre walk or taxi ride.

Northwest Jutland: Limfjordslandet and around

Limfjordslandet is the name given to the area around the western portion of the **Limfjorden**, the body of water that separates northern Jutland from the rest of the peninsula. In the northwestern half, both the North Sea coast and the shore of the Limfjorden itself – which here resembles a large inland lake – attract legions of holidaying northern Europeans during the summer months, at which time it's best to arrange accommodation in advance. At other times this is a rarely visited quarter of the country. There are fine beaches and plenty of opportunities to mess about in boats – and to catch them to Norway and beyond – and a number of small, neat old towns with a smattering of mildly diverting museums. But the weather here is unpredictable, with sharp winds blustering in off the North Sea, and getting around is difficult: trains only reach to the fringes, so you'll need to rely on buses if you're without your own transport.

For a quick taste of the area, take the train from Viborg and change at Struer for the short journey south to **HOLSTEBRO**, the largest town in the region, with an easy-going atmosphere and a small, walkable centre. There's a commendable **Art Museum** (July–Aug Tues–Sun 11am–5pm; Sept–June Tues–Fri noon–4pm, Sat & Sun 11am–5pm; 40kr, includes entry to Holstebro Museum; ⓦwww.holstebrokunst museum.dk) in the town park, with a strong contemporary Danish collection and some quality international pieces, including works by Matisse and Picasso. In the same building, the **Holstebro Museum** (same hours; 40kr, includes entry to the Art Museum; ®www.holstebro-museum.dk) has a fair local history collection. The **tourist office** at Slotsgade 2 (Mon–Fri 9.30am–5pm, Sat 10am–noon; ☎97 42 57 00; ®www.holstebro-tourist.dk) can supply information on travelling deeper into Limfjordslandet. For staying overnight, there's a **campsite** equipped with cabins and canoes at Birkevej 25 (☎97 42 20 68, ®www.mejdal.dk; April–Sept). The cheapest **hotel** by far, and most unusual, is the *Borbjerg Mølle Kro*, Borgbjerg Møllevej 3 (☎97 46 10 10, ®www.borbjergmill.dk; ❺), 12km northeast of town towards Hjerl Hede. Apart from the ordinary hotel rooms, it also has octagonal African-style reed huts and tents on offer.

Also reachable from Struer, **THISTED**, at the end of the local rail line, has access to good beaches and a youth hostel (☎97 92 50 42, ®www.danhostelnord .dk/thisted) with dorms (110kr) and doubles (❷), as well as a campsite at Iversensvej 3 (☎97 92 16 35, ®www.thisted-camping.dk; April–Oct), but little else of interest beyond its link (by bus #23, 40min) to **HANSTHOLM**, from where ferries leave for Egersund and Bergen in Norway. While waiting for the ferry, head over to the quaint *Basses Kro*, in the centre at Vestergade 28A, a perfect place for a Danish meal or a glass of the fine Thy Pilsner, brewed in Thisted and one of the country's best lagers.

Northeast Jutland

Much easier to get to and travel around than Limfjordslandet, **northeastern Jutland** is nonetheless another portion of Denmark often ignored by foreigners. This is a shame, as the region has a highly convivial major city in **Aalborg**, as well as ferries to Sweden and Norway departing from **Frederikshavn**. What's more, once you cross the Limfjorden, the northeast boasts a landscape wilder than anywhere else on the peninsula: lush green pastures giving way to strangely compelling views of bleak moorland and windswept dunes. The highlight here is **Skagen**, a uniquely atmospheric place whose unusual natural light has long attracted artists.

Aalborg

Hugging the south bank of the Limfjorden, **AALBORG** is the obvious place to spend a night or two before venturing into the wilder countryside further on. The country's fourth largest city and the main transport terminus for northern Jutland, it boasts a notable modern art museum, a well-preserved old section, and the brightest nightlife for miles around.

The profits from the seventeenth-century herring boom briefly made Aalborg the biggest and wealthiest Danish town outside Copenhagen, and much of what remains of **old Aalborg** – chiefly the area within Østerågade (commonly abbreviated to Østerå), Bispensgade, Gravensgade and Algade – dates from that era, standing in stark contrast to the new roads that slice through it to accommodate the traffic using the Limfjorden bridge.

Information and accommodation

The **tourist office** is centrally placed at Østerågade 8 (mid- to end-June & Aug Mon–Fri 9am–5.30pm, Sat 10am–1pm; July Mon–Fri 9am–5.30pm, Sat 10am–4pm; Sept to mid-June Mon–Fri 9am–4.30pm, Sat 10am–1pm; ☎99 30 60 90, ®www.visitaalborg.com).

Some years ago, it was officially decreed that the Danish double "Aa" would be written as "Å". The mayor of Aalborg, and many locals, resisted this change and eventually forced a return to the previous spelling of their city's name – though you may still see some maps and a few road signs using the "Å" form.

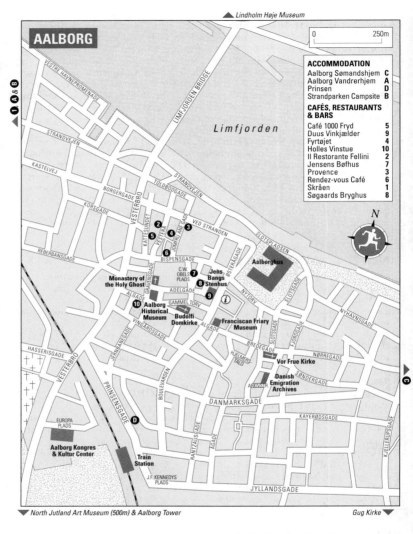

▲ Lindholm Høje Museum

AALBORG

0 _____ 250m

ACCOMMODATION
Aalborg Sømandshjem	C
Aalborg Vandrerhjem	A
Prinsen	D
Strandparken Campsite	B

CAFÉS, RESTAURANTS & BARS
Café 1000 Fryd	5
Duus Vinkjælder	9
Fyrtøjet	4
Holles Vinstue	10
Il Restorante Fellini	2
Jensens Bøfhus	7
Provence	3
Rendez-vous Café	6
Skråen	1
Søgaards Bryghus	8

Limfjorden

▼ North Jutland Art Museum (500m) & Aalborg Tower   Gug Kirke ▼

If you want **to stay** in Aalborg, be aware that bargain-priced hotels are hard to find. The tourist office has a list of private rooms in the Aalborg area that all go for a fixed rate of 325kr per night (plus a 25kr fee if you want the tourist office to make the booking). For a little more adventure, catch the half-hourly **ferry** (☎98 11 78 23; 6.30am–11.15pm; 14kr) from near the campsite (bus #13 from the centre) to Egholm, an island in Limfjord, where there's free camping under open-sided shelters.

Accommodation

Aalborg Sømandshjem Østerbro 27 ☎98 12 19 00, ⊛www.hotel-aalborg.com. This family-oriented former seaman's home is now among the city's cheapest year-round options. Its rather plain-looking, but the rooms are fully modernized and clean. 600m east of the centre, or take bus #11, #14, #17 or #19. ⑤

Aalborg Vandrerhjem Skydebanevej 50 ☎98 11 60 44, ⓦwww.bbbb.dk. Large youth hostel to the west of the town, beside the marina on the bank of the Limfjorden, which has dorms (120kr), doubles (❸) and rustic cabins sleeping up to five (520–600kr). Take bus #16 from the centre to Skydebanevej, from where it's a ten-minute walk.

Krogen Skibstedvej 4 ☎98 12 17 05, ⓦwww .krogen.dk. Homely place, some 2km west of the city centre, with a large leafy garden; some rooms have shared facilities. Buses #15 and #38 run

closest to the hotel; get off at Constancevej and continue along it for five minutes. ❹, en-suite ❺

Prinsen Prinsensgade 14–16 ☎98 13 37 33, ⓦwww.prinsen-hotel.dk. Comfortable, newly refurbished hotel across from the train station, with a range of rooms of different shapes and size, a cosy in-house bar and free parking. They also offer reduced rates for the fitness centre across the street. ❺

Strandparken Skydebanevej 20 ☎98 12 76 29, ⓦwww.strandparken.dk. Appealing campsite, about 300m from the youth hostel. Open mid-April to mid-Sept.

The Old Town

The tourist office on Østerågade is as good a place as any to start exploring, with one of the town's major seventeenth-century structures standing directly opposite. The **Jens Bangs Stenhus** is a grandiose five storeys of Dutch Renaissance style and, incredibly, has functioned as a pharmacy ever since it was built. Jens Bang himself was Aalborg's wealthiest merchant but was not popular with the governing elite, who conspired to keep him off the local council. The host of goblin-like figures carved on the walls allegedly represent the councillors of the time, while another figure, said to be Bang himself, pokes out his tongue towards the former Rådhus, next door, the predecessor to the present eighteenth-century building further down Østerågade.

The commercial roots of the city are further evidenced within **Budolfi Domkirke** (May–Sept Mon–Fri 9am–4pm, Sat 9am–2pm; Oct–April Mon–Fri 9am–3pm, Sat 9am–noon), just a few steps behind the Jens Bangs Stenhus and easily located by its bulbous spire. Inside, there's a list (rather than the more customary portraits of nobles) of the town's merchants during the 1660s. A small but elegant specimen of sixteenth-century Gothic, the cathedral itself is built on the site of an eleventh-century wooden church; only a few tombs from the original remain, embedded in the walls close to the altar. Apart from these, there's little to see inside, but plenty to hear when the electronically driven bells ring out each hour – sending a cacophonous racket across the old square of **Gammel Torv**, on which the cathedral stands.

After viewing the cathedral, drop into the **Aalborg Historical Museum**, across the square at Algade 48 (Tues–Sun 10am–5pm; 20kr; ⓦwww.aahm.dk). The first exhibit here is a dramatic one: the peat-preserved skeleton of a 40-year-old woman who died around 400 AD. In comparison, the rest of the prehistoric section is fairly routine; make instead for the local collections, which provide a good record of Aalborg's early prosperity. The museum also has an impressive glasswork collection, illustrating different designs from various Danish glass-working centres – look out for the armadillo-shaped bottle.

Just off Adelgade is the fifteenth-century **Monastery of the Holy Ghost** (*Helligåndsklostret*). Much of the building now serves as a senior citizens' home, and the remainder can be seen only on one of the guided tours which run during the summer (check details at the tourist office, as timings change frequently; 40kr). These take in the refectory, largely unchanged since the monks were thrown out in 1536, and the small Friar's Room, the only part of the monastery into which nuns (from the adjoining nunnery) were permitted entry. Indeed, this was one of the few monasteries where monks and nuns were allowed any contact at all, a fact which accounts for the reported hauntings of the Friar's Room – reputedly by the ghost of a nun who got too friendly with a monk, and as punishment was buried alive in a basement column (the monk was beheaded). Most interesting, however, are the **frescoes** of various biblical characters – dramatically posed images of Jesus,

Samson, Mary and St John the Baptist amongst others – that cover the entire ceiling of the chapel. In more recent times, the corridor outside the chapel was used for shooting practice by the so-called "Churchill Gang", a group of local schoolboys who organized Denmark's first resistance group against the Nazis.

The rest of old Aalborg lies to the east across Østerågade, and is a mainly residential area – with just a few exceptions. The sixteenth-century **Aalborghus** (grounds daily 8am–9pm; free) is technically a castle but looks much more like a country manor house, and has always had an administrative rather than a military function. Aside from the grounds, which make a scenic spot for a picnic and for the free theatrical productions staged here in summer, the castle is mainly worth visiting for the severely gloomy **dungeon** (May–Oct Mon–Fri 8am–3pm; free), to the right from the gateway, and the **underground passageways** (daily 8am–9pm; free) that run off it. From the castle, Slotsgade leads to the maze of narrow streets around **Vor Frue Kirke** (Mon–Fri 9am–2pm, Sat 9am–noon; ✺www.vorfrue.dk) a somewhat dull church that's surrounded by some meticulously preserved houses, many of which have been turned into upmarket craft shops. The best are along the oddly L-shaped Hjelmerstald: notice no. 2, whose ungainly bulge around its midriff has earned it the nickname "the pregnant house".

If you're of Danish descent, or particularly interested in Danish social history, visit the **Danish Emigration Archives**, nearby at Arkivstræde 1 (Mon–Thurs 9am–4pm, Fri 9am–2pm, plus until 8pm Mon May–Sept; ✺www.emiarch.dk). The story of Danish migration overseas is recorded through immense stacks of files and books; given enough background facts, details of individual migrants can be traced.

Also east of Østerågade, just past the Budolfi Domkirke on Algade 19, is the new **Franciscan Friary Museum** (Tues–Sun 10am–5pm; ✺www.aahm.dk). Set below ground, it's entered by way of an elevator which takes loads of up to 250kg down to the absorbing exhibit; insert 20kr into the machine. The remains of the Friary were discovered during archaeological excavations in the 1990s, and the foundations and walls that were unearthed, alongside skeletons from nearby graveyards, form the bulk of the display. Models, placards and information panels give an excellent introduction to Aalborg in the Viking and Middle Ages.

Outside the old centre

The old centre sets the pleasant tone of the city, but just outside it are a couple of other notable targets. One is the **North Jutland Art Museum** (Tues–Sun 10am–5pm; 40kr, Dec free; ✺www.nordjyllandskunstmuseum.dk), south from the centre on Kong Christians Allé, close to the junction with Vesterbro (bus #15 or a 15min walk from the centre). Housed in a building designed by the Finnish architect Alvar Aalto, this is one of the country's better modern art collections, strikingly contemporary in both form and content. Alongside numerous Danish contributions, it features works by Max Ernst, Andy Warhol, Le Corbusier and, imposingly stationed next to the entrance, Claes Oldenburg's wonderful *Fag-ends in a Colossal Ashtray*. After leaving the museum, you can get a Danish pastry and coffee plus a grand view over the city and the Limfjorden by ascending the **Aalborg Tower** (July daily 10am–7pm; April–June, Aug & mid- to late Oct daily 11am–5pm; 25kr), on the hill just behind.

From the tower, you may, on a very clear day, be able to spot what looks like a set of large concrete bunkers on a hill to the southeast of the city. This is the **Gug Kirke** (Mon–Fri 9am–4pm; ✺www.gugkirke.dk), designed by Inger and Johannes Exner and completed in the early 1970s. It's one of the most unusual churches in the country: except for the iron crucifix and the wooden bell tower, the whole thing, including the font, pulpit and altar (decorated by a collage of newspapers) is made of concrete. The idea was to blend the church into the mostly high-rise parish it serves, and for it to function also as a community centre: the perfectly square interior can be turned into a theatre, while the crypt doubles as a café and youth club. It's unique enough to merit a closer look; take bus #13 from the city centre.

Eating, drinking and nightlife

In pursuit of **food**, **drink** and most especially **nightlife**, almost everybody heads for Jomfru Ane Gade, a small street close to the harbour between Bispensgade and Borgergade. Jomfru Ane (literally "young maiden Anne") was a noblewoman and reputed witch who, because of her social standing, was beheaded rather than burnt at the stake – though the street nowadays, at least by night, is more synonymous with getting legless than headless. *Aalborg Kongres & Kultur Center*, Europa Plads 4 (☎99 35 55 65, ✪www.akkc.dk), is the city's theatre and concert venue. At the opposite end of the scale, several of the Jomfru Ane Gade bars host more lowbrow live acts; just walk along, listen, and decide which appeals.

Restaurants

Fyrtøjet Jomfru Ane Gade 17. Of the many restaurants along Jomfru Ane Gade, this enduring place is the most reliable, with traditional steak-and-two-veg lunches starting at 55kr.

Holles Vinstue Algade 57. The city's best *smørrebrød*, as well as filling traditional Danish meals, starting at 45kr.

Il Restorante Fellini Vesterå 13. Good-value pizzas and pastas.

Jensens Bøfhus C.W. Obels Plads 9. The usual steaks and salads, served up in a half-timbered merchants' house dating from 1585.

Provence Ved Stranden 11 ☎98 13 51 33. Around the corner from Jomfru Ane Gade, the tightly packed tables at this cosy French restaurant overlook the Limfjorden. Book ahead.

Søgaards Bryghus Obels Plads 1A. Excellent new combination of microbrewery, restaurant and butcher's shop, which does steaks (from 188kr) and homemade beer; you can also stock up on cold cuts for the picnic basket.

Cafés and bars

Café 1000 Fryd Kattesundet 10 ☎98 13 22 21, ✪www.1000fryd.dk. Popular music venue hosting alternative-type international acts.

Duus Vinkjælder Østerågade 9. This atmospheric wine bar in the cellar of the Jens Bangs Stenhus is the perfect place for a quiet evening drink. Closed Sun.

Rendez-vous Café Jomfru Ane Gade 5. A café-cum-bar and nightclub with live music on Saturdays; as well as cocktails, there's brunch, sandwiches and coffee on offer.

Skråen Strandvejen 19 ☎98 12 21 89, ✪www.skraaen.dk. A short walk from the centre, and a good place to catch gigs by better-known Danish rock acts; there's also a decent café.

Around Aalborg: Lindholm Høje and Rebild Bakker

A few kilometres north from Aalborg across the Limfjorden, **Lindholm Høje** was a major Viking and Iron Age burial ground, and is a captivating place, especially at dawn or dusk. There are a number of very rare Viking "ship monuments" here – burial places with stones arranged in the outline of a ship – as well as more than six hundred Iron Age cremation graves. Numerous burial sites and dwellings are reconstructed in the dedicated **Lindholm Høje Museum** (April–Oct daily 10am–5pm; Nov–March Tues & Sun 11am–4pm; 30kr), which also gives an insight into life during the Viking era. From Aalborg you can get to the site by bus #2 (every 30min for most of the day), or walk there in under an hour: go over the Limfjorden bridge, along Vesterbrogade into Thistedvej, right into Viaduktvej, and straight on until Vikingvej appears to the left.

About 30km south of Aalborg is **Rebild Bakker**, a heather-covered hill close to some scattered beech woods and the dense conifers that make up Rold Skov. The area is prime hiking territory, and has been a **national park** since a group of expatriate Danes in America purchased the land and presented it to the Danish government in 1912. It's also the site of the largest American Independence Day celebration outside the US, staged every July 4, and is home to the somewhat tacky **Lincoln's Log Cabin** (daily: June noon–4.30pm; July–Aug 11am–5pm; rest of the year open only on demand; ☎98 39 14 40, ✪www.rebildfesten.dk; 15kr), a re-creation of Abraham Lincoln's log cabin, filled with mundane articles from 49 American states alongside facts about Danish migration to the US. The Americana doesn't intrude on the natural beauty of the area, however, and the park can provide a couple of relaxing days. For an insight into the tough life of loggers and the region's infamous poachers (who were also known for their prowess as fiddle players), head for the **Rebild Fiddlers, Hunting and Forestry Museum** (*Spillemands- Jagt- og Skovbrugs-Museet i Rebild*; May–Aug daily 10am–5pm, Sept daily noon–5pm, Oct–April Sun 1–5pm; 20kr). It gives an excellent introduction into the cultural history of the region and its isolation from the rest of Denmark. To get to Rebild from Aalborg, take a train to Skørping, and then bus #104 to **REBILD**, where the quaint, newly renovated **youth hostel** at Rebildvej 23 (☎98 39 13 40, ⊛www.vandrerhjem .net; May–Sept) has dorm beds (120kr) and doubles (❸); the adjacent **campsite** (☎98 39 11 10, ⊛www.dk-camp.dk/safari) has four- and six-person cabins and is open year-round.

Continue 20km south of Rebild Bakker, via bus #104 to Skørping and then the train from Aalborg, and you'll reach the town of **HOBRO**, worth visiting for the 1000-year-old **Fyrkat** (daily: June–Aug 10am–5pm; April–May & Sept–Oct 10am–4pm; 55kr; ⊛www.fyrkat.dk), a fortress said to have been built by the Viking king Harald Bluetooth. Fyrkat is a good place to get an impression of life during Bluetooth's era: houses and farms have been reconstructed, and in summer there are demonstrations of traditional Viking activities like bronze casting. Fyrkat is two kilometres' walk from the centre of Hobro, which has a **hostel** at Amerikavej 24 (☎98 52 18 47, ⊛www.danhostelnord.dk/hobro; closed mid-Dec to mid-Jan) with dorm beds (120kr) and doubles (❷).

Frederikshavn

FREDERIKSHAVN, on north Jutland's east coast, is neither pretty nor particularly interesting, and as a major ferry port it's usually full of Swedes and Norwegians taking advantage of Denmark's liberal drinking laws. There's really not much of interest, and the main reason most stop here is for the ferry docks and the small train station, from where there are regular services to Skagen. And as it's at the end of the rail route from Aalborg, Frederikshavn is virtually unavoidable if you're heading north – if you've an international sailing to meet at Hirtshals, change for the private train at Hjørring (holders of InterRail, Eurail and Scanrail passes get half-price fares). If you're not catching a boat, speed straight on to Skagen (see p.203).

There are, however, a couple of things worth seeing in Frederikshavn. If you have half an hour, visit the **Krudttårnet** (June to mid-Sept daily 10.30am–5pm; 15kr), the squat, white tower near the train station, which has maps detailing the harbour's seventeenth-century fortifications (of which the tower was a part) and a collection of weaponry, uniforms and military paraphernalia from the seventeenth to the nineteenth centuries. With more time on your hands, take the fifteen-minute ride on bus #3 to Møllehuset at the edge of the Bangsbo estate and walk on through the beautifully groomed botanic garden to the **Bangsbo-Museet** (June–Aug daily 10am–5pm; Sept–May Tues–Sun 10am–5pm; 35kr; ⊛www .bangsbo-museum.dk), set in the manor building. Here, comprehensive displays chart the development of Frederikshavn from the 1600s, alongside a slightly grotesque, but very engrossing, collection of pictures, bracelets, rings and necklaces all made of human hair. The barns and outbuildings store an assortment of maritime articles, distinguished only by the twelfth-century *Ellingåskibet*, a ship found north of Frederikshavn, plus a worthwhile exhibition covering the German occupation during World War II and the rise of the Danish resistance movement. The estate also encompasses a large deer park and rock garden (daily dawn–dusk; free) with various viewpoints and picnic spots. **Bangsbo Fort** at the northern perimeter has cannon and gun emplacements last used during World War II against British planes – thankfully the users were all bad shots. You can also experience the claustrophobic living conditions inside the bunkers (same hours as the museum; 25kr; tours at 2pm included in the price).

Practicalities

Buses and **trains** both terminate at the train station; crossing Skippergade and walking along Denmarksgade brings you to the town centre in a few minutes. Arriving **ferries** dock near Havnepladsen, also near the centre, and close to the **tourist office** at Skandiatorv 1, on the corner of Rådhus Allé and Havnepladsen (July–Aug Mon–Sat 9am–6pm, Sun 9am–2pm; Sept–June Mon–Fri 9am–4pm, Sat 11am–2pm; ☎98 42 32 66, ⓦwww.frederikshavn-tourist.dk). Staff rent out **bicycles** (60kr/315kr per day/week; book in advance) and can help with **private accommodation**, from 320kr per room per night, plus a 25kr booking fee. If you'd rather stay in a **hotel**, *Discount Logi Teglgården*, slap-bang in the centre at Teglgårdsvej 3 (☎98 42 04 44, ⓦwww.discountlogi.dk; ❸), has some rooms with private and shared bathrooms, and a communal kitchen; breakfast isn't included in the rates. Equally central, *Hotel Herman Bang*, Tordenskjoldsgade 3 (☎98 42 21 66, ⓦwww.hermanbang.dk; ❹, en-suite ❻) also houses the *City Hostel* (☎98 42 14 21, ⓦwww.city-hostel.dk; 125kr per person in five-bed rooms) upstairs. There's also a **youth hostel** with dorms (100kr) and doubles (❶) at Buhlsvej 6 (☎98 42 14 75, ⓦwww.danhostel.dk/frederikshavn), 1500m from the train station (turn right), and a **campsite**, *Nordstrand*, at Apholmenvej 40 (☎98 42 93 50, ⓦwww.nordstrand -camping.dk; April to mid-Oct); the site is 3km north of the town centre, just off Skagensvej.

Skagen and around

Forty kilometres north of Frederikshavn, **SKAGEN** perches at the very top of Jutland amid a desolate landscape of heather-topped sand dunes, its houses painted a distinctive bright yellow. Its tranquil, remote setting makes it a popular holiday destination in the summer, when hotels and restaurants are packed to the limits and prebooking accommodation is essential. Visiting outside the peak period gives you a much better chance of experiencing the area's uniqueness. Skagen can be reached by a privately operated train (Scanrail, Eurail and InterRail passholders get half-price fares), which leaves from Frederikshavn train station roughly once an hour.

The Town

Sunlight seems to gain extra brightness as it bounces off the two seas that collide off Skagen's coast, something that attracted the **Skagen artists** in the late nineteenth century. Painters Michael Ancher and Peder Severin (P.S.) Krøyer and writer Holger Drachmann arrived in the small fishing community during 1873 and 1874, and were later joined by Lauritz Tuxen, Carl Locher, Viggo Johansen, Christian Krogh and Oscar Björck. The painters often met in the bar of ⚓ *Brøndum's Hotel*, off Brøndumsvej, and the owner's stepsister, Anna, herself a skilful painter, married Michael Ancher. The grounds of the hotel now house the **Skagens Museum** (May–Sept daily 10am–5pm; Oct–April Wed–Sun 10am–3pm; 60kr; ⓦwww .skagensmuseum.dk), which contains the most comprehensive collection of these artists' work anywhere in the world. The majority of the canvases depict local scenes, capturing subtleties of colour using the area's strong natural light. Many of the works, particularly those of Michael Ancher and Krøyer, are outstanding; but it's the work of Anna Ancher, though perhaps the least technically accomplished, which often comes closest to achieving the naturalism these artists sought.

A few strides away at Markvej 2-4, the **Michael & Anna Anchers Hus** (April & Oct daily 11am–3pm; May–June & Aug–Sept daily 10am–5pm; July daily 10am–6pm; Nov–March Sat 11am–3pm; 50kr; ⓦwww.anchershus.dk) has been restored with the intention of evoking the atmosphere of their time through an assortment of squeezed tubes of paint, sketches, paintings, books, ornaments and piles of canvases. On the other side of town, less essential is **Drachmanns Hus** (June to mid-Sept daily 11am–3pm; May & mid-Sept to mid-Oct Sat & Sun 11am–3pm; 25kr; ⓦwww.drachmannshus.dk), where Holger Drachmann lived from 1902. It's ten minutes' walk from the centre at Hans Baghs Vej 21, on the junction with Skt Laurentii Vej. Inside is a large collection of Drachmann's paintings and sketchbooks, although it was for his lyrical poems – at the forefront of the early twentieth-century Danish Neo-Romantic movement – that he was best known. Such was Drachmann's cultural importance that, on his death, the major Danish newspaper *Politiken* devoted most of its front page to him; facsimiles are on display.

The arrival and subsequent success of these artists inadvertently made Skagen fashionable, and the town continues to be a popular holiday destination. But it still bears many marks of its past as a fishing community, a history that is well documented in the **Skagens By og Egnsmuseum** at P.K. Nielsensvej 8–10 (July Mon–Fri 10am–6pm, Sat & Sun 11am–4pm; March–June & Aug–Oct Mon–Fri 10am–4pm, Sat & Sun 11am–4pm; Nov–Feb Mon–Fri 11am–3pm; 30kr; @www .skagen-bymus.dk), a fifteen-minute walk south along Skt Laurentii Vej (or the much nicer Vesterbyvej) from the town centre. Built on the tall dune where townswomen would watch for their husbands returning from sea during storms, the museum examines local fishing techniques in its main displays, reinforced by photos showing millions of fish strewn along the quay before being auctioned. Among the auxiliary buildings are reconstructions of rich and poor fishermen's houses: the rich house includes a macabre guest room kept cool to facilitate the storage of bodies washed ashore from wrecks, while the poor man's dwelling makes plain the contrast in lifestyles: it possesses just two rooms to accommodate the fisherman, his wife, and fourteen children.

Around Skagen: the Buried Church and Grenen

Amid the dunes to the south of town, about twenty minutes' walk along Skt Laurentii Vej, Damstedvej and Gammel Kirkestræde, then onto a signposted footpath, is **Den Tilsandede Kirke**, the "Buried Church" (June–Aug daily 11am–5pm; 10kr). The name is misleading, however, since all that's here is the tower of a fourteenth-century church, built in what was then a minor agricultural area. From the beginning of the sixteenth century the church was assaulted by vicious sandstorms; by 1775 the congregation could only reach the building with the aid of shovels. In 1810 the nave and most of the fittings were sold, leaving just the tower as a marker to shipping – while not especially tall, its white walls and red roof are easily visible from the sea. Still under the sands are the original church floor and cemetery. Although part of the tower is open to the public, the great fascination is simply looking at the thing from outside, and appreciating the incredible severity of the storms which covered it.

Returning to Skagen, and carrying on straight through to the other side of the town (five daily Skagen Bybus buses from the station during summer, or a halfhour walk), you'll reach Batterivej and the architecturally serene **Skagen Odde Naturcenter** (daily: mid-June to mid-Aug 10am–6pm; mid-Aug to mid-June 10am–4pm; 65kr; @www.skagen-natur.dk). Designed by Danish architect Jørn Utzon – best-known for the Sydney Opera House – this exploration of natural forces is beautifully centred around the themes of sand, water, wind and light, and how these different forces interact with each other – something very evident just outside.

The forces of nature can be further appreciated at **Grenen**, at the northernmost tip of Denmark some 4km north of Skagen (reachable via hourly Skagen Bybus bus during summer). From the bus stop and car park at the end of Fyrvej, the Sandormen tractor-drawn bus (April–Oct; 15kr return) runs along the beach to the tip, though it's nicer to walk the half-kilometre. This is the actual meeting point of two seas – the **Kattegat** and **Skagerrak** – and the spectacle of their clashing waves (the seas flow in opposing directions) is a powerful draw, although only truly dramatic when the winds are strong. On the way back, spare a thought for Holger Drachmann (see p.203), a man so enchanted by the thrashing seas that he chose to be buried in a dune close to them. His tomb is signposted from the car park.

Adjacent to the car park, the **Grenen Kunstmuseum** (daily: July 10am–5pm; early to mid-Aug 10am–4pm; mid-June to end June and mid-Aug to end Aug 11am–4pm; May to mid-June 11am–3pm; 40kr; ⊛www.grenenkunstmuseum.dk) is devoted to more recent Skagen artists such as Axel and Eva Lind, with Carl Milles' elegant bronze sculpture – a preliminary work for the UN building in New York – by the main entrance.

Practicalities

Buses stop at Skagen's **train station** on Skt Laurentii Vej, which also houses the **tourist office** (July Mon–Sat 9am–6pm, Sun 10am–4pm; June & Aug Mon–Sat 9am–5pm, Sun 10am–2pm; April–May & Sept–Oct Mon–Fri 9am–4pm, Sat 10am–2pm; Nov–March Mon–Fri 10am–4pm, Sat 10am–1pm; ⊛www.skagen-tourist.dk; ☏98 44 13 77). There is **bicycle** hire next door at Skagen Cykeludlegning (☏98 44 10 70, ⊛www.skagencykeludlejning.dk) for 75kr a day.

Staying overnight in Skagen is infinitely preferable to going back to Frederik-shavn, and there are a number of options. **Private accommodation** (from 325kr upwards) can be arranged through the tourist office for a steep 75kr booking fee. All rooms are within a 3km radius of the centre and come without breakfast. The **youth hostel** at Rolighedsvej 2 (☏98 44 22 00; ⊛www.skagenvandrerhjem.dk; closed Dec to mid-Feb) has dorms (120kr) and doubles (❹), and is only a couple of minutes west of the town centre. Of the many **campsites**, most accessible are *Grenen*, on the way to Grenen along Fyrvej (☏98 44 25 46, ⊛www.grenencamping .dk; May to mid-Sept), and *Poul Eeg's* (☏98 44 14 70; May to mid-Sept), on Bat-terivej (the road to Skagen Odde Naturcenter).

There are plenty of **eating** options in Skagen – all of the hotels have restaurants, though most of them are expensive. Of independent places, it's worth splashing out for a meal at the 🍴 *Skagen Fiskerestaurant*, a red wooden shack by the harbour at Fiskehuskaj 13. Superb fish dishes are on the menu upstairs, and there are equally delicious fishy snacks to be had in the less formal quayside setting downstairs, where there's live music in the summer. For Italian food, try *Firenze* or *Toscana*, both in Havnegade and serving reasonably priced pizza and pasta dishes. For superb Danish pastries, sandwiches and fresh bread head for the *Krages* café and bakery at Skt Laurentii Vej 104.

Accommodation

Badepension Marienlund Fabriciusvej 8 ☏98 44 13 20, ⊛www.marienlund.dk. A rustic thatched cottage a short walk from the centre with a small range of different rooms; those with a bathroom cost a little more. ❺

Brøndum's Hotel Anchervej 3 ☏98 44 15 55, ⊛www.broendums-hotel.dk. Known for its artistic associations, this is by far the most atmospheric spot around; the fact that few of the rooms have their own bathrooms and all are far from luxurious keeps the price of doubles down, but book well ahead in summer. ❺, en-suite ❻

Den Gamle Skibssmedie Vestre Strandvej 28 ☏98 44 67 16, ⊛www.den-gl-skibssmedie.dk. In the old ships' smithy near the harbour, rooms here are pleasant; most share bathrooms. ❹, en-suite ❺

Foldens Hotel Skt Laurentii Vej 41 ☏98 44 11 66, ⊛www.skaw.dk/foldens-hotel. Very comfort-able en-suite rooms a stone's throw from the train station and tourist office. ❻

Skagen Sømandshjem Østre Strandvej 2 ☏98 44 25 88, ⊛www.skaw.dk/soemandshjem. Next to the harbour, this former seaman's home has a range of basic rooms, some with shared bath-rooms. The downstairs cafeteria serves up bargain meals. ❺, en-suite ❻

Travel details

Trains

Aalborg to: Århus (34 daily; 1hr 30min); Frederikshavn (hourly; 1hr 11min).

Århus to: Aalborg (34 daily; 1hr 30min); Copenhagen (38 daily; 3hr 16min); Frederikshavn (16 daily; 2hr 40min); Grenå (hourly; 1hr 12min); Randers (roughly half-hourly; 35min); Silkeborg (roughly half-hourly; 46min); Struer (hourly; 2hr); Vejle (40 daily; 45min); Viborg (hourly; 1hr 14min).

Esbjerg to: Århus (10 daily; 2hr 12min); Copenhagen (9 daily; 3hr); Fredericia (hourly; 1hr 5min); Ribe (hourly; 33min).

Fredericia to: Århus (roughly half-hourly; 1hr 5min); Vejle (roughly every 20min; 15min).

Frederikshavn to: Skagen (20 daily; 35min).

Ribe to: Tønder (hourly; 50min).

Silkeborg to: Århus (roughly half-hourly; 46min).

Skagen to: Frederikshavn (20 daily; 35min).

Struer to: Holstebro (40 daily; 15min); Thisted (10 daily; 1hr 20min); Vejle (15 daily; 1hr 50min); Viborg (roughly half-hourly; 55min).

Tønder to: Ribe (hourly; 50min).

Vejle to: Århus (40 daily; 45min); Fredericia (roughly every 20min; 15min).

Viborg to: Struer (roughly half-hourly; 55min).

Buses

Aalborg to: Copenhagen (2–5 daily; 4hr 45min–5hr).

Århus to: Copenhagen (via Ebeltoft: 1 daily; 4hr 5min; direct: 5 daily; 2hr 50min); Ebeltoft (20 daily; 1hr 17min).

Ebeltoft to: Copenhagen (3 daily; 2hr 50min); Århus (20 daily; 1hr 17min).

Fjerritslev to: Copenhagen via Hobro, Randers and Grenå (2–5 daily; 6hr 15min).

Randers to: Ebeltoft (hourly; 1hr 28min); Grenå (32 daily; 1hr 30min); Viborg (26 daily; 45min–1hr).

Silkeborg to: Århus (38 daily; 1hr 10min); Viborg (30 daily; 1hr).

Sønderborg to: Fynshav (12 daily; 25–40min).

Thisted to: Aalborg (16 daily; 1hr 40min–2hr 10min); Hanstholm (19 daily; 40min).

Viborg to: Silkeborg (30 daily; 1hr).

Ferries

Århus to: Kalundborg (3–6 daily; 2hr 40min); Odden (5 daily; 1hr 5min).

Ebeltoft to: Odden (10–15 daily, 45min).

Frederikshavn to: Vesterø Havn (2–5 daily; 1hr 30min).

Fynshav to: Bøjden (8 daily; 50min).

Grenå to: Anholt (1–2 daily; 2hr 30min).

Hov to: Sælvig (5–10 daily; 1hr 15min).

Mommark to: Søby (2–5 daily in summer; 1hr).

International trains

Fredericia to: Flensburg (15 daily; 1hr 50min).

International ferries

Esbjerg to: Harwich (3–4 weekly in summer; 18hr).

Frederikshavn to: Gothenburg (up to 8 daily in summer; 3hr 15min); Oslo (1 daily; 8hr 30min); Larvik (1–3 daily; 6hr 15min).

Grenå to: Varberg (2 daily; 4hrs).

Hanstholm to: Egersund (4–7 weekly; 7hrs); Bergen (3 weekly; 16hr 30min).

Havneby to: List (July–Aug 11 daily; rest of the year 6 daily; 50min).

Hirtshals to: Oslo (1 daily; 8hr 30min); Kristiansand (2–5 daily; 4hr 30min); Stavanger/Bergen (3–4 weekly; 9hrs).

Norway

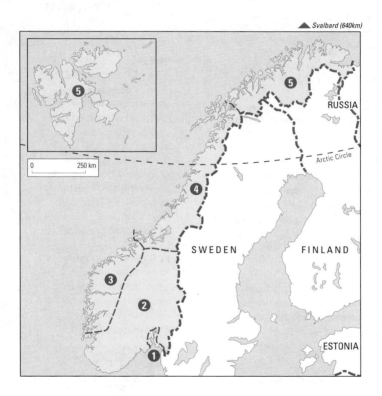

▲ Svalbard (640km)

❺

RUSSIA

0   250 km

Arctic Circle

❹

SWEDEN   FINLAND

❸

❷

ESTONIA

❶

Norway highlights

* **Oslo's Viking Ships Museum** See Viking longships at close hand in this excellent museum. See p.269

* **Oslo's Vigelandsparken** Whatever you do, don't miss this phantasmagorical open-air sculpture park. See p.272

* **Oslo's Munch Museum** A huge collection of works from Norway's finest artist. See p.274

* **Jotunheimen National Park** Craggy and severe, this mountain range is the most sumptuously beautiful example of Norway's wild mountain scenery. See p.291

* **Edvard Grieg's Troldhaugen** Norway's most celebrated composer, Grieg lived just outside Bergen and his old house makes for a delightful visit. See p.328

* **Urnes stave church** Viking carvings are seen to exquisite advantage at this country church. See p.345

* **Norangsfjord** The most immediately beautiful fjord, a serene band of blue-black water below dark and sharp ice-tipped peaks. See p.354

* **Trondheim** This easy-going, laid-back city with its stirring medieval cathedral provides a taste of urban life before the wilds of the north. See p.361

* **Å** Tiny village at the tip of the Lofoten that's hard to beat, both for its setting and its assortment of nineteenth-century buildings. See p.398

△ Puffin with fish

Introduction and basics

In many ways **Norway** is still a land of unknowns. Quiet for a thousand years since the Vikings stamped their distinctive mark on Europe, the country often seems more than just geographically distant even today. Beyond Oslo and the famous fjords, the rest of Norway might as well be blank for all many visitors know – and, in a manner of speaking, large parts of it are: vast stretches in the north and east are sparsely populated and starkly vegetated, and it is, at times, possible to travel for hours without seeing a soul.

Despite this isolation, Norway has had a pervasive influence on the world outside. Traditionally its inhabitants were explorers, from the **Vikings – the first Europeans to reach Greenland and North America** – to more recent figures like Amundsen, Nansen and Heyerdahl. And Norse traditions are common to many other isolated fishing communities, not least northwest Scotland and the Shetlands. At home, too, the Norwegian people have striven to escape the charge of national provincialism, touting the disproportionate number of acclaimed artists, writers and musicians (most notably Munch, Ibsen and Grieg) who have made their mark on the wider European scene. It's also a pleasing discovery that the great outdoors – great though it is – also harbours some lively historic towns.

Where to go

Beyond **Oslo**, one of the world's most prettily positioned capitals, the major cities of interest, in roughly descending order, are medieval **Trondheim**; **Bergen in the heart of the fjords**; hilly, southern **Stavanger**; and northern **Tromsø**. All are likeable cities, worth spending time in both for themselves and for the startlingly handsome countryside in which they're set. The perennial draw, though, is the **western fjords** – a must, and every bit as scenically stunning as they're cracked up to be. Dip into the region from

---

Norway on the Net

ⓦ**www.visitnorway.com** The official site of the Norwegian Tourist Board, with links to all things Norwegian and good sections on outdoor activities and events.

ⓦ**odin.dep.no** Government site of ODIN (Official Documentation and Information from Norway); despite the plain presentation this has everything you ever wanted to know about Norway and much more. Especially good on politics.

ⓦ**www.vandrerhjem.no** The official site of Norwegian Hostelling, providing clear and detailed information. You can make a reservation, order brochures and other publications, and there's a useful news section, too.

ⓦ**www.bike-norway.com** The best of the English-language cycling sites, with around a dozen suggested routes and lots of practical information about road conditions, traffic, cycle repair facilities and so forth.

ⓦ**www.turistforeningen.no** DNT – the Norwegian Mountain Touring Association – operates this excellent site detailing the country's most popular hiking routes, region by region. Also has comprehensive information on local affiliated hiking associations and DNT huts.

ⓦ**www.oslopro.no** Dedicated Oslo site with city listings and links.

ⓦ**www.unginfo.oslo.no** A comprehensive guide to Oslo specifically designed for young people. Strong on practical information geared to the budget traveller. In English and Norwegian.

Bergen or Åndalsnes, both accessible by direct train from Oslo, or take more time and appreciate the subtleties of the innumerable waterside towns and villages. The **south of** Norway, in particular the long southern coast with its beaches and whitewashed wooden towns, is popular with holidaying Norwegians; the central, more remote regions are ideal for hiking and camping.

To the **north**, Norway grows increasingly barren. The vast lands of **Troms** and **Finnmark** boast wild and untamed tracts of breathtaking proportions. Here you'll find the Sámi people and their herds of reindeer, which you'll see on the thin, exposed road up to the North Cape, or **Nordkapp** – (nearly) the northernmost point of mainland Europe. The Cape is the natural end to the long trek north, although there are still several hundred kilometres to be explored

further east, right the way to Kirkenes and the Russian border.

When to go

Norway is widely regarded as a remote, cold country – spectacular enough but climatically inhospitable. There is some truth in this – and winters are certainly cold, but **when to go** is not, however, as clear-cut a choice as you'd imagine. There are advantages to travelling during the long, dark **winters** with their reduced everything: daylight, opening times and transport services. If you are equipped and hardy enough to reach the far north, seeing the phenomenal **Northern Lights** (aurora borealis) is a distinct possibility; later, once the days begin to get lighter, **skiing** is excellent; while **Easter** is the time

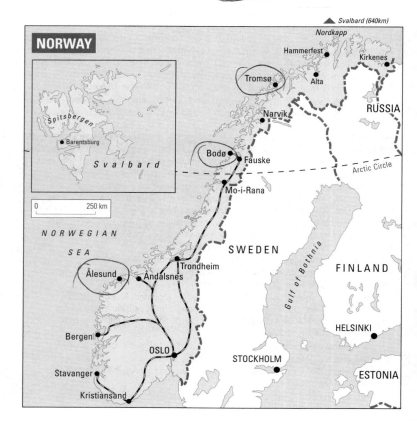

▲ Svalbard (640km)

The midnight sun

Alta: May 16–July 26
Bodø: May 30–July 12
Hammerfest: May 13–July 29
Nordkapp: May 11–July 31
Tromsø: May 18–July 26

of the colourful Sámi festivals. But – especially in the north – it is cold, often bitterly so, and this guide has been deliberately weighted towards the **summer** season, when most people travel and when it is possible to camp and hitch to keep costs down. This is the time of the Midnight Sun: the further north you go, the longer the day becomes, until at Nordkapp the sun is continually visible from mid-May to the end of July. (The box above lists the dates when the Midnight Sun is visible in different parts of the north.) Something worth noting is that the **summer season** in Norway is relatively short, stretching roughly from the beginning of June to mid-August. Come much later than 16–20 August and you'll find that tourist offices, museums and other sights cut back their hours, while buses, ferries and trains often switch to reduced schedules.

As regards **temperatures**, January and February are generally the coldest months, July and August the warmest; the Gulf Stream makes the coastal north surprisingly temperate during summer.

Getting there from the rest of Scandinavia

There's no problem in reaching Norway from the rest of **Scandinavia**. There are regular train services from Sweden, year-round ferry connections from Denmark and frequent flights from Denmark, Sweden and Finland.

By train

By train you can reach **Oslo** from both Stockholm (3 daily; 8–9hr) and Copenhagen (2–3 daily; 8hr 30min). There are also regular services from Stockholm to **Trondheim** (2 daily; 11hr) and **Narvik** (2 daily; 19hr).

InterRail, ScanRail and Eurail passes are valid – for train pass details see "Basics", p.35; for timetable details, consult RESPLUS, who bring all the international timetables together at ⓦwww.resplus.se. Note that there are no direct train services from Finland to Norway.

By bus

Two main **bus** companies provide regular daily services to Oslo from **Copenhagen**, **Gothenburg** and **Malmo**. They are Eurolines Scandinavia (ⓦ www.eurolines-travel .com) and Safflebussen (ⓦ www.saffle bussen.se). The main difference between the two is price: Safflebussen are almost always less expensive, but there again the Eurolines buses link into a much larger network of international and pan-Scandinavian bus routes; both are cheaper than the train. Safflebussen also operates a fast and frequent service from **Stockholm** to Oslo; there are no direct express buses to Norway from **Finland**, not even in the far north where the two countries share a common border.

By ferry

Of the several **car ferry** services shuttling across the Skagerrak **from Denmark** to Norway, one of the most useful is DFDS Seaways' ferry (ⓦwww.dfdsseaways.com) from Copenhagen to Oslo (1 daily; 16hr). Alternatively, Stena Line (ⓦ www.stenaline .com) links Frederikshavn with Oslo (1–2 daily; 8hr 30min–12hr), while Color Line (ⓦ www.colorline.com) ferries depart Hirtshals for Oslo (6–7 weekly; 8hr), Kristiansand (1–2 daily; 4hr 30min), and Stavanger and Bergen (3 weekly; 11hr/18hr). There's also a Color Line ferry service to Norway **from Sweden**, linking Strömstad, north of Gothenburg, with Sandefjord (2–6 daily; 2hr 30min).

Details of sailings and costs can be had via the company websites or from any major travel agent. Prices tend to rise sharply in summer, though this is partly offset by all sorts of special deals; rail-pass holders get discounts on some routes, too.

By plane

Norway has international **airports** at Oslo (Gardermoen), Bergen, Kristiansand,

Sandefjord (Torp), Stavanger, and Trondheim; most flights from elsewhere in Scandinavia are with SAS (®www.sas.no) or one of its subsidiaries, primarily Braathens (same website). Standard unrestricted tickets are very expensive, but discounts are legion, mostly with caveats about the length of stay and so forth. As examples of standard one-way fares, Stockholm to Oslo costs about 900Nkr, Copenhagen to Oslo up to 1200Nkr. SAS is also being pressured by a number of new **budget airlines**, primarily Snowflake (see p.430), Sterling (see p.330) and Norwegian Airlines (see Norwegian Air Shuttle, p.282). The latter, for example, charge as little as 400Nkr for a single fare from either Stockholm or Copenhagen to Oslo.

For details of pan-Scandinavian air discounts and deals, see "Getting around" (p.217).

Costs, money and banks

Norway has a reputation as one of the most **expensive** of European holiday destinations, and in some ways (but only some) this is entirely justified. Most of what you're likely to need – from a cup of coffee to a bottle of beer – is costly, though on the other hand certain major items are reasonably priced, most notably **accommodation**, which compared with other north European countries can be remarkably inexpensive: Norway's (usually) first-rate youth hostels, almost all of which have family, double and dormitory rooms, are particularly good value. **Getting around** is good news, too. Most travellers use some kind of rail pass, there are myriad discounts and deals, and the state subsidizes the more remote and longer bus hauls. Furthermore, **concessions** are almost universally available at attractions and on public transport, with infants (under 4) going everywhere free, children and seniors (over 67, sometimes 60) paying – on average at least – half the standard rate. **Food** is, however, a different matter. With few exceptions – such as tinned fish – it's expensive, while the cost of **alcohol** is enough to make even a heavy drinker contemplate abstinence.

Average costs, if you're prepared to buy your own picnic lunch, stay in youth hostels and stick to the less expensive cafés and restaurants, are around £30/$52 a day excluding the cost of public transport. Staying in three-star hotels, eating out in medium-range restaurants most nights (but avoiding drinking in a bar), you'll get through at least £50/$90 a day – with the main variable being the cost of your room. As always, if you're travelling alone you'll spend much more on accommodation than you would in a group of two or more: most hotels do have single rooms, but they're usually around sixty to eighty percent of the price of a double.

Currency and exchange rates

Norwegian currency consists of **kroner**, one of which, a krone (literally "crown"; abbreviated **kr** or **NOK**), is divided into 100 **øre**. Coins in circulation are 50 øre, 1kr, 5kr and 10kr; notes are for 50kr, 100kr, 200kr, 500kr and 1000kr.

At the time of writing the **exchange rate** was 11.45kr to one pound sterling; 6.50kr to one US dollar; 5.50kr to one Canadian dollar; 4.90kr to one Australian dollar; 4.55kr to one New Zealand dollar and 7.80kr to one euro.

Changing money

All but the tiniest of settlements in Norway have a **bank** or **savings bank**, and the vast majority will change foreign currency and travellers' cheques. **Banking hours** in Norway are usually Monday to Friday 8.15am–3.30pm, though they usually close thirty minutes earlier during the summer (June–Aug) and are open till 5pm, sometimes 6pm, on Thursday all year. All major **post offices** change foreign currency and travellers' cheques at rates that are competitive with those of the banks, and they have longer opening hours too, generally Monday to Friday 8am–4/5pm and Saturday 9am–1pm. Almost every bank and post office charges a small commission for changing currency and cheques; if commission is waived, it probably means you're getting a lower exchange rate instead.

Outside banking and post office hours, most major hotels, many travel agents and some hostels and campsites will change money at less generous rates and with variable commissions, as will the **exchange kiosks** to be found in Oslo. In addition, **ATMs**, from which you can withdraw local currency using a credit or debit card, are commonplace right across Norway.

Tax-free shopping

Taking advantage of their decision not to join the EU, the Norwegians run a **tax-free shopping scheme** for tourists. If you spend more than 308kr at any of the three thousand outlets in the tax-free shopping scheme, you'll get a voucher for the amount of VAT you paid. On departure at an airport, ferry terminal or frontier crossing, present the goods, the voucher and your passport and – provided you haven't used the item – you'll get an 11–18 percent refund, depending on the price of the item. There isn't a reclaim point at every exit from the country, however – pick up a leaflet at any participating shop to find out where they are – and note that many of the smaller reclaim points keep normal shop hours, closing for the weekend at 2pm on Saturday.

Mail and telecommunications

Postal and telephone systems are both very efficient in Norway, and things are made even easier by the prevalence of English-speaking staff.

Post offices are plentiful; usual opening hours are Monday to Friday

Useful numbers

International dialling code for Norway
☏0047
Directory enquiries (Scandinavia)
☏1881
Directory enquiries (international)
☏1882
Collect and reverse-call operator ☏115
Emergencies (fire) ☏110
Emergencies (police) ☏112
Emergencies (ambulance) ☏113

8/8.30am–4/5pm and Saturday 9am–1pm. Some urban post offices open longer hours. **Postage** costs are currently 5.5kr for either a postcard or a letter under 20g sent within Norway (7kr within Scandinavia, 9kr to the EU), and 10kr to countries outside. Mail to the USA takes a week to ten days, two to three days within Europe.

Domestic and international calls are easy to make from **public telephones**, which are plentiful and almost invariably work. They are of the usual Western European kind, where you deposit the money before you make your call. They take 1kr, 5kr, 10kr and 20kr coins, though the minimum charge for a call is 5kr. Most public telephones also accept **phonecards** (*TeleKorts*). These can be purchased at newsstands, Narvesen kiosks, post offices and some supermarkets, and come in a variety of denominations from 40kr to 140kr. An increasing number of public phones also accept major credit cards. Phone booths have English instructions displayed inside. Most hotel rooms have phones too, but note that they nearly always attract an exorbitant surcharge.

Domestic telephone calls **cost** a minimum of 5kr, while 10kr is enough to start an international telephone call, but not much more. Discounted rates on domestic and international calls (of around thirty percent) apply from 5pm to 8am on weekdays and all weekend. All Norwegian telephone numbers have eight digits and there's no area code.

You can access the **Internet** either at one of the country's growing number of Internet cafés (all major cities have at least a couple) or at public libraries. Library access is free, but Internet café charges vary wildly – 30kr per thirty minutes is a reasonable average. Most of Norway is on the **mobile network**, which works on the GSM 900/1800 system common across Europe.

Media

Most British and some American daily **newspapers**, plus the occasional periodical, are sold in every town and city from Narvesen kiosks, which are ubiquitous and always at train stations and airports. As for the **Norwegian media**, state advertising, loans and subsidized production costs sustain a wealth of smaller papers that would bite the dust elsewhere. Most are closely linked with political parties, although the bigger city-based titles tend to be independent. Highest circulations are claimed in Oslo by the independent *Verdens Gang* and the independent-conservative *Aftenposten*, and in Bergen by the liberal *Bergens Tidende*. There are no English-language titles.

The **television** network has expanded over the last few years, in line with the rest of Europe. Alongside the state channels, NRK1, NRK2 and TV2, there are satellite channels like TV Norge, while TV3 is a channel common to Norway, Denmark and Sweden; you can also pick up Swedish TV – though pornographic programmes are jammed. Many of the programmes are English-language imports with Norwegian subtitles, so there's invariably something on that you'll understand, though much of it is pretty unadventurous stuff. The big global cable and satellite channels like MTV and CNN are commonly accessible in hotel rooms.

Local tourist **radio**, giving details of events and festivals, is broadcast during the summer months; watch for signposts by the roadside and tune in. The BBC World Service is broadcast to all mainland Scandinavia. Frequencies vary according to area and often change every few months; visit Ⓦ www.bbc.co.uk/worldservice for updates.

Getting around

Norway's **public transport system** – a huge mesh of trains, buses, car ferries and passenger express ferries – is comprehensive and reliable. In the winter (especially in the north) services can be cut back severely, but no part of the country is unreachable for long. Bear in mind, however, that Norwegian villages and towns usually spread over a large distance, so don't be surprised if you end up walking a kilometre or two from the bus stop or train station to get where you want to go. It's this sprawling nature of the country's towns and, more especially, the remoteness of many of the sights, that encourages visitors to rent a **car**. This is a

very expensive business, but costs are manageable if you hire locally for a day or two rather than make a booking with one of the international companies for the whole trip.

Timetables for most of the principal air, train, bus and ferry services are detailed in the NRI Guide to Transport and Accommodation, a free and easy-to-use booklet available in your home country from the Norwegian Tourist Board. In Norway itself, almost every tourist office carries a comprehensive range of free local and regional public transport timetables. In addition, all major train stations carry the *NSB Togruter*, a brochure detailing Norway's principal train timetables, whilst long-distance bus routes operated by the national carrier, Nor-Way Bussekspress, are listed in the free *Rutehefte* (timetable), available at principal bus stations.

Trains

With the exception of the Narvik line into Sweden, operated by Connex (℡ 0046/771 260 000; Ⓦ www.connex.se), all Norwegian **train** services are run by the state railway company, Norges Statsbaner (NSB; ℡ 81 50 08 88, then dial 4 for English, Ⓦ www.nsb.no). Apart from a sprinkling of branch lines, NSB services operate on three main domestic routes, linking Oslo to Stavanger in the southwest, to Bergen in the west and to Trondheim and on to Bodø in the north. In places, the rail system is extended by a TogBuss (literally train-bus) service, with connecting coaches continuing on from train terminals. The nature of the country has made several of the routes engineering feats of some magnitude, worth the trip in their own right – the tiny **Flåm line** and the sweeping **Rauma line** from Dombås to Åndalsnes are exciting examples.

Prices are bearable, the popular Oslo–Bergen run, for example, costing around 700kr one-way, Oslo–Trondheim 770kr. Both journeys take around six and a half to seven hours. Costs can be reduced by purchasing a **rail pass** in advance (see p.35 & p.45) or, in the case of the Norway Rail Pass (see opposite), either in advance or within Norway, though in this case you're probably best off buying in advance too as sorting things out can be surprisingly time-consuming. Inside Norway, NSB offers a variety of **discount fares**. The main ticket scheme is the **Minipris** (mini-price), under which you can cut up to fifty percent off the price of long-distance journeys. In general, the further you travel, the more economic they become. The drawback is that Minipris tickets must be purchased at least one day in advance, are not available at peak periods and on certain trains, and stopovers are not permitted. In addition, NSB offers a variety of special deals and discounts – inquire locally (and ahead of time) for details on any specific route.

In terms of **concessionary fares**, there are group and family reductions; children under 4 travel free provided they don't take up a seat; under-16s pay half-fare and so do senior citizens (67+). It's worth noting that on many intercity trains and on all overnight and international services, an advance **seat reservation** (30kr) has to be made whether you have a rail pass or not. In high season it's wise to reserve a seat on main routes anyway, as trains can be packed. **Sleepers** are reasonably priced if you consider you'll save a night's hotel accommodation: a bed in a three-berth cabin costs around 175kr, two-berth from 270kr.

NSB have two main sorts of train – local (Lokaltog) and regional (Regiontog). There is one standard class on both, but certain regional trains have a more luxurious and spacious "Komfort" carriage, for which you pay a supplement of 75kr. NSB **timetables** are available free at every train station: there is a general timetable, the NSB Togruter, and this is supplemented by individual timetables and, in the case of the more scenic routes, by leaflets describing the sights as you go.

For further advance advice about passes, discounts and tickets, either contact NSB or the specialist agents listed in "Getting there" (p.211).

Rail passes

Both the **InterRail** and **Eurail** passes (see p.35) are valid for the Norwegian railway system, as is the **ScanRail** pass (see p.45). The other alternative is the **Norway Rail Pass**, which allows unlimited travel on the NSB railways of Norway (except the Oslo Airport Express) on a specified number of days within a specific period. Three days in one month costs 1370kr, with additional days costing 230kr each. The Norway Rail Pass can be bought from major train stations inside Norway (in theory at least) and from agents abroad (see "Basics", p.35). Children under 4 travel free, under-16s get a fifty percent discount and seniors (60-plus) twenty percent.

All rail-pass holders have to shell out a small additional surcharge on certain trains on certain routes, and also have to pay the compulsory seat reservation fee on most intercity trains and all overnight and international services. On the plus side, rail passes are good for travel on connecting Togbuss services, while two of them (ScanRail and InterRail) give a fifty-percent discount on scores of intercity bus and boat routes.

Buses

Where the train network won't take you, **buses** will – and at no great cost, either: a substantial fjord journey, like the ten-hour bus ride between Ålesund and Bergen, is a reasonable 548kr; even better, many of the long-distance express buses have a discounted maximum price – Oslo to Bergen, for instance, costs a maximum of 290k. All tolls and ferry costs are included in the price of a ticket, which can represent a significant saving. You'll need to use buses principally in the western fjords and the far north, though there are also lots of long-distance express services between major towns. Most long-distance buses are operated by the national carrier, **Nor-Way Bussekspress** (Norwegian-language info line ☎81 54 44 44, ⌨ www.nor-way.no), whose principal information office is at Oslo's main bus station. Their services are supplemented by a dense network of local buses, whose timetables are available at most tourist offices and bus stations. In general, most longer-distance routes tend to operate once or twice daily, with one bus leaving early in the morning, while shorter hauls, although more frequent, often tail off in the late afternoon. **Tickets** are usually bought on board, but bus stations and travel agents sell advance tickets on the more popular long-distance routes; be sure to keep your ticket till the journey is completed.

In terms of **concessionary fares**, there are group and family reductions, children under 3 travel free provided they don't take up a seat, youngsters under 16 pay half fare, and senior citizens over 67 get a 33 percent discount. Nor-Way Bussekspress offers InterRail and ScanRail pass holders a fifty percent reduction on certain services, and some local bus companies have comparable deals. Indeed, rail-pass and student-card holders should always ask about discounts when purchasing a ticket.

If you are going to travel much by bus, the Nor-Way Bussekspress **Nor-Way BussPass** is excellent value – 10 successive days of unlimited travel for 1300kr, 21 successive days for 2400kr. Valid on all Nor-Way Bussekspress services, the pass offers a guarantee of a seat without advance booking (except for groups of more than eight) – the idea is that if one bus gets full, they will lay on another. Again, all toll and ferry costs are covered, but not the majority of local bus services. Infants under 3 travel free; a pass for a child (4–15) is at 75 percent of the adult rate. The pass can be purchased at any of the larger bus stations in Norway, and a complimentary timetable detailing all Nor-Way Bussekspress services is included.

Ferries

Using a **ferry** is one of the highlights of any visit to Norway – indeed among the western fjords and around the Lofotens they are all but impossible to avoid. The majority are roll-on, roll-off **car ferries**. These represent an economical means of transport, with prices fixed on a nationwide sliding scale: short journeys (10–15min) cost foot passengers 18–25kr, whereas car and driver will pay 40–68kr. Ferry procedures are straightforward: foot passengers walk on and pay the conductor, car drivers usually wait in line with their vehicles on the jetty till the conductor comes to the car window to collect the money (although some busier routes have a drive-by ticket office). One or two of the longer car ferries – in particular Bodø–Moskenes – take advance reservations, but the rest operate on a first-come, first-served basis. In the off-season, there's no real need to arrive more than twenty minutes before departure – with the possible exception of the Lofoten Island ferries – but in the summer allow two hours, two and a half to be really safe.

Passenger express boats

Norway's **Hurtigbåt passenger express boats** are catamarans that make up in speed what they lack in enjoyment: unlike the ordinary ferries, you're cooped up and have to view the passing landscape through a window, and in choppy seas the ride can be disconcertingly bumpy. Nonetheless, they're a convenient time-saving option: it takes just four hours on the Hurtigbåt service from Bergen to Balestrand, for instance, the same from Narvik to Svolvær, and a mere two and a half hours from Harstad to Tromsø. Hurtigbåt services are concentrated on the west coast around Bergen and the neighbouring fjords; the majority operate all year. There's no fixed tariff table, so rates vary considerably, though Hurtigbåt boats are significantly more expensive per kilometre than car ferries – Bergen–Flåm, for instance, costs 560kr for the five and a half-hour journey, 630kr for the four-hour trip from Bergen to Stavanger. There are **concessionary fares** on all routes, with infants up to the age of 3 travelling free, and children (4–15) and senior citizens (over 67) getting a fifty percent discount. In addition, rail-pass holders and students are often eligible for a fifty percent reduction on the full adult rate.

The Hurtigrute

Norway's most celebrated ferry journey is the long and beautiful haul up the coast from Bergen to Kirkenes on the **Hurtigrute** (literally "rapid route") **coastal boat** – or "coastal steamer", in honour of its past rather than present means of locomotion. To many, the Hurtigrute remains the quintessential Norwegian experience, and it's certainly the best way to observe the drama of the country's extraordinary coastline. Fourteen ships combine to provide one daily service in each direction, and the boats stop off at over thirty ports on the way.

The whole trip lasts eleven days. **Tickets**, which include all meals, go for anything from 10,000kr to 25,000kr depending on whether you're sailing on one of the old or new vessels, where your cabin is on the boat and when you sail – departures between October and March are around forty percent cheaper than those in the summer. There are also **concessionary fares** offering fifty percent discounts for senior citizens (over 67), families, groups of ten or more, students and children (4–15). Infants up to 3 years old travel free providing they do not occupy a separate berth. Note that in the summertime these discounts are only valid for a limited number of cabins, which makes pre-booking pretty much essential. Further details are available from authorized travel agencies back home, whom you can also make bookings with – there's a list of agents on the Hurtigrute website (see below). Making a Hurtigrute booking once you've got to Norway is easy too, though some of the special deals may not be available. In Norway, the general Hurtigrute number is ☎810 30 000; the **website** is ⓦ www.hurtigruten .com. Most city and west-coast tourist offices have details of sailing schedules.

A **short or medium-sized hop** along the coast on a portion of the Hurtigrute route is also well worth considering. Fares are not particularly cheap, especially in comparison with the bus, but they are affordable. The standard, high-season, one-way passenger fare from Bergen to Trondheim (40hr), for example, costs about 1800kr; from Svolvær to Stokmarknes (3hr) 240kr. Last-minute bargains, however, can bring the rates down to amazingly low levels. All the tourist offices in the Hurtigrute ports have the latest details and should be willing to telephone the captain of the nearest ship to make a reservation on your behalf. Note that prices for shorter trips don't include meals.

As for specifics, you don't need to have a cabin, as sleeping in the lounges or on deck is allowed (though you would of course be nuts to sleep on deck in winter), and bikes travel free. There's a restaurant and a 24-hour cafeteria supplying coffee and snacks on all Hurtigrute boats; the restaurant is very popular, so book as soon as you board.

Planes

Internal flights can prove a surprisingly inexpensive way of hopping about the country, and are especially useful if you're short on time and want to reach, say, the far north: Tromsø to Kirkenes takes the best part of two days by bus, but it's just an hour by plane. Domestic air routes are serviced by several companies, but the only big player is **SAS Braathens** (ⓦ www.sas.no), a conglomerate with many (airline) subsidiaries, the most useful of which, for domestic flights, is Widerøe (ⓦ www.wideroe.no). You might also want to check out one up and coming budget airline, Norwegian Airlines (see Norwegian Air Shuttle, p.282). Regular standard fares with SAS Braathens are around 650kr one-way from Oslo to Bergen, 1000kr from Oslo to Tromsø, and 1100kr from Bergen to Trondheim. SAS/Braathens also offer all sorts of deals and discounts, especially on return fares, which often cost just ten percent more than single tickets, but these bargains usually come with restrictions, regarding, for example, advance booking and including a Saturday night away. In terms of **concessionary fares**, SAS/Braathens permit infants under 2 to travel free on most flights, while on others ten percent of the regular fare is charged. In addition, people over 65, and children under 16 travelling in a family group including at least one full-fare-paying adult, receive a 33 percent discount on most flights. The details of these various discounts vary year to year, so it's always worth checking them out.

With fares tumbling in recent years, **air passes** are much less tempting than they used to be, but SAS/Braathens do offer a reasonably economic **Visit Scandinavia AirPass** (see p.28) and **Widerøe** (ⓦ www .wideroe.no, ☎810 01 200), an SAS subsidiary, offer two competitively priced Norway-only passes – Explore Norway and Fly Norway. **Explore Norway** provides for two weeks unlimited travel between 35 Widerøe destinations during the summer (from late June to mid-August) at a cost of 3750kr; destinations include all of the country's cities. You can also opt for a southern, central or northern Norway Explore Norway pass, with travel within one area (or zone) costing 2600kr, or 3330kr for two zones; the zonal boundaries are drawn through Tromsø and Trondheim, both of which are counted in two zones – thus Tromsø is in the north as well as the central zones. Alternatively, the all-year **Fly Norway** pass offers heavily discounted fares for non-Scandinavians to all 35 Widerøe destinations. Under the scheme, there is a standard charge for any direct flight of between 470kr and 640kr, with some shorter routes costing even less.

Driving

Norway's **main roads** are excellent, especially when you consider the rigours of the climate; and nowadays, with most of the more hazardous sections either ironed out or tunnelled through, driving is comparatively straightforward. Nonetheless, you still have to be careful on some of the higher sections and in the longer, fume-filled tunnels. Once you leave the main roads for the narrow mountain byroads, however, you'll be in for some nail-biting experiences – and that's in the summertime. In winter the Norwegians close many roads and concentrate their efforts on keeping the main highways open, but obviously blizzards and ice can make driving difficult to dangerous anywhere, even with winter tyres, studs and chains. At any time of the year, the more adventurous the drive, the better equipped you need to be: on remote drives you should pack provisions, have proper hiking gear, check the car thoroughly before departure, carry a spare can of petrol and take a mobile phone.

Norway's main highways have an E prefix – E6, E18 etc; all the country's other significant roads (riksvei, or rv) are assigned a number and, as a general rule, the lower the number, the busier the road. In our guide, we've used the E prefix, but designated other roads as Highways, or "Hwy" (followed by the number). Don't be too amazed if the road number we've given is wrong – the Norwegians are forever changing the numbers.

Tolls are imposed on certain roads to pay for construction projects such as bridges and tunnels. Normally, the toll is removed once the costs are covered. The older projects levy a fee of around 20–30kr, but the toll for some of the newer works (like the tunnel near Fjaerland) runs to well over 100kr per vehicle. There's also a modest toll on entering the country's larger cities (15–20kr), but whether this is an environmental measure or a means of boosting city coffers is a moot point. To avoid getting flustered at a toll booth, Norwegians carry a supply of coins ready to hand.

Fuel is readily available, even in the north, though here the settlements are so widely separated that you'll need to keep your tank pretty full; if you're using the byroads extensively, remember to carry an extra can. Current fuel prices are 11–13kr a litre, and there are four main grades: unleaded (blyfri) 95 octane; unleaded 98 octane; super 98 octane; and diesel (the cheapest). It's worth remembering that some petrol stations don't accept credit cards, so be sure to double-check before filling up.

Documentation and rules of the road

EU **driving licences** are honoured in Norway, but other nationals will need an

---

Opening dates of major mountain passes

Obviously enough, there's no preordained date for the opening of **mountain roads** in the springtime – it depends on the weather, and the threat of avalanches is often much more of a limitation than actual snow falls. The dates below should therefore be treated with caution; if in doubt, seek advice from a local tourist office. If you do head along a mountain road that's closed, you'll sooner or later come to a barrier and have to turn round.

E6: Dovrefjell (Oslo–Trondheim). Usually open all year.

E69: Skarsvåg–Nordkapp. Closed late Oct to early April.

E134: Haukelifjell (Oslo–Bergen/Stavanger). Usually open all year.

Hwy 7: Hardangervidda (Oslo–Bergen). Usually open all year.

Hwy 51: Valdresflya. Closed Nov to early May.

Hwy 55: Sognefjellet. Closed Nov to early May.

Hwy 63: Grotli–Geiranger–Åndalsnes (Trollstigen). Closed late Oct to late May.

International Driver's Licence (available at minimum cost from your home motoring organization). No form of provisional licence is accepted. If you're bringing your own car, you must have vehicle registration papers, adequate insurance, a first-aid kit, a warning triangle and a green card (available from your insurers or motoring organization). Extra insurance coverage for unforeseen legal costs is also well worth having, as is an appropriate **breakdown policy** from a motoring organization. In Britain, for example, the RAC and AA charge members and non-members about £110 for a month's Europe-wide breakdown cover, with all the appropriate documentation, including green card, provided.

Rules of the road are strict: you drive on the right, with dipped headlights required at all times; seat belts are compulsory for drivers and front-seat passengers, and for back-seat passengers too, if fitted. There's a speed limit of 30kph in residential areas, 50kph in built-up areas, 80kph on open roads and 90kph on motorways and some other main roads. Cameras monitor hundreds of kilometres of road – watch out for the Automatisk Trafikk Kontroll warning signs – and they are far from popular with the locals: there are all sorts of folkloric (and largely apocryphal) tales of men in masks appearing at night with chain saws to chop them down. **Speeding fines** are so heavy that local drivers stick religiously within the speed limit. If you're filmed breaking the limit in a hire car, expect your credit card to be stung by the car hire company to the tune of at least 700kr. If you're stopped for speeding, large spot fines (700–3000kr) are payable; rarely is any leniency shown to unwitting foreigners. **Drunken driving** is also severely frowned upon. You can be asked to take a breath test on a routine traffic-check; if you're over the limit, you will have your licence confiscated and may face 28 days in prison.

If your **hired car** breaks down, you'll get roadside assistance from the particular repair company the car hire firm has contracted. The same principle works with your own vehicle's breakdown policy (see above). Two major **breakdown companies** in Norway are Norges Automobil-Forbund and Viking Redningstjeneste, who combine to operate a 24-hour emergency assistance line on ☎810 00 505. There are emergency telephones along some motorways, and NAF patrols on all mountain passes between mid-June and mid-August.

Car rental

All the major international **car rental** companies are represented in Norway – contact details are given in the "Listings" sections of larger cities, and in "Basics" (p.46). To rent a car, you'll need to be 21 or over (and have been driving for at least a year), and you'll need a credit card. Rental **charges** are fairly high, beginning at around 3500kr per week for unlimited mileage in the smallest vehicle, but include collision damage waiver and vehicle (but not personal) insurance. To cut costs, watch for the special deals offered locally by both large and small companies – a Friday to Monday weekend rental might, for example, cost you as little as 800kr. If you go to a smaller, local company (of which there are many, listed in the telephone directory under *Bilutleie*), you should proceed with care. In particular, check the policy for the excess applied to claims and ensure that it includes collision damage waiver (applicable if an accident is your fault). Bear in mind, too, that it's almost always cheaper to rent a car before you leave home (see p.45) and that one-way car rental **drop-off charges** are almost always wallet-searing, from 1000kr and up.

Cycling

Cycling is a great way to enjoy Norway's scenery – just be sure to wrap up warm and dry, and don't be over-ambitious in the distances you expect to cover. Cycle tracks as such are few and far between, and are mainly confined to the larger towns, but there's precious little traffic on most of the minor roads and cycling along them is a popular pastime. Furthermore, whenever a road is improved or rerouted, the old highway is usually redesigned as a cycle route. At almost every place you're likely to stay in, you can anticipate that someone will **rent bikes** – either the tourist office, a sports shop, youth hostel or campsite. Costs are pretty uniform: reckon on paying between

120kr and 200kr a day for a seven-speed bike, plus a refundable deposit of up to 1000kr; mountain bikes are about thirty percent more.

A few tourist offices have maps of recommended cycling routes, but this is a rarity. It is, however, important to check your itinerary thoroughly, especially in the more mountainous areas. Cyclists aren't allowed through the longer **tunnels** for their own protection (the fumes can be life-threatening), so discuss your plans with whoever you hire the bike from. Bikes mostly go free on car ferries and attract a nominal charge on passenger express boats, but buses vary. National carrier Nor-Way Bussekspress accepts bikes only when there is space and charges the appropriate child fare, whilst local rural buses sometimes take them free, sometimes charge and sometimes do not take them at all. There's a fee of 50–180kr to take bikes on NSB trains.

If you're planning a **cycling holiday**, your first port of call should be the Norwegian Tourist Board (see p.43), where you can get general cycling advice, a map showing roads and tunnels inaccessible to cyclists and a list of companies offering all-inclusive **cycling tours**. Obviously enough, tour costs vary enormously, but as a baseline reckon on about 5000kr per week all-inclusive. The Norwegian Cyclist Association Syklistenes Landsforening, Storgata 23D, Oslo (☎22 47 30 30, Norwegian-language only website ⊛www.slf.no) have an excellent range of specific cycling books and maps. Finally, Sykkelturisme i Norge (⊛www.bike-norway .com) has ideas for a dozen routes around the country from 100km to 400km, plus useful practical information about road conditions, repair facilities and places of interest en route.

Accommodation

Inevitably, **hotel accommodation** is one of the major expenses of a trip to Norway and indeed, if you're after a degree of comfort, it's going to be the costliest item by far. There are, however, **budget alternatives**, including private rooms, campsites and cabins, and an abundance of HI hostels.

Hotels

Almost universally, Norwegian **hotels** are of a high standard: neat, clean and efficient. Summer prices and impromptu weekend deals also make many of them, by European standards at least, comparatively economical. Another plus is that the price of a hotel room always includes a buffet breakfast – in mid- to top-range hotels especially, these can be sumptuous banquets. The only negatives are the sizes of rooms, which tend to be small – singles especially – and their sameness: Norway abounds in mundanely modern concrete and glass skyrise hotels. In addition to the places we've detailed in the guide, most Norwegian hotels, along with their room rates, summer discounts and facilities, are listed in the free booklet Transport and Accommodation, available from Norwegian tourist offices both inside the country and abroad (see p.43).

Summer is the best time to use one of the several **hotel discount and pass schemes** which operate throughout Norway. There are five main ones to choose from; each serves to cut costs, though often at the expense of a flexible itinerary – advance booking is the norm. Most Norwegian hotels are members of one discount/pass scheme or another, and you can usually join the scheme at one of the hotels, or at a tourist office; it's also worth checking what's available with your travel agent before leaving home. Amongst the options, perhaps the best is the **Fjord Pass** (⊛www.fjord-pass.com), which offers discounts of up to thirty percent at over 200 hotels with the Fjord Pass discount card; the card costs just 100kr and is valid for two adults and children under the age of fifteen.

Pensions, guesthouses and inns

For something a little less formal and anonymous than the average hotel, **pensions** (*pensjonater*) are your best bet – small, sometimes intimate boarding houses which can usually be found in the larger cities and more touristy towns. Rooms go for 350–450kr single, 450–550kr double; breakfast is generally extra. A *gjestgiveri* or *gjestehus* is a **guesthouse** or **inn**, charging similar prices. Facilities in all of these establishments are

Accommodation price codes

The hotels and guesthouses detailed in the Norway chapters of this guide have been graded according to the following price categories, based on the cost of the **least expensive double room during the high season** (usually June to mid-August). However, almost every hotel offers seasonal and/or weekend discounts, which can reduce the rate by one or even two grades. Wherever this is the case we've given two grades, separated by a forward slash, covering both the discounted and the regular rate.

❶ under 350kr	❸ 600–800kr	❺ 1000–1200kr	❼ over 1400kr
❷ 350–600kr	❹ 800–1000kr	❻ 1200–1400kr	

usually adequate without being overwhelmingly comfortable; at the cheaper places you'll share a bathroom with others. Some pensions and guesthouses also have kitchens available for the use of guests.

Hostels and private rooms

For many budget travellers, as well as hikers, climbers and skiers, the country's **hostels** (*vandrerhjem*) are the accommodation mainstay. There are almost a hundred in total, with handy concentrations in the western fjords, the central hiking and skiing regions and in Oslo. The Norwegian hostelling association, **Norske Vandrerhjem**, Torggata 1, Oslo (☎23 13 93 00, ⓦ www.vandrerhjem.no), issues a free booklet, *Norske Vandrerhjem*, which details locations, opening dates, prices and telephone numbers; bear in mind that it's possible to make bookings via their website. The hostels themselves are invariably excellent – the only quibble, at the risk of being churlish, is that those occupying schools tend to be rather drab and institutional.

Prices per night vary from 120–200kr, although the more expensive hostels nearly always include a grand breakfast. On average, reckon on paying 130kr a night for a bed, 50kr for breakfast and 80–100kr for a hot evening meal. Bear in mind also that almost all hostels have at least a few regular double and family rooms on offer: at 250–700kr a double, these are among the cheapest rooms you'll find in Norway. If you're not a member of Hostelling International (HI) you can still use the hostels, though it will cost you an extra 25kr or so a night – better to join up before you leave home. If you don't have your own sheet sleeping bag, you'll mostly have to rent one for around 40–50kr a time.

It cannot be stressed too strongly that **pre-booking** a hostel bed will save you lots of unnecessary legwork. Many hostels are only open from mid-June to mid-August and most close between 11am and 4pm. There's sometimes an 11pm or midnight curfew, though this isn't a huge drawback in a country where carousing is so expensive. Where breakfast is included – as it usually is – ask for a breakfast packet if you have to leave early to catch transport; otherwise note that hostel **meals** are nearly always tasty and excellent value. Most, though not all, hostels have small **kitchens**, but often no pots, pans, cutlery or crockery, so self-caterers should take their own.

Tourist offices in the larger towns and amongst the more touristy settlements can often fix you up with a **private room** in someone's house, which may include kitchen facilities. Prices are competitive – from 200–250kr per single, 300–350kr per double – though there's usually a booking fee (20–30kr) on top, and the rooms themselves are frequently some way out of the centre. Nonetheless, they're often the best bargain available and, in certain instances, an improvement on the local hostel. Where this is the case, we've said so in the guide. If you don't have a sleeping bag, check the room comes with bedding – not all of them do; and if you're cooking for yourself, a few basic utensils wouldn't go amiss either.

Campsites, cabins and mountain huts

Camping is a popular pastime in Norway, and there are literally hundreds of sites to choose from – anything from a field with a few tent pitches to extensive complexes with all mod cons. The Norwegian tourist authorities detail around 400 campsites in their free Camping brochure, classifying them on a one- to five-star grading depending on the facilities offered. Most sites are situated with the motorist (rather than the cyclist or walker) in mind, and a good few occupy key locations beside the main roads, though in summer these prime sites are occasionally inundated by seasonal workers. The majority of campsites are two- and three-star establishments, where prices are usually per tent, plus a small charge per person; on average expect to pay around 150kr for two people using a tent, with four- and five-star sites around twenty percent more. During peak season it can be a good idea to **reserve ahead** if you have a car and a large tent or trailer; contact details are listed in the free camping booklet and throughout the Guide.

Camping rough in Norway, as in Sweden, is a tradition enshrined in law. You can camp anywhere in open areas as long as you are at least 150m away from any houses or cabins. As a courtesy, ask farmers for permission to use their land – it is rarely refused. Fires are not permitted in woodland areas or in fields between April 15 and September 15, and camper vans are not allowed (ever) to overnight in lay-bys. A good sleeping bag is essential, since even in summer it can get very cold, and, in the north at least, mosquito repellent is vital.

The Norwegian countryside is dotted with thousands of timber **cabins/chalets** (called *hytter*), ranging from simple wooden huts through to comfortable lodges. They are usually two- or four-bedded affairs, with full kitchen facilities and sometimes a bathroom or even TV. Some hostels have them on their grounds, there are nearly always at least a handful at every campsite, and in the Lofoten islands they are the most popular form of accommodation, many occupying refurbished fishermen's huts called *rorbuer*. Costs vary enormously, depending on location, size and amenities, and there are significant seasonal variations, too. However, a four-bed *hytter* will rarely cost more than 600kr per night – a more usual average would be about 400kr. If you're travelling in

a group, they are easily the cheapest way to see the countryside – and in some comfort. Hundreds of *hytter* are also rented out as holiday cottages by the week.

One further option for hikers is the **mountain huts** (again called *hytter*), which are strategically positioned on every major hiking route. Some are privately run, but the majority are operated by **Den Norske Turistforening** (DNT), Storgata 7, Oslo (☎22 82 28 00, ⊛ www.turistforeningen.no), the Norwegian Mountain Hiking Association, and its affiliated regional hiking organizations. Membership of DNT costs 445kr a year, and although you don't have to be a member of DNT to use their huts, you'll soon recoup your outlay through reduced hut charges for members. For members staying in staffed huts, a bunk in a dormitory costs 155kr, a family or double room 195kr; meals start at 80kr for breakfast, 190kr for a three-course dinner. At unstaffed huts, where you leave the money for your stay in a box provided, an overnight stay costs 155kr.

Food and drink

At its best, **Norwegian food** can be excellent: fish is plentiful, and carnivores can have a field day trying meats like reindeer and elk or even, conscience permitting, seal and whale. Admittedly it's not inexpensive, and those on a tight budget may have problems varying their diet, but by exercising a little prudence in the face of the average menu (which is almost always in Norwegian and English), you can keep costs down to reasonable levels. Vegetarians, however, will have slim pickings (except in Oslo), and drinkers will have to dig very deep into their pockets to maintain much of an intake. Indeed, most drinkers end up visiting the supermarkets and state off-licences (*Vinmonopolet*) so that they can sup away at home (in true Norwegian style) before setting out for the evening.

Food

Many travellers exist almost entirely on a mixture of picnic food and by cooking their own meals, with the odd café meal thrown in to boost morale. Frankly, this isn't really necessary (except on the tightest of budgets), as there are a number of ways to eat out inexpensively. To begin with, a good self-service buffet breakfast, served in almost every hostel and hotel, goes some way to solving the problem, whilst special lunch deals will get you a tasty, hot meal for 70–90kr. Finally, alongside the regular restaurants – which are expensive – there's the usual array of budget pizzerias and cafeterias in most towns.

Breakfast, picnics and snacks

More often than not, **breakfast** (*frokost*) in Norway is a substantial self-service affair of bread, crackers, cheese, eggs, preserves, cold meat and fish, washed down with tea and ground coffee. It's usually first-rate at youth hostels, and often memorable in hotels, filling you up for the day for 70–100kr, on the rare occasions when it's not thrown in with the price of your room.

If you're buying your own **picnic food**, bread, cheese, yoghurt and local fruit are all relatively good value, but other staple foodstuffs – rice, pasta, meat, cereals and vegetables – can be way above the European average. Anything tinned is particularly dear (with the exception of fish), but coffee and tea are quite reasonably priced. **Supermarkets** are ten-a-penny.

Fast food offers the best chance of a hot takeaway snack. The indigenous Norwegian stuff, served up from **gatekjøkken** – street kiosks or stalls – in every town, consists mainly of rubbery hot dogs (*varm pølse*), while pizza slices and chicken pieces and chips are much in evidence too. American burger bars are also creeping in – both at motorway service stations and in the towns and cities. A better choice, and usually not much more expensive, is simply to get a sandwich, normally a huge open affair called a **smørbrød** (pronounced "smurrbrur"), heaped with a variety of garnishes. You'll see them groaning with meat or shrimps, salad and mayonnaise in the windows of bakeries and cafés, or in the newer, trendier sandwich bars in the cities.

Good **coffee** is available everywhere, rich and strong, and served black or with cream. **Tea**, too, is ubiquitous, but the local preference is for lemon tea or a variety of flavoured infusions; if you want milk, ask for it. All the familiar **soft drinks** are also available.

Lunch and dinner

For the best deals, you're going to have to eat your main meal of the day at lunch or possibly tea time, when **kafeterias** (often self-service restaurants) lay on daily specials, the *dagens rett*. This is a fish or meat dish served with potatoes and a vegetable or salad, often including a drink, sometimes bread, and occasionally coffee, too; it should go for 80–100kr. Dipping into the menu is more expensive, but not cripplingly so if you stick to omelettes and suchlike. Many department stores have *kafeterias*, as does every large railway station. You'll also find them hidden above shops and offices and adjoining hotels in larger towns, where they might be called kaffistovas. Most close at around 6pm, and many don't open at all on Sunday. As a general rule, the food these places serve is plain-verging-on-the-ordinary (though there are many excellent exceptions), but the same cannot be said of the continental-style **café-bars** which abound in Oslo and, increasingly, in all of Norway's larger towns and cities. These eminently affordable establishments offer much tastier and much more adventurous meals like pasta dishes, salads and vegetarian options for 90–130kr.

In all of the cities, but especially in Oslo, there are first-class **restaurants**, serving dinner (*middag*) in quite formal surroundings. Apart from exotica such as reindeer and elk, the one real speciality is the seafood, simply prepared and wonderfully fresh – whatever you do, don't go home without treating yourself at least once. In the smaller towns and villages, gourmets will be harder pressed – many of the restaurants are pretty mundane, though the general standard is improving rapidly. Main courses begin at around 120kr, starters and desserts at around 75kr. If in doubt, smoked salmon comes highly recommended, as does catfish and monkfish. Again, the best deals are at lunchtime.

In the towns, and especially in Oslo, there is also a sprinkling of **ethnic restaurants**, mostly Italian with a good helping of Chinese and Indian places. Other cuisines pop up

Glossary of Norwegian food and drink terms

Basics and snacks

Appelsin-marmelade	marmalade
brød	bread
eddik	vinegar
egg	egg
eggerøre	scrambled eggs
flatbrød	flat unleavened cracker, half barley, half wheat
fløte	cream
grøt	porridge
iskrem	ice cream
kaffefløte	single cream (for coffee)
kake	cake
kaviar	caviar
kjeks	biscuits
krem	whipped cream
melk	milk
mineralvann	mineral water
nøtter	nuts
olje	oil
omelett	omelette
ost	cheese
pannekake	pancakes
pepper	pepper
pommes-frites	chips
potetchips	crisps
ris	rice
rundstykker	roll
salat	salad
salt	salt
sennep	mustard
smør	butter
smørbrød	open sandwich
sukker	sugar
suppe	soup
syltetøy	jam
varm pølse	hot dog
yoghurt	yogurt

Meat (kjøtt) and game (vilt)

dyrestek	venison
elg	elk
kalkun	turkey
kjøttboller	meatballs
kjøttkaker	meat cakes
kylling	chicken
lammekjøtt	lamb
lever	liver
oksekjøtt	beef
pølser	sausages

postei	pâté
reinsdyr	reindeer
ribbe	pork rib
skinke	ham
spekemat	dried meat
stek	steak
svinekjøtt	pork

Fish (fisk) and shellfish (skalldyr)

ål	eel
ansjos	anchovies
blåskjell	mussels
brisling	sprats
hummer	lobster
hvitting	whiting
kaviar	caviar
krabbe	crab
kreps	crayfish
laks	salmon
makrell	mackerel
ørret	trout
piggvar	turbot
reker	shrimps
rødspette	plaice
røkelaks	smoked salmon
sardiner	sardines
sei	coalfish
sild	herring
sjøtunge	sole
småfisk	whitebait
steinbit	catfish
torsk	cod
tunfisk	tuna

Vegetables (grønsaker)

agurk	cucumber/gherkin/pickle
blomkål	cauliflower
bønner	beans
erter	peas
gulrøtter	carrots
hodesalat	lettuce
hvitløk	garlic
kål	cabbage
linser	lentils
løk	onion
mais	sweetcorn
nepe	turnip
paprika	peppers
poteter	potatoes
rosenkål	Brussels sprouts
selleri	celery
sopp	mushrooms

spinat	spinach	*sitron*	lemon
tomater	tomatoes	*solbær*	blackcurrants
		tyttbær	cranberries
Fruit (frukt)			
ananas	pineapple	**Food terms**	
appelsin	orange	*blodig*	rare, underdone
aprikos	apricot	*godt stekt*	well done
banan	banana	*grillet*	grilled
blåbær	blueberries	*grytestekt*	braised
druer	grapes	*kokt*	boiled
eple	apple	*marinert*	marinated
fersken	peach	*ovnstekt*	baked/roasted
fruktsalat	fruit salad	*røkt*	smoked
grapefrukt	grapefruit	*stekt*	fried
jordbær	strawberries	*stuet*	stewed
multer	cloudberries	*sur*	sour, pickled
pærer	pears	*syltet*	pickled
plommer	plums	*saltet*	cured

Norwegian specialities

brun saus	gravy served with most meats, meat cakes, fish cakes and sausages
fenalår	marinated mutton that is then smoked, sliced, salted, dried and served with crispbread, scrambled egg and beer
fiskekabaret	shrimps, fish and vegetables in aspic
fiskeboller	fish balls, served under a white sauce or on open sandwiches
fiskesuppe	fish soup
flatbrød	a flat unleavened cracker, half barley, half wheat
gammelost	a hard, strong smelling, yellow-brown cheese with veins
geitost/gjetost	goats' cheese, slightly sweet and fudge-coloured. Similar cheeses have different ratios of goats' milk to cows' milk
gravetlaks	salmon marinated in salt, sugar, dill and brandy
juleskinke	marinated boiled ham, served at Christmas
kjøttkaker med surkål	home-made burgers with cabbage and a sweet-and-sour sauce
koldtbord	a midday buffet with cold meats, herrings, salads, bread and perhaps soup, eggs or hot meats
lapskaus	pork, venison (or other meats) and vegetable stew, common in the south and east, using salted or fresh meat, or leftovers, in a thick brown gravy
lutefisk	fish (usually cod) preserved in an alkali solution and flavoured; an acquired taste
multer	cloudberries – wild berries, mostly found north of the Arctic Circle and served with cream (*med krem*)
mysost	brown whey cheese made from cows' milk
nedlagtsild	marinated herring
pinnekjøtt	western Norwegian Christmas dish of smoked mutton steamed over shredded birch bark, served with cabbage; or accompanied by boiled potatoes and mashed swede (*kålrabistappe*)
reinsdyrstek	reindeer steak, usually served with boiled potatoes and cranberry sauce

rekesalat	shrimp salad in mayonnaise
ribbe julepølse medisterkake	eastern Norwegian Christmas dish of pork ribs, sausage and dumplings
spekemat	various types of smoked, dried meat
Trondhjem-suppea	kind of milk soup with raisins, rice, cinnamon and sugar

Bread, cake and desserts

bløtkake	cream cake with fruit
fløtelapper	pancakes made from cream, served with sugar and jam
havrekjeks	oatmeal biscuits, eaten with goats' cheese
knekkebrød	crispbread
kransekake	cake made from almonds, sugar and eggs, served at celebrations
lomper	potato scones-cum-tortillas
riskrem	rice pudding with whipped cream and sugar, usually served with *frukt saus*, a slightly thickened fruit sauce
tilslørtbon-depiker	stewed apples and breadcrumbs, served with cream
trollkrem	beaten egg whites (or whipped cream) and sugar mixed with cloudberries (or cranberries)
vafle	waffles

Drinks

akevitt	aquavit	*te med melk/ sitron*	tea with milk/ lemon
appelsin saft/ juice	orange squash or juice	*vann*	water
brus	fizzy soft drink	*varm sjokolade*	hot chocolate
eplesider	cider	*vin*	wine
fruksaft	sweetened fruit juice	*søt*	sweet
kaffe	coffee	*tørr*	dry
melk	milk	*rød*	red
mineralvann	mineral water	*hvit*	white
øl	beer	*rosé*	rosé
sitronbrus	lemonade	*skål!*	cheers!

here and there, too – Japanese, Moroccan and Persian to name but three.

Vegetarians

Vegetarians are in for a hard time. Apart from a handful of specialist restaurants in the big cities, there's little option other than to make do with salads, look out for egg dishes in *kafeterias* and supplement your diet from supermarkets. If you are a **vegan** the problem is greater: when the Norwegians are not eating meat and fish, they are attacking a fantastic selection of milks, cheeses and yoghurts. At least you'll know what's in every dish you eat, since everyone speaks English. If you're self-catering, look for **health food shops** (*helsekost*), found in some of the larger towns and cities.

Drink

One of the less savoury sights in Norway – and especially common in the north – is the fall-over drunk: you can spot them at any time of the day or night zigzagging along the street, a strangely disconcerting counter to the usual stereotype of the Norwegian as a healthy, hearty figure in a wholesome woolly jumper. For reasons that remain obscure – or at least culturally complex – many Norwegians can't just have a drink or two, but have to get absolutely wasted. The majority of their compatriots deplore such behaviour and have consequently imposed what amounts to alcoholic rationing: thus, although booze is readily available in the bars and restaurants, it's taxed up to the eyeballs and the distribution of wines and spirits is strictly controlled by a state-run monopoly, **Vinmonopolet**. Whether this paternalistic type of control makes matters better or worse is a moot point, but the majority of Norwegians support it.

What to drink

If you decide to splash out on a few drinks, you'll find Norwegian **beer** is lager-like and comes in three strengths (class I, II or III), of which the strongest and most expensive is class III. Brands to look for include Hansa and Ringsnes. There's no domestically produced **wine** to speak of and most **spirits** are imported, too, but one local brew worth experimenting with at least once is **aquavit** (akevitt), a bitter concoction served ice-cold in little glasses and, at forty percent proof or more, real headache material – though it's more palatable with beer chasers: Linie aquavit is one of the more popular brands.

Where to buy alcohol

Beer is sold in supermarkets and shops all over Norway, though some local communities, particularly in the west, have their own rules and restrictions; at around 13kr per third of a litre, the supermarket price is about half what you'd pay in a bar. The strongest beer, along with **wines and spirits**, can only be purchased from the state-run **Vinmonopolet** shops. There's generally one branch in each medium-size town and many more in each of Norway's cities. Opening hours are usually Monday to Wednesday 10am–4/5pm, Thursday 10am–5/6pm, Friday 9am–4/6pm, Saturday 9am–1pm, though these times can vary depending on the location, and they'll be closed on public holidays. At *Vinmonopolet* stores, wine is quite a bargain, from around 80kr a bottle, and there's generally a wide choice.

Where to drink

Wherever you **go for a drink**, a third-litre of beer should cost between 35kr and 45kr,

and a glass of wine from 30kr. You can get a drink at most outdoor cafés, in restaurants and at bars, pubs and cocktail bars. That said, only in the towns and cities is there any kind of "European" bar life, and in many places you'll be limited to a drink in the local hotel bar or restaurant. However, in Oslo, Bergen, Stavanger, Trondheim and Tromsø you will be able to keep drinking in bars until at least 1am, 4am in some places.

Directory

Borders There is little formality at the Norway–Sweden border, slightly more between Norway and Finland. However, the northern border with Russia is a different story. Despite the break-up of the Soviet Union, border patrols (on either side) won't be overjoyed at the prospect of you nosing around. If you have a genuine wish to visit Russia, it's best to sign up for an organized tour from Kirkenes (see p.421).

Kids There are no real problems with taking children to Norway. They go for half-price (infants under 3 or 4 go free) on all forms of public transport, and get the same discount on an extra bed in their parents' hotel room. Family rooms are widely available in youth hostels, while many of the summer activities detailed in this book are geared up to cater for kids as well. There are also baby compartments (with their own toilet and changing room) for kids under 2 and their escorts on most overnight trains, and baby-changing rooms at most larger train stations. Many restaurants have children's menus; where they don't, it's always worth asking if there are cheaper, smaller portions.

Left luggage There are coin-operated lockers in most railway and bus stations and at all major ferry terminals.

Public holidays National public holidays are a noticeable feature of the Norwegian calendar and act as a unifying force in what remains an extremely homogeneous society. There are ten national public holidays per year, most of which are keenly observed, though the tourist industry carries on pretty much regardless. Some state-run museums adopt Sunday hours on the public holidays listed below, except on Christmas Day and

New Year's Day (and often December 26) when they close. Otherwise most businesses and shops close on these days, and the public transport system operates a skeleton or Sunday service. Most Norwegians take their holidays in the summer season, between mid-June and mid-August. Public holidays are: New Year's Day; Maundy Thursday; Good Friday; Easter Monday; Labour Day (May 1); Ascension Day (mid-May); National Day (May 17); Whit Monday; Christmas Day; Boxing Day.

Shopping hours Normal shopping hours are Monday to Friday 9am–4/5pm, with late opening on Thursdays till 6pm or 8pm, plus Saturdays 9am–1/3pm. Some urban supermarkets stay open much longer – until 8pm in the week and 6pm on Saturdays – and, in

addition, the majority of kiosks-cum-news-stands stay open till 9pm or 10pm every night of the week (including Sundays), especially in cities and larger towns. Many petrol stations sell a basic range of groceries and stay open till 11pm daily.

Smoking Smoking has long been prohibited in all public buildings, including train stations, as well as on flights and bus services. In June 2004, these restrictions were widened and smoking is now banned in restaurants, bars and cafés. A pack of twenty costs £6/$11, but nevertheless – and perhaps rather surprisingly – one in three Norwegians still puff away.

Tipping A service charge is automatically included in hotel and restaurant bills, so any additional tip is not expected – but always welcome.

History

Despite its low contemporary profile, **Norway** has a fascinating past. As early as the tenth century its people had explored – and conquered – much of northern Europe, and roamed the Atlantic as far as the North American mainland. Norway's salad days were as an independent state, but from the fourteenth century the country came under the sway of first Denmark and then Sweden. Independent again from 1905, Norway was propelled into World War II by the German invasion of 1940, an act of aggression that transformed the Norwegians' attitude to the outside world. Gone was the old insular neutrality, replaced by a liberal internationalism typified by Norway's leading role in the environmental movement.

Early civilizations

The earliest signs of human habitation in Norway date from the end of the last Ice Age, around 10,000 BC. In the Finnmark region of north Norway, the **Komsa** culture was reliant upon seal-fishing, whereas the peoples of the **Fosna** culture, further south near present-day Kristiansund, hunted seals and reindeer. Both these societies were essentially static, dependent upon flint and bone implements. At Alta, the Komsa people left behind hundreds of **rock carvings** and drawings, naturalistic representations of their way of life dating from the seventh to the third millennia BC.

As the edges of the ice cap retreated from the western coastline, so new migrants slowly filtered north. These new peoples, of the **Nøstvet-økser** culture, were also hunters and fishers, but they were able to manufacture stone axes, examples of which were first unearthed at Nøstvet, near Oslo. Beginning around 2700 BC, immigrants from the east, principally the semi-nomadic **Boat Axe** and **Battle-Axe peoples** – so-called because of the distinctive shape of their stone weapons/tools – introduced animal husbandry and agriculture. The new arrivals did not, however, overwhelm their predecessors; the two groups coexisted, each learning from the other how to survive in a land of harsh infertility. These late Stone Age cultures flourished at a time when other, more southerly countries were already using metal. Norway was poor and had little to trade, but the Danes and Swedes exchanged amber for copper and tin from the bronze-making countries of the Mediterranean. A fraction of the imported bronze subsequently passed into Norway, mostly to the Battle-Axe people, who appear to have had a comparatively prosperous aristocracy. This was the beginning of the Norwegian **Bronze Age** (1500–500 BC).

At around 500 BC Norway was affected by two adverse changes: the climate deteriorated, and trade relations with the Mediterranean were disrupted by the westward movement of the Celts across central Europe. The former encouraged the development of settled, communal farming in an attempt to improve winter shelter and storage; the latter cut the supply of tin and copper and subsequently isolated the country from the early **Iron Age**. Norway's isolation continued through much of the **classical period**, though the expansion of the Roman Empire in the first and second centuries AD did revive Norway's (indirect) trading links with the Mediterranean. Evidence of these renewed contacts is provided across Scandinavia by **runes**, carved inscriptions dating from around 200 AD whose 24-letter alphabet – the *futhark* – was clearly influenced by Greek and Latin capitals. Initially, runes were seen as having magical powers, but gradually their usage became more prosaic. Of the 800 or so runic inscriptions extant across southern Norway, most commemorate events and individuals: mothers and fathers, sons and slain comrades.

The renewal of trade with the Mediterranean also spread the use of **iron**. Norway's agriculture was transformed by the use of iron tools, and the pace of change accelerated in the fifth century AD, when the Norwegians learnt how to smelt the brown iron ore, limonite, that lay in their bogs and lakes – hence its common name, **bog-iron**. Clearing the forests with iron axes was relatively easy and, with more land available, the pattern of settlement became less concentrated. Family homesteads leapfrogged up the valleys, and a class of wealthy farmers emerged, their prosperity based on fields and flocks. Above them in the pecking order were local **chieftains**, the nature of whose authority varied considerably. Inland, the chieftains' power was based upon landed wealth and constrained by feudal responsibilities, whereas the coastal lords, who had often accumulated influence from trade, piracy and military prowess, were less encumbered. Like the farmers, these seafarers had also benefited from the iron axe, which made boat-building much easier.

By the middle of the eighth century, Norway had become a country of **small**, **independent kingships**, its geography impeding the development of any central authority.

The Vikings

Overpopulation, clan discord and the lure of commerce all contributed to the sudden explosion that launched the **Vikings** (from the Norse word *vik*, meaning "creek", and -*ing*, "frequenter of") upon an unsuspecting Europe in the ninth century. The patterns of attack and eventual settlement were dictated by the geographical position of the various Scandinavian countries: the Swedish Vikings turned eastwards, the Danes headed south and southwest, while the Norwegians sailed west to fall upon Scotland, Ireland and England.

The whole of Norway felt the stimulating effects of the Viking expeditions. The standard of living rose and the economy was boosted by the spoils of war. Farmland was no longer in such short supply; slaves assisted labour-intensive land clearance schemes; cereal and dairy farming extended into new areas in eastern Norway; new vegetables, such as cabbages and turnips, were introduced from Britain; and farming methods were improved by overseas contact – the Celts, for instance, taught the Norwegians how to thresh grain with flails.

The Vikings' brand of **paganism**, with its wayward, unscrupulous deities, underpinned their inclination to vendetta and clan warfare. Nevertheless, institutions slowly developed which helped regulate the bloodletting. Western Norway adopted the Germanic *wergeld* system of cash-for-injury compensation; every free man was entitled to attend the local **Thing** (a broadly democratic body which administered local law), while a regional *Lagthing* made laws and settled disputes. Justice was class-based, however, with society divided into three main categories: the lord, the freeman and the thrall or slave, the latter worth about eight cows. Viking **decorative art** was pan-Scandinavian, with the most distinguished work being the elaborate and often grotesque animal motifs that adorned their ships, sledges, buildings and furniture. This craftsmanship is seen at its best in the **ship burials** of Oseberg and Gokstad, both on display in Oslo's Viking Ships Museum.

Norway's first widely recognized chieftain was **Harald Hårfagri** (Fair-Hair), who gained control of the coastal region as far north as Trøndelag around 900. This sparked an exodus of minor rulers, most of whom left to settle in Iceland. Harald's long rule was based on personal pledges of fealty and when he died his kingdom broke up into its component parts. Harald did, however, leave an extremely important legacy: from now on every ambitious chieftain was not content to be a local lord, but strove to be ruler of Harald's whole kingdom. Harald's sons and grandsons warred over their inheritance for the rest of the tenth century, undermining Norway's independence by seeking military support in Denmark and Sweden. Meanwhile, Norwegian settlers were laying the foundations of independent Norse communities in the Faroes and Iceland, Erik the Red reached Greenland in about 985, and Leif Eriksson

the Lucky founded a colony he called Vinland on the shore of **North America** (probably Newfoundland) around 1000 AD.

The arrival of Christianity

In 1015, a prominent Viking chieftain, **Olav Haraldsson**, sailed for Norway from England, intent upon conquering his homeland. Significantly, he arrived by merchant ship with just 100 men, rather than with a fleet of longships and an army, a clear sign of the passing of the Viking heyday. Pledged to him was the support of the yeoman farmers of the interior – a new force in Norway that was rapidly supplanting the old warrior aristocracy – and Haraldsson was soon recognized as king of much of the country.

For twelve years, Olav ruled in peace, founding Norway's first national government. His authority was based upon the regional parliaments, or *Things*, and on his willingness to deliver justice without fear or favour. The king's most enduring achievement, however, was to make Norway **Christian**. Olav had been converted during his days in England, and vigorously imposed his new faith on his countrymen.

It was foreign policy rather than pagan enmity, however, that brought about Olav's downfall. By scheming with the Swedish ruler against **King Knut** (Canute) of Denmark and England, Olav provoked a Danish invasion. The Norwegian chieftains who had suffered at the hands of Olav could be expected to help Knut, but even the yeomen failed to rally to the cause. In 1028, Olav was forced to flee, first to Sweden and then to Russia, while Knut's son **Svein** and his mother, the English Queen Aelfgifu, took the Norwegian crown. Two years later, Olav made a sensational return at the head of a scratch army, only to be defeated and killed by an alliance of wealthy landowners and chieftains at **Stiklestad**, the first major Norwegian land battle.

The petty chieftains and yeoman farmers who had opposed Olav soon fell out with their new king: Svein had no intention of relaxing the royal grip, and his chieftains' subsequent rebellion seems also to have had nationalistic undertones – many Norwegians had no wish to be ruled by a Dane. Svein had to hightail it out of the country, and Olav's old enemies popped over to Sweden to bring back Olav's young son, **Magnus**, who became king in 1035.

The chastening experience of Svein's short rule transformed the popular memory of Olav. With surprising speed, he came to be regarded as an heroic champion of Norway, and there was talk of miracles brought about by the dead king's body. The Norwegian church, looking for a local saint to enhance its position, fostered the legends and had Olav canonized. The remains of **St Olav** were then reinterred ceremoniously at Nidaros, today's Trondheim, where the miracles increased in scope, hastening the conversion of what remained of heathen Norway.

On Magnus's death in 1047, **Harald Hardråda** (Olav's half-brother) became king. The last of the Viking warrior-chiefs, Hardråda dominated his kingdom by force of arms for over twenty years. Neither was Hardråda satisfied with being king of just Norway. In 1066, the death of Edward the Confessor presented Harald with an opportunity to press his claim to the English throne. The Norwegian promptly sailed on England, landing near York with a massive fleet, but just outside the city, at Stamford Bridge, his army was surprised and trounced by Harold Godwinson, the new Saxon king of England. Hardråda was killed in the battle and the threat of a Norwegian conquest of England had – though no one realized it at the time – gone forever. Not that the victory did much for Godwinson, whose weakened army trudged back south to be defeated by William of Normandy at the Battle of Hastings.

Medieval success

Harald's son, **Olav Kyrre** (the Peaceful) went on to reign as king of Norway for the next 25 years. Peace engendered economic prosperity, and treaties with Denmark ensured Norwegian independence. Three native bishoprics were established, and cathedrals built at Nidaros, Bergen and Oslo. It's from this period, too, that Norway's surviving **stave churches** date: wooden structures resembling an upturned keel, they were lavishly decorated with dragon heads and scenes from Norse mythology, proof that the traditions of the pagan world were slow to disappear.

The first decades of the twelfth century witnessed the further consolidation of Norway's position as an independent power, despite internal disorder as the descendants of Olav Kyrre struggled to maintain their influence. Civil war ceased only when **Håkon IV** took the throne in 1240, ushering in what is often called "The Period of Greatness". Secure at home, Håkon strengthened the Norwegian hold on the Faroe and Shetland islands, and in 1262 both Iceland and Greenland accepted Norwegian sovereignty. When his claim to the Hebrides was disputed by Alexander III of Scotland, Håkon assembled an intimidatory fleet, but died in 1263 in the Orkneys. Three years later the Hebrides and the Isle of Man (always the weakest links in the Norwegian empire) were sold to the Scottish crown by Håkon's successor, **Magnus the Lawmender** (1238–80).

Under Magnus, Norway prospered. Law and order were maintained, trade flourished and the king's courtiers even followed a code of etiquette compiled in the *King's Mirror* (*Konungs skuggsja*), in contrast to former rough-and-ready Viking ways. Neither was the power of the monarchy threatened by feudal barons as elsewhere in thirteenth-century Europe. Norway's scattered farms were not susceptible to feudal tutelage and, as a consequence, the nobility lacked local autonomy (castles remained few and far between) and were drawn into the centralized administration of the state. Norwegian **Gothic art** reached its full maturity in this period, as construction began on the nave at Nidaros Cathedral and on Håkon's Hall in Bergen.

Magnus was succeeded by his sons, first the undistinguished Erik and then by **Håkon V** (1270–1319), the last of medieval Norway's talented kings. Håkon continued the policy of his predecessors, making further improvements to central government and asserting royal control of Finnmark by the construction of a fortress at Vardø. His achievements, however, were soon to be swept away along with the independence of Norway itself.

Medieval failure

Norway's independence was threatened from two quarters. With strongholds in Bergen and Oslo, the **Hanseatic League** and its merchants had steadily increased their influence, holding a monopoly on imports and controlling inland trade to such an extent that Norway's royal household became dependent on the taxes they paid. The second threat was **dynastic**. When Håkon died in 1319 he left no male heir and was succeeded by his grandson, the 3-year-old son of a Swedish duke. The boy, **Magnus Eriksson**, was elected Swedish king two months later, marking the virtual end of Norway as an independent country until 1905.

Magnus assumed full power over both countries in 1332, but his reign was a difficult one. When the Norwegian nobility rebelled he agreed that the monarchy should again be split: his 3-year-old son, Håkon, would become Norwegian king when he came of age, while the Swedes agreed to elect his eldest son Erik to the Swedish throne. It was then, in 1349, that the **Black Death** struck, spreading quickly along the coast and up the valleys, and killing almost two-thirds of the Norwegian population. It was a catastrophe of almost unimaginable proportions, its effects compounded by the way the

country's agriculture was structured. Animal husbandry was easily the most important part of Norwegian farming, and the harvesting and drying of sufficient winter fodder was labour-intensive. Without the labourers, the animals died in their hundreds and famine conditions prevailed for several generations.

Many farms were abandoned and, deprived of their rents, the petty chieftains who had once dominated rural Norway were, as a class, almost entirely swept away. The vacuum was filled by royal officials, the *syslemenn*, each of whom exercised control over a large chunk of territory on behalf of a Royal Council. The collapse of local governance was compounded by the dynastic to-ing and fro-ing at the top of the social ladder. In 1380, Håkon died and Norway passed under Danish control with Olav, the son of Håkon and the Danish princess **Margaret**, becoming the ruler of the two kingdoms.

The Kalmar union

Despite Olav's early death in 1387, the resourceful Margaret persevered with the union. Proclaimed regent by both the Danish and (what remained of the) Norwegian nobility, she engineered a treaty with the Swedish nobles that not only recognized her as regent of Sweden but also agreed to accept any king she should nominate. Her chosen heir, **Erik of Pomerania**, was foisted on the Norwegians in 1389. When he reached the age of majority in 1397, Margaret organized a grand coronation with Erik crowned king of all three countries at Kalmar in Sweden – hence the **Kalmar Union**.

After Margaret's death in 1412, all power was concentrated in Denmark. In Norway, Danes were preferred in both state and church, and the country became impoverished by paying for Erik's wars. Incompetent and brutal in equal measure, Erik managed to get himself deposed in all three countries at the same time. In the meantime Sweden had left the union, and eventually a Danish count, Christian of

Oldenburg, was crowned king of Norway and Denmark in 1450. Thereafter, Norway ceased to take any meaningful part in Scandinavian affairs. Literature languished as Danish displaced the old Norse **language** in every official communication and within the governing class – and indeed Norse soon came to be regarded as the language of the ignorant and inconsequential. Only the Norwegian church retained any power, but this itself was overwhelmed by the Reformation.

Union with Denmark

In 1536 **Christian III** declared his kingdom Protestant and, although it was slow to take root among the Norwegian peasantry, **Lutheranism** soon came to be a powerful instrument in establishing Danish influence. The Bible, catechism and hymnal were all in Danish, the bishops were all Danes and, after 1537, so were all the most important provincial Norwegian governors. In many respects, Norway became simply a source of raw materials – fish, timber and iron ore – whose proceeds lined the royal purse. Naturally enough, the Swedes coveted these materials too, the upshot being a long and inconclusive war (1563–70), which saw much of Norway ravaged by competing bands of mercenaries. Among the Danish kings of the period, **Christian IV** (1588–1648) proved the most sympathetic to Norway. He visited the country often, improving the quality of its administration and founding new towns including Kongsberg, Kristiansand and Christiania (later Oslo).

At last, in the middle of the seventeenth century, the Norwegian economy began to pick up. The population grew, trade increased and, benefiting from the decline of the Hanseatic League, a native bourgeoisie began to take control of certain parts of the economy, most notably the herring industry. But Norwegian cultural self-esteem remained at a low ebb: the country's merchants spoke Danish, mimicked Danish manners and read Danish pot-boilers.

What's more, Norway was a constant bone of contention between Sweden and Denmark, the result being a long series of wars in which its more easterly provinces were regularly battered by the competing armies.

The year 1660 marked a turning point in the constitutional arrangements governing Norway. For centuries, the Danish Council of State had had the power to elect the monarch and impose limitations on his or her rule. Now, a powerful alliance of merchants and clergy swept these powers away to make **Frederik III** an absolute ruler. This was not a reactionary coup, but an attempt to limit the power of the conservative-minded nobility. In addition, the development of a centralized state machine would, many calculated, provide all sorts of job opportunities to the low-born but adept. Norway was incorporated into the administrative structure of Denmark, with royal authority delegated to the *Stattholder*, who governed through what soon became a veritable army of professional bureaucrats. There were positive advantages for Norway: the country acquired better defences, simpler taxes, a separate High Court and doses of Norwegian law, but once again power was exercised almost exclusively by Danes.

The eighteenth and early nineteenth centuries

The **absolute monarchy** established by Frederik III soon came to concern itself with every aspect of Norwegian life. The ranks and duties of minor officials were carefully delineated, religious observances tightly regulated and restrictions imposed on everything from begging and dress through to the food and drink that could be consumed at weddings and funerals. This extraordinary superstructure placed a leaden hand on imagination and invention. Neither was it impartial: there were some benefits for the country's farmers and fishermen, but by and large the system worked in favour of the middle class. The merchants of every small town were allocated the exclusive rights to trade in a particular area, and competition between the towns was forbidden. These local monopolies placed the peasantry at a dreadful disadvantage, nowhere more iniquitously than in the Lofotens, where the fishermen not only had to buy supplies and equipment at the price set by the merchant, but had to sell their fish at the price set by him, too.

In the meantime, there were more wars between Denmark and Sweden. In 1700, **Frederik IV** (1699–1730) made the rash decision to attack the Swedes at the time when their king, Karl XII, was generally reckoned to be one of Europe's most brilliant military strategists. Predictably, the Danes were defeated and only the intervention of the British saved Copenhagen from falling into Swedish hands. Undeterred, Frederik tried again, and this time Karl retaliated by launching a full-scale invasion of Norway. The Swedes rapidly occupied southern Norway, but after Karl was shot dead by a sniper, the two countries agreed the **Peace of Frederiksborg** (1720), which ended hostilities for the rest of the eighteenth century.

Peace favoured the growth of trade, but although Norway's economy prospered it was hampered by the trade monopolies exercised by the merchants of Copenhagen. In the 1760s, however, the Danes did a dramatic U-turn, abolishing monopolies, removing trade barriers and even permitting a free press – and the Norwegian economy boomed. Nonetheless, the bulk of the population remained impoverished and prey to famine whenever the harvest was poor. The number of landless agricultural labourers rose dramatically, partly because the more prosperous farmers were buying up large slices of land, and for the first time Norway had something akin to a lumpen proletariat.

Despite this, Norway was one of the few European countries little affected by the French Revolution. Instead of political action, there was a **religious revival**, with Hans Nielson Hauge emerging as an evangelical leader. The movement's characteristic hostility to officialdom caused concern, and Hauge was imprisoned, but in reality it posed little threat to the status quo. The end result was rather the foundation of a fundamentalist movement that is still a force to be reckoned with in parts of fjordland Norway.

The period leading up to the **Napoleonic Wars** was a good time for Norway: overseas trade, especially with England, flourished, with the demand for Norwegian timber and iron heralding a period of unparalleled prosperity. Denmark and Norway had remained neutral throughout the Seven Years' War (1756–63) between England and France, and renewed that neutrality in 1792. However, when Napoleon implemented a trade blockade – the Continental System – against Britain, he roped in the Danes. As a result, the British fleet bombarded Copenhagen in 1807 and forced the surrender of the entire Dano-Norwegian fleet. Denmark, in retaliation, declared war on England and Sweden. The move was disastrous for the Norwegian economy, which had suffered bad harvests in 1807 and 1808, and the English blockade of its seaports dented trade.

By 1811 it was obvious that the Danes had backed the wrong side in the war, and the idea of an equal union with Sweden, which had supported Britain, became increasingly attractive to many Norwegians. By latching on to the coat-tails of the victors, they hoped to restore the commercially vital trade with England. They also thought that the new Swedish king would be able to deal with the Danes if it came to a fight – just as the Swedes had themselves calculated when they appointed him in 1810. The man concerned, **Karl XIV Johan**, was, curiously enough, none other than Jean-Baptiste Bernadotte, formerly one of Napoleon's marshals. With perfect timing, he had helped the British defeat Napoleon at

Leipzig in 1813. His reward came in the **Treaty of Kiel** the following year, when the great powers instructed the Danes to cede all rights in Norway to Sweden (although Denmark did keep the dependencies of Iceland, Greenland and the Faroes). Four hundred years of union had ended.

Union with Sweden 1814–1905

The high-handed transfer of Norway from Denmark to Sweden did nothing to assuage the growing demands for greater independence. Furthermore, the Danish Crown Prince Christian Frederik roamed Norway stirring up fears of Swedish intentions. The prince and his supporters convened a Constituent Assembly, which met at Eidsvoll in April 1814 and produced a **constitution**. Issued on May 17, 1814 (still a national holiday), this declared Norway to be a "free, independent and indivisible realm" with Christian Frederik as its king. Not surprisingly, Karl XIV Johan would have none of this and, with the support of the great powers, he invaded Norway. Completely outgunned, Christian Frederik mounted barely any resistance. In exchange for Swedish promises to recognize the Norwegian constitution and the **Storting** (parliament), he abdicated as soon as he had signed a peace treaty – the so-called **Convention of Moss** – in August 1814.

The ensuing period was marred by struggles between the Storting and Karl XIV Johan over the nature of the union. Although the constitution emphasized Norway's independence, Johan had a veto over the Storting's actions; the post of *Stattholder* in Norway could only be held by a Swede; and foreign and diplomatic matters concerning Norway remained entirely in Swedish hands. Despite this, Karl XIV Johan proved popular in Norway, and during his reign the country enjoyed a fair amount of independence. From 1836 all the highest offices in Norway were filled exclusively by Norwegians, and democratic local councils were established, in part due to the rise of peasant farmers as a political force.

The gradual increase in prosperity had important **cultural implications**. The layout and buildings of modern Oslo – the Royal Palace, Karl Johans gate and the university – date from this period, whilst Johan Christian Dahl, the most distinguished Scandinavian landscape painter of his day, was instrumental in the moves to establish the National Gallery in Oslo in 1836. Other prominent members of the bourgeoisie championed all things Norwegian, but under both Oscar I (1844–59) and Karl XV (1859–72) it was **pan-Scandinavianism** that ruled the intellectual roost. This belief in the natural solidarity of Denmark, Norway and Sweden was espoused by the leading artists of the period, including Ibsen and Bjørnstjerne Bjørnson, but died a death in 1864, when the people of Norway and Sweden refused to help Denmark when it was attacked by Austria and Prussia (some of the loudest cries of treachery came from a young Henrik Ibsen, in his poetic drama *Brand*).

Domestic politics changed, too, with the rise to power in the 1850s of **Johan Sverdrup**, who started a long and ultimately successful campaign to wrest executive power from the king and transfer it to the Storting. By the mid-1880s, Sverdrup and his political allies had pretty much won the day, but a further bout of sabre-rattling between the supporters of Norwegian independence and the Swedish king, **Oscar II** (1872–1907), was necessary before both sides would accept a **plebiscite**. This took place in August 1905, when there was an overwhelming vote in favour of the **dissolution of the union**, which was duly confirmed by the Treaty of Karlstad. A second plebiscite determined that independent Norway should be a monarchy rather than a republic and, in November 1905, Prince Karl of Denmark (Edward VII of England's son-in-law) was elected to the throne as **Håkon VII**.

The dissolving of the union came at a time of further economic advance, largely engendered by the introduction of hydroelectric power. Social reforms also saw funds being made available for unemployment relief, accident insurance schemes and a Factory Act (1909). An extension to the franchise gave the vote to all men over 25 and, in 1913, to women too. The education system was reorganized, and substantial sums were spent on new arms and defence matters. This prewar period also saw the emergence of a strong trade union movement and of a Labour Party committed to radical change.

Culturally, the second half of the nineteenth century was fruitful for Norway, with the rediscovery of the Norwegian language and its folklore by a number of academics who formed the nucleus of a National Romantic movement, which did much to restore the country's cultural self-respect. Following on were well-known authors like **Alexander Kielland**, who wrote most of his works between 1880 and 1891, and **Knut Hamsun**, who published his most characteristic novel, *Hunger*, in 1890. In music, **Edvard Grieg** (1843–1907) made his debut in the first concert to consist entirely of works by Norwegian composers, and was himself inspired by old Norwegian folk melodies. The artist **Edvard Munch** was also active during this period, completing many of his major works in the 1880s and 1890s, while the internationally acclaimed dramatist **Henrik Ibsen** returned to Oslo after a prolonged, self-imposed exile in 1891.

The early years of independence up to 1939

Since 1814 Norway had had precious little to do with European affairs, and at the outbreak of **World War I** declared herself strictly neutral. Sympathy, though, lay largely with the Western Allies, and the Norwegian economy boomed since its ships and timber were in great demand. By 1916, however,

Norway had begun to feel the pinch, as German submarine action hit both enemy and neutral shipping, and by the end of the war Norway had lost half its chartered tonnage and 2000 crew. The Norwegian economy also suffered after the USA entered the war – the Americans imposed strict trade agreements in their attempt to prevent supplies getting to Germany, and rationing had to be introduced across Norway. Indeed, the price of neutrality was high: there was a rise in state expenditure, a soaring cost of living and, at the end of the war, no seat at the conference table. In spite of its losses, Norway got no share of the confiscated German shipping, although it was partly compensated by gaining sovereignty of **Spitsbergen** and its coal deposits – the first extension of the Norwegian frontiers for 500 years. In 1920 Norway also entered the new League of Nations.

Later in the 1920s, the decline in world trade led to a decreased demand for Norway's shipping. Bank failure and currency fluctuation were rife, and, as unemployment and industrial strife increased, a burgeoning Norwegian **Labour Party** took advantage. With the franchise extended to all those over 23 and the introduction of larger constituencies, it had a chance, for the first time, to win seats outside the large towns. At the 1927 election the Labour Party, together with the Social Democrats from whom they'd split, were the biggest grouping in the Storting. Nonetheless, because they had no overall majority and because many feared their radical leftist rhetoric, they were manoeuvred out of office after only fourteen days. **Trade disputes** and lockouts continued and troops were used to enable workers to cross picket lines.

During the war, **Prohibition** had been introduced as a temporary measure, and a referendum of 1919 showed a clear majority in favour of its continuation. But the ban did little to quell – and maybe even exacerbated – drunkenness, and it was abandoned in 1932, to be replaced by the government sales monopoly of wines and spirits that remains in force today. The 1933 election gave the Labour Party more seats than ever. Having shed its revolutionary image, a campaigning reformist Labour Party benefited from the increasing conviction that state control and a centrally planned economy were the only answer to Norway's economic problems. In 1935 the Labour Party, in alliance with the Agrarian Party, took power – an unlikely combination since the Agrarians were profoundly nationalist in outlook, so much so that their defence spokesman had been the rabid anti-Semite **Vidkun Quisling**. Frustrated by the democratic process, Quisling had left the Agrarians in 1933 to found the **Nasjonal Samling** (National Unification), a fascist movement which proposed, among other things, that both Hitler and Mussolini should be nominated for the Nobel Peace Prize. Quisling had good contacts with Nazi Germany but little support in Norway – local elections in 1937 reduced his local representation to a mere seven, and party membership fell to 1500.

The Labour government under **Johan Nygaardsvold** presided over an improving economy. By 1938 industrial production was 75 percent higher than it had been in 1914; unemployment had dropped as expenditure on roads, railways and public works increased. Social welfare reforms were implemented and trade union membership increased. When war broke out in 1939, Norway was lacking only one thing – adequate defence. A vigorous member of the League of Nations, the country had pursued disarmament and a policy of peace since the end of World War I, and it was determined to remain neutral.

World War II

In early 1940, despite the threatening rumblings of Hitler, the Norwegians were preoccupied with Allied minelaying off the Norwegian coast – part of the British attempt to prevent Swedish iron ore being shipped from Narvik to Germany. Indeed, such was Norwegian naivety that they made a formal protest to Britain on the day of the **German invasion**. Caught napping, the Norwegian army offered little initial resistance to the Germans and the south and central regions of the country were quickly overrun. King Håkon and the Storting were forced into a hasty evacuation of Oslo and headed north, eventually taking refuge in Britain where they formed the Norwegian government-in-exile. Norway was rapidly brought under Nazi control, Hitler sending **Josef Terboven** to take full charge of affairs. The fascist Nasjonal Samling was declared the only legal party and the media, civil servants and teachers were brought under German control. As **civil resistance** grew, a state of emergency was declared: two trade union leaders were shot, arrests increased and a concentration camp was set up outside Oslo. In February 1942 Quisling was installed as "Minister President" of Norway, but it was soon clear that his government didn't have the support of the Norwegian people. The church refused to cooperate, schoolteachers protested and trade union members and officials resigned en masse. In response, deportations increased, death sentences were announced and a compulsory labour scheme was introduced.

Military resistance escalated. A military organization (MILORG) was established as a branch of the armed forces under the control of the High Command in London. By May 1941 it had enlisted 20,000 men (32,000 by 1944) in clandestine groups all over the country. Arms and instructors came from Britain, radio stations were set up and a continuous flow of intelligence about Nazi movements sent back. Sabotage operations were legion, the most notable being the destruction of the heavy-water plant at **Rjukan**, foiling a German attempt to produce an atomic bomb.

The **government in exile** in London continued to represent free Norway to the world, mobilizing support on behalf of the Allies. Most of the Norwegian merchant fleet was abroad when the Nazis invaded, and by 1943 the Norwegian navy had seventy ships helping the Allied convoys. In Sweden, Norwegian exiles assembled in "health camps" at the end of 1943 to train as police troops in readiness for liberation.

When the Allies landed in Normandy in June 1944, overt action against the Nazis in Norway by the resistance was temporarily discouraged, since the Allies couldn't safeguard against reprisals. By late October, the Russians had crossed the border in the far north. The Germans, forced to retreat, burned everything in their path and drove the local population into hiding. To prevent the Germans reinforcing their beleaguered Finnmark battalions, the resistance – with renewed Allied encouragement – planned a campaign of mass railway sabotage, stopping three-quarters of the troop movements overnight. As their control of Norway crumbled, the Germans finally **surrendered** on May 7, 1945. King Håkon returned to Norway on June 7, five years to the day since he'd left for exile.

Terboven committed suicide and the Nasjonal Samling collaborators were rounded up. A caretaker government took office, staffed by resistance leaders, and was replaced in October 1945 by a majority **Labour government**. The Communists won eleven seats, reflecting the efforts of Communist saboteurs in the war and the prestige that the Soviet Union enjoyed in Norway after liberation. Quisling was shot, along with 24 other high-ranking traitors, and hundreds of collaborators were punished.

Postwar reconstruction

At the end of the war, Norway was on its knees: the far north – Finnmark – had been laid waste, half the mercantile fleet had been lost, and production was at a standstill. Recovery, though, fostered by a sense of national unity, was quick and it took only three years for GNP to

return to its prewar level. Norway's part in the war had increased her prestige in the world. The country became one of the founding members of the **United Nations** in 1945, and the first UN Secretary-General, Tryggve Lie, was Norway's Foreign Minister. With the failure of discussions to promote a Scandinavian defence union, the Storting also voted to enter **NATO** in 1949.

Domestically, there was general agreement about the form that social reconstruction should take. In 1948, the Storting passed the laws that introduced the Welfare State virtually unanimously. The 1949 election saw the government returned with a larger majority, and Labour administrations remained in power throughout the following decade, when the dominant political figure was **Einar Gerhardsen**. As national prosperity increased, society became much more egalitarian, levelling up rather than down. Subsidies were paid to the agricultural and fishing industries, wages were increased and a comprehensive social security system helped to eradicate poverty. The state ran the important mining industry, was the largest shareholder in the hydro-electric company and built an enormous steelworks at Mo-i-Rana to help develop the economy of the devastated northern counties. Rationing ended in 1952 and, as the demand for higher-level education grew, new universities were approved at Bergen, Trondheim and Tromsø.

Beyond consensus: modern Norway

The political consensus began to fragment in the early 1960s. Following changes in the constitution concerning the rural constituencies, the centre had realigned itself in the 1950s, with the outmoded Agrarian Party becoming the **Centre Party**. Defence squabbles within the Labour Party led to the formation of the **Socialist People's Party** (the SF), which wanted Norway out of NATO and sought a renunciation of nuclear weapons. The Labour Party's 1961 declaration that no nuclear weapons would be stationed in Norway except under an immediate threat of war did not placate the SF who, unexpectedly, took two seats at the election that year. Holding the balance of power, the SF voted with the Labour Party until 1963, when it helped bring down the government over the mismanagement of state industries. A replacement coalition collapsed after only one month, but the writing was on the wall. Rising prices, dissatisfaction with high taxation and a continuing housing shortage meant that the 1965 election put a **non-socialist coalition** in power for the first time in twenty years.

The new coalition's programme, under the leadership of **Per Borten** of the Centre Party, was unambitious. Nonetheless, living standards continued to rise, and although the 1969 election saw a marked increase in Labour Party support, the coalition hung on to power. Also in 1969, **oil and gas** were discovered beneath the North Sea and, as the vast extent of the reserves became obvious, so it became clear that the Norwegians were to enjoy a magnificent bonanza – one which was destined to pay about 25 percent of the government's annual bills. Meanwhile, Norway's politicians, who had applied twice previously for membership of the **European Economic Community** (EEC) – in 1962 and 1967 – believed that de Gaulle's fall in France presented a good opportunity for a third application, which was made in 1970. There was great concern, though, about the effect of membership on Norwegian agriculture and fisheries, and in 1971 Per Borten was forced to resign following his indiscreet handling of the negotiations. The Labour Party, the majority of its representatives in favour of EEC membership, formed a minority administration, but when the 1972 referendum narrowly voted "No" to joining the EEC, the government resigned.

With the 1973 election producing another minority Labour government,

the uncertain pattern of the previous ten years continued. Even the postwar consensus on **Norwegian security policy** broke down on various issues – such as the question of a northern European nuclear-free zone and the stocking of Allied material in Norway – although there remained strong agreement for continued NATO membership.

In 1983, the Christian Democrats and the Centre Party joined together in a non-socialist coalition, which lasted for just two years. It was replaced in 1986 by a minority Labour administration, led by **Dr Gro Harlem Brundtland**, Norway's first woman prime minister. She made sweeping changes to the way the country was run, introducing seven women into her eighteen-member cabinet, but her government was beset by problems for the three years of its life: tumbling oil prices led to a recession, unemployment rose (though only to four percent) and there was widespread dissatisfaction with Labour's high taxation.

At the **general election** in September 1989, Labour lost eight seats and was forced out of office – the worst result that the party had suffered since 1930. More surprising was the success of the extremist parties on both political wings – the anti-NATO Left Socialist Party and the right-wing, anti-immigrant Progress Party both scored spectacular results, winning almost a quarter of the votes cast, and increasing their representation in the Storting many times over. This deprived the Conservative Party (one of whose leaders, bizarrely, was Gro Harlem Brundtland's husband) of the majority it might have expected, the result being yet another shaky minority administration – this time a **centre-right coalition** between the Conservatives, the Centre Party and the Christian Democrats, led by Jan Syse.

The new government immediately faced problems familiar to the last Labour administration. In particular, there was continuing conflict over joining the **European Community**, a policy still supported by many in the

Norwegian establishment but flatly rejected by the Centre Party. It was this, in part, that signalled the end of the coalition, for after just over a year in office, the Centre Party withdrew its support and forced the downfall of Syse. In October 1990, Gro Harlem Brundtland was put back in power at the head of a **minority Labour administration**, remaining in office till her re-election for a fourth minority term in 1993. The 1993 elections saw a revival in Labour Party fortunes and, to the relief of the majority, the collapse of the Progress Party vote. However, it was also an untidy, confusing affair where the main issue, membership of the EU, cut across the traditional left versus right axis of the political parties.

Present-day Norway

Following the 1993 election, Norway tumbled into a long and fiercely conducted campaign over membership of the EU. Brundtland and her main political opponents wanted in, but despite the near unanimity amongst politicians, the Norwegians narrowly rejected the EU in a **referendum** on November 28, 1994. It was a close call (52.5 percent versus 47.5 percent), but in the end farmers and fishermen afraid of the economic results of joining, as well as women's groups and environmentalists who felt that Norway's high standards of social care and "green" controls would suffer, came together to swing opinion against joining. Afterwards, and unlike the Labour government of 1972, the Brundtland administration soldiered on, wisely soothing ruffled feathers by promising to shelve the whole EU membership issue until at least 2000. Nevertheless, the **1997 election** saw a move to the right, the main beneficiaries being the Christian Democratic Party and the ultra-conservative Progress Party. In itself, this was not enough to remove the Labour-led coalition from office – indeed Labour remained comfortably the largest party – but the right was dealt a trump card

by the new Labour leader, **Thorbjørn Jagland**. During the campaign, Jagland had promised that the Labour Party would step down from office if it failed to elicit more than the 36.9 percent of the vote it had secured in 1993. Much to the chagrin of his colleagues, Jagland's political chickens came home to roost when Labour only received 35 percent of the vote – and they had to go, leaving the government in the hands of an unwieldy right-of-centre minority coalition. Bargaining with its rivals from a position of parliamentary weakness, the new government found it difficult to cut a clear path – or at least one very different from its predecessor – apart from in managing to antagonize the women's movement by some of its reactionary social legislation during 1998 and 1999. In the spring of 2000, the government resigned and Labour resumed command – but not for long: in the elections of the next year, they took a drubbing and the right prospered, paving the way for another ungainly centre-right administrative coalition. The coalition battled on until October 2005 when the Labour Party, along with its allies the Socialist Left Party and the Centre Party, won a general election with the politically experienced **Jens Stoltenberg** becoming Prime Minister.

In the long term, quite what Norway will make of its splendid **isolation from the EU** is unclear, though the situation is mitigated by Norway's membership of the European Economic Agreement (EEA), a free-trade deal of January 1994 which covers both Norway and the EU. Whatever happens, and whether or not there is another EU referendum, it's hard to imagine that the Norwegians will suffer any permanent economic harm. They have, after all, a superabundance of natural resources and arguably the most educated workforce in the world. Which isn't to say the country doesn't collectively **fret** – a modest increase in the amount of drug addiction and street crime has produced much heart-searching, the theory being that an advanced and progressive social policy should be able to eliminate such barbarisms. This thoughtful approach, so typical of Norway, is very much to the country's credit, as is the refusal to accept a residual level of unemployment (of about 6–7 percent) that is the envy of many other western governments.

Books

M ost of the books listed below are in print and in paperback, and those that are out of print (o/p) should be easy to track down either in second-hand book shops or through Amazon's used and secondhand book service (ⓦwww.amazon.co.uk or ⓦwww.amazon.com). Note also that while we recommend all the books we've listed below, we do have favourites – and these have been marked with 🏃.

Travel and general

Thor Heyerdahl *The Kon-Tiki Expedition*. You may want to read this after visiting Oslo's Kon-Tiki Museum (p.271). The intrepid Heyerdahl's accounts of his expeditions aroused huge interest when they were first published, and remain ripping yarns – though surprisingly few people care to read them today.

🏃 **Mark Kurlansky** *Cod: A Biography of the Fish that Changed the World*. This wonderful book tracks the life and times of the cod and the generations of fishermen who have lived off it. There are sections on over-fishing and breeding habits, and recipes are provided too. Norwegians figure frequently – after all, cod was the staple diet of much of the country for centuries.

Constance Roos *Walking in Norway*. This well-researched and informative guide outlines hiking routes in almost every part of Norway, with useful sections on conditions in the mountains and equipment. It's the best of its type on the market, though the descriptions of some of the hiking routes lack detail.

Mary Wollstonecraft *Letters written during a Short Residence in Sweden,* *Norway and Denmark*. For reasons that have never been entirely clear, Wollstonecraft, the author of *A Vindication of the Rights of Women* and mother of Mary Shelley, travelled Scandinavia for several months in 1795. Her letters home represent a real historical curiosity, though her trenchant comments on Norway often get sidelined by her intense melancholia.

History and mythology

🏃 **Peter Christen Asbjørnsen and Jørgen Moe** *Norwegian Folk Tales*. Of all the many books on Norwegian folk tales, this is the edition you want – the illustrations by Erik Werenskiold and Theodor Kittelsen are delightful.

Fredrik Dahl *Quisling: A Study in Treachery*. A comprehensive biography of the world's most famous traitor, Vidkun Quisling – the man presented in all his unpleasant fullness.

Rolf Danielsen (et al) *Norway: A History from the Vikings to Our Own Times*. Thoughtful and well-presented account investigating the social and economic development of Norway – a modern and well-judged book that avoids the "kings and queens" approach to its subject.

241

Art and music

J.P. Hodin *Edvard Munch* (o/p). Excellent general introduction to Munch's life and work, with much interesting historical detail.

Robert Layton *Grieg* (o/p). Clear, concise and attractively illustrated book on Norway's greatest composer. Essential reading if you want to get to grips with the man and his times.

Marion Nelson (et al) *Norwegian Folk Art: The Migration of a Tradition*. Lavishly illustrated book discussing the whole range of folk art, from wood carvings through to bedspreads and traditional dress. It's particularly strong on the influence of Norwegian folk art in the USA, but the text sometimes lacks focus.

Literary fiction and biography

Kjell Askildsen *A Sudden Liberating Thought*. Short stories, in the Kafkaesque tradition, from one of Norway's most uncompromisingly modernist writers.

Jens Bjørneboe *The Sharks*. Set at the end of the last century, this is a thrilling tale of shipwreck and mutiny by a well-known Norwegian writer who had an enviable reputation for challenging authoritarianism of any description. Also recommended is his darker trilogy – *Moment of Freedom*, *The Powderhouse* and *The Silence* – exploring the nature of cruelty and injustice.

Karin Fossum *Calling out for You* and *Don't look Back*. Norway's finest crime writer, Fossum has written a string of superb thrillers in the Inspector Sejer series, and each gives the real flavour of contemporary Norway. These two novels are the best place to get started.

Jostein Gaarder *Sophie's World*. Hugely popular novel that deserves all the praise heaped upon it – it's beautifully and gently written, with puffs of whimsy all the way through. It bears comparison with Hawking's *A Brief History of Time*, though the subject matter here is philosophy, and there's an engaging mystery story tucked in here too. Also try *Through A Glass Darkly*.

Knut Hamsun *Hunger*. Norway's leading literary light in the 1920s and early 1930s, Hamsun was a writer of international acclaim until he disgraced himself by supporting Hitler. Of his many novels, *Hunger* (1890) made his name, a trip into the psyche of an alienated and angst-ridden young writer which shocked contemporary readers.

Henrik Ibsen *The Complete Major Prose Plays*. The key international figure of Norwegian literature, Ibsen was a social dramatist, keen to portray contemporary society, in all its forms and with all its hypocrisies, through his eerily haunting characters. Comparatively few of his plays are ever performed in Britain or the USA, apart perhaps from *A Doll's House* and *Hedda Gabler*. All his major plays are contained in this volume, of which there are several imprints.

Amalie Skram *Under Observation*. Confined to a mental hospital against her will, Skram (1846–1905) had a terrible time at the hands of her tyrannical male doctor, and based this chunky novel on her experiences. Similar themes are developed in her excellently written *Lucie*.

Herbjørg Wassmo *Dina's Book: A Novel*. Set in rural northern Norway in the middle of the nineteenth century, this strange but engaging tale has a plot centred on a powerful but tormented heroine.

A brief guide to Norwegian

There are two official Norwegian languages: *Riksmål* or *Bokmål* (book language), a modification of the old Dano-Norwegian tongue left over from the days of Danish dominance; and *Landsmål* or *Nynorsk*, which was codified during the nineteenth-century upsurge of Norwegian nationalism and is based on rural dialects of Old Norse provenance. Roughly eighty percent of schoolchildren have *Bokmål* as their primary language, and the remaining twenty percent, concentrated in the fjord country of the west coast and the mountain districts of central Norway, are *Nynorsk* speakers. Despite the best efforts of the government, *Nynorsk* is in decline – in 1944 one-third of the population used it. As the more common of the two languages, it is *Bokmål* we use here.

As elsewhere in Scandinavia, you don't really need to know any Norwegian to get by. Almost everyone speaks at least some English, and in the tourist industry many Norwegians are fluent. **Phrase books** are thin on the ground, but Berlitz's Norwegian–English dictionary has a useful grammar section and a menu reader.

Pronunciation

Pronunciation can be tricky. A **vowel** is usually long when it's the final syllable or followed by only one consonant; followed by two it's generally short. Unfamiliar ones are:

ae before an r, as in bad; otherwise as in say
ø as in fur but without pronouncing the r
å usually as in saw
øy between the ø sound and boy
ei as in say
consonants are pronounced as in English except:
c, q, w, z found only in foreign words and pronounced as in the original
g before i, y or ei, as in yet; otherwise hard
hv as in view
j, gj, hj, lj as in yet
rs usually as in shut
k before i, y or j, like the Scottish loch; otherwise hard
sj, sk before i, y, ø or øy, as in shut

Basic phrases

do you speak English?	**snakker du engelsk?**
yes	**ja**
no	**nei**
do you understand?	**forstår du?**
I don't understand	**jeg forstår ikke**
I understand	**jeg forstår**
please	**vær så god**
thank you (very much)	**takk (tusen takk)**
you're welcome	**vær så god**
excuse me	**unnskyld**
good morning	**god morgen**
good afternoon	**god dag**
good night	**god natt**
goodbye	**adjø**
today	**i dag**
tomorrow	**i morgen**
day after tomorrow	**i overmorgen**
in the morning	**om morgenen**
in the afternoon	**om ettermiddagen**
in the evening	**om kvelden**

Some signs

entrance	**inngang**
exit	**utgang**
gentlemen	**herrer** or **menn**
ladies	**damer** or **kvinner**
open	**åpen**
closed	**stengt**
arrival	**ankomst**
police	**politi**
hospital	**sykehus**
cycle path	**sykkelsti**
no smoking	**røyking forbudt**
no camping	**camping forbudt**
no trespassing	**uvedkommende forbudt**
no entry	**ingen adgang**
pull/push	**trekk/trykk**

243

departure	avgang
parking fees	avgift

Questions and directions

where? (where is/are?)	hvor? (hvor er?)
when?	når?
what?	hva?
how much/many?	hvor mye/hvor mange?
why?	hvorfor?
which?	hvilket?
what's that called in Norwegian?	hva kaller man det på norsk?
can you direct me to …?	kan de vise meg veien til …?
it is/there is (is it/is there)	det er (er det)?
what time is it?	hvor mange er klokken?
big/small	stor/liten
cheap/expensive	billig/dyrt
early/late	tidlig/sent
hot/cold	varm/kald
near/far	i nærheten/langt borte
good/bad	god/dårlig
vacant/occupied	ledig/opptatt
a little/a lot	litt/mye
more/less	mer/mindre
can we camp here?	kan vi campe her?
is there a youth hostel near here?	er det et vandrerhjem i nærheten?
how do I get to …?	hvordan kommer jeg til …?
how far is it to …?	hvor langt er det til …?
ticket	billett
single/return	en vei/tur-retur
can you give me a lift to …?	kan jeg få sitte på til …?
left/right	venstre/høyre
go straight ahead	kjør rett frem

Numbers

0	null
1	en
2	to
3	tre
4	fire
5	fem
6	seks
7	sju
8	åtte
9	ni
10	ti
11	elleve
12	tolv
13	tretten
14	fjorten
15	femten
16	seksten
17	sytten
18	atten
19	nitten
20	tjue
21	tjueen
22	tjueto
30	tretti
40	førti
50	femti
60	seksti
70	sytti
80	åtti
90	nitti
100	hundre
101	hundreogen
200	to hundre
1000	tusen

Days

Sunday	søndag
Monday	mandag
Tuesday	tirsdag
Wednesday	onsdag
Thursday	torsdag
Friday	fredag
Saturday	lørdag

Months

January	januar
February	februar
March	mars
April	april
May	mai
June	juni
July	juli
August	august
September	september
October	oktober
November	november
December	desember

(Note: days and months are never capitalized)

Glossary of Norwegian terms and words

stream or creek	å	church	kirke/kjerke
chemist	apotek	o'clock	klokken/kl.
hill	bakke	discount or price	moderasjon
bookshop	bokhandel	reduction	
bridge	bro/bru	Value Added Tax	MOMS or MVA
valley/dale	dal	museum	museet
cathedral	domkirke	Norwegian	NAF
taxi	drosje	Automobile Association	
AD	e.Kr	discount or price	rabatt
river/stream	elv/bekk	reduction	
ferry	ferje/ferge	town hall	rådhus
mountain	fjell/berg	city or town centre	sentrum
BC	f.Kr	sea	sjø
waterfall	foss	forest	skog
street	gate/gata (gt.)	castle, palace	slott
ocean	hav	parliament	Storting
harbour	havn	special offer	tilbud
cottage, cabin	hytte	main town square,	torget
lake	innsjø	often home to an	
railway station	jernbanestasjon	outdoor market	
Norwegian YMCA/	KFUM/KFUK	water or lake	vann/vatn
YWCA		road	vei/veg/vn

2.1

Oslo and the Oslofjord

Oslo is an enterprising city. Something of a poor relation to Stockholm until Norway's break with Sweden at the beginning of the twentieth century, it remained dourly provincial until the 1950s, since when it has developed into a go-ahead and cosmopolitan commercial hub of half a million people. The new self-confidence is plain to see in the vibrant and urbane city centre, whose easy-going atmosphere compares favourably with any other capital in Europe. Inevitably, Norway's big companies are mostly based here, as a rash of concrete-and-glass towers testify, though these monoliths rarely interrupt the stately Neoclassical lines of the late nineteenth-century **town centre**. It's here you should head first, as Oslo's handsome older quarters notch up some excellent museums and field a cosmopolitan street-life and bar scene that surprises many first-time visitors; furthermore, they're also within easy reach of the **Bygdøy peninsula**, home to the world-famous Viking Ships Museum.

Oslo is also the only major metropolis in the country (its nearest rival, Bergen, is less than half its size), a distinction which gives the city an unusually powerful – some say overweening – voice in the nation's affairs, whether political, cultural or economic. The centre itself is compact, but the city's vast boundaries (453 square kilometres) encompass huge areas of forest and coastline, reflecting the deep and abiding affinity which the inhabitants have for the wide open spaces that surround their city. The waters of the **Oslofjord** to the south and the forested hills of the **Nordmarka** inland to the north are immensely popular for everything from boating and hiking to skiing, and on all but the shortest of stays there's ample opportunity to join in. The **island beaches** just offshore in the Oslofjord and the open forest and ski jumps at **Holmenkollen** are obvious targets, both within easy reach by ferry or underground train.

Oslo

The oldest of the Scandinavian capital cities, **OSLO** (the name is made up from Ås, a Norse word for God, and Lo, meaning field) was founded, according to the medieval Norse chronicler Snorre Sturlason, around 1048 by Harald Hardråde. Harald's son, Olav Kyrre, established a bishopric and built a cathedral here, though the kings of Norway continued to live in Bergen – an oddly inefficient division of church and state, considering the difficulty of communications between the two settlements. At the start of the fourteenth century, Håkon V rectified matters by moving to Oslo, where he built himself the Akershus fortress. The town boomed until 1349 when the bubonic plague wiped out almost half the population, initiating a period of slow decline whose pace accelerated after Norway came under Danish control in 1397. No more than a neglected backwater, Oslo's fortunes were ultimately revived by the Danish king **Christian IV**, who in 1624 moved Oslo lock, stock and barrel, shifting it west to its present site and re-christening it

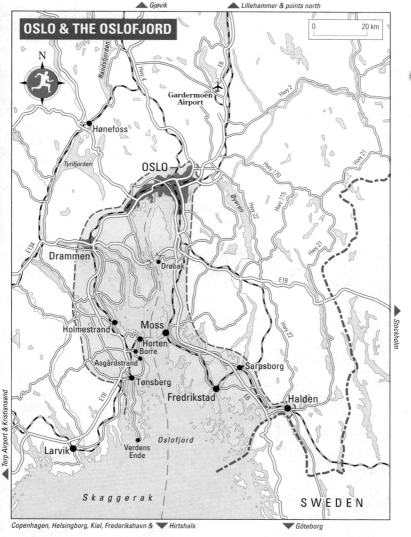

OSLO & THE OSLOFJORD

0   20 km

N

Randsfjorden

Hwy 4

E6

Hwy 2

Gardermoen
Airport

Hønefoss

Tyrifjorden

OSLO

Hwy 170

Hwy 21

Øyeren

Hwy 115

Hwy 22

E134

Drammen

Drøbak

E18

Hwy 21

▶ Stockholm

Holmestrand

Moss

Hwy 22

Horten
Borre

Sarpsborg

E18

Asgårdstrand

E6

Tønsberg

Fredrikstad

Halden

◀ Torp Airport & Kristiansand

Larvik

Verdens
Ende

Oslofjord

Skaggerak

SWEDEN

"Christiania". The new city prospered and by the nineteenth century, Christiania (indeed Norway as a whole) was clamouring for independence, which it finally achieved in 1905 – though the city didn't revert to its original name for another twenty years.

Today's **city centre** embodies the urban elegance of the late nineteenth and early twentieth centuries: wide streets, dignified parks and gardens, solid buildings and long, consciously classical vistas combine to lend it a self-satisfied, respectable air. Oslo's biggest single draw is its **museums**, which cover a hugely varied and stimulating range of topics: the fabulous Viking Ships Museum, the Munch Museum, the park devoted to the bronze and granite sculptures of Gustav

Vigeland, and the moving historical documents of the Resistance Museum are enough to keep even the most battle-weary museum-goer busy for a few days. There's also a decent **outdoor life** – Oslo is enlivened by a good range of parks, pavement cafés, street entertainers and festivals, and in summer, when virtually the whole population lives outdoors, the city is a real delight. It's also worth visiting in winter, when its prime location amid hills and forests makes it a thriving and affordable ski centre.

Arrival and information

Downtown Oslo is at the heart of a superb public transport system, which makes arriving and departing convenient and straightforward. The principal arrival hub is **Oslo Sentralstasjon** (usually shortened to Oslo S) on the Jernbanetorget, a square at the eastern end of the main thoroughfare, **Karl Johans gate**. This large complex includes the main train and bus stations, city tram, metro and bus stops, a tourist office and exchange facilities. The other transport hub is **Nationaltheatret** at the west end of Karl Johans gate, handier for most city centre sights and Oslo's main harbour. As well as the **tourist information** office in Oslo S, there's another close to Nationaltheatret, at Fridtjof Nansens plass 5.

△ Oslo tram

Arriving by air: Gardermoen airport

Opened in 1998, **Oslo Gardermoen airport** is a lavish affair designed in true pan-Scandinavian style, with acres of cool stone floor and lightly-varnished pine, soft angles, slender concrete pillars and high ceilings. Departures is on the upper level, Arrivals on the lower, where there are also currency exchange facilities, car rental offices (see p.282 for details) and a visitor information desk.

Gardermoen is located 45km north of the city centre, at the end of a 7km-long spur road off the E6 motorway. There are three ways to get from the airport to the centre of Oslo by **public transport**. The fastest and most expensive option is the **FlyToget** express train (daily 5.30am–12.30pm every 10–15 min; 160kr single; 320kr return; ◍www.flytoget.no), which takes twenty minutes to reach Oslo S, a couple more to Nationaltheatret. Alternatively, the once hourly Eidsvoll–Kongsberg **local train** links Gardermoen with Oslo S and Nationaltheatret; compared to the FlyToget, these trains take a bit longer (40–45min) and cost a lot less (77kr each way). Note also that there are express trains north from Gardermoen to a number of destinations, including Lillehammer, Røros and Trondheim; many of these services require a reservation – for details and bookings, head to the train ticket office in Arrivals.

By bus, **SAS Flybussen** (daily 5.20am–1am, every 20–30min; 110kr single; 170kr return; ◍www.flybussen.no) depart from outside the Arrivals concourse for the main downtown bus station, Oslo Bussterminalen, part of the Oslo S complex; the journey takes about 45 minutes, traffic depending. They then continue on to Jernbanetorget, Grensen and the *Radisson SAS Scandinavia Hotel*. **For Gardermoen departures**, the Flybussen follows the same route in the opposite direction. In addition, **Flybussekspressen** (☎177 from within Oslo, ☎81 50 01 76 from elsewhere; ◍www.flybussekspressen.no) operates a variety of bus services from the airport direct to the small towns surrounding Oslo at regular intervals and at reasonable rates. The **taxi fare** from Gardermoen to the city centre is 490kr. Finally, note that if you're heading into Oslo from Gardermoen by **car**, there is a 15kr toll on all approach roads into the city, so have some kroner handy.

Arriving by air: Oslo (Torp) airport

Oslo's second airport, **Oslo (Torp)**, is located just outside the town of Sandefjord, about 110km southwest of Oslo. The **Torp-Ekspressen bus** (3–6 daily; 130kr single; ☎177 from within Oslo, ☎81 50 01 76 from elsewhere; ◍www.torpekspressen.no) links this airport with the main downtown bus station, Oslo Bussterminalen, part of the Oslo S complex; the bus schedule to and from Torp, links with flight arrivals and departures. The bus journey takes just under two hours, and you buy tickets from the driver.

Arriving by train

International and domestic **trains** use **Oslo S** (train information and reservations ☎81 50 08 88, ◍www.nsb.no). There are money exchange facilities here, as well as a post office, a tourist office, and two **train information** offices – one for enquiries, the other for tickets and seat reservations. (The latter are compulsory on many long-distance trains – see p.254). Many domestic trains also pass through the Nationaltheatret station, at the west end of Karl Johans gate, which is slightly more useful for the city centre.

Arriving by bus

The central **Bussterminalen** (bus terminal) is part of the Oslo S complex; it's handily placed a short, signposted walk to the northeast of the train station on Schweigårdsgate. International and domestic long-distance buses arrive at and depart from here, as do services from Gardermoen Torp airports. For all bus enquiries, consult the Nor-Way Bussekspress Bussterminalen **information desk** (Mon–Fri

7am–10pm, Sat 8am–5.30pm & Sun 8am–10pm; ☎ 23 00 24 00 for services to and from Oslo; ☎ 81 54 44 44 for all other services; ⊛ www.nor-way.no), which also handles information on the airport buses (see p.249) and the Säfflebussen (☎ 81 56 60 10, ⊛ www.safflebussen.se) international services to Copenhagen and Stockholm.

Arriving by car ferry

DFDS Scandinavian Seaways **ferries** from Copenhagen and Helsingborg, and Stena ferries from Fredrikshavn in Denmark, arrive at the **Vippetangen quays**, a twenty-minute walk (1300m) south of Oslo S: to get to the station, take Akershus-stranda/Skippergata to Karl Johans gate and turn right. Alternatively, catch bus #60, marked "Jernbanetorget" (Mon–Fri 6am–11.30pm, Sat from 8.30am, Sun from 9am, every 20–30min; 5min). On Color Line services from Kiel and Denmark's Hirsthals, you'll arrive at the **Hjortneskaia**, some 3km west of the city centre. From here, bus #33 runs to the Nationaltheatret, plumb in the city centre, but not to Oslo S; it is an occasional bus service geared to meet incoming ferries. Failing that, a taxi to Oslo S will cost about 120kr.

Driving into the city and parking

Arriving in Oslo **by car**, you'll have to drive through one of the eighteen video-controlled **toll-points** that ring the city; it costs 15kr to enter and there are hefty spot fines if you're caught trying to dodge payment. The "Abonnement" lanes (with blue signs) are for passholders only and are always on the left; the "Mynt/Coin" lanes (with yellow signs) are for exact cash payments only and usually have a bucket-shaped receptacle where you throw your money; and the "Manuell" (grey) lanes are also used for cash payments, but provide change. Oslo's ring roads encircle and tunnel under the city; if you follow the signs for "Ring 1" you'll be delivered right into the centre and emerge (eventually) at the Ibsen P-Hus, a multi-storey car park a short distance from Karl Johans gate.

You won't need your car to sightsee in Oslo, so you'd do best to use a designated **car park**. There are half a dozen multi-storey car parks in the centre, though some of them operate restricted hours: both the Ibsen P-hus at CJ Hambros plass 1, two blocks north of Karl Johans gate, and Aker Brygge P-hus, Sjøgata 4, are open 24 hours. Costs begin at 15kr for 20 minutes during the day (Mon–Sat 7am–5pm), up to a maximum of 225kr for 24 hours; Sunday, evening and overnight rates are heavily discounted.

Alternatively, you can park in **pay-and-display car parks** and **on-street metered spaces** around the city. Identified by blue "P" signs, these metered spaces are owned and operated by the municipality, and are usually free of charge from Monday to Friday between 5pm and 8am and over the weekend after 3pm on Saturday. There is a maximum three-hour stay in pay periods. **Charges** vary considerably: a prime on-street parking spot (if you can get one) costs 106kr for three hours, half that further out. Oslo Pass holders get free parking in all municipal parking spaces, but have to abide by the posted regulations. Holders must be sure to write the vehicle registration number, date and time on the card in the space provided.

Information

The main **tourist information office** (Oct–March Mon–Fri 9am–4pm; April–May & Sept Mon–Sat 9am–5pm; June–Aug daily 9am–7pm; ☎ 81 53 05 55, ⊛ www.visitoslo.com) is in front of the Rådhus, at Fridtjof Nansens plass 5. Staff have a full range of information about Oslo and its environs, and they issue both free city maps and maps of the transport system. They also sell the Oslo Pass (see opposite), supply free copies of both the excellent and very thorough *Oslo Official Guide* and the listings brochure *What's On in Oslo*, and can make reservations on guided tours and book accommodation (see p.255). There's a second tourist office inside **Oslo S** (Oct–April Mon–Sat 8am–5pm; May–Sept daily 8am–11pm) and this offers the same services. Oslo also has a youth information shop, **Unginfo**, also known as **Use-it**, at Møllergata 3 (July–Aug Mon–Fri 9am–6pm; Sept–June Mon–Fri 11am–5pm; ☎24 14 98 20, ⊛www.use-it.no), They produce a free annual booklet, *Streetwise*, which provides an excellent city round up of everything from bars and clubs to museums and cafés.

The **Trafikanten** information office (see below) provides information on Oslo's public transport system.

City transport

Oslo's safe and efficient public transport system consists of buses, trams, a small underground rail system (the Tunnelbanen or T-bane) and local ferries. It's run by AS Oslo Sporveier, whose information office, **Trafikanten**, is beneath the distinctive, see-through clocktower outside Oslo S, on the Jernbanetorget (Mon–Fri 7am–8pm, Sat & Sun 8am–6pm; ☎177, ⊛www.trafikanten.no). The office sells all the tickets and passes detailed below, has racks of free timetables and gives away a useful **visitor's transit map**, the *Sporveiens besøskart*, though this is also available at the tourist office.

Flat-fare **single tickets** for all forms of Oslo's public transport cost 20kr if purchased before the journey (there are automatic ticket machines at all T-bane stations and ferry docks, most tram stops and many bus stops), 30kr if purchased from a bus or tram driver. They are valid for unlimited travel within the city boundaries for one hour; seniors and children four to sixteen years old travel half price, babies and toddlers free. There are several ways to cut costs. The best is to buy an **Oslo Pass** (see below), which is valid on the whole network and on certain routes into the surrounding *kommunes* – but not on trains or buses to the airport. If you're not into museums, however, a straight **travel pass** might be a better buy. A Dagskort (24hr pass) is valid for unlimited travel within the city limits and costs 60kr; a seven day pass costs 210kr, while a monthly pass will set you back 700kr. Alternatively, there's the Flexikort, which is valid for eight trips within the city limits and costs 150kr. As well as the Trafikanten office, all these passes and tickets can be bought at the automatic machines mentioned above.

All tickets and passes must be **stamped** when they are first used: buses, trams, ferries (except those to the Bygdøy) and T-bane stations all have automatic stamping machines. Ticket inspectors roam around in mufti and if you haven't got a valid, stamped pass or ticket, you will receive a hefty on-the-spot fine of 750kr.

Oslo Pass

The useful and money-saving **Oslo Pass** gives free admission to almost every museum in the city, unlimited free travel on the whole municipal transport system, and free parking in municipal car parks. It also provides some discounts in shops, hotels and restaurants, though in winter, when opening hours for many sights and museums are reduced, you may have to work hard to make the card pay for itself. Valid for 24, 48 or 72 hours, it costs 210kr, 300kr or 390kr respectively, with children aged four to fifteen charged 90kr, 110kr or 140kr. It's available at the city's two tourist offices, most hotels and campsites in Oslo, the Trafikanten office (see above) and some of the larger downtown Narvesen convenience stores. The card is valid for a set number of hours (rather than days) starting from the moment it is first used, at which time it should either be presented or stamped, or you should fill in the date and time yourself. A booklet detailing every advantage the Oslo Pass brings is issued when you buy one.

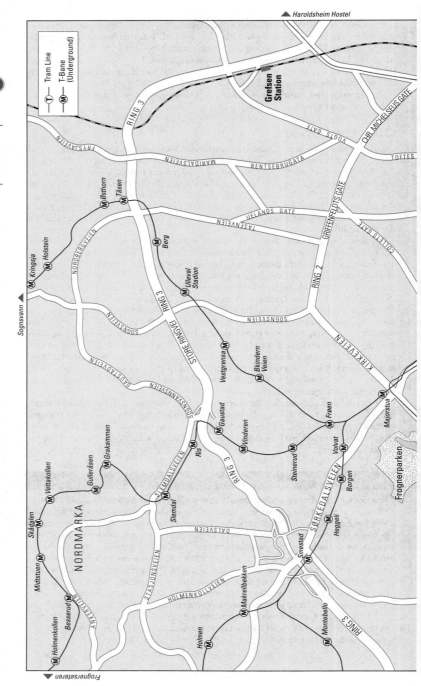

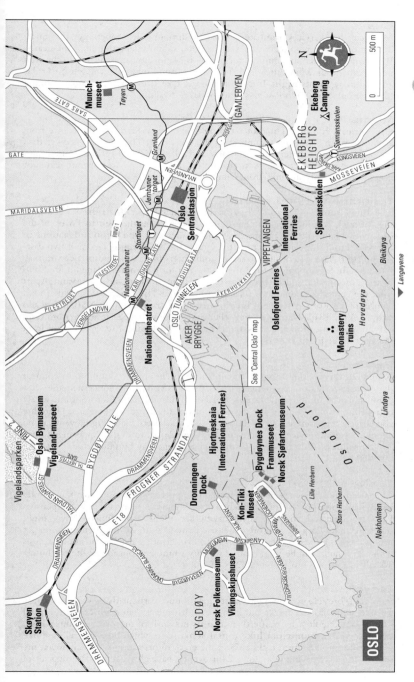

OSLO

Langøyene

Buses

Many city **bus** services originate at – or pass through – Jernbanetorget, the square in front of Oslo S, with many buses to the outer suburbs departing from the nearby Bussterminal. A second common port of call is Nationaltheatret, further to the west near the harbour. Most buses stop running at around midnight, though on Friday and Saturday nights **night buses** (*nattbussen*) take over on certain major routes (flat-rate fare 50kr; Oslo Pass and other passes not valid).

Trams

Oslo's **trams** run on eight routes through the city, crisscrossing the centre from east to west, and sometimes duplicating the bus routes. They are a bit slower than the buses, but are a rather more enjoyable and relaxing way of getting about. Major stops include Jernbanetorget, Nationaltheatret and Storgata. Most operate regularly: every ten or twenty minutes, from 6am to midnight.

Tunnelbanen and trains

The Tunnelbanen – **T-bane** – has five lines which converge to share a common slice of track crossing the city centre from Majorstua in the west to Tøyen in the east, with Nationaltheatret, Stortinget, Jernbanetorget and Grønland stations in between. From this central section, three lines run westbound (*Vest*) and two eastbound (*Øst*). The system mainly serves commuters from the suburbs, but you may find it useful for hopping around the centre and for trips out into the forested hills of the Nordmarka, and to Frognerseteren, Holmenkollen and Sognsvann. Apart from the central section, trains travel above ground. The system runs from around 6am until 12.30am. A series of **local commuter trains**, run by NSB, links Oslo with Moss, Eidsvoll, Drammen and other outlying towns; departures are from Oslo S, with many also stopping at Nationaltheatret. For details of services to and from the airport, see p.249.

Ferries

Numerous **ferries** shuttle across the northern reaches of the Oslofjord to connect the city centre with the outlying districts. As far as visitors are concerned, the most popular are the summertime ferries (April–Sept) leaving from Pier #3 immediately behind the Rådhus bound for the museums of the Bygdøy peninsula. There are also all-year ferry services to a number of Oslofjord islets, including Hovedøya, and a June to August service to Langøyene, but these depart from the Vippetangen quay, 1300m south of Oslo S. To get to the Vippetangen quay by public transport, take bus #60 from Jernbanetorget.

Taxis

The speed and efficiency of Oslo's public transport system means that you should rarely have to resort to a **taxi**, which is probably just as well as they are expensive. Fares are regulated, with the tariff varying according to the time of day – night times are about 25 percent more expensive than daytime – though on many longer routes there is a fixed tariff: central Oslo to Gardermoen airport, for instance, costs 490kr. Taxi ranks can be found round the city centre and outside all the big hotels. To call a cab ring Oslo Taxi ℡02323 or Taxi2 ℡02202.

Bicycles

Renting a **bicycle** is a pleasant way to get around, particularly as Oslo has a reasonable range of cycle tracks and many roads have cycle lanes; what's more, central Oslo is not engulfed by traffic thanks to its network of motorway tunnels. Even better, there is a **municipal bike rental scheme** in which bikes are released like supermarket trolleys from racks all over the city. Visitors can join the scheme at the tourist office by paying 60kr for a 24hr cycling pass, plus a refundable deposit of

500kr. Bikes can be used for up to three hours before they have to be dropped off (or swapped) at one of the bike racks; a map showing you the location of the racks is provided by the tourist office.

Accommodation

Oslo has the range of **hotels** you would expect of a capital city, as well as **B&Bs**, a smattering of **guesthouses** (*pensjonater*) and a quartet of **youth hostels**. To appreciate the full flavour of the city, you're best off staying on or near the western reaches of Karl Johans gate – between the Stortinget and the Nationaltheatret – though the well-heeled area to the north and west of the Royal Palace (Det Kongelige Slott) is enjoyable too. Many of the least expensive lodgings are, however, to be found in the vicinity of Oslo S, but this somewhat grimy district – along with the grey suburbs to the north and east of the station – hardly sets the pulse racing. That said, if money is tight and you're here in July and August, your choice of location may well be very limited as the scramble for **budget beds** becomes acute – or at least tight enough to make it well worth phoning ahead to check on space. For peace of mind, it is advisable to make an **advance reservation**, particularly for your first night.

One way to cut the hassle is to use the **accommodation service** provided by the tourist office, either online (@www.visitoslo.com) or in person at either of their branches (see p.250). Each office issues full accommodation lists and will make a booking on your behalf for a minimal fee, altogether a real bargain when you consider that they often get discounted rates; note also that the Oslo S office is especially good for B&Bs.

Hotels

In Oslo, 600–1000kr will get you a fairly small and simple en-suite room. You hit the comfort zone at about 1000kr, and luxury from around 1200kr. However, special offers and **seasonal deals** often make the smarter hotels more affordable than this. Most offer up to forty percent discounts at weekends, while in July and August – when many Norwegians leave town for their holidays – prices everywhere tend to drop radically. The price codes below give both the usual and the discounted rate where applicable. Also, most room rates are tempered by the inclusion of a good-to-excellent self-service buffet **breakfast**. The tourist office keeps lists of the day's best offers, or try the places on the following list – but always ring ahead first.

Central

Best Western Bondeheimen Rosenkrantz gate 8 ☏23 21 41 00, @www.bondeheimen.com. One of Oslo's most delightful hotels, its public areas and comfortable bedrooms tastefully decorated in a modern, pan-Scandinavian style, with polished pine everywhere. The inclusive buffet breakfast, served in the *Kaffistova* (see p.276) is substantial, and there's free coffee, soup and bread in the foyer throughout the evening. Look out for weekend and summer discounts of up to forty percent. ❸/❺

Bristol Kristian IV's gate 7 ☏22 82 60 00, @www.bristol.no. Plush establishment distinguished by its sumptuous public areas with ornate nineteenth-century chandeliers, columns and fancifully carved arches. The 200-odd bedrooms are decorated in lavish period(ish) style. ❻

City Skippergata 19 ☏22 41 36 10, @www.cityhotel.no. This modest but pleasant hotel, a long-time favourite with budget travellers, is located above shops and offices in a typical Oslo apartment block near Oslo S. The surroundings are a little seedy, but the hotel is cheerful enough, with small but perfectly adequate rooms. ❸

Continental Stortingsgata 24–26 ☏22 82 40 40, @www.hotel-continental.no. Arguably the classiest hotel in town, family-owned and with swish public areas that even boast some Munch paintings. The bedrooms are extremely comfortable and decorated in a fetching, almost Georgian style – all soft colours and delicate patterned wallpaper. The breakfast is a banquet. ❺

First Hotel Nobel House Kongens gate 5 ☏23 10 72 00, @www.firsthotels.com. Deluxe hotel with style – from the smart wooden floors to the

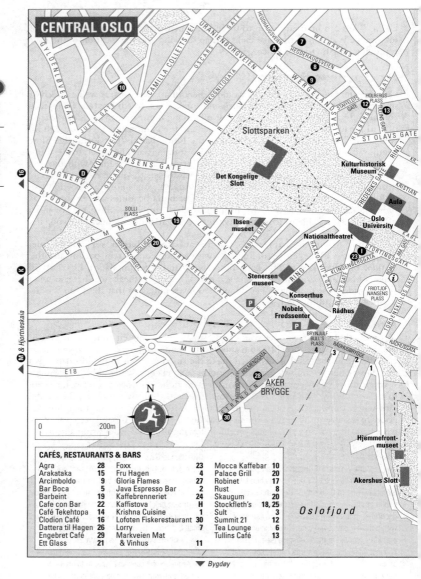

CENTRAL OSLO

Slottsparken

Det Kongelige Slott

Kulturhistorisk Museum

Aula

Oslo University

Ibsenmuseet

Nationaltheatret

Stenersen museet

Konserthus

Nobels Fredssenter

Rådhus

AKER BRYGGE

Hjemmefrontmuseet

Akershus Slott

Oslofjord

CAFÉS, RESTAURANTS & BARS			
Agra	28	Foxx	23	Mocca Kaffebar	10
Arakataka	15	Fru Hagen	4	Palace Grill	20
Arcimboldo	9	Gloria Flames	27	Robinet	17
Bar Boca	5	Java Espresso Bar	2	Rust	8
Barbeint	19	Kaffebrenneriet	24	Skaugum	20
Cafe con Bar	22	Kaffistova	H	Stockfleth's	18, 25
Café Tekehtopa	14	Krishna Cuisine	1	Sult	3
Clodion Café	16	Lofoten Fiskerestaurant	30	Summit 21	12
Dattera til Hagen	26	Lorry	7	Tea Lounge	6
Engebret Café	29	Markveien Mat		Tullins Café	13
Ett Glass	21	& Vinhus	11		

▼ Bygdøy

cool, modernist decor. Great downtown location too, close to the restaurants and art museums of Bankplassen. Hard to beat. ❹

Grand Karl Johans gate 31 ☎23 21 20 00, ⓦwww.grand.no. Once Norway's most prestigious hotel, its café the haunt of Ibsen and his chums,

the *Grand* remains one of Oslo's best, its 300 rooms mostly decorated in a modern rendition of early twentieth-century style. Hefty weekend and summertime discounts make the *Grand* much more affordable than you might perhaps expect. ❻

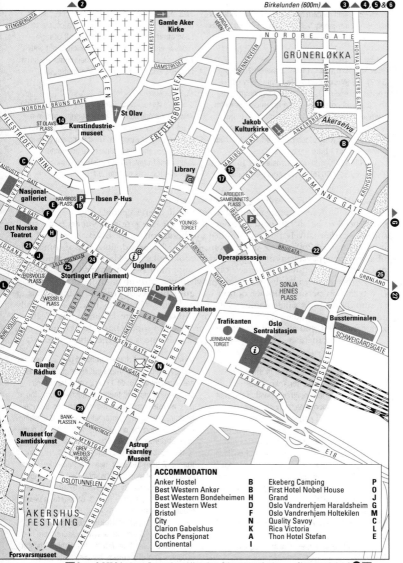

ACCOMMODATION

Anker Hostel	B	Ekeberg Camping	P
Best Western Anker	B	First Hotel Nobel House	O, J
Best Western Bondeheimen	H	Grand	J
Best Western West	D	Oslo Vandrerhjem Haraldsheim	G
Bristol	F	Oslo Vandrerhjem Holtekilen	M
City	N	Quality Savoy	C, L
Clarion Gabelshus	K	Rica Victoria	L
Cochs Pensjonat	A	Thon Hotel Stefan	E
Continental	I		

Map labels: Gamle Aker Kirke, GRÜNERLØKKA, St Olav, Kunstindustrimuseet, Jakob Kulturkirke, Akerselva, Library, Nasjonalgalleriet, Ibsen P-Hus, Det Norske Teatret, UngInfo, Operapassasjen, Stortinget (Parliament), Domkirke, SONJA HENIES PLASS, Basarhallene, Trafikanten, Oslo Sentralstasjon, Bussterminalen, Gamle Rådhus, JERNBANE-TORGET, Museet for Samtidskunst, Astrup Fearnley Museet, BANK-PLASSEN, AKERSHUS FESTNING, Forsvarsmuseet

▼ Stena & DFDS ferries to Denmark, and Hovedøya & Langøyene ferries   Sjømannsskolen & ❶ ❷ ▼

Quality Savoy Universitetsgata 11 ☎23 35 42 00, ⊛www.choicehotels.no/hotels/no060. Efficient chain hotel with 100 rooms decorated in brisk modern/minimalist style. In an interesting area too, near bookshops and cafés at the corner of Universitetsgata and Kristian Augusts gate. ❺

Rica Victoria Rosenkrantz gate 13 ☎24 14 70 00, ⊛www.rica.no. Justifiably popular with visiting business folk, this is a large, modern hotel whose spacious rooms have every convenience. ❻

Thon Stefan Rosenkrantz gate 1 ☎23 31 55 00, ⊛www.thonhotels.no. Unremarkable but spick-and-span modern hotel above the ground-floor shops in a five-storey building. Near the bottom of its price range, it's one of the city's better deals. ⑤/⑥

Westside

Best Western West Hotel Skovveien 15 ☎ 22 54 21 60, ⓦwww.bestwestern.com/no/west. Located in one of Oslo's ritziest neighbourhoods, this pleasant hotel occupies a revamped Victorian townhouse. Each of the comfortable bedrooms is decorated in an attractive contemporary style. One kilometre west of the centre off Frognerveien – take tram #12 from the centre. ⑤

🎿 **Clarion Gabelshus** Gabels gate 16 ☎ 23 27 65 00, ⓦwww.gabelshus.no.

This attractive, medium-sized hotel occupies an old villa in a smart residential area a couple of kilometres west of the city centre, off Drammensveien. The public areas are kitted out with antique furnishings, while the bedrooms are smart and efficient. Tram #10 from the centre. ④

Eastside

Best Western Anker Storgata 55 ☎ 22 99 75 00, ⓦwww.anker.oslo.no. A large budget hotel in a glum high-rise block beside the Akerselva River at the east end of Storgata. The clientele are mainly Norwegian, and the facilities are adequate, if somewhat frugal. Fifteen minutes' walk from Oslo S or five minutes by tram. ⑤

Hostels, B&Bs and guesthouses

There are two very popular HI **hostels** in Oslo, all open to people of any age, though you'll need to be an HI member to get the lowest rate – non-members pay a small surcharge. Alternatively, the tourist office can book you into a **B&B**, which will cost in the region of 250kr for a single room, 450–500kr for a double. This is something of a bargain, especially as many B&Bs have cooking facilities, but they do tend to be out of the city centre, and there is often a minimum two-night stay; note also that the tourist office will only arrange them when you turn up at either of their offices (see p.250) in person. Another option is a **guesthouse**, or *pensjonater*; these start at around 340kr for a single room, 450kr for a double. They offer basic but generally adequate accommodation, either with or without en-suite facilities, but breakfast is not included, and at some places you may need to supply your own sleeping bag. Unfortunately, there are very few in Oslo, and only one is near the city centre.

Anker Hostel Storgata 55 ☎ 22 99 72 10, ⓦwww.ankerhostel.no. Located in the same glum high-rise block as the *Anker Hotel* (see above), in a cheerless neighbourhood at the east end of Storgata. More positively, the rooms are plain and simple but perfectly adequate, with dorm beds at 175kr in a 4-bedded room, or 150kr in a 6-bedded room, and double rooms (②) too; breakfast costs an extra 60kr. Bed linen and towels can be hired; sleeping bags are not allowed. The hostel is fifteen minutes' walk from Oslo S, or five minutes by tram #11, #12, #13 or #17. Open all year.

Cochs Pensjonat Parkveien 25 ☎ 23 33 24 00, ⓦwww.cochspensjonat.no. Straightforward guesthouse occupying the third floor of an old apartment block, in a handy location behind Slottsparken at the foot of Hegdehaugsveien. There are several types of room: some have private bathrooms, others a kitchen, and triples and quadruples are available. ②, en-suite or with kitchen ②/③

🎿 **Oslo Vandrerhjem Haraldsheim** Haraldsheimveien 4, Grefsen ☎ 22 22 29 65, ⓦwww.haraldsheim.oslo.no. The best of Oslo's HI youth hostels (book ahead in summer), with

comfortable, attractively furnished public areas and 270 beds in 70 frugal but clean rooms; most are four-bedded (beds 175kr), some have their own bathrooms, and there are double rooms too (②); all rates include breakfast. Facilities include kitchen, a restaurant, Internet access and washing machines, and the only downside can be the presence of parties of noisy schoolchildren. The hostel is 4km northeast of the centre; to get there, take tram #17 from Storgata, near the Domkirke, to the Sinsenkrysset stop, from where it's a five-minute (signposted) walk. By road, *Haraldsheim* is close to – and signed from – Ring 3. Closed for a week around Christmas.

Oslo Vandrerhjem Holtekilen Micheletsvei 55, Stabekk ☎ 67 51 80 40, ⓦwww.vandrerhjem. no. Much smaller than *Haraldsheim*, this HI hostel occupies part of a college building in its own grounds some 8km west of the city centre off the E18, and has kitchen facilities, a restaurant and a laundry. Dorm beds cost 180kr, and there are single and double (②) rooms too; rates include breakfast. To get there from Oslo Bussterminalen, take bus #151, #153, #161, #162 or #252 the hostel is 200m from the Kveldsroveien bus stop. Open mid-May to Sept.

Camping and cabins

Camping is a fairly easy proposition in an uncrowded city, and of the sixteen-odd sites dotted within a 50km radius, the nearest to the centre is just 3km away. If you're out of luck with rooms in town, most sites also offer **cabins**, but ring ahead to check availability.

Ekeberg Camping Ekebergveien 65 ☎ 22 19 85 68, ⓦ www.ekebergcamping.no. Large, somewhat rudimentary but nonetheless popular campsite in a rocky, forested piece of parkland just 3km east of the city centre; to get there, take bus #34 from Jernbanetorget. Open June–Aug.
Langøyene Camping Langøyene island ☎ 22 36 37 98. Extremely popular, no-frills, semi-wilder-

ness camping among the low forested hillocks of Langøyene, one of the most agreeable – and least developed – of the islands of the inner Oslofjord. Langøyene also has the city's best beach, but that's not a great boast – it's no more than a narrow sliver of brownish sand. To get there, take ferry #94 (late May to Aug hourly 9am–7/8pm; 15min) from the Vippetangen quay.

Central Oslo

At the time of their construction, the grand late nineteenth- and early twentieth-century buildings that populate **central Oslo** provided the country's emerging bourgeoisie with a sense of security and prosperity, an aura that survives today. Largely as a result, most of downtown Oslo remains easy and pleasant to walk around, a humming, good-natured place whose airy streets and squares combine these appealing remnants of the city's earlier days with several good museums – in particular the Nasjonalgalleriet (National Gallery) and the Hjemmefrontmuseum (Resistance Museum) – plus dozens of lively bars, cafés and restaurants.

Despite the mammoth proportions of the Oslo conurbation, the **city centre** has remained surprisingly compact, and is easy to navigate by remembering a few simple landmarks. From the Oslo S train station, at the eastern end of the centre, the main drag, **Karl Johans gate**, heads directly up the hill, passing the **Domkirke** (Cathedral) and cutting a pedestrianized course until it reaches the **Stortinget** (Parliament building). From here it sweeps down past the **University** to **Det Kongelige Slott**, or Royal Palace, situated in parkland – the **Slottsparken** – at the western end of the centre. South of the palace, on the waterfront, sits the harbourside **Aker Brygge** shopping complex, across from which lies the distinctive twin-towered **Rådhus** (City Hall). South of the Rådhus, on the lumpy peninsula overlooking the harbour, is the severe-looking castle, **Akershus Slott**. The castle, the Stortinget and Oslo S form a triangle enclosing a tight, rather gloomy grid of streets and high tenement buildings that was originally laid out by Christian IV in the seventeenth century. For many years this was the city's commercial hub and although Oslo's burgeoning suburbs undermined its position in the 1960s, the district is currently making a comeback, re-inventing itself with specialist shops and smart restaurants.

Along Karl Johans gate

Heading west and uphill from Oslo S train station, **Karl Johans gate** begins unpromisingly with a clutter of tacky shops and hang-around junkies. But things soon pick up at the corner of Dronningens gate, where the curious **Basarhallene** is a circular, two-tiered building whose brick cloisters once housed the city's food market, but now hold shops and cafés. The adjacent **Domkirke** (daily 10am–4pm; free) dates from the late seventeenth century, though its heavyweight tower was remodelled in 1850. From the outside the cathedral appears plain and dour, but the elegantly restored interior is a delightful surprise, its homely, low-ceilinged nave and transepts awash with maroon, green and gold paintwork. At the central crossing, the flashy Baroque **pulpit**, where cherubs frolic among the foliage, faces a **royal box** that would look more at home at the opera. The **high altar** is Baroque too, its relief of the Last Supper featuring a very Nordic-looking sacrificial lamb.

△ Karl Johans gate

The brightly coloured **ceiling paintings** are also modern, with representations of God the Father above the high altar, Jesus in the north transept and the Holy Spirit in the south. Down below, the **crypt** is sometimes used for temporary exhibitions of religious fine and applied art. Outside the Cathedral, **Stortorvet** was once the main city square, but it's no longer of much account, its nineteenth-century **statue** of a portly Christian IV merely the forlorn guardian of a second-rate flower market.

Returning to Karl Johans gate, it's a brief stroll up to the **Stortinget** (Parliament), an imposing chunk of neo-Romanesque architecture whose stolid, sandy-coloured brickwork, dating from the 1860s, exudes bourgeois certainty. The Stortinget is open to the public during the summer (June–Sept Wed & Fri–Sun 11am–5pm, plus Tues & Thurs 11am–7pm; 45kr), but the interior is notably unexciting. In front of the Parliament, a narrow **park-piazza** runs west to the Nationaltheatret, filling in the gap between Karl Johans gate and Stortingsgata. In summer, the park brims with promenading city folk, who dodge between the jewellery hawkers, ice-cream kiosks and street performers; in winter the magnet is the dinky little open-air and floodlit **ice-skating rinks**, where skates can be rented at minimal cost.

Lurking at the western end of the park is the Neoclassical **Nationaltheatret**, built in 1899 and fronted by statues of Henrik Ibsen and Bjørnstjerne Bjørnson. Inside, the red-and-gold main hall, which seats eight hundred, has been restored to its turn-of-the-century glory; you can savour it during a performance – though these are usually in Norwegian – or by taking one of the occasional **guided tours** (ask for details at the box office or phone ☏22 00 14 00; theatre tickets on ☏81 50 08 11). It's also worth noting that Nationaltheatret is a useful transport interchange. A pair of tunnels round the back – one for points west, the other east – give access to NSB trains, the T-bane and the Flytoget, the airport express train. In addition, many city buses and trams as well as the Flybussen stop behind the Nationaltheatret, on Stortingsgata.

The University Aula

Opposite the Nationaltheatret, at the western end of Karl Johans gate, stand three of the **University**'s main buildings, grand nineteenth-century structures whose classical columns and imperial pediments fit perfectly with this monumental part of the city centre. The middle one of the trio is the **Aula** (late June to mid-Aug Mon–Fri 10am–2.45pm; free), where the imposing, deeply recessed entrance leads to a hall decorated with **murals** by Edvard Munch. The controversial result of a competition held by the university authorities in 1909, the murals weren't actually unveiled until 1916, after years of heated debate. Munch had just emerged (cured) from a winter in a Copenhagen psychiatric clinic when he started on the murals, and they reflect a new mood in his work – confident and in tune with the natural world they trumpet. All three main pieces feature a recognizably Norwegian land-scape, harsh and bleak and painted in ice-cold blues and yellowy whites. *History* focuses on an old, bearded man telling stories to a young boy and *Alma Mater* has a woman nourishing her children, but it is *The Sun* which takes the breath away, a searing globe of fire balanced on the horizon to shoot its laser-like rays out across a rocky landscape.

Det Kongelige Slott and the west end

Standing on the hill at the west end of Karl Johans gate, **Det Kongelige Slott** (the Royal Palace) is a monument to Norwegian openness. Built between 1825 and 1848, when the monarchs of other European nations were nervously counting their friends, it still stands without railings and walls, its grounds – the **Slottsparken** – freely open to the public. A snappy changing of the guard takes place daily outside the palace at 1.30pm, and there are guided tours of certain sections of the interior from late June to mid-August, though tickets (95kr) are hard to come by – ask at the tourist office. Directly in front of the palace is an equestrian statue of **Karl XIV Johan** (1763–1844) himself. Not content, seemingly, with the terms of his motto (inscribed on the statue), "The people's love is my reward," Karl Johan had this whopping palace built for his further contentment, only to die before it was completed.

The grand old mansions bordering the southern perimeter of the Slottsparken once housed Oslo's social elite. Here, in a fourth floor apartment at Arbins gate 1, **Henrik Ibsen** (1828–1906; see p.242) spent the last ten years of his life, strolling down to the *Grand Café*, in the *Grand Hotel* (see p.256) every day to hold court – a tourist attraction in his own lifetime. His old quarters are now incorporated within the brand new **Ibsen-museet** (Ibsen Museum), whose entrance is round the corner on Drammensveien (daily: May–Sept 11am–6pm; Oct–April 11am–4pm; 70kr). The museum provides a fascinating background to the great man's work, helping to explain the importance of the playwright to his emergent nation, and his apartment has been restored to its appearance as of 1895. Both Ibsen and his wife died here: Ibsen paralyzed in bed, but his wife, unwilling to expire in an undignified pose, dressed herself to die sitting upright in a chair.

From the Ibsen-Museet, it's a five-minute walk south to the **Stenersen museet**, Munkedamsveien 15 (Tues & Thurs 11am–7pm; Wed, Fri, Sat & Sun 11am–5pm; 45kr; ⓦwww.stenersen.museum.no), home to an eclectic collection of modern art, the bulk of which was gifted to the city in 1936 by the author and art collector Rolf Stenersen (the same man who gave a second collection to Bergen – see p.327). The first-floor entrance, across from the city's main concert hall, leads straight to the museum's pride and joy, its room of Munch paintings – Stenersen was a friend of Munch and bought many of his works. These include early paintings like *The Sick Room* and *Cabaret*, both dating from 1886, and disturbing later works, from the unnerving *Melancholy* to the forceful *Dance of Life*. Adjoining rooms hold an enjoyable sample of early- to mid-twentieth-century Scandinavian paintings, including the noteworthy *Small Girl on a Sofa* by **Alex Revold** and **Per Krohg**'s aloof but finely observed *Two Children*, *Actress*, and *Dressmaker*. Other rooms are devoted to Munch sketches, the soft-hued Norwegian landscapes of **Amaldus Nielsen** (1838–1932), bright burlesques of Oslo life by **Ludvig Ravensberg** (1871–1958), and two portraits of Stenersen himself. There's also a lively programme of temporary exhibitions.

North of Karl Johans gate

Returning to the west end of Karl Johans gate, follow Frederiks gate to get to Oslo's **Kulturhistorisk Museum** (Cultural Heritage Museum; May–Aug daily 10am–6pm; Sept–April Tues–Sun 11am–4pm; 40kr), which holds within its capacious walls the university's hotch-potch historical and ethnographical collections. The highlight is the **Viking and early medieval** section, on the ground floor: in the rooms to the left of the entrance are several magnificent twelfth- and thirteenth-century stave-church porches and gateposts, alive with dragons and beasts emerging from swirling, intricately carved backgrounds (for more on stave churches, see p.296). Here also are weapons, coins, drinking horns, runic stones, religious bric-a-brac and bits of clothing, as well as a superb **vaulted room** dating from the late thirteenth century and retrieved from the stave church in Ål, near Geilo.

The rest of the ground floor is taken up by a pretty average **Viking Age** exhibition geared towards school parties. The tiny dioramas are downright silly and detract from the exhibits, which attempt to illustrate various aspects of early Norwegian society, from religious beliefs and social structures through to military hardware, trade and craft. More positively, there is a fascinating sample of Viking decorative art, including the intensely flamboyant, ninth-century Oseberg and Borre styles and continuing into the Jellinge style, where greater emphasis was placed on line and composition. There's also a **skattkammeret** (treasure room) of precious objects – finger rings, crucifixes, pendants, brooches, buckles and suchlike – illustrating the sustained virtuosity of Norse goldsmiths and silversmiths.

On the first floor, the first part of the **etnografiske utstillingene** (ethnographic exhibition; same times) is devoted to the Arctic peoples and features an illuminating section on the Sámi, who inhabit the northern reaches of Scandinavia. Incongruously, there's a **myntkabinettet** (coin collection) here as well, while the top two floors contain a diverse collection of African and Asiatic pieces, from Samurai suits to African masks and everything in between.

The Nasjonalgalleriet

From the Kulturhistorisk Museum, it's a couple of minutes walk east to Norway's biggest and best art gallery, the **Nasjonalgalleriet** (National Gallery; Tues, Wed & Fri 10am–6pm; Thurs 10am–8pm; Sat & Sun 10am–5pm; free; ⓦwww .nationalmuseum.no), at Universitetsgata 13. Housed in a grand nineteenth-century building, the collection may be short on internationally famous painters – apart from a fine body of work by Edvard Munch – but there's compensation in the oodles of Norwegian art, including work by all the leading figures up until the end of World War II.

The first floor holds the kernel of the gallery's collection, including the work of the country's most important nineteenth-century landscape painters, **Johan Christian Dahl** (1788–1857) and his pupil **Thomas Fearnley** (1802–42). Dahl's giant-sized canvas *Stalheim* is typical of his work, the soft and dappled hues of the mountain landscape framing a sleepy village dotted with tiny figures. His *Hjelle in Valdres* of 1851 adopts the same approach, though here the artifice suffusing the apparent naturalism is easier to detect: the year before, Dahl had completed another painting of Hjelle, but he returned to the subject to widen the valley and heighten the mountains, sprinkling them with snow. Fearnley often lived and worked abroad, but he always returned to Norwegian themes, painting no fewer than five versions of the *Labrofossen ved Kongsberg* ("The Labro Waterfall at Kongsberg"), a fine, moody canvas of dark, louring clouds and frothing water.

On the same floor are paintings by **Gerhard Munthe** (1849–1929), whose cosy, folksy scenes are echoed by the work of **Erik Werenskiold** (1855–1938), well represented by *Peasant Burial* (1885). During this period, **Theodor Kittelsen** (1857–1914) defined the appearance of the country's trolls, sprites and sirens in his illustrations of Asbjørnsen and Moe's *Norwegian Folk Tales*, published in 1883. Two modest examples of his other work – a self-portrait and a fairytale landscape – are exhibited here. **Harald Sohlberg** (1869–1935) is represented by a series of sharply observed Røros streetscapes, and by more elemental themes such as the stunning *En blomstereng nordpå* ("A Northern Flower Meadow") and *Vinternatt i Rondane* ("Winter Night in the Rondane"). Also on this floor is the museum's star turn – its **Munch** collection, which comprises representative works from the 1880s through to 1916. Munch's early work is very much in the naturalist tradition of his mentor Christian Krohg, though by 1885 Munch was already pushing the boundaries in *The Sick Child*, a heart-wrenching evocation of his sister Sophie's death from tuberculosis. Other works with this same sense of pain include *Mother and Daughter, Moonlight* and one of several versions of *The Scream*, a seminal canvas of 1893 whose swirling lines and rhythmic colours were to inspire the Expressionists. This sample of Munch's work serves as a good introduction to the artist, but for a more detailed appraisal – and a more comprehensive selection of his work – check out the Munch Museum (see p.274).

The Kunstindustrimuseet

The **Kunstindustrimuseet** (Museum of Applied Art; Tues, Wed & Fri 11am–5pm, Thurs 11am–8pm, Sat & Sun noon–4pm; free, but admission charged for exhibitions; ⊛ www.nationalmuseum.no), at St Olavs gate 1, occupies an imposing nineteenth-century building some five minutes' walk from the Nasjonalgalleriet – continue to the far end of Universitetsgata, veer to the right and it's at the end of the street. Founded in 1876, it can lay claim to being one of the earliest applied art museums in Europe, and its multifaceted permanent collection is particularly strong on **furniture**, with examples of all the major styles – both domestic and imported – that have been popular in Norway from the medieval period to the present day.

The museum spreads over four floors with the first floor devoted to a lively programme of temporary exhibitions. The next floor up focuses on the development of **Modernism**, casting a wide net to start in 1905 and end a century later, and including keynote displays on Art Nouveau and postwar Scandinavian design. The third floor is devoted to the **History of Style 1100–1905** and, in the first room to the right of the stairs, there's an engaging hotchpotch of **medieval** paraphernalia, from brooches and crosses through to portable altars. Here also is the museum's top exhibit, the intricate and brightly coloured **Baldishol Tapestry**, one of the finest and earliest examples of woven tapestry in Europe, plus a charming selection of **bedspreads** decorated with religious and folkloric motifs. Using skills distantly inherited from Flemish weavers, the Norwegians took to pictorial bedspreads in a big way, their main modification being the elimination of perspective in the attempt to cover the seams. Of ceremonial significance, these bedspreads were brought out on all major occasions – weddings and festivals in particular. They began as fairly crude affairs at the start of the seventeenth century, but achieved greater precision and detail throughout the eighteenth century, after which the art went into a slow decline. Also on this floor is a sequence of **period interiors** illustrating foreign fashions from Renaissance and Baroque through to Rococo, Louis XVI, Jugendstil and Art Nouveau. There's also a curious little room kitted out in neo-Viking style, a medievalist fantasy dating from the late nineteenth century.

The top floor has ceramics and glassware from the early nineteenth century onwards, and displays on textiles and fashions. The highlight here is the collection of extravagant **costumes** worn by Norway's royal family at the turn of the twentieth century. Dresses is too prosaic a word for the fairy-tale affairs favoured by Queen Maud, daughter of England's Edward VII and wife of Haakon VII, not to mention Crown Princess Sonja's consecratory robe from the 1930s.

East from the Kunstindustrimuseet to Grünerløkka

Leaving the museum, walk round the dull, brown-brick pile of **St Olav Domkirke**, built for the city's Catholics in the middle of the nineteenth century, and follow Akersveien as far as the cemetery. There's a choice of routes here. If you keep straight on, it's a short stroll up the slope to the **Gamle Aker Kirke** (May–Sept Tues–Fri noon–2pm; free), a sturdy stone building still in use as a Lutheran parish church. It dates from around 1100, which makes it the oldest stone church in Scandinavia, although most of what you see today is the result of a heavy-handed nineteenth-century refurbishment.

Alternatively, back at the cemetery, turn right down **Damstredet**, a steep cobbled lane flanked by early nineteenth-century clapboard houses built at all kinds of odd angles. These are some of the few wooden buildings to have survived Oslo's developers and they make the street a picturesque affair, a well-kept reminder of how the city once looked. At the bottom of Damstredet, there's another choice of routes. If you stroll south along **Fredensborgveien**, you'll thread your way past office blocks, regaining the city centre in around fifteen minutes; heading southeast for about five minutes along Iduns gate and then Hausmanns gate, you'll reach the **Jakob Kulturkirke**, a disused church now housing a cultural centre where concerts, art exhibitions, and theatre productions are staged (call ☎22 99 34 50 or visit ⊛www.kkv.no for details).

Behind the church is the **Ankerbrua** (Anker bridge) across the **River Akerselva**. Sporting sculptures by Norwegian sculptor Per Ung – look out for Peer Gynt and his reindeer – the bridge marks the main approach to **Grünerløkka**. Formerly a run-down working-class district, Grünerløkka's recent regeneration has turned it into one of the most fashionable parts of the city, particularly amongst artists and students. Turn left just beyond the bridge, and you'll find yourself on **Markveien**, where there's a string of fashionable cafés, bars, restaurants and designer shops. At Olav Ryes plass, the first splash of greenery, turn right to reach the most interesting part of Grünerløkka's other main drag, **Thorvald Meyers gate**, which runs north to **Birkelunden**, a grassy square that's especially popular for hanging out in the summer.

The quickest way to get back to the centre is on tram #11 or #12, which both run along Thorvald Meyers gate.

To the water: the Rådhus and around

Back in the city centre, just a couple of minutes' walk south of Karl Johans gate, the **Rådhus** (daily: May–Aug 8.30am–5pm; Sept–April 9am–4pm; free: guided tours June–Aug 3 daily, Sept–May Mon–Fri 3 daily; 40kr) rears high above the waterfront. Nearly twenty years in the making, Oslo's once controversial City Hall

Scandinavian **style**

Whatever your aesthetic sensibilities, Scandinavia's ubiquitously high standards of design are sure to strike a chord. Even the most humdrum of public spaces – airport terminals, museum restrooms – command a few extra moments of appreciation, with simple and subtle touches that make bold statements without screaming for attention. And this says nothing of the finer hotels and restaurants, homages to exemplary design done out in the sleekest of furnishings. Comprising a remarkable smorgasbord of styles, Scandinavia's urban architecture provides another visual feast, from the magnificent thirteenth-century passageways of Stockholm's Gamla Stan to the imposing modernist structures by Alvar Aalto scattered all over Finland.

Gamla Stan, Stockholm

Arne Jacobsen's Swan chairs

Design

Employing simple lines, organic materials and a deft merging of function with form, Scandinavian style has a timeless appeal and the region's design traditions have become nothing short of iconic. Scandinavians have come to regard the fusion of a highly stylized aesthetic with basic utilitarian demands as central to modern living – hardly surprising in a region whose harsh climate can mean a lot of time spent indoors.

It was strikingly original pieces of furniture such as Arne Jacobsen's cradle-like Egg Chair that first got Scandinavian design noticed, and from the early 1950s onwards, objects from the region's designers became synonymous with outstanding craftsmanship, quality and innovative style. Since then, housewares and the applied arts – woodwork, glassmaking, metalwork and ceramics in particular – have been widely imitated for their simplicity and purity of line. Alongside Denmark's Jacobsen, revolutionary designers like Alvar Aalto (Finland) and Carl Malmsten (Sweden) created smooth, sensual motifs that stood out amongst the work of their overly-technical European counterparts, and were quickly heralded as masters in sculpting natural materials into shapes that evoked nature itself. Looking to the landscapes that surrounded them, they employed beech or cherry woods, and used muted, matte colours in uncomplicated, understated designs – decisions which made perfect sense in a region where standing out in a crowd has always been a social no-no. Today, classic works such as Hans Wegner's Round Chair (1949), Jacob Jensen's plastic matte-red bowls (1954), and Alvar Aalto's Paimio Chair (1933) take pride of place in design museums throughout Scandinavia.

But museums are not the only place to take in the best of Scandinavian design. Contemporary cutting-edge designers to look out for in shops across the region include Finnish crystaliers Iittala and Arabia, and the Norwegian furniture makers Stokke and Norway Says. The creations of industrial designers such as Knud Holscher and the gorgeous home entertainment equipment from Bang & Olufsen are well-known far outside Denmark's borders, while small Swedish groups like CKR and Ingegerd Råman continue a tradition of independent artisanal design.

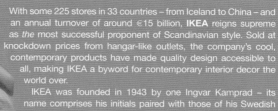

With some 225 stores in 33 countries – from Iceland to China – and an annual turnover of around €15 billion, **IKEA** reigns supreme as *the* most successful proponent of Scandinavian style. Sold at knockdown prices from hangar-like outlets, the company's cool, contemporary products have made quality design accessible to all, making IKEA a byword for contemporary interior decor the world over.

IKEA was founded in 1943 by one Ingvar Kamprad – its name comprises his initials paired with those of his Swedish home town (Eneryda Agunnaryd) – then a seventeen-year-old farm boy with a growing belief in both simple product design and corporate social responsibility. Kamprad started out selling pens, watches and nylon stockings from home, but after recognizing a need for low-cost furniture, he soon expanded. By the mid-1950s, IKEA was selling its own flat-packed furniture straight out of the company showroom, and its success grew steadily through its catalogue sales to Europe, America and beyond. Kamprad has since become one of the world's richest men, and his company, still privately owned, has made *haute* design available to all, combining great concepts and quality with simple production and distribution models that keep prices affordable. An almost exclusively Scandinavian team of designers conceive the company's 12,000 products, many of which take their names from the region's lakes, rivers and towns; unsurprisingly, IKEA also wants to be seen as responsible, using renewable resources and sourcing timber from managed forests.

Architecture

"The best standardization committee in the world is nature herself."
Alvar Aalto (1898–1976)

Perhaps the most striking thing about contemporary Scandinavian architecture is its simplicity. For hundreds of years, the region's landscape was defined by its ornate stave churches and magnificently turreted castles. But come the early twentieth century, modesty and understatement came to dominate: frill and showiness were out, restraint and clarity were in, and the rest of the world soon followed. While most European building design employed the old modernist standbys of glass, steel and concrete, Scandinavian architects – much like their furniture-building contemporaries – embarked upon an inventive incorporation of traditional forms with modern techniques, and a return to materials like wood and brick. Long before eco-friendly became a buzzword, this regressive move helped to designate Scandinavian architecture as some of the most forward-looking in the world, and set a global standard for architectural modernism. Early on, building design was profoundly influenced by Finnish architects Eliel Saarinen and Alvar Aalto, while more recent visionaries like Danes Jørn Utzon and Henning Larsen and the Swede Erik Asplund have wielded significant influence with their creations, both at home and abroad. Today, most Scandinavian towns and cities offer rich architectural pickings, and a stroll around most urban centres – from Copenhagen's Indre By district (see p.107) to the garden city of Tapiola (see p.712) just outside Helsinki – will provide hours of visual diversion.

The must-sees of Scandinavian style

▲ Central station, Helsinki

❏ **Bryggen**, Bergen. The medieval provenance of one of Norway's best preserved old quarters is strikingly evoked here by a string of gabled wooden warehouses that front the municipal wharf. See p.324

❏ **Central Train Station**, Helsinki. Guarded by four towering granite giants, Eliel Saarinen's bold Neoclassical edifice of 1909 is the defining structure of the cityscape. See p.695

❏ **Danish Design Centre**, Copenhagen. Scandinavia's most comprehensive design museum, where the newest industrial design objects are juxtaposed with timeless modernist classics. See p.115

❏ **Finlandia Hall**, Helsinki. Hidden behind an austere marble façade, the interior of Alvar Aalto's cubist-meets-modernist concert hall boasts grand, sweeping foyers and asymmetric curves. See p.698

▼ Øresunds Link

❏ **Øresunds Link**. Connecting Denmark to southern Sweden, the breathtaking steel swathes of this 16km-long road and rail bridge elegantly exemplify the confluence of form and function. See p.100

❏ **Smålands Museum**, Växjö. This superb permanent exhibition explores five hundred years of Swedish glassblowing history, with some remarkable pieces from modern masters Wilke Adolfsson and Jan-Erik Ritzman. See p.570

❏ **Stave churches**, Norway. With their characteristic vertical timbers, grooved sills and richly expressive carvings, these tiered medieval churches still dot the landscape of central Norway. See p.296

❏ **T-Bana stations**, Stockholm. The stations on the T-Bana's blue line are veritable art galleries of innovation in design and sculpture, each the work of a different local designer. See p.465

▲ T-Bana, Stockholm

finally opened in 1950 to celebrate the city's nine-hundredth anniversary. Designed by Arnstein Arneberg and Manus Poulsson, the Modernist, twin-towered building of dark brown brick was a grandiose statement of civic pride. At first, few people had a good word for what they saw as an ugly and strikingly un-Norwegian addition to the city, but with the passing of time the obloquy has fallen on more recent additions to the skyline – such as Oslo S – and the Rådhus has become one of the city's more popular buildings.

Initially at least, the ornamentation was equally contentious. Many leading Norwegian painters and sculptors contributed to the decorations, which were intended to celebrate all things Norwegian, but the themes they chose gave the hump to many of the country's Protestants. The **main approach** to the Rådhus is up along a wide ramp, whose side galleries are adorned by garish **wood panels** illustrating pagan Nordic myths with several featuring the Tree of the World, Yggdrasil or Yggdrask (see p.264). Inside, the principal hall, the **Rådhushallen**, is decorated with vast, stylized and very secular murals. On the north wall, Per Krohg's *From the Fishing Nets in the West to the Forests of the East* invokes the figures of polar explorer Fridtjof Nansen (on the left) and dramatist Bjørnstjerne Bjørnson (on the right) to symbolize, respectively, the nation's spirit of adventure and its intellectual development. On the south wall is the equally vivid *Work, Administration and Celebration*, which took Henrik Sørensen a decade to complete. The self-congratulatory nationalism of these murals is hardly attractive, although the effect is partly offset by the forceful fresco in honour of the Norwegian Resistance of World War II, running along the east wall.

Outside, at the back of the Rådhus, a line of six muscular **bronzes** represents the trades – builders, bricklayers and so on – who worked on the building. Behind them stand four massive granite female sculptures surrounding a fountain, and beyond is the busy central **harbour**, with the bumpy Akershus peninsula on the left and the islands of the Oslofjord filling out the backdrop. This is a delightful spot, one of the city's happiest moments.

Nobels Fredssenter and around

The brand new **Nobels Fredssenter** (Nobel Peace Centre; mid-June to Aug daily 9am–7pm; Sept to mid-June Tues–Sun 10am–6pm; 60kr; ⓦwww.nobelpeace center.org) was founded to celebrate and publicize the Nobel Peace Prize. Born in Sweden, Alfred Nobel (1833–96) invented dynamite in his thirties and went on to become extraordinarily rich, with factories in over twenty countries. In his will, Nobel established a fund to reward good works in five categories – physics, chemistry, medicine, literature and peace. The awards were to be made annually based on the recommendations of several Swedish institutions – with the exception of the Peace Prize, the recipient of which was to be selected by a committee of five, itself appointed by the Norwegian parliament. Inside, the Peace Centre's ground floor features a series of fancy screen displays designed to get visitors into thinking about conflict and peace with quotations from notorious thugs – Eichmann and so forth – set against those of the peaceable. Upstairs, there's a small display on the Nobel family, "wall papers" (broadly, information sheets) on all things to do with peace, and the so-called "Nobel Field", where each of the past holders of the Peace Prize is represented by a light bulb on a wispy stalk; taken together, and with the overhead lights dimmed down, the stalks make a sort of miniature electrical forest that looks rather effective. As for the winners of the Peace Prize themselves, there are many outstanding individuals – Martin Luther King, Desmond Tutu, Nelson Mandela and Willy Brandt to name but four – but some real surprises too, especially Theodore Roosevelt, who was part of the American invasion of Cuba in the 1890s, and Henry Kissinger, who was widely blamed for destabilizing Cambodia in the 1970s.

Behind the Peace Centre, the old Aker shipyard has been turned into the swish **Aker Brygge** shopping-cum-office complex, a gleaming concoction of walkways, circular staircases and glass lifts, all decked out with neon and plastic; the bars and restaurants here are some of the most popular in town.

East to Bankplassen

Running east from the Rådhus, **Rådhusgata** cuts off the spur of land on which the Akershus Castle (see opposite) is built. For the most part the street is flanked by ponderous late nineteenth-century high-rises, reminders of the time when this was the commercial heart of the city, but at the foot of Akersgata it bisects an elegant cobbled square framed by a handful of much older pastel-painted buildings, including the pint-sized **Gamle Rådhus**, Oslo's old town hall, though this was heavily restored after fire damage in 1996. It was here, in 1667, that Oslo's first theatrical performance took place – as recalled on the building's second floor in the mildly diverting **Teatermuseet** (Theatre Museum; Wed 11am–3pm, Thurs & Sun noon–4pm; 30kr), with posters, puppets and costumes.

Arguably the city's most attractive square, **Bankplassen** lies one block south of Rådhusgata, between Kongens gate and Kirkegata. Framed by Gothic Revival and Second Empire buildings, the square is a perfect illustration of the grand tastes of the Dano–Norwegian elite who ran the country at the start of the twentieth century. Bankplassen's proudest building is the former Norges Bank headquarters of 1907, a redoubtable Art Nouveau edifice with an imposing granite facade; it now houses the enterprising **Museet for Samtidskunst** (Contemporary Art Museum; Tues, Wed & Fri 10am–6pm, Thurs 10am–8pm, Sat & Sun 10am–5pm; free; ⓦ www.nationalmuseum.no). The museum owns work by every major post-war Norwegian artist and many leading foreign figures too, and for the most part the **displays** take the form of a series of temporary, thematic exhibitions spread over three floors. The works, some of which are massive, are each allowed a generous amount of space, so – given that the museum also hosts prestigious international exhibitions – only a fraction of the permanent collection can be shown at any one time. Nonetheless, Norwegian names to look out for include Bjørn Carlsen, Frans Widerberg, Erik Killi Olsen, Knut Rose and Bjørn Ransve.

About 200m to the east of Bankplassen at Dronningens gate 4, the **Astrup Fearnley Museet for Moderne Kunst** (Astrup Fearnley Modern Art Museum; Tues, Wed & Fri 11am–5pm, Thurs 11am–7pm, Sat & Sun noon–5pm; free; ⓦ www .afmuseet.no), occupies a sharp modern building of brick and glass, with six-metre-high steel entrance doors. It's meant to impress – a suitably posh setting for the display of several private collections and for prestigious temporary exhibitions. The latter often leave little space for the permanent collection, which includes examples of the work of most major post-war Norwegian artists, as well as a smattering of foreign works by such celebrated figures as Francis Bacon, Damien Hirst, Jeff Koons and Anselm Kiefer.

The Akershus Festning

Though very much part of central Oslo by location, the thumb of land that holds the sprawling fortifications of the **Akershus complex** (outdoor areas daily 6am–9pm; free) is quite separate from the city centre in feel. Built on a rocky knoll overlooking the harbour in around 1300, the original **Slott** (castle) was already

> ### The Arkitekturmuseet
>
> One of Oslo's four national museums, the **Arkitekturmuseet** (Museum of Architecture) was closed at the time of writing, but will move into new premises on Bankplassen sometime in 2007. It's a lavish redevelopment, costing millions of kroner, and will include a spanking new exhibition pavilion. For a progress update, visit ⓦ www .nationalmuseum.no.

the battered veteran of several unsuccessful sieges when Christian IV (1596–1648) took matters in hand. The king had a passion for building cities and a keen interest in Norway – during his reign he visited the country about thirty times, more than all the other kings of the Dano–Norwegian union together. When Oslo was badly damaged by fire in 1624, he took his opportunity and simply ordered the town to be moved round the bay from its location at the mouth of the River Alna beneath the Ekeberg heights. It was rebuilt in its present position, and renamed Christiania – a name which stuck until 1925 – and the medieval castle was transformed into a Renaissance residence. Around the castle, Christian also constructed a new fortress – the **Akershus Festning** – whose thick earth-and-stone walls and protruding bastions were designed to resist artillery bombardment. Refashioned and enlarged on several later occasions, and now bisected by Kongens gate, parts of the fortress have remained in military use until the present day.

There are several **entrances** to the Akershus complex, but the most appealing is at the west end of **Myntgata**, from where a footpath leads up to a side gate in the perimeter wall. Just beyond the gate is a dull museum-cum-information centre, which makes a strange attempt to tie in the history of the castle with modern environmental concerns, and frankly you're much better off keeping going along the signed **footpath** that worms its way up to the castle and the Hjemmefrontmuseum, offering the possibility of heady views over the harbour on the way.

Hjemmefrontmuseum

The **Hjemmefrontmuseet** (Resistance Museum; mid-April to mid-June & Sept Mon–Sat 10am–4pm, Sun 11am–4pm; mid-June to Aug Mon, Wed, Fri & Sat 10am–5pm, Tues & Thurs 10am–6pm, Sun 11am–5pm; Oct to mid-April Mon–Fri 10am–3pm, Sat & Sun 11am–4pm; 30kr) occupies a separate building just outside the castle entrance, an apt location given that the Gestapo tortured and sometimes executed captured Resistance fighters here in the castle. Labelled in English and Norwegian, the museum details the history of the war in Norway, from defeat and occupation through resistance to final victory. There are tales of extraordinary heroism here – notably the determined resistance of hundreds of the country's teachers to Nazi instructions and the sabotaging of German attempts to produce heavy water for an atomic bomb at Rjukan (see p.237), deep in southern Norway. There's also the moving story of a certain Petter Moen, who was arrested by the Germans and imprisoned in the Akershus, where he kept a diary by picking out letters on toilet paper with a nail: the diary survived, but he didn't. Another section deals with Norway's Jews, who numbered just 1800 in 1939; the Germans captured 760, of whom 24 people survived. There's also an impressively honest account of Norwegian collaboration: fascism struck a chord with the country's petit bourgeois, and hundreds of volunteers joined the Germany army.

Akershus Slott

Next door to the Resistance Museum, the severe stone walls and twin spires of the medieval **Akershus Slott** (May to early Sept Mon–Sat 10am–4pm, Sun 12.30–4pm; 40kr including frequent guided tour; out of season 1 guided tour in English weekly – call ☎23 09 35 53 for details) perch on a rocky ridge high above the zigzag fortifications that Christian IV added in the seventeenth century. The castle is approached through a narrow tunnel-gateway, beyond which lies a stone-flagged courtyard and then the main gate. So far so good, but thereafter the interior is a bit of a disappointment, mostly comprising a string of sparsely furnished rooms linked by bare-brick passageways. Nevertheless, there are one or two items of interest, primarily the royal chapel and **mausoleum**, holding the sarcophagi of Norway's current dynasty – not that there have been many of them, just two in fact, Haakon VII (1872–1957) and Olav V (1903–91).

Back outside, a **path** leads off the courtyard, running down the side of the castle with the walls pressing in on one side and views out over the harbour on the other.

At the foot of the castle, the path swings across a narrow promontory and soon reaches the **footbridge** over Kongens gate. Cross the footbridge for the Forsvars-museet (see below), or keep straight for the string of ochre-coloured barrack blocks that leads back to Myntgata (see p.267).

Forsvarsmuseet

On the far side of the Kongens gate footbridge, head southeast across the army parade ground to reach the **Forsvarsmuseet** (Armed Forces Museum; May–Aug Mon–Fri 10am–5pm, Sat & Sun 11am–5pm; Sept–April Mon–Fri 11am–4pm, Sat & Sun 11am–5pm; free), which tracks through Norwegian military history from the Vikings to postwar peace-keeping. The most interesting section deals with World War II, although otherwise it's hard to get enthralled by the museum's assortment of uniforms, rifles and guns, doubly so since the wars fought between the Scandi-navian countries are frequent and hard to disentangle one from the other.

From here, it's a short walk back to the main entrance of the Akershus complex at the foot of Kirkegata.

Southwest of the centre: the Bygdøy peninsula

Other than the centre, the place where you're likely to spend most time in Oslo is the **Bygdøy peninsula**, across the bay to the southwest of the main harbour, where five **museums** make for an absorbing cultural and historical trip. Indeed, it's well worth spending a full day or, less wearyingly, two half-days here. The most enjoyable way to reach Bygdøy is by **ferry**. These leave from the Rådhusbrygge (pier 3) behind the Rådhus every twenty to thirty minutes (April to mid-June & Sept daily 8.45am–6pm; mid-June to Aug daily 8.45am–8.45pm; 20kr), returning to a similar schedule. All the ferries to the peninsula perform a loop, calling first at the **Dronningen** dock (10min from Rådhusbrygge) and then the **Bygdøynes** dock (15min) before returning to the Rådhusbrygge; note that the ferries only go **one-way** – so there is no service from Bygdøynes to Dronningen. The two most popular attractions – the Viking Ships and Folk museums – are within easy walking distance of the Dronningen dock; the other three are a stone's throw from Bygdøynes. If you decide to walk between the two groups of museums, allow about fifteen minutes: the route is well signposted but dull. The alternative to the ferry is **bus** #30 (every 15–30min), which runs all year from Jernbanetorget and the Nationaltheatret to the Folk and Viking Ships museums.

Norsk Folkemuseum

About 700m uphill from the Dronningen dock – just follow the signs – the **Norsk Folkemuseum** (Norwegian Folk Museum; mid-May to mid-Sept daily 10am–6pm, 90kr: mid-Sept to mid-May daily 11am–3/4pm, 70kr; ⊛www.norsk folkemuseum.no), at Museumsveien 10, combines indoor collections on folk art, furniture, dress and customs with an extensive open-air display of reassembled buildings, mostly wooden barns, stables, storehouses and dwellings from the sev-enteenth to the nineteenth centuries. Look out also for the imaginative temporary exhibitions, for which the museum has a well-deserved reputation. Pick up a free **map** of the museum at the entrance.

The complex of buildings just beyond the entry turnstiles holds the indoor col-lections, both permanent and temporary. Of the former, the **folk art** section on the lower level is delightful, exhibiting samples of quilted bedspreads and painted furniture from the sixteenth century onwards. On the upper level, the **folk dress** section is excellent too. Rural customs specified the correct attire for every sort of social gathering, but it's the extravagant and brightly coloured bridal headdresses that grab the eye. The amount of effort that went into the creation of the folk costumes was quite extraordinary, although perhaps it should be remembered that the exhibits were mostly owned by wealthier Norwegians – many others could barely avoid starvation, never mind indulging in fancy dress.

The **open-air collection** consists of more than 150 reconstructed buildings. Arranged geographically, they provide a marvellous sample of Norwegian rural architecture, somewhat marred by inadequate explanations. That said, it's still worth tracking down the **stave church** (see box on p.296), particularly if you don't plan to travel elsewhere in Norway. Dating from the early thirteenth century but extensively restored in the 1880s, when it was moved here from Gol, near Geilo, the church is a good example of its type, with steep, shingle-covered roofs and dragon finials. The interior is cramped and gloomy, the nave preceding a tiny chancel painted with a floral design and sporting a striking *Last Supper* above and behind the altar. Elsewhere, the cluster of buildings from **Setesdal** in southern Norway holds some especially well-preserved dwellings and storehouses from the seventeenth century, while the **Numedal** section contains one of the museum's oldest buildings, a late thirteenth-century house from Rauland whose door posts are embellished with Romanesque vine decoration. In summer, many of the buildings are open for viewing, and costumed guides roam the site to both explain the vagaries of Norwegian rural life and demonstrate traditional skills, from spinning and carving to dancing and horn blowing.

Vikingskipshuset

A five-minute walk south along the main road is the **Vikingskipshuset** (Viking Ships Museum; daily: May–Sept 9am–6pm; Oct–April 11am–4pm; 40kr; ⊛www .khm.uio.no), a large hall specially constructed to house a trio of ninth-century Viking ships, with viewing platforms to enable you to see inside the hulls. The three oak vessels were retrieved from ritual burial mounds in southern Norway around the turn of the twentieth century, each embalmed in a subsoil of clay, which accounts for their excellent state of preservation. The size of a Viking **burial mound** denoted the dead person's rank and wealth, while the possessions buried with the body were designed to make the afterlife as comfortable as possible. Implicit was the assumption that a chieftain in this world would be a chieftain in the next – slaves, for example, were frequently killed and buried with their master or mistress – a belief that would subsequently give Christianity, with its alternative, less fatalistic vision, an immediate appeal to those at the bottom of the Viking pile. Quite how the Vikings saw the transfer to the after-life taking place is less certain. The evidence is contradictory: sometimes the Vikings stuck the anchor on board the burial ship in preparation for the spiritual journey, but at other times the vessels were moored to large stones before burial. Neither was ship burial the only type of Viking funeral – far from it. The Vikings buried their dead in mounds and on level ground, with and without grave goods, in large and small coffins, both with and without boats – and they practised cremation too.

The museum's star exhibits are the Oseberg and Gokstad ships, named after the places on the west side of the Oslofjord where they were discovered, in 1904 and 1880 respectively. The **Oseberg ship** is 22m long and 5m wide, and is probably representative of the type of vessel the Vikings used to navigate fjords and coastal waters. It has an ornately carved prow and stern, both of which rise high above the hull, where thirty oar-holes indicate the size of the crew. It's thought to be the burial ship of a Viking chieftain's wife, and much of the treasure buried with it was retrieved and is displayed behind it. The grave goods reveal an attention to detail and a level of domestic sophistication not traditionally associated with the Vikings. There are marvellous decorative pieces, like the fierce-looking animal-head posts, and exuberantly carved ceremonial items, including a sled and a cart, plus a host of smaller, more mundane articles such as shoes, rattles, agricultural tools and cooking pots. Here, also, are finds from the Gokstad ship, most memorably an ornate bridle and two dragonhead bedposts, though the Gokstad burial chamber was ransacked by grave robbers long ago and precious little has survived.

△ Vikingskipshuset

The **Gokstad ship** itself is slightly longer and wider than the Oseberg vessel, and quite a bit sturdier – its seaworthiness was demonstrated in 1893 when a replica sailed across the Atlantic to the USA. The third vessel, the **Tune ship**, is the smallest of the nautical trio and only fragments survive; these are displayed unrestored, much as they were discovered in 1867 on the eastern side of the Oslofjord.

The Frammuseet

Just up from the Bygdøynes dock stands the **Gjøa**, the one-time sealing ship in which **Roald Amundsen** (1872–1928) made the first complete sailing of the Northwest Passage in 1906. By any measure, this was a remarkable achievement and the fulfilment of a nautical mission that had preoccupied sailors for several centuries. It took three years, with Amundsen and his crew surviving two ice-bound winters deep in the Arctic, but this epic journey was soon eclipsed when, in 1912, the Norwegian dashed to the South Pole famously just ahead of the ill-starred Captain Scott. The ship that carried Amundsen to within striking distance of the

South Pole, the *Fram*, is displayed inside the mammoth triangular display hall that is the **Frammuseet** (Fram Museum; daily: May to mid-June 10am–5.45pm; mid-June to Aug 9am–6.45pm; Sept 10am–4.45pm; Oct–April 10am–3.45pm; 40kr; ⓦwww.fram.museum.no). Designed by Colin Archer, a Norwegian shipbuilder of Scots ancestry, and launched in 1892, the *Fram*'s design was unique, its sides made smooth to prevent ice from getting a firm grip on the hull, while inside a veritable maze of beams, braces and stanchions held it all together. Living quarters inside the ship were necessarily cramped, but – in true Edwardian style – the Norwegians found space for a piano. Look out also for the assorted knick-knacks the explorers took with them, exhibited in the display cases on the uppermost of the **three galleries** that run along the museum's walls. There are playing cards, maps, notebooks, snowshoes and surgical instruments – but this was nothing as compared to the equipment carted around by Scott, one of the reasons for his failure. Scott's main mistake, however, was to rely on Siberian ponies to transport his tackle. The animals were useless in Antarctic conditions and Scott and his men ended up pulling the sledges themselves, whereas Amundsen wisely brought a team of huskies.

The Kon-Tiki Museet

Across from the Frammuseet, the **Kon-Tiki Museet** (Kon-Tiki Museum; daily: April–May & Sept 10.30am–5pm; June–Aug 9.30am–5.30pm; Oct–March 10.30am–4pm; 40kr; ⓦwww.kon-tiki.no) displays the eponymous balsawood raft on which, in 1947, the Norwegian **Thor Heyerdahl** (1914–2002) made his famous journey across the Pacific from Peru to Polynesia. Heyerdahl wanted to prove the trip could be done: he was convinced that the first Polynesian settlers had sailed from pre-Inca Peru, and rejected prevailing opinions that South American balsa rafts were unseaworthy. Looking at the flimsy raft, you could be forgiven for agreeing with Heyerdahl's doubters – and for wondering how the crew didn't murder each other after a day – never mind several weeks – in such a confined space. Heyerdahl's later investigations of Easter Island statues and cave graves lent further weight to his ethnological theory, which has now received a degree of acceptance. The whole saga is outlined here in the museum, and if you're especially interested, the story is also told in his book, *The Kon-Tiki Expedition* (see p.241). Preoccupied with transoceanic contact between prehistoric peoples, Heyerdahl went on to attempt several other voyages, sailing across the Atlantic in a papyrus boat, *Ra II*, in 1970, to prove that there could have been contact between Egypt and South America. *Ra II* is also displayed here and the exploit recorded in another of Heyerdahl's books, *The Ra Expeditions*.

Norsk Sjøfartsmuseum

Across from the Kon-Tiki Museet, the **Norsk Sjøfartsmuseum** (Norwegian Maritime Museum; mid-May to Aug daily 10am–6pm; Sept to mid-May Mon–Wed & Fri–Sun 10.30am–4pm, Thurs 10.30am–6pm; 40kr; ⓦwww.norsk -sjofartsmuseum.no) occupies two buildings, the larger of which is a well-appointed, modern brick structure holding a varied collection of all things nautical. The ground floor is given over to temporary exhibitions, and the bulk of the permanent collection is upstairs. Here, among much else, there are pinpoint-accurate ship models, a peculiar-looking fog cannon dating to 1900, a section on shipwrecks, old passenger-ferry cabins, and even part of the deck of an old sailing ship from 1893. There's also the so-called **Gibraltar boat**, a perilously fragile canvas-and-board home-made craft on which a bunch of Norwegian sailors fled Morocco for British Gibraltar after their ship had been impounded by the Vichy French authorities during World War II, and what is reputed to be the oldest surviving Norwegian boat, a **carved-out tree trunk** that's about two thousand years old.

The museum's second building, the **Båthallen** (boat hall), holds an extensive collection of small and medium-sized wooden boats from all over Norway, mostly inshore sailing and fishing craft from the nineteenth century. Non-sailors may find it of limited interest – and head straight for the museum's fjordside café instead.

Northwest of the centre: Frognerparken

The green expanse of **Frognerparken** (Frogner Park), to the northwest of the city centre, incorporates one of Oslo's most celebrated and popular cultural targets, the open-air **Vigelandsparken** (Vigie Park) which, along with the nearby museum, commemorates a modern Norwegian sculptor of world renown, **Gustav Vigeland** (1869–1943). Between them, the park and the museum display a good proportion of his work, presented to the city in return for favours received by way of a studio and apartment during the years 1921–30.

Frogner Park is readily reached from the centre (two of the central tram stops are Jernbanetorget and Aker Brygge) on **tram #12**; get off at Vigelandsparken, the stop after Frogner plass.

The Vigelandsparken

A country boy, raised on a farm just outside Mandal on the south coast, **Gustav Vigeland** began his career as a woodcarver but later, when studying in Paris, he fell under the influence of Rodin and switched to stone and bronze. He started work on the open-air **Vigelandsparken** (daily dawn–dusk; free) in 1924, and was still working on it when he died almost twenty years later. It's a literally fantastic concoction, medieval in spirit and complexity, and it was here that he had the chance to let his imagination run riot. Indeed, when the place was unveiled, many city folk were simply overwhelmed – and no wonder. From the monumental wrought-iron gates on Kirkeveien, the central path takes you to the footbridge over the river and a world of frowning, fighting and posturing bronze figures – the local favourite is *Sinnataggen* ("The Angry Child"). Beyond, the **central fountain**, part of a separate commission begun in 1907, is an enormous bowl representing the burden of life, supported by straining, sinewy bronze Goliaths, while underneath, water tumbles out around figures engaged in play or talk, or simply resting or standing.

Yet it's the twenty-metre-high **obelisk** up on the stepped embankment just beyond that really takes the breath away. It's a deeply humanistic work, a writhing mass of sculpture which depicts the cycle of life as Vigeland saw it: a vision of humanity playing, fighting, teaching, loving, eating and sleeping – and clambering on and over each other to reach the top. The granite sculptures grouped around the obelisk are exquisite too, especially the children, little pot-bellied figures who tumble over muscled adults and provide the perfect foil to the real Oslo toddlers who splash around in the fountain below, oblivious and undeterred.

The Vigeland-museet

From the obelisk, it's a ten-minute walk south across the lawns of the Frognerpark – and over the river by a second footbridge – to the **Vigeland-museet** (Vigeland Museum; June–Aug Tues–Sun 11am–5pm; Sept–May Tues–Sun noon–4pm; 45kr; ⓦwww.vigeland.museum.no), on Halvdan Svartes gate. This was the artist's studio and home during the 1920s, built for him by the city, who let him live here rent free on condition that the building – and its contents – passed back to public ownership on his death. It's still stuffed with all sorts of items related to the sculpture park, including photographs of the workforce, discarded or unused sculptures, woodcuts, preparatory drawings and scores of plaster casts. Vigeland was obsessed with his creations during his last decades, and you get the feeling that given half a chance he would have had himself cast and exhibited. As it is, his ashes were placed in the museum tower.

North of the centre: the Nordmarka

Crisscrossed by **hiking trails** and **cross-country ski routes**, the forested hills and lakes that comprise the **Nordmarka** occupy a tract of land that extends deep inland from central Oslo, but is still within the city limits for some 30km. A network of byroads provides dozens of access points to this wilderness, which is extremely popular with the capital's outdoor-minded citizens. **Den Norske Turistforening** (DNT), the Norwegian hiking organization, maintains a handful of staffed and unstaffed huts here. Its Oslo branch, in the city centre at Storgata 3 (Mon–Wed & Fri 10am–5pm, Thurs 10am–6pm, Sat 10am–2pm; ☏22 82 28 22, ⊛www .dntoslo.no), has detailed **maps** and can sell a year's DNT membership for 445kr, which confers a substantial discount at its huts. See p.222 for more on DNT and hiking in general.

Frognerseteren and Holmenkollen

T-bane #1 delves deep into the Nordmarka, wriggling its way up into the hills to the **Frognerseteren terminus**, a thirty-minute ride north of the city centre. From the station, there's a choice of signposted trails across the surrounding countryside. The easiest is the squelchy 2.5km stroll to the **Tryvannstårnet TV Tower** (daily: May & Sept 10am–5pm; June 10am–6pm; July & Aug 10am–8pm; Oct–April 10am–4pm; 40kr), where a lift whisks you up to an observation platform. From here, there are panoramic views over to the Swedish border in the east, Oslo to the south and the forested hills of the Gudbrandsdal valley to the north. Labels inside the platform show where everything is, but it's not worth going up unless the weather is clear as even a light mist obscures the view. Alternatively, it's just a couple of hundred metres from the T-bane terminus to **Frognerseteren** (café: Mon–Sat 10.30am–10.30pm, Sun 10.30am–9pm; restaurant: daily noon–9pm; ☏22 92 40 40), a large and good-looking wooden lodge where the views from the terrace out over Oslo and the Oslofjord are more enjoyable than the café food.

Forest footpaths link Frognerseteren with Sognsvannet to the east (see below), an arduous and not especially rewarding trek over the hills of about 5km. Locals mostly shun this route in summer, but it's popular in winter with parents teaching their children to cross-country ski. There is also a longer and more interesting hiking route to Sognsvannet via **Ullevålseter**, where the lodge (Tues–Fri 9am–4pm, Sat & Sun 9am–5pm; ☏22 14 35 58) has a very good café serving excellent home-made apple cake. The whole route is about 9km long, and takes about three hours.

Alternatively, you can hop back on the T-bane for the five-stop journey back down the line to the flashy chalets and hotels of the **Holmenkollen ski resort**, whose main claim to fame is its international **ski-jump** – a gargantuan affair that dwarfs its surroundings; it's located 1km or so from the T-bane station. At the base of the ski-jump, the diligent **Skimuseet** (Ski Museum; daily: Jan–April & Oct–Dec 10am–4pm; May & Sept 10am–5pm; June–Aug 9am–8pm; 60kr) exhibits skiing apparel and equipment through the ages, from the latest in competition wear to the seemingly makeshift garb of early Polar explorers like Nansen and Amundsen. The museum also gives access to the mountain of metal steps that leads up the **ski-jump**, for a peek straight down at what is, for most people, a horrifyingly steep, almost vertical, descent. It seems impossible that the tiny bowl at the bottom could pull the skier up in time – or that anyone could possibly want to jump off in the first place. The bowl is also the finishing point for the 8000-strong cross-country skiing race that forms part of the Holmenkollrennene ski festival every March.

From Holmenkollen T-bane station (line #1), it's a 20-minute ride back to central Oslo.

Sognsvannet

It takes fifteen minutes for T-bane #3 to reach its northerly **Sognsvann terminus** from central Oslo. It's not as pleasant a journey as the T-bane to Frognerseteren (see above) – the landscape is flatter and you never really leave the city behind – but from the Sognsvann T-bane station, it's just five minutes' walk straight ahead down the slope to **Sognsvannet**, an attractive loch flanked by forested hills and encircled by an easy 4km-long hiking trail. The lake is iced over until the end of March or early April, but thereafter it's a perfect spot for swimming, though Norwegian assurances about the warmth of the water should be treated with caution. Forest footpaths link Sognsvannet with Frognerseteren.

Northeast of the centre: the Munch-museet

Nearly everyone who visits Oslo makes time for the **Munch-museet** (Munch Museum; June–Aug daily 10am–6pm; Sept–May Tues–Fri 10am–4pm, Sat & Sun 11am–5pm; 65kr; ⓦwww.munch.museum.no), and with good reason. In his will, Munch donated all the works in his possession to Oslo city council – a mighty bequest of several thousand paintings, prints, drawings, engravings and photographs, which took nearly twenty years to catalogue and organize for display in this pur-pose-built gallery. The museum is located to the east of the city centre at Tøyengata 53 and is reachable by T-bane – get off at Tøyen, from where it's a signposted five-minute walk.

The museum

The collection is huge, and only a small part of it can be shown at any one time – an advantage, since you don't feel overwhelmed by what's on display. The space required by visiting exhibitions also often confines the Munch paintings to one large gallery, which can appear cluttered, but at least you can reckon on seeing many of the more highly praised works.

In the main galleries, the landscapes and domestic scenes of Munch's **early paintings** – such as *Tête à Tête* (1885) and *At the Coffee Table* (1883) – reveal the perceptive, if deeply pessimistic, realism from which Munch's later work sprang. Even more riveting are the great works of the **1890s**, which form the core of the collection and are considered Munch's finest achievements. Among many, there's *Dagny Juel*, a portrait of the Berlin socialite Ducha Przybyszewska, with whom both Munch and his friend Strindberg were infatuated; the searing representations of *Despair* and *Anxiety*; the chilling *Red Virginia Creeper*, a house being consumed by the plant; and, of course, *The Scream* – of which the museum holds several of a total of fifty versions. Consider Munch's words as you view it:

I was walking along a road with two friends. The sun set. I felt a tinge of melan-choly. Suddenly the sky became blood red. I stopped and leaned against a railing feeling exhausted, and I looked at the flaming clouds that hung like blood and a sword over the blue-black fjord and the city. My friends walked on. I stood there trembling with fright. And I felt a loud unending scream piercing nature.

Munch's style was never static, however. **Later paintings** such as *Workers On Their Way Home* (1913), produced after he had recovered from his breakdown and had withdrawn to the tranquillity of the Oslofjord, reflect his renewed interest in nature and physical work. His technique also changed: in works like the *Death of Marat II* (1907) he began to use streaks of colour to represent points of light. Still later paintings, such as *Winter in Kragerø* and *Model by the Wicker Chair*, reveal at last a happier – if rather idealized – attitude to his surroundings, also evident in works like *Spring Ploughing*, painted in 1919.

The exhibition is punctuated by **self-portraits**, a graphic illustration of Munch's state of mind at various points in his career. There's a palpable sadness in his *Self-portrait with Wine Bottle* (1906), along with obvious allusions to his heavy drinking, while the telling perturbation of *In Distress* (1919) and *The Night Wanderer* (1923) indicate that he remained a tormented, troubled man even in his later years. One of his last works, *Self-portrait by the Window* (1940), shows a glum figure on the borderline of life and death, the strong red of his face and green of his clothing contrasted with the ice-white scene visible through the window.

Edvard Munch

Born in 1863, **Edvard Munch** had a melancholy childhood in what was then Christiania, overshadowed by the early deaths of both his mother and a sister from tuberculosis. After some early works, including several self-portraits, he went on to study in Paris, a city he returned to again and again, and where he fell (fleetingly) under the sway of the Impressionists. In 1892 he moved to Berlin, where his style developed and he produced some of his best and most famous work, though his first exhibition there was considered so outrageous it was closed after only a week – his painting was, a critic opined, "an insult to art". Despite the initial criticism, Munch's work was subsequently exhibited in many of the leading galleries of the day. Generally considered the initiator of the Expressionist movement, Munch wandered Europe, painting and exhibiting prolifically. Meanwhile overwork, drink and problematic love affairs were fuelling an instability that culminated, in 1908, in a nervous breakdown. Munch spent six months in a Copenhagen clinic, after which his health improved greatly – and his paintings lost the hysterical edge characteristic of his most celebrated work. It wasn't until well into his career, however, that he was fully accepted in his own country, where he was based from 1909 until his death in 1944.

South of the centre: the islands and beaches of the inner Oslofjord

The compact archipelago of low-lying, lightly forested **islands** to the south of the city centre in the **inner Oslofjord** is the capital's summer playground, and makes going to the **beach** a viable option. The ferry trip out there is fun too, especially on warm summer evenings when the less populated islands become favourite party venues for the city's preening youth. **Ferries** to the islands leave from the Vippetangen quay, at the foot of Akershusstranda – a twenty-minute walk or a five-minute ride on bus #60 from Jernbanetorget. Ferry tickets cost 20kr each way, though Oslo Pass and all other transport passes are valid; there's also a ferry day-pass allowing unlimited inter-island travel for 36kr.

Hovedøya and Langøyene

Conveniently, **Hovedøya** (ferry #92; daily mid-March to Sept 7.30am–6.30pm every hour to ninety minutes; Oct to mid-March 4 daily; 10min), the nearest island, is also the most interesting. Its rolling hills comprise both farmland and deciduous woods, and hold the overgrown ruins of a **Cistercian monastery** built by English monks in the twelfth century; there are also incidental remains from the days when the island was garrisoned and armed to protect Oslo's harbour. A map of the island at the jetty helps with orientation, but on an islet of this size – it's just ten minutes' walk from one end to the other – getting lost is pretty much impossible. There are plenty of footpaths to wander, you can swim at the shingle beaches on the south shore, and there's a seasonal café opposite the monastery ruins. Camping, however, is not permitted, as Hovedøya is a protected area – which is also why there are no summer homes.

The pick of the other islands is **Langøyene**, a pint-sized, H-shaped islet where a central meadow is flanked on either side by low, lightly forested rocky hills. There are no houses on the island and no roads to speak of, but there is a campsite (see p.259) and a long and narrow sandy(ish) beach. To get to Langøyene, take ferry #94 (late May to Aug hourly 9am–7/8pm; 15min) from the Vippetangen quay.

Eating and drinking

There was a time when eating out in Oslo hardly set the pulse racing, but things are very different today. At the top end of the market, the city possesses dozens of fine **restaurants**, the pick of which feature Norwegian ingredients, especially fresh north Atlantic fish, but also more exotic dishes of elk, caribou and salted-and-dried cod – for centuries Norway's staple food. Many of these restaurants have also assimilated the tastes and styles of other cuisines – Mediterranean foods are very much in vogue – and there's a reasonable selection of less expensive foreign restaurants too, everything from Italian to Vietnamese.

Even more affordable – and more casual – are the city's **cafés** and **café-bars**. These run the gamut from homely family places offering traditional Norwegian standbys to student haunts and ultra-trendy hang-outs. Nearly all serve inexpensive lunches, and many offer excellent, competitively priced evening meals as well, though many cafés close at 5pm or 6pm. In addition, downtown Oslo boasts a vibrant **bar** scene, boisterous but generally good-natured, and at its most frenetic on summer weekends when the city is crowded with visitors from all over Norway.

Finally, those carefully counting the kroner will find it easy to buy bread, fruit, **snacks** and sandwiches from stalls, supermarkets and kiosks across the city centre, while fast-food joints offering hamburgers and *pølser* (hot dogs) are legion. **Smoking** is forbidden in every Norwegian bar, café and restaurant.

Cafés, coffee houses and café-bars

For sit-down food, **cafés** represent the best value in town. Traditional *kafeterias* (often self-service) offer substantial portions of Norwegian food in pleasant surroundings, mostly decorated in crisp modern style. Oslo also has a slew of **café-bars** dishing up salads, pasta and the like in attractive, often modish premises. The best deals are generally at lunchtime, when there's often a dish of the day. In addition, Oslo now contains dozens of specialist **coffee houses**, both independents and chains – not that you should notice much difference. Most of the cafés listed below close around 8 or 9pm, while the café-bars stay open much later, till midnight and often beyond. The coffee houses tend to close between 5 and 7pm on weekdays, and around 5pm at weekends, though many are closed altogether on Sundays.

Central

Café Tekehtopa St Olavs plass 2. Known to all and sundry as *Apotheket*, this good-looking old building used to be a pharmacy, and has retained its high ceilings and old wooden fittings. It's now a highly recommended café-bar serving a wide range of food, from omelettes and pizzas to tapas and meze, all washed down by a good selection of beers. Prices are very competitive with omelettes costing 90kr, pizzas 100kr.

Ett Glass Karl Johans gate 33, but entrance round the corner on Rosenkrantz gate. Youthful, lively café-bar with an imaginative albeit short menu focusing on Mediterranean-influenced light meals and lunches; main courses are around 90kr.

Java Espresso Bar Ullevålsveien 45B, St Hanshaugen district. Coffee connoisseur's paradise patronized by Norwegian royals, but lacking any corresponding pomp. Delicious sandwiches too. Closed Sun.

Kaffebrenneriet 45 Grensen. One of the most central branches of this popular Norwegian coffee house chain. Serves particularly good espressos, as well as tasty snacks and great cakes. Closed Sun.

Kaffistova Rosenkrantz gate 8. Part of the *Hotell Bondeheimen* (see p.255), this spick-and-span self-service café serves quite tasty, traditional Norwegian cooking at very fair prices – reckon on 120kr for a main course. There's usually a vegetarian option, too.

Stockfleth's Lille Grensen, off Karl Johans gate, and CJ Hambros plass. Many locals swear by the coffee served at this small chain, which regularly wins awards for its brews. Both branches closed Sun.

Tullins Café Tullins gate 2. The building may be glum – it's a dull modern high-rise – but this ground floor café-bar is painted in exuberant modern style and furnished with an idiosyncratic mix of antiques. Pasta dishes are the mainstay – reckon on 100kr per main course – and there's inexpensive beer (at least by Norwegian standards) as the place morphs into a late-night bar. Handy central location, too.

Westside

Arcimboldo Wergelandsveien 17. Fashionable but unpretentious self-service café-bar located on the ground floor of the Kunstnernes Hus, an artist-run gallery facing the Slottsparken. Offers good-quality food with a Mediterranean slant; main courses average 160kr.

Clodion Café Bygdøy Allé 63, but entrance round the corner on Thomas Heftyes gate. Well to the west of the city centre, not far from Frognerparken, this café-bar, with its brightly-painted second-hand furniture, hosts regular art displays and serves good food: soups at around 55kr, bowls of pasta for 80kr. Bus #30, 31 or 32 from the centre.

Mocca Kaffebar Niels Juels gate 70. The only Oslo coffee house to roast its own beans – the results speak for themselves. Like its sister establishment, *Java* (see p.276), it also serves a good line in sandwiches. Closed Sun.

Rust Hegdehaugsveien 22. Smart, loungy kind of place that's good for lunches and light meals during the day and tapas in the early evening. Turns into a chic bar late at night – and one that boasts a fine selection of Calvados.

Eastside: Grønland and Grünerløkka

Dattera til Hagen Grønland 10. Extremely popular spin-off venture of *Fru Hagen* (see below), serving tasty snacks and light meals during the daytime and authentic tapas later on. Later still, the place turns into a happening bar with live DJs on the first floor (Mon–Sat). The outdoor area at the back is great on a hot summer's night.

Fru Hagen Thorvald Meyers gate 40. Colourful, long-standing joint; still trendy, and serving tasty meals from an inventive menu with a Mediterranean flavour, alongside filling sandwiches, salads and wok-cooked dishes at 80–130kr. The kitchen closes at 9.30pm, after which the drinking gets going in earnest. Very popular spot, so go early to be sure of a seat.

Restaurants

Dining out at one of Oslo's **restaurants** can make a sizeable dent in your wallet unless you exercise some restraint. In most places, a main course will set you back between 150kr and 220kr – not too steep until you add on a couple of beers (at about 50kr a throw) or a bottle of wine (at least 240kr). On a more positive note, Oslo's better restaurants have creative menus marrying Norwegian culinary traditions with those of the Mediterranean – and a lousy meal is a rarity. Restaurant decor is often a real feature too, ranging from fishing photos and nets to sharp modernist styles, all pastel walls and angular furnishings and fittings. As most places tend to be busy, it's a good idea to call and book in advance.

Central

Agra Stranden 3, Aker Brygge ☏ 22 83 07 12. Smart north Indian restaurant serving all the classics – chicken tikka and so forth – with main courses at 210–250kr. Decorated in traditional style, from the Moghul decorative arches to the deep-red tiles of the ceiling. It's a little difficult to find: take the first right – Grundigen – off the Aker Brygge boardwalk, then a left at the end.

Arakataka Mariboes gate 7 ☏ 23 32 83 00. This smart, modern bar and restaurant serves outstanding food, mostly fish, at unbeatable prices, both à la carte and with a set three-course menu for just 280kr. Highly recommended, though the service can be a tad patchy. A fifteen-minute walk north of the Domkirke on the way to Grünerløkka.

Engebret Café Bankplassen 1 ☏ 22 82 25 25. Across from the Museum of Contemporary Art, this smart and fairly formal restaurant occupies a fetching old building with oodles of wood panelling and Norwegian paintings on the wall. Specializes in local delicacies such as reindeer and fish, with mouthwatering main courses in the region of 250–350kr, less at lunchtime. In summer, there's seating outside on the pretty cobbled square. Reservations advised. Closed Sun.

Lofoten Fiskerestaurant Stranden 75, Aker Brygge ☏ 22 83 08 08. This smart, modern restaurant offers one of the city's best ranges of fish and shellfish, all immaculately prepared and served. It's located beside the harbour at the far end of the Aker Brygge jetty, which makes it popular with locals and tourists alike. Mains kick off at around 170kr, but some of the more unusual fish – including the wonderfully textured catfish (*steinbit*) – cost another 90kr or so.

Westside

Krishna Cuisine Kirkeveien 59B ☏ 22 60 62 50. Generally considered the best vegetarian joint in the city, the *dagens rett* (daily special) here costs 90kr and is always tasty and filling. Just east of Bogstadveien and the briefest of walks from the Majorstuen T-bane station. Closed Sun.

Grønland and Grünerløkka

Markveien Mat & Vinhus Torvbakkgata 12, Grünerløkka ☏ 22 37 22 97. This popular, top-quality restaurant and wine bar serves up Mediterranean-inspired dishes as well as traditional Norwegian favourites. Main courses average 220–250kr in the restaurant, half that in the wine bar, and the service is excellent. Also boasts one of the best wine cellars in the city. The entrance is on Markveien. Closed Sun.

Sult Thorvald Meyers gate 26, Grünerløkka ⊕22 87 04 67. One of the city's most popular restaurants – called "Hunger" after the novel by Knut Hamsun – the informal and very relaxed *Sult*

features a short but inventive menu using only the freshest of (local) ingredients. Main courses cost 170–200kr and include such delights as Hardanger trout and chicken from Stange. If that wasn't enough attraction, the adjacent bar *Tørst* ("Thirst") serves mouthwatering margaritas.

Bars

Bar-hopping in Oslo is an enjoyable affair. The more mainstream (meat market) bars are in the centre along and around Karl Johans gate, while the sharper, more alternative spots are concentrated to the east in the Grønland and Grünerløkka districts. The westside of the city has its chic spots too, mostly along and around Hegdehaugsveien and Bogstadveien. Most city bars stay **open** until around 1am on weekdays, often 3–4am on the weekend, and almost all of them are open daily. Drinks are uniformly expensive, so if you're after a big night out, it's a good idea to follow Norwegian custom and have a few warm-up drinks at home before you set out. A number of bars feature **live music**, blurring the lines between the bars listed here and the clubs listed on p.279.

Central

Foxx Olavs gate 2. Owned by the *Hotel Continental*, this bright and lively sidewalk bar is popular with the young(ish) and well-heeled.

Summit 21 Holbergs gate 30. On top of the *Radisson SAS Scandinavia Hotel*, this bar-lounge looks like the interior of a cruise ship – and neither can you fault the panoramic views over the city.

Westside

Barbeint Drammensveien 20, close to Parkveien. If you're familiar with Scandinavian bands and films, you may recognize a few faces in this jam-packed, fashionable bar. Loud sounds – everything from rap to rock.

Lorry Parkveien 12. Popular and enjoyable café-bar, with old-fashioned fittings, that attracts a mixed crowd. There's a wide choice of beers – well over one hundred – and outdoor seating in the summer.

Palace Grill Solligata 2. Popular New Age-meets-alternative café-bar with a roots, rock and jazz soundtrack. Good food too. In summertime, there's an outside bar, *Skaugum*, in the yard behind and beside the *Palace* – and it heaves.

Eastside: Grønland and Grünerløkka

Bar Boca Thorvald Meyers gate 30. Tiny 1950s-style bar serving the best cocktails in town. The bartenders take their work very seriously, and you need to get there early to avoid the crush. Live jazz once or twice weekly.

Cafe con Bar Brugata 11. Hip-as-you-like with retro interior and a long bar that can make buying a drink hard work. Good atmosphere, loungy decor and unisex toilets for those surprise meetings.

Gloria Flames Grønland 18 ⊕22 17 16 00, ⊕www.gloriaflames.no. Not the easiest bar-cum-club to find – there's just a small sign on the door – but worth searching out if you're into rock and rockabilly. Regular live acts and a summer rooftop bar.

Robinet Mariboes gate 7. Possibly the smallest bar in Oslo – 1950s retro kitsch combined with excellent drinks and an intellectual crowd.

Tea Lounge Thorvald Meyers gate 33B. Lounge-type café-bar with velvety red couches and big windows. As you might guess from the name, tea is a big deal here – all sorts and served to a soft house backtrack. Cocktails also.

Entertainment and nightlife

With bars staying open till the wee hours, Oslo's **nightclubs** struggle to make themselves heard – indeed there's often little distinction between the two – though there is still a reasonably good and varied nightclub scene. Live music is not perhaps Oslo's forte, and the domestic **rock** scene is far from inspiring, but **jazz** fans are well served, with several first-rate venues dotted round the city centre; **classical music** enthusiasts benefit from an ambitious concert programme. Most **theatre** productions are in Norwegian, but English-language theatre companies visit often, and at the **cinema** films are shown in the original language with Norwegian subtitles.

For **entertainment listings** it's worth checking out *Natt & Dag* (𝕨www .nattogdag.no), a Norwegian-language, bi-monthly broadsheet that carries thorough listings and reviews; it's available free from downtown cafés, bars, some shops and the tourist office. The main alternative is *What's On in Oslo*, a monthly English-language freebie produced by the tourist office. One other useful free publication is *Streetwise*, which is produced annually by Use-It, the city's youth information shop (see p.251); it carries descriptions of – amongst much else – the city's best bars and clubs.

For **tickets**, contact the venue direct or try Billettservice (℡81 53 31 33, 𝕨www .ticketmaster.no), who have an outlet in the Oslo Konserthus, Munkedamsveien 14, and employ the city's larger post offices as agents.

Nightclubs and live music

Oslo's hippest bars and **nightclubs** are located on the east side of the city, away from the centre in the Grønland and Grünerløkka districts, but there are also several clubs in the centre. Generally speaking, entry will set you back in the region of 100kr, and, surprisingly enough, drink prices are the same as anywhere else. Nothing gets going much before 11pm; closing times are generally around 3am. Many of the clubs also host a variety of **live music**, ranging from local home-grown talent to the big-name bands – check *Natt & Dag* (see above) for gigs.

Blå Brenneriveien 9C 𝕨www.blx.no. Creative, cultural nightspot in Grünerløkka, featuring everything from live jazz and cabaret through to poetry readings. Also features some of the best DJs in town, keeping the crowd moving until 3.30am at the weekend. In summer, there's a pleasant riverside terrace too.

Blue Monk St Olavs gate 23, at the corner of Pilestredet 𝕨www.clubbluemonk.no. Crowded, earthy nightspot noted for its eclectic programme of live music, from blues through to Estonian funk.

Café Mono Pløens gate 4 𝕨www.cafemono.no. Darkly lit bar with retro fixtures and fittings that attracts a student crowd, who appreciate the live,

mainly indie acts on several nights a week; diverse DJ sounds, too.

Last Train Karl Johans Gate 45, entrance on Universitetsgata 𝕨www.lasttrain.no. The best rock-pub/club in town, with good old-style rock played at volume to a leather and jeans clientele.

Oslo Spektrum Sonja Henies plass 2 𝕨www .oslospektrum.no. Major venue, close to Oslo S, showcasing big international acts, as well as small-fry local bands.

Smuget Rosenkrantz gate 22 𝕨www.smuget.no. Large, long-established and still popular nightclub with bars, a disco and regular live acts, mostly home-grown rock or blues bands.

Music festivals

Big-name rock bands often include Oslo on their tours, leavening what would otherwise be a pretty dull scene. The most prestigious annual event is **Norwegian Wood** (℡81 53 31 33, 𝕨www.norwegianwood.no), a four-day open-air rock festival held in June in the outdoor amphitheatre at Frogner Park, a ten-minute ride from the city centre on tram #12. Previous years have attracted the likes of Iggy Pop, Lou Reed, the Kinks and Van Morrison, and the festival continues to pull in some of the best international artists, supported by a variety of Norwegian acts. The arena holds around six thousand people, but tickets, costing around 400kr per day, sell out long in advance.

Oslo also hosts the more contemporary **Øyafestivalen** (𝕨www.oyafestivalen .com), a four-day event that showcases a wide range of artists, mostly Norwegian but with some imports too – 2005, for example, included Babyshambles and Diskaholics Anonymous. A club night traditionally kicks the whole thing off in style. The festival takes place in the middle of August in the open-air in Middelalderparken – a ten-minute ride on tram #18 from Jernbanetorget.

Jazz venues

Oslo has a strong **jazz** tradition, and in early or mid-August its week-long **Jazz Festival** attracts internationally renowned artists as well as showcasing local talent. The Festival Office, at Tollbugata 28 (☏22 42 91 20, ⓦwww.oslojazz.no) has full programme details of all the gigs, including those where there's an admission charge as well as the many free outdoor performances. At other times of the year, try one of the following for regular jazz acts.

Bare Jazz Grensen 8 ☏22 33 20 80, ⓦwww .barejazz.no. Slick and polished jazz shop with frequent live sounds, both homegrown and imported.
Herr Nilsen Jazzklubb CJ Hambros plass 5 ☏22 33 54 05, ⓦwww.herrnilsen.no. Small and intimate bar whose brick walls are decorated

with jazz memorabilia. Live jazz – often traditional and bebop – most nights. Air-conditioned; central location.
Original Nilsen Rosenkrantz gate 11 ⓦwww .original-nilsen.no. Popular bar featuring regular live jazz.

Classical music and opera

Oslo's major orchestra, the **Oslo Filharmonien** (☏22 01 49 02, ⓦwww .oslophil.com), gives regular concerts in the city's Konserthus, at Munkedamsveien 14. As you might expect, programmes often include works by Norwegian and other Scandinavian composers. Tickets for most performances cost around 300kr. In August and September, the orchestra traditionally gives a couple of free evening concerts in the Vigeland sculpture park, as part of the city's summer entertainment programme, which also sees classical performances at a variety of other venues, including the Domkirke, the Munch Museum and the University Aula; for details of the summer programme, contact the tourist office (see p.250).

In October, the ten-day **Ultima Contemporary Music Festival** (☏22 42 99 99, ⓦwww.ultima.no) gathers together more Scandinavian and international talent in an ambitious programme of concerts featuring everything from modern contemporary music to opera, ballet, classical and folk. The performances take place in a variety of venues throughout the city; for full details check Ultima's website.

Finally, **Den Norske Opera**, Norway's prolific opera company, offers a popular repertoire – Mozart, R. Strauss and the Italians – but also undertakes a number of contemporary works each year. Performances are usually held at the Opera House, Storgata 23 (☏81 54 44 88, ⓦwww.operaen.no).

△ Oslo Konserthus

Cinema

The ease with which most Norwegians tackle other languages is best demonstrated at the **cinema**, where films are shown in their original language with Norwegian subtitles. Given that American (and British) films are the most popular, this has obvious advantages for visiting English speakers. Oslo has its share of mainstream multi-screens, as well as a good art house cinema. Prices are surprisingly reasonable with tickets averaging 80–90kr.

Cinema listings – including information on late-night screenings – appear daily in the local press and the tourist office has details too. All the main cinemas share the **same telephone number** and website (☎82 03 00 01, ✆www.oslokino.no). The following is a selection of central screens.

Eldorado Torggata 9. Mainstream cinema showing the usual blockbusters.

Filmens Hus Dronningens gate 16 at Tollbugata ☎22 47 45 00, ✆www.nfi.no. Art house cinema with a varied programme mixing mainstream and alternative films. Tickets 70kr.

Filmteatret Stortingsgata 16. Old theatre

converted into a cinema, with wonderful decor. Shows mainstream and classic films.

Gimle Bygdøy allé 39. A sympathetically revamped old cinema with the most comfortable seats in town. A wine bar in the entrance adds a nice touch. Varied programme, mostly mainstream.

Saga Stortingsgata 28 at Olav V's gate. Mainstream cinema with six screens.

Theatre

Nearly all of Oslo's theatre productions are in Norwegian, making them of limited interest to (most) tourists, though there are occasional English-language performances by touring theatre companies. The principal venue is the **Nationaltheatret**, Stortingsgata 15 (☎81 50 08 11, ✆www.nationaltheatret.no), which hosts the prestigious, annual Ibsen Festival. Touring companies may also appear at the more adventurous **Det Norske Teatret**, Kristian IV's gate 8 (☎22 47 38 00, ✆www.detnorsketeatret.no).

Sports

Surrounded by forest and fjord, Oslo is very much an outdoor city, offering a wide range of **sports** and active pastimes. In **summer**, locals take to the hills to hike the network of trails that lattice the forests and lakes of the Nordmarka (see p.272), where many also try their hand at a little freshwater fishing, while others head out to the offshore islets of the Oslofjord (see p.275) to sunbathe and swim. In **winter**, the cross-country ski routes of the Nordmarka are especially popular, as is downhill skiing at Holmenkollen. Indeed skiing is such an integral part of winter life here that the T-bane carriages all have ski racks. Sleigh-riding is possible too, and so is ice skating, with the handiest rinks right in the middle of the city in front of the Stortinget (see p.282).

As regards **fishing**, the freshwater lakes of the Nordmarka are reasonably well stocked with such common species as trout, char, pike and perch. The Oslomarkas Fiskeadministrasjon, Sørkedalen 914 (☎22 49 90 04, ✆www.ofa.no) provides all the background information you need. In particular they will advise about fishing areas and have lists of where local licences can be bought. **Ice fishing** is another popular option, but follow what the locals do (or even better, keep them company) as it can be dangerous.

Winter sports

Skiing is extremely popular throughout Norway, and here in Oslo both cross-country and downhill enthusiasts might begin by calling in at the **Skiforeningen** (Ski Association) office, at Kongeveien 5 (☎22 92 32 00, ✆www.skiforeningen.no), near the Holmenkollen ski-jump, on T-bane #1. They have lots of information on Oslo's floodlit trails, cross-country routes, downhill and slalom slopes, ski schools (including one for children) and excursions to the nearest mountain resorts. Most Norwegians have their own skiing gear, but **equipment hire** is available from Skiservice Tomm Murstad, beside the Voksenkollen T-bane station (☎22 13 95 00, ⒲www.skiservice.no). For spectators, March sees the annual Holmenkollen Ski Festival: tickets and information from the Skiforeningen or the tourist office.

Every winter, from November to March, a floodlit **skating rink**, Narvisen, is created in front of the Stortinget, beside Karl Johans gate. Admission is free and you can hire skates on the spot at reasonable rates. In addition, **horsedrawn sleigh rides** in the Nordmarka can be arranged through Helge Torp, Sørbråten Gård, Maridalen, Oslo (☎22 23 22 21).

Listings

Airlines Air Lingus ☎24 14 87 50; British Airways ☎81 53 31 42; Finnair ☎81 00 11 00; KLM ☎22 64 37 52; Norwegian Air Shuttle ☎81 52 18 15; SAS/Braathens ☎05400; SN Brussels ☎23 16 25 68; Widerøe ☎81 00 12 00.

Banks and exchange ATMs are liberally distributed across the city, and at Gardermoen airport. Among Oslo's plethora of banks, Den Norske Bank (DnB) has downtown branches at Stranden 21, Aker Brygge, Stortingsgate 30 and Grensen 17. You can also change money and travellers' cheques at major post offices, where the rates are especially competitive. There are late-opening bureaux de change at the airports in arrivals (daily 8am–10.30pm) and departures (daily 5.30am–8pm). The money exchange company Forex has several outlets dotted across the city centre with one branch at Oslo S (Mon–Fri 9am–7pm), another at Øvre Slottsgate 12 (Mon–Fri 9am–7pm).

Car rental Bislet Bilutleie, Pilestredet 70 ☎22 60 00 00, ⒲www.bislet.no; Europcar, Haakon VII's gate 9 ☎22 83 12 42; Hertz, Jernbanetorget 1 ☎67 16 80 00, Holbergs gate 30 ☎67 16 80 00, and at the airport ☎67 16 80 00; National, at the airport ☎64 81 06 60, ⒲www.nationalcar.no. See also under *Bilutleie* in the Yellow Pages.

Dentist Municipal dental information on ☎22 67 30 00. Otherwise, see under *Tannleger* in the Yellow Pages.

Email and Internet Almost all city hotels and hostels provide Internet access for their guests at (fairly) reasonable rates. Net access is also available for free at the main city library, the Deichmanske bibliotek, at Henrik Ibsen gate 1 (June–Aug Mon–Fri 10am–6pm, Sat 9am–2pm; Sept–May Mon–Fri 10am–8pm, Sat 9am–3pm; ⒲www.deichman.no), and at Oslo's youth information shop, Use-it, Møllergata 3 (see p.251)

Embassies and consulates Canada, Wergelandveien 7 ☎22 99 53 00; Ireland, Haakon VII's gate, 15th floor ☎22 01 72 00; Netherlands, Oscars gate 29 ☎23 33 36 00; Poland, Olav Kyrres plass 1 ☎22 43 00 15; UK, Thomas Heftyes gate 8 ☎23 13 27 00; USA, Drammensveien 18 ☎22 44 85 50. For others, look under *Ambassadeur og Legasjoner* in the Yellow Pages. There is no Australian consulate or embassy.

Emergencies Ambulance and medical assistance ☎113; Police ☎112; Fire brigade ☎110.

Gay Oslo There's not much of a scene as such, primarily because Oslo's gays and lesbians are mostly content to share pubs and clubs with heteros. That said, gay men congregate at the *London Pub*, CJ Hambros plass 5 (⒲www .londonpub.no), with a pub/bar on one floor and a disco downstairs; and *SinPecado*, Øvre Vollgate 13 (closed Sun & Mon; ⒲www.sinpecado.no), is a popular lesbian bar. The main gay event is the *Skeive Dager* (Queer Days) festival, usually held over ten days in late June with parties, parades, political meetings, a film festival and incorporating Gay Pride. Norway's national gay and lesbian organization is *LLH* (Landsforeningen for lesbisk og homofil frigjøring; ⒲www.llh.no).

Laundry Majorstua Myntvaskeri, Vibes gate 15 ☎22 69 43 17; Snarvask, Thorvald Meyers gate 18, Grünerløkka ☎22 37 57 70. See under *Vaskerier* in the Yellow Pages.

Left luggage Coin-operated lockers (24hr) and luggage office at Oslo S.

Lost property (*hittegods*) Trams, buses and T-bane ☎22 08 53 61; NSB railways ☎23 15 40 47; police ☎22 66 98 65.

Medical treatment For emergencies, call ☎113. For lesser problems, either head for the nearest pharmacy (see "Pharmacy" below) or the Walk-In Clinic, to the rear of the Aker Brygge complex at the corner of Munkedamsveien and Sjøgata (☎22 83 10 83, ⒲www.walk-in-clinic.com). The clinic is fast, efficient, friendly – and expensive. For cheaper treatment, stick to the A&E departments of the nearest hospital.

Pharmacy A 24hr pharmacy – Vitusapotek Jernbanetorvet – is located across the street from Oslo S at Jernbanetorget 4b (☎23 35 81 00). See also "Medical Treatment".

Police In an emergency, ring ☏ 112.

Post offices The main post office is at the corner of Kirkegata and Prinsens gate (Mon–Fri 9am–5pm, Sat 10am–3pm). There are lots of other post offices dotted across the city, including a branch in Oslo S – for full details consult ⓦ www.posten.no. All post offices exchange currency and cash travellers' cheques at very reasonable rates.

Supermarkets There are lots of small supermarkets in central Oslo – Rimi, ICA and Kiwi are three of the larger chains. All of them sell at least a small selection of fresh fruit and veg. Rimi has a branch in Oslo S, ICA has one on Grensen near the corner with Akersgata 45.

Vinmonopolet There are lots of branches of this state-run liquor and wine store in Oslo, including one in Oslo S.

Travel details

Trains

Oslo to: Bergen (3–4 daily; 6hr 30min); Dombås (4–5 daily; 4hr); Geilo (3–4 daily; 3hr 20min); Hamar (7 daily; 1hr 30min); Hjerkinn (4–5 daily; 4hr 30min); Kongsberg (3–5 daily; 1hr 10min); Kristiansand (3–5 daily; 4hr 40min); Lillehammer (7 daily; 2hr); Myrdal (4–5 daily; 4hr 30min); Otta (4–5 daily; 3hr 30min); Røros (2–3 daily; 5hr); Stavanger (3–5 daily; 7hr 30min); Trondheim (4–5 daily; 6hr 50min); Voss (3–4 daily; 5hr 20min); Åndalsnes (2–3 daily; 5hr 30min).

Buses

Oslo to: Alta via Sweden (3 weekly; 27hr); Arendal (1 daily; 4hr 15min); Balestrand (3 daily; 8hr 15min); Bergen (1 daily; 11hr 40min); Grimstad (1 daily; 4hr 40min); Hamar (1 daily; 2hr); Hammerfest via Sweden (3 weekly; 30hr); Haugesund (1 daily; 10hr); Kongsberg (1 daily; 2hr); Kristiansand (1 daily; 5hr 40min); Lillehammer (1 daily; 3hr); Lillesand (1 daily; 5hr); Mundal, Fjaerland (3 daily; 7hr 50min); Odda (1 daily; 8hr); Otta (2 daily; 5hr); Sogndal (3 daily; 7hr); Stavanger (1 daily; 10hr); Stryn (1 daily; 8hr); Voss (1 daily; 10hr 30min).

2.2

South and central Norway

Preoccupied by the fjords and the long road to the Nordkapp, few tourists are tempted to explore **south and central Norway**. The Norwegians know better. Trapped between Sweden and the fjords, this great chunk of land boasts some of the country's finest scenery, with forested dales trailing north and west from Oslo towards the rearing peaks of the interior. It's here, within shouting distance of the country's principal train line and the E6 – the main line of communication between Oslo, Trondheim and the north – that you'll find three of Norway's prime **hiking areas**. These are made up of a trio of mountain ranges, each partly contained within a **national park** – from south to north, Jotunheimen, Rondane and the Dovrefjell. Each park is equipped with well-maintained walking trails and DNT huts; **Otta** and **Kongsvoll**, on both the E6 and the train line, are particularly good starting points for hiking expeditions.

Entirely different, but just as popular with the Norwegians, is the **south coast**, an appealing region whose myriad islets and skerries, beaches and coves punctuate the shoreline that extends west from the Oslofjord. This coast is at its prettiest in the east where a handful of old timber ports – **Arendal**, **Lillesand** and **Mandal** – sport bright-white, antique clapboard houses along their harbourfronts. **Kristiansand**, easily the largest town on the coast, is different again, a brisk, modern place that successfully combines its roles as a resort and as a major ferry port with connections to Denmark. Beyond Kristiansand lies **Mandal**, an especially fetching holiday spot with a great beach, but thereafter the coast becomes harsher and less absorbing, heralding a sparsely inhabited region with precious little to detain you before **Stavanger**, a lively oil town and port within easy striking distance of some fine fjord and mountain scenery.

The south coast is traversed by the E18 (and its continuation the E39), linking Oslo with Stavanger. In between the E18/39 and the E6, three major roads – the E134, Hwy 7 and, fastest of the lot, the E16 – cut across the interior from the capital to the central fjords and Bergen. These highways can make the whole region seem rather like a transport corridor, but, whichever way you're heading, it would be a great pity not to allow at least a couple of days for the south coast or the national parks in the north.

As you might expect, **bus** services along these main highways are excellent and **trains** are fast and frequent, too. Away from the highways, however, the bus system thins out and travelling becomes a pain without your own vehicle – it can be worth renting a car locally for a few days. In terms of **accommodation**, roadside campsites are commonplace, there's a reasonable supply of youth hostels and every major town has at least one hotel or guesthouse.

North to Kongsvoll and Røros

Hurrying from Oslo to Trondheim and points north, the **E6** remains the most important highway in Norway, and is consequently kept in excellent condition

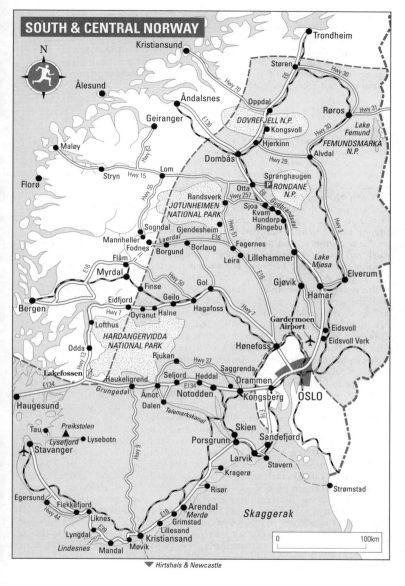

SOUTH & CENTRAL NORWAY

N

Trondheim

Kristiansund

Støren · Hwy 30

Ålesund · E6

Åndalsnes · Oppdal · Røros · Hwy 31

Geiranger · E136 · DOVREFJELL N.P. · Kongsvoll · Lake Femund · FEMUNDSMARKA N.P.

Måløy · Hjerkinn · Hwy 30

Florø · Stryn · Hwy 15 · Lom · Dombås · Alvdal

Hwy 63 · Hwy 29

Sprænghaugen

Otta · P · RONDANE N.P.

Randsverk · Hwy 257 · E6

JOTUNHEIMEN NATIONAL PARK · Sjoa · Kvam · Hundorp · Ringebu

Sogndal · Gjendesheim · Gudbrandsdal

Mannheller · Lærdal · E16

Fodnes · Borgund · Borlaug · Fagernes

Flåm · Leira · Lillehammer

Myrdal · Hwy 50 · Gol · Lake Mjøsa · Elverum

E16 · Finse · Geilo · Gjøvik · Hamar

Eidfjord · Dyranut · Halne · Hagafoss · Hwy 7 · Gardermoen Airport

Bergen · Hwy 7 · E16

Lofthus · Eidsvoll

HARDANGERVIDDA NATIONAL PARK · Eidsvoll Verk

Odda · Rjukan · Hønefoss

Lakefossen · Saggrenda

Haukeligrend · Seljord · Heddal · Drammen

E134 · Grungedal · Åmot · Notodden · Kongsberg · OSLO

Haugesund · Dalen · E18

Telemarkskanal

Tau · Preikstolen · Skien

Lysefjord · Lysebotn · Porsgrunn · Sandefjord

Stavanger · Larvik · Stavern

Kragerø

Risør · Strømstad

Egersund · Flekkefjord · Skaggerak

Hwy 44 · Liknes · Arendal · Merdø

Lyngdal · Grimstad

Lindesnes · Mandal · Møvik · Lillesand · Kristiansand

0 — 100km

▼ Hirtshals & Newcastle

– often with the roadworks to prove it. Inevitably, the road is used by many of the region's long-distance **buses**, and for much of its length it's also shadowed by Norway's principal **train** line. Heading out of Oslo, both the E6 and the railway thump northwards across the lowlands to clip along the north bank of Lake Mjøsa en route to **Lillehammer**, site of the country's best open-air folk museum. Thereafter, road and rail wriggle on between the **Jotunheimen** and **Rondane national** parks, whose magnificent mountains are both within easy reach of the amiable town of **Otta**. Further north still is the beautiful **Dovrefjell** range, which forms a third and equally stunning national park, and one that's best approached from tiny **Kongsvoll**. All three parks are famous for their hiking, and are criss-crossed by an extensive and well-planned network of **trails**. From Kongsvoll, the obvious route north is along the E6 to Trondheim (see p.361), though you might consider detouring east to the quaint old mining town of **Røros**.

Hamar

Beyond the flat farmlands north of Oslo, the E6 curves round the northern shore of Norway's largest lake, **Mjøsa**, a favourite retreat for Norwegian families, with the surrounding farmland, woods and pastures harbouring numerous second homes. Before the railroad arrived in the 1880s, the lake was an important transport route, crossed by boats during the summer and by horse and sleigh in winter. It's also halfway country: the quiet settlements around the lake give a taste of small-town southern Norway before the E6 plunges on into wilder regions further north. Midway round the lake, some 130km from Oslo, lies **HAMAR**, an easy-going little place of 25,000 souls, where marinas and waterside cafés make a gallant attempt to sustain a nautical flavour. The town was once the seat of an important medieval bishopric, and the substantial Gothic remains of the **Domkirke** are stuck out on the **Domkirkeodden** (Cathedral Point), a low, grassy headland towards the west end of town. The cathedral is thought to have been built by the "English pope" Nicholas Breakspear, who spent a couple of years in Norway as the papal legate before becoming Adrian IV in 1154, but the building, along with the surrounding episcopal complex, was ransacked during the Reformation, and local road-builders subsequently helped themselves to the stone. The ruins have now been incorporated into the **Hedmarksmuseet** (mid-May to mid-June Tues–Sun 10am–4pm; mid-June to mid-Aug daily 10am–5pm; mid-Aug to early Sept Tues–Sun 10am–4pm; 70kr; ⓦwww.hedmarksmuseet.no), which contains an archeological museum and an open-air folk museum. The latter holds around fifty buildings collected from across the region and, although it's not as comprehensive as the one in Lillehammer (see p.287), it does contain one or two particularly fine buildings, including the parsonage of Bolstad with its beautifully decorated log walls. The most scenic approach to the headland is along the pleasant lakeshore footpath, which stretches 2km north from the train station.

Hamar is also as good a place as any to pick up the 130-year-old **paddle steamer**, the *Skibladner* (ⓣ61 14 40 80, ⓦwww.skibladner.no), which shuttles up and down Lake Mjøsa between late June and mid-August: on Tuesdays, Thursdays and Saturdays the boat makes the return trip across the lake from Hamar to Gjøvik and on up to Lillehammer, while on Mondays, Wednesdays and Fridays it chugs down to Eidsvoll and back; there's no Sunday service. Departure details are available direct or at any local tourist office. Tickets are bought on board: return trips from Hamar to Eidsvoll cost around 280kr and last two and a half hours, those to Lillehammer cost 320kr and last eight hours. One-way fares cost a little over half these rates. Travellers heading north may find the trip to Lillehammer tempting at first sight, but the lake is not particularly scenic, and after four hours on the boat you'll feel like jumping overboard with tedium. The best bet is to take the short bus or train ride instead.

Practicalities

Hamar's **train station** is in the town centre beside the lake; **buses** stop outside. Some trains from Oslo pause here before heading up the secondary branch line to Røros (see p.293), a fine three-and-a-half-hour ride over the hills and through huge forests. Some 600m from the train station – turn left out of the terminal building and head along Stangevegen – is the jetty for the *Skibladner* ferry.

There's a fair choice of central **hotels**, one pleasant and reasonably priced option being the lakeshore *First Hotel Victoria*, Strandgata 21 (℡62 02 55 00, ⊛www .firsthotels.com; ➏), which also has a competent restaurant serving Norwegian favourites. There's also an all-year HI **hostel**, Åkersvikaveg 24 (℡62 52 60 60, ⊛www.vandrerhjem.no; doubles ➋, dorm beds 200kr), which occupies smart modern buildings about 2km south along the lakeshore from the train station. It's in the middle of nowhere, just across from the massive skating arena built for the 1994 Winter Olympics in the shape of an upturned Viking ship.

Lillehammer

LILLEHAMMER (literally "Little Hammer"), 50km north of Hamar and 180km from Oslo, is Lake Mjøsa's most worthwhile destination. In **winter**, it's *the* Norwegian ski centre, a young and vibrant place whose rural, lakeshore setting and extensive cross-country ski trails contributed to its selection as the main venue for the 1994 Winter Olympic Games. In preparation for the games, the Norwegian government spent a massive two billion kroner on the town's **sporting facilities**, which are now the best in the country. Spread along the hillsides above and near the town, these include a ski-jumping tower and chair lift; a ski-jumping arena with two jumping hills and chair lift; an ice hockey arena; a bobsleigh track and a cross-country skiing stadium which gives access to about 30km of cross-country ski trails. Several local companies, including Saga Arrangement, Gudbrandsdalsvegen 203 (℡61 26 92 44, ⊛www.sagaarrangement.no), operate all-inclusive winter sports and activity holidays, though if this is what you have in mind, you may as well book your holiday with an agent back home. As you would expect, most Norwegians arriving here in winter come fully equipped, but it's possible to rent (or purchase) equipment when you get here – the tourist office (see opposite) will advise.

Lillehammer remains a popular holiday spot in **summer** too. Hundreds of Norwegians hunker down in their second homes in the hills, dropping into the town centre for a drink or a meal. Cycling, walking, fishing and canoeing are popular pastimes at this time of year, with all sorts of possibilities for guided tours and equipment hire. But, however appealing the area may be to Norwegians, the countryside round here has little of the wonderful wildness of other parts of Norway, and unless you're someone's guest or bring your own family, you'll probably feel rather out on a limb. That said, Lillehammer is not a bad place to break your journey, and there are a couple of attractions to keep you busy for a day – but not two.

The Kunstmuseum and Maihaugen

Lillehammer's briskly efficient centre, just a few minutes' walk from one end to the other, is tucked into the hillside above the lake, the E6 and the railway. It has just one really notable attraction, the municipal art gallery, the **Kunstmuseum**, at Stortorget 2 (late June to late Aug daily 11am–6pm; late Aug to late June Tues–Sun 11am–4pm; 60kr; ⊛www.lillehammerartmuseum.com). Housed in a flashy modern building, the gallery's speciality is its temporary exhibitions of contemporary art (which attract an extra admission charge), but the permanent collection is also very worthwhile, with a small but representative sample of works by most major Norwegian painters, from Johan Dahl and Christian Krohg to Munch and Erik Werenskiold.

The much-vaunted **Maihaugen** open-air folk museum – the largest of its type in northern Europe – is located a twenty-minute walk or a quick bus ride southeast from the Skysstasjon along Anders Sandvigsgate (late May & late Aug to Sept Mon–Sat 9am–4pm, Sun 10am–2pm; June to mid-Aug Mon–Sat 9am–6pm, Sun noon–5pm; June to mid-Aug 90kr, rest of the year 75kr; ⊛www.maihaugen .no). Incredibly, the whole collection represents the lifetime's work of one man, a magpie-ish dentist by the name of Anders Sandvig. The Maihaugen holds around

140 reconstructed buildings, brought here from all over the region, including a charming seventeenth-century presbytery (*prestegårdshagen*), a thirteenth-century stave church from Garmo, log stores and smokehouses, summer grazing huts and various workshops. The key exhibits, however, are the two **farms** dating from the late seventeenth century, complete with their various outhouses and living areas.

The outside area is stocked with farmyard animals, while guides dressed in traditional costume give the lowdown on traditional rural life, and in the summertime there's often the chance to have a go at homely activities such as spinning, baking, weaving and pottery – good, wholesome fun. The main museum building features temporary exhibitions on folkloric themes. Allow a good half-day for a visit and take advantage of the free guided tour (in English every other hour, on the hour).

Practicalities

The E6 runs along the lakeshore about 500m below the centre of Lillehammer, where the ultramodern **Skysstasjon**, on Jernbanetorget at the bottom of Jernbanegata, incorporates the **train station** and the **bus terminal**. The **tourist office** is also here (Mon–Sat 8am–4pm, Sat 10am–2pm; ☎61 28 98 00, ⍾www .lillehammerturist.no). Staff have bucketloads of free brochures, information on local events and activities, and will help with finding accommodation. **Orientation** couldn't be easier, with all activity focused on the pedestrianized part of Storgata which runs north from Bankgata, across Jernbanegata to the tumbling River Mesnaelva; Anders Sandvigsgate and Kirkegata run parallel on either side to east and west respectively.

For a place to stay, *Gjestebu Overnatting* (☎61 25 43 21, ⍾gjestebu@lillehammer .online.no) offers **hostel**-style accommodation in a large house just north of the centre beyond the river at Gamleveien 110 and Løkkgata. There are mixed dorms at 120kr, doubles at 350kr and self-catering apartments from 550kr per night. If you're around for longer, you may want something rather more cosy: *Gjestehuset Ersgaard*, Nordseterveien 201 (☎61 25 06 84, ⍾www.ersgaard.no; ❸), a couple of kilometres above town (in the Nordseter direction), is a pleasant **guesthouse** which serves excellent breakfasts in its dining room overlooking the town and lake. In the centre, the *First Hotell Breiseth*, across from the Skysstasjon at Jernbanegata 3 (☎61 24 77 77, ⍾www.firsthotels.no; ❻), is a large chain **hotel** with comfortable rooms.

Downtown Lillehammer has a good supply of **restaurants** and **cafés**. The busy *Bøndernes Hus Kafeteria*, Kirkegata 68, is a big, old-fashioned sort of place with cheap and filling self-service meals. Moving up a rung, *Blåmann* at Lilletorvet 1 (down an alley off the pedestrianized part of Storgata) has a lovely leafy terrace suspended over the cascading river below, and does excellent steaks, grilled fish and the like. The town has an animated nightlife, with **bars** clustered around the western end of Storgata – try *Nikkers* at Elvegata 18 for lively low-key drinks; at the other end of the scale, *Brenneriet*, just over the road, is a swanky nightclub-cum-restaurant.

The Gudbrandsdal: Hundorp and Sjoa

Heading north from Lillehammer, the E6 and the railway leave the shores of Lake Mjøsa for the Gudbrandsdal, the 160-kilometre-long river valley which was for centuries the main route between Oslo and Trondheim. Enclosed by mountain ranges, the valley has a comparatively dry and mild climate, and its fertile soils have nourished a string of farming villages since Viking times – though there was some industrialization at the beginning of the twentieth century.

The first part of the Gudbrandsdal is fairly uninspiring, but after 70km the road swings past **HUNDORP**, where a neat little quadrangle of old farm buildings has been tastefully turned into a roadside tourist stop, with a café, art gallery and shop. There has been a farm here since prehistoric times, its most famous owner a Viking warrior by the name of Dalegudbrand, who became a bitter enemy of St Olav after his enforced baptism in 1021. With a little time to spare, you could ramble down towards the river from the compound and nose around a couple of Viking burial mounds. Three kilometres further north, amongst the orchards overlooking the E6, is ⚓ **Sygard Grytting** (☎61 29 85 88, ⊛www.grytting.com; mid-June to mid-Aug), an ancient farmstead whose eighteenth-century buildings are in an almost perfect state of preservation – a beautiful ensemble with assorted barns and outhouses facing onto a tiny courtyard. One barn dates from the fourteenth century, when its upper storey was used to shelter pilgrims on the long haul north to Trondheim – it now offers inexpensive dormitory accommodation (340kr per person), whilst the **rooms** in the main farmhouse (❹) provide some of the most attractive lodgings in the region. There is no train station at Hundorp – the nearest is at Ringebu – but **buses** stop in front of the hotel on the E6.

Pressing on, the E6 weaves north along the course of the river to reach, after 35km, **SJOA**, a scattered hamlet set beside the junction of the E6 and Highway 257. The latter cuts west along the Heidal valley, where the River Sjoa boasts some of the country's most exciting **whitewater rafting**. If you want to come to grips with the Sjoa's gorges and rapids, contact the local specialists Heidal Rafting (☎61 23 60 37, ⊛www.heidalrafting.no). An all-inclusive one-day rafting excursion costs around 800kr; a more strenuous two-day expedition inclusive of meals and lodgings will set you back just over twice that amount. The season lasts from May to September and reservations are recommended, though there's a reasonably good chance of being able to sign up at the last minute. Heidal Rafting are based at the Sjoa HI **hostel** (☎61 23 62 00, ⊛www.vandrerhjem.no; mid-May to Sept), itself worth a second look. Perched on a wooded hillside high above the river, the main building is a charming old log farmhouse dating from 1747 and, although visitors sleep elsewhere, you do eat here. Breakfasts are banquet-like and dinners (by prior arrangement only) are reasonably priced if rather less spectacular. The hostel offers no-frills dormitory accommodation (from 155kr) and a handful of spacious and comfortable double rooms and chalets (both   ). Advance reservations are recommended for the chalets at weekends. There's no train station – the nearest is at Otta 10km to the north – but buses stop on the E6 near the Hwy 257 intersection.

Otta and the Rondane and Jotunheimen national parks

Just 10km up the E6 beyond Sjoa lies **OTTA**, an unassuming and unexciting little town at the confluence of the rivers Otta and Lågen. It may be dull, but Otta makes a handy base for hiking in the nearby Rondane and Jotunheimen national parks, especially if you're reliant on public transport – though staying in one of the parks' mountain lodges is to be preferred. In Otta, everything you need is within easy reach: the E6 passes within 200m of the centre, sweeping along the east bank of the Lågen, while the **train station**, **bus terminal** and **tourist office** (July–Aug Mon–Fri 8.30am–7pm, Sat & Sun 11am–6pm; Sept–June Mon–Fri 8.30am–4pm; ☎61 23 66 50, ⊛www.visitrondane.com) are all clumped together on the west bank in the Skysstasjon, just 100m from the small grid of streets that pass for the town centre. There are no sights as such, but the stiff hike along the footpath up the forested slopes to the summit of nearby **Pillarguritoppen** (853m), across the Otta River south of the centre, is a popular outing.

Staff at Otta tourist office are exceptionally helpful, providing local bus timetables, booking accommodation, reserving boat tickets, selling DNT membership and fishing licences, offering hiking tips and selling a range of hiking maps. As for **accommodation**, the *Grand Gjestegård* (☎61 23 12 00; ❹), across from the train station at the corner of Ola Dahls gate, is a large pension-cum-hotel with simple but perfectly adequate rooms furnished in brisk modern style. If they're full, try the *Norlandia Otta Hotell* (☎61 21 08 00, ⊛www.norlandia.no/otta; ❹), which occupies a recently spruced up concrete block a few metres to the west along Ola Dahls

Moving on from Otta and the western fjords

Running west from Otta, **Hwy 15** sweeps along the wide and fertile Hjelledal river valley over to Lom (see p.346), where there's a choice of wonderful routes on into the western fjords. From Lom, **Hwy 55** climbs steeply to the south, travelling along the western flank of the Jotunheimen National Park and offering breathtaking views of its jagged peaks before careering down to Sogndal (see p.344). Alternatively, Hwy 15 forges ahead from Lom to Stryn (see p.350), passing the nerve-jangling **Ørnevegen** (Eagle's Highway) – Hwy 63 – turning to **Geiranger** (see p.354). In terms of public transport, the Oslo–Måløy Nor-Way Busseksspress **bus** (2–3 daily) passes through Otta and Lom en route to Stryn; from mid-June to August, one of the three buses connects at Grotli with the bus down to Geiranger. The journey time from Otta to Lom is one hour, three hours to Stryn. There are no bus services along Hwy 55.

gate. The nearest **campsite**, the all-year *Otta Camping* (☎61 23 03 09), occupies a small riverside site, with pitches and cabins (**②**), in a scenic spot on the wooded banks of the River Otta about 1500km from the town centre. To get there, cross the bridge on the south side of the centre, turn right and keep going. Otta doesn't have much in the way of **restaurants**, but the *Pillarguri Café* on Storgata musters a more-than-competent range of Norwegian standbys.

Rondane National Park

Spreading north and east from Otta towards the Swedish border, **Rondane Nasjonalpark** (Rondane National Park) was established in 1962 as Norway's first national park and is now one of the country's most popular hiking areas. Its 580 square kilometres, one-third of which are in the high alpine zone, appeal to walkers of all ages and abilities. The soil is poor, so vegetation is sparse and lichens, especially reindeer moss, predominate, but the views across this bare landscape are serenely beautiful, and a handful of lakes and rivers along with patches of dwarf birch forest provide some variety.

Wild mountain peaks divide the Rondane into three distinct areas. To the west of the centrally located lake, **Rondvatn**, are the wild cirques and jagged peaks of Storsmeden (2017m), Sagtinden (2018m) and Veslesmeden (2015m), while to the

△ Rondane National Park

east of the lake tower Rondslottet (2178m), Vinjeronden (2044m) and Storronden (2138m). Further east still, the park is dominated by Høgronden (2115m). Most of the mountains, ten of which exceed the 2000-metre mark, are accessible to any reasonably fit walker via a dense network of trails and hiking huts.

Buses to the park from Otta depart daily in summer (late June to mid-Aug 2 daily; 50min), travelling the 25km to the Spranghaugen car park, the starting point for hikes into the Rondane. One bus leaves in the morning, the other in the afternoon. If you opt for the latter, you'll need to overnight at Rondvassbu hut (see below). The return bus leaves Spranghaugen for Otta in the late afternoon. Taking a **taxi** is also a possibility, especially if you're in a group – enquire at the tourist office, where you can also get details of local **car rental** companies. Taxis are available from Otta Skysstasjon and rental cars from Otta Auto (T61 23 64 50).

Accommodation in the Rondane is limited to the **Rondvassbu hut** (T61 23 18 66; late June to mid-Sept) at the southern end of Rondvatn. This is a typical DNT staffed lodge, with over one hundred dorm beds, filling meals and pleasant service. If visibility is poor or you don't fancy a climb, there is a charming summer **boat service** (July to late Aug 2–3 daily; 1hr return; 45kr one-way, 70kr return) to the far end of Rondvatn, from where it takes about two and a half hours to walk back to Rondvassbu along the lake's steep western shore.

Jotunheimen National Park

Norway's most celebrated walking area, the **Jotunheimen Nasjonalpark** ("Home of the Giants" National Park) lives up to its name: pointed summits and undulating glaciers dominate the skyline, soaring high above river valleys and lake-studded plateaux. The park offers an amazing concentration of high peaks, more than two hundred of them rising above 1900 metres, including Norway's – and northern Europe's – two highest mountains, Galdhøpiggen (2469m) and Glittertind (2464m), while Norway's highest waterfall, the 275-metre-high Vettisfossen, is here too, a short walk from the Vetti lodge on the west side of the park. A network of foot-paths and mountain lodges lattices Jotunheimen, but be warned that the weather is very unpredictable and the winds can be bitingly cold – be cautious if you're new to mountain hiking and always come well-equipped (see "Basics", p.51).

There are no public roads into the park; visitors usually walk or ski into the interior from Hwy 55 in the west, or make the slightly easier approach via **GJENDESHEIM**, off Hwy 51 in the east of the park about 90km from Otta. In summer, there's an early-morning **bus** from Otta to Gjendesheim (late June to mid-Aug Mon–Sat 1 daily; 2hr) and another leaving around noon (late June to Aug 1 daily; 2hr). Gjendesheim is no more than a couple of buildings, one of which is the excellent DNT ⚔ **Gjendesheim lodge** (T61 23 89 10, Wwww.gjendesheim .no; mid-June to early Oct; dorm beds 105–195kr for DNT members, 225–260kr for non-members; doubles ❷), which sits at the eastern tip of long and slender Lake Gjende. **Boats** (late June to mid-Sept 1–3 daily; T61 23 85 09) travel the length of the lake, reaching deep into the park to connect with mountain trails, and dropping passengers off at two more lodges, the privately owned **Memurubu** (T61 23 89 99; Wwww.memurubu.no; late June to early Sept), halfway along the lake, with double rooms (❷) as well as dorms; and the DNT's **Gjendebu** (T61 23 89 44; mid-June to mid-Sept; same prices as Gjendesheim), right at the other end. It takes the boat twenty minutes to reach Memurubu, forty-five minutes to Gjendebu. Naturally, you can see a slice of the Jotunheimen and avoid a hike by riding the boat and sleeping at the lodges – a useful option in bad weather.

North along the E6 to Dovrefjell

If you avoid the temptation of heading west from Otta along Hwy 15 to the fjords, you might want to follow the E6 (and the railway) 45km north to **DOMBÅS**, a mundane crossroads settlement that has a couple of good places to **stay**, if not much else. Close to the train and bus station as well as the E6/E136 junction is the *Dombås Hotell* (☎61 24 10 01, ⊛www.dombas-hotel.no; ❹), whose distinctive high gables look back down the Gudbrandsdal. A hotel of two halves, most of the bedrooms are tucked away in the modern annexe round the back, but the old main building holds a handsome series of long public rooms dating from the beginning of the twentieth century. Also offering valley views is Dombås's HI **hostel** (☎61 24 09 60, ⊛www.vandrerhjem.no; dorm beds 190kr), a comfortable complex of mountain huts, which hold some double rooms (❷), way up on the hillside above the E6. To get there, head north out of town along the E6 for around 1km and follow the signs up the hill; on foot, it's a hard slog from the train and bus station, down in the valley below. Both routes out of Dombås offer tantalizing prospects: E136 leads the 110km west to Åndalsnes and the Romsdalsfjord (see p.316), whilst the E6 plunges north through the mountains towards Trondheim (see p.361); you can complete either journey by rail as well, though the Åndalsnes train only runs a couple of times a day.

Staying on the E6 north from Dombås, it's just 30km to the outpost of **HJERKINN**, stuck out on bare and desolate moorland, its pocket-sized military base battened down against the wind-blasted ice and snow of winter. The base overlooks the E6/Hwy 29 junction, as does the adjacent train station, a perky wooden affair with brightly painted window frames. There's been a mountain inn here since medieval times, a staging post on the long trail to Trondheim, now just 170km away. The present inn, the *Hjerkinn Fjellstue* (☎61 24 29 27, ⊛www .hjerkinn.no; ❺), continues this tradition in a becoming manner, with two expansive wooden buildings with big open fires and breezy pine furniture. The restaurant is good, too – try the reindeer culled from local herds – and there's horse-riding from the stables next door. The inn is set on a hill overlooking the moors just over 2km from the train station beside Hwy 29.

Kongsvoll

Beyond Hjerkinn, the E6 slices across the barren uplands before descending into a narrow ravine, the **Drivdal**. Hidden here, just 12km from Hjerkinn, is **KONGS-VOLL**, home of a tiny train station and the delightful 🏛 *Kongsvold Fjeldstue* (☎72 40 43 40, ⊛www.kongsvold.no; ❹), which provides some of the most charming accommodation in the whole of Norway. There's been an inn here since medieval times and the present complex, a huddle of tastefully restored old timber buildings with sun-bleached reindeer antlers tacked onto the outside walls, dates back to the eighteenth century. Dinner is served in the excellent, reasonably priced **restaurant**, and the complex also includes a **café** and a small **park information centre**. The inn is a lovely spot to break your journey and an ideal base for hiking into the Dovrefjell National Park, which extends to east and west. If you're arriving by **train**, note that only some of the Oslo–Trondheim trains stop at Kongsvoll station, 500m down the valley from the inn – and then only by prior arrangement with the conductor.

Beyond Drivdal, 35km north of Kongsvoll, **OPPDAL** is a crossroads town where Hwy 70 forks west for the coast, while the E6 presses on north the 120km to Trondheim (see p.361).

Dovrefjell National Park

Bisected by the railroad and the E6, **Dovrefjell Nasjonalpark** (Dovrefjell National Park) is one of the more accessible of Norway's national parks. Just 265 square kilometres in area, it comprises two distinct zones: the marshes, open moors and rounded peaks that characterize much of eastern Norway spread east from the E6, while to the west the mountains become increasingly steep and serrated as they approach the jagged spires of the Romsdal. Beyond the park's western limits, backing on to the Romsdalsfjord, is the greatest concentration of high peaks outside the Jotunheimen; this is a favourite destination for European mountaineers, who clamber up perpendicular rock faces reckoned to be some of the world's most difficult.

Hiking trails and **huts** are spread throughout the western part of the Dovrefjell. Kongsvoll makes an ideal starting point: it's possible to hike all the way from here to the coast at Åndalsnes, but this takes all of nine or ten days; a more feasible expedition for most visitors is the two-day hike there and back to one of the four snow-tipped peaks of mighty **Snøhetta**, at around 2200m. There's accommodation five hours' walk west from Kongsvoll at the unstaffed **Reinheim** hut (mid-Feb to mid-Oct). Further hiking details and maps are available at the park information centre in the *Kongsvold Fjeldstue*.

Røros and around

Located on a treeless mountain plateau 160km east of Kongsvoll, **RØROS** is a blustery place even on a summer's afternoon, when it's full of day-tripping tourists surveying the old part of town, little changed since its days as a copper-mining centre. Røros is a unique and remarkable survivor – until the mining company went bust a decade or two ago, mining had been the basis of life here since the seventeenth century. This dirty and dangerous work was supplemented by a little farming and hunting, and life for the average villager can't have been anything but hard. Surprisingly, Røros' wooden houses, some of them 300 years old, have escaped the fires that have devastated so many of Norway's timber-built towns, and consequently Røros is now on UNESCO's World Heritage List with firm regulations limiting changes to its grass-roofed cottages. Film companies regularly use the town as a backdrop for their productions – it featured as a labour camp in the 1971 film of *One Day in the Life of Ivan Denisovich*, starring Tom Courtenay.

In the town centre, **Røros kirke** (early to mid-June & mid-Aug to mid-Sept Mon–Sat 11am–3pm; mid-June to mid-Aug Mon–Sat 10am–5pm, Sun 1–3pm; mid-Sept to May Sat 11am–1pm; 25kr) is the most obvious target for a stroll, its heavy tower reflecting the wealth of the eighteenth-century mine owners. Built in 1784, and once the only stone building in Røros, the church is more like a theatre than a religious edifice. A huge structure capable of seating 1600 people, it was designed, like the church at Kongsberg (see p.298), to overawe rather than inspire. Its pulpit is built directly over the altar to emphasize the importance of the priest's word, and a two-tiered gallery runs around the nave. Mine labourers were accommodated in the gallery's lower level, while "undesirables" were compelled to sit above, and even had to enter via a separate, external staircase. Down below, the nave exhibited even finer distinctions: every pew nearer the front was a step up the social ladder, while mine managers vied for the curtained boxes, each of which had a well-publicized annual rent; the monarch (or royal representative) had a private box commanding views from the back. These byzantine social arrangements are explained in depth during the **guided tour** (late June to mid-Aug 1 daily in English), the cost of which is included in the admission fee.

Immediately below the church, on either side of the river, lies the oldest part of Røros, a huddle of sturdy cross-timbered smelters' cottages, storehouses and workshops squatting in the shadow of the **slegghaugan** (slagheaps) – more tourist attraction than eyesore, and providing fine views over the town and beyond. Here also, next to the river, the rambling main works – the Smelthytta (see p.295) – have been tidily restored and face on to **Malmplassen** ("ore-place"), the wide earthen square where drivers arrived from across the mountains to have their cartloads of ore weighed on the outdoor scales. Also in the square, hung in a rickety little tower, is the smelters' bell, which used to be rung at the start of each shift.

Malmplassen is at the top of Bergmannsgata which, together with parallel Kjerkgata, forms the heart of today's Røros. Conspicuously, the smaller artisans' dwellings, some of which have become **art and craft shops**, are set near the works, away from the rather more spacious dwellings once occupied by the owners and overseers,

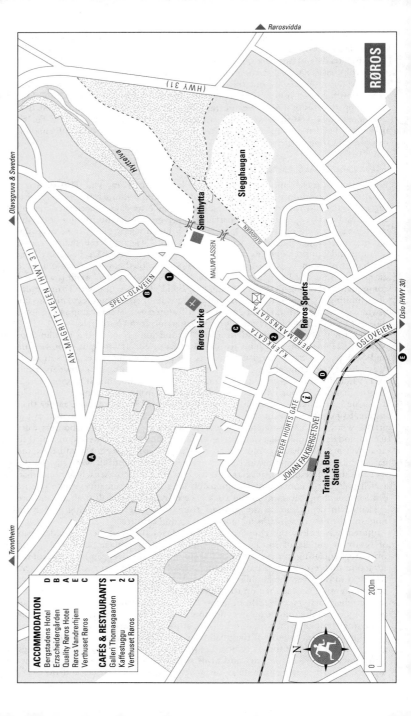

RØROS

▲ Rørosvidda

Hyttelva

(HWY 31)

Slegghaugan

Smelthytta

MALMPLASSEN

SLEGGVEIEN

▲ Olavsgruva & Sweden

AN-MAGRITT-VEIEN (HWY 31)

SPELL-OLAVEIEN

B

1

Røros kirke

C

KJERKGATA

BERGMANNSGATA

Røros Sports

2

D

OSLOVEIEN

i

PEDER HIORTS GATE

JOHAN FALKBERGETSVEI

Train & Bus Station

A

▲ Trondheim

E ▶ Oslo (HWY 30)

ACCOMMODATION
Bergstadens Hotel   D
Erzscheidergården   B
Quality Røros Hotel   A
Røros Vandrerhjem   E
Verthuset Røros   C

CAFÉS & RESTAURANTS
Galleri Thomasgaarden   1
Kaffestuggu   2
Verthuset Røros   C

200m

N

0

which cluster round the church. The main works, the **Smelthytta** (literally "melt-ing hut"; early June daily 11am–5pm; late June to mid-Aug daily 11am–7pm; mid-Aug to mid-Sept Mon–Fri 11am–5pm, Sat & Sun 11am–3pm; mid-Sept to May daily 11am–2/3pm; 60kr), has been converted into a museum, a large three-storey affair where most interesting section, set in the cavernous hall which once housed the smelter, explains the intricacies of copper production. Dioramas illuminate every part of the process, and there are production charts, samples of ore and a potted history of the company; pick up the comprehensive English-language leaflet available free at reception. There's actually not that much to look at – the building was gutted by fire in 1975 – and so the museum is perhaps for genuine copper enthusiasts only.

Practicalities

The adjacent **train** and **bus stations** are at the foot of the town centre, a couple of minutes' walk from the **tourist office** on Peder Hiorts gate (late June to mid-Aug Mon–Sat 9am–6pm, Sun 10am–4pm; mid-Aug to late June Mon–Fri 9am–3.30pm, Sat 10.30am–12.30pm; ☎72 41 11 65, ⓦwww.rorosinfo.com), where you can pick up a comprehensive free booklet on Røros and the surrounding region. They also have details of local **hikes** out across the uplands that encircle the town, one of the more popular being the five-hour trek east to the self-service DNT hut at Marenvollen. The uplands are also popular with **cross-country skiers** in the winter, and the tourist office has a leaflet mapping out several possible routes. To get around town, pick up one of the free municipal **bicycles** available at the train station and tourist office; for those venturing further afield, **mountain bikes** can be rented from Røros Sports, Bergmannsgata 13 (☎72 41 12 18), for around 150kr a day (plus 100kr deposit).

Because of the long drive here and the infrequency of trains to Trondheim and Oslo, you may well want to stay the night. Fortunately, there's a reasonable range of centrally located **accommodation**. Easily the best deal in town is the *Erzschei-dergården* guesthouse, Spell-Olaveien 6 (☎72 41 11 94, ⓦwww.erzscheidergaarden .com; ❹), with some charming, unassuming rooms in its wooden main building. Some rooms also have fine views over town, and there's an attractive subterranean breakfast area and a cosy lounge. Also worth considering is *Vertshuset Røros*, Kjerk-gata 34 (☎72 41 93 50, ⓦwww.vertshusetroros.no; ❸), a guesthouse with cramped doubles that's bang in the centre of town. There's also the *Røros Vandrerhjem*, Ørave-ien 25 (☎72 41 10 89, ⓦwww.vandrerhjem.no), an all-year HI **hostel** with dorm beds, 200kr and doubles (❷) in a plain wooden building about 800m south of the train station next to the sports ground.

When it comes to **food**, Røros is no gourmet's paradise, but there's just enough choice to get by. The unfussy homeliness at the restaurant in the *Verthuset Roros* makes for a good spot to enjoy an evening meal – choose from favourite traditional Norwegian dishes such as *Kjøttkaker i Brun Saus* (meatballs in brown sauce) from around 100kr. For a quicker bite, *Kaffestuggu*, Kjerkgata 19, has a suntrap of a courtyard and a series of elegant little rooms from where you can sample their cakes, sandwiches and reasonably priced daily specials. Tucked away, at Kjerkgata 48 is *Galleri Thomasgaarden*, a ceramics gallery that also houses the cosiest café in town, where you can avoid the crowds and get good home-cooked snacks.

Olavsgruva copper mine

Thirteen kilometres east of Røros off Highway 31, the **Olavsgruva**, one of the old copper mines, has been kept open as a museum, and there are guided tours of the workings (early June & late Aug 2 daily; early Sept Mon–Sat 2 daily, Sun 1 daily; late June to late Aug 6 daily; early Sept to Dec Sat 1 daily; 60kr). The temperature down the mine is a constant 5°C, so take something warm to wear – you'll need sturdy shoes, too.

West towards the fjords

The forested dales and uplands which fill the interior of southern Norway between Oslo and the western fjords rarely inspire: in almost any other European country, these elongated valleys would be attractions in their own right, but here in Norway they simply can't compare with the mountains and fjords of the north and west. Almost everywhere, the architecture is routinely modern and most of the old timber buildings that once lined the valleys are long gone – except in the ten-a-penny open-air museums that are a feature of nearly every town.

Of the three major trunk roads crossing the region, the **E16** is the fastest, a quick 350km haul up from Oslo to the fjord ferry point near Sogndal and the colossal 24km-long tunnel that leads to Flåm and ultimately Bergen. Otherwise, the E16's nearest rival, the slower **Hwy 7**, branches off the E16 at Hønefoss and, after a scenic wriggle along the edge of the Hardangervidda plateau, finally reaches the coast at Eidfjord near Hardangerfjord, a distance of 334km. Hwy 7 also intersects with Hwy 50, offering another possible route to Flåm. For most of its length, Hwy 7 is shadowed by the **Oslo–Bergen railway**, though they part company when the train swings north for its spectacular traverse of the mountains. The third road, the **E134**, stretches the 418km from Drammen near Oslo to Haugesund, passing near Odda on the Sørfjord (323km); it's another slower route, and has the advantage of passing through **Kongsberg**, an attractive town that makes for a pleasant overnight stay. There are regular long-distance **buses** along all three major roads.

West along the E16 to Leira and Borgund

Clipping along the **E16** from Oslo, it's 180km up through a sequence of river valleys to ribbon-like **LEIRA**, where you can break your journey economically – if not exactly thrillingly – at the HI **hostel** (℡61 35 95 00, ⊛www.vandrerhjem.no; June to mid-Aug), which occupies part of the high-school complex beside the road

---

Stave churches

Of the 29 surviving **stave churches** in Norway, all but a handful are in the southern and central areas. Together, they represent the country's most distinctive architectural legacy. Their key characteristic is that their timbers are placed vertically into the ground – in contrast to the log-bonding technique used by the Norwegians for everything else. Thus, a stave wall consists of vertical planks slotted into sills above and below, with the sills connected to upright posts – or **staves** (hence the name) – at each corner. The general design seems to have been worked out in the twelfth century and regular features include external wooden galleries, shingles and finials. However, the most fetching churches are those where the central section of the nave has been raised above the aisles to create – from the outside – a distinctive, almost pagoda-like effect. In virtually all stave churches, the **door frames** (where they survive) are decorated from top to bottom with surging, intricate carvings – fantastic long-limbed dragons, entwined with tendrils of vine – that clearly relate back to Viking design.

The **origins** of stave churches have attracted an inordinate amount of academic debate. Some scholars argue that they were originally pagan temples, converted to Christian use by the addition of a chancel, whilst others are convinced that they were inspired by Russian churches. In the nineteenth century, they also developed a symbolic importance as reminders of the time when Norway was independent. Many had fallen into a dreadful state of repair and were clumsily renovated – or even remodelled – by enthusiastic medievalists with a nationalist agenda. Undoing this repair work has been a major operation that continues today. For most visitors, seeing one or two will suffice – two of the finest are those at Heddal (see p.299) and Borgund (see p.297).

△ Borgund stave church

and has double rooms (❶) as well as dorm beds (120kr). Hwy 51 branches north at the next village of **Fagernes**, running along the eastern edge of the Jotunheimen National Park, passing near Gjendesheim and its lodge (see p.291) before finally joining Hwy 15 west of Otta (see p.290).

About 30km west of Fagernes along the E16, the scenery improves as you approach the coast. The road dips and weaves from dale to dale, slipping between the hills until it reaches the **Laerdal** valley, whose forested sides frame the stepped roofs and angular gables of the **Borgund stave church** (daily: May to mid-June & late Aug to Sept 10am–5pm; mid-June to late Aug 8am–8pm; 65kr). One of the best preserved stave churches in Norway, Borgund was built beside what was – until bubonic plague wiped out most of the local population in the fourteenth century – one of the major pack roads between east and west. The church has preserved much of its medieval appearance, its tiered exterior protected by shingles and deco-rated with finials in the shape of dragons and Christian crosses, culminating in a slender ridge turret. A rickety wooden gallery runs round the outside of the church, and the doors sport a swirling abundance of carved animals and foliage. Inside, the dark, pine-scented nave is framed by the upright wooden posts that define this style of church architecture. An adjacent visitor centre fills in some of the historical and architectural background.

Beyond the church, the valley grows wilder as the E16 travels the 45km down to Fodnes, where a 24hr car ferry zips over to Manheller, some 18km from Sogndal (see p.344). On the way, you'll pass the entrance to the 24.3km-long tunnel that extends the E16 to Flåm (see p.338) and Bergen (see p.316).

West along Highway 7 to Geilo

Highway 7 branches off the E16 about 60km from Oslo at **Hønefoss**, and then cuts an unexciting course along the **Hallingdal** valley, as does the main Oslo–Bergen railway. Some 180km from Hønefoss, the road forks at **Hagafoss**, with Hwy 50 descending the dales to reach, after 100km, the Aurlandsfjord just round the coast from Flåm. Meanwhile, Hwy 7 presses on west to the winter ski resort of **GEILO**, 250km from Oslo. Frankly, Geilo is a boring town out of the skiing season, but it does have several inexpensive places to stay, including an HI **hostel** (☎32 08 70 60, ⍟www.vandrerhjem.no; mid-June to Aug & Dec–April; dorm beds 180kr, doubles ❷), housed in large barrack-like buildings in the town centre just off the main drag. Details of other accommodation are available from the **tourist office** nearby (June & late Aug Mon–Fri 8.30am–6pm, Sat 9am–3pm; July to mid-Aug daily 8.30am–8pm; Sept–May Mon–Fri 8.30am–4pm; ☎32 09 59 00, ⍟www .geilo.no).

Just beyond Geilo, the rail line ceases to follow the road, breaking off to tunnel its way through the mountains to Finse, Myrdal (where you change for the scenic branch line down to Flåm; see p.338), and points to Bergen. Hwy 7 continues west for a further 100km, slicing across the peripheries of the Hardangervidda national park (see p.336). It's a lonely, handsome road and on the way you'll pass several places – such as **Halne** and **Dyranut** – where you can pick up the Hardangervidda's network of hiking trails (for more on hiking in the Hardangervidda, see p.336). On the far side of the plateau, Hwy 7 rushes down a steep valley to reach the fjords at Eidfjord (see p.334).

West along the E134: Kongsberg and around

A third main route west from Oslo to the fjords, the **E134** has the advantage of passing through **KONGSBERG**, about 80km from the capital and one of the most interesting towns in the region. A local story claims that the silver responsible for its existence was discovered by two goatherds, who stumbled across a vein of the metal laid bare by the scratchings of an ox. True or not, Christian IV, his eye on the main chance, was quick to exploit the find, sponsoring the development of mining here – the name means "King's Mountain" – at the start of what became a seventeenth-century silver rush. In the event, it turned out that Kongsberg was the only place in the world where silver was to be found in its pure form, and there was enough of it to sustain the town for a couple of centuries. Indeed, by the 1750s Kongsberg was the largest town in Norway, with half of its 8000 inhabitants employed in and around the 300-odd mine shafts that littered the area. The silver works closed in 1805, but by this time Kongsberg was also the site of a royal mint and then an armaments factory, which still employs people to this day.

To appreciate the full economic and political clout of the mine owners, visit the church they funded, **Kongsberg kirke** (mid-May to mid-Aug Mon–Fri 10am–4pm, Sat 10am–1pm & Sun 2–4pm; late Aug Mon–Fri 10am–noon; Sept to mid-May Tues–Thurs 10am–noon; 30kr), the largest and arguably the most beautiful Baroque church in Norway. It dates from 1761, when the mines were at the peak of their prosperity, and sits impressively in a square surrounded on three sides by period wooden buildings. The interior is a grand affair too, with an enormous and showily mock-marbled western wall incorporating altar, pulpit and organ. This arrangement was dictated by political considerations: the pulpit is actually *above* the altar, to ram home the point that the priest's stern injunctions to work harder on behalf of the mine owners were an expression of God's will.

Kongsberg itself is an agreeable if quiet place in summer, with plenty of green spaces. The **River Lågen** tumbles through the centre, and statues on the town bridge at the foot of Storgata commemorate various local activities, including foolhardy attempts to locate new finds of silver – one of them involving the use of divining rods. Enthusiasts will enjoy the **Norsk Bergverksmuseum**, Hyttegata 3 (Norwegian Mining Museum; daily: mid-May to Aug 10am–5pm; Sept to mid-May noon–4pm; 50kr), housed in the old smelting works at the river's edge; it shares its premises a pocket-sized ski museum and coin collection, but merely pottering around is as enjoyable a way as any of spending time in Kongsberg.

The **silver mines** themselves, the **Sølvgruvene**, are open for tours and make a pleasant excursion, especially if you have children to amuse. They're hidden in green surroundings 8km west of town in the hamlet of **SAGGRENDA** – drive along the E134 in the Notodden direction and look for the sign leading off to the right. The informative 90-minute **tour** includes a ride on a miniature train through black tunnels to the shafts. There are three to six tour departures daily from mid-May to August and two weekly in September and October; the tour costs 125kr – 50kr for kids – and the tourist office (see below) has the schedule. Remember to take a sweater as it's cold in them there mines. Back outside the mine, just 350m down the hill, the old ochre-painted timber workers' compound – the **Sakkerhusene** – has been restored and holds some rather half-hearted displays on the history of the mines, as well as a café.

Practicalities

Kongsberg **tourist office**, at Karsches gata 3 (early May to mid-June & late Aug to late Sept Mon–Fri 9am–4pm, Sat 10am–2pm; late June to late Aug Mon–Fri 9am–7pm, Sat & Sun 10am–4pm; mid-Sept to April Mon–Fri 9am–4pm; ☎32 29 90 50, ⊛www.visitkongsberg.no), is a brief walk from the **train and bus station**, and can help with accommodation – not that there's much of a decision to be made. The HI **hostel** at Vinjesgate 1 (☎32 73 20 24, ⊛www.kongsberg-vandrerhjem.no) is *the* place to stay, with both dorm beds (195kr) and comfortable en-suite double rooms (**②**) in an attractive timber lodge close to the town centre. Drivers need to follow the signs on the E134; train and bus users need to walk south from the station along Storgata, cross the bridge and walk round the back of Kongsberg kirke on the right-hand side. At the back of the church, head down the slope and over the footbridge – about a ten-minute walk in all. As for central **hotels**, there is just one appealing option, the *Quality Hotel Grand*, down near the river at Christian Augusts gate 2 (☎32 77 28 00, ⊛www.quality-grand.no; **⑥/④**), which also has a first-class **restaurant**. If the weather's good, head for the pleasant riverside terrace of the *Gamle Kongsberg Kro* café-restaurant below the church.

West of Kongsberg: Heddal, Seljord and Åmot

A few kilometres west of Kongsberg, the **E134** passes into **Telemark**, a county that covers a great forested chunk of southern Norway. Just inside its borders is industrial **Notodden** and, 6km beyond that, beside the main road, is the **stave church of Heddal** (daily: late May to late June & late Aug to early Sept 10am–5pm; late June to late Aug 9am–7pm; 35kr; ⊛www.heddal-stavkirke.no). Surrounded by a neat cemetery and rolling pastureland, Heddal is the largest surviving stave church in Norway. Its pretty tumble of shingle-clad roofs was restored to something like its medieval appearance in 1955, rectifying a heavy-handed nineteenth-century remodelling. The crosses atop the church's gables alternate with dragon-head gargoyles, a mix of Christian and pagan symbolism that is typical of many stave churches. Inside, the twenty masts of the nave are decorated at the top by masks, and there's some attractive seventeenth-century wall decoration in light blues, browns and whites. Pride of place, however, goes to the ancient bishop's chair in the chancel. Dating from around 1250, the chair carries a relief retelling the saga of Sigurd the Dragonslayer, a pagan story that Christians turned to their advantage by recasting the Viking as Jesus and the dragon as the Devil. Across from the church, there's a café and a modest museum illustrating further aspects of Heddal's history.

There's another fine church around 55km further west just off the E134 in **SELJORD**, a small industrial town of ancient provenance that spreads between forested hills and lake Seljordsvatnet. Dating from the twelfth century, the church (open for free guided tours in the summer, call ☎35 05 08 74) is built of stone, and as such is something of a medieval rarity. The town also seems to have attracted more than its fair share of "Believe It Or Not" stories: a monster is supposed to lurk in the depths of the lake; elves are alleged to gather here for some of their soirées; and the 570kg stone outside the church was, so the story goes, only lifted once, by an eighteenth-century strongman by the name of Nils Langedal. Elves and serpents apart, there's nothing much to delay you.

Beyond Seljord, it's a further 80km west along E134 to the handsome **Grungedal valley**, home to several antique farmsteads. Pushing on, the scenery bordering E134 becomes wilder and more dramatic as the road slips across the southern peripheries of the Hardangervidda plateau before tunnelling through the mountains to meet the coastal Hwy 13. Branching off to the north, Hwy 13 passes, in 5km, the waterfalls at **Latefossen**, two huge torrents that empty into the river with a deafening roar. From here, it's a further 14km to Odda, an ugly industrial centre that is a particularly unfortunate introduction to the fjords: try to allow enough time to avoid the place altogether and keep going north to the much more appealing hamlet of Lofthus (see p.334). Alternatively, if you ignore Hwy 13 and keep on along the E134, it's 115km from the crossroads to the coast at Haugesund.

The south coast

Stretching from the Oslofjord to Stavanger, Norway's **south coast** may have little of the imposing grandeur of other, wilder parts of the country, but its island-shredded eastern half, running down to Kristiansand, is undeniably lovely. Backed by forests, fells and lakes, it's this part of the coast that attracts Norwegians in droves, equipped not so much with bucket and spade as with boat and navigational aids – these waters, with their narrow inlets, islands and skerries, make for particularly enjoyable **sailing**. Camping on the offshore islands is easy too, the only restrictions being that you shouldn't stay in one spot for more than 48 hours, shouldn't get too close to anyone's home, or light a fire – either on bare rock or among vegetation. Leaflets detailing coastal rules and regulations are available at any local tourist office.

If boats and tents aren't your thing, the white-painted clapboard houses of tiny towns like **Lillesand**, **Arendal** and – to a lesser degree – **Grimstad** have an appropriately nautical, almost jaunty air. This portion of the coast is also important for Norway's international trade: it's just a short hop to Denmark from here, and larger towns such as Sandefjord, Larvik and Porsgrunn have kicked over their seventeenth-century traces as rustic timber ports to become modern industrial centres in their own right. Most of these manufacturing towns are run-of-the-mill, except for the biggest of them, **Kristiansand**, a lively port and resort with enough sights, restaurants, bars and beaches to while away a day, maybe two. Beyond Kristiansand lies **Mandal**, an especially fetching holiday spot with a great beach, but thereafter the coast becomes harsher and less absorbing, heralding a sparsely inhabited region with little to detain you. A possible exception is the old port of **Flekkefjord**, which does warrant a pit-stop, though most visitors push on to the bustling, oil-rich city of **Stavanger**, 250km from Kristiansand.

There are regular **trains** from Oslo to Kristiansand and Stavanger, but the rail line runs inland for most of its journey, only dipping down to the coast at the major resorts – a disappointing ride, the sea views shielded much of the time behind bony, forested hills. The same applies to the main **road and bus** route – the **E18/E39** – which also sticks stubbornly inland for most of the 300km from Oslo to Kristiansand (E18) and again for the 250km on to Stavanger (E39). It does, however, make for easy and fast travel to the main destinations, even if exploring the smaller coastal settlements is awkward without your own vehicle.

All the places in this section are easily accessed from the E18/E39, all offer accommodation in some form or other and most provide boat trips along the neighbouring coastline. Note, though, that the main season is short – from June to the end of August. At other times of the year, many museums are closed and boat trips curtailed.

Arendal

The first place that really merits a stop on the E18 is **ARENDAL**, 260km from Oslo and one of the most appealing spots on the coast, with its sheltered harbour curling right into the town centre, itself pushed up tight against the forested hills behind. The town's heyday was in the eighteenth century when its shipyards churned out dozens of the sleek wooden sailing ships that then dominated international trade. There's an attractive reminder of these boom times in the form of the elegant old merchants' buildings along the waterfront in the oldest part of town, known as **Tyholmen**. After a wander through Tyholmen, stroll north along the boardwalk flanking **Pollen**, the short rectangular inner harbour bordered by pavement cafés. For the architectural lowdown on Tyholmen, call in at the tourist office (see below) and sign up for one of their **walking tours** (late June to early Aug 3 weekly; 1hr 30min; 50kr).

The tourist office also has details of all sorts of **boat trips** which leave from Pollen. The most enjoyable excursion is to **Merdø**, a low-lying, lightly wooded islet in the Skagerrak. Footpaths network the island, there's a beach, a café and the **Merdøgaard Museum** (late June to mid-Aug daily noon–4pm; 30kr), which occupies a sprightly eighteenth-century sea captain's house, its period rooms liberally sprinkled with appropriate bygones. Ferries leave Pollen for Merdø every hour or so; the return fare is 30–35kr.

Practicalities

From Arendal **train station**, it's a five- to ten-minute walk west to the main square, Torvet – either up and over the steep hill along Iuellsklev and then Bendiksklev, or through the tunnel. Torvet is about 150m north of the Pollen inner harbour. **Buses** stop in the larger square, west of Torvet and across from the huge red-brick church with the copper-green steeple. Arendal **tourist office** (July Mon–Fri 9am–7pm, Sat & Sun 11am–6pm; Aug–June Mon–Fri 9am–7pm, Sat 11am–4pm; ☎37 00 55 44, ⓦ www.arendal.com) is alongside the bus station, in the combined new Rådhus and concert hall at Sam Eydes plass.

Easily the nicest place **to stay** is the luxurious ⚓ *Clarion Hotel Tyholmen*, Teaterplassen 2 (☎37 07 68 00, wwww.choicehotels.no; ⓺) which occupies a handsome wooden building in the style of an old warehouse on the Tyholmen quayside. The more modest *Thon Hotel Arendal*, Friergangen 1 (☎37 05 21 50, ⓦ www.thonhotels .no; ⓸/⓹), is a straightforward modern hotel with well-appointed rooms, just off the west side of Pollen. Alternatively, a hundred yards west of the *Clarion*, there are rooms with shared facilities in the pleasant *Høholthus Gjestehus*, Radhusgaten 6 (☎92 83 63 90, ⓦ www.kulturkompasset.com; ⓷). The rate includes the use of a kitchen, garden and a library with tiny balcony overlooking the water. For **food**, there are a couple of inexpensive cafés on Torvet and a string of more tempting places along and around Pollen, including *Madam Reiersen*, which offers delicious seafood and fresh pasta dishes from its harbourside premises at Nedre Tyholmsvei 3; mains average 140kr. The café-bars lining Pollen become lively **drinking** haunts till the early hours, especially on a warm summer's night.

Grimstad

From Arendal, it's a short 20km hop south on the E18 by bus or car to **GRIMSTAD**, a brisk huddle of white houses with orange-tiled roofs stacked up behind the harbour. At the beginning of the nineteenth century the town had no less than forty shipyards and carried on a lucrative trade with France. It wasn't particularly surprising, therefore, that when **Henrik Ibsen** left his home in nearby Skien in 1844 at the age of sixteen he should come to Grimstad, where he worked as an apprentice pharmacist for the next six years. The careless financial dealings of Ibsen's father had impoverished the family, and Henrik's already jaundiced view of Norway's provincial bourgeoisie was confirmed here in the port, whose worthies Ibsen mocked in poems like *Resignation* and *The Corpse's Ball*. It was here, too, that Ibsen picked up first-hand news of the Paris Revolution of 1848, an event that radicalized him and inspired his paean to the insurrectionists of Budapest, *To Hungary*, written in 1849. Nonetheless, Ibsen's stay on the south coast is more usually recalled as providing the setting for some of his better-known plays, particularly *Pillars of Society*. The pharmacy where Ibsen lived and worked, just up from the harbour in the centre of town on Henrik Ibsens gate, has been turned into the pocket-sized **Ibsenhuset og Grimstad Bymuseum** (Ibsen House and Grimstad Town Museum; June–Aug Mon–Fri 11am–5pm, Sat & Sun noon–5pm; Sept–May Mon–Fri 10am–2pm; 40kr). With creaking wooden floors and narrow-beamed ceilings, the building has maintained its nineteenth century appearance and comes complete with various Ibsen memorabilia – look out for the glass case displaying the playwright's hat, coat, umbrella and boots, as worn on his daily stroll down to Oslo's *Grand Hotel*.

Practicalities

Grimstad's **bus station** is at the south end of the harbour, a couple of hundred metres along from the **tourist office** (June–Aug Mon–Fri 9am–6pm, Sat 10am–4pm, plus Sun in July 10am–4pm; Sept–May Mon–Fri 8.30am–4pm; ☎37 25 01 68, ⍟www.grimstad.net), from where you can pick up all the usual bumph as well as detailed maps of the islands that dot the seaward approaches to Grimstad harbour. Many of the islands – or parts of them – are publicly owned and protected within the **Skjærgårdspark**. In the park, public access moorings are commonplace and so are picnic and bathing facilities, though you do need a boat to get there, of course. Boat hire is available from several local companies via the tourist office. In addition, there are a handful of **boat cruises** to choose from, though these don't stop at any of the islands. The most popular is a two-hour coastal jaunt around the offshore islands and skerries with the *M/S Bibben* (July Tues, Thurs & Sun 1 daily; 150kr); call ☎95 20 20 06 to sign up. Grimstad has an attractive and central **hotel**, the *Grimstad*, Kirkegaten 3 (☎37 25 25 25, ⍟www.grimstadhotell.no; ⓺), in an old and cleverly converted clapboard complex amongst the narrow lanes near the Ibsen house; the hotel has the best **restaurant** in town, too. Wine buffs can check out the fruit wines made by Fuhr, a local firm – with Fuhr Rhubarb and Fuhr Vermouth representing two daunting challenges for the palate.

Lillesand

Bright, cheerful **LILLESAND**, just 20km south of Grimstad, is one of the most popular holiday spots on the coast, the white clapboard houses of its tiny centre draped prettily round the harbourfront. One or two of the buildings, notably the sturdy **Rådhus** (1734), are especially good-looking, but it's the general appearance of the place which appeals, best appreciated from the terrace of one of the town's waterfront café-restaurants: the *Sjøbua*, midway round the harbour, does very nicely.

To investigate Lillesand's architectural nooks and crannies, sign up at the tourist office (see below) for one of their hour-long **guided walks** (1 daily mid-June to Aug; 30kr). The tourist office also has information on – and sailing schedules for – a wide variety of local **boat trips**, from fishing trips to cruises along the coast. One of the best is the three-hour cruise aboard *M/S Øya* (late June to mid-Aug Mon–Sat 10am; 200kr each way; ☎95 93 58 55), a dinky little passenger ferry which wiggles its way south to Kristiansand (see below) along a narrow channel separating the mainland from the offshore islets. Sheltered from the full force of the ocean, this channel – the **Blindleia** – was once a major trade route, but today it's trafficked by every sort of pleasure craft imaginable, from replica three-mast sailing ships to the sleekest of yachts. Other, faster, boats make the trip too, but the *M/S Øya* is the most charming.

Practicalities

Lillesand cannot be reached by train, but it is on the main Oslo–Arendal–Kristiansand bus route. **Buses** pull in near the south end of the harbour, a brief stroll from the **tourist office**, located in the old waterfront customs house (mid-June to mid-Aug Mon–Fri 10am–6pm, Sat 10am–4pm, Sun noon–4pm; mid-Aug to mid-June Mon–Fri 9am–4pm; ☎37 40 19 10, ⓦwww.lillesand.com). Lillesand has one central **hotel**, the first-rate *Norge*, Strandgaten 3 (☎37 27 01 44, ⓦwww.hotelnorge.no; ❻), which occupies a grand old wooden building near the bus stop. Refurbished in attractive period style, the interior holds some charming stained-glass windows and the rooms are named after some of the famous people who have stayed here – the novelist Knut Hamsun and the Spanish king Alfonso XIII for starters. Otherwise, *Tingsaker Familiecamping*, on Øvre Tingsaker (☎37 27 04 21, ⓦwww.tingsakercamping.no; May–Aug), is a well-equipped waterfront campsite with cabins (❷). Amongst its facilities, there's a communal kitchen, canoe hire, a pool and a playground; the site is about 1km north of the centre – take Storgata and keep going. For **food**, the *Hotel Norge* has an excellent **restaurant**, but with mains from around 250kr it's more expensive and formal than the harbourfront *Sjøbua*, where you can sample excellent fish dishes for around 180kr in breezily naff surroundings – the interior is kitted out like an old sailing ship.

Kristiansand and around

With 75,000 inhabitants, **KRISTIANSAND**, some 30km on along the E18 from Lillesand, is Norway's fifth largest town and a part-time holiday resort, a genial, energetic place which thrives on its ferry connections with Denmark, its busy marinas and its passable sandy beaches. In summer, the seafront and adjoining streets are a frenetic bustle of cocktail bars, fast-food joints and flirting holidaymakers, and even in winter Norwegians come here to live it up. Like so many other Scandinavian towns, Kristiansand was founded by and named after **Christian IV**, who saw an opportunity to strengthen his coastal defences here. Building started in 1641, and the town has retained the spacious quadrant plan that characterized all Christian's projects. There are few specific sights, but it's worth a quick look around, especially when everyone else has gone to the beach and left the central pedestrianized streets relatively empty. Kristiansand is also just a few kilometres from the **Kristiansand Kanonmuseum**, the forbidding remains of a large coastal gun battery built during the German occupation of World War II.

CAFÉS & RESTAURANTS

FRK Larsen	3
Lille-Dampen	1
Royal China	2
Sjøhuset	4

ACCOMMODATION

Centrum	C
Frobusdalen Rom	B
Kristiansand Vandrerhjem	E
Roligheden Camping	A
Thon Hotel Wergeland	D

Arrival and information

Trains, **buses** and Color Line **ferries** all arrive close to each other, by Vestre Strandgate on the edge of the town grid. The main regional **tourist office** is here too, at Vestre Strandgate 32 (mid-June to mid-Aug Mon–Fri 8am–6pm, Sat 10am–6pm, Sun noon–6pm; mid-Aug to mid-June Mon–Fri 8.30am–3.30pm; ☎38 12 13 14, ⓦwww.sorlandet.com). Staff issue free town maps, public transport timetables and information on boat times, free guided walks, island bathing and beaches. **Parking** is easy throughout town, with car parks concentrated along Vestre Strandgate. The best way to explore the centre is on **foot** – it only takes about ten minutes to walk from one side to the other – but **bike rental** is available at the edge of town at *Kristiansand Sykkelsenter*, Grim Torv 3 (☎38 02 68 35), where 21-gear bikes cost 150kr per day, 490kr for a week.

Accommodation

Kristiansand has a reasonably good choice of **accommodation** with a fair sprinkling of hotels, a guesthouse or two and a youth hostel and campsite – all are either in or fairly near the centre.

Accommodation

Centrum Motel Vestre Strandgate 49 ☎38 02 79 69, ⓦwww.motell.no. Right by the train station, and offering frugal lodgings at budget prices. Doubles are in the form of bunk beds, all rooms are en suite, and there's a kitchen and laundry. ②

Frobusdalen Rom Frobusdalen 2 ☎91 12 99 06, ⓔimsan@start.no. Undoubtedly the best option

in town, this delightful hotel is a family-run affair occupying a shipowner's mansion of 1917. Its interior has been sensitively restored and is crammed with period antiques. Though just five minutes' walk from the train station, it's hard to find: go northwest up Vestre Strandgate, straight on at the roundabout by the flyover (signed Evje), then take the path immediately to your right, and *Frobusdalen* is ten metres on the left. Drivers should head

north along Festningsgata and, at the traffic lights at the end, follow the sign to Evje. **②**
Kristiansand Vandrerhjem Skansen 8 ☎ 38 02 83 10, ⊛ www.vandrerhjem.no. An odd location a few hundred yards from the (busy) town beach in a light industrial estate. The building is an ugly 1960s prefab, but the facilities are quite good, with self-catering, a laundry and a café, and doubles (**②**) as well as dorm beds (195kr). The hostel is about fifteen minutes' walk east of the ferry terminal on the tiny peninsula, Tangen, edging the marina – take any street up to Elvegata, turn right and keep going: Skansen is on the left.

Roligheden Camping Framnesveien ☎ 38 09 67 22, ⊛ www.roligheden.no. Large and quite formal campsite 3km east of the town centre behind a yacht jetty. To get there, drive over the bridge at the end of Dronningens gate, turn right along Marviksveien, then right again near the end, following the signs. Open June–Aug.
Thon Hotel Wergeland Kirkegata 15 ☎ 38 17 20 40, ⊛ www.thonhotels.no. A converted nineteenth-century townhouse right in the middle the city, near the Domkirke, with comfortable, modern rooms. **❸/❺**

The Town

Neat and trim, the gridiron streets that make up Kristiansand's compact centre hold one architectural high point, the **Domkirke** (June–Aug Mon–Fri 10am–2pm; free), at the corner of Kirkegata and Rådhusgaten, an imposing neo-Gothic edifice dating from the 1880s and seating nearly 2000. Its only rival is the **Christiansholm Festning** on Strandpromenaden (mid-May to mid-Sept daily 9am–9pm; free), a squat fortress whose sturdy circular tower and zigzagging earth-and-stone ramparts overlook the marina in the east harbour. Built in 1672, the tower's walls are five metres thick, a precaution that proved unnecessary since it never saw action. These days it houses various arts and crafts displays.

If you fancy a **swim** one option is **Galgebergtangen** (Gallows' Point), an attractive rocky cove 2km east of the town centre with a small sandy beach. To get there, go over the bridge at the end of Dronningens gate, take the first major right (at the lights) and follow the signs. Closer still, head for the **Odderøya**, a tiny peninsula which curves off the city's southernmost corner, by the fish market (*fiskebrygga*). This wooded former military area is criss-crossed by tracks and is an ideal place for a barbecue or a summer swim from its rocks and beaches.

The Kristiansand Kanonmuseum

Despite the inveigling of the German admiralty, who feared the British would occupy Norway and thus trap their fleet in the Baltic, **Hitler** was lukewarm about invading Norway until he met Vidkun Quisling in Berlin in 1939. Hitler took Quisling's assurances about his military ability to stage a coup at face value, no doubt encouraged by the Norwegian's virulent anti-Semitism, and was thereafter keen to proceed. In the event it went smoothly enough – even if Quisling was soon discarded – but for the rest of the war Hitler overestimated both Norway's strategic importance and the likelihood of an Allied counter-invasion in the north. He garrisoned the country with nigh on half a million men and built several hundred artillery batteries round the coast – a huge waste of resources that were desperately needed elsewhere.

Work began on the coastal battery that is now conserved as the **Kristiansand Kanonmuseum** (April to mid-May & Oct daily 11am–5pm; mid-May to mid-June & mid-Aug to late Sept Mon–Wed 11am–3pm, Thurs–Sun 11am–5pm; mid-June to mid-Aug daily 11am–6pm; Nov–March daily noon–4pm; 50kr), in 1941, using (like all equivalent emplacements in Norway) the forced labour of POWs. Around 1400 men worked on the project, which involved the construction of protective housings for four big guns at the narrowest part of the Skagerrak. Guns on the Danish shore complemented those here, so that any enemy warship trying to slip through the straits could be shelled. Only a small zone in the middle was out of range, and this the Germans mined. The complex once covered 220 acres, but today the principal remains hog a narrow ridge, with a massive, empty artillery casement at one end, and a whopping 38cm-calibre **gun** in a concrete well

Moving on from Kristiansand

When it comes to **moving on from Kristiansand**, the obvious choice – the 240km trip west to Stavanger – is also the best. It's a journey that can be made by train as well as bus or car along the E39, though both the railway line and the highway afford only glimpses of the coast, travelling for the most part a few miles inland. It may not be a gripping journey, but it's certainly a lot more pleasant than the dreary 240km haul north to **Haukeligrend**, and then onto the Hardangervidda National Park, on Highway 9, to the E134. If, on the other hand, you're travelling north to Oslo between late June and mid-August, it might be worth considering the three-hour cruise up to Lillesand on the *M/S Øya* (see p.303).

at the other. The gun, which could fire a 500kg shell almost 55km, is in pristine condition, and visitors can explore the loading area, complete with the original ramrods, wedges, trolleys and pulleys. Below is the underground command post and soldiers' living quarters, again almost exactly as they were in the 1940s – including the odd bit of German graffiti.

If you want to **drive** to the Kanonmuseum, take Highway 456 out of Kristiansand to **Møvik**, then Highway 457 for the last 3km. Alternatively get **bus** M1 from Vestre Strandgate, heading west towards Flekkerøy; the Kanonmuseum is the penultimate stop.

Eating and drinking

There are lots of **restaurants** and **cafés** in the centre of Kristiansand, but the standard is very variable – we've listed a few of the choicer places below. There's also a fairly active nightlife based around a handful of **bars**, which stay open until 2am.

FRK Larsen Markens gate 5. Near the corner of Kongens gate, this laid-back café-bar is an appealing, fashionable place. Also serves meals, such as salted cod (*bacalao*), for a very reasonable 175kr.
Lille-Dampen Henrik Wergelands gate 15. First-rate and inexpensive bakery, with delicious takeaway baguettes from 40kr. Closed Sat & Sun.
Royal China Tollbodgaten 7. Surprisingly plush Chinese restaurant offering tasty main courses from as little as 110kr.
Sjøhuset Østre Strandgate 12A. In an old converted warehouse by the harbour at the east end of Markens gate, this excellent restaurant serves superb fish courses from 230kr (159kr at lunchtime). Nautical fittings and wooden beams set the scene. Open daily in summer; closed Sun rest of the year.

West to Flekkefjord

West of Kristiansand lies a sparsely inhabited region, where the rough uplands and long valleys of the interior bounce down to a shoreline that is pierced by a string of inlets and fjords. The highlight is undoubtedly **Mandal**, a fetching seaside resort with probably the best sandy beach in the whole of Norway, but thereafter it's a struggle to find much inspiration. The best you'll do is the old harbour town of Flekkefjord, though frankly there's not really much reason to pause anywhere between Mandal and Stavanger.

The **E39** weaves its way across the region, staying deep inland for the most part and offering views of not very much at all; the same applies to the Kristiansand–Stavanger **train line**, which doesn't include Flekkefjord on its itinerary.

Mandal

MANDAL, just 40km from Kristiansand along the E39, is Norway's southernmost town. This old timber port reached its heyday in the eighteenth century, when pines and oaks from the surrounding countryside were much sought-after by the Dutch to support their canal houses and build their trading fleet. Although it's now bordered by a modern mess, Mandal has preserved its quaint **old centre**, a narrow strip of white clapboard buildings spread along the north bank of the Mandalselva River just before it rolls into the sea. It's an attractive spot, well worth a short stroll; in summer, you can also drop by the municipal **museum** (late June to mid-Aug Mon–Fri 11am–5pm, Sat 11am–2pm, Sun 2–5pm; 20kr), whose rambling collection – from agricultural implements to seafaring tackle – occupies an old merchant's house overlooking the river. It's not its antiquities that make Mandal a popular tourist spot, however, but its fine beach, **Sjøsanden**. An 800-metre stretch of golden sand backed by pine trees and framed by rocky headlands, it's touted as Norway's best – and although this isn't saying a lot, it's a very enjoyable place to unwind for a few hours. The beach is about 1.5km from the town centre: walk along the harbour, past the tourist office to the end of the road and turn left; keep going until you reach the car park at the beach's eastern end. You can also explore a tiny wooded peninsular directly to the west of the beach, where a network of paths winds through the trees and rocks to reveal hidden sandy coves. The tourist office can provide you with a leaflet – complete with map – describing the area.

Practicalities

Mandal hasn't got a train station, but there is a fast and fairly frequent bus service from Kristiansand (2–4 daily; 40min) and Stavanger (1–3 daily; 3hr 30min). The town's ugly modern **bus station** is by the bridge on the north bank of the Man-dalselva River; from here it's a brief walk west to the old town centre, just beyond which is the **tourist office**, facing the river at Bryggegata 10 (June–Aug Mon–Fri 9am–7pm, Sat & Sun 10am–4pm; Sept–May Mon–Fri 9am–4pm; ☎ 38 27 83 00, ⓦ www.visitregionmandal.com). There are a couple of good places to **stay**, beginning with the handy and economical *Kjøbmandsgaarden Hotel* (☎ 38 26 12 76, ⓦ www.kjobmandsgaarden.com; ❹), which occupies an one of the old timber houses across from the bus station on Store Elvegate. All the dozen or so rooms are spick-and-span and the decor is bright and cheerful. Moving upmarket, the ⚜ *First Hotel Solborg*, Neseveien 1 (☎ 38 27 21 00, ⓦ www.firsthotels.com/Solborg; ❺), is an odd-looking but somehow rather fetching modern structure with every mod con; it's on the west side of the town centre, tight against a wooded escarpment, about a ten-minute walk from the bus station. Alternatively, you can camp or rent a cabin (❷) very close to the western end of the beach at the *Sjøsanden Feriesenter*, Sjøsandvei 1 (☎ 38 26 14 19), a signposted 2km from the town centre.

The *First Hotel Solborg* has the best **restaurant** in town, but for something less pricey and more informal, head into the centre where you'll find several places, including the lively pizzeria-restaurant, *Jonas B Gundersen*, Store Elvegate 25, where mains start at 120kr. The café-restaurant of the *Kjøbmandsgaarden* hotel comes highly recommended too, offering a tasty, inexpensive range of Norwegian dishes (from 110kr).

From Mandal, there are daily **express buses** along the E39 to Flekkefjord and Stavanger, respectively 80km and 210km away to the west. **Train** travellers have to return to Kristiansand to rejoin the rail network.

Flekkefjord

Moving on from Mandal, the **E39** hurries west, proceeding over the hills to worka-day **Lyngdal** and then **Liknes**, the latter an inconsequential village at the foot of Kvinesdal and the head of the slender Fedafjord. Thereafter the highway offers a rare glimpse of the ocean as it travels the western shore of the Fedafjord before turning inland again to snake over the hills to **FLEKKEFJORD**, 80km from Mandal. With a population of 6000, Flekkefjord is the big deal hereabouts, the old and picturesque timber houses of its tiny centre strung along the banks of a short (500m) channel that connects the Lafjord and the Grisefjord. Flekkefjord boomed in the sixteenth century on the back of its trade with the Dutch, who purchased the town's timber for their houses and its granite for their dykes and harbours. Later, in the 1750s, the herring industry came to prominence, along with shipbuilding and tanning, but the Flekkefjord economy had pretty much collapsed by the end of the nineteenth century when sailing ships gave way to steam. Recalling the Dutch connection by its nickname, "Hollenderbyen", the oldest and prettiest part of Flekkefjord lies on the west side of the channel. It only takes a few minutes to explore, though you can extend this pleasantly enough by visiting the nearby nineteenth-century period rooms of the **Flekkefjord Museum** (mid-June to Aug Mon–Fri 11am–5pm, Sat noon–3pm, Sun noon–4pm; 25kr) at Dr Kraftsgate 15–17.

Buses pull in on Løvikgata, about 200m east of the central waterway, while the **tourist office** is on the west side at Elvegaten 15 (mid-June to mid-Aug Mon–Fri 9am–5pm, Sat & Sun 10am–3pm; mid-Aug to mid-June Mon–Fri 9am–4pm; ☎38 32 21 31). There's no pressing reason to overnight here, but if you do want to **stay**, the best bet is the unassuming *Maritim Fjord Hotel* (☎38 32 58 00, ⓦwww.fjord hotellene.no; ❹/❺), overlooking the east side of the waterway at Sundgaten 15.

Stavanger and around

STAVANGER, 120km from Flekkefjord, is something of a survivor. While other Norwegian coastal towns have fallen foul of the precarious fortunes of fishing,

△ Stavanger harbour

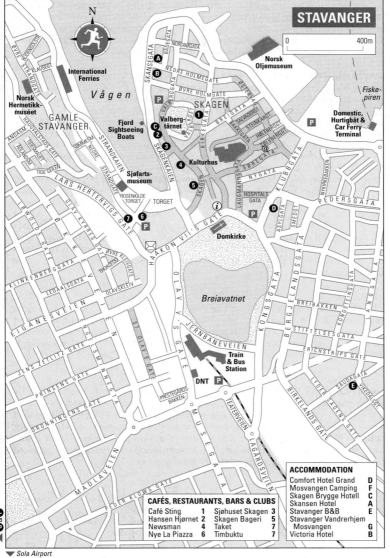

STAVANGER

0   400m

N

Norsk Oljemuseum

International Ferries

Vågen

Fiske-piren

Norsk Hermetikk-muséet

GAMLE STAVANGER

SKAGEN

Domestic, Hurtigbåt & Car Ferry Terminal

Fjord Sightseeing Boats

Valberg-tårnet **1**

2

Kulturhus

Sjøfarts-museum

ROSENKILDE TORGET

TORGET

i

D

HOSPITALS GATA

PEDERSGATA

Domkirke

Breiavatnet

E

Train & Bus Station

DNT

ACCOMMODATION

Comfort Hotel Grand	**D**
Mosvangen Camping	**F**
Skagen Brygge Hotell	**C**
Skansen Hotel	**A**
Stavanger B&B	**E**
Stavanger Vandrerhjem Mosvangen	**G**
Victoria Hotel	**B**

CAFÉS, RESTAURANTS, BARS & CLUBS

Café Sting	**1**	Sjøhuset Skagen	**3**	
Hansen Hjørnet	**2**	Skagen Bageri	**5**	
Newsman	**4**	Taket	**7**	
Nye La Piazza	**6**	Timbuktu	**7**	

G&F

Stavanger has grown and flourished, and is now the proud possessor of a dynamic economy which has swelled the population to over 100,000. It was the herring fishery that first put money into the town, crowding its nineteenth-century wharves with coopers and smiths, net makers and menders. When this industry failed, Stavanger moved into shipbuilding and ultimately oil: today, the port builds the rigs for Norway's offshore oilfields and refines the oil as well.

None of which is terribly enticing, and certainly no one could describe Stavanger as entirely picturesque. However, it's an easy city to adjust to, has a couple of enjoyable museums and a raft of excellent restaurants and lively bars. If you stay a while, you can sally out into the surrounding fjords, where the hike to the **Preikestolen** rock is one of the most popular jaunts in southern Norway.

Arrival, information and city transport

Stavanger's international **airport** is 14km southwest of the city centre at **Sola**. There's a Flybussen into Stavanger (Mon–Fri 5.10am–8.30pm, Sat 6am–7.30pm, Sun 8.30am–9pm; every 20–30min; 45kr), which stops at major downtown hotels, the ferry terminals and the bus and train stations. The adjacent **bus** and **train stations** (☎51 56 96 00) are on the southern side of the Breiavatnet, a tiny lake that's the most obvious downtown landmark. Also at the bus station is Rogaland Kollektivtrafikk Kolumbus, an agency run collectively by several transport companies (Mon–Fri 7am–8pm, Sat 8am–3.30pm, Sun 11am–6pm; ☎81 50 01 82, ⊛www.kolumbus.no), which provides comprehensive details of buses, boats and trains in the city and surrounding area.

The city's main square, Torget, is immediately northwest of the central lake. **International ferries** (☎81 53 35 00, ⊛www.fjordline.com) from Newcastle, Haugesund and Bergen – berth a five-minute walk away on the west side of the harbour at Strandkaien. All other **domestic ferries**, including **Hurtigbåt** passenger express boats and car ferries bound for the islands and fjords around Stavanger, use the Fiskepiren terminal, about 800m northeast of the train and bus stations. Finally, most **pleasure cruises** depart from Skagenkaien, on the east side of the main harbour.

Information

The **tourist office** is opposite the Domkirke, in the square at the top of Kongsgata (June–Aug daily 9am–8pm; Sept–May Mon–Fri 9am–4pm, Sat 9am–2pm; ☎51 85 92 00, ⊛www.regionstavanger.com). It publishes the useful, free *Stavanger Guide*, provides local bus and ferry timetables and free cycling maps of both the city and its surroundings; staff can also arrange a 15 percent reduction on some guided tours (see below).

City transport and tours

All of Stavanger's key attractions are clustered in or near the centre within easy walking distance of each other, while the town's watery surroundings can be reached by a variety of local boats and buses departing from the terminals detailed above. A number of operators also provide regular summertime **fjord sightseeing tours**, with the **Lysefjord** (see p.313) being the most popular trip. Most of the tours depart from Skagenkaien and prices start at around 280kr for a three- to four-hour excursion; tickets are available at the quayside.

Accommodation

There's plenty of choice of **accommodation** in Stavanger. Half a dozen **hotels** are dotted around the town's compact centre, each offering substantial weekend and summer discounts. Alternatively, there are a couple of convenient, no-frills **guesthouses** and, further afield, an HI **hostel** and **campsite**.

Hotels and guesthouses

Comfort Hotel Grand Klubbgata 3 ☎51 20 14 00, ⊛www.choicehotels.no. A good central option, close to all the bars and restaurants. The rooms are smart, modern and spacious, and the price includes a very good buffet breakfast and afternoon snacks. ❸/❻

Mosvangen Camping Tjensvollveien 1B ☎51 53 29 71, ⊛www.stavangercamping.no. By the lake, next door to the youth hostel, with cabins (❷) as well as spaces for tents and caravans. Open mid-May to mid-September.

Skagen Brygge Hotell Skagenkaien 30 ☎51 85 00 00, ⊛www.skagenbrygge hotell.no. A delightful quayside hotel, built in the style of an old warehouse but with lots of glass to allow great views over the harbour. The rooms are modern and tastefully decorated, the buffet breakfast outstanding and delicious mid-afternoon nibbles are on offer for free – cheese, pickled herring etc. The only quibble is noise from outside on summer weekends, when your best bet is to get a room at the back or on the top floor. ❹

Skansen Hotel Skansegata 7 ☎51 93 85 00, ⓦwww.skansenhotel.no. This recently revamped hotel-cum-guesthouse in an old wooden building on the east side of the harbour has 28 en-suite rooms, the best of which are kitted out in a brisk and pleasant modern style. ❸/❹

Stavanger B&B Vikdelsgata 1A ☎51 56 25 00, ⓦwww.stavangerbedandbreakfast.no. Straightforward modern place, with a hugely welcoming host, in a residential area five minutes' walk southeast of the central lake. Bright, pleasant rooms with showers and sinks; toilets are shared. An inexpensive option. ❸

Stavanger Vandrerhjem Mosvangen Henrik Ibsens gate 19 ☎51 54 36 36, ⓦwww .vandrerhjem.no. This plain HI youth hostel occupies a lakeside setting, a 3km walk from the centre: take Madlaveien west from near the station and turn left just beyond the lake, Mosvatnet, on to Tjensvollveien – Henrik Ibsens gate is its continuation. The hostel has doubles (❶) as well as beds 160kr, and self-catering and laundry facilities; advance reservations are advised. Open early June to mid-Aug.

Victoria Hotel Skansegata 1 ☎51 86 70 00, ⓦwww.victoria-hotel.no. Part of the *Rica* chain, this large hotel occupies a big old building with a fancy portico, overlooking the east side of the harbour. The foyer has kept much of its Victorian appearance, complete with wood panelling, leather sofas and ships' models, while the comfortable rooms beyond are also in a broadly period style. ❸

The City

Built with oil money, much of central Stavanger is modern, a flashy but surprisingly likeable ensemble of mini tower-blocks. The only relic of the medieval city is the twelfth-century **Domkirke** (June–Aug Mon–Sun 11am–7pm; Sept–May Tue, Thurs & Sat 11am–4pm; free), above the Torget, whose pointed-hat towers signal a Romanesque church that has suffered from several poorly conceived renovations. The simple interior, originally the work of English craftsmen, has fared badly too, spoilt by ornate seventeenth-century additions including an intricate pulpit and five huge memorial tablets adorning the walls of the aisles – a jumble of richly carved angels, crucifixes, death's-heads, animals and apostles. Organ recitals are held here every Thursday at 11.15am.

A brief stroll northeast, beyond the fresh fish and flower stalls of **Torget**, is the **Skagen** area, built on the bumpy promontory that forms the eastern side of the harbour. It's an oddly discordant district, a sometimes clumsy, sometimes charming mixture of old and new. Incorporating the town's main shopping zone, whose mazy street plan is the only legacy of the original Viking settlement, it takes on a funky feel around Øuvre Holmegate, with its designer stores and multi-coloured shopfronts. The spiky **Valbergtårnet** (Valberg tower), atop the highest point and guarded by three rusty cannons, is the one specific sight, a nineteenth-century firewatch offering sweeping views of the city and its industry.

Beside the waterfront on the far side of Skagen, the oil industry celebrates its achievements by way of the gleaming **Norsk Oljemuseum** (Norwegian Petroleum Museum; June–Aug daily 10am–7pm, Sept–May Mon–Sat 10am–4pm & Sun 10am–6pm; 80kr; ⓦwww.norskolje.museum.no). Housed in a hangar-like building, this excellent museum has displays on North Sea geology, oil extraction and the like, complete with drill bits and other oil-rig paraphernalia. There are several hands-on exhibits, too – including a diving bell – plus an honest account of the accidents and occasional disasters that have befallen the industry.

Gamle Stavanger

The city's star turn is the **Gamle Stavanger** (Old Stavanger) area, on the western side of the harbour. Though very different in appearance from the modern structures back in the centre, the buildings here were also the product of a late nineteenth-century boom. From 1810 until around 1870, herring turned up just offshore in their millions, and Stavanger took advantage of this slice of luck. The town flourished and expanded, with the number of merchants and ship owners increasing dramatically. Huge profits were made from the exported fish, which were salted and later, as the technology improved, canned. Today, some of the wooden stores and warehouses flanking the western quayside hint at their nineteenth-century pedigree, but it's the succession of narrow, cobbled lanes behind them that show Gamle Stavanger to best advantage. Formerly home to local seafarers, craftsmen and cannery workers, the area has been maintained as a residential quarter, mercifully free of tourist tat; the long rows of white-painted, clapboard houses are immaculately maintained, complete with gas lamps, picket fences and tiny terraced gardens.

The **Norsk Hermetikkmuséet** (Canning Museum; early June & late Aug Mon–Thurs 11am–3pm; mid-June to mid-Aug daily 11am–4pm; Sept–May Sun 11am–4pm; 40kr), right in the heart of Gamle Stavanger at Øvre Strandgate 88, occupies an old sardine-canning factory and gives a glimpse of the industry that saved Stavanger from collapse at the end of the nineteenth century. The herring largely disappeared from local waters in the 1870s, but the canning factories switched to imported fish, thereby keeping the local economy afloat. That remained Stavanger's main source of employment until as late as 1960: in the 1920s there were seventy canneries in the town, and the last one only closed down in 1983. A visit to an old canning factory may not seem too enticing, but actually the museum is very good, not least because of its collection of sardine tin labels. The variety of design is extraordinary – anything and everything from representations of the Norwegian royal family to surrealistic fish with human qualities. You can watch the museum smoking its own sardines on the first Sunday of every month and every Tuesday and Thursday from mid-June to mid-August – and very tasty they are too.

Eating

Although prices are marginally inflated by oil-industry expense accounts, Stavanger is a great place to **eat**, with several fine seafood restaurants clustered on the east side of the harbour along Skagenkaien. For something less expensive, the best option is to stick to the more mundane cafés and restaurants near the Kulturhus in the heart of the Skagen shopping area.

Cafés and restaurants

Café Sting Valbergjet 3. Right next to the Valbergtårnet, this laid-back café-bar is probably the coolest place in town; it also doubles as an art gallery and live music venue, hosting anything from indie through to rock. The food is tasty and inexpensive (mains from 100kr), with mostly Mediterranean and Norwegian dishes.

Nye La Piazza Rosenkildetorget 1. By the harbour, this smart Italian restaurant serves delicious pizzas, pasta and more, from 125kr for a main dish.

Sjøhuset Skagen Skagenkaien 16. Fine fish and seafood restaurant on the harbour, with monkfish a speciality. Main dishes from around 200kr.

Skagen Bageri Skagen 18. This pleasant coffee house, with its finely carved antique door and lintel, occupies the prettiest of the old wooden buildings on Skagen, one block up from the quayside. Great pastries, cakes and snacks at reasonable prices.

Drinking and nightlife

Stavanger is lively at night, particularly at weekends when a rum assortment of oil workers, sailors, fishermen, executives, tourists and office workers gather in the **bars and clubs** on and around Skagenkaien to live (or rather drink) it up. Most places stay open until 2am or later, with rowdy – but usually amiable – revellers lurching from one bar to the next.

For more subdued evenings, check out the programme at the concert hall, concert hall, **Stavanger Konserthus** (℡51 53 70 00, ℗www.stavanger-konserthus.no), in Bjergsted park, north of the centre beyond Gamle Stavanger, where there are regular concerts by the Stavanger Symphony Orchestra and visiting artists. There's an eight-screen **cinema**, Stavanger Kinematografer, inside the Kulturhus, Sølvberggaten 2 (℡820 51 00).

Bars and clubs

Hansen Hjørnet Skagenkaien 18. Down on the harbour, this is one of Stavanger's most popular spots, particularly on a sunny day when the outside terrace fills up fast.

Newsman Skagen 14. One block back from the east side of the harbour, this attractive, busy bar has papers to read and a well-heeled clientele.

Taket Nedre Strandgate 15. The best club in town, across the harbour from most of the bars, just metres from the tourist office; don't be surprised if you have to queue.

Timbuktu Nedre Strandgate 15. Flashy café-bar beneath *Taket* that's noted for its imaginative modern decor and trendy atmosphere.

Listings

Airlines Norwegian Air ☎81 52 18 15; SAS Braathens ☎05400; Widerøe ☎81 00 12 00.

Car rental Avis, at the airport ☎51 71 89 50; Hertz, Olav V's gate 13 ☎51 52 00 00.

Emergencies Ambulance ☎113; Fire ☎110; Police ☎112.

Exchange Competitive rates at the main post office (see below).

Ferries: Domestic: Rogaland Kollektivtrafikk Kolumbus, for regional boat, bus and train enquiries ☎81 50 01 82; locally also ☎177; Flaggruten, for Hurtigbåt passenger express boat services to Haugesund and Bergen ☎51 86 87 80.

Ferries: International: Fjord Line, Strandkaien ☎51 53 35 00.

Hiking The DNT-affiliated Stavanger Turistforening, Olav V's gate 18 (Mon–Wed & Fri 10am–4pm, Thurs 10am–6pm, Sat 10am–2pm; ☎51 84 02 00, ⊛www.stavanger-turistforening.no), will advise on local hiking routes and weather conditions, and sells a comprehensive range of hiking maps. It maintains around 900km of hiking trails and runs more than thirty cabins in the mountains east of Stavanger, as well as organizing ski schools on winter weekends.

Internet C@fe.com, Sølvberggata 15, just east of the Domkirke (Mon–Sat 11am–9pm, Sun noon–9pm)

Laundry There are coin-operated machines at Renseriet, Kongsgata 40, by Breiavatnet. (Mon–Wed & Fri 8am–4pm, Thurs 8am–7pm, Sat 9am–2pm)

Left luggage Fiskepiren Hurtigbåt terminal (Mon–Fri 6.30am–11.15pm, Sat 6.30am–8pm, Sun 8am–10pm); and at the bus station (daily 7am–10pm).

Pharmacist Løveapoteket, Olav V's gate 11 (daily 9am–11pm; ☎51 52 06 07).

Post office The main post office is at Haakon VII's gate 9 (Mon–Fri 9am–6pm & Sat 10am–3pm).

Taxis Norgestaxi ☎08000.

Vinmonopolet Nytorget 5, a few minutes walk north-east of the central lake.

Around Stavanger: Lysefjord

Stavanger sits on a long promontory that pokes a knobbly head north towards the Boknafjord, whose wide waters form a deep indentation in a coast speckled with islets and islands. To the east of the town, longer, narrower fjords drill far inland. The most diverting of these is the blue-black **Lysefjord**, famous for its precipitous cliffs and an especially striking rock formation, the **Preikestolen**. This distinctive 25-metre-square table of rock boasts a sheer 600m drop down to the fjord on three of its sides.

From Stavanger to Bergen

With great ingenuity, Norway's road builders have cobbled together the E39 coastal road, the **Kystvegen**, which traverses the west coast from Stavanger to Haugesund and Bergen – a distance of about 190km with two ferry trips breaking up the journey. The highway slips across a string of islands, which provide a pleasant introduction to the scenic charms of western Norway, and a hint of the sterner beauty of the fjords beyond.

By **car**, it takes between five and six hours to get from Stavanger to Bergen. A fast and frequent bus service – the Kystbussen – plies the E39 too, taking a little under six hours to get to Bergen (8–11 daily; 400kr); you'll get to see far more of the coast this way than by using the **Hurtigbat passenger express boat** on the same route (2–4 daily; 4hr; 590kr).

Along the Lysefjord to Lysebotn

There are several ways to visit Lysefjord by boat from Stavanger. One option is a round-trip halfway up the fjord with **Rødne Clipper Fjord Sightseeing** (☎51 89 52 70, ⊛www.rodne.no), departing from the Skagenkaien (Jan–April & Oct–Dec Sat only; May, June & Sept daily; July & Aug twice daily; 3hr 30min; 280kr). Despite the gushing multilingual commentary, the fjord seems disappointingly gloomy when seen from the bottom of its cliffs, and from this angle the Preikestolen hardly makes any impression at all. A rather more dramatic trip, run by **Stavangerske** (☎51 86 87 88), takes you the full length of the fjord to **Lysebotn**, where a connecting bus heads up the mountainside, tackling no less than 27 switchbacks, on its way to the minor road that leads back to Stavanger (mid-June to late Aug daily; 7hr; 490kr). If you want avoid the tours and cover the same ground on public transport, you'll need to be good at juggling timetables – check with the tourist information office to make sure you don't get stranded. The road from Lysebotn offers spectacular views as it wiggles its way up the mountainside, but adventurous souls may prefer the very demanding hiking trail which leads west from the car park of the **Øygardstøl** café and information centre, just above the last hairpin, to a much-photographed boulder, the **Kjeragbolten**, a chunk of rock is wedged between two cliff faces high above the ground. It's a tough route, so allow between five and six hours for the round trip – and steel your nerves for sights of the 1000m drop down to the fjord below.

Preikestolen

Lysefjord's most celebrated vantage point, **Preikestolen** ("Pulpit Rock"), offers breathtaking views, though on sunny summer weekends you'll share them with

△ Preikestolen (Pulpit Rock)

a fair crowd. To get to the rock, take the **ferry** east from Stavanger to **Tau** (every 30min to 1hr; 40min; passengers 33kr, car & driver 100kr) and then drive south along Highway 13 until, after about 14km, you reach the signed side road leading to Preikestolen. A local **bus** runs between Tau and Preikestolen, too (4 daily; 25min); check first with the tourist office which of the ferries it connects with. From the car park at the end of the road, it's a two-hour hike to the Preikestolen rock itself (and two hours back) along a clearly marked trail. The first half is steep in parts and paved with uneven stones, while the second half – over bedrock – is easier. The change in elevation is 350m; take food and water.

If you want to stay, a first-rate HI **hostel**, *Preikestolen Vandrerhjem* (☎97 16 55 51, ⓦwww.vandrerhjem.no; dorm beds 150kr, doubles ❷); mid-May to mid-Sept) is near the car park, perched high on the hillside, with great views over the surrounding mountains. Built on the site of an old mountain farm, the hostel is a small complex of turf-roofed lodges, each of which has a spick-and-span pine interior. There are self-catering facilities and boat rental, but no laundry. Reservations are advised as the place is popular with school groups.

Travel details

Trains

Kristiansand to: Oslo (3–5 daily; 4hr 40min); Stavanger (3–5 daily; 3hr).
Oslo to: Arendal, change at Nelaug (3–5 daily; 4hr 40min); Egersund (3–5 daily; 6hr 40min); Kristiansand (3–5 daily; 4hr 40min); Stavanger (3–5 daily; 7hr 30min).
Stavanger to: Kristiansand (3–5 daily; 3hr); Oslo (3–5 daily; 7hr 30min).

Long-distance buses

Arendal to: Lillesand (4–5 daily; 45min); Oslo (4–5 daily; 4hr).
Grimstad to: Lillesand (4–5 daily; 15min); Oslo (4–5 daily; 4hr 30min).
Kristiansand to: Flekkefjord (1–3 daily; 2hr); Mandal (Mon–Sat hourly, Sun 6 daily; 50min); Oslo (4–5 daily; 5hr 30min); Stavanger (1–3 daily; 4hr).
Oslo to: Arendal (4–5 daily; 4hr); Grimstad (4–5 daily; 4hr 30min); Kristiansand (4–5 daily; 5hr 30min); Lillesand (4–5 daily; 4hr 45min).
Lillesand to: Arendal (4–5 daily; 45min); Grimstad (4–5 daily, 15min); Kristiansand (4–5 daily; 45min); Oslo (4–5 daily; 4hr 45min).
Mandal to: Kristiansand (Mon–Sat hourly, Sun 6 daily; 50min); Stavanger (1–3 daily; 3hr 30min).
Stavanger to: Bergen (8–11 daily; 5hr 40min); Kristiansand (1–3 daily; 4hr); Mandal (1–3 daily; 3hr 30min).

Car ferries

Egersund to: Bergen (2–4 weekly; 8hr). With Fjord line; originates in Hantsholm, Denmark.
Stavanger to: Bergen (2–6 weekly; 7hr). With Fjord Line; originates in Newcastle, UK.

Hurtigbåt passenger express boats

Stavanger to: Bergen (2–4 daily; 4hr).

2.3

Bergen and the western fjords

I f there's one familiar and enticing image of Norway, it's the **fjords**: huge clefts in the landscape running from the coast deep into the interior. Wild, rugged and serene, these water-filled wedges are visually stunning; indeed, the entire fjord region elicits inordinate amounts of purple prose from tourist office handouts, and for once it's rarely overstated. The fjords are undeniably beautiful, especially around early May after the brief Norwegian spring has brought colour to the landscape.

The fjords run all the way up the coast to the Russian border, but are most easily – and impressively – seen on the west coast near **Bergen**, the self-proclaimed "Capital of the Fjords". Norway's second largest city, Bergen is a welcoming place with an atmospheric old warehouse quarter, a relic of the days when it was the northernmost port of the Hanseatic trade alliance. It's also a handy springboard for the nearby fjords, including the Flåmsdal valley to the east, where the inspiring **Flåmsbana** mountain railway trundles down to the **Aurlandsfjord**, a small arm of the mighty **Sognefjord**. Lined with pretty village resorts, the Sognefjord is the longest, deepest and most celebrated of the country's waterways, and is certainly one of the most beguiling. North of here lies the **Jostedalsbreen** glacier, mainland Europe's largest ice sheet, the relatively uninspiring **Nordfjord**, and the narrow, S-shaped **Geirangerfjord**, perhaps the most scenically impressive of all the fjords – though here, for once, the tourist hordes can be off-putting. Further north, towards the **Romsdalsfjord**, the landscape becomes more extreme still, reaching pinnacles of isolation in the splendid **Trollstigen** mountain highway, a stunning prelude to the amenable little town of **Åndalsnes**.

Bergen and around

As it has been raining ever since she arrived in the city, a tourist stops a young boy and asks him if it always rains here. "I don't know," he replies, "I'm only thirteen." The joke isn't brilliant, but it does tell at least part of the truth. Of all the things to contend with in **BERGEN**, the weather is the most predictable: it rains relentlessly even in summer, and the surroundings are often shrouded with mist. But despite its dampness, Bergen is one of Norway's most enjoyable cities. Its setting – between seven hills, sheltered to the north, south and west by a series of straggling islands and fjords – is spectacular. There's plenty to see in town too, from sturdy **medieval buildings** to a whole series of good **museums**; and just outside the city limits is **Troldhaugen**, Edvard Grieg's charming old home.

More than anything else, though, it's the general flavour of the place that appeals. Although Bergen has become a major port and minor industrial centre in recent

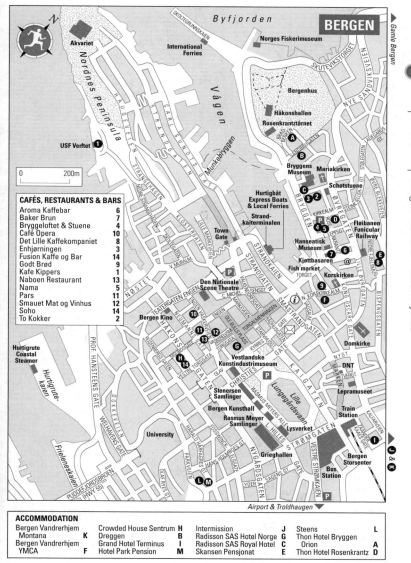

CAFÉS, RESTAURANTS & BARS

Aroma Kaffebar	6
Baker Brun	7
Bryggeloftet & Stuene	4
Café Opera	10
Det Lille Kaffekompaniet	8
Enhjørningen	3
Fusion Kaffe og Bar	14
Godt Brød	9
Kafe Kippers	1
Naboen Restaurant	13
Nama	5
Pars	11
Smauet Mat og Vinhus	12
Soho	14
To Kokker	2

ACCOMMODATION

Bergen Vandrerhjem Montana	**K**	Crowded House Sentrum	**H**	Intermission	**J**	Steens	**L**
Bergen Vandrerhjem		Dreggen	**B**	Radisson SAS Hotel Norge	**G**	Thon Hotel Bryggen	
YMCA	**F**	Grand Hotel Terminus		Radisson SAS Royal Hotel	**C**	Orion	**A**
		Hotel Park Pension	**M**	Skansen Pensjonat	**E**	Thon Hotel Rosenkrantz	**D**

decades, it remains a laid-back, easy-going town with a nautical air. Fishing continues to underpin the local economy, and the bustling main harbour, **Vågen**, is still very much the focus of attention. If you stay more than a day or two – perhaps using Bergen as a base for visiting the local fjords – you'll soon discover that the city also has the region's best choice of **restaurants**, some impressive art galleries, and a decent nightlife.

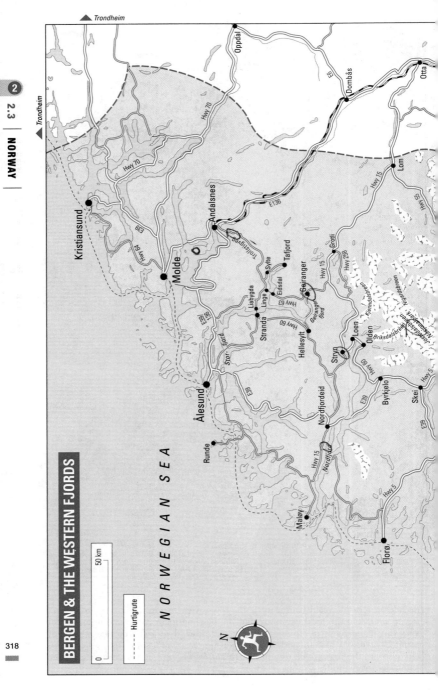

BERGEN & THE WESTERN FJORDS

N O R W E G I A N   S E A

------ Hurtigrute

0 _____ 50 km

Trondheim

Trondheim

Oppdal

Dombås

Otta

Lom

Hwy 15

Hwy 55

Kristiansund

Hwy 70

Hwy 70

Hwy 64

E39

Molde

Andalsnes

E136

E39

Trollstigveien

Valldal

Sylte

Tafjord

Linge

Liabygda

Stranda

Hwy 63

Eidsdal

Geiranger

Geiranger fjord

Hwy 15

Grotli

Hwy 258

Kronndalsbreen

Nigardsbreen

Jostedalsbreen Nasjonalpark

Hellesylt

Hwy 60

Loen

Olden

Briksdalsbræ

Stryn

Hwy 15

Nordfjordeid

Nordfjord

Byrkjelo

Skei

Hwy 5

E39

E39

Runde

Ålesund

Stor- fjord

Hwy 15

Maløy

Florø

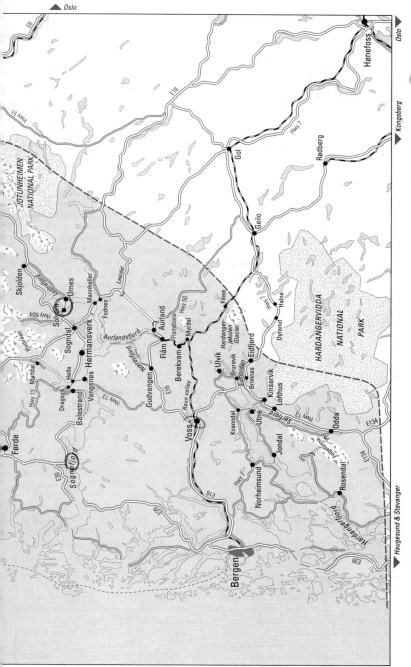

Arrival

Bergen's sturdy stone **train station** (local ☎55 96 69 00, national ☎81 50 08 88) is located on Strømgaten, just along the street from the entrance to the Bergen Storsenter shopping mall, within which is the **bus station** (☎177). From Strømgaten, it's a five- to ten-minute walk west to the most interesting part of the city, the waterfront at Bergen's main harbour, **Vågen**, via the pedestrianized shopping street Marken. The **airport** is 20km south of the city at Flesland, and is connected to the centre by the **Flybussen** (every 15–30min; Mon–Fri & Sun 4.15am–9pm, Sat 4.15am–5pm; 45min; 70kr). This pulls in beside the *SAS Norge* hotel on Ole Bulls plass and at the bus station before proceeding to the harbourfront *SAS Royal Hotel*. Taxis from the rank outside the airport arrivals hall charge 250–300kr for the same trip.

By boat

As well as being a hub for ferry and catamaran links with the fjords, Bergen is a busy international port. **Ferries** from Denmark, Iceland, Shetland and the Faroe Islands all arrive at Skoltegrunnskaien, the quay just beyond Bergenhus fortress, as do those from Newcastle, which call at Stavanger and Haugesund on the way here. **Hurtigbåt passenger express boats** from Haugesund, Stavanger and the Hardangerfjord, as well as those from the Sognefjord and Nordfjord, line up on the opposite side of the harbour at the Strandkaiterminalen; local **ferries** from islands and fjords immediately north of Bergen mostly arrive here too, though short sightseeing excursions round the Byforden, adjoining Bergen harbour, leave from beside Torget.

Bergen is also a port of call for the **Hurtigrute coastal boat**, which arrives at the Hurtigrutekaien harbour on the southern edge of the city centre, beyond the university; it's a brisk ten- to fifteen-minute walk from the centre, or a 60kr taxi ride.

For domestic ferry and boat **ticket and timetable information**, see "Ferries" under "Listings" (p.330); for international ferries to Bergen, see "Basics", p.36.

By car

If you're driving into Bergen, note that a **toll** (10kr) is charged on all vehicles over 50cc entering the city centre from Monday to Friday between 6am and 10pm; pay at the tollbooths. There's no charge for driving out of the city. In an attempt to keep the centre relatively free of traffic, there's a confusing and none-too-successful one-way system in operation, supplemented by rigorously enforced on-street parking restrictions. During peak periods (Mon–Fri 8am–5pm, Sat 8am–6pm), on-street parking for a maximum of two hours costs 18kr per hour (pay at the meters), and the best advice is to make straight for one of the four central **car parks**. The largest is the 24hr ByGarasjen on Vestre Strømkaien, a short walk from the centre behind the Storsenter shopping mall and bus station. The Parkeringshuset, on Rosenkrantzgaten (Mon–Fri 7am–11pm, Sat 8am–6pm, Sun 9am–6pm), has shorter opening hours but is handier for the harbourfront. To get there, follow the international ferry signs until you pick up the car park signs. **Tariffs** vary, but reckon on 15kr per hour up to a maximum of 150kr for 24hrs. Outside of peak periods, on-street parking is relatively easy and free.

Information

The **tourist office** is in a large, mural-decorated hall at Vågsallmenningen 1 (May & Sept daily 9am–8pm; June–Aug daily 8.30am–10pm; Oct–April Mon–Sat 9am–4pm; ☎55 55 20 00, ◍www.visitbergen.com), across the road from Torget, at the east end of Vågen, the main harbour. Staff give away copies of the *Bergen Guide*, an exhaustive listings booklet, and numerous other free brochures. Here you can also book hotels and rooms in private houses, reserve places on guided tours, buy tickets for fjord sightseeing boats, and change foreign currency – in high season, expect long queues. Bergen has one very good, and free, bi-monthly **newssheet** containing local news, entertainment listings and reviews – the Bergen edition of the Oslo-based *Natt & Dag*. Naturally enough, it's in Norwegian, but the listings section is still (fairly) easy to use. It's widely available across the city centre.

City transport

Most of Bergen's key attractions are located in the city centre, which is compact enough to be best explored **on foot**. For outlying sights and accommodation, however, you'll need to take a **bus**. Bergen and its surroundings are served by a dense network of local buses, whose hub is the bus station in the Storsenter shopping mall on Strømgaten (☎177). Within the city centre, flat-fare tickets, available from the driver, cost 12kr and are valid for an hour; outside the centre, fares are based on the distance travelled. In addition, a tiny **orange ferry** (Mon–Fri 7am–4.15pm; 15kr) bobs across Vågen to provide a shortcut between Munkebryggen, along Carl Sundts gate, and a point near the *SAS Royal Hotel* on the Bryggen.

Accommodation

Finding budget **accommodation** in Bergen is no great problem. There are three hostels, a choice of pensions and guesthouses, and some of the central hotels are surprisingly good value. Among the better deals are the **private rooms**, bookable through the tourist office. The vast majority provide self-catering facilities and some are fairly central, though most are stuck out in the suburbs. Prices are at a fixed nightly rate, currently 370kr for a double room without en-suite facilities (260kr single), or 440kr (300kr single) for an en-suite room. These private rooms are very popular, so in summer you'll need to arrive at the tourist office early to secure one for the night.

    Camping is also an option, and there are several campsites on the outskirts of the city, but you'll be far from the action at any of them. Most campsites have four-bunk timber **cabins**.

Hotels

Dreggen Sandbrugaten 3 ☎55 31 61 55, ⓦwww .hotel-dreggen.no. Modest place in a plain modern block, but with a great location just off the Bryggen. Thirty plain and fairly small rooms kitted out in routine modern style, both with shared facilities and, costing a bit more, en suite. Rates include breakfast. ④

Grand Hotel Terminus Zander Kaaes gate 6 ☎55 21 25 00, ⓦwww.grand-hotel-terminus.no. There was a time when the tweed-jacketed visitors of prewar England headed straight for the *Grand* as soon as they arrived in Bergen – and not just because the hotel is next door to the train station. Those ritzy days are long gone, but the hotel has reinvented itself, making the most of its quasi-baronial flourishes, notably its extensive wood panelling, chandeliers and stained glass. Breakfasts are superb and the bedrooms attractive and quiet, though some are rather pokey – if you can, have a look before you commit. ④/⑥

The Bergen Card

The **Bergen Card** is a 24-hour (170kr) or 48-hour (250kr) pass which provides free use of all the city's buses, free or substantially discounted admission to most of the sights, and reductions on many sightseeing trips. It also gives free on-street parking – if you can find a space and within the two-hour maximum parking time. The pass comes with a booklet listing all the various concessions. Obviously, the more diligent a sightseer you are, the better value the card becomes, doubly so if you're staying a bus ride from the centre. The card is sold at a wide range of outlets, including the tourist office, major hotels and the train station.

Hotel Park Pension Harald Hårfagres gate 35 ☎55 54 44 00, ⊛www.parkhotel.no. This excellent, family-run hotel occupies two handsome late nineteenth-century town houses on the edge of the town centre near the university. The charming interior is painted in soft pastel colours, the public areas are dotted with antiques and the bedrooms smart, neat and appealing. It's a very popular place, so advance reservations are advised. ❺

Radisson SAS Hotel Norge Ole Bulls plass 4 ☎55 57 30 30, ⊛www.radissonsas.com. Swish and swanky top-class hotel, right in the thick of things and with a full range of facilities from bar to heated swimming pool. ❻

Radisson SAS Royal Hotel Bryggen ☎55 54 30 00, ⊛www.radissonsas.com. Full marks here to the architects, who have built an extremely smart, first-rate hotel behind a brick facade that mirrors the style of the old timber buildings that surround it. All facilities – pool, health club and so forth, plus attractively appointed rooms. Popular with visiting business folk. ❹/❻

Steens Parkveien 22 ☎55 30 88 88, ⊛www.steenshotel.no. One of an attractive terrace of high-gabled town houses, overlooking a mini-lake on the edge of the town centre near the university, this well-established hotel offers inexpensive lodgings. The interior has lots of late Victorian flourishes, but the overall effect is a tad gloomy. ❹/❺

🏃 **Thon Hotel Bryggen Orion** Bradbenken 3 ☎55 30 87 00, ⊛www.thonhotels.no. Deservedly popular mid-range hotel with unassuming but perfectly comfortable modern rooms. A handy location, a stone's throw from the Bergenhus fort, and the breakfasts are magnificent banquets – with every type of pickled herring you can think of – and then some. Hard to beat. ❸/❻

Thon Hotel Rosenkrantz Rosenkrantzgaten 7 ☎55 30 14 00, ⊛www.thonhotels.no. Efficient and extremely competent mid-range hotel in an old building just behind the Bryggen. Rooms are tidy and trim, and the best ones on the upper floors have pleasing views over the harbour. Shame about the aluminium windows stuck in the attractive facade. ❹/❼

Guesthouses

🏃 **Crowded House Sentrum** Håkons gaten 27 ☎55 90 72 00, ⊛www.crowded-house.com.
Traditionally, Bergen's guesthouses have been a little dowdy, but this lively, appealing place is the opposite – from the pastel-painted foyer to the bright and airy (if admittedly spartan) bedrooms. There are thirty-three rooms in total – singles, doubles and triples, all with shared bathrooms, as well as self-catering facilities and a laundry, too. Located halfway along traffic-clogged Håkons gaten, about five minutes' walk from the city centre. ❸

Skansen Pensjonat Vetrlidsallmenningen 29 ☎55 31 90 80, ⓔpost@skansen-pensjonat.no. This simple little guesthouse occupies a nineteenth-century stone house of elegant proportions just above – and up the steps from – the terminus of the Fløibanen funicular railway, near Torget. It's a great location, in one of the most beguiling parts of town. The guesthouse has eight perfectly adequate if simple rooms, one of which is en suite. A real snip. ❷, en suite ❸

Hostels

Bergen Vandrerhjem Montana Johan Blyttsveien 30, Landås ☎55 20 80 70, ⊛www.montana.no. This large and comfortable HI hostel occupies lodge-like premises in the hills overlooking the city and is popular with school parties, who are (usually) housed in a separate wing. Great views and great breakfasts (included in rates), plus self-catering facilities, a laundry and Internet/email access. Dorm accommodation (150–200kr), family rooms and doubles (❸), the pick of which are en suite and in a newly added wing. The hostel is 6km east of the centre – 15min on bus #31 (stop Montana) from the train station. Closed Dec.

Bergen Vandrerhjem YMCA Nedre Korskirkealmenning 4 ☎55 60 60 55, ⊛www.vandrerhjem.no. No-frills HI hostel in the centre, a short walk from Torget, whose 170 beds (including dorms for 125–170kr, private singles and doubles, the latter ❸) fill up fast in summer. Facilities include a café, communal kitchen and a laundry; breakfast costs 50kr. Open all year.

Intermission Kalfarveien 8 ☎55 30 04 00. Christian-run private hostel in a two-storey, oldish wooden building five minutes' walk from the train station, just beyond one of the old city gates. Open mid-June to mid-Aug. Breakfast is 35kr; dorm beds 120kr.

The City

Founded in 1070 by King Olav Kyrre ("the Peaceful"), **Bergen** was the largest and most important town in medieval Norway, a regular residence of the country's kings and queens and, from the fourteenth century, a Hanseatic League port, connected to other European and Baltic cities by vigorous trading links. The League was controlled by German merchants, however, and although Hansa and local interests initially coincided, the picture slowly changed. Eventually, Germans came to dominate the region's economy, reducing the locals to a state of dependency by fixing the price of fish, the region's principal commodity – the Hansa trading station, which flourished on Bergen's main wharf, Bryggen, became wealthy and hated in equal measure. In the 1550s, with Hanseatic power evaporating, a local lord, one Kristoffer Valkendorf, finally reasserted Norwegian control. Unfortunately, Valkendorf and his cronies simply took over the monopolies that had enriched their German predecessors, operating a system that continued to pauperize the region's fishermen right down to the nineteenth century.

Very little of medieval Bergen has survived, although parts of the fortress – the **Bergenhus** – which commands the entrance to the harbour, date from the thirteenth century. The rest of the city centre divides into several distinct parts, the most interesting being the wharf area, Bryggen, which houses an attractive ensemble of eighteenth- and nineteenth-century merchants' trading houses. The Bryggen ends at the head of the central harbour, **Vågen**, where the **Torget** is home to an open-air fish market. East of here, stretching up towards the train station, is one of the city's older districts, a mainly nineteenth-century quarter at its prettiest along **Lille Øvregaten** and amongst the narrow lanes that clamber up the adjacent hillside.

NYKOKTE
KRABBE-
KLØR
Kr.60,-
Pr.1/2 kg

△ Torget fish market, Bergen

The main thoroughfare of this quarter, **Kong Oscars gate**, leads to Bergen's most endearing museum, the Leprosy Museum, itself little more than a stone's throw from the modern concrete blocks surrounding the city's central lake, **Lille Lungegårdsvann**. The high-rises here form the cultural focus of the city, holding Bergen's main concert hall and art galleries, whilst the main commercial area is just to the west along pedestrianized **Torgalmenningen**. The **university** crowns the steep hill to the south of Lille Lungegårdsvann.

Most of the main sights and museums are concentrated in these areas, but no tour of the city is complete without a stroll out along the **Nordnes peninsula**, where fine timber houses dot the bumpy terrain, and whose old USF sardine factory now contains a first-rate arts complex and café.

Torget

The nineteenth-century traveller Lilian Leland, writing about Bergen in 1890, complained that "Everything is fishy. You eat fish and drink fish and smell fish and breathe fish." Those days are long gone, but even now that Bergen is every inch the go-ahead, modern city, tourists still flock down to the **Torget** to seek out all things piscine. The nearest they get to those fishy days is the open-air **fish market** (June–Aug daily 7am–5pm; Sept–May Mon–Sat 7am–4pm), but frankly it's not a patch on the days when scores of fishing smacks moored up against the quayside to empty their bulging holds. That said, however, the stalls still display huge mounds of prawns and crab-claws, buckets of herring and a hundred other varieties of marine life on slabs, in tanks and under the knife. Load up or eat up and hang around for a while to assess the comings and goings of the local boats and ferries.

Bryggen

From Torget, central Bergen spears right and left around the Vågen, with the **Bryggen**, on the northerly side of the harbour, the obvious historical and cultural target. The site of the original settlement at Bergen, this is the city's best-preserved old quarter, containing, among other things, the distinctive wooden gabled trading posts that front the wharf. The area was once known as Tyskebryggen, or "German Quay", after the Hansa merchants who operated their trading station here, but the name was unceremoniously dumped at the end of World War II.

The medieval buildings of Bryggen were destroyed by fire in 1702, to be replaced by another set of wooden warehouses. In turn, many of these were later replaced by high-gabled stone warehouses in a style modelled on that of the Hansa period, but a small section of the eighteenth-century **timber buildings** has survived and now holds shops, restaurants and bars. It's well worth nosing around here, wandering down the passageways in between wherever you can. Interestingly, these eighteenth-century buildings carefully follow the original building line: the governing body of the Hansa trading station stipulated the exact depth and width of each merchant's building, and the width of the passage separating them – a regularity that's actually best observed from Øvregaten (see p.325). The planning regulations didn't end there. Trade had to be carried out in the front section of the building, with storage rooms at the back; above could be found the merchant's office, bedroom and dining room, and above that, on the top floor, the living quarters of the employees,

Guided tours of the Bryggen

Informative and amusingly anecdotal English-language **guided tours** of Bryggen start from the Bryggens Museum daily between June and August at 11am and 1pm, and take roughly an hour and a half. Tickets (80kr) are on sale at the Bryggens Museum, and after the tour you can re-use them to get back into the Bryggens and Hanseatic museums as well as the Schøtstuene – but only on the same day.

arranged by rank: merchants, journeymen/clerks and foremen, wharf hands and, last and least, house boys. At the near end of Bryggen, just off Torget, the **Hanseatisk Museum** (May & late Sept daily 11am–2pm; June–Aug daily 9am–5pm; early Sept daily 11am–3pm; Oct–April Tues–Sat 11am–2pm; 45kr) is the best preserved of the early eighteenth-century merchants' dwellings and, kitted out in late Hansa style, gives an idea of how things worked. Among the assorted bric-a-brac are the possessions and documents of contemporary families, including several fine pieces of furniture, but more than anything else it's the gloomy, warren-like layout of the place that impresses, as well as the all-pervading smell of fish.

Nearby, the basement of the **Bryggens Museum** (May–Aug daily 10am–5pm; Sept–April Mon–Fri 11am–3pm, Sat noon–3pm, Sun noon–4pm; 40kr) features all manner of things dug up in archeological excavations that started on the Bryggen in 1955. A wide range of artefacts – domestic implements, handicrafts, maritime objects and trade goods – illustrates the city's early history, and the whole Hansa caboodle is put into context by a set of twelfth-century foundations, left *in situ* where they were unearthed. The floors above are given over to temporary exhibitions, which explore other aspects of Bergen's past with panache.

Mariakirken and the Schøtstuene

Beside the Bryggens Museum, the perky twin towers of the **Mariakirken** (late June to late Aug Mon–Fri 9.30–11.30am & 1–4pm; rest of the year Tues–Fri 11–12.30pm; late May to Aug 10kr, otherwise free) are the most distinctive features of what is Bergen's oldest extant building, a Romanesque-Gothic church dating from the twelfth century. Still used as a place of worship, Mariakirken is now firmly Norwegian, but from 1408 to 1706 it was the church of the Hanseatic League merchants. Inside, several of the ecclesiastical bits and pieces exhibited in the nave and choir date from medieval times, most notably the choir's fifteenth-century altar reredos, a gaudy north German triptych with crude depictions of saints and apostles but exquisite framing.

Directly opposite at Øvregaten 50, the **Schøtstuene** (May & Sept daily 11am–2pm; June–Aug daily 10am–5pm; Oct–Dec & March–April Sun 11am–2pm; 45kr, includes Hanseatisk Museum) comprises the old Hanseatic assembly rooms where the merchants would meet to lay down the law or just relax – it was the only building in the trading post whose occupants were allowed to have heating. As you explore the comfortable rooms, it's hard not to conclude that the merchants cared not a jot for their employees shivering away nearby – though, to be fair, the wooden warehouses were a very real fire hazard.

Øvregaten and the Fløibanen funicular railway

Saving the mildly interesting Bergenhus fortress for later (see below), stroll east from the Schøtstuene along **Øvregaten**, an attractive cobbled street which has marked the boundary of the Bryggen for the last 800 years. The Hanseatic warehouses once stretched back from the quayside to this street, but no further, and in medieval times – despite the fulminations of the Hansa merchants – this was the haunt of the city's prostitutes. From Øvregaten, the old **layout** of the trading station is still easy to discern, a warren of tiny passages separating warped and crooked buildings. On the upper levels, the eighteenth-century loading bays, staircases and higgledy-piggledy living quarters are still much in evidence, while the overhanging eaves of the passageways were designed to shelter trade goods.

At the far end of Øvregaten, back near the Torget, stands the terminus of the infinitely quaint **Fløibanen** funicular railway (every 30min May–Aug Mon–Fri 7.30am–midnight, Sat 8am–midnight, Sun 9am–midnight; Sept–April Mon–Fri 7.30am–11pm, Sat 8am–11pm, Sun 9am–11pm; 60kr return), which shuttles up to the top of **Mount Fløyen** – "The Vane" – at 320m above sea level. When the weather is fine you get a bird's-eye view of Bergen and its surroundings from the top, where there's also a popular if rather staid café-restaurant. Several well-marked, colour-coded footpaths head off through the woods or you can hoof it back down to the city in about 45 minutes. Walking maps are displayed here and there, or you can pick up a free (and very simple) walking map from the tourist office.

From the funicular, you can either push on along Lille Øvregaten (see below) or double back to the Bergenhus.

The Bergenhus

Just to the west of the Bryggens Museum lies the **Bergenhus**, a large and roughly star-shaped fortification now used mostly as a park (daily 7am–11pm). Its thick stone-and-earth walls date from the nineteenth century, but they enclose the remnants of earlier strongholds – or rather their copies: the Bergenhus was wrecked when a German ammunition ship exploded just below the walls in 1944. Of the two main medieval replicas, the more diverting is the **Rosenkrantztårnet** (mid-May to Aug daily 10am–4pm; Sept to mid-May Sun noon–3pm; 25kr), a sturdy stone tower whose thirteenth-century spiral staircases, medieval rooms and low, rough corridors make an enjoyable gambol. A doughty exhibition on medieval life occupies the top floor and it's also possible to walk out onto the rooftop battlements, from where there's an attractive view out over the harbour.

Across the cobbled courtyard, flanked by nineteenth-century officers' quarters, is the **Håkonshallen** (mid-May to Aug daily 10am–4pm; Sept to mid-May Mon–Wed & Fri–Sun noon–3pm, Thurs 3–6pm; 25kr), a careful reconstruction of the Gothic ceremonial hall built for King Håkon Håkonsson in the middle of the thirteenth century. Surplus to requirements once Norway lost its independence, no-one knew quite what to do with the capacious hall for several centuries, but it was revamped in 1910 and rebuilt after the 1944 explosion – it's now in use once again for public ceremonies.

From the Bergenhus, it's a five-minute walk back to Torget and the Fløibanen terminal.

Along Lille Øvregaten and Kong Oscars gate to the Lepramuseet

Lille Øvregaten runs east from the Fløibanen terminal, lined by an appealing mix of expansive nineteenth-century villas and dinky timber houses, all bright-white clapboard and tiny windows. Soon the street curves round to the **Domkirke** (mid-June to Aug Mon–Sat 11am–4pm; Sept to mid-May Tues–Fri 11am–12.30pm; free), a solemn edifice whose stern exterior has been restored and rebuilt several times since its original construction in the thirteenth century. The interior doesn't set the pulse racing, but there's a noticeable penchant for fancy wooden staircases – two leading to the organ and one to the pulpit – which seems a little flippant given the dour surroundings.

Just up from the Domkirke at Kong Oscars gate 59, the fascinating **Lepramuseet** (Leprosy Museum; late May to Aug daily 11am–3pm; 30kr) is far more promising. This endearingly antiquated collection is housed in the eighteenth-century buildings of **St Jørgens Hospital**, ranged around a charming cobbled courtyard, and tells the tale of the Norwegian fight against leprosy. The disease first appeared in Scandinavia in Viking times and became especially prevalent in the coastal districts of western Norway, with around three percent of the population classified as lepers in the early nineteenth century. St Jørgens specialized in the care of lepers, assuming a more proactive role from 1830, when a series of Norwegian medics tried to find a cure for the disease. The most successful of them was Armauer Hansen, who in 1873 was the first person to identify the leprosy bacillus. The last lepers left St Jørgens in 1946 and the hospital has been left untouched, the small rooms off the central gallery revealing the patients' cramped living quarters. Also on display are medical implements (including cupping glasses for drawing blood) and a few gruesome sketches and paintings of sufferers. Dating from 1702, the adjoining hospital **chapel** is delightful, its rickety, creaking timbers holding a lovely folksy pulpit and altarpiece decorated with cherubs and dainty scrollwork. The two altar paintings are crude but appropriate – *The Ten Lepers* and the *Canaanite's Daughter Healed*.

Lille Lungegårdsvann: Bergen's art galleries

Bergen's central lake, **Lille Lungegårdsvann**, is a focus for summertime festivals and events, and its southern side is flanked by the city's four principal art galleries, three of which comprise the **Bergen Kunstmuseum** (Bergen Art Museum; mid-May to mid-Sept daily 11am–5pm; mid-Sept to mid-May Tues–Sun 11am–5pm; 50kr for entry to all three; ⊛www.bergenartmuseum.no). First up at Rasmus Meyers Allé 9 – and working east to west – is the **Lysverket**, where the ground floor is dominated by a wide range of contemporary international art, from installations through to paintings. The floor above zeroes in on Norwegian art from the 1930s to the 1980s and elsewhere is a mixed bag of older works, from seventeenth-century Dutch paintings to medieval Greek and Russian icons. Just along the street, the **Rasmus Meyers Samlinger** (Rasmus Meyer Collection) was gifted to the city by one of its old merchant families. The collection contains an extensive range of Norwegian painting, from early landscapes by Dahl and Fearnley (see p.263) through Christian Krohg to later figures such as Alex Revold and Henrik Sørensen. It is, however, for its large sample of the work of **Edvard Munch** that the museum is usually visited – if you missed out in Oslo (see p.274), this is the place to make amends. There are examples from all of Munch's major periods, with the disturbing – and disturbed – works of the 1890s stealing the spotlight from the calmer paintings that followed his recovery from the nervous breakdown of 1908. There's also a substantial collection of his woodcuts and lithographs.

Next door, at Rasmus Meyers Allé 5, stands the **Bergen Kunsthall** (Tues–Sun noon–5pm; 40kr; ⊛www.kunsthall.no), which has built itself an excellent reputation for the quality of its contemporary art exhibitions, and next door again is the Bergen Kunstmuseum's **Stenersens Samlinger** (Stenersen Collection; same hours and entry as Bergen Kunstmuseum), which features both changing exhibitions and the modern art collection of Rolf Stenersen. Something of a Renaissance man, Stenersen (1899–1978) – one-time athlete, financier and chum of Munch – seems to have had a successful stab at almost everything; he even wrote some highly acclaimed short stories in the 1930s. In 1936 he donated his first art collection to his hometown of Oslo (see p.262), and 35 years later he was in a similar giving mood, the beneficiary being his adopted town of Bergen. The collection is especially strong on one of Stenersen's favourites, the Bauhaus painter Paul Klee, and there's a smattering of work by other big names like Toulouse-Lautrec, Picasso, Miró, Ernst and Léger.

The Grieghallen and the Vestlandske Kunstindustrimuseum

Behind the museums lurks the **Grieghallen** concert hall, an ugly concrete structure that serves as the main venue for the annual Bergen Festival (see p.330). Close by, at the corner of Christies gate and Nordahl Bruns gate, is a fifth art museum, **Vestlandske Kunstindustrimuseum** (West Norway Decorative Art Museum; mid-May to mid-Sept daily 11am–5pm; mid-Sept to mid-May Tues–Sun noon–4pm; 50kr; ⊛www.vk.museum.no), which occupies the Permanenten building, a whopping neo-Gothic structure built to impress. A lively exhibition programme with the focus on contemporary craft and design brings in the crowds, and some of the displays are very good indeed – which is more than can be said for the permanent collection and its Chinese marble statues. Fans of Ole Bull (see below) will, however, be keen to gawp at one of the great man's violins, made in 1562 by the Italian Salò.

Torgalmenningen and the Nordnes peninsula

The broad sweep of pedestrianized **Torgalmenningen** is a suitable setting for the commercial heart of modern Bergen, lined with shops and department stores and decorated at its harbour end by a vigorous large-scale sculpture celebrating figures from the city's history. Around the corner, **Ole Bulls plass**, also pedestrianized, sports a rock pool and fountain, above which stands a rather jaunty statue of local boy Ole Bull, the nineteenth-century virtuoso violinist and heart-throb – his island villa just outside Bergen is the target of a popular day-trip. Ole Bulls plass stretches up to the municipal **theatre**, Den Nationale Scene, at the top of the hill, worth the short walk for a look at the fearsome, saucer-eyed statue of Henrik Ibsen that stands in front.

Beyond the theatre, the hilly **Nordnes peninsula** juts out into the fjord, its western tip accommodating the large **Akvariet** (Aquarium; May–Aug daily 9am–7pm; Sept–April daily 10am–6pm; ⊛www.akvariet.com; 100kr; bus #11) and a pleasant park. It takes about fifteen minutes to walk there from Ole Bulls plass – via Klostergaten/Haugeveien – but the effort is much better spent in choosing a different, more southerly route along the peninsula. This takes you past the charming timber villas of Skottegaten and Nedre Strangehagen before it cuts through the bluff leading to the old, waterside United Sardines Factory, imaginatively converted into an arts complex, the **USF Verftet** (see p.330), which incorporates a groovy café-bar (see p.329).

Out from the centre – Troldhaugen

The lochs, fjords and rocky wooded hills surrounding central Bergen have channelled the city's **suburbs** into long ribbons that trail off in every direction. These urban outskirts are not in themselves appealing, but tucked away among them is **Troldhaugen** (Hill of the Trolls; May–Sept daily 9am–6pm; Oct & Nov Mon–Fri 10am–2pm, Sat & Sun noon–4pm; mid-Jan to April Mon–Fri 10am–2pm; 60kr; ⊛www.troldhaugen.com), Edvard Grieg's lakeside home and one of the region's most popular attractions. Located about 8km south of downtown off the E39, it's accessible by public transport (see below), though this is a bit of a pain, and there are organized excursions from Bergen too, from about 250kr – ask at the tourist office for more information. Norway's only composer of world renown, Grieg has a good share of commemorative monuments in Bergen – a statue in the city park, the Grieghallen concert hall – but it's here that you get a sense of the man, an immensely likeable and much-loved figure of leftish opinions and disarming modesty: "I make no pretensions of being in the class with Bach, Mozart and Beethoven. Their works are eternal, while I wrote for my day and generation."

A visit begins at the **museum**, where Grieg's life and times are exhaustively chronicled and a short film provides yet further insights. From here, it's a brief walk to the **house**, a pleasant and unassuming villa built in 1885, and still pretty much as Grieg left it, with a jumble of photos, manuscripts and period furniture. Grieg didn't, in fact, compose much at home, but preferred to walk round to a tiny **hut** he had built just along the shore. The hut has survived, but today it stands beside a modern concert hall, the **Troldsalen**, where there are **recitals** of Grieg's works from mid-June through to October. Recital tickets (220kr), covering admission and transport, can be bought from Bergen tourist office.

To get to Troldhaugen, go to the city bus station and take any bus leaving from platform 20. Get off at the Hopsbroen stop, walk back along the road for about 200m and then turn left up Troldhaugsveien for a stiff and uninteresting twenty-minute walk.

Eating, drinking and nightlife

Bergen has a good supply of **restaurants**, the pick of which focus mostly on seafood – the city's main gastronomic asset. The pricier tourist haunts are concentrated on the Bryggen, but these should not be dismissed out of hand – several are first-rate. Other marginally less expensive restaurants dot the side streets behind the Bryggen and the narrow lanes east of Torget, though many locals prefer to eat more economically and informally at the city's **café-bars**, some of the best of which are in the vicinity of Ole Bulls plass. As regards **opening hours**, the city's restaurants mostly open daily from 4pm to 10pm or 11pm, though quite a few close one day a week – mostly Sunday – and a minority start at 11am; café-bars stay open much longer, usually daily from 11am to the early hours of the morning. Note that we've given phone numbers only for restaurants where you need to book.

Entertainment listings (in Norwegian), including club, restaurant and café reviews, are provided by *Natt & Dag* (www.nattogdag.no), a free monthly news-sheet widely available across the city centre.

Cafés, coffee houses, bars and café-bars

Aroma Kaffebar Rosenkrantzgaten 1. Specialist coffee house with a good line in lattés and cappuccinos; snacks are available, and the atmosphere's convivial.

Baker Brun Kjøttbasaren. There are several of these café-bakery franchises in Bergen, but this branch is probably the best, inside the covered market – the Kjøttbasaren – at the Torget end of Bryggen. Closed Sun.

Café Opera Engen Vaskerveien 24. Fashionable café-cum-bar in a rickety old wooden building near Ole Bulls plass, serving tasty, filling snacks from as little as 60kr. DJ sounds – mostly house – at weekends.

Det Lille Kaffekompaniet Nedre Fjellsmug 2. Many locals swear by the coffee here, reckoning it to be the best in town. Great selection of teas too, and charming premises – just one medium-sized room in an old wooden building one flight of steps above the funicular terminal.

Fusion Kaffe og Bar Håkons gaten 27. Snacks, salads, juices and coffees during the day, a busy bar at night. Attached to – and in the same stylistic vein as – the *Soho Restaurant* (see below).

Godt Brød Vestre Torggate 2. Eco-bakery and café (in that order), with great bread and good pastries, plus coffee and made-to-order sandwiches. Also at Nedre Korskirkealmenning 12. Closed Sun.

Kafe Kippers USF Verftet. Part of the city's adventurous contemporary arts complex on the Nordnes peninsula, this laid-back café-bar serves tasty, inexpensive food (the reindeer is especially delicious), lays on occasional barbecues and, with its sea views and terrace, is *the* place to come on a sunny evening, when it's jam-packed. Puts on live music, too.

Restaurants

Bryggeloftet & Stuene Bryggen ☎55 31 06 30. This restaurant may be a little old-fashioned, but it serves the widest range of seafood in town – delicious, plainly served meals featuring every North Atlantic fish you've ever heard of, and some you might not have heard of at all. Main courses around 200kr.

Enhjørningen Bryggen ☎55 32 79 19. On the second floor of a superbly restored eighteenth-century merchants' house – all low beams and creaking floors – this smart restaurant serves a mouthwatering range of fish and shellfish, with main courses from 220kr. Worth every krone for an indulgent evening out. The buffet lunch (June–Aug only) is a slightly more affordable alternative, with heaps of salmon, prawns and herring, along with salads, hot dishes, bread, cheese and desserts. Closed Sun.

Naboen Restaurant Sigurdsgate 4 ☎55 90 02 90. Easy-going restaurant featuring a lively, inventive menu that includes Swedish specialities and a wide range of fish dishes, including such extravagances as sea bass with blood-orange sauce; the pollack is especially good. Reckon on 170–200kr for a main course.

Nama Lodin Lepps gate 2B ☎55 32 20 10. Behind the Bryggen, this popular sushi and noodle restaurant is a modern affair, crisply decorated with pastel-painted walls and angular furniture. It may be popular, but it's not cheap – each piece of sushi will cost you some 25kr.

Pars Sigurdsgate 5 ☎55 56 37 22. First-rate Persian food in pleasantly kitsch surroundings. A good range of vegetarian dishes – aubergine casserole with rice, for instance, at 100kr; meat dishes are in the region of 130kr. Closed Mon.

Smauet Mat og Vinhus Vaskerelvsmuget, off Ole Bulls plass ☎55 21 07 10. Excellent, smart and fairly formal restaurant offering traditional Norwegian cuisine – including oodles of seafood – plus more exotic dishes like ostrich and antelope. Reckon on 220kr for a main course. From 4pm nightly, 5pm on Saturday.

Soho Håkons gaten 27 ☎55 90 19 60. Chic and ultra-modern restaurant with a creative and flexible menu – from full set meals to a one-course pit stop. Has a great line in traditional Norwegian dishes: try the klippfisk (dried and salted fish). Main courses average 200kr.

To Kokker Bryggen ☎55 32 28 16. Similar to – and metres from – the *Enhjørningen*, but without the buffet. First-class seafood, plus regional dishes – the oven-baked reindeer is a house speciality. Main courses around 230kr. Closed Sun.

Festivals and the performing arts

Bergen takes justifiable pride in its **performing arts**, especially during the **Festspillene i Bergen** (Bergen International Festival; ☎55 21 06 30, ☻www.festspillene.no), held over twelve days from the end of May and presenting an extensive programme of music, ballet, folklore and drama. The principal venue for the festival is the **Grieghallen**, on Lars Hilles gate (☎55 21 61 50, ☻www.grieghallen.no), where you can pick up programmes, tickets and information, as you can at the tourist office. The city's contemporary arts centre, the **USF Verftet**, down on the Nordnes peninsula (☎55 31 55 70, ☻www.usf.no), contributes to the festival by hosting **Nattjazz** (☎55 30 72 50, ☻www.nattjazz.no), a prestigious and long-established international jazz festival held over the same period.

The Bergen International Festival is also the main player in the wide-ranging programme of cultural events that are tabulated and promoted by the tourist office in their **Sommer Bergen** leaflet and website (☎55 55 39 39, ☻www.sommerbergen.no). Part of this summer programme is devoted to **folk music** and **folk events** – singing, dancing and costumed goings-on of all kinds. Catch folk dancing at either the Bryggens Museum (late June to early Aug, once weekly at 9pm; 95kr) or at **Fana Folklore**'s "country festivals" (☎55 91 52 40), a mix of Norwegian music, food and dancing held on a private estate outside the city. These take place at 7pm several times a week from June to August and cost 300kr per person, including meal and transport; tickets from hotels and Flølo, Torgalmenning 9. There are also **chamber music and organ recitals** at the Mariakirken in June, July and August, and **Grieg recitals** at Grieg's home, Troldhaugen, from mid-June to October.

Out the summer season, USF Verftet (see above) puts on an ambitious programme of concerts, art-house films and contemporary plays; the **Bergen Philharmonic** performs regularly in the Grieghallen from September to May (tickets on ☎81 03 31 33, ☻www.harmonien.no); and Bergen's main **theatre**, Den Nationale Scene, on Engen (☎55 54 97 00; ☻www.den-nationale-scene.no), offers a wide range of performances on three stages. Most productions are, of course, in Norwegian, but there are occasional appearances by English-speaking troupes. Finally, Bergen has one large city-centre **cinema**, Bergen Kino, Konsertpaleet, Neumanns gate 3 (premium line ☎82 05 00 05, ☻www.filmweb.no/bergenkino), a five-minute walk south of Ole Bulls plass. Predictably, American films rule the roost, so English speakers are at a linguistic advantage.

Listings

Airlines SAS/Braathens ☎81 52 04 00; Norwegian Airlines (including Norwegian Air Shuttle, see p.282) ☎81 52 18 15; Sterling ☎81 55 88 10; Widerøe ☎81 00 12 00.
Airport Bergen airport ☎55 99 81 55.
Bookshop Norli, right in the city centre at Torgalmenning 7 (Mon–Fri 9am–8pm, Sat 9am–6pm), is easily the best bookshop in town, with a wide range of English books and French, German and Spanish titles, too. The travel section is especially good and the staff extremely helpful. Very competitive prices also.
Bus enquiries Timetable information on ☎177.
Car rental Avis, Lars Hilles gate 20A ☎55 55 39 55; Hertz, Nygårdsgaten 89 ☎55 96 40 70. Car rental can also be arranged at the tourist office.
Emergencies Ambulance ☎113, Fire ☎110, Police ☎112.

Exchange The main post office (see p.331) offers competitive exchange rates for foreign currency and travellers' cheques, and has longer opening hours than any Bergen bank. There are ATMs dotted all over the city centre.
Ferries: Domestic: Hurtigbåt passenger express boats depart from the Strandkaiterminalen. The principal operators are HSD (south to Haugesund & Stavanger; north to Hardangerfjord; ☎55 23 87 80, ☻www.hsd.no) and FSF (Sognefjord & Nordfjord; ☎55 90 70 70, ☻www.fylkesbaatane.no). The Hurtigrute coastal boat (☎81 03 00 00, ☻www.hurtigruten.no) sails daily at 8pm from the Hurtigrutekaien on the southern edge of the city centre, about 1km from the train station. Tickets from local travel agents or the operator.

Ferries: International: Fjord Line, Skolteg-runnskaien (☎81 53 35 00, ⊛www.fjordline .com), operates a car ferry service to Haugesund, Stavanger and Newcastle, and another to Egersund and Hantsholm in Denmark; Smyril Line, Slottsgaten 1 (☎55 59 65 20, ⊛www.smyril-line.com), has car-ferry sailings from the Skoltegrunnskaien to Shetland, the Faroes, Denmark and Iceland.

Hiking The DNT-affiliated Bergen Turlag, Tvergaten 4–6 (Mon–Wed & Fri 10am–4pm, Thurs 10am–6pm 7 Sat 10am–2pm; ☎55 33 58 10, ⊛www.bergen-turlag.no), will advise on hiking trails in the region, sells hiking maps and arranges guided walks.

Internet The Cyberhouse Internet Café (Mon–Sat 9am–11pm & Sun noon–10pm) has lots of terminals and is located just northeast of the Torget at Hollendergaten 3. They charge, but the Central Library, metres from the train station on Strømgaten, doesn't (Mon–Thurs 10am–8pm, Fri 10am–4.30pm & Sat 10am–4pm).

Laundry Coin operated and service wash at Jarlens Vaskoteque, Lille Øvregate 17, near the funicular (☎55 32 55 04).

Pharmacy Apoteket Nordstjernen, at the bus station (Mon–Sat 8am–midnight, Sun 9.30am–midnight; ☎55 21 83 84).

Post office Main post office in the city centre on Småstrandgaten gate at Olav Kyrres gate (Mon–Fri 8am–6pm, Sat 9am–3pm).

Taxi Bergen Taxi ☎07000.

Trains National timetable information on ☎81 50 08 88.

Vinmonopolet Bergen Storsenter, Strømgarten.

The western fjords

Heading out from Bergen, the **western fjords** beckon. The most popular initial target is the **Hardangerfjord**, a delightful and comparatively gentle introduction to the wilder fjords that lie beyond. Also popular is **Voss**, inland perhaps, but still a sports centre of some renown, and a useful halfway house en route to **Flåm**, draped beside the **Aurlandsfjord** and at the end of a spectacularly exciting train ride down the valley from Myrdal. Nonetheless, scenic as all this is, it's the **Sognefjord**, further to the north, that captivates most visitors, its stirring beauty amplified by its sheer size, stretching inland from the coast for some 200km. Beyond, and running parallel, lies the **Nordfjord**, smaller at 120km long and less intrinsically enticing, though its surroundings are more varied with patches of the **Jostedalsbreen glacier** visible and visitable nearby. From here, it's another short journey to the splendid **Geirangerfjord** – narrow, sheer and rugged – whilst, hopping over a mountain range or two, the town of **Åndalsnes** boasts an exquisite setting with rearing peaks behind and the tentacular Romsdalsfjord in front. At the west end of the Romsdalsfjord is the region's prettiest town, **Ålesund**, whose centre is liberally sprinkled with charming Art Nouveau buildings courtesy of Kaiser Bill.

This is not a landscape to be hurried – there's little point in dashing from fjord to fjord. Stay put for a while, go for at least one hike or cycle ride, and you'll really appreciate the western fjords in all their grandeur. The sheer size is breathtaking – but then the geological movements that shaped them were on a grand scale. During the Ice Age, around three million years ago, the whole of Scandinavia was covered in ice, the weight of which pushed the bottom of what would become the fjords down to depths well below that of the ocean floor – the Sognefjord, for example, descends to 1250m, ten times deeper than most of the Norwegian Sea. Later, as the ice retreated, it left huge coastal basins that filled with seawater to become the fjords, which the warm Gulf Stream keeps free of ice.

Where to stay in the fjords
Bergen advertises itself as "Capital of the Fjords", and the tourist office does organize a barrage of excursions from the city. These are an expensive option, however, since most trips can be done independently and far more cheaply. Also, as Bergen is in fact on the western edge of the fjords, the bulk of the day-trips from here involve too much travelling for comfort. This is doubly true as the main road

east from Bergen – the E16 – is prone to congestion and possesses over twenty tunnels, many of which are horribly noxious. Avoid the E16 east of Bergen if you can, and certainly aim to branch off onto the relatively tunnel-free and much more scenic **Hwy 7** the first chance you get – about 30km east of the city. For all these reasons, the small towns that dot the fjords are far better as bases than Bergen, especially as distances once you're actually amidst the fjords are – at least by Norwegian standards – quite modest. In the Hardangerfjord, **Ulvik** and **Lofthus** are the most appealing places, Sognefjord has **Mundal** and **Balestrand**, while further north **Loen**, **Åndalsnes** and **Ålesund** all have their advantages.

Getting around the fjords

The convoluted topography of the western fjords has produced a dense and complex **public transport** system that's designed to reach all the larger villages and towns at least once every weekday, whether by train, bus, ferry, Hurtigrute coastal boat or Hurtigbåt express passenger boat. By **train**, you can reach Bergen and Flåm in the south and Åndalsnes in the north. For everything in between – the Nordfjord, Jostedalsbreen glacier and Sognefjord – you're confined to buses and ferries, and although virtually all services connect up with each other, it means that there is no set way of reaching or exploring the fjord region. General travel details for this chapter are given on p.330, and in the text itself we've included local connections where they are especially useful; this information should be used in conjunction with the timetables that are widely available across the region. Bear in mind also that although there may be a transport connection to the town or village you want to go to, many Norwegian settlements are scattered and you may be in for a long walk after you've arrived – a particularly dispiriting experience if it's raining.

We've covered the region **south to north** – from the Hardangerfjord to Sognefjord, Nordfjord, Geirangerfjord, Åndalsnes and Ålesund. There are certain obvious connections – from Bergen to Flåm, and from Geiranger over the Trollstigen to Åndalsnes, for example – but routes are really a matter of personal choice; the text lists the options. It's a good idea to pick up full **bus and ferry timetables** from the local tourist offices whenever you can. The shorter bus routes are often part of a longer chain of linked buses and ferries, so at least you shouldn't get stranded anywhere.

The Hardangerfjord

To the east of Bergen, the obvious initial target is the 100-kilometre **Hardangerfjord** (@www.hardangerfjord.com), whose wide waters are overlooked by a rough, craggy

Fjord ferries

Throughout the text there are numerous mentions of fjord **car ferries** and **Hurtigbåt passenger express boats**. The details given in parentheses concern the frequency of operation and the duration of the crossing: for example (hourly; 45min). Hurtigbåt services are usually fairly infrequent – three a day at most – whereas many car ferries shuttle back and forth every hour or two from around 7am in the morning until 10pm at night every day of the week; we've given times of operation where they are either different from the norm or particularly useful. **Hurtigbåt fares** are fixed individually, with prices starting at around 100kr for every hour travelled: the five and a half-hour trip from Bergen to Flåm, for example, will cost you around 550kr. ScanRail and Inter-Rail pass holders (see p.35 & p.45) are often entitled to discounts of up to fifty percent, and on some routes there are special excursion deals – always ask. **Car ferry fares**, on the other hand, are priced according to a nationally agreed sliding scale, with ten-minute crossings running at around 20kr per person and 47kr per car and driver, 25kr and 65kr respectively for a twenty-five minute trip.

shoreline and a scattering of tiny settlements. At its eastern end the Hardanger divides into several lesser fjords, and it's here you'll find the district's most appealing villages, **Utne**, **Lofthus** and **Ulvik**, each of which has an attractive fjordside setting and at least one especially good place to stay. To the east of these tributary fjords rises the **Hardangervidda**, a mountain plateau of remarkable, lunar-like beauty and a favourite with Norwegian hikers. The plateau can be reached from almost any direction, but one favourite starting point is **Kinsarvik**.

Of the two principal **car ferries** negotiating the Hardangerfjord, one shuttles in triangular fashion between Kvanndal, Utne and Kinsarvik, the other links Brimnes with Bruravik. There are no trains in the Hardangerfjord area but **buses** are fairly frequent, allowing you to savour the scenery and get to the three recommended villages without too much difficulty, except possibly on Sundays when services are reduced. Finally, if you're planning to travel south down Hwy 13 from Kinsarvik bound for either Stavanger or Oslo, be sure your itinerary does not involve an overnight stay at the eminently missable industrial town of **Odda**, at the head of the Sørfjord.

East from Bergen to Norheimsund and the Kvanndal ferry

Heading east from Bergen by bus or car along the **E16** bound for the Hardanger-fjord, the road first has to clear a string of polluted tunnels, an unpleasant 30km journey before you can fork off along **Hwy 7**. By contrast, Hwy 7 is a rattling trip, with the road twisting up over the mountains and down the valleys, gliding past thundering waterfalls and around tight bends before racing down to **NORHEIM-SUND** on the Hardangerfjord. A small-time port and furniture-making town, Norheimsund makes a gallant effort to bill itself as the gateway to the fjords, but in truth it's a modest little place and there's precious reason to hang around: like many fjord settlements, it's the travel in between that is the real attraction. Norheimsund does, however, have its uses as a minor transport hub, principally for its Hurtigbåt passenger express boat service to Utne, Kinsarvik, Lofthus, Ulvik and Eidfjord.

Leaving Norheimsund by road, Hwy 7 sticks to the rugged shoreline as it travels east to the ferry dock at **Kvanndal**, another pleasant journey with every turning bringing fresh mountain and fjord views as the Hardangerfjord begins to split into its various subsidiaries. There's a choice of routes from Kvanndal: you can either press on along the northern shore of the Hardangerfjord towards Ulvik and ulti-mately Voss (see p.336 and p.337), or take the Kvanndal **ferry** over to Utne and/or Kinsarvik (1 or 2 hourly; 20min/50min).

Utne

The tiny hamlet of **UTNE**, the Kvanndal ferry's midway point, occupies a splendid location, its huddle of houses overlooking the fjord from the tip of the rearing peninsula that divides the Hardangerfjord from the slender Sørfjord. Utne was long reliant on the orchards that still trail along the Sørfjord's sheltered slopes, its inhabit-ants making enough of a living to support themselves in some comfort, especially when supplemented by fishing and furniture-making: the brightly painted furniture that once hailed from the district made a popular export. Classic examples of this furniture are on display in the delightful *Utne Hotel* (☎53 66 64 00, ⑩www.utne hotel.no; ❸), whose twenty-four rooms, mostly en suite, occupy an immaculately maintained old clapboard complex metres from the ferry dock. It's a lovely place – family-owned and very relaxing – and the food, traditional Norwegian cuisine at its best, is top-notch too, served amidst the ancient panelling of the dining room.

Utne's heritage is celebrated at the **Hardanger Folkemuseum** (May–June daily 10am–4pm; July & Aug daily 10am–5pm; Sept–April Mon–Fri 10am–3pm; 40kr; ⑩www.hardanger.museum.no), a five-minute walk along the fjord from the hotel. One of the largest and best-appointed folk museums in the region, its collection begins with an assortment of displays on various aspects of traditional Hardanger life, from fishing and farming through to fruit growing and trade. There's also a large display on local **folk costume** – the women's headdresses hereabouts were amongst the most elaborate in Norway and a popular subject for the romantic painters of the nineteenth century, notably Adolph Tidemand and Hans Frederik gade. Outside, an assortment of old wooden buildings – farmhouses, cottages, storehouses and so forth – rambles over the hillside in an **open-air section** whose logic is hard to fathom, though in summertime, when there are demonstrations of farming and craft skills, things make much more sense.

Kinsarvik

From Utne, the car ferry (every 1–2hr; 30min) bobs over the mouth of the Sørfjord to **KINSARVIK**, a humdrum little town which was once an important Viking marketplace. The Vikings stored their boats in the loft of the town's sturdy stone **church** (May–Aug daily 10am–7pm; free), though the building was clumsily restored in the 1880s, leaving only hints of its previous appearance, most notably a series of faint chalk wall-paintings dating from the thirteenth century. Kinsarvik also lies at the mouth of the forested **Husedalen valley**, with its four crashing waterfalls. The valley makes an enjoyable hike in itself, though it's mostly used as an access route up to the Hardangervidda plateau. From Kinsarvik, it takes seven hours to reach the nearest DNT hut, the self-service **Stavali**, but be warned that the going is very steep and, in rainy conditions, intermittently very slippery. Hiking maps can be purchased at Kinsarvik **tourist office**, near the ferry jetty (late June to late Aug daily 9am–7pm; late Aug Mon–Fri 9am–5pm; Sept to late June Mon–Fri 9am–4pm; ☎53 66 31 12, ⍟www.ullensvang.herad.no).

Nearby Lofthus (see below) is a lot more enticing, but Kinsarvik does have a couple of places to **stay**, with the obvious choice being the *Best Western Kinsarvik Fjord Hotel* (☎53 66 31 00, ⍟www.kinsarvikfjordhotel.no; 5/6), which occupies a large and reasonably attractive ivy-clad modern block by the ferry dock.

Lofthus

Draped beside the Sørfjord 11km to the south of Kinsarvik, with the Folgefonna glacier glinting in the distance, **LOFTHUS** is an idyllic hamlet of narrow lanes and mellow stone walls, where a scattering of old grass-roofed houses sits among the orchards, pinky-white with blossom in the springtime. It's the overall impression which counts, though the **church** (May Mon–Fri 10am–3pm; June–Aug daily 10am–7pm; free), dating from 1250, is a good-looking stone structure with immensely thick walls and several bright but crude wall paintings. A stream gushes through the village, tumbling down the steep escarpment behind Lofthus to bubble past the delightful ⚘ *Ullensvang Gjesteheim* (☎53 66 12 36, ☏53 66 15 19; ❸), a huddle of antique timber buildings with thirteen cosy and unassuming rooms – and great food. Another option is the modern, plush but much less distinctive *Hotel Ullensvang* (☎53 67 00 00, ⍟www.hotel-ullensvang.no; ❺/❼), a massive, solitary affair plonked on the water's edge 1km to the north of Lofthus. As at Kinsarvik, a steep **hiking trail** leads up from Lofthus to the Hardangervidda plateau. It takes about four hours to reach the plateau at Nosi (950m above sea level) and part of the trail – at 650–700m – includes the **Munketreppene**, stone steps laid by the monks who farmed this remote area in medieval times. You can also hike up to the Stavali self-service DNT hut, a trek that takes about seven or eight hours.

North to Eidfjord

Heading north from Kinsarvik, **Hwy 13** fidgets along the coastline to reach, after 19km, Brimnes, where a **car ferry** (1–2 hourly; 10min) shuttles over the fjord to Bruravik, for Ulvik (see p.336) and Voss (see p.337). Beyond Brimnes, Hwy 13 becomes **Hwy 7**, whose first significant port of call, after another 11km, is the village of **EIDFJORD**, which straggles over a narrow and hilly neck of land in between the fjord and a large and deep lake, the Eidfjordvatnet. There's been a settlement here since prehistoric times, and for centuries the village prospered as a trading centre at the end of one of the main routes over the Hardangervidda – though this was a two-edged sword: from the seventeenth until the mid-nineteenth century, the villagers were obliged to build and repair foot and cart tracks up to the plateau, forced labour for which they weren't paid. Nowadays, Eidfjord and its environs rustle up a couple of good attractions, beginning with the **Hardangervidda Natursenter** in the village itself (daily: April–May & Sept–Oct 10am–6pm, June–Aug 9am–8pm; 80kr), whose displays focus on the plateau's natural history and geology. Secondly, a byroad leads northeast from Eidfjord up the **Simdal valley** to reach, after about 6km, the tortuous turning that wriggles up to the **Kjeåsen mountain farm**, a lonely complex of old farm buildings from where there are wondrous views over the Simadalsfjord rippling way down below. The road is much too narrow to take two-way traffic, but drivers can relax (a little) – you can only drive up to the farm on the hour and descend on the half hour.

The best **hotel** hereabouts is the *Eidfjord Hotell* (☎53 66 52 64, ✇www.eidfjordhotel .no; 4), a crisply designed, medium-sized modern place with tastefully furnished rooms that perches on a knoll high above the Eidfjord. The **restaurant** is very good here, too. In addition, the village **tourist office** (June to mid-Aug daily 10am–7pm; mid to late Aug Mon–Sat 10am–6pm; Sept Mon–Fri 9am–4pm; Oct–May Mon, Wed & Fri 9am–4pm; ☎53 67 34 00, ✇www.eidfjordinfo.com) has the details of a handful of **private rooms** as well as a veritable raft of information on the area as a whole.

Heading east from Eidfjord, Hwy 7 weaves and tunnels its way up to the Hardangervidda, the first part of its journey to Geilo (see p.298). En route, it passes the Hardangervidda hiking bases of Dyranut and Halne.

The Hardangervidda plateau

The **Hardangervidda** is Europe's largest mountain plateau, occupying a one-hundred-square-kilometre slab of land east of the Hardangerfjord and south of the Oslo–Bergen railway. The plateau is characterized by rolling fells and wide stretches of level ground, its rocky surfaces strewn with pools, ponds, lakelets and rivers. The whole plateau is above the treeline, and at times has an almost lunar-like appearance, although even within this elemental landscape there are variations. To the north, in the vicinity of Finse, there are mountains and a glacier, the **Hardangerjøkulen**, while the west is wetter – and the flora somewhat richer – than the

△ The Hardangervidda plateau

barer moorland to the east. The lichen that covers the rocks is savoured by herds of reindeer, who leave their winter grazing lands on the east side of the plateau in the spring, chewing their way west to their breeding grounds before returning east again after the autumn rutting season.

Stone Age hunters once followed the reindeer on their migrations and traces of their presence – arrowheads, pit-traps, etc – have been discovered over much of the plateau. Later, the Hardangervidda became one of the main crossing points between east and west Norway, with horse traders, cattle drivers and Danish dignitaries all cutting across along cairned paths. Some of these paths are still in use as part of a dense network of trails and tourist huts that has been developed by several DNT affiliates. Roughly one third of the plateau has been incorporated within the **Hardangervidda National Park**, but much of the rest is protected too, so hikers won't notice a great deal of difference between the park and its immediate surroundings. The entire plateau is also popular for winter cross-country hut-to-hut ski touring. Many hikers and skiers are content with a day on the Hardangervidda, but some find the wide-skied, lichen-dappled scenery particularly enchanting and travel from one end of the plateau to the other, a seven- or eight-day expedition.

In terms of **access**, the Oslo–Bergen **train** line cuts across the northern edge of the plateau, calling at Finse train station, from where hikers and skiers head off across the plateau in all directions. Finse is not, however, accessible by road, so motorists (and bus travellers) use **Hwy 7**, which runs across the plateau between **Eidfjord** (see p.334) and **Geilo** (see p.298). There's precious little in the way of human habitation on this lonely hundred-kilometer-long stretch of road, but you can pick up the plateau's hiking trails easily enough at several points. **Dyranut** and **Halne** are two such places, respectively 39km and 47km from Eidfjord. Some hikers prefer to walk eastwards onto the Hardangervidda from Kinsarvik and Lofthus (see p.334), but this does involve an arduous day-long trek up to the plateau from the fjord.

Ulvik

Tucked away in a snug corner of the Hardangerfjord, the pocket-sized village of **ULVIK** strings prettily along the shoreline, with orchards dusting the green hills behind. There's nothing specific to see – the town's main claim to fame as the place where potatoes were first grown in Norway in 1765 just about sums things up – but it's an excellent place to unwind, a popular little resort with a cluster of good hotels. **Hiking trails** lattice the rough uplands to the north of Ulvik and explore the surrounding shoreline. Indeed the local council have gone to some trouble here in their "kulturlandskapsplan" (culture landscape plan), in which four designated areas incorporate both footpaths and historic sights, most enjoyably the **Ljonakleiv crofter's farm** in the hills above the village; hiking maps are available at the tourist office (see below).

Practicalities

Ulvik is off the main **bus** routes, but there are regular local buses here from Voss (Mon–Sat 2–5 daily, Sun 1 daily; 1hr). These are routed via Bruravik to pick up passengers on the Brimnes–Bruravik ferry, coming from the likes of Odda, Lofthus, Kinsarvik and Eidfjord (1–4 daily). There are also summertime-only **Hurtigbåt passenger express boat** services to Ulvik from Norheimsund via Kinsarvik and Lofthus (1 daily; 2hr 10min). Buses pull into the centre of the village, metres from the jetty, from where it's a couple of minutes' walk along the waterfront to the **tourist office** (mid-May to mid-Sept Mon–Sat 8.30am–5pm, Sun 1–5pm; mid-Sept to mid-May Mon–Fri 9am–2pm; ☏56 52 63 60, ⦿www.visitulvik.com). Staff issue all the usual information, including bus and ferry timetables, sell detailed hiking maps and rent out bikes.

Among the **hotels**, the big deal hereabouts is the *Rica Brakenes* (☏56 52 61 05, ⦿www.brakanes-hotel.no; ❹/❺), a large and luxurious modern place occupying a lovely fjordside location in the centre of the village. If the *Brakenes* is a bit too big and domineering for your liking, the *Rica Ulvik* (☎56 52 62 00, ⊛www.rica.no; ④/⑤), five minutes' walk east along the waterfront, is a good deal less overpowering. Again, it's the setting rather than the architecture that appeals, with the fjord stretching out in front of the hotel, overlooked by the balconies of the fifty-odd modern bedrooms. Different again is the *Ulvik Fjord Pensjonat* (☎56 52 61 70, ⊛www.ulvikfjordpensjonat.no; 4), a well-maintained and appealing **guesthouse** situated a ten-minute walk west from the centre along the waterfront. The rooms in the main building are straightforward but very comfortable, and there's a modern annexe, too. Breakfasts are first-rate and evening meals are available by prior arrangement. Otherwise, **eat** at either of the *Rica* hotels – the *Ulvik* edges the other in terms of price and informality.

Voss

Travelling east from Bergen on either the E16 or the train, it's an enjoyable 100km jaunt over the hills and round the mountains to **VOSS**, which boasts an attractive lakeside setting and a splendid thirteenth-century church. Voss is, however, best known as an adventure sports and winter skiing centre, with everything from skiing and snowboarding through to summertime rafting, kayaking and horse riding. Consequently, unless you're here for a sweat, your best bet is to have a quick look round and then move on, though there is a caveat: Voss is the ideal base for a **day trip by train** east up the Raun Valley, an especially scenic part of the Bergen–Oslo rail line. The most popular target on this stretch of the line is the Myrdal junction, where you change for the dramatic train ride down to Flåm (see box on p.339).

The town

With the lake on one side and the River Vosso on the other, **Voss** has long been a trading centre on one of the main routes between west and east Norway – though you'd barely guess this from the modern appearance of the town centre. In 1023, King Olav visited to check that the population had all converted to Christianity,

---

Voss sports

Every summer, hundreds of Norwegians make a beeline for Voss on account of its **watersports**. The rivers near the town offer a wide range of conditions, suitable for everything from a quiet paddle to a finger-chewing whitewater ride. There are several operators, but **Voss Rafting Senter** (☎56 51 05 25, ⊛www.vossrafting.no) set the benchmark. Their four-hour whitewater rafting trips venture out onto three rivers – the relatively placid Vosso and the much rougher Stranda and Raundalen; the price, including swimming test and a snack, is 700kr, 750kr on Saturdays. Other options with the same operator and at about the same price include river-boarding (5hr), sports rafting, which is akin to canoeing (4hr), and whitewater rappelling (4hr). In addition, Nordic Ventures (☎56 51 00 17, ⊛www.nordicventures.com) offers all sorts of **kayaking** excursions as well as **tandem paragliding**; and Stølsheimen Fjellridning (☎56 51 91 66, ⊛www.fjellhest.com) specializes in mountain **horseback riding**.

Skiing in Voss starts in late November and continues until mid-April – nothing fancy, but good for an enjoyable few days. From behind and above the train station, a **cable car** – the Hangursbanen – climbs 700m to give access to several short runs as well as the first of three chair lifts which take you up another 300m. A one-day lift pass costs 265kr (200kr per half-day), and in January and February some trails are floodlit. There's a choice of red, green and blue downhill ski routes, and amongst the latter is a long and fairly gentle route through the hills above town. Full **equipment** for both downhill and cross-country skiing can be rented by the day from Voss Ski, at the upper Hangursbanen station (☎56 51 00 32). They also offer lessons in skiing and snowboarding techniques.

and stuck a big stone cross here to make his point. Two centuries later another king, Magnus Lagabøte, built a church in Voss to act as the religious focal point for the whole region. The church, the **Vangskyrkja** (June–Aug daily 10am–4pm; 20kr), still stands, its eccentric octagonal spire rising above stone walls which are up to two metres thick. The interior is splendid, a surprisingly flamboyant and colourful affair with a Baroque reredos and a folksy rood screen showing a crucified Jesus attended by two cherubs. The ceiling is even more unusual, its timbers painted in 1696 with a cotton-wool cloudy sky inhabited by flying angels – and the nearer you approach the high altar, the more of them there are. That's pretty much it as far as specific sights go, though you could take a stroll along the leafy Prestegardsalléen footpath, which heads south along the shore of **Vangsvatnet** lake from opposite the church; or wander the central shops and cafés – if you've come from the hamlets and villages further north, the shopping might seem something of a treat.

Practicalities

Buses stop outside the **train station** at the western end of the town centre. From here, it's a five-minute walk to the **tourist office** (June–Aug Mon–Fri 8am–7pm, Sat 9am–7pm & Sun 2–7pm; Sept–May Mon–Fri 9am–3.30pm; ☎56 52 08 00, ⓦ www.visitvoss.no) on the main street, Uttrågata – veer right round the Vangskyrkja church and it's on the right. They have oodles of information on hiking, rafting, skiing and local touring, the bones of which are detailed in the free *Voss Guide*.

To cater for all the visiting sportsfolk, Voss has lots of inexpensive **accommodation**, from guesthouses through to camping. The best budget bet is the excellent HI **hostel**, *Voss Vandrerhjem* (☎56 51 20 17, ⓦ www.vandrerhjem.no; Jan–Oct), which has both double rooms (**2**) and dorm beds (200kr), and is sited in a modern chalet/lodge complex overlooking the water about 700m from the train station. To get there, turn right outside the station building and head along the lake away from the town centre – a ten-minute walk. The hostel serves large, inexpensive evening meals and good breakfasts, has its own sauna, laundry, Internet access and a kitchen for guests to use; it also rents out bikes and canoes. Advance booking is strongly recommended. A second inexpensive option is the rudimentary *Voss Camping* (☎56 51 15 97, ⓦ www.vosscamping.no), located a short walk south of the Vangskyrkja church: turn left from the train station, take the right fork at the church and then turn right again, along the Prestegardsalléen footpath. It's open all year and has a few cabins (**2**), an outside pool and washing machines. As for the town's **hotels**, one or two barely pass muster and easily the best bet is *Fleischer's* (☎56 52 05 05, ⓦ www .fleischers.no; **6**), next door to the train station. Dating from the 1880s, the hotel's high-gabled and towered facade overlooks the lake and consists of the original building and a modern wing built in the same style. Parts of the hotel – and many of the bedrooms – have the whiff of real luxury, but others are more mundane. The **restaurant** serves the best food in town and there's a terrace bar as well. Their all-inclusive food-and-lodging deals offer substantial savings on the normal rate.

North to Flåm

Heading north along the E16 from Voss, it's a short, scenic hop to **Flåm**, one of the region's most visited villages and justifiably famous for its railway, the **Flåmsbana**. Flåm is also an excellent base for further explorations, whether it be the train ride up to – or down from – Myrdal, the ferry trip up along the **Nærøyfjord** or a day-long hike in the surrounding mountains. Nearing Flåm you'll pass through two spirited pieces of tunnelling, with stretches of 11km and 5km bored through the mountainside at colossal expense. However, these are but pip-squeaks when compared with the newly completed 24-kilometre-long **tunnel** that links Aurlandsdal – from a point just east of Flåm – with Lærdal and, more importantly, completes the fast road, the E16, from Bergen to Oslo. Even better, it's free.

As for public transport, **express buses** (2–5 daily) scuttle north from Voss bound for Flåm and points east. Eastbound **trains** from Voss stop at Myrdal, where you change for the branch line down to Flåm.

Flåm and the Nærøyfjord

Fringed by meadows and orchards, **FLÅM** village sits beside the Aurlandsfjord, a slender branch of the Sognefjord, with the mountains glowering behind. It's a splendid setting, but initially you could still be excused for wondering why you bothered coming here. The fjordside complex adjoining the train station is crass and commercial – souvenir trolls and the like – and on summer days the tiny village heaves with tourists, who pour off the train, have lunch, and then promptly head out by bus and ferry. But a brief stroll is enough to leave the crowds behind at the harbourside, while out of season or in the evenings when the day-trippers have all moved on, Flåm is a pleasant spot – and an eminently agreeable place to spend the night. If you're prepared to risk the weather, mid-September is perhaps the best time to visit: the peaks already have a covering of snow and the vegetation is just turning its autumnal golden brown.

Not only is Flåm the terminus for the Flåmsbana (see box below), but it's also the starting point for one of the most stupendous **ferry trips** in the fjords, the two-hour cruise up the Aurlandsfjord and down its narrow offshoot, the **Nærøyfjord** (1–4 daily; 195kr single, 230kr return) to Gudvangen (see p.338). With high rockfaces keeping out the sun throughout the winter, Nærøyfjord is the narrowest fjord in Europe, and its stern beauty makes for a magnificent excursion.

Practicalities

Flåm's harbourside complex may be ugly, but it is convenient, holding a supermarket, a train ticket office and the **tourist office** (daily: May & Sept 8.30am–4pm; June–Aug 8.30am–8pm; ☎57 63 21 06, ⊛www.alr.no), where you can pick up a very useful free booklet on Aurland, Flåm and Lærdal, which includes public transport timetables as well as all sorts of local information. Staff also provide hiking hints, sell hiking maps and will purchase fjord ferry tickets on your behalf. If you do decide to overnight here, *Flåm Camping og Vandrerhjem*, a couple of minutes' signposted walk

---

The Flåm railway – the Flåmsbana

Lonely **Myrdal**, just forty minutes by train from Voss, is the start of one of Europe's most celebrated branch rail lines, the **Flåmsbana** (⊛www.flaamsbana.no), a twenty-kilometre, 900-metre plummet down the Flåmsdal valley to **Flåm** – a fifty-minute train ride that's not to be missed under any circumstances. The track, which took four years to lay in the 1920s, spirals down the mountainside, passing through hand-dug tunnels and, at one point, actually travelling through a hairpin tunnel to drop nearly 300m. The gradient of the line is one of the steepest anywhere in the world and as the tiny train squeals its way down the mountain, past cascading waterfalls, it's reassuring to know that it has five separate sets of brakes, each capable of bringing it to a stop. The service runs all year round, a local lifeline during the deep winter months. There are ten departures daily from mid-June to mid-September, four the rest of the year; fares are 160kr single, 250kr return.

In the past, the athletic have risen to the challenge and undertaken the five-hour **walk** from the railway junction at Myrdal down the old road into the valley, instead of taking the train, but much the better option is to disembark about halfway down and walk in from there. **Berekvam** station, at an altitude of 343m, will do very nicely, leaving an enthralling two- to three-hour hike through changing mountain scenery down to Flåm. **Cycling** down the valley road is also perfectly feasible, though it's too steep to be relaxing.

Moving on from Flåm

From Flåm, there are daily **Hurtigbåt passenger express boat** services up the Aur-landsfjord and along the Sognefjord to Balestrand and Bergen. The one-way trip to Bergen takes five-and-a-half hours and costs 560kr; Balestrand is an hour and a half away and costs 160kr. By **train**, Myrdal, at the top of the Flåmsbana, is on the main Oslo–Bergen line, while Sognebussen **express buses** pass through Flåm bound for a variety of destinations, including Bergen, Voss and Sogndal (2–6 daily). Heading east by car, it's tempting to use the brand new free tunnel to Lærdal, but the 45km-long **mountain road** that the tunnel replaced has survived to provide splendid views and some hair-raising moments.

from the train station, incorporates a small and well-kept HI **hostel** (May–Sept; ☎57 63 21 21, ⊛www.vandrerhjem.no; doubles ❶, dorm beds 120k) plus tent spaces and cabins (❶). Alternatively, the *Heimly Pensjonat* (☎57 63 23 00, ⊛www.heimly.no; ❹) provides simple but adequate lodgings in a mundane modern block that overlooks the fjord, about 450m east of the train station along the shore. Set back from the water a couple of hundred metres from the station, Flåm's only **hotel** is the *Fretheim* (☎57 63 63 00, ⊛www.fretheim-hotel.no; ❺/❻), a rambling structure whose attractive older part, with high-pitched roofs and white-painted clapboard, is now flanked by a matching extension with well-appointed rooms furnished in brisk modern style. The hotel is the only good place to **eat** in town, with a banquet-like buffet every night; go early to get the pick of the buffet crop.

The Sognefjord

Profoundly beautiful, the **Sognefjord** drills in from the coast for some 200km, its inner recesses splintering into half a dozen subsidiary fjords. Perhaps inevitably, none of the villages and small towns that dot the fjord quite lives up to the splendid setting, but **Balestrand** and **Mundal**, on the Fjærlandsfjord, come mighty close and are easily the best bases. Both are on the north side of the fjord which, given the lack of roads on the south side, is where you want (or pretty much have) to be – Flåm (see p.339) apart. Mundal is also near two southerly tentacles of the Jostedalsbreen glacier: **Flatbreen** and easy-to-reach **Bøyabreen**.

Hwy 55 hugs the Sognefjord's north bank for almost the whole of its length and at **Sogndal** it slices northeast to clip along the lustrous **Lustrafjord**, which boasts a top-notch attraction in **Urnes stave church**, reached via a quick ferry ride from **Solvorn**. Further north, a side road leaves Hwy 55 to clamber up from the Lustrafjord to the east side of the Jostedalsbreen glacier at the **Nigardsbreen** nodule, arguably the glacier's finest vantage point. Thereafter Hwy 55 – as the **Sognefjellsveg** – climbs steeply to run along the western side of the **Jotunheimen mountains**, an extraordinarily beautiful journey even by Norwegian standards and one which culminates with the road thumping down to **Lom** on the flatlands beside Hwy 15.

Public transport to and around the Sognefjord is generally excellent. Operating about halfway along the fjord, perhaps the most useful of the **car ferries** plies between Vangsnes, Hella and Dragsvik (for Balestrand), and in the east another useful link is the 24-hour ferry shuttle between Mannheller and Fodnes, for points east and ultimately Oslo. **Hurtigbåt passenger express boat** services connect Bergen, Balestrand and Sogndal, and long-distance **buses** come up from Bergen to Sogndal via Voss, Flåm and the Fodnes–Mannheller ferry. At Sogndal, passengers change for onward services west along the north shore of the Sognefjord to Hella and Balestrand, or run east to Oslo; other buses run up Hwy 5 to the peripheries of Mundal and the Nordfjord (see p.348), and in the summertime local buses link Sogndal with Lom along the stirring Sognefjellsveg (Hwy 55; see p.346).

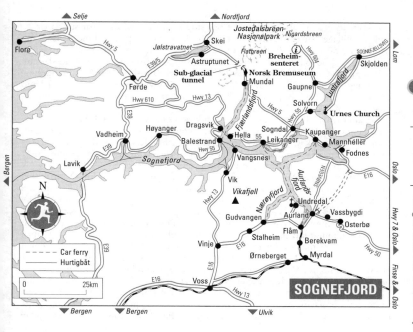

Balestrand

An appealing first stop along the Sognefjord, **BALESTRAND** has been a tourist destination since the middle of the nineteenth century, when it was discovered by European travellers in search of cool, clear air and picturesque mountain scenery. Kaiser Wilhelm II got in on the act too, becoming a frequent visitor and sharing his holiday spot with the tweeds and hobnail boots of the British bourgeoisie. These days, the village is used as a touring base for the immediate area, as the battery of small hotels and restaurants above the quay testifies, but it's all very small-scale, and among the 1500-strong population farming still remains the principal livelihood.

An hour or so will suffice to take a peek at Balestrand's two attractions. The **English church of St Olav** is a spiky brown-and-beige wooden structure built, in 1897, in the general style of a stave church at the behest of a British émigré, a certain Margaret Kvikne, who moved here after she married a local curate. In one of those curious hand-me-downs from Britain's imperial past, the church remains part of the Diocese of Gibraltar, which arranges English-language services during the summer. The Germans have left their mark, too. About 300m south of the church along the fjord are two humpy **Viking burial mounds**, supposedly the tombs of King Bele and his wife. On the larger of them is a statue of the king in heroic pose, plonked there by the Kaiser in 1913 to match the statue of Bele's son-in-law that stands tall across the fjord in Vangsnes (see below).

Practicalities

The only **car ferry** direct to Balestrand is the summertime service south from Mundal, on the Fjærlandsfjord (see p.343); otherwise, the nearest you'll get is Dragsvik, 9km along the fjord to the north of Balestrand, and reached by ferry from either Hella to the east or Vangsnes on the fjord's south shore (every 40min to 1hr). Both the Mundal ferry and **Hurtigbåt** services (from Bergen and Sogndal) dock at the village quayside, plumb in the centre. **Buses** stop beside the quayside too, but there no services direct from Bergen and Voss; coming from the south it's necessary to change at Sogndal. The bus stop is in front of the Spar supermarket, and the village **tourist office** is at the back of the shop (late June to late Aug Mon–Fri 7.30am–1pm & 3.30–9pm, Sat 7.30am–1pm & 3.30–6.30pm, Sun 8am–12.30pm & 3.30–6.30pm; early June & late Aug to Sept Mon–Fri 7.30am–1pm & 3.30–6pm, Sat 7.30am–1pm & 3.30–6.30pm, Sun 8am–12.30pm & 3.30–5.30pm; Oct–May Mon–Fri 9am–3pm; ☏57 69 12 55, ⊛www.sognefjord.no). Staff hand out a wide range of fjord leaflets, sell local hiking maps, issue bus and ferry timetables and rent bikes at 150kr per day.

For **accommodation**, the all-year *Midtnes Pensjonat* (☏57 69 11 33, ⊛www.midtnes.no; ❸, ❹ with fjord view), about 300m from the dock behind the English church, is a low-key, pleasantly sedate affair with a few workaday but spacious rooms in a modern wing adjoining the original clapboard house; make sure to get a room with a fjord view. Close by, the *Balestrand Hotel* (☏57 69 11 38, ⊛www.balestrand.net; May–Sept; ❹) is very similar, with thirty unassuming rooms kitted out in modern, modest style. Another good choice, just 150m uphill from the dock, is the HI **hostel** (☏57 69 13 03, ⊛www.vandrerhjem.no; late June to late Aug; doubles ❷, dorm beds 190kr), which is part of the neat and trim *Kringsjå Hotell* (same number; ⊛www.kringsja.no; ❷). This complex occupies a pleasant modern building and its long verandah overlooks the fjord; there's a communal kitchen, a more-than-competent café-restaurant and a laundry; rowing boat rental is available, too. The big deal hereabouts, though, is *Kvikne's Hotel* (☏57 69 42 00, ⊛www.kviknes.no; ❺; May–Sept), whose various buildings dominate much of the waterfront. It's worth popping into the bar to take a look at the fancy fittings – some of which are in a sort of Victorian Viking-baronial style – but don't take a room without having a gander first: the best and most expensive overlook the fjord, but some are at the back of the modern annexe. Finally, the town **campsite**, *Sjøtun*

Moving on from Balestrand

When it comes to **moving on from Balestrand**, you're spoiled for choice. In the summertime, one especially tempting proposition is the **car ferry** (late May to September 1–2 daily; 1hr 15min; passengers 160kr one-way 240kr return; car & driver 275kr one-way, 520kr return) north up along the stunningly beautiful Fjærlandsfjord to the eminently appealing hamlet of Mundal (see p.343), from where there's the possibility of an onward bus trip to the Norsk Bremuseum and the Bøyabreen glacier arm (see p.344). There is also a **Hurtigbåt passenger express boat** service linking Balestrand with Bergen in one direction, Sogndal in the other (2–3 daily). **Driving** north from Balestrand, **Hwy 13** cuts a scenic route over the mountains on its way to its junction with the E39 (near Førde), which itself proceeds north to the Nordfjord (see p.348), but **Hwy 55** to Sogndal and the eastern reaches of the Sognefjord has much more to offer – not least the Sognefjellsveg mountain road (Hwy 55; see p.340). To get to Sogndal from Balestrand, it's necessary to cross the mouth of the Fjærlandsfjord by ferry from Dragsvik, 9km along the coast to the north. This **Dragsvik car ferry** operates a triangular service shuttling both east across the fjord to Hella (15min; 20kr passengers, 50kr car & driver) and south to Vangsnes (25min; 25kr passengers, 65kr car & driver); sailings to both destinations are every forty minutes or so from mid-June to mid-August, hourly the rest of the year. The other significant cost for drivers is the 150kr toll payable on Hwy 5 just south of the Mundal turning.

Finally, the Sogn og Fjordane **express bus** travels west from Balestrand to Førde (1 daily; 2hr), where passengers change for Stryn and the Nordfjord (see p.348). This same bus also heads east (3 daily) from Balestrand to Sogndal and ultimately Oslo. At Sogndal, passengers change for Mundal and Lom (see p.344). Note, however, that connecting services are few and far between – mostly you'll have to hang around for an hour or two (at least) between buses.

Camping (☎57 69 12 23; June to mid-Sept) occupies a treeless field just beyond the burial mounds, a kilometre or so south of the dock; there are *hytter* (❶) as well as tent pitches.

For **food**, both the *Kringsjå* and the *Midtnes* serve tasty, excellent-value dinners, and there are competent snacks and light lunches at *Gekkens Café*, upstairs in the shopping centre on the quayside. The cream of the gastronomic crop, however, is the restaurant at *Kvikne's Hotel*, which serves up a banquet-sized buffet (300kr) every night – go early to get the pick and be sure to try the earth-shattering mousse.

North to the Fjærlandsfjord and Mundal

To the north of Balestrand, the **Fjærlandsfjord** is a wild place, its flanks blanketed by a thick covering of trees that extends down to the water's edge, with a succession of thundering waterfalls tumbling down vast clefts in the rock up above. The village of **MUNDAL** – sometimes inaccurately referred to as Fjærland – matches its surroundings perfectly, a gentle ribbon of old wooden houses edging the fjord, with the mountains as a backcloth. It's one of the region's most picturesque places, saved from the developers by its isolation: it was one of the last settlements on the Sognefjord to be connected to the road system, with Hwy 5 from Sogndal only being completed in 1986. Moreover, Mundal has eschewed the crasser forms of commercialism to become the self-styled "Norwegian Book Town", with a dozen old buildings accommodating antiquarian and secondhand bookshops. Naturally enough, most of the books are in Norwegian, but there's a liberal sprinkling of English editions, too. The bookselling season runs from mid-May to early September and the bookshops are mostly open daily from 10am to 6pm.

Bookshops aside, the village has two good-looking buildings, the first of which is the **Hotel Mundal** (see p.344), whose nineteenth-century turrets, verandahs and high-pitched roofs overlook the fjord from amongst the handful of buildings that amount to the village centre. Next door, the **church** (June–Aug daily 10am–6pm; free) is a serious affair dating from 1861, lacking in ornamentation but immaculately maintained; its graveyard hints at the hard but healthy life of the district's farmers – most of them seem to have lived to a ripe old age. Many locals are still farmers, but in summer hardly any of them herd their cattle up to the mountain pastures, as was the custom until the 1960s. The disused tracks to these summer farms (*støls*) now serve as **hiking trails** of varying length and difficulty – the tourist office (see below) will advise.

Around Mundal: the Flatbreen and Bøyabreen

About 2.5km north of the village, along the quiet byroad that links it with Hwy 5, is the **Norsk Bremuseum** (Norwegian Glacier Museum; daily: April, May, Sept & Oct 10am–4pm; June–Aug 9am–7pm; information and enquiries free but displays 80kr; ☎57 69 32 88, ⓦwww.bre.museum.no), which tells you more than you ever wanted to know about glaciers. It features several lavish hands-on displays – a simulated walk below a glacier, for example – and screens films about glaciers; package tourists turn up in droves.

The museum is one of the Jostedalsbreen National Park's three information centres (see p.348 for details of the others), and as such has the details of all the various **guided glacier walks** on offer across the park as outlined in their *Breturar* (glacier walks) leaflet. The usual target from Mundal is the **Supphellebreen**, the Jostedalsbreen's nearest hikeable arm, or, to be precise, that part of it called **Flatbreen**, but this is a challenging part of the glacier and neither is it easy to get to. Flatbreen excursions take between six and eight hours and take place in late July and early August. Advance reservations, at least a day beforehand, are essential on ☎57 69 32 33; the cost is 650kr per person. At the other extreme, you can get close to the glacier without breaking sweat just 10km north of Mundal on Hwy 5. Here, just before you enter the tunnel, look out for the signposted side road on the right, leading the 200m to the *Brævasshytta* restaurant (May–Sept daily 9am–5/8pm). This smart, modern place, a tour-package favourite, overlooks the slender glacial lake fed by the **Bøyabreen** arm of the glacier up above. It takes a couple of minutes to stroll down from the restaurant to the lake, close to the sooty shank of the glacier.

Practicalities

Arriving **by car** from the south, there's a whopping 150kr toll to pay on Hwy 5, just before you reach the turning for Mundal. The nearest you'll get to Mundal by regular **bus** is the Norsk Bremuseum on Hwy 5, from where it's an easy 2.5km stroll south along the fjord to the village. **Car ferries** arriving from Balestrand dock in the centre of Mundal and connect with special excursion buses – bookable either here or in Balestrand – which take passengers on to the Bremuseum and then, after a stop-off of over an hour, to the Bøyabreen. Mundal **tourist office**, metres from the boat dock (May–Sept daily 9.30am–5.30pm; ☎57 69 32 33, ⊛www.fjaerland .org), advises on local hiking routes, sells hiking maps and has bus and ferry timetables. **Cycle rental** is available from them too, at around 150kr per day.

There are two fjordside **hotels** in Mundal. The obvious choice is the splendid ⚲ *Hotel Mundal* (☎57 69 31 01, ⊛www.fjordinfo.no/mundal; May–Sept; ❻), a quirky sort of place dating back to 1891 whose public rooms display many original features, from the parquet floors and fancy wooden scrollwork through to the old-fashioned sliding doors of the cavernous dining room. The rooms are frugal and some show their age, but somehow it doesn't matter much. If you do stay, look out for the old photos on the walls of men in plus-fours and hobnail boots clambering round the glaciers – only softies bothered with gloves. Nearby, the ⚲ *Fjærland Fjordstue Hotell* (☎57 69 32 00, ⊛www.fjaerland.no; May–Sept; ❹) is very different – a well-tended family hotel with smart modern furnishings and a conservatory overlooking the fjord. A third option is *Bøyum Camping* (☎57 69 32 52) near the Bremuseum, which has huts (❸) as well as spaces for tents. Both hotels offer good, wholesome **food**.

Leaving Mundal, long-distance **buses** travelling along Hwy 5 can be picked up from the bus stop close to the Norsk Bremuseum. There are services south to Sogndal and Oslo along the E16 (3–4 daily) and north to Skei and Førde (3 daily). Change at Skei for onward services north to Stryn and the Nordfjord (see p.348).

East to Sogndal

From Balestrand it's 9km north along the fjord to **Dragsvik**, where ferries shuttle over to the jetty at **Hella**, which is itself 40km from **SOGNDAL** – bigger and livelier than Balestrand, but still hardly a major metropolis, with a population of just 6000. Neither is Sogndal as appealing: it has a pleasant fjord setting in a broad valley, surrounded by low, green hills dotted with apple and pear trees, but its centre is a rash of modern concrete and glass. Frankly, there are other much more agreeable spots within a few kilometres' radius and your best option is to keep going.

Buses drop passengers at the **bus station** – a major interchange – on the west side of the town centre near the end of Gravensteinsgata, the long main drag. From here, it's about 500m east along Gravensteinsgata to the **tourist office** (early June to late Aug Mon–Fri 9am–8pm, Sat 9am–5pm, Sun 3–8pm; late Aug to Sept Mon–Fri 9am–4pm; ☎57 67 30 83, ⊛www.sognefjorden.no), housed in one of the street's flashy modern buildings. Staff issue bus and ferry timetables, and have a list of local **accommodation**, though pickings are fairly slim. The nicest place to stay – though it's no great shakes – is the *Hofslund Fjord Hotel*, a stone's throw from the tourist office at Fjøregata 37 (☎57 62 76 00, ⊛www.hofslund-hotel.no; ❸). It comprises an old wooden building and a modern annexe; ask for a room with a fjord view. Another palatable and certainly economical option is the HI **hostel** (☎57 62 75 75, ⊛www.vandrerhjem.no; mid-June to mid-Aug; doubles ❶, dorm beds 100kr), which manages to feel quite homely despite being housed in a residential folk high school, *Folkehøgskule*. It's well signposted and situated near the bridge at the east end of town and about 400m beyond the roundabout that

Moving on from Sogndal

From Sogndal, there is a **Hurtigbåt passenger express boat** service to Balestrand, Vik and Bergen. There are also **express buses** northwest to Mundal and Skei (for Stryn) and southeast to Oslo via the E16. **Local buses** include a summer service north up along Hwy 55, the Sognefjellsveg (see p.346), the highest parts of which are closed by snow from late October to May, to Solvorn and the Nigardsbreen glacier nodule (late June to Aug 1 daily); and another to Solvorn, Turtagrø and Lom (late June to mid-Sept 1–2 daily).

Finally, drivers should remember that the road to Oslo is interrupted some 18km southeast of Sogndal by the round-the-clock Manheller–Fodnes **car ferry** (every 30min; 10min; passengers 30kr, car & driver 90kr).

---

marks the east end of Gravensteinsgata. This same roundabout is about 50m from the tourist office and it also marks the start of Fjøravegen, the town's other main drag, which cuts through the commercial heart of Sogndal. For **food**, the restaurant of the *Quality Hotel Sogndal*, Gravensteinsgata 5 (℡57 62 77 00), is reliable, offering tasty Norwegian dishes at affordable prices.

Northeast to Solvorn and Urnes stave church

Some 15km northeast of Sogndal on Hwy 55, a steep 3km-long turning leaves the main road to snake its way down to **SOLVORN**, an attractive little hamlet clustered beneath the mountains on the sheltered foreshore of the **Lustrafjord**. Solvorn is the site of the *Walaker Hotell* (℡57 68 20 80, ⊛www.walaker.com; ❹), the prettiest of which is the old house, a comely pastel-painted building with a lovely garden and first-rate period bedrooms.

From Solvorn, a local **car ferry** (early June to Aug Mon–Fri 10am–4pm hourly, plus Sat & Sun 11am–4pm hourly; Sept to early June Mon–Fri 2–4 daily, Sun 1 daily; 20min; 25kr passenger, 70kr car & driver; ℡91 79 42 11) shuttles across the Lustrafjord to the hamlet of **Ornes**, from where it's a stiff, ten-minute hike up the hill to **Urnes stave church** (early June–Aug daily 10.30am–5.30pm; 45kr). Magnificently sited with the fjord and the snow-dusted mountains as its backdrop, this is the oldest and most celebrated stave church in Norway. Parts of the building date back to the twelfth century, and its most remarkable feature is its wonderful medieval **carvings**. On the outside, incorporated into the north wall, are two exquisite door panels, the remains of an earlier church dating from around 1070 and alive with a swirling filigree of strange beasts and delicate vegetation. These forceful, superbly crafted panels bear witness to the sophistication of Viking woodcarving – indeed the church has given its name to this distinctively Nordic art form, found in many countries where Viking influence was felt and now generally known as the "Urnes" style. Most of the interior is seventeenth-century, but there is Viking woodcarving here too, notably the strange-looking figures and beasts carved on the capitals of the staves and the sacred-heart bench-ends. A small display in the neighbouring house-cum-ticket office fills in all the details and has photographic enlargements of carvings that are hard to decipher inside the (poorly-lit) church.

If you're driving, there's a choice of routes on from the church. You can head north along the minor road that tracks along the east shore of the Lustrafjord to rejoin Hwy 55 at Skjolden (see p.346), or retrace your steps back to Hwy 55 via Solvorn. The latter is the route you'll need to take if you're heading to the Nigards-breen arm of the Jostedalsbreen glacier.

Onto the Nigardsbreen

North from the Solvorn turning, it's about 15km along Hwy 55 to **Gaupne**, where Hwy 604 forks north for the delightful 34km trip up the wild, forested river valley leading to the **Breheimsenteret Jostedal information centre** (daily: May to late June & late Aug to Sept 10am–5pm; late June to late Aug 9am–7pm; displays 50kr; ☎57 68 32 50, ⍟www.jostedal.com). This angular, ultra-modern structure fits in well with the bare peaks that surround it and, as you sip a coffee on the terrace, you can admire the glistening glacier dead ahead – the **Nigardsbreen**, an eastern arm of the Jostedalsbreen. From the centre, it's an easy 3km drive or walk along the toll road (25kr) to the shores of an icy green lake, where a tiny **boat** (mid-June to Aug daily 10am–6pm; 30kr) shuttles across to the bare rock slope beside the glacier, a great rumpled and seamed wall of ice that sweeps between high peaks. It's a magnificent spectacle and most visitors are satisfied with the forty-minute hike up from the jetty to the glacier's shaggy flanks, but others plump for a **guided glacier walk**. There is a plethora to choose from, beginning with a quick and easy one- to two-hour jaunt suitable for children over 6 (daily July to mid-Aug; 140kr, children 70kr), and tougher four-hour trips (daily late May to mid-Sept; 300kr). Prices include equipment and the starting point is at the foot of the glacier on the far side of the lake. Tickets for the family walks can be purchased direct from the guides, but longer day-trip excursions need to be pre-booked and pre-paid at the information centre at least one hour before departure. Advance reservations for the longer, overnight trips are essential and must be made at least four weeks beforehand. For more on the Jostedalsbreen glacier, see p.348; further information on glacier walks is given on p.343.

Along the Sognefjellsveg

Back at Gaupne, Hwy 55 continues 26km northeast to **SKJOLDEN**, a dull little town that is both at the head of the Lustrafjord and at the start of the 85km-long **Sognefjellsveg** road over the mountains to Lom. Despite the difficulty of the terrain, the Sognefjellsveg marks the course of one of the oldest trading routes in Norway, with locals transporting goods by mule or, amazingly enough, on their shoulders: salt and fish went east, hides, butter, tar and iron went west. That portion of the road that clambers over the highest part of the mountains – 1434 metres above sea level – was only completed in 1938 under a Great Depression "make-work" scheme, which kept a couple of hundred young men busy for two years. Tourist literature hereabouts refer to the lads' "motivation and drive", but considering the harshness of the conditions and the crudeness of their equipment – pickaxes, spades and wheelbarrows – their purported enthusiasm seems unlikely.

Beyond Skjolden, the Sognefjellsveg worms its way up the valley to a mountain plateau which it traverses, providing absolutely stunning views of the jagged, ice-crusted Jotunheimen peaks to the east. En route are several roadside **lodges**, easily the best of which is the comfortable and very modern ⌘ *Turtagrø Hotel* (☎57 68 08 00, ⍟www.turtagro.no; hotel rooms ❻, dorm bunk beds in the annexe 260kr, 360kr with breakfast; Easter–Oct), just 15km out from Skjolden. The hotel is a favourite haunt for mountaineers, but it also provides ready access to the **hiking trails** that lattice the Jotunheimen National Park (see p.291). However, the terrain is unforgiving and the weather unpredictable, so novice hikers beware. In addition, the *Turtagrø* is a base for mountain guides, who offer an extensive programme of guided mountain and glacier walks as well as summer **cross-country skiing**; the season begins at Easter and extends until October.

Onto Lom

Pushing on along the Sognefjellsveg, it's another short hop to the *Bøverdalen* hostel (see p.347) and then the crossroads settlement of **LOM**, a long-time trading and transport centre, benefiting – in a modest sort of way – from the farms which dot the surrounding valleys. Today, with a population of just 700, it's hardly a boom town, but it does make a comfortable living from the passing tourist trade. Lom's eighteenth-century heyday is recalled by its **stave church** (daily: late May to mid-June & mid-Aug to mid-Sept 10am–4pm; mid-June to mid-Aug 8am–8pm; 40kr), an enormous structure perched on a grassy knoll above the river. The original church was built here about 1200, but it was remodelled and enlarged after the Reformation, when the spire and transepts were added and the flashy altar and pulpit installed. Its most attractive features are the dinky, shingle-clad roofs, adorned by dragon finials, and the Baroque acanthus vine decoration inside.

Nearby is the town's open-air museum, the **Lom Bygdamuseum Presthaugen** (late June & late Aug Tues–Sun 11am–4pm; July to mid-Aug daily 11am–5pm; 40kr), a surprisingly enjoyable collection of old log buildings in a forest setting. Norway teems with this type of museum – stay in the country long enough and the very sight of one will make you want to scream – but Lom's is better than most. It is distinguished by the Olavsstugu, a modest hut where St Olav is said to have spent a night, and also by what must be the biggest and ugliest Storstabburet (large storehouse) in the country. Museum enthusiasts will also want to visit the **Norsk Fjellmuseum** (Norwegian Mountain Museum; Jan–April & Oct–Dec Mon–Fri 9am–4pm; May to mid-June & mid-Aug to Sept Mon–Fri 9am–5pm, Sat & Sun 11am–5pm; mid-June to mid-Aug Mon–Fri 9am–7pm, Sat & Sun 10am–7pm; 50kr), a modern place which focuses on the Jotunheimen mountains. It's all here in admirable detail, from the fauna and the flora to the landscapes, farmers and past mountaineers.

Buses to Lom pull in a few metres west of the main crossroads, and most of what you're likely to need is within easy walking distance of here. The church and the open-air museum are across the bridge on the other side of the river, as is the mountain museum, which shares its premises with the **tourist office** (Jan–April & Oct–Dec Mon–Fri 9am–4pm; May & Sept Mon–Fri 9am–4pm, Sat & Sun 10am–5pm; early June & late Aug Mon–Fri 9am–6pm, Sat & Sun 10am–5pm; mid-June to mid-Aug Mon–Fri 9am–9pm, Sat & Sun 10am–8pm; ☏61 21 29 90, ⊛www.visitlom.com). The choicest **accommodation** is the *Fossheim Turisthotell* (☏61 21 95 00, ⊛www.fossheimhotel.no; ❹), about 300m east of the crossroads along Hwy 15. The main lodge here is neat and smart, with an abundance of pine, and behind, trailing up the wooded hillside, are some delightful little wooden cabins (also 4), some of which are very old and all of which are en suite. The hotel **restaurant** is excellent and reasonably priced; it specializes in traditional Norwegian cuisine. A palatable second-choice hotel is the modern *Fossberg* (☏61 21 22 50, ⊛www.fossberg.no; ❹), a large, mostly wooden place by the crossroads. For bargain-basement lodgings, the nearest HI **hostel**, *Bøverdalen Vandrerhjem* (☏61 21 20 64, ⊛www.vandrerhjem.no; June–Sept; doubles ❶, dorm beds 120kr) is about 20km back down the Sognefjellsveg and occupies a series of glum modern buildings right by the roadside.

Routes on from Lom

Heading west along Hwy 15, Lom is within comfortable striking distance of either the Geirangerfjord (see p.351) or the Nordfjord and the western flanks of the Jostedalsbreen glacier (see p.348). In the opposite direction, also along Hwy 15, it's another very manageable drive to Otta (see p.289) and the main E6 highway between Oslo and Trondheim. A tantalizing choice perhaps, but, if you're after more fjord scenery, the Geirangerfjord definitely has the edge.

By **bus** from Lom, there are daily express services west to Grotli and Stryn, and east to Otta, Lillehammer and Oslo. From mid-June to the end of August, you can change onto a local bus at Grotli for the Geirangerfjord – but check connections with Lom tourist office before you depart. **There is also a summer bus service south** along Hwy 55, the Sognefjellsveg to Turtagrø, Solvorn and Sogndal (late June to mid-Sept; 1–2 daily).

The Nordfjord and the Jostedalsbreen glacier

Heading north from Mundal (see p.343) along Hwy 5, you soon journey beneath the Jostedalsbreen glacier via the Fjærland tunnel, which somehow seems a bit of a cheek – and environmentally dubious. That said, the highway is the handiest way to get between the Sognefjord and the **Nordfjord**, the next great fjord system to the north. The inner recesses of the Nordfjord are readily explored along **Hwy 60**, which weaves a tortuous course through a string of unexciting little towns in between the fjord and the glacier. Amongst them, **Loen** is the best base for further explorations, including the glacier, though humdrum **Stryn** is larger and more important. Stryn is also close to where Hwy 60 meets **Hwy 15**. The former presses on north to Hellesylt (see p.353), the latter runs west along the Nordfjord, with the road dipping and diving along the northern shore in between deep-green reflective waters and severe peaks. It's a handsome enough journey, but the Nordfjord doesn't have the allure of its more famous neighbours, at least in part because its roadside hamlets lack much appeal.

High up in the mountains, dominating the whole of the inner Nordfjord region, lurks the **Jostedalsbreen glacier**, a five-hundred-square-kilometre ice plateau that creaks, grumbles and moans out towards the Sognefjord and the Jotunheim mountains. The glacier stretches northeast in a lumpy mass from Hwy 5, its myriad arms – or "nodules" – nudging down into the nearby valleys, the clay particles of its meltwater giving the local rivers and lakes their distinctive light-green colouring. Catching sight of the ice nestling between peaks and ridges can be unnerving – the overwhelming feeling being that somehow it shouldn't really be there.

For centuries, the glacier presented an impenetrable east–west barrier, crossed only at certain points by determined farmers and adventurers. It's no less daunting today, but access is much freer, a corollary of the creation of the **Jostedalsbreen Nasjonalpark** (Jostedalsbreen National Park) in 1991. Since then, roads have been

---

Guided glacier walks and national park information centres

Most **guided glacier walks** on the Jostedalsbreen are scheduled between late June and early September, though on some arms of the glacier the season extends from May until late September, even longer on parts of the Briksdalsbreen. The walks range from two-hour excursions to five-day expeditions. Day-trip prices start at 150–250kr per person for a two- to three-hour gambol, rising to 650kr for six to eight hours. A comprehensive leaflet detailing all the various walks is widely available across the region and at the national park's three **information centres**. These are the **Norsk Bremuseum**, on the south side of the glacier near Mundal (see p.343); the **Breheim-senteret Jostedal** on the east side at the Nigardsbreen (see p.345); and the **Jostedalsbreen Nasjonalparksenter** (daily: May to mid-June 9am–4pm; mid-June to mid-Aug 9am–6pm; mid-Aug to Sept 9am–4pm; exhibitions 70kr; ☎57 87 72 00, ⊛www .jostedalsbre.no) in Oppstryn, 20km east of Stryn on Hwy 15. Each of the centres has displays on all things glacial and sells books, souvenirs and hiking maps.

Booking arrangements for the shorter glacier walks vary considerably. On some of the trips – for example those at the Nigardsbreen – it's sufficient to turn up at the information centre an hour or two beforehand, but in general it's a good idea to make a reservation at least a day ahead. Sometimes this is best done through the informa-tion centre, sometimes direct with the tour operator. In the case of the overnight trips, however, advance booking is essential, often a minimum of four weeks beforehand. In all cases, basic **equipment** is provided, though you'll need to take good boots, water-proofs, warm clothes, gloves, hat, sunglasses – and your own **food** and **drink**.

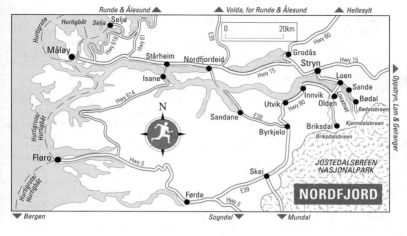

driven deep into the glacier's flanks, the comings (but mostly goings) of the ice have been closely monitored and there has been a proliferation of officially licensed **guided glacier walks** (*breturar*) on its various arms (see box on p.348). If that sounds too energetic and all you're after is a **close look at the glacier**, then this is possible at several places, with the easiest approach being the five-minute stroll to the Bøyabreen on the south side of the glacier near Mundal (see p.343). By contrast, the east side's Nigardsbreen (see p.345) requires much more commitment – getting to the ice involves a boat ride and a stiff forty-minute hike. Here on the west side, off Hwy 60, the **Briksdalsbreen** requires a forty-five minute walk from the end of the road, but is still the most visited approach by a long chalk, partly on account of its horse-and-carriage rides up towards the ice. Much less crowded and far prettier is the easy fifteen-minute walk to the **Kjenndalsbreen**, near Loen – a charming way to spend a morning or afternoon.

Travelling around the area by **bus** presents few problems if you stick to the main highways, but services from Hwy 60 to the glacier are limited. There's a once daily bus to and from Briksdalsbreen, which gives you three hours there, but nothing at all to Kjenndalsbreen – the bus, again once daily, stops at Bødalseter, about 8km short of the end of the road.

North to Olden and the Briksdalsbreen

From Mundal on the Fjærlandsfjord (see p.343), it's 90km north along Hwy 5, the E39 and then Hwy 60 to the hamlet of **OLDEN** on the shores of the Nordfjord. The village doesn't have much going for it, but it is at the start of the 24km byroad south to **BRIKSDAL**, a scattering of mountain chalets that serves as the starting point for the easy 45-minute walk to the **Briksdalsbreen** arm of the Jostedalsbreen glacier. The path skirts waterfalls and weaves up the river until you finally reach the glacier, surprisingly blue except for streaks of dust and dirt. It's a simple matter to get close to the ice as the only precaution is a flimsy rope barrier with a small warning sign – do be careful. Alternatively, you can hire a pony and trap at the café area at the start of the trail, something that will cost you about 250kr – steep considering that you still have to hike the last bit of the path. Guided glacier walks begin at the café area, too. There are several operators to choose from; Briksdal Breføring (☎57 87 68 00, ✆www.briksdalsbre.no) are as good as any.

Local **buses** link Stryn, Loen and Olden with Briksdal once daily throughout the year. Passengers get about three hours at Briksdal before the departure of the return service, again once daily.

Loen and the Kjenndalsbreen

LOEN spreads ribbon-like along the Nordfjord's low-lying, grassy foreshore, with ice-capped mountains breathing down its neck. The village is also home to one of Norway's most famous hotels, the outstanding ⅓ *Alexandra* (☎57 87 50 00, ⓦwww .alexandra.no; ❺/❼), whose exterior hardly does it justice. The hotel occupies a large and fairly undistinguished modern block overlooking the fjord, but inside the lodge-like public rooms are splendid – wide, open and extremely well-appointed. There's every convenience, including a sauna and solarium, while the bedrooms are spacious, infinitely comfortable and furnished in bright modern style. Breakfasts are banquet-like, but the evening **buffets** (from 7pm; 400kr) are even better, a wonderful selection that lays fair claim to being the best in the fjords. The *Alexandra* is, of course, fairly pricey, but across the road and right on the water's edge, the *Hotel Loenfjord* (☎57 87 57 00, ⓦwww.loenfjord.no; ❻) is an excellent and less expensive second choice. A happy cross between a motel and a lodge, the *Loenfjord* comprises a long and low modern building in a vernacular version of traditional Norwegian style. The public rooms are expansive, and the evening buffet very good.

From beside the *Hotel Alexandra*, a 21km-long byroad leads south to the **Kjenndalsbreen** nodule of the Jostedalsbreen glacier. The road starts by slipping up the river valley past lush meadows, before threading along the northerly shore of **Lovatnet**, a long and slender lake of glacial blue. After 4.4km, it reaches the ferry point for boat cruises along the lake (see box below) and then scuttles on to the hamlet of **Bødal**. There are guided glacier walks near Bødal on the **Bødalsbreen** (June to mid-Sept; ☎57 87 68 00) and the meeting point is **Bødalseter**, a DNT self-service hut about 5km from Bødal up along a bumpy, signposted mountain road and then a ten-minute walk from the car park. From the hut to the glacier, it's another 2.5-kilometre walk; there are no guided glacier walks on the Kjenndalsbreen itself.

Back on the Kjenndalsbreen road, it's a further 3km or so to a toll post (30kr) and a couple of hundred metres more to the **Kjendalstova café** (May–Sept) at the very end of the Lovatnet – and the spot where the boat docks. Pushing on, it's 5km more to the car park, from where it's an easy and very pleasant fifteen-minute ramble through rocky terrain to the **ice**, whose fissured, blancmange-like blue and white folds tumble down the rock face, with a furious white-green river, fed by plummeting meltwater, flowing underneath. If the weather holds, it's a lovely spot for a picnic.

There are no local **buses** to the Kjenndalsbreen; the nearest you'll get is the once daily service – in each direction – from Stryn and Loen to Bødal, though note that the bus to Bødal leaves early in the afternoon, the bus from Bødal early in the morning.

Stryn

STRYN, merely 12km around the fjord from Loen, is the biggest town hereabouts, though with a population of just 1200 that's hardly a major boast. For the most

---

Loen boat trips

From June to August, a small **passenger boat** (1 daily) weaves a leisurely course from one end of lake **Lovatnet** to the other, a delightful cruise through beguiling scenery. The departure point is the pint-sized **Sande** jetty, 4.4km down the Kjenndalsbreen road from the *Hotel Alexandra* in Loen, and the boat docks beside the *Kjendalsstova* café, 5km from the Kjenndalsbreen ice-face. The excursion costs 160kr, including onward transportation by bus from the café to the car park at the end of the Kjenndalsbreen road and the return journey – again by bus and boat – back to Sande; in total the round-trip takes four hours. The *Hotel Alexandra* (see above) issues tickets and takes bookings and will, at a pinch, give you a lift down to Sande, though the Stryn–Loen–Bødal bus connects with boat departures.

part, it's a humdrum modern sprawl straggling beside its long main street, but there is a pleasant pocket of antique **timber houses** huddled round the old bridge, down by the river on the west side of the centre, just to the south of the main drag; take a few moments to have a look.

The **bus station** is beside the river to the west of the town centre on Hwy 15/60. From here, it's a 600m walk to the **tourist office**, bang in the centre just off the main street, Tonningsgata (early June & late Aug Mon–Fri 8.30am–6pm & Sat 9.30am–5pm; late June & early Aug Mon–Fri 8.30am–6pm, Sat & Sun 9.30am–5pm; July daily 8.30am–7pm; Sept–Dec Mon–Fri 8.30am–3.30pm; Jan–May Mon–Fri 8.30am–3.30pm; ☎57 87 40 54, ⊛www.nordfjord.no). Staff issue free town maps, rent mountain bikes, have a wide range of local brochures and sell hiking maps. There's no strong reason to overnight here, but Stryn does have a better-than-average HI **hostel**, *Stryn Vandrerhjem* (☎57 87 11 06, ⊛www .vandrerhjem.no; June–Aug; doubles ❷, dorm beds 185kr), perched high above the centre at Geilevegen 14. The chalet-like building has self-catering facilities, a laundry and Internet access plus splendid views over Stryn and its surroundings – compensation for the lung-wrenching one-kilometre-long trek up here. The hostel is signposted from the main drag – north up Bøavegen – on the east side of the centre. Four-star *Stryn Camping* (☎57 87 11 36, ⊛www.stryn-camping.no) is handier, just a couple of hundred metres up Bøavegen; it's well-equipped and has tent pitches as well as cabins (❷).

Heading west out of Stryn, highways 15 and 60 share the same stretch of road until, after 16km, Hwy 60 spears north to reach, after about 30km, Hellesylt, on the Geirangerfjord.

The Geirangerfjord and Norangsdalen

The **Geirangerfjord** is one of the region's smallest fjords, but also one of its most breathtaking. A convoluted branch of the Storfjord, the Geirangerfjord cuts deep inland and is marked by impressive waterfalls, with a village at either end of its snake-like profile – **Hellesylt** in the west and **Geiranger** in the east. Of the two,

△ The Geirangerfjord

Geiranger has the smarter hotels as well as the tourist crowds, Hellesylt is smaller and quieter with the added bonus of its proximity to the magnificent **Norangsdal** valley, where the hamlet of **Øye** boasts one of Norway's most enjoyable hotels.

You can reach Geiranger in dramatic style from both north and south along the rip-roaring, nerve-jangling Hwy 63 – the aptly named **Ørnevegen** ("Eagle's Highway"). The approach to Hellesylt along Hwy 60 is comparatively demure, though taken as a whole this highway is an especially appealing route between the Nordfjord and Ålesund. In addition, **car ferries** (May–Sept 4–8 daily; 1hr; passengers 95kr one-way, car & driver 190kr) run between Hellesylt and Geiranger. This is one of the most celebrated trips in the entire region, the S-shaped waters about 300m deep and fed by a series of plunging waterfalls up to 250m in height. The falls are all named, and the multilingual commentary aboard the ferry does its best to ensure that you become familiar with every stream and rivulet. More interesting are the scattered ruins of abandoned farms, built along the fjord's sixteen-kilometre length by fanatically optimistic settlers during the eighteenth and nineteenth centuries. The cliffs backing the fjord are almost uniformly sheer, making farming of any description a short-lived and back-breaking occupation – and not much fun for the children either: when they went out to play, they were roped to the nearest boulder to stop them dropping off.

Long-distance **buses** travelling west along Hwy 15 link Otta (see p.289) and Lom (see p.346) with Grotli and Langvatn, at one of which – depending on the

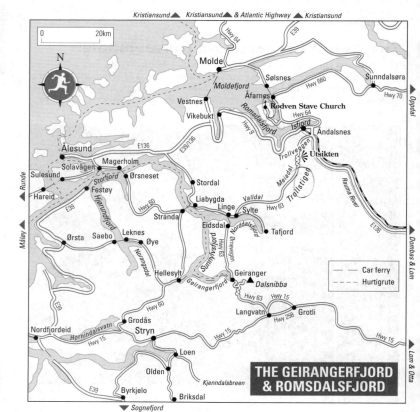

THE GEIRANGERFJORD & ROMSDALSFJORD

service – you change for the **local bus** north to Geiranger, though note that this connecting service only operates from mid-June to August. The same local bus pushes on from Geiranger to Åndalsnes (see p.356). Hellesylt is on the main Bergen–Ålesund bus route, which passes along Hwy 60 through Loen and Stryn; there are at least a couple of services daily. Finally, there's a limited local bus service from Hellesylt down along the Norangsdal valley to Øye and Leknes (late June to mid-Aug Mon–Fri 1 daily); it leaves at lunch times, whereas the bus from Leknes leaves mid-morning.

Hellesylt

An important and well-protected trading station since prehistoric times, **HELLESYLT** is now little more than a stop-off on tourist itineraries, with most visitors staying just long enough to catch the ferry down the fjord to Geiranger. For daytime entertainment, there is a tiny **beach** beyond the mini-marina near the ferry quay, the prelude to some very cold swimming. Or you could splash about (as many do) in the waterfall in the village centre, but by nightfall, when the day-trip-pers have departed, Hellesylt is quiet and peaceful.

The **tourist office** (June & late Aug to Sept Mon–Fri 9am–6pm, Sat & Sun noon–6pm; July to late Aug daily 9am–8pm; ☎70 26 38 85) is a five-minute walk from the jetty in a modern building that doubles as an **art gallery** (same times; 50kr). On display is a set of kitsch-meets-Baroque woodcarvings illustrating Ibsen's *Peer Gynt* by a certain Oddvin Parr from Ålesund. It's all rather strange, but good fun all the same. Hellesylt has one **hotel**, the *Grand* (☎70 26 51 00, ⊛www .grandhotel-hellesylt.no; May–Sept; ❹), whose fancy wooden scrollwork and high-pitched gables have been a local landmark since 1871. However, the interior has been patchily restored and guests are put up in the modern annexe next door. The main competitor is the HI **hostel** (☎70 26 51 28, ⊛www.vandrerhjem.no; June–Aug), pleasantly set on the hillside above the village beside Hwy 60 – a steep 350-metre walk up the signed footpath from the jetty. They have cabins (❷), which suit a family of four nicely, as well as both double rooms (❶) and dorm beds (125kr); facilities include self-catering and a bike store. Rowing boats can be rented at the *Grand*, which also sells fishing licences and rents out fishing equipment. Finally, *Hellesylt Camping* (☎90 20 68 85; April–Sept) fills out the shadeless field beside the fjord, about 400m from the quay.

The Norangsdal valley and Øye

A century ago, pony and trap took cruise-ship tourists from Hellesylt down through the majestic **Norangsdal** valley to what was then the remote hamlet of **ØYE**, a distance of 24km. By car, it's a simple journey today, but the scene appears not to have changed at all: steep, snow-tipped peaks rise up on either side of a wide, boulder-strewn and scree-slashed valley, dented by a thousand rock falls. Near the top of the valley, the road, 8km of which is gravel, slips through mountain pastures, where local women once spent every summer with their cows. The women slept in spartan timber cabins and today roadside plaques at a couple of surviving cabins flesh out the details. Pushing on, the road soon dips down into Øye, whose pride and joy is the splendid *Hotel Union* (☎70 06 21 00, ⊛www.unionoye.no; April–Oct; ❻), a delightfully restored High Victorian establishment, built in 1891 to accom-modate touring gentry. Its interior is crammed with period antiques and bygones seemingly hunted down from every corner of the globe by the present owner. Each of the bedrooms is individually decorated in elaborate style and most celebrate the famous people who stayed here, like King Haakon VII and Kaiser Wilhelm II, not to mention the Danish author Karen "*Out of Africa*" Blixen: enthusiasts might be pleased to see a pair of her lover's boots. It's a great place to spend the night – though you do have to turn a blind eye to the occasional period excesses, like the four-posters – and the food is first-rate, too. Telephones are banned, which is inducement enough to sit on the terrace and watch the weather fronts sweeping in off the glassy green **Norangsfjord**, or have a day's fishing – the hotel sells licences and dispenses advice.

Geiranger

Any approach to **GEIRANGER** is spectacular. Arriving by ferry slowly reveals the little village tucked in a hollow at the eastern end of the fjord, while approaching from the north by road involves thundering along a fearsome set of switchbacks on the Ørnevegen (Hwy 63) for a first view of the village and the fjord glinting in the distance. Similarly, the road in from Hwy 15 to the south begins innocuously enough, but soon you're squirming round and down the zigzags to arrive in Geiranger from behind. It's a beautiful setting, one of the most magnificent in western Norway, the only fly in the ointment being the excessive number of tourists at the peak of the season. That said, the congestion is limited to the centre of the village and it's easy enough to slip away to appreciate the true character of the fjord, hemmed in by sheer rock walls interspersed with hairline waterfalls, with tiny-looking ferries and cruise ships bobbing about on its blue-green waters.

The only specific sight is the **Norsk Fjordsenter** (daily: mid-June to mid-Aug 10am–7pm, May to mid-June & mid-Aug to Sept 10am–5pm; 75kr; ⑩www .fjordsenter.info), just across from the *Union Hotel* (see below). The centre follows the usual pattern of purpose-built museums, with separate sections exploring different aspects of the region's history from communications and transportation through to fjord farms and the evolution of tourism. Perhaps the most interesting display examines the problem of fjordland avalanches – whenever there's a major rock fall into a fjord, the resulting tidal wave threatens disaster.

The fjord centre is, however, small beer when compared with the scenery. A network of **hiking trails** lattices the mountains that crimp and crowd Geiranger: some make their way to thundering waterfalls, while others visit abandoned mountain farmsteads or venture up to vantage points where the views over the fjord are exhilarating if not downright scary. One popular excursion, to the mountain farm of **Skageflå**, involves both a boat ride – on one of the sightseeing boats – and a stiff hour-long hike up from the fjord to the farm, followed by a three-hour trek back to Geiranger. There's also the short but precarious trail to the **Flydalsjuvet**, an overhanging rock high above the Geirangerfjord that features in a thousand leaflets. To get there, drive south up from the Geiranger jetty and watch for the sign after about 5km; the car park offers extravagant views, but the Flydalsjuvet is about 200m away, out at the end of a slippery and somewhat indistinct track.

Practicalities

Buses to Geiranger stop a stone's throw from the waterfront and a couple of hundred metres from the **ferry terminal**. The latter is used by both the ferry from Hellesylt and the **Hurtigrute**, which detours from – and returns to – Ålesund on its northbound route between the middle of April and the middle of September only; it leaves Geiranger at 1.30pm. The nearby **tourist office** (mid-June to mid-Aug daily 9am–7pm; mid-May to mid-June & mid-Aug to mid-Sept 9am–5pm; ☎70 26 30 99, ⑩www.geiranger.no) is also on the waterfront, beside the sightseeing boat dock. Staff issue bus and ferry timetables, sell hiking maps and supply free village maps, which usefully outline local hiking routes. They also promote expensive boat tours of the fjord, though the car ferry from Hellesylt is perfectly adequate.

There are several **hotels** to choose from, but advance reservations are strongly advised in July and August. Cream of the crop is the large and lavish *Union* (☎70 26 83 00, ⑩www.union-hotel.no; ❺/❼; March to late Dec), high up the hillside but just 300m up the road from the jetty. There's been an hotel here since 1891 and although the present building, with its retro flourishes, is hardly startling, the public rooms are large and lodge-like, and there's a sauna and both indoor and outdoor pools. In addition, the bedrooms are pleasantly furnished in modern style and the best have fjord-view balconies; those on floor four are the pick. In addition, the *Union* does a first-rate help-yourself buffet dinner at 350kr – easily the best **food** around. Another good hotel option is the ultramodern timber-built *Grande Fjordhotell* (☎70 26 94 90, ⊛www.grandefjordhotel.com; ❹; May–Sept), which has a pleasant fjordside location about 2km north of the centre on the road to Eidsdal. They also have **cabins** (❸) and a **campsite**, which is adjacent to the very similar *Grande Hytteutleige og Camping* (☎70 26 30 68; May–Sept). The main campsite, *Geiranger Camping* (☎ & ☎70 26 31 20; late May to early Sept), sprawls along the fjordside fields a couple of hundred metres to the east of the tourist office. In summer it's jam-packed with caravans, cars and motorbikes – not much fun at all.

From mid-June to August, local **buses** run north into Geiranger from either Grotli or Langvatn on Hwy 15 – it depends on the service. There are two buses daily, one going straight into Geiranger (1hr), the other (2hr) making a dramatic detour up a rough mountain toll-road to the **Dalsnibba viewpoint**, overlooking the Geirangerfjord at 1476m. This same local bus pushes north out of Geiranger heading for Åndalsnes (see p.356) via the Trollstigen, a journey that takes just over three hours. Åndalsnes can also be reached by a number of other routes, including trains from Oslo.

North to Åndalsnes via the Trollstigen

Promoted as the "Golden Route", the 80km journey **from Geiranger to Åndalsnes** along Hwy 63 is famous for its mountain scenery – no wonder. Even by Norwegian standards, the route is of outstanding beauty, the road bobbing past a whole army of austere peaks whose cold severity is daunting. The journey also incorporates a ferry ride across the Norddalsfjord, a shaggy arm of the Storfjord, but the most memorable section is the **Trollstigen**, a mountain road that cuts an improbable course between the Valldal valley and Åndalsnes. At the end of the trip, small-town **Åndalsnes** is an ideal base for further fjordland explorations and has a couple of smashing places to stay. It's also the northern terminus of the dramatic **Rauma train line** (see p.214) from Dombås to the east.

Twice-daily from mid-June to August, a special **bus** travels the length of the Golden Route, taking the sweat out of driving round its hairpins and hairy-scary corners. The higher parts of the road are generally closed from early October to mid-May – earlier/later if the snows have been particularly heavy.

Over the Trollstigen

Heading north from Geiranger, the first part of the Golden Route is the 22-kilometre, knuckle-whitening jaunt up and over the **Ørnevegen** (Hwy 63) to **Eidsdal** on the Norddalsfjord. From here, a **car ferry** (every 30–45min; 10min; passengers 20kr, car & driver 50kr) shuttles over to the **Linge** jetty, from where it's just 3km east to **SYLTE**, a shadowy, half-hearted village that straggles along the fjord. More importantly, Sylte marks the start of the road over the **Trollstigen** ("Troll's Ladder"), a dramatic trans-mountain route that is equally compelling in either direction. The road negotiates the mountains by means of eleven hairpins with a maximum gradient of 1:12, but it's still a pretty straightforward drive until, that is, you meet a tour bus coming the other way – followed by a bit of nervous backing up and re-positioning. Drivers (and cyclists) should also be particularly careful in wet weather.

From Sylte, the southern end of the Trollstigen starts gently enough with the road rambling up the **Valldal** valley, passing dozens of fresh strawberry stalls in June and July – many Norwegians reckon these are the best strawberries in the country, some say the world. Thereafter, the road swings north, building up a head of steam as it bowls up the **Meiadal** valley bound for the barren mountains beyond. It's here that the road starts to climb in earnest, clambering up towards the bleak and icy plateau-pass marking its high point. At the top, there are the inevitable cafés and souvenir shops, but it's all pretty low-key and a fast-flowing river muffles every untoward sound as it rushes off the plateau to barrel down the mountain below. A five-minute walk leads over to the **Utsikten** (viewing point), from where there's a magnificent panorama over the surrounding mountains and valleys. From here, the sheer audacity of the road becomes apparent, zigzagging across the face of the mountain and somehow managing to wriggle round the tumultuous, 180-metre **Stigfossen Falls**. Clearly visible to the west are some of the region's most famous mountains peaks: Bispen and Kongen (the "Bishop" and the "King") are the nearest two, at 1462m and 1614m respectively. If you're feeling extremely energetic, the pass is one place you can pick up the **Kløvstien**, the original drovers' track over the mountains – abandoned when the road was completed in 1936. It is not, however, an easy route to follow and parts are very steep with chains to assist. Consequently, most hikers prefer to undertake more manageable outings west to nearby peaks and mountain lakes. By contrast, the mountains to the east are part of the **Trollveggen** mountain wall and remain the preserve of climbers. As usual, prospective hikers should come properly equipped and watch for sudden weather changes.

Beyond the hairpins on the north side of the Trollstigen, the road resumes its easy ramblings, scuttling along the Isterdal to meet the E136 just 6km from Åndalsnes.

Åndalsnes

Almost six hours by train from Oslo, **ÅNDALSNES** is, for many travellers, their first – and sometimes only – contact with the fjord country, a distinction it doesn't really warrant. Despite a wonderful setting between lofty peaks and chill waters, the town itself is unexciting: small (with a population of just 3500), modern and industrial, and sleepy at the best of times. That said, Åndalsnes is an excellent place to orientate yourself and everything you're likely to need is near at hand, not least some first-rate accommodation. Åndalsnes also makes an ideal base for further fjord explorations. Within easy reach by ferry, bus and/or car is some wonderful scenery, from the stern peaks that bump away inland through to the fretted fjords that stretch towards the open sea. There's also the matter of **Rødven stave church** (late June to mid-Aug daily 11am–4pm; 30kr), just half an hour's drive away – from Åndalsnes, head east round the Isfjord and after 22km take the signed turning which covers the final 10km. In an idyllic setting amid meadows, by a stream and overlooking a slender arm of the Romsdalsfjord, the church dates from around 1300, though its distinctive wooden supports may have been added in 1712 during the first of several subsequent remodellings. Every inch a country church, the place's creaky interior holds boxed pews, a painted pulpit and a large medieval crucifix, but it's the bucolic setting which most catches the eye.

Practicalities

Buses all stop outside the **train station**, where you'll also find the **tourist office** (mid-June to mid-Aug Mon–Fri 9am–6pm, Sat & Sun 11am–6pm; mid-Aug to mid-June Mon–Fri 8am–3.30pm; ☎71 22 16 22, ⊛www.visitandalsnes.com). Staff here provide bus and train timetables, regional guides and a wide range of local information geared to make you use Åndalsnes as a base. Their free *Dagsturer* (day-trips) booklet gives details of all sorts of motoring excursions, and most of their recommendations include a short hike. They also have details of fishing trips out on the fjord (300kr), local day-long hikes and guided climbs (from 1500kr), not to mention fixed-rate sightseeing expeditions with Rauma Taxi (☎71 22 15 55), who charge, for example, 500kr for a brief scoot down the Trollstigen, or 650kr for the return trip to Rødven church. This is, however, hardly a bargain when you consider the special deals offered by local car hire firms. Åndal Bil (☎71 22 22 55), for instance, charge around 650kr for a 24-hour car rental. The tourist office has all the latest information on local deals. Local **hiking maps** are sold at *Romsdal Libris*, a couple of minutes' walk from the tourist office in the centre of town.

The tourist office has a small supply of en-suite **private rooms** which go for 350–500kr per double per night, with self-catering facilities often provided, though most are a good walk from the town centre. Alternatively, Åndalsnes has a delightful HI ⚲ **hostel** (late May to Aug; ☎71 22 13 82, ☯www.vandrerhjem.no; doubles ②, dorm beds 200kr, both including breakfast), a two-kilometre hike west out of town on the E136. To get there, head up the hill out of the centre, keep straight onto the E136 at the traffic island at the top, go past the turning to Dombås, staying on the E136 in the direction of Ålesund; cross the river and it's signed on the left-hand side. The hostel has a pleasant rural setting and its simple rooms, set in a group of modest wooden buildings, are extremely popular, making reservations pretty much essential. The buffet-style **breakfast**, with its fresh fish, is one of the best hostellers are likely to get in the whole country. Note that the hostel doesn't do evening meals (though there are cooking facilities) and reception is closed from 11am to 4pm. Bikes can also be rented here. The other excellent choice, the *Grand Hotel Bellevue*, Åndalsgata 5 (☎71 22 75 00, ☯www.grandhotel.no; ⑤), occupies a large whitewashed block, with attractive Art Deco touches, on a hillock just up from the train station; it's the second hotel here – its predecessor was bombed to bits in 1940. The rooms on the top floors – four and five – have great views, well worth the extra 100kr or so. Among several local **campsites**, *Åndalsnes Camping og Motell* (☎71 22 16 29, ☯www.andalsnescamp.no) has a fine riverside setting about 3km from the town centre – follow the route to the youth hostel but turn first left immediately after the river. It's a well-equipped site with cabins (③) as well as bikes, boats and canoes available for rent.

For **food**, the *Buona Sera* pizzeria, a brief walk from the station up the hill out of town, serves filling Italian food at reasonable prices, but much better is the evening buffet served at the *Grand Hotel Bellevue* for 200kr from 6pm to 9.45pm; go early to catch the best of the spread.

From Åndalsnes, there are regular **express buses** to Ålesund (3–4 daily; 2hr 25min).

Ålesund

On the coast at the end of the E136, some 120km west of Åndalsnes, the fishing and ferry port of **ÅLESUND** is immediately – and distinctively – different from any other Norwegian town. Neither old clapboard houses nor functional concrete and glass is much in evidence, but instead the centre boasts a proud conglomeration of pastel-painted facades, lavishly decorated and topped off by a forest of towers and turrets. There are dragons and human faces, Neoclassical and mock-Gothic facades, decorative flowers and even a pharaoh or two, the whole ensemble set amid the town's several harbours. These architectural eccentricities sprang from disaster: in 1904, a dreadful fire left 10,000 people homeless and the town centre destroyed, but within three years a hectic reconstruction programme saw almost the entire area rebuilt in a bizarre **Art Nouveau** style, which borrowed heavily from the German Jugendstil movement. Many of the Norwegian architects who undertook the work had been trained in Germany, so the Jugendstil influence is hardly surprising, but this was no simple act of plagiarism: the Norwegians added all sorts of whimsical, often folkloric flourishes to the Ålesund stew. The result was – and remains – an especially engaging stylistic hybrid and Kaiser Wilhelm II, who footed the bill, was mightily pleased.

Arrival and information

From north to south, Ålesund's town centre is about 700m wide. The **bus station** is situated on the southern waterfront and from beside it local ferries depart for points south along the coast; northbound ferries leave from the other side of the harbour, just metres from both the **tourist office**, on Skateflukaia (June–Aug Mon–Fri 8.30am–7pm, Sat 9am–5pm, Sun 11am–5pm; Sept–May Mon–Fri 8.30am–4pm; ☎70 15 76 00, ☯www.visitalesund.com), and the quay for the **Hurtigrute coastal boat** (southbound 12.45am, northbound 3pm – but 9.30am for Geiranger and 6.45pm for Trondheim from mid-April to mid-Sept).

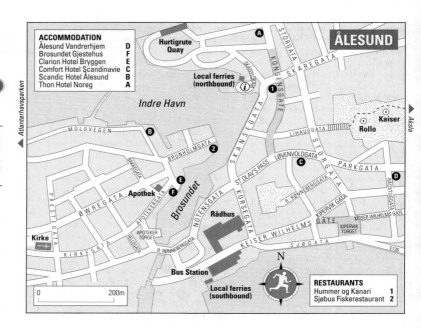

Accommodation

One of Ålesund's real pleasures is the quality of its downtown **hotels**, but the town is equipped with other, less expensive options too, most temptingly a waterfront **guesthouse** and an HI **hostel**.

Ålesund Vandrerhjem Parkgata 14 ☎70 11 58 30 ⊛www.vandrerhjem.no. Small, clean and verging on the cosy HI hostel, right in the thick of things and with Double rooms (②) as well as dorm beds (170kr). May–Sept.

Brosundet Gjestehus Apotekergata 5 ☎70 12 10 00, ⊛www.brosundet.no. Excellent guesthouse, occupying an attractively converted waterside warehouse, with a sauna, washing machines and self-catering facilities, and offering an excellent breakfast (included in the rates) too. ③/④

Clarion Hotel Bryggen Apotekergata 1 ☎70 12 64 00, ⊛www.choicehotels.no. Smart hotel in a carefully modernized old waterside warehouse, with good facilities and well-appointed rooms. ④/⑦

Comfort Hotel Scandinavie Løvenvoldgata 8 ☎70 15 78 00, ⊛www.choicehotels.no. Efficient chain hotel inhabiting a grand old Art Nouveau edifice, unfortunately spoiled by an especially horrid set of automatic front doors. Brisk, uncomplicated bedrooms. ③/④

Scandic Hotel Ålesund Molovegen 6 ☎21 61 45 00, ⊛www.scandic-hotels.com. It may be one of a chain and occupy a modern block, but there's something very appealing about this relaxed and friendly hotel. The rooms are bright and cheerful – but be sure to ask for one with a sea view. ④/⑦

Thon Hotel Noreg Kongensgate 27 ☎70 12 29 38, ⊛www.thonhotels.no. Suffers by comparison with its more atmospheric rivals, but the upper floors of this modern block do offer sea views and the rooms are perfectly adequate. ④/⑥

The town

Pedestrianized **Kongensgate**, the main drag, features several of the town's architectural highlights, as does neighbouring **Apotekergata**, where the old "Apothek" (pharmacy) building, at the corner of Bakkegata, has, with its bay windows and sturdy circular tower, a decidedly neo-baronial appearance. Adjoining Apotekergata is **Kirkegata**, perhaps the most harmonious street of all, its long line of Art Nouveau houses decorated with playful turrets and towers reminiscent of a Ruritanian film set. Up along this street is Ålesund's finest building, its **kirke** (church; June–Aug Tues–Sun 10am–2pm; free), which was completed in 1909 to a decidedly Romanesque style, from the hooped windows through to the roughly dressed stone blocks and the heavy-duty tower. Inside, the high altar is flanked by the most wonderful of **frescoes**, a blaze of colour that fair takes the breath away; it was the work of one Enevold Thømt in the 1920s.

Further architectural intricacies are covered in the free but verbose *On Foot in Ålesund*, available at the tourist office (see p.357), though you'd be much better off signing up for one of their **guided walking tours** (mid-June to mid-Aug 1 daily; early May to early June & late Aug to late Sept Sat only; 1hr 30min; 70kr). The other obvious objective in the town centre is the **park** at the top of Lihauggata, which runs from Kongensgate. It's a surprise to find monkey puzzle and copper beech trees here, as well as a large statue of **Rollo**, a Viking chieftain born and raised in Ålesund, who seized Normandy and became its first duke in 911; he was an ancestor of William the Conqueror. Nearby, there's also a much smaller bust of the town's benefactor, the kaiser, in which – if you're used to images of him as a grizzled older figure in a helmet – he looks disarmingly youthful. From the park, several hundred steps lead to the top of the **Aksla hill**, where the view out along the coast and its islands is fabulous. Otherwise, Ålesund's lively centre, which drapes around its oldest harbour, the **Brosundet**, makes for a pleasant stroll, and you can watch the ferries and Hurtigbåt coming and going to the islands just offshore.

Ålesund also possesses one of those prestige tourist attractions so beloved of development boards and councillors. It's the **Atlanterhavsparken** (Atlantic Sea Park; June–Aug Mon–Fri & Sun 10am–7pm, Sat 10am–4pm; Sept–May daily 11am–4pm; 90kr; ⑩www.atlanterhavsparken.no), a large-scale recreation of the Atlantic marine environment that includes several enormous fish tanks; there's also an outside area with easy footpaths and bathing sites. The Sea-Park is located 3km west of Ålesund on a low-lying headland.

Eating and drinking

For **food**, the 🍴 *Sjøbua Fiskerestaurant*, Brunholmgata 1 (☎70 12 71 00; closed Sun), round the corner from the *Clarion Hotel Bryggen*, serves wonderful seafood in chic surroundings and even has its own lobster tank. It's expensive but very popular, so reservations are advised. Similarly excellent is *Hummer og Kanari*, Kongensgate 19 (☎70 12 80 08), where a house speciality is *klippfisk* (salted and dried cod) cooked every which way.

Travel details

Trains

Åndalsnes to: Dombås (2 daily; 1hr 30min); Oslo (2 daily; 6hr 30min).
Bergen to: Geilo (4–5 daily; 3hr); Myrdal (4–5 daily; 1hr 50min); Oslo (4–5 daily; 6hr 30min); Voss (4–5 daily; 1hr 10min).
Dombås to: Åndalsnes (2 daily; 1hr 30min); Trondheim (3–4 daily; 2hr 30min).
Myrdal to: Flåm (June to late Sept 11–12 daily; Oct–May 2–4 daily; 50min).

Buses

Ålesund to: Bergen (1–2 daily; 10hr); Hellesylt (1–2 daily except Sat; 2hr 40min); Stryn (1–2 daily except Sat; 4hr); Trondheim (1–2 daily; 8hr 10min); Åndalsnes (3–4 daily; 2hr 20min).
Åndalsnes to: Geiranger (mid-June to late Aug 2 daily; 3–4hr); Kristiansand (2 daily; 3hr); Ålesund (3–4 daily; 2hr 20min).
Balestrand to: Oslo (3 daily; 8hr 15min); Sogndal (2 daily; 1hr 10min).

Bergen to: Dombås (1 daily; 12hr); Grotli (1 daily; 8hr); Hellesylt (1–2 daily; 8hr 15min); Kinsarvik (2 daily; 2hr 40min); Loen (3 daily; 6hr 30min); Lofthus (2 daily; 3hr); Norheimsund (3 daily; 2hr); Oslo (1 daily; 11hr); Skei (3 daily; 5hr); Sogndal (3 daily; 4hr 15min); Stavanger (1–5 daily; 5hr 40min); Stryn (3 daily; 6hr 45min); Trondheim (1 daily; 14hr); Utne (2 daily; 2hr 45min); Voss (4 daily; 1hr 45min); Ålesund (1–2 daily; 10hr).
Mundal to: Oslo (3 daily; 7hr 50min).
Geiranger to: Åndalsnes (mid-June to late Aug 2 daily; 3–4hr).
Sogndal to: Balestrand (2 daily; 1hr 10min); Bergen (3 daily; 4hr 15min); Mundal (3 daily; 35min); Oslo (3 daily; 7hr); Stryn (1–2 daily; 4hr 30min); Voss (3 daily; 3hr).
Stryn to: Bergen (2 daily; 7hr); Hellesylt (1–2 daily; 1hr); Oslo (1 daily; 8hr 30min); Trondheim (1 daily; 8hr).
Ulvik to: Voss (2–4 daily; 1hr).
Voss to: Bergen (4 daily;1hr 45min); Norheimsund (3 daily; 2hr); Sogndal (2 daily; 3hr); Ulvik (2–4 daily; 1hr).

Boats

A plethora of boats shuttles between the settlements dotting the western fjords. There are two main types of service, **car ferries** and **Hurtigbåt express passenger boats**. They are supplemented by the **Hurtigrute coastal boat**.

Principal car ferries

Balestrand to: Mundal, Fjærland (late May to early Sept 2 daily; 1hr 25min).
Bruravik to: Brimnes (1–2 hourly; 10min).
Dragsvik to: Hella (every 30min; 15min); Vangsnes (hourly; 25min).
Fodnes to: Manheller (every 30min; 15min).
Geiranger to: Hellesylt (May–Sept 4–8 daily; 1hr).
Hella to: Dragsvik (every 30min; 15min); Vangsnes (hourly; 15min).
Utne to: Kinsarvik (2 hourly; 25min).

Hurtigbåt

Bergen to: Balestrand (1–2 daily; 4hr); Sogndal (1–2 daily; 5hr).
Bergen to: Kinsarvik (1–3 daily; 2hr 20min); Lofthus (1–3 daily; 2hr 35min); Utne (1–3 daily; 1hr 50min).

Hurtigrute

Mid-April to mid-Sept:
Northbound departures: daily from Bergen at 8pm; Ålesund at 9.30pm & 6.45pm; Trondheim at noon.
Southbound departures: daily from Trondheim at 10am; Ålesund at 12.45am; arrives Bergen, where the service terminates, at 2.30pm.
Mid-Sept to mid-April:
Northbound departures: daily from Bergen at 10.30pm; Ålesund at 3pm & Trondheim at noon.
Southbound departures: daily from Trondheim at 10am; Ålesund at 12.45am; arrives Bergen, where the service terminates, at 2.30pm.

2.4

Trondheim to the Lofoten

M arking the transition from the rural south to the blustery north is the 900-kilometre-long stretch of Norway that extends from Trondheim to the island-studded coast near Narvik. Easily the biggest town hereabouts is **Trondheim**, a charming place of character and vitality, which boasts an imposing cathedral – the finest medieval building in the country. Trondheim is also the capital of the **Trøndelag** province, whose sweeping valleys are – by Norwegian standards at least – very fertile, and it is, to boot, readily accessible from Oslo by train. But travel on one of the express trains that thunder further north, and you begin to feel far removed from the more intimate south. Distances between places grow ever greater, the travelling becomes more of a slog, and as Trøndelag gives way to the province of **Nordland** the scenery becomes ever wilder and more forbidding – "Arthurian", thought Evelyn Waugh.

The **E6** thrashes north from Trondheim over the hills and down the dales, but with the exception of the rugged landscape there's not much to detain you until you reach **Mo-i-Rana**, an industrial town that has partly – and successfully – rejigged and reinvented itself to attract the passing tourist. Just north of Mo-i-Rana on the E6, you cross the **Arctic Circle** – one of the principal targets for many travellers – at a point where the cruel and barren scenery seems strikingly appropriate. The circle marks the southernmost point at which the sun does not sink below the horizon in summer, or rise above it in winter – the Midnight Sun and the Polar Night. Here, they occur on one day each every year – at the summer and winter solstices – but the further north you go, the longer the phenomena last.

Beyond the Arctic Circle, the mountains of the interior lead down to a fretted, craggy coastline where even the towns, the largest of which is the port of **Bodø**, have a feral quality about them. The iron-ore port of **Narvik**, in the far north of Nordland, has perhaps the wildest setting of them all, and was the scene of some of the fiercest fighting between the Allied and Axis forces in World War II. To the west lies the offshore archipelago that makes up the **Vesterålen and Lofoten islands**. In the north of the Vesterålen, between **Harstad** and **Andenes**, the coastline of this island chain is mauled by massive fjords, whereas to the south, the Lofoten are backboned by a mighty and ravishingly beautiful mountain wall – a highlight of any itinerary. Among a handful of idyllic fishing villages the pick is the economically named **Å**, though **Henningsvær** and **Stamsund** come a very close second.

Transport is good, which is just as well given the isolated nature of much of the region. The **Hurtigrute coastal boat** stops at all the major settlements on its route up the Norwegian coast from Bergen to Kirkenes, while the islands are accessed by a variety of **ferries** and **Hurtigbåt passenger express boats**. The **E6** – sometimes known as the "Arctic Highway" – is the major road north from Trondheim; it's kept in excellent condition, though caravans can make the going very slow. The **train** network reaches as far north as Fauske and nearby Bodø, from either of which **buses** make the trip on to Narvik, itself the terminal of a separate rail line that runs the few kilometres to the border and then south through Sweden. The only real problem is likely to be **time**. It's a day or two's journey from Trondheim to Fauske, another to Narvik, and without time to spare you should think twice before venturing further: the travelling can be arduous, and in any case it's pointless if done at a hectic pace.

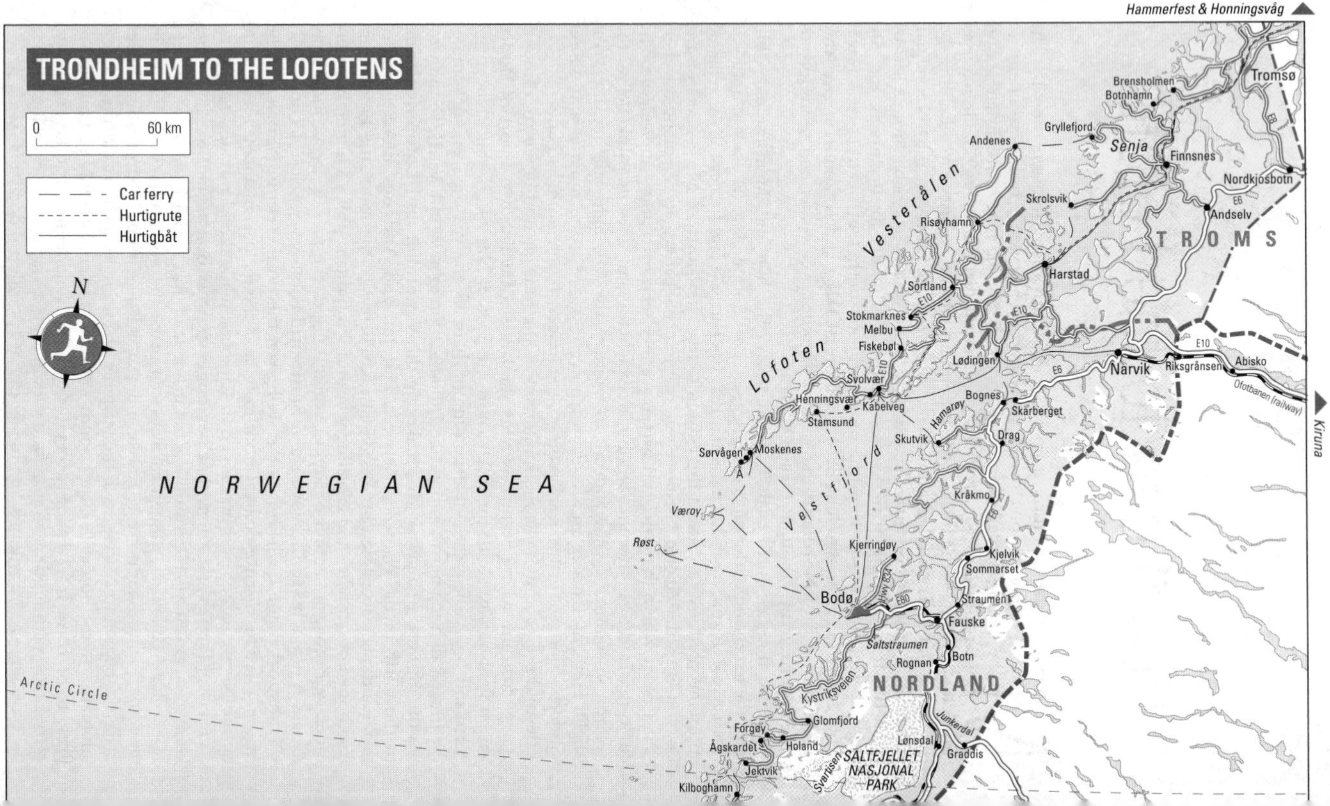

TRONDHEIM TO THE LOFOTENS
0 60 km
Car ferry
Hurtigrute
Hurtigbåt
N
Hammerfest & Honningsvåg
Kiruna
NORWEGIAN SEA
Arctic Circle
TROMS
NORDLAND
SALTFJELLET NASJONAL PARK
Vesterålen
Lofoten
Vestfjord
Senja
Tromsø
Brensholmen
Botnhamn
Gryllefjord
Finnsnes
Nordkjosbotn
Andselv
Skrolsvik
Andenes
Risøyhamn
Harstad
Sortland
Stokmarknes
Melbu
Fiskebøl
Lødingen
Narvik
Riksgrånsen
Abisko
Ofotbanen (railway)
Svolvær
Henningsvær
Kabelvåg
Stamsund
Bognes
Skarberget
Hamarøy
Skutvik
Drag
Sørvågen
Moskenes
Å
Værøy
Røst
Kråkmo
Kjelvik
Sommarset
Kjerringøy
Bodø
Straumen
Fauske
Saltstraumen
Botn
Rognan
Kystriksveien
Glomfjord
Forgøy
Ågskardet
Holand
Jektvik
Kilboghamn
Svartisen
Lønsdal
Junkerdal
Graddis
E6
E8
E10
E80
Hwy 834

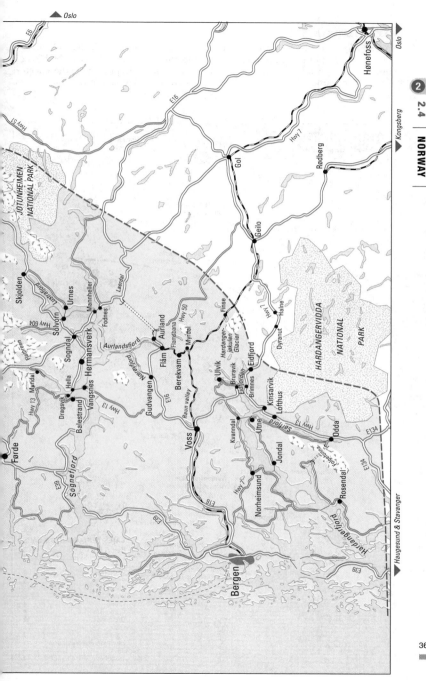

Trondheim

An atmospheric city with much of its antique centre still intact, **TRONDHEIM** was known until the sixteenth century as Nidaros ("mouth of the river Nid"), its importance as a military and economic power base underpinned by the excellence of its harbour and its position at the head of a wide and fertile valley. The

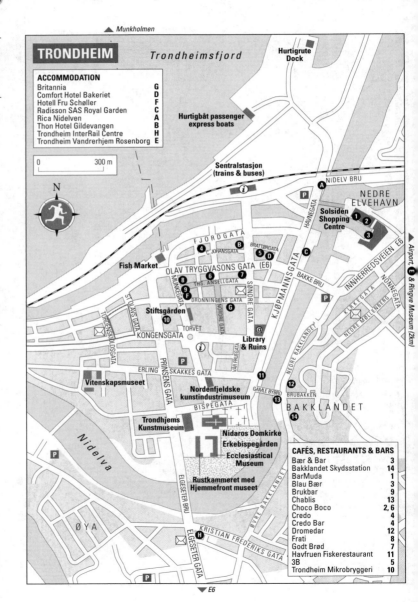

▲ Munkholmen

TRONDHEIM

Trondheimsfjord

Hurtigrute Dock

ACCOMMODATION

Britannia	G
Comfort Hotel Bakeriet	D
Hotell Fru Schøller	F
Radisson SAS Royal Garden	C
Rica Nidelven	A
Thon Hotel Gildevangen	B
Trondheim InterRail Centre	H
Trondheim Vandrerhjem Rosenborg	E

0   300 m

N

Hurtigbåt passenger express boats

Sentralstasjon (trains & buses)

NIDELV BRU

A NEDRE ELVEHAVN

HAVNEGATA

Solsiden Shopping Centre 1 2 3

INNHERREDSVEIEN E6

KIRKEGATA

NEDRE MØLLENBERG

NONNEGATA

► Airport, E & Ringve Museum (2km)

FJORDGATA

C. JOHANSGATA **B**

BRATTØRGATA 5 **D**

4

C

Fish Market

OLAV TRYGGVASONS GATA (E6)

8 THS. ANGELLGATA 7

9 6

F DRONNINGENS GATA

SØNDRE GATA

BAKKE BRU

KJØPMANNSGATA

P

Stiftsgården 10

NORDRE GATA

G

TORVET

KONGENSGATA

@ **Library & Ruins**

NEDRE BAKKLANDET

ST. OLAVS GATA

TORDENSKIOLDSGATA

i

ERLING SKAKKES GATA

P

PRINSENS GATA

VÅR FRUEGATA

11

GAMLE BYBRO

12 BRUBAKKEN

13

BAKKLANDET

Vitenskapsmuseet

Nordenfjeldske kunstindustrimuseum

BISPEGATA

14

Trondhjems Kunstmuseum

Nidaros Domkirke

Erkebispegården

Ecclesiastical Museum

N i d e l v a

P

Rustkammeret med Hjemmefront museet

ØYA

ELGESETER BRU

ØVRE BAKKLANDET

P

KRISTIAN FREDERIKS GATA

H

ELGESETER GATA

P

▼ E6

CAFÉS, RESTAURANTS & BARS

Bær & Bar	3
Bakklandet Skydsstation	14
BarMuda	1
Blau Bær	3
Brukbar	9
Chablis	13
Choco Boco	2, 6
Credo	4
Credo Bar	4
Dromedar	12
Frati	8
Godt Brød	7
Havfruen Fiskerestaurant	11
3B	5
Trondheim Mikrobryggeri	10

early Norse parliament, or *Ting*, met here, and the cathedral was a major pilgrimage centre at the end of a route stretching all the way back to Oslo. After a fire destroyed much of the city in 1681, Caspar de Cicignon, a military engineer from Luxembourg, rebuilt Trondheim on a gridiron plan, with broad avenues radiating from the centre to act as firebreaks. Cicignon's layout has survived intact, giving the city centre an airy, elegant air, though most of the buildings date from the commercial boom of the late nineteenth century. With timber warehouses lining the river and doughty stone structures dotting the main streets, the centre is a suitably dignified and prosperous setting for the cathedral, one of Scandinavia's finest medieval structures.

Trondheim is now Norway's third city, but the pace is slow and easy and the main sights are best appreciated in leisurely fashion over a couple of days. Genial and eminently likeable, Trondheim is also a pleasant place to wave goodbye to city life if you're heading for the wilds of the north.

Arrival, information and city transport

Trondheim is on the E6 highway, seven or eight hours' drive (500km) from Oslo. It's a major stop for the **Hurtigrute coastal boat** (⊛ www.hurtigruten.com), which docks at the harbour north of the centre, from where it's a dull fifteen-minute walk to **Sentralstasjon**, the gleaming bus and train terminal, where there's an **information kiosk** (☎177) dealing with all transport enquiries. A taxi from the Hurtigrute quay to the city centre is 60kr. The all-year **Kystekspressen passenger express boat** from Kristiansund docks at the Hurtigbåt dock, which is also behind Sentralstasjon. From Sentralstasjon, you simply cross the bridge to reach the triangular island that holds all of central Trondheim.

If you're **driving**, a toll of 35kr is levied in either direction on the E6 near Trondheim, and there's another municipal toll of 15kr (Mon–Fri 6am–6pm) as you approach the city itself. **Parking** can be a pain. On-street parking during restricted periods (mostly Mon–Fri 8am–8pm, Sat 7am–7pm) is expensive and hard to find, so it's best to head for a car park: try the handy Torvet P-hus, in the centre at Erling Skakkes gate 16, or the marginally cheaper (and slightly less convenient) Bakke P-hus, east across the bridge from the centre at Nedre Bakklandet 60. Rates are around 15kr an hour. At other times, on-street parking is free and spaces are easy to find.

Trondheim **airport** is 35km northeast of the city at Værnes. From here, Flybussen buses (Mon–Fri 4.30am–9pm every 15min, Sat 5am–5.10pm every 30min, Sun 6.45am–9.25pm every 15–30min; 65kr) run to Sentralstasjon and points in the city centre, including the *Radisson SAS Royal Garden* hotel; journey time is about 45 minutes.

Information

The **tourist office**, Munkegata 19, sits right in the centre of town on the corner of the main square, Torvet (mid-May to early June & late Aug Mon–Fri 8.30am–6pm, Sat & Sun 10am–4pm; mid- to late June & mid-Aug Mon–Fri 8.30am–8pm, Sat & Sun 10am–6pm; early Aug Mon–Fri 8.30am–10pm, Sat & Sun 10am–8pm; Sept to mid-May Mon–Fri 9am–4pm, Sat 10am–2pm; ☎73 80 76 60, ⊛www.trondheim .com). Staff provide the free and very useful *Trondheim Guide* (also available from the information racks at Sentralstasjon) and a wide range of other free tourist literature, including a cycle map of the city and its surroundings; they also have a limited supply of private rooms (see p.366). You can also buy hiking maps of the surrounding area.

City transport

The best way of exploring the city centre is **on foot** – it only takes about ten minutes to walk from one end to the other. For longer excursions, **mountain bikes** can be rented from Ila Sykkelsenter, Steinberget 1 (☎73 51 09 40), at about

170kr a day. Otherwise, transport in town is by **buses** and **trams** with flat-fare tickets, from the driver, costing 22kr. If you need to travel outside town, to one of the outlying museums or the campsite, it might be worth buying the unlimited 24-hour public transport ticket, the *dagskort*, which costs 55kr from bus drivers and is valid on all local buses and trams.

Accommodation

Accommodation is plentiful in Trondheim, with a choice of private rooms, two hostels and a selection of reasonably priced hotels and guesthouses (*pensjonater*). What's more, most of the more appealing places are dotted round the city centre, though the private rooms booked via the tourist office are usually on the outskirts. These **private rooms** are good value, however, at a fixed rate of 400–450kr per double per night (250–340kr single), plus a 20kr booking fee and a 30kr deposit.

Hotels

Britannia Dronningens gate 5 ☏73 80 08 00, ⓦwww.britannia.no. Right in the middle of town, this long-established hotel has a magnificent Art Nouveau breakfast room, complete with a Moorish fountain, Egyptian-style murals and Corinthian columns. The comfortable rooms are heavily discounted in summer. ➎/➏

Comfort Hotel Bakeriet Brattørgata 2 ☏73 99 10 00, ⓦwww.choicehotels.com. Competent chain hotel in a pleasantly modernized former bakery. Central location. ➍/➎

Hotell Fru Schøller Dronningens gate 26 ☏73 87 08 00, ⓦwww.scholler.no. Spick and span hotel in a central location above a café, with just 25 rooms. Modern furnishings and fittings. ➌/➍

🏃 **Radisson SAS Royal Garden** Kjøpmanns-gata 73 ☏73 80 30 00, ⓦwww .radissonsas.com. Stylish modern hotel with sweeping architectural lines and wonderfully comfortable beds. Good summer deals make this more affordable than you might expect. Banquet-like breakfasts, too. Highly recommended. ➍/➏

Rica Nidelven Hotell Havnegata 1–3 ☏73 56 80 00, ⓦwww.rica.no. Shiny, spacious new hotel pushing out over the river, with lots of glass to maximize the views. Smooth service and stylish touches, but ultimately a bit soulless. ➍/➏

Thon Hotel Gildevangen Søndre gate 22B ☏73 87 01 30, ⓦwww.thonhotels.no. In a sturdy Romanesque Revival stone building, a couple of minutes' walk northeast of Torvet, this chain hotel offers eighty or so comfortable, modern rooms with a touch of style. ➌/➍

Hostels

Trondheim InterRail Centre Elgeseter gate 1 ☏73 89 95 38, ⓦwww.tirc.no. In the unusual, big, red and round building – the Studentersamfundet (university student centre) – just over the bridge at the south end of Prinsens gate, a five-minute walk from the cathedral. Offers basic mixed dormitory bed-and-breakfast accommodation at 135kr per person per night; there's an inexpensive café, too. Mid-June to mid-Aug.

Trondheim Vandrerhjem Rosenborg Weidemannsvei 41 ☏73 87 44 50, ⓦwww .trondheim-vandrerhjem.no. Mostly parcelled up into four-bed dorm rooms (dorms 210kr) and with some doubles (➋), this large and well-equipped HI hostel looks more like a hospital than somewhere you'd want to stay from the outside, but the interior is pleasant enough – especially the comfortable, newer rooms. There are self-catering facilities, a laundry and a canteen. A twenty-minute, 2km hike east from the centre: cross the Bakke bru onto busy Innherredsveien (the E6) and walk uphill; turn right onto Wessels gate and it's on the left at the fourth crossroads. To save your legs, take any bus up Innherredsveien and ask the driver to let you off as close as possible. Open all year.

The City

The historic centre of Trondheim sits on a small triangle of land bordered by the River Nidelva, with the curve of the long and slender Trondheimsfjord beyond. **Torvet** is the main city square, a spacious open area anchored by a statue of St Olav perched on a tall stone pillar like some medieval Nelson. The broad avenues that radiate out from here were once flanked by long rows of wooden buildings, which served all the needs of the small town and administrative centre. Most of these older structures are long gone, replaced for the most part by uninspiring modern constructions, though one notable survivor is the **Stiftsgården**, a fine timber

△ Nidaros Domkirke, Trondheim

mansion erected in the late eighteenth century. Nevertheless, this is small beer compared with the **Nidaros Domkirke** (cathedral), an imposing, largely medieval structure that is the city's architectural high point. The cathedral dominates the southern part of the centre and close by are the much-restored **Erkebispegården** (Archbishop's Palace) and the pick of Trondheim's several museums, the **Nordenfjeldske Kunstindustrimuseum** (Museum of Decorative Arts) and the **Trondheim Kunstmuseum** (City Art Gallery). Near here too, on the far side of the **Gamle Bybro** – the old town bridge – is a clutter of old warehouses and timber dwellings that comprises the prettiest and most fashionable part of town, **Bakklandet**, home to its best restaurants and bars.

Nidaros Domkirke

The goal of Trondheim's pilgrims in times past was the colossal **Nidaros Domkirke** at the south end of Munkegata (May to mid-June & mid-Aug to mid-Sept Mon–Fri 9am–3pm, Sat 9am–2pm, Sun 1–4pm; mid-June to mid-Aug Mon–Fri 9am–6pm, Sat 9am–2pm, Sun 1–4pm; mid-Sept to April Mon–Fri noon–2.30pm, Sat 11.30am–2pm, Sun 1–3pm; 40kr, includes entry to Erkebispegården coronation museum). Scandinavia's largest medieval building, it has been gloriously restored following several fires and the upheavals of the Reformation, it remains the focal point of any visit to the city and is best explored in the early morning, when it's reasonably free of tour groups. The building, still known by Trondheim's former name, is dedicated to King – later Saint – Olav. Born in 995, **Olav Haraldsson** followed the traditional life of the Viking chieftain from the tender age of 12, "rousing the steel-storm" as the saga writers put it from Finland to Ireland. He also served as a mercenary to both the duke of Normandy and King Ethelred of England, and it was during this time that he was converted to Christianity. In 1015 he invaded Norway, defeated his enemies and became king, though his zealous imposition of Christianity alienated many of his followers and the bribes of Olav's rival Knut (Canute), King of England and Denmark, did the rest: Olav's retainers deserted him and he was forced into exile in 1028. Two years later, he was back in the Trøndelag, but the army he had raised was far too weak to defeat his enemies, and Olav was killed in battle near Trondheim.

Olav may have lost his kingdom, but the nationwide church he founded had no intention of losing ground. Needing a local **saint** to consolidate its position, the church carefully nurtured the myth of Olav, a beatification assisted by the oppressive rule of the "foreigner" Knut. After the final battle, Olav's body had been spirited away and buried on the banks of the River Nid at what is today Trondheim. There were rumours of miracles in the vicinity of the grave and, when the bishop arrived to investigate these strange goings-on, he exhumed the body and found it, lo and behold, perfectly uncorrupted. Olav was declared a saint, his body was placed in a silver casket and Olav Kyrre, who became King of Norway in 1066, started work on the grand church that was to house the remains in appropriate style. Over the years the church was altered and enlarged to accommodate the growing bands of medieval tourists; it achieved cathedral status in 1152 and subsequently became the traditional burial place of Norwegian royalty.

The cathedral is a magnificent blue- and green-grey soapstone edifice, with a copper-green spire and roof and a fancy set of gargoyles on the choir. It's also a true amalgam of architectural styles. The original eleventh-century church was a simple basilica, but subsequent alterations enlarged it considerably. The Romanesque transepts, with their heavy hooped windows and dog-tooth decoration, were built by English stonemasons from Lincoln in the twelfth century, while the early Gothic choir, with its flying buttresses and intricate tracery, is clearly influenced by contemporaneous churches in England. The nave was built in the early thirteenth century, also in the early Gothic style, but was destroyed by fire in 1719; the present structure is a painstakingly accurate late nineteenth-century replica.

Inside, the gloomy half-light hides much of the lofty decorative work, but it is possible to examine the striking **choir screen**, whose wooden figures are the work of Gustav Vigeland. The other item of particular interest is a famous fourteenth-century **altar frontal** (the front panel of an altar painting) displayed in a chapel off the ambulatory, directly behind the high altar. This is the earliest surviving representation of Olav's life and times, created during a period when few Norwegians could read or write and the saint's cult had to be promoted visually.

What you won't see, however, is St Olav's silver casket-coffin, which was taken to Denmark and melted down for coinage in 1537; but you can see the **Norwegian crown jewels** in the new coronation museum next to the Archbishop's palace. The lavish display of crowns, orbs, sceptres and the anointing horn is a permanent fixture, as coronations were abolished in 1908.

Two other features are the English-language **guided tours** of the cathedral (mid-June to mid-Aug at 11am, 1.30pm, 3pm & 4pm; 30min), and the climb up the cathedral **tower** (every half-hour late June to late Aug Mon–Fri 10am–5pm, Sat 10am–12.30pm, Sun 1–3.30pm). From the top, there's a fine view of the city and the forested hills that surround it, with the fjord trailing away in one direction, the river valley in the other.

Archbishop's Palace

Behind the Domkirke lies the heavily restored **Erkebispegården** (Archbishop's Palace). This courtyard complex was originally built in the twelfth century for the third archbishop, Øystein, but two stone-and-brick wings are all that survive of the original quadrangle – the others were added later. After the archbishops were kicked out during the Reformation, the palace became the residence of the Danish governors. It was subsequently used as the city armoury, and many of the old weapons are now displayed in the **Rustkammeret med Hjemmefrontmuseet** (Army and Resistance Museum; March–May & Sept–Oct Sat & Sun 11am–4pm; June–Aug Mon–Fri 9am–3pm, Sat & Sun 11am–4pm; free), which occupies the west wing. The first floor gives the broad details of Norway's involvement with the interminable Dano-Swedish wars that wracked Scandinavia from the fifteenth to the nineteenth century. Of more general interest, the second floor describes the German invasion and occupation of Norway during World War II, dealing honestly with the sensitive issue of collaboration. There are also some intriguing displays on the daring antics of the Norwegian Resistance, notably in an extraordinary – perhaps hair-brained – attempt to sink the battleship *Tirpitz* as it lay moored in an inlet of the Trondheimsfjord in 1942. This escapade, like so many others, involved **Leif Larsen**, the Resistance hero who is commemorated by a statue on the Torget in Bergen. Larsen worked closely with the Royal Navy, who organized covert operations in occupied Norway from their base in the Shetlands. Supplies and personnel were transported across the North Sea by Norwegian fishing boats – a lifeline known, in that classically understated British (and Norwegian) way, as the "Shetland bus".

Moving on, the **south wing** now holds a smart ecclesiastical **museum** (May to mid-June & mid-Aug to mid-Sept Mon–Fri 9am–3pm, Sat 9am–2pm; mid-June to mid-Aug Mon–Fri 9am–5pm, Sat 9am–2pm, Sun 1–4pm; mid-Sept to April Mon–Sat 11am–3pm Sun noon–4pm; 40kr or free with cathedral ticket), which is largely devoted to a few dozen medieval statues originally retrieved and put away for safekeeping during the nineteenth-century reconstruction of the nave and west facade. Many of the statues are too battered and bruised to be engaging, but they are well displayed and several are finely carved. In particular, look out for a life-size sculpture of poor old **St Denis**, his head in his hands (literally) in accordance with the legend that, after he was beheaded, he irritated his executioners no end by carrying his head to his grave. Downstairs, an assortment of finds unearthed during a lengthy 1990s archeological investigation of the palace demonstrates the economic power of the archbishops: they employed all manner of skilled artisans – from glaziers and shoemakers to rope-makers, armourers and silversmiths – and even minted their own coinage.

From the back of the Archbishop's Palace, you can stroll out onto the grassy lawns beside the **River Nidelva**. A trio of rusting bastions offers a reminder of the military defences that once protected this side of town, while footpaths snake round to the sturdy old tombs and wild flowers of the **graveyard**, just to the east of the cathedral's main entrance.

The Museum of Decorative Arts and City Art Museum

A couple of museums close to the Domkirke provide some varied entertainment, in particular the delightful **Nordenfjeldske Kunstindustrimuseum** (Museum of Decorative Arts; June to late Aug Mon–Sat 10am–5pm, Sun noon–5pm; late Aug to May Tues–Wed & Fri–Sat 10am–3pm, Thurs 10am–5pm, Sun noon–4pm; 50kr; ⍵www.nkim.museum.no), at Munkegata 5. The museum's collection is too extensive to be shown in its entirety at any one time, so displays are rotated regularly, and there's also an ambitious programme of temporary exhibitions focusing on contemporary arts, craft and design. Start in the basement, where bourgeois life in Trøndelag from the sixteenth century to 1900 is illustrated via an eclectic assemblage of furniture, faïence, glassware and silver, along with some twentieth-century pieces, notably a fine selection of **Art Nouveau** ceramics and furniture. The domestic theme is developed on the ground floor, where there's a room kitted out by the Belgian designer and architect Henri van de Velde. An unusual display of folkloric tapestries produced in Trondheim in the early years of the twentieth century is also usually displayed on this floor – they're modelled on original paintings by the Norwegian Gerhard Munthe, one of whose specialities was the portrayal of medieval folk tales. More modern works can be found on the first floor, but the highlight here is the room devoted to fourteen stunning tapestries by **Hannah Ryggen**, each done in a naive style with flair and vigour.

The **Trondhjems Kunstmuseum** (City Art Museum; June–Aug daily 10am–5pm; Sept–May Tues–Sun 11am–4pm; 40kr), near the cathedral at Bispegata 7B, is quite small, but features an enjoyable selection of works by Johan Dahl and Thomas Fearnley, the leading figures of nineteenth-century Norwegian landscape painting, as well as the romantic canvases of Hans Gude and his chum Adolph Tidemand.

Also displayed is the first overtly political work by a Norwegian artist: *Streik* (*The Strike*), was painted in 1877 by the radical Theodor Kittelsen, better known for his illustrations of the folk tales collected by Jorgen Møe and Pieter Asbjørnsen. The bad news is that the museum's substantial collection of works by Edvard Munch has been permanently removed from display amid fears of the dreaded Munch thieves, who, in broad daylight, stole a copy of *The Scream* from Oslo's Munch Museum in 2004.

From the Stiftsgården to Bakklandet

One conspicuous remnant of old timber-town Trondheim survives in the city centre – the **Stiftsgården** (June to late Aug Mon–Sat 10am–5pm, Sun noon–5pm; guided tours every hour on the hour till 1hr before closing: 50kr), which stretches out along Munkegata just north of Torvet. Built in 1774–78, this good-looking yellow creation is claimed to be the largest wooden building in northern Europe. These days it serves as an official royal residence – a marked social improvement on its original function as home to the provincial governor. Inside, a long series of period rooms with fanciful Italianate wall-paintings and furniture comes in a range of late eighteenth- to early nineteenth-century styles, from rococo to Biedermeier, that reflect the genteel tastes of the early occupants. The anecdotal guided tour brings a smile – but not perhaps 50kr wide.

From the Stiftsgården, it's a couple of minutes' walk east to the **medieval church ruins** discovered under the library at the far end of Kongens gate. A twelfth-century relic of the days when Trondheim had fifteen or more religious buildings, it is thought to have been a chapel dedicated to St Olav, although the evidence for this is a bit shaky. Excavations revealed nearly 500 bodies in the immediate area, which was once the church graveyard, and the skeletons on display are neatly preserved under glass. Entry is free and the site is accessible during library opening hours (July to mid-Aug Mon, Tues, Thurs & Fri 9am–4pm, Wed 9am–7pm, Sat 10am–3pm; mid-Aug to June Mon–Thurs 9am–7pm, Fri 9am–4pm, Sat 10am–3pm; plus Sept–April Sun noon–4pm).

Following the river south from the library, it's a short walk to the **Gamle Bybro** (Old Town Bridge), an elegant wooden reach with splendid views over the early eighteenth-century gabled and timbered warehouses which flank Kjøpmannsgata. Most of these are now restaurants and offices, and there are more restaurants and several groovy bars at the far end of the bridge in the brightly painted old timber houses of the **Bakklandet** area, Trondheim's own "Left Bank".

Out from the centre: the Ringve museum

The **Ringve Museum** (mid-May to June & Aug to mid-Sept daily 11am–3pm; July daily 11am–5pm; mid-Sept to mid-May Sun 11am–4pm; 70kr; ℗ www.ringve.com) occupies a delightful eighteenth-century country house and courtyard complex on the hilly Lade peninsula, some 4km northeast of the city centre. Devoted to musical history and to musical instruments from all over the world, the museum is divided into two sections. In the main building, the collection focuses on **antique European instruments** in period settings, with several demonstrations included in a lengthy – and obligatory – guided tour. The second section, in the old barn, contains an **international selection of musical instruments** and offers a self-guided zip through some of the key moments and movements of **musical history**. There are themes like "the invention of the piano" and "pop and rock", not to mention the real humdinger, "the marching band movement in Norway". Immaculately maintained, the surrounding **botanical gardens** (daily; free) make the most of the scenic setting. To get there, take bus #3 or #4 to Lade from Munkegata.

Eating and drinking

As befits Norway's third city, Trondheim has a healthy selection of first-rate **restaurants**, but although they offer a variety of cuisines, the Norwegian places almost always have the gastronomic edge. In the particular, there's a cluster of excellent places in the **Bakklandet** district, by the east end of the Gamle Bybro; this area also holds a string of laid-back and fashionable **café–bars**, where the food is usually very good and much less expensive than in the restaurants. There's another cluster of very recommendable café–bars and **bars** – Trondheim boasts a hectic weekend scene – in the **Brattørgata** district, in the centre near the west end of Bakke bru, and yet more of both in **Nedre Elvehavn**, an imaginatively revamped old industrial area on the water's edge near the east end of Bakke bru, and the location of the whopping Solsiden shopping centre. Note that we've included phone numbers only for places where you need to book a table. As for **opening hours**, some restaurants open for a couple of hours at lunch times and then in the evening, but many just stick to the evenings and some are closed one day a week. Café–bars and bars almost invariably stay open from 11am or noon till the early hours of the morning – or at least until there's no-one left. Note that we've included phone numbers only for places where you'll need to book a table.

Finally – if needs must – the city's mobile **fast-food** stalls are concentrated around Sentralstasjon and along Kongens gate, on either side of Torvet.

Cafés

Choco Boco Olav Tryggvassons gate 29, and TMVKaia 3. Of this mini-chain's several locations, the pick is the TMVKaia branch in Nedre Elvehavn, with plenty of indoor and outdoor seating, plus entertainingly arty decor. Serves coffee, cakes and light meals – salads, sandwiches and so forth. Patchy service, but still a good place to hang out.

Dromedar Nedre Bakklandet 3A. A few metres north of the Gamle Bybro, this modern café-bar offers a laid-back atmosphere and the best coffee in the city. There's also snacks and light meals – filled bagels, sandwiches and the like – plus tasty salads.

Godt Brød Thomas Ansellgata 16. The aroma of baking bread, rolls and pastries, all organic, wafts around as you enjoy the coffee and sample the baked goods at this specialist bakery.

Restaurants

Bakklandet Skydsstation Øvre Bakklandet 33. Friendly, intimate old coaching inn with a warren of homely dining rooms and a small courtyard. The reasonably priced menu features home-cooked staples, including the renowned bacalao (Portuguese salt-cod stew) and a super cheesecake. Main courses around 110kr.

Blau Bær Innherredsveien 16. The excellent value stone-baked pizzas and *blau bær* (blueberry) tart at this relaxed dockside place affirm its status as one of Trondheim's best options for a leisurely evening of grazing and people-watching. Pizzas from 80kr.

Chablis Øvre Bakklandet 62 ☎73 87 42 50. Just metres from the Gamle Bybro, this polished brasserie-restaurant with its modish furnishings and fittings serves up excellent food: Norwegian but with a Mediterranean slant. A floating pontoon

river terrace makes a lovely spot for a meal in summer. Moderate prices, with main courses from around 90kr.

Credo Ørjaveita 4 ☎73 53 03 88. Smart and very popular Mediterranean/Spanish influenced place, with delicious daily specials at very competitive prices (80kr).

Frati Munkegata 25. Favoured by locals, the Italian food here is plentiful and authentic – it should be, as the same Italian family have run it for years and it's always deservedly busy. Main courses from 120kr.

Havfruen Fiskerestaurant Kjøpmanns- gata 7 ☎73 87 40 70. This excellent fish restaurant near the cathedral is one of the best in town, with prices to match: main courses from 200kr. Try to book well in advance. Closed Sun.

Bars

Bær & Bar Innherredseien 16. The pick of the bars in this buzzy dockside area; sister bar of *Blau Bær* (see above), it shares much the same philosophy – quality sounds and quality cocktails for a discerning unpretentious crowd.

BarMuda TMV-Kaia 11, Nedre Elvehavn. Relaxed cocktail bar with comfortable couches and an arty, punk-meets-New-Age clientele.

Brukbar Munkegata 26. Interesting, colourful bar catering for just about everyone – from business folk dropping in for an after-work snifter through to hardcore student boozers. Note the peculiar bee-shaped wall-lamps.

Credo Bar Ørjaveita 4. Modish first-floor bar above the *Credo* restaurant (see above).

3B Brattørgata 3B ☎73 51 15 50. Rock'n'roll/indie club-cum-bar for drinking well into the wee hours.

Trondheim Mikrobryggeri Prinsens gate 39. Mainstream bar serving its own microbrewery ales. Filling pub food too, and a friendly atmosphere.

Listings

Car rental Avis, Kjøpmannsgata 34 ☎73 84 17 90; Budget, Elgeseter gate 21 ☎73 94 10 25; and at the *Radisson SAS Royal Garden Hotel*, Kjøpmannsgata 73 ☎73 52 69 20; Europcar, Trondheim airport ☎74 82 67 00.

Consulates UK, Beddingen 8 ☎73 60 02 00; Poland, TMV-Kaia 23 ☎73 87 69 00.

Emergencies Ambulance ☎113; Fire ☎110; Police ☎112.

Hiking Trondhjems Turistforening, just west of the centre at Sandgata 30 (☎73 92 42 00, ⊛www .tt.no), is the DNT's local branch, offering advice on the region's hiking trails and huts. Guided walks and cross-country skiing trips, with activities concentrated in the mountains to the south and east of the city, are also available, from one-day excursions to longer expeditions that suit different levels of skill and fitness.

Internet access Free Internet access at the library, Peter Egges plass 1 (☎72 54 75 00;

July to mid-Aug Mon, Tues, Thurs & Fri 9am–4pm, Wed 9am–7pm, Sat 10am–3pm; mid-Aug to June Mon–Thurs 9am–7pm, Fri 9am–4pm, Sat 10am–3pm; plus Sept–April Sun noon–4pm).

Pharmacy The main late- and weekend-opening pharmacy is St Olav Vakt-apotek, Solsiden, Beddingen 4 (☎73 88 37 37). Also Løveapoteket Byhaven, Olav Tryggvasons gate 28 (☎73 83 32 83).

Police station Kongens gate 87 ☎73 89 90 90.

Post office Main office, with poste restante, at Dronningens gate 10 (Mon–Fri 8am–5pm, Sat 9am–2pm).

Taxis Eight ranks in and around the city centre including those at Torvet, Sentralstasjon, Søndre gate and the *Radisson SAS Royal Garden Hotel*, or call Trønder Taxi ☎07373.

Vinmonopolet There's a city-centre branch at Kjøpmannsgata 32.

North from Trondheim to Fauske

North of Trondheim, it's a long haul up the coast to the next major places of interest: Bodø (see p.376), the main ferry port for the Lofoten, and the gritty but likeable town of Narvik (see p.380), respectively 720km and 910km distant. The easiest way to make the bulk of the trip is by **train**, a rattling good journey with the scenery becoming wilder and bleaker the further north you go – and you'll usually get a blast from the whistle as you cross the **Arctic Circle** thrown in. The train takes nine hours to reach **Fauske**, where the line reaches its northern limit and turns west for the last 65-kilometre dash to Bodø. Fauske has little of interest other than its **bus** connections north to Narvik, a further five-hour drive, but many travellers take an overnight break here – though in fact nearby Bodø is a far more pleasant place.

If you're **driving**, you'll find the E6 – which runs all the way from Trondheim to Narvik and points north – too slow to make more than three or four hundred kilometres comfortably in any one day – more, and the journey becomes a tiresome thrash. Fortunately, there are several pleasant places to stop, beginning with Trøndelag's **Snåsa**, a relaxing village beside the E6 with somewhere good to stay. Further on, in Nordland, the next region up, lies **Mo-i-Rana**, once a grimy steel town, but now attractively rehashed and the obvious starting point for a visit to the **Svartisen glacier**, which crowns the coastal peaks close by.

The only alternative to the E6 is the coastal Highway 17, the **Kystriksveien**, an ingenious and extremely scenic cobbling together of road, tunnel, bridge and ferry that negotiates the shredded coastline from **Steinkjer**, just north of Trondheim, all the way up to Bodø, a distance of nigh on 700km. Join the Kystriksveien just west of Mo-i-Rana for the best of the scenery.

Hell to Snåsa

Leaving Trondheim, the **E6** tunnels and twists its way round the Trondheimsfjord to **Hell**, a busy rail junction where one line forks north to slice through the dales and hills of Trøndelag en route to Fauske, while the other heads east for the seventy-kilometre haul to the Swedish frontier, with Östersund (see p.623) beckoning beyond. Just beyond Hell, the road forks too, with the E6 thumping north and the

E14 zipping east. Hell itself has nothing to recommend it, except its name, though even this is a bit of a let-down when you realise that *hell* in Norwegian means good fortune: don't despair, the locals still sell postcards of the train station's freight depot tagged "Hell – gods ekspedisjon" ("have a good journey"). Pressing on along the E6, it's about 160km to **SNÅSA**, a sleepy, scattered hamlet, whose farms roll over the gentle, lightly wooded countryside. It looks as if nothing much has happened here for decades, yet there is one sight of note, a pretty little hilltop **church** of softly hued grey stone, dating from the Middle Ages and very much in the English style. On the west side of the village – 6km from the E6 – is the *Snåsa Hotell* (⊕74 15 10 57, ⊛www.snasahotell.no; ❹/❸), where the decor may be somewhat dated, but the bedrooms are comfortable and it boasts a lovely setting overlooking the lake; it's a peaceful spot, ideal if you want to rest after a long drive. The hotel also operates a small **campsite** (same numbers; all year) with cabins (❷) as well as spaces for tents and caravans. There's a restaurant here too, serving mundane but filling Norwegian staples, but note that if you're likely to arrive hungry and late (after 7pm), you should telephone ahead to check it will still be open.

Mo-i-Rana and around

Beyond Snåsa, the E6 leaves the wooded valleys of the Trøndelag for the wider, harsher landscapes of **Nordland**. The road bobs across bleak plateaux, scuttles along rangy river valleys and eventually – after 300km – reaches **MO-I-RANA**, or "Mo", which hugs the head of the Ranafjord. A minor port and market town until World War II, the construction of a large steel plant transformed Mo in the postwar period. The plant dominated proceedings until the 1980s, when there was some economic diversification and the town began to clean itself up. The fjord shore was cleared of its industrial clutter and the E6 was rerouted to create the pleasantly spacious and surprisingly leafy town centre of today. Most of Mo is resolutely modern, but look out for the pretty **Mo kirke**, a good-looking structure of 1832 with a pitched roof and onion dome, perched on a hill on the eastern edge of the town centre. Otherwise, Mo is first and foremost a handy base for visiting the east side of the Svartisen glacier (see p.375) and/or exploring the region's lakes, fjords and mountains, though it does possess a couple of minor surprises: it's home to the main archives of the **Nationalbiblioteket** (National Library), and its waterfront sports an Antony Gormley sculpture, the contemplative **Havmannen** (*Man of the Sea*) who stands in the shallows gazing down the fjord.

Practicalities

Mo's **bus** and **train stations** are close together, down by the fjord on Ole Tobias Olsens gate. The compact town centre lies east of this street, with the foot of the main pedestrianized drag, Jernbanegata, opposite the bus station. The **tourist office** is about 300m to the south of the bus and train stations, also on Ole Tobias Olsens gate (mid-Aug to mid-June Mon–Fri 9am–4pm; mid-June to mid-Aug Mon–Fri 9am–8pm, Sat 9am–4pm, Sun 1–7pm; ⊕75 13 92 00, ⊛www.arctic-circle.no). Staff have the usual local leaflets, provide free town maps and issue the free booklet that details the Kystriksveien (the Highway 17 Coastal Route; see box on p.374). Bus timetables are available, too, but local services are much too patchy to allow you to explore the town's environs without your own transport. In this regard, there's **car rental** – at around 750kr a day – from Avis, located at the Hydro Texaco Røssvoll gas station (⊕75 14 81 57). If that looks too expensive, note that the tourist office is usually able to arrange a shared taxi ride to the most popular local attraction, the Svartisen glacier – there are no buses – and while you're here be sure to check that the boats that give access to the glacier are running.

The best of the town's several **hotels** is the *Meyergården*, at the north end of Ole Tobias Olsens gate (⊕75 13 40 00, ⊛www.meyergarden.no; ❹/❸), with smooth service and an excellent restaurant. Most of the building is modern, but the original lodge has survived and is maintained in period style, with stuffed animal heads on the wall and elegant panelled doorways. Much less expensive – and much plainer – is the tour group favourite *Fjordgården Hotell Mo i Rana*, down by the waterfront at Søndregate 9 (☎75 15 28 00, ⓦwww.fjordgarden.no; open May–Aug; ❸). Also, tucked into a back street at Elias Blix's gate 5, is the *Mo Gjestegaard* (☎75 15 22 11, ⓦwww.mo-gjestegaard.no; ❸/❷), which is a little heavy on the pine finishings, but peaceful and pleasant nonetheless. A fourth and final option, is *City Camping* (☎75 15 28 11; mid-May to mid-Sept), a pretty riverside site, a ten-minute walk east of the centre, with cabins (❷) as well as tent pitches.

For **food**, first choice must be the *Meyergården Hotell*, where the restaurant serves an excellent range of Norwegian dishes featuring local ingredients; main courses average around 150kr. There's also the *China Kro*, in the centre of town at Nordahl Griegs gate 9 (☎ 75 15 15 93), where the Chinese food is surprisingly good, even if the surroundings are a little drab; main courses are around 100kr. Alternatively, the *Abelone mat & vinstue*, Ole Tobias Olsens gate 6, does competent pizzas and steaks, whilst *Babettes*, in the centre at Ranheimgata 2, is good for light meals and coffee.

The Svartisen glacier

Norway's second largest glacier, **Svartisen** – literally "Black Ice" – covers roughly 370 square kilometres of mountain and valley between the E6 and the coast. It's actually divided into two sections – east and west – by the Vesterdal valley, though this cleft is a recent phenomenon: when it was surveyed in 1905, the glacier was one giant block, about 25 percent bigger than it is today; the reasons for this change are obscure. The highest parts of the glacier lie at around 1500m, but its tentacles

---

The Kystriksveien Coastal Route on Highway 17

Branching off the E6 just beyond Steinkjer, the tortuous **Kystriksveien** – the coastal route along Highway 17 – threads its way up the west coast, linking many villages that could formerly only be reached by sea. This is an obscure and remote corner of the country, but apart from the lovely scenery there's little of special appeal, and the seven ferry trips that interrupt the 688-kilometre drive north to Bodø (there are no buses) make it both expensive and time-consuming in equal measure. A free **booklet** describing the Coastal Route can be obtained at tourist offices throughout the region – including Mo – and it contains all of Highway 17's car-ferry timetables. You can also get information online at ⓦwww.rv17.no.

Conveniently, the stretch of Highway 17 between **Mo-i-Rana** and **Bodø** takes in (most of) the scenic highlights, can be negotiated in a day and saves a packet on ferry fares to boot. To sample this part of the route, drive 37km west from Mo along the E12 to the Highway 17 crossroads, from where it's some 60km north to the **Kilboghamn–Jektvik** ferry (4–9 daily; 1hr; driver and car 127kr) and a further 30km to the ferry linking **Ågskardet** with **Forgøy** (7–9 daily; 10min; driver and car 49kr). On the first ferry you cross the Arctic Circle with great views of the beautiful **Melfjorden**, and on the second, after arriving at Forgøy, you get a chance to see a westerly arm of the **Svartisen** glacier (see box on p.374), viewed across the slender Holandsfjorden. For an even closer look at the glacier, stop at the information centre in **HOLAND**, 12km beyond Forgøy, and catch the **passenger boat** (June to early Sept Mon–Fri 8am–9pm, Sat–Sun 10.30am–5.30pm; every 45min to 1hr 30min; 15min; 60kr return; ☎94 86 55 16), which zips across the fjord to meet a connecting bus; this travels the couple of kilometres up to the Svartisen Turistsenter (June to Mid-Aug daily 10am–5pm; ☎75 75 00 11, ⓦwww.svartisen.no), merely 250m from the ice. The Turistsenter has a café, rents cabins (❷) and is the base for four-hour guided **glacier walks** (mid-June to mid-Aug only; prior booking is essential). For more on glacier walks see p.381. From Holand, it's 140km to the Saltstraumen (see p.379) and then 30km more to Bodø (see p.370).

reach down to about 170m – the lowest-lying glacial arms in mainland Europe. Mo is within easy reach of one of the glacier's eastern nodules: to get there, drive north from town on the E6 for about 12km and then take the signed turning to the glacier, a straightforward 23-kilometre trip ending beside the ice-green, glacial lake **Svartisvatnet**. Here, **boats** (early June & late Aug 11am & 1pm, mid-June to mid-Aug hourly 10am–4pm; 20min each way; 90kr return) shuttle across the lake, but note that services can't begin until the ice has melted – usually by late June, so check with Mo tourist office before you set out. Viewed from the boat, the great convoluted folds of the glacier look rather like bluish-white custard, but close up, after a stiff three-hour hike past the rocky detritus left by the retreating ice, the sheer size of the glacier becomes apparent: a mighty grinding and groaning wall of ice edged by a jumble of ice chunks, columns and boulders.

The west side of the Svartisen can be seen and visited via the coastal highway, the Kystriksveien (see box on p.374).

The Arctic Circle

Given its appeal as a travellers' totem, and considering the amount of effort it takes to actually get here, crossing the **Arctic Circle**, about 80km north of Mo, is a bit of a disappointment. Uninhabited for the most part, the landscape is undeniably bleak, but the gleaming **Polarsirkelsenteret** (Arctic Circle Centre; daily: May to early June & Aug 9am–8pm; late June to July 8am–10pm; early Sept 10am–6pm; free; ⓦwww.polarsirkelsenteret.no) only serves to disfigure the scene: it's a giant lampshade of a building plonked by the roadside and stuffed with every sort of tourist bauble imaginable. You'll whizz by on the bus, the train toots its whistle as it passes by, and drivers can, of course, shoot past too – though the temptation to brave the crowds is strong and, even if you resist the Arctic exhibition, you'll probably get snared by either the "Polarsirkelen" certificate, or the specially stamped postcards. Outside the centre, a couple of simple stone memorials are poignant reminders of crueller times: they pay tribute to the Yugoslav and Soviet POWs who laboured under terrible conditions to build the Arctic railroad (Nordlandsbanen) to Narvik for the Germans in World War II.

Fauske

But for a brief stretch of line from Narvik into Sweden further north, **FAUSKE** marks the northernmost point of the Norwegian rail network and is, consequently, an important transport hub. Along with Bodø, the town is a departure point of the **Nord-Norgeekspressen**, the express bus service that carries passengers to Narvik and Tromsø, where you change – and stay overnight – before embarking on the next leg of the journey up to Alta (for Honningsvåg and Nordkapp). The bus leaves twice daily from beside Fauske train station, and tickets can be purchased from the driver or at any bus station. There are left-luggage lockers at train station, and you can pick up information on the region's ferries there too from a leaflet-stuffed rack. Note that there is a fifty percent discount for InterRail and Scanrail pass holders on the route to Narvik (see p.380), a gorgeous five-hour run past fjords, peaks and snow. Most northbound **train travellers** spend the night in Fauske rather than making a quick change onto the connecting bus to Narvik or travelling on by train to Bodø, just forty minutes away to the west and a much more palatable place to stay.

From Fauske's **train station**, it's a five- to ten-minute walk down the hill and left at the T-junction to the local bus station, and a few metres more to the main drag, **Storgata**, which doubles as the E6. Storgata runs parallel to the fjord and holds the handful of shops that pass for the town centre. There's no tourist office, and there's no strong reason to linger here except in so far as Fauske is a handy accommodation stopover point. Storgata holds the better of the two **hotels**, the *Fauske Hotell*, Storgata 82 (ⓣ75 60 20 00, ⓦwww.rica.no; ❹/❸), a chunky square block whose interior is made slightly sickly by a surfeit of salmon-coloured streaky marble.

Quarried locally, the marble is exported all over the world, but is something of an acquired taste. Marble apart, the hotel rooms are comfortable enough, and the big, tasty breakfast is a real snip at 80kr. The most popular budget choice is the hostel-like *Seljestua*, just 500m from the train station at Seljeveien 2 (☎90 73 46 96; late June to mid-Aug; ❷), but much, much better is the *Lundhøgda* **campsite** (☎75 64 39 66, ✉lundhogda@c2i.net; May–Sept). This occupies a splendid location about 3km west of the town centre, overlooking the mountains and the fjord: head out of town along the E80 (the Bodø road), turn off down a signposted country lane, ablaze with wild flowers in the summertime and flanked by old timber buildings. The campsite takes caravans, has spaces for tents and also offers cabins (❷).

Bodø and around

Readily reached by train or bus from Fauske, **BODØ**, 63km west of Fauske along the E80, is the terminus of the Trondheim train. Founded in 1816, the town struggled to survive in its early years, but was saved from insignificance by the herring boom of the 1860s. It later accrued several industrial plants and became an important regional centre, but was then heavily bombed during World War II, and nowadays there's precious little left of the proud nineteenth-century buildings that once flanked the waterfront. Nonetheless, Bodø manages a cheerful modernity, a bright and breezy place within comfortable striking distance of the old trading post of **Kjerringøy**, one of Nordland's most delightful spots. Bodø is also a regular stop on the Hurtigrute coastal boat route and, importantly, much the best place from which to hop over to the most interesting parts of the Lofoten Islands.

Arrival and information

Bodø's **train station** is at the eastern end of the town centre, just off the long main street, Sjøgata. The southern **Lofoten ferry** (to and from Moskenes plus the islets of Værøy and Røst) and the **Hurtigrute coastal boat** use the docks (respectively) 500m and 700m northeast along the waterfront from the train station. The **bus station** is 700m west along Sjøgata from the train station, across from the gigantic *Radisson SAS Hotel Bodø*. Adjoining the bus station is the dock handling **Hurtig-båt passenger express boat** services for the Lofoten, most usefully to and from Svolvær.

The **tourist office** (June–Aug Mon–Fri 9am–8pm, Sat 10am–6pm, Sun noon–8pm; Sept–May Mon–Wed & Fri 9am–4pm, Thurs 9am–6pm, Sat 10am–3pm; ☎75 54 80 00, ✆www.bodoe.com) shares the Hurtigbåt and bus station terminal building at Sjøgata 3; information on connections to the Lofoten Islands is available, as is an excellent town and district guide (free) and bike rental.

Accommodation

Bodø has a reasonable supply of **accommodation**, including half a dozen hotels, a hostel and a couple of guesthouses. In addition, the tourist office has a small supply of **private rooms** in the town and its environs, with a fixed tariff of 400–500kr per double, plus a modest booking fee. Finally, the town's **campsite**, *Bodøsjøen Camping*, Bodøsjøen (☎75 56 36 80, ☎75 56 36 89), has a pleasant lakeside setting about 3.5km to the southeast of the centre, not far from the Bodin kirke. It has tent pitches, caravan hook-ups and cabins (❷).

Bodø Gjestegård Storgata 88–90 ☎75 52 04 02, ✉johansst@online.no. Bargain accommodation in this pleasant twenty-room guesthouse not far from the railway station. ❷

Bodø Hotell Professor Schyttes gate 5 ☎75 54 77 00, ✆www.bodohotell.no. Reasonably priced, mid-sized, mid-range hotel in a five-storey block

right in the centre of town. Well-kept rooms with the usual mod cons, plus oodles of pine in the Scandinavian style. ❸/❹

Bodø Vandrerhjem Storgata 88–90 ☎75 52 04 02, ✉bodo.hostel@vandrerhjem.no This HI hostel occupies a modest, modern building with sunny balconies and a garden. It shares its reception with

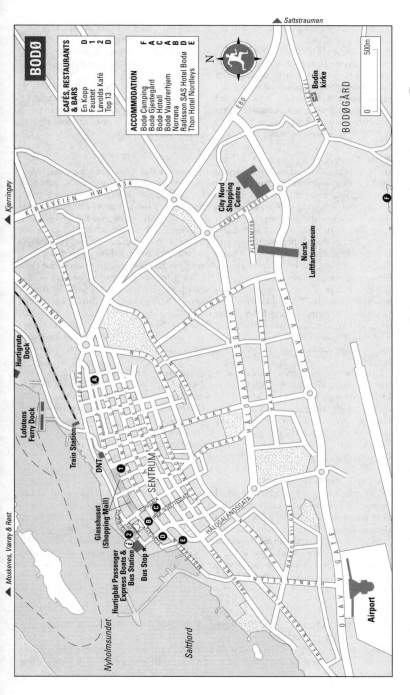

BODØ

CAFÉS, RESTAURANTS & BARS

En Kopp	D
Faustet	1
Løvolds Kafé	2
Top 13	D

ACCOMMODATION

Bodø Camping	F
Bodø Gjestegård	A
Bodø Hotell	C
Bodø Vaudrerhjem	A
Norrøna	B
Radisson SAS Hotel Bodø	D
Thon Hotel Nordleys	E

▲ Saltstraumen

N

0   500m

BODØGÅRD

Bodin kirke

E80

GAMLE RIKSVEI

City Nord Shopping Centre

GAMLE RIKSVEI

PLASSMYRA

Norsk Luftfartsmuseum

▲ Kjerringøy

KIRKEVEIEN   HWY   834

RØNVIKVEIEN

BANKGATA

OLAV V GATE

HÅLOGALANDSGATA

HAAKON VII GATE

Hurtigrute Dock

Lofotens Ferry Dock

Train Station

DNT

A

Glasshuset (Shopping Mall)

Hurtigbåt Passenger Express Boats & Bus Station

Bus Stop

1

B C

D

E

SENTRUM

TORVGATA

Nyholmsundet

▲ Moskenes, Værøy & Røst

Saltfjord

Airport

OLAV V GATE

HAAKON VII GATE

the Bodø Gjestegård (see below). Doubles (**②**) as well as dorm beds (150kr).
Norrøna Storgata 4B ☎ 75 52 55 50, ⊛ www .radissonsas.com. Standard-issue hotel in a large modern block just metres from the bus station; it's run by the neighbouring *Radisson* as an overflow, so guests enjoy all of its facilities. At the lower end of the market, but still reliably comfortable. **②/③**
Radisson SAS Hotel Bodø Storgata 2 ☎ 75 52 41 00, ⊛ www.radissonsas.com. The best hotel in town. Occupies an overly large, modern concrete and glass tower block, but has commodious and well-appointed rooms – and those on the upper floors have great views out to sea. **④/⑥**
Thon Hotel Nordleys Moloveien 14 ☎ 75 53 19 00, ⊛ www.thonhotels.no. The newest hotel in Bodø, this suave establishment is right on the harbourfront, and most of the rooms have some kind of sea view. **④/⑤**

The Town

Bodø rambles over a low-lying, tapering peninsula that pokes out into the Saltfjord, its long and narrow **centre** marked by two parallel main streets, Sjøgata and Storgata. The town is short of specific sights, but on the outskirts, on Olav V gate, there is the imaginative **Norsk Luftfartsmuseum** (Norwegian Aviation Museum; mid-June to mid-Aug Sun–Fri 10am–7pm, Sat 10am–5pm; mid-Aug to mid-June Mon–Fri 10am–4pm, Sat & Sun 11am–5pm; 90kr; ⊛ www.aviation-museum .com), which tracks through the general history of Norwegian aviation. It's housed in a building shaped like a two-bladed propeller: one blade houses air force and defence exhibits, the other concerns itself with civilian displays. The hub of the two blades straddles the outer ring road – Olav V's gate – and is topped by part of the old Bodø airport control tower. Among the planes to look out for are a Spitfire, a reminder that two RAF squadrons were manned by Norwegians during World War II, a rare Norwegian-made Hønningstad C-5 Polar seaplane and an American U2 spy plane – the US air force made regular use of Bodø throughout the Cold War. The museum is situated about 2km southeast of the centre, a dreary walk that you can avoid by catching one of several city buses – details from the bus station or the tourist office.

From the museum, it's a short drive east along the ring road to the Gamle Riksvei roundabout, where you turn right for the detour south to the onion-domed **Bodin kirke** (late June to mid-Aug Mon–Fri 10am–3pm; free), a pretty little stone church sitting snugly among clovery meadows. Dating from the thirteenth century, the church was modified after the Reformation by the addition of a tower and the widening of its windows; dark, gloomy churches were then associated with Catholic "superstition". It is, however, the colourful seventeenth-century fixtures that catch the eye, plus the lovingly carved Baroque altarboard and pulpit.

Eating and drinking

Bodø is hardly a gourmet's paradise, but there are one or two very competent **cafés** and **restaurants**, kicking off with the traditional and inexpensive Norwegian menu of *Løvolds Kafé* (closed Sun), down by the quay at Tollbugata 9; main courses here feature local ingredients and average around 120kr, daily specials 100kr. Alternatively, the first-rate *Faustet*, Storgata 11, specializes in uncomplicated, excellent fish dishes which are a real treat considering their low prices – and the homemade chocolate ice cream is worth the visit alone; main courses are around 110kr. In addition, the *Radisson SAS Hotel* chimes in with both the *En Kopp* coffee bar, which makes the best coffee in town, and the **bar** with the best view, the swish *Top 13*.

Out from Bodø: Kjerringøy, Saltstraumen and the Svartisen glacier

There are three obvious excursions from Bodø: one northeast to the old trading station at **Kjerringøy**, another southeast to the tidal phenomenon known as the **Saltstraumen**, and a third south to the **Svartisen glacier**. The first two can be done by public transport, but are much easier with your own vehicle, while Bodø tourist office coordinate bus and ferry day-trips to Svartsen from June to August, every day except Saturdays. Excursions take twelve hours, departing Bodø bus station at 7.45am and arriving at the glacier at 11.30am; the cost is 425kr, but this doesn't include food. Be sure to have warm clothing. The glacier and the Saltstraumen can also be reached by car or bike on Highway 17 – the Kystriksveien – between Bodø and Mo-i-Rana (see p.374).

Kjerringøy

The **Kjerringøy trading post** (late May to mid-Aug daily 10am–5pm; 45kr; ⓦwww.saltenmuseum.no), just 40km north along the coast from Bodø by road and ferry, boasts a superbly preserved collection of nineteenth-century timber buildings set beside a slender, islet-sheltered channel. This was once the domain of the Zahl family, merchant suppliers of everything from manufactured goods, clothes and farmyard foodstuffs to the fishermen of Lofoten. It was not, however, an equal relationship: the Zahls, who operated a local monopoly until the 1910s, could dictate the price they paid for the fish, and many of the islanders were permanently indebted to them. This social division is still very much in evidence at the trading post, where there's a marked distinction between the guestrooms of the main house and the fishermens' bunkbeds in the boat- and cookhouses. Indeed, the family house is remarkably fastidious, with its Italianate busts and embroidered curtains – even the medicine cabinet is well-stocked with formidable Victorian remedies like the bottle of "Sicilian Hair Renewer". There are enjoyable, hour-long **guided tours** around the main house throughout the summer (late May to mid-Aug daily, every hour on the hour; 25kr) and afterwards you can nose around the reconstructed general store, drop in at the café and stroll the fine sandy beach.

Getting here by car is easy enough – a straightforward coastal drive along Highway 834 with the added treat of a ferry ride (Festvåg to Misten, every half-hour or hour, less frequently on Sun; 10min; passengers 20kr return, car and driver day return 49kr; ☎94 89 42 88). **By bus** (1–2 Mon–Fri & Sun; 78kr return including ferry), things are a tad more complicated, but a day-return trip beginning at Bodø bus station is possible Monday through Friday, but only in July and August – pick up a combined bus-and-ferry schedule from Bodø tourist office. There's **accommodation** in Kjerringøy in the old parsonage, *Kjerringøy prestegård*, about 1km north of the trading post along the main road (☎75 51 07 80, ⓔkirkevergen@kirken.bodo.no). There are simple double rooms in the main building (❶) and slightly more pleasant ones in the renovated cowshed next door (❷).

Saltstraumen

Less interesting, but more widely publicized, is the maelstrom known as the **Saltstraumen**, 33km southeast of Bodø round the bay on Hwy 17. Billions of gallons of water are forced through this narrow, 150m-wide channel four times daily, making a headlong rush between inner and outer fjord. The creamy water is at its most turbulent at high tide, and its most violent when the moon is new or full – a timetable is available from Bodø tourist office. However, although scores of tourists troop here for every high tide, you can't help but feel they wish they were somewhere else – the scenery is, in Norwegian terms at least, flat and dull, and the view from the bridge which spans the channel unexciting. There's a local **bus** service from Bodø to the Saltstraumen (Mon–Sat 5–7 daily, Sun 1 daily; 1hr), but the times rarely coincide with high tides, which means you'll end up hanging around. To pass the time you might drop by the **Saltstraumen Opplevelsessenter** (Saltstraumen Experience Centre; May–Aug daily 11am–6pm; Sept Sat & Sun 11am–6pm; 60kr), housed in two adjoining buildings near the east end of the bridge. The centre tells you all you'd ever wanted to know about tidal currents and also has several pools where you can take a close look at local fish, seals and tidepool life.

North to Narvik

The 240-kilometre journey north from Fauske to Narvik is spectacular, with the **E6** rounding the fjords, twisting and tunnelling through the mountains and rushing over high, pine-studded plateaux. This stretch of the highway presents two opportunities to catch a **car ferry** to the Lofoten – one at Skutvik, the other at Bognes. The more southerly of the two is **Skutvik**, 37km to the west of the E6, with ferries to Svolvær. At **Bognes**, where the E6 is interrupted by the Tysfjord, there's a choice of ferries. One sails to Lødingen and the E10 on the Lofoten, while a second hops over to **Skarberget** for the E6 and, after a further 80km, Narvik. Long-distance **buses** link Bodø, Fauske and Narvik twice daily.

Narvik

NARVIK, six hours from Fauske by bus along the E6, is a relatively modern town established less than a century ago to handle the iron ore brought by train from northern Sweden. It makes no bones about its main function: the **iron ore docks** are immediately conspicuous, slap bang in the centre of town and totally overwhelming the whole waterfront. Yet, for all the mess, the industrial complex is strangely impressive, its cat's cradle of walkways, conveyor belts, cranes and funnels oddly beguiling and giving the town a frontier, very Arctic feel. Not content with its iron, Narvik has also had a fair old stab at re-inventing itself as a **sports** centre with the emphasis on the extreme, becoming a popular destination for skiers, paragliders and scuba divers – and developing a good range of guesthouses to match.

Arrival and information

Fifteen minutes' walk from one end to the other, Narvik's sloping centre straggles along the main street, **Kongens gate**, which doubles as the E6. The **train station** is at the north end of the town, and from here it's a five- to ten-minute walk along

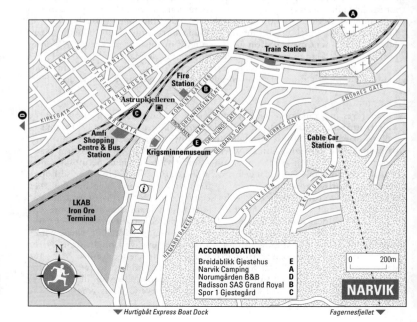

ACCOMMODATION

Breidablikk Gjestehus	E
Narvik Camping	A
Norumgården B&B	D
Radisson SAS Grand Royal	B
Spor 1 Gjestegård	C

0   200m

NARVIK

▼ Hurtigbåt Express Boat Dock   Fagernesfjellet ▼

Kongens gate to the **bus station**, in the basement of the Amfi shopping centre on the west side of the street. A few metres further along Kongens gate on the main square, the **tourist office** (early June Mon–Fri 9am–5pm, Sat & Sun 11am–5pm; mid-June to mid-Aug Mon–Fri 9am–5pm, Sat 10am–5pm, Sun 11am–5pm; late Aug Mon–Fri 9am–5pm, Sat 10am–3pm; Sept–May Mon–Fri 8.30am–3.30pm; ℡76 94 33 09, ⊛www.narvikinfo.no) has a full range of bus and ferry timetables, and can provide lots of information on outdoor pursuits; staff will also assist with ferry and activity reservations. Amongst many outdoor options, there's **mountain climbing** and guided **glacier walking** with Nord-Norsk Klatreskole (℡76 95 13 53), who also rent out the appropriate tackle, and **scuba diving** amidst the wreck-studded local waters with Narvik Dykk & Eventyr (℡99 51 22 05); they rent out equipment too, and provide diving tuition. From the tourist office, it's another five-minute walk down along Kongens gate to the south end of the town centre and the dock for the **Hurtigbåt passenger express boat** service to Svolvær on the Lofoten.

Accommodation

Narvik is a tad short of **hotels**, but it does have several very recommendable **guesthouses** and a reasonably convenient **campsite**, *Narvik Camping*, about 2km north of the centre on the E6 at Rombaksveien 75 (℡76 94 58 10, ⊛www .narvikcamping.com), It's open all year and has tent and caravan pitches, hook-ups and cabins (❶).

Breidablikk Gjestehus Tore Hunds gate 41 ℡76 94 14 18, ⊛www.breidablikk.no. Pleasant, unassuming guesthouse with homely, neat and trim en-suite rooms. Those on the upper floors have attractive views over town, and a good, hearty breakfast is included in the rates. It's located at the top of the steps at the end of Kinobakken, a side road leading east off Kongens gate, just up from the main town square. ❷

Norumgården B&B Framnesveien 127 ℡76 94 48 57, ⊛norumgaarden.narviknett.no. Lavish B&B in a fancy 1920s timber villa. The Germans used the place as an officers' mess during the war, and today, tastefully restored, it holds three large guest rooms, two of which have kitchenettes. Antiques

are liberally distributed and breakfast is included in the (surprisingly low) room rate. ❸

Radisson SAS Grand Royal Kongens gate 64 ℡76 97 77 00, ⊛www.radissonsas.com. Some of Narvik's hotels have seen better days, but the *Grand*, just up from the tourist office, puts on a good show of wood-panelled elegance and has perfectly adequate rooms. ❹/❺

Spor 1 Gjestegård Brugata 2A ℡76 94 60 20, ⊛www.spor1.no. Set in a creatively recycled railway building just below the main town bridge, this trim guesthouse is the pick of the budget/backpacker options, with clean and comfortable double rooms in brisk, modern style; quads and a larger dorm room are also available. Kitchen facilities, a sauna and a bar on site. ❷

The town

Narvik's first modern settlers were the labourers who built the railway line to the mines in Kiruna, over the border in Sweden – a herculean task commemorated every March by a week of singing, dancing and drinking, when the locals dress up in nineteenth-century costume. The town grew steadily up to World War II, when it was demolished during fierce fighting for control of the harbour and iron ore supplies. Rebuilt, the town centre is, perhaps inevitably, rather lacking in appeal, with modern concrete buildings replacing the wooden houses that went before. Nevertheless, try to devote an hour or so to the **Nordland Røde Kors Krigsminnemuseum** (Red Cross War Memorial Museum; May Mon–Sat 10am–4pm; June to late Aug Mon–Sat 10am–9pm, Sun noon–6pm; 50kr), just along from the tourist office. Run by the Red Cross, the museum documents the wartime German saturation bombing of the town, and the bitter and bloody sea and air battles in which hundreds of foreign servicemen died alongside a swathe of the local population. In total, the fight for Narvik lasted two months, a complicated campaign beginning with the German invasion of April 1940, followed by an

Moving on from Narvik

There's a choice of several routes on from Narvik. By **bus**, the Nord-Norgeekspressen (North Norway Express bus; 1–3 daily) makes the four-hour hop north to Tromsø (see p.403), where you change (and stay overnight) before embarking on the next leg of the journey up to Alta (see p.409). There's also a bus direct from Narvik to Alta (Mon–Fri & Sun 1 daily; 9hr 30min). Both trips give sight of some wonderfully wild and diverse scenery, from craggy mountains and blue-black fjords to gentle, forested valleys, though it's not perhaps quite as scenic a journey as the E6 from Fauske to Narvik. A third bus service, the Narvik-Lofoten Ekspressen (1–2 daily; 6hr 40min), runs west from Narvik to Sortland, Stokmarknes and eventually Svolvær in the Lofoten Islands (see p.387). On all these buses, plus the bus trip south from Narvik to either Fauske (for connecting trains to Trondheim) or Bodø, rail-pass holders get a fifty percent discount. Narvik's **Hurtigbåt passenger express boat** service to Svolvær operates all year (Mon–Fri & Sun 1 daily; 3hr 30min; 310kr one-way). Again, rail-pass holders get a fifty percent discount.

One of the real treats of a visit to Narvik is the **train ride** into the mountains that edge the town and spread east across the Swedish border. Called the **Ofotbanen**, the rail line passes through some wonderful scenery, slipping between hostile peaks before reaching the barren, loch-studded plateau beyond. Operated by a private company, Tågkompaniet (℡0046/690 69 10 17; ✆www.tagkompaniet.se), trains leave Narvik two or three times daily and take fifty minutes to reach the Swedish border settlement of **Riksgrånsen** (see p.640), a hiking outdoor sports centre on the plateau; the fare is 80kr each way. You can either nose around here before returning by train to Narvik or travel east on to Kiruna and, ultimately, Stockholm; the ride to Stockholm takes around eighteen hours.

allied counterattack spearheaded by the Royal Navy. The Allies actually recaptured Narvik, driving the Germans into the mountains, but were hurriedly evacuated when Hitler launched the invasion of France. The story is movingly related by the museum, which then tracks through the German occupation of Norway until liberation in 1945.

There are also guided tours (mid-June to mid-Aug daily 3pm; 50kr) of the LKAB mining company's **ore-terminal complex**, interesting if only for the opportunity to spend ninety minutes amid such giant, ore-stained contraptions. After its arrival by train, the ore is carried on the various conveyor belts to the quayside, from where some thirty million tons of it are shipped out each year. Sign up for the tours at the tourist office.

Fagernesfjellet

Located a stiff fifteen-minute walk up above the town behind the train station, Narvik's **cable car** (daily: mid-June to July noon–1am; Aug 1–9pm; 100kr return) whisks passengers up the first 650m of the mighty mount **Fagernesfjellet**. There's a restaurant and viewing point at the top of the cable-car run and from here, on a clear day, you can spy the Lofoten Islands on the horizon and, from the end of May to mid-July, experience the Midnight Sun in all its glory. In addition, **hiking trails** that delve further into the mountains start here and, even more adventurously, **hang- and paragliders** have established a designated take-off point metres from the restaurant. Indeed, there's even a local club to advise on conditions: the Hang og Paragliderklubb (℡90 61 81 15). The cable car also provides a shuttle service for **skiers and snowboarders** during the season (late November to early June). The network of skiing slopes and trails includes five ski lifts, 7km of prepared courses and unlimited off-piste skiing; everywhere – including some cross country tracks – is floodlit. For further details contact Narvik ski centre (℡76 96 04 94,

Eating

Things are likely to change, but at present Narvik is very short of recommendable
cafés and **restaurants**. The best bet is the *Astrupkjelleren*, Kinobakken 1, where the
mostly meaty main courses start at 170kr.

The Vesterålen islands

A raggle-taggle archipelago in the Norwegian Sea, the **Vesterålen**, and their neighbours the Lofoten, are like western Norway in miniature: the terrain is hard and
unyielding, the sea boisterous and fretful, and the main – often the only – industry
is fishing. The weather is temperate but wet, and the islanders' historic isolation has
bred a distinctive culture based, in equal measures, on Protestantism, the extended
family and respect for the ocean.

The islands were first settled by semi-nomadic hunter-agriculturalists some 6000
years ago, and it was they and their Iron Age successors who chopped down the
birch and pine forests that once covered the coasts. It was **boat-building**, however,
which brought a brief golden age: by the seventh century, the islanders were able
to build ocean-going vessels, a skill that enabled them to join in the bonanza
of Viking exploration. In the early fourteenth century, the islanders **lost their
independence** and were placed under the control of Bergen: by royal decree, with
all fish caught by islanders having to be shipped to Bergen for export. This may have
suited the economic interests of the Norwegian monarch and the Danish governors
who succeeded them, but it put the islanders at a terrible disadvantage. With their
monopoly guaranteed, Bergen's merchants controlled both the price they paid
for the fish and the price of the goods they sold to the islanders – a truck system
that was to survive, increasingly under the auspices of local merchants, until the
early years of the twentieth century. Since World War II, improvements in fishing
techniques and, more latterly, the growth in tourism and the extension of the road
system have all combined to transform island life.

The Vesterålen are the less rugged of the two island groups: greener, gentler and
less mountainous than the Lofoten to the south, with more of the land given over to
agriculture, though this gives way to vast tracts of peaty moorland in the far north.
The villages are less appealing too, often no more than formless ribbons straggling
along the coast and across any available stretch of fertile land. Many travellers simply
rush through on their way to the Lofoten, demoralized by the sheer mediocrity of
the main settlements, a mistake primarily in so far as the fishing port of **Andenes**,
tucked away at the far end of the island of Andøya, has a strange but enthralling
back-of-beyond charm and is noted for its whale-watching expeditions. The other
highlight is the magnificent but extremely narrow **Trollfjord**, where cruise ships
and the Hurtigrute coastal boat perform some nifty manoeuvres.

Harstad

Just 130km northwest of Narvik, and easily reached by bus and the Hurtigrute
coastal boat, **HARSTAD** is easily the largest town on the Vesterålen. It's home to
much of northern Norway's engineering industry, its sprawling docks a tangle of
supply ships, repair yards and cold-storage plants spread out along the gentle slopes
of the Vågsfjord. This may not sound too enticing, and it's true that Harstad wins
few beauty competitions, but the town does have the odd attraction and, if you're
tired of sleepy Norwegian villages, it at least provides a bustling interlude.

The main item of interest, the **Trondenes kirke** (guided tours early June to
mid-Aug Mon 10am, 2pm & 4pm; Tues, Wed & Sun 2pm, 4pm & 6pm; Thurs &
Fri 2pm & 4pm; 35kr), occupies a lovely, leafy location beside the fjord 3km north
of the town centre at the end of a slender peninsula. The original wooden church

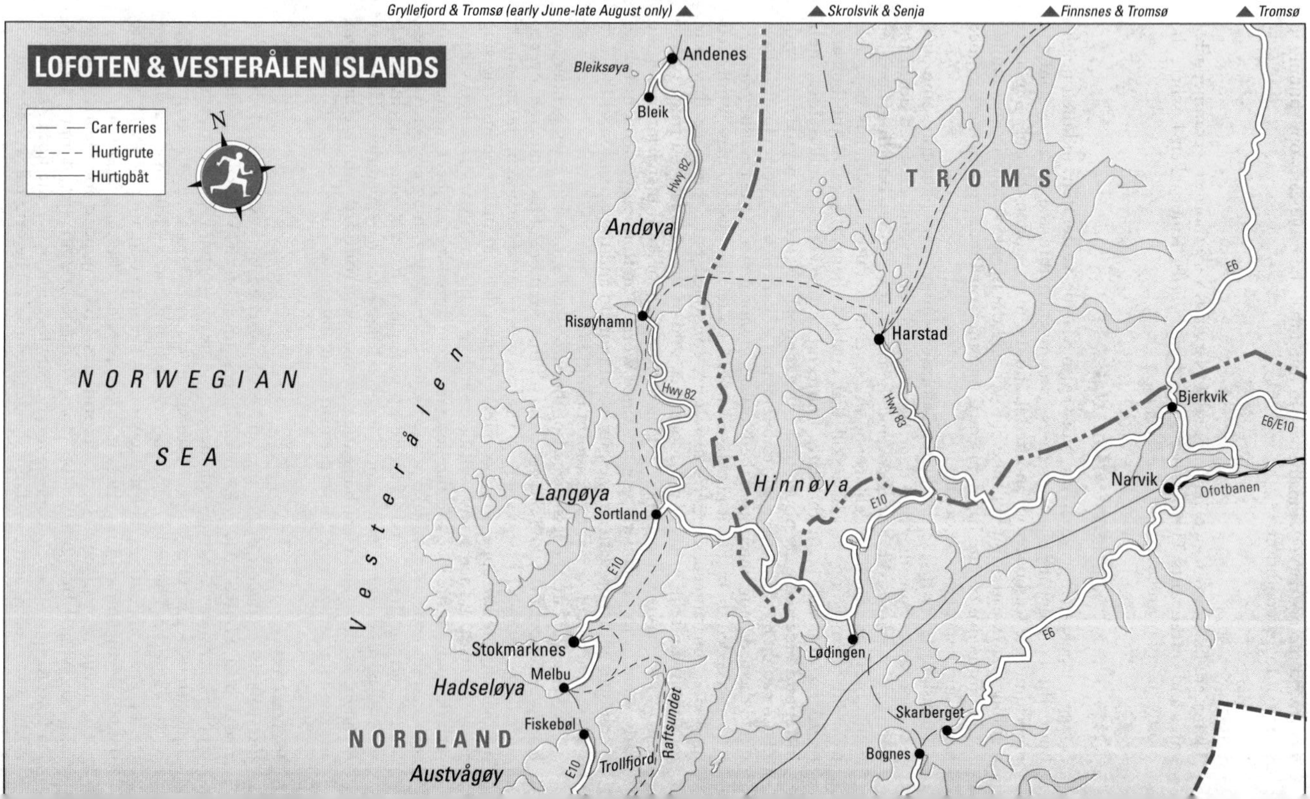

LOFOTEN & VESTERÅLEN ISLANDS

Key
- —— Car ferries
- ---- Hurtigrute
- —— Hurtigbåt

N

◀ Tromsø

◀ Finnsnes & Tromsø

◀ Skrolsvik & Senja

◀ Gryllefjord & Tromsø (early June–late August only)

T R O M S

Bjerkvik

Narvik

Ofotbanen

E6/E10

E6

Harstad

Hwy 83

Skarberget

Bognes

Hinnøya

Lødingen

E10

Andenes

Bleik

Bleiksøya

Andøya

Hwy 82

Risøyhamn

Hwy 82

Langøya

Sortland

E10

Raftsundet

NORDLAND

Austvågøy

E10

Trollfjord

Fiskebøl

Stokmarknes

Melbu

Hadseløya

Vesterålen

N O R W E G I A N

S E A

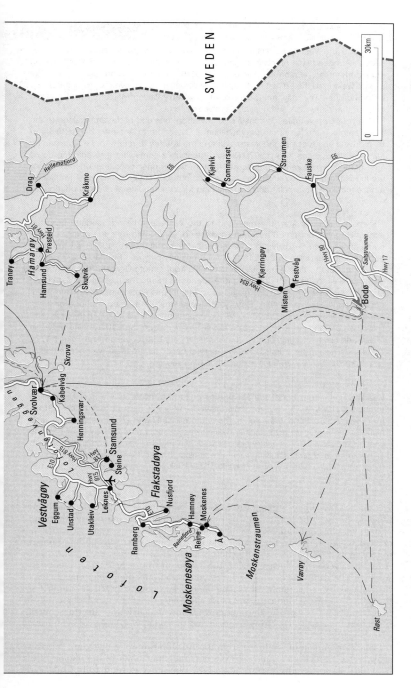

SWEDEN

30km

0

Hellemofjord

Drag

Kråkmo

E6

Kjelvik

Sommarset

Straumen

Fauske

E6

Tranøy

Hamarøy

Presteid

Hamsund

Skutvik

Saltstraumen

Hwy 17

Kjerringøy

Festvåg

Misten

Bodø

Hwy 80

Hwy 834

Skrova

Kabelvåg

Svolvær

Henningsvær

Stamsund

Hwy 815

Hwy 815

E10

Steine

Flakstadøya

Eggum

Unstad

Utakleiv

Leknes

Nusfjord

E10

Vestvågøy

Ramberg

Reinefjord

Hamnøy

Moskenes

Reine

Å

Lofoten

Moskenesøya

Moskenstraumen

Værøy

Røst

Getting to and around the Vesterålen Islands

Getting to the Vesterålen Islands from the mainland by **public transport** is easy enough – indeed, the number of permutations is almost bewildering – but getting around them can be more troublesome. The **E10** is the main island road, running the 370km west from the E6 just north of Narvik across the Vesterålen to the southern tip of the Lofoten. The only interruption is the **car ferry** linking Melbu, on the southern edge of the Vesterålen, with Fiskebøl in the Lofoten.

With your own **vehicle** it's possible to drive from one end of the archipelago to the other, catching the ferry from the mainland at Gryllefjord to Andenes (see p.391) and then driving south across the Vesterålen and the Lofoten to return to the mainland by ferry from Moskenes (see p.392). Drivers intent on a somewhat less epic trip could investigate the **car rental** outlets at Harstad, which offer special short deals from around 650kr a day. No single itinerary stands out, but Andenes has most to offer as a base thanks to its whale- and birdwatching trips and choice of accommodation.

By car ferry

The main **car ferry** from the mainland to the Vesterålen Islands departs from the jetty at **Bognes**, on the E6 between Fauske and Narvik, and sails to **Lødingen** (first-come, first-served 5–7daily; 1hr; passengers 41kr, car and driver 133kr; ☏177). From Lødingen, it's just 4km to the E10 at a point midway between Harstad and Sortland. A second, but this time seasonal, car ferry runs from remote **Gryllefjord**, 110km west of the E6 well to the north of Narvik, to **Andenes** at the northern tip of the Vesterålen (early to late June & mid- to late Aug 2 daily; late June to early Aug 3 daily; 1hr 40min; passengers 120kr, car 330kr). Reservations are strongly advised – phone or email Andøy Reiseliv in Andenes (☏76 14 18 10, ✉booking@whaleroute.no). A third car ferry links the Lofoten with the Vesterålen about halfway along the E10, running between Melbu and Fiskebøl (every 90min; 25min; passengers 28kr, driver and car 70kr; ☏177). Tickets are issued on a first-come, first-served basis, so get there twenty minutes or so before departure – an hour and a half in high season.

By boat: Hurtigrute and Hurtigbåt

Heading north from Bodø, the **Hurtigrute coastal boat** threads a scenic route up through the Lofoten to the Vesterålen Islands, where it calls at four places: **Stokmarknes** and **Sortland** in the south, **Risøyhamn** in the north and **Harstad** in the east. None of the four is an especially appealing destination, but workaday Risøyhamn is well on the way to Andenes, while Harstad is a regional centre and transport hub with a fine old church. Cruising southwards from Tromsø (see p.403), the Hurtigrute follows the same itinerary, but in reverse. Scenically, the highlight is the **Raftsundet**,

was built at the behest of King Øystein (of *rorbuer* fame – see p.394) at the beginning of the twelfth century and had the distinction of being the northernmost church in Christendom for several centuries. The present stone structure was erected in the 1300s, its thick walls and the remains of its surrounding ramparts reflecting its dual function as both church and fortress – these were troubled times. After the necessarily stern exterior, the warm and homely interior comes as a surprise. The dainty arches of the rood screen lead into the choir, where each of the three altars is surmounted by a late medieval wooden triptych in bas relief. Of the trio, the central triptych is the most charming: the main panel, depicting the Holy Family, is fairly predictable, but down below is a curiously cheerful sequence of biblical figures, each wearing a turban and sporting a big, bushy and exquisitely carved beard.

There's a reminder of World War II in the **Adolfkanonen** (Adolf Gun), a massive artillery piece stuck on a hilltop to the north of the church in the middle of the peninsula. It's inside a military zone, and the obligatory **guided tour** (daily: early a narrow sound between Svolvær and Stokmarknes, off which branches the magnificent Trollfjord. Unfortunately, though, the Hurtigrute leaves Svolvær heading north at 10pm, so the Raftsundet is only visible during the period of the Midnight Sun (late May to mid-July); things are, however, easier in the opposite direction with boats leaving Stokmarknes at a much more convenient 3.15pm. This stretch of the journey takes three hours and costs 312kr for passengers, and 331kr for cars.

Sailing north, the Hurtigrute leaves Bodø for the Lofoten and the Vesterålen at 3pm daily and departs Tromsø heading south at 4am daily. Passenger tickets are reasonably priced, with the sixteen-hour journey from Bodø to Harstad costing around 835kr, Tromsø to Harstad (6.5hr) 563kr in summer, with significant off-season discounts. The fare for transporting a car from Bodø to Harstad is 472kr, from Tromsø to Harstad 425kr. Advance reservations are essential (℡81 03 00 00, www.hurtigruten.com), but can be made just a few hours beforehand by telephoning the captain – ask down at Bodø harbour or at the port's tourist office for assistance, as all the boats have individual phone numbers. Special deals, which can reduce costs dramatically, are advertised at local tourist offices.

Hurtigbåt passenger express boat services provide a speedy and economic alternative to the car ferries and Hurtigrute. Principal Hurtigbåt services are **Tromsø to Harstad** (2 daily; 2hr 45min; 390kr); **Narvik to Svolvær** in the Lofoten (Mon–Fri & Sun 1 daily; 3hr 30min; 310kr); and **Bodø to Svolvær** (Mon–Fri & Sun 1 daily; 3hr 30min; 350kr). In all cases, advance booking – most easily done via the local tourist office – is recommended.

By bus

A long-distance **bus** leaves **Narvik** once or twice daily to run along the E6 and then the E10 as far as Sortland. Here, passengers can usually – but not always – change, after an hour or two's wait, for the onward bus to **Stokmarknes**, the Melbu–Fiskebøl ferry and then **Svolvær**. Once daily, another long-distance bus runs up the E6 from **Bodø** and **Fauske** to meet the **Bognes–Lødingen** car ferry. At Lødingen, there's a choice of two onward connecting buses: one service continues north to **Harstad**, the other heads west for **Stokmarknes**, the Melbu–Fiskebøl ferry and **Svolvær**. As examples of journey times, Narvik to Sortland takes three hours, Bodø to Sortland seven, Bodø to Svolvær ten.

Generally speaking, **local buses** across the Vesterålen are no more than reasonable in the summer and very patchy out of season. Most are operated by Nordtrafikk (℡177 in Nordland, otherwise ℡75 77 24 10). One of their most useful services links Sortland with Andenes (1–3 daily; 2hr).

June to mid-Aug 11am, 1pm & 3pm; late Aug 1pm & 3pm; 55kr), which begins at the gate of the compound 1km up the hill from the church, stipulates that you have to have your own vehicle to cross from the gate to the gun, a distance of 3km. Once you've arrived, there's not much to see apart from the gun's underground loading area with displays of the huge shells and the gun itself. A third attraction, near the church and just south along the fjord, is the **Trondenes Historiske Senter** (Trondenes Historical Centre; mid-June to early Aug daily 10am–5pm; early Aug to mid-June Mon–Fri 10am–noon, Sun 11am–5pm; 70kr), a plush modern complex with exhibitions on the history of the locality – dioramas, mood music, incidental Viking artefacts and the like.

Frankly, **downtown Harstad** doesn't have much going for it, though the comings and goings of the ferry boats are a diversion. In late June, the ten-day **North Norway Arts Festival** (*Festspillene i Nord-Norge*; www.festspillnn.no) provides a spark of interest with its concerts, drama and dance, but there again the town's hotels are full to overflowing throughout the proceedings.

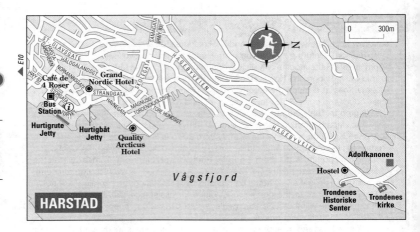

Practicalities

Although Harstad is easy to reach by bus or boat from Sortland, Tromsø and Narvik, it's actually something of a cul-de-sac for car drivers, who have to leave the E10 for the final thirty-kilometre drive north into town along Highway 83, though in summertime the ferry to Skrolsvik does offer another route out (see box below), in addition to the Hurtigbåt and Hurtigrute. Once you've arrived, however, you'll find almost everything you need in the immediate vicinity of the **bus station**. Jetties for the **Hurtigbåt passenger express** and **Hurtigrute coastal boat** services are just metres away, and next to the bus station at Torvet 8, the **tourist office** (early June to mid-Aug Mon–Fri 8am–6pm, Sat & Sun 10am–3pm; mid-Aug to May Mon–Fri 8am–3.30pm; ☎77 01 89 89, ⓦwww.destinationharstad.no) has a wide selection of tourist literature on the Vesterålen.

As regards **accommodation**, the centre is dotted with modern chain hotels. Among them, the *Quality Arcticus* has an attractive quayside location a short walk from Torvet at Havnegata 3 (☎77 04 08 00, ⓦwww.choicehotels.no; ❸/❹). A good alternative is the neat and trim *Grand Nordic*, a couple of minutes' walk from Torvet at Strandgata 9 (☎77 00 30 00, ⓦwww.nordic.no; ❸/❻). The HI **hostel** (June to late Aug; ☎77 07 28 00, ⓔharstad.hostel@vandrerhjem.no; reception closed 4–6pm) has the advantage of a pleasant fjordside location, near the Trondenes kirke. It's easy to reach by the local "Trondenes" bus from the station (Mon–Sat 1 hourly; 10min), has self-catering facilities, washing machines, and large, comfortable and pleasantly furnished double rooms (❶) as well as dorm beds (170kr); the only problem is that the building is a school for most of the year and so has a rather cold, institutional feel.

Harstad is no gastronomic nirvana, but the saving grace is the *Café de 4 Roser*, Rikard Kaarbøs plass 4 (☎77 06 12 16), which covers all the culinary bases by

Moving on from Harstad

From Harstad, the **Hurtigrute** sails north for Tromsø at 8am and south for points in the Vesterålen and Lofoten Islands at 8.30am. Alternatively, there's a **Hurtigbåt** service to Tromsø (1–3 daily; 2hr 45min; 380kr) and frequent **buses** to Narvik, Sortland (for Andenes) and the Lofoten. In Harstad, several local **car rental** firms offer special short-term deals: try Europcar, Samagata 33 (☎77 01 86 10), or Hertz, Torvet 8 (☎77 06 13 46).

offering light meals downstairs at the café-bar and first-rate French-influenced cuisine in the restaurant up above (book ahead); the café-bar is also the best place in town for an evening drink.

Sortland, Stokmarknes, the Trollfjord and Melbu

Back on the E10 south of Harstad, it's 50km southwest along the fjord to the turning for the Lødingen ferry, and 50km more to **SORTLAND**, an unappetizing modern sprawl straggling along the shore near the bridge linking the islands of Langøya and Hinnøya. Sortland's location makes it something of a transport centre: bus travellers have to change here for the onward journey south to Stokmarknes and the Lofoten, or to catch the local bus north to Andenes, which originates here. If you've a little time to spare, visit the **tourist office** (mid-June to late Aug Mon–Fri 10am–6pm, Sat & Sun 11am–5pm; Sept to mid-June Mon–Fri 10am–5pm; ☎76 11 14 80, ⊛www.visitvesteralen.com), a five-minute walk from the bus station in the centre of town at Kjøpmannsgata 2; they have the full range of regional information.

Pushing south along the E10 from Sortland, the road hugs the shoreline for 30km before shooting over the two bridges that span the straits to reach **STOKMARKNES** on Hadseløya. The main reason for stopping in Stokmarknes is to catch the Hurtigrute south to Svolvær via the Trollfjord. The boat leaves at 3.15pm, sailing down the narrow sound – the Raftsundet – separating the harsh, rocky shanks of Hinnøya and Austvågøy. Towards the southern end of the sound, the ship usually makes the short detour to the **Trollfjord**, a majestic, two-kilometre-long tear in the landscape. Slowing to a mere chug, the vessels inch up the narrow gorge, smooth stone towering high above and blocking out the light. At the Trollfjord's head, the boats effect a nautical three-point turn and then crawl back to rejoin the main waterway. It's very atmospheric, and the effect is perhaps even more extraordinary when the weather is up. One caution: the Hurtigrute does not enter the Trollfjord when there's the danger of a rock fall, but pauses at the fjord's mouth instead. Check locally before you embark, though this is most likely to happen in spring. The Hurtigrute cruise from Sortland to Svolvær takes three hours and costs 241kr per passenger.

If you stay the night in Stokmarknes awaiting the Hurtigrute, you'll find most things conveniently close, with **buses** pulling in near the harbourfront **tourist office** (mid-June to late Aug Mon–Fri 10am–5pm; ☎76 15 00 00, ⊛www.tourist office.com). Staff here have details of local **accommodation**, though there's not much on offer. The obvious choice is the *Hurtigrutens Hus* (☎76 15 29 99, ⊛www .hurtigrutenshus.com; ❺), a brassy, modern hotel-cum-conference centre plonked on the Børøya islet, about fifteen minutes' walk from the tourist office and at the end of the first of the two bridges back over to Langøya.

From Stokmarknes, it's 15km along the E10 to **MELBU**, from where there's a **car ferry** (every 90min; 25min; passengers 28kr, driver and car 81kr; ☎177) over to Fiskebøl on the Lofoten; Melbu is on the main bus routes to Svolvær from Fauske, Narvik and Tromsø.

North to Andenes

From Sortland, Hwy 82 begins its 100-kilometre trek north, snaking along the craggy peripheries of the ocean before crossing the bridge over to humdrum **RISØYHAMN**, the only Hurtigrute stop on **Andøya**, itself the most northerly of the Vesterålen Islands. Beyond Risøyhamn, the scenery is much less dramatic, as the mountains give way to hills in the west and a vast, peaty moor in the east. Hwy 82 crosses this moorland and, despite fine panoramic views of the mountains back on the mainland, it's an uneventful journey on to Andenes.

At the old fishing port of **ANDENES**, lines of low-slung buildings trail up to the clutter of wooden warehouses and small boat repair yards that edge the harbour and its prominent breakwaters. Andenes is famous for its **whale safaris**, three to four-hour cruises off the coast with a marine biologist on board to point out sperm, killer and minke whales, as well as various species of porpoise; male sperm whales populate the area all year round, and there's a 99 percent chance of seeing at least one, if not more. Other species are not quite so reliable, but still make frequent appearances. Trips take place daily between late May and mid-September, with departures at 11.30am and 3.30pm (subject to demand, there are additional departures at 9.30am & 5.30pm); tickets are 725kr each and cover both lunch and a guided tour of the Whale Centre (see below) beforehand. The trip isn't recommended for children under five as the sea can get rough; warm clothing and sensible shoes are essential. **Booking** (☎76 11 56 00, ⊛www.whalesafari.no) at least a day in advance is strongly advised as the trips are popular, and indeed some are booked up weeks beforehand.

The **Whale Centre** (*Hvalsenter*; daily: late May to mid-June & mid-Aug to mid-Sept 8am–4pm; mid-June to mid-Aug 8am–7.30pm; 60kr), metres from the harbour, is actually a somewhat disappointing way to start. Its incidental museum displays on the life and times of the animal hardly fire the imagination, and neither does the massive – and deliberately dark and gloomy – display of a whale munching its way though a herd of squid. Much more diverting is the **Hisnakul/Northern Lights Centre** (mid-June to mid-Aug daily 10am–6pm; 30kr), in a refurbished timber warehouse near the Whale Centre, which explores various facets of Andøya life. It's short on historical artefacts, plumping instead for imaginative displays such as the two hundred facial casts of local people made in 1994 and an assortment of giant replica bird beaks. There's also a comprehensive explanation of the northern lights (see the box in "The Great Outdoors" colour insert) – Andenes is a particularly good spot to see them – illustrated by first-class photographs and a slide show.

The other recommended **boat trip** is a cruise round the **bird island of Bleiksøya** (June to late Aug 1 daily at 1pm & 3pm, additional departures as required; 1hr 30min; 300kr; bookings through the tourist office or direct on ☎97 19 52 75), a pyramid-shaped hunk of rock populated by thousands of puffins, kittiwakes, razorbills and, sometimes, white-tailed eagles. Cruises leave from the jetty at **Bleik**, an old and picturesque fishing hamlet around 7km southwest of Andenes; a local bus often makes the trip from Andenes to coincide with sailings.

Practicalities

Bisecting the town, Andenes' long and straight main street, Storgata, ends abruptly at the seafront. The **bus station** is just a few metres to the east of Storgata, just back from the seafront, and the **tourist office** (June–Aug daily 8am–8pm; Sept–May

△ Whale-watching off Andenes

The coastal route north from Andenes to Tromsø

From early June to late August, two **car ferries** operated by Senjaferries (☎76 14 18 00, ⊛www.senjafergene.no) make it possible to head up the coast from **Andenes to Tromsø** without having to double back inland. This scenic coastal route begins with the (often choppy) ferry ride from Andenes to the remote fishing village of **Gryllefjord** (early June to late Aug 2–3 daily; 1hr 40min; passengers 120kr, cars 330kr), on the island of **Senja**. From here, Highway 86 weaves a handsome route across the island's mountains to reach, after about 70km, the main town hereabouts, the boring Hurtigrute port of **FINNSNES**. Keep going – or rather turn north along Highway 861 just before Finnsnes – for the lovely 55 kilometre-long fjordside drive that leads up to **BOTNHAMN**, where a second **car ferry** crosses over to **BRENSHOLMEN** (June to late Aug 4–7 daily; 40min; passengers 60kr, cars 150kr). Brensholmen is within easy driving distance of Tromsø (see p.403). The whole journey is easily completed in a day – Gryllefjord to Tromsø is 230km.

Mon–Fri 8am–4pm; ☎76 14 18 10, ⊛www.andoy.net) shares the same building as the Northern lights centre. The office has a comprehensive range of local information and can make reservations for bird-island boat trips, whale safaris and the car ferry to Gryllefjord; there's a booking fee for the car ferry, but not the others.

Andenes has a fair sprinkling of inexpensive **accommodation** and several households offer **private rooms** – look out for the signs – but, considering how isolated a spot this is, you'd be well advised to make an advance reservation either directly or via the tourist office. One of the nicest places to stay is the *Sjøgata Gjestehus*, Sjøgata 4 (☎76 14 16 37, ✉tovekhan@online.no; May–Sept; ❹), which provides simple, inexpensive rooms in a pleasant old timber building just 200m east of the tourist office. Nearby, on the seafront, is the green-timbered *Grønnbua* (☎76 14 1 99, ⊛www.rorbucamping.no) comprising of two *sjøhus* (see p.394), one a cosy, modern affair (❸), the other older and slightly tattier (❷); both have rooms overlooking the water. There's also a very small and very spartan HI **hostel** (☎76 14 28 50; June–Aug), with a few doubles (❶) as well as dorm beds (190kr). There are two **hotels**, the better of which is the *Norlandia Andrikken*, about 900m from the harbour at Storgata 53 (☎76 14 12 22, ⊛www.norlandia.no; ❹/❺), whose main building is a routine modern concrete block with rooms to match. More positively, the hotel **restaurant** is easily Andenes' best place to eat – the Arctic char is superb – and prices are reasonable. For daytime snacks, head for *Juhl Nilsens Bakeri*, close to the bus station at Kong Hansgata 1.

Leaving Andenes by **bus**, there are daily services south to Risøyhamn and Sortland, though the latter are few and far between on the weekend. In the summer, there's also the possibility of catching the **ferry** north to Gryllefjord (see box, above).

The Lofoten Islands

A skeletal curve of mountainous rock stretched out across the Norwegian Sea, the **Lofoten Islands** are the focal point of northern Norway's winter fishing season. At the turn of every year, cod migrate from the Barents Sea to spawn here, where the coldness of the waters is tempered by the Gulf Stream. The season lasts from February to April, though it impinges on all aspects of the islands' life and is impossible to ignore at any time of year. At almost every harbour stand the massed ranks of wooden racks used for drying the catch; full and odiferous in winter, empty in summer like so many abandoned climbing frames.

Sharing the same history, but better known and more beautiful than their neighbours the Vesterålen, the Lofoten Islands have everything from seabird colonies in

The Lofoten can be reached by car ferry, Hurtigbåt passenger express boat and the Hurtigrute coastal boat, but once you've got there you'll find **public transport** thin on the ground. What local **bus** services there are stick almost exclusively to the **E10**, the islands' only main road. Leave the main highway, however, and you'll mostly have to **walk** – hardly an onerous task in such beautiful surroundings. Alternatively, **bike rental** is available at the Svolvær tourist office (see p.394), as well as at many hotels, campsites and hostels, while the detailed *Cycling in Lofoten* booklet, which includes route maps, is sold at all tourist offices.

If you have your own **vehicle**, village-hopping is easy and quick, but do allow time for at least one walk or sea trip. Conversely, if you don't have a vehicle and want to reach the islands' remoter spots, it's worth considering renting a car, an inexpensive option if a few people share the cost. There are local **car rental** outlets at Svolvær, Stamsund and Leknes airport, and special short-term deals can bring costs down to around 650kr a day.

For **timetable enquiries** for all public transport in the province of Nordland, which covers the Lofoten, call ☎177 from within Nordland, or ☎75 77 24 10 from other parts of Norway; alternatively, visit ⌨www.177nordland.com.

By car ferry

From the mainland, the principal **car ferry** service to the Lofoten connects tiny Skutvik, 40km west of the E6 midway between Fauske and Narvik, with Svolvær (June to mid-Aug 8 daily; mid-Aug to May 2–3 daily; 2hr; passengers 78kr, car and driver 214kr; ☎177). Queues are commonplace and, as it's a first-come first-served ferry, it's best to arrive about two hours before departure to make sure of a place. A second car ferry service links **Bodø** with three destinations in the southern peripheries of the Lofoten: **Moskenes**, a tiny port just a few kilometres from the end of the E10, and the islets of Røst and Værøy. The route varies, but there's almost always one ferry a day (and sometimes more) to Moskenes throughout the year, with marginally less frequent services to Røst and Værøy. Moskenes is usually the first port of call. The trip from Bodø to Moskenes takes about four hours; allow a further two hours to Værøy and two more for Røst. Don't be surprised if it's a turbulent crossing. The fare from Bodø to Moskenes is 125kr for passengers, 440kr for a car and driver. These ferries are operated by OVDS (☎177 from within Nordland, ☎76 11 82 45 from out-

---

the south to beaches and fjords in the north, not to mention the 160-kilometre **Lofotenveggen** (Lofoten Wall), a chain of rearing mountains whose grandeur simply takes your breath away. The Lofoten have their own relaxed pace, and are perfect for a simple, uncluttered few days. For somewhere so far north, the weather is exceptionally mild: summer days can be spent sunbathing on the rocks or hiking around the superb coastline, and when it rains – as it does frequently – life focuses on the *rorbuer* (fishermen's huts), where freshly caught fish are cooked over wood-burning stoves, stories are told and time gently wasted. If that sounds rather contrived, in a sense it is – the way of life here is to some extent preserved like this for tourists, but it's rare to find anyone who isn't less than completely enthralled by it all.

The **E10** weaves a scenic route across the Lofoten, running the 170km from Fiskebøl in the north to Å in the south, hopping from island to island by bridge and causeway and occasionally tunnelling through the mountains and under the sea. The highway passes through or within a few kilometres of all the islands' main villages, amongst which **Henningsvaer** and **Å** are breathtakingly beautiful, with **Stamsund** coming in just behind; all three also make great bases for further exploration. **Boat trips** along the coast (with or without birdwatching and fishing) side; ⓦwww.ovds.no). **Advance reservations** can be made online, or through Bodø tourist office for a fee of 100kr (ferry staff don't always speak English); otherwise drivers should arrive at least two hours before departure to make sure of a place. If you're driving to the Lofoten on the **E10**, which branches off the E6 north of Narvik, you'll use a third car ferry linking **Melbu** on the Vesterålen Islands with **Fiskebøl** on the Lofoten (first-come, first served; every 90min; 25min; passengers 28kr, driver and car 81kr; ⊕177).

By Hurtigrute and Hurtigbåt

Heading north from Bodø at 3pm, the **Hurtigrute coastal boat** calls at two ports in the Lofoten – Stamsund and Svolvær – before nudging through the Raftsundet en route to Stokmarknes. Advance reservations for cars are essential (ⓦwww.hurtigruten .com, ⊕76 81 03 00 00), though these can be made up to a few hours before departure by telephoning the captain – ask down at the harbour or at the port's tourist office for assistance, as each boat has a different number. Special deals, which can reduce costs dramatically, are commonplace.

Hurtigbåt passenger express boats operate from **Bodø to Svolvær** (Mon–Fri & Sun 1 daily; 3hr 30min; 350kr) and **Narvik to Svolvær** (Mon–Fri & Sun 1 daily; 4hr; 292kr). In both cases, advance booking (via the local tourist office) is recommended.

Buses

There are two long-distance **bus** services linking the mainland with the Lofoten. One is from **Fauske to Å** via Svolvær (1 daily; 12hr; one-way 642kr) via the Bognes–Lødingen and Melbu–Fiskebøl ferries; you can also start the journey in **Bodø**. The second service runs from **Narvik to Leknes** via Svolvær (1 daily; 7hr 45min; 476kr) via the Melbu–Fiskebøl ferry.

On the Lofoten, there are at least a couple of **local buses** on weekdays between most of the larger villages, but often nothing at all on Sunday, and sometimes Saturday as well. One useful service travels south from Svolvær to Leknes and Å (Mon–Sat 1–2 daily). To avoid getting stuck, be sure to pick up a bus and ferry **timetable** from any island tourist office or bus station. Both Avis (⊕76 07 11 40) and Europcar (⊕76 06 83 33) offer some economic short-term, car-hire deals (from around 650kr per day) and have offices in Andenes, Svolvær, Leknes Airport, Stockmarknes and Stamsund.

are popular, as is **mountaineering** – Austvågøy island has the finest climbing, with the best climbing school at the village of Henningsvaer. There's **walking**, too: the islands do not have a well-developed system of huts and hiking trails, but the byroads are quiet and delve into the heart of the scenery.

As regards **accommodation**, the Lofoten have a sprinkling of **hotels** as well as four HI **hostels** and numerous **campsites**, along with the local speciality, the *rorbuer* (see box below).

Svolvær

On the east coast of **Austvågøy**, the largest of the Lofoten, the town of **SVOLVÆR** provides a disappointing introduction to the islands. The administrative and transport centre of the Lofoten, it has all the bustle but little of the charm of the other fishing towns, though it does have more accommodation than its neighbours and, despite the poor aspect of the town itself, Svolvær's surroundings are delightful. Two local **boat trips** provide an excellent taster. Every day (mid-May to Aug) several **cruises** leave Svolvær for the **Trollfjord** (for more on which, see p.389), an impossibly narrow, two-kilometre-long stretch of water up and down which countless excursion boats inch a careful way. The excursion takes three hours, and costs around 300kr. You can also pick up the Hurtigruten here (daily at 3.15pm) for the three hour trip ending in Stockmarknes which costs 241kr.

Svolvær also boasts one of the archipelago's most famous **climbs**, the haul up to the top of the **Svolværgeita** (the "Svolvær goat"), a twin-pronged peak that rises high above the E10 just to the northeast of town. The lower slopes of the mountain are difficult enough, but the last 40m – up the horns of the "goat" – require considerable expertise. Daring-daft mountaineers then finish it off by jumping from one pinnacle to the other.

Practicalities

Ferries to Svolvær from Skutvik dock on the edge of town, about 1km from the centre, whereas the Hurtigrute docks in the centre, the briefest of walks from both the **bus station** and the busy **tourist office**, which is beside the main town square by the harbour (late May to mid-June Mon–Fri 9am–4pm, Sat 10am–2pm; mid- to late June Mon–Fri 9am–4pm & 5–7.30pm, Sat 10am–2pm, Sun 4–7pm; late June to mid-Aug Mon–Fri 9am–4pm & 5–9.30pm, Sat 9am–4pm & 5–8pm, Sun 10am–9.30pm; mid-Aug to late Aug Mon–Fri 9am–7pm, Sat 10am–2pm; Sept to mid-May Mon–Fri 9am–4pm; ☎76 06 98 00, ☻www.lofoten-tourist.no). Staff will reserve accommodation anywhere in the Lofoten (for a 50kr booking fee) and can book ferry tickets for a fee of 120kr. Svolvær is also a good place to **rent a car**. Budget have an outlet in the centre at Sivert Nilsens gate 43 (☎76 07 00 00), and there's Europcar at Avisgaten 11 (☎76 06 83 33)

Svolvær's flashiest **accommodation** is the gleaming and justifiably popular *Rica Hotel Svolvær* (☎76 07 22 22, ☻www.rica.no; ④), whose various buildings, in the style of the traditional *sjøhus*, occupy a prime location on a tiny islet at the end of a causeway in the middle of the harbour. Not to be outdone, a longer causeway now leads out from the east end of the harbour to the slender islet of Svinøya, where *Svinøya Rorbuer* (☎76 06 99 30, ☻www.svinoya.no) has everything from plain and simple *rorbuer* (③) through to the deluxe models (⑥), all in a modern version of

Staying in a rorbu or sjøhus

Right across the Lofoten, **rorbuer** (fishermen's shacks) are rented out to tourists for both overnight stays and longer periods. Traditionally, *rorbuer* were built on the shore, often on poles sticking out of the sea, and usually coloured with a red paint based on cod-liver oil. They consisted of two sections, a sleeping and eating room and a smaller storage area. At the peak of the fisheries in the 1930s, some 30,000 men were accommodated in *rorbuer*, but in the 1960s the fishing boats became more comfortable and since then many fishermen have preferred to sleep aboard. Most of the original *rorbuer* disappeared years ago and, although a few have survived, visitors today are much more likely to stay in a modern version, mostly prefabricated units churned out by the score. At their best, they are comfortable and cosy seashore cabins, sometimes a well-planned conversion of an original *rorbu* with bunk beds and wood-fired stoves; at their worst, they're little better than prefabricated hutches – or even garages – in the middle of nowhere. Most have space for between four and six guests and the charge for a hut is in the region of 600kr per night – though some cost as little as 400kr, while others rise to about 1200kr. Similar rates are charged for the islands' **sjøhus** (literally, sea-houses), bigger buildings that originated in the quayside halls where the catch was processed and the workers slept. Inside, they're similar to the *rorbuer*, with varying degrees of comfort; but sjøhus are much more spacious, sleeping anything from eight to twenty, and often have windows directly over the sea making fishing from your armchair a distinct possibility.

A full list of *rorbuer* and *sjøhus* is given in the *Lofoten Info-Guide*, a free pamphlet that you can pick up at any local tourist office.

traditional style. Back in town, there are more modest rooms at the long-established – and much smaller – *Svolvær Sjøhus*, by the seashore at the foot of Parkgata (☎76 07 03 36, ⊛www.svolver-sjohuscamp.no; ❷): to get there from the square, turn right up the hill along Vestfjordgata and it's to the right, past the library. Svolvær also has a handful of **hotels**, for the most part surly modern blocks that hardly set the architectural pulse racing, though the *Norlandia Royal Hotel* (☎76 07 12 00, ⊛www.norlandia.no; ❹), a few metres up from the main square at the end of Torggat, has comfortable (if decoratively confused) rooms, a mini health spa and a convenient location.

There are several good **eating** options. Down on the quay, *Café Bacalao* is a spacious café-restaurant with snappy service and a menu that mixes Mediterranean and Norwegian cuisine with flair and imagination – the salads are especially splendid. Lunches and main courses in the evening hover around 100kr, and at night the place turns into the town's liveliest **bar**, jam-packed on the weekend. In addition, the restaurants of the *Rica Hotel Svolvær* and the *Svinøya Rorbuer* are both highly competent, with seafood their forte, but the classiest and smartest restaurant is *Du Verden*, in the centre at J.E. Paulsens gate 12 (☎76 07 70 99), where a creative menu features the freshest of local ingredients. In the evening, prices are high, but not unreasonable – either à la carte, with main courses costing around 130kr, or with a set menu for around 160kr. At lunch time the place is a bit of a snip – try the mouthwatering, taste-bud-symphony-making fish soup.

Henningsvær

A beguiling headland village, **HENNINGSVÆR** lies 24km southwest of Svolvær, its cobweb of cramped and twisting lanes lined with brightly painted wooden houses. These frame a tiny inlet that literally cuts the place in half, forming a sheltered, postcard-pretty harbour. Almost inevitably, coach parties are wheeled in and out, despite the narrowness of its two high-arched bridges, but for all the tourist hustle and bustle the village is well worth an **overnight stay**.

The smartest **hotel** is the quayside *Heningsvær Bryggehotell* (☎76 07 47 50, ⊛www.dvgl.no; ❻), an attractive modern building in traditional style right on the waterfront, but the more economical – and frugal – choice is *Den siste Viking*, Misværveien 10 (☎76 07 49 11, ✉postmaster@nordnorskklatreskole.no; ❷), which provides unadorned lodging right in the centre, on the main street just back from the waterfront. The latter doubles as the home of the Lofoten's best **mountaineering school**, Nord Norsk Klatreskole (same number; ⊛www.nordnorskklatreskole .no). The school operates a wide range of all-inclusive climbing holidays in the mountains near Henningsvær, catering to various degrees of fitness and experience. Prices vary greatly depending on the trip, but a three-day, one-climb-a-day holiday costs in the region of 4500kr per person, including equipment, food and accommodation.

Much less strenuous are **fishing trips**, a morning or afternoon's excursion for around 300kr, booked down at the harbour, or you could drop by the **Galleri Lofoten Hus** (daily: March noon–3pm, late May to early June & mid-Aug 10am–6pm, mid-June to early Aug 9am–7pm; late Aug 11am–4pm; 70kr), which exhibits and sells the work of the contemporary artist Karl Erik Harr alongside a scattering of earlier local paintings.

For **food**, the *Klatrekafeen* at *Den siste Viking* serves up a good range of Norwegian standbys from 90kr, plus soup and salads and some killer chocolate cupcakes, all washed down with first-rate coffee. Much classier, however, is the waterside *Fiskekrogen Restaurant*, Dreyersgate 19, where the fish soup in particular and the seafood in general are simply superb; main courses from 180kr.

Vestvågøy: Stamsund

It's the next large island to the southwest of Austvågøya, **Vestvågøy**, that captivates many travellers to the Lofoten. This is due in no small part to the laid-back charm of **STAMSUND**, whose older buildings string along the rocky, fretted seashore in an amiable jumble of crusty port buildings, wooden houses and *rorbuer*. There have been some recent additions to the Stamsund stew, but it's all pretty low-key and the new art gallery, **Galleri 2**, about 100m from the Hurtigrute dock (mid-June to mid-Aug Tues–Sun noon–4pm & 7–9.30pm; 20kr), is well worth a quick rummage. Stamsund is also the first port at which the **Hurtigrute coastal boat** docks on its way north from Bodø, and is much the best place to stay on the island. Getting there **by bus from Austvågøya** is reasonably easy too, with several buses making the trip daily, though you do have to change at **LEKNES**, 15km away to the west and the site of the island's airport. Leknes itself is the dull and boring administrative centre of Vestvågøy – something you're likely to discover fairly immediately as you wait the hour or two it usually takes to change buses.

Stamsund's HI **hostel** (℡76 08 93 34, ℻76 08 97 39; mid-Dec to mid-Oct; dorm beds 90kr, doubles ❶) is located about 1km down the road from the port and 200m from the nearest bus stop – ask to be let off. The warden, who is something of a one-off, knows everything there is to know about Vestvågøy and then some, from hiking through to fishing and beyond, and he presides over several *rorbuer* and a *sjøhus* perched over a bonny, pin-sized bay. The **fishing** hereabouts is first-class: the hostel lends out rowing boats and lines to take out on the (usually still) water, or you can head off on an organized half-day fishing trip for just 200kr. Afterwards you can barbecue your catch and eat alfresco on the veranda overlooking the bay. Unsurprisingly, many travellers return time and again – though no one could say the hostel was spick or span and the general sense of chaos is not to everyone's taste. The safer and smoother option is *Skjærbrygga* (℡76 05 46 00, ☻www.skjaerbrygga .no; ❺), a combined **hotel**, *sjøhus* and *rorbuer* facility right in the centre of Stamsund by the harbour. Most of the nineteen *rorbuer* (❺) are tastefully revamped old cabins dating back to the 1910s; others are more modern but all are comfortable. The *Skjærbrygga* itself is a pleasantly recycled former warehouse that now contains a café and a very good **restaurant**, with main courses, featuring local ingredients, costing around 150kr.

Cars can be hired from Avis at the *Stamsund Hotel*, an unforgiving concrete edifice just back from the centre (℡76 08 93 00, ☻post@lofoten-tour.com).

The west coast and the Lofotr Vikingmuseum

Admirers of wild scenery should consider heading out to Vestvågøy's blustery **west coast**, where a few hardy fishing villages hung on until they were finally abandoned and left to the birds, the wind and the sea in the 1950s. This coast is accessed by a series of turnings off the **E10** as it slices across Vestvågøy's drab central valley: from Stamsund, follow the Hwy 817/815 for a hilly 15km to **Leknes** (see above) and then go north along the E10 until you come to the second signposted byroad which leads to **UNSTAD**, a huddle of houses in a diminutive river valley set right beneath the mountains and with wide views out to sea. A popular and comparatively straightforward nine-kilometre-long **hiking trail** runs north along the seashore from Unstad, with mountains and lakes on one side and the surging ocean on the other, until it slips into **EGGUM**. This tiny hamlet is an especially pretty spot, its handful of houses hanging onto a precarious headland dwarfed by the mountains behind and with a whopping pebble beach in front. Eggum can also be reached by road off the E10 – it's the next turning along from the Unstad turn – but note that without a car, all these places are difficult to reach: cyclists will face stiff gradients and often strong winds and, although there is a limited bus service along the E10, there are no buses off it to the west coast. More accessible, in that it's on the E10 between the Unstad and Eggum turnings, some 14km from Leknes, is the flashy **Lofotr Vikingmuseum** (mid-May to Sept daily 10am–7pm; 90kr; 80kr in May & Sept; ☻www.lofotr.no), where the accidental discovery of the site of a Viking chieftain's house by a local farmer in 1981 has inspired the creation of a full-blooded Viking museum. The 83-metre Viking house has been reconstructed and all sorts of gimcrackery – flickering lights, wood tar smells and so forth – add to the atmosphere, though some visitors prefer the permanent exhibition of actual archeological finds. "Viking" animals graze the grounds and the boathouse contains a full-size replica of the Gokstad ship displayed in Oslo (see p.269).

South to Nusfjord

By any standard the next two islands of the archipelago, **Flakstadøya** and **Moske-nesøya**, are extraordinarily beautiful. As the Lofoten taper towards their southerly conclusion, the rearing peaks of the Lofotenveggen crimp the sea-shredded coast-line, providing a thunderously scenic backdrop to a necklace of tiny fishing villages. The E10 travels along almost all of this shoreline, leaving Leknes to tunnel west under the sound separating Vestvågøy from Flakstadøya (toll 90kr). About 20km from Leknes, an even more improbable byroad manages somehow to worm its way 6km up through the mountains to **NUSFJORD**, an extravagantly picturesque fishing village in a tight and forbidding cove. Unlike many *rorbuer* elsewhere in the Lofoten, the ones here are the genuine nineteenth-century article, and the general store, with its wooden floors and antique appearance, fits in nicely, too. Inevitably, it's tourism that keeps the local economy afloat, and the village is firmly on the day-trippers' itinerary, but it's still an incredibly beguiling place. **Accommodation** is available in more than thirty comfortably refurbished – and chain-hotel owned – ⚡ *rorbuer*. The standard and prices vary from the very basic one-bedroomed affairs (sleeping two to four people) with water from a tap outside, no shower and a dry toilet (from 500kr), to the two-bedroom ones, which have space for up to eight (from 900kr) and have toilets, kitchens and showers. There's also a **bar-restaurant**. Advance reservations are strongly advised (☎76 07 22 22, ⊛www.rica-lofoten.no).

Hamnøy and Reine

Back on the E10, it's a further 5km to the **Flakstad kirke**, a distinctive onion-domed, red-timber church built of driftwood in 1780. The church marks the start of **RAMBERG**, the island's administrative centre – if that's what you can call the smattering of services (garage, supermarket and suchlike) straggling the sandy beach. Pressing on south, over the first of several narrow bridges, you're soon on **Moskenesøya**, where the road squeezes along the coast before squirming across the mouth of the Reinefjord, hopping from islet to islet to link **HAMNØY**, on the north side of the inlet, with **REINE** to the south. Both villages boast impos-sibly picturesque settings, and Hamnøy also lays claim to an excellent restaurant, *Hamnøy Mat & Vinbu* (early March to Sept), which offers traditional Norwegian cuisine at its best. The menu is short, but the food is first-rate and this is as good a place as any to try a traditional island delicacy, fried cods' tongues. Hamnøy also holds the very plain *Hamnøy Rorbuer* (☎76 09 23 20, ⓕ76 09 21 54; ❸), but these are not nearly as appealing as those on the tiny islet of **Sakrisøya**, midway between Hamnøy and Reine, where the pretty yellow cabins of *Sakrisøy Rorbuer* (☎76 09 21 43, ⊛www.rorbu.as; ❸) are well-kept and cosy.

Stuck on a promontory just off the E10 immediately to the south of Sakrisøya, **REINE** conspires to look a tad seedy despite the scenery. It is, however, very useful as the departure point for a variety of **boat trips**. These include Midnight Sun cruises (late May to mid-July 1 weekly; 5hr; 470kr), coastal voyages (June to mid-Aug 1 weekly; 4hr; 350kr), fishing expeditions (late May to mid-Aug; 500kr) and excursions to the Moskenstraumen (see p.399). Further information about these trips, including sailing schedules, is easy to come by locally – phone or visit the Moskenes tourist office (see below), or ask at wherever you're staying.

Moskenes

From Reine, it's about 5km to **MOSKENES**, the main island port from Bodø – not that there's much here beyond a handful of houses dotted round a horseshoe-shaped bay. There is, however, a helpful **tourist office** by the jetty (early to late

△ Hamnøy, Lofoten islands

June Mon–Fri 10am–5pm; late June to early Aug daily 10am–7pm; early to mid-Aug Mon–Fri 10am–5pm; mid-Aug to early June Mon–Fri 10am–2pm; ☎76 09 15 99; ⊛www.lofoten-info.no), and a basic **campsite** (☎76 09 13 44; June–Aug), a five-minute walk away some 400m up a gravel track. A local **bus** runs along the E10 linking Leknes, Moskenes and Å (see below) at least once or twice daily from late June to late August, less frequently the rest of the year. Times do not usually coincide with ferry sailings, however.

Å

Five kilometres further south the road ends abruptly at the tersely named **Å**, one of the Lofoten's most delightful villages, its old buildings rambling along a foreshore that's wedged in tight between the grey-green mountains and the surging sea. Unusually, so much of the nineteenth-century village has survived that a goodly portion has been incorporated into the **Norwegian Fishing Village Museum** (*Norsk Fiskevaersmuseum*; late June to late Aug daily 11am–6pm; late Aug to late June Mon–Fri 11am–3pm; 50kr), an engaging attempt to recreate life here at the end of the nineteenth century. There are about fifteen buildings to examine – though some seem to be permanently closed – including a boathouse, forge, cod-liver oil processing plant, *rorbuer* and the houses of the two traders who dominated things hereabouts and the fishermen who did their bidding. The museum has a series of displays detailing every aspect of village life – and very well presented it is, too. Afterwards, you can extend your knowledge of all things fishy by visiting the **Stockfish Museum** (*Tørrfiskmuseum*; early to late June daily 11am–5pm; late June to late Aug daily 10am–5pm; 40kr), stockfish being the air-dried fish that was the staple diet of most Norwegians well into the twentieth century.

Å also weighs in with several **boat trips**. There are day-long fishing expeditions (June–Aug Mon–Sat 1 daily; 3hr; 300kr) and, weather and tides permitting, regular cruises (June to mid-Aug 1 weekly; 4hr; 400kr) to the **Moskenstraumen**, the maelstrom at the southern tip of Moskenesøya. There are other places to see similar phenomena in Norway – the Saltstraumen near Bodø (see p.379) springs to mind – but the swirling, hissing, spinning waters of the Moskenstraumen are the most dramatic.

Practicalities

Reachable by local **bus** at least once or twice daily from late June to late August, less frequently the rest of the year, Å is at the very end of the E10. Irritatingly, bus times do not usually coincide with the Moskenes ferry sailings to and from the mainland, so to get from Moskenes to Å you'll either have to walk – it's an easy 5km – or take a taxi.

Most of the **accommodation** in Å is run by one family. They own the all-year HI **hostel**, which has doubles (❶) and dorm rooms (160kr); the assortment of smart three- to ten-bedded *rorbuer* (800–1350kr per *rorbu*) surrounding the dock; and the adjacent ✹ *sjøhus*, which offers very comfortable and equally smart, hotel-standard rooms (from ❷). The family also permit some informal **camping** within the Norsk Fiskevaersmuseum and operate Å's cosy **bar** and only **restaurant**, where the seafood is first-rate and main courses average around 120kr. **Bookings** for all the above are on ☎76 09 11 21, though off-season (September–May) you may have better luck on ☎22 50 97 84 or via ⊛www.lofoten-rorbu.com. Finally, Å has a grocery store, an old-style bakery and bikes can be rented at 150kr per day.

Travel details

Trains

Narvik to: Riksgränsen (2–3 daily; 50min); Stockholm (1 daily; 18hr).
Trondheim to: Bodø (2–3 daily; 11hr); Dombås (3–4 daily; 2hr 30min); Fauske (2–3 daily; 9–10hr); Mo-i-Rana (2–3 daily; 6–7hr); Oslo (3–5 daily; 6hr 30min); Otta (3 daily; 3hr); Røros (1–2 daily; 2hr 30min); Steinkjer (hourly; 2hr); Stockholm (2 daily; 12hr).

Principal buses

Bodø to: Fauske (6–7 daily; 1hr 10min); Harstad (1 daily; 7hr 30min); Narvik (1–3 daily; 7hr 30min); Sortland (1–2 daily; 7hr); Svolvær (1 daily; 10hr 40min).
Fauske to: Bodø (6–7 daily; 1hr 10min); Harstad (1 daily; 6hr 30min); Narvik (1–3 daily; 5hr 30min); Sortland (1–2 daily; 6hr); Svolvær (1 daily; 9hr).
Harstad to: Fauske (1 daily; 6hr 30min).
Narvik to: Alta (Mon–Fri & Sun 1–3 daily; 9hr); Bodø (1–3 daily; 7hr); Fauske (1–3 daily; 5hr 30min); Sortland (1–2 daily; 4hr); Svolvær

(1–2 daily; 6hr 40min); Tromsø (1–3 daily; 4hr 10min).
Sortland to: Andenes (1–3 daily; 2hr 15min).
Svolvær to: Å (Mon–Fri 1–2 daily; 3hr 20min).
Trondheim to: Bergen (2 daily; 14hr); Kristiansund (1–3 daily; 5hr); Otta (2 daily; 4hr 30min); Stryn (2 daily; 7hr 20min); Ålesund (1–3 daily; 8hr).

Nord-Norgeekspressen

The **Nord-Norgeekspressen** (North Norway Express Bus) complements the railway system. It runs north from Bodø and Fauske to Narvik and Tromsø, where you change – and stay overnight – before embarking on the next leg of the journey up to Alta. In Alta, passengers change again for the connecting **Nordkappekspressen** bus onto Honningsvåg and Nordkapp. For further details of the northern parts of this epic bus journey, see "Travel details" at the end of the North Norway chapter.

Car ferries

Andenes to: Gryllefjord (early June to late Aug 2–3 daily; 1hr 40min).
Bodø to: Moskenes (June–Aug 5–6 daily; Sept–May Mon–Fri & Sun 1–3 daily; 3hr 30min); Røst (1–2 daily; 7hr 20min); Værøy (1–2 daily; 5hr 15min).
Bognes to: Lødingen (10–12 daily; 1hr); Skarberget (20–21 daily, usually every 1hr or 1hr 15min; 25min).

Botnhamn to: Brensholmen (June to late Aug 4–7 daily; 35min).
Fiskebøl to: Melbu (every 90min; 25min).
Harstad to: Skrolsvik (early June to late Aug 2–4 daily; 1hr 50min).
Skutvik to: Svolvær (June to mid-Aug 9 daily; mid-Aug to May 3–4 daily; 2hr).
Svolvær to: Skutvik (June to mid-Aug 9 daily; mid-Aug to May 3–4 daily; 2hr).

Hurtigbåt passenger express boats

Bodø to: Svolvær (Mon–Fri & Sun 5 daily; 5hr 30min).
Harstad to: Tromsø (1–2 daily; 2hr 45min).
Narvik to: Svolvær (Tues–Fri & Sun 2 daily; 2hr 20min).
Trondheim to: Kristiansund (1–3 daily; 3hr 30min).

Hurtigrute coastal boat

Northbound departures: daily from Trondheim at noon; Bodø at 3pm; Stamsund at 7.30pm; Svolvær at 10pm; Stokmarknes at 1am; Sortland at 3am and Harstad at 8am.
Southbound departures: daily from Harstad at 8.30am; Sortland at 1pm; Stokmarknes at 3.15pm; Svolvær at 7.30pm; Stamsund at 9.30pm; Bodø at 4am and Trondheim at 10am.
Journey time Trondheim–Harstad 43hr, Trondheim–Tromsø 51hr.

2.5

North Norway

Baedeker, writing 100 years ago about Norway's remote **northern provinces**, Troms and Finnmark, observed that they "possess attractions for the scientific traveller and the sportsman, but can hardly be recommended for the ordinary tourist" – a comment which isn't too wide of the mark even today. These are enticing lands, no question, the natural environment they offer stunning in its extremes, but the travelling can be hard, the specific sights well distanced and, when you reach them, subtle in their appeal.

Troms's intricate, fretted coastline has shaped its history since the days when powerful Viking lords operated a trading empire from its islands. Indeed, over half the population still lives offshore in dozens of tiny fishing villages, but the place to aim for is **Tromsø**, the so-called "Capital of the North" and a lively university town where King Håkon and his government proclaimed a "Free Norway" in 1940 before fleeing into exile. Beyond Tromsø, the long trek north begins in earnest as you enter **Finnmark**, a vast wilderness covering 48,000 square kilometres, but home to just two percent of the Norwegian population. Much of the land was laid waste during World War II, the combined effect of the Russian advance and the retreating German army's scorched-earth policy, and it's now possible to drive for hours without coming across a building more than sixty years old. The first obvious target in Finnmark is **Alta**, a sprawling settlement that's famous for its prehistoric rock carvings. Alta is also an important crossroads. From here, most visitors head straight for the steely cliffs of **Nordkapp** (the North Cape), mainland Europe's northernmost point, with or without a detour to the likeable port of **Hammerfest**, and leave it at that; but some doggedly press on to **Kirkenes**, the last town before the Russian border, which feels as if it's about to drop off the end of the world. From Alta, the other main alternative is to travel inland across the eerily endless scrubland of the **Finnmarksvidda**, where winter temperatures plummet to -35°C. This high plateau is the last stronghold of the **Sámi**, northern Norway's indigenous people, many of whom still live a semi-nomadic life tied to the movement of their reindeer herds. You'll spot Sámi in their brightly coloured traditional gear all across the region, but especially in the remote towns of **Kautokeino** and **Karasjok**, strange, disconsolate places in the middle of the plain.

Finally, and even more adventurously, there is the **Svalbard** archipelago, whose icy mountains rise out of the Arctic Ocean 640km north of mainland Norway. Once the exclusive haunt of trappers, fishermen and coal miners, Svalbard now makes a tidy income from adventure tourism – everything from guided glacier walks to snowmobile excursions and whale-watching. You can fly there independently from

---

Finnmark: the midnight sun and polar night

On clear nights, the **Midnight Sun** is visible at Alta, Hammerfest and Nordkapp from mid-May until the end of July; the long **Polar Night** runs from the last week in November until the third week in January.

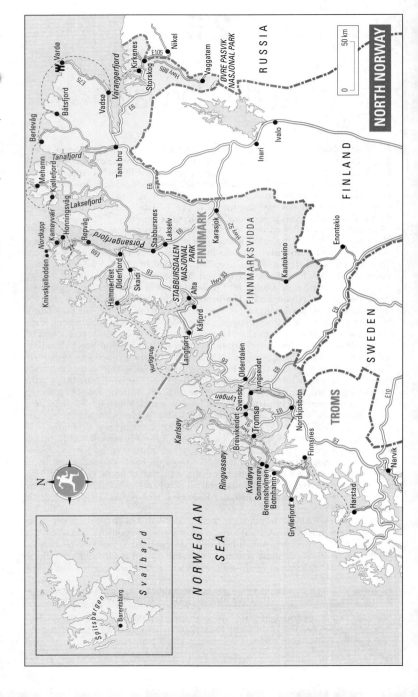

NORTH NORWAY

50 km

0

RUSSIA

FINLAND

SWEDEN

NORWEGIAN SEA

N

Svalbard

Spitsbergen

Barentsburg

most of Norway's larger towns, including Tromsø, at prices that are bearable, though most people opt for a package tour.

Transport and accommodation

Public transport in Troms and Finnmark is by bus, Hurtigrute coastal boat and plane – there are no trains. For all but the most truncated of tours, the best idea is to pick and mix these different forms of transport – for example by flying from Tromsø to Kirkenes and then taking the Hurtigrute back, or vice versa. It's best to avoid endless doubling back on the E6, though this is often difficult, as this is the only road to run right across the region. To give an idea of the distances involved, it's 400km from Tromsø to Alta, 600km to Nordkapp and 950km to Kirkenes.

The principal long-distance bus is the **Nord-Norgeekspressen**, which links Tromsø with Alta, from where there are onward services to Honningsvåg and – from late June to mid-August – Nordkapp. Alta is also handy for local buses to Karasjok and Kirkenes. North of Alta, just about every bus uses the E6 to pass through Skaidi, where you change for Hammerfest and Olderfjord. The bus linking Hammerfest with Karasjok and Kirkenes also runs through Olderfjord. Bus **time-tables** are available at most tourist offices and bus stations. On the longer rides, it's a good idea to buy **tickets** in advance as empty seats can get scarce.

The main **highways** are all well-maintained, but **drivers** will find the going a little slow as they have to negotiate some pretty tough terrain. You can cover 250–300km in a day without any problem, but much more and it all becomes rather wearisome. Be warned also that in July and August, the E6 north of Alta can get congested with caravans and motor homes on their way to Nordkapp. You can avoid the crush by starting early or, for that matter, by driving overnight – an eerie experience when it's bright sunlight in the wee hours of the morning. In **winter**, driving conditions can be appalling and, although the Norwegians make a spirited effort to keep the E6 open, they don't always succeed. If you're not used to driving in these sorts of conditions, don't start here – especially during the Polar Night. If you intend to use the region's **unpaved roads**, be prepared for the worst and certainly take food and drink, warm clothes and, if possible, a mobile phone. Keep an eye on the fuel indicator too, as petrol stations are confined to the larger settlements and these are often 100–200km apart. Car repairs can take time since workshops are scarce and parts often have to be ordered from the south.

Much more leisurely is the **Hurtigrute coastal boat**, which takes the best part of two days to cross the huge fjords between Tromsø and Kirkenes. En route, it calls at eleven ports, mostly remote fishing villages, but also Hammerfest and Honningsvåg, where it pauses for two or three hours so that special buses can cart passengers off to Nordkapp and back. With regard to **air travel**, the region has several **airports**, including those at Alta, Hammerfest, Honningsvåg, Kirkenes and Tromsø, as well as Longyearbyen on Svalbard. Via its subsidiary, Widerøe, SAS flies in and out of a string of small northern airstrips; summer discounts and special deals and passes making flying an economic possibility.

As for **accommodation**, all the major settlements have at least a couple of hotels and the main roads are sprinkled with campsites. If you have a tent and a well-insulated sleeping bag you can, in theory, bed down more or less where you like, but the hostility of the climate and the ferocity of the mosquitoes, which breed in marshy areas of the Finnmarksvidda, make most people think (at least) twice. There are HI **hostels** at Tromsø, Alta, Lakselv and Karasjok.

Tromsø

TROMSØ has been called, rather preposterously, the "Paris of the North", and though even the tourist office doesn't make any pretence to such grandiose titles today, the city is without question the effective capital of northern Norway. Easily the region's most populous town, Tromsø received its municipal charter in 1794,

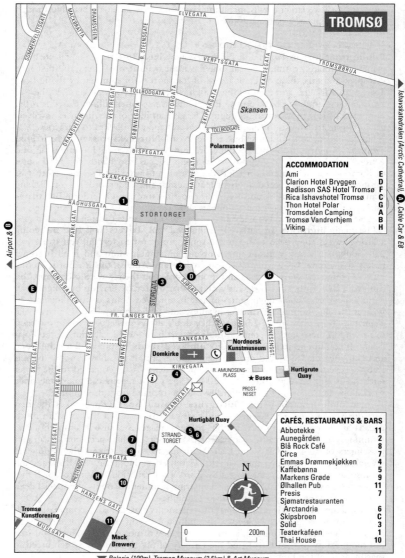

▲ Airport & B

▶ Ishavskatedralen (Arctic Cathedral), ⓐ Cable Car & E8

TROMSØ

Skansen

Polarmuseet

STORTORGET

ACCOMMODATION
Ami	E
Clarion Hotel Bryggen	D
Radisson SAS Hotel Tromsø	F
Rica Ishavshotel Tromsø	C
Thon Hotel Polar	G
Tromsdalen Camping	A
Tromsø Vandrerhjem	B
Viking	H

Domkirke

Nordnorsk Kunstmuseum

R. AMUNDSENS-PLASS

★ Buses

Hurtigrute Quay

PROST-NESET

Hurtigbåt Quay

STRAND-TORGET

CAFÉS, RESTAURANTS & BARS
Abbotekke	11
Aunegården	2
Blå Rock Café	8
Circa	7
Emmas Drømmekjøkken	4
Kaffebønna	5
Markens Grøde	9
Ølhallen Pub	11
Presis	7
Sjømatrestauranten Arctandria	6
Skipsbroen	C
Solid	3
Teaterkaféen	1
Thai House	10

N

Tromsø Kunstforening

Mack Brewery

0   200m

▼ Polaria (100m), Tromsø Museum (2.5km) & Art Museum

when it was primarily a fishing port and trading station, and flourished in the middle of the nineteenth century when its seamen ventured north to Svalbard to reap rich rewards hunting arctic foxes, polar bears and, most profitable of all, seals. Subsequently, Tromsø became famous as the jumping-off point for a string of arctic expeditions, its celebrity status assured when the explorer Roald Amundsen flew from here to his death somewhere on the Arctic ice cap in 1928. Since those heady days, Tromsø has grown into an urbane and likeable small city, with a population of 60,000 employed in a wide range of industries and at the university. Give or take the odd museum, Tromsø is short on specific sights, but its amiable atmosphere and fine mountain and fjord setting more than compensate. It also possesses a clutch of good restaurants, lively bars and several enjoyable hotels.

Arrival and information

At the northern end of the E8, 73km from the E6 and 250km north of Narvik, Tromsø's compact centre slopes up from the waterfront on the hilly island of Tromsøya. The island is connected to the mainland by bridge and tunnel. The **Hurtigrute** docks in the town centre at the foot of Kirkegata; **Hurtigbåt** boats arrive at the quay about 150m to the south. Long-distance **buses** arrive and leave from the car park a few metres away. The **airport** is 5km west of the centre on the other side of Tromsøya. From the airport, frequent Flybussen airport buses (Mon–Fri hourly 8.25am–7.50pm, Sat 7 daily 8.25am–8.30pm, Sun 10 daily 11am–12.40pm; 45kr) run into the city, stopping at the *Radisson SAS Hotel Tromsø* on Sjøgata and at several other central hotels; the taxi fare is 100–130kr.

Tromsø's **tourist office**, Storgata 61 (mid- to late May & mid-Aug to mid-Sept Mon–Fri 8.30am–4pm, Sat & Sun 10.30am–2pm; June to mid-Aug Mon–Fri 8.30am–6pm, Sat 10am–5pm & Sun 10.30am–5pm; mid-Sept to mid-May Mon–Fri 8.30am–4pm, Sat 10.30am–2pm, closed Sun; ☎77 61 00 00, ⊛www .destinasjontromso.no), is a couple of minutes' walk straight up Kirkegata from where the long-distance buses stop. Staff can supply free town maps and oodles of local information, and also sell a one- or two-day **tourist ticket** (60kr/120kr, valid 24/48hr from when it's first used) offering unlimited city bus travel, though most places of interest can easily be reached on foot.

It only takes five minutes to walk from one side of the centre to the other, but for the outlying attractions you can either catch a local bus or **rent a bike** from Sportshuset, Storgata 87 (Mon–Fri 9am–5pm, Sat 10am–4pm; ☎77 66 11 00). There's **Internet** access at the *Amtmannens Datter* café-bar, Grønnegata 81 (Mon–Thurs noon–2am, Fri & Sat noon–3.30am, Sun 3pm–2am).

△ Hurtigrute passengers

Accommodation

Tromsø has a good supply of modern, central **hotels**, though the majority occupy chunky concrete high-rises. Less expensive are the town's **guesthouses** (*pensjonater*), the HI **hostel** and the campsite.

Note that advance booking is a very good idea for all the options listed here, especially in the summer.

Ami Skolegata 24 ☎77 68 22 08, ⊛www
.amihotel.no. With seventeen simple rooms, this
guesthouse/hotel has wide views over the city
from the hillside behind the town centre. ❷/❸

Clarion Hotel Bryggen Sjøgata 19–21 ☎77 78
11 00, ⊛www.choicehotels.no. Polished, super-
modern chain hotel down on the waterfront, with
small but tastefully furnished rooms. The fifth-floor
jacuzzi offers fine sea (and sky) views. Substantial
weekend and summer discounts. ❻

Radisson SAS Hotel Tromsø Sjøgata 7 ☎77
60 00 00 ⊛www.radissosnsas.com. This plush
downtown high-rise offers smart and comfortable
modern rooms, and ultra-efficient service. ❺/❻

Rica Ishavshotel Tromsø Fr. Langes gate
2 ☎77 66 64 00, ⊛www.rica.no. Perched
on the harbourfront, this imaginatively designed
hotel is partly built in the style of a ship, complete
with a sort of crow's nest bar. Lovely rooms and
unbeatable views of the waterfront. Best place in
town. ❻

Thon Hotel Polar Grønnegata 45 ☎77 75 17
00, ⊛www.thonhotels.no. Small, modern rooms

decorated in typical chain-hotel style, but summer
and weekend discounts make this place a real
bargain; central location, too. ❸/❹

Tromsdalen Camping Elvestrandvegen ☎77 63
85 24, ⊜post@tromsocamping.no. Reasonably
handy site about 2km east of the Arctic cathedral
(Ishavskatedralen), on the mainland side of the
main bridge, with cabins (❶) as well as tent
pitches. Open all year.

Tromsø Vandrerhjem Åsgårdsveien 9, Elverhøy
☎77 65 76 28, ⊛www.vandrerhjem.no. Basic,
barracks-like HI hostel with dorm beds (150kr)
and doubles (❶). It's located some 2km west of
the centre in Elverhøy, a stiff thirty-minute walk
from the centre; it's also reachable by local bus
– ask at the bus station. No food is available, but
there's a store close by and communal kitchens.
Reception is closed 11am–5pm. Open late June
to late Aug.

Viking Grønnegata 18 ☎77 67 44 30, ⊛www
.viking-hotell.no. Simple and straightforward
hotel-cum-B&B, centrally located and with very
good prices. ❸

The City

Completed in 1861, the **Domkirke** (Tues–Sat 10am–4pm, Sun 10am–2pm; free), bang in the centre on Kirkegata, bears witness to the prosperity of Tromsø's nine-teenth-century merchants, who became rich on the back of the barter trade with Russia. They part-funded the cathedral's construction, resulting in the large and handsome structure of today, whose imposing spire pokes high into the sky. Behind the church, at Sjøgata 1, stands the **Nordnorsk Kunstmuseum** (Art Museum of Northern Norway; mid-June to mid-Aug daily noon–6pm; mid-Aug to mid-June Tues, Wed & Fri 10am–5pm, Thurs 10am–7pm, Sat & Sun noon–5pm; 30kr; ⊛www.museumsnett.no/nordnorsk-kunstmuseum), a well-presented collection of fine art and northern handicrafts from the 1850s onwards. It's not a large ensemble, but it does contain the work of many Norwegian painters, from lesser-known figures like Axel Revold and Christian Krohg to a handful of works by Edvard Munch (for more on whom, see p.274). There are also several Romantic peasant scenes by Adolph Tidemand and a couple of ingenious landscapes by both the talented Thomas Fearnley and Johan Dahl. The permanent collection is enhanced by frequent loans from the National Gallery in Oslo, and by a lively programme of temporary exhibitions.

Back at the front of the Domkirke, it's a gentle five-minute stroll north past the shops of Storgata to the main square, **Stortorget**, site of a daily open-air flower and knick-knack **market**. The square nudges down to the waterfront, where fresh fish and prawns are sold direct from inshore fishing boats throughout the summer. Follow the harbour round to the north and you're in the heart of old Tromsø: the raised ground close to the water's edge was the centre of the medieval settlement, and it was here that the locals built the first fortifications. Nothing now remains of the medieval town, but you can discern the shape of a later, eighteenth-century **fort** in the modest knoll, Skansen, at the end of Skansegata.

Close by, in an old wooden waterfront warehouse, is the city's most enjoyable museum, the **Polarmuseet** (Polar Museum; daily: mid-May to mid-June & mid-Aug to mid-Sept 11am–5pm; mid-June to mid-Aug 10am–7pm; mid-Sept to mid-May 11am–3pm; 50kr; ⊛www.polarmuseum.no). The collection begins with a rather unappetizing series of displays on trapping in the Arctic, but beyond is an outstanding section on Svalbard, including archeological finds recently retrieved from an eighteenth-century Russian trapping station – most come from graves in which they were preserved by permafrost. Two other sections on the first floor focus on seal hunting, an important part of the local economy until the 1950s. Upstairs, on the second floor, a further section is devoted to the polar explorer **Roald Amundsen** (1872–1928). Amundsen spent thirty years searching out the secrets of the polar regions, and on December 14, 1911, he and four of his crew became the first men to reach the South Pole, famously just ahead of his British rival Captain Scott. The museum exhibits all sorts of oddments used by Amundsen and his men – from long johns and pipes through to boots and ice picks – but it's the photos that steal the show, both for the fascinating insight they give into the expeditions and their hardships, and for their images of a heroically posed Amundsen, complete with the finest set of eyebrows north of Oslo.

To the south of the city centre, the eminently profitable **Mack brewery**, at the corner of Storgata and Musegata, proudly lays claim to being the northernmost brewery in the world – and dreams up all sorts of bottle labels with ice and polar bears to hammer home the point. Nearby, just up Musegata, the **Tromsø Art Institute** (*Kunstforening*; Tues–Sun noon–5pm; 30kr) occupies part of a large and attractive late nineteenth-century building that started out as the municipal museum. Today, the gallery showcases imaginative temporary exhibitions of Norwegian contemporary art with the emphasis on the work of Nordland artists; most of the works are on sale.

Doubling back down Musegata, it's a couple of hundred metres south along Storgata to **Polaria** (daily: mid-May to mid-Aug 10am–7pm; mid-Aug to mid-May noon–5pm; 80kr; ⊛www.polaria.no), a lavish waterfront complex which deals with all things Arctic. There's an aquarium filled with Arctic species, a 180-degree cinema showing a gripping film on Svalbard and several exhibitions on polar research.

Eating and drinking

With a clutch of first-rate **restaurants**, several enjoyable **cafés** and a good supply of late-night **bars**, Tromsø is certainly as well served as any comparable Norwegian city. The best of the cafés and restaurants are concentrated in the vicinity of the tourist office, on Storgata, and most of the livelier bars – many of which sell Mack, the local brew – are in the centre, too. We've given phone numbers only for places where you need to book.

Cafés and restaurants

Aunegården Sjøgata 29. Large(ish) café-restaurant within the listed Aunegården building. All the Norwegian standard dishes are served, at moderate prices, but these are as nothing when compared with the cakes, wonderful confections which are made at their own bakery. Weep with pleasure as you nibble at the cheesecake.

Emmas Drømmekjøkken Kirkegata 8 ☎77 63 77 30. Much praised in the national press as a gourmet treat, "Emma's dream kitchen" lives up to its name, with an imaginative and wide-ranging menu centred around Norwegian

produce. The grilled Arctic char with chanterelle risotto is a treat and, giving reindeer a wide berth, a delicious venison dish with rowanberries is handled with finesse. Main courses are 190kr and up. Closed Sun.

Kaffebønna Strandtorget 1. Smart, specialist coffee house with definitively the best brew in town, plus tasty snacks from their own bakery.

Markens Grøde Storgata 30 ☎77 68 25 50. Classy and expensive Norwegian cuisine featuring innovative preparations of local fish and game, and lots of seasonal specialities. Main courses from 200kr. Closed Mon.

Presis Storgata 30. Norwegian-style tapas that really works, in super-cool surroundings upstairs from the *Circa* bar (see below). If you choose carefully you can fill up while keeping the prices reasonable (90kr or less).

Sjømatrestauranten Arctandria Strandtorget 1 ☎77 60 07 20. Some of the best food in town. The upstairs restaurant serves a superb range of fish, with the emphasis on Arctic species, and there's also reindeer and seal; main courses start at around 220kr. Prices are about twenty percent less at the café-bar *Skarven*, downstairs, where there's a slightly less varied menu. Closed Sun.

Solid Storgata 73. Brisk, modern café in the daytime, with tasty snacks and light meals, and a busy bar at night.

Thai House Storgata 22. Decent Thai cooking with the welcome inclusion of some excellent fish and vegetable dishes; the Thai spicy salads are especially good, and prices are moderate (mains from around 150kr).

Bars

Abbotekke Storgata 4. Fresh, inventive cocktails and an array of whiskeys attracts a classy crowd.

There isn't room to swing a cat, but drinkers revel in the intimacy.

Blå Rock Café Strandgata 14. Definitely the place to go for loud rock music – with and without the roll. Occasional live acts too, not to mention the best burgers in town.

Circa Storgata 36. With DJs Thursday to Saturday and intimate jazz concerts at least once a week, the sense of fun in this laid-back bar makes it one of the best in town.

Skipsbroen Fr. Langes gate 2. Inside the *Rica Ishavshotel* (see p.406), this smart little bar overlooks the waterfront from on high – it occupies the top of a slender tower with wide windows that afford sea views. Relaxed atmosphere; lots of tourists.

Teaterkaféen Grønnegata 87, corner of Stortorget. Inside the Kulturhus, this arts-centre café-bar is long on conversation and (student) style. Open until 1am daily.

Ølhallen Pub Storgata 4. Solid (some would say staid) pub adjoining the Mack brewery, whose various ales are its speciality. It's the first pub in town to start serving, and so pulls in the serious drinker. Closed Sun.

Into Finnmark: Alta

Northeast of Tromsø, the vast sweep of the northern landscape slowly unfolds, with silent fjords gashing deep into the coastline beneath ice-tipped peaks which themselves fade into the high plateau of the interior. This forbidding, elemental terrain is interrupted by the occasional valley where those few souls hardy enough to make a living in these parts struggle on – often by dairy farming. In summer, cut grass dries everywhere, stretched over wooden poles that form long lines on the hillsides like so much washing drying.

Slipping along the valleys and traversing the mountains in between, the **E8** and then the **E6** follow the coast pretty much all the way to Alta, some 420km – about nine hours' drive – to the north. Drivers can save around 120km (although not necessarily time, and certainly not money) by turning off the E8 25km south of Tromsø onto **Highway 91** – a quieter, arguably even more scenic route, offering extravagant fjord and mountain views. Highway 91 begins by cutting across the rocky peninsula that backs onto Tromsø to reach the **Breivikeidet–Svendsby car ferry** (every 1–2hr: Mon–Thurs 6am–8pm, Fri 6am–9pm, Sat 8am–8pm, Sun 10am–9pm; 25min; 68kr car and driver) over to the glaciated Lyngen peninsula. From the Svensby ferry dock it's just a 22-kilometre drive across the Lyngen to

Routes north from Tromsø

Northbound, the **Hurtigrute** leaves Tromsø daily at 6.30pm, taking eleven hours to reach Hammerfest. The **Nord-Norgeekspressen** (North Norway Express Bus) runs north from Tromsø to Alta, where passengers change again for the connecting **Nordkappekspressen** bus onto Honningsvåg. The Nord-Norgeekspressen operates all year, the Nordkappekspressen from late June to mid-August, when FFR, the local transport company, operates a bus onto Nordkapp. FFR also operates a bus service, weather permitting, from Alta to Honningsvåg, from mid-August to late June.

the **Lyngseidet–Olderdalen car ferry** (every 1–2hr: Mon–Thurs 7am–7pm, Fri 7am–9pm, Sat 9am–7pm, Sun 11am–9pm; 40min; 95kr car and driver), by means of which you can rejoin the E6 at **Olderdalen**, some 220km south of Alta. This is the route used by most long-distance buses.

Beyond Olderdalen, the E6 enters **Finnmark** as it approaches the hamlet of **Langfjordbotn**, at the foot of the long and slender Langfjord. Thereafter, the road sticks tight against the coast to reach, after another 60km, the tiny village of **KÅFJORD**, whose recently restored nineteenth-century church was built by the English company who operated the area's copper mines until they were abandoned as uneconomic in the 1870s. From here, it's just 20km further to Alta.

Alta

Despite the long haul to get here, first impressions of **ALTA** are not encouraging. With a population of just 16,000, the town spreads unenticingly along the E6 for several kilometres, at its ugliest in **Alta Sentrum**, now befuddled by a platoon of concrete blocks. Alta was at least interesting once, and for decades was not Norwegian at all, but Finnish and Sámi, and host to an ancient Sámi fair. World War II polished off the fair and destroyed all the old wooden buildings that once clustered together in Alta's **Bossekop**, where Dutch whalers settled in the seventeenth century.

For all that, Alta does have one remarkable feature, the most extensive area of **prehistoric rock carvings** in northern Europe, the **Helleristningene i Hjemmeluft**, which has been designated a UNESCO World Heritage site. The carvings are located beside the E6 as you approach Alta from the southwest, some 2.5km before the Bossekop district, and form part of **Alta Museum** (May daily 9am–6pm; early June and late Aug daily 8am–8pm; mid-June to mid-Aug daily 8am–11pm; Sept daily 9am–6pm; Oct–April Mon–Fri 9am–3pm, Sat & Sun 11am–4pm; 80kr May–Sept, otherwise 40kr; ⓦwww.alta.museum.no). The **museum** itself provides a wealth of background information on the carvings and on prehistoric Finnmark in general, as well as a potted history of the Alta area, with exhibitions on the salmon-fishing industry, copper mining and so forth. Outside, the **rock carvings** extend down the hill from the museum building to the fjordside. A clear and easy-to-follow footpath and boardwalk circumnavigate the site, taking in all the carvings in about an hour. On the trail, there are **thirteen vantage points** offering close-up

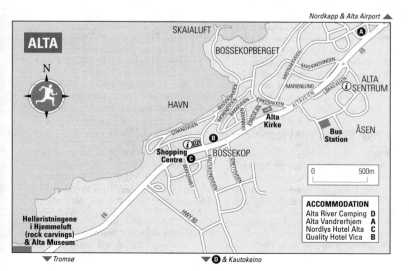

views of the carvings, recognizable though highly stylized representations of boats, animals and people picked out in red pigment (the colours have been retouched by researchers). They make up an extraordinarily complex tableau, whose minor variations – there are **four identifiable bands** – in subject matter and design indicate successive historical periods. The carvings were executed between 6000 and 2500 years ago, and are indisputably impressive: clear, stylish and touching in their simplicity, offering an insight into a prehistoric culture that was essentially settled and largely reliant on the hunting of land animals.

Practicalities

Long-distance **buses** make two stops in Alta – one at Alta Sentrum, where they pause at the **bus station**, the other at Alta airport, further north along the E6 in the Elvebakken district. Get off at Alta Sentrum for the rock carvings, which are reachable via a 4.5-kilometre walk back along the E6. Alternatively, you can catch a **local bus** (every half-hour Mon–Fri 6am–8pm, Sat 10am–3pm) from the bus station (or the airport) to Bossekop, from where you walk the final 2.5km. If you want to call a taxi, ring Alta Taxi on ☏78 43 53 53.

Alta has two **tourist offices**, one in the shopping centre in Alta Sentrum (Mon–Fri 8.30am–4pm, Sat 10am–2pm; ☏78 44 50 50, ⊕www.destinasjonalta.no), the other a seasonal office near the Coop supermarket in the Bossekop shopping centre (early June Mon–Fri 8am–4pm; mid-June to early Aug Mon–Fri 8am–6pm, Sat 10am–4pm, Sun noon–4pm; early Aug to end Aug Mon–Fri 8am–4pm & Sat 10am–3pm; ☏78 45 77 77). Both offer public Internet access (3kr per minute, minimum charge 50kr for 30min), will advise on hiking the Finnmarksvidda (see p.411) and help with finding **accommodation**.

Alta's best hotel by far is the *Quality Hotel Vica*, a couple of minute's walk from the Bossekop tourist office at Fogdebakken 6I (☏78 43 47 11, ⊕www.vica.no; ❺/❻). It's a small, cosy place decorated in the style of a mountain lodge, with lots of pine panelling, a sun-trap of a terrace and free Internet access. Alternatively, opposite the Bossekop tourist office is *Nordlys Hotell Alta*, Bekkefaret 3 (☏78 45 72 00, ⊕www .nordlyshotell.no; ❹/❺) a rather uninviting mish-mash of styles, but with large, comfortable rooms nonetheless. Less costly by far is the HI **hostel**, *Alta Vandrerhjem*, in a plain chalet about 700m north of Alta Sentrum at Midtbakkveien 52 (☏78 43 44 09, ⊕www.vandrerhjem.no; mid-June to mid-Aug), which has doubles (❶) as well as dorm beds (140kr). To get there from Alta Sentrum, drive or walk east up the E6 to the next roundabout, where you turn left and then first left again – a fifteen-minute stroll. Food isn't available, but there are self-catering facilities. There are also several **campsites** in the vicinity of Alta. The best is the well-equipped, four-star *Alta River Camping* (☏78 43 43 53, ✉annjenss@online.no), by the river about 4km out of town along Highway 93, which cuts off the E6 in between Bossekop and the rock paintings.

Easily the best **restaurant** in town is at the *Hotel Vica*, which specializes in regional delicacies – cloudberries, reindeer and the like. Prices are very reasonable (mains around 90kr) and traditional Sámi dishes are often on the menu, too.

The Finnmarksvidda

Venture far inland from Alta and you enter the **Finnmarksvidda**, a vast mountain plateau which spreads southeast up to and beyond the Finnish border. Rivers, lakes and marshes criss-cross the region, but there's barely a tree, let alone a mountain, to break the contours of a landscape whose wide skies and deep horizons are eerily beautiful. Distances are hard to gauge – a dot of a storm can soon be upon you, breaking with alarming ferocity – and the air is crystal-clear, giving a whitish lustre to the sunshine. A couple of roads cross this expanse, but for the most part it remains the preserve of the few thousand semi-nomadic **Sámi** who make up the majority of the local population. Many still wear traditional dress, a brightly coloured affair of red bonnets and blue jerkins or dresses, all trimmed with red, white and yellow embroidery. You'll see permutations on this traditional costume all over Finnmark, but especially at roadside souvenir stalls and on Sundays outside Sámi churches.

Setting aside the slow encroachments of the tourist industry, lifestyles on the Finnmarksvidda have remained remarkably constant for centuries. The main occupation is **reindeer-herding**, supplemented by hunting and fishing, and the pattern of Sámi life is mostly still dictated by the movements of their animals. During the winter, the reindeer graze the flat plains and shallow valleys of the interior, migrating towards the coast in early May as the snow begins to melt. By October, both people and reindeer are journeying back from their temporary summer quarters.

The Sámi

The northernmost reaches of Norway, Sweden and Finland, and the Kola peninsula of northwest Russia, are collectively known as **Lapland**. Traditionally, the indigenous people were called "Lapps", though in recent years this name has fallen out of favour and been replaced by the term **Sámi**, although the change is by no means universal. The new name comes from the Sámi word *sámpi*, meaning both the land and its people, of whom there are around 70,000 spread across the whole of the region. Among the oldest peoples in Europe, the Sámi are probably descended from prehistoric clans who migrated here from the east by way of the Baltic. Their **language** is closely related to Finnish and Estonian, though it's somewhat misleading to speak of a "Sámi language" as there are, in fact, three distinct versions, and each of these breaks down into a number of markedly different regional dialects. All three share many common features, however, including a superabundance of words and phrases to express variations in snow and ice conditions.

Originally, the Sámi were a semi-nomadic people, living in small communities (*siidas*), each of which had a degree of control over the surrounding hunting grounds. They mixed hunting, fishing and trapping, but it was the wild reindeer that supplied most of their needs. This changed in the sixteenth century when the Sámi switched over to **reindeer herding**, with communities following the seasonal movements of the animals.

What little contact the early Sámi had with other Scandinavians was almost always to their disadvantage, but these early depredations were nothing compared with the **dislocation of Sámi culture** that followed the efforts of Sweden, Russia and Norway to control and colonize Sámi land from the seventeenth century onwards. Things got even worse for the Norwegian Sámi towards the end of the nineteenth century, when the government, influenced by the Social Darwinism of the day, embarked on an aggressive policy of **"Norwegianization"**. New laws banned the use of the Sámi languages in schools, and stopped Sámi from buying land unless they could speak Norwegian. This policy was only abandoned and slowly replaced by a more considerate and progressive approach in the 1950s.

Since the international anti-colonial struggles of the 1960s, the Norwegians have been obliged to re-evaluate their relationship with the Sámi. In 1988, the country's **constitution** was amended with an article that stated "It is the responsibility of the authorities of the state to create conditions enabling the Sámi people to preserve and develop its language, culture and way of life", and the following year the **Sameting** (Sámi Parliament) was opened in Karasjok. Certain deep-seated problems do remain and, in common with other aboriginal peoples marooned in industrialized countries, there have been heated debates about land and mineral rights and the future of the Sámi as a people, above and beyond one country's international borders. Neither is it clear quite how the Norwegian Sámi will adjust to having something akin to dual citizenship – but at least Oslo is asking the right questions.

The long, dark winter is spent in preparation for the great **Easter festivals**, when weddings and baptisms are celebrated in the region's two main settlements, Karasjok and, more especially, Kautokeino. As neither settlement is particularly engaging in itself, Easter is without question the best time to be here – a celebration of the end of the Polar Night and the arrival of spring. There are folk-music concerts, church services and traditional sports, including the famed reindeer races – not, thank goodness, reindeers racing each other (they would never cooperate), but reindeer pulling passenger-laden sleighs. Details of these Easter festivals are available at any Finnmark tourist office, and there's a **Kautokeino festival website** (@www .saami-easterfestival.org). Summer visits, on the other hand, can be disappointing, since many families and their reindeer are at coastal pastures and there is precious little activity.

From Alta, the only direct route into the Finnmarksvidda is south along Highway 93 to **Kautokeino**, a distance of 130km. Just short of Kautokeino, about 100km from Alta, Highway 93 connects with Highway 92, which travels east the 100km or so to **Karasjok**, where you can rejoin the E6 – but well beyond the road to Nordkapp. **Bus** services across the Finnmarksvidda are patchy: there are one or two buses from Alta to Kautokeino every day except Tuesday and Saturday, and a limited service along the E6 from Alta to Karasjok (late June to mid-Aug Mon–Fri & Sun 2 daily; late Aug to early June 1–2 daily on 4 variable days a week). A further service links Karasjok with Hammerfest once or twice daily except on Saturdays, but there is only a twice-weekly bus between Karasjok and Kautokeino, on Friday and Sunday. Local buses are operated by FFR (@78 43 36 77, @www.ffr.no).

The best time to **hike** in the Finnmarksvidda is in August and early September – after the peak mosquito season and before the weather turns cold. For the most part the plateau vegetation is scrub and open birch forest, which makes the going fairly easy, though the many marshes, rivers and lakes often impede progress. There are a handful of clearly demarcated **hiking trails** and a smattering of appropriately sited but unstaffed huts; for detailed information, ask at Alta tourist office.

Kautokeino

It's a two- and a half-hour drive or bus ride from Alta across the Finnmarksvidda to **KAUTOKEINO** (Guovdageaidnu in Sámi), the principal winter camp of the Norwegian Sámi and the site of a huge reindeer market in spring and autumn. The Sámi are not, however, easy town dwellers and although Kautokeino is very useful to them as a supply base, it's still a desultory, desolate-looking place that straggles along the banks of the Kautokeinoelva River. Nevertheless, the settlement has become something of a tourist draw on account of the **jewellers** who have moved here from the south. Every summer, their souvenir booths line long main street, attracting Finnish day-trippers like flies. The jewellery bigwigs hereabouts are **Frank and Regine Juhls**, who braved all sorts of difficulties to set up their workshop here in 1959. It was a bold move at a time when the Sámi were very much a neglected minority, but the Juhls had a keen interest in nomadic cultures and, although the Sámi had no tradition of jewellery-making, they did adorn themselves with all sorts of unusual items traded in from the outside world. The Juhls were much influenced by the Sámi style of self-adornment, repeating and developing it in their own work, and their business prospered – perhaps beyond their wildest dreams. As testimony to the Juhls' commercial success, the plain and simple workshop they first built has been replaced by the **Juhls' Silver Gallery** (daily: early June to early Aug 9am–7pm; mid-Aug to May 9am–6pm; ring in winter to confirm hours on @78 48 61 89, @www.juhls.no), an extensive complex of low-lying showrooms and workshops with pagoda-like roofs are derived from the Sámi. Exquisitely beautiful, high-quality silver work is made and sold here alongside a much broader range of classy craftwork. The complex's **interior** (regular, free guided tours; 30min) is intriguing in its own right, with some rooms decorated in crisp, modern pan-Scandinavian style, others done out in an elaborate version of Sámi design. The gallery is located on a ridge above the west bank of the Kautokeinoelva, 2.5km south from the handful of buildings that passes for the town centre – follow the signs.

Practicalities

Doubling as Highway 93, Kautokeino's main street is 1500m long, and most of the town's facilities are clustered on the north side of the river, about 350m south of the **bus stop** in the vicinity of the **tourist office** (daily: June 9am–4pm, July & Aug 9am–6pm; ☏78 48 65 00, ✆www.kautokeino.info), which marks what is effectively the town centre. The tourist office provides town maps and has details of local events and activities, from fishing and hiking through to "**Sami adventures**", which typically include a boat trip and a visit to a *lavvo* ("tent") where you can sample traditional Sámi food and listen to *joik* (rhythmic song poems), from around 300kr. The main local tour operator is Cavzo Safari (☏78 48 75 88, ✆www.samitour.no).

The only **hotel** as such, is the modest and modern *Villmarkssenter* (☏78 48 76 02; ❸), across the highway from the tourist office. There are also a couple of **campsites** near the river on the southern edge of town, primarily *Kautokeino Camping og Motell* (☏78 48 54 00, ☏78 48 75 05), with cabins (❶) and a few frugal motel rooms (❷). **Eating** establishments are thin on the ground, but there's good coffee, cakes and sandwiches at *Kaffe Galleriet*, behind the tourist office.

Karasjok

The only other settlement of any size on the Finnmarksvidda is **KARASJOK** (*Kárásjohka* in Sámi), Norway's Sámi capital, which straddles the E6 on the main route from Finland to Nordkapp and consequently sees plenty of tourists. Spread across a wooded river valley, it has none of the desolation of Kautokeino, yet it still conspires to be fairly mundane despite the presence of the Sámi parliament and the country's best Sámi museum. The busiest place in town is the **tourist office** (early June & late Aug daily 9am–4pm; mid-June to late Aug daily 9am–7pm; Sept–May Mon–Fri 9am–4pm; ☏78 46 88 10, ✆www.koas.no), located on the north side of the river beside the E6 and Highway 92 crossroads, which is, to all intents and purposes, the centre of town. Staff issue free town maps, book overnight accommodation and organize authentic(ish) Sámi expeditions. The office is also incorporated within a miniature Sámi theme park, **Sámpi Park** (same times; 95kr), which offers a fancy multimedia introduction to the Sámi in the Stálubákti ("Magic Theatre"), as well as examples of traditional dwellings, Sámi shops and a restaurant. It also features displays of various ancient Sámi skills with the obligatory reindeer brought along as decoration or to be roped and corralled.

You may also want to take a peek at the **Gamle kirke** just off Highway 92 on the south side of the river and not to be confused with the more modern church on the north side. Gamle kirke was the only building left standing here at the end of World War II. Of simple design, it dates from 1807, making it easily the oldest surviving church in Finnmark.

Practicalities

There is a limited **bus** service to Karasjok along the E6 from Alta and Kirkenes (late June to mid-Aug Mon–Fri & Sun 2 daily; late Aug to early June 1–2 daily 4 variable days a week), and another bus links Hammerfest with Karasjok once or twice daily except on Saturdays; there's also a twice-weekly service from Kautokeino (Fri & Sun). Schedules mean that it's often possible to spend a couple of hours in Karasjok before moving on, which is quite enough to see the sights, but not nearly long enough to get the real flavour of the place. Buses pull in at the **bus station** on Storgata. From here, it's a signposted five- to ten-minute walk west to the **tourist office** (see above).

The best **hotel** in town is the *Rica Hotel Karasjok* (☏78 46 74 00, ✆www.rica .no; ❻/❹), a breezy modern establishment a short stroll north of the tourist office along the E6. More modest and less expensive accommodation is provided by the unassuming *Annes Overnatting og Motell* (⊕78 46 64 32; ❷), east of the tourist office along the E6 towards Kirkenes. There's also the all-year *Karasjok Camping*, a ten-minute walk west from the tourist office on the Kautokeino road (⊕78 46 61 35, ⊕78 46 66 97); the latter has cabins (❷) as well as spaces for tents. Some 7km out of town on the Kautokeino road (Highway 92), *Engholm Husky Vandrerhjem* (⊕78 46 71 66, ⊛www.engholm.no) is a fantastic all-year HI **hostel**, which has cosy home-made four- to six-bed **cabins** (350kr per night plus 150kr per person; dorm bed 175kr). The hostel is open all year and offers self-catering facilities, a sauna and Arctic dinners, sitting on reindeer skins around an open fire. The owner, the illustrious Sven, is an expert dog-sled racer and keeps about forty huskies; he uses them on a variety of winter guided tours – dog sledding and so forth – and in summer organizes everything from fishing trips and guided wilderness hikes to horseback riding. He will pick up guests from Karasjok by prior arrangement, too.

For **food**, the *Rica Hotel Karasjok* has the unusual *Gammen* restaurant, a set of turf-covered huts where Sámi-style meals are served. It's all good fun, but the choices are pretty much limited to reindeer or salmon plus delightful cloudberries with sweetened cream.

From Karasjok, it's 130km west to Kautokeino; 270km north to Nordkapp; 220km northwest to Hammerfest and 330km east to Kirkenes.

Hammerfest

Some 150km north of Alta, **HAMMERFEST** is, as its tourist office takes great pains to point out, the world's northernmost town. It was also, they add, the first town in Europe to have electric street-lighting. Hardly fascinating facts perhaps, but both give a glimpse of the pride that the locals take in making the most of what is, indisputably, an inhospitable location. Indeed, it's a wonder the town has survived at all: a hurricane flattened the place in 1856; it was burnt to the ground in 1890; and the retreating Germans mauled it at the end of World War II. Yet, instead of being abandoned, Hammerfest was stubbornly rebuilt for a third time. Nor is it the grim industrial town you might expect from the proximity of the offshore oil wells, but a bright, cheerful port that drapes around a horseshoe-shaped harbour sheltered from the elements by a steep rocky hill. But don't get too carried away: Bill Bryson, in *Neither Here Nor There*, hit the nail on the head with his description of Hammerfest as "an agreeable enough town in a thank-you-God-for-not-making-me-live-here sort of way".

The Town

Running parallel to the waterfront, **Strandgata**, Hammerfest's principal street, is a busy, 500-metre-long run of supermarkets, clothes and souvenir shops, partly inspired by the town's role as a stop-off for cruise ships on the way to Nordkapp. However, most of the activity takes place on the **town quay**, off Sjøgata, with tourists emerging from the liners to beetle around the harbourfront, eating shellfish from the stalls along the wharf or buying souvenirs in the small summertime Sámi market. The Hurtigrute spends a couple of hours here too, arriving at an unsociable 5.15am on its way north, 11.15am heading south.

Beyond that, it's the general atmosphere of the place that appeals rather than any specific sight, though Hammerfest's tiny town centre does muster a couple of attractions, beginning with the **Isbjørnklubben** (Royal and Ancient Polar Bear Society; Jan to mid-May & Sept–Dec Mon–Fri 11am–1pm, Sat & Sun 10.30am–1.30pm; mid-May to late June & late Aug daily 9am–5pm; 40kr) in the main quayside building. The pint-sized museum here tells the story of Hammerfest as a trapping centre and also relates the Society's own history as an organization that hunted and trapped polar bears, eagles and arctic foxes. Make

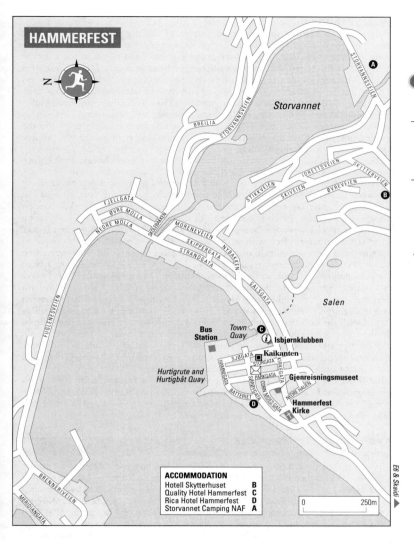

HAMMERFEST

N

Storvannet

STORVANNSVEIEN

A

BREILIA

STORVANNSVEIEN

SKYTTERVEIEN

IDRETTSVEIEN

STIKKVEIEN

SKIVEIEN

ØVREVEIEN

B

FJELLGATA

ØVRE MOLLA

NEDRE MOLLA

SKOLEBAKKEN

MORENEVEIEN

SKIPPERGATA

NYBAKKEN

STRANDGATA

SALSGATA

Salen

FUGLENESVEIEN

Bus Station

Town Quay

C

i **Isbjørnklubben**

SJØGATA

Kaikanten

HAMNEGATA

STORGATA

KIRKEGATA

PARKGATA

Hurtigrute and Hurtigbåt Quay

SIRMAGATA

BATTERIET

CHR. MOES GA.

NEDRE HAUEN

Gjenreisningsmuseet

D

Hammerfest Kirke

BRENNERIVEIEN

MERIDIANGATA

E6 & Skaidi ►

ACCOMMODATION

Hotell Skytterhuset	**B**
Quality Hotel Hammerfest	**C**
Rica Hotel Hammerfest	**D**
Storvannet Camping NAF	**A**

0   250m

sure you avoid the ceremony of being "knighted" with a Walrus' penis bone – not only will it set you back 250kr, but will make you cringe with embarrassment for weeks. Of more general interest is the purpose-built **Gjenreisningsmuseet** (Museum of Postwar Reconstruction; mid-June to Aug daily 10am–4pm; Sept to mid-June by appointment on ☎78 42 26 30; 40kr), a five-minute walk west of the main quay up Kirkegata. This begins with a fascinating section on the hardships endured by the inhabitants of Finnmark during the German retreat, in the face of the advancing Russians in late 1944, then goes on to deal with postwar reconstruction. As the labelling is only in Norwegian, it's worth investing 30kr for the English-language guidebook.

Practicalities

Hammerfest is situated on the western shore of the rugged island of Kvaløya, which is linked to the mainland by bridge. Buses pull into Hammerfest **bus station** at the foot of Sjøgata; the **Hurtigrute coastal boat** docks at the adjacent quay, as does the **Hurtigbåt express passenger boat** from Alta (1 daily Mon–Fri & Sun; 1hr 30min). The **tourist office** (Jan to mid-May & Sept–Dec Mon–Fri 11am–1pm, Sat & Sun 10.30am–1.30pm; mid-May to late June & late Aug daily 9am–5pm; ☎78 41 21 85, ⊛www.hammerfest-turist.no) occupies the same building as the Isbjørnklubben (see p.414). Staff issue free town maps and have details of local excursions, easily the most popular of which are the fishing trips and the summertime sea cruises to local nesting cliffs, squawking with guillemots, gannets, kittiwakes and many other types of seabird.

Hammerfest is light on places to stay, but there are two good **hotels**. First choice should be the enjoyable *Quality Hotel Hammerfest*, Strandgata 2–4 (☎78 42 96 00, ⊛www.hammerfesthotel.no; ④/⑤), which occupies a prime spot just metres from the main quay; it's housed in a routine modern block, but the cosy interior has a pleasant, slightly old-fashioned air, the rooms equipped with chunky wooden fittings that pre-date the chipboard craze of the 1960s onwards. Equally appealing is the *Rica Hotel Hammerfest*, Sørøygata 15 (☎78 41 13 33, ⊛www.rica.no; ③/④), an attractive modern place with sea views that sits on a grassy knoll a couple of minutes' walk west of the main quay. The only budget option is the unprepossessing *Hotell Skytterhuset*, Skytterveien 24 (☎78 41 15 11, ℱ78 41 19 26; ③), in a large prefabricated block up on a hillside, some 3km from the town centre. To get there by car, head east from the main quay along Strandgata and, after about 400m, just over the stream, turn right along Skolebakken. This road becomes Storvannsveien as it leads round a lake, Storvannet, which lies at the bottom of a steep-sided valley dotted with the houses of Hammerfest's one and only suburb. The road then climbs up the east side of Salen hill to run past the hotel. On the way to the hotel, you'll pass the tiny lakeshore *Storvannet Camping NAF* (☎78 41 10 10; June to mid-Sept), with tent spaces and a few cabins (①). Unless you're particularly energetic, you'll not want to walk to either of these places from the centre – take a taxi.

For **food**, the *Rica Hotel Hammerfest* possesses the best **restaurant** in town, with ocean views and delicious seafood; main courses start at around 200kr. More economical is *Kaikanten*, just up from the Hurtigrute quay at Sjøgata 19, where you'll find solid pub food in an amenable atmosphere.

Moving on from Hammerfest

Except on Saturdays, there's a once- or twice-daily **bus** from Hammerfest to Karasjok and Kirkenes. This passes through Skaidi, on the E6, as does the bus from Hammerfest to Alta (1–2 daily Mon–Fri & Sun). Both these services are operated by Finnmark Fylkesrederi og Rutesselskap (FFR; ☎78 40 70 00, ⊛www.ffr.no). At Skaidi, you change for either the Nordkappekspressen service to Honningsvåg and Nordkapp, or FFR's Skaidi–Honningsvåg bus (see below). Note that not all the buses make the connection, so be sure to check at Hammerfest bus station before you set out. The **Hurtigrute coastal boat** departs Hammerfest heading south daily at 12.45pm and takes 11 hours to reach its next port of call, Tromsø (passengers 829kr one-way, car 378kr). Sailing north, the Hurtigrute departs at 6.45am and reaches Honningsvåg at 11.45am (passengers 422kr, car 354kr). At Honningsvåg, it stops for three and three-quarter hours, plenty time enough for special connecting buses to make the return trip to Nordkapp. Finally, Hammerfest has several **car rental** companies and these frequently offer attractive short-term deals from around 700kr a day; try Hertz, Rossmollgate 48 (☎78 41 71 66). If, however, Nordkapp is your goal, comparable rental deals are available at Honningsvåg (see p.418), 180km north from Hammerfest.

Magerøya and Nordkapp

At the northern tip of Norway, the treeless and windswept island of **Magerøya** is mainly of interest to travellers as the location of the **Nordkapp** (North Cape), generally regarded as mainland Europe's northernmost point – though in fact it isn't; that distinction belongs to the neighbouring headland of **Knivskjellodden**. Somehow, everyone seems to have conspired to ignore this simple fact of latitude and now, whilst Nordkapp has become one of the most popular tourist destinations in the country, there isn't even a road to Knivskjellodden. Neither has the development of the Nordkapp as a tourist spot been without its critics, who argue that the large and lavish visitor centre – **Nordkapphallen** – is crass and grossly overpriced; their opponents simply point to the huge number of people who visit. Whatever, it's hard to imagine making the long trip to Magerøya without at least dropping by Nordkapp, and the island has other charms too, notably a bleak, rugged beauty that's readily appreciated on the E69 as it threads across the mountainous interior from Honningsvåg, on the south coast, to Nordkapp, a distance of 34km.

The obvious base for a visit to Nordkapp is **Honningsvåg**, the island's main settlement and a middling fishing village with a clutch of chain hotels. More appealing, however, is the tiny hamlet of **Kamøyvær**, nestling beside a narrow fjord just off the E69 between Honningsvåg and Nordkapp, and with a couple of family-run guesthouses. Bear in mind also that Nordkapp is within easy striking distance of other places back on the mainland, including the picturesque fishing station-cum-hotel at **Repvåg** – and maybe even Alta and Hammerfest, respectively 210km and 240km distant.

Getting to Magerøya and Nordkapp

Arriving by bus from Alta and/or Skaidi (for Hammerfest), even on the Nordkappekspressen, you must change at Honningsvåg for the FFR service onto Nordkapp (mid-June to late Aug 2 daily, 10.45am & 9.30pm; late Aug to mid-June 1 daily, 10.45am). The schedule is such that if you catch the second bus in summer, you'll have two hours at Nordkapp, from 10.15pm to 12.15am – which means, of course, that you can view the Midnight Sun. If Honningsvåg is as far as you can get by bus, the best way of proceeding onto Nordkapp is to rent a car or take a taxi. Honningsvåg tourist office has the details of local **car hire** companies offering special deals – reckon on 800kr for a five-hour rental. The **taxi fare** to Nordkapp, including an hour's waiting time after you get there, is 900kr return and 500kr one-way; contact Nordkapp Taxisentral (☎78 47 22 34).

Arriving by car, bear in mind that the last stretch of the Honningsvåg–Nordkapp road is closed by snow in winter, roughly from November to early April, and is only open to buses. To stand a chance of seeing the northern lights, try to go when the weather's clear.

North from Skaidi to Repvåg and Nordkapp

At the **Skaidi** crossroads at the end of Highway 94 from Hammerfest, the **E6** veers east to clip across a bleak plateau that brings it, 23km later, to the turning for Nordkapp. This turning, the **E69**, scuttles north along the shore of the **Porsangerfjord**, a deep and wide inlet flanked by bare, low-lying hills whose stone has been fractured and made flaky by the biting cold of winter. After 48km, the E69 zips past the byroad to **REPVÅG**, an old timber fishing station on a promontory just 2km off the main highway. A rare and particularly picturesque survivor from prewar days, the station is painted red in the traditional manner and perches on stilts at the water's edge. The whole complex has been turned into the 🍴 *Repvåg Fjordhotell og Rorbusenter* (☎78 47 54 40, ⓦwww.repvag-fjordhotell.no; April–Oct), with simple, unassuming rooms (❸) in the main building, as well as a cluster of old fishermen's shacks – *rorbuer* (❷). It's a charming place to stay and an ideal base from which to reach Nordkapp. Almost inevitably, the hotel **restaurant** specializes in seafood – and very good it is, too.

Back on the E69, it's about 25km to the ambitious – and amazingly expensive – series of tunnels and bridges (140kr toll) that spans the straits between the mainland and Honningsvåg, on the island of **Magerøya**; you'll see the island long before you arrive, a hunk of brown rock looking like an inverted blancmange.

Honningsvåg

HONNINGSVÅG, 180km from Hammerfest, is officially classified as a village, which robs it of the title of the world's northernmost town – hard luck considering it's barely any smaller or less hardy in the face of adversity than its neighbour. Largely made up of a jumble of well-worn modern buildings, the village straggles along the seashore, sheltered from the blizzards of winter by the surrounding crags – though, given the conditions, sheltered is a comparative term. Its prettiest area is at the **head of the harbour**, where an assortment of timber warehouses,

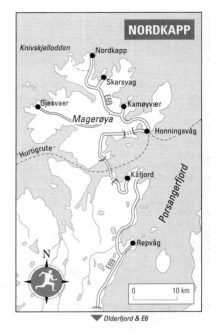

dating back to the days when the village was entirely reliant on fish, makes an attractive ensemble.

Honningsvåg strings out along its main drag, Storgata, for about one kilometre. Buses from the mainland, including the long-distance Nord-Norgeekspressen, pull in to the **bus station** at the west end of Storgata. **Hurtigrute coastal boats** dock at the adjacent jetty and are met by special Nordkapp excursion buses. The **tourist office** is here, too (mid-June to mid-Aug Mon–Fri 8.30am–8pm, Sat & Sun noon–8pm; mid-Aug to mid-June Mon–Fri 8.30am–4pm; ☎78 47 70 30, ⦿www.northcape.no).

All of Honningsvåg's **hotels** are along or near Storgata. Walking east from the bus station, it's a few metres to the first, the *Rica Hotel Honningsvåg* (☎78 47 23 33, ⦿www.rica.no; mid-May to Aug; ❹), a routine block with nearly two hundred modern rooms. Its sister hotel, the all-year *Rica Bryggen* (☎78 47 28 88, ⦿www.rica.no; ❺), occupies a much more attractive fishing warehouse about 500m to the east, down at the head of the harbour. Again, the rooms are bright, modern and comfortable. More appealing is the adjacent *Honningsvåg Brygge Hotel* (☎78 47 64 64, ⦿www.hvg.brygge.no; ❹), a tasteful and intelligent conversion of a set of wooden warehouses perched on one of the old jetties. The rooms here are smart and cosy – and advance reservations are strongly advised. Alternatively, *NAF Nordkapp Camping* (☎78 47 33 77, ✉nordkapp.camping@nordkapp.com; late May to mid-Sept), comprising a **campsite** and **cabins** (❷), is located about 8km from Honningsvåg on the road to Nordkapp. Right next door is the sprawling, chalet-style *Rica Hotel Nordkapp* (☎78 47 33 88, ⦿www.rica.no; June to mid-Aug; ❺).

For **food**, the ⋔ *Honningsvåg Brygge Hotel*'s *Sjøhuset* is the best **restaurant** by far: seafood is delicious and main courses hover around 190kr; reservations are advised.

North from Honningsvåg

The E69 winds out of Honningsvåg staying close to the shore and, just beyond the conspicuous *Rica Hotel Nordkapp* (see above), some 9km on, passes the turning for **KAMØYVÆR**, a pretty little village 2km from the main road, tucked in tight between the sea and the hills. Here, right on the jetty, the old timber fishing station has been converted into the charming *Havstua* (☎78 47 51 50, ⊛www.havstua.no; ❸; May to mid-Sept), with five simple but smart and extraordinarily cosy rooms. It's a delightful spot and the food is also first-rate – but note that it's advisable to book dinner in advance. A few metres away, just back from the jetty, is the *Árran Nordkapp Gjestehus* (☎78 47 51 29, ⊛www.arran.as; ❹; May to mid-Sept), not quite as appealing perhaps, but still a pleasant, family-run guesthouse in a brightly painted and well-tended house.

Beyond the Kamøyvær turning, the E69 twists a solitary course up through the hills to cross the high-tundra plateau, the mountains stretching away on either side. It's a fine run, with snow and ice lingering well into the summer and impressive views over the treeless and elemental Arctic terrain. From June to October this is pastureland for herds of reindeer, who graze right up to the road, paying little heed to the passing vehicle unless they wander too close. The Sámi, who bring them here by boat, combine herding with souvenir selling, setting up camp at the roadside in full costume to peddle clothes, jewellery and antler sets, which some motorists are daft enough to attach to the front of their vehicles. About 29km from Honningsvåg, the E69 passes the start of the well-marked **hiking trail** that leads to the tip of Europe, the headland of **Knivskjellodden**, stretching about 1500m further north than its famous neighbour. The 16-kilometre-long hike – there and back – takes between two and three hours each way, but the terrain is too difficult and the climate too unpredictable for the inexperienced or poorly equipped.

Nordkapp

Many visitors, when they finally reach **Nordkapp**, feel desperately disappointed – it is, after all, only a cliff and, at 307 metres, it isn't even all that high. But for others there's something about this greyish-black hunk of slate, stuck at the end of a bare, wind-battered promontory, that exhilarates the senses – and some such feeling must have inspired the prehistoric Sámi when they established a sacrificial site here.

The "North Cape" was actually named by the English explorer Richard Chancellor in 1553, as he drifted along the Norwegian coast in an attempt to find the Northeast Passage from the Atlantic to the Pacific. He failed, though the name stuck, and the visit of the Norwegian king Oscar II in 1873 opened the tourist floodgates. Nowadays the lavish **North Cape Hall** (*Nordkapphallen*; daily: April to late May & Sept to early Oct noon–4pm; late May to mid-June noon–1am; mid-June to early Aug 9am–2am; early Aug to end Aug 9am–midnight; 190kr for 48 hours, including parking), cut into the rock of the Cape, entertains hundreds of visitors every day, who all pay handsomely for the pleasure of standing at mainland Europe's supposed northernmost extremity. Fronted by a statue of King Oscar II, the main building contains a restaurant, cafés, souvenir shops, a post office where you can get your letters specially stamped, and a cinema showing – you guessed it – films about the cape. There's a viewing area too, but there's not much to see except the sea – and, weather permitting, the Midnight Sun (May 11 to July 31). A **tunnel** runs from the main building to the cliff face. It's flanked by a chapel, where you can get married, and a series of displays detailing past events and visitors, including the unlikely appearance of the King of Siam in 1907, who was so ill that he had to be carried up here from his boat on a stretcher. At the far end, the cavernous **Grotten Bar** offers caviar and champagne, long views out to sea through the massive glass wall and (of all things) a mock bird cliff. Alternatively, to escape the hurly-burly, you may decide to walk out onto the surrounding headland, though this is too bleak a spot to be much fun.

East to Kirkenes

East of Nordkapp the landscape is more of the same: a relentless expanse of barren plateaux and ocean. Occasionally the picture is relieved by a determined village commanding sweeping views over the fjords that slice into the mainland, but generally there's little for the eyes of a tourist. Nor is there much to do in what are predominantly fishing and industrial settlements, and few tangible attractions beyond the sheer impossibility of the chill wilderness.

The **E6** weaves a circuitous course across this vast territory, travelling close to the Finnish border for much of its length. The only obvious target is the Sámi centre of **Karasjok** (see p.413), 270km from Nordkapp and 220km from Hammerfest and easily the region's most interesting town. Frankly, there's not much reason to push on further east unless you're intent on picking up the **Hurtigrute coastal boat** as it bobs along the remote and spectacular shores of the Barents Sea. Amongst the Hurtigrute's several ports of call, perhaps the most diverting is **Kirkenes**, 320km to the east of Karasjok near the Russian frontier, and a town that comes close to defining remoteness. Kirkenes is actually the northern terminus of the Hurtigrute, from where it begins its long journey back to Bergen. Taking the boat also means that you can avoid the long haul back the way you came – and by the time you reach Kirkenes you'll probably be heartily sick of the E6. The other shortcut is to **fly** – SAS's Braathens (☎91 50 54 00, ☯www.braathens.no) operates regular flights between Kirkenes and various Norwegian cities including Alta, Oslo and Tromsø; as a sample fare, a single economy ticket from Kirkenes to Alta currently goes for around 1000kr. Incidentally, if you are using a car hire, note that Norwegian one-way dropoff charges are exorbitant. The main **long-distance bus** links Alta with Kirkenes via Skaidi, Karasjok and Tana Bru three times weekly, and takes eleven hours to do it.

Accommodation in this part of Norway is very thin on the ground, with campsites being the main option; they usually have cabins, but the sites are mostly stuck in the middle of nowhere.

East from Nordkapp: by land

Beyond the junction of the E69 Nordkapp road, the **E6** bangs along the western shore of the **Porsangerfjord**, a wide inlet that slowly shelves up into the sticky marshes and mudflats at its head. After about 45km, the road reaches the hamlet of **STABBURSNES**, which is home to the small but enjoyable **Stabbursnes Naturhus og Museum** (Stabbursnes Natural History Museum; early June & mid-to late Aug daily 10am–6pm; mid-June to early Aug daily 9am–8pm; Sept–May Tues & Thurs noon–3pm, Wed noon–6pm; 50kr), which provides an overview of the region's flora and fauna.

From Stabbursnes, it's about 15km to **LAKSELV**, an inconsequential fishing village at the head of the Porsangerfjord, and another 80km to Karasjok (see p.413), the best place to spend the night. Pushing on, the E6 weaves its way northeast along the Finnish border to reach, in 180km, **TANA BRU**, a Sámi settlement clustered round the suspension bridge over the River Tana, one of Europe's best salmon rivers, which sweeps down to the Tanafjord and the Barents Sea. Beyond the village, the E6 follows the southern shore of the **Varangerfjord**, a bleak, weather-beaten run, with all colour and vegetation confined to the opposite coastline with its scattered farms and painted fishing boats. As the road swings inland, it's something of a relief to arrive in Kirkenes.

East from Nordkapp: by sea

Beyond Nordkapp, the **Hurtigrute** steers a fine route round the top of the country, nudging its way between tiny islets and craggy bluffs and stopping at a series of remote fishing villages. Amongst these, the prettiest is **BERLEVÅG**, which sits amidst a landscape of eerie greenish-grey rock, splashes of colour in a land otherwise stripped by the elements. It's a tiny village, with a population of just 1200, but its cultural traditions and tight community spirit were deftly explored in Knut Jensen's documentary film *Heftig og Begeistret* ("Cool & Crazy"), released in 2001. The film received rave reviews both here in Norway and across Europe, a welcome fillip to Berlevåg in general and the subject of the film – the local men's choir, the **Berlevåg Mannsangforening** – in particular.

From Berlevåg, it's five hours more to **VARDØ**, Norway's most easterly town, built on an island a couple of kilometres from the mainland, to which it's connected by a tunnel. Like every other town in Finnmark, Vardø was savaged in World War II and subsequently rebuilt. Its present population is just 3000 and its main attraction, located about 500m to the west of the Hurtigrute quay, is the **Vardø fortress** (Vardøhus Festning; daily: mid-June to mid-Sept 8am–9pm, mid-Sept to mid-June 8am–6pm; 25kr), a well-preserved – if tiny – star-shaped fortress built in the 1730s at the behest of Christian VI.

Northbound, the **Hurtigrute** reaches Vardø at 4am and leaves just fifteen minutes later; heading south, it docks here at 4pm and hangs around for an hour – quite enough time to make it to the fortress and back.

Kirkenes

During World War II, the mining town and ice-free port of **KIRKENES** was bombed more heavily than any other place in Europe apart from Malta. The retreating German army torched what was left as they fled in the face of liberating Soviet soldiers, who found 3500 locals hiding in the nearby iron-ore mines. The mines were finally closed in 1996, threatening the future of the 6000-strong community, which is desperately trying to kindle trade with Russia to keep itself afloat.

Kirkenes is almost entirely modern, with long rows of uniform houses spreading out along the Bøkfjord. If that sounds dull, it's not to slight the town, which makes the most of its inhospitable surroundings with some pleasant public gardens, lakes and residential areas – it's just that it seems an awfully long way to come for not very much. That said, once you've finally got here it seems churlish to leave quickly and it's certainly worth searching out the **Savio Museum** (*Saviomuseet*; late June to late Aug daily 10am–6pm; late Aug to late June Mon–Fri 10am–3pm; 35kr), housed in the old library about 300m south of the tourist office at Kongensgate 10B. This small museum displays the work of the local Sámi artist, **John Savio** (1902–38). Savio's life was brief and tragic – orphaned at the age of three, he was ill from childhood onwards and died in poverty of tuberculosis aged 36 – a fact which lends poignancy to his woodcuts and paintings, with their lonely evocations of the Sámi way of life and the overbearing power of nature. The museum also hosts travelling contemporary art exhibitions.

Practicalities

Kirkenes is the northern terminus of the **Hurtigrute coastal boat**, which arrives here at 10am and departs for Bergen at 12.45pm. It uses the quay just over 1km east of the town centre; a local bus shuttles between the two. Kirkenes **airport** is 14km southwest of town; Flybussen (Mon–Fri hourly, Sat 5 daily, Sun 1 daily; 65kr) connect the airport with the centre, or you can take a taxi. Long-distance and local buses share the same **bus station** on the west side of the town centre, at the end of Kirkegata. From here, it's about 300m east to the **tourist office** (early June to mid-Aug Mon–Fri 8.30am–6pm, Sat & Sun 10am–5pm; mid-Aug to early June Mon–Fri 8.30am–4pm; ☎78 99 25 44, ⓦwww.kirkenesinfo.no), in the centre at Presteveien 1. They issue free town maps, have lots of ideas as to how to while away the time here and provide general information about excursions to Russia.

The town's best **hotel** is the *Rica Arctic*, whose eighty well-appointed rooms occupy a smart modern block in the centre at Kongensgate 1 (☎78 99 59 00, ⓦwww.rica.no; ⑤). More affordable is *Barents Frokost Hotell*, metres from the tourist office at Presteveien 3 (☎78 99 32 99, ⓔgcelsius@frisurf.no; ②) and equipped with frugal rooms, both en suite and with shared facilities. As for **food**, the *Rica Arctic Hotel* has a very competent restaurant, though it's slightly bettered by *Vin og Vilt*, Kirkegata 5 (☎78 99 38 11), where they serve up an excellent range of Arctic specialities from reindeer to char and beyond. Main courses at both hover at around 120kr.

Svalbard

During the long Arctic winter, the **Svalbard archipelago** is one of the most hostile places on earth. Some 640km north of the Norwegian mainland (and just 1300km from the North Pole), two-thirds of its surface is covered by glaciers, the soil frozen to a depth of up to 500m. It was probably discovered in the twelfth -century by Icelandic seamen, though it lay ignored until 1596 when the Dutch explorer Willem Barents named the main island, **Spitsbergen**, after its needle-like mountains. However apart from a smattering of determined adventurers, few people ever lived here until, in 1899, rich coal deposits were discovered, the geological residue of a prehistoric tropical forest. The first **coal mine** was opened by an American seven years later and passed into Norwegian hands in 1916. Meanwhile, other countries, particularly Russia and Sweden, were getting into the coal-mining act and when, in 1920, Norway's sovereignty over the archipelago was

△ Polar bear, Svalbard

ratified by international treaty, it was on condition that those other countries who were operating mines could continue to do so. It was also agreed that the islands would be a demilitarized zone.

Despite the hardships, there are convincing reasons to make a trip to this oddly fertile land, covering around 63,000 square kilometres. Between late April and late August there's continuous daylight, with temperatures regularly bobbing up into the late teens of degrees centigrade (the snow has virtually all melted by July, leaving the valleys covered in flowers); and there's an abundance of wildlife – over a hundred species of migratory birds, arctic foxes, polar bears and reindeer on land, and seals, walruses and whales offshore. In winter, it's a different story: the polar night, during which the sun never rises above the horizon, lasts from late October to mid-February; and the record low temperature is a staggering -46°C, not counting the wind-chill factor.

Getting there and getting around

The simplest way to reach Svalbard is to **fly** to the archipelago's airport at Long-yearbyen on the main island, Spitsbergen. SAS/Braathens (℡79 15 54 00, ⊛www .braathens.no) operates services there from a variety of Norwegian cities, including Oslo, Bergen, Trondheim, Alta and Tromsø, on average four or five times weekly. The Tromsø–Longyearbyen flight takes an hour and thirty-five minutes and a ticket with no restrictions is roughly 2500kr return, though special deals are commonplace and reduce this to 1500–1800kr. However, before you book your flight, you'll need to reserve accommodation in Longyearbyen (see below) and – unless you're happy to be stuck in your lodgings – you'd be well-advised to pre-book one of the **guided excursions** too. There's a wide range on offer, from hiking and climbing through to kayaking, snowmobiling, glacier walking, helicopter rides, Zodiac boat trips, wildlife "safaris" and ice caving. In the first instance, further **information**, including details of all the tour companies, is available from the tourist office in Longyearbyen (℡79 02 55 50, ⊛www.svalbard.net). Also in Long-yearbyen, Spitsbergen is a very good travel and tour agency (℡79 02 61 00, ⊛www .spitsbergentravel.com). You can, of course, take pot luck when you get there, but be warned that wilderness excursions are often fully booked weeks in advance.

Otherwise, there are **adventure cruises** around Svalbard, involving polar-bear spotting and the like. A five-day package with four days' cruising and one night in a Longyearbyen hotel costs anywhere between 7000kr and 16000kr, depending on the standard of the boat – seven nights works out at between 18000kr and 33000kr. (Prices don't include the flight to Longyearbyen.) In addition, adventure tour operators abroad offer all sorts of Svalbard **holidays**; one of the best is Britain's Arctic Experience (see p.29 for address and details), which runs an excellent range of all-in camping and hiking tours to the archipelago in July and August; prices vary with the itinerary and length of stay, but a ten-day trip costs around £2000.

Finally, if you are determined to strike out into the wilderness **independently**, you first have to seek permission from, and log your itinerary with, the governor's office in Longyearbyen (℡79 02 43 00, ⊛www.sysselmannen.svalbard.no); they will certainly expect you to carry a gun on account of the polar bears. Note also that there are no road connections between any of Svalbard's settlements, though there's about 45km of road around Longyearbyen.

Spitsbergen

The main island of the Svalbard archipelago, **Spitsbergen**, is the only one that is permanently inhabited; its settlements (three Norwegian and one Russian) have a total population of around 3000. With just over 1500 inhabitants, the only Norwegian settlement of any size is **LONGYEARBYEN**, which huddles on the narrow coastal plain below the mountains and beside the Isfjord, roughly in the middle of the island. It was founded in 1906, when John M. Longyear, an American mine owner, established the Arctic Coal Company here. Longyearbyen is now well equipped with services, including shops, cafés, a post office, bank, swimming pool, several tour companies, a campsite, a couple of guesthouses and three hotels – but note that advance reservations are essential for all accommodation.

Longyearbyen practicalities

Longyearbyen **airport** is 5km west of town and an **airport bus**, the Flybussen (March–Sept; 50kr) links the two; a **taxi** will cost 90–100kr. The settlement itself trails inland from the Isfjorden for a couple of kilometres. The few buildings that pass for the centre are located about 600m in from the fjord; one of them contains the all-year **tourist office** (Mon–Fri 8am–6pm, Sat 9am–4pm, Sun noon–4pm; ☎79 02 55 51, ⓦwww.svalbard.net), which has a full range of leaflets on the archipelago as well as information on a wide range of trips.

Longyearbyen has a healthy supply of **accommodation**. Cream of the crop is the plush *Radisson SAS Polar Hotel* (☎79 02 34 50, ⓦwww.radisson.com; ❻) just to the north of the tourist office. More distinctive, if frugal, lodgings are available in old miners' quarters to the west of the centre, across the river, at the *Mary-Ann's Polar Riggen* guesthouse (☎79 02 37 02, ⓦwww.polarriggen.com; ❹). Similarly economic, though not perhaps as agreeable, is the *Spitsbergen Nybyen Gjestehus*, on the southern edge of town (☎79 02 63 00, ⓔguesthouse@spitsbergentravel.no; ❹). Finally, *Longyearbyen Camping* (☎79 02 14 44, ⓦwww.longyearbyen-camping .com; late June to early Sept), out near the airport, charges just 80kr per person per night. Surprisingly, they don't have any cabins, but there is a kitchen, laundry and (thank goodness) heated toilets. Obviously enough, you must come fully equipped to survive what can be, at any time of the year, a cruel climate.

For **food**, the *Radisson SAS Polar Hotel's Restaurant Nansen* is the best place in town, serving all manner of Arctic specialities from char through to seal and (like it or not) whale. For **drinking**, the liveliest hangout is the *Funken Bar*, part of the *Spitsbergen Hotel* and situated just to the south of the centre. The *Radisson SAS Polar Hotel's Barents Pub* is both smarter and more sedate.

Travel details

Buses

Alta to: Hammerfest (1–3 daily except Sat; 2hr 30min); Honningsvåg (1–3 daily; 4hr 15min); Karasjok (1–2 daily; 4hr 30min); Kautokeino (1–2 daily except Tues, Thurs & Sat; 2hr 15min); Kirkenes (1 daily except Thurs, Sat & Sun; 13hr); Skaidi (1–3 daily except Sat; 1hr 40min); Tromsø (1–2 daily; 6hr 30min).

Hammerfest to: Alta (1–3 daily except Sat; 2hr 30min); Karasjok (1–2 daily except Sat & Sun; 4hr 15min); Kirkenes (1 daily Mon, Wed & Fri; 10hr 20min); Skaidi (1–2 daily except Sat; 1hr).

Honningsvåg to: Alta (1–3 daily; 4hr 15min); Nordkapp (mid-June to late Aug 2 daily, late Aug to mid-June 1 daily; 45min).

Karasjok to: Hammerfest (1–2 daily except Sat & Sun; 4hr 15min); Kirkenes (1 daily except Tues, Thurs & Sat; 5hr 15min).

Kautokeino to: Alta (1–2 daily except Tues, Thurs & Sat; 2hr 15min).

Kirkenes to: Alta (1 daily except Thurs, Sat & Sun; 13hr); Hammerfest (1 daily Mon, Wed & Fri; 10hr 20min); Karasjok (1 daily except Tues, Thurs & Sat; 5hr 15min); Vadsø (1–2 daily except Sat; 3hr).

Skaidi to: Alta (1–3 daily except Sat; 1hr 40min); Hammerfest (1–2 daily except Sat; 1hr).

Tromsø to: Alta (1–2 daily; 6hr 30min); Narvik (3–4 daily; 4hr).

Hurtigrute coastal boat

Northbound from: Tromsø at 6.30pm; Hammerfest at 6.45am; Honningsvåg at 3.15pm; terminates at Kirkenes at 10am.

Southbound from: Kirkenes at 12.45am; Honningsvåg at 6.15pm; Hammerfest at 12.45pm; Tromsø at 1.30am.

The Tromsø–Kirkenes journey time is 42hrs.

Hurtigbåt passenger express boats

Alta to: Hammerfest (1–2 daily; 1hr 30min).
Tromsø to: Harstad (1–3 daily; 2hr 45min).

3

Sweden

Sweden highlights

* **Gamla Stan, Stockholm** Stroll through the beautiful Baroque old town. See p.461

* **Fürstenburg Galleries, Gothenburg Art Museum** Gloriously evocative paintings by Sweden's finest nineteenth-century artists. See p.513

* **Kalmar castle** A sensational twelfth-century stronghold remodelled into a Renaissance palace. See p.560

* **Gotland** Amble through the remarkable walled old town of Visby and cycle though Gotland's beautiful landscapes. See p.582

* **Gammelstad parish village, Luleå** Dozens of superbly preserved wooden cottages around a beautiful church. See p.610

* **Inlandsbanan** This single-track railway traverses some dramatic landscapes and crosses the Arctic Circle. See p.619

* **Gallivare mine tour** Take a bus 1000m underground to see mammoth machines in a high-tech working iron ore mine – and your mobile works down here, too. See p.634

* **Abisko national park** Take the cable car up Mount Nuolja for stunning arctic views, or hike along the wild Kungsleden trail. See p.640

△ Visby, Gotland

Introduction and basics

In geographical terms, Sweden is easily the biggest of the Scandinavian countries – a massive 450,000 square kilometres, larger than California and twice as big as Britain – although its population numbers barely nine million. Essentially one vast coniferous forest punctuated by some 100,000 crystal-clear lakes, Sweden reposes contentedly within an endless natural beauty. Remote, austere, cold – all these generalizations may be partly true, but Sweden is also friendly and efficient and, as it boasts no single concentration of sights (other than in Stockholm and Gothenburg), you're as likely to fetch up on a sunny Baltic beach as camp in the forest or hike through the national parks of Swedish Lapland.

One aspect of the country most likely to impinge on the cluttered eye of Europeans is the sense of space. Away from the relatively densely populated south, it's easy to travel for miles without seeing a soul, and taking in these vast, unpopulated stretches in a limited time can be exhausting and unrewarding. Better, on a short trip, to delve into one or two regions and experience the natural beauty that pervades and shapes the Swedes' attitude to life: once you've broken through the oft-quoted reserve of the people there's a definite emotive feel to the country. And initial contact is easy, as almost everyone speaks English.

Where to go

The **south and southwest** of the country are flat holiday lands. For so long territory disputed with Denmark (which the landscape closely resembles), the provinces now harbour a host of historic ports – including **Gothenburg**, **Helsingborg** and **Malmö** – and less frenetic beach towns, all old and mostly fortified. Off the **southeast** coast, the Baltic islands of **Öland** and **Gotland** are the country's most hyped resorts – and with good reason, supporting a lazy beach-life to match that of the best southern European spots, but without the hotel blocks, crowds and tat.

Central and northern Sweden is the stuff of tourist brochures: great swathes of forest, inexhaustible lakes ideal for nude bathing and some of the best wilderness hiking in Europe. Two train routes link north with south. The eastern run, close to the **Bothnian coast**, passes old wood-built towns and is handy for the city of **Umeå**, with its ferry connections to Vaasa in

Sweden on the net

ⓦ **www.visitsweden.com** The official site of the Swedish tourist board with links to tourism, transport and accommodation resources, and a useful search engine.

ⓦ **www.eniro.net** This combination of the Yellow Pages, a search engine and an incredibly detailed interactive map allows you to find anything, anywhere.

ⓦ **www.resplus.com** Excellent site for finding public transport links across the country, including all train and regional bus connections.

ⓦ **www.sj.se** Home page of Sweden's main rail company, with timetables, pricing and advance online ticket sales.

ⓦ **www.stfturist.se** Details of all of Sweden's youth hostels and mountain cabins, with opening times and prices.

ⓦ **www.stockholmtown.com** Copious amounts of information on the Swedish capital from the city's tourist board.

ⓦ **www.abbasite.com** Official shrine to Stockholm's fab four, with picture galleries, sound clips and assorted Eurovision trivia.

Finland. In the centre of the country, the trains of the **Inlandsbanan** (inland railway) strike off through some remarkably changing landscapes of lakelands to mountains, clearing reindeer off the track as they go. Both routes meet in Sweden's **far north**, home of the Sami, the oldest indigenous Scandinavian people, and of the **midnight sun**, which in high summer never sets.

Of the cities, **Stockholm** is supreme. A bundle of islands housing regal and monumental architecture, fine museums and the country's most active culture and nightlife, it's a likely point of arrival and a vital stop-off. Two university towns, **Uppsala** and **Lund**, also demand a visit, while nearly all the other major cities – chiefly Östersund, Umeå, and Kiruna – can make some sort of cultural claim on your attention. Time is rarely wasted in humbler towns, either, as the

beauty of the local surroundings adequately compensates for any lack of specific sights.

When to go

Summer in Sweden is short and hectic. Generally speaking, Swedes consider summer to run from mid-June to mid-August, and during this time accommodation is reduced in price (to fill rooms occupied by business people during the rest of the year) and most of the country's attractions are open for business. Conversely, though, summer also sees something of a shutdown: many bus timetables are at their most skeletal, and facilities such as swimming pools and cinemas in sparsely populated parts of the country close completely. Most Swedes take their holidays during the summer, with

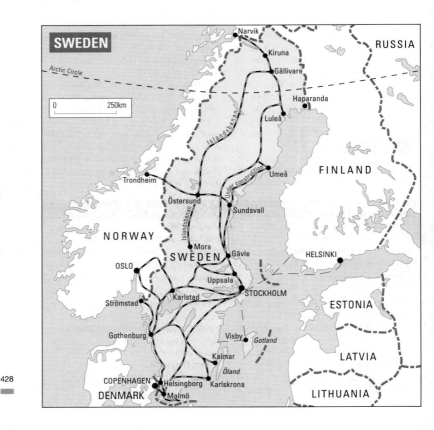

the result that popular destinations such as Dalarna can be tediously overcrowded. From rowdy Midsummer's Night (June 21) onwards, accommodation is scarce and trains packed as Swedes head out into the country and to the beaches. Outside the peak month of **July**, however, things are noticeably quieter; by mid-August, most Swedes have returned to work and the feeling of summer has gone – by late August, some parts of northern Sweden see their first frost. To avoid the rush, try visiting in September or late May – both are usually bright and warm. The **midnight sun** extends the days in June and July, and north of the Arctic Circle it virtually never gets dark. Elsewhere it stays light until very late, up to midnight and beyond. Thanks to the Gulf Stream, temperatures in Sweden are surprisingly high – see the temperature chart on p.8 – and on the south coast it can be as hot as any southern European resort.

Winter, on the other hand, can be a miserable experience. It lasts a long time (November to April solid) and gets very cold indeed: temperatures of -15°C and below are not unusual even in Stockholm. Further north it's positively arctic. Days are short and dark (in the far north the sun barely rises at all) and biting winds cut through the most elaborate of padded coats. On the plus side, the snow stays crisp and white, the air is clean, the water everywhere frozen solid: a paradise for skaters and skiers. Stockholm, too, is particularly beautiful with its winter covering of snow and ice.

Getting there from the rest of Scandinavia

The cheapest **Scandinavian connection** with Sweden is from Denmark, by bus and ferry, and regular trains and ferries connect other mainland countries.

By train

There are four possible **train** routes into Sweden **from Norway**. Cheapest are the five-hour run from Oslo to Gothenburg and

the slightly longer route from Oslo to Stockholm; the other options are the eleven-hour ride from Trondheim to Stockholm and the day-long (20hr) haul from Narvik. Through-trains **from Denmark** (Copenhagen and Kastrup airport) to Malmö, Gothenburg or Stockholm use the Öresunds Link between the Danish coast and Malmö. **Rail passes** (InterRail, Eurail and ScanRail) are valid on all these routes.

By bus

There are several **bus** routes into Sweden from other Scandinavian cities, though the frequent services **from Denmark** are the only ones that will get you there quickly. The easiest – and cheapest – connection is on one of the several daily buses **from Copenhagen** to Stockholm (9hr) or Oslo (8hr), via the Oresund bridge and Malmö. **From Norway** there are several daily buses from Oslo to Gothenburg, the journey taking four hours, and four daily buses from Oslo to Stockholm, a seven-hour ride. **From Finland** most routes converge upon Helsinki or Turku and then use the ferry crossings to Stockholm.

By ferry

Ferry or **fast ferry** (**HSS**) services to Sweden are plentiful, but can be confusing – not least because several operators run rival services on the same route. To make any sense of the routes, timetables and prices, which change from year to year, check the ferry company websites, or consult their brochures at any tourist office. You'll find other details – frequencies and journey times – in the "Travel details" at the end of each chapter. In addition, rail passes give **discounts and free travel** on some of the ferry routes. The ScanRail pass currently gives free passage on ferries between Helsingør and Helsingborg, and thirty to fifty percent discounts on several other routes, including Frederikshavn–Gothenburg, Turku–Stockholm and Helsinki–Stockholm.

From Denmark

The shortest and cheapest ferry crossing is **Helsingør–Helsingborg** (⊛www.scandlines .com; 20min; foot passengers 17Dkr, cars

230Dkr); just walk on board and go. There are also year-round HSS sailings and slower connections via regular ferry to Gothenburg **from Frederikshavn** (⊛www.stenaline.com; 2hr HSS, foot passengers 160Dkr, cars 775Dkr; 3hr 15min regular ferry; foot passengers 115Dkr, cars 610Dkr). Stena Line also sail daily to Varberg **from Grenå** (4hr; foot passengers 115Dkr, cars 610Dkr). The other approach from Denmark is to come via the Danish island of **Bornholm**; ferries and catamarans (⊛www.bornholmferries.dk; foot passengers 162Dkr; cars from 717Dkr) cross from Rønne to Ystad, on the Swedish coast.

From Finland

Longer ferry journeys link Sweden with Finland, the major crossing being the **Helsinki–Stockholm** route, a sixteen-hour trip with either Silja (⊛www.silja.com; foot passengers from €32, cars from €55) or Viking (⊛www.vikingline.fi; foot passengers from €32, cars from €36). There are also regular crossings **from Turku** and **from Mariehamn** in the Finnish Åland Islands to Stockholm (both Silja and Viking; 4hr; foot passengers from €11, cars from €7). If you're aiming for the north of Sweden, you might be better off crossing **from Vaasa** (⊛www.rgline .com; foot passengers from €30; cars from €50): there are year-round four-hour services to Umeå, as well as to Sundsvall (foot passengers and cars from €60).

From Norway

There's one year-round crossing from Norway to Sweden, **from Sandefjord** to Strömstad, north of Gothenburg (⊛www .colorline.com; 2hr 30min; foot passengers 125Nkr, cars 132Nkr).

By plane

The cost of **flying** to Sweden from the other Scandinavian countries has decreased dramatically thanks to the competition offered to SAS (⊛www.scandinavian.net) by several **budget airlines**, notably Blue1 from Finland (⊛www.blue1.com); Sterling (⊛www.sterling ticket.com), FlyNordic (⊛ www.flynordic .com) and FlyMe (⊛ www.flyme.se) from Denmark; ⊛www.whichbudget.com gives a good overview of who currently flies where.

SAS has its own no-frills airline, Snowflake (⊛www.flysnowflake.com), which uses SAS aircraft. If you shop around and book far in advance, a flight within Scandinavia including taxes can cost as little as €25. However, the sudden bankruptcy of the SweFly airline in the summer of 2005 – leaving passengers stranded and with no hope of reclaiming any money – is proof that the smaller budget airlines aren't always reliable.

SAS operates regular daily flights from its hub **Copenhagen** to Gothenburg, Jönköping, Stockholm, and Västerås. Sterling flies from Copenhagen to Gothenburg three times per week and to Stockholm daily, while FlyNordic has two flights weekly to Gothenburg and daily flights to Stockholm. **From Oslo**, SAS operates hourly flights to Stockholm and five daily services to Gothenburg, and FlyNordic has several daily flights to Stockholm. Finnair (⊛www.finnair.com) flies daily between Oslo and Stockholm, and three times a week from Bergen to Stockholm.

Of all the Scandinavian countries, **Finland** has the greatest number of regional flights to Sweden. Most services are operated by SAS, Finnair, Blue1 and FlyMe, but are too numerous to list here. Information on most of Sweden's commercial airports including airlines and timetables can be found at ⊛www.lfv.se.

Costs, money and banks

Sweden is not much more expensive than, say, France or Germany, and certainly much cheaper than neighbouring Norway. If you don't already have a rail pass, using budget airlines or flying on standby with SAS (for under-25s) is a fast and affordable option in cutting travel **costs**, while city and regional discount travel passes ease what could otherwise be a burden. Accommodation, too, can be good value: a bed in one of Sweden's well-appointed STF youth hostels costs an average of 140kr (£10/$17) per night for members (plus another 45kr for non-members), while campsites are plentiful and cheap. Virtually every hotel in Sweden halves its prices in summer, bringing even the most palatial places within reach of most travellers, and the cost of eating is made bearable by the three-course daily *dagens rätt* lunch offers found throughout the country on weekdays – around £6/$9 for a main dish with a side salad, bread, coffee and a soft drink.

Put all this together and you'll find you can exist – camping, self-catering, hitching, no drinking – on around £15/$26 a day. Stay in hostels, eat lunch, get out and see the sights and this will rise to at least £25/$44. Add on £3/$5 for a drink in a bar, around £2/$3 for coffee and cake and £40/$70 minimum a night in a hotel (for a double room) and you're looking at a figure of more like £60–75/$105–130 a day. Remember, though, that the countryside (and much of your camping) is free, museums usually have low (or no) admission charges, and that everything everywhere is clean, bright and works.

Swedish **currency** is the **krona** (plural kronor), made up of 100 öre. It comes in coins of 50 öre, 1kr, 2kr, 5kr and 10kr; and notes of 20kr, 50kr, 100kr, 500kr and 1000kr. The **exchange rates** at time of writing were: 14kr for £1; 7.88kr for $1 and 9.49kr for €1.

The easiest way to get local currency is to use your debit card in one of thousands of **ATMs** (for more on which, see "Basics", p.38); it's also the cheapest method, as Swedish banks won't charge for ATM transactions. Alternatively, you can change money in **banks** all over Sweden, which open Monday to Friday from 9.30am until 3pm (plus late opening on Thursdays until 5.30pm), or in **exchange offices** at airports and ferry terminals, where rates are generally a little better than at banks – though still not as good as the interbank rate used for ATMs. Both the banks and Forex (view rates at ⓦ www.forex.se), Sweden's leading exchange office chain, charge roughly 30–40kr commission.

Mail and communications

Communications within Sweden are good, and as most people speak at least some English, you won't go far wrong in the post or telephone office.

Post offices are gradually being phased out in Sweden – those remaining are open Monday to Friday from 9am until 6pm and on Saturday from 10am to 1pm. Most newspaper kiosks, supermarkets, tobacconists and hotels sell **stamps** for letters and light parcels; a letter under 20g costs 7kr to Europe and 8kr to the rest of the world. **Poste restante** is available at all main post offices; take your passport along to claim mail.

For international **telephone calls** dial direct from public **cardphones** – payphones accepting coins no longer exist in Sweden. This is very easy: buy a card from a newsagent for 120 units (100kr) for the best value for money (the larger the card's denomination, the cheaper the cost per unit). English instructions on how to use a cardphone are generally displayed inside each booth. You can also pay for calls using your credit card – look out for phones marked "CCC". International dialling codes for calling **from and to Sweden** are given on p.40. For **directory enquiries**, dial ☏ 118 118 for domestic numbers, ☏ 118 119 for international enquiries.

If you have a GSM mobile phone, it's easy to buy a Swedish **SIM card** with which you can call at local rates – phoning to Swedish land-line number costs from 0.89kr to 3.75kr per minute – rather than pay expensive roaming costs to and from your home country. Telia, 3, Vodafone and Comviq offer several options, with a *startpaket* costing around 100kr, after which you need to buy recharge cards to start making calls. SIM cards are best bought from a Phone House shop (in thirty towns across Sweden; ☏ 0200/11 00 11, ⓦ www.phonehouse.se); these sell the full range of SIM cards and can advise on which option suits your needs best.

Internet cafés are thin on the ground, restricted primarily to the bigger cities and charging around 40–60kr per hour. However, libraries usually have free Internet access, and it's a good idea to book a timeslot. Also look for the expanding number of Sidewalk Express coin-operated terminals (ⓦ www .sidewalkexpress.se, 19kr/hr), which are currently found in airports, train stations and 7-Eleven shops.

The media

You'll easily be able to keep in touch with home by tuning into the TV – which relies heavily on English and American programmes – or listening to one of the English-language radio stations. Assuming that you don't read Swedish, you can also keep abreast of world events by buying **foreign newspapers** in the major towns and cities, sometimes on the day of issue, more usually the day after. Of **Swedish newspapers**, the *Dagens Nyheter* broadsheet is the best source of non-biased Swedish-language news. Its main competitor, *Svenska Dagbladet*, is another serious source of news, albeit with a slight right-of-centre slant. *Aftonbladet* and *Expressen* are Sweden's two tabloids.

Swedish **television** is fairly unchallenging. On top of the two state channels, SVT1 and 2, there are two commercial stations, TV4 and TV5, while the dire cable station TV3 is shared with Denmark and Norway. On the **radio**, there's national (Swedish) news in English on **Radio Sweden** (@www.sr.se /rs/red/ind_eng.html). Their English-language programming can be heard daily in Stockholm on 89.6FM, which also broadcasts some BBC World Service programmes.

Getting around

Sweden's internal **transport** system is quick, efficient and runs in all weather. Services are often reduced in the winter (especially on northern bus routes), but it's unlikely you'll ever get stranded. In summer, when everyone is on holiday, trains and, to a lesser extent, buses are packed, making seat reservations a good idea on long journeys.

All train, bus, ferry and plane schedules are contained within the giant **Rikstidtabellen** ("timetable"); every tourist office and travel agent has a copy. It costs 80kr and isn't worth buying and carrying around; just ask for photocopies of the relevant pages.

Keep an eye out for city and regional **discount cards**. One payment gets a card valid for anything from a day up to a week, and it usually covers **unlimited local travel** (bus, tram, ferry, sometimes train), museum entry

and other discounts and freebies. Cards are often only available during the summer (valuable exceptions being the Stockholm, Gothenburg and Malmö cards), and where useful are detailed in the relevant accounts within the Guide. Otherwise it's worth asking at tourist offices, as schemes change frequently.

Trains

Apart from flying, **trains** are the quickest way to get around Sweden's vast expanses. The service is excellent, especially on the main routes, and prices not too expensive – a standard-class single from Stockholm to Gothenburg, for example, starts at 320kr if booked in advance. Several companies operate trains in Sweden (see below); if you're trying to work out a train-and-bus journey and want to ensure smooth connections, visit @www.resplus.se. It's worth picking up the Resplus **timetable**, free from any train station. Published twice yearly, this is an accurate and comprehensive list of the most useful train services in the country. Otherwise, each train route has its own timetable leaflet, also available free from any station.

SJ (*Statens Järnvägar* – Swedish State Railways; @0771/75 75 75, @www.sj.se) has an extensive network of routes, running right from the far south of the country up to Östersund and Sundsvall in central Sweden. Their high-speed X2000 train services can often shave a couple of hours off the normal journey time, particularly on the Stockholm–Gothenburg run, though prices are higher. **Connex** (@0771/26 00 00, @www .connex.se) operates the Norrlandståget service from Gothenburg via Stockholm, Gävle and Boden to Gällivare and Kiruna in Swedish Lapland, and across the border to Narvik in Norway. **Tågkompaniet** (@0771/44 41 11, @www.tagkompaniet.se) runs trains on several smaller lines in central Sweden, including Sundsvall–Östersund and Gävle–Falun–Borlänge–Mora. Tickets for Connex and Tågkompaniet trains can be bought at no extra cost at any SJ sales point (though not on the SJ website), and rail passes are valid.

In Skåne in southern Sweden, **Pågatåg** (@www.sj.se) operates trains between Helsingborg, Lund, Malmö and Ystad. Finally,

Inlandsbanan (☎ 063/19 44 12, ⊕ www .inlandsbanan.se) runs trains on the summer-only (mid-June to early Sept) route between Kristinehamn near Karlstad via Mora and Östersund to Gällivare in Swedish Lapland, and if you're in the country during the summer months, then travelling at least a section of the Inlandsbanan is a must. Inter-Rail holders under 26 travel free; ScanRail pass holders get a 25 percent discount on the **Inlandsbanankort** (Inland Railway Card; full price 1195kr). Available on board the trains, this card gives unlimited travel on the line for fourteen days. Individual tickets cost 108kr per 100km and seat reservations are free if booked in advance, otherwise 50kr.

Tickets and reservations

Buying individual **train tickets** is easy and can be done online, at the ticketing machines you'll see at most stations or, for a slightly higher fare, at the station counters. Rail travel on SJ services are most expensive when buying a ticket last-minute, whether you choose a specific train or buy an **öppen 2 klass** (open second class) ticket in advance – these are valid for any departure. **Discounts** are given for travelling off-peak and for buying tickets in advance. The **just nu** tickets – valid for a specific departure time, and sold up to the day before departure – are great value, offering considerable savings if booked well in advance. However, there's only a limited amount available per train, and refunds can only be made up to a week before the travel date. **Under-26s** are entitled to a thirty percent discount on most fares, but must bring ID to prove their age. SJ has an excellent system for **buying tickets in advance from abroad**; select the ticket on the SJ website and pay for it by credit card, and you'll get a code that can later be punched into any SJ machine to print out your actual ticket. If you need more assistance, the Sweden Booking rail travel agency can book your trip for you (☎ 0046/498 20 33 80, ⊕ www.sweden booking.com).

Unless you can use their Swedish-language website, **Connex tickets** can only be purchased over the phone (call ☎ 0771/26 00 00) or at the Connex and SJ stations. Fares for daytime tickets are as follows: Luleå–Gällivare 150kr; Luleå–Kiruna 221kr; Umeå–Luleå 258kr.

On long **overnight** train journeys it's worth paying for a couchette (*bädd* or *liggplats*) or a sleeping car (*säng* or *sovplats*) in mixed or women-only compartments. There are several night-train connections within Sweden, as well as daily services from Oslo to Malmö and to Stockholm, and from Malmö to Berlin. Prices are low: the cost of either a couchette in a six-berth cabin or a sleeping berth in a two- or three-person cabin depends on the length of the journey: from Stockholm to Malmö, for example, a ticket including a couchette costs 739kr, while 937kr buys a berth in a three-berth cabin, and 1135kr in a two-berth (with *just nu* prices about half of these fares). Fares on overnight Connex trains are similar, with a Stockholm–Kiruna ticket costing 599kr for a couchette, 799kr for a sleeping car, up to 1699kr for a bed in a two-person sleeping cabin with private shower.

Rail passes

If you're planning to travel a lot by train, you're generally better off buying a **train pass**, such as a multicountry InterRail, Eurail or ScanRail pass, which needs to be purchased before you leave home (for details, see "Basics", p.35 & p.45). If you're planning to travel only in Sweden, then it might be worth buying a Sweden Railpass; you need to pre-purchase before arriving in Sweden, and the pass currently costs 1820kr for three days second class travel in one calendar month, up to 2990kr for eight days. Reservations cost extra for X2000 (60kr) and Intercity (30kr) seats, and for night train couchettes (90kr) and beds (variable costs). The Sweden Railpass is available from Sweden Booking and from the train ticket agents detailed in "Basics", p.34.

Buses

The main **long-distance bus** companies in the southern half of Sweden are Swebus Express (from Sweden ☎ 200/21 82 18, from abroad ☎0046/362 90 80 00; ⊕www .swebusexpress.se) and the smaller Svenska Buss (☎0771/67 67 67, ⊕www.svenska buss.se). The main routes and one-way fares are: Stockholm–Gothenburg 350kr

(6hr 45min); Stockholm–Malmö 435kr (9hr 30min); and Gothenburg–Malmö 260kr (3hr). Return tickets are cheaper than two singles, and both companies have cheaper tickets for those who book in advance online, by phone or at a sales point. Reservations are not necessary for Swebus Express as you're always guaranteed a seat, even if you turn up last minute.

In the north, there are a number of smaller companies, including **Y-buss** (☎0771/33 44 44; ⊛www.ybuss.se), which operates services from Stockholm to Sundsvall (220kr), the High Coast (300kr) and Umeå (350kr), as well as inland to Östersund (290kr); there's a 25 percent discount for travelling at off-peak times (look for the *röd avgång* buses). Connex (☎0771/10 01 10, ⊛www .ltnbd.se) runs the **Kustbussen** (#10 and #20) and the express **Norrlandskusten** (#100) buses from Sundsvall to Härnösand, the High Coast, Umeå, Skellefteå, Luleå and Haparanda at the Finnish border, charging about 100kr per 100 km. There are also many regional bus companies in the north, charging similar rates. Major routes are listed in the "Travel details" at the end of each chapter, and you can pick up comprehensive **timetables** at bus terminal or tourist office, or view them online.

Local buses, too, are frequent and regular, and budget travellers will need them to reach hostels and campsites, which are often a fair distance from town centres. Flat **fares** are 15–20kr, with tickets usually valid for an hour. Most large towns operate some sort of discount system where you can buy cheaper books of tickets – these are detailed in the text where useful, and more information is available from tourist offices.

Ferries and cruises

Unlike Norway and Finland, there are few domestic long-distance **ferry** services in Sweden. The various archipelagos on the southeast coast are served by small ferries, the most comprehensive network being within the **Stockholm archipelago**, for which you can buy a boat pass (see p.493). The other major link is between the Baltic island of **Gotland** and the mainland at Nynäshamn and Oskarshamn, both very popular routes for which you should book ahead in summer:

all routes are operated by Destination Gotland ☎0771/22 33 00; ⊛www.destinationgotland .se); see p.584 for more details.

Planes

The **domestic flight** network is operated by SAS (⊛www.scandinavian.net) and an increasing number of budget airline companies, whose competition has forced SAS to offer cheap one-way fares as well. Useful budget operators are: DirektFlyg (⊛www .direktflyg.com); FlyMe (⊛www.flyme.se); FlyNordic (⊛www.flynordic.com); Gotlands-flyg (⊛www.gotlandsflyg.se); KullaFlyg (⊛www.kullaflyg.se); Malmö Aviation (⊛www .malmoaviation.se); Nordic Regional (⊛www .nordicregional.se); Swedline (⊛www .swedline.com); and Umeåflyg (⊛www .umeaflyg.se). For the latest overview of who flies where, visit ⊛www.whichbudget.com.

Flying can be a real steal, depending on when the ticket is booked. A single trip from Stockholm to Gothenburg costs around 420kr with SAS, 470kr with FlyNordic, 250kr with FlyMe, and 450kr with Malmö Aviation. Flying from Stockholm to Kiruna can be a bargain, at around 399kr with Flynordic, while the cheapest Stockholm to Gällivare flight with Swedline costs about 700kr. Stockholm to Östersund is in the region of 400kr with FlyNordic, 250kr with FlyMe, and 1450kr with SAS. The only way to get reliable **timetable** information and the lowest prices is to visit the relevant websites and book online, rather than call the premium-rate phone lines.

Under-26s can fly on standby with SAS anywhere in Sweden – the standby fare from Stockholm to Luleå, for example, can be as little as 350kr one-way. If you buy eight single standby tickets, you also get two free single standby tickets within Sweden; buy sixteen single tickets and you're entitled to a free return ticket from Sweden to any SAS European destination north of the Alps. You can avoid lengthy waits at airports by checking seat availability; phone ☎0770/72 78 88, or visit ⊛www.sas.se/ungdom (both Swedish-language only). **Children** under two travel free. It's also worth considering an **air pass**, which you'll need to buy in conjunction with your ticket to Scandinavia – SAS and Skyways offer a "Visit Scandinavia" pass that's valid on all their routes in Sweden, Denmark, Norway and Finland. See "Basics", p.28, for more information.

Driving

Driving presents few problems: roads are excellent, and the only real dangers are the reindeer and elk that can wander onto the tarmac. Keep to the speed limits and watch out around dawn and dusk particularly – if you hit one you'll know about it; every year, dozens of drivers are hospitalized or killed after hitting elk. As for **documentation**, you need a full licence and the vehicle registration document; an international driving licence and insurance "green card" are not essential. **Speed limits** are 110kph on motorways, 90kph and 70kph on other roads, 50kph in built-up areas; note that there are hundreds of speed cameras across Sweden, mainly in the south. It's compulsory to use **dipped headlights** during daylight hours (on rented cars they will probably come on automatically) and, if you are taking your own car from Britain, remember to get the beam of your headlights adjusted to suit **driving on the right**. If you're motoring into northern Sweden then it's recommended that you fit mud flaps to your wheels and stone guards on the front of caravans. Swedish **drink-driving laws** are among the toughest in Europe and random breath tests the norm. Even the smallest amount of alcohol can lead to lost licences (always), fines (often) and prison sentences (not infrequently).

If you **break down** or are in an **accident**, call either the police or the Larmtjänst (☏ 112), a 24-hour rescue organization run by Swedish insurance companies. If you're heading into a city for the first time, keep an eye out for the excellent **information points** along the motorways, usually a few kilometres before the turnoff; apart from listing tourist information, some now have machines that spit out free city or regional maps. Town centre tourist offices are usually well indicated, and those in larger towns and cities often have special spaces where you can park free of charge for 15–30 minutes.

Car rental and petrol

Car rental is uniformly expensive, though most companies have special weekend tourist rates – from around 600kr, Friday to Monday, for a small car. It's worth checking out local tourist offices in the summer, as they sometimes recommend or operate reasonable weekly deals; otherwise, expect to pay around 3500kr a week, unlimited mileage, for a VW Golf or similar-sized car. Both Avis (☏0046/317 25 67 11, in Sweden ☏0770/82 00 82, ⊛www.avis.se) and Hertz (☏ 0046/960 47 30 0, ⊛ www.hertz.se) are represented in all the large towns and cities, and there are also numerous outlets of the cheaper local rental company, Mabi (☏0046/86 1260 90, ⊛www.mabihyrbilar. se). **Petrol** currently costs around 12kr per litre, diesel 9.90kr per litre; lead-free fuel is widely available. Most filling stations are self-service (*tanka själv*) and lots of them have automatic pumps (*sedel automat*), where you can fill up at any time using your credit card (international cards usually accepted) at a slightly lower price.

Cycling

A much better way to get around Sweden independently is to **cycle**. Some parts of the country were made for it, the southern provinces (and Gotland in particular) being ideal for a leisurely pedal. Many towns are best explored by bike, too – there are even public air pumps for soft tyres – and tourist offices, campsites and youth hostels often **rent** bicycles from around 100kr a day to 400kr a week; you may have to pay a returnable deposit as well. If you're touring, be prepared for long-distance hauls in the north and for rain in summer. **Taking a bike on a train** is possible on selected routes and will cost you up to 350kr extra; phone ☏0771/75 75 75 for more information. You need to check bikes in ahead of your journey – the Swedish word for this is *pollettera*.

The Svenska Cykelsällskapet (Swedish Cycling Association, ☏08/751 62 04, ⊛www.svenska-cykelsallskapet.se), sign-post cycle routes in southern and central Sweden and can provide maps of these routes as well as general information. The STF can also advise on cycling package holidays in Sweden, which usually include youth hostel accommodation, meals and bike rental.

Accommodation

Finding somewhere cheap to sleep is not difficult provided you're prepared to do some advance planning. There's an excellent network of **youth hostels**, **pensions** and **campsites**, while **private rooms** and **bed-and-breakfast** places are common in the cities. Year-round discounts even make **hotels** affordable, an option certainly worth considering in the large cities where a city discount card is thrown in as part of the package.

Hotels and pensions

Hotels and **pensions** (the latter usually family-run B&B-type places) come cheaper than you'd think in Sweden. Although there's little chance of a room under 450kr a night anywhere, you'll find that rates vary according to season and the day of the week. Outside the summer period (roughly mid-June to mid-Aug), rates are reduced at weekends (usually Fri and Sat), while a higher price is applied from Sunday to Thursday to take advantage of business travellers. During the summer, the winter weekend rates generally apply throughout the week. Bear in mind, though, that this is a general rule that varies from place to place.

In summer and at weekends outside of summer, expect to pay from 450kr for a single, 600kr for a double room with a TV and private bathroom. From Sunday to Thursday outside of summer, prices average at around 700kr for a single and 1000kr for a double. Nearly all hotels include a self-service buffet breakfast in the price – which, given its size, can make for a useful saving.

The best local **package deals** are available through the tourist offices in Malmö, Stockholm and Gothenburg: 400–500kr (minimum) gets you a double room for one night, breakfast and the relevant city discount card thrown in. These schemes are generally valid from mid-June to mid-August and at weekends throughout the rest of the year; see the accommodation details under the city accounts within the guide for more detailed information.

The other option to consider is buying into a **hotel pass** scheme, where you pay in advance for a series of vouchers or cheques which then allow discounts or "free" accommodation in various hotel chains throughout the country. Further details can be found in the free booklet *Hotels in Sweden*, available from the Swedish Tourist Board, which also lists every hotel in the country.

Youth hostels

The biggest choice (indeed, quite often the only choice) of accommodation lies with the country's huge chain of youth hostels (*vandrarhem*), operated by the Swedish Tourist Association (STF, ☎08/463 21 00, ⓦ www.stfturist.se). There are over 300 hostels in the country, mainly in southern and central Sweden, but also at regular and handy intervals throughout the north. Forget any preconceptions about youth hostelling: in Sweden rooms are family-oriented, modern, clean and hotel-like, existing in the unlikeliest places – old castles, schoolrooms, country manors, and even in old prisons and on boats. Virtually all have well-equipped self-catering kitchens and serve a buffet breakfast, and many offer free use of a washing machine. Prices are low, at 130–200kr for a bed; depending on the hostel, the bed can be either in a room (generally shared with one to three others), or in a larger dorm. Most hostels will charge you about 50kr extra for the use of **sheets** (some expressly forbid the use of sleeping bags, though they won't check), so if you're planning to stay in more than one hostel it pays to bring your own. Some hostels have cheap private double rooms, and we've given price codes for these where they exist. Note that non-members of *Hostelling International* (see p.47) pay an extra 45kr per night, and that some hostels apply the same seasonal reductions to rates as hotels (see p.46). It would be impossible to list every hostel in this guide, so consult the Hostelling International handbook, or the useful *Bo hos STF* guide, available free from hostels, tourist offices and large bookshops.

Apart from the STF establishments, there are a number of independently run hostels, some of them united under the Swedish Youth Hostel Association, **SVIF** (☎0413/55 34 50, ⓦwww.svif.se). These usually charge similar prices to STF hostels; local tourist offices will have details, and we've included the best places in the Guide.

Bear in mind that hostels are used by Swedish families as cheap, hotel-standard accommodation and can fill quickly, so always **book ahead** in the summer; it's also worth noting that hostels are sometimes closed between 10am and 5pm, and some have curfews around 11pm/midnight.

Private rooms and B&Bs

A further option are **private rooms** in people's houses. Affordable and usually pleasant, these have access to showers and/or baths, sometimes a kitchen too, and hosts are rarely intrusive. Where rooms are available they are mentioned in the text, or look for the words *rum* or *logi* by the roadside. In any reasonably sized town, though, the tourist office can book private rooms for you or give you an overview of options so you can book yourself; rates are anything from 100kr to 2000kr per person per night, plus a 30–50kr booking fee.

Farms throughout Sweden offer B&B accommodation and self-catering facilities; rooms can be booked directly via the website of *Bo på Lantgård* (ⓦwww.bopalantgard.org), or from local tourist offices. Farm accommodation costs roughly 250–300kr per night per person, with discounts for children. If you want to book before you leave, the Swedish

Tourist Board should be able to point you in the right direction.

Campsites

Practically every town or village has at least one **campsite**. These are generally of a high standard and will usually have a shower block, though you may have to pay for hot water. The larger campsites may have outdoor pools, too. Pitching a tent costs 80–160kr a night and there's often a charge of 10–25kr per person, too. Most sites are open from June to September; some (in winter sports areas) throughout the year. The bulk of the sites are approved and classified by the Swedish Tourist Board, and a comprehensive listings book, *Camping Sverige*, is available at larger sites and most Swedish bookshops (or, in advance, try one of the map outlets listed in "Basics"). The Swedish Tourist Board also puts out a short free list. Note that you'll need a **camping card** (60kr from your first stop) at most sites and that **camping gaz** can be tricky to get hold of in Sweden – take your own if possible.

Thanks to a tradition known as *Allemansrätt* ("everyman's right"), it's perfectly possible to **camp rough** throughout the country. This gives you the right to pitch a tent anywhere for one night without asking permission, provided you stay a reasonable distance (100m) away from other dwellings. In practice (and especially if you're in the north) no-one will object to discreet camping for longer periods, although it's as well, and polite, to ask first. The wide open spaces within most town and city borders make free camping a distinct possibility in built-up areas, too.

Cabins and mountain huts

Many campsites also boast **cabins** (look for the word *stugor*), usually decked out with bunk beds, kitchen and equipment, but not sheets. For groups or couples, these make an excellent alternative to camping; cabins go for 350–500kr for a four-bed affair. Again, it's wise to ring ahead to secure one. Sweden also has a whole series of **chalet villages**, which – on the whole – offer high-standard accommodation at prices to match. If you're interested in a package along these lines, contact the Swedish Tourist Board for more details.

In the more out-of-the-way places, STF operate a system of **mountain huts** (*fjällstationer* or *fjällstugor*), strung along hiking trails and in national parks. Usually staffed by a warden, and with cooking facilities, the huts cost 130–300kr per person per night for STF and HI members, and 45–100kr more for non-members. All huts are listed in the *Bo hos STF* guide (see p.437).

Food and drink

There's no escaping the fact that **eating** and **drinking** is going to take up a large slice of your daily budget in Sweden. However, if

Glossary of Swedish food and drink terms

Basics and snacks

Ägg	Egg
Bröd	Bread
Glass	Ice cream
Grädde	Cream
Gräddfil	Sour cream
Gröt	Porridge
Jus	Fruit juice
Kaffe	Coffee
Knäckebröd	Crispbread
Mineralvatten	Mineral water
Mjölk	Milk
Olja	Oil
Omelett	Omelette
Ost	Cheese
Pastej	Pâté
Peppar	Pepper
Ris	Rice
Salt	Salt
Senap	Mustard
Småkakor	Biscuits
Smör	Butter
Smörgås	Sandwich
Socker	Sugar
Soppa	Soup
Strips	Chips
Sylt	Jam
Te	Tea
Våfflor	Waffles
Vinäger	Vinegar

Meat (Kött)

Älg	Elk
Biff	Beef steak
Fläsk	Pork
Kalvkött	Veal
Korv	Sausage
Kotlett	Cutlet/chop
Köttbullar	Meatballs
Kyckling	Chicken
Lammkött	Lamb
Lever	Liver
Oxstek	Roast beef

Renstek	Roast reindeer
Skinka	Ham

Fish (Fisk)

Ål	Eel
Ansjovis	Anchovies
Blåmusslor	Mussels
Fiskbullar	Fishballs
Forell	Trout
Hummer	Lobster
Kaviar	Caviar
Krabba	Crab
Kräftor	Freshwater crayfish
Lax	Salmon
Makrill	Mackerel
Räkor	Shrimps/prawns
Rödspätta	Plaice
Sardiner	Sardines
Sik	Whitefish
Sill	Herring
Strömming	Baltic herring
Torsk	Cod

Vegetables (Grönsaker)

Ärtor	Peas
Blomkål	Cauliflower
Bönor	Beans
Brysselkål	Brussels sprouts
Gurka	Cucumber
Lök	Onion
Morötter	Carrots
Potatis	Potatoes
Rödkål	Red cabbage
Sallad	Salad
Spenat	Spinach
Svamp	Mushrooms
Tomater	Tomatoes
Vitkål	White cabbage
Vitlök	Garlic

Fruit (Frukt)

Ananas	Pineapple
Apelsin	Orange
Äpple	Apple

you choose to eat your main meal of the day at lunchtime, as the Swedes do, you'll save a small fortune.

At its best, **Swedish food** is excellent. It's largely meat-, fish- and potato-based, but varied for all that, and generally tasty and filling. There are unusual northern delicacies to look out for as well – reindeer and elk meat, and wild berries – while herring comes in so many different guises that fish fiends will always be content. **Drinking** is more uniform, the lager-type beer and imported wine providing no surprises, although the local spirit, *akvavit*, is worth trying at least once – it comes in dozens of different flavours. Note that **smoking** is banned in all restaurants, bars and clubs.

Aprikos	Apricot		*Lagom*	Medium
Banan	Banana		*Pocherad*	Poached
Citron	Lemon		*Rökt*	Smoked
Hallon	Raspberry		*Stekt*	Fried
Hjortron	Cloudberry		*Ugnstekt*	Roasted/baked
Jordgrubbar	Strawberries		*Varm*	Hot
Lingon	Cranberries			
Päron	Pear		**Drinks**	
Persika	Peach		*Apelsin juice*	Orange juice
Vindruvor	Grapes		*Choklad*	Hot chocolate
			Citron	Lemon
General terms			*Frukt juice*	Fruit juice
Ångkokt	Steamed		*Kaffe*	Coffee
Blodig	Rare		*Mineralvatten*	Mineral water
Filé	Fillet		*Mjölk*	Milk
Friterad	Deep-fried		*Öl*	Beer
Genomstekt	Well-done		*Saft*	Squash
Gravad	Cured		*Te*	Tea
Grillat/Halstrad	Grilled		*Vatten*	Water
Kall	Cold		*Vin*	Wine
Kokt	Boiled		*Skål!*	Cheers!

Swedish specialities

Ål	Eel, smoked and served with creamed potatoes or scrambled eggs (*äggröra*).
Ärtsoppa	Yellow pea soup with pork; a winter dish traditionally served on Thursdays.
Björnstek	Roast bear meat; fairly rare; but occasionally served at Orsa.
Bruna bönor	Baked, vinegared brown beans, usually served with bacon.
Fisksoppa	Fish soup.
Getost	Goat's cheese.
Gravadlax	Salmon marinated in dill, sugar and seasoning, and served with mustard sauce.
Hjortron	A wild berry served with fresh cream and/or ice cream.
Köttbullar	Meatballs served with a brown sauce and cranberries.
Kryddos	Hard cheese with caraway seeds.
Lövbiff	Sliced, fried beef with onions.
Mesost	Brown, sweet cheese; a breakfast favourite.
Potatissallad	Potato salad.
Pytt i panna	Cubes of meat and fried potatoes with a fried egg.
Sillbricka	Various cured and marinated herring dishes; often appears as a first course at lunchtime in restaurants.
Sjömansbiff	Beef, onions and potato stewed in beer.

Food

Eating well and cheaply in Sweden are often mutually exclusive aims, at least as far as a sit-down restaurant meal is concerned. The best strategy is to fuel up on breakfast and lunch, both of which offer good-value options. There's also a large number of foreign restaurants – principally pizzerias and Chinese restaurants – which are more likely to serve decently priced evening meals. In the Guide, we've included telephone numbers only for places where you need to **book a table**. Note that quite a few small restaurants close in July; we've stated where this is the case in the Guide.

Breakfast, snacks and self-catering

Breakfast (*frukost*) in most youth hostels and hotel restaurants is almost invariably a help-yourself buffet; it usually costs around 50kr in hostels, and is free in hotels. If you can eat vast amounts between 7am and 10am, it's nearly always good value. Juice, milk, cereals, bread, jam, boiled eggs, salami, tea and coffee appear on even the most limited tables. Swankier venues will also add herring, porridge, yoghurt, pâté and fruit. Something to watch out for is the jug of *filmjölk* next to the ordinary milk – it's thicker, sour milk for pouring on cereals. **Coffee** in Sweden is always freshly brewed and very good; often it's free after the first cup, or at least greatly reduced in price – look for the word *påtår*. **Tea** is less exciting – weak Lipton's as a rule – but costs around the same: 15kr a cup.

For **snacks** and lighter meals the choice expands, although availability is inversely related to health value. A *gatukök* (street kitchen) or *korvstånd* (hot-dog stall) will serve a selection of hot-dogs, burgers, pizza slices, chicken bits, chips, ice cream, Coke, crisps and ketchup – something and chips will cost around 50kr. These stalls and stands are on every street in every town and village. A hefty burger-and-chips meal in a **burger bar** goes for around 55kr.

It's often nicer to hit the **konditori**, a coffee shop with succulent pastries and cakes. They're not particularly cheap (coffee and cake cost 35–50kr) but are generally as good as they look, and the coffee is often free after you've paid for the first cup. This is also where you'll come across *smörgåsar*, open **sandwiches** piled high with an elaborate variety of toppings. Favourites include shrimps, smoked salmon, eggs, cheese, pâté and mixed salad – around 50–60kr a time. *Konditoris* often make delicious **ice cream**, too; if you see it, try the unique *lakrits* (salty liquorice) flavour.

Restaurants: lunch and dinner

Eating in a **restaurant** (*restaurang*) needn't be out of your price range, but remember that **lunch** is always around a third cheaper than dinner. Most restaurants offer something called the **dagens rätt** ("daily dish") at 60–75kr, an excellent way to sample real Swedish *husmanskost* – "home cooking". Served Monday to Friday between 11am and 2pm, *dagens rätt* is simply a choice of main meal (usually one meat and one fish dish) which comes with bread/crispbread and salad, sometimes a soft drink or light beer, and usually coffee. Some Swedish dishes, like *pytt i panna* and *köttbullar*, are standards. On the whole, though, more likely offerings in the big cities are pizzas, basic Chinese meals and meat or fish salads. If you're travelling **with kids**, look out for the word *barnmatsedal* (children's menu).

More expensive – but good for a blowout – are restaurants and hotels that put out the **smörgåsbord** at lunchtime. Following the breakfast theme, you help yourself to unlimited portions of herring, hot and cold meats, eggs, fried and boiled potatoes, salad, cheese, desserts and fruit for 150–250kr. To follow local custom you should start with *akvavit*, drink beer throughout and finish with coffee, although this will add to the bill unless it is a fancier all-inclusive spread (usually found on Sundays). A variation on the buffet theme is the **sillbricka**, a specialist buffet where the dishes are all based on cured and marinated herring – it might simply be called the "herring table" on the menu.

If you don't eat the set lunch, meals in restaurants, especially at **dinner** (*middag*), can be expensive. Expect to pay at least 400kr per head for a three-course affair, to which you can add 40–50kr for a beer, and 150kr for the cheapest bottle of house wine. The food in Swedish restaurants is generally *husmanskost*, although the latest trend is for "crossover" cuisine: Swedish cooking with an international edge that's usually delicious.

Swedes eat early and lunch in most restaurants is served from around 11am, dinner from around 6pm.

Ethnic restaurants

For years the only **ethnic** choice in Sweden was between the pizzeria or the odd Chinese restaurant, and these still offer the best-value dinners. In **pizzerias** you'll get a large, if not strictly authentic, pizza for around 50kr, usually with free coleslaw and bread, and the price generally remains the same whether it's lunch or dinner. **Chinese** restaurants nearly always offer a set lunch or buffet for around 50kr, and though pricier in the evenings (80–100kr a dish), a group of people can usually put together quite a good-value meal.

Vegetarians

It's not too tough being **vegetarian** in Sweden, given the preponderance of buffet-type meals, most of which are heavy with salads, cheeses, eggs and soups. The cities, too, have salad bars and sandwich shops where you'll have no trouble feeding yourself, and if all else fails the local pizzeria will always deliver the meat-free goods. At lunchtime you'll find that the *dagens rätt* in many places has a vegetarian option; don't be afraid to ask.

Drinking

Drinking in Sweden is no longer the notoriously pricey pursuit it once was – in fact, a beer in Stockholm now costs roughly the same as in London. Nonetheless, it's still cheaper to forgo bars every once in a while and buy your booze from the state-licensed **Systembolaget** liquor stores – though doing so is, of course, not nearly as enjoyable. Swedes still perceive drinking to be an expensive activity: consequently, you won't find yourself stuck buying rounds at the bar which demand a bank loan to pay off, and it's perfectly acceptable to nurse your drink as long as you like. It's worth noting, though, that some bars have happy hours, when half a litre of beer goes for around half-price.

What to drink

If you drink anything alcoholic in Sweden, a good choice is **beer**, which, while expensive, at least costs the same almost everywhere, be it a café, bar or restaurant. For 40–45kr, you'll get a half-litre of good, lager-type brew – unless you specify, it will be *starköl*, the strongest Class III beer; cheaper will be *folköl*, Class II and weaker; whilst cheapest (around half the price of *folköl*) is *lättöl*, a Class I concoction notable only for its virtual absence of alcohol. Classes I and II are available in supermarkets, although the real stuff is only on sale in the *Systembolaget* liquor stores – see p.442 – where it's around a third of the price you'll pay in a bar. **Wine** is good value when bought in the *Systembolaget* but can be expensive in restaurants and bars, where you'll pay around 45kr for a glass and upwards of 150kr for a bottle. **Spirits** are the most expensive alcoholic drinks; vodka, for example, costs around 50kr a shot. For experimental drinking, **akvavit** – clear and tasteless – is a good bet. Served ice cold in tiny shots, it's washed down with beer: hold onto your hat. There are various different "flavours" too, in which spices and herbs are added to the finished brew to produce some unusual headaches. Or try **glögg**: served at Christmas, it's a mulled red wine with cloves, cinnamon, sugar and more than a dash of *akvavit*.

Where to drink

You'll find **bars** in all towns and cities and most villages. In Stockholm and the larger cities the move is towards brasserie-type places – smart and flash – and fast-expanding chains of British-style pubs. Elsewhere, you still come across more down-to-earth drinking dens, often sponsored by the local union or welfare authority, but the drink's no cheaper and the clientele heavily male and drunk. Either way, the bar is not the centre of Swedish social activity – if you really want to meet people, you'd be better off heading for the campsite or the beach.

In the summer, **café-bars** spread out onto the pavement, better for kids and handy for just a coffee. In out-of-the-way places, when you want a drink and can't find a bar, head for a hotel. Things close down at

11pm or midnight except in Gothenburg and Stockholm where – as long as your wallet is bottomless – you can drink all night.

Systembolaget

Venturing into a **Systembolaget** (a state-run off-licence) used to be a move into a twilight world, with buying alcohol made as unattractive as possible. Things are changing though, and *Systembolaget* is making moves towards becoming a service-oriented, responsible and knowledgeable retail enterprise before the EU – or loss of income because of Swedes shopping abroad – forces it to lose its monopoly. Many Swedes don't mind being mothered by the state, and are convinced that *Systembolaget*'s purchasing policy gets them a better and cheaper selection of wine and liquor than in normal market circumstances. Responsibility is more important than profit at *Systembolaget*, and the list of actions taken against corrupt managers and employees makes for sobering reading for would-be racketeers (see ⓦ www.systembolaget.se). Buying from the *Systembolaget* is the only option for many budget travellers, although apart from strong beer (15kr or so for a third of a litre), the only bargain is the wine – from around 50kr a bottle for some surprisingly good European and New World imports. *Systembolaget* shops are open Monday to Saturday only (10am–6pm or 7pm, Sat until 2pm); minimum age for being served is 20, and you may need to show ID, although in bars and pubs the age limit is 18. Some bars and clubs, however, have a **minimum age** requirement (often 19 or 21), indicated by the word *aldersgräns*; depending on the sort of event, this can change according to the day of the week.

Directory

Customs Coming from another European Union country where tax has been paid, your customs allowance for your own use is 10 litres of spirits, 90 litres of wine and 110 litres of strong beer; under-20s are not allowed to import alcohol into Sweden.

Emergencies Dial ☏ 112 for police (*polis*), fire brigade (*brandkår*) or ambulance (*ambulans*), free of charge from any public phone.

Public holidays Banks, offices and shops are closed on the following days and may shut early on the preceding day: January 1, January 6 (Epiphany), Good Friday, Easter Monday, May 1 (Labour Day), Ascension Day (fortieth day after Easter), Whit Monday (eighth Monday after Easter), Midsummer's Day, All Saint's Day, Christmas Day, Boxing Day.

Shops Opening hours are Mon–Fri 9am–6pm, Sat 9am–4pm. Some department stores stay open until 8–10pm in cities, and may open on Sunday afternoons as well.

Tipping Hotels and restaurants include their service charge in the bill, though a small 5–10 percent tip for good service is not unusual. You should tip cloakroom attendants in bars and discos around 10kr a time.

History

S weden has one of Europe's longest documented histories, but for all the upheavals of the Viking times and the warring of the Middle Ages, during modern times the country has seemed to delight in taking an historical back seat. The murders of prime minister Olof Palme in 1986 and of foreign minister Anna Lindh in 2003 briefly thrust Sweden into the international limelight, but since then, the country regained its poise, even though the current situation is fraught. Political infighting and domestic disharmony are threatening the one thing that the Swedes have always been proud of and that other countries aspire to: the politics of consensus. The passing of this, arguably, is of far greater importance than even the murders of their politicians.

Early civilizations

It wasn't until around 6000 BC that the **first settlers** roamed north and east into Sweden, living as nomadic reindeer-hunters and herders. By 3000 BC people had settled in the south of the country and were established as farmers; whilst from around 2000 BC a development in burial practices occurred, with **dolmens** and **passage graves** being found throughout the southern Swedish provinces. Traces also remain of the **Boat Axe People**, named after their characteristic tool/weapon shaped like a boat. The earliest Scandinavian horse-riders, they quickly held sway over the whole of southern Sweden.

During the **Bronze Age** (1500–500 BC) the Boat Axe People traded furs and amber for southern European copper and tin. Large finds of ornaments and weapons attest to a comparatively rich culture, exemplified by elaborate burial rites, with the dead laid in single graves under mounds of earth and stone.

The deterioration of the Scandinavian climate in the last millennium before Christ coincided with the advance across Europe of the Celts, which halted the flourishing trade of the Swedish settlers. With the new millennium, Sweden made its first mark upon the classical world when Pliny the Elder (23–79 AD), in the *Historia Naturalis*, mentioned the "island of Scatinavia" far to the north. Tacitus was more specific: in 98 AD he referred to a powerful people, the Suinoes, who were strong in men, weapons and ships: a reference to the **Svear**, who were to form the nucleus of an emergent Swedish kingdom by the sixth century.

Rulers of the whole country except the south, the Svear settled in the rich land around Lake Mälaren. The modern Swedish name for Sweden, *Sverige*, is a derivation "Svear rike", meaning the kingdom of the Svear; more importantly, the Svear gave their first dynastic leaders a taste for expansion, trading with Gotland and holding suzerainty over the Åland Islands.

The Viking period

The Vikings – raiders and warriors who dominated the political and economic life of Europe and beyond from the ninth to the eleventh centuries – came from all parts of southern Scandinavia. But there is evidence that the **Swedish Vikings** were among the first to leave home, impelled by a rapid population growth, domestic unrest and a desire for new lands. The raiders (and, later, traders) turned their attention largely eastwards, and by the ninth century trade had developed along well-established routes, with Swedes reaching the Black and Caspian seas and making valuable contact with the **Byzantine Empire**. Although more commercially inclined than their Danish and Norwegian counterparts, Swedish Vikings were quick to use force if profits were slow to materialize. From 860 onwards Greek and

Muslim records relate a series of raids across the Black Sea against Byzantium, and across the Caspian into northeast Iran.

But the Vikings were settlers as well as traders and exploiters, and their long-term influence was marked. Embattled Slavs to the east gave them the name **Rus**, and their creeping colonization gave the area in which the Vikings settled its modern name, Russia. Russian names today – Oleg, Igor, Vladimir – can be derived from the Swedish – Helgi, Ingvar, Valdemar.

Domestically, **paganism** was at its height. Freyr was "God of the World", a physically potent god of fertility from whom dynastic leaders would trace their descent. It was a bloody time. Nine **human sacrifices** were offered at the celebrations held every nine years at Uppsala. Adam of Bremen recorded that the great shrine there was adjoined by a sacred grove where "every tree is believed divine because of the death and putrefaction of the victims hanging there".

Viking **law** was based on the **Thing**, an assembly of free men to which the king's power was subject. Each largely autonomous province had its own assembly and its own leaders: where several provinces united, the approval of each Thing was needed for any choice of leader. For centuries in Sweden the new king had to make a formal tour to receive the homage of each province.

The arrival of Christianity

Christianity was slow to take root in Sweden. Whereas Denmark and Norway had accepted the faith by the beginning of the eleventh century, Swedish contact was still with the peoples to the east, who remained largely heathen. Missionaries met with limited success and no Swedish king was converted until 1008, when **Olof Skötonung** was baptized. He was the first known king of both Swedes and Goths (that is, ruler of the two major provinces of Västergötland and Östergöt-

land) and his successors were all Christians. Nevertheless, paganism retained a grip on Swedish affairs, and as late as the 1080s the Svear banished their Christian king, Inge, when he refused to take part in the pagan celebrations at Uppsala. By the end of the eleventh century, though, the temple at Uppsala had gone and a Christian church was built on its site. In the 1130s Uppsala replaced Sigtuna – original centre of the Swedish Christian faith – as the main episcopal seat and, in 1164, Stephen (an English monk) was made the first archbishop.

The warring dynasties

The whole of the early Middle Ages in Sweden were characterized by a succession of struggles for control of a growing central power. Principally two families, the Sverkers and the Eriks, waged battle throughout the twelfth century. **King Erik the Holy** was the first notable Sverker ruler to make his mark: in 1157 he led a crusade to heathen Finland, but was killed at Uppsala in 1160 by a Danish pretender to his throne. Within a hundred years he was to be recognized as patron saint of Sweden, and his remains interred in the new Uppsala Cathedral.

Erik was succeeded by his son **Knut**, whose stable reign lasted until 1196 and was marked by commercial treaties and strengthened defences. Following Knut's death, virtual civil war weakened the royal power with the result that the king's chief ministers, or **Jarls**, assumed much of the executive responsibility for running the country; so much so that when Erik Eriksson (last of the Eriks) was deposed in 1229, his administrator **Birger Jarl** assumed power. With papal support for his crusading policies, Jarl confirmed the Swedish grip on the southwest of Finland. His son Valdemar succeeded him, but proved a weak ruler and didn't survive the family feuding after Birger Jarl's death. Valdemar's brother Magnus assumed power in 1275.

Magnus Ladulås represented a peak of Swedish royal power not to be repeated for three hundred years. His enemies dissipated, he forbade the nobility to meet without his consent and began to issue his own authoritative decrees. Preventing the nobility from claiming maintenance at the expense of the peasantry as they travelled from estate to estate earned him his nickname Ladulås or "Barn-lock". He also began to reap the benefits of conversion: the clergy became an educated class upon whom the monarch could rely for diplomatic and administrative duties. By the thirteenth century, there were ambitious Swedish clerics in Paris and Bologna, and the first stone churches were appearing in Sweden, among them the monumental early Gothic cathedral at Uppsala.

The nobility, meanwhile, had come to form a military class, exempted from taxation on the understanding that they would defend the crown. In the country the standard of living was still low, although a burgeoning population stimulated new cultivation. The forests of Norrland were pushed back, southern heathland was turned into pasture, and crop rotation introduced. Noticeable, too, was the increasing **German influence** within Sweden as the Hanseatic League traders spread. Their first merchants settled in Visby and, by the mid-thirteenth century, in Stockholm.

The fourteenth century – towards unity

When Magnus died in 1290, power shifted to a cabal of magnates led by **Torgil Knutsson**. As Marshal of Sweden, he pursued an energetic foreign policy, conquering western Karelia to gain control of the Gulf of Finland and building the fortress at Viborg, which was lost only with the collapse of the Swedish Empire in the eighteenth century.

Magnus's son Birger came of age in 1302 but soon quarrelled with his brothers Erik and Valdemar. They had Torgil Knutsson executed, then rounded on Birger, who was forced to divide

Sweden among the three of them. An unhappy arrangement, it lasted until 1317, when Birger had his brothers arrested and starved to death in prison – an act that prompted a shocked nobility to rise against Birger and force his exile to Denmark. The Swedish nobles restored the principle of elective monarchy by calling on the 3-year-old **Magnus** (son of a Swedish duke and already declared Norwegian king) to take the Swedish crown. While Magnus was still a boy, a treaty was concluded with Novgorod (1323) to fix the frontiers in eastern and northern Finland. This left virtually the whole of the Scandinavian peninsula (except the Danish provinces in the south) under one ruler.

Yet Sweden was still anything but prosperous. The **Black Death** reached the country in 1350, wiping out whole parishes and killing around a third of the population. Subsequent labour shortages and troubled estates meant that the nobility found it difficult to maintain their positions. German merchants had driven the Swedes from their most lucrative trade routes and even the copper and iron-ore **mining** that began around this time in Bergslagen and Dalarna relied on German capital.

Magnus soon ran into trouble, threatened further by the accession of Valdemar Atterdag to the Danish throne in 1340. Squabbles over the sovereignty of the Danish provinces of Skåne and Blekinge led to Danish incursions into Sweden and, in 1361, Valdemar landed on Gotland and sacked **Visby**. The Gotlanders, refused refuge by the Hanseatic League, were massacred outside the city walls.

Magnus was forced to negotiate and his son **Håkon** – now King of Norway – was married to Valdemar's daughter Margrethe. With Magnus later deposed, power fell into the hands of a group of magnates, who shared out the country. Chief of the ruling nobles was the Steward **Bo Jonsson Grip**, who controlled virtually all Finland and central and southeast Sweden. Yet on his death, the nobility turned to Håkon's wife **Margrethe**, already regent in Norway (for her son Olof) and in Denmark since the death of her father, Valdemar. In 1388 she was proclaimed "First Lady" of Sweden and, in return, confirmed all the privileges of the Swedish nobility. They were anxious for union, to safeguard those who owned frontier estates and strengthen the crown against any further German influence. Called upon to choose a male king, Margrethe nominated her nephew, **Erik of Pomerania**, who was duly elected king of Sweden in 1396. As he had already been elected to the Danish and Norwegian thrones, Scandinavian unity seemed assured.

The Kalmar Union

Erik was crowned King of Denmark, Norway and Sweden in 1397 at a ceremony in **Kalmar**. Nominally, the three kingdoms were now in union but, despite Erik, real power remained in the hands of Margrethe until her death in 1412.

Erik was at war throughout his reign with the Hanseatic League. Vilified in popular Swedish history as an evil and grasping ruler, the taxes he raised went on a war that was never fought on Swedish soil. He spent his time instead directing operations in Denmark, leaving his queen Philippa (sister to Henry V of England) behind. Erik was deposed in 1439 and the nobility turned to **Christopher of Bavaria**, whose early death in 1448 led to the first major breach in the union.

No one candidate could fill the three kingships satisfactorily, and separate elections in Denmark and Sweden signalled a renewal of the infighting that had plagued the previous century. Within Sweden, unionists and nationalists skirmished, the powerful unionist **Oxenstierna** family opposing the claims of the nationalist **Sture** family until 1470, when **Sten Sture** (the Elder) became "Guardian of the Realm". His victory over the unionists at the **Battle of Brunkeberg** (1471)

– in the middle of modern Stockholm – was complete, gaining symbolic artistic expression in the statue of St George and the Dragon that still adorns the Great Church in Stockholm.

Sten Sture's primacy fostered a new cultural flowering. The first **university** in Scandinavia was founded in Uppsala in 1477, and the first printing press appeared in Sweden six years later. Artistically, German and Dutch influences were great, traits seen in the decorative art of the great Swedish medieval churches. Only remote **Dalarna** kept alive a native folk-art tradition.

Belief in the union still existed, though, particularly outside Sweden, and successive kings had to fend off almost constant attacks and blockades emanating from Denmark. With the accession of **Christian II** to the Danish throne in 1513, the unionist movement found a leader capable of turning the tide. Under the guise of a crusade to free Sweden's imprisoned archbishop Gustav Trolle, Christian attacked Sweden and killed Sture. After Christian's coronation, Trolle urged the prosecution of his Swedish adversaries who, gathered together under an amnesty, were found guilty of heresy. Eighty-two nobles and burghers of Stockholm were executed and their bodies burned in what became known as the **Stockholm Bloodbath**. A vicious persecution of Sture's followers throughout Sweden ensued, a move that led to widespread reaction and, ultimately, the downfall of the union.

Gustav Vasa and his sons

Opposition to Christian II was vague and unorganized until the appearance of the young **Gustav Vasa**. Initially unable to stir the locals of the Dalecarlia region into open revolt, he left for exile in Norway, but was chased on skis and recalled after the people had had a change of heart. The chase is celebrated still in the **Vasalopet** race, run each year by thousands of Swedish skiers.

Gustav Vasa's army grew rapidly and in 1521 he was elected regent, and subsequently, with the capture of Stockholm in 1523, king. Christian had been deposed in Denmark and the new Danish king, Frederik I, recognized Sweden's de facto withdrawal from the union. Short of cash, Gustav found it prudent to support the movement towards religious reform propagated by Swedish Lutherans. More of a political than a religious **Reformation**, the result was a handover of church lands to the crown and the subordination of church to state. It's a relationship that is still largely in force today, the clergy being civil servants paid by the State. In 1541 the first edition of the Bible in the vernacular appeared. Suppressing revolt at home, Gustav Vasa strengthened his hand with a centralization of trade and government. On his death in 1560 Sweden was united, prosperous and independent.

However, Gustav Vasa's heir, his eldest son **Erik**, faced a difficult time, not least because the Vasa lands and wealth had been divided among him and his brothers Johan, Magnus and Karl (an atypically imprudent action of Gustav's before his death). The Danes, too, pressed hard, reasserting their claim to the Swedish throne in the inconclusive **Northern Seven Years' War**, which began in 1563. Erik was deposed in 1569 by his brother, who became **Johan III**: his first act was to end the war at the **Peace of Stettin**. At home, Johan ruled more or less with the good will of the nobility, but upset matters with his Catholic sympathies. He introduced the liturgy and Catholic-influenced Red Book, and his son and heir Sigismund was the Catholic king of Poland. On Johan's death in 1592, Sigismund agreed to rule Sweden in accordance with Lutheran practice but failed to do so. When Sigismund returned to Poland the way was clear for Duke Karl (Johan's brother) to assume the regency, a role he filled until declared King **Karl IX** in 1603.

Karl had ambitions eastwards but, routed by the Poles and staved off by the Russians, he suffered a stroke in 1610 and died the year after. The last of Vasa's sons, his heir was the 17-year-old Gustav II Adolf, better known as Gustavus Adolphus.

The rule of Vasa and his sons made Sweden a nation, culturally as well as politically. The courts were filled with men of learning and the arts flourished. The **Renaissance** style appeared for the first time in Sweden, with royal castles remodelled – Kalmar being a fine example. Economically, Sweden remained mostly self-sufficient, its few imports being luxuries like cloth, wine and spices. With around 8000 inhabitants, Stockholm was its most important city, although **Gothenburg** was founded in 1607 to promote trade to the west.

Gustav II Adolf: the rise of the Swedish empire

During the reign of **Gustav II Adolf**, Sweden became a European power. Though still a youth, he was considered able enough to rule, and proved so by concluding peace treaties with Denmark (1613) and Russia (1617), the latter isolating Russia from the Baltic and allowing the Swedes control of the eastern trade routes into Europe.

In 1618 the **Thirty Years' War** broke out in Germany. It was vital for Gustavus that Germany should not become Catholic, given the Polish king's continuing pretensions to the Swedish crown, and the possible threat it could pose to Sweden's growing influence in the Baltic. The 1629 Altmark treaty with a defeated Poland gave Gustavus control of Livonia and four Prussian sea ports, and the income this generated financed his entry into the war in 1630 on the Protestant side. After several convincing victories Gustavus pushed through Germany, delaying an assault upon undefended Vienna. It cost him his life. At the **Battle of Lützen** in 1632 Gustavus was killed, his body stripped and battered by the enemy's soldiers. The war dragged on until the **Peace of Westphalia** in 1648.

With Gustavus away at war for much of his reign, Sweden ran smoothly under the guidance of his friend and chancellor, **Axel Oxenstierna**. Together they founded a new Supreme Court in Stockholm (and the same, too, in Finland and the conquered Baltic provinces); reorganized the national assembly into four Estates of nobility, clergy, burghers and peasantry (1626); extended the university at Uppsala (and founded one at Åbo – modern Turku); and fostered the mining and other industries that provided much of the country's wealth. Gustavus had many other accomplishments, too: he spoke five languages and designed a new light cannon, which assisted in his routs of the enemy.

The Caroleans

The Swedish empire reached its territorial peak under the **Caroleans** – yet the reign of the last of them was to see Sweden crumble.

Following Gustav II Adolf's death and the later abdication of his daughter Christina, **Karl X** succeeded to the throne. War against Poland (1655) led to some early successes and, with Denmark espousing the Polish cause, gave Karl the opportunity to march into Jutland (1657). From there his armies crossed the frozen sea to threaten Copenhagen; the subsequent **Treaty of Roskilde** (1658) broke Denmark and gave the Swedish empire its widest territorial extent.

However, the long regency of his son and heir, **Karl XI**, did little to enhance Sweden's vulnerable position, so extensive were its borders. On his assumption of power in 1672, Karl was almost immediately dragged into war: beaten by a smaller Prussian army at Brandenberg in 1675, Sweden was suddenly faced with war against both the Danes and Dutch. Karl rallied, though, to drive out the Danish invaders, the war ending in 1679 with the reconquest of Skåne and the restoration of most of Sweden's German provinces.

In 1682 Karl XI became **absolute monarch** and was given full control over legislation and *reduktion* – the resumption of estates previously alienated by the crown to the nobility. The armed forces were reorganized too, and by 1700 the Swedish army had 25,000 soldiers and twelve regiments of cavalry; the naval fleet was expanded to 38 ships and a new base built at **Karlskrona** (nearer than Stockholm to the likely trouble spots).

Culturally, Sweden began to benefit from the innovations of Gustav II Adolf. *Gymnasia* (grammar schools) continued to expand and a second university was established at **Lund** in 1668. A national literature emerged, helped by the efforts of **George Stiernhielm**, "father" of modern Swedish poetry, while the same period saw the work of **Olof Rudbeck** (1630–1702), a Nordic polymath whose scientific reputation lasted longer than his attempt to identify the ancient Goth settlement at Uppsala as Atlantis. Architecturally, this was the age of **Tessin**, both father and son. Tessin the Elder was responsible for the glorious palace at **Drottningholm**, work on which began in 1662, as well as the cathedral at **Kalmar**. His son, Tessin the Younger, succeeded him as royal architect and was to create the new palace at Stockholm.

In 1697 the 15-year-old **Karl XII** succeeded to the throne, and under him the empire collapsed. Faced with a defensive alliance of Saxony, Denmark and Russia, there was little the king could have done to avoid eventual defeat. However, he remains a revered figure for his valiant (often suicidal) efforts to prove Europe wrong. Initial victories against Peter the Great and Saxony led him to march on Russia, where he was defeated and the bulk of his army destroyed. Escaping to Turkey, where he remained as guest and then prisoner for four years, Karl watched the empire disintegrate. With Poland reconquered by Augustus of Saxony, and Finland by Peter the Great, he returned to Sweden only to have England declare war on him.

Eventually, splits in the enemy's alliance led Swedish diplomats to attempt peace talks with Russia. Karl, though, was keen to exploit these differences in a more direct fashion. In order to strike at Denmark, but lacking a fleet, he besieged Fredrikshald in Norway in 1718 and was killed by a sniper's bullet. In the power vacuum thus created, Russia became the leading Baltic force, receiving Livonia, Estonia, Ingria and most of Karelia from Sweden.

The age of freedom

The eighteenth century saw absolutism discredited in Sweden. A new constitution vested power in the Estates, who reduced the new king **Fredrik I**'s role to that of nominal head of state. The chancellor wielded the real power and under **Arvid Horn** the country found a period of stability. His party, nicknamed the "Caps", was opposed by the hawkish "Hats", who forced war with Russia in 1741, a disaster in which Sweden lost all of Finland and had its whole east coast burned and bombed. Most of Finland was returned with the agreement to elect **Adolf Fredrik** (a relation of the crown prince of Russia) to the Swedish throne on Fredrik I's death, which duly occurred in 1751. During his reign Adolf repeatedly tried to reassert royal power, but found that the constitution was only strengthened against him. The resurrected "Hats" forced entry into the **Seven Years' War** in 1757 on the French side, another disastrous venture as the Prussians repelled every Swedish attack.

The aristocratic parties were in a state of constant flux. Although elections of sorts were held to provide delegates for the Riksdag (parliament), foreign sympathies, bribery and bickering were hardly conducive to a democratic administration. Cabals continued to rule Sweden, the economy was stagnant, and reform delayed. It was, however, an age of intellectual and scientific advance, surprising in a country that had lost much of its cultural impetus. **Carl von Linné** (better known by the Latinized version of his name, Linnaeus), the botanist whose classification of plants is still used, was professor at Uppsala from 1741 to 1778. **Anders Celsius** initiated the use of the centigrade temperature scale; **Carl Scheele** discovered chlorine. A royal decree of 1748 organized Europe's first full-scale census, and by 1775 the census had become a five-yearly event. Other fields flourished, too. **Emmanuel Swedenborg**, the philosopher, died in 1772, his mystical works encouraging new theological sects; and the period encapsulated the life of **Carl Michael Bellman** (1740–95), the celebrated Swedish poet, whose work did much to identify and foster a popular nationalism.

With the accession of **Gustav III** in 1771, the crown began to regain the ascendancy. A new constitution was forced upon a divided Riksdag, and proved a balance between earlier absolutism and the later aristocratic squabbles. A popular king, Gustav founded hospitals, granted freedom of worship and removed many state controls over the economy. His determination to conduct a successful foreign policy led to further conflict with Russia (1788–90) in which, to everyone's surprise, he managed to more than hold his own. But with the French Revolution polarizing opposition throughout Europe, the Swedish nobility began to entertain thoughts of conspiracy against a king whose growing powers they now saw as those of a tyrant. In 1792, at a masked ball in the Stockholm Opera House, the king was shot by an assassin hired by the disaffected aristocracy. Gustav died two weeks later and was succeeded by his son **Gustav IV**, the country led by a regency for the years of his minority.

The battles waged by revolutionary France were at first studiously avoided in Sweden but, pulled into the conflict by the British, Gustav IV entered the **Napoleonic Wars** in 1805. However, Napoleon's victory at Austerlitz two years later broke the coalition and Sweden found itself isolated. Attacked by

Russia the following year, Gustav was later arrested and deposed, his uncle elected king.

A constitution of 1809 established a liberal monarchy in Sweden, responsible to the elected Riksdag. Under this constitution **Karl XIII** was a mere caretaker, his heir a Danish prince who would bring Norway back to Sweden – some compensation for finally losing Finland and the Åland Islands to Russia (1809) after five hundred years of Swedish rule. On the prince's sudden death, however, Marshal Bernadotte (one of Napoleon's generals) was invited to become heir. Taking the name of **Karl Johan**, he took his chance in 1812 and joined Britain and Russia to fight Napoleon. Following Napoleon's first defeat at the Battle of Leipzig in 1813, Sweden compelled Denmark (France's ally) to exchange Norway for Swedish Pomerania.

By 1814 Sweden and Norway had formed an uneasy union. Norway retained its own government and certain autonomous measures. Sweden decided foreign policy, appointed a viceroy and retained a suspensive (but not absolute) veto over the Norwegian parliament's legislation.

The nineteenth century

Union under Karl Johan, or **Karl XIV** as he became in 1818, could have been disastrous. He spoke no Swedish and, until just a few years previously, had never visited either kingdom. However, under him and his successor **Oscar I**, prosperity ensued. The **Göta Canal** (1832) helped commercially, and liberal measures by both monarchs helped politically. In 1845 daughters were given an equal right of inheritance, a poverty law was introduced in 1847, restrictive craft guilds were reformed and an education act passed.

The 1848 revolution throughout Europe cooled Oscar's reforming ardour, and his attention turned to reviving **Scandinavianism**. There was still a hope, in certain quarters,

that closer cooperation between Denmark and Sweden–Norway could lead to some sort of revived Kalmar Union. With the **Crimean War** of 1854, expectations were raised that Russia – Sweden's main enemy in the eighteenth century – could be weakened for good. But peace was declared too quickly (at least for Sweden) and there was still no real guarantee that Sweden would be sufficiently protected from Russia in the future. With Oscar's death, talk of political union faded.

His son **Karl XV** presided over a reform of the Riksdag that put an end to the Swedish system of personal monarchy. The Four Estates were replaced by a representative two-house parliament along European lines. This, together with the end of political Scandinavianism (following the Prussian attack on Denmark in 1864 in which Sweden refused to offer assistance), marked Sweden's entry into modern Europe.

Industrialization was slow to take root in Sweden. No real industrial revolution occurred, and developments such as mechanization and the introduction of railways were piecemeal. One result was widespread **emigration** amongst the rural poor, who had been hard hit by famine in 1867 and 1868. Between 1860 and 1910, over one million people left for America (in 1860 the Swedish population was only four million). Given huge farms to settle, the emigrants headed for land similar to that they had left behind – to the Midwest, Kansas and Nebraska.

At home, Swedish **trade unionism** emerged to campaign for better conditions. Dealt with severely, the unions formed a confederation (1898) but largely failed to make headway – even peaceful picketing carried a two-year prison sentence. Hand in hand with the fight for workers' rights went the **temperance movement**. The level of spirit consumption was alarming and various abstinence programmes attempted to educate the drinkers and, where necessary, eradicate the stills. Some towns made the selling of spirits a municipal monopoly – not a big step away from the state monopoly that exists today.

With the accession of **Oscar II** in 1872, Sweden continued on an even, if uneventful, keel. Keeping out of further European conflict (the Austro–Prussian War, Franco–Prussian War and various Balkan crises), the country's only worry was a growing dissatisfaction in Norway with the union. Demanding a separate consular service, and objecting to the Swedish king's veto on constitutional matters, the Norwegians brought things to a head and, in 1905, declared the union invalid. The Karlstad Convention confirmed the break and Norway became independent for the first time since 1380.

The late nineteenth century was a happier time for Swedish culture. **August Strindberg** enjoyed great critical success and artists like **Anders Zorn** and **Prince Eugene** made their mark abroad. The historian **Artur Hazelius** founded the Nordic and Skansen museums in Stockholm; and the chemist, industrialist and dynamite inventor **Alfred Nobel** left his fortune to finance the Nobel Prizes. Nobel hoped that the knowledge of his invention would help eradicate war – optimistically believing that mankind would never dare unleash the destructive forces of dynamite.

Two world wars

Sweden declared a strict neutrality on the outbreak of **World War I**, tempered by much sympathy within the country for Germany sponsored by long-standing language, trade and cultural links. It was a policy agreed with the other Scandinavian monarchs, but a difficult one to pursue. Faced with British demands to enforce a blockade of Germany and the blacklisting and eventual seizure of Swedish goods at sea, the economy suffered grievously; rationing occurred and inflation mushroomed. The **Russian Revolution** in 1917 brought further problems to Sweden. The Finns immediately declared independence, waging civil war against the Bolsheviks, and Swedish volunteers enlisted in the White army. But a conflict of interest arose when the Swedish-speaking Åland Islands wanted a return to Swedish rule rather than stay with the victorious Finns. The League of Nations overturned this claim, granting the islands to Finland who remain in control of them today.

After the war, a Liberal–Socialist coalition remained in power until 1920, when **Branting** became the first socialist prime minister. By the time of his death in 1924, the franchise had been extended to all men and women over 23 and the state-controlled alcohol system (*Systembolaget*) set up. Following the Depression of the late 1920s and early 1930s, conditions began to improve after a Social Democratic government took office for the fourth time in 1932. A **welfare state** was rapidly established, meaning unemployment benefit, higher old-age pensions, family allowances and paid holidays. The **Saltsjöbaden Agreement** of 1938 drew up a contract between trade unions and employers to help eliminate strikes and lockouts. With war again looming, all parties agreed that Sweden should remain neutral in any struggle and rearmament was negligible, despite Hitler's apparent intentions.

World War II was slow to affect Sweden. Unlike in 1914, there was little sympathy for Germany, but neutrality was again declared. The Russian invasion of Finland in 1939 brought Sweden into the picture, providing weapons, volunteers and refuge for the Finns. Regular Swedish troops were refused, though, fearing intervention from either the Germans (then Russia's ally) or the Allies. Economically, the country remained sound – less dependent on imports than in World War I and with no serious shortages. The position became stickier in 1940 when the Nazis marched into Denmark and Norway, isolating Sweden. Concessions were made – German troop transit allowed, iron ore exports continued – until 1943–44 when Allied threats became more convincing than the failing German war machine. Sweden became the recipient of countless refugees from the rest of Scandinavia and the Baltic. Instrumental, too, by rescuing Hungarian Jews from the SS, was **Raoul Wallenberg**, who persuaded the Swedish government to give him diplomatic status in 1944. Unknown thousands (anything up to 35,000) of Jews in Hungary were sheltered in "neutral houses" (flying the Swedish flag), fed and clothed by Wallenberg. But when Soviet troops liberated Budapest in 1945, Wallenberg was arrested as a suspected spy and disappeared – he was later reported to have died in prison in Moscow in 1947, although unconfirmed accounts had him alive in a Soviet prison as late as 1975.

The end of the war was to provide the country with a serious crisis of conscience. Physically unscathed, Sweden was now vulnerable to **Cold War** politics. Proximity to the Soviet Union meant that Sweden refused to follow the other Scandinavian countries into **NATO** in 1949. The country did, however, much to Conservative disquiet, return most of the Baltic and German refugees who had fought against Russia during the war into Stalin's hands – their fate is not difficult to guess.

Postwar politics

The wartime coalition quickly gave way to a purely **Social Democratic** government committed to welfare provision and increased defence expenditure – non-participation in military alliances didn't mean a throwing down of weapons.

Sweden regained much of its international moral respect (lost directly after World War II) through the election of **Dag Hammarskjöld** as Secretary-General of the United Nations in 1953. His strong leadership greatly enhanced the prestige (and effectiveness) of the organization, participating in the solution of the Suez crisis in 1956 and the Lebanon–Jordan affair in 1958. He was killed in an air crash in 1961, towards the end of his second five-year term.

Throughout the 1950s and 1960s, domestic reform continued unabated. It was in these years that the country laid the foundations of its much-vaunted social security system, although at the time it didn't always bear close scrutiny. A **National Health Service** gave free hospital treatment, but only allowed for a small refund of doctor's fees, medicines and dental treatment – hardly as far-reaching as the British system introduced immediately after the war.

The Social Democrats stayed in power until 1976, when a **non-Socialist coalition** (Centre–Liberal–Moderate) finally unseated them. In the 44 years since 1932, the Socialists had been an integral part of government in Sweden, tempered only by periods of war and coalition. It was a remarkable record, made more so by the fact that modern politics in Sweden has never been about ideology so much as detail. Socialists and non-Socialists alike shared a broad consensus on foreign policy and defence matters, and even on the need for the social welfare system.

Olof Palme

The Social Democrats regained power in 1982, subsequently devaluing the krona, introducing a price freeze and cutting back on public expenditure, but they lost their majority in 1985, and had to rely on Communist support to get their bills through. Presiding over the party since 1969, and prime minister for nearly as long, was **Olof Palme**. Assassinated in February 1986, his death threw Sweden into modern European politics like no other event. Proud of their open society (Palme was returning home unguarded from the cinema), the Swedes were shocked by the gunning down of a respected politician, diplomat and pacifist. Shock turned to anger and then ridicule as the months passed without his killer being caught. Police bungling was criticized and despite the theories – Kurdish extremists, right-wing terror groups – no one was charged with the murder.

Then, finally, the police came up with **Christer Pettersson**, who – despite having no apparent motive – was identified by Palme's wife as the man who had fired the shot that night. Despite pleading his innocence, claiming he was elsewhere at the time of the murder, Pettersson was convicted of Palme's murder and jailed. There was great disquiet about the verdict, however, both at home and abroad: the three legal representatives in the original jury had voted for acquittal at the time; and it was believed that Palme's wife couldn't possibly be sure that the man who fired the shot was Pettersson, since by her own admission she had only seen him once, on the dark night in question and then only very briefly. In 1989, on appeal, Pettersson was acquitted and released. The Swedish police appear to believe that they had the right man but not enough evidence to convict; more recent evidence has pointed to South African involvement, Palme having been a vocal opponent of apartheid.

Carlsson and Bildt

Ingvar Carlsson was elected prime minister after Palme's murder, a position confirmed by the **1988 general election** when the Social Democrats – for the first time in years – scored more seats than the three non-Socialist parties combined. However, Carlsson's was still a minority government, the Social Democrats requiring the support of the Communists to command an overall majority – support that was usually forthcoming but that, with the arrival of the **Green Party** into parliament in 1988, could no longer be taken for granted. The Greens and Communists jockeyed for position as protectors of the Swedish environment, and any Social Democrat measure seen to be anti-environment cost the party Communist support. Perhaps more worryingly for the government, a series of **scandals** swept the country, leading to open speculation about a marked decline in public morality. The Bofors arms company was discovered to

be involved in illegal sales to the Middle East, and early in 1990 the Indian police charged the company with paying kickbacks to politicians to secure arms contracts in the subcontinent. In addition, there was insider dealing at the stock exchange and the country's ombudsman resigned over charges of personal corruption.

The real problem for the Social Democrats, though, was the **state of the economy**. With a background of rising inflation and slow economic growth, the government announced an austerity package in January 1990 which included a two-year ban on strike action, and a wage, price and rent freeze – measures whose severity astounded most Swedes. The Greens and Communists would have none of it and the Social Democrat government resigned a month later. Although the Social Democrats were soon back in charge of a minority government, having agreed to drop the most draconian measures of their programme, the problems didn't go away.

The **general election of 1991** merely confirmed that the consensus model of politics had finally broken down. A four-party centre-right coalition came to power, led by **Carl Bildt**, which promised tax cuts and economic regeneration, but the recession sweeping western Europe didn't pass Sweden by. Unemployment hit a postwar record and in autumn 1992 – as the British pound and Italian lira collapsed on the international money markets – the krona came under severe pressure. Savage austerity measures did little to help: VAT on food was increased, statutory holiday allowances were cut, welfare budgets were slashed, and – after a period of intense currency speculation – short-term marginal interest rates raised to a staggering 500 percent. In a final attempt to steady nerves, prime minister Bildt and the leader of the Social Democratic opposition, Ingvar Carlsson, made the astonishing announcement that they would ignore party lines and work together for the good of Sweden – and then proceeded with drastic public expenditure cuts.

However, it was too little too late. Sweden was gripped by its worst **recession** since the 1930s, and unemployment reached record levels of fourteen percent. Poor economic growth coupled with generous welfare benefits, runaway speculation by Swedish firms on foreign real estate, and the world recession, all contributed to Sweden's economic woes. With the budget deficit growing faster than that of any other western industrialized country, Sweden also decided it was time to tighten up its asylum laws and introduced controversial new visa regulations to prevent a flood of Bosnian refugees.

To the millennium

Nostalgia for the good old days of Social Democracy swept the country during the general election of September 1994 and Carl Bildt's minority Conservative government was pushed out, allowing a return to power by Sweden's largest party, headed by **Ingvar Carlsson**. Social Democracy was well and truly back, with Carlsson choosing a cabinet composed equally of men and women. New social reforms were implemented, most significantly the 1995 law allowing gay couples to marry, which gives them virtually equal rights with heterosexual couples.

During 1994, negotiations on Sweden's planned membership of the **European Union** were completed and put to a referendum that saw public opinion split right down the middle. While some thought that EU membership would allow Sweden a greater influence within Europe, others were concerned that the country's standards would be forced downwards, affecting the quality of life Swedes had come to expect. However, in November the vote for membership was won, albeit by the narrowest of margins – just five percent – and Sweden joined the Union as of January 1, 1995.

Meanwhile, the welfare state was further trimmed back and new taxes announced to try to rein in the spiralling debt: unemployment benefit was cut to 75 percent of previous earnings, sick-leave benefits reduced, and lower state pension payments came into force, though finance minister **Göran Persson** did at least reduce taxes on food from 21 percent to 12 percent, in an attempt to retain some public support. Just when everything appeared to be under control, Carlsson announced his resignation in order to spend more time with his family, to be replaced by the domineering Persson.

Following elections in September 1998, Göran Persson clung on to power but with a much reduced majority. The election was a disaster for Sweden's Social Democrats, who recorded their worst result since World War II after losing support to the far left. Many voters complained that the Social Democrats had slashed the welfare state too far in an effort to revive the flagging economy.

Sweden today

Sweden's export-led **economy** has rendered the country extremely susceptible to changes in world finances. As globalisation has gathered momentum since the turn of the millennium, the country has faced a number of difficult choices which would have been totally unthinkable during the heady days of Social Democracy. During recent years privatizations, mergers and general cost-cutting measures – most visibly the virtual disappearance of the post office from Swedish high streets and the much-lamented fragmentation of the national rail network – have brought Sweden more into line with countries that went through equally painful economic change decades ago. Some economists argue that it's this enforced shaking up of the business environment from outside, rather than any direct government measures, that is responsible for Sweden's improved economic fortunes since 1998 – today, Swedish markets are once again flourishing.

In 2003, this renewed growth and prosperity was at the centre of discussions in the months leading up to the referendum on adopting the **euro** as Sweden's currency, with the no-voters eventually claiming a clear majority. The referendum went ahead despite the shocking murder of the popular foreign minister and pro-euro campaigner **Anna Lindh** in a Stockholm department store, just days before (see p.477).

After the 2002 elections, the Social Democratic Party went on to form a minority government – dependent on the support of the anti-EU Left and Greens – with Goran Persson starting his third term as prime minister. In a environment where consensus politics is less obvious than ever in Sweden, his main challenges are to reign in the mounting costs of the welfare system, and to make Sweden's voice heard in an ever-globalised international environment.

Books

There's a surprisingly small number of books available in English on all matters Swedish, but what follows is a summary of some of the more readily available publications. Titles that are out of print (listed as "o/p") may be available secondhand, or on websites such as ⓦwww.amazon.com. For books on Scandinavia in general, see "Basics", p.53. Titles marked with 🏃 represent essential reads.

History and politics

🏃 **Sheri Berman** *The Social Democrat Movement*. A comparison of the Swedish and German social democratic system between the First and Second World Wars.

Eric Elstob *Sweden: A Traveller's History* (o/p). An introduction to Swedish history from the year dot, with useful chapters on art, architecture and cultural life.

Lee Miles *Sweden and European Integration*. A political history of Sweden focusing on the period 1950–66, and the accession to the European Union in 1995.

Vilhem Moberg *The Emigrants*. A series of emotionally poignant historical novels, centred on a husband and wife, that tell the story of the one million Swedes who emigrated to the United States in the late nineteenth and early twentieth centuries. Moberg himself chose to stay in Sweden, and is recognised as a major social chronicler of his time.

Alan Palmer *Bernadotte* (o/p). First English biography for over fifty years of Napoleon's marshal, later Sweden's King Karl Johan XIV. It's lively and comprehensive, though probably for enthusiasts only.

Michael Roberts *The Early Vasas: A History of Sweden 1523–1611* (o/p). This general account of the period is complemented by Roberts' more recent *Gustavus Adolphus and the Rise of Sweden* (Addison Wesley) which, more briefly and enthusiastically, covers the period from 1612 to the king's death in 1632.

Franklin Daniel Scott *Sweden: The Nation's History*. A good all-round account of Sweden's history from a poor, backward warrior nation to the prosperous modern one of today.

Literature

Stig Dagerman *The Games of Night*. Intense short stories by a prolific young writer who had written four novels, four plays, numerous short stories and travel sketches by the time he was 26. He committed suicide in 1954 at the age of 31. This is some of the best of his work.

Kerstin Ekman *Under the snow*. In a remote Lapland village, a police constable investigates the death of a teacher following a drunken brawl – the dark deeds of winter finally come to light under the relentless summer sun. An excellent means of getting to grips with the mentality of northern Swedes.

Robert Fulton (trans.) *Preparations for Flight*. Eight Swedish short stories from the last 25 years, including two rare prose outings from the poet Niklas Rådström.

P.C. Jersild *A Living Soul*. Social satire based around the "experiences" of an artificially produced, bodiless human brain floating in liquid. Entertaining, provocative reading from one of Sweden's best novelists.

Sara Lidman *Naboth's Stone*. A novel set in 1880s Västerbotten, in Sweden's far north, charting the lives of settlers and farmers as the industrial age – and the railway – approaches.

Astrid Lindgren *Pippi Longstocking, The Brothers Lionheart*. Delightful and essentially Swedish children's books featuring independent, unconventional and, in the case of Pippi, slightly anarchist children.

Henning Mankell *Faceless Killers, Sidetracked*. Cracking yarns from Scandinavia's leading crime writer featuring Inspector Kurt Wallander, a shambolic and melancholic middle-aged police officer in Ystad struggling to make sense of it all in small-town southern Sweden.

Agneta Pleijel *The Dog Star*. Powerful tale of a young girl's approach to puberty. One of Pleijel's finest novels, full of fantasy and emotion.

Clive Sinclair *Augustus Rex* (o/p). August Strindberg dies in 1912 – and is then brought back to life by the devil in 1960s Stockholm. Bawdy,

imaginative and very funny treatment of Strindberg's well-documented neuroses.

Hjalmar Söderberg *Short Stories*. Twenty-six short stories from the stylish pen of Söderberg (1869–1941). Brief, ironic and eminently ripe for dipping into.

August Strindberg *Strindberg Plays: Two*; *Strindberg Plays: Three*; *Three Plays*; *Inferno/From an Occult Diary; By the Open Sea*. Strindberg is now seen as a pioneer in both his subject matter and style. His early plays were realistic in a manner not then expected of drama, and confronted themes that weren't considered suitable viewing at all, with psychological examinations of the roles of the sexes both in and out of marriage. A fantastically prolific writer, only a fraction of his sixty plays, twelve historical dramas, five novels, short stories, numerous autobiographical volumes and poetry has ever been translated into English.

Criticism and biography

Peter Cowie *Ingmar Bergman*. New edition of a well-written and sympathetic account of the director's life and career.

Michael Meyer *Strindberg on File* (o/p). A useful brief account of Strindberg's life and work, though for a more stirring biography the same author's *Strindberg* (o/p) is the best and most approachable source.

Art and architecture

Henrik O. Andersson and Frederic Bedoure *Svensk Arkitektur* (o/p). Seminal book on Swedish architectural history from 1640 to 1970, with text in English and Swedish. Colour plates illustrate the works of each architect. One to borrow from the library.

Barbro Klein and Mats Widbom (eds) *Swedish Folk Art – All Tradition*

Is Change (o/p). Lavishly produced volume on the folk art movement, illustrating the influences of local culture on art and design up to and including IKEA.

Roger Tanner (trans.) *A History of Swedish Art* (o/p). Covers architecture, design, painting and sculpture, ranging from prehistoric rock carvings to post-modernism. Well illustrated.

A brief guide to Swedish

Nearly everyone, everywhere in Sweden speaks English, and the tourist offices are often staffed with what appear to be native English speakers. Still, knowing the essentials of Swedish is useful, and making an effort with the language certainly impresses. If you already speak either Danish or Norwegian you should have few problems being understood; if not, then a basic knowledge of German is a help too. Of the phrasebooks, most useful is *Swedish for Travellers* (Berlitz), or use the section in *Travellers' Scandinavia* (Pan).

Pronunciation

Pronunciation is more difficult than Danish or Norwegian. A **vowel** sound is usually long when it's the final syllable or followed by only one consonant; followed by two it's generally short. Unfamiliar combinations are:

ej as in m**a**te.
y as in **ewe**.
å when short as in h**o**t; when long as in r**a**w.
ä when before r as in m**a**n; otherwise as in g**e**t.
ö as in f**ur** but without the r sound.
Consonants are pronounced as in English except:
g usually as in **y**et; occasionally as in **sh**ut.
j, dj, gj, lj as in **y**et.
k before i, e, y, ä, or ö, like the Scottish lo**ch**; otherwise hard.
qu as **kv**.
sch, skj, stj as in **sh**ut; otherwise hard.
tj like lo**ch**.
z as in **s**o.

Basics

Hej	Hello
God morgon	Good morning
God middag	Good afternoon
God natt	Good night
Hejdå	Goodbye
Talar du engelska?	Do you speak English?
Ja	Yes
Nej	No
Jag förstår inte	I don't understand
Var så god	Please
Tack (så mycket)	Thank you (very much)
Var så god	You're welcome
I dag	Today
I morgon	Tomorrow
I övermorgon	Day after tomorrow
På morgonen	In the morning
På eftermiddagen	In the afternoon
På kvällen	In the evening

Some signs

Ingång	Entrance
Utgång	Exit
Herrar	Men
Damer	Women
Öppen, öppet	Open
Stängt	Closed
Skjut	Push
Drag	Pull
Ankomst	Arrival
Avgång	Departure
Rökning förbjuden	No smoking
Tältning förbjuden	No camping
Tillträde förbjudet	No trespassing
Ingen ingång	No entry
Polis	Police

Questions and directions

Var är... ?	Where is ... ?
När?	When?

Vad?	What?	femton	15
Skulle du kunna	Can you direct	sexton	16
visa mig vägen till	me to ...	sjutton	17
Det är/det finns	It is/There is	arton	18
(Är det/Finns det?)	(Is it/Is there?)	nitton	19
Hur mycket är	What time is it?	tjugo	20
klockan?		tjugoett	21
Stor/liten	Big/small	tjugotvå	22
Billig/dyr	Cheap/expensive	trettio	30
Tidig/sen	Early/late	fyrtio	40
Varm/kall	Hot/cold	femtio	50
Nära/avlägsen	Near/far	sextio	60
Bra/dålig	Good/bad	sjuttio	70
Vänster/höger	Left/right	åttio	80
Ledig/upptagen	Vacant/occupied	nittio	90
Lite/en mängd	A little/a lot	hundra	100
Jag skulle vilja ha ...	I'd like	hundraett	101
... ett enkelrum	... a single room	tvåhundra	200
... ett dubbelrum	... a double room	femhundra	500
Vad kostar det?	How much is it?	tusen	1000
Får vi tälta här?	Can we camp here?		
Campingplats	Campsite		
Tält	Tent		
Finns det något	Is there a youth		
vandrarhem	hostel near here?		
i närheten?			

Days and months

måndag	Monday
tisdag	Tuesday
onsdag	Wednesday
torsdag	Thursday
fredag	Friday
lördag	Saturday
söndag	Sunday
januari	January
februari	February
mars	March
april	April
maj	May
juni	June
juli	July
augusti	August
september	September
oktober	October
november	November
december	December

(Days and months are never capitalized)

Numbers

noll	0
ett	1
två	2
tre	3
fyra	4
fem	5
sex	6
sju	7
åtta	8
nio	9
tio	10
elva	11
tolv	12
tretton	13
fjorton	14

Glossary of Swedish terms and words

Bastu	Sauna	Dal	Valley
Berg	Mountain	Domkyrka	Cathedral
Bokhandel	Bookshop	Drottning	Queen (as in
Bro	Bridge		Drottninggatan,
Cykelstig	path		Queen Street)

Färja	Ferry	**Sjö**	Lake
Gamla	Old (as in Gamla Stan, old town)	**Skog**	Forest
		Slott	Castle
Gata (gt)	Street	**Spår**	Track/platform (at railway station)
Hamnen	Harbour		
Järnvägsstation	Railway station	**Stadshus**	Town hall
Klockan (kl)	o'clock	**Stora**	Great/big (as in Storatorget, main square)
Kyrka	Church		
Lilla	Little (as in Lilla Torget, small square)		
		Strand	Beach
Muséet	Museum	**Stugor**	Chalet, cottage
Pressbyrå	Newsagent	**Torg**	Central town square, usually the scene of daily/weekly markets
Rabatt	Rebate/discount		
Rea	Sales (and Vrakpriser, bargain)		
		Universitet	University
Riksdagshus	Parliament building	**Väg (v)**	Road

3.1

Stockholm and around

tockholm is one of the most beautiful cities in Europe. Built on no fewer than fourteen islands, where the fresh water of Lake Mälaren meets the brackish Baltic Sea, it has clean air and open space in plentiful supply: one-third of the area inside the city limits is made up of water, another third of parks and woodland, and it's easy to find a quiet corner to enjoy what's one of Europe's saner and more civilized capitals. Broad boulevards lined with elegant buildings are reflected in the deep blue water of the Baltic, while the world's first urban national park offers a unique opportunity to swim and fish virtually in the city centre.

You can appreciate Stockholm's unique geography by taking one of a number of boat trips around the city and through the **Stockholm archipelago** – a

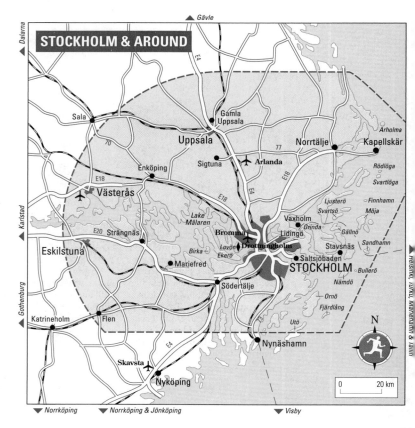

STOCKHOLM & AROUND

staggering 24,000 islands, rocks and skerries, as the Swedish mainland slowly dissolves into the Baltic Sea. A boat trip inland along the serene waters of Lake Mälaren is another easy day-trip, with the target of seventeenth-century **Drottningholm**, the Swedish royal residence, right on the lakeside. Also within day-trip range is the ancient Swedish capital and medieval university town of **Uppsala**, easily reached from Stockholm by frequent trains, as well as the odd boat.

Stockholm

"It is not a city at all," he said with intensity. "It is ridiculous to think of itself as a city. It is simply a rather large village, set in the middle of some forest and some lakes. You wonder what it thinks it is doing there, looking so important."

Ingmar Bergman interviewed by James Baldwin.

STOCKHOLM often feels like two cities. Its self-important status as Sweden's most forward-looking commercial centre can seem at odds with the almost pastoral feel of its open spaces and expanses of water. First impressions can be of a distant and unwelcoming place – provincial Swedes call it the Ice Queen – but stick around for the weekend, when the population really lets its hair down, and you'll see another side to Stockholm.

Gamla Stan (meaning Old Town) was the site of the original settlement of Stockholm. Today it's an atmospheric mixture of pomp and history, with ceremonial buildings surrounded by a lattice of medieval lanes and alleyways. Close by to the east is the tiny island of **Skeppsholmen**, with fantastic views of the curving waterfront, while to the north is the modern centre, **Norrmalm**, with its shopping malls, huge department stores and conspicuous wealth, plus the lively Kungsträdgården park and the transport hub of Central Station. East of Norrmalm is the grand residential area of **Östermalm**, southeast of which is the green park island of **Djurgården**, home to two of Stockholm's best-known attractions: the extraordinary seventeenth-century warship, **Vasa**, and **Skansen**, Europe's oldest open-air museum. South of Gamla Stan, the island of **Södermalm** was traditionally Stockholm's working-class area; it's known today for its cool bars and restaurants and lively streetlife. To the west of the centre is **Kungsholmen** island, which is coming to rival its southern neighbour with its trendy eateries and drinking establishments.

Arrival and information

Most planes – international and domestic – arrive at **Arlanda airport**, 45km north of Stockholm. A high-speed rail link, the **Arlanda Express**, connects the airport with the city every fifteen minutes (daily from 4.35am to 12.35am; 20min; 190kr; @www.arlandaexpress.com), and is the easiest way to get into Stockholm. A cheaper option is to take the **airport buses**, Flygbussarna (daily 4.50am–11.45pm; 40min; 89kr; @www.flygbussarna.se), which run every ten minutes from the airport to Cityterminalen (Stockholm's central bus station; see p.462); buy your ticket in the airport arrivals hall or from the driver. **Taxis** into Stockholm should cost around 350kr, an affordable alternative for a group – choose the ones that have prices displayed in their back windows to avoid being ripped off.

Some flights arrive at the more central **Bromma airport**, 10km to the west of the city centre near Brommaplan T-bana station. Bromma is also connected to the Cityterminalen by Flygbussarna – buses run in connection with flight arrivals and departures (20min; 70kr). Some budget airlines arrive at **Skavsta airport**, 100km to the south of the capital close to the town of Nyköping, as well as at **Västerås**,

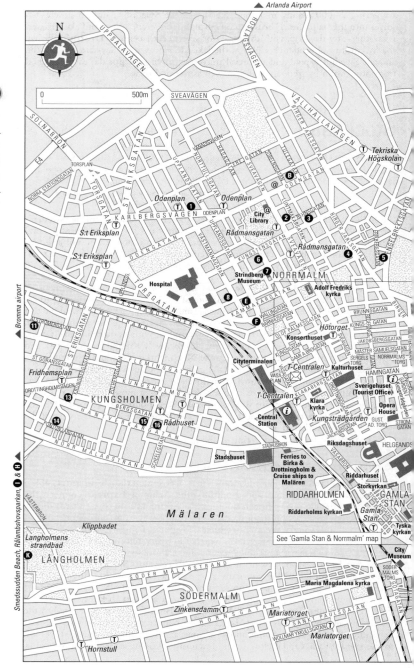

▲ Arlanda Airport

N

0 ────────── 500m

SVEAVÄGEN

UPPSALAVÄGEN

ROSLAGSVÄGEN

VALLHALLAVÄGEN

BIRGER JARLSGATAN

ENGELBREKTSGATAN

Ⓣ Tekniska Högskolan

SOLNABRON

E4

TORSPLAN

NORRA STATIONSGATAN

TORSGATAN

S:t ERIKSGATAN

UPPLANDSGATAN

NORRTULLSGATAN

VANADISVÄGEN

FREJGATAN

SVEAVÄGEN

DÖBELNSGATAN

TEGNERGATAN

ODENGATAN

Ⓑ

@

Odenplan   *Odenplan*
          Ⓣ❶   Ⓣ

KARLBERGSVÄGEN   ODENPLAN

City
Library @

S:t Eriksplan
Ⓣ

ODENGATAN   VÄSTMANNASGATAN

Rådmansgatan   ❷   Ⓣ ❸

S:t Eriksplan
Ⓣ   KUNGSTENSGATAN

Rådmansgatan
Ⓣ   ❹

TEGNERGATAN   ❺

KUNGSHOLMSSTRAND

Hospital

TORSGATAN

KLARASTRANDSLEDEN

Strindberg
Museum ❼ **NORRMALM**

❻

❽ Ⓔ
KAMMAKARGATAN

WALLINGATAN
Ⓕ BARNHUSGATAN

Adolf Fredriks
kyrka

OLOF PALMESGATAN

Hötorget
Ⓣ

BRUNNSGATAN

KUNGSGATAN GATAN
JAKOBSBERGSGATAN

Konserthuset Ⓣ

GAMLA BROGATAN

Cityterminalen

VASAGATAN
VASAPLAN

T-Centralen Ⓣ
Kulturhuset

SERGELS
TORG

MASTER SAMUELSGATAN

NORRMALMS-
TORG

HAMNGATAN

Ⓣ **T-Centralen**

Klara
kyrka

Central
Station

Ⓣ
Ⓘ

KLARABERGSGATAN

Sverigehuset
(Tourist Office) ⓘ

Kungsträdgården GUST.
AD. TORG.

Opera
House Ⓣ

STRÖM-
GATAN

KUNGSBROGATAN

ALMROMSROGATAN

ALSTROMERGATAN ❶❶

Fridhemsplan
Ⓣ

ST GÖRANSGATAN

S:t ERIKSGATAN

FLEMINGGATAN

DROTTNINGHOLMSVÄGEN ❶❸

KUNGSHOLMEN

KUNGSHOLMGATAN

BERGSGATAN Ⓣ

HANTVERKARGATAN

❶❹

PILGATAN

POLHEMSGATAN

SCHEELEGATAN ❶❺ ❶❻
Rådhuset Ⓣ

NORR MÄLARSTRAND

Stadshuset STADSHUSBRON

▲ Bromma airport

Smedsudden Beach, Rålambshovsparken, ❶ & ❷ ◀

VÄSTERBRON

Riksdagshuset

VASABRON

Ferries to
Birka &
Drottningholm &
Cruise ships to
Malären

RIDDARHOLMEN

Riddarholms kyrkan

HELGEANDS-

Riddarhuset

Storkyrkan **GAMLA
STAN**

*Gamla
Stan* Ⓣ

Tyska
kyrkan

Mälaren

Klippbadet

Langholmens
strandbad

Ⓚ **LÅNGHOLMEN**

SÖDER MÄLARSTRAND

SÖDERMALM

Zinkensdamm Ⓣ
HORNSGATAN

Ⓣ *Hornstull*

WOLLMAR YXKULLSGATAN

SANKT PAULSGATAN

Mariatorget
Ⓣ

Maria Magdalena kyrka

SÖDER-
MALMS-
TORG

City
Museum

See 'Gamla Stan & Norrmalm' map

Mariatorget

GÖTGATAN

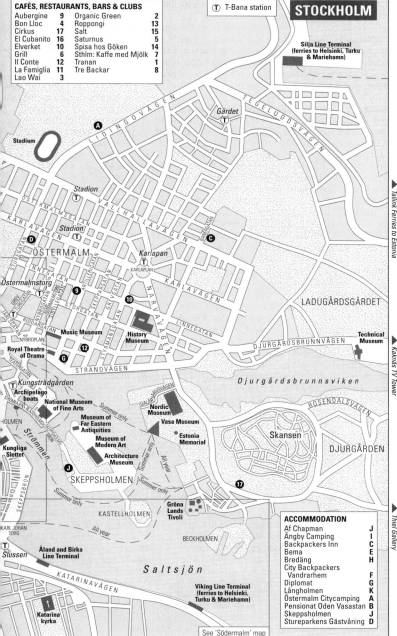

CAFÉS, RESTAURANTS, BARS & CLUBS

Aubergine	9	Organic Green	2
Bon Lloc	4	Roppongi	13
Cirkus	17	Salt	15
El Cubanito	16	Saturnus	5
Elverket	10	Spisa hos Göken	14
Grill	6	Sthlm: Kaffe med Mjölk	7
Il Conte	12	Tranan	1
La Famiglia	11	Tre Backar	8
Lao Wai	3		

Ⓣ T-Bana station

STOCKHOLM

Silja Line Terminal (ferries to Helsinki, Turku & Mariehamn)

Stadium

Ⓐ IDINGÖVÄGEN

Gärdet Ⓣ

TEGELUDDSVÄGEN

Stadion Ⓣ

VALLHALLAVÄGEN

ÖSTERMALMSGATAN

Stadion Ⓣ

BANÉRGATAN

Ⓒ

Ⓓ

KARLAVÄGEN

STUREGATAN

ÖSTERMALM

Karlapan
KARLAPLAN

LINNÉGATAN

KARLAVÄGEN

LADUGÅRDSGÄRDET

Östermalmstorg Ⓣ

ARTILLERIGATAN

STORGATAN

GREVGATAN

NARVAVÄGEN

LINNÉGATAN

Ⓣ
NYBROPLAN

RIDDARGATAN

STRANDVÄGSKAJEN

Ⓣ
RÖDA
ENGELBREKTSGATAN

Ⓣ

Ⓣ

Ⓣ

Ⓖ

Ⓢ

Ⓣ

9

10

Music Museum

STRAMSMANSGATAN

History Museum

DJURGÅRDSBRUNNSVÄGEN

Technical Museum

Royal Theatre of Drama

Ⓖ

12

STRANDVÄGEN

Kungsträdgården

Archipelago boats

STRÖMKAJEN
BLASIEHOLMSHAMNEN
SKEPPSHOLMSBRON

National Museum of Fine Arts

Museum of Far Eastern Antiquities

Museum of Modern Art

Architecture Museum

Ⓙ

SKEPPSHOLMEN

Summer only

Nordic Museum

GALÄRVÄGEN

Vasa Museum

Estonia Memorial

Djurgårdsbrunnsviken

ROSENDALSVÄGEN

Skansen

DJURGÅRDEN

Summer only

All year

Summer only

HOLMEN

Kungliga Slottet

Strömmen

SKEPPSBRON

KARL JOHAN TORG

Ⓣ
Slussen

KASTELLHOLMEN

All year

BECKHOLMEN

Gröna Lunds Tivoli

17

Åland and Birka Line Terminal

KATARINAVÄGEN

Saltsjön

Katarina kyrka

Viking Line Terminal (ferries to Helsinki, Turku & Mariehamn)

See 'Södermalm' map

ACCOMMODATION

Af Chapman	J
Ängby Camping	I
Backpackers Inn	C
Bema	E
Bredäng	H
City Backpackers Vandrarhem	F
Diplomat	G
Långholmen	K
Östermalm Citycamping	A
Pensionat Oden Vasastan	B
Skeppsholmen	J
Stureparkens Gästvåning	D

Ⓑ Tallink Ferries to Estonia

Ⓑ Kaknäs TV Tower

Ⓑ Thiel Gallery

Ⓓ 3

3.1 | SWEDEN

463

100km west of Stockholm (see p.494); Flygbussarna buses to and from Stockholm's Cityterminalen operate in conjunction with flights from both airports (both 80min; 130kr).

By **train**, you'll arrive at and depart from **Central Station**, a cavernous structure on Vasagatan in the Norrmalm district. Inside there are **ATM**s, a Forex **money exchange** office, and a very useful **tourist information office** and **room-booking service**, Hotellcentralen (see "Accommodation", p.467). From the station, it's a ten-minute walk across a pedestrian bridge to Gamla Stan, and another ten minutes uphill along Götgatan to central Södermalm.

By **bus**, your arrival point will be the huge glass structure known as **Cityterminalen**, a bus terminal adjacent to Central Station and reached by a series of escalators and walkways from the northern end of the main hall. It handles all bus services: airport and ferry shuttle services, and domestic and international buses. There are ATMs, an exchange office and Sidewalk Express Internet terminals here.

There are two main **ferry** companies connecting Stockholm with Helsinki, Turku and Mariehamn in Finland. **Viking Line** (☎08/452 20 00, ⊛www .vikingline.fi) ferries dock at Vikingterminalen on the island of Södermalm, from where you can catch a bus or walk to Slussen or Gamla Stan for the T-bana. **Silja Line** (☎08/22 21 40, ⊛www.silja.com) ferries dock at Värtahamnen on the northeastern edge of the city; it's a short walk to the Gärdet T-bana station, or hop on bus #76, departing from beneath the pedestrian walkway, to Gamla Stan and Södermalm. **Tallink** (⊛www.tallink.se) sailings from Tallinn in Estonia arrive at Frihamnen at the end of the #1 bus route, which passes Hötorget and Cityterminalen. If you're leaving Stockholm by ferry, note the Swedish names for destinations: Helsinki is "Helsingfors"; Turku is "Åbo".

Information

You should be able to pick up a map of the city at most points of arrival, but it's still worth dropping in to Sweden House or *Sverigehuset*, the city's **tourist office** at Hamngatan 27, on the corner of Kungsträdgården (Jan–Feb Mon–Fri 9am–6pm, Sat & Sun 10am–3pm; March–Dec Mon–Fri 9am–7pm, Sat 10am–5pm, Sun 10am–4pm; ☎08/50 82 85 08, ⊛www.stockholmtown.com). Fistfuls of free information are available, and you'll find good **maps** in some of the brochures and booklets – though it's worth paying 25kr for the larger plan of Stockholm and the surrounding area produced by the Stockholm Visitor Board. These are on sale at the office, as are Stockholm Cards (see p.466). Look out also for *What's On*, the free listings and entertainment guide.

From the tourist office it's a short walk to the **Sweden Bookshop**, next to the royal palace at Slottsbacken 10 (Mon–Fri 10am–6pm, July–Sept also Sat & Sun 10am–6pm; ☎08/453 78 00, ⊛www.swedenbookshop.com), which has an unsurpassed stock of English-language books on Sweden as well as calendars, videos and souvenirs.

City transport

Stockholm winds its way across islands, over water and through parkland: the best way to get to grips with it is to equip yourself with a map and walk – it only takes about half an hour to cross central Stockholm on foot. Sooner or later, though, you'll have to use some form of **transport** and, while routes are easy enough to master, there's a bewildering array of passes available. One thing to try to avoid is paying as you go on the city's transport system – a very expensive business. The city is zoned, a trip within one zone costing 30kr, with single **tickets** valid within that zone for one hour; cross a zone and it's another 15kr. See p.466 for more on tickets and travel passes.

City bus, local train and T-bana **timetables** are easily obtained from the SL-Centers dotted around the city (see p.465); timetables for mainline trains operated by Swedish Railways (SJ) can be found at Central Station, or online at ⊛www.sj.se

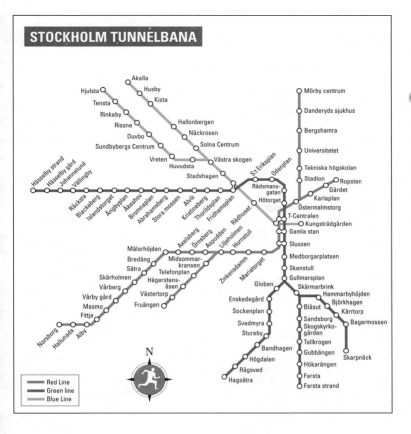

STOCKHOLM TUNNELBANA

Akalla
Hjulsta
Husby
Tensta
Kista
Rinkeby
Rissne · Hallonbergen
Duvbo · Näckrosen
Sundbybergs Centrum · Solna Centrum
Vreten · Västra skogen
Huvudsta
Hässelby strand
Hässelby gård
Johannelund
Vällingby
Stadshagen

Mörby centrum
Danderyds sjukhus
Bergshamra
Universitetet
Tekniska högskolan
Stadion · Ropsten
Gärdet
Karlaplan
Östermalmstorg
Kungsträdgården
Gamla stan
Slussen
Medborgarplatsen
Skanstull
Gullmarsplan
Skärmarbrink · Hammarbyhöjden
Björkhagen
Blåsut · Kärrtorp
Sandsborg · Bagarmossen
Skogskyrko-gården
Tallkrogen
Gubbängen · Skarpnäck
Hökarängen
Farsta
Farsta strand

Räcksta
Blackeberg
Islandstorget
Ängbyplan
Åkeshov
Brommaplan
Abrahamsberg
Stora mossen
Alvik
Kristineberg
Thorildsplan
Fridhemsplan
S:t Eriksplan
Odenplan
Rådmansgatan
Hötorget
T-Centralen

Axelsberg
Örnsberg
Aspudden
Liljeholmen
Hornstull
Rådhuset
Mälarhöjden
Bredäng
Sätra
Skärholmen
Vårberg
Vårby gård
Masmo
Fittja
Midsommar-kransen
Telefonplan
Hägerstens-åsen
Västertorp
Fruängen
Zinkensdamm
Mariatorget

Norsborg
Hallunada
Alby

Enskedegård
Sockenplan
Svedmyra
Stureby
Bandhagen
Högdalen
Rågsved
Hagsätra

Globen

N

Red Line
Green line
Blue Line

(Swedish-language only). For general public transport **information**, consult the English-language website ⓦwww.resplus.se, or call ☎08/600 10 00.

Storstockholms Lokaltrafik (SL; ⓦwww.sl.se) operate a comprehensive system of buses and trains (underground and regional) that extends well out of the city centre. For information and timetables, the main **SL-Center** (Mon–Fri 7am–6.30pm, Sat & Sun 10am–5pm) is at Sergels Torg, just by the entrance to T-Centralen (see "Listings", p.489, for other branches), and has timetables for the city's buses, metro, regional trains and archipelago boats.

The quickest and most useful form of transport both around the centre and out to the suburbs is Stockholm's metro system, the Tunnelbana or **T-bana**. There are three main lines (red, green and blue) and a smattering of branches; station entrances are marked with a blue letter "T" on a white background. Trains run from early morning until around midnight (and all through the night on Fridays and Saturdays). All branches of the T-bana meet at **T-Centralen**, the metro station below Central Station. The **Pendeltågen** regional trains that run throughout Greater Stockholm leave from the main train platforms on ground level. The T-bana is something of an artistic venture, too, with all stations decorated in some way: the most impressive are on the blue line – the T-Centralen station is a huge blue cave, while Kungsträdgården station is littered with statues, spotlights and fountains.

Bus routes can be less direct due to Stockholm's islands and central pedestrianization – consult the route map on the back of the *Stockholms innerstad* bus timetable for help. You board buses at the front, get off at the back or in the middle, and can buy tickets from the driver, though this is more expensive than purchasing in advance. **Night buses** replace the T-bana after midnight, except on Friday and Saturday nights.

From outside the *Grand Hotel* on Strömkajen, **ferries** provide access to the sprawling archipelago and also link some of the central islands: Djurgården is connected with Skeppsholmen and Nybroplan (summer-only), the latter a small square behind the *Grand* in Norrmalm, and with Slussen in Gamla Stan (year-round). **Cruises** on Lake Mälaren leave from outside the Stadshus at the southeastern tip of Kungsholmen, and city boat tours leave from outside the *Grand Hotel* and from around the corner on Nybroplan.

For the ultimate Swedish experience, hop on the free bus to IKEA from Regeringsgatan 17 (Mon–Fri 11am–5pm).

Travel passes and tickets

If you're planning to do any sightseeing, the best pass to have is the **Stockholm Card** (*Stockholmskortet*), which gives unlimited travel on city buses, T-bana, regional trains and the Djurgården tram and ferry, as well as free sightseeing tours, museum entry and parking. Cards are valid for 24, 48 or 72 hours (260kr/390kr/540kr respectively, children aged 7–17 100kr/140kr/190kr respectively, children under 7 free). They're sold undated, and are valid from first use. You can buy the card from the tourist office, from Hotellcentralen (see p.467) in Central Station, from SL Centers or online at ⊛www.stockholmtown.com/shop. Note that now many museums have free admission, it may make sense to buy only a transport card if you only plan on visiting a few.

In terms of passes that cover transport only, the reduced-price SL **ticket coupons** (*rabattkuponger*) are a good idea for infrequent journeys. They're available at any T-bana station (ten coupons 80kr, twenty coupons 145kr), and you have them stamped at the T-bana entrance or by the bus driver before each trip. Among the other options, the **24-hour SL Card** (95kr) and the **72-hour SL Card** (180kr) cover unlimited travel by bus, T-bana and regional trains, plus travel on the Slussen to Djurgården ferry and the tram line to Djurgården. Discounts for under-18s or over-65s bring the cost down to 55kr (24 hours) and 110kr (72 hours). These cards can be bought from Pressbyrå newsagents or SL travel centres and are valid from the minute you buy them, unless you specify otherwise. Serious sightseers should consider investing in the Stockholm Card (see above).

If you're staying in Stockholm for a week or more it's worth considering a **monthly card** (*Månadskort*), which allows unlimited travel on virtually everything that moves throughout the whole of Greater Stockholm for a mere 600kr. If you're spending several months in the city it's probably worth buying a **season card** (*Säsongskort*) – prices vary depending on the time of year. Both these cards can be bought from any SL-Center.

One-way tickets for the **ferries** to Djurgården cost a basic 20kr, and for longer trips into the **archipelago** up to 100kr. Tickets can be bought on board or in advance from the offices of the main ferry company, Waxholms Ångfartygs AB (known as *Waxholmsbolaget*), on Strömkajen in Norrmalm, outside the *Grand Hotel*. If you intend to spend a week or so exploring the islands of the archipelago, it may be worth buying a special pass – see p.493 for details.

Bikes, taxis and parking

Bike rental is available from Cykeluthyrningen at Kajplats 24 along Strandvägen in Norrmalm (☎08/660 79 59), Sjöcafé at Galärvarvsvägen 2 (☎08/660 57 57), just across the Djurgården bridge, or from Servicedepån at Scheelegatan 15 (☎08/651 00 66) on Kungsholmen. Reckon on paying 200kr per day or 800kr per week.

To get a **taxi**, either try to hail one in the street or, more reliably, call one of the four main operators: Taxi Stockholm (☎08/15 00 00), Taxi Kurir (☎08/30 00 00) or Taxi 020 (☎020/20 20 20). If you do phone for a cab, the meter will show around 35kr before you even get in, and will continue to race upwards at an alarming speed – a trip across the city centre should be in the region of 150–200kr.

If you're driving, be warned that **parking** in Stockholm is a hazardous business. First, it's forbidden to park within ten metres of a road junction, however small; nor can you park within the same distance of a pedestrian crossing; and on one particular night of the week (as specified on the rectangular yellow street signs) no parking is allowed, to permit street cleaning and, in winter, snow clearance. You should never stop in a bus lane or in a loading zone. Also, the closer to the city centre you park the more expensive it will be, though it's free at the clearly signed municipality-run lots for Stockholm Card users. For details on **car rental**, see p.489.

Accommodation

Stockholm has **accommodation** to suit all tastes and budgets, from elegant hotels with waterfront views to some unusual youth hostels. Demand is high, however, particularly from mid-June to mid-August, and it's always advisable to book at least your first night's accommodation in advance.

Between mid-June and mid-August and at weekends year-round, the excellent **Stockholm à la Carte Package** (☎08/663 00 80, ⊛www.destination-stockholm .com) offers reduced rates on accommodation at some forty hotels: deals for a twin room with breakfast start at a very economical 399kr per person in a basic hotel, rising to 875kr per person in more upmarket places. There is no charge for cancellation or changes to reservations, you pay for rooms on the day of departure, and the package includes a free **Stockholm à la Carte Card** for each person, which is slightly different from the Stockholm Card but also covers free local transport and reduced or free museum entry for the duration of your stay.

Alternatively, **Hotellcentralen**, the room-booking service in the main hall of Central Station (daily: June–Aug 8am–8pm; Sept–May 9am–6pm; ☎08/50 82 85 08, ⊛www .stockholmtown.se) has comprehensive hotel and hostel listings, information on the latest special offers and also sells the Stockholm à la Carte Package. Booking in advance online or by telephone pays off, as they charge a fee of 60kr per hotel room, 100kr for the à la Carte Package and 25kr for a hostel room if you show up in person.

Unless otherwise stated, for hotels and pensions in **Södermalm** see the map on p.482; for those in **Gamla Stan and Norrmalm**, see the map on p.570; all other places are on the main Stockholm map, pp.462–463. All hostels are on the main Stockholm map.

Hotels and pensions

In summer, when business trade dwindles, it's a buyer's market in Stockholm, with double rooms going for as little as 600kr. The cheapest **hotels** and **pensions** are generally found to the north of Cityterminalen in the streets to the west of Adolf Fredriks kyrka, but don't rule out the more expensive places either – there are some attractive weekend and summer prices that can make a spot of luxury a little more affordable. All the following places include breakfast in the price unless otherwise stated and, where applicable, we've given the lower summer and non-summer weekend rate followed by the higher weekday rate outside of summer.

Bema Upplandsgatan 13, Norrmalm (see Stockholm map) ☎08/23 26 75, ℮hotell .bema@stockholm.mail.telia.com. Small pension-style hotel ten minutes' walk north of the station. Twelve en-suite rooms, with modern Swedish decor and beechwood furniture. Bus #47 or #69 from Central Station. ❸/❹

Central Vasagatan 38, Norrmalm ☎08/56 62 08 00, ⊛www.profilhotels.se. Modern hotel that's one of the least expensive of those around the station. T-bana T-Centralen. ❺/❻

Columbus Tjärhovsgatan 11, Södermalm ☎08/50 31 12 00, ⊛www.columbushotell.se. Simple rooms with shared bathrooms, set in a building that looks like a school. T-bana Medborgarplatsen. ③/⑤

Diplomat Strandvägen 7C ☎08/459 68 00, ✆www.diplomathotel.com. Art Nouveau hotel with top-of-the-range suites and views out over Stockholm's grandest boulevard and inner harbour. It's not cheap, though much better value than the cheaper rooms at the *Grand* (see below). Out of season, rooms start at 2455kr, but there are summer and weekend reductions. T-bana Östermalmstorg. ⑤/⑥

First Hotel Reisen Skeppsbron 12, Gamla Stan ☎08/22 32 60, ✆www.firsthotels.se. Traditional place with a heavy wood-panelled interior. All rooms have baths; some also have excellent views over the Stockholm waterfront. T-bana Gamla Stan. ⑤/⑥

Grand Södra Blasieholmshamnen 8, Norrmalm ☎08/679 35 00, ✆www.grandhotel.se. Set in a late nineteenth-century harbourside building overlooking Gamla Stan, Stockholm's most refined hotel provides the last word in luxury at world-class prices (even with the summer and weekend reductions). Only worth it if you're staying in the best rooms – otherwise, the *Diplomat* has suites with a view for the same price as rooms here. Out-of-season double rooms start at 3600kr. T-bana Kungsträdgården. ⑥

🏃 **Lydmar** Sturegatan 10, Norrmalm ☎08/56 61 13 00, ✆www.lydmar.se. Well located for the nightlife options around Stureplan, with functional rooms overlooking the park, and one of the city's trendiest bars in the lobby (see p.486). ⑥

Mälardrottningen Riddarholmen (see Gamla Stan map) ☎08/54 51 87 80, ✆www.malardrottningen.se. This elegant white ship moored by the side of the island of Riddarholmen was formerly American millionairess Barbara Hutton's gin palace. Its cabin-style rooms can be tiny, but still represent good value for such a central location. T-bana Gamla Stan. ④/⑤

Nordic Sea and Nordic Light Vasaplan, Norrmalm ☎08/50 56 30 00, ✆www.nordichotels.se. Right next to Cityterminalen, the *Light* has incredibly sleek if somewhat overdesigned interiors with fabulous lighting, while the slightly cheaper *Sea* has green-blue colours throughout, plus huge fish tanks and the novelty *Icebar* (see p.486) downstairs. ⑤/⑥

Pensionat Oden Söder Hornsgatan 66B, Södermalm ☎08/796 96 00, ✆www.pensionat.nu. A good-value choice in the heart of Södermalm, with tastefully decorated rooms at excellent prices. T-bana Mariatorget. ③

Pensionat Oden Vasastan Odengatan 38 ☎08/796 96 00, ✆www.pensionat.nu. A good, central location and modern rooms. T-bana Rådmansgatan. ③

Queen's Drottninggatan 71A, Norrmalm ☎08/24 94 60, ✆www.queenshotel.se. Mid-range pension-style hotel, with some en-suite rooms and a breakfast buffet. T-bana Hötorget. ③

Rica City Gamla Stan Lilla Nygatan 25, Gamla Stan ☎08/723 72 59, ✆www.rica.se. Wonderfully situated, elegant building with rooms to match; all 51 are individually decorated. T-bana Gamla Stan. ⑥

🏃 **Rival** Mariatorget 3, Södermalm ☎08/54 57 89 00, ✆www.rival.se. A funky boutique hotel, owned by Benny of ABBA fame, with film- and music-themed designer rooms, a bar, café, bakery and cinema. ⑤/⑥

Scandic Continental Vasagatan/Klara Vattugrand 4, Norrmalm ☎08/51 73 42 00, ✆www.scandic-hotels.com. Right next to Central Station, this business-orientated eco-hotel has good deals in summer and at weekends; the cabin rooms are excellent value. ⑤/⑥

🏃 **Stureparkens Gästvåning** Sturegatan 58, Östermalm (see Stockholm map) ☎08/662 72 30, ✆www.stureparkens.nu. Charming bed and breakfast with just nine rooms, shared bathrooms and a communal kitchen. T-bana Stadion. ②/③

Tre Små Rum Högbergsgatan 81, Södermalm ☎08/641 23 71, ✆www.tresmarum.se. Seven small semi-basement rooms, all clean, modern and simple, with a help-yourself breakfast from the kitchen fridge. Very popular and often full. T-bana Mariatorget. ②

Zinkensdamm Zinkens Väg 20, Södermalm ☎08/616 81 10, ✆www.zinkensdamm.com. Pleasant hotel rooms in a separate wing of the youth hostel (see p.469). T-bana Hornstull or Zinkensdamm. ④/⑥

Hostels and private rooms

Stockholm has a wide range of good, well-run **hostel** accommodation, costing from 150kr to 200kr a night per person. There are several STF youth hostels in the city, two of which – *Af Chapman* and *Långholmen* – are among the best in Sweden, and you'll have to plan ahead if you want to stay at most of the hostels listed below, particularly in summer.

Several agencies can help book a **private room**, though some close during the summer months when business travel dwindles. Try Hotelltjänst, Nybrogatan

44 (☎08/10 44 37, ✆www.hotelltjanst.com); Bed & Breakfast agency (☎08/643 80 28, ✆www.bba.nu); or Stockholm Guesthouse (no phone; ✆www.stockholm guesthouse.com). Somewhere central with a fridge and cooking facilities, or with breakfast included, will cost 200–400kr per person per night.

Abbes Skeppsbron 40, Gamla Stan ☎08/30 03 50, ✆www.abbes.se. Stockholm's most central hostel, with comfortable dorm rooms in three historic buildings across Gamla Stan.

Af Chapman Flaggmansvägen 8, Skeppsholmen ☎08/463 22 66, ✆www .stfchapman.com. Beautiful rigged 1888 ship that offers (at least for the price) unsurpassed views over Gamla Stan from the deck and some dorms. Double rooms are also available (❶). Open all year; book well in advance. Note that it's scheduled to close for a few months in 2006. T-bana Kungsträdgården or bus #65 from Central Station.

Backpackers Inn Banérgatan 56, Östermalm ☎08/660 75 15, ✆665 40 39. Reasonably central former school residence with 300 beds in large dorms, plus laundry facilities. Open late June to early Aug. T-bana Karlaplan (Valhallavägen exit) or bus #4.

City Backpackers Vandrarhem Upplandsgatan 2A ☎08/20 69 20, ✆www .citybackpackers.se. Five minutes from central station, this is a friendly, conveniently located non-HI hostel with 84 beds and some double rooms (❶). The owners and staff have travelled widely, and can provide lots of advice for backpackers; Internet access, coffee, tea and sauna. Open all year. T-bana T-Centralen.

City Lodge Klara Norra Kyrkogata 15, Norrmalm ☎08/22 66 30, ✆www.citylodge.se. Some 200m east of Cityterminalen, this compact 40-bed hostel offers central lodging, and free Internet access.

Långholmen Långholmsmuren 20, Långholmen ☎08/720 85 10, ✆www.langholmen.com. Stockholm's grandest STF hostel is set on the island of Långholmen inside a 1724 prison building, the cells converted into smart dorms and private rooms (❷) with their original small and high windows. It's not very central, but the beach and the whole of Södermalm are on the doorstep. T-bana Hornstull, then a ten-minute walk, crossing over the small bridge onto the island.

Skeppsholmen Flaggmansvägen 8, Skeppsholmen ☎08/463 22 66, ✆www.stfchapman.com. Located at the foot of the gangplank to *Af Chapman*, this is an immensely popular hostel housed in the former royal firewood storehouse – you're unlikely to get in without a reservation. Kitchen or laundry facilities are shared with *Af Chapman*, and there's no lockout. T-bana Kungsträdgården or bus #65.

Zinkensdamm Zinkens väg 20, Södermalm ☎08/616 81 00, ✆www.zinkensdamm.com. Huge hostel with 490 beds and kitchen and laundry facilities. It's in a good location for exploring Södermalm, though a thirty–minute walk from the city centre. T-bana Zinkensdamm.

Camping

With only one summer option near the city centre, **camping** in Stockholm can prove a bit of a drag. The tourist offices provide free booklets detailing facilities at all Stockholm's campsites, and the sites below represent the best the city has to offer. With the exception of the site in Östermalm, they're all a 45min (or thereabouts) T-bana ride from the city centre. In July and August it costs around 100kr for two people to pitch a tent; half that the rest of the year.

Ängby ☎08/37 04 20, ✆www.angbycamping.se. West of the city on the lakeshore, with cabins (❶) and camping beneath the trees. Open all year, but book ahead between Sept and April. Five minutes' walk from T-bana Ängbyplan.

Bredäng ☎08/97 70 71, ✆www.camping.se. Large campsite southwest of the city with views over Lake Mälaren. Open all year, but phone ahead to book between November and April. Five minutes' walk from T-bana Bredäng.

Östermalm Citycamping Fiskartorpsvägen 2, Östermalm ☎08/10 29 03, ✆www.camping.se. The most centrally located of all Stockholm's campsites but only open from mid-June to mid-Aug. Walkable from the city centre in around 20min. T-bana Stadion or bus #55 from Slussen/Gamla Stan.

The City

Visitors have been responding to Stockholm's charms for 150 years, and today the combination of elegant Old Town architecture, wide tree-lined boulevards and

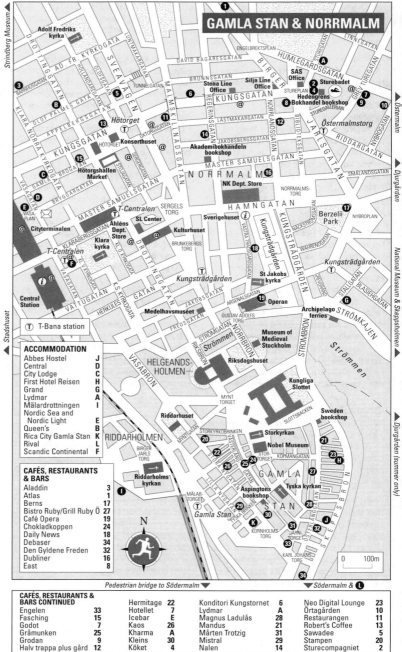

GAMLA STAN & NORRMALM

Strindberg Museum ◀

Stadshuset ◀

Östermalm ▶

Djurgården ▶

National Museum & Skeppsholmen ▶

Djurgården (summer only) ▶

Södermalm & ⓛ ▶

Pedestrian bridge to Södermalm ▼

ⓣ T-Bana station

ACCOMMODATION

Abbes Hostel	**J**
Central	**D**
City Lodge	**C**
First Hotel Reisen	**H**
Grand	**G**
Lydmar	**A**
Mälardrottningen	**I**
Nordic Sea and Nordic Light	**E**
Queen's	**B**
Rica City Gamla Stan	**K**
Rival	**L**
Scandic Continental	**F**

CAFÉS, RESTAURANTS & BARS

Aladdin	3
Atlas	1
Berns	17
Bistro Ruby/Grill Ruby Ö	27
Café Opera	19
Chokladkoppen	24
Daily News	18
Debaser	34
Den Gyldene Freden	32
Dubliner	16
East	8

CAFÉS, RESTAURANTS & BARS CONTINUED

Engelen	33	Hermitage	22	Konditori Kungstornet	6	Neo Digital Lounge	23
Fasching	15	Hotellet	7	Lydmar	A	Örtagården	10
Godot	7	Icebar	E	Magnus Ladulås	28	Restaurangen	11
Gråmunken	25	Kaos	26	Mandus	21	Robert's Coffee	13
Grodan	9	Kharma	A	Mårten Trotzig	31	Sawadee	5
Halv trappa plus gård	12	Kleins	30	Mistral	29	Stampen	20
		Köket	4	Nalen	14	Sturecompagniet	2

great expanses of open water right in the centre all conspire to offer an unparalleled city panorama. Seeing the sights is straightforward: everything is easy to get to, opening hours are long, and the city is a relaxed and spacious place to wander. There's also a bewildering range of galleries and museums, many of which are now free to enter.

Old Stockholm: Gamla Stan and Riddarholmen

The islands of Riddarholmen, Staden and Helgeandsholmen make up the **oldest part of Stockholm**, a historic cluster of seventeenth- and eighteenth-century Baroque and Renaissance buildings backed by narrow alleys. Here, on these three adjoining polyps of land, Birger Jarl erected the first fortification in 1255, and for centuries this was the nucleus of the first city of Stockholm. Rumours abound about the derivation of the name Stockholm, but it's generally thought that it means "island cleared of trees" – trees on the island that is now home to Gamla Stan were probably felled to make way for settlers. Incidentally, today the words *holm* ("island") and *stock* ("log") are still in common use.

Strictly speaking, the **Gamla Stan** or Old Town area refers only to the streets of the largest island, **Staden**, although in practice the name is usually applied to all three islands. Nowadays Gamla Stan is primarily a tourist enclave, a rich tableau of cultural history embodied by the royal palace, parliament and cathedral. The central spider's web, especially if you approach it over the bridges of Norrbron or Riksbron, invokes potent images of the past, with sprawling, monumental buildings and airy churches forming a protective girdle around the narrow streets. The tall, dark houses in the centre were mostly those of wealthy merchants, still picked out today by intricate doorways and portals bearing coats of arms. Some of the alleys in between are the skinniest thoroughfares imaginable, steeply stepped between battered walls; others are covered passageways linking leaning buildings. It's easy to spend hours wandering around here, although the atmosphere these days is not so much medieval as mercenary: there's a dense concentration of antique shops, art showrooms and chichi cellar restaurants, though the frontages don't really intrude upon the otherwise light-starved streets. Not surprisingly, this is the most exclusive part of Stockholm in which to live.

The Riksdagshuset and the Museum of Medieval Stockholm

Entering or leaving the Old Town, you're bound to pass the Swedish parliament building, the **Riksdagshuset** (July–Aug Mon–Fri guided tours in English at 12.30pm & 2pm; free). Despite the assassinations of former Swedish prime minister Olof Palme and foreign minister Anna Lindh (see p.477), Politicians still go freely about their business here, and you'll often see them nipping in and out of the building or lunching in one of the nearby restaurants. The Riksdagshuset itself was completely restored in the 1970s (though only seventy years old even then), and today the grand columned front entrance, seen to best effect from Norrbron, is hardly ever used, the business end concentrated in the new glassy bulge at the back. This being Sweden, the building contains a crèche, and the seating in the chamber itself is in healthy, non-adversarial rows, with members grouped by constituency rather than party.

In front of the Riksdagshuset, accessible by a set of steps leading down from Norrbron, the **Museum of Medieval Stockholm** (*Medeltidsmuseum*; July–Aug Mon, Tues & Thurs–Sun 11am–4pm, Wed 11am–6pm; Sept–June Mon, Tues & Thurs–Sun 11am–4pm, Wed 11am–6pm; 60kr; ⊛www.medeltidsmuseet.stockholm .se) showcases the medieval ruins, tunnels and walls discovered during excavations under the parliament building. These remains have been incorporated into a fascinating walk-through underground exhibition, with reconstructed houses to poke around in, models and pictures, boats, skeletons and street scenes, all with detailed English-language labels.

Kungliga Slottet

South across a second section of bridges is the most distinctive monumental building in Stockholm, **Kungliga Slottet** (the Royal Palace; ✪ www.royalcourt.se), a low, yellowy-brown structure whose two front arms stretch down towards the water. Stockholm's old Tre Kronor (Three Crowns) castle burned down at the beginning of King Karl XII's reign, leaving his architect, Tessin the Younger, with a clean slate on which to design his simple but beautiful Renaissance structure. Finished in 1754, the palace is a striking achievement: uniform and sombre from the outside, its magnificent Baroque and rococo interior is a swirl of state rooms and museums. A combination ticket costing 120kr valid for all the various parts of the palace can be bought at any entrance.

The **Apartments** (mid-May to end June & mid-Aug to end Aug daily 10am–4pm; July to mid-Aug daily 10am–5pm; Sept to mid-May Tues–Sun noon–3pm; 80kr) form a relentlessly linear collection of furniture and tapestries. It's all basically Rent-a-Palace stuff, too sumptuous to take in and inspirational only in terms of its colossal size. The **Treasury** (same times; 80kr), on the other hand, is certainly worthy of the name, with its ranks of jewel-studded crowns: the oldest is that of Karl X (1650); the most charming are intricately worked crowns belonging to princesses Sofia (1771) and Eugéne (1860). Also worth catching is the **Armoury** (June–Aug daily 10am–5pm; Sept–May Tues, Wed & Fri–Sun 11am–5pm, Thurs 11am–8pm; free; ✪ www.lsh.se/livrustkammaren), which is less to do with weapons and more to do with ceremony, featuring suits of armour, costumes and horse-drawn carriages from the sixteenth century onwards. It certainly couldn't be accused of skipping over historical detail. King Gustav II Adolf died in the Battle of Lützen in 1632 and the museum displays his horse (stuffed) and the blood- and mud-spattered garments retrieved after the enemy had stripped him down to his underwear on the battlefield. For those with the energy, the **Museum Tre Kronor** (same times as Apartments; 80kr) contains part of the older Tre Kronor castle, whose ruins lie beneath the present building, and exhibitions on the castle's role as a medieval stronghold.

Into Gamla Stan: Stortorget and around

Beyond the Royal Palace, the streets get narrower and darker and you're in Gamla Stan proper. Here, the highest point of old Stockholm is crowned by **Storkyrkan** (mid-May to mid-Sept daily 9am–6pm; 25kr; rest of the year daily 9am–4pm; free), the "Great Church", consecrated in 1306. Pedantically speaking, Stockholm has no cathedral, but this rectangular brick church fulfils the same role and is the place where the monarchs of Sweden are married and crowned. Storkyrkan gained its present shape at the end of the fifteenth century, with a Baroque remodelling in the 1730s. Inside, twentieth-century restoration has removed the white plaster from the red-brick columns, and although there's no evidence that this was intended in the original, it lends a warm colouring to the rest of the building. Much is made of the fifteenth-century sculpture of St George and the Dragon, though this is easily overshadowed by the golden, throne-like royal pews and the monumental black-and-silver altarpiece. Organ recitals take place here on winter Saturdays at 1pm.

Stretching south from the church is **Stortorget**, Gamla Stan's handsome and elegantly proportioned main square, fringed by eighteenth-century buildings and surrounded by narrow shopping streets. In 1520 Christian II used the square as an execution site during the "Stockholm Bloodbath", dispatching his opposition en masse with gory finality. Housed in the former stock exchange overlooking the square, the **Nobel Museum** (mid-May to mid-Sept daily 10am–5pm, Tues till 8pm; mid-Sept to mid-May Tues 11am–8pm, Wed–Sun 11am–5pm; 50kr; ✪ www .nobel.se/nobelmuseum) is an innovative presentation of the history of Alfred Nobel and the six Nobel prizes, with fascinating short films about the laureates' creativity and their milieus.

△ Stortorget café, Gamla Stan

Gamla Stan's busiest thoroughfares, **Västerlånggatan**, **Österlånggatan**, **Stora Nygatan** and **Lilla Nygatan** run the length of the Old Town, and today their time-worn buildings hold a succession of art and craft shops and restaurants. Happily, though, the consumerism is largely unobtrusive and in summer, buskers and evening strollers clog the narrow alleyways, making it an entertaining area in which to wander and to eat and drink. There are few real targets, though at some stage you'll probably pass the copy of the George and Dragon statues in the small **Köpmantorget** square (off Österlånggatan). Take every opportunity too to scuttle up side streets, where you'll find fading coats of arms, covered alleyways and worn cobbles at every turn.

Just off Västerlånggatan, on Tyska Brinken, the **Tyska kyrkan** (German Church; daily noon–4pm) was originally owned by Stockholm's medieval German merchants, when it served as the meeting place of the Guild of St Gertrude. A copper-topped red-brick building atop a rise, it abandoned its secular role in the seventeenth century when Baroque decorators got hold of it: the result, a richly fashioned interior with the pulpit dominating the nave, is outstanding. Sporting a curious royal gallery in one corner, designed by Tessin the Elder, it comes complete with mini palace roof, angels and the three crowns of Swedish kingship.

Riddarhuset and Riddarholmen

If Stockholm's history has gripped you, it's better to head west from Stortorget towards the handsome Baroque **Riddarhuset** (daily Mon–Fri 11.30am–12.30pm; free; ⊛www.riddarhuset.se), the seventeenth-century "House of Nobles". It was in the Great Hall here that the Swedish aristocracy met during the Parliament of the Four Estates (1668–1865) and their coats of arms – 2326 of them – are splattered across the walls. Some six hundred of the noble families survive; the last ennoblement was in 1974. Take a look downstairs, too, at the Chancery, which stores heraldic bone china by the shelfload, and racks full of fancy signet rings – essential accessories for the eighteenth-century noble-about-town.

From Riddarhuset it takes only seconds to cross the bridge onto **Riddarholmen** (Island of the Knights), to visit the **Riddar holmskyrkan** (mid-May to June & mid to end Aug daily 10am–4pm; July to mid-Aug daily 10am–5pm; first week of Sept Tues–Sun noon–3pm; mid to end Sept Sat & Sun noon–3pm; 20kr), the burial place for Swedish royalty ever since Magnus Ladulås was sealed up here in 1290. Amongst others, you'll find the tombs of Gustav II Adolf (in the green marble sarcophagus), Karl XII, Gustav III and Karl Johan XIV, plus other innumerable and unmemorable descendants. There's a daily English-language tour at 1pm. Walk around the back of the church for stunning views of Stadshuset, the City Hall and Lake Mälaren. Incidentally, the island to the left of Västerbron (the bridge in the distance) is Långholmen; in winter people skate and even take their dogs for walks on the ice along here, as the water freezes solid right up to the bridge and beyond.

Skeppsholmen

A ten-minute walk east from Stortorget lie the islands of **Skeppsholmen** and the microscopic **Kastellholmen**, connected by a bridge to the south. Originally settled by the Swedish Navy – some of whose old barracks are still visible – in the nineteenth century, Skeppsholmen is now home to two of the city's youth hostels and an eclectic clutch of museums, the most impressive of them just by the Skeppsholmsbron, the bridge onto the island.

The National Museum of Fine Arts

As you approach the bridge it's impossible to miss the striking waterfront **National Museum of Fine Arts** (*Nationalmuseum*; June–Aug Tues 11am–8pm, Wed–Sun 11am–5pm; Sept–May Tues & Thurs 11am–8pm, Wed & Fri–Sun 11am–5pm; free; ⊛www.nationalmuseum.se), looking right out over the Royal Palace. The impressive collection is contained on three floors: the **ground floor** is taken up by changing exhibitions of prints and drawings, and there's a shop and café here too, as well as luggage lockers. So much is packed into the museum that it can quickly become overwhelming – it's worth splashing out on the guidebook.

The **first floor** is devoted to applied art, and if it's curios you're after, this museum has the lot – beds slept in by kings, cabinets leaned on by queens, plates eaten off by nobles – mainly from the centuries when Sweden was a great power. There's modern work alongside the ageing tapestries and furniture, including Art Nouveau coffee pots and vases, and examples demonstrating the intelligent simplicity of Swedish chair design.

It's the **second floor**, however, that's most engaging, featuring a plethora of European and Mediterranean sculpture and some mesmerizing sixteenth- and seventeenth-century Russian icons. The paintings are equally wide ranging and of a similarly high quality, including pieces by El Greco, Canaletto, Gainsborough and, most notably, Rembrandt's *Conspiracy of Claudius Civilis*, one of his largest monumental works, a bold depiction of well-armed Roman chieftains. There are also minor paintings by other later masters (most notably Renoir and Gauguin) and some fine sixteenth- to eighteenth-century works by Swedish artists.

Skeppsholmen's museums

One of the better collections in Europe, Stockholm's **Museum of Modern Art** (*Moderna Muséet*; Tues & Wed 10am–8pm, Thurs–Sun 10am–6pm; free; @www .modernamuseet.se), is one of the city's must-see museums, with enthusiastic attendants and a comprehensive selection of works by some of the leading artists of the twentieth century. Highlights include Dali's monumental *Enigma of William Tell*, showing the artist at his most conventionally unconventional, and Matisse's striking *Apollo*. Look out also for Picasso's *Guitar Player*, a whole host of Warhol, Lichtenstein, Kandinsky, Miró and Magritte; and the provocative video-painting *In Orgia* by Lars Nillson. Sharing the same building, the **Architecture Museum** (*Arkitekturmuseet*; same times; free) showcases Swedish architectural models and sketches through the centuries, focusing on the post-war social city planning projects that were meant to promote democracy and welfare through egalitarian building practices.

A steep climb up the northern tip of the island brings you to the **Museum of Far Eastern Antiquities** (*Östasiatiska Muséet*; Tues 11am–8pm, Wed–Sun 11am–5pm; free; @www.ostasiatiska.se), which holds an array of objects displaying incredible craftsmanship – fifth-century Chinese tomb figures, delicate jade amulets, an astounding assembly of sixth-century Buddhas, Indian watercolours and gleaming bronze Krishna figures – and that's just one room.

Norrmalm and Kungsholmen

Modern Stockholm lies immediately to the north and east of Gamla Stan, and is split into two distinct sections. **Norrmalm**, to the north, is the buzzing commercial heart of the city, packed with restaurants, bars, cinemas and shops, while to the east is the more sedate Östermalm, a well-to-do area of classy boulevards. The island of **Kungsholmen**, linked by bridge to the west of Norrmalm, is a mostly residential and administrative district, though with one positive draw in Stockholm's landmark City Hall.

Around Gustav Adolfs Torg

Down on the waterfront, at the foot of Norrbron, is **Gustav Adolfs Torg**, more a traffic island than a square these days, with the nineteenth-century **Opera** (Opera House) its proudest, most notable building. It was here in an earlier opera house on the same site, at a masked ball in 1792, that King Gustav III was shot by one Captain Ankarström, an admirer of Rousseau and member of the aristocratic opposition. The story is recorded in Verdi's opera *Un ballo in maschera*, and you can see Gustav's ball costume, as well as the assassin's pistols and mask, on display in the royal palace Armoury in Gamla Stan.

A statue of King Gustav II Adolf marks the centre of the square, between Opera and the Foreign Office opposite. Look out hereabouts for fishermen pulling salmon out of **Strömmen**, the fast-flowing tributary that winds its way through the centre of the city. Stockholmers have had the right to fish this outlet from Lake Mälaren to the Baltic since the seventeenth century; it's not as difficult as it sounds and there's usually a group of hopefuls on one of the bridges around the square trying their luck.

Just off the square, at Fredsgatan 2 in the heart of Swedish government land, is the **Mediterranean Museum** (*Medelhavsmuséet*; Tues & Wed 11am–8pm, Thurs & Fri 11am–4pm, Sat & Sun noon–5pm; free; @www.medelhavsmuseet.se), a sparkling collection devoted to ancient Mediterranean cultures, notably Egypt, Cyprus, Greece and Rome. Its enormous Egyptian section covers just about every aspect of life in Egypt up to the Christian era, with several whopping great mummies and some attractive bronze weapons, tools and domestic objects from the time before the pharaohs. The Cyprus collections are the largest outside Cyprus itself, spanning a period of over six thousand years, and there are also strong displays of Greek, Etruscan and Roman art. A couple of rooms examine Islamic culture through pottery, glass and metalwork, as well as decorative elements of architecture, Arabic calligraphy and Persian miniature painting.

Walk back towards the Opera and continue across the main junction onto Arsenalsgatan to reach the red **St Jakobs kyrka** (Mon–Wed, Fri & Sat 11am–4pm, Thurs 11am–6pm, Sun 9am–8pm), one of the many easily overlooked churches in Stockholm. It's the pulpit that draws the eye, a great, golden affair, while the date of the church's consecration – 1642 – is stamped high up on the ceiling in gold figures. There are weekly classical music recitals here, with organ and choir recitals on Saturdays at 3pm.

Kungsträdgården

Just beyond St Jakobs kyrka and Opera, Norrmalm's eastern boundary is marked by **Kungsträdgården**, most fashionable and central of the city's numerous squares, reaching from the water northwards as far as Hamngatan. The name means "the king's gardens", though if you're expecting neatly trimmed flower beds and rose gardens you'll be sadly disappointed – it's actually a great expanse of concrete with a couple of lines of trees. The area may once have been a royal kitchen garden, but nowadays it serves as Stockholm's main meeting place, especially in summer when there's almost always something happening, with free evening gigs, theatre and other performances taking place on the central open-air stage. Look out too for the cafés on the square, packed out in spring with winter-weary Stockholmers soaking up the sun. In winter the square is equally busy, particularly at the Hamngatan end where there's an open-air ice rink, the **Isbanan** (mid-Nov to March daily 9am–6pm; skate rental 40kr). The main tourist office is here, too, in the Sverigehuset at the corner of Hamngatan (see p.464). Hamngatan runs east to **Birger Jarlsgatan**, the main thoroughfare that divides Norrmalm from Östermalm, and now a mecca for eating and drinking.

Sergels Torg to Hötorget

At the western end of Hamngatan, beyond the enormous NK department store, lies **Sergels Torg**, the ugliest part of modern Stockholm. It's an unending free show centred on the five seething floors of **Kulturhuset** (Mon–Fri 11am–7pm, Sat & Sun 11am–5pm, ⊛www.kulturhuset.stockholm.se), a cultural centre whose windows look down upon the milling concrete square. Inside are temporary art and craft exhibitions together with workshops open to anyone willing to get their hands dirty. Admission to Kulturhuset is free, but you have to pay to get into specific exhibitions or performances; check the information desk as you come in for details of the programme of poetry readings, concerts and theatre performances. The reading room (*läsesalongen*) and the adjoining *World News Café* on the second floor are stuffed with foreign newspapers, books, records and magazines, and you can also watch foreign TV news reports. Check out the *Stockholms Terassen* café on the top floor for delicious apple pie with custard and views of central Stockholm, an area that saw massive demolition and construction from the 1930s to the 1970s, with all the usual results. From the café terrace you'll get a bird's-eye view of the tall glass column that dominates the square, and the surrounding spewing fountain. Down the steps, below Sergels Torg, is **Sergels Arkaden**, a set of grotty underground walkways home to buskers, brass bands and demented lottery ticket vendors; look out for the odd demonstration or ball game, too. There are also entrances down here into **T-Centralen**, the central T-bana station, and Stockholm's other main department store, Åhléns, not quite as posh as NK and easier to find your way around.

A short walk west from Kulturhuset along Klarabergsgatan will bring you to **Central Station** and **Cityterminalen**, hub of virtually all Stockholm's transport. The area around here is given over to unabashed consumerism, and as you explore the streets around the main drag, **Drottinggatan**, you'll find little to get excited about – run-of-the-mill clothing stores and twee gift shops punctuated by *McDonald's* and the odd sausage stand. In summer the occasional busker or jewellery stall livens up what is essentially a soulless grid of pedestrianized shopping streets. The only point of culture is the **Klara kyrka** (Mon–Fri 10am–6pm, Sat 10am–7pm, Sun 8.30am–6pm), just to the right off Klarabergsgatan, opposite the station. Hemmed in on all sides, with only the spires visible from the surrounding streets, it's a particularly delicate building, with a light and flowery eighteenth-century painted interior and an impressive golden pulpit. Out in the churchyard, a memorial stone commemorates eighteenth-century Swedish poet Carl Michael Bellman, whose popular, lengthy ballads are said to have been composed extempore.

Three blocks further up Drottinggatan, the cobbled square of **Hötorget** holds a fruit and veg market on weekdays, as well as the wonderful indoor **Hötorgshallen** market, an orgy of Middle Eastern smells and sights and a good place to pick up ethnic snacks. Grab something to eat and plonk yourself on the steps of the **Konserthuset** (Concert House), one of the venues for the presentation of the Nobel Prizes, and a good place to hear classical music recitals (often free on Sunday afternoons). The tall building opposite is a former department store where Greta Garbo once worked as a sales assistant in the hat department. Today, though, Hötorget is better known for its superb cinema complex, Filmstaden Sergel, the capital's biggest; to the east, canyon-like **Kungsgatan**, which runs down to Stureplan and Birger Jarlsgatan, holds more cinemas, interspersed with some agreeable cafés (see p.483).

North to the Strindberg Museum

From Hötorget the two main streets of Drottinggatan and Sveavägen run parallel uphill and north as far as Odengatan and the cylindrical **Stadsbiblioteket** (City Library), in its own little park. Close by, set in secluded gardens between the two roads, sits the eighteenth-century **Adolf Fredriks kyrka**. Although it has a noteworthy past – the French philosopher Descartes was buried here in 1650 before his body was moved to France – the church would be insignificant today were it not the final resting place for the assassinated Swedish prime minister, **Olof Palme**:

The murders of Olof Palme and Anna Lindh

The assassination of **Prime Minister Olof Palme** in February 1986 sent shockwaves through a society unused to political extremism of any kind. As for most Nordic leaders, Palme's fame was his security, and he died unprotected, shot down in front of his wife on their way home from the cinema on Sveavägen. Sweden's biggest ever **murder inquiry** was launched and as the years went by so the allegations of police cover-ups and bungling grew. **Christer Pettersson** was eventually jailed for the murder in July 1989 (see "History", p.453), but was released after five months for lack of evidence. Recent theories have suggested that the regime in South Africa was behind the killing – Palme was an outspoken critic of apartheid, leading calls for an economic blockade against Pretoria.

In September 2003, another brutal killing shook Sweden. The popular foreign minister **Anna Lindh** was stabbed whilst shopping in the NK department store, just four days before Sweden's referendum on joining the euro, for which she had been campaigning. The police had learnt from earlier mistakes, and this time there was no bungling, with the murderer – the 25-year-old psychiatric patient **Mijailo Mijailovic** – soon arrested and sentenced to life imprisonment. The motive for the killing remains unknown, and it seems Lindh was the random victim of a deranged man. Ironically, it was Lindh's party that earlier supported reforms of Sweden's psychiatric system that saw many patients reintegrated into society and others refused treatment.

a simple headstone and flowers mark his grave. A plaque now marks the spot on Sveavägen, at the junction with Tunnelgatan, where the prime minister was gunned down; the assassin escaped up the nearby flight of steps (see box on p.477).

Continue north along Drottninggatan and you'll come to the "Blue Tower" at no. 85, the last building in which the writer August Strindberg lived, now turned into the **Strindberg Museum** (*Strindbergsmuséet*; June–Aug Tues–Sun noon–4pm; Sept–May Tues noon–7pm, Wed–Sun noon–4pm; 40kr; ✆www.strindbergsmuseet .se). Strindberg lived here between 1908 and 1912, and his house has been preserved to the extent that you must put plastic bags on your feet to protect the floors and furnishings. The study remains as he left it on his death, a dark and gloomy place – he would work with both Venetian blinds and heavy curtains closed against the sunlight. Upstairs is his library, a musty room with all the books firmly behind glass, which is a shame because Strindberg wasn't a passive reader: he underlined heavily and made notes in the margins as he read, though these are rather less erudite than you'd expect: "Lies!", "Crap!", "Idiot!" and "Bloody hell!" seem to have been his favourite comments. Good explanatory notes in English are available.

Kungsholmen: Stadshuset

Take the T-bana back to T-Centralen and it takes only a matter of minutes to cross the Stadshusbron bridge to the island of **Kungsholmen** and Stockholm's **Stadshuset** (City Hall; guided tours, daily June–Aug at 10am, 11am, noon, 2pm & 3pm; Sept–May 10am, noon & 2pm; 60kr, tower 20kr; ✆www.stockholm .se/stadshuset). Finished in 1923, the Stadshuset is a landmark of the modern city. Its simple exterior, comprising some eight million bricks, is no preparation for the intricate decor within. Visiting heads of state are escorted from their boats up the elegant waterside steps, but for lesser mortals, the only way to view the innards is on one of the guided tours, which reveal the kitschy Viking-style legislative chamber and impressively echoing Golden Hall. The quay just across the Stadshusbron bridge is the departure point for **boats** to destinations around Lake Mälaren: Birka and Drottningholm. Venture further into Kungsholmen and you'll discover a rash of excellent bars and restaurants that have sprung up here – see p.485 – and an excellent **beach** at Smedsudden (buses #1, #4 or #62 to Västerbroplan, then a short walk). Another attraction is the popular **Rålambshovsparken**, a large expanse of open grassland gently sloping down to the waters of Lake Mälaren, where you can take a swim with fantastic views of the City Hall and Old Town.

Östermalm

East of Birger Jarlsgatan, the streets become noticeably broader and grander as you enter the district of **Östermalm**, one of the last areas of central Stockholm to be developed. The first place to head for is the waterside square, **Nybroplan**, just east along Hamngatan from Sergels Torg, and dominated by the white, relief-studded **Royal Theatre of Drama** (*Kungliga Dramatiska Teatern*; ✆www.dramaten.se), Stockholm's showpiece theatre. The curved harbour in front is the departure point for all kinds of archipelago **ferries** and tours (see p.490), and for the ferry service (May–Aug 10am–8pm every 20min; single 35kr) via the Nordic and Vasa museums and Skeppsholmen to Gröna Lunds Tivoli (see opposite); some ferries stop at the royal palace as well.

Behind the theatre at Sibyllegatan 2 is the innovative **Music Museum** (*Musik-muséet*; July & Aug daily 10am–5pm; Sept–April Tues–Sun noon–5pm; free; ✆stockholm.music.museum), containing a range of instruments that visitors are allowed to experiment with. The collection charts the history of music in Sweden via photographs, instruments and sound recordings. Best are the sections that deal with the late nineteenth century (a time when *folkmusik* was given fresh impetus by the growing labour movement), and the space given over to ABBA.

Near the museums, up the hill of Sibyllegatan, **Östermalmstorg** is an absolute find: the square is home to the **Östermalms saluhallen**, an indoor market hall not unlike Norrmalm's Hötorgshallen, but selling more refined delicatessen – reindeer hearts and the like – and attracting a clientele to match. Wander round at lunchtime and you'll spot any number of fur-coated Stockholmers, sipping Chardonnay and munching shrimp sandwiches.

History Museum
As you plod your way around Östermalm's affluent streets, you're bound to end up at the circular **Karlaplan** sooner or later, full of media types coming off shift from the Swedish Radio and Television buildings at the end of Karlavägen. From here it's a short walk down Narvavägen to the impressive **History Museum** (*Historiska Muséet*; May–Sept daily 10am–5pm; Oct–April daily 11am–5pm, Thurs until 8pm; free; ⓦwww.historiska.se); from Norrmalm, take bus #56 via Stureplan and Linnégatan. The most wide-ranging historical display in Stockholm, it's really two large collections: a museum of National Antiquities and the underground Gold Room, with its magnificent fifth-century gold collars and other fine jewellery. Ground-floor highlights include a Stone Age ideal home – flaxen-haired youth, stripped pine benches and rows of neatly labelled herbs – and a mass of Viking weapons, coins and boats, much of it labelled in English. Upstairs there's a worthy collection of medieval church art and architecture, with odds and ends turned up from all over the country, evocatively housed in massive vaulted rooms. If you're heading to Gotland, be sure to look out for the reassembled bits of stave churches uncovered on the Baltic island – some of the few examples that survive in Sweden.

Djurgården
When you tire of pounding the streets, there's respite at hand in the form of Stockholm's so-called National City Park, and in particular the section just to the east of the centre, **Djurgården**. Originally royal hunting grounds from the sixteenth to eighteenth centuries, it is actually two distinct park areas separated by the water of **Djurgårdsbrunnsviken** – popular for swimming in summer and skating in winter, when the channel freezes over. Djurgården also holds some of Stockholm's finest **museums**: the massive open-air Skansen village museum, and the impressive Vasa warship at the Vasa museum.

You can walk to Djurgården through the city centre out along Strandvägen, but it's quite a hike; in summer, trams (30kr) trundle regularly between Norrmalmstorg in Norrmalm and Djurgården. Alternatively, take bus #44 from Karlaplan, or buses #47 and #69 from Norrmalm to the bridge, Djurgårdsbron, which crosses over onto the island. There are also ferries from Skeppsbron in Gamla Stan (all year) and Nybroplan in Östermalm (May–Aug only).

The Nordic Museum, Skansen and Gröna Lunds Tivoli
A full day is just about enough to see everything on Djurgården. Just over Djurgårdsbron from Strandvägen is the palatial **Nordic Museum** (*Nordiska Muséet*; Mon–Fri 10am–4pm, Sat & Sun 11am–5pm; free; ⓦwww.nordiskamuseet.se). The displays attempt to represent Swedish cultural history from the past 500 years in an accessible fashion, and an audioguide (20kr) is available to guide you past the best exhibits – including 1950s furniture design and a collection of toys and doll's houses – in an hour. On the ground floor of the cathedral-like interior is Carl Milles's phenomenal statue of Gustav Vasa, the sixteenth-century king who drove out the Danes and whose inspirational qualities summoned the best from the sculptor (for more on Milles, see p.491).

However, it's for **Skansen** (daily: May 10am–8pm; June–Aug 10am–10pm; Sept 10am–5pm; Oct–April 10am–4pm; 70kr June–Aug, 50kr rest of the year; ⓦwww.skansen.se) that most people come here: a great open-air museum with 150 reconstructed buildings ranging from an entire town to windmills and farms. They're all laid out on a region-by-region basis, with each section boasting its own daily activities – traditional handicrafts, games and displays – that anyone can join in. The best of the buildings are the small Sámi dwellings, warm and functional, and the craftsmen's workshops in the old town quarter. You can also potter around a small **zoo** and a bizarre **aquarium**, where fish live cheek by jowl with crocodiles, monkeys and snakes. Partly because of the attention paid to accuracy, partly due to the admirable lack of commercialization, Skansen manages to avoid the tackiness associated with similar ventures in other countries. Even the snack bars dole out traditional foods and in winter serve up great bowls of warming soup.

Immediately opposite Skansen's main gates (and at the end of the tram and the #44 bus route; bus #47 also goes by), **Gröna Lunds Tivoli** (May to mid-Sept daily noon–midnight; 60kr entrance, or 235kr unlimited rides; ⓦ www.gronalund .com) is not a patch on its more famous namesake, Copenhagen's Tivoli Gardens. It's definitely more of a place to stroll through rather than indulge in the rides, which are generally rather tame. One notable exception is the Fritt Fall – a hair-raising vertical drop of 80m in just six seconds – do lunch later. At night, the emphasis shifts as the park becomes the stomping ground for Stockholm's youth, with raucous music, cafés and some enterprising chat-up lines to be heard.

Vasa Museum

In a new building close to the Nordic Museum, the **Vasa Museum** (*Vasamuséet*; daily: mid-June to mid-Aug 9.30am–7pm; mid-Aug to mid-June 10am–5pm, Wed until 8pm; 80kr; ⓦ www.vasamuseet.se) is head and shoulders above anything else that Stockholm has to offer in the way of museums. Built on the orders of King Gustav II Adolf, the *Vasa* warship sank in Stockholm harbour on her maiden voyage in 1628 – built to a design that was both too tall and too narrow, it keeled over and sank as soon as it was put afloat. Preserved for over 300 years by the Baltic's brackish waters – not salty enough for the taste of wood-boring worms – the ship was raised along with 12,000 objects in 1961, and now forms the centrepiece of a startling, purpose-built hall on the water's edge.

Though the building itself is impressive, nothing prepares you for the sheer size of the **ship** itself: 62m long, with a main mast which was originally 50m above the keel, it sits virtually complete in the hall. Surrounding walkways bring you nose to nose with cannon hatches and restored decorative relief, the gilded wooden sculptures on the soaring prow designed to intimidate the enemy and proclaim Swedish might. Faced with its frightening bulk, it's not difficult to understand the terror that such ships must have generated. Adjacent **exhibition halls** and presentations on several levels take care of all the retrieved bits and bobs. There are reconstructions of life on board, detailed models of the *Vasa*, displays relating to contemporary social and political life, an hourly English-language film about the history of the *Vasa*, excellent explanations and regular English-language **guided tours** (included in the entrance fee).

Adjacent to the museum, an altogether more frightening reminder of the power of the sea deserves your attention. At the edge of the pretty seaman's graveyard, the three-metre-high granite walls of the **Estonia Memorial**, arranged in the form of a triangle bear the engraved names of the 852 people who died when the *Estonia* ferry sank in the Baltic Sea in September 1994 whilst crossing from the Estonian capital, Tallinn, to Stockholm.

Thiel Gallery

At the far eastern end of Djurgården (take bus #69 from Norrmalm) is one of Stockholm's major treasures, the **Thiel Gallery** (*Thielska Galleriet*; Mon–Sat noon–4pm, Sun 1–4pm; 50kr; ⓦ www.thielska-galleriet.se), a fine example of Swedish architecture and art. The house was built by Fredinand Boberg at the beginning of the twentieth century for a banker, Ernet Thiel, who then sold it to the state in 1924, after which it entered its present incarnation. Thiel, who knew many contemporary Nordic artists, gathered an impressive collection of paintings over the years, including works by Carl Larsson, Anders Zorn, Edvard Munch, Bruno

Liljefors and even August Strindberg. The views back towards the city alone are attractive enough to warrant a visit.

The Kaknäs TV Tower

Bus #69 from Norrmalm will take you directly to Stockholm's landmark TV tower, in the northern stretch of parkland known as **Ladugårdsgärdet** (or, more commonly, Gärdet); it's also possible to walk here from Djurgården proper – head northwards across the island on Manillavägen over Djurgårdsbrunnsviken. At 160m, the **Kaknäs TV Tower** (*Kaknästornet*; daily: May–Aug 9am–10pm; Sept–April 10am–9pm; 30kr) is one of the highest buildings in Scandinavia, allowing fabulous views over the city and archipelago; there's a restaurant about 120m up, should you fancy a vertiginous cup of coffee or lunch (65kr). If you come here by bus, you'll pass a gaggle of sundry (and eminently missable) museums – Dance, Maritime, Technical and Ethnographical – while north of the tower beyond Ladugårdsgärdet, where windmills used to pierce the skyline, lies first Frihamnen, where the Tallink ferry from Estonia docks and, just beyond that, Värtahamnen and the Silja Line ferry terminal for Finland.

Södermalm and Långholmen

Whatever you do in Stockholm, don't miss the delights of the city's southern island, **Södermalm**, whose craggy cliffs, turrets and towers rise high above the traffic interchange at Slussen. The perched buildings are vaguely forbidding, but venture beyond the main roads skirting the island and a lively and surprisingly green area unfolds, one that's emphatically working-class at heart, though Swedish-style – there are no slums here. To get here, take bus #43 or #55 to Mariatorget, or the #53 to Folkungagatan; alternatively, ride the T-bana to Slussen or, to save an uphill trek, Medborgarplatsen or Mariatorget.

On foot, you reach the island over a double bridge from Gamla Stan into Södermalmstorg – the square around the entrance to the T-bana at Slussen. Just to the south of the square is the rewarding **City Museum** (*Stadsmuséet*; June–Aug daily 11am–5pm, Thurs until 8pm; rest of the year Tues–Sun 11am–5pm, Thurs until 9pm; 60kr; ⊛www.stadsmuseum.stockholm.se), hidden in a basement courtyard. The Baroque building, designed by Tessin the Elder and finished by his son in 1685, was once the town hall for this part of Stockholm; it now houses a set of collections relating to the city's history as a seaport and industrial centre. Uphill and to the east, the Renaissance-style **Katarina kyrka** on Högbergsgatan stands on the site where the victims of the Stockholm Bloodbath – the betrayed nobility of Sweden who opposed King Christian II's Danish invasion – were buried in 1520. Their bodies were burned as heretics outside the city walls and it proved a vicious and effective coup, Christian disposing of the opposition in one fell swoop. The murdered politician Anna Lindh (see box on p.477) lies buried in the graveyard behind the church.

The church about as far as specific sights go on Södermalm, although it's worth wandering westwards towards **Mariatorget**, a spacious square of Art Nouveau-influenced buildings. This is one of the most desirable places to live in the city, within easy reach of a glut of stylish bars and restaurants where trendy Stockholmers simply have to be seen. To the southeast of Medborgarsplatsen square, the young and hip **SoFo** area ("South of Folkungagatan", around Bondegatan, Skånegatan and Nytorget) is full of trendy shops, fashion boutiques and cafés. You'll probably end up back here after dark too, since there are some good bars and restaurants (see p.483).

Södermalm is also home to one of Stockholm's most popular parks, **Tantolunden**, located close to the Hornstull T-bana at the end of Lignagatan, complete with open-air theatre in summer. It's also the place to come for **swimming pools** – there are three of them – Forgrénskabadet (Medborgarplatsen T-bana), Erikdalsbadet (Skanstull T-bana) and the wonderful little Liljeholmsbadet (Hornstull

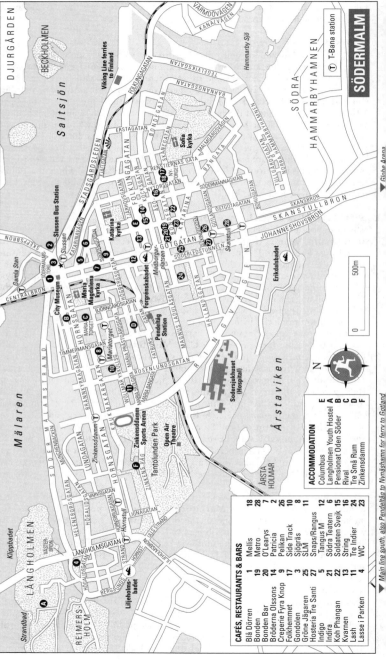

SÖDERMALM

(T) T-Bana station

▶ *Main line south, also Pendeltåg to Nynäshamn for ferry to Gotland*

▶ *Globe Arena*

ACCOMMODATION

Columbus	E
Langholmen Youth Hostel	A
Pensionat Oden Söder	B
Rival	C
Tre Små Rum	D
Zinkensdamm	F

CAFÉS, RESTAURANTS & BARS

Blå Dörren	1		Mellis	18
Bonden	19		Metro	28
Bonden Bar	20		O'Learys	7
Bröderna Olssons	14		Patricia	2
Creperie Fyra Knop	9		Pelikan	26
Folkhemmet	17		Side Track	10
Gondolen	3		Sjögräs	8
Gröne Jägaren	25		SLM	11
Hosteria Tre Santi	27		Snaps/Rangus	12
Indigo	21		Tangus M	6
Indira	22		Södra Teatern	15
Koh Phangan	13		Soldaten Svejk	16
Kvarnen	11		String	24
Lash	4		Tre Indier	23
Lasse i Parken			WC	

482

T-bana) a floating pool in a boat-like pontoon contraption from the 1920s: there's single-sex nude swimming here on Mondays and Fridays, and the water is never less than 30°C.

Långholmen

The name translates as "long island" and **Långholmen** is just that, a skinny finger of land off the northwestern tip of Södermalm, spanned by the mighty Västerbron bridge which links Södermalm with Kungsholmen. There are a couple of popular **beaches** here: **Långholmens strandbad** to the west of the bridge and rocky **Klippbadet** to the east; if you don't fancy swimming, take a leisurely stroll through the trees instead for some stunning views over the water towards the City Hall and Gamla Stan.

You may well find yourself staying on Långholmen, as the island's large prison building has been converted into one of the better hostels in Sweden (see p.469). There's a café here in the summer, and you can sit outside and have a drink in what used to be the prison's exercise yard – narrow, bricked-up runs with iron gates at one end.

Långholmen is best reached by taking the T-bana to Hornstull and then following the signs to the youth hostel; bus #4 is also handy as it crosses Västerbron on its way between Södermalm, Kungsholmen, Vasastaden and Östermalm – a good budget way of seeing much of the city.

Eating

Eating out in Stockholm needn't be outrageously expensive. If money is tight, switch your main meal of the day to lunchtime, at least on weekdays, when almost every café and restaurant offers an excellent-value set menu, or **dagens rätt**, for 60–70kr. In the evening, look around for the best deals but don't necessarily assume that Italian and Chinese places will be the least expensive; more often than not they're overpriced and the food is tasteless. Having said that, there are plenty of other foreign cuisines on offer, particularly Japanese and Thai, plus, of course, a number of traditional Swedish places.

Breakfast, snacks and shopping for food

Stockholmers don't usually go out for **breakfast**, so there are very few places open in the early morning. Hotels provide help-yourself buffet breakfasts which go a long way to filling you up for the day, and are the best place to go early in the morning – most will allow non-guests to have breakfast for 40–50kr. In terms of **snacks**, don't bother with burgers unless you're desperate – you'll pay around 50kr for a large burger and fries at *McDonald's*, only 10–20kr less than the lunchtime *dagens rätt* elsewhere. If the nibbles strike, it's much more economical to pick up a *korv*, a grilled or fried sausage in bread, for 10–20kr from a street vendor.

Of the indoor **markets** (both closed Sun), Hötorgshallen in Hötorget is cheaper and more varied than the Östermalms saluhallen on Östermalmstorg. The former is awash with small cafés and ethnic snacks, but buy your fruit and veg outside where it's less expensive. The latter is posher and pricey – while it's pleasant for a wander, you'll find most things cost less in the city's biggest **supermarket** in the basement of the Åhléns department store on Sergels Torg. In summer, **fruit and veg** stalls spring up outside many of the T-bana stations, especially those out of the centre.

Cafés and restaurants

For decent eating, day or night, head for the city-centre area bounded by Norrmalmstorg, Birger Jarlsgatan and Stureplan; Grev Turegatan in Östermalm; and around Folkungagatan, Skånegatan and Bondegatan on Södermalm. Kungsholmen's restaurants are more spread out, so it's best to have a destination in mind before setting out. Although prices for main dishes usually cost 120–180kr, restaurants in Gamla Stan tend to be 50–100kr more. **Vegetarians** shouldn't have too much difficulty in finding something to eat. Note that in Sweden as a whole there's a fine distinction between cafés, restaurants and bars, with many places offering music and entertainment in the evening as well as serving food throughout the day. Bear in mind, too, that Swedes eat early: lunch is served from 11am to 2pm and dinner from 6pm to around 9pm. Advance booking is generally not required (we've given numbers for places where you do need to book), but as many restaurants don't take bookings at all, it's often a case of just waiting until a table becomes free. Note that we list some gay-friendly restaurants and cafés on p.489.

Unless otherwise stated, for places in **Gamla Stan and Norrmalm**, see the map on p.570; for those in **Södermalm** see the map on p.482; those in **Östermalm**, **Kungsholmen** and **northern Norrmalm** appear on the main Stockholm map, pp.462–463.

Gamla Stan

Bistro Ruby/Grill Ruby Österlånggatan 14. A French bistro, tastefully done out in Parisian style, but pricey. Main dishes go for 200–300kr, though there's a daily 150kr dinner special (5–7pm). *Grill Ruby*, next door, serves up more reasonably priced American-style grills and weekend brunches.

Den Gyldene Freden Österlånggatan 51. Stockholm's oldest restaurant, *The Golden Peace* was opened in 1772, and its vaulted cellars edged with elegant wall paintings remain marvellously atmospheric. Expect to pay around 350kr for two courses of Swedish fare, without drinks.

Hermitage Stora Nygatan 11. Vegetarian restaurant well worth checking out for its hearty, moderately priced food – look out for the spicy Middle Eastern dishes in particular. Closes at 8pm (Sun 7pm).

Mårten Trotzig Västerlånggatan 79. Known throughout Sweden for excellent and stylish food served in a beautiful setting – attracts luvvies and business types from across Stockholm, though it's expense-account stuff.

Mistral Lilla Nygatan 21 ☎08/10 12 24. Excellent, award-winning crossover cuisine served in a cosy atmosphere. Splash out on a set menu for the best taster of the chef's skills (700–900kr).

Norrmalm

Berns Berzelii Park, Nybroplan. One of the more chic brasseries in town (mains around 250kr), with interior design by Britain's Sir Terence Conran, and with a menu of Swedish and international dishes.

East Stureplan 13. One of the city's finest restaurants. Trendy to a T, and serving some excellent food – lots of fish and Asian-style dishes. Dinner 150–190kr.

Grill Drottninggatan 89 (see Stockholm map) ☎08/31 45 30. Pricey, trendy Swedish cuisine in an eclectic set of rooms and lounge spaces. The 97kr all-you-can-eat lunch is an excellent way to sample some of their culinary talent.

Grodan Grev Turegatan 16. "The Frog" serves up great French cuisine (mains around 130kr) and transforms into a popular club with dancing later on in the night. The terrace is also good for people-watching in the summer.

Halv trappa plus gård Lästmakargatan 3. Very popular eatery, with moderately priced modern European dishes, particularly fish, served outside in summer. Bursting with fashion victims.

Konditori Kungstornet Kungsgatan 28. Popular 1950s-style coffee house with excellent cakes and sandwiches from 40kr.

Restaurangen Oxtorgsgatan 14. Run by one of Stockholm's top chefs, this is the place for Swedish home cooking with an added international flavour at moderate prices. No starters or main courses – you simply put together a meal from three or five excellent smaller dishes.

Robert's Coffee Kungsgatan 44. Just inside the door of the Kungshallen food hall, and a popular place to meet for a good cup of coffee, muffins or a light lunch.

Sawadee Olofsgatan 6. Next to Hötorget T-bana. Attractive Thai restaurant with a wonderful 150kr special dinner and reasonably priced drinks.

Sthlm: Kaffe med Mjölk Drottninggatan 73c (see Stockholm map). Relaxed café serving sandwiches, cakes, great breakfasts, of both the fried and healthy varieties, and pasta dishes (65–75kr).

Södermalm

Blå Dörren Södermalmstorg 6. Beer hall and restaurant serving excellent, but expensive, Swedish food.

Bonden Bondegatan 1C. Small and cosy restaurant with rough brick walls and moderate prices; the *Bondenbar* next door gets lively with DJs and bands from Wednesday to Saturday.

Bröderna Olssons Folkungagatan 84. A scruffy, fun restaurant with a black-and-white tiled butcher-shop look, specializing in garlic-laced dishes, accompanied by shots of vodka.

Creperie Fyra Knop Svartensgatan 4. Excellent crêpes at affordable prices (around 80kr).

Folkhemmet Renstiernas gata 30. Very popular place serving Swedish home cooking and international dishes (mains around 120kr) to young trendies. Packed at weekends.

Gondolen Stadsgården 6. Breathtaking views over Stockholm from this high-level place serving up local dishes right on the waterfront at the top of the Katarina lift. Choose the smaller of the two restaurants here and prices fall dramatically.

Hosteria Tre Santi Blekingegatan 32. One of Södermalm's better Italian restaurants and excellent value for money – always busy.

Indigo Götgatan 19. The ideal place to stop off for an afternoon cappuccino. Good pastries, too – the carrot cake is a house speciality. After serving a moderately priced evening menu, the place turns into a lively bar.

Indira Bondegatan 3B. The area's biggest Indian restaurant, with a good, inexpensive tandoori-based menu. Takeaway food, too.

Koh Phangan Skånegatan 57. Swedes love Thailand, and this is a small chunk of paradise 11,070km from Bangkok – a crammed, heaving bar-restaurant with great food (mains around 150kr), lots of bamboo and imitation tropical storms.

Kvarnen Tjärhovsgatan 4. A wonderful beer hall serving Swedish food: lunch for around 50kr, meatballs for 115kr and *pytt i panna* mash for 98kr. Open till 3am, kitchen until 11pm.

Lasse i Parken Högalidsgatan 56. Daytime café (June–Aug only) housed in an eighteenth-century house with a pleasant garden. Very popular in summer; also handy for the beaches at Långholmen.

Mellis Skånegatan 83–85. Popular place on this busy restaurant street. Greek, French and Swedish dishes at around 120kr, and good coffee and cakes, too.

Pelikan Blekingegatan 40. Atmospheric, working-class beer hall with excellent traditional food, such as *pytt i panna* for 98kr.

Sjögräs Timmermansgatan 24. A modern approach to Swedish cooking, influenced by world cuisines, and offering mains at 180–220kr. Always packed.

Snaps/Rangus Tangus Medborgarplatsen. Good, old-fashioned and expensive Swedish food served in a 300-year-old building. Very popular.

Soldaten Svejk Östgötagatan 35. Lively Czech-run joint that draws in a lot of students, with a simple menu at around the 100–125kr mark. Large selection of Czech beers – a Staropramen goes for 45kr.

String Nytorgsgatan 38. Trendy daytime café, good for people-watching from the large windows, which churns out moderately priced cakes and snacks.

Tre Indier Åsögatan 92. Lively, moderately priced Indian restaurant, slightly tucked away in a tiny street off Åsögatan, but well worth hunting out.

Östermalm

Aubergine Linnégatan 38. Upmarket and expensive place, decked out with lots of wood and glass and located on one of Östermalm's busiest streets. Mostly serves Mediterranean cuisine; the separate bar menu brings prices within reach.

Elverket Linnégatan 69. Moderately priced Swedish "crossover" food (international dishes given a Swedish flavour with use of local produce and flavours), served up in a restaurant attached to a theatre. Spacious lounge for drinks before dinner or relaxation afterwards.

Godot Grev Turegatan 36, corner Linnégatan. Calm, stylish brasserie with imaginative French dishes such as mussels with cauliflower sauce or steaks, for 165–275kr. Excellent wine list, too.

Il Conte Grevgatan 9. One of the best Italian restaurants in town, doling out excellent pasta dishes for around 120kr.

Örtagården Nybrogatan 31. Expensive, top-notch vegetarian restaurant, with food dished up under a huge chandelier in c.1900 surroundings. Dozens of different salads, warm dishes and soups.

Kungsholmen

El Cubanito Scheelegatan 3. Delicious Spanish food (mains around 180kr) that deservedly attracts people from across Stockholm.

La Famiglia Alströmergatan 45. One of Kungsholmen's better Italian places (even Frank Sinatra once ate here), and a good one for that first date. Mains 100–180kr.

Roppongi Hantverkargatan 76. Great sushi and other Japanese delights, at a price: main dinner dishes are around 235kr, while lunch goes for 130kr.

Salt Hantverkaregatan 34. Inexpensive, stodgy traditional Swedish fare, including salted, oven-baked moose. The name is no joke – drink lots of water if you're eating the slabs of pork they serve up.

Spisa hos Göken Pontonjärgatan 28. An excellent choice for modern Swedish food served up in a small neighbourhood restaurant. Mains around 100kr.

Northern Norrmalm

Atlas Birger Jarlsgatan 41. Trendy café-restaurant with fresh vegetarian dishes from 60kr and meat and fish mains from around the world for about 110kr. The weekend brunches are excellent, and there's outside seating on comfy sofas.

Bon Lloc Regeringsgatan 111 ☏08/660 60 60. Expensive Euro-Latino dishes with a hint of Swedish home cooking, prepared by award-winning chefs. Mains from 395kr.

Lao Wai Luntmakargatan 74. A Szechuan and Thai restaurant serving 40kr servings of dim sum. Main dishes cost around 150kr; for cheaper

fare, head next door for the snackbar/takeaway department.

Organic Green Rehnsgatan 11. A new-agey organic café serving vegan fare such as home-made bread, soups, a vegetable buffet and freshly pressed juices, for 55–78kr. Closed Sun.

Saturnus Erikbergsgatan 6. Café food during the day, including good, reasonably priced pasta, huge cakes and massive sandwiches, with more substantial dishes on offer in the evening.

Drinking, nightlife and entertainment

There's plenty to keep you entertained in Stockholm, from pubs, gigs and clubs to the cinema and theatre. There's a particularly good **live music** scene in the bars and pubs, but you'll generally have to pay a cover charge of around 60–80kr. Wear something other than jeans and trainers if you don't want to feel very scruffy – many places won't let you in dressed like that anyway – and be prepared to cough up around 20kr to leave your coat in the cloakroom, a requirement at many bars, discos and pubs, particularly in winter. As well as the weekend, Wednesday is a busy night in Stockholm – there's usually plenty going on and queues to get into the more popular places.

Bars, brasseries and pubs

The scourge of Swedish **nightlife** – high alcohol prices – is gradually being neutralized and beer prices have dropped considerably; these days, you'll pay roughly the same as in most Western European capitals. On Södermalm especially there are some very good deals. **Happy hours** also throw up some bargains – look out for signs outside bars and pubs. Like clubs, most bars and pubs have long queues and evil bouncers at the doors; dress up and arrive before 11pm for easy entry. Many Stockholmers do their drinking over a meal, or tank up before hitting the streets, and several of the places listed below are primarily cafés or restaurants.

Most places listed below are open until around 1am, and till 2am at weekends; we've indicated which stay open later. Unless otherwise stated, for places in **Gamla Stan** and **Norrmalm**, see the map on p.570; for those in **Södermalm** see the map on p.482; those in **Östermalm**, **Kungsholmen** and **northern Norrmalm** appear on the main Stockholm map, pp.462–463.

Norrmalm and Östermalm

Café Opera Gustav Adolfs Torg, Norrmalm. If your Gucci gear isn't too crushed and you can stand just one more Martini, join the queue outside the Opera House. Daily till 3am.

Dubliner Smålandsgatan 8. One of the busiest Irish pubs in town, with live music most evenings.

Icebar *Nordic Sea* hotel, Vasaplan, Norrmalm. Icy, pricey but unique. Constructed from Jukkasjärvi river ice, this bar serves vodka cocktails and lingonberry juice in ice glasses. The entrance fee (95/140kr) includes a warm cape and a drink (alcoholic and non-alcoholic respectively); refills are 85kr.

Lydmar *Lydmar* hotel, Sturegatan 10, Norrmalm. A very popular, very elegant bar with occasional jazz and soul music.

Sturecompagniet Sturegatan 4. Three floors of heaving bars, with something for everybody.

Tranan Karlbergsvägen 14, Östermalm (see Stockholm map). Atmospheric old workers' beer hall.

Gamla Stan

Gråmunken Västerlånggatan 18. Cosy café-pub, usually busy and sometimes with live music to jolly things along.

Kaos Stora Nygatan 21. DJs at weekends and unpretentious people out for a fun time.

Kleins Kornhamnstorg 51. One of the better bars in Gamla Stan, generally full of young professional Stockholmers dying to practise their English.

Magnus Ladulås Österlånggatan 26. Rough brick walls and low ceilings make this bar-cum-restaurant an appealing place for a drink or two.

Södermalm

Bonden Bar Bondegatan 1B. Just along from the *Bonden* restaurant and down a series of steps. A good choice for an evening beer before strutting your stuff on the adjoining dance floor.

Folkhemmet *Folkhemmet* hotel, Renstiernas gata 30. Trendy hangout for twenty- to thirty-somethings. Inordinately popular at weekends.

Gröne Jägaren Götgatan 64. Some of the cheapest beer in Stockholm; *storstark* is just 24kr until 9pm. Perhaps inevitably, the clientele tends to get raucously drunk.

Kvarnen *Kvärnen* hotel, Tjärhovsgatan 4. Busy beer hall with two bars.

O'Learys Götgatan 11–13. Södermalm's most popular Irish pub – great fun and within stumbling distance of the nearby T-bana at Slussen.

Pelikan *Pelikan* hotel, Blekingegatan 40. A fantastic old beer hall full of character – and characters.

Sjögräs *Sjögräs* hotel, Timmermansgatan 24. Wonderful bar specializing in rum, and playing bebop, reggae and world music to chilled-out locals.

WC Skånegatan 51. Very busy at weekends with people from across town, and handy for the restaurants around Skånegatan and Blekingegatan.

Clubs

The **club scene** in Stockholm is limited, with several places doubling as bars or restaurants (where you have to eat). Entrance charges aren't too high (around 100kr), but beers sometimes get more expensive as the night goes on, reaching as high as 55kr. For gay venues, see p.489.

Aladdin Barnhusgatan 12, Norrmalm ☎08/10 09 32. One of the city's most popular dance restaurants, often with live bands. Expensive.

Dailys Kungsträdgården, Norrmalm ☎08/21 56 55, ⊛www.dailys.nu. The *G-Klubben* inside this cheesy nightclub complex, complete with striplights on the stairs, is where you'll find Stockholm's movers and shakers. Be young, beautiful and trendy.

Hotellet Linnégatan 18, Östermalm ☎08/442 89 00. The hottest club in town, with plenty of mingling going on until the early hours. Dress up.

Köket Sturegatan 4 ☎08/611 65 79. The party at this place on Stureplan goes on till 5am, way beyond the usual closing hours. Also popular for very late eats.

Metró Götgatan 93, Södermalm, ☎08/442 03 30. The area's newest, sleekest and most popular lounge bar, with a restaurant (closed summer), bar and club with nicely priced drinks. Closed Sun.

Patricia Stadsgårdskajen, Slussen, Södermalm ☎743 05 70, ⊛www.patricia.st. Formerly the royal yacht of Britain's Queen Mother, today a restaurant-disco-bar with good views of the city across the harbour. Swedish stand-up comedy nights; and fantastic food. Arrive early. Wed–Sun.

Sturecompagniet Sturegatan 4, Norrmalm. Strut to house and techno and a fantastic light show or work your way through three floors of bars. Very popular.

Live music: rock and jazz

Apart from the cafés and bars already listed, there's no shortage of specific venues that put on **live music**. Most of the performers will be local bands, for which you'll pay 60–70kr entrance, but nearly all the big names make it to Stockholm, playing at a variety of seated halls and stadiums – naturally, tickets for these are much more expensive. The main venue is the Stockholm Globe Arena (T-bana Globen; ☎08/600 3400, ⊛www.globearenas.se), supposedly the largest spherical building in the world – ring for programme details or ask at the tourist offices.

Cirkus Djurgårdsslätten 43, Djurgården (see Stockholm map) ☎08/587 987 00, ⊛www.cirkus.se. Occasional rock and R&B performances.

Daily News Kungsträdgården, Norrmalm ☎08/21 56 55, ⊛www.dailys.nu. Part of the Dagens Nyheter complex, this central rock venue hosts the most consistent range of live music in town – everything from grunge to techno.

Debaser Karl Johans torg , Gamla Stan ☎08/30 56 20. Perhaps Stockholm's best rock club, with live performances on most days.

Engelen Kornhamnstorg 59, Gamla Stan ☎08/20 10 92, ⊛www.wallmans.com. Live jazz, rock or blues nightly until 3am, but arrive early to get in; the music starts at 8.30pm (9pm Sun).

Fasching Kungsgatan 63, Norrmalm ☎08/21 62 67, ⊛www.fasching.se. Local and foreign contemporary jazz; a good place to go dancing too. Closed Sun.

Nalen Regeringsgatan 74, Norrmalm ☎08/566 398 00, ⊛www.nalen.com. Once *the* place to hear music in the city (even the Beatles were booked to play here), now offering jazz, swing and big band.

Södra Teatern Mosebacke torg 3, Södermalm ☎08/556 972 30. This is one of the best places in the capital for world music, hip hop, rock and pop – if it's happening anywhere, it's happening here. Weekends only.

Stampen Stora Nygatan 5, Gamla Stan ☎08/20 57 93. Long-established and rowdy jazz club, both trad and mainstream; occasional foreign names, too.

Tre Backar Tegnérgatan 12–14, Norrmalm (see Stockholm map) ☎08/673 44 00. Good, cheap pub with a cellar for live music performances. Rock and blues nightly Mon–Sat until midnight.

Classical music, theatre and cinema

For up-to-date **information** about what's on where, check the special Saturday supplement of the *Dagens Nyheter* newspaper, "På stan". *What's On*, free from the tourist office, is also indispensable for **arts listings**, with day-by-day information about a whole range of events – gigs, theatre, festivals, dance – sponsored by the city, many of which are free and based around Stockholm's many parks. Popular venues in summer are Kungsträdgården and Skansen, where there's always something going on.

Classical music and opera

Classical music is always easy to find. Many museums – particularly the History Museum (see p.479) – have regular programmes, and there's generally something on at one of the following venues: Konserthuset, Hötorget, Norrmalm (☎08/10 21 10); Berwaldhallen, Strandvägen 69, Östermalm (☎08/784 18 00, ⓦwww.sr.se /berwaldhallen); Gamla Musikaliska Akademien, Blasieholmstorg 8, near the National Art Museum (☎08/20 68 18); and Myntet, Hantverkargatan 5 (☎08/652 03 10). The Opera House (☎08/24 82 40, ⓦwww.operan.se) is Sweden's most famous **operatic** venue; for less rarefied presentations of the classics, check the programme at the Folkoperan, Hornsgatan 72, Södermalm (☎08/658 53 00). If you're after **church music**, you'll find it in Norrmalm at Adolf Fredriks kyrka, Gustav Wasa kyrka on Odenplan, and at St Jakobs kyrka; in Gamla Stan, try Storkyrkan and Tyska Kyrkan. For more details, consult *What's On*.

Theatre and cinema

There are dozens of **theatres** in Stockholm, but only one has regular performances of **English-language productions**: Vasa Teatern, Vasagatan 19 (☎08/24 82 40), just north of the Cityterminal. If you want tickets for anything else theatrical, it's often worth waiting for reduced-price standby tickets, available from the kiosk in Norrmalmstorg.

Cinema-going is an incredibly popular pastime in Stockholm, with screenings of new releases nearly always full. The largest venue in the city centre is Filmstaden Sergel in Hötorget (☎08/562 600 00, ⓦwww.sf.se), but there's also a good number of cinemas along the entire length of Kungsgatan between Sveavägen and Birger Jarlsgatan, always very lively on Saturday night. Tickets cost around 80kr and films are never dubbed into Swedish.

Finally, **Kulturhuset** in Sergels Torg (see p.476) has a full range of artistic and cultural events, most of them free; the information desk on the ground floor gives away programmes.

Gay Stockholm

Stockholm's **gay scene** is surprisingly small and closeted. Attitudes in general are tolerant, but you won't see gay couples walking hand in hand or kissing in the street – just one of the false perceptions of Sweden. Until just a few years ago, when the country freed itself from restrictive tax rules imposed on bars and restaurants, there was only one specifically gay hangout in the whole city. Thankfully today things have changed and bars are springing up all over the place, although a kneejerk reaction by the government in response to AIDS has forced all gay saunas to close. The main bars and clubs to be seen at are listed below, but beware that all are male-dominated – lesbians have an extremely low profile in Stockholm.

For **information**, visit ⓦwww.stockholmtown.com/gay or pick up the free *QX* monthly (ⓦwww.qx.se/english) from the tourist office or venues across town; look out for their useful yearly Gaymap. The *Chokladkoppen* café is perhaps the best place to stock up on brochures and tips for events. You can also contact the **RFSL**, the National Association for Sexual Equality (☏08/736 02 12, ⓦwww.rfsl.se), the city's main gay centre at Sveavägen 57 (T-bana Rådmansgatan). The centre offers HIV advice (☏08/736 02 11) and runs a bookstore, a restaurant and radio station. **Stockholm Pride Week** (ⓦwww.stockholmpride.org) takes place during the second week of August.

Restaurants, bars and clubs

Chokladkoppen Stortorget 18. Excellent, gay-friendly café with a sunny terrace overlooking the bustling square. Good for lunch, coffee, hot chocolate and Indian chai.

Kharma Sturegatan 10. Popular gay men's club on Friday nights, at the *Lydmar* bar.

Mandus Österlånggatan 7 ☏08/20 60 55. The best gay restaurant in Stockholm, serving up tiger prawns, beef and chicken wok dishes and delicious home-made burgers. Deservedly known for its vibrant bar staff, too.

Neo Digital Lounge Brunnsgränd 2, Gamla Stan, ⓦwww.neoslounge.com. A central Thursday night gay club with a lounge bar and heaving dancefloor.

Rio Sveavägen 57, Norrmalm ⓦwww.riostock holm.com. The largest mixed gay club in town, on four floors. Closed Sun.

Roxy Nytorget 6, Södermalm ⓦwww.roxysofo.se. A cosy and warm Mediterranean restaurant that turns into a bar after dinner.

Side Track Wollmar Yxkullsgatan 7, Södermalm ⓦwww.sidetrack.nu. Dark and smoky British-style pub, popular with leather and denim boys. Men only.

SLM & LASH Wollmar Yxkullsgatan 18, Södermalm ⓦwww.slm.a.se & ⓦwww.lash.tk. Two popular leather club nights, the former for men, the latter for women only.

Torget Mälartorget 13, Gamla Stan, ⓦwww .torgetbaren.com. Opposite Gamla Stan T-bana, this is an elegant place for a drink at any time of the evening. Always busy and full of beauties.

Listings

Airlines Scheduled: American Airlines ☏08/78 03 55; British Airways ☏0770/11 00 20; Delta Air Lines ☏08/587 691 01; Finnair ☏0771/78 11 00; Icelandair ☏08/690 98 00; KLM and Northwest ☏08/587 997 57; SAS Stureplan 8 ☏0770/727 727; United Airlines ☏020/79 54 02. Budget airlines: Blue1 ☏0900/102 58 31, ⓦwww.blue1 .com; FlyMe ☏0770/790 790, ⓦwww.flyme.com; FlyNordic ☏08/528 068 20, ⓦwww.flynordic.com; Kullaflyg ☏042/244 222, ⓦwww.kullaflyg.se; Ryanair ☏0900/20 20 240, ⓦwww.ryanair.com; Snalskjutsen ☏040/660 23 40, ⓦwww.snalsk jutsen.com; Snowflake ☏0770/727 727, ⓦwww .flysnowflake.com; Sterling ☏08/58 76 91 48, ⓦwww.sterlingticket.com; Swedline ☏0495/24 90 50, ⓦwww.swedline.com.

Airport enquiries Arlanda ☏08/797 61 00; SAS domestic flights to and from Arlanda ☏08/797 50 50; Bromma ☏08/797 68 00; Skavsta ☏0155/28 04 00; Västerås ☏021/80 56 00.

ATMs, banks and exchange There are ATMs at the airport, train stations and the banks dotted all over the city. Forex branches can be found in the main hall at Central Station (daily 7am–9pm); Cityterminalen (Mon–Fri 7am–8pm, Sat & Sun 8am–5pm); Vasagatan 14 (Mon–Fri 9am–7pm, Sat 9am–4pm); in the Sverigehuset (Mon–Fri 8am–7pm, Sat & Sun 9am–5pm); and at Arlanda airport (three offices; daily 6am–9pm).

Bookshops Akademibokhandeln, corner of Regeringsgatan & Mäster Samuelsgatan, Norrmalm; Aspingtons (secondhand), Västerlånggatan 54, Gamla Stan; Hedengrens Bokhandel, Sturegallerian, Stureplan 4, Norrmalm; Sweden Bookshop, Slottsbacken 10, Gamla Stan.

Bus enquiries For SL bus information see "SL travel information" below; for long-distance bus information call Swebus Express on ☏0200/218 218 or visit ⓦwww.swebusexpress.se; for Svenska Buss call ☏0771/67 67 67.

Car rental Avis, Vasagatan 10B, and Arlanda and Bromma airports ☏020/78 82 00; Budget, Klarabergsviadukten 92 ☏08/411 15 00; Europcar, Tegelbacken 6 ☏08/611 45 60; Hertz, Vasagatan 26 ☏020/211 211.

Dentist Emergency dental care at St Eriks

Hospital, Fleminggatan 22; daily 8am–8.30pm. Out of hours ring Stockholm Care on ☎08/672 24 00.

Doctors Tourists can get emergency outpatient care at the hospital for the district they are staying in; check with Stockholm Care ☎08/672 24 00, ✺www.stockholmcare.se.

Embassies and consulates Australia, Sergels Torg 12 ☎08/613 29 00; Canada, Tegelbacken 4 ☎08/453 30 00; Ireland, Östermalmsgatan 97 ☎08/661 80 05; New Zealand – use the Australian Embassy; UK, Skarpögatan 6–8 ☎08/671 30 00; USA, Dag Hammarskjöldsväg 31 ☎08/783 53 00.

Emergencies Ring ☎112 for police, ambulance or fire services.

Ferries For Finland from Silja Line at Stureplan or Värtahamnen ☎08/22 21 40, ✺www.silja.com; and Viking Line at Stadsgårdsterminalen ☎08/452 40 00, ✺www.vikingline.se; for Estonia from Tallink, Frihamnen (☎08/666 60 01, ✺www.tallink.se); for the archipelago from Waxholms Ångfartygs, Strömkajen ☎08/679 58 30, ✺www.waxholmsbolaget.s, or Strömma, Skeppsbron 22 ☎08/587 140 00, ✺www.strommakanalbolaget.com.

Internet access The excellent Sidewalk Express (coin-operated terminals at 19kr per hour) can be found at Central Station, Cityterminalen and Hötorget Sergel Cinema as well as inside Pressbyra and 7–Eleven stores at Drottninggatan 33 & 81, Götgatan 57, Humlegårdsgatan 11, Kungsgatan 9, Sveavägen 73, Vasagatan 22 and Västerlånggatan 38. Other options, costing 40–60kr per hour, are: Café Access, Kulturhuset, Sergels torg and Café Zenit, Sveavägen 20.

Laundry Self-service launderette at Västmannagatan 61 (☎08/34 64 80), or try the youth hostels.

Left luggage There are lockers at Central Station, the Cityterminalen bus station and the Silja and Viking ferry terminals. Locker prices start at 30kr per day.

Lost property Östra Kyrkogatan 4, Central Station ☎08/412 69 60.

Newspapers There are newspaper kiosks at Central Station and Cityterminalen, and you can read papers for free at the Stadsbibliotek (City Library), Sveavägen 73, or at Kulturhuset, Sergels Torg.

Pharmacy 24hr service at C.W. Scheele, Klarabergsgatan 64 ☎08/454 81 30.

Police ☎08/401 00 00, ☎112 for emergencies.

The main station is at Kungsholmsgatan 37, Kungsholmen.

Post office The most useful office is in the Central Station (Mon–Fri 7am–10pm, Sat 10am–7pm); take your passport if collecting poste restante mail.

SL travel information Bus, T-bana and regional train (*pendeltåg*) information on ☎08/600 10 00. There are SL-Centers at Sergels Torg (Mon–Fri 7am–6.30pm, Sat & Sun 10am–5pm); Slussen (Mon–Fri 7am–6pm, Sat 10am–1pm); Gullmarsplan, Södermalm (Mon–Thurs 7am–6.30pm, Fri 7am–6pm, Sat 10am–5pm); and Fridhemsplan, Kungsholmen (Mon–Fri 7am–6.30pm, Sat 10am–5pm).

Systembolaget Norrmalm: Klarabergsgatan 62; Regeringsgatan 44; Sveavägen 66; Vasagatan 25; Odengatan 58 and 92. Gamla Stan: Lilla Nygatan 18. Södermalm: Folkungagatan 56 & 101 and inside the Söderhallarna shopping centre in Medborgarplatsen. Opening hours are generally Mon–Wed 10am–6pm, Thurs & Fri 10am–7pm, Sat 10am–2pm.

Toilets There are central public toilets at T-Centralen, Cityterminalen, the Gallerian shopping centre, Åhléns and NK department stores.

Train information For tickets and information for domestic and international routes with SJ (Swedish State Railways), call ☎0771/75 75 75; for Tågkompaniet call ☎0771/444 111.

Travel agents Kilroy, Kungsgatan 4 (☎0771/54 57 69) and STA Travel, Kungsgatan 30 (t0771/61 10 10), for discounted rail and air tickets and ISIC cards.

Around Stockholm

Such are Stockholm's attractions, it's easy to overlook the city's surroundings; yet only a few kilometres from the centre the countryside becomes noticeably leafier, the islands less congested and the water brighter. As further temptation, some of the country's most fascinating sights are within easy reach, like the spectacular **Millesgården** sculpture museum at **Lidingö** and **Drottningholm**, Sweden's greatest royal palace. Other trips from Stockholm – out into the stunning **archipelago** or to the university town of **Uppsala** – really merit more time, although if you're pressed it's possible to travel to each and return the same day.

Bear in mind that while the Stockholm Card and 1- and 3-day cards are valid on bus, T-bana and regional train services within Greater Stockholm, you can't use them on the more enjoyable boat services to Drottningholm or in the archipelago.

Lidingö and Millesgården

A residential island just northeast of the city centre, **Lidingö** is where the well-to-do of Stockholm live – you'll already have glimpsed it if you arrived from Finland or Estonia on the Silja or Tallink ferries, as they dock immediately opposite. It's worth visiting for the statues in the startling **Millesgården** at Carl Milles väg 2 (mid-May to Aug daily 10am–5pm; Sept to mid-May Thurs–Sun noon–5pm; 75kr; ⓦ www.millesgarden.se), the outdoor sculpture collection of **Carl Milles** (1875–1955), one of Sweden's greatest sculptors and collectors. To **get there**, take the T-bana to Ropsten, then bus #207.

The statues are placed on terraces carved from the island's steep cliffs, with many of Milles's animated, classical figures perching precariously on soaring pillars, overlooking the distant harbour. A huge *Poseidon* rears over the army of sculptures, the most remarkable of which, *God's Hand*, has a small boy delicately balanced on the outstretched finger of a monumental hand. If you've been elsewhere in Sweden much of the work may seem familiar – copies and casts of the originals adorn countless provincial towns. If this collection inspires, it's worth tracking down three other pieces by Milles in the capital: his statue of *Gustav Vasa* in the Nordic Museum on Djurgården, the *Orpheus Fountain* in Norrmalm's Hötorget and, at Nacka Strand (reached most enjoyably by Waxholmsbolaget boats from Strömkajen), the magnificent *Gud på Himmelsbågen*, a claw-shaped vertical piece of steel topped with the figure of a boy – a stunning marker at the entrance to Stockholm harbour.

Drottningholm and Birka

Even if your time in Stockholm is limited, it's worth saving a day for a visit to the harmonious Unesco-listed royal palace of **Drottningholm** (May–Aug daily 10am–4.30pm; Sept daily noon–3.30pm; Oct–April Sat & Sun noon–3.30pm; 60kr; ⓦ www.royalcourt.se), beautifully located on the shores of leafy Lovön island, 11km west of the city centre. The fifty-minute boat trip there is part of the experience, with hourly departures from Stadhusbron (May to mid-Sept daily 9.30am–6pm; 90kr one-way, 120kr return); alternatively, take the T-bana to Brommaplan and then any bus numbered between #301 and #323 from there – a less thrilling ride, but one that's covered by the SL transport cards and the Stockholm Card.

Drottningholm is perhaps the greatest achievement of the architects **Tessin**, father and son. Work began in 1662 on the orders of King Karl X's widow, Eleonora, Tessin the Elder modelling the new palace in a thoroughly French style – leading to that tired and overused label of a Swedish Versailles. Apart from anything else it's considerably smaller than its French counterpart, utilizing false perspective and trompe l'oeil to boost the elegant, rather narrow interior. On Tessin the Elder's death in 1681, the palace was completed by his son, already at work on Stockholm's Royal Palace. Inside, good English notes are available to help you sort out each room's detail, a riot of Rococo decoration largely dating from the time when Drottningholm was bestowed as a wedding gift on Princess Louisa Ulrika (a sister of Frederick the Great of Prussia). Since 1981 the Swedish royal family has slummed it out at Drottningholm, using the palace as a permanent home, a move that has accelerated efforts to restore parts of the palace to their original appearance – so that the monumental **Grand Staircase** is now exactly as envisaged by Tessin the Elder.

Nearby in the palace grounds is the **Court Theatre** (*Slottsteater*; May–Sept, guided tours only, every 30min; 60kr), dating from 1766. Its heyday came a decade later when Gustav III imported French plays and acting troupes, making

Drottningholm the centre of Swedish artistic life. Take a guided tour and you'll get a flowery though accurate account of the theatre's decoration: money to complete the building ran out in the eighteenth century, meaning that not everything is quite what it seems, with painted papier-mâché frontages masquerading as the real thing. The original backdrops and stage machinery are still in place, though, and the tour comes complete with a display of eighteenth-century special effects – wind and thunder machines, trapdoors and simulated lighting. If you're in luck you might catch a **performance** of drama, ballet or opera here (May–Sept): the cheapest **tickets** cost around 170kr, though decent seats are in the region of 300–600kr – ask at the tourist offices in the city. With time to spare, the extensive palace grounds also yield the **Chinese Pavilion** (May–Aug daily 11am–4.30pm; Sept daily 11am–3.30pm; 50kr), an eighteenth-century royal summer house.

Birka

Further into Lake Mälaren lies the island of **Björkö**, known for its rich flora and good swimming beaches. Its real draw, though, are the remnants of Sweden's oldest town, **BIRKA**, founded in around 750 AD, and now listed by Unesco as a World Heritage site. A Viking trading centre at its height during the tenth century, a few obvious remains lie scattered about, including the fragments of houses and a vast cemetery. Major excavations were carried out between 1990 and 1995 and a museum, **Birka the Viking Town** (May to mid-Sept daily 10am–5pm; 50kr), now displays rare artefacts recovered during the excavations as well as scale models of the harbour and craftsmen's quarters. You can get there from Stadshusbron in Stockholm on a Strömma boat (departures May to mid Sept daily 9.30am, return trip from Birka at 3pm; July & Aug daily at 1.15pm, return at 6.45pm); tickets can be bought on board or booked by calling ☎08/587 140 00 and cost 255kr return, which includes admission to the museum.

Stockholm archipelago

If you arrived in Stockholm by ferry from Finland or Estonia, you'll already have had a tantalizing glimpse of the **Stockholm archipelago**, a unique array of hundreds upon hundreds of pine-clad islands and islets. The archipelago can be split into three distinct sections: inner, centre and outer. In the inner section there's

△ Stockholm archipelago

more land than sea; in the centre it's pretty much fifty-fifty; while in the outer archipelago distances between islands are much greater – out here, sea and sky merge into one and the nearest island is often no more than a dot on the horizon. It's worth knowing that if it's cloudy in Stockholm, chances are that the sun will be shining somewhere out on the islands. Even if your trip to the capital is short, don't miss the chance to come out here.

Practicalities

Getting to the islands is easy and cheap, with Waxholmsbolaget (☎08/679 58 30, ◉www.waxholmsbolaget.se) operating the majority of sailings and Strömma (☎08/587 140 00, ◉www.strommakanalbolaget.com) offering regular cruises. Most boats leave from Strömkajen in front of the *Grand Hotel*; others leave from just round the corner at Nybrokajen, next to the Royal Theatre of Drama. Buy tickets either from the Waxholmsbolaget office on Strömkajen or on the boats themselves; you can also pick up free timetables from the office to help you plan your route – timetables are also posted on every jetty. **Departures** to the closest islands are more frequent (often around four daily) than those to the outer archipelago; if there's no direct service connections can often be made at the island of Vaxholm. Ticket prices are reasonable, ranging from 65kr to 120kr depending on the length of the journey, though if you're planning to visit several islands it might be worth buying the **Interskerries Card** (*båtluffarkort*), which gives five days' unlimited travel on all Waxholmsbolaget lines for 300kr.

Though there are few hotels in the archipelago, **accommodation** is most easily available in a number of several well-equipped and comfortable **youth hostels** – the most useful are at **Finnhamn** (☎08/542 462 12, ◉www.finnhamn.nu; open all year; dorm beds 230kr, rooms ❶); **Grinda** (☎08/542 490 72; May to late Oct; dorm beds 170, rooms ❶); **Gällnö** (☎08/571 661 17; May–Sept; dorm beds 175kr, rooms ❶); and **Utö** (☎08/504 203 00, ◉www.uto-vardshus.se May–Sept, dorm beds 280kr), which also has luxury year-round cabins and rooms (❹). It's also possible to rent **cottages** on the islands during summer, though you'll need to book way in advance – get hold of the Stockholm hotel's brochure from the city tourist office. **Campsites** are surprisingly hard to find – you'll be much better off camping rough, as a few nights' stay in most places won't cause any problems. Remember, though, that open fires are prohibited all over the archipelago.

Archipelago highlights

Of the vast number of islands in the archipelago, several are firm favourites with Stockholmers, **Vaxholm** in particular; others offer more secluded beaches and plenty of opportunity for lovely walks. The following are a few of the better islands to make for.

Inner and central archipelago

Lying just an hour's ferry ride northeast of Stockholm, **Vaxholm** is a popular weekend destination. The main settlement on the island, **Vaxholm town**, has an atmospheric wooden harbour with an imposing fortress which once guarded the waterways into the city, successfully staving off attacks from Danes and Russians in the seventeenth and eighteenth centuries; it's now an unremarkable museum of military bits and pieces. Also within easy reach is **Grinda**, two hours or so east, a thickly wooded island typical of the inner archipelago, whose magnificent sandy beaches are much favoured by families.

In the central archipelago, low-lying **Gällnö** is covered with dense pine forest. One of the most beautiful islands, it has been designated a nature reserve, with deer and eider duck the most likely wildlife you'll spot. Ferries take about two hours to get here from Stockholm.

Also two hours by boat from Stockholm, **Svartsö**, near the island of Möja (see p.494), lies in the most scenic part of the archipelago, where dozens of surrounding islands give the impression of giant stepping stones leading to the mainland. Known for its fields of grazing sheep, virgin forest and crystal-clear lakes, Svartsö's good roads make the island ideal for cycling or walking.

Outer archipelago

If you're heading into the outer archipelago from Stockholm, you can sometimes cut the journey time by taking a bus or train to a further point on the mainland and picking the boat up there – where this is the case, we've given details below.

Three hours from Stockholm, the tiny island of **Finnhamn** lies in the outer reaches of the archipelago, where the islands start to become fewer and where the sea takes over. It's a good place for walking, through forests, meadows and along cliff tops.

Möja (pronounced roughly as "Murr-ya"), three and a half hours from the city, is one of the most popular islands, home to around three hundred people, who make their living from fishing and farming. There's a small craft museum in the main town, **Berg**, and even a cinema, though as there are no beaches (private houses line the entire shoreline), it's not the place to come if you want to go swimming.

In the southern stretch of the archipelago, the beautiful island of **Bullerö** is home to a nature reserve with walking trails and an exhibition on the archipelago's plentiful flora and fauna. The journey takes three hours in total: get the train from Slussen to Saltsjöbaden, and from there a boat to the island of Nämdö, where you can take the shuttle service to Bullerö.

Sandhamn has been a destination for seafarers since the 1700s and remains so today, its tiny harbour packed full of sailing yachts of all shapes and sizes. The main village is a haven of narrow alleyways, winding streets and overgrown verandas. It takes three and a half hours to get here from Stockholm by boat, or you can save time by taking bus #434 from Slussen to Stavsnäs – the furthest point on the mainland – and picking up a boat for the hour-long sailing to Sandhamn.

Lying far out in the southern reaches of the archipelago, **Utö** is ideal for cycling, with the sandy beaches at Ålö storsand perfect for a picnic stop. You can also walk along Utö's cliffs at Rävstavik. The journey time from Stockholm is three hours.

Västerås

Around 100km inland from Stockholm, **VÄSTERÅS**, Sweden's sixth biggest city and capital of the county of Västmanland, is an immediately likeable mix of old and new. Today the lakeside city carefully balances its dependence on industrial technology giant ABB with a rich history dating back to Viking times – and it's also home to two very wacky hotels.

Arrival, information and accommodation

The **airport**, served by direct Ryanair flights from London Luton, is 6km east of the centre and is connected to the centre by bus #941; Ryanair flights are met by the Flygbussarna bus which drives directly to Stockholm's T-Centralen (80mins, 130kr). The airport has no ATM or exchange office. The **train** and **bus stations** are located together on Södra Ringvägen, a ten-minute walk through Vasaparken from the **tourist office** at Stora Gatan 40 (mid-June to mid-Aug Mon–Fri 9am–7pm, Sat 9am–3pm, Sun 10am–2pm; mid-Aug to mid-June Mon–Fri 9.30am–6pm, Sat 10am–3pm; ☎021/10 38 30, ⊛www.vasterasturism.se). The lakeside Lövudden **youth hostel** (☎021/18 52 30, ⊛www.lovudden.nu; dorm beds 150kr, private rooms ❶ is 5km west of the city; take bus #25 from the bus station.

Hotels

Aaros Metro Vasagatan 22 ☎021/18 03 30. One of the cheapest best-value hotels in town, and very centrally located. ❷/❸

Elite Stadshotellet Stora Torget ☎021/10 28 00, ⊛www.vasteras.elite.se. A Västerås fixture: good-quality modern rooms right in the heart of the city. ❸/❺

First Hotel Plaza Karlsgatan 9A ☎021/10 10 10, ⓦwww.firsthotels.se. Known locally as the "skyscraper", this 25-storey glass-and-chrome structure is the last word in Scandinavian chic, and offers good value in summer. ❸/❺

Klipper Kungsgatan 4 ☎021/41 00 00. Charming rooms in the old town, close to the Svartån River. If you're prepared to "bädda själv" – put the sheets on the bed yourself – you can avail yourself of the lowest room rates in town. Breakfast is included, as is lunch on weekdays. ❷/❸

Utter Inn & Hackspett Lake Mälaren & Vasapark ☎070/77 55 393 or mobile 0739/64 45 52, ⓦwww.mikaelgenberg.com. Built by a local artist, the *Utter Inn* is a double room hanging three metres below a tiny hut floating on Lake Mälaren, with windows on all sides for observing the fish. The *Hackspett* ("woodpecker") consists of a one-bed tree hut perched in an oak tree in the middle of the city park. Open April to mid-Oct; book well in advance. ❻, ❺ if you bring your own sheets and food.

The City

From the tourist office, it's a short stroll up Köpmangatan to the twin cobbled, squares of **Bondtorget** and **Stora Torget**. A narrow lane leads from the southwestern corner of Bondtorget to the narrow **Svartån River**, which runs right through the centre of the city; the bridge across it affords great views of the old wooden cottages which nestle eave to eave along the riverside. Although it may not appear so significant, the Svartån was a decisive factor in making Västerås the headquarters of one of the world's largest engineering companies, **Asea-Brown-Boveri** (ABB), which needed a ready source of water for production. North of the two main squares is the thirteenth-century brick **Domkyrkan** (Mon–Fri 8am–5pm, Sat & Sun 9.30am–5pm), last resting place of Erik XIV, who died an unceremonious death in Örbyhus castle in 1577 after eating pea soup laced with arsenic. His tomb lies to the right of the altar; local rumour has it that his feet had to be cut off in order to fit his body into its coffin. Beyond the cathedral is the most charming district of Västerås, **Kyrkbacken**, a hilly area with steep cobblestone alleys winding between well-preserved old wooden houses where the craftsmen and the petit bourgeoisie lived in the 1700s.

A quick walk past the restaurants and shops of Vasagatan will bring you back to Stora Gatan and eventually to the modern **Stadshuset**, a far cry from the Dominican monastery which once stood on this spot. Although home to the city's administration, the building is best known for its 47 **bells**, the largest of which (known as "The Monk") can be heard across Västerås at noon. Across Fiskartorget square, the **castle** was under renovation at time of writing and it's uncertain if the **county museum** inside will reopen, but if it does, don't miss the Viking boat grave from nearby Tuna, Badelunda – the richest female burial yet discovered in Sweden.

Eating and drinking

Västerås has a good selection of **restaurants**, with numerous cuisines represented: from Thai to Greek, traditional Swedish to British-style pub food. The city also has a lively **drinking** scene, including one cocktail bar 24 floors up, from where there are unsurpassed views of the lake.

Atrium Corner of Smedjegatan and Sturegatan. Greek favourites from 89kr, and starters from 20kr.

Bellman Stora Torget 6. Elegant restaurant in a yellow wooden house overlooking the main square, with Swedish fare from 120kr.

Bill o Bob Stora Torget 5. A bustling restaurant on the main square, with all the usual meat and fish dishes for around 130kr.

Bishops Arms Östra Kyrkogatan 1. British-style drinking hole with a large selection of beers, single-malt whisky and pub grub.

Brogården Stora Gatan 42, next to the tourist office. Riverside café with good views of the water and old wooden houses.

Kalle på Spången Kungsgatan 2. Great old-fashioned café with outdoor seating close to the river. *The* place for coffee, cakes, grilled baguettes and fresh orange juice.

Karlsson på taket Karlsgatan 9A. Chichi restaurant and café on the 24th floor of the Skrapan skyscraper, which also houses the *First Hotel Plaza*. Expensive, but fantastic views.

Kina Thai Gallerian 36. Chinese and Thai evening meals for around 150kr, and lunch for 69kr.

Piazza di Spagna Vasagatan 26. The best pizzeria in town and a very popular place for lunch (69kr). Otherwise, pizzas and pasta are from around 70kr, and meat dishes start at 180kr.

Real Mälargatan 6D. Excellent Mediterranean-inspired mains for around 200kr, served overlooking the new Östra Hamnen harbour.

Varda Vasagatan 14. Trendy, above-average restaurant with international dishes for around 180kr. A great spot for lunch.

Around Västerås: the Anundshög burial mound

Six kilometres northeast of Västerås, **Anundshög** is the largest royal burial mound in Sweden. Dating from the sixth century, it's thought to be the resting place of King Bröt-Anund and the stash of gold with which he was buried. Several other smaller burial mounds are located close by, suggesting that the site was an important Viking meeting place for several centuries. Beside the main mound lie a large number of **standing stones** arranged end to end in the shape of two ships. Bus #12 (19kr) leaves the centre of town two to four times an hour; the mound is a twenty-minute walk from its final stop, Bjurhovda.

Uppsala

First impressions as the train pulls into **UPPSALA**, less than an hour north of Stockholm, are encouraging. The red-washed **castle** looms up behind the railway sidings, while the **cathedral** dominates the foreground. A sort of Swedish Oxford, Uppsala clings to the past through a succession of striking buildings connected with and scattered about its cathedral and **university**. Regarded as the historical and religious centre of the country, it serves as a tranquil daytime alternative to Stockholm – with an active student-oriented nightlife.

Arrival and information

Uppsala's **train** and **bus stations** are adjacent to each other off Kungsgatan. **Boats** to and from Stockholm use the pier south of the centre, at the end of Bävernsgränd. If you're flying in or out of Sweden, you can bypass Stockholm entirely by using the #801 bus between Uppsala bus station and **Arlanda airport** (daily 4am–midnight every 15–30min; 40min; 75kr). A short walk from the train and bus stations, the **tourist office** is at Fyristorg 8 (Mon–Fri 10am–6pm, Sat 10am–3pm, also Sun noon–4pm end June to mid-Aug; ☎018/727 48 00, ⊛www.uppsalatourism.se). You can pick up the free *What's On* guide, or buy the Uppsala Card (125kr; valid for three days), which allows free admission to most sights, as well as free parking and use of local buses.

Accommodation

Though Uppsala can easily be seen as a day-trip from Stockholm, you may want to stay around a little longer. Contact the tourist office to book the excellent-value Uppsala Package; an Uppsala Car, and a hotel room with breakfast, starting at 400kr per person in a double room. As well as a fair range of hotels, there's a new *City* **youth hostel** at Kungsgatan 27 (☎018/480 50 55, ⊛www.uppsalavandrarhem.se).

For **camping**, head a few kilometres north to the open spaces of Gamla Uppsala (see p.498), or use the regular site, *Sunnersta Camping* (☎018/727 60 84), 7km from town by Lake Mälaren (bus #20).

Årsta Gård Jordgubbsgatan 14 ☎018/25 35 00. This large cottage-style building on the outskirts is the cheapest hotel in town; take bus #7 (daytime) or #56 (evenings) to Södra Årsta (15min). **②**

Comfort Hotel Svava Bangårdsgatan 24 ☎018/13 00 30, ⊛www.hotelsvava.com. Modern hotel with all mod-cons, offering good summer discounts. **③/⑥**

Grand Hotell Hörnan Bangårdsgatan 1 ☎018/13 93 80, ⊛www.grandhotellhornan.com. Wonderfully elegant place with large, old-fashioned rooms and a restaurant. **④/⑤**

Radisson SAS Gillet Dragarbrunnsgatan 23 ☎018/68 18 00, ⊛www.radisson.com. A stone's throw from the cathedral but with average, over-priced rooms. **④/⑥**

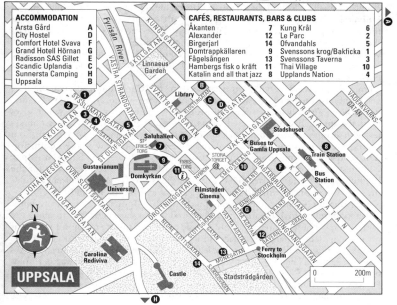

Within the map image:

ACCOMMODATION

Årsta Gård	A
City Hostel	D
Comfort Hotel Svava	F
Grand Hotell Hörnan	G
Radisson SAS Gillet	E
Scandic Uplandia	C
Sunnersta Camping	H
Uppsala	B

CAFÉS, RESTAURANTS, BARS & CLUBS

Åkanten	7	Kung Krål	6
Alexander	12	Le Parc	2
Birgerjarl	14	Ofvandahls	5
Domtrappkällaren	9	Svenssons krog/Bakficka	1
Fågelsången	13	Svenssons Taverna	3
Hambergs fisk o kräft	11	Thai Village	10
Katalin and all that jazz	8	Upplands Nation	4

Gamla Uppsala (5km)

UPPSALA

Scandic Uplandia Dragarbrunnsgatan 32 ☎018/495 26 00, ⊛www.scandic-hotels.com. A modern business hotel in the heart of the city, 500 metres from the station in the centre of town, with free wi-fi throughout. Good summer prices. ③/⑤

Uppsala Kungsgatan 27 ☎018/480 50 00, ⊛www.profilhotels.se. Simple, bright and clean rooms with en-suite bathrooms and a tiny kitchen. ③/⑤

The City

The centre of the medieval town is the great Gothic **Domkyrkan** (daily 8am–6pm; free; ⊛www.uppsaladomkyrka.se), Scandinavia's largest cathedral. Built to show the people of Trondheim in Norway that even their mighty church could be overshadowed, it loses out to its competitor by reason of the building material – local brick rather than imported stone – and only the echoing interior remains impressive, particularly the French Gothic ambulatory, bordered by tiny chapels and bathed in a golden glow. One chapel contains a lively set of restored fourteenth-century wall paintings that recount the legend of Saint Erik, Sweden's patron saint: his coronation, crusade to Finland, eventual defeat and execution at the hands of the Danes. The relics of Erik, encased in a golden coffin, are zealously guarded in a chapel off the nave: poke around and you'll also find the tombs of Reformation rebel Gustav Vasa and his son Johan III, and that of Linnaeus, the botanist, who lived in Uppsala. Time and fire have resulted in the rebuilding of the rest of the cathedral, now scrubbed and painted to the extent that it resembles a historical museum more than a thirteenth-century spiritual centre; even the characteristic twin spires are late nineteenth-century additions.

The buildings grouped around the Domkyrkan can all claim a purer historical pedigree. Opposite the towers, the onion-domed **Gustavianum** (Tues–Sun 11am–4pm; 40kr), built in 1625 as part of the university, is much touted for its **Augsburg Art Cabinet**, an ebony treasure chest presented to Gustav II Adolf, and for its tidily preserved anatomical theatre from 1663. The same building houses a couple of small collections of Egyptian, classical and Nordic antiquities. The current **University** building is the imposing nineteenth-century Renaissance edifice over the way. Originally a seminary, it's used today for lectures and seminars and hosts the graduation ceremonies each May. The more famous of its alumni include Carl von Linné (Linnaeus) and Anders Celsius, inventor of the temperature scale. No one will mind if you stroll into the entrance hall for a quick look, but the rest of the building is not open to the public.

From the university, Övre Slottsgatan leads to the **Carolina Rediviva**, the university library. On April 30 each year the students meet here to celebrate the first day of spring (usually in the snow), all wearing a traditional student cap, which gives them the appearance of disaffected sailors. This is one of Scandinavia's largest libraries, with around five million books. It's most valuable treasures – some stolen from Poland and Bohemia in the seventeenth century – are on show in the **exhibition hall** (mid-June to mid-Aug Mon–Fri 9am–5pm, Sat 10am–5pm, Sun 11am–4pm; 20kr; rest of the year Mon–Fri 9am–8pm, Sat 10am–4pm; free). Look out for the beautiful sixth-century Silver Bible, Mozart's drafts for *The Magic Flute* and Ptolemy's 1477 map of the world. There's also a pretty café on the ground floor.

After this, the **Castle** (guided tours June–Aug 1 & 3pm; 60kr) up on the hill is a disappointment. In 1702 a fire that destroyed three-quarters of the city did away with much of the building, and only one side and two towers remain of what was once an opulent rectangular palace. Inside, admission also includes access to the castle's art museum but, quite frankly, it won't make your postcards home.

Seeing Uppsala's central sights will take up a good half day. If the weather holds out, use the rest of your time to stroll from the lush Stadsträdgården park along the Fyrisån River through the centre of town. One beautiful spot worth lingering in is the **Linnaeus Garden** (daily: May–Sept 9am–9pm; rest of the year 7am–7pm; 30kr; @www.linnaeus.uu.se) over the river on Svartbäcksgatan. Sweden's oldest botanical gardens, established in 1655 by Olof Rudbeck the Elder, they were relaid by Linnaeus (Carl von Linné) in 1741, and some of the species he introduced and classified still survive. The adjoining **museum** (same times; 20kr) was once home to Linnaeus and his family, and it attempts to re-create his life through a partially restored library, writing room and a collection of natural-history specimens.

Gamla Uppsala

Five kilometres to the north of the present city, and a pleasant walk or bike ride from the centre, three huge **barrows** – royal burial mounds dating back to the sixth century – mark the original site of Uppsala, **Gamla Uppsala** (@www.raa.se/olduppsala), a pagan settlement and a place of ancient sacrificial rites. Every ninth year the festival of Fröblot demanded the death of nine people, hanged from a nearby tree until their corpses rotted. The pagan temple where this bloody sacrifice took place is now marked by the Christian **Gamla Uppsala kyrka** (daily: April–Sept 9am–6pm; rest of the year 9am–4pm), built over pagan remains when the Swedish kings were first baptized into the new faith. What survives is only a remnant of what was, originally, a cathedral – look inside for the faded wall paintings and the tomb of Celsius, of thermometer

△ Carved stone, Gamla Uppsala

fame. An eleventh-century rune stone is set into the wall outside, and others can be found nearby.

Arriving by bus from Uppsala (#2 or #210 from Vaksalagatan), first cross the train tracks to see the worthwhile **Old Uppsala Museum** (May–Aug daily 11am–5pm; Sept–April Wed, Sat & Sun noon–3pm; 50kr). The exhibitions illustrate the origin of local myths from Roman times as well as Uppsala's era of greatness until the thirteenth century. There's little else to Gamla Uppsala, and perhaps that's why the site remains so mysterious and atmospheric. If the nibbles strike after an afternoon of pillaging and plundering, there's a **restaurant**, *Odinsborg*, near the museum, and snacks are served in the museum itself.

Eating, drinking and nightlife

Commensurate with its status as one of Sweden's largest cities and major university centres, Uppsala boasts an impressive range of sophisticated **restaurants** and **bars**. Almost all of them are located in the grid of streets bordered by the Fyrisån River, St Olofsgatan and Bangårdsgatan and, though many places get pretty busy in the summer, it's not necessary to book a table. For affordable snacks, visit the Saluhallen on St Eriks torg, where there are sushi, kebab and sandwich bars. If you're travelling north from here into the Swedish provinces, it's a good idea to splurge and make the most of the city's eateries, while the bars, often packed with pub-crawling students, are usually pretty lively.

Cafés and restaurants

Åkanten St Eriks torg. Outdoor café right by the river; a delightful place to relax in summer.

Alexander Östra Ågatan 59. Completely OTT Greek place with busts of famous personalities from the ancient world at every turn. Mains at 100–165kr.

Birgerjarl Nedre Slottsgatan 3. More than just a playground for students, this large, ramshackle wooden-built restaurant and bar is a must. There's a range of burgers for around 115kr, and wild partying later at night. Outdoor tables in summer.

Domtrappkällaren St Eriks Gränd 15. One of the most chichi places in town, with an old vaulted roof and great atmosphere. The Swedish mains go for around 250kr, and lunch for 110kr, though the pub lunch is only 75kr.

Fågelsången Munkgatan 3. Café and lunch place with cheap sandwiches (15–40kr) and a pleasant terrace overlooking the park.

Hambergs fisk o kräft Fyristorg 8. Very good fresh fish and seafood, from a reasonable 135kr per main dish.

Kung Krål St Persgatan 4. Across the river from the tourist office, in an old stone building with outdoor seating in summer. Swedish home cooking and international dishes for 130–200kr.

Le Parc Torsgatan 15. Set in a small park, this delightful cottage with outdoor seating is an excellent place for a Swedish lunch or dinner.

Ofvandahls Sysslomansgatan 3–5. A lively café dating from 1878 furnished with shabby old wooden tables and sofas. Don't leave town without trying the home-made cakes.

Svenssons krog/Bakficka Sysslomangatan 15. A wonderful restaurant decked out in wood and glass with everything from Swedish home cooking to top-class salmon. The cheaper *Bakficka* ("back pocket") bar serves good pasta dishes.

Svenssons taverna Sysslomangatan 14. One of Uppsala's best eateries, with a large outdoor seating area under the shade of huge linden trees, and an international menu with main courses at around 130kr.

Thai Village Smedsgränd 9. Asian food served at reasonable prices in pleasant surroundings. Mains 110–160kr.

Nightlife

At night, most of Uppsala's action is generated by the **students** in the "nation" houses in the grid of streets behind the university, backing onto St Olofsgatan. Not unlike college fraternities, each house organizes dances, gigs and parties of all hues and, most importantly, all boast very cheap bars. The official line is that if you're not a Swedish student you won't get into most of the things; in practice, being foreign and being nice to the people on the door generally yields entrance, while with an ISIC card it's even easier. Since many students stay around during the summer, functions are not strictly limited to term time. A good choice to begin with is *Upplands Nation*, at St Larsgatan 11, which has a summer outdoor café open until 3am. Otherwise, *Birgerjarl* (see above) is a sure bet for a party, as is *Katalin and all that jazz*, open late and with jazz nights – it's in the old goods shed just behind the train station.

Listings

Banks and exchange Handelsbanken, Vaksalagatan 8; Nordea, Stora Torget; SEB, Kungsängsgatan 7–9. There's a Forex exchange near the tourist office at Fyristorg 8 (Mon–Fri 9am–7pm, Sat 9am–3pm).
Bus enquiries Uppsalabuss ☎018/27 37 00. City buses leave from Stora Torget and Vaksalagatan; long-distance buses from the bus station adjacent to the train station (see Stockholm "Listings", p.489, for phone numbers).
Car rental Avis, Stålgatan 8 ☎018/15 16 80; Europcar, Kungsgatan 103 ☎018/17 17 30; Hertz, Kungsgatan 97 ☎018/16 02 00.

Internet There are coin-operated *Sidewalk Express* terminals (19kr/hr) in the station and at *Saffets* café, Stora Torget 1.
Pharmacy at Bredgränd Mon–Fri 9am–6.30pm, Sat 10am–3pm ☎020/66 77 66.
Police Svartbäcksgatan 49 ☎018/16 85 00.
Systembolaget at Svavagallerian, Bredgränd (Mon–Wed 10am–6pm, Thurs & Fri 10am–7pm, Sat 10am–2pm).
Taxis Taxi Kurir ☎018/12 34 56; Uppsala Taxi ☎018/10 00 00.
Train enquiries Information on ☎018/65 22 10.

Travel details

Trains

Stockholm to: Falun (17 daily; 2hr 40min); Gällivare (2 daily; 16hr); Gävle (hourly; 1hr 20min); Gothenburg (hourly; 3–6hr); Helsingborg (hourly; 5hr); Kalmar (hourly; 4hr 30min); Kiruna (2 daily; 17hr); Luleå (2 daily; 14–15hr); Malmö (hourly; 4hr 30min); Mora (6 daily; 4hr); Norrköping (hourly; 1hr 20min); Örebro (hourly; 2hr); Östersund (6 daily; 6hr); Sundsvall (8 daily; 3hr 20min); Umeå (1 daily; 10hr); Uppsala (hourly; 40min).
Uppsala to: Falun (17 daily; 2hr); Gällivare (2 daily; 15hr); Gävle (6 daily; 1hr); Kiruna (2 daily; 16hr); Luleå (2 daily; 13hr); Mora (6 daily; 3hr); Östersund (6 daily; 5hr); Stockholm (hourly; 40min); Sundsvall (8 daily; 2hr 45 min); Umeå (1 daily; 9hr).

Buses

Stockholm to: Gävle (2 daily; 2hr 45min); Gothenburg (6 daily, 7hr); Helsingborg (2–3 daily; 7hr

30min); Jönköping (8 daily; 4hr); Kalmar (3 daily; 6hr); Malmö (2–3 daily; 8hr); Norrköping (8 daily; 2hr 10min); Östersund (1–2 daily; 7hr 40min); Umeå (2 daily; 10hr).

International trains

Stockholm to: Copenhagen (hourly, via Malmö; 5hr 20min); Narvik (2 daily; 20–21hr); Oslo (3 daily via Gothenburg; 7hr 30min).
Uppsala to: Narvik (2 daily; 19–20hr).

International buses

Stockholm to: Copenhagen (2 daily, 8hr 40min); Oslo (4 daily, 7hr 30min).

International ferries

Stockholm to: Helsinki (2 daily; 16hr 30min); Mariehamn (7 daily; 4hr); Tallinn (1 daily; 17hr); Turku (3 daily; 11hr).

3.2

Gothenburg and around

othenburg is Sweden's second city and the largest seaport in Scandinavia – facts that have been enough to persuade many travellers arriving here by ferry to move quickly on to the surrounding countryside. But beyond the gargantuan shipyards, Gothenburg's Dutch-designed cityscape of broad avenues, elegant squares, trams and canals is one of the prettiest in Sweden, and with its well-established café society and rich cultural life, it's worth a lot more time than most visitors give it. The city's image has also suffered from the inevitable comparisons with the capital, and while there is a certain resentment on the west coast that Stockholm wins out in the national prestige stakes, many Swedes far prefer Gothenburg's more relaxed atmosphere and its closer proximity to Western Europe, particularly since the Öresund Bridge near Malmö has put it within three hours of Copenhagen.

The counties to the north and east of the city are prime targets for domestic tourists. The closest highlight to Gothenburg is the glorious fortress island of **Marstrand**, an easy and enjoyable day-trip away, while heading further towards Norway, the uninhabited islands, tiny fishing villages and clean beaches of the craggy **Bohuslän coastline** attract thousands of holidaymakers. To the northeast of the city, the vast and beautiful lakes of **Vänern** and **Vättern** provide the setting for a number of

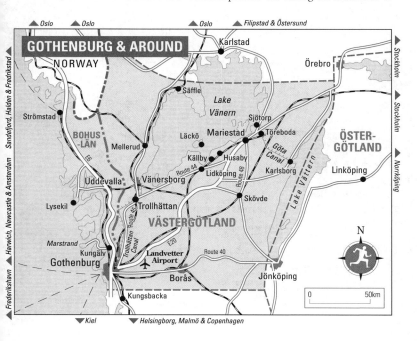

historic towns, fairytale castles and some splendid scenery, all within an hour's train journey from Gothenburg. The lakes are connected to each other (and to the east and west coasts) by the cross-country **Göta Canal**, and if you're inspired by the possibilities of water transport you could always make the four-day voyage from Gothenburg to Stockholm, or opt for a day-trip along the prettiest stretch of the canal near picturesque medieval **Mariestad**, on the eastern shore of Lake Vänern.

GOTHENBURG

RESTAURANTS, CAFÉS, BARS & CLUBS

28+	43	Publik	27
Ahlstroms Konditori	3	Rondo	39
Beefeater Inn	37	The Rover	21
Bishops Arms	J	Ruby Nuevo Latino Bar	L
Brasserie Lipp	14	Rumpanbar	46
Café Kringlan	32	Sjöbaren	35
Café Teatergatan	25	Smaka	17
Cigarren	22	Solrosen	29
Condeco	10	Stars & Stripes	23
Cyrano	40 & 41	Studs	44
Diamond Dogs	15	Tai Pak	34
Dubliners	6	Thai Garden	28
E.t.c.	16	Tintin	33
Eva's Paley	31	Trädgårn	9
Frågetecknet	26	Valand	38
Froken Olssons Kafe	4	Vasastan	M
Gabriel at Feskekörka	12		
Gillestugan	22		
Grande E.t.c.	8		
Greta's	5		
Hard Rock Café	11		
Hemma Hos	30		
Hos Pelle	47		
Jacob's Café	30		
Java Café	36		
Junggrens Café	19		
Klara	18		
Kompaniet	7		
Krakow	45		
Lai Wa	24		
Linné Terassen	42		
Louice	20		
Mauritz Kaffehus	2		
Nivå	13		
The Palace	1		
Pasta Gambero	48		

HISINGEN

Docks

N

Stenpiren

Göta River

Stena Line Ferry Terminal

ANDRÉEGATAN

ESPERANTO PLATSEN

Feskekörkan

STORA RADHUS

SKEPPSBRON

JÄRN-TORGET

Saluhallen
Briggen

Hagabadet

SÖDRA

HAGA

HAGA ÖSTER-

HAGA NYGATAN

VARLANDS-
FÖRSTA LÅNGGATAN
MAST-
HUGGSTORGET
ANDRA LÅNGGATAN
TREDJE LÅNGGATAN

STIGBERGSLIDEN

Fiskhamnen

BANGATAN

FJÄLLGATAN

JUNGMANS-

VÄGEN

LINNÉ

NORDHEMS-
GATAN

PILGATAN

LANDSVÄGS-
GATAN

PRINSGATAN

OLIVEDALS-
GATAN

LINNÉGATAN

Skansparken

SKANS-
TORGET

ROSENGATAN

OLIVEDALSGATAN

ÖVRE HUSARGATAN

VEGAGATAN

HOTELS & PENSIONS

Allén	M
Barken Viking	B
City	K
Eggers	F
Elite Plaza	J
Europa	E
Hotel 11	U
Lilton	T
Maria Erikssons Pensionat	P
Rica City Hotel	D
Robinson	H
SAS Radisson Scandinavia	G
Scandic Rubinen	L

HOSTELS & CAMPSITES

Askims Strand Camping	V
Göteborgs Minihotel	Q
Karralund Camping	R
Kviberg	C
Lilleby Camping	A
Masthuggsterrassen	O
Partille	I
Slottsskogen	S
Stigbergssliden	N
Torrekulla	W

Stena Line Ferry Terminal for Kiel, Klippan ◀ & Saltholmen & Gay Centre ◀ Frederikshavn

Slottsskogsparken

Natural History Museum

▼ Botanical Gardens

▼▼ V

Gothenburg

With its long history as a trading centre, **GOTHENBURG** (Göteborg in Swedish, pronounced "Yur-te-boy") is a truly cosmopolitan city. Founded on its present site in the seventeenth century by Gustav Adolf, it was the last in a long line of attempts

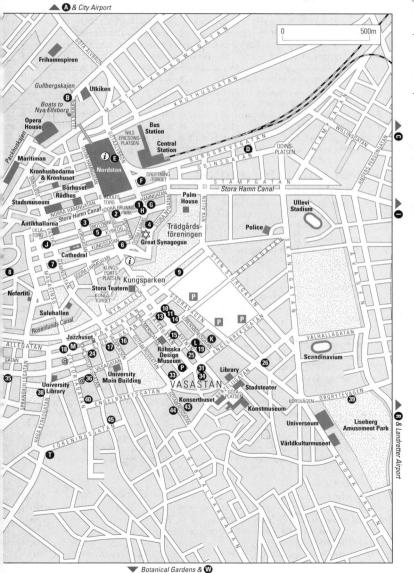

to create a trade centre free from Danish influence – Denmark had enjoyed control of Sweden's west coast since the Middle Ages, extracting extortionate tolls from all water traffic travelling into Sweden. An original medieval settlement was sited 40km up the Göta River, but was later moved to a location north of the present city in order to avoid these tolls; a third attempt was built on the island of Hisingen, but this fell to the Danes during the Battle of Kalmar in 1611. Six years later, Gustav Adolf founded a new city on the site of today's main square.

Although Gothenburg's reputation as an industrial and trading centre has been severely eroded in recent years – as evidenced by the motionless cranes in the shipyards – the British, Dutch and German traders who settled here during the eighteenth and nineteenth centuries left a rich architectural and cultural inheritance. The city is graced with terraces of grand merchant houses, all carved stone, stucco and painted tiles, while the trade between Sweden and the Far East brought an Oriental influence, still visible in the chinoiserie detail on many buildings. This vital trading route was monopolized for over eighty years by the hugely successful Swedish East India Company, whose auction house, selling exotic spices, tea and fine cloth, attracted merchants from all over the world.

Today, the city remains a regular port of call for business travellers, though the flashy central hotels that accommodate them say much less about Gothenburg than the restrained opulence of the older buildings, which reflect not only the city's bygone prosperity but also the understatement of its citizens.

Arrival and information

From **Landvetter airport** (☎031/94 10 00, ⌨www.landvetter.lfv.se), 25km east of the city, Flygbussarna buses run every fifteen minutes to the bus station. The journey takes around thirty minutes (daily 5am–11.15pm; 60kr; ⌨www.flygbussarna.se;). The **City airport** (☎31/92 60 60, ⌨www.goteborgcityairport.se) is 15km north of Gothenberg; the Flygbussarna airport bus (50kr; 30min) to the bus station meets all flights, and it leaves the bus station 2hr 20min before each flight. A taxi from either airport to the centre will cost about 300kr. For airline and airport information numbers, see p.518.

All **trains** arrive at Central Station, on Drottningtorget in the centre of the city. Just behind, the modern glass **bus** station handles all regional, national and international bus services. Swebus (Mon–Fri 7.15am–6.15pm, Sat 7.15am–3pm, Sun 9.30am–6.15pm; ☎0200/21 82 18, ⌨www.swebus.se) and Säfflebussen (Mon–Fri 9am–6pm, Sat & Sun 10am–3pm; ☎0771/15 15 15, ⌨www.safflebussen .se) both have offices here, selling tickets for destinations in Sweden, as well as Oslo, Trondheim and mainland Europe. For regional bus tickets, visit the **Tidpunkten** office (Mon–Fri 7.30am–5.45pm, Sat 8am–2pm; there's another office located in Brunnsparken). DFDS Seaways **ferries** arrive at Frihamnspiren on Hisingen, north of the river (☎031/650 650, ⌨www.dfdsseaways.se); special buses shuttle from here to the bus station (40kr) – walking across the high Göta Älvbron bridge is a long slog. When leaving, buses return to Frihamnspiren ninety minutes before sailings. Stena Line (☎031/704 06 50, ⌨www.stenaline.com) ferries from Frederikshavn in Denmark dock close to Masthuggstorget, twenty minutes' walk or a tram (#3, #9 or #11) ride west of the city centre, while those from Kiel in Germany dock 3km outside Gothenburg – take bus #491 or tram #3 or #9 into the centre.

Information

Gothenburg has two **tourist offices**. Handiest for new arrivals is the kiosk in the middle of the Nordstan shopping centre, linked to the train and bus stations by a pedestrian tunnel (Mon–Fri 9.30am–6pm, Sat 10am–5pm, Sun noon–4pm). The busy **main tourist office** is on the canalfront at Kungsportsplatsen 2 (May Mon–Fri 9.30am–6pm, Sat & Sun 10am–2pm; June & mid- to late Aug daily 9.30am–6pm; July to mid-Aug daily 9.30am–8pm; Sept–April Mon–Fri 9.30am–

The Gothenburg Pass

Buying a **Gothenburg Pass** is an excellent money-saver if you're planning to do any sightseeing. Available from tourist offices, Pressbyrån kiosks and hotels, or online at Ⓦ www.goteborg.com, it gives unlimited bus and tram travel within the city (airport and ferry buses excluded), free entry to all city museums except the Volvo Museum, admission to the Liseberg amusement park (not including rides), free car parking (see p.513), boat excursions and various other reductions, including free bike rental. Passes are available for either 24hr (210kr) or 48hr (295kr).

5pm, Sat 10am–2pm; ☏ 031/61 25 00; Ⓦ www.goteborg.com). From the train station, it's five minutes' walk across Drottningtorget and along the canal. Both offices can provide information and sell the Gothenburg Pass. You can also pick up a free copy of the trilingual, annually updated *Göteborg Guide*, which details sights, events, music and nightlife, and contains city and transport maps.

City transport

Apart from excursions north of the river or to the islands, almost everywhere of interest in Gothenburg is within easy walking distance of the centre. The wide streets are pedestrian-friendly, and the canals and grid layout of the avenues make orientation simple. If you're staying further out, however, some sort of transport may be necessary; consult the maps in the *Göteborg Guide*.

Public transport

The most convenient form of public transport are the **trams**, which clunk around the city and its outskirts on a colour-coded, eight-line system, passing all the central areas every few minutes – you can tell at a glance which line a tram is on as the route colour appears on the front. The main pick-up points are outside Central Station and in Kungsportsplatsen. During summer, there's the chance to ride on **vintage trams** (18kr, free with Gothenburg Pass), some dating from 1902, which trundle through the city centre to Liseberg. Gothenburg also has a fairly extensive **bus** network, using much the same routes as the trams, although central pedestrianization can lead to some odd and lengthy detours. You shouldn't need to use them in the city centre; routes are detailed in the text where necessary.

If you have a Gothenburg Pass, all public transport within the city is free; otherwise, you need to stamp two **coupons** per adult for a trip within the centre. These can be bought on board for 10kr each from tram and bus drivers, though it's cheaper to buy them in advance from Pressbyrån kiosks or from the Tidpunkten travel information offices (see opposite) – a seven- to eight-trip ticket card costs 100kr. Stick these in the machines on a tram or bus, and press twice for an adult, once for a child. Trams run from 5am to midnight, after which there is a night service at double the price. **Fare-dodging** carries an instant fine of 600kr – since all the ticket information is posted in English at bus and tram stops, ignorance is no defence.

Finally, a good way to get to grips with the city is to take a **paddan boat tour**, an hour-long trip around the canals and harbour; tours leave regularly from moorings on the canal by Kungsportsplatsen (daily: May & June 10am–5pm; July to mid-Aug 10am–9pm; mid- to late Aug 10am–7pm; Sept to early Oct 11am–3pm; 95kr, free with Gothenburg Pass after 3pm; Ⓦ www.paddan.com).

Cars, taxis and bikes

There's no shortage of **car parks** in the city, with a tariff of 20–30kr per hour in the centre. Buying a Gothenburg Pass gets you a free parking card, though this is not valid in privately run or multistorey car parks. The most useful car parks are the huge multistorey car parks in the Nordstan shopping centre near Central Station and the four car parks on the Heden field, near Avenyen. For information on **car rental** see p.518.

There are several **taxi** companies in Gothenburg: Kurir (☎031/27 27 27), VIP (☎031/27 16 11) and Göteborg (☎031/65 00 00) are the most reliable, with fixed prices to and from the airport. The latter offers a ten- to twenty-percent reduction for anyone travelling alone at night; check with the driver first.

Cycling is a popular and easy way to get around, since Gothenburg boasts a comprehensive series of cycle lanes and plenty of bike racks. The most central place to **rent a bike** (around 150kr per day, free with Gothenburg Pass; bring ID) is Cykelverkstan, near the main tourist office, at Parkgatan 29 (daily 10am–6pm; ☎031/711 97 70); there are only about twenty bikes, so arrive early. Alternatively, there's Millennium Cykel at Chalmersgatan 19 (☎031/18 43 00; 150kr per day), just south of Avenyn, or you can rent bikes from either Slottsskogen or Stigbergssliden youth hostels (see p.507) for 50kr per day. Serious cyclists should ask the tourist office for the excellent *Cykelkarta* (20kr), showing all cycle routes through the city and out to the archipelago.

Accommodation

Gothenburg has plenty of decent accommodation options, with no shortage of comfortable **youth hostels**, a couple of which are very central, along with **private rooms** and a number of big, city-centre **hotels**. Most of these are clustered together around the train station, and offer a high standard of service, if with fairly uniform and uninspiring decor. Summer and weekend reductions mean that even the better hotels can prove surprisingly affordable, and most places also take part in the **Gothenburg Package** scheme, which can cut costs further (see below).

Whenever you turn up, you shouldn't have any trouble finding accommodation, though in summer it's a good idea to book ahead if you're aiming to stay in one of the cheaper hotels, or in the most popular youth hostels.

Hotels and pensions

The **Gothenburg Package** scheme, coordinated by the tourist office, is a real bargain, as it bundles together accommodation, breakfast and a 24-hour Gothenburg Pass for as little as 485kr per person in a twin bedroom, with discounts for children sharing. Around forty good, central hotels take part in the scheme, which operates all week, all year. Unless otherwise stated, all the places listed below are part of the Gothenburg Package scheme, and all include breakfast in the price. Bookings for the Gothenburg Package have to be made by phoning or visiting the tourist office (60kr per booking surcharge), or online at www.goteborg.com; you can't get this offer by contacting the hotels direct.

Allén Parkgatan 10 ☎31/10 14 50, ℮hotel .allen@telia.com. Very central, sensibly priced hotel close to Avenyn and the Old Town. Rates include room-service breakfasts and parking. ❷/❸

Barken Viking Gullbergskajen ☎31/63 58 00, ℮barken.viking@liseberg.se. Moored by the Opera House, this 1906 Danish-built training ship is a charismatic and comfortable choice, with dark, cosy rooms and good service. ❷

City Lorensbergsgatan 6 ☎31/708 40 00, ⓦwww.cityhotelgbg.se. A cheapish and popular hotel, excellently positioned close to Avenyn. En-suite rooms cost 300kr more than those with shared facilities. Not in the Gothenburg Package. ❶

Eggers Drottningtorget ☎31/80 60 70, ⓦwww.bestwestern.se. The original station hotel and now part of the Best Western chain, this very characterful establishment has individually furnished bedrooms and a wealth of grand original features. One of the best-value central hotels, especially if you stay here using the Gothenburg Package. ❹/❻

Elite Plaza Västra Hamngatan 3 ☎31/720 40 40, ℮reservations@gbgplaza.elite.se. With its magnificently opulent facade, painted ceilings and mosaic floors, this is the perfect place if money is no concern: a stunning blend of contemporary and classical design. ⑤/⑥

Europa Köpmansgatan 38 ☏ 31/751 65 00, ⓦwww.scandic-hotels.com. Reputedly the biggest hotel in Sweden, with 460 rooms and a massive facade attached to the Nordstan shopping centre. Very plush – all rooms are en suite with bath tubs – and breakfasts are huge. ③/⑥

Hotel 11 Maskingatan 11 ☏31/779 11 11, ⓦwww .hotel11.se. At the harbour, on the site of an old shipbuilding yard, with views across to Hisingen, this is one of the city's most interesting and stylish options. Take the *Älv Snabben* boat (Mon–Fri 6am–11.30pm every 30min, shorter hours on weekends; 16kr, free with Gothenburg Pass) in the direction of Klippan from in front of the Opera House at Lilla Bommen – get off at Eriksberg. ③/⑤

Lilton Föreningsgatan 9 ☏31/82 88 08, ⓔhotel .lilton@acrewoodab.se. Close to the Haga district, this is a small, old, ivy-covered place set among trees with very friendly, informal service. 100kr reduction at weekends; not in the Gothenburg Package. ③

Maria Erikssons Pensionat Chalmersgatan 27a ☏31/20 70 30, ⓕ16 64 63. Just ten rooms, but

well positioned on a road running parallel with Avenyn. Breakfast isn't included, and you can't stay as part of the Gothenburg Package. ①

Rica City Hotel Burggrevegatan 25 ☏31/771 00 80, ⓦwww.rica.se. Comfortable hotel close to Central Station; en-suite rooms with cable TV, plus a solarium (30kr) and a free sauna. ③

Robinson Södra Hamngatan 2 ☏31/80 25 21, ⓦwww.hotelrobinson.com. Facing Brunnspark, this cheap central hotel has classically furnished rooms, and still boasts its original facade – the building was part of the old Furstenburg Palace. Not part of the Gothenburg Package scheme. ②/③

SAS Radisson Scandinavia Södra Hamngatan 59–65 ☏31/80 60 00, ⓦwww.radissonsas.com. Opposite the train station, and exuding all the usual glitz: the atrium foyer is like a shopping mall with glass lifts and fountains; bedrooms are all pastel shades and birch wood. ④/⑥

🏃 **Scandic Rubinen** Avenyn 24, ☏031/751 54 00, ⓦwww.scandic-hotels.com. Completely renovated, with pleasant, modern rooms, and now boasting an excellent restaurant/bar (see p.516). ④/⑥

Hostels and private rooms

Gothenburg's cheapest accommodation options are either a **private room** (from 175kr per person in a double, 225kr for a single), bookable through the tourist office (60kr booking fee), or a bed in one of the **youth hostels**. All the hostels listed below are run by the STF and are open all year unless otherwise stated. Other than *Partille*, they all have private double rooms (①), too. It's wise to book ahead in summer.

Göteborgs Minihotel Tredje Långgatan 31 ☏31/24 10 23, ⓦwww.minihotel.se. Open all year, this uninspiring hostel is nevertheless well placed for the alternative scene around the Linné area.

Kärralund Olbergsgatan 1 ☏31/84 02 00, ⓦwww.liseberg.se. Four kilometres from the centre, close to Liseberg amusement park – take tram #5 to Welandergatan, in the direction of Torp. Non-smoking rooms available, plus cabins and a campsite (see p.508). Breakfast can only be ordered by groups.

Kviberg Kvibergsvägen 5 ☏31/43 50 55, ⓦwww .vandrarhem.com. In Gamlestad, 10min by tram #6, #7 or #11 from Central Station. Cheap private rooms (sleeping 1–6) with bunk beds and shared facilities.

Masthuggsterrassen Masthuggsterrassen 8 ☏31/42 48 20, ⓔmasthuggsterrassen .vandrarhem@telia.com. Up the steps from Masthuggstorget and a couple of minutes' walk from the Stena Line ferry terminal from Denmark.

Partille Landvettervagen, Partille ☏ 31/44 65 01,

ⓦwww.partillevandrarhem.com. Fifteen kilometres east of the city (bus #513 to Åstebo; 30min), this hostel has a solarium and day room with TV.

🏃 **Slottsskogen** Vegatan 21 ☏31/42 65 20, ⓔemail@Slottsskogenvh.se. Superbly appointed and well-designed family-run hostel, just two minutes' walk from Linnégatan and not far from Slottsskogparken. Take tram #1 or #6 to Olivedalsgatan.

Stigbergssliden Stigbergssliden 10 ☏31/24 16 20, ⓦwww.hostel-gothenburg.com. Excellent hostel, well placed for ferries to or from Denmark, being just west of the Linné area, down Första Långgatan. All rooms have basins, and there's disabled access, laundry facilities (20kr) and pleasant back courtyard. Breakfast is 40kr, and bike rental costs 50kr per day.

Torrekulla Kallered ☏31/795 14 95, ⓦwww .stfturist.se. Pleasantly situated 15km south of the city, with lots of room, a free sauna and a nearby bathing lake. A ten-minute train journey from Central Station to Mölndal, then bus #760.

Campsites and cabins

Two of the following campsites also provide **cabins**, which are worth considering, especially if there are more than two of you. Facilities are invariably squeaky clean and in good working order – there's usually a well-equipped kitchen, too – but you'll have to pay extra for bedding. Prices for cabins are given below; if you want to **camp**, you'll pay around 100kr for two people in July or August (50kr the rest of the year).

Askims Strand ☏ 31/28 62 61, ⊚ www .liseberg.se. Set beside sandy beaches 12km from the centre: bus #80, or the Blå Express bus. Open early May to late Aug (office daily 9am–noon & 3–6pm, slightly later Thurs–Sat); four-bed cabins cost 615kr in high season, 495kr in low.

Kärralund Olbergsgatan ☏ 31/84 02 00, ⊚ www .liseberg.se. Four kilometres from the centre, close

to Liseberg amusement park – take tram #5 to Welandergatan, in the direction of Torp. Set among forest and lakes, it's open all year; four-bed cabins cost 615kr; 695kr with your own toilet (50kr discount outside June–Aug).

Lilleby Havsbad ☏ 31/56 50 66, ⊛ 56 16 05. Take bus #25 and change to the #23 at Lilleby-vägen. It takes forty minutes to reach, but has a splendid seaside location.

The City

Everything of interest in Gothenburg lies south of the **Göta River**, and there's rarely any need to cross the water. This is a fairly compact city, and easy to get around, so you can cover most of the sights in just a day or two, although to get the most from your stay, allow a few more days and slow your pace down to a stroll – which will put you in step with the locals.

At the heart of the city is the historic **Old Town**, and while Gothenburg's attractions are by no means restricted to this area, its picturesque elegance makes it the best place to start. Tucked between the Göta River to the north and the zigzagging Rosenlunds Canal to the south, old Gothenburg's tight grid of streets are lined with impressive facades and boast an interesting food market and a couple of worthwhile museums – the **City Museum** and, up by the harbour, the Maritiman **maritime museum**. Just across the canal that skirts the southern edges of the Old Town is **Trädgårdsföreningen** park, in summer full of picnicking Gothenburgers.

Heading further south, **Avenyn** (officially Kungsportsavenyn) is Gothenburg's showcase boulevard, alive with showy restaurants and bars. However, it's the roads off Avenyn that hold the area's real interest, with trendy 24-hour café-bars and some of Gothenburg's best museums: in a small area called **Vasastan** to the southwest, you'll find the **Röhsska Design Museum** and, further south in **Götaplatsen**, the city **Konstmuseum**. For family entertainment day or night, the famous **Liseberg amusement park**, just to the southeast of Avenyn, has been pulling in the crowds (and throwing them about) since the 1920s.

Vasastan stretches west to **Haga**, the city's old working-class district, now thoroughly gentrified and fashionable. Haga Nygatan, the main thoroughfare, heads towards Linnégatan, the arterial road through the **Linné** district. The area is home to Gothenburg's most interesting evening haunts, with cafés, bars and restaurants dotted amongst long-established antique emporiums and sex shops. Further out, the rolling **Slottsskogsparken** holds the **Natural History Museum**, but is perhaps most appealing as a place to relax and enjoy the sun.

The Old Town and harbour

The **Old Town** is divided in two by the **Stora Hamn Canal**, to the north of which are most of the main sights and the harbour, where the decaying shipyards make for a dramatic backdrop. The streets south of the Stora Hamn, stretching down to the Rosenlunds Canal, are perfect for an afternoon's leisurely stroll, with some quirky cafés, food markets and junk shops to dip into, as well as Sweden's oldest synagogue. Overlooking the Stora Hamn is Gothenburg's main square, **Gustav Adolfs Torg**, the best place to start your explorations.

North of the Stora Hamn Canal

At the centre of stately **Gustav Adolfs Torg**, a copper statue of the city's founder, Gustav Adolf, points ostentatiously at the ground where he reputedly declared "Here I will build my city." The statue is a copy, however: the German-made original was kidnapped on its way to Sweden and the Gothenburgers commissioned a new one rather than pay the ransom.

To the west of the square stands the **Rådhus**. Beyond its rather dull classical colonnaded facade, the interior of its extension was designed by the innovative functionalist architect E.G. Asplund in 1936 and retains its original glass lifts, mussel-shaped drinking fountains and huge areas of laminated aspen. Facing the canal is the white, double-columned 1842 **Börshuset**, the former stock exchange. If you can persuade the attendants to let you in, you'll be rewarded with magnificent banqueting and concert halls, and smaller rooms with a riot of red and blue stucco inspired by the eighteenth-century excavations at Pompeii.

△ Gothenburg harbour, from Lilla Bommen

Heading north from the square along the filled-in canal of Östra Hamngatan leads you to the **Nordstan shopping centre**, Sweden's biggest. Despite several attempts to jazz it up, it remains a depressingly bland design; the shopping is good, though, and you might also venture inside to visit the tourist kiosk or one of the ferry company offices. It's worth cutting through Nordstan to see the city's impressive **Central Station**. One of the oldest in the country, dating from 1856, it retains its original facade and boasts a grand and marvellously preserved interior. Look out for the wood beam-ends in the ticket hall, each one carved into the likeness of a city council member of the day.

At its far end, Östra Hamngatan runs into **Lilla Bommen** (until the completion of the large traffic tunnel that will divert the ring road under the city centre, it may be better to use the pedestrian bridge from the northern end of the Nordstan shopping centre). Here, Gothenburg's industrial decline comes together with its artistic regeneration to dramatic visual effect: to the west, the cranes of dormant shipyards loom across the sky, a backdrop to industrial-themed sculptures in bronze and pink granite dotted along the waterfront. The **Opera House** (⊕031/10 82 03, ⊛www .opera.se) to the left was designed with conscious industrial styling; phone ahead or contact the tourist office for information about tours. To the right, **Utkiken** ("The Lookout"; June–Aug daily 10am–4pm; Sept–May Mon–Fri 10am–4pm; 30kr, free with Gothenburg Pass), designed by the Scottish architect Ralph Erskine in the late 1980s, is an 86-metre-high office block taking the form of a half-used red lipstick. Its top storey offers panoramic views of the city and harbour.

Boats leave Lilla Bommen harbour for the popular half-hour excursion to the island fortress of **Nya Elfsborg** (mid-May to Aug, 6 daily between 9.30am–4.30pm; 110kr, free with Gothenburg Pass; ⊕031/60 96 70, ⊛www.borjessons.com). Built in the seventeenth century to defend the harbour and the city, the surviving buildings have been turned into a **museum** and café. There are tours in English (included in the price of the boat trip) given by guides in period dress around the square tower, chapel and prison cells.

Just west along the quay is **Maritiman** (March–Oct daily 10am–4pm, May–Aug until 8pm; Nov Fri–Sun 10am–4pm; ⊛www.maritiman.se; 60kr, free with Gothenburg Pass), the self-proclaimed "biggest floating marine museum in the world". An interesting experience, even for non-enthusiasts, it comprises 19 boats, including a 1915 lightship, a submarine and a fire float, giving a glimpse of how seamen lived and worked on board, plus exhibits on Gothenburg's long-gone shipbuilding era. There's a good café and restaurant here, too.

From Maritiman, it's a short walk to Gothenburg's oldest secular building, the **Kronhuset** on Kronhusgatan, currently a concert hall. Built by the Dutch in 1642 as an artillery depot for the city's garrison, this was where the five-year-old Karl XI was proclaimed king in 1660. Set in the eighteenth-century wings that flank the original building are the **Kronhusbodarna** (Mon–Fri 10am–5pm, Sat 10am–2pm), a cluster of small, pricey shops specializing in gold, silver and glasswork, and an atmospheric vaulted café with seating in the courtyard.

A couple of blocks further south, the **Stadsmuseum** (City Museum; May–Aug daily 10am–5pm; Sept–April Tues–Sun 10am–5pm, Wed until 8pm; 40kr; ⊛www .stadsmuseum.goteborg.se) is Gothenburg's primary museum. Located at Norra Hamngatan 12, it's housed in Ostindiska Huset, the offices, store and auction house that were constructed in 1750 for the enormously influential **Swedish East India Company**. Granted sole Swedish rights to trade with China in 1731, the company monopolized Far East commerce for over eighty years, the only condition being that the spices, silk and porcelain it brought back were to be sold in Gothenburg. The museum itself is well worth a browse, not least for its rich interior, a mix of stone pillars, stained glass and frescoes. Head first to the third floor, where there are exhibitions on the East India Company, allowing a look at the renovated auction hall. The section devoted to industry here is also impressive, a well-designed exhibition relating Gothenburg's twentieth-century history, with displays on shipping and working conditions in the textile factories at the beginning of the century.

South of the Stora Hamn Canal

Across Stora Hamn just to the west of the Stadsmuseum lies **Lilla Torg**, with its statue of Jonas Alstromer, who introduced the potato to Sweden in the eighteenth century. Walk on to the quayside at **Stenpiren**, the spot where hundreds of emigrants said their last goodbyes before sailing off to the United States. The original granite **Delaware Monument** was carted off to America in the early twentieth century, and it wasn't until 1938 that celebrated sculptor Carl Mille cast a replacement in bronze, which stands here looking out to sea.

Back at Lilla Torg, walk down Västra Hamngatan, which leads off the southern side of the square, to the city's cathedral; on the way you'll pass **Antikhallarna** (Mon–Fri 10am–6pm, Sat 10am–2pm), a clutch of pricey antique shops set in a fantastic building with a gilded ceiling and regal marble stairs leading up to a café. A few blocks south of here, to the left off Västra Hamngatan, is the classically styled **Cathedral** (Mon–Fri 8am–5pm, Sat 8am–3pm, Sun 10am–3pm). Built in 1827 (the two previous cathedrals were destroyed by fires at a rate of one a century), four giant sandstone columns stand at the portico, and inside there's an opulent gilded altarpiece. The plain white walls concentrate your eyes on the unusual post-Resurrection cross, devoid of a Jesus, whose gilded grave clothes are strewn below. Another quirky feature are the twin glassed-in verandas that run down either side, designed for the bishop's "private conversations".

Continuing east past the cathedral and north, on Östra Hamngatan, towards Stora Hamn Canal, the leafy square known as **Brunnspark** soon comes into view, with Gustav Adolfs Torg just across the canal. The sedate house facing the square (now the snazzy *Palace* restaurant and nightclub) was once home to Pontus and Gothilda Furstenburg, the city's leading arts patrons in the late nineteenth century, who converted the top floor into an art gallery, the first in Gothenburg to be lit with electric light. They later donated their entire collection – the biggest batch of Nordic paintings in the country – to the city's Konstmuseum. As a tribute to the Furstenburgs, the museum has made over the *Palace*'s top floor into an exact replica of the original gallery (see p.513) – you can wander upstairs and see the richly ornate plasterwork and gilding much as it was.

Along Roselunds Canal

Marking the southern perimeter of old Gothenburg, the meandering Rosenlunds Canal follows the spiky contours of the former city walls, and its banks make for a fine twenty-minute stroll past pretty waterside views and a number of interesting diversions.

Just east of Brunnspark, **Stora Nygatan** wends its way south along the canal's most scenic stretch, with classical buildings stuccoed in cinnamon and cream on one side, and the green expanse of Trädgårdsföreningen park (see p.508) on the other. Among all the architectural finery sits mainland Sweden's oldest synagogue, the **Great Synagogue**, inaugurated in 1855. This simple domed structure hides one of the most exquisite interiors of any European synagogue: the ceiling and walls are a rich mixture of blues, reds and gold, with Moorish patterns stunningly interwoven with Viking leaf designs. An impressive restoration programme has brought the original colours into brilliant relief. Sadly, security concerns mean that it can only be visited by calling ☏031/10 94 00 first.

Heading south from the synagogue, you'll pass **Kungsportsplatsen**, in the centre of which stands a useful landmark, a sculpture known as the *Copper Mare* – though whoever gave it its name obviously knew more about metallurgy than physiology. Also on the square is the main tourist office. A few minutes further on, and a block in from the canal at Kungstorget (the square adjacent to Kungsportsplatsen) is **Saluhallen** (Mon–Fri 9am–6pm, Sat 9am–2pm), a pretty, barrel-roofed indoor market built in the 1880s. Busy and full of atmosphere, it's a great place to wander around; there's a flower market outside.

Five minutes from here is another food market, the neo-Gothic **Feskekörkan**, or "Fish Church" (Tues–Thurs 9am–5pm, Fri 9am–6pm, Sat 9am–1.30pm). Despite its undeniably ecclesiastical appearance, the closest this 1874 building gets to religion is in the devotion shown by the fish lovers who come to buy and sell here. Inside, every kind of fish lies gaping in gleaming, pungent mounds of silver, pink and black flesh; there's a very small, very good restaurant in the gallery upstairs (see p.515).

The Trädgårdsföreningen

Before you merge into the crowds of Avenyn, take time out to visit the **Trädgårds- föreningen**, or Garden Society Park (May–Aug daily 7am–9pm, 15kr, free with Gothenburg Pass; Sept–April 7am–7.30pm, free), whose main entrance is just over the canal bridge from Kungsportsplatsen. For once, this park really does lives up to its blurb – "a green oasis in the heart of the city". Among the trees and lawns are a surprising number of experimental sculptures, designed to blend in with their natural surroundings. Within the park, the **Palm House** (daily: June–Aug 10am–6pm; Sept–May 10am–4pm; 20kr, ticket covers entry to the Botanical Gardens), built in 1878, looks like a huge English-style conservatory and contains a wealth of very un-Swedish plant life.

Avenyn and around

From the park, the wide cobbled length of Kungportsavenyn runs all the way southeast to Götaplatsen. Known more simply as **Avenyn**, this is the city's liveliest – if most blandly showy – thoroughfare, lined with nineteenth-century buildings, almost all of their ground floors converted into cafés, bars or restaurants. Gothenburg's young and beautiful strut up and down and sip overpriced drinks at tables that spill onto the street from mid-spring till September. It's enjoyable to sit here and watch life go by, but for all its glamour most of the tourist-oriented shops and brasseries are interchangeable and the grandeur of the city's industrial past is better evoked in the less spoiled mansions along roads such as Parkgatan, at right angles to Avenyn.

Vasastan, Götaplatsen and Liseberg

Once you've had your fill of Avenyn, take one of the roads off to the west and wander into the district of Vasastan, where the streets are lined with fine nineteenth-century and National Romantic architecture, and the cafés are cheaper and more laid-back. On Vasagatan, the main street through the area, is the excellent **Röhsska Design Museum** at 37–39, Sweden's only museum of applied arts (Tues noon–8pm, Wed–Fri noon–5pm, Sat & Sun 11am–5pm; 40kr, free with Gothenburg Pass; ⓦwww.designmuseum.se). Built in 1916, this is an aesthete's Aladdin's cave, each floor concentrating on different areas of decorative and functional art, from early dynasty Chinese ceramics to European arts and crafts of the sixteenth century. The first floor holds an especially interesting section devoted to twentieth-century design (from garden gnomes to the Absolut vodka bottle) – enough to send anyone on a nostalgia trip. The exhibition ends with a brilliant film about consumerism and the need for anarchy in order to achieve true happiness.

At the top of Avenyn, **Götaplatsen** is modern Gothenburg's main square, its focal point Carl Milles' **Poseidon**, a giant bronze nude with the physique of a body-builder and a staggeringly ugly face; the size of the figure's penis caused outrage when the sculpture was unveiled in 1930 and it was subsequently dramatically reduced. From the front, Poseidon appears to be squeezing the daylights out of a large fanged fish – a symbol of local trade – but if you climb the steps of the **Konserthuset** (Concert House) to the right, it becomes clear that Milles won the battle over Poseidon's manhood to stupendous effect.

Behind Poseidon looms the impressive **Konstmuseum** (Art Museum; Tues & Thurs 11am–4pm, Wed 11am–9pm, Fri–Sun 11am–5pm; 40kr, free with Gothenburg Pass; ⓦwww.konstmuseum.goteborg.se), whose massive, symmetrical facade is reminiscent of 1930s Fascist architecture. One of the city's finest museums, it is easy to spend half a day absorbing the diverse and extensive collections. The **Hasselblad Centre** (ⓦwww.hasselbladcenter.se) on the ground floor shows excellent changing photographic exhibitions, while upstairs there are postwar and contemporary Scandinavian paintings, a room full of French Impressionists, and a collection of Italian and Spanish paintings from the sixteenth to eighteenth centuries. Best of all, though, are the **Fürstenburg Galleries** on the sixth floor, which celebrate the work of some of Scandinavia's most prolific and revered artists from the early twentieth century. Well-known paintings by Anders Zorn and Carl Wilhelmson depict the seasons and landscapes of the Nordic countries and evoke a vivid picture of life a hundred years ago. Keep an eye out for Ernst Josephson's sensitive portraits and a couple of Hugo Birger paintings depicting the interior of the Fürstenburg Gallery. Also worth a look is the room of Carl Larsson's fantastical and bright wall-sized canvases.

Just a few minutes' walk southeast from Götaplatsen lies Sweden's largest amusement park, **Liseberg** (late April to June & late Aug daily 3–11pm; July to mid-Aug daily noon–11pm, some Fri & Sat evenings until midnight; Sept Sat 1–11pm, Sun noon–8pm; 60kr, under-7s free, free with Gothenburg Pass; all-day ride pass 265kr, or 15-60kr per ride). Dating from 1923, it's a league away from today's neon and plastic entertainment complexes, with flowers, trees, fountains and clusters of lights – more Hansel and Gretel than Disneyland. Old and young dance to live bands, and while the young and raucous predominate at night, it's all good-humoured. The two newest attractions are the "Kanonen" roller coaster, which shoots you from 0 to 75km/hr in under two seconds, and a traditional wooden big dipper, "Balder".

Near Liseberg, a glass, wood and concrete building draped against a hill holds the impressive **Universeum** nature and science discovery centre (early June to mid Aug daily 10am–8pm; rest of year Tues–Sun 10am–6pm; 135kr, free with Gothenburg Pass; ⓦwww.universeum.se). Water is the main theme: starting with a glacier at the top of the building, 3km of paths follow its journey through a variety of Swedish landscapes to the Baltic Sea. There are detailed English texts about the flora and fauna of each environment. The tour ends in a tropical rainforest with free-flying birds and butterflies. Huge sharks glide around the walk-through oceanarium, while an open tank nearby allows you to stroke a friendly ray. There are good-value cafés on the roof or in the atrium.

Next door stands the brand new **Världkulturmuseet** (Museum of World Culture; Tues, Sat & Sun noon–5pm, Wed–Fri noon–9pm; free; ⓦwww .varldskulturmuseet.se), a successful blend of public meeting place and museum. The changing exhibitions focus on current themes seen from an international perspective, and are very well done. There's a good café, a theatre and a cinema, too; check the website for the programme.

Haga and Linné

West of Avenyn, and a ten-minute stroll up Vasagatan (or tram #3, #6, #9 or #11 to Hagakyrkan), lies the district of **Haga**, the city's oldest working-class area, now transformed into the Greenwich Village of Gothenburg. Centred on **Haga Nygatan**, Haga is one of the city's most picturesque quarters, its cobbled streets lined with pricey alternative-type cafés and antique clothes shops, frequented by right-on and well-off twenty- and thirty-somethings. Although there are a couple of good restaurants along Haga Nygatan, this is really somewhere to come during the day, when tables are put out on the street and the atmosphere is friendly and villagey, if a little self-consciously fashionable. An opportunity for a break in your wanderings is provided by the beautifully renovated **Hagabadet** (Mon–Thurs 6.30am–9.30pm, Fri 6.30am–8.30pm, Sat 9am–6pm, Sun 10am–6pm) on Södra Allégatan 3, a former bathhouse for the working classes that's been glammed up into a very fine health spa, with the prettiest of pools in an Art Nouveau-style setting, as well as a Roman bath, gym and massage area. A one-day card to use the Roman bath complex including sauna and pool costs a steep 360kr, or 100kr between 6.30am and 9am.

West of Haga is the cosmopolitan district of **Linné**, named after the botanist Carl von Linné (better known by the Latinized version of his name, Linnaeus), who originated the system of plant classification that's used the world over. Recent years have seen so many new cafés and restaurants spring up along **Linnégatan** – which runs along the western end of Haga Nygatan – that this street of tall, Dutch-style buildings has become a second Avenyn, but without the attitude.

Five minutes' walk south of Linnégatan (or tram #1 or #6 to Linnéplatsen) is the huge, tranquil mass of greenery that constitutes the **Slottsskogsparken**. Home to farm animals and a variety of birds, including pink flamingos in summer, there's plenty here to entertain children. The rather dreary **Natural History Museum** (daily 11am–5pm; 60kr, 20kr with Gothenburg Pass; ®www.gnm.se) within the grounds prides itself on being the city's oldest, dating from 1833. Its endless cases of stuffed birds seem particularly depressing after the squawking, living ones outside, and the only worthwhile item is the world's only stuffed blue whale, which stranded on a nearby beach in 1865 and now contains a Victorian sitting room complete with red velvet sofas (open just once a year). On the south side of Slottsskogsparken are the large **Botanical Gardens** (daily 9am–dusk; greenhouses May–Aug daily 10am–5pm, Sept–April daily 10am–4pm; free; greenhouses 20kr, free with Gothenburg Pass), which holds some 12,000 species of plants; highlights are the Japanese valley and the rock gardens.

Eating

Gothenburg has a multitude of **eating** places catering for every taste and budget. The foreign restaurants that opened here in the early 1990s are now less prevalent than the host of simpler, pan-European eateries that draw on Swedish staples such as herring and salmon dishes, good breads and, in summer, glorious soft fruits. The emphasis now is much more on casual eating: Gothenburgers are as likely to munch on filled ciabattas served with substantial salads as sit down to three-course meals. Naturally, there are great fish restaurants, including some of the most exclusive establishments in town, while for less costly eating there are a growing number of low-priced pasta places, alongside the staple pizza parlours and burger bars.

Café life has really come into its own in Gothenburg, with a profusion of places throughout the city joining the traditional *konditori* (bakeries with tearoom attached). Nowadays, it's easy to stroll from one café to another at any time of day or night, and tuck into enormous sandwiches and gorgeous cakes. Cafés also offer a wide range of light meals, and are the best option for good food at reasonable prices; the most interesting places are concentrated in the fashionable Haga and Linné districts.

Markets and supermarkets

The bustling, historic **Saluhallen** at Kungstorget is a delightful sensory experience, with a huge range of meat, fish, fruit, vegetables and delectable breads; there are also a couple of cheap coffee and snack bars here. **Saluhall Briggen**, on the corner of Tredje Långgatan and Nordhemsgatan in the Linné area, is more continental and much smaller than Saluhallen, specializing in high-quality meats, fish, cheeses and mouthwatering deli delights. Also in Linné, at Övra Husargatan 12, Delitalia is a terrific Italian delicatessen selling anything you could want for a picnic. The Konsum supermarket at Avenyn 26 (daily 9am–11pm, Sun from 11am) has a wide range of the usual staples and a good deli counter.

Cafés and restaurants

If you want to avoid paying over the odds, it's generally a good idea to steer clear of Avenyn itself (where prices are much higher than in Haga or Linné), and to eat your main meal at **lunchtime**, when you can fill up on *dagens rätt* deals for 55–75kr. Otherwise, expect to pay 80–150kr for a main dish in most restaurants, a lot higher in the more exclusive places. It's not usually necessary to **book** tables, but we've given numbers for places where you might need to; things get especially busy between the peak hours of 7 and 9pm.

The Old Town

Ahlstroms Konditori Korsgatan 2. Dating from 1901, this traditional-style café/bakery is very much of the old school, as are many of its patrons. While modernization has watered down the original features, it's still worth a visit for its good selection of cakes, plus lunches for 72kr.

Froken Olssons Kafe Östra Larmgatan 14. Heaps of sandwiches, salads and sumptuous desserts served up in a rural-style atmosphere. Look out for the mountains of giant meringues on tiered, silver cake trays. Sandwiches for 30–60kr, and a good-value lunchtime vegetarian salad buffet for 50kr.

Gabriel at Feskekörka Feskekörkan fish market ☏31/13 90 51. Excellent fish restaurant overlooking the stalls below, with mains from 145kr.

Grande E.t.c. Kungsgatan 12 ☏031/701 77 84. Big brother to *E.t.c.* at Vasaplatsen (see below), serving similar, very fresh pasta dishes from 95kr.

Greta's Drottninggatan 35. Stylish, casual and popular bar-restaurant drawing a mixed gay and straight clientele. The wide-ranging menu has fish, meat and vegetarian options. Small salads start at 60kr, with more substantial meals of meat, fish or shellfish costing 130–170kr.

Mauritz Kaffehus Fredgatan 2. Small and unassuming café run by the great grandson of its founder, who began importing coffee into Gothenburg in 1888. Come here for espressos and cappuccinos; there's hardly room to sit down, but the owner will tell you that standing makes the ambience more Italian.

Avenyn and around

28+ Götabergsgatan 28 ☏31/20 21 61. Very fine French-style gourmet restaurant, whose name refers to the fat percentage of its renowned cheese, sold in the shop near the entrance (9am–11pm). Service is excellent. Closed Sun.

Café Dali Vasagatan 42. Friendly, studenty and stylish basement café with good sandwiches and cakes.

Café Teatergatan Teatergatan 36. Somewhat artsy place where you can sit at one of the black-and-white swivel chairs and try sandwiches and salads.

Condeco Avenyn 4. Excellent café with its own bakery. Worth visiting for the funky toilets alone.

E.t.c. Vasaplatsen 4. This cool, elegant grey-painted basement is the best place in town for superb home-made pasta. Lunch 55kr; dinner menu also offers meat and fish dishes.

🏃 **Eva's Paley** Avenyn 39. A popular sprawling café/bar with great cakes and muffins, reasonably priced food and Avenyn's largest and nicest terrace.

Frågetecknet Södravägen 20. Very popular spot just a minute's walk from Götaplatsen, with a name that translates as "the question mark". Eat out in the conservatory, or inside to watch the chefs at work, carefully preparing Balkan-influenced food. Steak at 230kr is the most expensive thing on the menu, but there's also pasta for 89kr.

Java Café Vasagatan 23. Studenty, bookshelf-filled Parisian-style coffee house decorated with such things as a collection of thermos flasks. Serves a wide range of coffees, and breakfasts for 39kr – a good Sunday morning hangout.

Junggrens Café Avenyn 37. One of only a couple of decently priced Avenyn cafés, with good snacks and sandwiches. Atmospheric and convivial, it's been run for decades by a charismatic old Polish woman and her sulky staff.

Lai Wa Storgatan 11. One of Gothenburg's better Chinese restaurants, with a wide variety of dishes (from 90kr) – try the Peking soup. Good lunch for just 45kr.

🏃 **Smaka** Vasaplatsen 3 ☏31/13 22 47. Traditional Swedish dishes (mains 140–180kr) enjoyed by a lively, young crowd in a striking blue interior.

Tai Pak Arkivsgatan 4, just off Avenyn near Götaplatsen. Decent Chinese restaurant serving a three-course special for 69kr, and individual dishes for 80–120kr.

Tintin Engelbrektsgatan 22. Very busy 24hr café with mounds of food and cheap coffee, and a laid-back, student atmosphere.

Haga and Linné

Café Kringlan Haga Nygatan 13. The best spot in town for wonderful chocolate pies, bagels, strudels, generous open sandwiches and people-watching. Great breakfast (50kr) and lunch (59kr) deals.

🏃 **Cyrano** Prinsgatan 7 ☏31/14 31 10. This superb, authentic Provençal bistro is a must, specializing in wood-fired pizzas and French cooking with three-course pizza (145kr) and meat (195kr) menus. There's a smaller, more central sister restaurant at Viktoriagatan 26.

Hemma Hos Haga Nygatan 12 ☏31/13 40 90. Popular restaurant full of quaint old furniture, serving upmarket Swedish food including fish dishes (mains from 145kr) till midnight. Closed Sun.

Hos Pelle Djupedalsgatan 2 ☏31/12 10 31. Sophisticated wine bar off Linnégatan, not cheap at over 259kr for a main course, but serving snacks as well as more economical bar meals, and decorated with intriguing abstract artwork. Closed mid-June to mid-Aug.

Jacob's Café Haga Nygatan 10. *The* place to sit outside and people-watch; inside, the decor is fabulous, with some fine Art Nouveau lamps.

Krakow Karl Gustavsgatan 28 ☏31/20 33 74. Burly staff serving big, basic and very filling Polish food in a large, dark restaurant. Cheap, too, with mains from 95kr. Closed Sun & July.

Linné Terassen Corner of Linnégatan and Landsvägsgatan ☏31/24 08 90. Sit at polished tables beneath chandeliers in this beautifully restored wooden house nestling in rough-hewn rock. Fish and meat dishes go for 160–180kr, and there's a wide drinks list and terrace seating.

Louice Värmlandsgatan 18. Justifiably popular and unpretentious neighbourhood restaurant, with occasional live music. Standard main courses are expensive, but look out for the excellent-value specials at 79kr. There's a full children's menu (35kr) in English, too. Closed July.

Pasta Gambero Övre Husargatan 5 ☏31/13 78 38. The best of a number of good, reasonably priced Italian eateries on this long street just south of Skansparken. The servings are generous and the service very obliging.

Publik Andra Långgatan 20. Young, funky and unashamedly retro place where people come to drink and lounge, with old velvet sofas and scores of LPs to leaf through on a nostalgia trip. Coffee and muffins, or nachos and ciabattas, cost 35–50kr.

Rumpanbar Linnégatan 38b, ☏031/775 83 00. Lovely café/restaurant on the up-and-coming section of Linnégatan, with outdoor seating and great-value meals (mains from 90kr, pizza from 50kr).

Sjöbaren Haga Nygatan 27. Small fish and shellfish restaurant on the ground floor of a traditional Governor's house building. Moderate Prices (*dagens* 75kr).

Solrosen Kaponjargatan 4a ☏31/711 66 97. The oldest vegetarian restaurant in Gothenburg, this is the place to come for well-prepared veggie and vegan delights; snacks from 40kr and mains from 90kr. The *dagens* costs 65kr.

Thai Garden Andra Långgatan 18. Nothing special to look at, but big portions and excellent service at good prices – stuff yourself silly at the 65kr lunch buffet.

Drinking

There's an excellent choice of places to **drink** in Gothenburg, but aside from a small number of British- and Irish-style pubs, even the hippest bars also serve food, and have more of a restaurant atmosphere. Listed below are some of the most popular pubs and bar-restaurants in the city, but note that many of the cafés and restaurants listed in the previous section are also good places for a beer, especially those around Avenyn and in Linné. Although there are a number of long-established bars in the Old Town, the atmosphere in this area is generally a bit low-key at night.

The Old Town

Bishops Arms Västra Larmgatan 1 (and Avenyn 36). Attached to the glamorous *Elite Plaza* hotel, this pub boasts a wide range of beers. It's all faux "olde Englishe" inside, but very nicely done.

Dubliners Östra Hamngatan 50b. For a while now, Swedes have been overtaken with a nostalgia for all things old and Irish – or at least a Swedish interpretation of what's old and Irish. This is the most popular exponent.

The Palace Brunnsparken. The rather splendid former home of the Furstenburgs and their art galleries (see p.511) is a very popular spot, with live bands on Thursdays.

Avenyn and around

Brasserie Lipp Avenyn 8. No longer the hippest place on Avenyn, *Lipp* is expensive and so attracts a slightly older crowd – but a crowd it is, especially during summer.

Hard Rock Café Avenyn 10. A very loud young crowd fills this outpost of T-shirt fame. Not a place for a drink and a chat, unless you want to stand out on the street.

Nivå Avenyn 9. Stylish, popular bar with a modern interior heavy on mosaic decor, and a bar and restaurant on different levels.

Ruby Nuevo Latino Bar Avenyn 24. The glitzy restaurant/bar of the *Scandic Rubinen* hotel serves up great Mediterranean food and tapas snacks.

Studs Götabergsgatan 17, off Engelbrecksgatan behind Vasa Church. This is the hub of Gothenburg student life, with a pub, bar and restaurant serving cheap beer. If you haven't got student ID, friendly bluffing should get you in.

Haga and Linné

Beefeater Inn Plantagegatan 1. One of the bevvy of British-oriented neighbourhood pubs that are very in-vogue with Swedes generally. This one really goes overboard, with a stylistic mishmash of red-telephone-box doors, tartan walls and staff in kilts.

Cigarren Järntorget 6, opposite the Folketshus. Looks as if it's been here forever, but has actually only existed since the revamping of this classic,

old workers' square. Huge range of cigars, and lots of coffees and teas alongside the beers and wines.

Gillestugan Järntorget 6. Cosy and panelled without being over the top, this bar has plenty of outdoor seating, and offers full meals such as beef fillet at 98kr or seafood burgers at 125kr.

Stars & Stripes Järntorget 4. Though rather unappealing on the outside and slightly rough within, *Stars & Stripes* boasts some remarkable painted ceilings and a very down-to-earth atmosphere.

The Rover Andra Långgatan 12. Run-of-the-mill Anglo-Irish pub selling Boddingtons, with other lagers, ales and cider on tap, plus a wide range of bottled beers. Lamb, steaks and trout dishes from 70kr.

Nightlife and entertainment

There are plenty of other things to do in Gothenburg at night besides drink. The city has a brisk **live-music scene** – jazz, rock and classical – as well as the usual cinema and theatre opportunities and, despite the fact that Gothenburg has never been particularly noted for its **club** scene, a range of hangouts that make for an appealing and lively night out. The details below should give you some ideas, but it's worth picking up the Friday edition of the *Göteborgs Posten*, which has a weekly listings supplement, *Aveny* – it's in Swedish but not very difficult to decipher.

Clubs

During the past few years, Gothenburg's old, mediocre **clubs** have been usurped in popularity by a cluster of smaller, laid-back joints around Viktoriagatan and Storgatan in Vasastan.

Diamond Dogs Avenyn 15. Popular rock 'n roll club that's open daily till 3am.

Klara Viktoriagatan 1a. A long-established and likeable bar with live music and a more varied mix of people and conversation – when the latter can be heard at all. Mondays are 1980s nights, Tuesday has reggae and Wednesday sees jamming sessions with local DJs.

Kompaniet Kungsgatan 19. A top-floor pub/bar, and a downstairs club playing alternative and dance music. Open until 3am daily in summer (winter Wed–Sat only).

Rondo Liseberg amusement park. Reputedly has Sweden's biggest dance floor, packed out

with locals of all ages, and blends contemporary bands with foxtrot evenings, the latter usually encouraging the whole place onto the dance floor. Great fun.

Trädgår'n Nya Allén. Doesn't look too promising outside, but has a stylish pale-wood interior and a restaurant run by the revered Dahlbom brothers. It's also one of the liveliest haunts, with five bars, a casino, disco and live bands.

Valand Vasagatan 3. Perhaps the most popular place in town, with three bars and a club floor.

Vasastan Victoriagatan 2a. A very popular, suave club where confident twenty- to thirty-somethings bask in the mellow atmosphere.

Live music

Gothenburg's large student community means there are plenty of local **live bands**. The best **venue** is *Kompaniet* (see above), while **jazz** enthusiasts should head for the trendy *Nefertiti* club at Hvitfeldtsplatsen 6 (Thurs–Sat; ☎031/711 99 46) – you may have to queue. *Jazzhuset*, Eric Dahlbergsgatan 3 (Wed–Sat; ☎031/13 35 44), puts on trad, Dixieland and swing, but is fairly staid and something of an executive pick-up joint.

International bands perform at some sizeable stadium-type venues in the city, notably **Scandinavium** (☎031/81 10 20) and the colossal **Ullevi Stadium** (☎31/ 61 20 50). Both are off Skånegatan to the east of Avenyn; take tram #1, #3 or #6.

Classical music, cinema and theatre

Classical music concerts are performed regularly in the Konserthuset, Götaplatsen (℡031/726 53 10, ⓦwww.gso.se), and the Stora Teatern, Avenyn (ⓦwww.storan .sami.se). Programme details are available from the tourist office.

There are plenty of **cinemas** around the city, screening mostly English-language movies with Swedish subtitles. The most unusual is the ten-screen Bio Palatset, on Kungstorget, originally a meat market and then a failed shopping mall. Its interior is now painted in clashing fruity colours, and the foyer has been excavated to reveal floodlit rocks studded with Viking spears. Another multi-screener is Filmstaden, behind the cathedral at Kungsgatan 35. Hagabion on Linnégatan is a fine **art-house cinema**, showing a wide range of alternative films. If you're around in January or February, look out for the **Gothenburg Film Festival** in cinemas across town, with a remarkable range of films.

Theatre in Gothenburg is mostly Swedish-language; ask at the tourist office for any English-language shows.

Gay Gothenburg

Gothenburg's **gay scene** is surprisingly half-hearted. Though things have been looking up in the past couple of years, and there's now something approaching choice, options remain very limited compared to most cities of this size. Sweden's official gay rights group, the **RFSL** (*Riksförbundet för Sexuellt Likaberättigande*), have an inconveniently located branch with a café at Karl Johansgatan 31 (℡031/775 40 10, ⓦwww.rfsl.se/goteborg). More appealing is the friendly and well-designed *Greta's* at Drottninggatan 35 (see p.515), the city's first gay restaurant and bar; it hosts the *Matahari* club on Friday and Saturday nights. Gothenburg's other gay **clubs** emerge and disappear at an alarming rate; ask the tourist office for the latest roll call. For lesbians, there's the *Zapphobar* club night (ⓦwww.zapphobar.com), on the last Sunday of every month at the *Trappan* restaurant on Järntorget, and the *Rainbow* club night at the *Pharmacy* restaurant, Västra Hamngatan 15, which attracts a mixed crowd. Alternatively, *Club Cosmopolitan* plays every Saturday at the *Enter Lounge* bar on Vasaplatsen, with guest DJs each week, two bars and two dance floors.

Listings

Airlines British Airways, Landvetter airport ℡20/78 11 44; Finnair, Fredsgatan 6 ℡20/78 11 00; KLM, Landvetter airport ℡31/94 16 40; Lufthansa, Fredsgatan 1 ℡31/80 56 40; SAS, Landvetter airport ℡20/91 01 10; Ryanair, City airport ℡0900/202 02 40; Sterling, ℡08/58 76 91 48.

Airport enquiries Landvetter airport ℡31/94 10 00, ⓦwww.landvetter.lfv.se; City airport ℡31/92 60 60, ⓦwww.goteborgcityairport.se.

ATMs, banks and exchange ATMs can be found at all points of arrival and throughout the city. Most banks are open Mon–Fri 9.30am–3pm, and are found on Östra Hamngatan, Södra Hamngatan and Västra Hamngatan. There are several Forex exchange offices, which accept American Express, Diners Club and travellers' cheques: central ones include Central Station (daily 7am–9pm), Avenyn 22, Nordstan shopping centre, and Kungsportsplatsen (all Mon–Fri 9am–7pm, Sat 10am–4pm), and there's also one at Landvetter airport.

Buses Reservations are recommended for buses to Stockholm, Helsingborg and Malmö; reserve seats at the Swebus (℡0200/21 82 18, ⓦwww .swebus.se) or Säfflebussen (℡0771/15 15 15, ⓦwww.safflebussen.se) offices in the bus station.

Car rental Avis, Central Station ℡31/80 57 80, Landvetter airport ℡31/94 60 30, City airport ℡031/91 61 95; Budget, Kristinelundsgatan 13 ℡31/20 09 30, Landvetter airport ℡31/94 60 55; Europcar, Stampgatan 22d ℡31/80 53 90, Landvetter airport ℡31/94 71 00, City airport ℡031/80 53 90; Hertz, Stampgatan 16a ℡31/80 37 30, Landvetter airport ℡31/94 60 20, City airport ℡031/80 37 30.

Dentist Akuttandvården (Dental Emergency Care), Stampgatan 2, near Central Station ℡31/80 78 00.

Doctor Medical Counselling Service and Information ℡31/41 55 00; Sahlgrenska Hospital at Per Dubbsgatan ℡31/60 10 00.

Emergencies For ambulance, police and fire services, call ℡112.

Internet access Sidewalk Express has coin-operated Internet terminals (19kr/hr) inside the bus and train stations, and there's free Internet access at the City Library, Götaplatsen. Alternatively, try GameOnLine, Magasinsgatan 26 or IT-Grottan, Chalmersgatan 27.

Laundry Service Centre, in Nordstan shopping centre (daily 9am–10pm; 115kr per load).

Left luggage at Nordstan Service Centre inside the shopping mall, or at Central Station.

Newspapers International newspapers from the Press Centre in Nordstan shopping centre or Central Station; or read them for free at the City Library, Götaplatsen.

Pharmacy Apoteket Vasen, Nordstan shopping centre (daily 8am–10pm; ☏31/80 44 10).

Police Headquarters at Ernst Fontells Plats (☏31/114 14).

Post offices The main office for poste restante is in the Nordstan shopping centre (daily 10am–6pm), but you can buy stamps at any newsagent or supermarket. For sending parcels, visit *Mail Boxes Etc.* at Lilla Kungsgatan 2 (☏701 88 10) or the *Konsum* supermarket at Avenyn 26.

Systembolaget Nordstan shopping centre or Avenyn 18.

Taxis Taxi Göteborg ☏31/650 000; Flygtaxi ☏31/710 30 00; Taxi Kurir ☏31/27 27 27.

Train enquiries Central Station ☏1.

Travel agents Kilroy, Vasagatan 7 (Mon–Fri 9.30am–5pm; ☏1).

Around Gothenburg

North of Gothenburg, the rugged and picturesque **Bohuslän coast** attracts countless Scandinavian and German tourists each summer. However, the crowds can't detract from the wealth of natural beauty and the many dinky fishing villages that make this stretch of country well worth a few days' exploration. The most popular destination is the island town of **Marstrand**, with its impressive fortress and richly ornamental ancient buildings.

Northeast of the city, the wooded county of **Västergötland** encompasses the southern sections of Sweden's two largest lakes, **Vänern** and **Vättern**. The attractive town of **Mariestad**, easily reached from Gothenburg, lies on the southeastern shore of Lake Vänern and is a good base from which to venture out into the forested countryside and onto the **Göta Canal**. The waterway connects the lakes to each other (and, in its entirety, the North Sea to the Baltic). With energy and time to spare, **renting a bike** offers a great alternative for exploring Västergötland, using the canal's towpaths, countless cycling trails and empty roads. Nearly all tourist offices, youth hostels and campsites in the region rent out bikes for around 90kr a day or 400kr a week.

The Bohuslän coast

A chain of **islands** linked by a thread of bridges and short ferry crossings make up the county of **Bohuslän** and, despite the summer crowds, it's still easy enough to find a private spot to swim or bathe. Sailing is a popular pastime among the Swedes, many of whom have summer cottages here, and you'll see yachts gliding through the water all the way along the coast. Another feature of the Bohuslän landscape you can't fail to miss is the large number of **churches** – for long stretches these are the only buildings of note. Dating from the 1840s to 1910, these are mostly simple white structures with little variation in design.

Travelling up the coast by **train** is feasible, and though **buses** also cover the coast, services are sketchy and infrequent. If you really want to explore Bohuslän's most dramatic scenery, you need a **car**. From Gothenburg, the E6 motorway is the quickest route north, with designated scenic routes leading off it every few kilometres.

Kungälv

Just under 20km north of Gothenburg on the E6, and reached in 25 minutes on the Grön Express regional bus, the quaint old town of **KUNGÄLV**, overshadowed by the fourteenth-century ruins of Bohus Fortress, is a gem of a place to stop for a few hours. Rebuilt after the Swedes razed it in 1676 to prevent the Danes finding useful shelter, the town now consists of sprawling cobbled streets with pastel-painted wooden houses, all leaning as if on the verge of collapse. The **tourist office**, in the Fästnungsholmen building (Jan to mid-June & mid-Aug to Dec Mon 9.30am–6pm, Tues–Fri 9.30am–5pm, plus June Sat & Sun noon–4pm; mid-June to mid-Aug Mon–Fri 9.30am–6pm, Sat 10am–5pm, Sun noon–4pm; ☎0303/23 92 00, ☜www.kungalv.se), in the square below the fortress, will provide you with a map of a walking tour detailing the history of almost every seventeenth-century property.

The main reason most people visit Kungälv is to see the remains of **Bohus Fortress**. The first wooden fort was built here by the Norwegian king Håkon in the early fourteenth century, on what was then Norway's southern border. This was replaced by a solid stone building, surrounded by deep natural moats, which managed to withstand six Swedish attacks in the 1560s and, once it became Swedish, a remarkable fourteen sieges by the Danes in the following century. Where attack failed, Swedish weather has succeeded, however, and today the building is very much a ruin. The fortress is open daily from May to September and on weekends only in April and October, with guided tours, concerts and opera performances in July and August; for full details, contact the tourist office.

There's little else to do here once you've seen the fortress and wandered round the town, but if you do want **to stay** there's a STF youth hostel a stone's throw from the fortress at Färjevägen 2 (☎0303/189 00, ☜www.kungalvsvandrarhem.se; ❶), with dorm beds from 150kr.

Marstrand

About 25km west of Kungälv, the island town of **MARSTRAND** buzzes with summer activity, as holidaymakers flock in to sail, bathe and take tours around the impressive castle. With ornate wooden buildings lining the bustling harbour, Marstrand is a delightful place and is easily visited on a day-trip from Gothenburg.

Founded under Norwegian rule in the thirteenth century, the town achieved remarkable prosperity through herring fishing in the following century; rich

△ Fishing harbour, Bohuslän coast

herring pickings, however, eventually led to greed and corruption, and Marstrand became known as the most immoral town in Scandinavia. The murder of a cleric in 1586 was seen as an omen: soon after, the whole town burned to the ground and the herring mysteriously disappeared. The fish – and Marstrand's prosperity – eventually returned in the 1770s, only to disappear again, for good, forty years later. By the 1820s, the old herring salting houses had been converted into bath houses, and Marstrand had been reborn as a fashionable bathing resort.

From the harbour, turn left, and it's a lovely walk up a cobbled lane, past the Renaissance-style *Grand Hotel*, to a small square surrounded by exquisite wooden houses painted in pastel shades. Across the square is the squat, white **St Maria kyrka**; beyond, the streets climb steeply to the castle, **Carlstens Fästning** (mid-June to mid-Aug daily 11am–6pm; early June & late Aug daily 11am–4pm; rest of the year Sat & Sun 11am–4pm; 60kr; Ⓦwww.carlsten.se; for English-language tours, call ☎0303/602 65), an imposing sweep of stone walls solidly wedged into the rough rock. You could easily spend half a day clambering around the walls and down the weather-worn rocks to the sea, where there are always plenty of places to bathe in private. The most interesting tales spun by the **tour guides** are related down in the grim prison cells: Carlstens' most noted prisoner was **Lasse Maja**, a thief who got rich by dressing as a woman and seducing rich farmers. A sort of Swedish Robin Hood, Maja was known for giving his spoils to the poor. Once incarcerated here, he ingratiated himself with the officers via his impressive cooking skills, a talent that, after 26 years, won him a pardon from the king.

Some of the tours (depending on the guide; ask in advance) lead up through the castle's hundred-metre tower, built in 1658. The views from the top are stunning, but you'll have to be fit to get there, as the steep, spiral climb is quite exhausting. Once a year, at the end of July, the fortress hosts a huge **festival**, with an eighteenth-century-style procession and live theatrical performances. It's a colourful occasion and well worth catching.

Practicalities

Gothenburg Pass holders can get a two-for-one ticket deal on the **day-trip by boat** from Gothenburg; boats leave from Lilla Bommen at 9.30am, arriving in Marstrand at 12.30pm (July & Aug daily; May & June selected dates, ask at Gothenburg tourist office, p.504). Otherwise, take **bus** #312; buy a 100kr carnet from Tidpunkten inside the bus station, which also covers the ferry journey from the mainland (2min; 23kr return). By car, take the E6 north out of Gothenburg, then road 168, which leads right to the ferry. No cars are allowed on the island, and parking on the mainland costs 25kr per day.

The **tourist office** at Hamngatan 33 (June Mon–Fri 9.30am–4.30pm, Sat & Sun noon–4pm; late June to early Aug Mon–Fri 9am–6pm, Sat & Sun 11am–5pm; mid-Aug to May Mon–Fri 10am–4pm; ☎0303/600 87, Ⓦwww.marstrand.se) can book **private rooms** in old barracks for a minimum of two people from 370kr per room, and apartments at 600kr for two people.

The island's **youth hostel**, *Båtellet* (☎0303/600 10, Ⓔmarstrandsvarmbadhus@telia .com; ❷), has dorm beds from 195kr, and is situated in an atmospheric old bath house overlooking the sea, and has a sauna, washing facilities, a swimming pool and a restaurant (see overleaf). Of the several very pleasant **hotels** on the island, the finest is the 1892-built *Grand* at Rådhusgatan (☎0303/603 22, Ⓦwww.grand marstrand.se; ❻). *Nautic*, Långgatan 6 (☎0303/610 30, Ⓦwww.hotelnautic.com; ❹), is rather simpler in style, but perfectly adequate.

Eating out is a major sport on Marstrand, but it comes at a price. About the most interesting place to eat on the island is the *American Bar*, opened in 1919, overlooking the harbour, which serves good but pricey meat and fish meals with mains costing 150–250kr. Alternatively, you could try the glamorous, if more formal, *Oscar's*, next door. Another very popular choice is *Lasse Maja's Krog*, in a jolly, yellow-painted house on the harbourfront, whose wide-ranging meat and fish menu has mains at 140–250kr, as well as pizzas at around 120kr. Decent meals are also served in *Drott*, the rather fine restaurant attached to the youth hostel: pasta dishes cost around 50kr; meat and seafood 100–200kr. Or try the gourmet restaurant in the classic old *Societetshuset* (☎0303/606 00), close to the youth hostel. The cheapest place to eat is the *Skepps Handel*, at the harbour at the corner of Drottninggatan. At night, the *American Bar* and *Oscar's* (which doubles as a nightclub) are good **drinking** haunts.

Mariestad and around

The small, pretty lakeside town of **MARIESTAD**, with its splendid medieval quarter and harbour area, is just over two hours by train from Gothenburg, and an excellent base for a day or two's exploration. It's also worth visiting for the extraordinary range of building styles crammed into its centre – Gustavian, Carolean, Classical, Swiss-chalet style and Art Nouveau – like a living museum of architectural design. Have a look, too, at the **cathedral**, on the edge of the centre, which was built by Duke Karl (who named the town after his wife, Maria of Pfalz) in an attempt to compete with his brother King Johan III's Klara kyrka in Stockholm (see p.477). To help you explore the town's compact centre, pick up a copy of the walking-tour map from the tourist office (10kr), or join one of the Swedish-language guided tours that start at the office (mid-June to mid-Aug Mon & Thurs 6.30pm; 40kr); ask in advance if the guide can do the tour in English as well.

Mariestad is also a good base from which to **cruise** on the Göta Canal. There are 21 **locks** between nearby Sjötorp and Karlsborg, with the most scenic section up to **Lyrestad**, just a few kilometres east of Sjötorp and 20km north of Mariestad on the E20. **Canal cruises** on the *MS Bellevue* take five hours to wend their way through sixteen locks and cost 300kr including a bus ride back to the starting point (mid-May to Aug: from Sjötorp on Wed & Sat at 10.30am; from Töreboda on Tues & Thurs at 10.30am). Ask the tourist office or visit ✪www.gotakanal.se/en for alternative cruises. There are no lake cruises, since Lake Vänern has been classified as an inland sea, such is its size, and sea-cruising licences are too expensive for the local boating companies.

The **tourist office**, by the harbour on Hamngatan (June–Aug Mon–Fri 9am–7pm, Sat & Sun 9am–6pm; Sept–May Mon–Fri 8am–4pm; ☎0501/100 01, ✪www.turism.mariestad.se), is opposite the hugely popular STF **youth hostel** (☎0501/104 48, ✪www.stfvandrarhemmariestad.se; book in advance mid-Aug to mid-June; ❶), with dorm beds from 140kr. Built after the fire of 1693, the hostel is a former tannery with galleried timber outbuildings and an excellent garden **café**. For a **hotel**, the small *Bergs Hotell* of 1698, in the old town, at Kyrkogatan 18 (☎0501/103 24, ✪www.bergshotel.com; ❷), is plain, but comfortable enough. Much grander is the classical *Stadshotellet* overlooking the main square at Nygatan 10 (☎0501/138 00, ✪www.stadtshotelletmariestad.com; ❹). Other good-value central options include the mundane *Hotell Aqva*, Viktoriagatan 15 (☎0501/195 15, ✪www.aqva.se; ❷), or the far cosier *Hotel Vänerport*, Hamngatan 32 (☎0501/771 11, ✪www.vanerport.se; ❸). The nearest **campsite** is *Ekudden*, 2km west along the lake (☎0501/106 37, ✪www.ekuddenscamping.se; May–Sept).

Mariestad's trendiest **eating** place is *Café Ströget* at Österlånggatan 10. The *St. Michel* restaurant at Kungsgatan 1 (☎0501/199 00) has good views of the river Tidan, and serves some of the best food in town, with main courses starting at 140kr. One possibility for evening fun is at *Björnes Magasin*, Karlsgatan 2 (Mon–Fri 11am–2.30pm, Tues–Thurs 6–11pm, Fri & Sat 6pm–1am; ☎0501/180 50), which serves good food all day and hosts weekly club nights – it's an enjoyable place for a 26-plus age group. Reasonable **pubs** are *Buffalo*, at Österlånggatan 16, and *Hjorten*, Nygatan 21.

Travel details

Trains

Gothenburg to: Helsingborg (10 daily; 2hr 20min); Kalmar (8 daily; 4–5hr); Kiruna (2 daily; 21hr 30min); Luleå (daily; 20hr); Malmö (hourly; 3hr); Mariestad (6 daily; 3hr); Östersund (daily; 11hr); Stockholm (hourly; 3hr by Express, 5–6hr by InterCity); Umeå (daily; 14hr 40min); Växjö (5 daily; 3hr).

Buses

Gothenburg to: Falun/Gävle (1–2 daily; 8–10hr 30min); Halmstad (5 daily; 3hr 40min); Jönköping (8 daily; 2hr 10min); Karlstad (3 daily; 4hr); Norrköping (6 daily; 4hr 40min); Mariestad (3 daily; 2hr 40min); Stockholm (6 daily; 7hr).

Mariestad to: Jönköping (2–4 daily; 2hr); Karlstad (3 daily; 3hr); Örebro (3 daily; 1hr 30min).

International buses

Gothenburg to: Copenhagen (3–6 daily; 4hr); Oslo (4–7 daily; 3hr 40min).

International trains

Gothenburg to: Copenhagen, via Copenhagen airport (7 daily; 4hr); Oslo (3 daily; 4hr).

International ferries

Gothenburg to: Frederikshavn (7–9 daily; 3hr 15min); Kiel (daily; 14hr); Newcastle (2 weekly; 24hr).

The southwest

T
here is a real historical interest to the **southwestern** provinces of Halland, Skåne and Blekinge, not least in the towns and cities that line the coast. The flatlands and fishing ports south of Gothenburg were traded almost constantly between Denmark and Sweden from the fourteenth to seventeenth centuries, and several fortresses today bear witness to the region's medieval buffer status.

Halland, facing Denmark, has a coastline of smooth sandy beaches and bare, granite outcrops, punctuated by a number of small towns. Most charismatic is the old

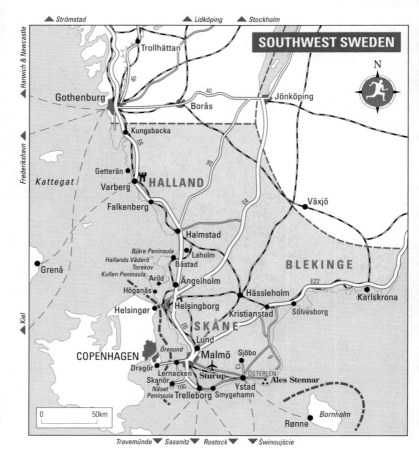

society bathing resort of **Varberg**, dominated by its tremendous thirteenth-century fortress. The small, beautifully intact medieval core of **Falkenberg** is also notable, while for beaches and nightlife, regional capital **Halmstad** is a popular base.

Further south, in the ancient province of **Skåne**, the coastline softens into curving beaches backed by gently undulating fields. This was one of the first parts of the country to be settled, and the scene of some of the bloodiest battles during the medieval conflict with Denmark. Although Skåne was finally ceded to Sweden in the late seventeenth century, the Danish influence died hard, and is still evident today in the thick Skåne accent, often incomprehensible to other Swedes, and in the province's architecture. The latter has also been strongly influenced by Skåne's agricultural economy, whose centuries of profitable farming have left the countryside dotted with **castles** – though the continued income from the land means that most of these palatial homes are still in private hands and not open to the public.

The popular perception of Skåne is as a fertile but largely flat and uniform landscape; however, it's worth taking a day or two to appreciate the subtle variety of the countryside – blocks of yellow rape, crimson poppy and lush-green fields interspersed with castles, charming white churches and black windmills. Skåne's glamorous tennis capital of **Båstad** is a good base to explore the region, while to the south, both **Helsingborg**, with its laid-back, cosmopolitan atmosphere, and Sweden's third city, bustling **Malmö**, are only a stone's throw from Denmark. Between these two centres, the university town of **Lund** has some classic architecture and a unique atmosphere.

Sweeping east towards the pretty medieval town of **Ystad**, the coastline holds some minor resorts with excellent beaches. Beyond here, you enter the splendid countryside of the **Österlen** area, whose pastoral scenery is studded with Viking monuments such as the Swedish Stonehenge at **Ales Stennar**, and whose coast is lined with some brilliant white beaches backed by nature reserves. In the northeast of the county, **Kristianstad**, built as a flagship town by the Danes, retains its fine, Renaissance church.

Beyond here to the east, the ledge of land running to the Baltic is **Blekinge**. Among the province's small run of fairly undistinguished resorts, **Karlskrona** stands out. Centred on a number of islands forming a small archipelago, Sweden's second city in the eighteenth century still exudes an air of regal and naval grandeur.

Getting around

The national **train** network follows the coast south from Gothenburg, with frequent trains stopping at all towns as far as Ystad, where the line cuts northeast to Kristianstad. Comfortable express trains run east and west across the country, linking Malmö, Helsingborg and Lund with Kristianstad and Karlskrona. However, some of the most beautiful and less-frequented areas are not covered by the train network, and the **bus** service can be skeletal along the south coast – it's a good idea to equip yourself with timetables from the train and bus stations or tourist offices in Gothenburg and Malmö.

With no really steep hills, the southwest is wonderful country for **cycling**, and bike rental outlets are numerous; most tourist offices, youth hostels and campsites also rent out bikes. There are also several recognized **walking trails**, mentioned in the text.

Varberg

More atmospheric than any other town in Halland, the fashionable little nineteenth-century bathing resort of **VARBERG** boasts surprisingly varied sights – most obviously its imposing fortress – plus a laid-back atmosphere, opportunities to swim and plenty of good places to eat.

Varberg's attractions are concentrated along or near the seafront, with the thirteenth-century moated **fortress** set on a rocky promontory. Home to the Swedish

△ Varberg Kallbadhuset

king Magnus Eriksson, important peace treaties with Valdemar of Denmark were signed here in 1343. Standing outside, it's easy to imagine how impenetrable the fortress must have appeared to attackers in the past, as the way in is hardly more obvious today: enter on the sea-facing side by climbing the uneven stone steps to a delightful terrace café, or approach through the great archways towards the central courtyard.

Although **tours** in English (July to mid-Aug hourly 11am–4pm; on request at other times; 40kr) take you into the dungeons and among the impressive cocoa-coloured buildings that make up the inner courtyard, it's the **museum** that deserves most of your attention (mid-June to mid-Aug daily 10am–5pm; mid-Aug to mid-June Mon–Fri 10am–4pm, Sat & Sun noon–4pm; mid-June to mid-Aug 50kr, mid-Aug to mid-June 30kr). The most unnerving exhibit is the **Bocksten Man**, a 600-year-old murder victim who was garrotted, drowned, impaled and buried in a local bog until 1936, when a farmer dug him up. His entire outfit preserved by the bog, Bocksten Man sports the Western world's most complete medieval wardrobe, made up of a cloak, a hood, shoes and stockings. His most shocking feature is the thick, red ringletted hair that cascades around his puny skull, while the three stakes thrust through his body were supposed to ensure that his spirit never escaped to seek out his murderers. Much of the rest of the museum is missable, with sections on farming and fishing in Halland, though the room devoted to the works of the so-called **Varberg School** is worth viewing. This small colony of artists – Richard Bergh, Nils Kreuger and Karl Nordström – who joined together in the last years of the nineteenth century, developed a national painting style reflecting the moods and atmosphere of Halland, Varberg in particular. Night scenes of the fortress beneath the stars show the strong influence of Van Gogh, but in other paintings, the misty colours create a more melancholy effect.

Overlooking the sea, the cream-painted **fortress prison** from 1850 looks incongruously delicate in the shadow of the looming fortress. The first Swedish jail to be built with individual cells, it housed life prisoners until the last one ended his days here in 1931. Today, you can stay in a youth hostel in the fortress, which has been carefully preserved to retain most of its original features (see opposite).

A minute or so from the fortress lie a couple of fine remnants from Varberg's time as a spa resort. Facing the town just behind the fortress is the grand **Societeshuset**, a confection of cream-and-green carved wood where upper-class ladies took their meals after bathing in the splendid – and now beautifully restored – **Kallbadhuset** (cold bathhouse), just to the north of the fortress and overlooking the harbour. This dainty bathhouse (mid-June to mid-Aug Mon, Tues & Thurs–Sun 10am–5pm, Wed 1–8pm; 45kr for cold bath and sauna) has separate-sex naked-bathing areas and is topped at each corner by Moorish cupolas, lending it an imperial air.

Although the Halland coastline is still a little rocky around here, there are several excellent spots for bathing. Head down Strandpromenaden for about five minutes to get to a couple of well-known **nudist beaches**: Goda Hopp for men, and Kärringhålan for women. Alternatively, a few kilometres further north at **Getterön**, a fist of land jutting into the sea, there's a nature centre (July & Aug daily 10am–4pm; free) and an extensive bird reserve, as well as a series of secluded coves, reached by regular buses from town.

Just 10km east of Varberg, the impressive **Grimeton transmitter station** (July & Aug Tues–Sun 11am–5pm; free; ⓦwww.grimetonradio.se) makes an interesting trip for technology buffs: the neoclassical transformer building and its six 127m-high radio masts were erected in 1924 to transmit telegrams to the USA – the location was chosen as there is nothing but open water along the transmission path to New York. The station, a World Heritage site, is the last of its kind worldwide, and, incredibly, the 1920s technology is still in full working order. There are hourly English-language **tours** (40kr) from the information centre, which also has a **café**. From Varberg, bus #661 goes to the visitor centre (20min; confirm the schedule with the tourist office beforehand).

Practicalities

Varberg is a handy entry point into southern Sweden, linked by a year-round **ferry** (pedestrians 155kr one-way; car and 4 people 855kr; 4hr) to Grenå in **Denmark**. Regular **trains** run down the coast from Gothenburg. From the **train and bus stations**, turn right down Västra Vallgatan and the town centre is off to the left, the harbour to the right. The **tourist office** at Brunnsparken, just off Västra Vallgatan (April & May Mon–Fri 9am–5pm, Sat 10am–1pm; June–Aug Mon–Sat 9.30am–7pm, Thurs till 9pm, Sun 3–7pm; Sept–March Mon–Fri 9am–5pm; ☏0340/868 00, ⓦwww.turist.varberg.se) provides free maps of the town. Varberg is easy to walk around, but to explore the nearby coast, it might be worth **renting a bike** from Erlan Cykel och Sport, Västra Vallgatan 41 (☏0340/144 55; 80kr per day, 250kr per week) or from *Getteröns Camping* (see below; 50kr per day).

It's worth booking well in advance for the fortress prison **youth hostel** (☏0340/887 88, ⓦwww.turist.varberg.se/vandrarhem; ❶), with dorm beds from 150kr; outside the summer, you have to book through the tourist office. Aside from being spotlessly clean, the prison is much as it was, with original cell doors (each has its own key) complete with spy-holes. If it's full, try the other very central hostel, *Varberg's Vandrahem* at Villagatan 13 (☏0340/61 16 40, ⓦwww.varbergsvandrarhem .info.se; ❶), with dorm beds for 180kr. Alternatively, a couple of excellent-value and appealing family-run **hotels** are just a few steps away. At Norrgatan 16, *Varberg* (☏0340/161 25, ⓦwww.hotellvarberg.nu; ❸) is an excellent choice for its very friendly atmosphere, quality service and value. Built in 1899, it retains plenty of character and serves a great breakfast. *Hotel Gåstis*, Borgmästaregatan 1 (☏0340/180 50, ⓦwww.hotellgastis.nu; ❹–❺), includes an evening meal in its rates and offers cycle hire at just 25kr per day for guests; there's also a sauna and spa pool. *Hotel Fregatten* (☏0340/67 70 00, ⓦwww.fregattenhomehotel.se; ❺), in a former cold-storage warehouse overlooking the harbour, is quite luxurious, boasting a Jacuzzi, sauna and spa. There are a number of **campsites** in the area, the nearest being *Apelvikens Camping* (☏0340/141 78, ⓦwww.apelviken.se), 3km south of the fortress along Strandpromenaden. To the north, near the nature reserve, is *Getteröns Camping* (☏0340/168 85, ⓦwww.getteronscamping.se). Alternatively, there are plenty of places to put up a tent for free beyond the nudist beaches.

There's no problem finding a good place to **eat** in Varberg, with most of the options north of the main square along Kungsgatan. The best café in town, and great for breakfast, is *Blå Dörren* on the corner of Norrgatan and Västra Vallgatan. Nearby, *Zorba's* at Västra Vallgatan 37 serves up great Greek food (100–185kr). The relaxed ♣ *Paganini* bakery, overlooking the main square at Kungsgatan 28, is an excellent place for sandwiches or pasta dishes (from 70kr). For lunch, try the grand *Societet* in Societets Park, directly behind the fortress, where daily specials go for 80kr, or visit on Friday evenings, when it comes alive with foxtrotting Swedes, or Saturday, when there's live bands and a disco. Finally, head to the *Oscar Bar & Club* and the attached *Sophia's Lounge* restaurant at Borgmästaregatan 15 (Fri & Sat from 9pm; ☎0340/67 68 00) for the town's liveliest **nightlife**.

Falkenberg

It's a twenty-minute train ride south from Varberg to the well-preserved medieval town of **FALKENBERG**, named after the falcons that were once hunted here. With a long beach and a pleasing old quarter, it's a likeable little town, though it only really comes alive in July and August. Sir Humphrey Davy, inventor of the mining safety lamp, visited in the 1820s to go **fly-fishing** in the River Ätran that runs through town, and as its reputation for salmon spread, a succession of wealthy English countrymen followed him here, leaving their mark on the town. Today, the waters have been so overfished that it costs relatively little to try your hand in the two-kilometre stretch from the splendid stone **Tullbron** toll bridge of 1756 – permits are available from the tourist office (see opposite) from March to September, cost 80kr and allow you to catch up to three fish a day.

The **old town**, to the west of the curving river, comprises a dense network of low, wooden cottages and cobbled lanes. Nestling among them is the fine fourteenth-century **St Laurentii kyrka**, its interior awash with seventeenth- and eighteenth-century wall and ceiling paintings. When the town acquired a solid new neo-Gothic church in the late nineteenth century, the church was only saved from demolition by being used variously as a shooting range, a cinema and a gymnasium, until being reconsecrated in the 1920s. Contact the tourist office or call ☎0346/552 00 for guided tours.

Bypassing the pedestrian **Local History Museum** on St Lars Kyrkogatan, head straight for the **Falkenbergs Museum** (June–Aug Tues–Fri noon–4pm; mid-Sept to May Tues–Fri & Sun noon–4pm; 20kr) in an old grain store near the main bridge. Displays cover Falkenberg's development over the past one hundred years, with original interiors of a shoe repair shop and a stylized café. The town also boasts the rather unusual **Olympia Photography Museum** at Sandgatan 13 (late June to Aug Tues–Thurs 1–7pm, Sun 1–5pm; Sept to late June Tues–Thurs 5–7pm, Sun 2–5pm; 40kr; ☎0346/879 28, ☜www.fotomuseet-olympia.com), housed in what was originally Falkenberg's first purpose-built cinema. Among the thousand or so cameras and other cinematic paraphernalia, there are some superb local peasant portraits, taken in 1898 by Axel Aurelius.

Less demanding is a tour of the local **Falken Brewery** (July & Aug Mon–Thurs 10am & 1.15pm; 20kr, bookable at the tourist office): Sweden's most popular beer, Falcon, has been brewed here since 1896 and is available for sampling at the end of the tour.

Over the river and fifteen minutes' walk south there's a fine, four-kilometre stretch of sandy beach, **Skrea Strand**. At its northern end is the large bathing and tennis complex of **Klitterbadhuset** (mid-June to mid-Aug Mon–Fri 9am–7pm, Tues & Thurs from 6am, Sat 9am–5pm, Sun 9am–4pm; mid-Aug to mid-June Tues & Thurs 6–9am & noon–8pm, Wed noon–8pm, Fri 9am–noon; 35kr plus 15kr for gym), which offers a fifty-metre saltwater pool and shallow children's pool, a vast sauna, Jacuzzi and steam rooms. If you walk all the way down past the wooden holiday shacks at the southern end of the beach, you'll come across some secluded coves; in early summer, the marshy grassland around here is full of wild violets and clover and is a great place for birdwatching.

Practicalities

Regular **buses** and **trains** drop you close to the centre on Holgersgatan, just a couple of minutes from the **tourist office** in Stortorget (mid-June to Aug Mon–Sat 9.30am–6pm, Sun 2–6pm; Sept to mid-June Mon–Fri 10am–5pm; ☎0346/8861 00, ⊛www.falkenbergsturist.se). They provide information about **private rooms** (from 160kr per person); a list of available rooms is posted on the door every day at noon.

The comfortable and well-equipped **youth hostel** (☎0346/171 11, ⊛www .falkenbergsturist.se/fbgvandrarhem; mid-March to mid-Oct; ❶), with dorm beds from 150kr, is 3km south of town on Hansagårdvägen, near Skrea beach. It's just a few minutes' walk through the neighbouring **campsite** (☎0346/171 07, ⊛www .skreacamping.se) at the southern end of the beach. The best-located **hotel** for the beach is the sprawling *Strandbaden* (☎0346/71 49 00, ⊛www.strandbaden.elite.se; ❹); rooms are large and luxurious, and rates include entry to the Klitterbadhuset complex. More interesting is the charming eighteenth-century *Hvitan* at Storgatan 24 (☎0346/820 90, ⊛www.hwitan.se; ❸), which hosts a popular **jazz and folk festival** in mid-July (⊛www.jazz.falkenberg.net; tickets from the tourist office; 200kr per day). The cheapest option is *Hotel Steria*, a ten-minute walk up from the river, at Arvidstorpsvägen 28 (☎0346/155 21, ⊛www.hotelsteria.se; ❷).

About the best place for **lunch** is the atmospheric *Falkmanska Caféet*, Storgatan 42 (closed Sun) in the oldest secular building in town; try the huge baguettes and decadent cakes. For outdoor eating, the *Café Rosengården* enjoys a great location just above the old bridge at Doktorspromenaden, while the trendy ℋ *Zäta's* restaurant/bar at Storgatan 37 attracts a younger crowd, with international dishes priced from 130kr. The poshest restaurant is *Gustav Bratt*, Brogatan l, near Tullbron bridge, serving good fish dishes and with prices from 200kr; it turns into a **club** on weekend nights. The restaurants at the *Hvitan* and *Strandbaden* hotels both offer at least one vegetarian option alongside meat and fish dishes, all of which are priced at 140–190kr.

Halmstad

The principal town in Halland, **HALMSTAD** was once a grand walled city and important Danish stronghold. Today, although most of the original buildings have disappeared, the town boasts a couple of cultural and artistic points of interest, most notably the works of the Halmstad Group, Sweden's first Surrealists, as well as extensive beaches and a wide range of good places to eat.

In 1619, Halmstad's **castle** was used by Danish king Christian IV to entertain the Swedish king Gustav II Adolf; records show that there were seven days of solid festivities. The bonhomie didn't last much longer than that, and Christian was soon building great stone and earth fortifications around the city, surrounded by a moat with four stone gateways. Shortly after, a fire all but destroyed the city; the only buildings to survive were the castle and church. Undeterred, Christian took the opportunity to create a modern Renaissance town with a grid of straight streets – the charming high street, Storgatan, still contains a number of impressive merchants' houses from that time. After the final defeat of the Danes in 1645, Halmstad lost its military significance and the walls were torn down. Today, just one of the great gateways, Norre Port, remains, while Karl XIs Vägen runs directly above the filled-in moat.

The Town

At the centre of the lively market square, **Stora Torg**, is Carl Milles' *Europa and the Bull*, a fountain with mermen twisted around it, all with Milles' characteristically muscular bodies and ugly faces. Flanking one side of the square, the grand four-teenth-century **St Nikolai kyrka** (daily 8.30am–3.30pm) is testimony to the town's former importance, but today, the only signs of its medieval origins are the splodges of bare rock beneath the plain brick columns. Leading north from the square, pedestrianized **Storgatan** holds some creaking old houses built in the years following the 1619 fire, as well as most of the town's restaurants and nightlife venues. The great stone arch of **Norre Port** marks the street's end: through here and to the right is the splendid **Norre Kattparken**, a delightful, shady place, with mature beech and horse chestnut trees sloping down to the river bank.

By the river at the northernmost edge of the park is the fine **county museum** (Tues–Sun noon–4pm, Wed till 8pm, ⊛www.hallmus.se; 40kr). While the archeo-logical finds on the ground floor are unlikely to set many pulses racing, there are some home interiors from the seventeenth, eighteenth and nineteenth centuries upstairs, including exquisitely furnished dolls' houses, and a room of glorious Gustavian harps and square pianos from the 1780s. The top floor contains a decent sample of the work of the Halmstad Group.

A few kilometres north of the town centre, heading out along Karlsrovägen past the tiny airport, **Mjellby Art Centre** (July to mid-Aug Tues–Sun 1–6pm; mid-March to June & mid-Aug to Oct Tues–Sun 1–5pm; Nov to mid-Dec Sat & Sun 1–5pm; 50kr) is home to the largest collection of works by the **Halmstad Group**, a body of six local artists who championed Cubism and Surrealism in 1920s Sweden. Their work caused considerable controversy in the 1930s and 1940s, and a quick glance shows how strongly they were influenced by Magritte and Dali. Reputedly the only group of its type to have stayed together in its entirety for fifty years, they sometimes worked together on a single project: you can see a good example at the Halmstad City Library at Fredsgatan 2 (Mon–Fri 10am–8pm, Sat 10am–4pm, Sun 1–5pm), where an impressive fourteen-metre-long, six-section work adorns the wall above the shelves. To get to the art centre, take bus #350 (every 2hr) from the centre of town, which will drop you just after the turnoff, from where it's a ten-minute walk. It's also a very enjoyable twenty-minute cycle ride.

Practicalities

From the **train station**, follow Bredgatan to the Nissan River and cross Österbro (East Bridge) to get to the coral-red castle on the opposite bank that contains the **tourist office** (May, June & late Aug Mon–Fri 10am–6pm, Sat 10am–3pm; July to mid-Aug Mon–Sat 9am–7pm, Sun 11–6pm; Sept–April Mon–Fri 9am–5pm; ☎035/13 23 20, ⊛www.halmstad.se/turist). Staff can book **private rooms** (from 125kr per person, plus 25kr booking fee in person, 50kr by phone). Renting a **bike** is a good way to get out to the Mjellby Arts Centre or the beaches on the coast hereabouts: Arvid Olsson Cykel, Norra Vägen 11 (Mon–Fri 9.30am–6pm, Sat 9.30am–1pm; ☎035/21 22 51), is the only outlet in the town centre, and charges 120kr per day for a five-speed bike. A cheaper though less central option is *Krono-camping*, 10km west of the town centre at Tylösand (☎035/305 10; 100kr per day).

The *PatriksHill* **youth hostel** (☎035/27 12 00, ⊛www.patrikshill-hostel.se; mid-June to mid-Aug; ❶), with dorm beds from 185kr, is 300m southwest of the castle, at Neptunigatan 3, and has showers and toilets in all rooms.

The best of the central **hotels** is the very comfortable old *Norre Park*, Norra Vägen 7 (☎035/21 85 55, ⊛www.norrepark.se; ❺), through the Norre Port Arch north of Storgatan, overlooking the park. Along the river and convenient for the city centre, the *Scandic Hallandia* at Rådhusgatan 4 (☎035/295 86 00, ⊛www.scandic .se; ❹) is a large business-oriented hotel, while just south of the castle, the rooms of the new *Gula Briggen* at Södra Vägen 3 (☎035/22 75 01, ⊛www.gulabriggen.com; ❸) are set in the small cells of a former prison. The nearest **campsite** is *Hagöns Camping* (☎035/12 53 63, ⊛www.hagonscamping.se), 4km east of the centre, next to a nature reserve bordering a **nudist beach**; the site's cabins cost 4200–6000kr per week for up to five people.

Eating, drinking and nightlife possibilities abound along Storgatan, ranging from casual cafés to glamorous gourmet joints. *Gaston*, at no.31, does pizzas for around 80kr, though most other dishes are priced from 200kr. Next door at no.33, *Pio* is a lovely place with a massive drinks list and a speciality of steak with piles of mashed potato served on wooden planks for 185kr. For a real splurge, ☕ *Lilla Helfwetet* ("Little Hell"), on the corner of Hamngatan and Bastiongatan, is the most stylishly contemporary restaurant in town, serving up lamb, halibut and beef dishes (all from 200kr) in a stunningly designed old turbine engine room overlooking the river. For **cafés**, try the old-fashioned *Skånska Hembageriet* at Bankgatan 1; the popular, chilled-out *Espresso House*, inside the Drottning Christina Passage just off Storgatan, has good coffee and snacks, and a courtyard terrace.

Båstad

The most northerly town in the ancient province of Skåne, **BÅSTAD** has a character markedly distinct from the other towns along the coast. Cradled by the Bjäre peninsula, which bulges westwards into the Kattegat (the water separating Sweden and Jutland), Båstad is Sweden's elite **tennis centre**, home of the annual Swedish Open (☎0431 750 75, ☻www.swedishopen.org; tickets 150–500kr) at the beginning of July, and boasting sixty tennis courts, five eighteen-hole golf courses and the Drivan Sports Centre. With a horizon of forested hills to the south, Båstad is pretty scenic, too; less pleasant, however, is the fact that ever since King Gustav V chose to take part in the 1930 tennis championships, wealthy retired Stockholmers and social climbers from all over Sweden have flocked here to bask in the social glow, with droves of well-heeled young men in expensive sports cars overspending and drinking to excess. The down-to-earth and friendly locals grin and bear it for the sake of their local economy.

The **harbour** makes a pretty spot for a picnic or stroll; to get there, follow Tennisvägen off Köpmansgatan through a luxury residential district until you reach Strandpromenaden; to the west, the old bathhouses have been converted into restaurants and bars.

Practicalities

From the **train station**, it's a half-hour walk east along Köpmansgatan to the main square, where the **tourist office** (mid-June to mid-Aug Mon–Fri & Sun 10am–6pm, Sat 10am–4pm; mid-Aug to mid-June Tue–Fri 10am–4pm, Sat 11am–4pm; ☎0431/750 45, ☻www.bastad.com) can book **private rooms** from 150kr per person. They can also give information on booking tennis courts and renting out sports equipment. The main **bike rental** place is Svenn's Cykel, Tennisvägen 31

Skåne Sommarkort and Öresunds Rundt

If you're spending a significant amount of time in Skåne, buying a **Skåne Sommarkort** can be an excellent way to save money. Covering travel on buses and trains throughout the county, the card is usable between June 15 and August 15, and costs 415kr for any 25 days within that period. Up to two children under 6 travel free with one adult holder. Before each journey, you simply insert your card into the readers on board trains and buses.

The two-day **Öresunds Rundt** ticket (Round the Öresund; from 199kr) covers any route (or part of it) by ferry and train between Helsingborg and Malmö, via Lund; the ferry to Helsingør and the Öresund Bridge (once) to Copenhagen.

The Skåne Sommarkort and the Öresunds Rundt ticket are available at the Skånetrafiken offices at Knutpunkten in Helsingborg, at Lund Station, and on Gustav Adolfs Torg in Malmö, or at the office near platform 9 in Malmö's Central Station; call ☎0771/77 77 77 or visit ☻www.skanetrafiken.se for more information.

(Mon–Fri 8am–noon & 1–5pm, Sat 8am–noon), which charges 100kr per day. The **youth hostel** (℡0431/685 00, @drivan@bastad.com; dorm beds from 150kr) is next to the Drivan Sports Centre on Korrödsvagen, signposted off Köpmansgatan. It's open all year, but tends to be reserved for groups in winter, and the sporty young guests can make it noisy. For a really excellent **bed and breakfast**, try *Falken*, Hamngatan 22 (℡0431/36 95 94; ❷), a lovingly maintained 1916-built villa set just above the harbour in delightful gardens, with lots of art on the walls and a welcoming atmosphere. The cheaper **hotels** are mostly around the station end of town; note that prices in Båstad increase dramatically during the summer due to the tennis. Try *Bed & Breakfast Malengården*, Åhusvägen 41 (℡ & ℡0431/36 95 67; ❶) – take the turning off Köpmansgatan towards the youth hostel. For a luxurious and beautifully designed alternative, try the harbourside *Hotel Skansen* (℡0431/55 81 00, @www.hotelskansen.se; ❹/❺). **Camping** is not allowed at the waterside.

Eating and drinking is as much a pastime as tennis in Båstad, and most of the waterside restaurants and hotels both here and on the peninsula offer two-course dinners for around 150kr, with menus changing weekly. *Pepe's Bodega* is a popular pizza place at the harbour, but for value, it's hard to beat *Sveas Skafferi*, a wooden hut at the harbour's edge serving smoked salmon and other fish goodies on paper plates from 70kr, as well as home-baked pies and cake. *Caffe & Torta*, opposite the church at the harbour end of Köpmansgatan, is a fine daytime **café** offering fresh-baked bread (from 6am daily), gazpacho, big salads and the best coffee and cake in town.

Ängelholm and the Kullen peninsula

The best aspects of peacefully uneventful **ÄNGELHOLM** are its justifiably popular 7km of golden beach and its proximity to everywhere else in the region – Helsingborg is just thirty minutes away by train. With a range of accommodation and some agreeable restaurants, it's not a bad base, and there's also a surprisingly lively nightlife scene, too. Ängelholm's efforts to sell itself, however, concentrate not on its beaches but on the town mascot, a musical clay cuckoo (on sale everywhere), and UFOs. The latter have been big business here since 1946, when a railway worker, Gösta Carlsson, convinced the authorities that he had encountered tiny people from another world. Today, Ängelholm hosts international UFO conferences, and the tourist board runs tours to the "landing site" of Carlsson's aliens throughout the summer.

From the train station, it's just a few minutes' walk over the Rönneå River to the main square, Stortorget and tourist office. Should you want to see more of the surrounding area, the least strenuous way is on a **boat trip** up the river from the harbour (℡0431/203 00; early June to mid-Aug); there are four forty-minute trips (70kr) and one two-hour cruise daily (90kr). For more freedom of movement, Skåne Marin (℡0431/203 00, @www.skanemarin.se), the company that runs the tours, also rents out boats (300kr for 3hr; 400kr per day) and canoes (150kr for 3hr; 200kr per day). If none of this appeals, head left from the station for some 4km to get to the **beaches**. A free bus runs there from the market square (late June to mid-Aug hourly 10am–4pm).

Jutting like a stiletto heel into the Kattegat, the **Kullen peninsula**, west of Ängelholm, is a highlight along this stretch of coast. It makes for good cycling, but still undulates enough to ensure some great vistas. Head to the picture-perfect village of **Arild**, from where it's just a couple of kilometres northwest to the eighteenth-century farmstead of **Himmelstorp**, with its remarkable and authentic eighteenth-century interiors. You can go in and have a look (May–Sept; free), though opening hours are variable – check with the owners on ℡042/34 60 06. From Himmelstorp, it's well worth the twenty-minute scramble to the coast to the remarkable "living" sculpture, **Nimis**. Created by Lars Vilks out of seventy tonnes of driftwood, Nimis forms corridors and stairways into the sea, providing a spectacular foreground to the backdrop of the Kattegat.

To get to Kullen by car or bike, take Järnvägsgatan from Ängelholm, following directions to Höganäs, then take the scenic northern coastal road at Utvälinge. **Bus** #225 runs from Ängelholm to Höganäs almost hourly until after midnight.

Practicalities

There are regular **trains** to Ängelholm from Båstad (25min), plus **buses** from Båstad and Torekov. It's a short distance from the train station to the **tourist office** in the main square (May & Sept Mon–Fri 9am–5pm, Sat 10am–1pm; June & Aug Mon–Fri 9am–6pm, Sat 10am–2pm; July Mon–Fri 9am–6pm, Sat 9am–3pm, Sun 10am–3pm; Oct–April Mon–Fri 9am–5pm; ☎0431/821 30, ⓦwww.turist.engelholm.se). For **bike rental**, head to Harry's Cykel, Södra Kyrkogatan 9 (☎0431/143 25; 100kr per day or 450kr per week). The tourist office can also book hotels (30kr booking fee) or **private rooms** (from 110kr, plus 30kr booking fee). There's an STF **youth hostel** (☎0431/45 23 64; booking necessary Nov–March; ❶), with dorm beds for 130kr, at the beach at Magnarp Strand, 10km north of the train station and reached by local bus.

Of several **campsites**, the most convenient for the beach is *Råbocka*, at the end of Råbockavägen (☎0431/105 43, ⓕ161 44). For a good-value and friendly **hotel**, try the *Lilton* (☎0431/44 25 50, ⓦwww.hotel-lilton.se; ❸), a few steps from the square at Järnvägsgatan 29, which has a great garden café in summer. Another stylish option is the *Klitterhus Pensionat* (☎0431/135 30, ⓦwww.klitterhus.com; ❸/❹), with elegant rooms, big en-suite bathrooms and a gorgeous bar area, located in the beautifully renovated premises of the classic old *Klitterhus* restaurant down by the beach.

The best place to look for **food** is the harbour. *Hamn Krogen* doesn't look anything special from the outside, but it serves the best fish dishes in Ängelholm – their speciality is "Toast Skagen", shrimps and red caviar on toast. A few metres up the beach, in a whitewashed wartime bunker, *Bunken* restaurant and bar serves barbecue food alongside more lavish seafood dishes (from around 200kr), and puts on regular live music. The most popular **nightclub** is *Bahnhof Bar* (ⓦwww.bahnhofbar.com; Thurs–Sat), a cavernous, industrial-looking place occupying old railway buildings just beyond the train station. If you have your own transport and want a taste of something different, *Ekebo*, in the suburb of Munka-Ljungby around 15km east of town, is a popular place to indulge the Swedish obsession with **foxtrots** on Saturday nights. In July, it hosts Sweden's biggest foxtrot festival (☎0431/43 22 30, ⓦwww.ekebonoje.se) – it's quite an eye-opener.

Helsingborg and around

Long gone are the days when the locals of **HELSINGBORG** joked that the most rewarding sight here was Helsingør, the Danish town whose castle (best known as the "Elsinore" of Shakespeare's *Hamlet*) is clearly visible just 4km away over the Öresund. With its beautifully developed harbour area, an explosion of brilliantly styled bars, cafés and restaurants both at the water's edge and among the warren of cobbled old-town streets, and an excellent museum, Helsingborg is one of the best urban bases Sweden has to offer: bright, pleasing and basking in a tremendous sense of buoyancy.

Past links between Denmark and this likeable city have been less than convivial, though – in fact, Helsingborg has a particularly bloody and tragic history. After the Danes fortified the town in the eleventh century, the Swedes conquered and lost it again on six violent occasions, finally winning out in 1710 under the leadership of Magnus Stenbock. By this time, the Danes had torn down much of the town, and on its final recapture the Swedes razed its twelfth-century castle, except for the five-metre-thick walled keep (*kärnen*) that still dominates the centre. By the early eighteenth century, war and epidemics had reduced the population to just 700, and only with the onset of industrialization in the 1850s did Helsingborg wake up to

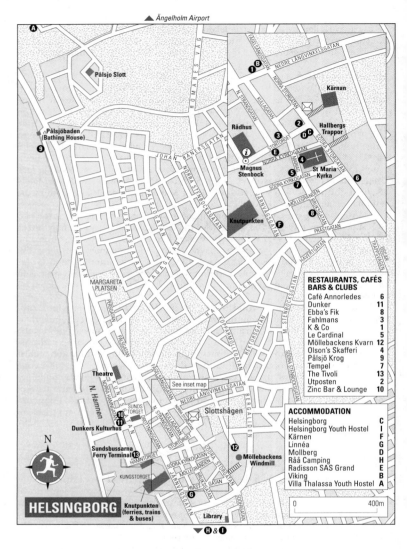

▲ *Ängelholm Airport*

Ⓐ

◆ **Pålsjo Slott**

Pålsjöbaden
(Bathing House)
Ⓘ

ⒾⒷ

NEDRE LÄNGVINKELSGATAN

Kärnan

Rådhus Ⓘ
Ⓘ
STORTORGET Ⓘ ◆ Ⓘ **Hallbergs**
Trappor
Ⓘ Ⓘ
Magnus St Maria
Stenbock Ⓘ **Kyrka** Ⓘ
Ⓘ
Ⓘ
Ⓘ

Knutpunkten Ⓕ
PRÄSTGATAN

MARGARETA
PLATSEN

RESTAURANTS, CAFÉS
BARS & CLUBS
Café Annorledes   6
Dunker   11
Ebba's Fik   8
Fahlmans   3
K & Co   1
Le Cardinal   5
Möllebackens Kvarn   12
Olson's Skafferi   4
Pålsjö Krog   9
Tempel   7
The Tivoli   13
Utposten   2
Zinc Bar & Lounge   10

Theatre

See inset map

Slottshågen

SUNDS
TORGET
Dunkers Kulturhus

Sundsbussarna
Ferry Terminal ⑬
HAMNTORGET

KUNGSTORGET

ACCOMMODATION
Helsingborg   C
Helsingborg Youth Hostel I
Kärnan   F
Linnéa   G
Mollberg   D
Råå Camping   H
Radisson SAS Grand   E
Viking   B
Villa Thalassa Youth Hostel A

⑫ ● **Möllebackens**
Windmill

N

HELSINGBORG **Knutpunkten**
(ferries, trains
& buses)

Library

▼ ⒽⒾ

0   400m

a new prosperity. Shipping and the railways turned the town's fortunes around, as evidenced by the formidable late nineteenth-century commercial buildings in the centre and some splendid villas to the north overlooking the Öresund. After decades out of the limelight, Helsingborg's fortunes now seem very much on the up.

Arrival, information and city transport

Unless you approach by car on the E6, the chances are that you'll arrive at the harbourside **Knutpunkten**, the vast, glassy expanses of which incorporate the bus, train and Scandlines passenger **ferry** terminals. The **bus station** is on the ground floor behind the main hall, while the ticket and transport information offices are in the front of the complex. Below ground level is the combined **train station** for the national SJ trains and the lilac-coloured local Pågatåg trains, which run south down the coast to Lund and Malmö. One floor up are a Forex **currency exchange** office (daily 7am–9pm) and the ferry ticket office. The Sundsbussarna passenger-only ferry to Helsingør uses the quayside at Hamntorget, 100m north. For ferry ticket details, bus and train information, see p.538.

The **tourist office** (mid-June to Aug Mon–Fri 9am–8pm, Sat 9am–5pm, Sun 10am–3pm; Sept to mid-June Mon–Fri 10am–6pm, Sat 10am–2pm; ☏042/10 43 50, ✆www.helsingborg.se) is inside the Rådhus (town hall) at the bottom of the Stortorget boulevard. It organizes hour-long **walking tours** of the city (daily except Sun at 10am; 35kr) and hands out free maps, the *Helsingborg This Month* listings guide and the useful *Helsingborg & Helsingør Guide*.

Central Helsingborg is compact enough to explore on foot, although for the *Villa Thalassa* youth hostel and outlying sights such the Pålsjöbaden bathing house on Drottninggatan, 3km north of the centre, you'll need to take a **bus**. Tickets are bought on board, cost 16kr and are valid for two changes within an hour. **Cycling** is an enjoyable option – the tourist office has a monopoly on bike rental and charges a steep 125kr per day plus a 50kr returnable deposit, though the bikes are at least new and good.

Accommodation

There are plenty of central **hotel** options in Helsingborg. Booking via the tourist office or their website will often result in better room prices; they can also book **private apartments** sleeping up to five, from 3500kr per week plus 100kr booking fee. The *Villa Thalassa* **youth hostel** at Dag Hammarskjöldsväg (☏042/38 06 60, ✆www.villathalassa.com), 2.5km north of the town centre, is superbly set around a one-hundred-year-old villa – unfortunately, the rooms (❶) and dorm beds (from 180kr) aren't in the villa itself, but in cabins behind; there are also some holiday cottages (doubles ❶). Bus #219 runs north from Knutpunkten (every 20min) to the Pålsjöbaden bathing house, from where it's a one-kilometre walk through forest. The *Helsingborg Youth Hostel* at Järnvägsgatan 39 (☏042/14 58 50, ✆www.hbgturist.com; ❶), with dorm beds for 185kr, is a more central though less interesting hostel choice, five minutes' walk from Knutpunkten. The nearest **campsite** is 5km south of town, by the sea in Råå (☏042/10 76 80, ✆www.camping .se/m03); take bus #209, #219 or #220.

Helsingborg Stortorget 20 ☏02/37 18 00, ✆www.rica.se. Lovely hotel with marble stairs, comfortable rooms and a perfect location at the foot of the steps up to the castle keep. ❸/❹

Kärnen Järnvägsgatan 17 ☏042/12 08 20, ✆www.hotelkarnan.se. Opposite Knutpunkten, this comfortable hotel prides itself on "personal touches", including ominous English-language homilies on each room door (no.235, for instance, has "He who seeks revenge keeps his wounds open"). There's a small library, cocktail bar and sauna. ❸/❺

Linnéa Prästgatan 4 ☏042/37 24 00, ✆www .hotell-linnea.se. Reasonably priced, central and pleasant, with agreeable standard rooms, as well as apartments for three people at 5000kr per week. ❸/❹

Mollberg Stortorget 18 ☏042/37 37 00, ✆www .elite.se. Every bit the premier hotel, with a grand nineteenth-century facade, elegant rooms and a brasserie. ❺/❸

Radisson SAS Grand Stortorget 8–12 ☏042/38 04 00, ✆www.radissonsas.com. A distinguished city-centre hotel dating from 1926, with a large period café. Big summer reductions make it much more affordable. ❸/❺

Viking Fågelsångsgatan 1 ☏042/14 44 20, ✆www.hotellviking.se. This appealing, quiet, old hotel in a good location, close to some of the finest old buildings in town, is the place to try first. Excellent service, cosy atmosphere and good breakfasts. ❸/❺

The Town

The most obvious place to start exploring is the waterfront, by the copper statue of Magnus Stenbock on his charger. Facing in the direction of the Öresund and

△ Helsingborg harbour

Denmark, the **Rådhus** (July & Aug Mon & Fri 40min tours at 11am; 25kr) is to your right, a heavy-handed neo-Gothic pile complete with turrets and towers designed by an architect whose admiration for medieval Italy is perhaps a little too obvious. It's worth a look inside to enjoy the extravagances of nineteenth-century provincial wealth and the fabulous stained-glass windows that tell the entire history of the town.

Crossing the road from the statue and turning right, you can't fail to notice the exceptional **Dunkers Kulturhus** cultural centre (Tues, Wed & Fri–Sun 10am–5pm, Thurs till 8pm; ⓦ www.dunkerskulturhus.com; 70kr) at the harbour to your left. This white building, roofed in waves of aluminium and opened in 2002, holds the **city museum** on its ground floor, which explores the Helsingborg's history – via the theme of water – from ice-age to present day with plenty of dramatic lighting and sound effects, plus a hall of artefacts. A good café/restaurant on the ground floor (see opposite) overlooks the harbour. The new **art museum** on the spacious upper floors has changing exhibitions. Henry Dunker, whose foundation funded the centre, was a pioneer of galoshes, and his brand, Tretorn, was a world leader till its demise in 1979.

Returning to the Stenbock statue at the bottom of **Stortorget**, you can walk up the slope to meet the steps leading to the massive castellated bulk of the medieval castle keep, **Kärnan** (daily: April, May & Sept 9am–4pm; June–Aug 11am–7pm; Oct–March 10am–2pm; 20kr). Shaped simply as a huge upturned brick, it's worth climbing more for its views than the historical exhibitions housed within. The keep and St Maria kyrka (see below) were the sole survivors of the ravages of war, but the former lost its military significance once Sweden finally won the day. In the mid-nineteenth century it was destined for demolition and only survived because seafarers found it a valuable landmark. Where cannon fire failed, neglect and the weather succeeded, and the keep fell into ruin before restoration began in 1894.

From the fine parkland around the keep, you can wander down rhododendron-edged stairs, the Hallbergs Trappor, to the **St Maria kyrka** (Mon–Sat 8am–6pm, Sun 9am–6pm), which squats in its own square by an avenue of beech trees. The church was begun in 1300 and completed a century later; its rather plain facade belies a striking interior, with a clever contrast between the early seventeenth-century Renaissance-style ornamentation of its pulpit and gilded reredos, and multi-coloured contemporary stained-glass windows. The square is surrounded by a cluster of quaint places to eat and some excellent **shops** for picnic food (see below).

Walking back to Stortorget, **Norra Storgatan** and **Södra Storgatan** (the streets that meet at the foot of the steps to Kärnen) formed Helsingborg's main thoroughfare in medieval times, and are today lined with the town's oldest merchants' houses. Heading south along Södra Storgatan, pass through the gate to the left of the old cream-painted brick building at no.31 (opposite no.20); from the courtyard here, a flight of steps leads up to the handsome nineteenth-century Möllebackens windmill, surrounded by a number of exquisite farm cottages. A further reward for the climb is to be found at the *Möllebackens Kvarn* restaurant (see below).

Eating, drinking and nightlife

Helsingborg has a range of excellent **restaurants** and some great daytime **cafés** and *konditori*. The harbour restaurants offer some stylish settings overlooking the water, though they're all pretty similar. There are also some superb food shops near St Maria kyrka, useful for picnic fare: notably Maratorgets on the south side of the square, which sells fruit; the adjacent Bengtsons Ost, a cheese shop; and to the east, for exquisite indulgence, the Peter Beier Chocalatier, a chocoholic's dream with a molten chocolate fountain in the window behind which you can consume the delicious products with a coffee.

Cafés and restaurants

Café Annorledes Södra Storgatan 15. A friendly atmosphere with jumble sale memorabilia and serving a 40kr weekday breakfast.

Dunker Kungsgatan 11. A bright and modern self-service café inside the Dunkers Kulturhus and overlooking the harbour, with light meals from 80kr, delicious cakes, and a high-tech paging system to alert you when your food is ready.

Ebba's Fik Bruksgatan 20. The most fun café in town, with authentic 1950s styling and great music to match. A must.

Fahlmans Stortorget 11. Helsingborg's classic *konditori*, this has been serving elaborate cakes and pastries since 1914. Try the coconut marzipan confections or the sumptuous apple meringue pie.

K & Co Nedre Långvinkelsgatan 9. Very friendly, with great muffins, cakes and filling ciabattas and baguettes.

Möllebackens Kvarn Bergaleden 11 ☎042/127275. Tiny, atmospheric restaurant in a historic wooden building next to Möllebackens windmill. Dishes cost 80–170kr; specialities include the fish stew with saffron and aioli (163kr), and the waffles with raspberry jam and cream (32kr). It's quickest reached via the steps in the courtyard at Södra Storgatan 31. Mon–Wed & Sun till 5pm, Thurs–Sat till 8pm; closed Jan & Feb.

Olson's Skafferi Mariagatan 6 ☎042/14 07 80. The city's best Italian restaurant, right outside St Maria kyrka. Wonderfully prepared, authentic Italian dishes with fish, meat and pasta options, and zabaglione to drool over. Prices between 90 and 190kr.

Pålsjö Krog ☎042/14 97 30. Attached to the lovely old Pålasjöbaden bathhouse 2km north of the centre, and run by an architect who has designed it to feel like a Swedish country house. It's a special-occasion place serving traditional, well-presented Swedish food with main courses at around 180kr.

Utposten Stortorget 17. Very stylish decor – a mix of the rustic and industrial – at this great, varied Swedish restaurant beneath the post office at the steps to Kärnen. A two-course meal will cost around 140kr. Try the delicate and filling seafood and salmon stew at 90kr. Open till 1am.

Bars and clubs

The glamorous **bars** along Norra hamnen (the North Harbour) have provided a stylish foil to Helsingborg's traditional night-time haunts and music venues. These newer bars overlooking the Öresund are more for wine- and beer-drinking than eating, though they do serve food along new-European lines. The *Zinc Bar & Lounge* takes over the *Dunker* café (see p.537) after hours, with regular live music.

You might want to indulge in the **Tura**, the classic Helsingborg activity of taking the ferry to Helsingør and going back and forth all night rather than getting off in Denmark. The entertainment is the boat itself and the characters on it; hang at the bar all night to take advantage of the low prices (beer 25kr). Scandlines, on the first floor of Knutpunkten, sells special Tura tickets for 71kr (includes 50kr worth of food and drink); booking a bar or table seat a day or two in advance is recommended.

Le Cardinal Södra Kyrkogatan 9. Piano bar and nightclub with a steak-oriented restaurant. The first-floor disco is usually busy, while the second-floor piano bar is quieter, with a roulette table. Cover is 60–70kr and you need to be 25 to get in. Often closed during summer; call ☎042/18 71 71 to check.
Tempel Bruksgatan 2, ☎042/32 70 20, ⊛www .tempel.dj. A trendy "loungeclub", a combination of fusion restaurant, bar, lounge and club that successfully manages to lure in the beautiful people. Thurs–Sat.
The Tivoli Hamntorget; ⊛www.thetivoli.nu. Lively place occupying the main part of the former train station opposite Knutpunkten, where you'll find lots of concerts and events. There's also a restaurant, *Vinyl Baren*, which is indeed filled with red vinyl bench seats and 1960s pop art.

Listings

Airport The nearest airport for domestic flights is at Ängelholm, 30km north of town and served by SAS and Kullaflyg (☎042/24 42 22, ⊛www .kullaflyg.se), flying to Stockholm Bromma. To get there, take bus #270 from Knutpunkten (1hr before flight departure). For international services, you'll need to go to Copenhagen's Kastrup airport; to get there costs 82kr using the ferry to Helsingør and a connecting train (but just 65kr if you buy the combined ticket from the Scandlines ferry office), or 153kr by train via Malmö and the Öresund Bridge; both routes take 2hr.
Buses Direct buses to Stockholm (3 daily; 280–311kr) and Gothenburg (7 daily; 147–174kr) leave from Knutpunkten. Tickets can be bought from the bus information section at the train booking office; the cheaper fares are valid when paid 24hrs in advance.
Car rental Avis, Garnisonsgatan 2 ☎042/15 70 80; Budget, Gustav Adolfsgatan 47 ☎042/12 50 40; Europcar, Muskötgatan 1 ☎042/17 01 15; Hertz, Bergavägen 4 ☎042/17 25 40.
Exchange Forex in Knutpunkten (first floor) or Järnvägsgatan 13. Both open June–Aug 7am–9pm & Sept–May 8am–9pm.
Ferries to Helsingør Scandlines car and foot-passenger ferries (☎042/18 60 00,
⊛www.scandlines.se) depart every 10–20min during the day from Knutpunkten, and every half hour at night; HH-Ferries (☎042/19 80 00, ⊛www .hhferries.se) sail every half hour during the day, every hour at night. Sundsbussarna foot-passenger ferries (☎042/38 58 80, ⊛www.sundsbussarna. se) leave every half hour to hour from Hamntorget between 6am and 7.30pm (weekends 8am–6.30pm). The crossing takes 20min and tickets for all companies cost 22kr one-way, 40kr return. You are allowed to take 110 litres of beer and 90 litres of wine across the border, and trolleys are for rent at Knutpunkten for that purpose.
Internet You can quickly check email for free at the tourist office; alternatively, use the eight coin-operated Sidewalk Express terminals at the 7-Eleven shop inside Knutpunkten (daily 6am–1am; 19kr/hr).
Pharmacy Björnen, Drottninggatan 14 (Mon–Fri 9am–6pm, Sat 9am–3pm), or Kärnan. Lasarett Hospital (Mon–Fri 8.30am–8pm, Sat 3–8pm, Sun 11am–8pm).
Post office Stortorget 17 (Mon–Fri 9.30am–5.30pm).
Trains The Pågatåg trains from Knutpunkten require a ticket bought from machines on the platform or in the main hall; international rail passes are valid. It's 72kr one-way to Lund and 84kr one-way to Malmö.

Lund

Only 20km from Malmö and 50km south of Helsingborg is the celebrated university city of **LUND**. Like England's Oxford, with which it is often and aptly compared, there's an eccentric and bohemian atmosphere to the place – a mass of students' bikes will probably be the first image to greet you. Cultural attractions aside, it's the mix of architectural grandeur and the buzz of student life that lends Lund its unique charm, and with its justly revered twelfth-century Romanesque cathedral, its medieval streets and numerous museums, the town could easily keep you busy for a couple of days.

Arrival, information and city transport

Frequent **trains** from Malmö (12min) and Helsingborg (30min) arrive at the train station on Bangatan at the western edge of town, which is also the terminus for **buses** and within easy walking distance of everything of interest. The **tourist office** (May & Sept Mon–Fri 10am–5pm, Sat 10am–2pm; June–Aug Mon–Fri 10am–6pm, Sat & Sun 10am–2pm; Oct–April Mon–Fri 10am–5pm; ☎046/35 50 40, ⓦwww.lund.se), opposite the Domkyrkan at Kyrkogatan 11, hands out free maps and copies of *I Lund*, a monthly English- and Swedish-language diary of events with museum and exhibition listings. There's an **Internet café**, Noll Ett, at Lilla Gråbrödersgatan 2 (Mon–Fri 10am–midnight, Sat noon–1am, Sun 1–11pm). Though none of the sights is more than ten minutes' walk away, you might want to consider renting a **bike** from the shop in the bus station building on Bangatan (☎046/35 57 42; 20kr/day).

Accommodation

There's a decent range of **accommodation** on offer in Lund, nearly all of it in the centre, and the tourist office can book **private rooms** for 225–250kr per

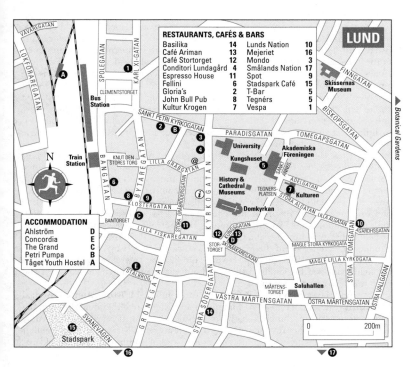

person, plus a 50kr booking fee. Lund's STF **youth hostel**, *Tåget*, at Vävaregatan 22, through the tunnel behind the train station (⌖046/14 28 20, ⍟www.trainhostel .com; dorm beds 130kr), is housed in the carriages of a 1940s train; unfortunately, the novelty quickly wears off when you find yourself crammed in three deep bunks with rope hoists.

Ahlström Skomakaregatan 3 ⌖046/211 01 74, ⍟www.hotellahlstrom.se. Average, very central cheapie with the option of en-suite rooms. Closed June to mid-Aug. ❷/❸

Concordia Stålbrogatan 1 ⌖046/13 50 50, ⍟www.concordia.se. A couple of streets southwest of Stortorget, this former student hostel has been upgraded into a very homely hotel with attentive service, though it's rather plain inside. There's a guest sauna, too. ❹/❻

🏃 **The Grand** Bantorget 1 ⌖046/280 61 00, ⍟www.grandilund.se. This imposing nineteenth-century pink-sandstone edifice straddles an entire side of a small, stately and central square. Unpretentious and comfortable, with a fantastic breakfast buffet. ❺/❻

Petri Pumpa Sankt Petri Kyrkogatan 7 ⌖046/13 55 19, ⍟www.petripumpa.se. A small but exclusive hotel with rooms full of character, some with private sauna. ❹/❻

The Town

It's only a short walk east from the train station to the magnificent **Domkyrkan** (Mon, Tues & Fri 8am–6pm, Wed & Thurs 8am–7.15pm, Sat 9.30am–5pm, Sun 9.30am–7.30pm; guided tours 3pm; free), whose storm-cloud charcoal and white stone gives it an unusual monochrome appearance. Before entering, head around the back, past the grotesque animal and bird gargoyles over the side entrances; at the very back is the most beautiful part of the exterior: the three-storey apse above the crypt, crowned with an exquisite gallery.

Beyond the great carved entrance, the majestic **interior** is surprisingly unadorned, an elegant mass of watery-grey, ribbed stone arches and stone-flagged flooring. One of the world's finest masterpieces of Romanesque architecture, the cathedral was built in the twelfth century when Lund became the first independent archbishopric in Scandinavia, laying the foundation for a period of wealth and eminence that lasted until the advent of Protestantism. There are several interesting features, such as the elaborately carved fourteenth-century choir stalls depicting Old Testament scenes, with grotesque carvings hidden beneath the seats, but most striking is the amazing astronomical clock just to the left of the entrance. Dating from the 1440s, it shows hours, days, weeks and the courses of the sun and moon in the zodiac; if you're here at noon or 3pm, you'll get to see an ecclesiastical Punch and Judy show, as two knights pop out and clash swords as many times as the clock strikes, followed by little mechanical doors opening to trumpet-blowing heralds and the three wise men trundling slowly around the Virgin Mary.

Don't miss the dimly lit and dramatic **crypt**, which has been left almost untouched since the twelfth century. Most of the tombstones are actually memorial slabs, with just one proper tomb containing the remains of Birger Gunnarsson, Lund's last archbishop. A short man from a poor family, Gunnarsson dictated that his stone effigy should be tall and regal. Two pillars are gripped by stone figures – one of a man, another of a woman and child. Legend has it that Finn the Giant built the cathedral for Saint Lawrence; in return, the saint was to guess the giant's name, or failing that, give him the sun, the moon or his eyes. Preparing to end his days in blindness, Lawrence heard the giant's wife boasting to her baby, "Soon Father Finn will bring some eyes for you to play with". On hearing Lawrence declare his name, the livid giant and his family rushed to the crypt to pull down the columns and were instantly turned to stone.

Just behind the cathedral on Krafts torg 1, the combined **History and Cathedral Museums** (Tues–Fri 11am–4pm, Sun noon–4pm; free) are rather dull, although the statues from Skånian churches in the medieval exhibition deserve a look, mainly because of the way they're arranged – a mass of Jesuses and Marys bunched together in groups, with the crowd of Jesuses on crosses looking ominously Hitchcockian.

A few minutes' walk east of nearby Tegnerplatsen is the town's best museum, the open-air **Kulturen** (daily: mid-April to Sept 11am–5pm; Oct to mid-April noon–4pm; 50kr; ❽www.kulturen.com). Despite the lack of labelling in English, it's easy to spend the best part of a day just wandering around this virtual town of perfectly preserved cottages, farms, merchants' houses, gardens and even churches, brought from seven regions around Sweden and from as many centuries.

Head north from the square along Sankt Annegatan, continue up Sandgatan and then take a right on to Finngatan to reach another rather special museum, the **Skissernas Museum** (Museum of Sketches; Tues–Sun noon–5pm; 30kr), with a fascinating collection of preliminary sketches and original full-scale models of artworks from around the world. One room is full of work by all the major Swedish artists, while in the international room you'll find sketches by Chagall, Matisse, Léger, Miró and Dufy, and sculptural sketches by Picasso and Henry Moore.

As an antidote to museum fatigue, the **Botanical Gardens** (daily 6am–8pm; greenhouses noon–3pm; free), a few minutes' stroll further southwest down Finngatan (turn left at the end of the street into Pålsjövågen and right into Olshögsvägen), are as much a venue for picnicking and chilling out as a botanical experience.

Eating, drinking and nightlife

There are plenty of appealing places to eat and drink in Lund, most associated with the university. Certain **cafés** are student institutions and a number of the better **restaurants** are attached to student bodies or museums – which serves to keep prices low, especially for beer. If you want to buy your own provisions, the **Saluhallen** market at Mårtenstorget sells a range of fish, cheeses and meats, including Lund's own tasty speciality sausage, *knake*. Opposite the library on Sankt Petri Kyrkogatan, Widerbergs Charkuteri is a long-established foodie shop brimming with all the ingredients for a picnic.

When it comes to **nightlife**, it's worth knowing that the university is divided into "nations", or colleges, named after different geographical areas of Sweden and with strong identities. Each nation has its own bar that's active two nights a week, and there are also regular discos. *Lunds Nation* (❽www.lundsnation.se) is the biggest, based in the red-brick house at Agardhsgatan 1, while *Smålands Nation* (❽www.smalands.lu.se) at Kastanjegatan 7 is the trendiest; both are known for hosting **live bands**.

Cafés and restaurants

Café Ariman Kungsgatan 2. A nineteenth-century red-brick building housing a classic, deliberately shabby left-wing coffee house – goatees, pony tails and blond dreadlocks predominate. Cheap meals and coffee, and club nights at weekends.

Café Stortorget Stortorget 1. Housed in a National Romantic-style former bank, with walls covered in dramatic black-and-white shots of actors, this café/restaurant is a prime meeting spot and has the town's best terrace for people-watching. Closed Sun.

Conditori Lundagård Kyrkogatan 17. Classic student *konditori*, with caricatures of professors adorning the walls. Justly famous for its apple meringue pie.

Espresso House Stora Grabrodersgatan 4. Part of the popular chain, this stylish café is good for breakfast (8–11am) as well as filled baguettes and cakes. The decor is contemporary, and there

are lots of lifestyle magazines (in English) to read while munching muffins and ciabatta.

Fellini Bangatan 6 ☎046/13 80 20, ❽www .fellini.se. Stylish and popular (book ahead) Italian restaurant that's stood the test of time, decked out in dull chrome and stripped wood. The lunch buffet with unlimited pizza and pasta is excellent value at 65kr; mains cost 120–200kr.

Gloria's Sankt Petri Kyrkogata 9. Good-value American and Cajun food, from burgers to big salads, and very popular with students and tourists. Sports games are shown on TVs. Local bands play Fri & Sat nights when *Gloria's* is open till 3am, and there's a big, lively garden area at the back.

Kultur Krogen In front of the Kulturen museum, beneath a giant beech tree, this busy café, bar and restaurant is a great place to relax, with a youngish crowd drinking cheap beer (28kr). Good lunch with vegetarian choice (60kr).

Mondo Kyrkogatan 23. Set in a quaint, beamed house, this café serves bagels, cheesecake, brownies and the like; the large baguettes are good value.

Spot Klostergatan 14. A splendid choice: downstairs offers à la carte Italian lunches, while upstairs there's delicious Swedish food (120–140kr). Closed Sun.

Stadspark Café Stadspark. Right at the end of Nygatan in an old wooden pavilion fronted by a sea of white plastic garden furniture, this place is always busy with families munching on snacks. Big baguettes fill you up for 35–40kr.

Tegnérs Sandgatan 2. Occupying the building next to the student union, with a main hall resplendent with gilded Ionic columns. Forget any preconceptions about student cafés being tatty, stale sandwich bars. Self-service lunch for 55–70kr allows you as much as you like from a choice of delicious gourmet dishes. There's seating inside or on the terrace. Daily 11.30am–2.30pm.

Vespa Karl XI vägen 1. Chic, well-priced restaurant with Italian styling in Vespa red; more of a post-grad hangout than the usual student haunts. Good pizzas (65–95kr).

Bars and clubs

Basilika Stora Södergatan 13 ☎046/211 66 60. Hip and firmly established place, just a few steps south of Stortorget. There's a café, and a bar with a huge drinks list, while events (comedy nights, cabaret) and concerts are also staged; there's a minimum age of 20 for these. Closed Sun.

John Bull Pub Bantorget, adjacent to the *Grand Hotel*. British-style traditional pub.

Mejeriet Stora Södergatan 64, ☎046/18 98 99. A lively music and cultural centre in a century-old dairy building, with a stylish café, concert hall and arts cinema. A few minutes walk from the cathedral.

T-Bar Sandgatan 2 ☎046 13 13 33, ⊕www.t-bar .nu. A student nightclub set in the Tegnérs building next to the student union. With a student card, people aged eighteen and over can get in, otherwise it's strictly over-23s only. Thurs 7pm–3am; free entry till midnight, then 20kr.

Malmö

Founded in the late thirteenth century, **MALMÖ** rose to become Denmark's most important city after Copenhagen. The high density of herring in the sea off the Malmö coast – it was said that the fish could be scooped straight out with a trowel – brought ambitious German merchants flocking to the city, an influence that can be seen in the striking fourteenth-century St Petri kyrka. Eric of Pomerania gave Malmö its most significant medieval boost when, in the fifteenth century, he built the castle and mint, and gave the city its own flag – the gold-and-red griffin of his family crest. It wasn't until the Swedish king Karl X marched his armies across the frozen belt of water to within striking distance of Copenhagen in 1658 that the Danes were forced into handing back the counties of Skåne, Blekinge and Bohuslän to the Swedes. For Malmö, this meant a period of stagnation, cut off from nearby Copenhagen and too far from its own uninterested capital. Not until the full thrust of industrialization, triggered by the tobacco merchant Frans Suell's enlargement of the harbour in 1775, did Malmö begin its dramatic commercial recovery, and the city's fortunes remained buoyant over the following two centuries. The 1990s saw a further commercial crisis after Malmö had invested heavily in the shipping industry that had been in decline since the 1970, but since the turn of the millennium, there's been a heartwarming reversal of the city's fortunes, with the new university and the opening of the Öresund Bridge, which links Malmö with Copenhagen, attracting an influx of investment that visitors can't fail to notice and creating an upbeat, energetic and likeable atmosphere. The attractive medieval centre, delightful parks and sweeping beach are all major draws, while the plentiful restaurants and bars and a lively nightlife serve as another inducement to stay a while.

Arrival, information and city transport

If you've driven over from Denmark via the Öresund Bridge, simply follow the signs north that take you into the centre of Malmö. All trains arrive at the **train station**, bang in the centre of town. The frequent local Pågatåg trains to and from Helsingborg, Lund and Ystad use platforms 9–13 at the back. Catch a city bus from the square outside, Centralplan. Buses from Stockholm, Helsingborg, Gothenburg and Copenhagen/Kastrup airport arrive at the **long-distance bus terminal** at the end of Skeppsbron.

MALMÖ

▲ **A** ▲ *Sturup Airport*

◀ *Long-distance Bus Terminal (50ml)*

◀ *Western Harbour (500ml)*, **1** & **2**

ACCOMMODATION

Baltzar	H
Clarion	I
Formule 1	A
Hilton Malmö City	K
Kramer	F
Malmö Camping	D
The Mayfair	E
Radisson SAS Malmö	C
Royal	G
Savoy	B
Villa Hilleröd Youth Hostel	J

RESTAURANTS, CAFÉS, BARS & CLUBS

Ambiance	8
Årstiderna	3
Buddha Lounge	5
Café Systrar och Bröder	14
Club Indigo	15
Club Wonk	13
Conditoria Hollandia	12
Espresso House	1
Grappa	7
Gustav Adolf	10
Mellow Yellow	6
Moosehead	6
Rådhuskällaren	4
Salt och Brygga	2
Schlagerbaren	9
The Tunnel	E
Vespa	11
Victor's	6

Central Station

Bus Station

Caroli Kyrka **C**

St Petri Kyrka

Mattssons Musikpub **E**

Rådhus

Rooseum

Malmö Synagogue ☆

Form Design Centre

Saluhall

Malmöhus

Kommendanthus

Library @

Kungsparken

Slottsparken

Mariedalspark

▶ Ribersborg Park & Kallbadhuset ▶ Öresund Bridge & **D**

▶ 15. Folketspark, Möllevångstorget, Jeriko & Kulturbolaget

▶ Konsthall, Pildammsvägen, **K** & **14**

0 — 250m

543

The Öresund Link

Connecting Malmö with Copenhagen in Denmark, the **Öresund Link** (ⓦwww
.oresundsbron.se) was finally completed in the summer of 1999 after nearly half a
century of debate between those who believed it would have a negative environmental impact on the Baltic Sea and those who felt it would be Sweden's most beneficial
and significant construction of the twentieth century. The completion was marked by
the symbolic embrace, halfway along the new bridge, of Sweden's Crown Princess
Victoria and Denmark's Crown Prince Frederick.

The sixteen-kilometre-long fixed link consists of three parts; most visible is the massive eight-kilometre-long suspension bridge, with two decks for the motorway and the
railway lines, and a 490m main span, raised 60m above the busy waterway by four
two-hundred-metre-high pylons. The bridge ends on the four-kilometre-long artificial
island of Peberholm, from where a four-kilometre-long tunnel dips under the sea to
surface in Denmark, near Copenhagen airport. Around 12,000 vehicles and 17,000
train passengers per day cross the bridge, and every June a half marathon is held
between Peberholm and Malmö stadium. This is Sweden's only toll road and crossing
by car costs 285kr, significantly more than the ferry connection from Malmö, which
still survives. Taking a train from Copenhagen to Malmö will be even quicker once a
new rail tunnel underneath Malmö's city centre, including an underground station at
Triangeln, is completed in 2011.

From Sturup **airport**, 30km east of Malmö, you can take the airport bus (*fly-
gbuss;* ⓦwww.flygbussarna.se) to Central Station (Mon–Fri 7.20am–11.50pm, Sat
10.20am–4.50pm, Sun 8.40am–11.50pm; 1–2 buses per hour; 40min; 90kr). Passengers landing in Trelleborg on the TT-Line **ferry** from Travemünde or Rostock
in Germany can take bus #146 to Malmö from the Trelleborg Övre stop.

Information and discount cards

The **tourist office** (June–Aug Mon–Fri 9am–7pm, Sat & Sun 10am–5pm; Sept &
May Mon–Fri 9am–5pm, Sat & Sun 10am–3pm; Oct–April Mon–Fri 9am–5pm,
Sat & Sun 10am–2pm; ☏040/34 12 00, ⓦwww.malmo.se) is inside the Central
Station. Here you can pick up a wealth of free information, including several good
maps, the *Malmö Guide* and the *Malmö What's On* events brochure. You can also buy
the very useful **Malmökortet** (Malmö Card; available for 1, 2 or 3 days for 130kr,
160kr or 190kr respectively), which gives free museum entry, car parking, a guided
bus tour and unlimited city bus journeys, plus various other discounts on transport,
cinemas, concerts and trips around the city. The **Öresunds Rundt card** (see box
on p.531), offering discounts on regional transport, can also be worth investing in.

There are ATMs in the train station, and Forex **money exchanges** just opposite
the tourist office (daily 8am–9pm), on Norra Vägen 60 (daily 7am–9pm) and
Gustav Adolfs Torg (daily 9am–7pm).

City transport

Although the city centre is easy to walk around, you'll need to use **buses** to reach
some of the sights and some accommodation. Individual tickets cost 15kr and are
valid for an hour; a 200kr magnetic card is also available and can be used by several
people at the same time. All tickets are sold on the bus. If you want to use **taxis**, it's
worth comparing rates. In summer, **bicycle rental** is available from Rent-a-Bike,
inside the tourist office (☏0707/49 94 22, ⓦwww.rent-a-bike.se; 90kr per day).

Between May and August, ninety-minute guided **sightseeing bus tours** (daily;
100kr, free with Malmö Card) leave at noon from the tourist office, and are a good
way to get your bearings. Alternatively, between May and October you can join
the hourly **boat tour** (☏040/611 74 88, ⓦwww.rundan.se; 50min; 75kr) of the

city's canals and harbour, departing from opposite the Central Station. Note that the construction of a new railway tunnel from the Central Station to the Öresund Bridge will cause traffic diversions until 2011.

Accommodation

There are some excellent and surprisingly affordable **hotels** in Malmö. Being a city that attracts business travellers as well as tourists, competition between the hotels can be fierce. Prices plummet at the weekend and most hotels have good summer rate reductions, too. Booking via the tourist office website (Ⓦ www.malmo.se/hotel) can be cheaper than booking directly with the hotel. Malmö's new year-round **youth hostel**, Villa Hilleröd, is housed in a quaint old house just southwest of the city centre at Ängdalavägen 38 (Ⓣ 040/26 56 26, Ⓦ www.villahillerod.se); dorm beds cost from 190kr and there are also has some private rooms (❶); get there by bus #3 to the Mellanheden stop. The nearest **campsite**, *Malmö Camping* at Strandgatan 101 in Limhamn (Ⓣ 040/15 51 65, Ⓦ www.camping.se/plats/m08), is in a picturesque spot, close to the bridge to Copenhagen and can be reached with bus #34.

Baltzar Södergatan 20 Ⓣ 040/665 57 00, Ⓦ www.baltzarhotel.se. Very central (between the two main squares), this is a swanky place done out in swags and flourishes that owe more to British posh hotel design than Swedish style. ❺/❻

Clarion Engelbrektsgatan 16 Ⓣ 040/710 20, Ⓕ 30 44 06. Pleasant central hotel; the price includes a big buffet breakfast. ❹

Formule 1 Lundavägen 1, 1km east of the city centre Ⓣ 040/93 05 80, Ⓦ www.hotelformule1.com. The cheapest hotel in town, with functional rooms sleeping up to three people (330kr). ❶

Hilton Malmö City Triangeln 2 Ⓣ 040/693 47 00, Ⓦ www.hilton.com. Towering over the southern part of the city centre, the top-floor rooms and fitness centre of this swanky business hotel offer unsurpassed views of Malmö and its environs. ❺/❻

Kramer Stortorget 7 Ⓣ 040/693 54 00, Ⓦ www.scandic-hotels.com. Beautiful white-stuccoed, French-turreted hotel from the 1870s on the main square, once Malmö's top hotel and still very luxurious. ❹/❻

The Mayfair Adelgatan 4 Ⓣ 040/10 16 20, Ⓦ www.mayfairtunneln.com. Very central Danish-owned place, and one of the finest of Malmö's more intimate hotels. Rooms are well furnished in cherry or Gustavian pastels. Good breakfasts and weekend discounts. ❸/❺

Radisson SAS Malmö Östergatan 10 Ⓣ 040/698 40 00, Ⓦ www.radissonsas.com. Just beyond the Caroli kyrka, this hotel's unimposing facade opens into a delightful interior. The rooms are large and stylish, and breakfast is eaten inside one of Malmö's oldest houses, cunningly incorporated into the building. ❹/❻

Royal Norra Vallgatan 94 Ⓣ 040/664 25 00, Ⓦ www.hotellroyal.com. Small, family-run hotel just up from the train station. Price includes breakfast, which is served in the garden in summer. ❸

Savoy Norra Vallgatan 62 Ⓣ 040/664 48 00, Ⓦ www.savoy.elite.se. Nicely priced during summer, and just opposite the train station, this is where the likes of Lenin, Bardot and Dietrich have stayed, with a brass plaque to prove it. The rooms are big and very comfortable. ❸/❻

The City

Standing outside the nineteenth-century train station with its ornate red-brick arches and curly-topped pillars, the **canal** in front of you, dug by Russian prisoners, forms a rough rectangle encompassing the **Old Town** directly to the south and the moated castle, the **Malmöhus**, to the west, surrounded by a series of attractive interconnecting parks. First off, though, head down Hamngatan to the main square, Stortorget. On the way you'll pass the striking sculpture of a twisted revolver, a monument to non-violence, which stands outside the grand former Malmö Exchange building from the 1890s.

The Old Town

Stortorget, the proud main square, is home to a series of elaborate sixteenth- to nineteenth-century buildings, amongst which the **Rådhus** of 1546 draws the most attention. A pageant of architectural fiddling and statuary, the building's original design was destroyed during remodelling in the nineteenth century, which left the present, finicky Dutch Renaissance exterior. It's impressive, nonetheless, and to add to the pomp, the red-and-gold Skånian flag, of which Malmö is so proud, hangs from the eaves. There are occasional tours of the interior; check with the tourist office. The cellars, home to *Rådhus Källaren Restaurant* (see p.549), have been used as a tavern for more than four hundred years.

The step-gabled red-brick building on the opposite side of the square was once the home of sixteenth-century mayor and Master of the Danish Mint, Jörgen Kocks. Danish coins were struck in Malmö on the site of the present Malmöhus, until irate local Swedes stormed the building and destroyed it in 1534. In the cellars here you'll find the *Kockska Krogan* restaurant, the only part of the building accessible to visitors. In the centre of the square, a statue of chubby King Karl X Gustav, high on his charger, presides over the city he liberated from centuries of Danish rule.

Head a block east, behind the Rådhus, to reach the Gothic **St Petri kyrka** on Göran Olsgatan (daily 10am–6pm), dark and forbidding on the outside, but light and airy within. The church has its roots in the fourteenth century and, although Baltic in inspiration, the final style owes much to German influences, for it was beneath its unusually lofty and elegantly vaulted roof that the German community came to pray – probably for the continuation of the "sea silver", the herrings that brought them to Malmö in the first place. The ecclesiastical vandalism of white-washing over medieval roof murals started early at St Petri – almost the whole interior was turned white in 1553 – and consequently your eyes are drawn to the pulpit and four-tiered altarpiece, both of striking workmanship and elaborate embellishment. The only part of the church left with its original artwork is a side chapel, the **Krämare Chapel**. Added to the church in the late fifteenth century as a Lady Chapel, it was considered redundant at the Reformation and sealed off, thus protecting the paintings from the zealous brushes of the reformers. Best preserved are the paintings on the vaulted ceiling, mainly depicting New Testament figures surrounded by decorative foliage, while underfoot the chapel floor is a chessboard of tombs in black, white and red stone.

Södergatan, Malmö's main pedestrianized shopping street, leads south of Stortorget down towards the southern canal. At the Stortorget end there's a jaunty troupe of sculptured bronze musicians, and a collection of lively cafés and restaurants further down. On the corner of the square, take a peek inside **Apoteket Lejonet**. Gargoyled and balconied on the outside, the pharmacy interior is a busy mix of inlaid wood, carvings and etched glass.

Despite the size of Stortorget, it still proved too small to suffice as the sole city square, so in the sixteenth century **Lilla Torg**, formerly marshland, was sewn on to the southeast corner. Looking like a film set, this little square with its creaky, old half-timbered houses, flowerpots and cobbles, is everyone's favourite part of the city. During the day, people congregate here to take a leisurely drink in one of the many bars, and wander around the summer jewellery stalls. At night, Lilla Torg explodes in a frenzy of activity, with people from all over the city converging on the square to visit the bars or promenade over the cobbles.

Walk through an arch on Lilla Torg and you'll reach the **Form Design Centre** (Tues, Wed & Fri 11am–5pm, Thurs 11am–6pm, Sat & Sun 10am–4pm; free), housed in a seventeenth-century grain store and celebrating Swedish design in textiles, ceramics and furniture. From the beginning of the twentieth century until the 1960s, the whole of Lilla Torg was a covered market, and the sole vestige of those days, **Saluhallen**, is diagonally opposite the Design Centre. Mostly made up of specialist fine food shops and snack bars, it makes for a pleasant, cool retreat on a hot afternoon.

A few streets away to the east, but well worth a visit if you're interested in contemporary art, is the **Rooseum** (Wed 2pm–8pm, Thurs–Sun noon–6pm, guided tours Wed 6pm, Thurs–Fri 4pm, Sat & Sun 2pm; 30kr, free with Malmö Card) on

Gasverksgatan 22. Space is imaginatively used in this elaborate building from 1900, originally constructed to house the Malmö Electricity Company's steam turbines. The main turbine hall forms the central gallery, displaying experimental installations and interesting photographic works.

Malmöhus and around

Take any of the streets running west from Stortorget or Lilla Torg and you soon come up against the edge of **Kungsparken**, within striking distance of the fifteenth-century castle, **Malmöhus** (daily: June–Aug 10am–4pm; Sept–May noon–4pm; 40kr, includes entry to Kommendanthus, free with Malmö Card. Free guided tours in English at 3pm). For a more dramatic approach, walk west (away from the station) up Citadellsvägen; from here, the low castle with its grassy ramparts and two circular keeps is straight ahead over the wide moat.

Originally Denmark's mint, the building was destroyed by the Swedes in 1534. Two years later, a new fortress was built on the site by the Danish king Christian III, only to be of unforeseen benefit to his enemies who, once back in control of Skåne, used it to repel an attacking Danish army in 1677. Serving as a prison for a time (the Earl of Bothwell, Mary Queen of Scots' third husband, was its most notable inmate), the castle's importance waned once back in Swedish hands, and it was used for grain storage until opening as a **museum** in 1937.

Passing swiftly through the natural history section – a taxidermal Noah's Ark – the most rewarding part of the museum is the ambitious series of furnished rooms that takes you from the mid-sixteenth-century Renaissance through Baroque, Rococo, pastel-pale Gustavian and Neoclassical. A stylish jugend (Art Nouveau) interior is equally impressive, while other rooms feature Functionalist and post-Functionalist interiors. Just as interesting are the spartan but authentic interiors of the castle itself. Finally, the modern art section has a large collection of twentieth-century Nordic art, with changing exhibitions.

Just beyond the castle to the west along Malmöhusvagen is the **Kommendan- thus** (Governor's House; same hours as Malmöhus, and included in Malmöhus entry fee), containing a strange combination of military and toy museums. The military section is a fairly lifeless collection of neatly presented medals, rifles and swords, along with the usual dummies sporting eighteenth- and nineteenth-century uniforms. The toy museum is more fun – the link between the two being a brigade of toy British soldiers. A little further west, running off Malmöhusvagen, is a tiny walkway, **Banerkajen**, lined with higgledy-piggledy fishing shacks selling fresh and smoked fish.

Once you've had your fill of museums, the castle **grounds** are good for a stroll, peppered with small lakes and an old windmill. The paths lead all the way down to Regementsgatan past the striking eighteen-metre-high reading room of the City Library in the southeastern corner of the park. You can continue walking through the greenery as far as Gustav Adolfs Torg by crossing Gamla Begravnings Platsen, a pretty graveyard.

Out from the centre

Tourists rarely head further south of the city than the canal banks that enclose the old town, yet with a few hours to spare, the areas around Amiralsgatan give an interesting insight into Malmö's mix of cultures. A few hundred metres down Amiralsgatan, the copper-domed Moorish building standing out on Föreningsgatan is the restored **Malmö Synagogue**. Designed and built in 1894, the synagogue is decorated with concentric designs in blue and green glazed brick. Strict security measures mean the unrenovated interior is closed to visitors.

Back on Amiralsgatan, it's a ten-minute walk to **Folketspark**, Sweden's oldest working people's park, once the pride and joy of the community. Now renovated with an attractive fountain, Folketspark contains a basic amusement park and, at its centre, the **Moriskan**, an odd, low building with Russian-style golden minarets topped with sickles and housing a ballroom. Amusement park and ballroom are both now privately owned, a far cry from the original aims of the park's Social Democratic founders, carved busts of whom are dotted all over the park.

South of the park, the multicultural character of Malmö becomes apparent. Middle Eastern, Asian and Balkan emigré families predominate, and strolling from the park's southern exit down Möllevången to **Möllevångstorget**, you enter an area populated almost entirely by non-Swedes, with Arabic and Urdu the main languages. The large Möllevångstorget square, boasting a poignant and impressive statue at its centre depicting Malmö workers straining under the weight of their toils, is a haven of cafés and exotic food shops, along with shops selling pure junk.

The Western Harbour and along the beach to Limhamn

Formerly home to the Kockum shipyard, the high-tech **Western Harbour** district, a ten-minute walk north of the Malmöhus, or bus #2 from the train station, is a popular spot for sunbathing and swimming, and for gazing across to the Öresund Bridge from its marina-side cafés and restaurants. Towering over it all, and visible for miles around, is the fantastic new 190m-high **Turning Torso skyscraper** (ⓦwww.turningtorso.com; closed for visitors; designed by the Spaniard Santiago Calatrava. This revolutionary residential tower, the highest building in Scandinavia, consists of nine stacked cubes that make a ninety-degree twist from base to top.

Malmö's long stretch of sandy **beach** reaches all the way from the Western Harbour to Limhamn, fringed by Ribersborgs Park (bus #32 runs along the park to Limhamn). At the town end of the beach is the **Ribersborgs kallbadhuset** (mid-April to mid-Sept Mon–Fri 8.30am–7pm, Sat & Sun 8.30am–4pm; mid-Sept to mid-April Mon–Fri noon–7pm, Sat & Sun 9am–4pm; 35kr), a cold-water bathhouse with a sauna and café.

LIMHAMN (Limestone Harbour), 3km to the southwest of the city, has an unusual history. Once a quiet limestone-quarrying village, Limhamn was taken by storm by a local man with big ambitions called Fredryk Berg. At the end of the nineteenth century, Berg had a train line constructed between the village and Malmö, and built up a huge cement works. Using waste concrete, Berg created the small island of **Ön**, building on it a couple of churches, and apartment houses for factory workers. A strongly religious man, he was fond of saying that the two best things in life were making corporations and attending church, earning him the nickname "Concrete Jesus". The huge canyon-like open limestone mine near Limhamn, now owned by HeidelbergCement, is part of the tourist office's bus tour (see p.544) and may in future feature housing projects on its steep slopes.

Eating

Most of Malmö's **eating places** are concentrated in and around its central squares, with Lilla Torg attracting the biggest crowds. By day, several cafés serve good lunches and sumptuous cakes; there's also a wide choice of places for dinner, from budget diners to romance-exuding restaurants. If you want a change of scene (and price), head south of the centre to Möllevångstorget, the heart of Malmö's immigrant community. Alternatively, to cut costs, stock up at the food shops within Saluhallen, on Lilla Torg.

Cafés and restaurants

Ambiance Engelbrektsgatan 17, ⓣ040/30 01 95. Upmarket Lebanese food from 130kr served in pleasant surroundings. Open from 5pm; closed Mon.

Årstiderna Suellsgatan 2, corner of Stortorget ⓣ040/23 09 10. This is a very fine – but rather pricey – old cellar restaurant in the former home of Malmö's sixteenth-century mayor, Jörgen Kock.

Daily lunch specials of traditional Swedish fare from 89kr. Closed Sun.

Bageri Café Saluhallen, Lilla Torg. Excellent bagels, baguettes, pies and health foods – with outside seating, too. Closed Sun.

Café Systrar och Bröder Östra Ronneholmsvägen 26. With leatherette bench seats and 1960s ambience, this bakery is the haunt of hip Malmöites. Superb breads, cakes and sandwiches, and a great-value breakfast buffet at 45kr.

Conditoria Hollandia Södra Förstadsgatan 8. Traditional, pricey *konditori* south of the canal, with a window full of delicious chocolate fondants.

Espresso House Sundspromenaden, Western Harbour. An outlet of the coffeehouse chain, with an excellent terrace sporting bridge views, and serving excellent chocolate cake, muffins, ciabattas and Indian *chai* (24kr), milky tea with cardamom.

Grappa Lilla Torg 4 ☎040/12 50 65. A designer restaurant with a pleasant terrace, serving innovative Italian dishes from 110kr.

Gustav Adolf Gustav Adolfs Torg 43. Long-established, slightly staid café-restaurant, but still a popular spot in a grand, white-stuccoed building with outside seating. Open late at weekends.

Krua Thai Möllevångtorget 12 ☎040/12 22 87. In the big square south of the city centre, this place serves good Thai food with an informal atmosphere that's more domestic than haute cuisine.

Rådhus Källaren Stortorget. Gloriously decorative setting beneath the town hall, with dishes at around 200kr, though there's also a well-cooked and beautifully served daily economy meal at 65kr. Outside seating in summer.

Salt och Brygga Sundspromenaden 7 ☎040/611 59 40, ☻www.saltobrygga.se. The stylish *Salt and the Bridge* serves up acclaimed ecological food with prime views of the Öresund Bridge. Lunch 89kr, dinner 135–250kr. Closed Sat & Sun in winter.

Vespa Kanalgatan 3. A small, cosy restaurant with pizzas from 65kr, pastas from 90kr and a good lunch buffet.

Drinking, nightlife and entertainment

The best place to head for an evening **drink** is **Lilla Torg**: the square buzzes with activity, the smell of beer wafts between the old, beamed houses, and music and chatter fill the air. It's a largely young crowd, and the atmosphere is like a summer carnival. It doesn't make a huge difference which of the ten or so bars that you go for (and expect to wait for a seat), but as a basic pointer, *Mellow Yellow* and *Victor's* are for the 25-plus age group and *Moosehead* for a younger crowd, although all are fun.

A striking **nightlife** option is *The Tunnel*, in the same building as the *Mayfair Hotel* at Adelgatan 4 (first Fri of each month and every Sat; closed July; ☻www.tunneln.com; 100kr cover). Designed as a futuristic metallic tunnel by Argentinian designer Aberlardo Gonzalez, it welcomes a wide age-range and boasts a cellar bar with a wild dance floor of silver and mirrors. Just south of the St Petri kyrka at Djäknegatan 9, the *Buddha Lounge* has a great lounge and dancing area. For fun, corny Swedish karaoke and disco, try the *Schlagerbaren* at Generalsgatan 1.

Gay nightlife

Though most gay Malmöites head off to Copenhagen for a good night out, Malmö's own **gay nightlife** is livelier than in any other Swedish city outside Stockholm. The RFSL-run gay centre (☎040/611 99 62, ☻www.rfsl.se/malmo) is south of the city centre at Monbijougatan 15 (head down Amiralsgatan and turn off to the right just before the Folketspark). It's home to *Club Indigo* (Fri & Sat from 10pm); first Saturday of each month is women-only, and there's a pub night on Wednesdays (9pm–midnight). Entry is 80kr, or 40kr for RFSL members. Otherwise, try *Club Wonk*, Amiralsgatan 20, on Saturday nights. In September, RFSL organizes the Rainbow Festival, nine days of non-stop parties, pub nights and a film festival.

Music and festivals

If you know where to look, you'll find there are some decent **live-music** venues in Malmö. *Mattsons Musikpub* (☎040/23 27 56), behind the Rådhus at Göran Olsgatan 1, puts on a variety of Scandinavian R&B and rock bands every night. Another good venue is *Jeriko*, near the Folketspark at Spångatan 38 (☎040/10 30 20, ☻www.jeriko.info), a concert hall with daily live performances, including jazz, pop, world music and dance. Nearby, the *Kulturbolaget* club at Bergsgatan 18 (☎040/30 20 11, ☻www.kulturbolaget.se) stages bigger bands and hosts parties.

Classical music performances take place at the Konserthuset, Föreningsgatan 35 (☎040/34 35 00, ⊛www.mso.se), home of the Malmö Symphony Orchestra, and at the Musikhögskolan, Ystadvägen 25 (☎040/32 54 50); check with the tourist office for programme details.

The main annual **festival** in town is the week-long **Malmö Festival** (⊛www.malmofestivalen.nu) in August, which takes place throughout the city centre. Huge tables are set out and free crayfish tails served on the first night, with revellers bringing their own drinks. In Gustav Adolfs Torg, stalls are set up by the immigrant communities, with Pakistani, Somali and Bosnian goodies and dance shows. In **winter**, there's a Winterland Festival for children in the Folkspark.

Listings

Airlines Direktflyg ☎021/80 06 45, ⊛www.direktflyg.com; FlyMe ☎0770/79 07 90, ⊛www.flyme.se; Malmö Aviation ☎020/55 00 10, ⊛www.snalskjutsen.com; Ryanair ☎0900/20 20 240, ⊛www.ryanair.com; SAS, Baltzarsgatan 18 ☎040/35 72 00, ⊛www.sas.se; Wizz Air ⊛www.wizzair.com.

Buses From Centralplan to Lund (#130), Kristianstad/Kalmar (#1) and Ystad (#330); others from the long-distance bus terminal on Skeppsbron.

Car rental Avis, Skeppsbron 13 ☎040/778 30; Europcar, Mäster Nilsgatan 22 ☎040/716 40; Hertz, Jörgen Kocksgatan 1b ☎040/33 07 70.

Doctor On call daily 7am–10pm, ☎040/33 35 00; at other times, ring ☎040/33 10 00.

Exchange Forex branches are at Norra Vallgatan 60 (Mon–Sat 8am–7pm), Gustav Adolfs Torg 12 (Mon–Fri 10am–7pm), and by the tourist office at Central Station (daily 7am–9pm).

Internet Coin-operated Sidewalk Express terminals (19kr/hr) can be found in the Central Station hall, at Sturup airport, inside the *Smaklokalen*

café at Lilla Torg 1 and in the 7-Eleven at Södra Förstadsgatan 78. There's also Cyberspace at Engelbrektsgatan 13 (Mon–Thurs 11am–11pm, Fri 11am–midnight, Sat 1pm–midnight, Sun 1–11pm; 30kr/hr); Twilight Zone, Stora Nygatan 15 (daily noon–3am; 20kr/hr); and 10 minutes free Internet at the city library, Regementsgatan 3 (Mon–Thurs 10am–2pm, Fri 10am–6pm, Sat & Sun noon–4pm).

Pharmacy There's 24hr service at Apoteket Gripen, Bergsgatan 48 (☎040/19 21 13) or Lejonet in Stortorget (Mon–Fri 9am–6pm, Sat 10am–2pm; ☎040/712 35).

Post office Skeppsbron 1 (Mon–Fri 8am–6pm, Sat 9.30am–1pm).

Taxis ☎040/70 000 or ☎040/33 03 30.

Train enquiries The SJ offices are next to the tourist information centre in the Central Station; the Skånetrafiken information office is near platform 9 (Mon–Fri 7am–6pm, Sat 8am–3pm, Sun 9am–3pm; ☎0771/77 77 77, ⊛www.skanetrafiken.se).

Southeastern Skåne: the coast to Ystad

The local **Pågatåg train** and the E6 and E14 highways cut directly east from Malmö towards Ystad, missing out some picturesque minor resorts and a couple of the region's best beaches along Sweden's most southwesterly tip. If you have your own transport, this quieter part of the south makes for a delightful few days' exploration. Thirty kilometres south of Malmö (by car, or bus #100), you cross an expanse of heathland to which bird-watchers flock every autumn to spot nesting plovers and terns, as well as millions of migratory birds fleeing the Arctic for the Stevns Peninsula, south of Copenhagen.

Skanör

Some 25km south of Malmö, route 100 leads west to the fan-shaped southwest tip of the country. Here, at the westernmost reach of the Näset Peninsula, is the seaside resort of **SKANÖR** (⊛www.skanor.se), a Hanseatic centre founded to take advantage of the abundance of herring off this stretch of the coast. In the first years of the twentieth century, Skanör became a fashionable bathing resort for rich Malmö families and, although it has since gone in and out of vogue, it's currently a desirable destination for much the same set. There's not much to see in Skanör, but its **beaches** are superb, with long ribbons of white sand bordering an extensive bird and nature reserve. From the beach, you can see across the reserve to the town's medieval **church**. Once the herring had moved on to waters new in the sixteenth century, the church never received its intended extensions, making it all the more appealing. From the little harbour, it's a pleasant walk to the town square and the lovely old cottages lining Mellangatan. If you want **to stay** – and the beach is worth it – *Hotell Gässlingen* (☏040/45 91 00; ⓦwww.hotel-gasslingen.com; ⑤) at Rådhustorget 6, is a simple but lovely place. If you're **camping**, there are plenty of places to throw down a tent for free, though be careful to avoid the protected bird reserves. The little harbour at Skanör boasts one of the best **restaurants** in this corner of the country, *Skanörs Fiskrögeri* (☏040/47 40 50, ⓦwww.rogeriet.se), where you can sample superb fish dishes in the simple, elegant setting, or choose from a remarkable range of smoked and pickled fish and have them made up into a picnic (around 90kr) – try herring roe marinated in rum or hot smoked salmon with black bread.

Foteviken Viking Museum

Just to the east of Skanör, signs point to the **Foteviken Viking Museum** (June–Aug daily 10am–4pm; May & Sept to mid-Oct Mon–Fri 10am–4pm; ⓦwww .foteviken.se; 60kr, includes free guided tour at 11am, 1pm & 2.30pm). Foteviken, an ancient coastal village and a centre of herring fishing from late Viking times, was the scene of a bloody battle in June 1134 between the Danish king and the would-be king of Skåne. Today, the whole area has been transformed into a working – and remarkably authentic – Viking village, which attempts to re-create the way of life as it existed here at the time of the battle. The complex includes houses, workshops, a sacrificial temple and shipbuilding yard, creating a virtually self-sufficient settlement – the atmosphere is like a sort of twelfth-century commune, with unemployed Skånians and others from all over Europe living and working in an eight-hundred-year-old time warp. All food, clothes and belongings are respectively cooked, woven and made on site, from curing leather to dying wool, and the houses are built authentically. The most dramatic time to come is the weekend closest to June 10, when the battle is re-enacted, while the last week of June and start of July sees hundreds of people participating in similar Viking-style living projects converge here from all over Northern Europe for an international get-together.

Ystad

Forty-five minutes by Pågatåg train from Malmö lies the well-preserved medieval market town of **YSTAD**, boasting a core of quaint cobbled lanes lined with hundreds of half-timbered cottages and a central square oozing rural charm. With the beautiful coastal region of Österlen stretching northeast from town in the direction of Kristianstad, and some excellent walking to the north, Ystad is a splendid place to base yourself for a day or so. It's also literary home of the popular fictional detective Kurt Wallander, and a dozen new episodes are to be filmed in and around town in 2006. Ystad is the departure point for **ferries** to Copenhagen, the Danish island of Bornholm, and to Poland.

Arrival and information

From the harbourside **train station**, cross the tracks to St Knuts Torg, where the **tourist office** (May–June Mon–Fri 9am–5pm, Sat 11am–2pm; July & Aug Mon–Fri 9am–7pm, Sat & Sun 10am–6pm; Sept Mon–Fri 9am–5pm, Sat 11am–2pm; Oct–May Mon–Fri 9am–5pm; ☏0411/776 81, ⓦwww.ystad.se/turism) is next door to the Art Museum. St Knuts Torg is also where Skåne Express **buses** from Lund (#6) and Kristianstad (#4) pull in, and where buses leave for destinations along the coast and into the rest of Skåne. Regular Pågatåg trains connect Ystad to Malmö and on to Copenhagen; to get to Kristianstad by train, you need to return to Malmö first.

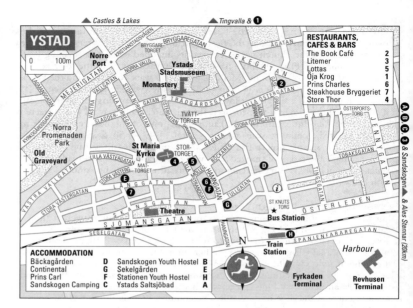

Ferries to the island of Bornholm depart from the Fyrkaden terminal right behind the train station, while those to Poland depart from the Revhusen terminal a few hundred metres to the east. One-way tickets to Rønne on **Bornholm** (☎0045-56/95 18 66, ⓦwww.bornholmstrafikken.dk) cost from 190kr (catamaran 1hr 20min, ferry 2hr 40min; both take cars). Tickets to Świnoujście in **Poland** cost from 450kr one-way (7–9hr crossing), with both Unity Line (☎0411/55 69 00, ⓦwww.unityline.se) and Polferries (☎040/12 17 00, ⓦwww.polferries.pl) offering daily departures; the latter also has a ferry connection to **Copenhagen** (from 380kr), which may be a cheaper option than driving across the Öresund Bridge if you're travelling by car. **Cycling** is a great way to see the surrounding landscape, and bikes can be rented from Roslins Cykelaffär, Jennygatan 11, just east of the bus and train terminals (☎0411/123 15; 40kr/day or 195kr/week).

Accommodation

There are several good and reasonably priced **hotels** in Ystad, and one at the beach. There are also two central **youth hostels**, one on the beach at Sandskogen (☎0411/665 66; ①), with dorm beds for 140kr, served by buses #570 and #304. The other, *Stationen*, is much more conveniently situated in the old station building at the train station (☎0708/57 79 95, ⓦwww.turistlogi.se; dorm beds 185kr). *Sandskogen Camping*, with four-bed **cabins** (from 135kr per person), is next to the youth hostel at Sandskogen (☎0411/192 70).

Bäckagården Dammgatan 36 ☎0411/198 48, ⓦwww.backagarden.nu. Small-scale guesthouse-type place in a converted home just behind the tourist office. ②

Continental Hamngatan 13 ☎0411/137 00, ⓦwww.hotelcontinental-ystad.se. Classic hotel touted as Sweden's oldest, with a grand lobby of marble, Corinthian pillars and crystal chandeliers. Rooms are modern

Italian-style, and the cold breakfast buffet is a treat. ④

Prins Carl Hamngatan 8 ☎0411/737 50, ⓦwww.hotellprinscarl.com. A mid-range, non-smoking place, with rooms adapted for people with disabilities or allergies. ②

Sekelgården Långgatan 18 ☎0411/739 00, ⓦwww.sekelgarden.se. The best place to stay in town, this small family-run hotel in an eighteenth-century merchant's house is friendly and informal, with a sauna, cobbled courtyard and flower garden. There are en-suite rooms in both the main house and the old tannery at the back, and excellent breakfasts are served under the trees or in the charming dining room. ❸

Ystads Saltsjöbad Saltsjöbadsvägen 6 ☎0411/136 30, ⊛www.ystadssaltsjobad .se. Renowned for its beachside position, just east of town, this large, one-hundred-year-old hotel (though with endless modern extensions tacked on) has an excellent new spa complex and a restaurant in the original saltwater bathing house. ❹

The Town

Turning left from the station and ferry terminals then right up Hamngatan brings you to the well-proportioned **Stortorget**, a grand old square encircled by picturesque streets. The **St Maria kyrka** is a handsome centrepiece, with additions from nearly every century since it was begun in the thirteenth. In the 1880s, changing tastes saw many of the church's rich decorative features removed, and only the most interesting ones were returned during a restoration programme forty years later. Inside, the early seventeenth-century Baroque pulpit is worth a look for the fearsome face carved beneath it and, opposite, the somewhat chilling medieval crucifix, which was placed here on the orders of Karl XII to remind the preacher of Christ's suffering.

If you stay in Ystad, you'll soon become acquainted with a tradition that harks back to the seventeenth century: from a room in the church's watchtower, a night watchman blows a haunting tune on a bugle every fifteen minutes from 9.15pm to 1am, as a safeguard against the outbreak of fire. The idea was that if one of the thatched cottages went up in flames, the bugle would sound repeatedly for all to go and help extinguish the blaze. The sounding through the night was to assure the town that the watchman was still awake; until the mid-nineteenth century, if he slept on duty he was liable to be executed.

From Stortorget, it's a short stroll up Garvaregränd, past art and craft workshops, and on up Klostergatan to the **Ystads Stadsmuseum** (June–Aug Tues–Fri 10am– 5pm, Sat & Sun noon–4pm, Sept–May Tues–Fri noon–5pm, Sat & Sun noon–4pm; 20kr). Set in the thirteenth-century Gråbröder ("Greyfriars") Monastery, it contains the usual local history collections, given piquancy here by their preserved medieval surroundings. After the monks were driven out during the Reformation, the monastery was at various times a hospital, a poorhouse, a distillery and, finally, a dump. A decision to demolish it in 1901 was overturned, and today it's definitely worth a visit. The monastery gardens (open 24hr; tours available in summer) consist of spice, vegetable and medicinal herb gardens and a wonderful rose garden.

Not far from the St Maria kyrka on the western side of town, **Norra Promenaden**, a strip of mature horse chestnut trees and parkland, is good for a stroll. Here you'll find *Café Norra Promenaden*, a white pavilion built in the 1870s to house a genteel café and dance hall.

Eating, drinking and nightlife

There's a fair selection of places to eat in Ystad, including some atmospheric **cafés** and fine **restaurants**, most of the latter around Stortorget. For **nightlife**, head to the *Starshine* club at Österportstorg (☎0411/100 95, ⊛www.starshine.se), east from Stortorget along Stora Östergatan, though the funkiest place to party is *Litemer* (☎0411/55 50 95, ⊛www.litemer.se), set in an old military complex a kilometre east of the centre at Björnstjernegatan 6; it has parties for all ages on Thursdays and Fridays, and over-23s and -30s club nights every other Saturday. In summer, there are several parties held out of town at the *Öja Krog* (⊛www.ojakrog.se); ask the tourist office for dates. Otherwise, locals tend to take a bus thirty minutes north to **Tingvalla**, where there are a couple of dance halls.

Lottas Stortorget 11, ☎0411/788 00, ⊛www .lottas.se. Justifiably the most popular restaurant in town, packed each evening in summer and

serving beautifully presented, scrumptious fish and meat dishes. Closed Sat & Sun. *Lottas Källare* in the cellars below is a cosy bar with several

English beers including the so-called Manchester United.

Prins Charles Hamngatan 8. Next door to the *Prins Carl Hotel*, this English-style pub and restaurant serves meat and fish dishes in the evenings, with live music on Fri and Sat nights.

Steakhouse Bryggeriet Långgatan 20 ☎0411/699 99, ⊛www.steakhousebryggeriet .com. The rough, beamed interior dominated by two copper beer casks creates a welcoming ambience at this fine restaurant. The well-cooked fish and meat dishes, with one vegetarian option, cost between 130 and 180kr.

Store Thor Stortorget 1, ⊛www.storethor.se.

Located in the cellars of the former Rådhus, and adding a breath of life to Stortorget in summer when tables are brought into the square itself. At weekends, and out of the high season, the elegant interior serves as a fitting backdrop to the less touristy Swedish menu.

The Book Café Gåsegränd. Down a tiny, cobbled street off Stora Östergatan, this precariously leaning wooden house has books – many in English – to read while you feast on the home-baked focaccia or sample one of the varieties of coffee. The gardens are delightful, too, and retain their 1778 layout. Closed Sun & Mon.

Ales Stennar

Twenty kilometres out of Ystad, near the hamlet of Kåseberga, is the Viking site of **Ales Stennar** ("Ale's Stones"). Believed to have been a Viking meeting place, this awe-inspiring monument consists of 58 stones forming a 67-metre-long boat-shaped edifice, the prow and stern denoted by two larger monoliths. The site was hidden beneath earth for centuries, and was only restored in 1958. Buried several metres into the sand, it's difficult to imagine how these great stones, which aren't native to the region and weigh 4–5 tonnes each, were transported here. Ales Stennar stands on a windy, flat-topped hill overlooking the sea, and despite the tourists snapping away at the rocks, there's a majestic timelessness at the top that more than rewards the climb.

To get to Ales Stennar from Ystad, take the infrequent bus #392 (20min) or rent a bike and follow the coastal cycle track through pine forests and past white sandy beaches, following the signs to Kåseberga.

Kristianstad

Ninety kilometres northeast of Malmö, quiet **KRISTIANSTAD** (for its correct pronunciation, try a guttural "Krwi-chwan-sta") is a Renaissance town created in 1614 by Christian IV, Denmark's seventeenth-century "builder-king". A good

△ Ales Stennar

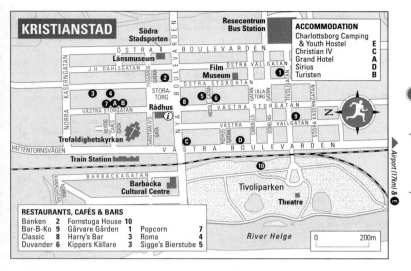

KRISTIANSTAD

Södra Stadsporten

Resecentrum Bus Station

ACCOMMODATION

Charlottsborg Camping & Youth Hostel	E
Christian IV	C
Grand Hotel	A
Sirius	D
Turisten	B

Östra Boulevarden

Länsmuseum

J.H. DAHLSGATAN

Film Museum

Tygårdsgatan

Stora-Torg

Rådhus

Västra Storgatan

Trefaldighetskyrkan

Vattentornsvägen

Train Station

Barbackagatan

Barbacka Cultural Centre

Tivoliparken

Theatre

River Helge

Airport (17km & E)

0   200m

RESTAURANTS, CAFÉS & BARS

Banken	2	Fornstuga House	10		
Bar-B-Ko	9	Gårvare Gården	1	Popcorn	7
Classic	8	Harry's Bar	3	Roma	4
Duvander	6	Kippers Källare	3	Sigge's Bierstube	5

example of the king's architectural preoccupations, with proportioned central squares and broad gridded streets, it was only to remain in Danish hands for another 44 years before being permanently ceded to Sweden during the Skånian Wars.

Arrival, information and accommodation

Buses from Ystad (1hr 45min) stop at the Resecentrum bus station on Östra Boulevarden, although the quickest and most comfortable way here is by **train** from Malmö (1hr 10min) or Karlskrona (1hr 30min). You might arrive at the sparkling little **airport**, 17km south of the city centre, on a domestic service (for flights from Stockholm Arlanda, see ⊛www.skyways.se). Buses leave the airport for the city twenty minutes after each flight arrival (20min; 40kr).

The **tourist office** on Nya Boulevarden (mid-June to mid-Aug Mon–Fri 10am–7pm, Sat 10am–3pm, Sun 10am–2pm; mid-Aug to mid-June Mon–Fri 10am–5pm; ☎044/13 53 35, ⊛www.kristianstad.se/turism) books **private rooms** from 150kr. There's a **campsite** with attached **youth hostel** at *Charlottsborg Camping* (☎044/21 07 67, ⊛www.charlottsborgsvandrarhem.se; dorm beds 135kr), 3km west of the town centre (bus #2 or #10).

Two of Kristianstad's **hotels** are side by side, just a few steps from the train station. At Västra Storgatan 17 is the appealing family-run *Turisten* (☎044/12 61 50, ⊛www.turisten.se; ❸/❹), while at no.15, the ironically unassuming *Grand Hotel* (☎044/28 48 00, ⊛www.choicehotels.com; ❸/❻) offers friendly service and particularly comfortable beds. The *Sirius* at Västra Boulevarden 35 (☎044/21 77 40, ⊛www.hotellsirius.se; ❸/❹) has very comfortable rooms overlooking the park, but the most glamorous place to spend the night is the *Christian IV*, Västra Boulevarden 15 (☎044/20 38 50, ⊛www.firsthotels.com; ❸/❺) – a grand, castle-like confection in the old Sparbank building, its beautifully renovated features include original fireplaces and parquet floors.

The Town

The obvious starting point is the **Trefaldighetskyrkan** (Holy Trinity Church; daily 9am–5pm), opposite the train station, which stands as a symbol of all that was glorious about Christian IV's Renaissance ideas. The grandiose exterior has seven magnificent spiralled gables, and the high windows allow light to flood the white interior. This being Sweden, there's a children's play area between the aisles. Diagonally across from the church, the main square, **Storatorg**, hosts the late nineteenth-century **Rådhus**, itself built in imitation of Christian's Renaissance style. Inside the entrance, a bronze copy of the king's 1643 bust is something of a revelation, with Christian sporting a goatee beard, one earring and a single dreadlock, his one exposed nipple decorated with a flower motif. Back outside in the square, Palle Pernevi's splintered *Icarus* fountain depicts the unfortunate Greek aeronaut falling from heaven into a scaffolded building site.

North of Storatorg, on Östra Boulevarden, is the **Länsmuseum** (County Museum; June–Aug Mon–Fri 10am–5pm; Sept–May Tues–Sat noon–5pm; Wed till 6pm year round; free), housed in a building that was begun as a royal palace by Christian in 1616, but soon became an arsenal for Danish partisans during the bloody Skånian Wars. Aside from the historical exhibits, there are some interesting textile and art collections on the top floor. If you've time on your hands, it's a pleasant stroll behind the museum to **Södra Stadsporten**, the 1790s southern town gate on Östra Boulevarden, one of the few remaining pieces of fortification.

Walking back through the town centre, a few minutes east of the Storatorg, the **Film Museum**, Östra Storgatan 53 (mid-June to mid-Aug daily 1–4pm; mid-Aug to mid-June Sun noon–5pm; free), is heralded by a bronze early movie camera outside the door. This was Sweden's first film studio, where the country's earliest movies were recorded between 1909 and 1911; some of these flickering works can now be viewed on videotape inside. From here, wander down any of the roads to the south and you'll reach **Tivoliparken**, where you can stroll beneath avenues of horse chestnuts; at the park's centre is a green-pained Art Nouveau **theatre**, designed by Kristianstad-born Axel Anderberg, who also created the Stockholm Opera House. Recently listed as a biosphere reserve, the **wetlands** around Kristianstad – the *vattenriket*, or "water kingdom" – are well worth a visit for their natural beauty and birdlife; in summer, sightseeing boats splash their way up the river to the area on two-hour trips from behind the theatre (May to mid-June & mid-Aug to mid-Sept 3 daily at 11am, 2pm & 6pm; 90kr, book at the tourist office); serious nature lovers can opt for four-hour tours (small-boat "safari" for 280kr/person or a kayak tour for 350kr/person including guide and lunch).

At the northwestern edge of Tivoliparken, there's an art gallery showing temporary exhibitions and housing the **Barbacka Cultural Centre** (Sept to mid-July Mon–Fri 9am–5pm, Sat noon–4pm; ☎044/13 56 50), where you can get information on musical events around the town and take in the hands-on science experiment rooms, live snakes in glass columns and mountains of toys –an ideal stop-off if you're travelling with children.

Eating, drinking and entertainment

Kristianstad has a number of good **places to eat**. Of the **cafés**, best are *Fornstuga House*, an elaborately carved Hansel-and-Gretel lodge in the middle of Tivoliparken, and the more central *konditori, Duvander*, Hesslegatan 6.

Among the town's **restaurants**, *Kippers Källare*, Östra Storgatan 9, is in an atmospheric cellar, and specializes in pricey steaks, while the nearby *Roma*, Östra Storgatan 15, is an inexpensive Italian restaurant serving big pizzas at 65kr. *Bar-B-Ko*, Tivoligatan 4, is an inviting place specializing in grilled meats, with main courses for 110kr and a huge range of whiskies, spirits, ale and cider. Greek cuisine can be sampled at *Classic*, Nya Boulevarden 6, with main courses from just 75kr. *Popcorn*, Västra Storgatan 17 next to the *Grand Hotel*, is a fun, movie-themed restaurant in homage to Sweden's first film studios, with seats taken from an old cinema. Fish and meat dishes (120–175kr) are served with a surprisingly varied wine list.

For a central **drinking** place, check out the 250 or so beers at *Banken* in the old Riksbank on Storatorg, or try the German-owned-and-themed *Sigge's Bierstube* on Hesslegatan. *Harry's Bar*, next to *Kippers Källare* at Östra Storgatan 9, is a small but lively place with loud rock music. Best bet, though, is *Gårvare Gården*, a lovely old house just up from the park on Tivoligatan, with good food and beers.

The town hosts two annual festivals: **Kristianstadsdagarna**, a seven-day cultural festival in the second week of July (during which the tourist office stays open till 8pm), while the annual **Kristianstad Jazz Festival** (℡044/12 68 05, ⓦwww .bluebird.m.se) takes place throughout June and October.

East into Blekinge

The county of **Blekinge** is something of a poor relation to Skåne in terms of tourism, though there are some good beaches, plentiful fishing, several fine walking trails and enough cultural diversions to make for an enjoyable few days. The landscape is much the same as in northeastern Skåne: forests and hills with fields fringing the sea, along with a number of islands and a small archipelago south of Karlskrona that make a picturesque destination for short boat trips.

Karlskrona

Blekinge county's most appealing destination is the regal county capital **KARL-SKRONA**, located on the largest link in a chain of breezy islands. Founded by Karl XI in 1680, who picked it as an ice-free southern harbour for his Baltic fleet, the town revolves around its unique maritime heritage, listed as a UNESCO World Heritage site (see ⓦwww.navalcity.org). The wide avenues and stately squares were built to accommodate the king's naval parades, and cadets in uniform still career around streets named after Swedish admirals and battleships. However, even if you're not a naval fan, Karlskrona has plenty to offer, particularly the picturesque old quarter around the once-busy fishing port at Fisktorget and some short cruises

around the islands in the archipelago; however, due to military restrictions no bathing is allowed on them (there's good swimming off the nearby island of Dragsö or at the fine bathhouse in town).

The town centre is on the former island of Trossö, connected to the mainland by the Österleden main road. Climb uphill from the train station past Hoglands Park to the main square, **Stortorget**, at the highest point and geographical centre of the island. It's a vast and beautiful space, dominated by two complementary **churches**, both designed by Tessin the Younger and stuccoed in burnt orange, with dove-grey stone colonnades. **Fredrikskyrkan** (June–Sept Mon–Fri 11am–4pm, Sat 9.30am–2pm) is elegant enough, but the interior of the circular domed **Trefaldighetskyrkan** (same times) holds more interest. Built for the town's German merchant community in 1709, the domed ceiling is its most remarkable feature, painted with hundreds of rosettes and brilliantly shaded to look three-dimensional. The altar is also distinctive, with golden angelic faces peering out of a gilded meringue of clouds.

Head between the churches, down the cobbled Södra Kungsgatan, which is divided down the centre by the railway that once carried trains to the harbour. The leafy square ahead is **Amiralitetstorget** and perched at its centre is the huge, apricot-and-grey wooden bell tower of the **Amiralitetskyrka**. To get to the church itself, head down Vallgatan, and the beautifully proportioned wooden church is up on your right. Built in 1685, it's the largest wooden church in Sweden (visits by appointment only; ☎0455/103 56). Outside the entrance, take a look at one of the city's best-known landmarks: the wooden statue of **Rosenbom**, a local beggar who one night forgot to raise his hat to thank the wealthy German carver, Fritz Kolbe. When admonished for this, Rosenbom retorted, "If you want thanks for your crumbs to the poor, you can take my hat off yourself!" Enraged, Kolbe struck him between the eyes and sent him away, but the beggar froze stiff and died in a snowdrift by the church. Next morning, Kolbe found the beggar's body and, filled with remorse, carved a figure of Rosenbom to stand at the spot where he died, designing it so that you have to raise his hat yourself to give some money.

Karlskrona's best museums are set on the island of Stumholmen, connected to the mainland by road five minutes' walk east of Stortorget down Kyrkogatan. The excellent **Marinmuseum** (Maritime Museum; June–Aug daily 10am–6pm, Sept–May Tues–Sun 11am–5pm; free; ⍟www.marinmuseum.se) has a facade like a futuristic Greek temple, while its exhibits (including several ships moored alongside the building) thoughtfully and evocatively bring seafaring ways to life. Close by is Karlskrona's good **art gallery** (Tues–Fri noon–4pm, Wed till 7pm, Sat & Sun noon–5pm; free), set in the splendid old Seamen's Barracks (*Båtmanskasern*). The highlight is the poignant work of local artist Erik Langemark, who chronicled the city in his paintings and drawings – modern photographs alongside show how the city has changed since.

For more of a feel of old Karlskrona, wander west past the military hardware towards the **Björkholmen** area. Here a couple of tiny wooden early eighteenth-century houses in little gardens survive, the homes built by the very first craftsmen at the naval yard. Nearby **Fisktorget**, originally the site of a fish market, is pleasant for a stroll, and is also the terminal for boat and river trips.

Practicalities

Trains from Malmö, Växjö and Kalmar stop at Emmaboda, from where there are five daily trains to Karlskrona. Stena Line **ferries to Gdynia** in Poland (☎0455/36 63 00, ⍟www.stenaline.se; 1–2 daily; 10hr 30min) depart from the ferry terminal to the east of the centre; one-way tickets cost from 305kr.

Karlskrona's **tourist office** (June–Aug Mon–Fri 9am–7pm, Sat & Sun 9am–4pm; Sept–May Mon–Fri 10am–5pm, Sat 10am–2pm; ☎0455/30 34 90, ⍟www.karlskrona.se/tourism) is at Stortorget 2. Staff can book you **private rooms** for around 125kr per person, and cheap one-gear **bikes** are available to rent for 30kr a day. The best place for new rental bikes (55kr/day) is the Q8 petrol station near the train station at Järnvägstorget (☎0455/819 93). The cheapest bed is to be had at the Trossö **youth hostel**,

centrally located at Bredgatan 16 (⊕0455/100 20, ⊛www.karlskronavandrarhem
.se; ❶), where dorm beds cost dorm beds from 125kr. The nearest **camping** is 2km
away on Dragsö island (⊕0455/153 54, ⊛www.dragsocamping.se; April–Oct): take
bus #7 from the bus station to Saltö, from where it's a short walk. In terms of **hotels**,
try the pleasant, modern ⅔ *Park Inn Karlskrona*, close to the station at Skeppsbrokajen
(⊕0455/36 15 00, ⊛www.karlskrona.parkinn.se; ❸/❺), while the *First Hotel Ja*,
Borgmästaregatan 13 (⊕0455/555 60, ⊛www.firsthotels.se; ❸), is another good
choice, with a very homely atmosphere. Within the same chain, the considerably more
expensive *First Hotel Statt*, Ronnebygatan 37 (⊕0455/555 50, ⊛www.firsthotels.se;
❹/❺), is supposed to be its glamorous sister, but in reality it's only a smattering of
Empire styling and a bit more gilt to differentiate the two. If these are out of your
range, *Hotel Conrad* on Västra Köpmangatan (⊕0455/36 32 00, ⊛www.hotelconrad.se;
❷/❹), halfway up the hill towards Stortorget, is plain and reasonable.

Most of the town's **konditori** are indistinguishable, an exception being *Systrarna
Lindkvists Café*, Borgmästaregatan 3, across from the tourist office – all fine old
gilded tea cups and silver sugar tongs. The Maritime Museum's café/restaurant
Jarramas Brygga is worth looking up for its good-value lunch, and view towards the
museum boats. *Glass* next to the tourist office on Stortorget serves up fist-sized
scoops of home-made ice-cream – you'll see them being eaten all over town by
the marine cadets.

The majority of Karlskrona's unremarkable **restaurants** are along central
Ronnebygatan. The Greek *Taverna Santorini*, Rädhusgatan 11, serves all the usual
choices, plus several vegetarian options, with no dish over 120kr. For a real treat,
though, try next door at the deli and café *Nya Skäfferiet*, a really fine place for filled
baguettes and luscious meats, cheeses and other picnic delights (closed Sun).

Travel details

Trains

Frequent daily express trains operate throughout
the region, in particular Oslo–Copenhagen (via
Gothenburg, Varberg, Halmstad, Helsingborg and
Malmö) and Stockholm–Copenhagen (via Helsingborg and Malmö).

Helsingborg to: Gothenburg (10 daily; 2hr 20min);
Lund (2 hourly; 30min); Malmö (2 hourly; 40min),
Stockholm (hourly; 5hr).

Karlskrona to: Emmaboda (for Kalmar, Stockholm
& Växjö; 5 daily; 40min); Växjö (3 daily; 1hr 30min)

Malmö to: Gothenburg (hourly; 3hr); Helsingborg (2
hourly; 40min); Kalmar (9 daily; 3hr); Kristianstad
(hourly; 1hr 10min); Lund (3–10 hourly; 13min);
Norrköping (13 daily; 3hr 10min); Stockholm
(hourly; 4hr 30min); Ystad (1–2 hourly; 50min).

Buses

Helsingborg to: Båstad (8 daily; 1hr 15min);
Halmstad (5–6 daily; 1hr).

Karlskrona to: Kalmar (1–2 daily; 1hr 15min);
Lund (1–2 daily; 2hr 45min), Malmö (1–2 daily;
3hr 10min).

Kristianstad to: Kalmar (1–2 daily; 3hr); Malmö
(1–2 daily; 1hr 30min), Stockholm.

Malmö to: Gothenburg (7–8 daily; 3hr 30min);
Halmstad (4 daily; 2hr 20min); Helsingborg (5–6
daily; 1hr); Jönköping (4–5 daily; 4hr); Kalmar
(1–2 daily; 4hr 25min); Karlskrona (1–2 daily; 3hr
10min); Kristianstad (1–2 daily; 1hr 30min); Lund
(4 daily; 25min); Stockholm (2–3 daily; 8hr); Trelleborg (hourly; 45min).

Ystad to: Kristianstad (9 daily; 1hr 35min); Lund
(hourly; 1hr 20min).

International buses

Malmö to: Copenhagen, via Copenhagen airport
(6 daily; 1hr).

International ferries

Halmstad to: Grenå (2 daily; 4hr).

Helsingborg to: Helsingør (2–5 hourly; 25min).

Karlskrona to: Gdynia (1–2 daily; 10hr
30min–12hr).

Trelleborg to: Rostock (3 daily; 5hr 30min); Sassnitz
(5 daily, 3hr 45min); Travemünde (4 daily; 7–9hr).

Varberg to: Grenå (1–2 daily; 4hr).

Ystad to: Rønne, Bornhom (3–5 daily; catamaran
1hr 20min, ferry 2hr 30min); Świnoujście (2–3
daily; 7–9hr).

3.4

The southeast

Although a less obvious target than the coastal cities and resorts of the south-west, Sweden's **southeast** certainly repays a visit. Impressive castles, lakeside sites and numerous glass-making factories hidden amongst forests are some of the mainland attractions, while off the east coast, Sweden's largest islands offer beautifully preserved medieval towns and fairytale landscapes. Train transport, especially between Stockholm and the towns close to the eastern shore of Lake Vät-tern, is good; you can even visit some places as day-trips from the capital.

Småland county in the south encompasses a varied geography and some strik-ingly varied towns. The glorious historic fortress town of **Kalmar** is an essential stop, and is also the jumping-off point for the island of **Öland**. Further inland, great swaths of dense forest are rescued from monotony by the **Glass Kingdom**, a region that continues the county's famous tradition of glass production. By the mid-nineteenth century, agricultural reforms and a series of bad harvests in Småland saw mass emigration to America, and in **Växjö**, the largest town in the south, the art of glass-making and the history of Swedish emigration are the subjects of two superb museums. At the northern edge of the county, **Jönköping** is a good base for exploring the beautiful shores of **Lake Vättern**.

The idyllic pastoral landscape of **Östergotland** stretches from the shores of the lake east to the Baltic. Popular with domestic tourists, the small lakeside town of **Vadstena** is one of the highlights, its medieval streets dwarfed by a Renaissance castle and an imposing abbey. Just to the north, bustling **Norrköping** grew up around the textile industry, a background that's preserved in a collection of hand-some red-brick and stuccoed factories.

Sweden's largest islands are in the Baltic: Öland and Gotland, adjacent slithers of land with unusually temperate climates, sandy beaches and impressive historic (and prehistoric) sights. **Gotland** is one of Sweden's highlights, with its medieval Hanseatic capital, **Visby**, a stunning backdrop to the carnival atmosphere that pervades the town in summer, when ferry-loads of young Swedes come here to sunbathe and party. It's also one of the most popular places for Swedes to celebrate **Midsummer's Night**. The rest of the island, however, is little visited by tourists, and all the more worthwhile for that. **Öland** – smaller and closer to the mainland – is less celebrated, but its mix of dark forest, UNESCO-listed landscapes and flowering meadows make it a tranquil spot for a few days' exploration. Both islands are ideal for cycling, and it's easy to rent bikes.

Kalmar

Delightful, breezy **KALMAR**, set on a huddle of islands at the southeastern edge of the county of Småland, has treasures enough to make it one of southern Sweden's most delightful towns – a fact sadly missed by most visitors, who have their sights set on the Baltic island of Öland, to which Kalmar is joined by a six-kilometre bridge. Surrounded by fragments of fortified walls, the seventeenth-century **town centre**, set on the Kvarnholmen islet and connected to the mainland by several bridges, is a mass of cobbled streets and lively squares, lined with some lovely old buildings. Close by is the exquisite castle, **Kalmar Slott**, scene of the

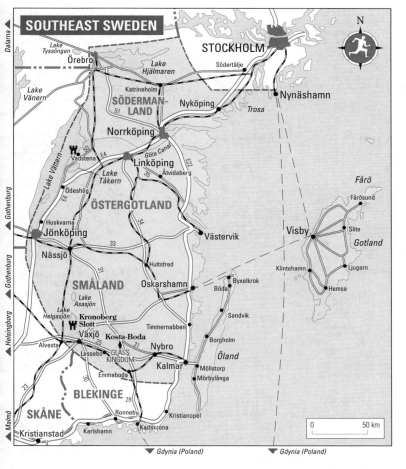

Kalmar Union, which brought Sweden, Norway and Denmark together as a single kingdom in 1397, and now one of Scandinavia's most finely preserved Renaissance palaces. Just a short walk in the other direction, there's the fascinating exhibition on the **Kronan**, one of the world's biggest warships, which sunk off Öland over three hundred years ago. Even now, new finds are being discovered, helping to piece together the world's most complete picture of seventeenth-century maritime life.

Arrival, information and accommodation

Flights from Stockholm and Copenhagen are met at the **airport** by a bus to the centre (15min; 25kr). The **bus terminal** and **train station** (from where there are several trains daily to Växjö, Malmö and Copenhagen) are within spitting distance of Kalmar's **tourist office**, at Ölandskajen 9 (May & Sept Mon–Fri 9am–5pm, Sat 10am–1pm; June & late Aug Mon–Fri 9am–7pm, Sat & Sun 10am–4pm; July to mid-Aug Mon–Fri 9am–9pm, Sat & Sun 10am–5pm; rest of year Mon–Fri 9am–5pm; ☎ 480/41 77 00, ✆www.kalmar.se/turism). Staff hand out maps and copies of the useful *Kalmar Guide*, and have information about Öland. Kalmar

can be explored easily on foot, but if you want to strike out into the surrounding countryside you can rent a **bike** from Team Sportia, Södra vägen 2 (℡0480/212 44; Mon–Fri 10am–6pm, Sat 10am–2pm; 40kr per day). Students from the local Maritime Academy give hour-long **boat tours** around the town moat and castle (mid-June to mid-Aug, 4–5 tours per day; 60kr), which is a great way to get your bearings; departures are from outside the tourist office.

In summer, the tourist office arranges **private rooms** from 200kr per person, 300kr for a double, plus a 50kr booking fee. More popular are the cottages that the tourist office rents out by the week from 3000kr for four people. From mid-June to mid-August, the central *Sjöfartsklubb* **youth hostel** at Ölandsgatan 45 (℡0480/180 10; **1**) has dorm beds for 175kr; alternatively, there's the year-round *Svanen* hostel on Ängö island, 1km north of the centre at Rappegatan 1 (℡0480/255 60, ⓦwww .hotellsvanen.se; **2**), with dorm beds for 205kr. The nearest **campsite** is 3km from the centre on Stensö island (℡0480/888 03, ⓦwww.stensocamping.se), which also has cheap cabins sleeping up to four people; bus #411 drops you off near here. Kalmar boasts several very attractive central **hotels**, such as the castle-like *Frimurarehotellet*, Lärmtorget 2 (℡0480/152 30, ⓦwww.frimurarehotellet.com; **3**/**5**), or the well-positioned and friendly *Kalmarsund*, Fiskaregatan 5 (℡0480/181 00, ⓦwww .kalmarsundhotel.se; **4**), which has comfortable, en-suite rooms, and a sauna and roof garden. If you fancy splashing out, the best-located choice is ⚜ *Slottshotellet*, Slottsvägen 7 (℡0480/882 60, ⓦwww.slottshotellet.se; **5**/**6**), right opposite the lovely park and castle, with a grand and very tasteful interior. For something cheaper, the *Hotel Svanen* at Rappegatan 1 (☎0480/255 60, ✆www.hotellsvanen.se; ❷), a kilometre north of the centre, on Ängö island, has comfortable rooms as well as a youth hostel (❶) with dorm beds from 205kr.

Kalmar Slott

Beautifully set on its own island, a short way from the train and bus stations, the first stones of **Kalmar Slott** (daily: April, May, Sept to mid-Oct 10am–4pm; late Oct Sat & Sun 10am–4pm; June & Aug 10am–5pm; July 10am–6pm; guided tours in English June & Aug 11.30am & 2.30pm, July also 3.30pm; 75kr) were probably laid in the twelfth century. A century later, it became the most impenetrable castle in Sweden under King Magnus Ladulås when it was reinforced to defend the nearby border between Sweden and Denmark. The biggest event to take place within its walls was in 1397, when Erik of Pomerania (under the protection of his aunt, the powerful Danish queen, Margarethe) was crowned king of Denmark, Sweden and Norway, instigating the **Kalmar Union**, in which the whole of Scandinavia was united under a single monarch. Subsequently, the castle passed repeatedly between Sweden and Denmark, but despite eleven sieges, remained almost unscathed. By the time Gustav Vasa became king of Sweden in 1523, Kalmar Slott was beginning to show signs of stress and strain, and the king set about rebuilding it, while his sons Eric XIV and Johan III continued with the decoration of the interior. The fine Renaissance palace that was the eventual result of their efforts well illustrates the Vasa family's concern with maintaining Sweden's prestige in the eyes of foreign powers.

Unlike many other southern Swedish castles, this one is picture-perfect, with turrets, ramparts, moat, drawbridge, dungeon, and a furnished interior that's fascinating to wander through; especially with the excellent guides who dress in period clothing. Among the many highlights is the bed – stolen from Denmark – in the **Queen's Suite**; it's decorated with carved faces, but with all the noses chopped off – it was general belief that the nose contained the soul, and so the faces were disfigured to prevent the avenging spirits of the rightful owners from taking revenge. However, it's King Eric's bedroom, the **King's Chamber**, which is the most intriguing room, with its wall frieze of vividly painted animals and a secret door to a toilet with two escape routes – Eric was convinced that his younger brother Johan wanted to kill him. This isn't as paranoid as it sounds: Eric's death in 1577 is widely believed to have been caused by eating pea soup poisoned with arsenic.

The rest of the town

In the 1640s, a fire devastated the nearby **Gamla Stan** (Old Town) – after which the town was moved to its present-day site on the island of Kvarnholmen – but the area still retains some winding old streets that are worth a look. On Slottsvägen, opposite the castle, Kalmar's **Konstmuseum** (Art Museum; daily 11am–5pm, Thurs till 8pm except in July; 40kr; ✆www.kalmarkonstmuseum.se) displays changing exhibitions of contemporary works, with an emphasis on late 1940s and 1950s Expressionism. The collection is shifted around to make way for temporary exhibitions, but one floor usually contains a gallery of impressive nineteenth- and twentieth-century Swedish nude and landscape paintings.

Head back into the elegantly laid out Renaissance town centre, focused on the grand **Domkyrkan** (daily 9am–6pm) in Stortorget, still named so even though Kalmar has had no bishop since 1915. This vast and airy, Italian Renaissance-style church was designed in 1660 by Nicodemus Tessin the Elder (as was the nearby Rådhus) after a visit to Rome. Inside, the altar, designed by Tessin the Younger, shimmers with gold, as do the sculptures of *Faith* and *Mercy* around it.

The Royal Ship Kronan Exhibition

Housed in a refurbished steam mill on Skeppsbrongatan, a few minutes' walk from the Domkyrkan, the awe-inspiring **Royal Ship Kronan Exhibition** is the main attraction of the **Läns Museum** (County Museum; mid-June to mid-Aug daily 10am–6pm; mid-Aug to mid-June, Tues–Fri 10am–4pm, Sat & Sun 11am–4pm, ⓦwww.kalmarlansmuseum.se; 50kr). The navy flagship *Kronan*, built by the British naval designer Francis Sheldon, was one of the world's three largest ships, twice the size of the *Vasa*, which sank near Stockholm in 1628 (see p.480). The *Kronan* went down in 1676, blown apart by an explosion in its gunpowder magazine – 800 of its 850 crew were killed, their bodies preserved for more than three hundred years on the Baltic seabed.

It wasn't until 1980 that super-sensitive scanning equipment detected the whereabouts of the ship, 26m down off the coast of Öland. A salvage operation was led by a descendant of the ship's captain, Admiral Lorentz Creutz, and the amazing finds are displayed in an imaginative walk-through reconstruction of the gun decks and admiral's cabin, accompanied by sound effects of cannon fire and screeching gulls. While the ship's treasure trove of gold coins is displayed at the end of the exhibition, it's the incredibly well-preserved clothing – hats, jackets, buckled leather shoes and even silk bows and cuff links – that brings this exceptional show to life. Other rooms detail the political background to the wars between the Swedes, Danes and Dutch at the time of the sinking. New discoveries are continuously being made, and added to the exhibition, and one day the museum hopes to raise and display the intact port side of the hull.

Eating and drinking

There's a generous number of good places **to eat** in Kalmar. The liveliest area is **Lärmtorget**, where restaurants, cafés and pubs serve Swedish, Indonesian, Chinese, Greek, Italian and English food. When it comes to **nightlife**, in summer, the *Vallen* club at Lärmtorget 4 (☎0480/233 37) is the best place to party, while in winter the hip crowd heads just west of the centre to *Palace* at Unionsgatan 14 (ⓦwww.palacekalmar.com) to boogie.

Cafés and restaurants

Byttan Slottsallén, Stadspark. Well situated in the lovely park between the New Town and the castle, this functionalist-style restaurant from 1939 serves up Swedish and international dishes (from 90kr).

Ernesto Salonger Lärmtorget 4, ⓦwww.ernesto-kalmar.com. Extremely popular place serving a huge range of very good pizzas and pastas (70–100kr), as well as traditional Italian salads, antipasti and meat dishes (90–190kr) in quite upmarket surroundings. Live music at weekends.

Krögers Lärmtorget 7. A popular pub/restaurant with a pleasant terrace, serving light Swedish meals from 69kr.

Kullzenska Caféet Kaggensgatan 26. Kalmar's best café by far, this is an exceptional *konditori* occupying the first floor of a nineteenth-century wooden house. Its eight interconnecting rooms are awash with stoves, Indian carpets, mahogany furnishings and crumbling royal portraits – exactly as they were during the reign of the twin sisters who lived here for the best part of a century before the building was opened as a tea house. Great coffee and cakes.

Ming Palace Fiskaregatan 7. The premier Chinese restaurant in town, with lunch specials for 66kr and an excellent-value all-you-can-eat buffet.

T&T Unionsgatan 20. Kalmar's hippest eatery, this place serves unusual (and delicious) pizzas with toppings such as banana, onion, curry and pineapple (60–80kr), along with meat dishes (sold by weight). Big range of wines and some great desserts.

Znaps Bar och Kök Corner of Södra Vallgatan and Kaggensgatan. A hip joint with a well-designed interior, attracting a youngish crowd. Lots of schnapps and other drinks, and the food is good – the likes of fish soup, salads, wok dishes and pastas at reasonable prices.

Öland

Linked to mainland Sweden by a six-kilometre bridge, the island of **Öland** is the kind of place a Swedish Famous Five would come on holiday: mysterious forests and flat, pretty meadows to cycle through, miles of mostly unspoilt beaches, wooden cottages with candy-striped canopies, windmills and ice-cream parlours. Swedes have been coming here in droves for over a century, but since becoming

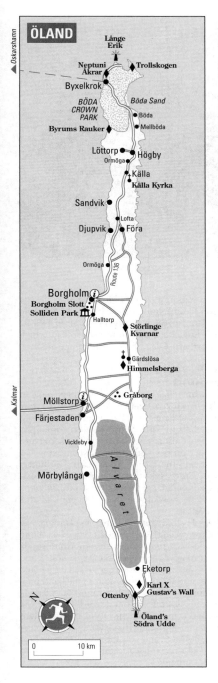

ÖLAND

Långe Erik
Neptuni Åkrar
Trollskogen
Byxelkrok
BÖDA CROWN PARK
Böda Sand
Böda
Mellböda
Byrums Rauker
Löttorp
Högby
Ormöga
Källa
Källa Kyrka
Sandvik
Lofta
Djupvik
Föra
Ormöga
Route 136
Borgholm
Borgholm Slott
Solliden Park
Halltorp
Störlinge Kvarnar
Gärdslösa
Himmelsberga
Gråborg
Möllstorp
Färjestaden
Vickleby
Alvaret
Mörbylånga
Eketorp
Karl X Gustav's Wall
Ottenby
Öland's Södra Udde

Oskarshamn
Kalmar

0   10 km

popular with foreign tourists, it's now visited by 55,000 people every July and August. Despite this onslaught, which clogs the road from the bridge north to the main town, Borgholm, this long, splinter-shaped island retains a likeably old-fashioned holiday atmosphere, with a labyrinth of walking trails and bicycle routes and some of the best bathing opportunities in Sweden.

A royal hunting ground from the mid-sixteenth century until 1801, Öland was ruled with scant regard for its native population. Peasants were forbidden from chopping wood or owning dogs or weapons, while Kalmar's tradesmen exploited the trade restrictions to force low prices for the islanders' produce. Danish attacks on Öland saw seven hundred farms destroyed, and following a succession of disastrous harvests in the mid-nineteenth century, a quarter of the population packed their bags for a new life in America. Today, Öland's young are just as likely to migrate to the Swedish mainland.

The island's attractions include numerous ruined castles, Bronze and Iron Age burial cairns, runic stones and forts, all set amid rich and varied fauna and flora and a striking landscape. To the south is a massive limestone plain known as the Alvaret, whose thin covering of soil is pierced by tiny flowers in summer. In central Öland, the Ice Age left the limestone more hidden and the area is blanketed with forest, while to the north, the coastline is craggy and irregular, with dramatic-looking *rauker* – stone pillars, weathered by the waves into jagged shapes.

Getting to the island

If you're **driving**, head north of Kalmar and over the bridge to Möllstorp on Öland. **Cycling** over the bridge during the day is forbidden from mid-June to August, but there's a free hourly bike bus from Jutnabben on the mainland, which drops you off outside the island's main tourist office in Möllstorp. **Bus**

△ Windmills, Öland

#101 runs almost hourly from Kalmar bus station to Borgholm (55min), while the equally frequent #103 serves Färjestaden (20min), hub of the island's bus network. If you're coming from the north, it's quicker to catch the **ferry** (☎0499/449 20, 🔵www.olandsfarjan.nu; mid-June to mid-Aug; 2hr 20min; one-way 150kr), which connects Oskarshamn to Byxelkrok in northern Öland twice daily; there are very few buses from there, however.

Information and getting around

Öland's main **tourist office** is the sprawling *Träffpunkt Öland* complex next to the end of the bridge in **Möllstorp** (Jan–April & Oct–Dec Mon–Fri 9am–5pm; May, June & early Aug Mon–Fri 9am–6pm, Sat 9am–4pm, Sun 10am–4pm; July to mid-Aug Mon–Sat 8.30am–8.30pm, Sun 9.30am–7pm; Sept Mon–Fri 9am–5pm, Sat 10am–3pm; ☎0485/56 06 00, 🔵www.olandsturist.se). Staff can book **private rooms** across the island from 150kr per person per night (plus 75kr booking fee, 175kr by phone). Pick up a bus timetable and the *Ölands Karten* (80kr), a hugely detailed and excellent, if costly, map that shows hiking routes and coastal treks. While you're at the tourist office complex, pop into the **Naturum** centre, where a twenty-metre model of the island lights up to show all the areas of interest. There's also a pleasant **café** here with well-priced meals.

It's worth noting the shape and size of Öland before forming ambitious plans to cover it all by bike; although the island is geared for cycling, with endless cycle tracks along the flat roads, you're looking at 130km if you want to explore it from north to south. **Bike rental** is available in Borgholm and at most of the island's campsites, hostels and the odd farm, for 45–80kr per day, 250kr per week. If you have a **car**, orientation could not be simpler: there is just one main road, Route 136, which runs from the lighthouse at the island's northernmost tip to the lighthouse in the far south; for most of its length, it runs close to the west coast. A smaller road runs off the 136 down the east of the island, south from Föra. A **bus** network connects most places in Öland: there are hubs at Färjestaden, south of the bridge with the mainland; Mörbylånga, 10km further south; and at Bornholm; the service is infrequent, however, and you should be prepared for a lot of waiting around, particularly in the south – you need to time trips carefully to avoid being stranded, though **hitching** is not impossible.

Borgholm

Walking the simple grid of streets that makes up **BORGHOLM**, Öland's "capital", it's clear that tourism is the lifeblood of this villagey town. Although swamped well beyond its capacity each July by tens of thousands of visitors, cramming its pizzerias and bars and injecting a riotous carnival atmosphere, Borgholm is in no way the tacky resort it could be. Encircled by the flaking, turreted villas that were the pride of the town during its first period as a holiday resort in the nineteenth century, most of the centre is a friendly, if bland, network of shops and restaurants leading to a pleasant harbour.

The only real attraction here is the **Borgholm Slott ruin** (daily: April & Sept 10am–4pm; May–Aug 10am–6pm; 50kr; ⓦwww.borgholmsslott.se), just to the southwest of the centre. A colossal stone fortification with rows of huge arches and corridors open to the skies, it can be reached either through a nature reserve (a signposted five-minute walk from the town centre) or from the first exit south off Route 136. Virtually destroyed by the wars of the 16th century, the medieval castle was rebuilt as a Renaissance palace, only to be damaged again during the 1611 Kalmar War. Plans to restore it again, this time in Baroque style, were never finalized, and the castle's deathblow was dealt by a devastating fire in 1806.

A few hundred metres south of the castle is the present royal family's summer residence, **Solliden Park**, an Italian-style villa built to a design specified by Swedish Queen Victoria (the present king's great-grandmother) in 1903. A huge, austere red-granite bust of Victoria rises out of scrubland at the entrance car park. She faces south, away from Sweden – which she was reputed to have loathed – and towards Italy – which she adored. The villa itself is closed to the public but the **gardens** (daily: mid-May to mid-Sept 11am–6pm; 50kr) make for a pleasant stroll, or you could just head for the delightful thatch-roofed café, *Kaffetorpet*, by the car park.

Just to the north of the town centre, **Blå Rör** is Öland's largest Bronze Age cairn, a huge mound of stones excavated when a coffin was discovered here in 1849. In the 1920s, burnt bones indicating a cremation grave were also discovered, along with bronze swords and tweezers – common items in such tombs. However, there's nothing much to see there now and you're better off visiting **Forngård**, Köpmangatan 23 (mid-June to Aug Mon–Sat 11am–5pm; 20kr), a museum of Öland life whose most interesting exhibits come from the historical sites around the island. The ground-floor displays include bits of ancient skulls, some Viking glass, Bronze Age jewellery and grave finds.

Practicalities

Borgholm's small **tourist office** (Jan–May & late Aug to Dec Mon–Fri 9am–12.15pm & 1–5.30pm; June to early July Mon–Fri 9am–6pm, Sat 10am–3pm; mid-July to early-Aug Mon–Sat 9am–6pm; early to late August Mon–Fri 9am–5.30pm, Sat 10am–3pm; ☎0485/890 00, ⓦwww.olandsturist.se) is tucked away out of the hubbub at Sandgatan 25, a couple of streets back from the main Storgatan. The only place to **rent a bike** is Hallbergs Hojjar, Köpmangatan 10 (☎0485/109 40; 60kr per day or 300kr per week). The *Ebbas* **youth hostel** at Storgatan 12 (☎0485/103 73, ⓦwww.ebbas.se; May–Sept) in the city centre is situated above a lively garden café and has cheap double rooms (❶) as well as dorm accommodation (220kr per bed). The tourist office will book **private rooms** from 150kr per person (booking fee 25kr; no telephone bookings). The local **campsite**, *Kapelludden* (☎0485/101 78, ⓦwww.kapelludden.se), is on a small peninsula five minutes' walk from the centre, though there's no shortage here, as on the rest of the island, of beautiful spots in which to camp rough.

The best of the **hotels** in the centre of town is *Villa Sol*, at Slottsgatan 30 (☎0485/56 25 52, ⓦwww.villasol.nu; ❶/❷). A charming old pale-yellow house set in a fruit tree-filled garden, it's beautifully furnished, with stripped floors, old tiled fireplaces and a sun-filled veranda; rooms in the basement are even cheaper, and perfectly comfortable, though less bright. Book early for July, when the place fills up. *Hotell Borgholm*, Trädgårdsgatan 15 (☎0485/770 60, ⓦwww.hotellborgholm .com; ❹), has smart en-suite rooms, while the vast *Strand Hotell*, overlooking the harbour at Villagatan 4 (☎0485/888 88, ⓦwww.strand.borgholm.se; ❸/❹), includes a nightclub, pool and sauna, though if you're not looking to be awake all night (see below), it's best avoided. Eight kilometres south of Borgholm on Route 136 lies one of the few really fine hotels on the island, *Halltorps Gästgiveri* (☎0485/850 00, ⓦwww.halltorpsgastgiveri.se; ❷/❹), with contemporary, neutrally decorated rooms set in a beautiful eighteenth-century manor house.

There's a pronounced summer-holiday feel to the town's **restaurants** and bars, though standards aren't always very high. Pizza places abound around Stortorget and down to the harbour, all much the same and not cheap at 65–85kr for a pizza. *Hemma Hos*, just behind the main church at Kvarngatan 13, serves good pizzas (80kr) and meat dishes (from 130kr) on a pleasant terrace. On the northern side of the harbour, *Skeppet* is a jolly little Italian restaurant, hidden behind a group of silos. For the finest food on the island (with prices to match – the multi-course menus start at 400kr), head for *Bakfickan* at the *Hotell Borgholm* (see above), whose chef, Karin Fransson, is something of a celebrity in Sweden. For good ice-cream, make for *Ölands Glass* on Storgatan, where you can eat the home-made sorbets and ices (try the salty liquorice variety for something completely different) in the pleasant back garden.

For **drinking**, *Pubben*, Storgatan 18, is a cosy pub run by a friendly local who knows his malts, offering 46 varieties of whiskey. Otherwise, try the fun *Robinson Crusoe*, jutting into the water at the harbour but with overpriced food. For night-time drinking, *Znaps*, at Södra Långgatan 18, occupies a building that was formerly a hospital for venereal diseases and a church; these days, you'll find R&B, house music and occasional live bands (50kr cover charge on Fri & Sat nights). Otherwise, a raucous young crowd invariably swarms past the gorilla bouncers into the *Strand* night club in the *Strand Hotell* every evening, turning it into a sort of Baltic Ibiza throughout the summer nights (cover charge 100kr).

North Öland

The north of the island holds Öland's most varied landscape, with some unexpected diversions to boot. Heading up Route 136, there's no shortage of idyllic villages, dark woods and flowery fields. At **FÖRA**, about 20km north of Borgholm, there's a good example of a typical Öland church, which doubled as a fortress in times of war. About 12km north of here is **KÄLLA**, 2km outside which sits proud, forlorn **Källa kyrka**, empty since 1888 and now sitting in splendid isolation. Surrounded by brightly flowering meadows, this medieval church is bounded by dry-stone walls, its grounds littered with ancient, weathered tombs. Continue north and west off Route 136 across the island to the striking **Byrums Rauker**: solitary limestone pillars formed by the sea at the edge of a sandy beach. The best **beaches** in northern Öland are along the east coast; the most popular stretch is a couple of kilometres north of Böda Sand.

There are some gorgeous areas of natural beauty in the far north. The nature reserve of **Trollskogen** ("Trolls Forest") – exactly the kind of place you would imagine trolls to inhabit, with twisted, gnarled trunks of ancient oaks shrouded in ivy – offers some excellent walking. On a tiny island at the tip of the north coast stands **Långe Erik Lighthouse**, a handsome obelisk of 1845 and a good goal for a walk or cycle ride. Three kilometres along the western coast is the ridged land formation of **Neptuni Åkrar** ("Neptune's Ploughland"), named by Carl von Linné for its resemblance to ploughed fields, and covered with lupin-like flowers during summer, which form a sheet of brilliant blue to rival the sea beyond. The only town in this region is **BYXELKROK**, a quiet place with an attractive harbour and a ferry to Oskarshamn in summer (see p.584).

The great outdoors

With their vast coniferous forests, rolling hills and duned beachfronts, the four countries of mainland Scandinavia boast some of the most diverse geography in Europe. This variety makes for a marvellous array of outdoor activities: from plunging into icy waters off an Arctic icebreaker, pitching a tent in a quiet birch forest, riding a husky-drawn sled or kayaking along the banks of a placid lake, the permutations for adventure are endless.

Cross-country skiers, Norway

Winter

There's no denying that the Scandinavian climate can be unforgivingly frigid: in the far reaches of the Arctic, where snow can remain on the ground well into June, winter temperatures can reach as low as -45°C/-49°F; in most parts, though, they hover around 0°C/32°F. However, visiting during the cold season doesn't only mean woolly underwear, stories in front of the fire and mugs of spicy glög wine – far from shrinking away from the subzero temperatures, locals make the best of them: office workers trade trainers for skis, while frozen lakes and rivers become playgrounds for skaters, snowmobilers and ice-fishermen. Visitors, too, will find several unique ways to exploit the winter weather. Both Northern Sweden (Jukkasjärvi) and Finland (Kemi) are home to spectacular ice hotels (see p.639 & 772), sculpted out of snow and ice and complete with requisite vodka bars; Kemi is also the departure point for unique icebreaker cruises through the Gulf of Bothnia's dense winter icefields. Husky safaris (see p.790) aboard dog-drawn sleds are an unusual way to explore the region's stark, frozen landscape, while throughout Scandinavia you'll find ample opportunity for solo or guided trekking and hiking, especially in Finland's national parks (see p.786 & 788) and on Norway's Jostedalsbreen glacier (see p.348). Cross-country skiing is something of an institution in Norway, where a network of trails (some floodlit) make exploring the backwoods a cinch – you'll have no trouble renting gear at ski resorts such as Geilo (see p.298) or Holmenkollen (see p.273). And everywhere in Finland, you'll be encouraged to experience the curative national ritual of hopping from steamy sauna into bone-chilling lake, a great way to unwind both body and mind.

Göta canal, Sweden

Summer

Though it's best known as a winter playground, Scandinavia does of course thaw out during the summer months. You'll want a pullover for the occasional chilly evening, but the climate is temperate in most parts from May to September. From June to August, temperatures hover around a comfortable 20°C/68°F (though they can reach as high as 35°C/95°F in some inland regions). These comparatively balmy climes combined with longer days see the locals excitedly making up for the long months of winter darkness. Walking is the transportation of choice when the weather's good, and the region's well-maintained, well-trodden hiking trails are peppered with campsites and huts in which to bed down for the night – Karhunkierros in northern Finland (see p.778), Kungsleden in Swedish Lapland (see p.640) and the Jotunheimen or Rondane national parks in central Norway (see p.290) offer some of the best walks. Hopping on a bicycle is an equally rewarding way to see the countryside, particularly in Denmark, where gorgeous scenery and an absence of hills have made cycling particularly popular – the island of Bornholm (see p.144) is one of the best places for two-wheeled excursions.

Beaches and swimming

You could be forgiven for not immediately associating **beaches** or tan-lines with a visit to Scandinavia, but the region does have plenty of places to laze around on a sandy strand, go for a dip in the pristine sea or indulge in some watersport. Of all the countries, **Denmark**, with more than 8000 kilometres of coastline, offers the best bathing opportunities, the most appealing spots being the long, duned beaches of southern Bornholm, northern Zealand and eastern Jutland (see p.144, 141 & 189). Elsewhere, **Norway**'s west coast fjords (see p.331) offer ample opportunity for swimming under towering mountainscapes (though the waters may not be as "warm" as locals suggest), while in **Sweden**, head for the Baltic island of Gotland (see p.582), or Halland on the so-called Swedish Riviera (see p.524), which gets more hours of sunshine per year than anywhere else in the country. In **Finland**, the southern Bothnian coast and Åland islands (see p.765 & 729) hold a number of great beach resorts where you can bake under the midnight sun, broil in a waterside sauna, cool off with a dip in the water and then repeat the ritual ad infinitum. In most of these locales, swimming is clean and safe, and if you fancy getting an all-over tan, you'll find plentiful nude beaches – though these aren't always marked as such, so bring a towel for backup.

Ærø island beach, Denmark

Arctic fox

Summer is also an opportune time to get acquainted with Scandinavia's immense diversity of fauna, most notably deer, wolf, bear and a multitude of birdlife. Reindeer and elk – about two million of them – prance about the northern stretches of forest and fell, as do Arctic foxes, wolverines and lemmings. In Finland, bird-watching is the pastime of choice for many, though Denmark and Norway also have their share of birdlife, mostly migratory waterbirds like the godwit, avocet and dunlin. Superb reel and fly fishing can be found all over the region and whale-watching excursions from Andenes in Norway are understandably popular (see p.389), given you've a 99 percent chance of at least one sighting.

Solar spectacle: midnight sun and northern lights

The midnight sun and its binary opposite – permanent darkness – are defining characteristics of the Scandinavian Arctic. From late May to mid-July, the **midnight sun** provides 24 hours of daylight, and the effect of this phenomenon can be downright unsettling, with routine scenes straight out of a B-movie horror: driving without headlamps at 10pm, a glowing red sunset at midnight and waking up to a "dawn" chorus of birdsong at 3am. To see the full effect, where the whole sun is visible at midnight, you'll need to be above the Arctic Circle, the "line" drawn at 66° 33' latitude which stretches across Norway, Sweden and Finland – the further north you are, the more extreme the effect.

Conversely, though northern winters often see 24 hours of darkness, the night sky is frequently illuminated courtesy of the bright, fiery tapestries of the **aurora borealis** or **northern lights**. These undulating ribbons of hazel, green and amber that flicker and stretch across the heavens may shimmer for hours or last no more than ten minutes, twisting and turning in bursts of colour before fading away. Created by the collision of solar particle emissions with the earth's atmosphere, the aurora is at its most dazzling on clear evenings in between September and October and February to March, when the nights are long and the sky at its darkest. The effect is most intense away from cities, since light pollution decreases the intensity, and the further north you are, the bigger and brighter the spectacle – Muonio in Finland (see p.789) and anywhere in Norway's Finnmark county (see p.102) are particularly good viewing spots.

Aurora borealis from Korsnes harbour, Lofoten islands

Practicalities

There's not much in the way of proper hotels north of Borgholm, but high-standard **campsites** abound, mostly beside the beaches. The most extensive site is *Krono Camping* at Böda Sand (☎0485/222 00, ⓦwww.kronocamping-oland.se; mid-May to Sept), 2km off the main road at the southern end of the beach. The STF **youth hostel**, *Vandrarhem Böda* at Mellböda (☎0485/220 38, ☞221 98; ❶), just south of *Krono Camping*, is big and well equipped and has dorm beds from 110kr. Just 6km northwest of Mellböda at **Byxelkrok**, *Solö Wärdhus* (☎0485/283 70, ⓦwww .wardshus.nu; ❸) is a pleasant enough **hotel**; the town also has the only decent **nightlife** venue in the north of Öland, the restaurant, pub and disco *Sjöstugan* (☎0485/283 30, ⓦwww.sjostugan.nu; closed Sept–March), right by the shore. The food is good and varied, with fish, meat and vegetarian dishes (100–180kr); while troubadours sing every evening in June and Swedish dance bands appear throughout July.

Central Öland

Cutting eastwards from Borgholm (take bus #102) and following signs to Räpplinge brings you to **Störlinge**, where you'll find a row of seven windmills (*kvarnar*) by the roadside. This is the island's longest line of postmill-type windmills, and they make an impressive sight. Almost opposite, *Hus och Hem* (closed Jan & Feb) is a very pleasant **café**. A couple of kilometres south, **GÄRDSLÖSA** has the island's best-preserved medieval church. It's the interior that's well worth a look for its 1666 pulpit and thirteenth-century ceiling paintings; these were whitewashed over in 1781, but uncovered in 1950. A few kilometres further south in a gorgeous setting is the preserved village of **Himmelsberga**, now an **open-air museum** (mid-May to mid-Aug daily 10am–5.30pm; 50kr; ⓦwww.olandsmuseum.com). Following the decline of farming in the middle of the twentieth century, most of Öland's thatched farmhouses were rather brutally modernized; Himmelsberga, however, escaped, and two of its original farms opened as museums in the 1950s. Buildings were subsequently brought from all over the island, and the collection now includes an extensive assortment of crofters' farms, a smithy and a windmill. **Gråborg**, passed by bus #102, another 10km south of Himmelsberga, is Öland's largest ancient castle ruin, with 640-metre-long walls. Built around 500 AD and occupied throughout the Middle Ages (when the Gothic entrance arch was built), the walls today encircle little more than a handful of hardy sheep.

South Öland

Dominated by **Alvaret**, the giant limestone plain on which no trees can grow, the south of the island is sparsely populated. You won't see any bare rock, however, only a meadow landscape sprouting rare alpine plant life that has clung on stoically since the Ice Age. The unique agricultural landscape of southern Öland – continuously inhabited and little changed in 5000 years – is listed as a heritage site by UNESCO, and there are plenty of signposted walks and viewpoints along Route 136. **Buses** run so infrequently here that you'll need to check times carefully at Färjestaden and Mörbylånga; **hitching** is also a feasible option here. There are fewer facilities as a whole than in the north, so it's worth stocking up before you head off. The great advantage of travelling in southern Öland, however, is that summer crowds thin out here, allowing you to explore the most untouched parts of the island in peace.

The prettiest village is **VICKLEBY**, the site of a remarkable art and design school, **Capella Gården**, the brainchild of furniture designer Carl Malmsten. An idealist, Malmsten's dream was to create a school that stimulated mind, body and soul. In 1959, he bought a range of picturesque farmhouses at Vickleby and opened an art and design school for adults, which still runs today. The students' work, including some lovely ceramic and wood pieces, is sold in an annual exhibition. If you want to visit, call the studios beforehand (☎0485/361 32).

Of all the ruined forts on Öland, the one most worth a visit is at the village of **EKETORP**, reachable twice daily by bus from Mörbylånga. The site (May to early Sept daily 10am–6pm, late Sept Sat & Sun only; guided tours in English 1.15pm; 70kr; ⊛www.eketorp.se) includes a reconstructed prehistoric ring fort and an archeological museum containing the finds of a major excavation in the 1970s. Three settlements were discovered, including a marketplace from the fourth century and an agricultural community dating from 1000 AD. The result is a wonderful achievement in speculative archeology, actual physical evidence being thin on the ground. The best of the finds, such as jewellery and weapons, are on show in the museum, and the Iron Age houses in the fort have workshops where you can have a go at leatherwork or ancient cookery.

If you head south from here, you'll come to a stone wall that cuts straight across the island. Called **Karl X Gustav's Wall**, it was built in 1650 to fence off deer and so improve hunting. **Ottenby**, in the far south of the island, is a birdwatcher's paradise, with a huge nature reserve and the Ottenby **bird station**.

Practicalities

The *Mörby* **youth hostel** (☎0485/493 93, ⊛www.svif.se; dorm beds from 135kr), 15km south of the bridge, has some hotel rooms as well (❶/❷). Bus #105 stops right outside. *Haga Park* (May–Sept; ☎0485/360 30, ⊛www.hagaparkcamping.se), 10km south of the bridge at Haga Park, has basic hotel rooms (❶) and a **campsite**. For a regular **hotel**, try the popular ⅔ *Bo Pensionat* at Vickleby (☎0485/360 01, ⊛www .bopensionat.nu; ❸), with an excellent garden café – book ahead in high season.

Inland Småland

Thickly forested and studded with lakes, **Småland county** makes up the southeastern wedge of Sweden – a region of appealing, if uniform, scenery. It's a part of the country that people frequently travel through – from Stockholm to the southwest, or from Gothenburg to the Baltic coast – yet beneath the canopy of greenery, there are a few spots of interest, along with opportunities for hiking, trekking, fishing and cycling.

Historically, Småland has had it tough. The simple, rustic charm of the pretty painted cottages belies the intense economic misery endured by generations of local peasants; in the nineteenth century, this led to a massive surge of emigration for America. Their plight is vividly retold at the **House of Emigrants** exhibition in **Växjö** – a town that makes an excellent base for exploring the region – but the county's most marketed tourist attraction remains the many **glass factories** hidden away in the forest. Further north and perched at the southern tip of Lake Vättern, industrial **Jönköping** has historically been the centre of Swedish match production.

Växjö and around

Founded by Saint Sigfrid in the eleventh century, **VÄXJÖ** (pronounced "veh-quer") is by far the handiest place to base yourself if you are interested in touring the region's glassworks. Deep in the heart of Småland county (110km from Kalmar), the town itself boasts two superb museums: the extensive **Smålands Museum**, notable for being home to the **Swedish Glass Museum**, and the fascinating **House of Emigrants**, which explores the mass emigration from Sweden in the nineteenth and early twentieth centuries. While the town centre doesn't hold much else of appeal, the romantic castle ruin of **Kronoberg** is within easy reach, just 4km to the north.

The Town

The **Smålands Museum**, behind the train station (June–Aug Mon–Fri 10am–5pm, Sat & Sun 11am–5pm; Sept–May Tues–Fri 10am–5pm, Sat & Sun 11am–5pm;

40kr; ⓦwww.smalandsmuseum.se), contains two permanent exhibitions: an intelligently displayed history of Småland's manufacturing industries and the more appealing "five hundred years of Swedish glass". The latter's exhibits range from sixteenth-century place settings to eighteenth- and nineteenth-century etched and coloured glass, along with stylish Art Nouveau-inspired pieces. Most appealing, though, are the wide-ranging displays of contemporary glass. If you're intending to visit any of the glassworks (see p.573), it's a good idea to come here first to gauge the different styles.

The plain building directly in front of the museum contains the inspired **House of Emigrants** (May–Aug Mon–Fri 9am–5pm, Sat & Sun 11am–4pm; Sept–April Mon–Fri 9am–4pm, Sat 11am–4pm; 40kr; ⓦwww.swemi.se), with its moving "Dream of America" exhibition. The museum presents a living picture of the intense hardship faced by the Småland peasant population from the mid-nineteenth century onwards. Due to agricultural reforms and a series of bad harvests, a million Swedes emigrated to America between 1860 and 1930, most of them from Småland. Most boats left from Gothenburg and, until 1915, sailed to Hull in Britain, where passengers crossed to Liverpool by train to board the transatlantic ships. Conditions on board were usually dire: the steamer *Hero* left Gothenburg in 1866 with 500 emigrants, nearly 400 oxen and 900 pigs, calves and sheep sharing the accommodation. Today, the tables have turned and new texts in the museum detail the experiences of the many immigrants in Sweden.

The attached **research centre** charges 150kr per half day or 200kr for a full day to help interested parties trace their family roots, using passenger lists from ten harbours, microfilmed church records from every Swedish parish, and records of bodies such as the Swedish New York Society, Swedes in Australia and the Swedish Congo Veterans Association. It's worth booking ahead during the summer season.

There's not much else to see in Växjö's centre, but take a quick look at the very distinctive **Domkyrkan** (daily 9am–5pm; book ahead for guided tours in June–Aug at ℡0470/70 48 24), with its unusual twin green towers and apricot-coloured facade. Regular restorations, the most recent in 1995, together with a catalogue of sixteenth-century fires and a lightning strike in 1775, have left nothing of note except a unique 1775 organ and some brilliant modern glass ornaments by Göran Wärff, one of the best known of the contemporary Glass Kingdom designers. The newest addition is a striking glass altar triptych by equally celebrated Bertil Vallien. The cathedral is set in the **Linné Park**, named after Carl von Linné, who was educated at the handsome school next door (closed to the public).

Kronoberg Slott

Set on a tiny island in Lake Helgasjön, the ruins of **Kronoberg Slott** lie 4km north of the town centre in a beautiful and unspoilt setting – follow the signs for Evedal, or take the hourly bus #1B from the bus station. The bishops of Växjö erected a wooden fortress here in the eleventh century, but it was Gustav Vasa who built the present stone version in 1540. Entered over an old wooden bridge set at a narrow spot in the lake, it's a perfect ruin, leaning precariously and complete with rounded tower and deep-set lookouts. Some new brick archways and a couple of reinforced roofs, added in the 1970s, stop the whole thing collapsing. The grass-roofed *Café Ryttmästargården*, set in an eighteenth-century cottage overlooking the castle, serves lunch and snacks among quaint old furnishings. The old paddle steamer *Thor* makes regular excursions from here around Lake Helgasjön, the perfect way to appreciate the lakeland scenery. There's an evening trip to Lake Asasjön and the Asa Herragård country house (400kr including dinner), or opt for the less expensive "coffee trips" (125kr) to the sluice gates between Helgasjön and Asasjön, which leave most Wednesdays at 6pm, and on Saturdays and Sundays at 1pm and 4.30pm; call ℡0470/70 42 00 to book.

Practicalities

Växjö's **train** and **bus stations** are alongside one another in the middle of town. The **tourist office**, inside the city library at Västra Esplanaden 7 (mid-June to Aug Mon–Fri 9.30am–6pm, Sat 10am–2pm, July to mid-Aug also Sun 10am–2pm; mid-Aug to mid-June Mon–Fri 9.30am–4.30pm; ☎0470/414 10, ⊛www.turism .vaxjo.se), can book **private rooms** from 150kr per person, plus a 50kr booking fee). You can use **Internet** for free in the library.

The splendid STF **youth hostel** (☎0470/630 70, ⊛www.vaxjovandrarhem .nu; ❶), with dorm beds for 155kr, is at Evedal, 6km north of the centre, in an eighteenth-century house set in parkland on tranquil Lake Helgasjön (with its own beach). To get there, take bus #1C from the bus station (last bus is at 4.15pm, 3.15pm on Sat & Sun), or bus #1A, which leaves you with a 1.5-kilometre walk, but runs daily till 8.15pm. Next to the hostel is a **campsite**, *Evedal Camping* (☎0470/630 34, ⊛www.evedalscamping.com), with four-person cabins from 600kr.

Of the town's **hotels**, the most striking is the *Quality Hotel Konserthuset*, in the central Concert Hall building at Västra Esplanaden 12 (☎0470/70 22 00, ⊛www .teaterparken.se; ❸/❺). Otherwise, try the no-frills *Esplanad*, Norra Esplanaden 21a (☎0470/225 80, ⊛www.hotell-esplanad.com; ❷), or the good-value *Värend*, Kungsgatan 27 (☎0470/77 67 00, ⊛www.hotellvarend.se; ❷/❸).

Växjö is a good place to eat traditional Småland cuisine, which features lots of berries, potatoes and game. For a **café** with strong gourmet leanings, try *Café Momento* in the Smålands Museum, which serves tasty Småland and Italian food, plus salads and soups. The central *PM & Friends* at Storgatan 24 (☎0470/70 04 44) is one of the very best **restaurants** in Sweden, with an emphasis on fine modern European cuisine using lake-caught fish; main dishes cost 180–350kr. It gets packed on Friday and Saturday nights. Set in Växjö's oldest house at Sandgärdsgatan 19, *Wibrowski* (☎0470/74 04 10) serves excellent lamb, Wienerschnitzel and pepper steak, starting at 180kr. Next door, ☆ *Kafé de Luxe* (⊛www.kafedeluxe.se), a fun 1950s-style eatery furnished with formica tables, tube metal chairs and wooden radios, has an excellent Swedish-influenced tapas menu (145–165kr) and regular live music.

The Glass Kingdom

Within the landscape of dense birch and pine forests, threaded by lakes, that stretches between Kalmar and Växjö, lie the bulk of Småland's celebrated **glassworks**. The area is dubbed Glasriket (⊛www.glasriket.se), or the "**Glass Kingdom**", with each glassworks signposted clearly from the spidery main roads. This seemingly odd and very picturesque setting for the industry is no coincidence. King Gustav Vasa pioneered glass-making in Sweden when he returned from Italy in the mid-sixteenth century and decided to set up a glassworks in Stockholm. However, it was only Småland's forests that could provide the vast amounts of fuel needed to feed the furnaces, and so a glass factory was set up here in 1742, named Kosta after its founders, Koskull and Stael von Hostein – today, under the name Kosta Boda, it's the largest glassworks in Småland.

Visiting the glassworks

All the fifteen or so glassworks still in operation in Småland put on captivating glass-blowing **demonstrations**, usually Monday to Friday between 9am and 2.30pm, sometimes longer hours; Kosta and Orrefors also have glass blowing on Saturdays (10am–4pm) and Sundays (noon–4pm). Several also have permanent **exhibitions** of contemporary work or pieces from the firm's history, and, without exception, all have a **shop**. **Bus** services to (or to within walking distance of) the glassworks are extremely limited, and without your own transport it is almost impossible to see more than a couple in a day – although you'll probably find this is enough. Glass fanatics can purchase the **Glasriket Pass** (95kr), which gives reductions on entrance fees and gift-shop sales, and free guided tours of eleven participating factories; it's available from the glassworks, tourist offices and hotels in the area.

While each glassworks has characteristic individual designs, the Kosta Boda and Orrefors works give the best picture of what is available. **Orrefors** (late April to Aug Mon–Fri 9am–6pm, Sat 10am–5pm, Sun 11am–5pm; Sept to mid–April Mon–Fri 10am–6pm, Sat 10am–4pm, Sun noon–4pm; tours 50kr; ☎0481/341 95, ⓦwww.orrefors.se) is easily reached by public transport from Växjö in one to two hours; take a train to Nybro, then bus #139, #140, #141 or #315 to the factory. The **Kosta Boda** and **Åfors** glassworks (June–Aug Mon–Fri 9am–6pm, Sat 10am–5pm, Sun 11am–5pm; Sept–May Mon–Fri 10am–6pm, Sat 11am–4pm, Sun noon–4pm; free; ☎0478/345 00, ⓦwww.kostaboda.se) are operated by the same team, with the biggest collection at Kosta. The historical exhibition here contains some delicate c.1900 glassware designed by Karl Lindeberg, while if you're looking for simple modern works, Anna Ehrener's bowls and vases are the most elegant pieces. Some of the most brilliantly innovative creations are by Göran Wärff – examples of his expressive work are found in Växjö's cathedral. These can be bought in the adjacent shop, alongside current designs that tend towards colourful high-kitsch. Ulrica Hydman Vallien's name is bandied around all over the place, and the marketing of her work is fierce, though in reality, the painted-on faces and crude flower motifs are far less innovative than the tourist blurbs would have you believe. To get to Kosta from Växjö, take Route 25 to Lessebo then follow signs to the left. By public transport, bus #218 makes the hour-long trip from Växjö bus station to Kosta. Åfors is just ten kilometres south of Kosta on Route 28, but there's no direct public transport connection; it can be reached in about fifty minutes from Växjö by taking a train to Emmaboda and then bus #135 to the factory.

Studioglass Strömbergshyttan (☎0481/310 75, ⓦwww.studioglas.se), near Hovmantorp, is the best bet for a short trip from Växjö; with both Kosta and Orrefors displays, it's more comprehensive than nearby Sandvik, an Orrefors company. To get there, head southeast down Route 25 from Växjö, or take bus #218 (the Kosta bus; 40min). If you're driving, continue on to the small, traditional **Bergdala** works (☎0478/316 50, ⓦwww.skruf-bergdala.se), 6km north of Hovmantorp, which produces Sweden's distinctive blue-rimmed glassware.

Glass-making and buying glass

Demonstrations of the **glass-making process** can be mesmerizing to watch. The process involves a plug being fished out of a shimmering lake of molten glass (heated to 1200°C) and then turned and blown into a graphite or steel mould. In the case of wine glasses, a foot is then added, before the piece is annealed (heated and then slowly cooled) for several hours. It all looks deceptively simple and mistakes are rare, but it nevertheless takes years to become a servitor (glass-maker's assistant), working up through the ranks of stem-maker and bowl-gatherer. In smaller works, all these processes are carried out by the same person, but in many of Småland's glassworks, you'll see the bowl-gatherer fetching the glowing gob for the master blower, who then skilfully rolls and shapes the syrupy substance. When the blower is attaching bases to wine glasses, the would-be stem will slide off or sink right through if the glass is too hot; if too cold, it won't stick – and the right temperature lasts a matter of seconds.

If you want to **buy glassware**, which is marketed with a vengeance, don't feel compelled to snap up the first thing you see. The same batch of designs appears at most of the glassworks, a testament to the fact that the Kosta Boda and Orrefors outfits are owned by the same umbrella company, and that most of the smaller works have been swallowed up by it, too, even though they retain their own names. This makes price comparison easier, but don't expect many bargains; the best pieces go for thousands of kronor.

Jönköping

Perched at the southernmost tip of Lake Vättern, **JÖNKÖPING** (pronounced "Yun-shu-ping") is one of the oldest medieval trading centres in the country, having won its town charter in 1284. Today, it's famous for being the home of the matchstick, the nineteenth-century manufacture and worldwide distribution of which made the town wealthy. Although just one Swedish company controlled sixty percent of the global matchstick industry a century ago, matches are no longer made here. In 1932, the town's match magnate, Ivar Kruger, shot himself rather than face bankruptcy, bringing a swift end to the industry in its home town. Despite the town's unspectacular centre, Jönköping's location and accommodation and eating possibilities make it a viable base for touring the lake. In late August, Jönköping hosts a five-day **film festival** (@www.filmfestival.nu) showing arthouse movies from Scandinavia and Europe.

The Town

Between Jönköping's historic core and the lake is the biggest of the town's match factories, built in 1847. It now houses the **Tändsticksmuséet** (Match Museum; June–Aug Mon–Fri 10am–5pm, Sat & Sun 10am–3pm; Sept–May Tues–Sat 11am–3pm; 40kr, free in winter) at Tändsticksgränd 27, with exhibitions on matchmaking machines, matchbox labels, and on the lives of the matchmakers, who suffered from phosphorus necrosis – the collapse of the facial bone structure – after inhaling too many poisonous fumes. Opposite, the **Radiomuseum** (Tues–Fri 10am–5pm, Sat 10am–1pm; 20kr; @www.radiomuseet.com) displays every type of radio from early crystal sets to Walkmans. A couple of metres away, and set in another old match factory, is **Kulturhuset**, a trendy centre with a good, cheap café and alternative bookshops. Next door is the stylish Bio art-house cinema. From September to May, there's also a bustling early-morning Saturday market on the street outside the Kulturhuset. The only other museum to bother with is the **Länsmuseum** (County Museum; Tues–Sun 11am–5pm, Wed till 8pm; 40kr; @www.jkpglm.se), on Dag Hammarskjölds Plats, across the canal between lakes Vättern and Munksjön. The main reason to come here is the well-lit collection of paintings and drawings by **John Bauer**, a local artist who enthralled generations of Swedes with his Tolkienesque representations of gnomes and trolls in the *Bland Tomtar och Troll* books.

Practicalities

The **train** and **bus stations** are next to each other on Lake Vättern's edge. Within the complex, the **tourist office** (mid-June to mid-Aug Mon–Fri 9.30am–7pm, Sat 9.30am–3pm, Sun 9.30am–2pm; mid-Aug to mid-June Mon–Fri 9.30am–6pm, Sat 9.30am–2pm, Sun 9.30am–4.30pm; ☎036/10 50 50, @www.jonkoping.se) can arrange a **private room** for 200–250kr per person. Just across the highway southeast of the centre, the new A6 *Vandrarhem* **youth hostel** at Bataljonsgatan 10 (☎036/34 00 41, @a6vandrarhem@hotmail.com; dorm beds from 150kr) can be reached by bus #3 or 26. The *Villa Björkhagen* **campsite** (☎36/12 28 63, @www.swecamp.se) is 3km east of the centre, near the Elmia Exhibition Centre at Rosenlund (bus #1 towards Huskvarna).

For style, value and atmosphere, the best **hotel** is the classic *Victoria* at F.E. Elmgrens gata 5 (☎036/71 28 00, @www.victoriahome.com; ❸/❺), which includes afternoon tea and a buffet supper in its price and even boasts its own radio and match museums in the corridors. The comfortable city-centre *Scandic Portalen* is a few minutes walk from the train station at Barnarpsgatan 6 (☎036/585 42 00, @www.scandic-hotels.com; ❸/❺). Another good bet is the *Familjen Ericsson's City Hotel*, just three minutes from the station at Västra Storgatan 25 (☎036/71 92 80, @www.cityhotel.nu; ❹/❷). A cheap option is the spartan *Formule 1*, Huskvarnavägen 76 (☎036/30 25 65, @www.hotelformule1.com; ❶) next to the Elmia Exhibition Centre, charging a flat 310kr for bare rooms sleeping up to three people.

Jönköping has plenty of good and lively places to **eat** and **drink**. However, some close for the summer, when many of the townsfolk head off to the coast, while others shut on Fridays and Sundays.

The best **café** is *Mackmakeriet*, five minutes' walk east of the station at Smedjegatan 26. In a lovely eighteenth-century building with an original painted ceiling, this place survived a huge fire in 2000 that devastated much of the area. Photos of the conflagration by local man Andreas Joakimson adorn the walls and are worth a visit in themselves, though the fresh-filled baguettes (45kr) and cakes are delicious and served in a thoroughly friendly atmosphere.

Bernard's at Östra Storgatan 12 is a *konditori* with great cakes and an ideal summer terrace for people-watching. On the main shopping street on the west side of the centre, *Johan's Coffee & Shop* at Barnarpsgatan 16 offers superb salads and home-baked pies as well as excellent-value lunches at 69kr. Among the town's **restaurants**, try *Anna-Gretas Matsal*, in a former market traders' café on Västra Torget, for its eclectic and frequently changing menu, or splash out at the excellent *Svarta Börsen Krogen* at Kyrkogatan 4 (℡036/71 22 22), which serves creative dishes with lamb, game and fish at 110–325kr.

Many of the town's **bars** also serve food: *Hemma*, Smedjegatan 36, is the most popular venue for laid-back live music, with very friendly service and a wide-ranging menu that includes some vegetarian options. *Karlsonn's*, Västra Storgatan 9, gets very busy and has a good cheap bar menu (up to 100kr); its rooftop terrace, *På Taket*, is very popular on warm nights. Jönköping's **pier** has a lively waterside run of summer bars and restaurants; the *Saltkråkan* ship at the end (℡036/12 53 53) serves great seafood and has a fine whisky bar, too.

Vadstena

With its beautiful lakeside setting, 95km north of Jönköping, **VADSTENA** is the most evocative town in Östergotland county, and a fine place for a day or two's stay. At one time a royal seat and an important monastic centre, the town's main attraction nowadays is its gorgeous moated castle, **Vadstena Slott**, planned in the sixteenth century by Gustav Vasa as part of his defensive ring to protect the Swedish heartland around Stockholm. Vadstena's cobbled, twisting streets, lined with cottages covered in climbing roses, also hold an impressive **abbey**, whose existence

△ Vadstena Slott

is the result of the passionate work of fourteenth-century Saint Birgitta, Sweden's first female saint.

The castle and abbey

Vadstena boasts a number of ancient sites and buildings, notably the Rådhus, which contains Sweden's oldest courthouse, but the town's top attraction is its castle, **Vadstena Slott** (early May Mon–Fri 11am–3pm; late May daily 11am–4pm; June & early Aug daily 10am–6pm; July daily 10am–7pm; late Aug daily 10am–5pm; early Sept Mon–Fri 10am–4pm; mid-Sept to early May Mon–Fri 11am–2pm; 50kr). With four seven-metre-thick round towers and a grand moat (which now doubles as the local marina), it was originally built in 1545 as a fortification to defend against Danish attacks, but was then prettified into a palace to house Gustav Vasa's mentally ill third son, Magnus. His elder brother, Johan III, was responsible for its lavish decorations, but fire destroyed it all just before completion, and to save on costs, the post-fire decor was merely painted on the walls, right down to the swagged curtains that can still be seen today.

From the end of the seventeenth century, the building fell into decay and was used as a grain store; the original hand-painted wooden ceilings were chopped up to make into grain boxes. As a result, there wasn't much to see inside until recently, when the acquisition of period furniture from all over Europe has created more of an atmosphere. Portraits of the Vasa family have also been crammed in, displaying some very unhappy and ugly faces that make for entertaining viewing. English-language **guided tours** of the furnished apartments and the royal chapel with its seventeen-second echo are included in the entrance fee (June & July 1.30pm; early Aug 2pm; late Aug 3pm; 45min). The second floor of the castle is used for **opera performances** in July (ask the tourist office for the schedule, or see @www.vadstena-akademien.org).

A few minutes' walk away at the water's edge stands Vadstena's **abbey church** (daily: May 9am–5pm; June & Aug 9am–7pm; July 9am–8pm), the architectural legacy of Saint Birgitta. Birgitta came to Vadstena as a lady-in-waiting to King Magnus Eriksson and his wife, Blanche of Namur, who lived at Bjälbo Palace. After being married at the age of 13, and having given birth to eight children, she began to experience visions and convinced her royal employers to give up their home in order to set up a convent and monastery. Unfortunately, she died abroad before her plans could be completed, and the work was continued by her daughter, Katarina, with the church finally being consecrated in 1430. Birgitta's specification that the church should be "of plain construction, humble and strong" is fulfilled from the outside, but the sombre, grey exterior hides a celebrated collection of medieval artwork. More memorable than the crypts of various royals is the statue, now devoid of hands, of Birgitta "in a state of ecstasy". To the right, the rather sad "Door of Grace and Honour" was where each Birgittine nun entered the abbey after being professed – the next time she passed through the doorway would be in a coffin on her funeral day. Birgitta's bones are encased in a red velvet box, decorated with silver and gilt medallions, in a glass case down stone steps in the monks' choir stalls. The excellent new **Sancta Birgitta Convent Museum** next to the abbey (daily: June & late Aug 11am–4pm; July to early Aug 11am–6pm; Sept & early Oct Sat & Sun 11am–4pm; 50kr; @www.sanctabirgitta.com) shows the humble cells of the Birgittine Order nuns who inhabited the convent from 1384, and displays rich textiles and books manufactured here.

Two more minor but fascinating museums are just a few steps outside the abbey graveyard gates (visited on tours only; daily: July 1.15pm & 3.15pm; early Aug 3pm; 50kr). The **Hospital Museum**, in the former "Great Madhouse" and part of Sweden's oldest hospital complex, displays alarming contraptions for "curing" the mad, including electroshock equipment and a spinning chair – dizzy patients were easier to handle. **Mårten Skinnare's house** next door, an amazingly preserved medieval home to a wealthy furrier, boasts an intact first floor privy overhanging the back wall.

Practicalities

Reaching Vadstena by **public transport** is a bit of a hassle as there are no trains – the nearest station is 30km east at Mjölby – and the bus system is lamentably poor; see www.resplus.se for timetables. By **car**, it's a straight run along the E4 and Route 50. **Bikes** can be rented from Sport Hörnen, on Storgatan by Rådhustorget (100kr per day, 300kr per week). Opening hours and tour times change regularly in Vadstena, so check first with the helpful **tourist office** inside the castle (May daily 9am–5pm; June & Aug daily 9am–7pm; July daily 9am–8pm; Sept Mon–Fri 9am–5pm, Sat 10am–2pm; Oct–April Mon–Fri 9am–5pm; ☏0143/315 70, ⊛www.vadstena.com).

The tourist office can make reservations for **private rooms** (from 165kr per person; 50kr booking fee), while Vadstena's STF **youth hostel** is in the town centre at Skänningegatan 20 (☏0143/103 02 or ☏0143/765 62, ⊛www.va-bostaelle.se; ❶), and has dorm beds for 170kr; always phone ahead. The lakeside *Vätterviksbadet* **camping** (☏0143/127 30, ⊛www.vadstenacamping.se) is 2km north of the centre and has two- and four-bed cabins (300kr and 550kr respectively).

The town's **hotels**, most of them housed in converted historic buildings, are fairly expensive. The *Vadstena Klosterhotell*, in the medieval nunnery next to the abbey (☏0143/315 30, ⊛www.klosterhotel.se; ❺), has comfortable rooms and very atmospheric public areas, including the original Kings Hall, where breakfast is served. A better-value option is the **B&B** *Pensionat Solgården*, Strågatan 3 (☏0143/143 50, ⊛www.pensionatsolgarden.se; mid-May to Sept; ❸/❹), a beautifully maintained villa from 1905, in a quiet, central little street.

Vadstena has a decent selection of places to eat. The pick of the **cafés** is *Micasa*, Rådhustorget 9, where a young, laid-back crowd comes for the relatively cheap light meals from 65kr. Also popular is *Gamla Konditoriet* at Storgatan 18, while the best **restaurant** in town is *Vadstena Valven*, in the same building, does lunch for 85kr and fish specialities in the evening (closed Sun outside summer). An interesting alternative is *På Hörnet*, next to a medieval tower at Skänningegatan 1, a neighbourhood **pub** serving well-thought-out dishes, such as marinated mushrooms and herrings. It's a great place for all-day brunch. The *Rådhuskällaren*, (☏0143/121 70, ⊛www.radhuskallaren.com) in the cosy cellars of the sixteenth-century courthouse on Rådhustorget, with lunch for 69kr and dinner from 130kr, also doubles as a pub, and is particularly busy on Thursday and Saturday evenings.

Örebro

One hundred and sixteen kilometres north of Vadstena and strategically located on the main route from southwest Sweden to Stockholm, the lively and youthful town of **ÖREBRO** lies near the shores of the country's fourth largest lake, Hjälmaren. While its light industrial hinterland promises little, the heart of Örebro comes as a pleasant surprise, its much-fortified thirteenth-century **castle** forming a magnificent backdrop for the water lily-studded River Svartån. Aside from the town's attractions, **Lake Tysslingen**, a few kilometres west, makes for a good afternoon excursion by bike, while in spring the several thousand whooper swans that settle here on their way to Finland provide spectacular viewing.

Arrival, information and accommodation

Örebro is two hours from Stockholm on the main east–west train line. From the train and bus stations it's a short walk to the **tourist office** in the castle (June–Aug Mon–Fri 10am–6pm, Sat & Sun 10am–4pm; Sept–May Mon–Fri 10am–6pm, Sat & Sun 11am–2pm; ☏019/21 21 21, ⊛www.orebro.se/turism). The town centre is easy to see on foot, but if you want to get out into the countryside, you can **rent a bike** from the boat moored along Kanalvägen near *Harry's Bar* (☏019/21 19 09; 20kr per hour, 50kr per day); there are also tandems at 80kr per day. Another option is take a **boat trip** around nearby Lake Hjälmaren on *M/S Gustaf Lagerbjelke* (☏019/10 71 91; 2hr trip 70kr, day cruise 275kr).

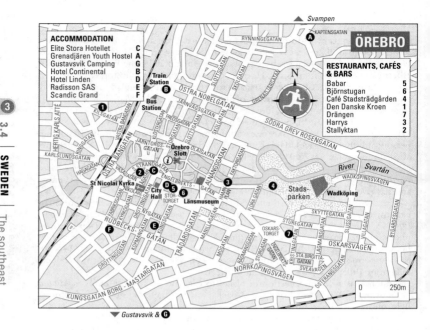

Private rooms can be booked at the tourist office for 135kr per person. The *Grenadjären* **youth hostel** (☎019/31 02 40, ⓦwww.hepa.se), which has double rooms (**1**) as well as dorm beds (from 150kr), is in a set of appealing old army barracks just to the north of the centre on Kaptensgatan 1; take bus #16 or #31. The huge *Gustavsvik* **camping site** (☎019/19 69 50, ⓦwww.gustavsvik.se; May to mid-Sept) is 2km south of town and features Scandinavia's biggest bathing complex – take bus #31.

Of Örebro's **hotels**, the best traditional option is the central *Elite Stora Hotellet*, Drottninggatan 1 (☎019/15 69 00, ⓦwww.elite.se; **4**/**5**), which is supposedly haunted by the ghost of a young woman and her mother. Near the castle, the superb *Radisson SAS*, Kungsgatan 14 (☎019/670 67 00, ⓦwww.radissonsas.com; **3**/**5**) has large and sumptuous bedrooms, while the high-quality *Scandic Grand* is 500m south of the station at Fabriksgatan 23 (☎019/767 43 00, ⓦwww.scandic-hotels .com; **3**/**6**). *Hotel Linden*, Köpmangatan 5 (☎019/611 87 11, ⒻF13 34 11; **1**), is basic but perfectly adequate.

The Town

A fort has defended Örebro ever since a band of German merchants settled here in the thirteenth century, attracted by the presence of iron ore in the area. Enlarged by King Magnus Eriksson, **Örebro Slott** on its own island in middle of the Svartån, was further fortified by Gustav Vasa, whose son Karl IX turned it into a splendid Renaissance palace, raising the walls to the height of the medieval towers and plastering them in cream stucco. After the town lost its importance, the castle fell into disuse and was turned into a storehouse and prison.

The fairytale exterior you see today is the result of renovation in the 1890s, when the castle was restored to reflect both its medieval and Renaissance grandeur. The same cannot be said for the interior: there is no original furniture, and today many of the rooms are used by the county governor or for conferences. The few features of interest are some finely inlaid doors and floors dating from the 1920s, depicting historical events at Örebro, and a large portrait of Karl XII and his family, all their faces painted to look the same – all have popping eyes, the result of using arsenic to whiten their faces. The only way to see the interior is to join the lively "Secrets of the Vasa fortress" **tour** (June–Aug 5 daily, English tour at 1pm; 60kr; ⓦ www.orebro .se/slottet), a mix of traditional tour and play, with guides dressed as kings, servants and prisoners. The southern tower holds an exhibition about the history of the castle (June–Aug Mon–Fri 10am–6pm, Sat & Sun 10am–4pm; Sept–May Mon–Fri 10am–6pm, Sat & Sun 10am–2pm; free).

Nearby, at the top of the very oblong Stortorget, the neo-gothic **city hall** – built after a fire destroyed its predecessor in 1854 – features a chime with mythological figures that pop out of the facade daily a few minutes past noon and 6pm (summer also 9pm). The adjacent **St Nicolai kyrka** (Mon–Fri 10am–5pm, Sat 11am–3pm) originates from 1260, but lost most of its original medieval character during extensive restoration in the 1860s. Recent renovations have tried to undo the damage, but today it's the contemporary art exhibitions on show here that catch the eye. Historically, however, the church is significant, as it was here in 1810 that Napoleon's unknown marshal, Jean Baptiste Bernadotte, was elected successor to the Swedish throne. The present royal family are descendants of this new king, Karl Johan, who never spoke a word of Swedish.

Just east of the castle, the **Länsmuseum** (County Museum; daily 11am–5pm, Wed till 9pm; free, fee for special exhibitions; ⓦ www.orebrolansmuseum.se) has a spacious series of galleries, with a good collection by the late nineteenth-century local artist, Axel Borg. Further east along the river, past the appealing Stadsparken, stands **Wadköping** (May–Aug Tues–Sun 11am–5pm; Sept–April Tues–Sun 11am–4pm; free), an entire village of centuries-old wooden cottages and shops brought to the site from the city centre to form a living open-air museum. It's all extremely pretty, but a little staged. Some of the cottages have been reoccupied, and the twee little shops sell pastel-coloured wooden knick-knacks.

Eating and drinking

Örebro boasts plenty of atmospheric places in which to **eat**. If you're here in July, though, bear in mind that some of the smaller restaurants close for the holidays.

Cafés, restaurants and bars

Babar Kungsgatan 4. The hippest bar in town for some years, and also worth a visit for its restaurant, which serves up meat and fish dishes from 120kr.

Björnstugan Kungsgatan 3. Opposite *Babar*, this is almost as popular and attracts the same hip young crowd. There's a restaurant, too.

Café Stadsträdgården Floragatan 1. With an unusual setting in the greenhouses at the park entrance, this is a wonderful daytime café offering fine, fresh sandwiches, home-baked cakes and superb pies, all organic.

Den Danske Kroen Kilsgatan 8. Danish bar and restaurant with a lively but relaxed and down-to-earth atmosphere, serving cheap, simple meals and a wide selection of beers.

Drängen Oskarstorget 9 ☎ 19/32 32 96, ⓦ www .drangen.se. Consistently superb locals' pub and restaurant of long standing.

Harrys Hamnplan. A popular, bustling pub overlooking the river, with Swedish and international food.

Stallyktan Södra Strandgatan 3. This pleasingly rustic pub, just a couple of minutes' walk west of the castle, is perfect for a quiet drink and dinner, with fish and meat dishes for 60–120kr. Closed July.

Norrköping

It is with good reason that the dynamic, youth-oriented town of **NORRKÖPING** calls itself Sweden's Manchester. Like its British counterpart, Norrköping's wealth came from its textile industry, which thrived in the eighteenth and nineteenth centuries (the Swedish word for corduroy is *manchester*). The legacy from this period is the town's most appealing feature: it's one of Europe's best-preserved **industrial**

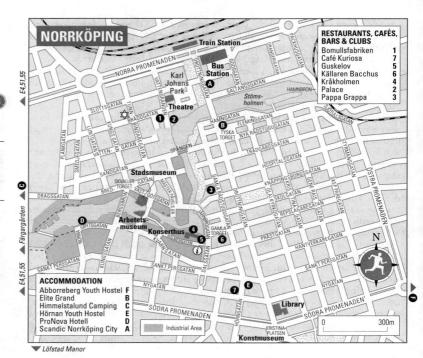

NORRKÖPING

Train Station

Bus Station Ⓐ

NORRA PROMENADEN

Karl Johans Park

Theatre

Stömsholmen

❶ ❷

Ⓑ TYSKA TORGET

Stadsmuseum

❸

Arbetets-museum

Konserthus ❹
❺ ❻ GAMLA TORGET

Ⓓ

ⓘ

Ⓔ

❼

Library

Konstmuseum

KRISTINA PLATSEN

N

RESTAURANTS, CAFÉS, BARS & CLUBS	
Bomullsfabriken	1
Café Kuriosa	7
Guskelov	5
Källaren Bacchus	6
Kråkholmen	4
Palace	2
Pappa Grappa	3

ACCOMMODATION	
Abborreberg Youth Hostel	F
Elite Grand	B
Himmelstalund Camping	C
Hörnan Youth Hostel	E
ProNova Hotell	D
Scandic Norrköping City	A

Industrial Area

0   300m

▼ Löfstad Manor

urban landscapes, with handsome red-brick and stuccoed mills reflected in the waters of Motala Ström.

It was this small, rushing river that attracted the Dutch industrialist **Louis De Geer** to the town in the late seventeenth century, and his paper mill, still in operation today, became the biggest factory in the city, to be followed by numerous wool, silk and linen factories. Today, many buildings are painted a strong, tortilla-chip yellow, as are the trams – De Geer's favourite colour has become symbolic of the town. Textiles kept Norrköping booming until the 1950s, when foreign competition began to sap the market, and the last big textile mill closed its doors in 1992.

Like Manchester, Norrköping has also become a nucleus for music-inspired **youth culture** – the city is home to the country's best-known working-class rock band, Eldkvarn, while its charms have been eulogized by Ulf Lundell, one of Sweden's most famous singer-songwriters. In addition, Norrköping has one of the highest immigrant populations in Sweden. The first to come here were the Jews in the mid-eighteenth century; today's immigrant communities are mostly from Asian and Arab countries, though in the past few years there's been a considerable influx from the former Yugoslavia.

Arrival, information and accommodation

Five minutes' walk from the **train** and **bus** terminals, inside the old paper mill gate at Dalsgatan 9, is the helpful **tourist office** (late April to June & late Aug Mon–Fri 10am–5pm, Sat 10am–2pm; July to mid-Aug 10am–6pm, Sat & Sun 10am–2pm; Sept to mid-April Mon–Fri 10am–5pm; ☎011/15 50 00, ⍟ www.destination .norrkoping.se), where you can buy tickets for the interesting **guided tour** of town (Wed at 7pm; 40kr); get a wealth of maps and brochures, including the useful

Upplev Norrköp!ng Guide; and use the **Internet** (30kr for 15min). Norrköping's **airport** only serves Stockholm, but international flights land at Skavsta airport, just 60km away and served by direct bus (up to 6 daily; 50min; 110kr). Ask at the tourist office about the 1902 **vintage tram**, which circles around the city on a sightseeing tour during summer. Ordinary yellow trams run on two lines all over the town centre, with tickets costing a flat 15kr, including any tram changes made within the hour. **Bicycles** can be rented from the Kungsgallerians Sko & Nyckelservice at Kungsgatan 32 (☎011/13 45 75; 100kr per day).

The central *Hörnan* **youth hostel** at Hörngatan 1 (☎011/16 58 90, ⊛www .hotellhornan.com) has cheap hotel rooms (❷), as well as dorm beds from 200kr. The picturesque *Abborreberg* STF hostel is 5km east of town (☎011/31 93 44, ⊛www.abborreberg.se; April–Oct; ❶) and has dorm beds for 175kr; take the Lindö bus (#116) from near the Konstmuseum. The closest **campsite**, *Himmelstalund* (☎011/17 11 90, ⊛www.norrkopingscamping.com) is 2km from the centre on Campingvägen; take the Klockaretorget tram (#3) to Folketpark, then walk for fifteen minutes. You can book **cottages** at the tourist office or via their online booking system; in high season, a central Norrköping cottage sleeping up to six costs from 1800kr per week.

Among the town's **hotels**, *ProNova Hotell* at Norra Grytsgatan 10 (☎011/42 45 20, ⊛www.pronovahotell.se; ❸) is set in the heart of the renovated industrial landscape; ask for a room with a view of the river. For a more upmarket experience, get a room at the grand old *Elite Grand*, bang in the centre at Tyska Torget 2 (☎011/36 41 00, ⊛www.grandhotel.elite.se; ❹/❻), or at the *Scandic Norrköping City*, near the train station at Slottsgatan 99 (☎011/495 52 00, ⊛www.scandic-hotels.se; ❸/❹).

The Town

Norrköping's main avenue, **Drottninggatan**, runs north–south from the train station through the city centre. Just a few steps down from the station, the small **Karl Johans Park** boasts (in summer) the unusual feature of 25,000 cacti, all formally arranged in thematic patterns. Continuing over the river and following the tram lines up Drottninggatan, a right turn into Repslagaregatan leads into **Gamla Torget**, overlooked by a charismatic sculpture of Louis De Geer by Carl Milles (see p.491). From here, the steely, modern riverside **Konserthus** is fronted by trees; it's worth stepping inside for a gander at its strikingly contemporary and naturally-lit interior, which belies the fact that this was once one of De Geer's paper factories. You can pick up information on the symphony orchestra's concerts (Sept to late May; tickets 80–210kr; ⊛www.louisdegeer.com) while you're here.

Go through the impressive, eighteenth-century paper mill gates to the left of the concert hall and you'll find yourself in Norrköpings fabulous **industrial landscape**, with old paper and textile factories crammed around a series of waterfalls along the Motala Ström, whose waters powered the mills before steam engines took over. The area was nearly bulldozed in the 1970s but has been beautifully restored and today houses the university, offices and a conference centre.

Down the steps next to the wooden bridge there's a huge turbine pipe that has been turned into a platform from where you can watch the waterfalls; in winter, there's a colourful lightshow here every half hour (from dusk till 9pm). Beyond the bridge stands the **Arbetetsmuseum** (Work Museum; daily Sept–June 11am–5pm, Tues till 8pm; free), housed in a triangular, yellow-stuccoed factory from 1917. Known as "The Iron" – though its shape and colour are more reminiscent of a wedge of cheese – the building was considered by Carl Milles to be Europe's most beautiful factory. It's a splendid place, with seven floors of exhibitions on living conditions, workers' rights and daily life in the mills. Take the stairs down, rather than the lift, to see a touching exhibition in the stairwell about the life of Alva, a woman who spent 35 years as a factory worker here.

Next door, over another little bridge, is the excellent **Stadsmuseum** (City Museum; Tues–Fri 10am–4pm, Sat & Sun 11am–4pm; free). Set in an interconnecting (and very confusing) network of old industrial properties, the permanent exhibitions include textile machines, examples of Swedish textile design, a model of the area in 1941 and a cute trade street featuring the workplaces of a milliner, confectioner and chimney sweep.

Three streets north of the Stadsmuseum, on Bråddgatan, stands the **synagogue**, spiritual home to Sweden's oldest Jewish community. The present synagogue, the city's third, was built in 1858. Beautifully restored, highlights of this grand old building include an enormous central chandelier and the pulpit, finely painted in blues, reds and yellows, and with a magnificent ark. Unfortunately, visits are difficult to arrange; ask at the tourist office.

Head back south across the river and follow the bank west for ten minutes into the countryside to reach **Färgargården**, an open-air dyeworks museum (May–Aug Tues–Sun noon–4pm; free), ranged in a huddle of wooden nineteenth-century houses. Better reasons to come here than the exhibitions are the outdoor café, open during summer whenever the weather is good, and the free **open-air cinema** (July & Aug; ❽www.flimmer.se).

Retracing your steps back into the town centre, any interest you have in Swedish art can be satisfied at the **Konstmuseum** (Art Museum; late May to mid-Aug Tues–Sun noon–4pm, Wed till 8pm; late Aug to mid-May Tues–Sun 11am–5pm, Tues & Thurs till 8pm; 40kr) on Kristinaplatsen, which displays some of the country's best-known modernist works. Founded by a local snuff manufacturer around the beginning of the twentieth century, the galleries offer a fine, well-balanced progression from seventeenth-century Baroque through to contemporary paintings. Coming out of the Konstmuseum, the bunker-like concrete building to the right is the town **library** (Mon–Fri 8am–8pm, Fri 8am–7pm, Sat 10am–4pm), more interesting and user-friendly than most, with a big range of international newspapers and free Internet access.

Eating and drinking

There's a fair selection of eating places in Norrköping, most of them doubling as bars. However, it's the Norrköping custom to have a drink at home before heading out to the pubs, so the city only starts coming alive from 10pm or so.

For an old-fashioned neighbourhood **café**, try *Café Kuriosa*, in the centre of town at Hörngatan 6, which serves home-baked cakes, savoury pies and ice-cream in an old living room-style environment. The *Kråkholmen* café, with a lovely setting overlooking the water next to the concert hall, serves lunch and drinks on weekdays in summer. The most sensational **restaurant** in town is ⅍ *Pappa Grappa*, Gamla Rådstugugatan 26 (☎011/18 00 14, ❽www.pappagrappa.se), a terrific Italian place offering inventive and original combinations of fresh ingredients in a mellow atmosphere; mains start at 120kr. Just east of the theatre at Bråddgatan 19, ⅍ *Bomullsfabriken* (Textile Factory; ☎011/10 59 10, ❽www.bomullsfabriken.se; closed July) is worth a visit for its factory-themed interior and excellent Swedish fish and meat specialities (140–210kr), while *Guskelov*, at Dalsgatan 13 by the concert hall (☎011/13 44 00; closed Sun & Mon), is an Art Deco-style restaurant specializing in similarly priced fish dishes. For **drinking** and dancing, try *Källaren Bacchus* at Gamla Torget 4, a cellar restaurant serving traditional Swedish food (from 125kr) with a long cocktail list. Alternatively, the *Palace* near the theatre at Bråddgatan 13 (☎011/18 96 00, ❽www.palacenorrkoping.se) is a huge restaurant, bar, club and casino with space for 2000 revellers.

Gotland

Rumours about good times on **Gotland** are rife. Wherever you are in Sweden, one mention of this ancient Baltic island will elicit a typically Swedish sigh followed by an anecdote about what a great place it is. You'll hear that the short summer season is an exciting time to visit; that it's hot, fun and lively. Largely, this is all true: the island has a distinctly youthful feel as young Stockholmers desert the capital for a boisterous summer spent on the beaches. During summer, the island (with a population of 29,000) plays host to some 750,000 tourists; bars, restaurants and campsites are packed, the streets swarm with revellers, and the sands are awash with bodies. It's not everyone's cup of tea: to avoid the hectic summer altogether, come in late May or September when, depending on your bravado, you can still swim.

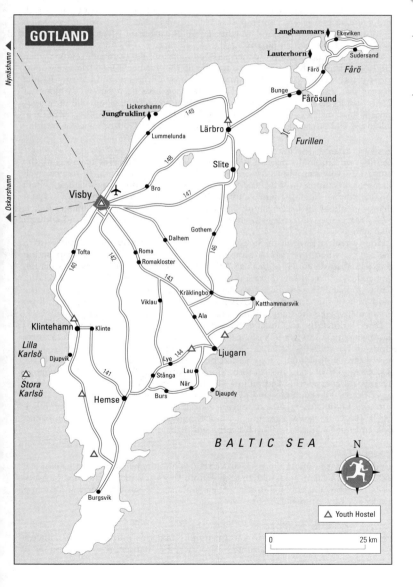

Gotland itself, and in particular its capital, **Visby**, has always seen frenetic activity of some kind. A temperate climate and fortuitous geographical position attracted the Vikings as early as the sixth century, and the lucrative trade routes they opened, through to Byzantium and western Asia, guaranteed the island its prosperity. With the ending of Viking domination, a golden age followed, during which Gotland's inhabitants maintained trading posts and signed treaties with European and Asian leaders. However, by the late twelfth century the island's autonomy had been undermined by the growing power of the Hanseatic League, under whose influence Visby became one of the great cities of medieval Europe, famed for its wealth and strategic power – a contemporary ballad had it that "The Gotlanders weigh their gold with twenty-pound weights. The pigs eat out of silver troughs and the women spin with golden distaffs."

This romantic notion of prosperity persisted right into the twentieth century, when Gotlanders began relying on tourism to prop up the traditional industries of farming, forestry and fishing. Modern hype makes great play of the sun, and it's true that the flowers that give Gotland its "Island of Roses" tag have been known to bloom at Christmas. It's not all just tourist brochure fodder, however: nowhere else in Scandinavia is there such a concentration of unspoilt medieval country churches, 92 of them still in use and providing the most permanent reminder of Gotland's ancient wealth.

Getting there: ferries and planes

Destination Gotland runs fast and comfortable daytime **ferries** to Gotland; the numerous daily departures can get booked solid in summer, so try to plan well ahead (reservations on ☎0771/22 33 00 or ⊛www.destinationgotland.se, where you can find an English-language timetable). Crossings take 3hr 15min from Nynäshamn or 3hr from Oskarshamn; one-way tickets cost 228–511kr, budget tickets 174–384kr (booked 21 days in advance). Return prices are double, and taking a bike across costs 41kr.

Hourly **trains** leave from Stockholm to **NYNÄSHAMN**, the nearest port to the capital, where the *Nicksta* camping and youth hostel is near the train station at Nickstabadsvägen 17 (☎08/520 127 80; dorm beds from 175kr). Destination Gotland also has **buses** (80kr in advance, otherwise 110kr) leaving Stockholm Cityterminalen 1hr 45min before the ferry's departure. From Gothenburg or the southwest of the country, **OSKARSHAMN** is the more convenient port; from Gothenburg, take the train to Växjö and then bus #310 (5hr 30min in total).

Three airlines **fly** to Gotland: Skyways (☎0771/95 95 00, ⊛www.skyways.se) has several daily services to Visby from Stockholm's Arlanda and Bromma airports; Gotlandsflyg (☎0498/22 22 22, ⊛www.gotlandsflyg.se) has slightly less frequent services from Stockholm Bromma; and, on weekdays, DirektFlyg (☎0234/44 47 00, ⊛www.direktflyg.com) flies to Visby from Linköping, 40km west of Norrköping. Tickets are cheapest booked online – a one-way trip costs from 400kr with Skyways, from 300kr with Gotlandsflyg and from 1100kr with DirektFlyg.

In Stockholm, the Gotland tourist association runs the Gotland City office (☎08/406 15 00, ⊛www.gotlandcity.se) at Kungsgatan 57, which provides information and can make reservations for ferry and flight tickets.

Visby

Undoubtedly the finest approach to **VISBY** is by ship, when you can take in the old trading centre as it should be seen – from the sea. With its fine medieval city walls, churches and cobbled streets, Visby is a pleasure to stroll through, and is quite unlike any town in mainland Sweden.

Arrival and information

Visby **airport** is 5km from town; a five-minute **taxi** ride into the centre will cost 70kr; in summer, there's an airport bus to Visby bus station (⊛www.flygbussarna .se; 49kr).

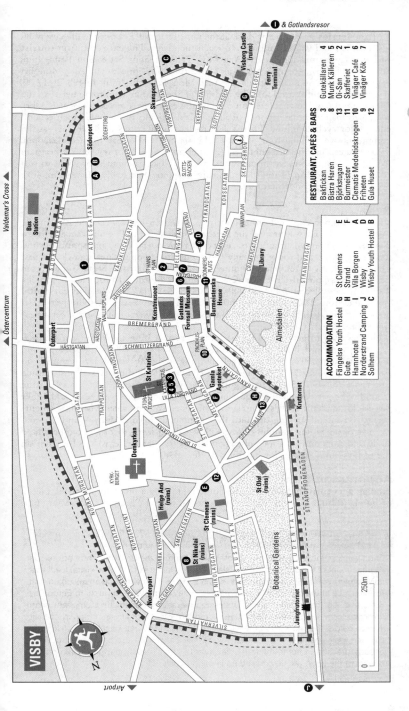

VISBY

RESTAURANT, CAFES & BARS

Bakfickan	3
Bistra Haren	8
Björkstugan	13
Burmeister	11
Clematis Medeltidskrogen	10
Friheten	9
Gula Huset	12
Gutekällaren	4
Munk Källeren	5
Oi-San	2
Skafferiet	1
Vinäger Café	6
Vinäger Kök	7

ACCOMMODATION

Fängelse Youth Hostel	G	St Clemens	E
Gute	I	Strand	F
Hamnhotell	H	Villa Borgen	A
Norderstrand Camping	C	Wisby	J
Solhem	D	Wisby Youth Hostel	B

▲ ❶ & Gotlandsresor

Ferry Terminal

Visborg Castle (ruins)

◀ Valdemar's Cross

◀ Östercentrum

Bus Station

Österport

Söderport

Skansport

FÄRJELEDEN

Gotlands Fornsal Museum

Konstmuseet

Burmeisterska House

Library

Almedalen

St Katarina

Gamla Apoteket

Domkyrkan

KYRK-BERGET

Helge And (ruins)

St Olof (ruins)

St Clemens (ruins)

St Nikolai (ruins)

Norderport

Botanical Gardens

Jungfrutornet

Kruttornet

▼ Airport

250m

N

0

All the **ferries** serving Visby dock at the same terminal, just outside the city walls. Just turn left and walk 10 minutes to reach the centre. The excellent main **tourist office** (May to mid-June & late Aug Mon–Fri 8am–5pm, Sat & Sun 10am–4pm; Sept Mon–Fri 8am–5pm, Sat & Sun 11am–2pm; mid-June to late Aug Mon–Fri 8am–7pm, Sat & Sun 8am–6pm; Oct–April Mon–Fri 8am–4pm); ☎0498/20 17 00, ⊛www.gotland.info) overlooks the harbour at Skeppsbron 4, en route between the ferries and the old town. Here you can buy the excellent *Turistkarta Gotland* (30kr), a detailed map with descriptions of all the island's points of interest, which is good enough for cycling around. There's also a selection of **tours** available, such as the comprehensive walking tour of Visby (2hr 45min; Wed & Sat 10am & 12.30pm; 85kr). You can use the **Internet** here (2kr per min), at the **library** on Cramergatan (Mon–Fri 10am–7pm, Sat noon–4pm), where a 20kr payment allows you to surf all day, or at SurfZon in the Östercentrum shopping area (daily 11am–9pm; 40kr per hr; ⊛www.gotlandsenergi.se).

Getting around

Visby itself is best explored on foot. Despite its warren-like appearance, it's a simple matter to find your way around the narrow, cobbled streets. The main square, **Stora Torget**, is signposted from almost everywhere. Modern Visby has spread beyond its old city walls, and today the ugly Östercentrum shopping area sprawls out past **Österport** (East Gate), a few minutes' walk up the hill from Stora Torget. From here, the **bus station** serves the rest of Gotland; the tourist office has timetables. **Taxis** can be called at ☎498/50 000 and ☎498/20 02 00. The cheapest **car rental** is available from *Mickes Old Cars* (☎0498/26 62 62, ⊛www.mickesbiluthyrning.se; 300kr per day). Renting a **moped** costs 340kr per day from the shop at Strandgatan 36 (☎0498/27 63 77).

The best way to get around the island is to **rent a bike**, available from *Gotlands Cykeluthyrning*, just behind the tourist office (☎0498/21 00 56, ⊛www.gotland scykeluthyrning.com); O´hoj Cykeluthyrning opposite the ferry terminal on Färjeleden (☎0498/20 12 60) and *Visby Hyrcykel*, along the city wall just outside Österport (☎0498/25 66 10, ⊛gotland.net/visbyhyrcykel). Most places charge around 65kr per day for three-gear bikes, 80kr per day for seven gears, and 125kr per day for tandems; rentals shops are usually open daily between May and September. If you intend striking out into the countryside beyond Visby – undiscovered by most of the young summer crowd – it's worth knowing that bikes can be rented easily, and sometimes cheaper, elsewhere. Bikes (but no tandems) can be taken on the island's buses, space allowing, for a flat fee of 40kr.

Accommodation

Finding **accommodation** in Visby should seldom be a problem. There are plenty of hotels (though few are particularly cheap), several campsites and cabins, plus

---

Medieval Week

For a week at the beginning of August, Visby becomes the backdrop for a boisterous re-enactment of the conquest of the island by the Danes in 1361. The visual feast that is **Medieval Week** (⊛www.medeltidsveckan.com) sees music in the streets, medieval food on sale in the restaurants (no potatoes – they hadn't been brought to Europe by then) and, on the first Sunday, a procession recreating Valdemar's triumphant entry through Söderport to Stora Torget. Here, modern-day burghers are stripped of their wealth before the procession moves on to the Jungfrutornet. Locals and visitors to Gotland really get into this festival – you'll see crowds on the boats over to Visby already dressed in home-made medieval garb, and at least half the people on the streets of the town will be dressed up in period costume.

three good youth hostels. Both the tourist office and the Gotlandsresor office at the *Hamnhotell* at Färjeleden 3 (☏0498/20 12 60, ⓦwww.gotlandsresor.se) can help with **private rooms** (from 285kr per person, 425kr for doubles), and **cottages** both in and outside Visby.

Of Visby's **youth hostels**, all of which have double rooms (❶) as well as regular dorms (beds from 150kr), the two most central are the *Wisby Jernvägshotell*, Adelsgatan 9 (☏0498/20 33 00 ⓦwww.gtsab.se/jernvagshotellet), and the more interesting and well-placed ⚑ *Fängelse Vandrarhem* (☏498/20 60 50; doubles ❶, dorm beds from 200kr), situated in a former prison building just opposite the ferry terminal. There's a café and sauna here, and it's lively in the evenings.

Chiefly, though, Gotland is a place for **camping**. After the success of Ulf Lundell's youth-culture novel *Jack*, which extolled the simple pleasure of getting wasted on a beach, Gotland became the place to go for wild summer parties: at many campsites, the most exercise you'll get is cycling to and from the *Systembolaget*. The closest campsite, *Norderstrand* (☏0498/21 21 57, ⓦwww.norderstrandscamping.se; late April to mid-Sept), is 1km outside the city walls – follow the cycle path that runs from the Botanical Gardens along the seafront.

Gute Mellangatan 29 ☏0498/20 22 60, ⓦwww.hotellgute.se. Very central and reasonably comfortable classical-style hotel with en-suite rooms. ❹/❺

Hamnhotell Färjeleden 3 ☏0498/20 12 50, ⓦwww.gotlandsresor.se. Hotel complex centred around the yellow building visible 200m south of the ferry terminal. All rooms have TV, shower and toilet, with a good breakfast in the on-site restaurant. ❸/❺

Solhem Solhemsgatan 3 ☏0498/25 90 00, ⓦwww.hotellsolhem.se. Just outside the city walls near Skansporten, this large, comfortable hotel has a basement sauna and is quieter than the more central places. ❹/❺

Strand Strandgatan 34 ☏0498/25 28 00, ⓦwww.strandhotel.net. A rather glamorous place in the heart of town, with a sauna, steam bath, indoor pool and a stylish atmosphere. ❺/❻

🏃 **St Clemens** Smedjegatan 3 ☏0498/21 90 00, ⓦwww.clemenshotell.se. A quiet hotel with a pleasant garden, and beautifully furnished rooms in five old buildings next to the ruins of St Clemens church. ❸/❹

Villa Borgen Adelsgatan 11 ☏0498/27 99 00, ⓦwww.guteinfo.com/villaborgen. Attractive family hotel in the middle of the action, yet with lovely, peaceful gardens. En-suite rooms, sauna and solarium. ❹/❺

Wisby Strandgatan 6 ☏0498/25 75 00, ⓦwww.wisbyhotell.se. Splendid, central hotel in a building dating back to the Middle Ages. Fine breakfasts. ❺/❻

The City

Visby is much older than its medieval remnants suggest – the name derives from its status as a Stone Age sacrificial site: "the settlement" (*by*) at "the sacred place" (*vi*). The magnificent **defensive wall** that encircles Visby is the most obvious manifestation of its previous importance. It was hardly a new idea to fortify trading centres against outside attack, although this land wall, built around the end of the thirteenth century, was actually constructed to separate the city's foreign traders from the rest of the island's inhabitants. Annoyed at having all their old trade monopolized, the Gotlanders saw something sinister in the wall's erection. They didn't have to wait long to be vindicated: in 1361, during the power struggle between Denmark and Sweden, the Danish king, Valdemar III, took Gotland by force and advanced on Visby. The burghers and traders, well aware of the wealth of their city, shut the gates and sat through the slaughter outside. Excavations during the twentieth century revealed the remains of two thousand bodies, more than half of them women and children. **Valdemar's Cross**, a few hundred metres east of Söderport (South Gate), marks their mass grave. Erected by the survivors of the carnage, it reads: "In 1361 on the third day after St James, the Goths fell into the hands of the Danes. Here they lie. Pray for them."

Back inside the city walls, the merchants surrendered, and a section of the wall near Söderport was broken down to allow Valdemar to ride through as conqueror.

Valdemar's Breach is recognizable by its thirteen crenellations representing, so the story goes, the thirteen knights who rode through with the Danish king. Valdemar soon left clutching booty and trade agreements, and Visby continued to prosper while the island's countryside around it stagnated, its people and wealth destroyed.

The old **Hanseatic harbour** at Almedalen is now a public park, and nothing is much more than a few minutes' walk from here. Pretty **Packhusplan**, the oldest square in the city, is bisected by curving Strandgatan, which runs southwards to the fragmentary ruins of **Visborg Castle** – blown up by the Danes in the seventeenth century – and northwest towards the sea and the lush **Botanical Gardens** (unrestricted access), just beyond which is the **Jungfrutornet** (Maiden's Tower), where a local goldsmith's daughter was walled up alive – reputedly for betraying the city to the Danes. **Strandgatan** itself is notable for the impressive, step-gabled merchants' houses looming over the narrow street, with storerooms above the living quarters and cellars below – the **Burmeisterska house** is particularly striking. One of the most picturesque buildings is the old pharmacy, **Gamla Apoteket**, a lofty place with gloriously higgledy-piggledy windows.

The fine **Gotlands Fornsal Museum** at Strandgatan 14 (mid-May to mid-Sept daily 10am–5pm; mid-Sept to mid-May Tues–Sun noon–4pm; 60kr; ⊛www .lansmuseetgotland.se) provides comprehensive coverage of Visby's past. Housed in an eighteenth-century distillery and a medieval warehouse, it holds five storeys of exhibition halls covering eight thousand years of history, as well as a good courtyard café and bookshop. Among the most impressive sections are the **Hall of Picture Stones**, a collection of richly carved stones dating mostly from the fifth to eleventh centuries, and the display of the **Spillings Hoard** – the richest of Gotland's seven hundred hoards. Found in 1999, this treasure, mostly from the Arab world, England and Germany, weighs 85 kilos. The **Hall of Prehistoric Graves** is equally fascinating, its glass cases displaying skeletons dating back six thousand years. Other rooms trace the history of **medieval Visby**, with exhibits including a trading booth, where the burghers of Visby and foreign merchants dealt in commodities – furs, lime, wax, honey and tar – brought from all over Northern Europe. A series of tableaux brings the exhibition up to 1900, starting with Erik of Pomerania, the first resident of Visborg Castle, and leading on through the years of Danish rule, up to the island's sixteenth-century trading boom. A couple of streets up, **Konstmuseet**, at St Hansgatan 21 (May to mid-Sept 10am–5pm, late Sept–April noon–4pm; 40kr), puts on innovative temporary exhibitions of contemporary painting, sculpture and installations that really tease the eye. The permanent work is not so exciting, but does include some twentieth-century local art.

Strolling aimlessly around the rest of the twisting streets is rewarding enough in itself, but if you need a focus, aim for **Norra Murgatan**, above the cathedral, once one of Visby's poorest areas. At the end nearest Norderport (North Gate) – the highest point in the old town – you'll be treated to the best view of the walls and city rooftops. **Kruttornet**, the dark, atmospheric tower back on Strandgatan (June–Aug daily 10am–5pm; free), affords grander views, while the roof of the **Helge And** church ruin (May–Sept daily 10am–5pm; free), which has been reinforced to allow access to the second floor, provides another central vantage point. Alternatively, head for **Strandpromenaden**, the path along the water's edge, a popular spot for picnicking and watching the magnificent sunsets.

Eating, drinking and nightlife

Visby's centre is small enough to wander around and size up the eating options. Near Österport, **Wallersplats** and adjoining **Hästgatan** are both busy at lunchtime, while neighbouring **Adelsgatan** is lined with cafés and snack bars – a good area to look for the island speciality, *saffranspannkaka*, baked rice pudding with saffron. Visby's restaurants and bars see plenty of life during the day, but at night they positively heave with young bodies – many of them drunk. **Stora Torget** and **Strandgatan** are the focus of the town's evening parade. Alternatively, head down to the **harbour**, where forests of masts make a pretty backdrop to the loud, happy beat of music and revellers grooving away on the dance floors. Note that many of Visby's discos open in the late afternoon, from around 4pm onwards, for "After Beach" sessions where you can get relatively cheap beer.

Gotlanders also enjoy a unique licence from the state to brew their own **beer**, the recipe differing from household to household. It's never on sale, but summer parties are awash with the murky stuff – be warned, it is extremely strong. There are central off-licences on Stora Torget and at Östervägen 3; the island's other *Systembolagets* are found at Hemse, Slite, Klintehamn, Färösunds and Burgsvik.

Daytime cafés

Björkstugan Speksgränd. In a fabulous, lush garden on Visby's prettiest cobbled street, this little café serves tasty pies and coffee. Open till 5pm.

Gula Huset Tranhusgatan 2. Close to the Botanical Gardens and a favourite amongst locals: cosy and serving delightful home-baked port-wine cake and concoctions of almonds, chocolate and fruit in an unspoiled garden setting outside a vine-covered cottage. Open noon–5pm.

Skafferiet Adelsgatan 38. A lovely eighteenth-century house turned into an appealing café, which boasts a lush garden at the back. Baked potatoes, great cakes and vast, generously filled baguettes that suffice for a full meal.

Vinäger Café Hästgatan 3. Great place for giant muffins, terrific cakes and pies and a relaxed, mellow atmosphere, all in an anachronistically modern former pharmacy dating from 1896. Its bakery, directly opposite, has fresh loaves from 6am, and the café is open till 9pm.

Restaurants and bars

Bakfickan St Katarinagatan. A relaxed little restaurant with a tiled interior, specializing in some of the best seafood in town (100–200kr). Also good for a drink.

Bistra Haren Smedjegatan 17. Excellent grilled dishes served in a medieval cellar or in the delightful garden right next to the St Nicholai ruins. From 5pm.

Burmeister Strandgatan 9, ☎0498/21 03 73, ⊕www.burmeister.se. Busy place serving a full à la carte menu with starters around 80kr, pasta 90kr and main courses 160kr.

Clematis Medeltidskrogen Strandgatan 20, ⊕www.clematis.se. No reservations. Set in the vaulted cellars of a thirteenth-century house, this is Visby's most brilliantly atmospheric and evocative restaurant by far, lit with candles only, with mead served in flagons and food in rough ceramic bowls and on wooden platters. The full medieval banquet (260kr) includes nuts, rose petals, honey-fried cabbage, and pear toffee. From 6pm.

Friheten Strandgatan 6. A lively pub attached to the *Wisby Hotel*. Loud, live bands reverberate on Fri & Sat evenings.

Gutekällaren Lilla Torggränd. Fronting onto Stora Torget, this is less frenetic than the other nearby restaurants, cleverly designed with striking primary-colour paintings to complement the vivid harlequin chairs. Excellent food, but quite costly, with mains from 140kr.

Munk Källaren Lilla Torggränd, ☎0498/27 14 00. Massively fashionable, and subsequently crowded. There's an extensive à la carte menu.

Oi-San St Hansgatan 51, ☎0498/25 65 50. Fantastic, innovative European and Asian crossover cuisine with mains from 200kr and three-course menus from 350kr.

Vinäger Kök Hästgatan 4. Just opposite its sister-café (see p.589), with a garden, great lighting and comfortable low seating, this is an excellent place for pasta dishes or a drink. Summer only.

The rest of the island

There's a real charm to the rest of Gotland – rolling green countryside, forest-lined roads, fine beaches and small fishing villages, and everywhere the rural skyline is dominated by churches, the remnants of medieval settlements destroyed in the Danish invasion. The **south** of the island, in particular, boasts numerous wonderful villages and beaches, and with Gotland's many bronze-age stone ships and remains of prehistoric farmsteads signposted off the road. **Cycling** around the island is immensely enjoyable, since the main roads are quiet and minor roads are positively deserted. Gotland's **buses** are very few; outside Visby, they tend to run only twice daily. Plan your trip carefully with the free *busstidstabell* timetable, available from the tourist office in Visby or online at ⊛www.gotland.se/kollektivtrafiken. **Hitching** is an accepted means of transport, and unless you have a specific destination in mind, it's often just as well to go wherever the driver is heading. As you go, keep an eye out for the waymarkers erected in the 1780s to indicate the distance in *mils* (10km units) to *Wisby* (the old spelling).

Southern Gotland

Near to Visby, **ROMAKLOSTER** has some impressive monastery ruins that are used for (Swedish-language) Shakespeare performances; the village shops here are the best on the island for local handicrafts. The so-called "capital" of the south, **HEMSE**, around 50km from Visby (buses ply the route almost hourly), is little more than a main street, but there are a couple of banks and a good local café, *Bageri & Conditori Johansson*, on Storgatan – this is the place to stock up with food. You can rent **bikes** from Ondrell's, on Ronevägen (40kr per day, 160kr per week). Travelling northeast along Route 144, the countryside is a glorious mix of wild, flowering meadows, medieval farmholdings with ancient windows and carved wooden portals, and dark, mysterious forest. Tiny **BURS**, east of Hemse, has a gorgeous thirteenth-century saddle church, so-called because of its low nave and high tower and chancel. Inside there's a fabulously decorated ceiling, medieval stained-glass windows and ornately painted pews. Nearby, *Burs Café* is a friendly locals' joint serving cheap, filling meals. The next place you come to is the tranquil and pretty hamlet of **NÄR**, notable for its church, set in an immaculate churchyard. The tower originally served as a defensive fortification in the thirteenth century, but more arresting are the bizarre portraits painted on the pew ends right the way up the left side of the church. All depict women with demented expressions and bare, oddly placed breasts. Follow Route 144 from Hemse and you'll pass through **STÅNGA,** worth a stop for its fourteenth-century church with unusual wall tablets running down the facade, and **LYE**, a charming if sleepy hamlet with an antique shop and café. A few kilometres further east, the village of **LAU** has another beautiful church.

For good **beaches**, and the nearest thing Gotland has to a resort, the slow-paced and relaxing village of **LJUGARN** (⊛www.ljugarn.com) makes a decent base. The

△ Limestone stacks, Gotland

village, 50km from Visby and served by several buses a day, manages to retain an authentic feel. This is a place where it's easy to find a range of eateries to suit most tastes, and accommodation, unlike most of the island, is not restricted here to camping or hostels. *Rums* (**rooms**) are advertised in several appealing-looking cottages, and start at 125kr per person; some are listed on the village website and the map handed out at local shops and kiosks. There's an STF **youth hostel** overlooking the beach at the end of Storgatan (☎0498/49 31 84, ⓔstf.ljugarn@gamma.telenordia. se; ❶), with dorm beds from 130kr, as well as Gotland's oldest **B&B**, *Badpensionatet* (☎0498/49 32 05, ⓦwww.badpensionatet.com; ❸), which first opened its doors in 1921. *Café Espegards* at Storvägen 58 has excellent coffee and cakes. The best place for food is the *Strandcafe* (May–Aug; ☎0498/49 33 78, ⓦwww.strandcafe .se), overlooking the beach from Strandvägen, near the end of Louis Ebbesvägen. A delightful cycle or stroll north from the restaurant follows the coastline through woods and clearings carpeted in *blåeld*, the electric-blue flowers for which the area is known, to the *Folhammar rauker* – tall limestone pillars rising up from the beach. There's a Konsum supermarket on Storvägen 27, and bike rental from Hallins at Storvägen 91 (☎0498/49 34 16; 50kr per day).

Northern Gotland

There's an interesting natural phenomenon 23km north of Visby near Lickershamn, where you'll see the highest of Gotland's *raukar*, coastal **limestone stacks** that are the remnants of reefs formed over four hundred million years ago. This stack, 11.5m high and known as **Jungfruklint**, is said to look like the Virgin and Child – something you'll need a fair bit of faith and imagination to deduce.

On the whole, though, it's far better to press on north, where **BUNGE** is worth visiting for its bright fourteenth-century fortified church and open-air museum (mid-May to mid-Aug daily 10am–6pm; 30kr); the small island of Furillen, south of Bunge, makes an interesting place to stay up here, boasting one of Sweden's more unusual hotels, the *Fabriken Furillen* (☎0498/22 30 40; ❹), with sleek designer rooms inside the silos of a former limestone quarry; you'll need private transport to get there.

Fårö (Sheep Island), at the northern tip of Gotland, is mostly flat limestone heath, with shallow lakes and stunted pines much in evidence. In winter (and sometimes in summer, too), the wind whips off the Baltic, justifying the existence of the local windmills – and of the sheep shelters, with their steeply pitched reed roofs, modelled on traditional Fårö houses. The five-kilometre white sand arc at **Suder-sandsviken** is a popular destination; swimming can also be done at **Ekeviken**. The remainder of the coastline is rocky, spectacularly so at **Lauterhorn** and, particularly, **Langhammars**, where *raukar*, limestone stacks, are grouped together on the beach. The island can be reached by taking a bus to the town of Fårösund (where there's a cafe, supermarket and bicycle rental) and making the ten-minute ferry crossing (departures every 30min; free) from the quay ten minutes' walk to the south, on the main road. Note that there's no public transport on Fårö.

Travel details

Trains

Jönköping to: Stockholm (hourly; 3hr 30min); Gothenburg (hourly; 2hr).
Kalmar to: Gothenburg (8 daily; 4–5hr); Malmö (9 daily; 3hr); Stockholm (hourly; 4hr 30min); Växjö (11 daily; 1hr 10min).
Norrköping to: Malmö (13 daily; 3hr 10min); Stockholm (hourly; 1hr 20min).
Örebro to: Falun (6 daily; 2hr 30min); Stockholm (hourly; 2hr).
Växjö to: Gothenburg (5 daily; 3hr); Kalmar (11 daily; 1hr 10min); Karlskrona (3 daily; 1hr 30min).

Buses

Jönköping to: Gothenburg (8 daily; 2hr 10min); Stockholm (8 daily; 4hr); Växjö (Mon–Fri 2 daily; 2hr).

Kalmar to: Lund/Malmö (1–2 daily; 4hr–4hr 25min); Oskarshamn (3 daily, 1hr); Stockholm (3 daily; 6hr).
Norrköping to: Gothenburg (6 daily; 4hr 40min); Jönköping (8 daily; 2hr 20min); Kalmar (3 daily; 3hr 50min); Stockholm (8 daily; 2hr 10min).
Växjö to: Jönköping (2 daily; 2hr).

Ferries

Nynäshamn to: Visby (mid-June to late Aug 5 daily, rest of the year 2 daily; 3hr 15min, **Oskarshamn** to: Visby (mid-June to late Aug 2 daily, rest of the year 1 daily; 3hr); Byxelkrok (mid-June to Aug 2 daily; 2hr 20min).

International ferries

Nynäshamn to: Gdynia (4 weekly; 18hr).

3.5

The Bothnian coast

Facing Finland across the waters of the Gulf of Bothnia, Sweden's **east coast** forms a corridor of land that, with its jumble of erstwhile fishing towns and squeaky-clean modern cities, is quite unlike the rest of the north. The coast is dominated by towns and cities, the endless forest so characteristic of other parts of northern Sweden having been felled here to make room for the settlements that dot almost the entire coastline. Some, such as **Gävle**, still have their share of old wooden houses, offering evocative images of the past, though much was lost during the Russian incursions of the eighteenth century. Others, such as **Sundsvall, Umeå** and **Luleå**, are more typical – modern, bright and airy. Throughout the north you'll also find traces of the religious fervour that swept the region in centuries past: **Skellefteå** and, particularly, **Luleå** boast excellently preserved *kyrkstäder*, or parish villages, clusters of wooden cottages dating from the 1700s, where villagers from outlying districts would spend the night after making the lengthy journey to church in the nearest town.

The highlight of the Bothnian Coast, however, is undoubtedly **Höga Kusten**, or the High Coast, north of Härnösand – an indented stretch of shimmering fjords, tall cliffs and a string of pine-clad islands on which it's possible to island-hop up the coast. The weather may not be as reliable as further south, but you're guaranteed clean beaches – often all to yourself – crystal-clear waters and some fine walking.

Getting around

The **train** line hugs the coast until Härnösand, where services terminate. There are regular trains between Stockholm and Sundsvall, via Gävle, with just one daily service pressing on for Härnosand. Beyond Sundsvall, it's easier to continue by regular Norrlandskusten and Ybuss **buses**, which run to Härnösand, and then north – via the High Coast – to Umeå, Skellefteå and Luleå, or inland to Långsele, on the main line to Swedish Lapland and Narvik in Norway. There's a handy rail link from Sundsvall to Östersund, and other train connections are available in Umeå and Luleå. Island-hopping by **ferry** along the High Coast is a wonderful way to take in one of northern Sweden's most beautiful regions. Ferries between the Bothnian coast and **Finland** are limited to the year-round links from Umeå and Sundsvall to Vaasa.

Gävle and around

It's only a on-hour thirty-minute train ride north from Stockholm to **GÄVLE** (pronounced "Yev-luh"), capital of the district of Gästrikland and the southernmost city in Norrland, the region that makes up two-thirds of Sweden and covers more or less everything north of Uppsala. Gävle is an old city – its town charter was granted in 1446 – although this is hardly obvious from the brutally modern centre, with its large squares, broad avenues and monumental buildings. Almost completely rebuilt after a devastating fire in 1869, the spacious layout of present-day Gävle reflects its industrial success in the late nineteenth century, when it was the export centre for locally produced iron and timber.

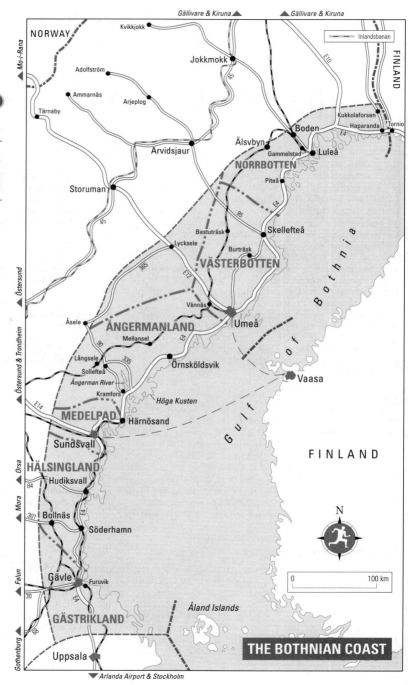

NORWAY

▲ Moi-i-Rana

Kvikkjokk

Gällivare & Kiruna ▲   ▲ Gällivare & Kiruna

FINLAND

Inlandsbanan

Jokkmokk

Adolfström

Ammarnäs

Arjeplog

Tärnaby

45

E10

Kukkolaforsen

Boden

Tornio

Älsvbyn

Gammelstad

Luleå

Haparanda

E4

Arvidsjaur

NORRBOTTEN

Piteå

◄ Östersund

Storuman

95

E4

Skellefteå

Bastuträsk

Lycksele

Burträsk

45

365

VÄSTERBOTTEN

E12

◄ Östersund & Trondheim

Åsele

ÅNGERMANLAND

Vännäs

Umeå

Bothnia

Mellansel

E4

90

Långsele

335

Sollefteå

Ångerman River

Örnsköldsvik

Vaasa

Kramfors

Höga Kusten

Gulf

of

E14

MEDELPAD

Härnösand

Sundsvall

FINLAND

HÄLSINGLAND

◄ Orsa

Hudiksvall

84

◄ Mora

301

Bollnäs

E4

Söderhamn

N

◄ Falun

Gävle

Furuvik

30

0   100 km

◄ Gothenburg

GÄSTRIKLAND

88

Åland Islands

Uppsala

THE BOTHNIAN COAST

▼ Arlanda Airport & Stockholm

Arrival, information and accommodation

The city centre is concentrated in the grid of streets that spreads southwest from the **train station**. The **bus station**, for both local and long-distance services, is on the east side of the train station, and connected to it by a tunnel. The small **tourist office** is a ten-minute walk away, inside the Gallerian Nian shopping mall at Drottninggatan 9, on the corner of Stortorget (Mon–Fri 10am–7pm, Sat 9am–2pm, Sun noon–4pm; ⊛www.gavle.se). Staff hand out free maps and the useful *Gävleguiden* booklet, and can help book private **apartments** from Gästrikland Turism (☏026/66 00 26; from 225kr per night). **Internet** access is available for free from the library on Södra Strandgatan (Mon–Thurs 10am–7pm, Fri 10am–5pm, Sat & Sun 10am–2pm).

Gävle has two **youth hostels**: the *Gamla Gefle* hostel is superbly located in the old quarter at Södra Rådmansgatan 1 (☏026/62 17 45, ⓔstf.vandrarhem@telia .se; closed mid-Dec to mid-Jan; doubles ❶, dorm beds from 135kr); while the *Engeltofta* hostel is near the **beach** in Engeltofta, 6km northeast of the city on bus #95 from the Rådhus (☏026/961 60, ⓔinfo_engeltoft@swipnet.se; May–Aug; doubles ❶, dorm beds 150kr). The nearest **campsite** (☏026/17 73 16, ⊛www.furuvik.se) is at Furuvik amusement park, a twelve-kilometre ride southeast on bus #838.

Aveny Södra Kungsgatan 31 ☏026/61 55 90, ⊛www.aveny.nu. Small and comfortable family-run hotel south of the river. ❸/❹

Boulogne Byggmästargatan 1 ☏026/12 63 52, ⊛www.hotellboulogne.com. Close to Boulognerskogen park, this is a cosy, basic hotel with the feeling of staying in a private home – breakfast is presented on a tray in the room. ❷

Järnvägshotellet Centralplan 3 ☏026/12 09 90, ⊛www.jarnvagshotellet.nu. Another cheap option, located on a busy corner opposite the train station. Toilets and showers are in the corridor. ❷

Park Inn Norra Slottsgatan 9 ☏026/64 70 00, ⊛www.rezidorparkinn.com. Another smart hotel, with its own pool, sauna and sunbeds. Rooms are tasteful if bland, with neutral colours and wooden floors. ❸/❺

Scandic CH Nygatan 45 ☏026/495 84 00, ⊛www.scandic-hotels.com. Recently renovated, this is one of the smartest hotels in town, with classically furnished en-suite rooms. ❸/❻

The City

Central Gävle is easy to navigate, with the broad, straight streets of the modern city bisected by a stretch of park that runs roughly north–south. To the south, across the river, lies Gamla Gefle, the only part of the city that survived the fire of 1869, and the first place to head for.

Gamla Gefle

The part of the city known as **Gamla Gefle** passes itself off today as the old town, though unfortunately there's not much left of it. The few remaining narrow cobbled streets – notably Övre Bergsgatan, Bergsgränd and Nedre Bergsgatan – are lined with pastel-coloured wooden cottages complete with window boxes bursting with summer flowers. For a glimpse of social conditions a century ago, visit the **Joe Hill Museum** (June–Aug Tues–Sat 11am–3pm; other times by arrangement on ☏026/61 20 22; free) at Nedre Bergsgatan 28. Joe Hill, born in the house as Joel Hägglund in 1879, emigrated to the United States in 1902, where with a new name he went on to become a working-class hero whose songs and speeches served as rallying cries to comrades everywhere. Framed for murder in Salt Lake City, he was executed in 1915. The syndicalist organization to which he belonged runs the museum, a collection of standard memorabilia – pictures and belongings – given piquancy by the telegram announcing his execution.

The county museum, **Länsmuséet Gävleborg**, is at Södra Strandgatan 20 (June–Aug Mon–Fri 10am–4pm, Sat & Sun noon–4pm; Sept–May Tues–Fri 10am–4pm, Wed till 9pm, Sat & Sun noon–4pm; 40kr; ⊛www.lansmuseetgavleborg.se). Its

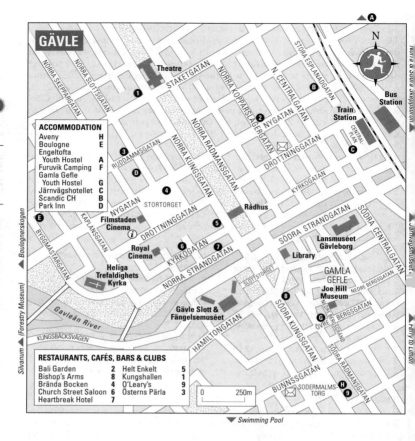

extensive displays of artworks by most of the great Swedish artists from the 1600s to the present day, including Nils Kreuger and Carl Larsson, make this a rarity among provincial museums, and attract visitors from across the country. Also on show are displays on the area's ironworks and fisheries, as well as work by local artist Johan-Erik Olsson (popularly known as Lim-Johan), whose vivid imagination and naive technique produced some strangely childlike paintings.

The rest of the city

The modern city lies over the Gavleån River, its wide streets and tree-lined avenues originally designed to prevent fires from spreading. A central boulevard of parks, trees and fountains runs from the sculpture-spiked **Rådhus** up to the beautiful nineteenth-century **theatre**, neatly dividing the modern city into two, while the concrete expanse of **Stortorget** has the usual open-air fruit and veg market (Mon–Sat).

Gävle's other sights – none of them major – are out of the centre but close enough to reach on foot. Back at the river by the main double bridge, **Gävle Slott**, the seventeenth-century residence of the county governor, lost its ramparts and towers years ago and now lurks behind a row of trees like some minor country house. You can't go inside, although you can visit the **Fängelsemuséet** (Prison Museum; tours on Sun at noon, 1pm & 2pm; 30kr; book on ☎026/65 44 30). From Gävle

Slott, a short walk along the river leads to a wooden bridge, across which is Kaplansgatan and the **Heliga Trefaldighets kyrka**, the Church of the Holy Trinity, a seventeenth-century masterpiece of wood-carved decoration. Check out the pulpit, towering altarpiece and screen – each the superb work of a German craftsman, Ewardt Friis. Cross back over the river and take a stroll down **Kungsbäcksvägen**, a narrow street lined with old wooden houses painted yellow, green and orange, with tulips and wild roses growing outside their front doors. Continue and you'll come to the rambling **Boulognerskogen**, which opened in the mid-nineteenth century and still provides an oasis of trees, water and flowers just outside the city centre – a good place for a picnic and a spot of sunbathing.

On a rainy day, you may find yourself contemplating the **Järnvägsmuséet** (Railway Museum) at Rälsgatan 1 (June & Aug daily 10am–4pm; Sept–May Tues–Sun 10am–4pm; 40kr; ⊛www.jarnvagsmuseum.se), a fifteen-minute walk south from the station following the train tracks. The old engine shed houses fifty or so locomotives, some of them over 100 years old. If you walk here from behind the train station, you'll pass the red wooden fronts and fading company names of the old dockside **warehouses** off Norra Skeppsbron, a reminder of the days when ships unloaded coffee and spices in the centre of Gävle. Today, the city is still well known for Gevalia coffee, widely available across Sweden.

If you're here in December, be quick to see the biggest traditional **yule goat** in Sweden, as it's usually destroyed by the locals long before Christmas, sometimes even before it makes it on to Stortorget. Since the tradition of erecting a huge straw goat started in 1966, it has been burnt down at least twenty times, vandalized four times and hit by a car once – despite its very own protective guards.

Around Gävle

In summer, the locals head for the beaches of **ENGELTOFTA**, 6km northeast of the city on bus #95 from the Rådhus. The island of **Limön**, 12km from Gävle, has more good beaches and is also a pleasant place for some gentle walks, with paths criss-crossing the island. It can be reached via a summer ferry, *MS Drottning Silvia* (daily 9.30am, 11.30am & 4.40pm; 40min; 40kr), which departs east along the river from Södra Skeppsbron.

Eating, drinking and entertainment

There's a fair choice of **eating places** in Gävle, but for the best options stick to the central grid of streets around Stortorget. Nearly all cafés and restaurants double up as bars, and some also mutate into nightclubs, too.

Bali Garden Corner of Nygatan and Norra Kopparslagergatan. Good Indonesian food, with dishes from 90kr.

Bishop's Arms Södra Kungsgatan 7. Popular but somewhat pricey English-style pub and restaurant near the youth hostel; dinner from 140kr.

Brända Bocken Stortorget. Young and fashionable eatery, with outdoor seating in summer. Lunch for 70kr, and beef and pork dishes, hamburgers and salmon from around 90kr.

Church Street Saloon Kyrkogatan 11. Fun, loud Western-style bar and restaurant. Closed Sun.

Heartbreak Hotel Norra Strandgatan 15. Pub, bar and nightclub – worth checking out.

Helt Enkelt Norra Kungsgatan 3. Excellent, stylish restaurant/bar serving Swedish fare from 130kr.

Kungshallen Norra Kungsgatan 17, next to the theatre. Mammoth-sized pizzas for 40–56kr and cheap beer.

O'Leary's Södra Kungsgatan 31. An incredibly busy bar catering for a young crowd. *The* place to do your boozing and boogying. A ten-minute walk south from the centre. Closed Mon.

Österns Pärla Ruddammsgatan 23. Chinese restaurant, serving all the usual favourites for 80–90kr.

Sundsvall

The capital of the tiny province of Medelpad, **SUNDSVALL**, known as "Stone City", is immediately and obviously different. Once home to a rapidly expanding

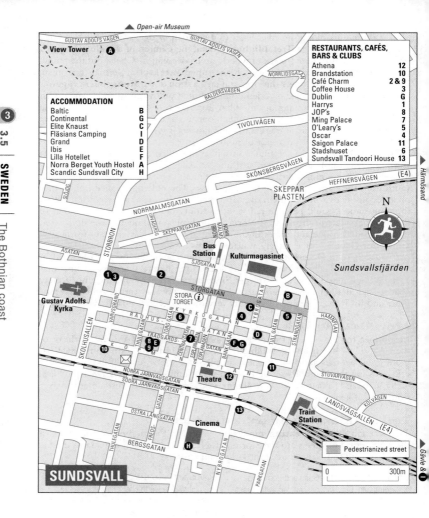

Open-air Museum

View Tower Ⓐ

Härnösand

Sundsvallsfjärden

N

SKEPPAR
PLASTEN

Bus
Station

Kulturmagasinet

**Gustav Adolfs
Kyrka**

STORA
TORGET ⓘ

Theatre

Cinema

Train
Station

Pedestrianized street

0   300m

SUNDSVALL

Gävle &

nineteenth-century sawmill industry, the whole city burned to the ground in June
1888, and nine thousand people lost their homes. Rebuilding began at once, and
within ten years a new centre constructed of stone had emerged. The result is a
living document of late nineteenth-century neo-Renaissance architecture, based
around wide esplanades intended to serve as fire breaks and designed and crafted by
the same architects who were involved in rebuilding Stockholm's residential areas
at the same time. However, the reconstruction was achieved at a price: the workers
who had laboured on the new buildings were shifted from their homes in the centre
and moved south to a poorly serviced suburb, highlighting the glaring difference
between the wealth of the new centre and the poverty of the surrounding districts.

Arrival and information

From the **train station**, it's a five-minute walk to the city centre. The helpful **tourist office** (Mon–Fri 10am–6pm, Sat 10am–2pm; ☎060/61 04 50,

www.sundsvallturism.com) is in the main square, Stora Torget. The **bus station** is at the northern end of Esplanaden, where you can buy Länstrafiken Norrlandskusten bus tickets north towards Haparanda on the Finnish border (☎0711/10 01 10, www.ltnbd.se); Ybuss (for buses to Stockholm, Umeå and Östersund) has its office nearby at Sjögatan 7 (☎060/17 19 60, www.ybuss.se). The weekly **ferry** from Vaasa in Finland (☎090/18 52 00, www.rgline.com; Sat; 10hr; 540kr) docks 5km east of town and is not met by bus; for a **taxi**, call ☎060/19 90 00. **Internet** can be used for free at the library inside the Kulturmagasinet complex.

Accommodation

There's no shortage of reasonably priced **hotels** in Sundsvall. It's worth contacting the tourist office first about their special offers (❷/❺) in several quality hotels. For budget accommodation, try the **youth hostel** (☎060/61 21 19, www.gaffelbyn.se; dorm beds 195kr), a twenty-minute uphill walk north of town on Norra Berget, the hill overlooking the city (phone to order a bus in advance on ☎060/744 90 10 or a fixed-price taxis on ☎060/19 90 00); it also has double rooms (❷). The nearest **campsite** is *Fläsians Camping* (☎060/55 44 75, www.camping.se/y26; mid-May to Aug), 4km outside town and reached by bus #2 or #20.

Baltic Sjögatan 5 ☎060/14 04 40, www.baltichotell.com. Cheap, and centrally located near the Kulturmagasinet and the harbour, with perfectly adequate rooms. ❶/❷

Continental Rådhusgatan 13 ☎060/15 00 60, ⊜15 75 90. Fairly cheap hotel between the station and the main square; all rooms are en suite. Sun terrace and cable TV in all rooms. ❸

Elite Knaust Storgatan 13, ☎060/608 00 00, www.elite.se. Newly renovated top-class hotel, known for its glamorous marble staircase, and boasting very comfortable rooms. ❹/❻

Grand Nybrogatan 13 ☎060/64 65 60, www.grandsundsvall.se. Good value in summer, and

there's an excellent sauna and Jacuzzi suite in the basement. ❸/❹

Ibis Trädgårdsgatan 31 ☎060/64 17 50, www.ibishotel.com. Excellent value for such a central location, though breakfast is an extra 50kr. All rooms are en suite. ❷

Lilla Hotellet Rådhusgatan 15 ☎060/61 35 87, home.swipnet.se/lilla-hotellet. One of the most reasonably priced places in town, with just eight rooms, all en suite and with cable TV. ❷

Scandic Sundsvall City Esplanaden 29 ☎060/785 62 00, www.scandic-hotels.com. Top-range hotel with good views, and winter prices to match the opulence. There's a cinema complex in the same building. ❸/❻

The City

The sheer scale of the rebuilding that followed the fire of 1888 is clear as you walk into town from the train station. The style is simple, uncluttered limestone and brick, the dimensions often overwhelming, with palatial four- and five-storey buildings serving as offices as well as homes. As you stroll the streets you can't help but be amazed by the tremendous amount of space right in the heart of Sundsvall – it's hard to believe that this is the most densely populated city in northern Sweden.

Several of the buildings in the centre are worth a second look, not least the sturdy bourgeois exterior of the **Kulturmagasinet** ("Culture Warehouse") four connected nineteenth-century warehouses down by the harbour. The buildings stood empty for twenty years before being turned into the complex now housing a museum, a library and a café. Inside, the **Sundsvall Museum** (Mon–Thurs 10am–7pm, Fri 10am–6pm, Sat & Sun 11am–4pm; July–Aug 20kr, Sept–June free) is worth a quick look for the models and photos of the city centre and the sawmills before the fire. Towards the other end of town, follow the main pedestrian street of Storgatan to its far end to the soaring red-brick **Gustav Adolfs kyrka** (daily: June–Aug 11am–4pm; Sept–May 11am–2pm; summer concerts on Wed from 7pm), where the friendly wards welcome visitors with free coffee and biscuits.

Beyond the city's design, the most attractive diversion is the tiring three-kilometre climb to the heights of **Gaffelbyn** on Norra Berget, the hill that overlooks the city to the north; walk up Storgatan, cross over the main bridge and follow the sign to the youth hostel. On a clear day, the panorama from the **view tower** is fantastic, giving a fresh perspective on the city's planned structure and the restrictive nature of its location, hemmed in on three sides by hills and the sea. From here you can see straight across to Södra Berget, the southern hill, with its ski slopes. Also here is the **Norra Bergets** park (daily 11am–5pm; 20kr; ⓦwww.norraberget.se), an open-air museum with the usual selection of twee wooden huts and assorted activities; in the handicrafts area you can try your hand at baking some *tunnbröd*, the thin bread that's typical of northern Sweden.

Eating, drinking and entertainment

Sundsvall has a good choice of **restaurants** – something you may want to make the most of if you're heading further north. The town's **bars** generally have a good atmosphere, though nightclubs are rather thin on the ground.

Cafés and restaurants

Athena Köpmangatan 7. All the Greek favourites, from *tzatziki* to *souvlakia*, as well as pizzas, from 110kr.

Brandstation Köpmangatan 29, ☎060/12 39 36, ⓦwww.brandstation.org. Swedish fare and luxury pizzas served in an atmospheric old fire station; mains from 150kr.

Café Charm Storgatan 34 and Köpmangatan 34. Good choices for coffee and naughty-but-nice cream cakes.

Coffee House Storgatan 31. *The* coffee house in Sundsvall, with dozens of varieties of coffee and excellent sandwiches and cakes.

Ming Palace Esplanaden 10. A good choice for Chinese, with dishes from 60kr to eat in or take away. Closed July.

Saigon Palace Trädgårdsgatan 5. Vietnamese and Chinese restaurant with some well-priced dishes, including a buffet lunch for 69kr and such delights as chicken in peanut sauce for dinner (around 90kr).

Stadshuset Rådhusgatan 22, ☎060/12 92 60.

Exquisite Swedish food served inside the grand town hall; lunch is 85kr, dinner from 120kr.

Sundsvall Tandoori House Södra Järnvägsgatan 9, ☎17 59 59. One of Sweden's best Indian restaurants, serving up first-class Indian meals (mains 120–150kr) in a basement restaurant near the centre.

Bars and nightlife

Dublin Nybrogatan 16. Irish pub with Irish food and music, darts and a broad selection of different beers, including Caffrey's and Kilkenny's.

Harrys Storgatan 33. Another in the chain of popular American-style bars. This one's a pub, restaurant and nightclub all rolled into one.

JOP's Trädgårdsgatan 35. Popular place for a mid-evening tipple.

O'Leary's Storgatan 5. Sports pub with a good choice of beer, and pub grub with a Tex-Mex flavour. Big screens show football and hockey matches.

Oscar Bankgatan 11. Good, lively restaurant and nightclub. Try the excellent cocktails, if your pocket can take the strain – staff are happy to make any concoction.

Härnösand

From Sundsvall, it's less than an hour by bus or train north along the coast to **HÄRNÖSAND**, a quiet little place at the mouth of the River Ångerman. Founded in 1585, the town has had its fair share of disasters – two great fires in 1710 and 1714, followed by a thorough ransacking by invading Russians in 1721 – yet despite this it preserves some architectural delights. Härnösand marks the beginning of the beautiful province of **Ångermanland**, one of the few areas in Sweden where the countryside resembles that of neighbouring Norway, with its low mountains, craggy coastlines and long fjords reaching far inland. The town is a good jumping-off point for the nearby High Coast (see opposite), or from which to head inland to connect with the main train line north at Långsele.

The Town

For such a small and provincial place, the proud civic buildings of Härnösand reek of grandeur and self-importance. The town centre is on the island of **Härnön**, and its main square, **Stora Torget**, was once chosen by local worthies as the most beautiful in Sweden. Its western edge is proudly given over to the governor's residence, built in neoclassical style using local brick; this rubs shoulders with the Renaissance former provincial government building on the southwestern edge. From the square's southern edge, take a stroll up Västra Kyrkogatan to the Neoclassical **Domkyrkan** (daily 10am–4pm), which dates from the 1840s, though it incorporates bits and pieces from earlier churches that stood on the site (the Baroque altar is eighteenth-century, as are the VIP boxes in the nave). Trivia lovers will be delighted to learn that this is the smallest cathedral in Sweden, and also the only one painted white. Turn right from here and follow the road round and back down the hill until you come to the narrow old street of **Östanbäcksgatan**, where the painted wooden houses date back to the 1700s. For a taste of the town's architectural splendour, take a walk up the main street, **Nybrogatan**, where the grand building with the yellow ochre facade that houses the Länsstyrelsen (Provincial Administration) at the corner with Brunnhusgatan is particularly beautiful.

The impressive **open-air museum** just north of the town centre at Murberget (June–Aug daily 11am–5pm, closed Mon; free) is a thirty-minute walk from the town centre, or reachable on bus #2. Around eighty buildings have been transplanted to the site, including traditional Ångermanland farmhouses and the old Murberget church.

Practicalities

The **tourist office** (June–Aug Mon–Fri 8am–7pm, Sat & Sun noon–4pm; Sept–May Mon–Fri 8am–5pm; ☎0611/881 40, ⊛www.harnosand.se) is opposite the train station at Järnvägsgatan 2, inside the building marked "Spiran"; the helpful staff can advise on transport, and book private **apartments** from 500kr.

Härnösand's **youth hostel** (☎0611/104 46, ⊜vhemmet@harnosandshus.se; mid-June to early Aug; ❶), where the only accommodation is in self-contained apartments, is a fifteen-minute walk from the centre up Nybrogatan and then left into Kastellgatan. *Sälstens Camping* (☎0611/181 50, ⊜salsten@telia.com) is around 2km from the centre, next to a string of pebble beaches; it also has a small selection of four-bed cabins for 300kr per night per person, and rents out bikes to guests.

Of the town's three **hotels**, the *Royal*, close to the train station at Strandgatan 12 (☎0611/204 55; ❷/❸), is the cheapest, and offers a fish dinner plus drink for 100kr to its guests. The *City* at Storgatan 28 (☎0611/277 00, ⊛www.kajutan.com; ❷/❸) is only marginally more expensive when discounted. The *First Hotel Stadt*, Skeppsbron 9 (☎0611/55 44 40, ⊛www.firsthotels.com; ❸/❺), is much bigger and a lot plusher, but can be worth it when summer rates kick in.

An atmospheric **restaurant** choice is *Apotequet*, located in an old pharmacy at Nybrogatan 3, serving northern Swedish delicacies (mains from 200kr) and later turning into a popular club (Wed & Sat). The summer-only *Hamnkrogen* restaurant in the wooden buildings next to the yacht marina is popular for its fish dishes (from 130kr) and the views of the town centre across the water. Other eateries include the Greek favourite, *Mykonos*, at Storgatan 20, with moussaka for 100kr; and the *Rutiga Duken* café at Västra Kyrkogatan 1, which does reasonably priced lunches and delicious home-baked pastries and pies. For **drinking**, the *O'Leary's* chain outlet at Storgatan 28 is the best place to head for a pint; on Saturdays, the *Nybrokälleren* at Nybrogatan 5 is a good **nightclub**.

The Höga Kusten (High Coast)

Between Härnösand and Örnsköldsvik lies the **Höga Kusten** or High Coast (⊛www.highcoast.net), the beautiful stretch of Bothnian coastline characterized by rolling hills and verdant valleys that plunge precipitously into the Gulf. During the Ice Age, the region sank some 800m under the weight of the three-kilometre-thick sheet of ice; the rebound has caused the High Coast to rise slowly but dramatically

△ Höga Kusten scenery

ever since, creeping back up at a rate of 8mm per year. The resulting dynamic landscape has recently been added to the World Heritage list: the rugged shoreline is composed of sheer cliffs and craggy outcrops of rock, along with some peaceful sandy coves. Offshore are dozens of islands, some just skerries no more than a few square metres in size, others much larger and covered with dense pine forest – it was on these that the tradition of preparing the foul-smelling *surströmming* (fermented Baltic herring) is thought to have first started.

The coastline is best seen from the sea, and a trip out to one of the islands gives a perfect impression of the scale of things; however, it's also possible to walk virtually the entire length of the coast on the **Höga Kusten leden**, a long-distance hiking path that extends 130km from the Golden Gate-style suspension bridge just north of Härnösand – one of the longest in the world – to Örnsköldsvik; accommodation is in huts, farmhouses and villages along the way, and can be booked at the High Coast's tourist offices. The path crosses through the small but untamed **Skuleskogen National Park**, whose 30km of marked paths traverse lush forest, boulder fields, sharp peaks and the impressive Slåtterdalsskrevan gorge, a sharp gouge into the mountain 40m deep and just 7m wide; Skuleskogen can be also be visited on a day trip with your own transport.

Drop by one of the regional **tourist offices** to purchase the detailed *High Coast Trail* booklet and map (80kr). The office along the E4 at Skuleberget near Docksta (☎0613/401 71, ⓦwww.skulenaturum.se) has a good café and can arrange guided hikes in the nearby Skuleskogen National Park; if you're just passing through the area you could stop off to climb Skuleberget mountain, secured with a safety wire (daily: June & Aug 10am–4pm, July 10am–7pm; ☎073/84 85 601; 100kr; 2–3hr). Twenty kilometres north of Härnösand, the Hornöberget tourist office (daily early June & late Aug 9.30am–5pm, mid-June to mid-Aug 9.30am–6.30pm; ☎0613/504 80, ⓦwww.turistinfo.kramfors.se) is inside the ⚔ *Höga Kusten* **hotel** (☎0613/72 22 70, ⓦwww.hotellhoga-kusten.se; ❸/❹), whose functional, modern rooms provide spectacular views over the massive Höga Kusten suspension bridge and the fjord beyond. From Härnösand or Örnsköldsvik, there are regular Norrlandskusten **buses** that stop at the bridge and the Skuleberget tourist office, and pass through the tiny villages of Ullånger and Docksta (jumping-off points for the island of Ulvön; see p.603). Alternatively, you can take the bus to Bönhamn (see p.603 for details), from where a small boat leaves for the island of Högbonden.

The islands

A trip out to the islands off the High Coast has to rank as the highlight of any trip up the Bothnian Coast. Using a combination of buses and boats, you can make your way to three of the most beautiful islands in the chain: **Högbonden**, **Ulvön** and **Trysunda**.

Högbonden

After just ten minutes' boat ride from the mainland, the steep sides of the tiny round island of **Högbonden** (ⓦ www.hogbonden.se) rise up in front of you. There are no shops, hotels or flush-toilets – in fact, the only building on Högbonden is a lighthouse situated at the highest point on a rocky plateau where the pine and spruce trees have been unable to get a foothold. The lighthouse has now been converted into a **youth hostel** (☎0613/230 05; May to mid-Oct; pre-book on ☎0613/231 00; dorm beds from 100kr), with stunning views and just thirty beds. To make the most of it, you need to stay a couple of nights, exploring the island's gorge and thick forest by day, and relaxing in the traditional wood-burning **sauna** down by the sea in the evenings.

To **get there** from Härnösand, take an early bus to Ullånger, change on to the bus for Nordingrå, then change again to get to Bönhamn (2hr in total from Härnösand), from where the *M/S Högbonden* (mid-June to mid-Aug daily 10am, noon, 3pm & 6pm; 80kr return) makes the trip out to the island.

Ulvön

The largest island in the chain, **Ulvön** ("Wolf Island"; ⓦ www.ulvon.com) is really two islands: Norra Ulvön and, across a narrow channel, the uninhabited Södra Ulvön. Before the last war Ulvön boasted the biggest fishing community along the High Coast, but many islanders have since moved to the mainland, leaving around forty permanent residents.

All boats to the island dock at the main village, **Ulvöhamn**, a picturesque one-street affair with red-and-white cottages and tiny boathouses on stilts. The island's only **hotel**, Ulvö Skärgårdshotell (☎0660/22 40 09, ⓦ www.ulvohotell.se; ❸; May to mid-Oct), is at one end of the street, just to the right of where the boats from Ullånger and Docksta put in. Walk a short distance to the left of the quay and you'll come to a tiny wooden hut that functions as a summer **tourist office** (mid-June to mid-Aug daily 11am–3.30pm; ☎0660/23 40 93) – you can also rent bikes here (30kr/4hr). Continue and you'll soon reach a seventeenth-century fishermen's chapel, decorated with flamboyant murals; the road leading uphill to the right just beyond here leads to the **youth hostel** (☎0660/22 41 90; June–Aug; doubles ❶, dorm beds from 130kr). At the other end of the main street is the village shop.

To **get to Ulvön**, make your way to **Docksta**, from where M/S Kusttrafik (☎0613/105 50, ⓦ www.hkship.se; 150kr same-day return; reservation recommended) leaves daily June–August at 10.15am, arriving in Ulvöhamn at 11.30am, and returning at 3pm. From **Härnösand**, there are frequent bus services to Docksta. To get to Docksta from Högbonden, take the bus from Bönhamn via Nordingrå to Gallsäter, where you can connect with the frequent Norrlandskusten buses that stop there on their way between Sundsvall and Umeå (for bus information, ring Din Tur on ☎0771/51 15 13 or see ⓦ www.dintur.se). The year-round M/S Ulvön runs to Trysunda and Ulvön from Köpmanholmen, 25km south of Örnsköldsvik, daily at 10.40am and 7.10pm, with return trips at 6.45am and 3.45pm; out of summer, there's generally one departure daily, depending on ice – check at the tourist office. Alternatively, there's also a private boat taxi (☎070/224 04 40) to zip you around the islands. From late June to early August, it's also possible to reach Ulvön from Örnsköldsvik on the M/S Otilia II (☎0660/22 34 31; 110kr single; daily 9.30am, returning 3pm).

Trysunda

Boats from Ulvön, just an hour away, dock in **Trysunda**'s narrow U-shaped harbour, around which curves the island's tiny village. This is the best-preserved fishing village in Ångermanland: a charming little spot with forty or so red-and-white houses right on the waterfront, and a seventeenth-century chapel with wonderful murals. The island's gently shelving rocks make it ideal for bathing and there's no shortage of secluded spots. Trysunda is also criss-crossed with walking paths leading through the gnarled and twisted dwarf pines. You can stay on the island in the STF **youth hostel** (☎0660/430 38; mid-May to mid-Sept; doubles ❶, dorm beds 140kr), at the harbour entrance.

Getting here from Ulvöhamn is simple: the *M/F Ulvön* (☎020/51 15 13; 45kr one-way) makes the trip at least once a day year round, before continuing on to **Köpmanholmen** back on the mainland (35kr), where there's a youth hostel (☎0660/22 34 96; doubles ❶, dorm beds 130kr) and regular buses to Örnsköldsvik, 25km to the north.

Umeå

UMEÅ is the biggest city in northern Sweden, with a population of around 105,000. Demographically, it's probably Sweden's most youthful city, with an average age of just 36, no doubt influenced by the presence of Norrland University and its 25,000 students. Strolling around the centre, you'll notice that those who aren't in pushchairs are pushing them, while the cafés and city parks are full of teenagers. With its fast-flowing river and wide, stylish boulevards, Umeå is a distinctly likeable city, and it's no bad idea to spend a couple of days here sampling some of the bars and restaurants – the variety of which you won't find elsewhere in Norrland.

Arrival, information and accommodation

It's a ten-minute walk from either the **train station** or **long-distance bus station** (☎0771/10 01 10, ⊛www.lanstrafikeniac.se) on Järnvägsallén to the centre, down one of the many parallel streets that lead in the general direction of the river. **Ferries** to Vaasa in Finland dock at Holmsund, 20km southeast of town (☎090/18 52 00, ⊛www.rgline.com; 1–2 daily except Sat; 4hr; 360kr); bus #125 has inconvenient departures so you'll probably need a **taxi** (Direkt Taxi ☎090/10 01 00; Umeå Taxi ☎090/77 00 00).

A good first stop is the helpful **tourist office** (May to mid-June & mid-Aug to late Sept Mon–Fri 10am–6pm, Sat 10am–2pm; mid-June to mid-Aug Mon–Fri 8.30am–7pm, Sat 10am–4pm, Sun noon–4pm; Oct–April Mon–Fri 10am–5pm; ☎090/16 16 16, ⊛www.umea.se) in the ugly concrete square of Renmarkstorget. The staff dish out maps and the *Summerguide* (also available online); sell the 60kr *Sevärt Kort* card, which gives reductions on museums and sights throughout the region; and offer a free guided **city walk** (Sat 2pm, mid-June to early Sept). They can also provide a list of **private rooms** from 160kr per night, while booking hotel rooms via the tourist office website can get you good deals. Umeå's bright and modern STF **youth hostel** (☎090/77 16 50, ⊛www.stfturist.se; doubles ❶, dorm beds from 130kr) is in the centre at Västra Esplanaden 10; alternatively, there's a new YMCA hostel, *KFUM Umeå*, just north of the centre at Järnvägsallén 20 (mid-June to mid-Aug; ☎090/18 57 18, ⊛hostel.kfum.nu; doubles ❶, dorm beds 160kr). The nearest **campsite** is the lakeside *First Camp Umeå* (☎090/70 26 00, ⊛www.firstcamp.se), 5km northeast of town along E4 at Nydala; it also has **cabins** for four people from 580kr, individual double rooms (❶) in other cabins and tiny two-bed huts called *trätält* (❶); facilities include washing machines and bike rental. Take bus #67 or #69, get off at Nydala and the campsite is about a five-minute walk towards Nydalabadet.

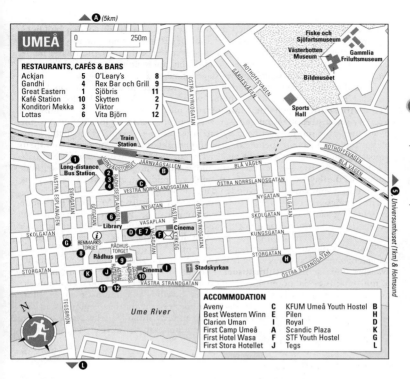

UMEÅ

0   250m

RESTAURANTS, CAFÉS & BARS			
Ackjan	5	O'Leary's	8
Gandhi	4	Rex Bar och Grill	9
Great Eastern	1	Sjöbris	11
Kafé Station	10	Skytten	2
Konditori Mekka	3	Viktor	7
Lottas	6	Vita Björn	12

Fiske och
Sjöfartsmuseum

Västerbotten
Museum

Gammlia
Friluftsmuseum

Bildmuséet

Sports
Hall

Train
Station

Long-distance
Bus Station

Library

Cinema

Rådhus

Cinema

Stadskyrkan

Ume River

ACCOMMODATION			
Aveny	C	KFUM Umeå Youth Hostel	B
Best Western Winn	E	Pilen	H
Clarion Uman	I	Royal	D
First Camp Umeå	A	Scandic Plaza	K
First Hotel Wasa	F	STF Youth Hostel	G
First Stora Hotellet	J	Tegs	L

Accommodation

Aveny Rådhusesplanaden 14 ☎ 090/13 41 42, ⓦ www.profilhotels.se. Brand new, upmarket hotel with comfortable, large rooms. ❹/❺

Best Western Winn Skolgatan 64 ☎ 090/71 11 00, ⓦ www.winnhotel.se. Modern rooms in a quaint central building. ❸/❹

Clarion Uman Storgatan 52 ☎ 090/12 72 20, ⓦ www.choicehotels.se. Comfortable, modern rooms, with evening coffee and newspapers for all guests. ❸/❺

First Hotel Wasa Vasagatan 12 ☎ 090/77 85 40, ⓦ www.firsthotels.com. A comfortable hotel in a lively, central location, though its rooms have a chain-hotel feel. ❹

First Stora Hotellet Storgatan 46 ☎ 090/77 88 70, ⓦ www.firsthotels.com. Newly renovated and rather chic, right in the heart of town. ❸/❹

Pilen Pilgatan 5 ☎ 090/14 14 60, ⓔ hotellpilen@spray.se. One of the cheaper smaller hotels with clean and basic rooms, and weekend and summer doubles for 500kr. ❷/❸

Royal Skolgatan 62 ☎ 090/10 07 30, ⓦ www.royalhotelumea.com. Pleasant, centrally located hotel with sauna, whirlpool and solarium. ❸/❹

Scandic Plaza Storgatan 40 ☎ 090/205 63 00, ⓦ www.scandic-hotels.com. Voted one of the best hotels in Sweden, this is very smart, with marble washbasins in the bathrooms and superb views from the sauna suite on the fourteenth floor – all at excellent rates. ❸/❹

Tegs Verkstadsgatan 5 ☎ 090/12 27 00, ⓦ www.tegshotell.se. The cheapest hotel in town – in summer, the dingy doubles are as little as 490kr – though it's south of the river and some way from the action. ❶/❷

The City

Umeå is known as the "City of Birches" for the trees that were planted along every street following a devastating fire in 1888. Most of the city was wiped out in the blaze, but rebuilding began apace, and two wide esplanades, together forming Rådhusesplanaden, were constructed to act as firebreaks should a similar disaster occur again. You'll be hard pushed to find any of the original wooden buildings, but around the little park in front of the former **Rådhus**, lingering bits of c.1900 timber architecture still look out over the river responsible for the town's name: *uma* means "roar" and refers to the sound of the rapids along the River Ume, now put to use by the hydroelectric power station further upstream.

Umeå also offers one terrific museum complex, **Gammlia**, which merits a good half-day. The original attraction around which everything else developed is the **Friluftsmuseum** (Open-Air Museum; mid-June to mid-Aug daily 10am–5pm; free; ⊕www.vasterbottensmuseum.se), a group of twenty regional buildings, the oldest being the seventeenth-century gatehouse on the way in. As usual, the complex is brought to life by people dressed in period costume – you can watch them preparing traditional unleavened *tunnbröd* in the bakery – while cows, pigs, goats, sheep and geese are kept in the yards and farm buildings. Look for the summer traditional **dance** evenings (Tues from 7pm), where the locals will be sure to whisk you off for a spin around the wooden dancefloor.

The main collection is housed in the indoor **Västerbotten Museum** (mid-June to mid-Aug daily 10am–5pm; mid-Aug to mid-June Tues–Fri 10am–4pm, Sat noon–4pm, Sun noon–5pm; free): a number of exhibitions canter through the county's development, from prehistory (including the oldest ski in the world, dated at 5200 years old) to the Industrial Revolution. It's all good stuff, well laid out and complemented by an array of videos and recordings, with a useful English leaflet available. Next door, the **Bildmuséet** (mid-June to mid-Aug noon–5pm; mid-Aug to mid-June Tues–Sat noon–4pm, Sun noon–5pm; free; ⊕www.umu.se/bildmuseet) houses interesting displays of contemporary Swedish and international art, photojournalism and visual design. Back outside, county history continues in the separate **Fiske och Sjöfartsmuseum** (Fish and Maritime Museum; same times as Friluftsmuséet; free), an attempt at a maritime museum that is really no more than a small hall clogged with fishing boats.

Eating and drinking

Umeå's **eating and drinking** possibilities are enhanced by the number of students in the city; they have their own lively bar serving 35kr beers in the Universumhuset, a twenty-minute walk east of town. Most of the restaurants can be found around the central pedestrianized Kungsgatan and Rådhusesplanaden; for a quick bite, the best **café** in town is *Konditori Mekka*, close to the train station at Rådhusesplanaden 17, serving heavenly pastries and free coffee refills. Otherwise, try *Kafé Station*, Östra Rådhusgatan 2, next to the Filmstaden cinema, with its rough brick walls and wooden floors; or the *Vita Björn*, the white boat moored down from the Rådhus.

Restaurants

Ackjan Strömpilsplatsen ☎090/70 14 15, ⊕www .ackjan.se. For a taste of Lapland, head 3km south of the centre along the river to sample Sámi specialities (from 120kr), including the delicious 150kr *Jokkmokkspanna*; reindeer with mushrooms and wild berries.

Gandhi Rådhusesplanaden 17. Despite its dingy basement, Gandhi offers excellent Indian food and is good value, too, with dishes around 150kr. Closed July.

Great Eastern Magasinsgatan 17. The best Chinese restaurant north of Stockholm. With a 70kr deal, it's busy at lunchtime, while in the evening there's chicken and beef dinners from 92kr, as well as a Mongolian barbecue.

Lottas Nygatan 22. This British-style pub is a great place to go drinking. The adjoining restaurant has fish and chips for 145kr, lobster for 115kr and good-value lunches for 75kr.

O'Leary's Kungsgatan 50. A huge outlet of the popular sportsbar, with bar food from 90–150kr and outdoor seating.

Rex Bar och Grill Rådhustorget ☎090/12 60 50, ⊕www.rexbar.com. Inside the town hall, this is the most popular – and stylish – place to eat. A pricey à la carte menu in which northern Swedish specialities are supplemented with bar meals from 90kr.

Sjöbris Kajplats 10. Excellent fish restaurant on board an old white fishing boat moored off Västra Strandgatan.

Skytten Rådhusesplanaden 17, ☎090/13 56 60, ⓦwww.skytten.se. A friendly restaurant with great grilled meat and fish dishes (125–250kr).

Viktor Vasagatan 11 ☎090/71 11 15, ⓦwww.restaurangviktor.com. Umeå's best – and priciest – restaurant specializes in exquisite Swedish cuisine, including imaginative fish dishes; mains from 280kr.

Skellefteå

"In the centre of the plain was Skellefteå church, the largest and most beautiful building in the entire north of Sweden, rising like a Palmyra's temple out of the desert." So enthused the nineteenth-century traveller Leopold von Buch, for there used to be a real religious fervour about **SKELLEFTEÅ**. In 1324, an edict in the name of King Magnus Eriksson invited "all those who believed in Jesus Christ or wanted to turn to Him" to settle between the Skellefte and Ume rivers. Many heeded the call and parishes mushroomed on the banks of the Skellefte. By the end of the eighteenth century, a devout township was centred on the monumental church, which stood out in stark contrast to the surrounding plains and wide river. Nowadays, more material occupations support the town, and the tourist office makes the most of modern Skellefteå's gold and silver refineries, while admitting that the town centre doesn't have much to offer: concentrate instead on the church and its nearby *kyrkstad*, or parish village.

Skellefteå's church and parish village, **Bonnstan**, are within easy striking distance of the centre: head west along Nygatan and keep going for about fifteen minutes. It consists of five long rows with 119 weatherbeaten log houses with battered wooden shutters. The houses are protected by law and any modernization is forbidden, including the installation of electricity. Take a peek inside, but bear in mind that they're privately owned by local people who use them as summer cottages. Beyond the parish village you'll find the **kyrka** (Mon–Fri 10am–4pm), a proud white neoclassical building with four mighty pillars supporting the domed roof. Inside there's an outstanding series of medieval sculptures, including the eight-hundred-year-old *Virgin of Skellefteå*, a walnut carving on the reverse side of the altar and one of the few remaining Romanesque images of the Virgin in the world.

On the way to the parish village you'll pass the **Nordanå Kulturcentrum**, a large and baffling assortment of buildings that's home to a theatre, a twee period grocer's shop (*lanthandel*) and a dire museum. Tucked away to the side of the *lanthandel* is *Nordanå Gårdens Värdshus*, a pleasant restaurant serving lunches for around 70kr.

To hold down the tourists a little longer, the **world's biggest moose** (ⓦwww .storalgen.se) is under construction on top of the 511metre-high Vithatten mountain, 15km south of Skellefteå. The wooden structure will be 45m high, with a viewing platform on top of its antlers and a restaurant inside its head; the monster moose will be nibbling at a huge fake pine tree, within which a lift will whisk people up to the restaurant. The moose is scheduled to be finished by December 2006; get there before Gävle's goat-burners do (see p.597).

Practicalities

Skellefteå's small centre is based around a modern square flanked by Kanalgatan and Nygatan; at the top of the square is the **bus station**, at the bottom the **tourist office** (late June to early Aug Mon–Fri 9am–6pm, Sat 10am–4pm, Sun 10am–4pm; early Aug to late June Mon–Fri 9am–5pm, Sat 10am–4pm; ☎0910/73 60 20, ⓦwww.turistinfo.skelleftea.se), at Trädgårdsgatan 7, which can provide all the usual information and help with accommodation. You can use Internet for free here, as well as at the library at Kanalgatan 73.

Of the central **hotels**, cheapest is the *Hotell Stensborg* at (☎0910/105 51, ⓦwww .hotell-stensborg.se; ❷/❸), just north of the train station, at Vinkelgränd 4. Near the main square, the *First Hotel Statt* at Stationsgatan 8 (☎0910/141 40, ⓦwww .firsthotels.se; ❸/❹) has comfortable rooms and the happening *Station 8* club downstairs (see overleaf). The smartest hotel is the *Scandic* (☎0910/75 24 00, ⓦwww.scandic -hotels.com; ❸/❺), just east of the centre at Kanalgatan 75. The STF **youth hostel**,

Parish villages

Consisting of rows of simple wooden houses grouped tightly around a church, **parish villages** are common throughout the provinces of Västerbotten and Norrbotten. After the break with the Catholic Church in 1527, the Swedish clergy were determined to teach their parishioners the Lutheran fundamentals. Church services became compulsory: in 1681, it was decreed that those living within 10km of the church should attend every Sunday, those between 10km and 20km every fortnight and those between 20km and 30km every three weeks. Within a decade parish villages had appeared throughout the region to provide the travelling faithful with somewhere to spend the night after attending church. The biggest and most impressive is in Gammelstad near Luleå (see below); another good example can be seen in Skellefteå (see p.607), while the parish village in Arvidsjaur (see p.630) is crowded with Sámi huts. They're no longer used in their traditional way, but people still live in the old houses, especially in summer, and sometimes even rent them out to tourists.

at Brännavägen 25 (℡0910/72 57 00, ⊛www.stfturist.se; doubles ❶, dorm beds from 240kr) – a rustic red two-storey building that's part of the luxury Stiftsgården conference centre by the banks of the Skellefte, 2km west of the centre – is well worth seeking out; take bus #4. For **campers**, *Skellefteå Campingplats* (℡0910/188 55, ⊛skecamp.mammon.se) is 2km north of the centre, just off the E4; it also has four-bed summer **cabins** costing 450kr per night, and heated year-round two-bed cabins for 320kr.

The best spot for **lunch** is *Carl Viktor*, Nygatan 40, or the twee *Lilla Mari* at Köpmangatan 13; both at around 70kr. Skellefteå's **restaurants** aren't exactly impressive, though the *M/S Norway* at Kanalgatan 58 does gorgeous, if somewhat pricey, Nordic specialities, such as fillets of ptarmigan or reindeer, from 280kr. Three blocks west of the main square, *Balzac* at Tjärhovsgatan 14 (℡0910/156 05, ⊛www .balzac.se) serves upmarket Swedish dishes from 140kr. Among the usual cluster of pizzerias, the best and most popular is *Monaco*, Nygatan 31, which also does takeaways. **Drinking** is best done at *O'Leary's* at Kanalgatan 31 or at *Old Williams Pub* in the main square, while the trendiest **club** in town is *Station 8* at Stationsgatan 8 (Fri & Sat; ⊛www.station8.se; entrance from Storgatan).

Luleå

The last city on the Bothnian Coast, **LULEÅ** lies at one end of the Malmbanan, the iron-ore railway that connects the ice-locked Gulf of Bothnia with the ice-free Norwegian port of Narvik in the Norwegian Sea. If you're heading north for the wilds of Gällivare and Kiruna, or to the sparsely populated regions inland, it's a good idea to spend a day or so here enjoying the lively atmosphere, the sights and the impressive range of bars and restaurants: Luleå is the last oasis in a frighteningly vast area of forest and wilderness spreading north and west.

Luleå was founded in 1621 around the medieval church and parish village of nearby Gammelstad (meaning Old Town; see p.610). Even in those days trade with Stockholm was important, and Gammelstad's tiny harbour soon proved inadequate to the task. In 1649, by royal command, the city was moved lock, stock and barrel to its present site – only the church and parish village remained behind. Shipping is still an important part of the local economy (in summer, you'll see a fleet of huge icebreakers resting in the harbour), but over recent years Luleå has become the high-tech centre of northern Sweden, specializing in metallurgy, research and education.

Arrival and information

The **train** and **bus** stations are about 500m apart at one end of the grid of parallel streets that make up the city centre. Luleå's **tourist office** is a short walk away in the Ebeneser Kulturcentrum at Storgatan 43b (mid-June to mid-Aug Mon–Fri 9am–7pm, Sat & Sun 10am–4pm; mid-Aug to mid-June Mon–Fri 10am–6pm, Sat 10am–2pm; ☏0920/29 35 00, ⊛www.lulea.se). Ask here about boat trips to some of the hundreds of mostly uninhabited islands in the archipelago off the coast. You can use the **Internet** here (10kr per 15min), or head for the city library at Kyrkogatan 15 (Mon–Thurs 10am–7pm, Fri 10am–6pm, Sat 11am–3pm) for free access. For information on **long-distance buses**, contact Länstrafiken (☏0771/10 01 10, ⊛www.ltnbd.se); for **taxis**, phone Taxi Luleå (☏0920/100 00) or 6:ans Taxi (☏0920/666 66).

Accommodation

The tourist office can provide a list of **private rooms** costing about 200kr per person per night. The **youth hostel** (☏ 0920/22 26 60, ⊛ web.telia .com/~u92017710; 150kr) in the centre at Sandviksgatan 26 is open year-round and has some single and double rooms (**❶**). The *Arcus* **campsite** (☏0920/43 54 00) is 5km east of the city centre, in Karlsvik.

Amber Stationsgatan 67 ☏0920/102 00, ⊛www .amber-hotell.nu. Small and cosy family-run place in an old wooden building near the train station. **❷**/**❸**

Aveny Hermelinsgatan 10 ☏ 0920/22 18 20, ⊛www.hotellaveny.com. Small, modern and

comfortable hotel, with reasonable prices in summer. **❷**/**❹**

Best Western Arctic Sandviksgatan 80 ☏0920/109 80, ⊛www.arctichotel.se. A recently renovated, smart little hotel with en-suite rooms. **❸**/**❹**

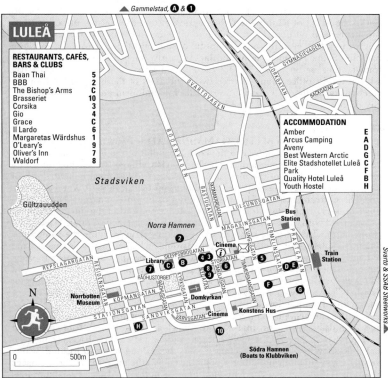

▲ *Gammelstad,* **A** & **❶**

LULEÅ

RESTAURANTS, CAFÉS, BARS & CLUBS

Baan Thai	5
BBB	2
The Bishop's Arms	C
Brasseriet	10
Corsika	3
Gio	4
Grace	C
Il Lardo	6
Margaretas Wärdshus	1
O'Leary's	9
Oliver's Inn	7
Waldorf	8

ACCOMMODATION

Amber	E
Arcus Camping	A
Aveny	D
Best Western Arctic	G
Elite Stadshotellet Luleå	C
Park	F
Quality Hotel Luleå	B
Youth Hostel	H

Stadsviken

Gültzauudden

Norra Hamnen

Bus Station

Cinema

Library

Train Station

Svartö & SSAB Steelworks

N

Norrbotten Museum

Domkyrkan

Cinema

Konstens Hus

Södra Hamnen
(Boats to Klubbviken)

0 — 500m

Elite Stadshotellet Luleå Storgatan 15
☎0920/27 40 00, ⊛www.elite.se. The oldest and
smartest of the city's hotels, right in the centre
of town, with tasteful, old-fashioned rooms and a
huge breakfast buffet. ❸/❺
Park Kungsgatan 10 ☎0920/21 11 49, ⊛www
.parkhotell.se. The least expensive of Luleå's
central hotels, basic but perfectly adequate, with
very cheap doubles (not en suite) in summer. ❷/❸
Quality Hotel Luleå Storgatan 17 ☎0920/20
10 00, ⊛www.choicehotels.se. A modern but
overpriced hotel with a seafaring theme – the
restaurant is a copy of the saloon of Gustaf III's
galleon. ❷/❺

The City

Luleå only really has one main street, the long **Storgatan**, south of which, past
the main square, Rådhustorget, is the **Domkyrkan**. The medieval original disappeared centuries ago and the current edifice, built in 1893, contains a modern
barrage of copper chandeliers hanging like Christmas decorations. Walking west
up Köpmangatan from the domkyrkan you'll find the **Norrbotten Museum**
(Tues–Fri 10am–4pm, Sat & Sun noon–4pm; free; ⊛www.norrbottensmuseum
.nu) at Storgatan 2. Among the humdrum resumé of county history are some good
displays on the Sámi culture that begins to predominate northwest of Luleå. Just
south of the Domkyrkan, **Konstens hus**, at Smedjegatan 2 (Tues–Fri 11am–6pm,
Sat & Sun noon–4pm; free), is worth a look for some interesting works by local
and not-so-local artists and sculptors.

If the weather's good, the next stop should be the **Gültzauudden** – a wooded
promontory with a sandy beach that's easily reached on foot from the centre by
heading west from Norra Hamnen. Gültzauudden's odd name derives from the
German shipbuilder, Christian Gültzau, who helped to make Luleå a shipbuilding
centre. For more room to stretch out, you're better off taking the *M/S Stella Marina*
out to the island of **Klubbviken**, the prettiest of the score of tiny islets that lie in
the archipelago offshore. Here you'll find an enormous sandy beach and enough
privacy to satisfy even the most solipsistic of souls. Boats leave from the southern
harbour (Södra Hamnen) from late June to early August; information from the
tourist office or on ☎070/565 07 61. For something different on a rainy day,
ask the tourist office about the free two-hour tours of the huge SSAB Tunnplåt
steelworks, on the aptly named Svartö (Black Island) peninsula 3km south of the
city centre.

Gammelstad

The original settlement of Luleå, **GAMMELSTAD** is 10km northwest of the city
centre. When the town moved to the coast a handful of the more religious stayed
behind to tend the church, and the attached **parish village** (see the box on p.608)
remained in use. One of the most important places of historical interest north of
Uppsala, the site proudly boasts inclusion on the UNESCO World Heritage
List. The **church** itself (mid-June to mid-Aug daily 9am–8pm, mid-Aug to mid-
June Mon–Fri 10am–2pm; free) was completed at the end of the fifteenth century
and adorned with the work of church artists from far and wide: both the decorated
choir stalls and the ornate triptych are medieval originals, while the sumptuous
pulpit is a splendid example of Bothnian Baroque, trimmed with gilt cherubs and
red and gold bunches of grapes. Look out for the opening above the south door,
through which boiling oil was generously poured over unwelcome visitors. Around
450 well-kept cottages are gathered around the church, making this the biggest
parish village in Sweden, though nowadays they're mostly unoccupied except
during important religious festivals.

Near the church at Kyrktorget 1 is Gammelstad's **visitor centre** (mid-June to
mid-Aug daily 9am–6pm; mid-Aug to mid-June Tues–Thurs 10am–noon and
1–4pm; ☎0920/29 35 81, ⊛www.lulea.se/gammelstad), which has an exhibition
and slide show about the village and is also the starting point of **guided walks**
(hourly 10am–4pm during summer; 30kr). Just down the hill is the **Friluftsmuséet
Hägnan** (Hägnan Open-Air Museum; June to mid-Aug daily 11am–5pm; free;

△ Gammelstad parish church

Ⓦwww.lulea.se/hagnan), an open-air heritage park whose main exhibits are two old farmstead buildings from the eighteenth century. During the summer there are demonstrations of rural skills such as sheep husbandry, the crafting of traditional wooden roof slates and the baking of *tunnbröd*, northern Sweden's unleavened bread. **Getting to Gammelstad** from Luleå is straightforward: bus #9 runs twice-hourly from the main bus stop on Smedjegatan.

Eating and drinking

Storgatan is stuffed with **restaurants** and **bars**, and you'll find that during the light summer evenings many young people simply drink their way from one end of the street to the other. As usual, you can happily order a beer in any of the restaurants listed below, with no obligation to eat there, too. For **drinking**, *Brasseriet* and *The Bishop's Arms* inside the *Elite* hotel are good places, while *Grace*, also inside the *Elite*, is the best **club** in town (open Wed, Fri & Sat).

Baan Thai Kungsgatan 22. Authentic and extensive Thai menu with all meat dishes at 89kr. Vegetarian and noodle dishes are 79kr; a strong beer is just 40kr. Don't miss it.

BBB Norra Hamnen ☎0920/22 00 00. On a boat in the northern harbour, the *Bar Bistro Brygga* is popular with a thirtysomething crowd for international food (150–250kr) and partying.

Brasseriet Södra Hamnen. Housed in the orange warehouse building by the southern harbour, this is one of the cheaper restaurants in town, and a popular drinking hole in the evenings. Pasta and other simple dishes for around 110kr.

Corsika Nygatan 14. Dark and dingy interior but worth seeking out for its traditional Corsican dishes (which you won't find anywhere else in Norrland), along with lots of steak and pizzas, all at 70–120kr. Lunch is popular at 60kr.

Gio Storgatan 27. One of Luleå's trendsetting bars. Wear your sharpest clothes, darkest shades and sip a chilled foreign beer before going clubbing. There's a predictably stylish yet surprisingly good-value menu of modern Swedish dishes for around 140kr.

Il Lardo Storgatan 40 ☎0920/22 29 99. Very trendy Italian restaurant/bar where pasta and meat dishes (from 130kr) and cocktails are served in minimalist white surroundings.

Margaretas Wärdshus Lulevägen 2, Gammelstad. Fine food, including Norrbotten delicacies at around 160kr, served in a beautiful old wooden house close to the church.

O'Leary's Köpmangatan 31. Tex-Mex mains for around 130kr, and a good selection of beer.

Oliver's Inn Storgatan 11. Pub grub and a good selection of beer. Known for its 1970s and 1980s music, which attracts a large crowd at weekends.

Waldorf Wasa City shopping centre, Storgatan 33. Renowned for its pizzas (from 60kr), and also serving Chinese and Japanese food.

Haparanda

Hard by the Finnish border and at the very north of the Gulf of Bothnia, **HAPARANDA** is not an easy place to like. The train station sets the tone of the place – an austere and rather grand-looking building reflecting Haparanda's aspirations to be a major trading centre. That never happened, and walking up and down the streets around the main square, Torget, can be a pretty depressing experience.

To fully understand why Haparanda is so grim, you need to know a little history: the key is the neighbouring Finnish town of **Tornio** (Torneå in Swedish). From 1105 to 1809, Finland was part of Sweden and Tornio was an important trading centre, serving markets across northern Scandinavia. But things began to unravel when Russia attacked and occupied Finland in 1807; the Treaty of Hamina then forced Sweden to cede Finland to Russia in 1809 – thereby losing Tornio. It was decided that Tornio had to be replaced, and so in 1821 the trading centre of Haparanda was founded, on the Swedish side of the new border along the River Torne. However, it proved to be little more than an upstart compared to its neighbour across the water. Nearly two hundred years on, with Sweden and Finland both now members of the European Union, Haparanda and Tornio have declared themselves a "Eurocity" – one city made up of two towns from different countries.

There are only a couple of sights in town: the train station building from 1918 and the peculiar **Haparanda kyrka**, a monstrous modern construction that looks like a cross between an aircraft hangar and a block of flats topped off in dark-coloured copper. When the church was finished in 1963 it caused a public scandal and has even been awarded a prize for being the ugliest church in Sweden. Then, after noting that Haparanda has the world's only golf course that crosses an international border, it's time to move on.

Practicalities

There are no **border formalities** and you can simply walk over the bridge to Finland and wander back whenever you like; it's worth remembering that Finland is an hour ahead of Sweden.

Haparanda's **tourist office** (June to mid-Aug Mon–Fri 8am–7pm, Sat & Sun 11am–7pm; mid-Aug to June Mon–Fri 9am–noon & 1–4pm; from Sweden ☎0922/120 10, from Finland ☎016/432 733, ⓦwww.haparandatornio.com) is actually in Finland, hence the above times are in **Finnish time**. The building is just over the bridge to Tornio in the Green Line Welcome Center. From June to August, it's also possible to get basic information from the *Stadshotel* in Haparanda's main square. Haparanda's STF **youth hostel** (☎0922/611 71; ⓦwww.haparanda vandrarhem.net; doubles ❶, dorm beds from 120kr) is a smart riverside place at Strandgatan 26 and has the cheapest beds in town, with good views across to Finland. Alternatively, there's the cheap-and-cheerful pension, *Resandehem*, in the centre of Haparanda at Storgatan 65b (☎0922/120 68; ❶). *Haparanda Stadshotel*, at

---

Moving on to Finland

It's perfectly feasible to **walk over the bridge to Finland**; indeed, the locals do this several times daily without batting an eyelid. However, with luggage, you may want to make use of the local Ringlinjen **bus** #2 that connects Haparanda with Tornio every hour or so. Additionally, the three daily Norrlandskusten buses that connect Sundsvall with Haparanda terminate at Tornio; departures from Haparanda to Tornio are at 6.35pm, 8.50pm and 10.50pm; in the other direction, buses leave Tornio at 6.10am, 8.10am, and 12.10pm (Finnish time). In Tornio, you can hop on a Finnish bus to Kemi and Oulu. Remember that Finland is one hour ahead of Sweden.

Torget 7 (☎0922/614 90, ⊛www.haparandastadshotell.se; ❸/❺), is the only **hotel** in town, an elegant and sumptuous place, dating from 1900, full of squeaky parquet floors and chandeliers.

Tornio (see p.612) has many more **bars** and **restaurants** than its Swedish neighbour, so you may want to do what the locals do and nip over into Finland for a bit of high life, especially at the weekend. In Haparanda, however, *Rickards Kök och Bar* next to the hostel at Strandgatan 26 is a good place for Swedish *dagens rätt* lunch and also **dinner** (from 90kr), while *Hasans Pizzeria* at Storgatan 88, close to Torget, does lunch for 55kr. Lunch and pizzas are also served at the Chinese restaurant *Leilani*, Köpmangatan 15, as well as a range of Chinese and Thai dishes in the 85–120kr bracket. *Nya Konditoriet* on Storgatan does decent coffee and cakes. For **drinking** in Haparanda, head for the pub *Ponderosa* at Storgatan 82, or try the *Gulasch Baronen* pub attached to the *Stadshotel*.

Travel details

Trains

Gävle to: Falun (11 daily; 1hr); Gällivare (2 daily; 15hr); Härnösand (daily; 2hr 50min); Kiruna (2 daily; 16hr); Luleå (2 daily; 12hr); Östersund (2 daily; 4hr); Stockholm (hourly; 1hr 20min); Sundsvall (11 daily; 2hr); Umeå (daily; 8hr 30min); Uppsala (6 daily; 1hr).
Härnösand to: Gävle (daily; 2hr 50min); Stockholm (daily; 4hr); Sundsvall (daily; 40min).
Luleå to: Gällivare (3 daily; 2hr 20min); Gävle (2 daily; 12hr); Gothenburg (daily; 20hr); Kiruna (3 daily; 3hr 30min); Stockholm (2 daily; 14–15hr); Umeå (daily; 4hr 30min); Uppsala (2 daily; 13hr).
Sundsvall to: Gävle (11 daily; 2hr); Härnösand (daily; 40min); Östersund (5 daily; 2hr 20min); Stockholm (8 daily; 3hr 20min), Uppsala (8 daily; 2hr 45 min).
Umeå to: Gällivare (daily; 5hr 40min); Gävle (daily; 8hr 30min); Gothenburg (daily; 14hr 40min); Luleå (daily; 4hr 30min); Stockholm (daily; 10hr); Uppsala (daily; 9hr).

Buses

Norrlandskusten express buses run seven times daily between Sundsvall and Umeå – three daily as far as Haparanda – and they're usually scheduled to connect with trains to and from Sundsvall. From Sundsvall, buses call at Härnösand (1hr); Ullånger (1hr 40min); Umeå (4hr); Skellefteå (6hr), Luleå (8hr 20min) and Haparanda (10hr 45min). Additionally, two daily **Ybuss** express buses run between Stockholm and Umeå, stopping at Sundsvall, Härnösand, Ullånger, Docksta, and Umeå, with onward connections from Sundsvall to Östersund.
Haparanda to: Kiruna (1–3 daily; 6hr).
Luleå to: Arvidsjaur (2–4 daily; 2hr 30min); Gällivare (4 daily; 3hr 15min); Jokkmokk (3 daily; 3hr); Kiruna (2 daily; 4hr 45min).
Skellefteå to: Arvidsjaur (3 daily; 1hr 50min).
Sundsvall to: Östersund (3 daily; 2hr 30min).
Umeå to: Storuman (2–4 daily; 3hr 40min); Tärnaby/Hemavan (Mon–Sat 3–4 daily; Sun daily; 6hr).

International trains

Luleå to: Narvik (2 daily; 7hr).
Gävle to: Narvik (2 daily; 18hr).

International buses

Haparanda to: Bodø (daily; 11hr 30min), Tornio (hourly; 5min).
Luleå to: Bodø (daily; 9hr).
Skellefteå to: Bodø (daily; 9hr).
Umeå to: Mo-i-Rana (daily; 7hr 50min).

International ferries

Umeå to: Vaasa (1–2 daily except Sat; 4hr).
Sundsvall to: Vaasa (weekly; 10hr).

3.6

Central and northern Sweden

I n many ways, the long wedge of land that comprises **central and northern Sweden** – from the shores of **Lake Vänern** up to the Finnish border north of the Arctic Circle – encompasses all that is most typical of the country. Rural and underpopulated, it fulfils the image most people have of Sweden: lakes, pine forests, wooden cabins and reindeer – a vast area of land that is really one great forest broken only by the odd village or town.

Folklorish **Dalarna** province is the most intensely picturesque region. Even a quick tour around one or two of the more accessible places gives an impression of the whole: red cottages with white doors and window frames, sweeping green countryside and water that is bluer than blue. Dalarna's inhabitants maintain a cultural heritage (echoed in contemporary handicrafts and traditions) that goes back to the Middle Ages. And the province is *the* place to spend midsummer, particularly Midsummer's Eve, when the whole region erupts in a frenzy of celebration featuring the age-old tradition of dancing around the maypole (an ancient fertility symbol), countless impromptu musical gatherings and much beer drinking.

The privately owned **Inlandsbanan**, the great inland railway, cuts right through central and northern Sweden and links most of the towns and villages covered in this chapter. Running from **Mora** to **Gällivare**, above the Arctic Circle, it ranks amongst the best European train journeys, an enthralling two-day, 1100-kilometre adventure. It's certainly a much livelier approach to the north than the east-coast run up from Stockholm. Buses connect the rail line with the **mountain villages** that snuggle alongside the Norwegian border – the Swedish *fjäll*, or fells, not only offer some of the most spectacular scenery in the country but also some of the best, and least spoilt, hiking in Europe. North of Mora, **Östersund** is the only town of any size, situated by the side of Storsjön, the "Great Lake", reputed to be home to Sweden's very own Loch Ness Monster. From here, trains head in all directions: west to Norway through the country's premier ski resort, **Åre**, south to Mora and Stockholm, east to Sundsvall on the Bothnian Coast, and north to Swedish Lapland.

The wild lands of the **Sámi** people make for the most fascinating trip in northern Sweden. Omnipresent reindeer are a constant reminder of how far north you are, but the enduring Sámi culture, which once defined much of this land, is now under threat. The problems posed by tourism are escalating, making the Sámi increasingly economically dependent on selling souvenirs and handicrafts. Further north, around industrial **Gällivare** and **Kiruna**, and as far as the Norwegian border near **Abisko**, the rugged **national parks** offer a chance to hike and commune with nature in Europe's last great wilderness.

Karlstad

Capital of the province of Värmland, **KARLSTAD** is named after King Karl IX, who granted the place its town charter in 1584. The town has had its fair share of

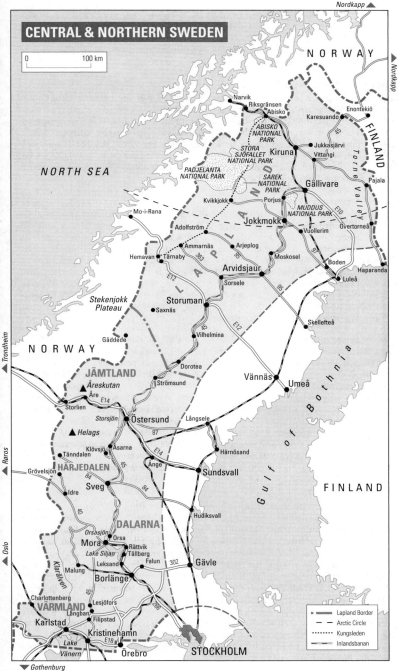

CENTRAL & NORTHERN SWEDEN

0   100 km

Nordkapp ▲

N O R W A Y

▶ *Nordkapp*

FINLAND

Narvik
Riksgränsen
Abisko
Enontekiö
Karesuando
45

ABISKO NATIONAL PARK

STORA SJÖFALLET NATIONAL PARK

Jukkasjärvi
Kiruna
Vittangi

NORTH SEA

PADJELANTA NATIONAL PARK

SAREK NATIONAL PARK

Gällivare

Pajala

Kvikkjokk
Porjus
MUDDUS NATIONAL PARK
E10

Mo-i-Rana
Adolfström
Jokkmokk
Vuollerim
Övertorneå

Torne Valley

Hemavan
Tärnaby
Ammarnäs
Arjeplog
Moskosel
Boden
Haparanda

363
Arvidsjaur
97
Luleå

E12
Sorsele

Stekenjokk Plateau
Storuman
Saxnäs

Skellefteå

45
Vilhelmina
E12

Gäddede

N O R W A Y

Dorotea

Vännäs
Umeå

Strömsund

JÄMTLAND
▲ *Åreskutan*
Åre
E14
Storlien

Gulf of Bothnia

▶ *Trondheim*

Långsele

Storsjön
Östersund
87

▲ Helags
Klövsjö
Åsarna
Härnösand

Tänndalen
HÄRJEDALEN
Änge
E14

FINLAND

▶ *Röros*

Grövelsjön
84

Idre
Sveg
84
Sundsvall

40

DALARNA
Hudiksvall

Orsasjön
Mora
Orsa
Rättvik
Tällberg

▶ *Oslo*

Klarälven
Malung
Lake Siljan
Leksand
Falun
302
Gävle
Borlänge

Charlottenberg
Lesjöfors
VÄRMLAND
Långban
Filipstad
286

Karlstad
Kristinehamn
Lake Vänern
E18
Örebro
STOCKHOLM

▼ *Gothenburg*

Legend:
▪▪▪ Lapland Border
– – – Arctic Circle
······ Kungsleden
—··— Inlandsbanan

disasters: devastating fires ripped through the centre in 1616, 1729 and, most cata-
strophically, in 1865, when a blaze that started in a bakery burnt virtually the entire
town, including the cathedral, to the ground. Rebuilding began apace, with an
emphasis on wide streets and large open squares to guard against another tragedy.
The result is an elegant and thoroughly likeable town.

Arrival and information

Draped along the shores of Lake Vänern roughly halfway between Stockholm
and Oslo, Karlstad is served by **trains** between the two capitals as well as services
along the western side of the lake from Gothenburg. Karlstad is also linked by
Swebus Express **bus** with Gothenburg and Gävle. The **tourist office** is inside
the library at Västra Torggatan 26 (June–Aug Mon–Fri 9am–7pm, Sat 10am–6pm,
Sun 11am–4pm; Sept–May Mon–Fri 9am–5pm, Sat 11am–3pm; ☎054/29 84 00,
⊛www.karlstad.se), where you can also access Internet for free. Ask here about
boat trips on Lake Vänern.

Accommodation

Karlstad's STF *Ulleberg* **youth hostel** (☎054/56 68 40, ⊛www.stfturist.se; doubles
❶, dorm beds from 135kr) is located 3km west of the centre in a rambling old
three-storey house, and is reachable on buses #32 and #92 towards Bellevue. The
nearest **campsites** are a seven-kilometre drive out of town west along the E18:
Skutbergets Camping (☎054/53 51 20, ⊛www.camping.se/s10) is open all year,
whereas *Bomstad Badens camping* (☎054/53 50 68, ⊛www.bomstad-baden.se) 2km
further away and beautifully situated on the lakeshore, is open only June–August.
From mid-June to mid-August, the campsites can be reached on the daily Badbus-
sen (#18; hourly 10.30am–5.30pm; 25min), which runs from Stora Torget via
Drottninggatan to the beaches at Bomstad.

Carlton Järnvägsgatan 8 ☎054/673 77 00,
⊛www.carltonhotel.se. Located in the pedestrianized centre, this is one of the cheaper hotels in
Karlstad. ❷/❸

Drott Järnvägsgatan 1 ☎054/10 10 10, ⊛www
.drotthotel.se. Smart, elegant place dating from
1908; it's next to a busy road just 50m from the
train station. ❸/❻

Freden Fredsgatan 1a ☎054/21 65 82, ⊛www
.fredenhotel.com. Cheap and cheerful place close
to the train station, also offering dorm beds from
160kr. ❶/❷

Ibis Hotel Karlstad City Västra Torggatan 20
☎054/17 28 30, ⊛www.ibishotel.com. Good-
value hotel in the centre of town with a large
breakfast buffet and free evening parking. ❶/❷

Radisson SAS Plaza Västra Torggatan 2
☎054/10 02 00, ⊛www.plaza-karlstad.nu. Large,
modern and plush with fantastic views over the
city from its panoramic sauna. ❸/❺

Scandic Winn Norra Strandgatan 9–11
☎054/776 47 00, ⊛www.scandic-hotels.com.
Central, upmarket hotel with good views over the
river, and a large new sauna area. ❸/❺

The Town

It's best to start your wanderings around town from the airy main square, Stora
Torget, one of the largest market squares in the country. The rather austere **Peace
Monument** in front of the Town Hall commemorates the peaceful dissolution of
the union between Sweden and Norway in 1905, which was negotiated in Karlstad.
Unveiled fifty years after the event, it portrays an angry woman madly waving a
broken sword whilst planting her right foot firmly atop a dismembered soldier's head:
"feuds feed folk hatred, peace promotes people's understanding" reads the inscription.
The Neoclassical **Rådhuset** was the cause of much local admiration upon its completion in 1867, just two years after the great fire – town worthies were particularly
pleased with the two fearsome Värmland eagles that adorn the building's roof, no
doubt hoping they would ward off another devastating blaze. Across Östra Torggatan,
the nearby **Domkyrkan** was consecrated in 1730, although only its arches and walls
survived the flames of 1865. Its most interesting features are the altar, made from
Gotland limestone with an Orrefors crystal cross, and the crystal font.

Continuing east along Kungsgatan and over the narrow Pråmkanalen, the road swings left and changes its name to Nygatan ahead of the longest arched stone bridge in Sweden, **Östra Bron**. Completed in 1811, this massive construction spans 168m across the eastern branch of the Klarälven River. It's claimed that the builder, Anders Jacobsson, threw himself off the bridge and drowned, afraid his life's work would collapse – his name is engraved on a memorial stone tablet in the centre of the bridge. On sunny days (and Karlstad is statistically one of the sunniest places in Sweden) the nearby wooded island of **Gubbholmen**, reached by crossing the stone bridge and turning right, is a popular place for catching the rays; take a picnic and dip your toes in the refreshing waters of the river.

Back in town, at the junction of Norra Standgatan and Västra Torggatan, the two-storey yellow wooden building with the mansard roof dates from 1781, one of the handful of dwellings that weren't destroyed in the great fire. This building, the **Biskopsgården** (Bishop's Residence), owes its survival to the massive trees on its south side, which formed a natural firebreak, as well as to the sterling fire-fighting efforts of the bishop of the time. The only other houses that survived are located in the **Almen district**, next to the river at Älvgatan; the oldest parts of these wooden buildings date from the 1700s, but their facades are all nineteenth-century.

A half-hour walk along Jungmansgatan, Hööksgatan and then Rosenborgsgatan will bring you to **Mariebergsskogen** (June–Aug daily 7am–10pm; free; ⊛www .mariebergsskogen.se). Originally modelled on the Skansen open-air museum in Stockholm, this contains a number of old wooden buildings from across Värmland. There's also a petting zoo, a children's train and a small nature museum.

Eating and drinking

Eating and **drinking** in Karlstad is a joy, with a good selection of restaurants specializing in everything from Spanish to vegetarian dishes. For a Swedish provincial town, **bars** are also thick on the ground – the *Bishop's Arms* is particularly popular.

Ankdammen Magasin 1, in the inner harbour just across the railway line. Pleasant restaurant specializing in fish (mains from 160kr), with seating on a wooden jetty. Open June to mid-Aug.

Bishop's Arms Kungsgatan 22. Classic British-style pub with a wide range of beers. A great location overlooking the river, with outdoor seating in summer.

Blå Kungsgatan 14. One of the more upmarket bar/restaurants facing the Stora Torget, with tapas, quality Swedish dishes from 220kr and a pleasant summer terrace.

Casa Antonio Drottninggatan 7. Good Spanish restaurant with tapas from 39kr and paella for two for 298kr.

Glada Ankan Kungsgatan 12. Lively first-floor restaurant and bar with a balcony overlooking Stora Torget. It serves Tex-Mex and Swedish dishes (130–230kr) and is a nice place for coffee.

Harrys Kungsgatan 16. American-style bar, café and restaurant in the main square, popular with drinkers in the evening, and with open-air seating in summer. Pub grub from 85kr, other main dishes from 130kr.

Legends Drottninggatan 4. Karlstad's trendiest restaurant and bar, serving fusion food priced between 105–200kr. Closed Sun.

Rådhuscafeet Tingvallagatan 8. Elegant café in the town hall; enter from the left side of the building.

Listings

Banks FöreningsSparbanken, Kungsgatan 8; Handelsbanken, Tingvallagatan 17; Nordea, Tingvallagatan 11–13; S-E Banken, Drottninggatan 24.

Beaches Sundstatjärnet, in the centre of town by the swimming pool on Drottning Kristinas väg; Mariebergsviken, take bus #12, #14 or #35; Bomstad, take bus #18.

Bus station Drottninggatan. Information on buses in Värmland on ☎054/19 09 09 or at ⊛www .kollplatsen.com.

Car rental Avis, Hamngatan 24 ☎054/15 26 60; Europcar, Hagalundsvägen 29 ☎054/18 23 20.

Police Nya Infanterigatan 22 ☎054/14 50 00.

Systembolaget Drottninggatan 26 (Mon–Wed 10am–6pm, Thurs & Fri 10am–7pm, Sat 10am–2pm).

Taxi Taxi Kurir ☎054/15 02 00.

Train station Hamngatan. For information, call ☎054/14 33 50 or 0771/75 75 75.

Around Lake Siljan

Swedes consider the area around **Lake Siljan** (@www.siljan.se) to be the heartland of the sizeable **Dalarna** province, itself perhaps the most typically "Swedish" area of the country. The idyllic landscape here is one of verdant cow pastures, gentle rolling meadows sweet in summer with the smell of flowers, and tiny rural villages nestling on the lakeshore. The lush vegetation of the Siljan region, enriched by the waters of the lake and benefiting from the relative lack of forest, has produced what the Swedes call *öppna landskap* (literally, "open landscapes"). Indeed, the temperate surroundings of Lake Siljan, coupled with age-old traditions and local handicrafts, weave a subtle spell on many visitors, too, and it certainly all adds a pleasing dimension to the small, low-profile towns and villages of this part of Dalarna. **Mora** and **Leksand** are the best of the lakeside towns; **Orsa**, on the other hand, with its massive bear park, is a must for all animal lovers and makes a perfect stop on any journey north from Dalarna.

Trains operated by Tågkompaniet call at the towns around the lake and terminate in Mora. **Inlandsbanan trains** (see opposite) call at Orsa on their way north from Mora, but it's easier to reach by bus. Another good way to get around Lake Siljan is to rent a **bike** from one of the tourist offices, which also dole out the handy, free *Siljanskartan* cycling map of the region. Since Lake Siljan and its surrounding districts are popular Swedish holiday destinations, there's no shortage of **accommodation** – though it can be a good idea to book ahead in the peak season of mid-June to mid-August.

Mora

If you've only got time to see part of the area, then **MORA** is the place to head for, especially if you're travelling further north with the Inlandsbanan (see opposite). The largest of the lakeside settlements, Mora's main draw is the work of Sweden's best-known artist, **Anders Zorn** (1860–1920), who moved here in 1896 and whose paintings are exhibited in the excellent **Zorn Museum** at Vasagatan 36 (mid-May to mid-Sept Mon–Sat 9am–5pm, Sun 11am–5pm; mid-Sept to mid-May Mon–Sat noon–5pm, Sun 1–5pm; 50kr, @www.zorn.se) – look out for the self-portrait and the especially pleasing *Midnatt* (*Midnight*) from 1891, which depicts a woman rowing on Lake Siljan, her hands blue from the cold night air. You might also want to wander across the lawn and take in his home, **Zorngården** (mid-May to mid-Sept Mon–Sat 10am–4pm, Sun 11am–4pm; mid-Sept to mid-May Mon–Sat noon–3pm, Sun 1–4pm; 50kr; guided tours only), where he lived with his wife, Emma, during the early 1900s. However, what really makes this place unusual is the cavernous ten-metre-high hall where the couple lived out their roles as darlings of local society, with its steeply V-shaped roof, entirely constructed from wood and decked out in traditional Dalarna designs and patterns. Also on Vasagatan, but on the other side of the church, is the **Vasaloppsmuséet** (Vasaloppet Museum; mid-June to mid-Aug daily 10am–5pm; mid-Aug to mid-June Mon–Fri 10am–5pm; 30kr; @www.vasaloppet.se), with an exhibition on the history of the Vasaloppet cross-country ski race, which started 500 years ago with the attempts of two Mora men to catch up with King Gustav Vasa, who was fleeing from the Danes. Held every March, the ninety-kilometre race attracts 14,000 skiers.

Once you've covered the town's sights, you might want to take a **cruise** (mid-June to mid-Aug only) on the lake aboard the lovely old steamship *M/S Gustaf Wasa* (timetables vary; info on ☎010/252 32 92, 070/542 10 25 or @www.wasanet.nu); it costs 120kr for a round-trip to Leksand or 80kr for a two-hour lunch cruise.

Practicalities

Mora's **tourist office** (mid-June to mid-Aug Mon–Fri 9am–7pm, Sat & Sun 10am–5pm; mid-Aug to mid-June Mon–Fri 10am–5pm, Sat 10am–1pm; ☎0250/56 76 00, @www.mora.se) is at Stationsvägen 3 inside Mora train station (not Mora

Inlandsbanan practicalities

The **Inlandsbanan** – the great inland railway that links central Sweden with Swedish Lapland – is a mere shadow of its former self today. In 1992, spiralling costs and low passenger numbers forced Swedish Railways to sell the line to the municipalities the route passes through, and a private company, Inlandsbanan AB, was launched. It now operates only as a tourist venture in summer – generally from mid-June to mid-September. The Inlandsbanan line officially starts in Kristinehamn, just east of Karlstad; however, much of the route from there to Mora (operating from late June to mid-August only) is by bus rather than by train, and you're best off starting in Mora.

Every day, one train trundles each way on the **Mora–Östersund** (6hr; 347kr) and **Östersund–Gällivare** (14hr; 697kr) sections – if you want to travel the line in one go, the distances are such that it'll take two days, with an overnight stop in Östersund. However, you'll get much more out of it if you make a couple of stops on the way and take in some of the stunning scenery passing by your train window first-hand – special guides available on board contain commentaries and information about places along the route. Timetables are approximate and the train is likely to stop whenever the driver feels like it, maybe for a spot of wild strawberry picking or to watch a beaver damming a stream. It's certainly a fascinating way to reach the far north of the country, but isn't recommended if you're in a rush.

Tickets cost 108kr per 100km. Under-26 InterRail passes (see p.35) give free travel, while ScanRail pass holders get a 25-percent discount on the **Inlandsbanankort** (full price 1195kr). Available on board, this card gives unlimited travel on the line for fourteen days. For **timetables** and other **information**, ask at any tourist office along the line, call ☎063/19 44 12 or visit ⬤www.inlandsbanan.se.

Strand station). SJ and Tågkompaniet **trains** terminate at the latter; **buses** (⬤www .dalatrafik.se), including the surrogate Inlandsbanan services from Kristinehamn (see box above), use the bus station opposite, actually on Moragatan, but just off the main Strandgatan. The cheapest place to stay is the *Kristineberg* **youth hostel**, right opposite the Mora train station at Kristinebergsgatan 1 (☎0250/150 70, ⬤www.trehotell.nu; doubles ❶, dorm beds 130kr); its reception is inside the *Hotell Kung Gösta* (see below). Mora's **campsite**, *Mora Camping* (☎0250/276 00, ⬤www .moraparken.se), is a ten-minute walk from the centre along Hantverkaregatan, which begins near the bus station: there's a good beach here. Among the **hotels**, the biggest and best is the *First Hotel Mora* at Strandgatan 12 (☎0250/59 26 50, ⬤www .firsthotelmora.com; ❸/❺), opposite Mora Strand train station, with a choice of modern and traditional rooms. *Hotel St Mikael*, Fridhemsgatan 15 (☎0250/150 70, ⬤www.trehotell.nu; ❸/❻), is small, with tasteful rooms, while *Hotell Kung Gösta*, Kristinebergsgatan 1, is handy for Mora train station (☎0250/150 70, ⬤www .trehotell.nu; ❸/❹).

As for **eating and drinking**, all the hotels serve up a decent *dagens rätt* for around 60kr – there's little to choose between them. 🍴 *Wasastugan*, a huge log building overlooking the lake at Tingnäsvägen 6, is particularly lively in the evenings, with Tex-Mex dishes from 90kr, and regular club nights. Alternatively, *Pizzeria Prima* at Fridhemsplan 2d or *Pizzeria Torino* at Älvgatan 73 serve up virtually any pizza you can think of, all at reasonable prices. In summer, coffee and cakes can be enjoyed al fresco at *Helmers Konditori* at Kyrkogatan 10.

Orsa and the bear park

North of Mora, the Dalarna landscape becomes more mountainous and less populous, and the only place of any note, **ORSA**, is also the last town of any significance for miles around. Sitting aside Orsasjön, a northerly adjunct of Lake Siljan, Orsa is right in the heart of Sweden's bear country: it's reckoned that there are several hundred

△ Brown bear, Orsa

brown bears roaming the dense forests around town, though few sightings are made, except by the hunters who cull the steadily increasing numbers. Your best chance of seeing one is to visit the bear park, **Orsa Grönklitt Björnpark** (mid-May to mid-June & mid-Aug to mid-Sept daily 10am–3pm; mid-June to mid-Aug daily 10am–6pm; 75kr; ⓦwww.orsa-gronklitt.se), 13km outside town and reachable by twice-daily bus #118 from Mora, which stops at Orsa train station. The bears here are not tamed or caged, but wander around the nine hundred square kilometres of the forested park at will; instead, it's the humans who are restricted, having to clamber up viewing towers and along covered-in walkways. Funny, gentle and vegetarian for the most part, the bears are occasionally fed the odd dead reindeer or moose that's been killed on the roads. Out of season, they hibernate in specially constructed lairs that are monitored by closed-circuit television cameras.

From the train station on Järnvägsgatan, it's a short walk to Orsa's **tourist office** at Dalagatan 1 (mid-June to mid-Aug Mon–Fri 10am–7pm, Sat & Sun 10am–5pm; mid-Aug to mid-June Mon–Fri 10am–5pm, Sat 10am–1pm; ☎0250/55 25 50, ⓦwww.siljan.se). If you need to stay, try the atmospheric *Orsa Stadshotell* (☎0250/409 40, ⓦwww.orsahotell.se; ❸) in the old station building at Järnvägs-gatan 4. Alternatively, the STF **youth hostel** (☎0250/421 70, Ⓔstfvandrarhem. orsa@telia.com), located 1km east of the centre at Gillevägen 3, has private rooms (❶) and dorm beds for 150kr.

Leksand

Located at the southernmost point of Lake Siljan, three hours from Stockholm, **LEKSAND** is perhaps the most popular and traditional of Dalarna's lakeside villages and is certainly worth making the effort to reach at Midsummer, when **festivals** recall age-old dances performed around the maypole (Sweden's maypoles, incidentally, aren't erected until June: spring comes late here, and in May there are few leaves on the trees and often some lingering snow). Celebrations culminate in the **kyrkbåtsrodd**, or church boat races, an aquatic procession of sleek wooden longboats that the locals once rowed to church every Sunday. The race starts on Midsummer's Day in nearby Siljansnäs and continues for ten days around the lake, reaching Leksand on the first Saturday in July. Between twenty and twenty-five teams take part, all cheered on by villagers at the water's edge. Another event worth coming here for is **Musik vid Siljan** (Music by Lake Siljan; ☎0248/102 90, ⊛www.musikvidsiljan.se) in the first week of July: nine days of nonstop classical, jazz and dance-band music performed in churches, on the lakeside and at various locations in the surrounding forest – check with the tourist office for the latest details on this and the boat races.

At other times, there's little to do in Leksand other than take it easy for a while. Stroll along the riverside down to **Leksands kyrka**, which enjoys a magnificent setting overlooking the river and the lake. One of the biggest churches in the country, it has existed in its present form since 1715, although the oldest parts date back to the thirteenth century.

All **trains** to Mora stop in Leksand; the **tourist office** (mid-June to mid-Aug Mon–Fri 9am–7pm, Sat & Sun 10am–5pm; mid-Aug to mid-June Mon–Fri 10am–5pm, Sat 10am–1pm; ☎0247/79 61 30, ⊛www.siljan.se) is at the train station. Leksand's comfortable **youth hostel**, one of the oldest in Sweden, is over the river, around 2km from the train station in Parkgården (☎0247/152 50, ⓔstf .vandrarhem.leksand@brevet.nu; doubles ❶, dorm beds 130kr). Otherwise, there are two **hotels** to choose between: *Moskogen*, at Insjövägen 50 (☎0247/146 00, ⊛www .moskogen.com; ❹), with luxury cottages decked out with traditional wooden wall panelling and woven textiles in Dalarna colours; and the beautiful *Korstäppan* at Hjortnäsvägen 33 (☎0247/123 10, ⊛www.korstappan.se; ❹), also tastefully done out in traditional styles. The nearest **campsite**, *Leksands Camping*, is a twenty-minute walk from the tourist office along Tällbergsvägen (☎0247/803 13, ⊛www .leksand.se/camping_stugby). The best place **to eat** is at *Siljans Konditori & Bageri*, facing the main square at Sparbanksgatan 5, with excellent open sandwiches, light snacks and salads for 50kr – in summer there are a couple of tables on the front terrace. Alternatively, try *Bosporen*, just opposite at Torget 1, a passable place serving pizzas and meat and fish dishes, which does lunch for 60kr and is also a good spot for a **drink**.

Falun

If you're in Dalarna for more than a couple of days, the copper-mining town of **FALUN** can be a relief after the folksiness of the lakeside and the visiting hordes that dominate the area in summer. Interestingly, this is where a 14-year-old Osama bin Laden spent two summers with his family in the early 1970s, driving around in a Rolls Royce flown in from Saudi Arabia, and staying at a cheap hotel. The best time to be in Falun is mid-July, when musicians from all over the world take over the town for a four-day **International Folk Music Festival** – check dates with the tourist office or visit ⊛www.falufolk.com.

Just twenty minutes northeast of Borlänge, Dalarna's biggest – and dullest – town, Falun is essentially an industrial settlement, though a surprisingly pleasant one at that. At its peak in the seventeenth and eighteenth centuries the mine here produced two-thirds of the world's copper ore, and Falun acquired buildings and a layout commensurate with its status as Sweden's second largest town. In 1761, however, two devastating fires wiped out virtually all of central Falun – the few old wooden houses to survive can be found in the areas of Elsborg (south of the centre), Gamla Herrgården and Östanfors (both north of the centre), which are worth seeking out for an idea of the cramped conditions the mineworkers had to live in.

The **mine** itself, 1km west of town at the end of Gruvgatan, was said by the botanist Carl von Linné to be as dreadful as hell itself. An unnerving element of eighteenth-century mining was the omnipresence of copper vitriol gases, a strong preservative: one case is recorded of a young man known as Fat Mats whose body was found in the mines in 1719. He'd died 49 years previously in an accident, but the corpse was so well preserved that his erstwhile fiancee, by then an old woman, recognized him immediately. The famous "Falun red" paint, which is made from the copper mine's waste materials, also contains the wood-preserving vitriol, which explains why millions of Swedes paint their timber houses deep red.

The mine and the surrounding industrial landscape is a UNESCO World Heritage site, and there's a new **visitor centre** (May, June, Aug & Sept daily 10am–5pm; July daily 10am–6pm; Oct–April Mon–Fri 11am–5pm; free; @www.kopparberget.com) highlighting the area's history. Hour-long **guided tours** of the mine (5–6 daily; July 10am–6pm; Sept Mon–Fri noon–4.30pm, Sat noon–4pm; Oct–July 12.30pm & 2pm; 90kr) begin with a lift ride that takes you 55m down to a network of old mine roads and drifts – be warned that the temperature drops to 6°C. Make sure you also walk around the various old mining buildings and peer into the one-hundred-metre-deep "Great Pit", **Stora Stöten**, which appeared on Midsummer's Day in 1687 – the result of a huge underground collapse caused by extensive mining and the unplanned driving of galleries and shafts.

Apart from the mines, Falun's attractions boil down to the **Dalarnas Museum** at Stigaregatan 2–4 (Mon–Fri 10am–5pm, Sat & Sun noon–5pm; Sept–April Wed till 9pm; 40kr; @www.dalarnasmuseum.se), which includes sections on the county's folk art, and, 2km east of the centre on the hill overlooking town, Sweden's **Riksskidstadion** (National Ski Stadium), where you can take a **lift** (mid-May to Aug daily 10am–6pm; 20kr) up to the top of the ninety-metre ski jump for a terrifying peek down.

Practicalities

From the **train** and **bus stations**, east of the centre, take the underpass beneath the main road and head towards the shops in the distance and Falun's **tourist office** (mid-June to mid-Aug Mon–Fri 9am–7pm, Sat 9am–6pm, Sun 11am–5pm; mid-Aug to mid-June Mon–Fri 9am–6pm, Sat 10am–2pm; ☎023/830 50 @www.visitfalun.se), opposite the *First Hotel Grand* on Trotzgatan.

The nearest **youth hostel** (☎023/105 60, @www.stfvandrarhemfalun.com), a modern affair with dorm beds from 140kr, is 3km east of the train station, at Vandrarvägen 3 – take bus #701 or #712 from the centre. The nearest **campsite** (☎023/835 63) is up by the Riksskidstadion, about fifteen minutes' walk from town, or take bus #705. **Hotels** include the upmarket *Scandic Lugnet Falun*, east of the centre and near the ski stadium at Svärdsjögatan 51 (☎023/669 22 00, @www.scandic-hotels.com; ❸/❻); the newly renovated *First Hotel Grand* at Trotzgatan 9–11 (☎023/79 48 80, @www.firsthotels.se; ❸/❺); and the more homely *Park Inn*, near the train station, at Bergskolegränd 7 (☎023/70 17 00, @www.falun.parkinn.se; ❸/❺).

In terms of **eating and drinking**, Falun far outstrips the towns around Lake Siljan in quality as well as choice. Next to the mine's visitor centre, the *Geschwornergården* restaurant is a good place for lunch (from 65kr). In town, the most popular place is *Banken* at Åsgatan 41, housed in an old bank building and serving grilled meat, fish and hamburgers from 130kr. Downstairs in the same building is the posh but cosy *Två rum och kök*, where meat and fish dishes start at 200kr. Another popular spot is *Rådhuskällaren*, a cellar under the town hall in the main square, Stora Torget, serving delicious, if somewhat pricey, food – reckon on 260kr upwards. The *Bakfickan* **bar** next door is the place to hang out among Falun's trendy young things, while the excellent *Pub Engelbrekt*, at Stigaregatan 1 also serves bar food (from 90kr) and has regular live rock music.

Sveg and around

From Mora and Orsa, the Inlandsbanan chugs through the northern reaches of Dalarna, offering breathtaking vistas of the vast forested hillsides that comprise some of the emptiest tracts of land in the whole of Sweden. Indeed, it's a good three hours before the train finally reaches the first place of any significance: **SVEG**, Härjedalen's uneventful main town, a sparsely populated fell region that belonged to Norway until 1645, something that has left its mark in the local dialect. The area offers excellent terrain for walking, as well as some of Sweden's most magnificent scenery – more than thirty mountains exceed 1000m, the highest peak being **Helags** (1796m), whose icy slopes support Sweden's southernmost glacier. Härjedalen is also home to the largest single population of brown bears in the country, as well as a handful of shaggy musk oxen, ferocious creatures that have wandered across the border from Norway.

In 1273, Sveg was the site of a parliament called to hammer out a border treaty between Sweden and Norway. Since then, things have quietened down considerably and even on a Friday night in midsummer you're likely to find yourself alone in the wide streets lined with grand old wooden houses. A graceful river runs right through the centre of town and there are some delightful meadows and swimming spots just a few minutes' walk from the centre.

Sveg's **tourist office** (mid-June to mid-Aug Mon–Fri 9am–4pm; mid-Aug to mid-June Mon–Fri 1–5pm; ☎0680/107 75, ⊕www.herjedalsporten.se) is in the centre of town at Kyrkgränd 1, next to the campsite. If you're keen to **stay overnight**, try the old-fashioned *Hotell Härjedalen* at Vallarvägen 11 (☎0680/103 38, ⊕www.hotellharjedalen.se; ❷); or the more upmarket *Hotell Mysoxen* (☎0680/170 00, ⊕www.sveg.info/logi/mysoxen.php; ❷/❸), close to the train station at Fjällvägen 12. The *Mysoxen* also houses the local STF **youth hostel** (same contact details; doubles ❶, dorm beds 175kr). The **campsite** (☎0680/130 25) is located right on the river. Your best chances of not **eating** alone are at the greasy-spoon *Inlandskrogen* café next to the bus and train stations on Järnvägsgatan, or at the *Knuten* pizzeria at Berggatan 4.

Klövsjö

From Sveg, the Inlandsbanan veers northeast to skirt a large area of marshland separating northern Härjedalen from neighbouring Jämtland, a province known, amongst Swedes at least, as the location of one of the country's most beautiful villages, **KLÖVSJÖ**. There's some justification to this – it's a thoroughly charming place of log cabins set amid rolling pastures, while the distant lake and forested hills that enclose the settlement on all sides create the feeling that it's in a world of its own. Ten farms continue to work the land much as in days gone by – ancient grazing rights still in force mean that horses and cows are free to roam through the village at will – while flowering meadows, trickling streams, wooden barns and the smell of freshly mown hay drying on frames in the afternoon sun cast a wonderful spell. Once you've taken a look at the old wooden buildings of the seventeenth-century farm estate, **Tomtangården** (July to mid-Aug daily; free), there's not much else to do except take in the bitingly clean air and admire the beauty – you won't find anywhere in Sweden as picturesque as this. Unfortunately, there are no rooms to let in the village itself, but the **tourist office** on the main road (Mon–Fri noon–3.30pm; ☎0682/41 36 60, ⊕klovsjo.utveckling.ab@telia.com) has cabins to rent in the vicinity (around 500kr per cabin for up to four people).

To **reach Klövsjö**, get off the train at **Åsarna**, a low-key cross-country skiing centre, from where buses make the twenty-minute trip to the village five times a day (note that only the southbound train has a good connection). There's a well-equipped **campsite** (☎0687/302 30, ⊕www.asarnaskicenter.se) and **youth hostel** behind the ski centre (same phone and website; doubles ❶, dorm beds from 120kr). There's a **tourist office** in the same ski centre (daily: June–Aug 8am–8pm; Sept–May 8am–7pm; ☎0687/301 93, ⊕staffan@ucab.se). Opposite the train station, the *Åsarna Hotell* (☎0687/300 04; ❷) has basic rooms; there's a restaurant and bar on site.

Östersund

North of Åsarna, the Inlandsbanan hugs the shores of the enormous Storsjön lake before pulling into one of central Sweden's most agreeable towns, **ÖSTERSUND**.

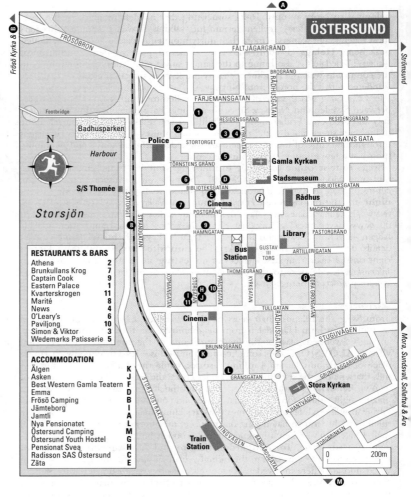

ÖSTERSUND

RESTAURANTS & BARS

Athena	2
Brunkullans Krog	7
Captain Cook	9
Eastern Palace	1
Kvarterskrogen	11
Marité	8
News	4
O'Leary's	6
Paviljong	10
Simon & Viktor	3
Wedemarks Patisserie	5

ACCOMMODATION

Älgen	K
Asken	J
Best Western Gamla Teatern	F
Emma	D
Frösö Camping	B
Jämteborg	I
Jamtli	A
Nya Pensionatet	L
Östersund Camping	M
Östersund Youth Hostel	G
Pensionat Svea	H
Radisson SAS Östersund	C
Zäta	E

It's well worth spending a day or two in what is the last large town until Gällivare, some 700km to the north inside the Arctic Circle – if you're heading north this is your final chance to indulge in a bit of high life, since the small towns and villages beyond have few of the entertainment or culinary possibilities available here. Östersund is also a major **transport hub**: the E14 highway cuts through town, offering good links to Sundsvall and west to Trondheim in Norway, while as well as the summer Inlandsbanan service there are trains west to Åre, Storlien and on to Trondheim in Norway, east to Sundsvall and south to Stockholm and Gothenburg, plus express buses north to Gällivare, which run all year and are a better option than the Inlandsbanan if you're in a hurry.

Arrival and information

From the **train station** on Strandgatan it's a five-minute walk north to the town centre; the **bus station**, off Rådhusgatan, is more central. A couple of blocks to the north, the excellent **tourist office** (June Mon–Fri 9am–7pm, Sat & Sun 9am–3pm; late June to early Aug Mon–Sat 9am–9pm, Sun 9am–7pm; Aug Mon–Fri 9am–5pm, Sat & Sun 9am–3pm; Sept–May Mon–Fri 9am–5pm; ☎063/14 40 01, ⊛www.turist.ostersund.se) is opposite the minaret-topped Rådhus at Rådhusgatan 44, and sells the **Östersund Card** (140kr), which includes free transport on city buses, and free parking and museum entry – good value if you're in town for a couple of days. You can use the **Internet** for free at the city library (Mon–Thurs 10am–7pm, Fri 10am–6pm, Sat 11am–3pm), opposite the bus station at Rådhusgatan 25.

Accommodation

For accommodation, the modern STF **youth hostel** (☎063/341 30, ⊛www .stfturist.se; late June to early Aug) is ten minutes' walk north of the train station at Södra Gröngatan 32 and has some double rooms (❶) as well as dorm beds for 165kr. More atmospheric, though, is the ⚑ *Jamtli Vandrarhem* (☎063/12 20 60, ⊛www.stfturist.com; doubles ❶, dorm beds from 140kr), another STF hostel, set amid the old buildings in the open-air museum grounds. **Campers** can stay either at *Östersunds Camping* (☎063/14 46 15, ⊛www.camping.se/z11), 3km south down Rådhusgatan (bus #2, #6 or #9); or over on Frösön at *Frösö Camping* (☎063/432 54, ⊛www.ncsab.se; mid-June to mid-Aug) – take bus #3 from the centre.

Älgen Storgatan 61 ☎063/51 75 25, ⊛www.hotelalgen.se. Small, central and handy for the train station, with comfortable en-suite rooms. ❷/❹

Asken Storgatan 53 ☎063/51 74 50, ⊛www .jamteborg.se. Only eight non-smoking rooms, all en suite but rather bland and simple. ❷/❸

Best Western Gamla Teatern Thoméegränd 20 ☎063/51 16 00, ⊛www.gamlateatern.se. An atmospheric hotel in an early twentieth-century theatre with sweeping wooden staircases, tall doorways and wide corridors, but with disappointingly plain rooms. ❸/❺

Emma Prästgatan 31 ☎063/51 78 40, ⊛www .hotelemma.com. Large, nicely renovated en-suite rooms in an old building on the main shopping street. ❷/❹

Jämteborg Storgatan 54 ☎063/51 01 01, ⊛www.jamteborg.se. Cheap, simple rooms in a central location; the price includes parking and a solarium and sauna. ❷/❸

Nya Pensionatet Prästgatan 65 ☎063/51 24 98, ✉britishblue@spray.se. Near the train station, this tastefully decorated house, dating from around 1900, has just six rooms, with a shared toilet and shower in the corridor. ❶/❷

Pensionat Svea Storgatan 49 ☎063/51 29 01, ⊛www.jamteborg.se. Seven tweely decorated rooms with shared toilet and shower. Discounted rates for long-term stays. ❷

Radisson SAS Östersund Prästgatan 16, ☎063/55 60 00, ⊛www.ostersund.radissonsas .com. The most luxurious hotel in the city, just north of Stortorget. ❸/❺

Zäta Prästgatan 32 ☎063/51 78 60, ⊛www .hotel-z.se. Simple, plain but comfortable rooms, with cable TV and sauna. ❷/❹

The Town

Östersund's position on the eastern shore of the mighty **Storsjön** (Great Lake) lends the town a seaside holiday atmosphere, unusual this far inland. An instantly likeable place, it's made up of the familiar grid of parallel streets. Strolling through the pedestrianized centre is a relaxed experience; take time out and sip a coffee around the wide open space of Stortorget and watch Swedish provincial life go by, or amble along one of the many side streets that slope down to the still, deep waters of the lake. Here you may be lucky enough to spot Sweden's own Loch Ness Monster, **Storsjöodjuret** (⊛www.storsjoodjuret.com), a huge dog-headed creature of which sightings are numerous if unsubstantiated.

The main attraction in town is **Jamtli** (late June to mid-Aug daily 11am–5pm; mid-Aug to late June Tues–Fri 10am–4pm, Sat & Sun 11am–5pm; 90kr late June to mid-Aug, otherwise 60kr; ⊛www.jamtli.com), an impressive open-air museum a quarter of an hour's walk north of the centre along Rådhusgatan. For the first few minutes it's a bit bewildering, full of people milling around in traditional country costume, farming much as their ancestors did. They live here throughout the summer and everyone is encouraged to join in – baking, tree-felling, grass-cutting. Kids, naturally, love it, and you'd have to be pretty cynical not to enjoy the enthusiastic atmosphere. Some intensive work has been done on getting the settings right: the restored and working interiors are gloomy and dirty, with no hint of the usual pristine historical travesty. You'll see women milking cows, and children running around barefoot in dimly lit farm cottages. Outside, even the planted crops and roaming cattle are historically accurate, while there's an old-fashioned local store, Lanthandel, among the wooden buildings around Jamtli's bustling main square. The indoor **museum** on the same site shows off the county collections: a rambling houseful of local exhibits that includes monster-catching gear devised by nineteenth-century lakeside worthies. The museum's prize exhibits are the awe-inspiring Viking **Överhogdal tapestries**, which date from the ninth or tenth centuries – discovered in an outhouse in 1910, the tapestries are crowded with brightly coloured animals and buildings.

Back in the centre, apart from the **Stadsmuseum** (City Museum; Mon–Fri 10am–4pm, Sat & Sun 1–4pm; 30kr) – a crowded two hundred years of history in a building the size of a shoebox – on Rådhusgatan, and the neighbouring **Gamla kyrkan** (Mon–Fri 8.30am–5pm), there's not a vast amount in the way of sights. Take a look though, at the **harbour**, with its fleet of tiny boats and the occasional seaplane bobbing about on the clean water. Immediately to the north of the harbour is the tiny **Badhusparken** – an inordinately popular spot in summer for catching a few rays.

Finally, it's possible to go monster-spotting on a **lake cruise** on board *S/S Thomée* – a creaking old wooden steamship built in 1875. Routes and timetables vary but always include a two-hour trip around the lake (June to early September; 80kr), amongst other destinations; contact the tourist office for information and bookings.

Frösön

Take the foot- or road-bridge across the lake and you'll come to the island of **Frösön**. People have lived here since prehistoric times – Frösön's name derives from the Viking settlement on the island and its association with the pagan god of fertility, Frö. There's plenty of good walking here, as well as a couple of historical stops. Just over the footbridge, look out for the eleventh-century **rune stone** that tells of a man called Östmadur (East Man), son of Gudfast, who brought Christianity to the people of Jämtland – presumably from some point to the east. From here you can clamber up the nearby hill of Öneberget, where you'll find the remains of the fourth-century settlement of Mjälleborgen – the most extensive in Norrland.

Follow the main road west and up the hill for about 5km (or take bus #3 from the centre of Östersund) to the beautiful **Frösö kyrka**, an eleventh-century church with a detached wooden belltower. In 1984, archeologists digging under the church's altar came across a bit of birch stump surrounded by the bones of bears, pigs, deer and squirrels – evidence of the cult of ancient gods, the *Aesir*, and an indication that the site has been a place of worship for almost two thousand years. Today, the church is one of the most popular in Sweden for marriages – especially at midsummer, for which you have to book years in advance.

Eating, drinking and nightlife

Gastronomically, Östersund has more to offer than any town further north. For **breakfast**, the train station café is good value and always busy, while **coffee** and cakes are best had at *Wedemarks Patisserie*, Prästgatan 27, where you can also make up your own sandwiches.

Athena Stortorget 3. Pompously decorated place tucked away in a corner of Stortorget, offering tasty pizzas from 65kr and dinner mains around 200kr.

Brunkullans Krog Postgränd 5. This old-fashioned restaurant, with polished lanterns and a heavy wooden interior, is Östersund's premier eating place, offering traditional Swedish fare as well as more international fish and meat dishes. In summer, there are tables in the garden at the rear.

Captain Cook Hamngatan 9. A selection of delicious Australian-style grilled delights (around 180kr) that really draw in the crowds – also a popular place for a drink, with an extensive beer and whisky selection.

Eastern Palace Storgatan 15. The best option for Chinese and Mongolian food, with all the usual dishes for around 100kr; the lunch buffet is great value at 62kr.

Kvarterskrogen Storgatan 54, ☎063/10 68 68. Upmarket restaurant, with tables decked out in fresh linen and high prices to match. Lamb, entrecôte, beef and sole dishes, as well as northern Swedish delicacies, start at 180kr.

Marité Sjötorget 3, ☎063/12 42 26, ⊛www .marite.nu. This trendy serving with fusion food

(140–230kr) transforms into a club popular with a mature crowd at weekends.

News Samuel Permans gata 9. Good-value international food for around 100kr, and a bar specializing in cocktails and whiskey. You can puff away on a hookah pipe, too.

O'Leary's Storgatan 28. Popular American sports pub offering a large selection of beer and a Tex-Mex menu with mains around 125kr.

Paviljong Prästgatan 50b. The best Thai and Indonesian restaurant in central northern Sweden – make the most of it. Main courses go for around 120kr (try the excellent chicken with garlic chilli and Thai basil), or there's a lunch for 60kr.

Simon & Viktor Prästgatan 19. An English-style watering hole at the top end of Stortorget serving upmarket pub grub for around 190kr.

Listings

Bike rental The kiosk in Badhuspark rents out bikes for 100kr per day; alternatively, Cykelogen, Kyrkogatan 45 (☎063/12 20 80), has similar prices.

Bus enquiries For information on all buses, call ☎0771/10 01 10 or visit ⊛www.lanstrafiken-z .se. The express bus, Inlandsexpressen (#45), leaves from the bus station north to Gällivare (2 daily); there's no need to book as seats are guaranteed. Tickets for the Ybuss express service to Stockholm are sold at the *Puck* handbag shop on Hamngatan 13; call 063/51 00 21 for information.

Car rental Avis, Bangårdsgatan 9 ☎063/10 12

50; Europcar, Hovvallsgränd 1 ☎063/57 47 50; Hertz, Fagerbacken 55 ☎063/14 94 00.

Left luggage Lockers at the train station for 15kr.

Pharmacy Prästgatan 51 (Mon–Wed & Fri 9am–6pm, Thurs 10am–7pm, Sat 9am–4pm, Sun 11am–4pm).

Police Köpmangatan 24 ☎063/15 25 00.

Systembolaget Kyrkgatan 66 (Mon–Wed & Fri 10am–6pm, Thurs 10am–7pm, Sat 10am–2pm).

Taxi Taxi Östersund ☎063/19 90 00.

Trains For SJ information, call ☎0771/75 75 75. The Inlandsbanan leaves daily (late June to early Aug), heading south for Mora at 3.10pm and north to Gällivare at 7.10am.

West to the Norwegian border

The E14 highway and the train line from Östersund follow the route trudged by medieval pilgrims on their way to Nidaros (now Trondheim) over the border in Norway, a twisting course that threads its way through sharp-edged mountains rising high above a bevy of fast-flowing streams and deep, cold lakes. Time and again the eastern Vikings assembled their armies beside the holy Storsjön lake to begin the long march west, most famously in 1030 when King Olaf of Norway collected his mercenaries for the campaign that led to his death at the Battle of Stiklestad. The Vikings always crossed the mountains as quickly as possible, and so today – although the scenery is splendid – there's nothing much to stop for en route, other than the skiing and walking centres of **Åre** and **Storlien**.

Åre

The alpine village of **ÅRE**, just over one hours' train ride from Östersund, is Sweden's most prestigious ski resort, with 44 lifts and snow guaranteed between December and May. Recently, the already excellent facilities have been upgraded to host the FIS World Ski Championships (⊛ www.worldcupare.com) in 2007. During the snowbound season, rooms are like gold dust and prices sky-high: if you do come to ski, book accommodation well in advance through the tourist office or, better still, come on a package tour. Equipment rental isn't too expensive: downhill and cross-country gear starts at 190kr per day – contact the tourist office.

In summer, the village is a haven for ramblers, sandwiched as it is between Åresjön lake and a range of craggy hills overshadowed by the mighty 1420-metre-high Åreskutan mountain. A network of **walking tracks** criss-crosses the hills or, for a more energetic scramble, take the **Kabinbanan**, Sweden's only cable-car (100kr return), up to a viewing platform, from where it's a thirty-minute clamber to the summit. The view is stunning – on a clear day you can see over to the border with Norway and a good way back to Östersund. Bear in mind, though, that even the shortest walk back to Åre takes two hours and requires some stamina.

The **tourist office** (May to mid-June & late Sept to early Dec Mon–Fri 9am–5pm, Sat & Sun 10am–3pm; mid June to early Sept & early Dec to April daily 9am–6pm; ☎0647/177 20, ⊛www.visitare.se) is 100m up the steps opposite the train station at St Olavsväg 35. It has detailed mountain maps and endless information on hiking and mountain biking in the nearby mountains and further afield – ask for the excellent *Hiking in Årefjällen* booklet.

When it comes to **hotels**, the cheapest option is the new *Åre Ski Lodge* hostel along the main road (☎0647/510 29, ⊛www.areskilodge.se), which has comfortable private rooms (❷) and some dorm beds (from 180kr); there's also the Brattlandsgården **youth hostel** (☎0647/301 38, ⊛www.brattlandsgarden.com; doubles ❶, dorm beds from 130kr), 8km south of town along the main road. The nearest **campsite** is at Såå (☎0647/321 22; late June to mid-August only), 7km east of Åre along the road to Östersund. Åre's **eating** possibilities aren't up to much, but there are several cheap places around the square: try the cheerful *Café Bubblan*, which does reasonable lunches of pies and sandwiches, or the more substantial dishes and pizzas served at nearby *Werséns*. At the cable-car terminus, *Bykrogen* does decent main meals from 100kr.

Storlien

Just 6km from the Norwegian border and a favourite feasting spot for the region's mosquitoes, **STORLIEN** is the place to stop if you plan to do some hiking, which is good and rugged around here. The countryside hereabouts is also prime berry-picking territory (the rare cloudberry grows here), while mushrooms, in particular chanterelles, can be found in great number. There's not much else here though, apart from a **tourist office** inside the train station (Mon–Fri 9.30am–2.30pm; ☎0647/705 70, ⊛www.storlienfjallen.se), a supermarket and a couple of **hotels**, the best of which is *Storliens Högfjällshotell* (☎0647/701 70, ⊛www.storliens hogfjallshotell.se, ❻), ten minutes' walk from the tourist office, a luxury affair with nearly two hundred well-appointed rooms and a swimming pool.

Storlien's **youth hostel** (☎0647/700 50, ⊛ww.stfstorvallen.se; doubles ❶, dorm beds from 150kr) is a four-kilometre walk across the railway tracks to the E14 and then left down the main road towards Storvallen. **Eating and drinking** is limited, the best option being the *Flamman* at Vintergatan 46, serving Swedish main dishes from 120kr; otherwise, coffee, pizzas and burgers are available at *Sylvias Kanonbar* on the main road.

Moving on from Storlien, trains leave twice daily for Trondheim in Norway. In the opposite direction, there are three daily trains to Östersund as well as direct night trains to Stockholm and Gothenburg.

North to Swedish Lapland

Beyond Östersund the **Inlandsbanan** slowly snakes its way across the remote Swedish hinterland heading for **Swedish Lapland** (⊛turism.norrbotten.se), known in Swedish as the province of Lappland; a truly enormous region stretching from just south of the town of Vilhelmina to the Finnish and Norwegian borders in the north, and east towards (but not including) the Bothnian Coast. This is a vast and

△ Swedish Lapland

scarcely populated region where the train often has to stop for moose and reindeer – and occasionally bears – to be cleared from the tracks. On the other occasions that the train comes to a halt with no station in sight, it's usually for a reason – a spot of berry-picking, perhaps – while at the Arctic Circle everyone jumps off for photos.

Route 45, the **Inlandsvägen**, shadows the train line on its way north to Gällivare. It's easy to drive and well surfaced, though watch out for suicidal reindeer – once they spot a car hurtling towards them they'll do their utmost to throw themselves underneath it. **Bus** travellers on the Inlandsexpressen from Östersund to Gällivare will also take this route. A direct bus, the Lapplandspilen, also links Vilhelmina and Storuman with Stockholm.

Vilhelmina and Storuman

Four hours up the Inlandsbanan from Östersund, **VILHELMINA** is a pretty little town that was formerly an important forestry centre. The timber business moved out of town some ten years ago, however, and the main source of employment nowadays is a telephone-booking centre for Swedish Railways. Sweden's coldest temperature on record was set in a small village near here in December 1941, when it plummeted to -53°C. Despite the grandeur hinted at by the town's name (from Fredrika Dorotea Vilhelmina, the wife of King Gustav IV Adolf), Vilhelmina remains a quiet little place with just one main street. The principal attraction is the **parish village**, nestling between Storgatan and Ljusminnesgatan, whose thirty-odd wooden cottages date back to 1792 when the first church was consecrated. It's since been restored, and today the cottages can be rented out via the **tourist office**, a five-minute walk from the **train and bus stations** (mid-June to mid-Aug Mon–Fri 9am–7pm, Sat & Sun 10am–1pm and 3–6pm; mid-Aug to mid-June Mon–Fri 9am–5pm; ☎0940/152 70, ⊛www.vilhelmina.se).

Vilhelmina's **campsite**, *Rasten Saiva Camping* (☎0940/107 60), is about ten minutes' walk from the centre and has two- and four-berth cabins for rent for 250kr and 300kr respectively, as well as a great sandy **beach**; head down Volgsjövägen from the centre and take the first left. There are two central **hotels** in town: the ostentatious *Wilhelmina* (☎0940/554 20, ⊛www.hotell.vilhelmina.com; ❸/❹), at Volgsjövägen 16, and the friendly *Lilla* (☎0940/150 59, ⊛www.lillahotellet. vilhelmina.com; ❸) at Granvägen 1.

There isn't exactly a multitude of **eating and drinking** options: try the à la carte restaurant at the *Hotell Wilhelmina* for traditional northern Swedish dishes and

65kr lunches, or the plain *Pizza Quinto*, Volgsjövägen 27. Coffee, cakes and lunch (60kr, including cake) can also be had at *Stenmans Konditori*, Volgsjövägen 21. In the evenings, locals gravitate towards *Svanen* opposite *Lilla Hotellet* for a **drink** or two.

Storuman

STORUMAN, an hour up the line from Vilhelmina, is a transport hub for this part of southern Lapland. **Buses** run northwest up the E12, skirting the Tärnafjällen mountains, to Tärnaby and Hemavan, before wiggling through to Mo-i-Rana on the Norwegian coast and, in the opposite direction, down to Umeå via Lycksele, where there's a connection with the main coastal rail line.

There's not much to Storuman itself apart from the large **statue** of the red Wildman at the northern edge of town, an old symbol for Lapland representing strength and determination – the centre consists of one street supporting a couple of shops and banks. The **tourist office** (late June to mid-Aug Mon–Fri 9am–8pm, Sat & Sun 10am–5pm; mid-Aug to late June Mon–Fri 9am–5pm; ☎0951/333 70, ⓦwww.entrelappland.se) is 50m right of the **train station** on Järnvägsgatan.

While it's possible to stay here – the **youth hostel** (☎0951/333 80; ❶) and the luxurious *Hotell Toppen* (☎0951/777 00, ⓦwww.hotelltoppen.se; ❸/❹) are both only a ten-minute walk up the hill at Blåvägen 238 – it's much better to head off into the mountains for some good **hiking** and **fishing**.

If you do stay, try the **restaurant** at *Hotell Toppen*, which has a lunch buffet for 65kr; alternatively, there's the basic, reasonably priced *Blå Stjärnan* at Blåvägen 246, behind the Konsum supermarket in the main square, and the *Kina Restaurang* opposite the train station, which does Chinese food, pizzas and lunch deals.

Arvidsjaur

Three hours north of Storuman on the Inlandsbanan, **ARVIDSJAUR** is by far the largest town you'll have passed since Östersund – though that's not saying much. For centuries this was where the region's Sámi gathered to trade and debate, until their agenda was hijacked by the Protestant missionaries who established their first church here in 1606. Arvidsjaur's success was secured when silver was discovered in the nearby mountains and the town flourished as a staging point and supply depot. Despite these developments, the Sámi continued to assemble here on market days and during religious festivals, building their own parish village, the **Lappstaden** (daily tours from mid-June to mid-August at 5pm, 30kr; at other times you can walk in for free), of simple wooden huts at the end of the eighteenth century. About eighty of these have survived at the north end of town; they're still used today for the Storstämningshelgen festival over the last weekend in August. There are still around twenty Sámi families in Arvisdjaur, making their living from reindeer husbandry.

The **tourist office** (mid-June to mid-Aug daily 9.30am–6pm; mid-Aug to mid-June Mon–Fri 8.30am–noon and 1–4.30pm; ☎0960/175 00, ⓦwww .arvidsjaurlappland.se) is at Östra Skolgatan 18c, just off Storgatan and five minutes' walk from the train station up Lundavägen. They can advise on activities in the surroundings, such as pedalling down a disused railway line on a trolley bicycle (70kr for 5hr, includes picnic), or white-water rafting on the nearby Pite River. They'll also fix you up with a **private room** for around 150kr per person. The best place to stay, however, is *Rallaren* (☎070/682 32 84; late June–Aug), a wonderful old wooden house near the train station, tastefully restored by a local artist, that operates as a luxury **youth hostel** with dorm beds for 135kr. There's also the cosy *Lappugglan* hostel, conveniently situated at Västra Skolgatan 9 (☎0960/124 13, ⓔlappugglan@hem.utfors.se) with dorm beds for 150kr; or you could try *Camp Gielas* (☎0960/556 00), which also has **cabins** (495kr for up to 4 people) set beside Tvättjärn, one of the town's many lakes, a few minutes' walk along Storgatan from the tourist office. The best **hotel** in town is *Hotell Laponia* at Storgatan 45

The Arctic Circle

Ten kilometres south of Jokkmokk, Route 45 and the Inlandsbanan finally cross the **Arctic Circle**, the imaginary line marking the southernmost latitude where the Midnight Sun can be seen at the summer solstice. On the train, this is occasion enough for a bout of whistle-blowing as it pulls up to allow everyone to take photos of the hoardings announcing the crossing. Due to the fluctuating inclination of Earth's axis, the line moves north and south within a 180-kilometre-wide area in a forty-thousand-year-cycle, and is currently creeping northwards at a rate of up to 15m a year. The actual place of the circle is now around 1km north, but for argument's sake this spot is as good as any (though it will be back at the marked spot in the year 22,000, if you can wait). Painted white rocks curve away over the hilly ground, a crude but popular representation of the circle: one foot on each side is the standard photographic pose.

(☎0960/555 00, ⊛www.hotell-laponia.se; ❸/❺), with a swimming pool and comfortable, modern en-suite rooms, some of which are in a budget annex (❶). Be warned that in winter much of the town's accommodation is booked by Europe's leading car companies, who come to the area to test-drive new models on the frozen lakes – book well in advance to secure a room.

For **snacks** and **coffee**, try *Kaffestugan* at Storgatan 21, which has sandwiches and salads for around 50kr. There's a small choice of **restaurants**: for pizzas and Greek food, try *Afrodite* at Storgatan 10, which has a 65kr lunch deal. For finer food, head for the *Hotell Laponia*, which serves delicious Lappish, including local reindeer, for 120–150kr; or, from mid-June to August, their new Sámi hut-style 🦌 *Laponiakåtan* restaurant, overlooking Nyborgstjärnen lake. A good place for a **drink** is the Scottish-themed *Old Duck Inn* at Stationsgatan 9, with Murphy's on tap and a good selection of Scotch malt whisky; just down the street at number 18, *Stalo Krog* is a cheaper bar, with beer from 30kr. If you're self-catering, consider visiting the Renomera shop at Larstorpsvägen 22, which sells delicious fresh reindeer products such as sausages and smoked meat.

Jokkmokk

During his journey through Lapland, the botanist Carl von Linné said "If not for the mosquitoes, this would be earth's paradise"; his comments were made after journeying along the river valley of the Lilla Luleälven during the short summer weeks when the mosquitoes are at their most active. **JOKKMOKK**'s Sámi name comes from one particular bend (*mokk*) in the river (*jokk*), which runs through a densely forested municipality the size of Wales with a population of just 6500; needless to say, the town is a welcome oasis, though not an immediately appealing one. Once wintertime Sámi quarters, a market and church heralded a permanent settlement by the beginning of the seventeenth century. Today, as well as being a well-known handicrafts centre, the town functions as the Sámi capital and is home to the Samernas Folkhögskola, the only further education college teaching handicrafts, reindeer husbandry and ecology in the Sámi language.

Jokkmokk's fantastic **Ájtte Museum** (*ájtte* means "storage hut" in Sámi), a brief walk east of the centre on Kyrkogatan, off Storgatan (mid-June to mid-Aug daily 9am–6pm; mid-Aug to mid-June Mon–Fri 10am–4pm; May to early June & Sept also Sat & Sun noon–4pm; 50kr; ⊛www.ajtte.com), is the place to really mug up on the Sámi. Displays and exhibitions recount the tough existence of the original settlers of northern Scandinavia and show how things have slowly improved over time – today's Sámi are more dependent on snow scooters and helicopters to herd their reindeer than on the age-old methods employed by their ancestors. There are some imaginative temporary exhibitions on Sámi culture and local flora and fauna (including mosquitos), and the museum staff can also arrange day-trips into the surrounding marshes for a spot of mushroom-picking. Close to the museum on Lappstavägen, the **alpine garden** (late June to early Aug Mon–Fri 10am–4pm, Sat & Sun 10am–3pm; other times by arrangement on ☎0971/101 00; 25kr) is home to moor king, mountain avens, glacier crowfoot and other vegetation to be found on the fells around Jokkmokk.

Have a look, too, at the **Lappkyrka**, off Stortorget, a recent copy of the eighteenth-century church that stood on this site. The octagonal design and curiously shaped tower betray a Sámi influence, but the surrounding graveyard wall is all improvisation: the space in between the coarsely hewn timbers was used to store coffins during winter until the thaw in May, when the Sámi could go out and dig graves again – temperatures in this part of Sweden regularly plunge to -30°C and below in winter.

Practicalities

Arriving by **Inlandsbanan**, it's a short walk south up Stationsgatan to Stortorget, the central square where you'll find the main bus stop. If you're here for the winter market (when the Inlandsbanan isn't running), you'll need to take the Inlandsexpressen **bus**, or alternatively get off the coastal train at Murjek (between Boden and Gällivare), from where buses run west to Jokkmokk five times a day. Two buses a day leave Jokkmokk for Kvikkjokk (for the Padjelanta Trail; see p.636).

Jokkmokk's **tourist office**, at Stortorget 4 (mid-June to mid-Aug daily 9am–7pm; mid-Aug to mid-June Mon–Fri 8.30am–4pm; ☎0971/222 50, ✪www.turism.jokkmokk.se), is a few minutes' walk from the train station along Stationsgatan. The **youth hostel** (☎0971/559 77, ✪www.jokkmokkhostel.com; doubles ❶, dorm beds from 160kr) is located in a wonderful old house with a garden at Åsgatan 20, behind the tourist office. The *Jokkmokk-Camping-Center* **campsite** (☎0971/123 70, ✪www.jokkmokkcampingcenter.com) is a three-kilometre walk southeast of town on the Lilla Lule River, off Route E97 to Luleå. Of the town's two **hotels**, ⚐ *Jokkmokk* has a convenient and attractive lakeside setting at Solgatan 45 (☎0971/777 00, ✪www.hoteljokkmokk.se; ❸/❺), large en-suite rooms and a big sauna area; *Hotell Gästis* at Herrevägen 1 (☎0971/100 12, ✪www.hotell-gastis.com; ❸/❹) is nothing to write home about, with simple, modern en-suite rooms.

Jokkmokk has a limited number of **eating** and **drinking** possibilities. The cheap and cheerful *Restaurang Kowloon* at Föreningsgatan 3 has lunch for 65kr and Chinese meals for around 90kr at other times, while pizzas from 65kr and simple fry-ups are available at *Restaurang Opera* at Storgatan 36. For traditional Sámi dishes

---

The Jokkmokk Winter Market

Now over 400 years old, the great **Jokkmokk Winter Market** (*Jokkmokks Vintermarknad*; ✪www.jokkmokksmarknad.com) is held in the first week of February (Thurs–Sun), and sees 30,000 people force their way into town, increasing the population tenfold. It's the best and coldest time of the year to be in Jokkmokk – there's a Wild West feeling in the air – with lots of drunken stall holders trying to flog reindeer hides and other unwanted knick-knacks to even more drunken passers-by – and all in, literally, Arctic temperatures. The **reindeer races** can be a real spectacle: held on the frozen Talvatissjön lake behind the *Jokkmokk* hotel, man and beast battle it out on a specially marked track on the ice; however, the reindeer often have other ideas and frequently veer off with great alacrity into the crowd, sending spectators fleeing for cover. Staying in town at this time of year means booking accommodation a good year in advance (although some private rooms become available in the autumn before the market). A smaller and less traditional autumn fair is held at the end of August (around the 25th) – an easier though poorer option.

such as reindeer, head for the restaurant at the Ájtte Museum, where lunch costs 60kr – the cloudberries and ice cream here are simply divine. The best place to drink is the *Restaurang Opera*; failing that, try the bar inside the *Jokkmokk* hotel – if you've drunk your way round Jokkmokk this far you won't mind the inebriated late-night company here.

Gällivare

Last stop on the Inlandsbanan and by far the biggest town since Östersund, **GÄL-LIVARE** is far more pleasant than you'd imagine from its industrial surroundings. Strolling around its open centre is a great antidote to the small inland villages along the train route. There's a gritty ugliness to Gällivare that gives the place a certain charm: a steely grey mesh of modern streets that has all the hallmarks of a city, although on a scale that's far too modest for the title to be applied with any justification. It's also a good base for hiking in the nearby national parks (see p.635).

Arrival, information and accommodation

Swedline (⊛www.swedline.se) flies between Gällivare's Lapland **airport**, 10km east of the centre, and Stockholm. Gällivare's **train station** is right next to the **tourist office** at Centralplan 3 (mid-June to mid-Aug 8am–10pm; mid-Aug to mid-June

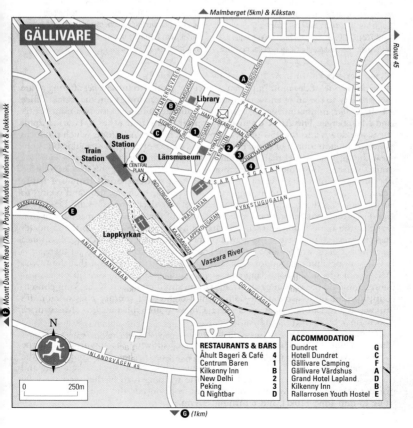

▲ Malmberget (5km) & Kåkstan

GÄLLIVARE

▶ Route 45

Library

Bus Station

Train Station

Länsmuseum

CENTRAL-PLAN

Lappkyrkan

Vassara River

◀ F Mount Dundret Road (7km); Porjus; Muddus National Park & Jokkmokk

N

INLANDSVÄGEN 45

0   250m

RESTAURANTS & BARS	
Åhult Bageri & Café	4
Centrum Baren	1
Kilkenny Inn	B
New Delhi	2
Peking	3
Q Nightbar	D

ACCOMMODATION	
Dundret	G
Hotell Dundret	C
Gällivare Camping	F
Gällivare Värdshus	A
Grand Hotel Lapland	D
Kilkenny Inn	B
Rallarrosen Youth Hostel	E

633

▼ G (1km)

Mon–Fri 9am–4pm; ☎0970/166 60, ⊛www.visit.gellivare.se), which stays open until the Inlandsbanan train from Östersund arrives. Here you can get good free maps, hiking information and tickets for the mine tours (see below). They can also fix you up with a **private room** for around 150kr per person, plus a booking fee of 25kr. The popular *Rallarrosen* **youth hostel** (☎0970/143 80, ⊛www.explore lapland.com; bookings required) is behind the train station at Barnhemsvägen 2, just across the river; it has dorm beds (150kr) in several cabins as well as private rooms (❶). The hostel doubles as an adventure centre and rents out bikes and canoes, and can arrange dog-sledding and snow scooter safaris. Nearby, *Gällivare Camping* (☎0970/100 10, ⊛www.gellivarecamping.com) has year-round cabins (450kr for 2 people). If you have your own transport, the most interesting place to stay is in the simple wooden huts at the reconstructed shanty town, **Kåkstan**, on Malmberget, the hill just to the north of the town centre, where a four-berth hut costs around 350kr; contact the tourist office.

Dundret ☎0970/145 60, ⊛www.dundret.se. At the foot of Dundret mountain and next to the ski slopes. Comfortable hotel rooms and cabins in the town's most luxurious hotel, a short taxi ride from the station. ❺

Hotell Dundret Per Högströmsgatan 1 ☎0970/550 40. Actually a small pension, with just seven rooms and shared shower and toilet. ❷/❸

Gällivare Värdshus Hellebergsvägen 5 ☎0970/162 00, ⊛home.swipnet.se/vardshuset. A German-run cheapie that's an excellent central

choice and a good place to meet backpackers. ❷/❸

Kilkenny Inn Per Högströmsgatan 9 ☎0970/77 22 80, ⊛www.kilkenny.nu/hotellet. Decent en-suite rooms in the same building as the lively *Kilkenny Inn* bar. ❷/❸

Grand Hotel Lapland Lasarettsgatan 1 ☎0970/77 22 90, ⊛www.grandhotellapland .com. Opposite the station, this is the best central hotel, with tastefully decorated rooms and the *Q Nightbar*. ❸/❹

The Town

Gällivare is one of the most important sources of **iron ore** in Europe, offering a rare opportunity to see an open working mine. Bus tours, starting from the tourist office (3.5hr; 200kr; minimum age 13; book ahead outside summer), visit two mines: Aitik and Malmberget. The **Aitik open-cast copper mine** tour (Tues & Thurs at 2pm) takes you down into the 350-metre-deep pit, the biggest in Europe, which produces nineteen million tonnes of copper ore and two tonnes of gold per year. The bus stops near the gigantic shovel machines and bulldozers (often operated by women – the mine's statistics prove they're better, more efficient drivers), and you may be allowed to climb into one. The tour of the **Malmberget underground iron-ore mine** (daily at 9.30am) is even more impressive: descending over one thousand metres to an ear-popping depth of 315m below sea level (the deepest outside the Dead Sea), you'll see rock-crusher stations crunching some of the eight million tonnes of iron ore that the mine produces each year. In winter, it's a balmy 15°C in the mine. It's hard to imagine that before the arrival of the railway, iron ore was dragged to Luleå on reindeer sleds, with one load of 100kg taking up to two months to get there.

Gällivare occupies the site of a Sámi village and one theory has it that the town's name comes from the Sámi language – *djelli* (a crack or gorge) *vare* (in the mountain). Down by the river near the train station, you'll come across the Sámi church, **Lappkyrkan** (June–Aug 10am–3pm), a mid-eighteenth-century construction. It's known as the Ettöreskyrkan (One Öre Church) after the one öre charity drive throughout Sweden that paid for it.

There's precious little else to see or do in Gällivare and you'd be wise to use your time strolling up the **Dundret** mountain, overshadowing the town, which is the target of Midnight Sun spotters. You can walk up to the *Björnfällan* restaurant (the name means "bear trap"), about a five-kilometre hike on a well-marked path, and the views are magnificent. Buses head up the winding road further west specially for the Midnight Sun, leaving daily at 11pm from outside the tourist office (mid-June to mid-July; 120kr), and returning at 1am.

Eating and drinking

If you're arriving from one of the tiny villages on the Inlandsbanan, the wealth of **eating and drinking** possibilities in Gällivare will make you quite dizzy; if you're coming from Luleå, grit your teeth and bear it. Good places for lunch are the *Åhult Bageri & Café* at Lasarettsgatan 19, serving great cakes and sandwiches, and the *Centrum Baren* at Storgatan 9, which has a good buffet. For more exotic food, *New Delhi* at Storgatan 19 does Indian dishes for around 120kr, while *Peking* at Storgatan 21b serves pizzas and reasonable Chinese food from 65kr. As for **drinking**, the places to be seen are the *Centrum Baren*, the Irish-themed *Kilkenny Inn* at Per Högströmsgatan 9, or the *Q Nightbar* inside the *Grand Hotel Lapland*.

Around Gällivare: the national parks

Gällivare is surrounded by some of Sweden's remotest and most beautiful terrain, and the town is within easy striking distance of no less than four **national parks**, which provide a ready taste of the wild side of Swedish Lapland – Europe's last wilderness.

Hemmed in by the Inlandsbanan on one side and the train line from Boden to Gällivare on the other, **Muddus National Park** (Ⓦwww.fjallen.nu/parker /muddus.htm) is ideal for beginners, a pine forest and marshland park between Jokkmokk and Gällivare that's home to bears, lynx, martens, weasels, hares, elk and, in summer, reindeer; the whooper swan is one of the most commonly sighted

birds. With your own transport, Muddus is easy to reach: the park's western edges are skirted by Route 45, and the easiest approach is to leave the highway at the Liggadammen dam and then follow the small road 12km to Skaite; otherwise, the Jokkmokk bus can drop you off at the dam. You can also reach the park from the southeast, via Nattavaara and Messaure. From Skaite, easy hiking trails head into the park – it's possible to do a daytrip, returning to Skaite on a circular route, or longer hikes, staying at cabins placed about 10km apart (150kr per person, book at Jokkmokk's tourist office; see p.632).

Sjaunjamyren marsh, on Muddus' northern fringes, is an apt location for the world's only **mosquito museum**: the area is something of a haven for the little beasties, with densities of over 3000 per square metre recorded here. The Inlandsbanan makes a short stop at the museum, which has displays on the benefits of the 1000 species of mosquito in Sweden, the development of mosquito repellents through the ages, and on how to avoid the critters – though staying on the train may be the best method.

Beginning about 120km northwest of Gällivare, the tract of wilderness edging Norway contains three of the country's wildest national parks, with the low fells, large lakes and moors of Padjelanta and Stora Sjöfallet parks framing the sheer face of the mountainous and inhospitable Sarek park. **Padjelanta** (ⓦwww.fjallen. nu/parker/padje.htm) is the largest national park in Sweden; the Sámi name means "the higher country", an apt description for an elevated tableland almost exclusively above the treeline and home to thousands of reindeer. A 150-kilometre hiking route, the **Padjelanta Trail**, runs from Kvikkjokk (reached by bus from Jokkmokk; see p.631) north through Padjelanta to Vaisaluokta, from where a boat (late Feb to mid-May & late June to late Sept; ☎0973/420 30) crosses the Akkajaure lake to and from Ritsem. Padjelanta is a good option for inexperienced walkers, but allow at least a week to do the trail. From Ritsem, there are buses back to Gällivare.

The real baddie of the parks is **Sarek** (ⓦwww.fjallen.nu/parker/sarek.htm), the terrain being officially classed as "extremely difficult". There are no tourist facilities, trails, cabins or bridges; the rivers are dangerous and the weather rotten – definitely not for anyone without Chris Bonington-type experience.

Hiking in the national parks

It's not a good idea to go hiking in the national parks of northern Sweden on a whim. Even for experienced walkers, the going can be tough and uncomfortable in parts, downright treacherous in others. Mosquitoes are a real problem: it's difficult to imagine the utter misery of being covered in a blanket of insects; your eyes, ears and nose full of the creatures. Yet this is one of the last wilderness areas left in Europe: the map of this part of the country shows little more than vast areas of forest and mountains; roads and human habitation are the exception rather than the norm. Reindeer are a common sight since the parks are breeding grounds and summer pasture, and Sámi settlements are dotted throughout the region – at Ritsem and Vaisaluokta, for example. Although there are some good short trails in the national parks, suitable for beginners, the goal for more ambitious hikers is the northern section of the Kungsleden trail (see p.640), which crosses several parks.

The best **time** to go hiking in the Swedish mountains is from late June to September. During May and early June, the ground is very wet and boggy due to the rapid snow melt. Once the snow has gone, wild flowers burst into bloom to make the most of the short summer months. The **weather** is very changeable – one moment it can be hot and sunny, the next cold and rainy – snow showers are by no means uncommon, even in summer. It goes without saying that you'll need to be **well equipped** with hiking gear, a sleeping bag, decent boots and Lantmateriet (Swedish National Survey) hiking maps.

Kiruna and around

KIRUNA was at the hub of the battle for the control of the iron ore supply during World War II. Ore was transported north from Kiruna by train to the great harbour at Narvik over the border in Norway, and much German fire-power was expended in an attempt to interrupt the supply to the Allies and wrest control for the Axis. In the process, Narvik suffered grievously, whilst Kiruna – benefiting from supposed Swedish neutrality – made a packet selling to both sides. Today, the train ride to Kiruna rattles through sidings, slag heaps and ore works, a bitter contrast to the surrounding wilderness. A brooding reminder of Kiruna's prosperity, the **LKAB iron-ore mine**, which churns out 13 million tonnes of ore a year, dominates the town: despite the new central buildings and open parks, Kiruna retains a gritty industrial air. **Guided tours** of the mines are arranged by the tourist office (July to mid-Aug 5 daily; June & late Aug 2 daily; 220kr). A coach takes visitors through the underground road network and then stops off at a "tourist mine", a closed-off section of a leviathan structure containing service stations, restaurants, computer centres, trains and crushing mills – an interesting, but far less authentic experience than the iron-ore mine tours in Gällivare (see p.633).

All the other sights in town are firmly wedded to the all-important metal in one way or another. The tower of the **Stadshus** on Hjalmar Lundbohmsvägen (June–Aug daily 8am–4pm; Sept–May Mon–Fri 8am–5pm) is obvious even from the train station, a strident metal pillar harbouring an intricate latticework clock face and sundry bells that chime raucously at noon. It was designed by Bror Mark-

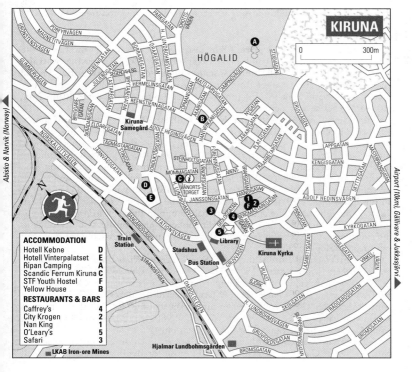

lund, and the whole hall unbelievably won the 1964 award for the most beautiful Swedish public building. Inside, there's a tolerable art collection and Sámi handicraft displays in summer.

Only a few minutes up the road, **Kiruna kyrka** (daily 11am–4.45pm; July till 6pm) raises a few eyebrows. Built in the style of a Sámi hut, it's a massive origami creation of oak beams and rafters the size of a small aircraft hangar, with an impressive 3500-pipe organ. LKAB, the mining company that to all intents and purposes *is* Kiruna, and which paid for church's construction, was also responsible for the nearby **Hjalmar Lundbohmsgården** (June–Aug Sun–Fri 10am–6pm; Sept–May Mon–Fri 10am–4pm; 30kr), a country house once used by the managing director of the company and "founder" of Kiruna. Displays inside mostly consist of early twentieth-century photographs featuring the man himself and assorted Sámi in their winter gear. Visit before going down the mine and everything will take on an added perspective – without the mine, Kiruna would be a one-reindeer town instead of the thriving place it is today. The **Kiruna Samegård**, at Brytaregatan 14 (mid-June to Sept Mon–Fri 7am–noon & 1–4pm; 20kr), is the most rewarding exhibition of Sámi culture in town. The handicrafts may be familiar but what won't be is the small display of really very good Sámi art featuring scenes from everyday life.

Strolling through the town's centre, you'll notice the adaptations made to withstand the **extreme conditions in winter**, when snow covers the ground for seven months, and when temperatures regularly plummet as low as -20°C, and sometimes down to -35°C; the modern, quadruple-glazed apartment blocks are insulated to keep the winter freeze at bay, and the colourful rounded buildings are designed to avoid snow falling from the roof. The streets are arranged in an unusual grid pattern to stop the biting wind from howling through town, and the flow of traffic is directed downhill through one-way streets to minimize fuel consumption.

Practicalities

Most flights to Kiruna's **airport**, 10km east of town, are met by the bus to the centre of town; otherwise, you'll need a taxi (⊕0980/120 20). Arriving by **train**, it's a brisk five-minute walk from the station uphill to the **tourist office** on the central square, Vänortstorget (mid-June to Aug Mon–Fri 8.30am–8pm, Sat & Sun 8.30am–6pm; Sept to mid-June Mon–Fri 8.30am–5pm, Sat 8.30am–2pm; ⊕0980/188 80, ⊛www.lappland.se).

Kiruna's city centre STF **youth hostel** (⊕0980/171 95, ⊛www.kirunahostel .com; doubles ❶, dorm beds from 150kr) is 900m from the train station at Bergmästaregatan 7. It fills quickly in summer, as does the other hostel in town, the ⚐ *Yellow House* at Hantverkaregatan 25 (⊕0980/137 50, ⊛www.yellowhouse .nu), which has double rooms (❶) and dorm rooms from 150kr per person. The *Ripan* **campsite** (⊕0980/630 00, ⊛www.ripan.se), a twenty-minute walk north on Campingvägen, has year-round cabins (❸) available. In winter, you can sleep in an **ice igloo** (Dec–Apr; ❸), with a window in the roof for watching the northern lights, a much better-value and more romantic option than the *Icehotel* (see opposite); the price includes a flask of warm lingonberry juice, breakfast and a sauna in the morning. The reception rents out skis for the nearby cross-country trails and can organize dog-sledding.

Of Kiruna's central **hotels**, the large *Scandic Ferrum Kiruna* next to the tourist office at Lars Janssonsgatan 15 (⊕0980/39 86 00, ⊛www.scandic-hotels.com; ❸/❺) has superb views of the Midnight Sun from its excellent sixth-floor sauna area, while the *Hotell Vinterpalatset* at Järnvägsgatan 18 (⊕0980/677 70, ⊛www .vinterpalatset.se; ❸/❺), is a smaller upmarket option. Round the corner at Konduktörsgatan 7, the cosy *Hotell Kebne* (⊕0980/681 80, ⊛www.hotellkebne .com; ❷/❹) is a handy option for the train station.

Kiruna is hardly a centre of haute cuisine, but there are several decent places to **eat**: the best is *City Krogen* next to the STF hostel at Bergmästaregatan 7, which serves up some excellent reindeer and salmon dishes from 130kr. *Nan King* at Mangigatan 26 is an inexpensive Chinese place (lunch 65kr), while *Caffreys*, at the corner of Föreningsgatan and Bergmästaregatan, does pizzas and pasta dishes, both around 90kr. Coffee and cakes are served up at *Safari*, Geologgatan 4. At the time of writing, the *O'Leary's* chain was set to expand beyond the Arctic Circle with a new bar and restaurant in an old wooden building at Föreningsgatan 11, and judging by its success elsewhere in Sweden, it will soon be the best place for a **drink**.

Around Kiruna: Jukkasjärvi

Just 15km east of Kiruna, the tiny village of **JUKKASJÄRVI** is a Mecca for many tourists travelling in Lapland in winter – albeit a disproportionately expensive one for the dubious pleasure of spending a night in subzero temperatures. The **Icehotel** (☎0980/668 00, ✆www.icehotel.com) that is built here every October is the world's biggest igloo and stands proudly by the side of the frozen River Torne until it melts in May. Thousands of tons of ice and snow are used to make the igloo, after which artists decorate the interior with elaborate carvings and lighting. Inside, there are bedrooms with compacted snow beds covered with reindeer hides, a bar, an exhibition hall, a cinema and a wedding chapel. Winter temperatures are generally around -20 to -30°C, which means that inside the igloo it's a positively balmy -5°C. Guests are provided with special sleeping bags, warm coats, hats and gloves. There are two types of room here: a standard **double room** containing nothing more than a reindeer-hide-swathed block of snow and ice for a bed costing 2800kr, and the more stylish **decorated suites** featuring ice carvings for an outrageous 3800–6000kr. If you chicken out, there are also warm cabins for rent on the site (2500kr for a two-berth cabin). A hotel bus picks up customers from the airport or train station (100kr per person), but undoubtedly the best way to arrive at the *Icehotel* is by **dog sled** from the airport; for a hefty 5125kr, you and three friends can be met from your plane and pulled to your

△ *Icehotel* bar, Jukkasjärvi

room. At the southern end of the village, there's a small wooden Sámi **church** from 1608, next to which is the *Nutti Sámi Siida* travel agency (☎0980/213 29, ⓦ www.nutti.se), which organizes Sámi-related adventures including dog- and reindeer sledding and accommodation in Sámi tepees. In **summer**, Jukkasjärvi is a good place for river-rafting, fishing and hiking – ask the *Icehotel* for details. In the *Icehotel's* Art Center (open year round), you can also see ice sculptures and the massive blocks of ice cut from the river in March in readiness for the next season's construction.

The two **eating** options in the village are both run by the hotel; the *Icehotel restaurant* (July–Aug & Dec–Apr) right across the road serves pricey gourmet Lapland dishes (200–290kr) and good-value lunches (95kr); 800m away, the *Hembygdsgården* restaurant has a 65kr lunch menu and more Lappish dishes, from 150kr.

From Kiruna to the Norwegian border

Quite amazingly, it's only since 1984 that there's been a choice of ways to continue your journey towards Norway: until then, only the train covered the last leg of the long run from Stockholm or Luleå towards Narvik. Today, though, there's the **Nordkalottvägen** road, which runs parallel to the railway, threading its way across the barren plateaux (the lakes up here are still frozen in mid-June) before slicing through the mighty Norwegian mountains. It's an exhilarating run that passes the start of the **Kungsleden** trail at Abisko (see box below): get off the train at Abisko Turiststation (not Abisko Östra, which is the village) where the adjoining fell station and ⚑ STF lodge (☎0980/40200, ⓦ www.abisko.nu; doubles ❷, dorm beds from 190kr) offers advice for hikers, rents out "hiking sets" (a small rucksack with a map and packed lunch) and has a good restaurant. Take the **linbana** (seat lift; 110kr return, 90kr for STF members) and walk a few kilometres to reach Nuolja peak, with fantastic views of the surrounding wilderness, including the spectacular U-shaped valley of Lapporten, the seventy-kilometre-long Torneträsk lake and the vast wooded expanses of Abisko National Park. Instead of taking the lift down, you could walk down a marked path that crosses through woods and ends up at the impressive canyon near the fell station.

Both train line and road continue on to **RIKSGRÄNSEN**, the last settlement in Sweden, a popular ski resort with good snow right up to late June. There's a **hotel** here, the *Hotell Riksgränsen* (☎0980/400 80, ⓦ www.riksgransen.nu; ❸/❺), opposite the train station, which has information about **hiking**, **mountain biking** and **canoeing** in the area. This is Sweden's wettest area, with the wind that whips off the Atlantic rising against the mountains here – intriguingly, Abisko, just 30km away, is the country's driest spot, sitting in the rain shadow of these mountains.

The Kungsleden

The **Kungsleden** is the most famous and popular of Sweden's hiking trails, a five-hundred-kilometre route from **Abisko** in the north to **Hemavan**, near Tärnaby, in the south. From Abisko to Kvikkjokk, north of the Arctic Circle, and in the south between Ammarnäs and Hemavan there are STF cabins and fell stations. Huts are placed at intervals of 15 to 20km, a distance that can be covered in one day, while shelter from the wind is provided at various places along the route. The Kungsleden is an easy trail to walk: it's well-marked; all the streams en route are crossed by bridges and patches of marshy ground overlaid with wooden planks; and there are also boat services or rowing boats for crossing the several large lakes on the way. If you're looking for total isolation this is not the trail for you – it's the busiest in the country. Avoid July and you'll find it easier going.

Travel details

Trains

The **Inlandsbanan** (see box on p.619) runs from Mora to Gällivare via Östersund from mid-June to mid-Sept. Timetables change slightly from year to year, but the following is a rough idea. Northbound trains leave Mora daily at 8am, calling at Orsa and Sveg and many other wayside halts en route for Östersund, where they arrive at 2.20pm; in the other direction, trains depart daily from Östersund at 3.10pm, arriving in Mora at 9pm. From Östersund, trains leave daily for Gällivare at 7.10am, calling at Vilhelmina, Storuman, the Arctic Circle and Jokkmokk before arriving in Gällivare at 9.15pm. Southbound trains leave Gällivare daily at 8.50am, arriving in Östersund at 11.10pm.

Falun to: Gävle (11 daily; 1hr); Örebro (6 daily; 2hr 30min); Stockholm (17 daily; 2hr 40min); Uppsala (17 daily; 2hr).

Gällivare to: Gävle (2 daily; 15hr); Gothenburg (2 daily; 19hr 30min–21hr); Kiruna (3 daily; 1hr); Luleå (3 daily; 2hr 20min); Stockholm (2 daily; 16hr); Umeå (daily; 5hr 40min); Uppsala (2 daily; 15hr).

Karlstad to: Stockholm (9 daily; 2hr 20min–3hr).

Kiruna to: Abisko (2 daily; 1hr 10min); Gällivare (3 daily; 1hr); Gävle (2 daily; 16hr); Gothenburg (2 daily; 21hr 30min); Luleå (3 daily; 3hr 30min); Riksgränsen (2 daily; 2hr); Stockholm (2 daily; 17hr); Uppsala (2 daily; 16hr).

Mora to: Leksand (9 daily; 45min); Stockholm (6 daily; 4hr); Uppsala (6 daily; 3hr).

Östersund to: Åre (3 daily; 1hr 15min); Gävle (2 daily; 4hr); Gothenburg (daily; 11hr); Stockholm (6 daily; 6hr); Storlien (3 daily; 2hr); Sundsvall (5 daily; 2hr 20min); Uppsala (6 daily; 5hr).

Buses

The **Inlandsexpressen** (#45) runs north from Östersund to Gällivare via Vilhelmina, Storuman, Arvidsjaur and Jokkmokk. It operates daily all year, leaving Östersund at 7.20am for Gällivare (arriving at 6.25pm), and at 5.30pm for Arvidsjaur (arriving at 12.20am). Heading south, a bus leaves Gällivare at 9.15am for Östersund (arriving at 8.20pm), and from Arvidsjaur at 8.35am for Östersund (arriving 3.30pm). **Ybuss** runs a daily express service between Stockholm and Östersund (8hr 30min), with one or two morning or early afternoon departures each way.

Åsarna to: Klövsjö (5 daily; 20min); Mora (2 daily; 4hr); Östersund (6 daily; 1hr 10min).

Gällivare to: Jokkmokk (5 daily; 1hr 30min); Kiruna (4 daily; 1hr 30min); Luleå (4 daily; 3hr 15min); Ritsem (2 daily; 3hr 20min).

Jokkmokk to: Gällivare (5 daily; 1hr 30min); Luleå (3 daily; 3hr); Kvikkjokk (2 daily; 1hr 50min).

Karlstad to: Stockholm (7 daily; 4hr 10min).

Kiruna to: Abisko (2 daily; 1hr 20min); Gällivare (4 daily; 1hr 30min); Jukkasjärvi (7 daily; 30min); Luleå (2 daily; 4hr 45min); Riksgränsen (daily; 2hr 10min).

Kvikkjokk to: Jokkmokk (2 daily; 1hr 50min).

Mora to: Åsarna (2 daily; 4hr); Leksand (hourly; 1hr 20min); Orsa (hourly; 20min); Östersund (2 daily; 5hr 10min); Stockholm (3 daily; 4hr 30min); Sveg (2 daily; 2hr 5min).

Östersund to: Åre (2 daily; 1hr 30min); Åsarna (6 daily; 1hr 10min); Mora (2 daily; 5hr 10min); Sveg (3 daily; 2hr 40min); Umeå (2 daily; 6hr).

Storuman to: Hemavan (4 daily; 2hr 30min); Tärnaby (5 daily; 2hr); Umeå (2–4 daily; 3hr 40min).

International buses

Arvidsjaur to: Bodö (daily; 7hr).
Karlstad to: Oslo (4–5 daily; 3hr).
Kiruna to: Narvik (daily; 2hr 30min).
Storuman to: Mo i Rana (daily; 4hr 15min).

International trains

Åre to: Trondheim (2 daily; 2hr 30min).
Gällivare to: Narvik (2 daily; 3hr 45min).
Kiruna to: Narvik (2 daily; 2hr 45min).
Östersund to: Trondheim (2 daily; 4hr).

Finland

Finland highlights

* **Travel by tram, Helsinki** The best way to see the capital's diverse and striking architecture – from Art Nouveau to ultra-modernist. See p.688

* **Pihlajasaari island, Helsinki** A great day-trip and the perfect place to work on your all-over tan. See p.701

* **Turku Castle, Turku** Delve into Finland's often uneasy relationship with neighbouring Sweden at this former seat of power. See p.724

* **Åland Islands** A summer paradise of verdant flower meadows, sheltered swimmable creeks and rolling countryside perfect for biking. See p.729

* **Savonlinna Opera Festival, Savonlinna** One of Europe's most sought-after musical affairs, performed in a spectacular fifteenth-century fortress. See p.749

* **Sauna, Kuopio** Experience the real thing in the world's biggest woodsmoke sauna, and get tips from the locals on technique. See p.758

* **Hiking the Karhunkierros trail** A must for serious hikers, traversing some of Lapland's most beautiful Arctic stretches. See p.778

* **Rovaniemi, Lapland** No matter what time of year, catch sight of some Nordic wild reindeer and visit Santa Claus to place your order for Christmas. See p.778

* **Inari, Lapland** Pan for gold or deepen your knowledge of Sámi history and culture at the excellent village museum. See p.787

△ Swimmer, Åland Islands

Introduction and basics

Mainland Scandinavia's most culturally isolated and least understood country, Finland has been independent only since 1917, having been ruled for hundreds of years by imperial powers: first the Swedes and then the tsarist Russians. Much of its history involves a struggle simply for recognition and survival.

Today, though, the battle has been won and the Finns are the proudest of all the Nordic nations, trumpeting the fact that this little-known country on the very edge of Europe is truly one of the continent's best kept secrets. Finland is without a doubt the most welcoming of all of the Scandinavian countries; Finns of all ages are inordinately proud of their nation's achievements (it is, after all, only by a quirk of history that Finland was not invaded by the Soviet Union and well and truly taken in to Moscow's sphere of influence) and are anxious that visitors learn more about their country, where a joy in all things Finnish goes hand in hand with eager participation in the European Union. Forget any lingering perceptions that Finland is mundane, grey or even Communist – today it's a welcoming, honest and prosperous society keen to make up for years of living on the sidelines and, in the capital at least, one whose nightlife scene rivals that of any cosmopolitan European centre.

During the Swedish period, the Finnish language (one of Europe's least familiar and most difficult) was regarded as fit only for peasants – which the majority of Finns were – and attempts were later made to forcibly impose Russian. All publications were in Swedish until the *Kalevala* appeared in the early nineteenth century. A written collection of previously orally transmitted folk tales telling of a people close to nature, living by hunting and fishing, the *Kalevala* instantly became regarded as a truly Finnish history, and formed the basis of the **National Romantic** movement in the arts that flourished from the mid-nineteenth century, stimulating political initiatives towards Finnish nationalism.

It's not surprising, therefore, that modern-day Finns have a well-developed sense of their own culture, and that the legacy of the past is strongly felt in the still widely popular Golden Age paintings of Gallen-Kallela, Edelfelt and others; the music of Sibelius; and the National Romantic architecture which paved the way for modern, modernist greats like Alvar Aalto. Equally in evidence, even among city dwellers, are the deeply ingrained, down-to-earth values of rural life, along with a sense of spirituality epitomized by the **sauna**, which for Finns is as much a meaningful social ritual as it is a health and fitness activity.

Finland on the net

Ⓦ **www.festivals.fi** Listings and descriptions of the country's biggest and most popular music and culture festivals.

Ⓦ **www.finland-tourism.com** The official tourist board site, with bundles of info in a functional layout.

Ⓦ **www.outdoors.fi** The Finnish Forest Service's website, offering hundreds of pages of information in English on hiking and staying in and around Finland's national parks.

Ⓦ **www.sauna.fi** Home of the Finnish Sauna Society, with indispensable practical advice on sauna do's and don'ts.

Ⓦ **www.santaclaus.fi** Old Saint Nick's "official" site, with stories, interviews and even a webcam so you can keep an eye on where all that brandy really goes.

Ⓦ **virtual.finland.fi** News and views, facts and figures from the Finnish Foreign Ministry.

Some elderly rural dwellers are prone to suspicion of anything foreign, but in general the Finnish population is much less staid than its Nordic neighbours, and the disintegration of its once powerful neighbour, the Soviet Union, has allowed it to form closer ties with Europe through membership of the European Union. By the end of the 1990s Finland's **economy** was buoyant enough to allow it to join the first wave of countries in the European Monetary Union. It's currently the only one of the three Nordic EU members to have introduced the euro, and with the success of Finnish telecommunications giant Nokia and a flourishing IT sector, the country reached the millennium with renewed confidence and self-belief. However, unemployment is still high in some places, particularly in rural areas, and some sections of the country's society are being left behind in Finland's drive to become a technological world leader.

Where to go

Topographically, Finland is mainly flat, and filled by huge forests and lakes – you'll need to travel around a lot to appreciate the country's wide regional variations. The **south** contains the least dramatic scenery, but the capital, **Helsinki**, more than compensates, with its brilliant architecture and superb museum collections. Stretching from the Russian border in the east to the industrial city of **Tampere**, the water systems of the **Lake Region** provide a natural means of transport for the timber industry – indeed, water here is a more common sight than land.

On most maps and many transport timetables cities and towns are given their **Finnish names** followed by their **Swedish names** in parentheses. Both Swedes and Finland-Swedes will frequently use the Swedish rather than the Finnish names. The main places in question are listed below, with the Finnish name first.

Helsinki (Helsingfors)	Iisalmi (Idensalmi)
Porvoo (Borgå)	Tampere (Tammerfors)
Turku (Åbo)	Mikkeli (St Michel)
Pori (Björneborg)	Savonlinna (Nyslott)
Hamina (Fredrikshamn)	Vaasa (Vasa)
Lappeenranta (Villmanstrand)	Kokkola (Gamla Karleby)
Kajaani (Kajana)	Oulu (Uleåborg)

Ostrobothnia, the upper portion of the west coast, is characterized by near-featureless farmlands and long sandy beaches which are – to Finns at least – the region's main draw. Here, too, you'll find the clearest Swedish influence: in parts up to a third of the population are Swedish-speaking – known as "Finland-Swedes" – and there's a rich heritage from the days of Swedish trading supremacy. **Kainuu** is the thickly forested heart of the country, much of its small population spread among scattered villages. The land begins to rise as you head north from here, folding into a series of fells and gorges that are ripe for spectacular hiking and cross-country skiing. Completely devoid of large towns, **Lapland** – or Sápmi to the region's indigenous people – contains the most alluring terrain of all, its stark and haunting landscapes able to absorb any number of visitors on numerous hiking routes. This region is home to the Sámi people, sedentary reindeer herders whose traditional ways of life meld relatively smoothly with modern Finnish society.

When to go

The official **holiday season** for Finns is early July to mid-August, ignited by the Midsummer celebrations of *Juhannus* in late June; during these weeks there's a nationwide exodus from the towns to the country. The best time to visit the rural regions is either side of these dates, when things will be less crowded and hectic – though no cheaper.

In **summer**, regarded as being from June to early September, Helsinki, the south and the Lake Region enjoy mild and sunny weather, while areas further north are on the whole cooler – though recent years have experienced significant variation in the length and intensity of the warm season. On average, temperatures are usually 18–24°C (65–75°F), sometimes reaching 32°C (90°F) in the daytime, but they drop swiftly in the evening, when you'll need a light jacket. The north is always a few degrees cooler and often quite cold at night, so carry a thick jumper at least. The Midnight Sun can be seen from Rovaniemi northwards for two months over midsummer; the rest of the country experiences a night-long twilight from mid-June to mid-July.

Winter, roughly from late October to early April in the south, plus a few weeks more on either side in the north, is painfully cold. Helsinki generally fluctuates between 0°C and -20°C (32°F and -4°F), the harshest months being January and February; in the north it's even colder, with just a few hours of daylight; and in the extreme north the sun doesn't rise at all. The snow cover generally lasts from November to March in the south, a few weeks longer in the north. On the plus side, Finland copes easily with low temperatures and transport is rarely disrupted.

Thanks to its relatively flat terrain, Finland is one of the most enjoyable countries in Scandinavia to go **hiking**, one of the Finns' favourite pastimes. The best time for hiking is from May to September in the south and from June to September in the north. You'll need a good-quality tent, a warm sleeping bag, rainwear, spare warm clothing, thick-soled waterproof boots, mosquito repellent, a compass and detailed maps, all of which can be bought in tourist centres close to the hiking routes. See p.51 for more on hiking.

Getting there from the rest of Scandinavia

Finland's geographical position – effectively separated from the rest of Scandinavia by the Gulf of Bothnia – means that except in the extreme north of the country the easiest approaches are usually by ferry or plane. Crossing from the east coast of Sweden is easy, with regular **ferry** services from a number of points and (usually) good onward links once you've arrived. Further north, Sweden and Norway both have land borders with Finland and these are no fuss to cross by **bus**, although in a few spots you may have to wait a day between connections. From Denmark, it's impossible to get to Finland without passing through Sweden unless you **fly**, although there's a direct bus–ferry service and fairly frequent trains.

By train

There are no direct **train** connections between Finland and other Scandinavian countries. The nearest railhead is at Boden in Sweden, at the northern end of the Gulf of Bothnia, around 100km before the Finnish border at Haparanda–Tornio (ScanRail, Inter-Rail and Eurail passes are valid on buses from Luleå/Boden to Haparanda). Other train connections, such as those between Helsinki and Stockholm or Copenhagen (1–2 daily; 25hr), make use of ferry crossings for much of their route.

By bus

In the Arctic North, **buses** connect the Norwegian–Finnish border towns of **Karasjok–Karigasniemi** and **Skibotn–Kilpisjärvi**, as well as the Finnish border villages of **Utsjoki**, **Polmak** and **Nuorgam**; fares and sched-

ules, beyond what we've included under the "Travel Details" at the end of the relevant chapters, can be checked at any tourist office or bus station, though on the whole these infrequent services don't change too much from year to year. There are also regular services from points in northern Sweden via the twin border towns of **Haparanda–Tornio**, at the northern end of the Gulf of Bothnia.

Long-distance bus-and-ferry connections to Finland are also fairly frequent. The service **from Copenhagen** to Finland runs four times a week to Helsinki, via **Stockholm** and **Turku**. Naturally, it's a fairly exhausting journey, taking 25 hours.

By ferry

The most frequent **ferries** from Sweden to Finland run between **Stockholm** and Helsinki and are operated by Silja Line (@www.silja.com; 16hr; €26 deck passenger, €125 cabin, €55 car) and Viking Line (@www.vikingline.fi; 16hr; €32 deck passenger, €56 cabin, €100 car), though frequent discounts are offered by both throughout the year, and you can occasionally land a bed in a four-person cabin for under €30. Both companies have a year-round overnight service, leaving at 5pm and arriving at 9.30am, and both also run a twice-daily service from Stockholm to **Turku**, which takes ten or eleven hours (Silja foot passenger €20, car €65; Viking Line foot passenger €18, car €58). Quicker still (4hr) are the daily services between Stockholm and **Mariehamn**, run by Viking (passengers €11, car €6.50) and Silja Line (€15, car €35). Prices for all the routes are usually cheapest outside of the summer months and during the week. There are no ferries from Denmark to Finland.

As these routes are extremely popular among Finns and Swedes, it's a good idea to plan ahead, though you shouldn't have a problem getting hold of a last-minute place on the boat, assuming you don't mind foregoing a cabin. For current details on timetables and the numerous discounts available – ranging from 50 percent reductions for holders of InterRail or Eurail cards to other generous concessions for children and senior citizens – check with a travel agent or the relevant ferry office.

By plane

Finnair (⊛www.finnair.com) and Scandinavian Airlines (⊛www.scandinavian.net) both have daily nonstop flights to Helsinki from **Copenhagen** (hourly; 1hr 30min), **Stockholm** (hourly; 1hr) and **Oslo** (5–6 daily; 1hr 30min). Both also offer flights between Stockholm and a number of Finnish regional cities including **Tampere** (6 daily; 1hr), **Oulu** (3 daily; 1hr 20min), **Vaasa** (4 daily; 1hr 15min) and **Turku** (3 daily; 1hr), though getting to these cities from Copenhagen or Oslo involves flying via Stockholm or Helsinki. Blue1 (⊛www.blue1.com), the budget arm of Scandinavian, operate direct flights between all the Scandinavian capitals, as well as less-travelled, direct daily routes like Copenhagen–Oulu and Gothenburg–Helsinki; prices start at €72 return, but last-minute flights can be frighteningly expensive. Check with a travel agent or visit the airlines' websites for occasional bargain fares.

Costs, money and banks

Though the cost of a meal or the bill for an evening's drinks can occasionally come as a shock, prices in Finland are generally comparable with those in most European capitals, and there is no shortage of places catering for those on tighter budgets, even in the more far-flung locales. Bargain lunchtime "specials" are common and travelling costs, in particular, can come as a pleasant surprise – travel by train, for example, is cheaper (though less efficient) in Finland than in the other Scandinavian countries.

There are ways to cut **costs**, which we've detailed where relevant, but as a general rule you'll need £20–30/US$35–55 a day even to live fairly modestly – staying mostly at youth hostels or campsites, eating out every other day and supplementing your diet with food from supermarkets, visiting only a few selected museums and socializing fairly rarely. To live well and see more, you'll be spending closer to £50/US$90.

Finnish **currency** is the **euro** (€), which comes in coins of 5 to 50 cents, €1 and €2,

and notes of €5 to €500. Note that Finland no longer circulates 1- and 2-cent coins as the government considered them too low a value; as a result any such coins are now collectors items and examples in good condition can fetch well over 1,000 times the face value. The **exchange rate** at the time of writing was €1.48 to £1, €0.82 to US$1, €0.70 to CAD$1, €0.63 to AUD$1 and ₵0.57 to NZD$1. For up-to-date rates, visit the web site ⊛www.oanda.com.

Credit cards are one of the best ways to pay for goods – in addition to being easy to carry around securely, they offer the most competitive exchange rates and few Finnish establishments will charge any over-and-above commission for you to use one. Major credit and charge cards – Amex, MasterCard, Visa, Diner's Club – are usually accepted by hotels, car rental offices, department stores, restaurants and sometimes even by taxis. However, it's still advisable to check beforehand.

For **cash**, your best bet is withdrawing money from ATMs using your home bank **debit card**. Nearly all foreign bank cards will work in a Finnish ATM/cash machine (known as a *pankkiautomaatti*), and banks usually give good exchange rates and charge 1–3 percent commission for foreign cash withdrawals. Note that there may be a minimum charge, so it could be worth taking out a larger amount when you use the machine; check with your bank for the charges they apply. Though they are much less convenient, **traveller's cheques** still remain a popular way to access cash; they also make a good backup in the event that you lose or damage your card. These can be changed at most **banks**, which open Monday to Friday from 9.15am to 4.15pm; the charge is usually €2 (though several people changing money together need only pay the commission once). You can also change money at hotels, though normally at a much worse rate than at the banks. In a country where every cent counts, it's worth looking around for a better deal: in rural areas some banks and hotels are known not to charge any commission at all. Outside normal banking hours, the best bet for changing money are the **currency exchange desks** at transport terminals which open to meet international arrivals, where commission is likely to be €3–5, roughly the same as at banks, though airport exchange rates are often a little more generous.

There are no restrictions on the amount of money you can take into or out of Finland.

Mail and telecommunications

In general, **communications** in Finland are dependable and quick, although in the far north, and in some sections of the east, minor delays arise due simply to geographical remoteness.

Unless you're on a hiking trek through the back of beyond, you can rest assured your letter or postcard will arrive at its destination fairly speedily. The cost of mailing anything weighing under 20g internationally is 65 cents. You can buy **stamps** from **post offices** (Mon–Fri 9am–5pm; longer hours at the main post office in Helsinki), street stands or R-Kiosks, and at some hotels. **Poste restante** is available at the main post office in every large town.

An out-of-order **public phone** is virtually unheard of in Finland. Most, however, only take **phonecards**, which you can buy in denominations of €5–15 from the R-Kiosk chain and some other outlets. If you intend to use the phone frequently, it may be worth stocking up on phonecards, since it can sometimes be impossible to buy them late at night or in out-of-the-way places. Also note that each municipality runs its own phonecard system, which may or may not be compatible with systems in other areas. Your best bet is probably to invest in a Sonera phonecard, since their telephones can be found pretty much everywhere. The minimum cost of a **local call** is €1. **International calls** are cheapest between 10pm and 8am. The bill for using a hotel phone is often dramatically more expensive.

Another option for making calls is using your **mobile phone** (for general advice on which, see "Basics", p.40). If you plan to make a lot of calls while in Finland, you might also invest in a Finnish SIM card for use in your phone. For around €20 you'll get

a Finnish number plus about sixty minutes of domestic calling time and a number of text messages.

International dialling codes for calling from and to Finland are given on p.40. Operator numbers are ☎118 for domestic calls and ☎92020 for reverse-charge international calls.

Finland comes second only to the USA in terms of per-person home **Internet** use, a fact made poignantly clear by the near absence of public Internet points in many towns. For web and email access, the most reliable option should be a public library – terminals are always free, and but in the busier ones you may need to book a slot the day before, although most have short-use walk-up terminals. You may need to show some kind of ID when booking a terminal, which you may also have to leave as a deposit while using it. Another source of Internet access is tourist offices, where terminals are sometimes free, while the larger towns will have cafés with free Internet access for customers; otherwise, you'll usually pay €3–5 per hour.

The media

The biggest-selling **Finnish newspaper**, and the only one to be distributed all over the country, is the daily *Helsingin Sanomat* (€2), whose online edition (⊛www.helsingin sanomat.fi) also includes a small section in English. Most other papers are locally based and sponsored by a political party; however, all carry entertainment listings – only the cinema listings (where the film titles are translated into Finnish) present problems for non-Finnish speakers. A better bet may be the Swedish language tongue-twister, *Hufvudstadsbladet*, a quality daily that can be found in Helsinki. The best information about **what's on**, if you're in Helsinki, Tampere or Turku, is the free *City* (appearing fortnightly in Helsinki, monthly in Turku and Tampere), which carries regional news, features and entertainment details in Finnish and English; it's available at tourist offices.

Overseas newspapers, including most British and some US titles, can be found, often on the day of issue, at the Academic

Bookstore, Pohjoisesplanadi 39, Helsinki. Elsewhere, foreign papers are harder to find and less up-to-date, though they often turn up at the bigger newsagents and train stations in Helsinki, Turku, Tampere and, to a lesser extent, Oulu.

Finnish **television**, despite its four channels (one of which is called MTV, but is unrelated to the music station), isn't exactly inspiring and, as usually goes off the air at midnight, shouldn't keep you off the streets for long. Moderately more interesting is the fact that, depending on where you are, you might be able to watch Swedish, Norwegian, Estonian and Russian programmes. A few youth hostels have TV rooms, and most hotel-room TVs have the regular channels plus a feast of cable and satellite alternatives. As with films shown in the cinema, all TV programmes are broadcast in their original language with Finnish subtitles.

The only **radio station** that non-Finnish speakers are likely to find interesting and useful is YLE Mondo (ⓦwww.yle.fi/ylemondo), a multi-language channel which relays programmes from foreign broadcasters including the BBC, NPR and CBC; a large part of the day's programming is given over to English material, and generally between 4pm and 6.30pm, and 11.30pm to 7.30am, there'll be a series of news programmes in English. Broadcast on 97.5FM in Helsinki, the channel also transmits a short English-language news summary (Mon–Fri 7.30am & 8.55am) put together by the Finnish national broadcaster YLE. This bulletin can also be heard at the same time in Lahti on 90.3FM, Jyväskylä 87.6FM, Kuopio 88.1FM, Tampere 88.3FM and in Turku on 96.7FM.

Getting around

Save for the fact that traffic tends to follow a north–south pattern, you'll have few headaches **getting around** the more populated parts of Finland. The chief form of public transport is the train, backed up, particularly on east–west journeys, by long-distance coaches. For the most part trains and buses integrate well, and you'll only need to plan with care when travelling through sparsely inhabited areas such as the far north and

east. Feasible and often affordable variations come in the form of ferries, planes, bikes, and even hitching – though car rental is strictly for the wealthy or densely car-pooled.

The complete **timetable** (*Suomen Kulkuneuvot*) for train, bus, ferry and air travel within the country is published every four months; it's sold primarily at large bookshops for €28. This is essential for plotting complex routes; for simplified details of the major train services, pick up the *Rail Pocket Guide* booklet, available at most train stations for around €1.

Trains

The swiftest land link between Finland's major cities is invariably the reliable **train service**, operated by the state railway company, VR. Large, comfortable express trains, super-smooth IC (inter-city trains) and an increasing number of state-of-the-art tilting *pendolino* trains serve the principal **north–south** routes several times a day, reaching as far north as Rovaniemi on the Arctic Circle, although occasional services penetrate as far north as Kemijärvi. Elsewhere, especially on east–west hauls through sparsely populated regions, rail services tend to be skeletal and trains are often tiny two-carriage affairs. The Arctic North has a very limited network of services. More details on Finnish Railways can be found at ⓦwww.vr.fi.

InterRail, BIJ and ScanRail **passes** are valid on all trains; if you don't have one of these and are planning a lot of travelling, get a **Finnrail Pass** before arriving in Finland (you can't buy it in Finland itself) from a travel agent or Finnish Tourist Office (for addresses, see p.43). This costs €168 for three days' unlimited travel within a month, €222 for five days, or €300 for ten days. Another option is the summer-only **Lomapassi**, available for purchase within Finland at all train stations and many travel agencies from June to August. This allows for three days of unlimited travel within one month and costs €109.

Otherwise, train **fares** are surprisingly reasonable. As a guide, a one-way, second-class ticket from Helsinki to Turku (a trip of around 200km) costs around €24; Helsinki to Kuopio (465km) €52, and Helsinki to Rovaniemi (900km) €72. If you've brought a car with you, car sleeper services are a convenient way of covering long distances. A one-way trip from Helsinki to Rovaniemi for a car and up to six passengers (including sleeping berths) costs between €317 and €448, depending on the time of year.

Tickets are purchased for specific dates and times, though there is no fee if you want to change the date or routing. Some journeys also allow you to break your journey en route – check when you purchase. You should **buy tickets** from station ticket offices (*lippumyymälä*), although you can also pay the inspector on the train. If there are three or more of you travelling together, **group tickets**, available from a train station or travel agent, can cut the regular fares on journeys over 80km by at least 20 percent (25 percent for parties of 11 or more). **Senior citizens** with Finnish Senior Citizens railcards (€9) are entitled to a 30 percent discount on regular tickets, or 50 percent if they are over 65. The cost of **seat reservations** depends on the distance travelled but is generally around €5 – remember that although they are not necessary on express trains, reservations can be a good idea if you're travelling over a holiday period or on a Friday or Sunday evening.

Buses

Run by local private companies but with a common ticket system, **buses** cover the whole country, and are often quicker and more frequent than trains over the shorter east–west hops, and essential for getting around the remoter regions; they are not necessarily cheaper than trains, however. In the Arctic North there is a very limited railway network, so almost all public transport is by road; hence it's here that you'll find buses most useful. The main operators are Gold Line (☎ 016/334 5500, ⊛ www.goldline.fi) and Eskelisen Lapin Linjat (☎016/342 2160, ⊛ www.eskelisen-lapinlinjat.com). The free bus **timetable**, *Suomen Pikavuorot*, lists all the routes in the country and can be picked up at most long-distance bus stations but is not very user-friendly, especially if you're not fluent in Finnish. Schedules and detailed information in English on travel in Finland by

coach and bus can also be found at ⊛ www .matkahuolto.fi. South of the Arctic Circle, you're more likely to use the excellent network of rail services than hassle with buses.

All **fares** are calculated according to the distance travelled: Helsinki to Lahti (100km) costs around €17, Helsinki to Kuopio (400km) around €44. Express buses charge a supplement of €2.40 per journey and are worth it for the correspondingly faster journey times. All types of ticket can be purchased at bus stations or at most travel agents; only ordinary one-way tickets can be bought on board the bus, though on journeys of 80km or less there's no saving in buying a return anyway. On return trips of over 80km, expect a reduction of ten percent.

Ferries

As **lake travel** is aimed more at holidaying families than the budget-conscious traveller, **prices** are high considering the distances, and progress is slow as the vessels chug along the great lake chains. If you have the time, money and inclination, though, it can be worth taking one of the shorter trips simply for the experience. There are numerous routeings and details can be checked at any tourist office in the country and at Finnish Tourist Offices abroad; we've detailed some of the more scenic routes in the Guide.

Planes

With their range of discounts, domestic **flights** can be comparatively cheap as well as time-saving if you want to cover long distances, such as from Helsinki to the Arctic North. That said, travelling by air means you'll miss many interesting parts of the country. Finnair (⊛www.finnair.com) and Blue1 (⊛www.blue1.com) offer a variety of off-peak summer reductions which can be checked online or at travel agents and airline or tourist offices in Finland. Youth **fares** are available for 17–24-year-olds and offer a fifty percent discount on the normal fare, though it's usually cheaper to look for special offers or to buy a weekend ticket which is always cheaper than the standard fare. Flights operate daily between most large cities, and one-way fares start at €36, though to ensure seats this cheap you must book several weeks in advance at least.

Driving and hitching

Renting a car is extremely expensive in Finland (as is petrol), and with such a good public-transport network, it's only worth considering if you're travelling as a group of four or five. The big international companies (detailed in "Basics", p.46) have offices in most Finnish towns and at international arrival points. If you're in Helsinki it's also worth checking the local company Transvell (☎08000/7000, ☻www.transvell.fi). They all accept major credit cards; if paying by cash, you'll need to leave a substantial deposit. You'll also need a valid driving licence, at least a year's driving experience, and to be a minimum of 19–24 years old, depending on the company you rent from.

Rates for a medium-sized car are €30–50 per day, with reductions for longer periods – you'll pay around €400 for a fortnight's use. On top of this, there can be a surcharge of up to 75 cents per kilometre (which may be waived on long-term rentals) and a drop-off fee of €50–100 if you leave the car somewhere other than the place from which it was rented. For more details on car rental before arriving in Finland, visit the website of one of the international companies mentioned above, or ask at a Finnish Tourist Board office.

If you **bring your own car** to Finland, it's advisable (though not compulsory) to have a Green Card as proof that you are comprehensively insured in the event of an accident. Some insurers in EU countries will offer you a Green Card for free as part of your insurance package, whilst others will charge a premium. Further **information** about driving in Finland can be obtained from Autoliitto, the Automobile and Touring Club of Finland, Hämeentie 105A, 00550 Helsinki (☎09/7258 4400, ☻www.autoliitto.fi).

Once underway, you'll find the next financial drain is **fuel**, which costs around €1.20 a litre (unleaded), though bear in mind that in rural areas, especially in Lapland, fuel is considerably more expensive than in Helsinki. Except in the far north, **service stations** are plentiful and usually open from 7am to 9pm between Monday and Saturday, and are often closed on Sunday – although in busy holiday areas many stay open round the clock during the summer. Larger towns will also have automatic pumps which function round-the-clock and accept cash and credit cards, though many of these machines do not recognize foreign cards. Though fuel prices may well impoverish you, take some consolation in the fact that you can drive on all Finnish motorways for free, as there are no tolls. Though **roads** are generally in good condition there can be problems with melting snows, usually during April and May in the south and occasionally early June in the far north. Finnish **road signs** are similar to those throughout Europe, but be aware of bilingual place names; one useful sign to watch for is *Keskusta*, which means "town centre". **Speed limits** vary, though generally the legal limit is between 30kph and 40kph in towns, and from 80kph to 100kph on major roads – if it's not signposted, the basic limit is always 80kph. On motorways the maximum speed is 120kph in summer, 100kph in winter.

Other **rules of the road** include using headlights all the time when driving outside built-up areas, as well as in fog and in poor light, and the compulsory wearing of seatbelts by drivers and all passengers. As elsewhere in Scandinavia, penalties for drink-driving are severe – the police may stop and breathalyze you if they think you've been driving erratically. In some areas in the north of the country, reindeer and elk are liable to take a stroll across a road, especially around dusk. These are sizeable creatures and damage (to the car) is likely to be serious; all such collisions should be reported at the nearest police station and the Finnish Motor Insurers' Centre (*Liikennevakuutuskeskus*), Bulevardi 28, 00120 Helsinki (☎09/680 401, ☻www.vakes.fi/lvk), which can also help with local breakdown companies.

Hitching is generally easy, and sometimes the quickest means of transport between two spots. Finland's large student population has helped accustom drivers to the practice, and you shouldn't have to wait too long for a ride on the busy main roads between large towns. Make sure you have a decent road map and emergency provisions/shelter if you're passing through isolated regions.

While many Finns speak English, it's still handy to memorize the Finnish equivalent of "let me out here" (*jään pois tässä*).

Cycling

Cycling can be an enjoyable way to see the country at close quarters, particularly because the only appreciable hills are in the far north and extreme east. Villages and towns may be separated by several hours' pedalling, however, and the scenery can get monotonous. You can take your bike along with you on an InterCity train for a €9 fee – as this isn't too common a practice you shouldn't need to reserve a spot ahead of time. Finnish **roads** are of high quality in the south and around the large towns, but are much rougher in the north and in isolated areas; beware the springtime thaw when the winter snows melt and sometimes cover roads with water and mud. All major towns have bike shops selling spares – Finland is one of the few places in the world where you can buy bicycle snow tyres with tungsten steel studs. Most youth hostels, campsites and some hotels and tourist offices offer **bike rental** from €10 per day, €45 per week; there may also be a deposit of around €30.

Accommodation

Whether you're at the end of one of Finland's long-distance hiking trails or in the centre of a city, you'll find some kind of **accommodation** to suit your needs. You will, however, have to pay dearly for it: prices are high, and only by making use of special offers and travelling during low season will you be able to sleep well on a budget.

Hotels

Finnish **hotels** (*hotelli*) are rarely other than polished and pampering: TV, phone and private bathroom are standard fixtures, breakfast is invariably included in the price, and there's often free use of the sauna and swimming pool, too. Chain hotels dominate mid-to-upper level accommodations in all cities, and rooms seem to follow a very strict, homogenous layout. Costs can be formidable – frequently in excess of €90 for a double – but planning ahead and taking advantage of various discount schemes and seasonal reductions can cut prices, often to as little as €50.

Room rates commonly move up and down depending on the season and whether there is a town festival being staged; on the whole, though, accommodation is much more expensive on weekdays and in winter. In major cities, particularly Helsinki, there are frequent bargains in business-oriented hotels during July and August, and on Fridays, Saturdays and Sundays throughout the year. Exact details of these change frequently, but it's worth checking the current situation at a local tourist office. Reductions are also available to holders of Helsinki Cards and the similar cards issued for Turku and Tampere. Otherwise, between July and August you're unlikely to find anything under €50 by turning up on spec. Hotels in country areas are no less comfortable than those in cities, and often a touch less costly, typically €40–50. However, space is again limited during summer.

Expense can be trimmed a little by using the **Finncheque** system: you buy an unlimited number of €36 or €45 vouchers, each valid for a night's accommodation for one person (double occupancy), plus breakfast, in any of the 140 participating hotels from June to September. The two price categories correspond to the quality of room. You can only buy Finncheques outside Finland at a Finnish Tourist Board office (see p.43) or a specialist travel agent, who will also supply addresses of the hotels involved. Don't worry about buying more vouchers than you might need – they are refundable at the place of purchase. Another discount is offered by the Scanhotel chain's Scandic Holiday Cheque vouchers. They're valid at all Scandic hotels (@ www.scandic-hotels.com) in Finland (as well as the group's hotels in other European countries) throughout the year and cost from €93 per double room including breakfast, though beware that some hotels add on a "quality surcharge". The cheques are widely available from travel agents outside Finland.

In many towns you'll also find **tourist hotels** (*matkustajakoti*) or **guesthouses** (*majatalot*), more basic types of family-run hotels, though the qualitative difference

Accommodation price codes

The hotels and guesthouses listed in the Finland chapters of this guide have been graded according to the following price bands, based on the cost of the **least expensive double room in summer**, usually mid-June to mid-August. However, many hotels offer summer and/or weekend discounts, and in these instances we've given two grades, covering both the discounted and the regular rate (eg ❶/❸).

❶ Under €30   ❸ €51–70   ❺ €91–110
❷ €31–50   ❹ €71–90   ❻ Over €111

between these and standard hotels may only be that they're not owned by a chain. They charge €30–45 per double room and sometimes have cheaper wood cabins out back, but may well be full throughout the summer. The facilities of **summer hotels** (*kesähotelli*), too, are more basic than regular hotels, since the accommodation is in student blocks which are vacated from June to the end of August: there are universities in all the major cities and in an impressive number of the larger towns. Reservable with any Finnish travel agent, summer hotel prices are around €35 per person. Bear in mind that identical accommodation – minus the bed linen and breakfast – comes a lot cheaper in the guise of a youth hostel.

Youth hostels

The easiest and cheapest place to rest your head is often a **youth hostel** (*retkeilymaja*). These exist throughout the country, in major cities (which will have at least one) and isolated country areas, and are run by the Finnish Youth Hotel Association, *Suomen Retkeilymajajärjestö* (SRM). It's always a good idea to phone ahead and reserve a place, which many hostel wardens will do for you, or book online at the address below. If you're arriving on a late bus or train, say so when booking and your bed will be kept for you; otherwise bookings are only held until 6pm and reception often closes around 8pm, though you can usually make arrangements to check in later, provided you let staff know in advance. Hostels are busiest during the peak Finnish holiday period, roughly mid-June to mid-August. Things are quieter after mid-August, although a large number of hostels close soon after this date – check that the one you're aiming for doesn't. Similarly, many hostels don't open until June.

Overnight **charges** are generally around €18 per person, depending on the type of accommodation, with hostels ranging from the basic dormitory type to those with two- and four-bed rooms and at least one bathroom for every three rooms. Bed linen, if not already included, can be rented for an extra €3–5. With a Hostelling International Card (see p.47; not obligatory) you can get a €2.50 reduction per person per night. The SRM publishes a useful free guide, *SRM Hostels in Finland*, available directly from them at Suomen Retkeilymajajärjestö, Yrjönkatu 38B, 00100 Helsinki (☎09/565 7150, ⊕www.srmnet.org), listing all Finnish hostels, and the very helpful staff there can also provide a free map showing locations.

All youth hostels have wardens to provide general assistance and arrange **meals**: most hostels offer breakfast, usually for €4–5, and some serve dinner as well (around €7.50). Hostel breakfasts, especially those in busy city hostels, can be rationed affairs and – hunger permitting – you'll generally be better off waiting until you can find a cheapish lunch somewhere else (see "Food and Drink", overleaf). The only hostel breakfasts really worth taking advantage of are those offered at summer hotels, where hostellers can mingle with the hotel guests and, for €5–7, partake of the help-yourself spread.

Campsites and holiday villages

There are some 200 official **campsites** (*leirintäalue*) in Finland, and several hundred more operating on a less formal basis. Most open from May to September, although around seventy stay open all year. The approved sites, marked with a blue and white tent sign in a letter C, are classified by a star system: one-star sites are in rural areas and usually pretty basic, while on a five-star site you can expect excellent cooking and laundry facilities and sometimes a well-stocked shop. The cost for two people sharing is €5–15 per pitch, depending on the site's star rating. Campsites outside major towns are frequently very big (a 2000-tent capacity isn't uncommon), and they're very busy at weekends during July and August. Smaller and more remote sites (except those serving popular hiking routes) are, as you'd imagine, much less crowded.

Holiday villages have been sprouting up throughout Finland in the last few years and there are now well over 200 of them. Standards vary considerably, with accommodation ranging from basic cabins to luxurious bungalows. All provide fuel, cooking facilities, bed linen and often a sauna – but you'll need to bring your own towels. Costs range from €100 to €450 per week for a cabin sleeping up to four people, though for a luxury bungalow you might be pay up to €900.

To camp in Finland, you'll need a Scandinavian Camping Card, available at every site for €6 and valid for a year. The card is valid in all four Nordic countries and offers discounts on many campsites all over Finland. If you're considering **camping rough**, remember it's illegal without the landowner's permission – though in practice, provided you're out of sight of local communities, there shouldn't be any problems.

Hiking accommodation

Hiking routes invariably start and finish close to a campsite or a youth hostel, and along the way there will usually be several types of basic accommodation. Of these, a *päivätupa* is a cabin with cooking facilities which is opened during the day for free use; an *autiotupa* is an unlocked hut which can be used by hikers to sleep in for one night only – there's no fee but often no space either during the busiest months. A *varaustupa* is a locked hut for which you can obtain a key at the Tourist Centre at the start of the hike – there's a smallish fee and you'll almost certainly be sharing. Some routes have a few *kämppä* – cabins originally erected for forest workers but now used mainly by hikers; check their exact location with the nearest

tourist centre. On most hikes there are also marked spots for pitching your own tent and building fires.

Food and drink

Contrary to the scathing potshots made in 2005 by Italian prime minister Silvio Berlusconi, Finnish **food** is full of surprises and demands investigation. It's pricey, but you can keep a grip on the expenses by using markets and Finland's many down-to-earth dining places, saving restaurant blowouts for special occasions. Though tempered by many regulations, alcohol is more widely available here than in much of Scandinavia: there are many places to **drink** but also many people drinking, most of them indulging moderately but quite a number doing it to excess on a regular basis.

Food

Though it may at first seem a stodgy, rather unsophisticated cuisine, **Finnish food** is an interesting mix of western and eastern influences. Many dishes resemble those you might find elsewhere in Scandinavia – an enticing array of delicately prepared fish (herring, whitefish, salmon and crayfish), together with some unusual meats like reindeer, elk and bear – while others bear the stamp of Russian cooking: solid pastries and casseroles, strong on cabbage, pork and mutton.

All Finnish restaurants will leave a severe dent in your budget, as will the foreign places, although the country's innumerable pizzerias are relatively cheap by comparison. The golden money-saving rule is to treat **lunch** (*lounas*, usually served 11am–2pm) rather than the much dearer **dinner** (*päivällinen*, usually from 6pm) as your main meal. Also, eke out your funds with stand-up snacks and by selective buying in supermarkets. If you're staying in a hotel, don't forget to load up on the inclusive **breakfast** (*aamiainen*) – often an open table laden with herring, eggs, cereals, porridge, cheese, salami and bread.

Snacks, fast food and self-catering

Economical **snacks** are best found in market halls (*kauppahalli*), where you can get basic foodstuffs along with local and national specialities. Adjoining these halls are cafeterias, where you're charged by the weight of food on your plate. Look out for *karjalan piirakka* – oval-shaped Karelian pastries containing rice and mashed potato, served hot with a mixture of finely chopped hard-boiled egg and butter for around €2. Also worth trying is *kalakukko*, a chunk of bread with pork and whitefish baked inside it – legendary around Kuopio but available almost everywhere. Expect to spend around €4 for a chunk big enough for two. Slightly cheaper but just as filling, *lihapiirakka* are envelopes of pastry filled with rice and meat – ask for them with mustard (*sinappi*) and/or ketchup (*ketsuppi*). Most train stations and the larger bus stations and supermarkets also have cafeterias proffering a selection of the above and other greasier nibbles.

Less exotically, the big **burger** franchises are widely found, as are the Grilli and Nakkikioski roadside fast-food stands turning out burgers, frankfurters and hot dogs for €2–3; they're always busiest when the pubs shut.

Finnish **supermarkets** – Sokos, K-Kaupat, Pukeva and Centrum are widespread names – are fairly standard affairs. In general, a substantial oval loaf of dark rye bread (*ruisleipä*) costs €1.75, ten *karjalan piirakkas* €2.50, a litre of milk €1, and a packet of biscuits around €2. A usually flavoursome option containing hunks of meat and vegetables, Finnish tinned **soup** (*keitto*) can be an excellent investment if you're self-catering.

Coffee (*kahvi*) is widely drunk – per capita, more than anywhere else in the world, in fact – and costs €1–1.50 per cup; in a *baari* or *kahvila* (bar or coffee shop) it's sometimes consumed with a *pulla* – a kind of doughy bun. It's normally drunk black, although milk is always available if you want it; you'll also commonly find espresso and cappuccino, although these are more expensive. **Tea** (*tee*) costs around €1, depending on where you are and whether you want to indulge in some exotic brew. In rural areas, though, drinking it is considered a bit effete. When ordering tea, it's a good idea to insist that the water is boiling before the teabag is added – and that the bag is left in for more than two seconds.

Lunch and dinner

If you're in a university town, the campus cafeteria or **student mensa** is the cheapest place to get a hot dish. Theoretically you have to be a student, but outside of Helsinki you are unlikely to be asked for ID. There's a choice of three meals: *Kevytlounas* (KL), the "light menu", which usually comprises soup and bread; *Lounas* (L), the "ordinary menu", which consists of a smallish fish or meat dish with dessert; and *Herkkulounas* (HL), the "delicious menu" – a substantial and usually meat-based plateful. All three come with bread and coffee, and each costs €2–3. Prices can be cut by half if you borrow a Finnish student ID card from a friendly diner. The busiest period is lunchtime (11.30am–12.30pm); later in the day (usually 4–6pm) many *mensas* offer price reductions. Most universities also have cafeterias where a small cup of coffee can cost as little as 45 cents.

If funds stretch to it, you should sample at least once a **ravintola**, or restaurant, offering a lunchtime buffet table (*voileipäpöytä* or *seisova pöytä*), which will be stacked with tasty traditional goodies that you can feast on to your heart's content for a set price of around €12. Less costly Finnish food can be found in a **baari**. These are designed for working people, generally close at 5pm or 6pm, and serve a range of Finnish dishes and snacks (and often the weaker beers; see "Drink", overleaf). A good day for traditional Finnish food is Thursday, when every *baari* in the country dishes up *hernekeitto ja pannukakut*, thick pea soup with black rye bread, followed by oven-baked pancakes with strawberry jam, and buttermilk to wash it down – all for around €6. You'll get much the same fare from a *kahvila*, though a few of these, especially in the big cities, fancy themselves as being fashionable and may charge a few euro extra.

Although *ravintola* and *baaris* are plentiful, they are often outnumbered by **pizzerias**. They're as varied in quality here as they are in any other country, but especially worthwhile for their lunch specials, when a set price (€6–8) buys a pizza, coffee and everything you can carry from the bread and salad

Glossary of Finnish food and drink terms

Basics

Juusto	Cheese
Kakku	Cake
Keitto	Soup
Keksit	Biscuits
Leipä	Bread
Maito	Milk
Makeiset	Sweets
Perunat	Potatoes
Piimä	Buttermilk
Piirakka	Pie
Riisi	Rice
Voi	Butter
Voileipä	Sandwich

Meat (lihaa)

Häränfilee	Fillet of beef
Hirvenliha	Elk
Jauheliha	Minced beef
Kana	Chicken
Kinkku	Ham
Lihapyörykat	Meatballs
Nauta	Beef
Paisti	Steak
Sianliha	Pork
Poro	Reindeer
Vasikanliha	Veal

Seafood (äyriäisiä) and fish (kala)

Ankerias	Eel
Graavilohi	Salted salmon
Hauki	Pike
Hummeri	Lobster
Katkaravut	Shrimp
Lohi	Salmon
Makrilli	Mackerel
Muikku	Small whitefish
Rapu	Crayfish
Sardiini	Sardine
Savustettu lohi	Smoked salmon
Savustettut silakat	Smoked Baltic herring
Siika	Large, slightly oily, white fish
Silakat	Baltic herring
Silli	Herring
Suolattu	Pickled herring
Taimen or forelli	Trout
Tonnikala	Tuna
Turska	Cod

Egg dishes (munaruoat)

Hillomunakas	Jam omelette
Hyydytetty muna	Poached egg
Juustomunakas	Cheese omelette
Keitetty muna	Boiled eggs
Kinkkumunakas	Ham omelette
Munakas	Omelette
Munakokkeli	Scrambled eggs
Paistettu muna	Fried egg
Pekonimunakas	Bacon omelette
Perunamunakas	Potato omelette
Sienimunakas	Mushroom omelette

Vegetables (vihannekset)

Herneet	Peas
Kaali	Cabbage
Kurkku	Cucumber
Maissintähkät	Corn on the cob
Paprika	Green pepper
Pavut	Beans
Peruna	Potato
Pinaatti	Spinach
Porkkana	Carrot
Sieni	Mushroom
Sipuli	Onion
Tilli	Dill
Tomaatti	Tomato

Fruit (hedelmä)

Appelsiini	Orange
Aprikoosi	Apricot
Banaani	Banana
Greippi	Grapefruit
Kirsikka	Cherries
Luumu	Plums
Mansikka	Strawberry
Meloni	Melon
Omena	Apple
Päärynä	Pear
Pähkinä	Nuts

bar. Many of the bigger pizza chains offer discounts for super-indulgence – such as a second pizza for half-price and a third for free if you can polish off the first two. **Vegetarians** are likely to become well acquainted with pizzerias – specific vegetarian restaurants are thin on the ground, even in major cities.

Drink

Finland's **alcohol** laws are as bizarre and almost as repressive as those of Norway

Persikka	Peach	*Sitruuna*	Lemon
Raparperi	Rhubarb	*Viinirypäle*	Grapes

Sandwiches (voileipä)

Kappelivoileipä	Fried French bread topped with bacon and a fried egg
Muna-anjovisleipä	Dark bread with slices of hard-boiled egg, anchovy fillets and tomato
Oopperavoileipä	Fried French bread with a hamburger patty and egg
Sillivoileipä	Herring on dark bread, usually with egg and tomato

Finnish specialities

Kaalikääryleet	Cabbage rolls: cabbage leaves stuffed with minced meat and rice
Kaalipiirakka	Cabbage and minced meat
Karjalanpaisti	Karelian stew of beef and pork with onions
Kurpitsasalaatti	Pickled pumpkin served with meat dishes
Lammaskaali	Mutton and cabbage stew or soup
Lasimestarin silli	Pickled herring with spices, vinegar, carrot and onion
Lihakeitto	Soup made from meat, potatoes, carrots and onions
Lindströmin pihvi	Beefburger made with beetroot and served with a cream sauce
Lohilaatikko	Potato and salmon casserole
Lohipiirakka	Salmon pie
Makaroonilaatikko	Macaroni casserole with milk and egg sauce
Maksalaatikko	Baked liver purée with rice and raisins
Merimiespihvi	Casserole of potato slices and meat patties or minced meat
Piparjuuriliha	Boiled beef with horseradish sauce
Porkkanalaatikko	Casserole of mashed carrots and rice
Poronkäristys	Sautéed reindeer stew
Sianlihakastike	Gravy with slivers of pork
Silakkalaatikko	Casserole with alternating layers of potato, onion and Baltic herring, with an egg and milk sauce
Stroganoff	Beef with gherkins and onions, browned in a casserole and braised in a tomato and sour cream stock
Suutarinlohi	Marinated Baltic herring with onion and peppers
Tilliliha	Boiled veal flavoured with dill sauce
Venäläinen silli	Herring fillets with mayonnaise, mustard, vinegar, beetroot, gherkins and onion
Wieninleike	Fried veal cutlet

Drinks

Appelsiinimehu	Orange juice	*Olut*	Beer
Gini	Gin	*Tee*	Tea
Kahvi	Coffee	*Tonic vesi*	Tonic water
Kivennäisvesi	Mineral water	*Vesi*	Water
Konjakki	Cognac	*Viini*	Wine
Limonaati	Lemonade	*Viski*	Whisky

and Sweden, although unlike those countries, boozing is tackled enthusiastically, and is even regarded by some as an integral part of the national character. Some Finns, men in particular, often drink with the sole intention of getting paralytic; younger people these days are on the whole more inclined to regard the practice simply as an enjoyable social activity, though spend a few nights in any town and you're sure to witness your share of plastered, stumbling Finnish youth – boys and girls alike.

What to drink

Finnish spirits are much the same as you'd find in any country. **Beer** (*olut*), on the other hand, falls into three categories: "light beer" (*I-Olut*) – more like a soft drink; "medium-strength beer" (*Keskiolut*, *III-Olut*) – more perceptibly alcoholic and sold in many food shops and cafés; and "strong beer" (*A-Olut* or *IV-Olut*), which is on a par with the stronger international beers, and can only be bought at the ALKO shops and fully licensed (Grade A) restaurants and nightclubs.

The main – and cheapest – outlet for alcohol of any kind are the state-run **ALKO** shops (Mon–Thurs 10am–5pm, Fri 10am–6pm, Sat 9am–2pm). Even the smallest town will have one of these, and prices don't vary. In 2004, in an effort to ensure that Finns would buy their alcohol at home instead of cheaper places like Estonia, the government slashed the excise tax on hard liquor, resulting in a price decrease of up to 30 percent in ALKO shops. In these shops, strong beers like Lapin Kulta Export – an Arctic-originated mind blower – and the equally potent Karjala, Lahden A, Olvi Export, and Koff porter, cost around €1.30 for a 300ml bottle. Imported beers such as Heineken, Carlsberg and Becks go for €1.90 a bottle. As for **spirits**, Finlandia vodka and Jameson's Irish Whiskey are €16 and €23 respectively per 75cl bottle. There's also a very popular rough form of vodka called Koskenkorva, ideal for assessing the strength of your stomach lining, which costs €13 for 75cl. The best **wine** bargains are usually Hungarian or Bulgarian, and cost around €15 per bottle in a restaurant, though you can buy bottles in ALKO for under €5. ALKO's French wines range from €6.50 to €50 a bottle.

Where to drink

Continental-style **brasseries** or British-influenced **pubs** are the most pleasant places to have a drink. Frequented by both men and women of all ages, you're most likely to feel more at home in these familiar environments than in the smoky, generally all-male bars which proliferate in many of the small towns away from Helsinki, especially in the north – these charmless drinking dens are nothing more than places to get seriously hammered.

Most **restaurants** have a full licence, and some are actually frequented more for drinking than eating; it's these that we've listed under "Drinking" throughout the text. They're often also called bars or pubs by Finns simply for convenience. Just to add to the confusion, some so-called "pubs" are not licensed; neither are *baari*.

Along with ordinary restaurants, there are also **dance restaurants** (*tanssiravintola*). As the name suggests, these are places to dance rather than dine, although most do serve food as well as drink. They're popular with the over-40s, and before the advent of discos were the main places for people of opposite sex to meet. Even if you're under 40, dropping into one during the (usually early) evening sessions can be quite an eye-opener. Expect to pay an €3–5 admission charge.

Once you've found somewhere to drink, there's a fairly rigid set of **customs** to contend with. Sometimes you have to queue outside the most popular bars, since entry is permitted only if a seat is free – there's no standing. Only one drink per person is allowed on the table at any one time except in the case of porter (a stout which most Finns mix with regular beer). There's always either a doorman (*portsari*) – whom you must tip (around €1) on leaving – or a cloakroom into which you must check your coat on arrival (again around €1). Bars are usually open until midnight or 1am, though a handful may stay open till 2am or, in the case of discos and clubs, 4am. Last call is announced half an hour before the place shuts by a winking of the lights – the *valomerkki*.

Some bars and clubs have **waitress/waiter service**, whereby you order, and pay when your drinks are brought to you. A common order is *iso tuoppi* – a half-litre glass of draught beer, which costs €3–4 (up to €6 in some nightclubs). This might come slightly cheaper in **self-service** bars, where you select your tipple and queue up to pay at the till. Though saying "beer" and pointing to the tap will generally work, you might get a more friendly response by offering up *Saisinko yhden oluen?*, Finnish for "Might I have a pint, please?".

Wherever you buy alcohol, you'll have to be of **legal age**: at least 18 to buy beer and wine, and 20 or over to have a go at the spirits. ID will be checked if you look too young – or if the doorman's in a bad mood.

Directory

Canoeing With many lakes and rivers, Finland offers challenges to every type of canoe enthusiast, expert or beginner. There's plenty of easy-going paddling on the long lake systems, innumerable thrashing rapids to be shot, and abundant sea canoeing around the archipelagos of the south and southwest coast. Canoe rental (available wherever there are suitable waters) costs around €3 per hour, €8–20 per day, or €60 per week, with prices dependent on the type of canoe. Many tourist offices have plans of local canoeing routes, and you can get general information from the Finnish Canoe Federation, Olympiastadion, Eteläkaarre, 00250 Helsinki (☎ 09/494 965, ✆ www .kanoottiliitto.fi).

Customs There are few, if any, border formalities when entering Finland from another Scandinavian country by land; many of the old customs booths and checkpoints are these days largely abandoned, ramshackle edifices. The same applies when crossing by sea; only by air do you usually need to show your passport. Much more a headache are crossings into Russia, still full-on bureaucratic nightmares with rubber stamps, scrupulous passport checks and askance eyes cast towards your baggage. In any event you'll need to plan well ahead to obtain the visa paperwork for a visit – the one exception being the cruises along the Saimaa canal into Karelian Russia (see box on p.717 for details).

Dentists Seeing a dentist can be very expensive: expect to spend a minimum of €25. Look under *Hammaslääkari* in the phone book, or ask at a tourist office.

Doctors Provided you're insured, you'll save time by seeing a doctor at a private health centre (*lääkäriasema*) rather than queueing at a national health centre (*terveyskeskus*). You are required to present a doctor's referral and a written statement confirming that

you will pay the bill in order to stay in hospital.

Emergencies For police, ambulance and fire service, dial ☎ 112.

Fishing Although angling and ice-fishing are considered public rights in Finland and require no permit, non-Scandinavians do need a General Fishing Licence if they intend to fish with a lure in Finland's waterways; this costs €6 for a seven-day period from post offices. In certain parts of the Arctic North and the Åland Archipelago you'll need an additional licence costing between €5–10 per day and obtainable locally. Throughout the country you'll also need the permission of the owner of the particular stretch of water, usually obtained by buying a permit on the spot. The nearest campsite or tourist office will have details of this, and advise on the regional variations on national fishing laws.

Markets In larger towns, markets usually take place every day except Sunday from 7am to 2pm. There'll also be a market hall (*kauppahalli*) open weekdays 8am–5pm. Smaller places have a market once or twice a week, usually including Saturday.

Nude bathing Finns are uptight and very un-Scandinavian in their attitude to public nudity. Hence, sections of some Finnish beaches are designated nude bathing areas, more often than not sex-segregated and occasionally with an admission charge of around €1.50. The local tourist office or campsite will part with the facts – albeit rather reluctantly. However, you should encounter no problem sunbathing naked by a secluded lake or in the forest.

Pharmacies *Kemikaalikauppa* sell only cosmetics; for medicines you need to go to an *apteekki*, generally open daily 9am–6pm.

Public holidays On the following days, shops and banks close and most public transport operates a Sunday schedule; museum opening hours may also be affected. Holidays are: January 1, May 1, December 6, December 24, 25 and 26; variable dates are Epiphany (between Jan 6 and 12), Good Friday and Easter Weekend, the Saturday before Whit Sunday, Midsummer's Eve, and All Saint's Day (the Saturday between Oct 31 and Nov 6).

Saunas These are cheapest at a public swimming pool, where you'll pay €2–3 for a session. Hotel saunas, which are sometimes better equipped than public ones, are more expensive (€5–7) but free to guests. Many Finnish people have saunas built into their homes and it's common for visitors to be invited to share one. Note that the sauna – and subsequent bathing in the nearest lake – is the one locale where nudity is commonly and publicly practised; it's fine to take along a towel or bathing suit, but bear in mind that your Finnish host will probably remain *au natural*.

Shops Supermarkets are usually open Mon–Fri 9am–8pm, Sat 9am–6pm. Some in cities keep longer hours, for example 8am–10pm. In Helsinki the shops in Tunneli are open until 10pm. In the weeks leading up to Christmas some stores and markets are open on Sunday, too.

History

I nextricably bound with the medieval superpowers, Sweden and Russia, and later with the Soviet Union, Finland's history is a stirring tale of a small people's survival – and eventual triumph – over what have often seemed impossible odds. It's also a story that's full of powerful contemporary resonances – the Finns' battle to regain their independence has not gone unnoticed on the other side of the Baltic Sea, having served as a model for the three ex-Soviet Baltic states in their fight for sovereignty and, more recently, EU membership.

First settlements

As the ice sheets of the last Ice Age retreated, parts of the Finnish Arctic coast were settled by tribes from eastern Europe. They hunted bear and reindeer, and fished the well-stocked rivers and lakes: relics of their existence have been found and dated to around 8000 BC. Pottery skills were introduced around 3000 BC, and trade with Russia and the east flourished. At the same time, other peoples were arriving and merging with the established population. The **Boat Axe** culture (1800–1600 BC), which originated in central Europe, spread as Indo-Europeans migrated into Finland. The seafaring knowledge they possessed enabled them to begin trading with Sweden from the Finnish west coast, as indicated by **Bronze Age** findings (around 1300 BC) concentrated in a narrow strip along the seaboard. The previous settlers withdrew eastwards and the advent of severe weather brought this period of occupation to an end.

The arrival of the Finns

The antecedents of the Finns were a race from central Siberia, from where they moved outwards in two directions. One tribe went south, eventually to Hungary; the other westwards to the Baltic, where it mixed with Latgals, Lithuanians and Germans. The latter, the "**Baltic Finns**", were migrants who crossed the Baltic around 400 AD to form an independent society in Finland. In 100 AD the Roman historian Tacitus described a wild and primitive people called "the Fenni". This is thought to have been a reference to the earliest **Sámi**, who occupied Finland before this. With their more advanced culture, the Baltic Finns absorbed this indigenous population, although some of their customs were maintained. The new Finns worked the land, utilized the vast forests and made lengthy fishing expeditions on the lakes.

The pagan era

The main Finnish settlements were along the west coast facing Sweden, with whom trade was established, until the Vikings' opening up of routes further to the east forced these communities into decline. Meanwhile, the Finnish south coast was exposed to seaborne raiding parties and most Finns moved inland and eastwards, a large number settling around the huge Lake Ladoga in **Karelia**. Eventually the people of Karelia were able to enjoy trade in two directions – with the Varangians to the east and the Swedes to the west. Groups from Karelia and the more northern territory of Kainuu regularly ventured into Lapland to fish and hunt. At the end of the pagan era Finland was split into three regions: Varsinais-Suomi ("Finland proper") in the southwest, Häme in the western part of the lake region, and Karelia in the east. Although they often helped one another, there was no formal cooperation between the inhabitants of these areas.

The Swedish era (1155–1809)

At the start of the tenth century, pagan Finland was caught between two opposing religions: Catholicism in Sweden on one side and the Orthodox Church of Russia on the other. The Russians wielded great influence in Karelia, but the west of Finland began to gravitate towards Catholicism on account of its high level of contact with Sweden. In 1155 King Erik of Sweden launched a "crusade" into Finland – although its real purpose was to strengthen trade routes – which swept through the southwest and established Swedish control, leaving the English **Bishop Henry** at **Turku** to establish a parish. Henry was killed by a Finnish yeoman, but became the patron saint of the Turku diocese and the region became the administrative base of the whole country. Western Finland generally acquiesced to the Swedes, but Karelia didn't, becoming a territory much sought after by both the Swedes and the Russians. In 1323, under the **Treaty of Pähkinäsaari**, an official border was drawn up, giving the western part of Karelia to Sweden while the Russian principality of Novgorod retained the eastern section around Lake Ladoga. To emphasize their claim, the Russians founded the Orthodox **Valamo Monastery** on an island in the lake.

Under the Swedish crown, Finns still worked and controlled their own land, often living side by side with Swedes, who came to the west coast to safeguard sea trade. Finnish provincial leaders were given places among the nobility and in 1362 King Håkon gave Finland the right to vote in Swedish royal elections. When the Swedish throne was given to the German Albrecht of Mecklenburg, in 1364, there was little support for the new monarch in Finland, and much violent opposition to his forces who arrived to occupy the Swedish-built castles. Once established, the Mecklenburgians imposed forced labour and the Finnish standard of living swiftly declined. There was even a proposal that the country should be sold to the Teutonic Order of Knights.

In a campaign to wrest control of the Swedish realm, a Swedish noble, **Grip**, acquired control of one Finnish province after another, and by 1374 was in charge of the whole country. In doing this he was obliged to consider the welfare of the Finns and consequently living conditions improved. Another effect of Grip's actions was to underline Finland's position as an individual country – under the Swedish sovereign but distanced from Sweden's political offices.

Grip had intended to ensure that Finnish affairs would be managed by the Swedish nobility irrespective of the wishes of the monarch. The nobility, however, found themselves forced to look for assistance to Margrethe, Queen of Denmark and Norway. She agreed to come to the Swedes' aid provided they recognized her as sovereign over all the Swedish realm, including Finland. This resulted in the **Kalmar Union** of 1397.

While the Finns were barely affected by the constitution of the Union, there was a hope that it would guarantee their safety against the Russians, whose expansionist policies were an increasing threat. Throughout the fifteenth century there were repeated skirmishes between Russians and Finns in the border lands and around the important Finnish Baltic trading centre of Viipuri (now Russian Vyborg).

The election of King Charles VIII in 1438 caused a rift in the Union and serious strife between Sweden and Denmark. He was forced to abdicate in 1458 but his support in Finland was strong, and his successor, Christian I, sent an armed column to subdue Finnish unrest. While Turku Castle was under siege, the Danish noble **Erik Axelsson Tott**, already known and respected in the country, called a meeting of representatives from every Finnish estate where it was agreed that Christian I would be acknowledged as king of the Union.

Tott went on to take command of Viipuri Castle and was able to function almost independently of central government. Although he planned to make Viipuri the major centre for east–west trade, resources had to be diverted to strengthen the eastern defences. During the 1460s Novgorod was sucked into Moscow's sphere of influence and finally absorbed altogether. This left Finland's eastern edge more exposed than ever before. Novgorod had long held claims on large sections of Karelia, and the border situation was further confused by the Finnish peasants who had drifted eastwards and settled in the disputed territories. Part of Tott's response to the dangers was to erect the fortress of **Olavinlinna** (in the present town of Savonlinna) in 1475, actually inside the land claimed by Russia.

Tott died in 1481 and **Sten Sture**, a Swedish regent, forced the remaining Axelssons to relinquish their family's domination of Finland. By 1487 Sture had control of the whole country, and appointed bailiffs of humble birth – instead of established aristocrats – to the Finnish castles in return for their surplus revenue. These monies were used to finance Sture's ascent through the Swedish nobility. As a result, nothing was spent on maintaining the eastern defences.

Strengthened by an alliance with Denmark signed in 1493, Russia attacked

Viipuri on November 30, 1495. The troops were fended off by the technically inferior Finns, an achievement perceived as a miracle. After further battles it was agreed that the borders of the Treaty of Pähkinäsaari would remain. However, the Swedes drew up a bogus version of the treaty in which the border retained its fifteenth-century position, and it was this forgery which they used in negotiations with the Russians over the next hundred years.

Within Finland, a largely Swedish-born nobility became established. Church services were conducted in Finnish, although Swedish remained the language of commerce and officialdom; because the bulk of the population was illiterate, any important deed had to be read to them. In the thirteenth and fourteenth centuries, any Finn who felt oppressed simply moved into the wild lands of the interior – out of earshot of church bells.

By the time **Gustav Vasa** took the Swedish throne in 1523, many villages had been established in the disputed border regions. Almost every inhabitant spoke Finnish, but there was a roughly equal division between those communities who paid taxes to the Swedish king and those who paid them to the Russian tsar. In the winter of 1555, a Russian advance into Karelia was quashed at Joutselkä by Finns using skis to travel speedily over the icy roads, a victory that made the Finnish nobility confident of success in a full-scale war. While hesitant, Vasa finally agreed to their wishes: 12,000 troops from Sweden were dispatched to eastern Finland, and an offensive launched in the autumn of 1556. It failed, with the Russians reaching the gates of Viipuri, and Vasa retreating to the Åland Islands, asking for peace.

In 1556 Gustav Vasa made Finland a Swedish Grand Duchy and gave his son, Johan, the title Duke of Finland. It was rumoured that **Duke Johan** not only spoke Finnish but was an advocate of Finnish nationalism. These claims may have been somewhat exaggerated, but the duke was certainly pro-Finnish, surrounding himself with Finnish nobles and founding a chancery and an exchequer. He moved into Turku Castle and furnished it in splendour. However, the powers of his office, as defined by the Articles of Arboga, were breached by a subsequent invasion of Livonia and he was sentenced to death in 1563 by the Swedish Diet, the governing legislative body, although the king's power of pardon was exercised. Finland was divided between loyalty towards the friendly duke and the need to keep on good terms with the Swedish crown, now held by Erik XIV. The Swedish forces sent to collect Johan laid siege to Turku castle for three weeks, executing thirty nobles before capturing the duke and imprisoning him.

The war between Sweden and Denmark over control of the Baltic took its toll on Erik. He became mentally unbalanced, slaying several prisoners who were being held for trial and, in a moment of complete madness, releasing Johan from detention. The Swedish nobles were incensed by Erik's actions and rebelled against him – with the result that Johan became king in 1568.

In 1570 Swedish resources were stretched when hostilities again erupted with Russia, now ruled by the aggressive Tsar Ivan ("the Terrible") IV. The conflict was to last 25 years, a period known in Finland as "**The Long Wrath**". It saw the introduction of a form of conscription instead of the reliance on mercenary soldiers, which had been the norm in other Swedish wars. Able-bodied men aged between fifteen and fifty were rounded up by the local bailiff and about one in ten selected for military service. Russia occupied almost all of Estonia and made deep thrusts into southern Finland. Finally the Swedish–Finnish troops regained Estonia and made significant advances through Karelia, capturing an important eastern European trading route. The war was formally concluded in 1595 by the **Treaty of Täyssinä**. Under its terms, Russia recognized the lands gained by

Sweden and the eastern border was altered to reach up to the Arctic coast, enabling Finns to settle in the far north.

Sweden was established as the dominant force in the Baltic, but under Gustav II, crowned king in 1611, Finland began to lose the special status it had previously enjoyed. Its administration was streamlined and centralized, causing many Finnish nobles to move to Stockholm. Civic orders had to be written rather than passed on orally, and many ambitious Finns anointed themselves with Swedish surnames. Finnish manpower supported Swedish efforts overseas – the soldiers gaining a reputation as wild and fearless fighters – but brought no direct benefit to Finland itself. Furthermore, the peasants were increasingly burdened by the taxes needed to support the Swedish wars with Poland, Prussia and Germany.

Conditions continued to decline until 1637, when **Per Brahe** was appointed governor-general. Against the prevailing mood of the time, he insisted that all officers should study Finnish, selected Turku as the spot for a university – the country's first – and instigated a successful programme to spread literacy among the Finnish people. After concluding his second term of office in 1654 he parted with the terse but accurate summary: "I was highly satisfied with this country and the country highly satisfied with me."

A terrible harvest in 1696 caused a **famine** that killed a third of the Finnish population. The fact that no aid came from Sweden intensified feelings of neglect and stirred up a minor bout of Finnish nationalism led by **Daniel Juslenius**. His book, *Aboa Vetus Et Nova*, published in 1700, claimed Finnish to be a founding language of the world, and Finns to be descendants of the tribes of Israel.

In 1711 Viipuri fell to the Russians. Under their new tsar, Peter ("the Great"), the Russians quickly spread across the country, causing the nobility to flee to Stockholm and Swedish commanders to be more concerned with salvaging their army than saving Finland. In 1714, eight years of Russian occupation – "**The Great Wrath**" – began. Descriptions of the horrors of these times have been exaggerated, but nonetheless the events confirmed the Finns' longtime dread of their eastern neighbour. The Russians saw Finland simply as a springboard to attack Sweden, and laid waste to anything in it which the Swedes might attempt to regain.

Under the **Treaty of Uusikaupunki**, in 1721, the tsar gave back much of Finland but retained Viipuri, east Karelia, Estonia and Latvia, and thus control of the Baltic. Finland now possessed a new eastern border that was totally unprotected; Russian occupation was inevitable but would be less disastrous if entered into voluntarily. The Finnish peasants, with Swedish soldiers forcibly billeted on them, remained loyal to the king but with little faith in what he could do to protect them.

The aggressive policies of the Hats in the Swedish Diet led to the 1741 declaration of war on Russia. With barely an arm raised against them, Russian troops again occupied Finland – the start of "**The Lesser Wrath**" – until the **Treaty of Turku** in 1743. Under this, the Russians withdrew, ceded a section of Finland back to Sweden but moved their border west.

The Russian era (1809–1917)

In an attempt to force Sweden to join Napoleon's economic blockade, Russia, under Tsar Alexander I, attacked and occupied Finland in 1807. The **Treaty of Hamina**, signed in September of that year, legally ceded all of the country to Russia. The tsar had been in need of a friendly country close to Napoleon's territory as a reliable ally in case of future hostilities between the two leaders. To gain Finnish favour, he guaranteed beneficial terms at the Porvoo-based Swedish Diet, which at the time still exercised control (the Finns had yet to establish their own Diet and Senate), and subsequently Finland became an **autonomous Russian Grand Duchy**. There was no conscription and taxation was frozen, while realignment of the northern section of the Finnish–Russian border gave additional land to Finland. Finns could freely occupy positions in the Russian empire, although Russians were denied equal opportunities within Finland. The long period of peace that ensued saw a great improvement in Finnish wealth and well-being.

After returning Viipuri to Finland, the tsar declared Helsinki the **capital** in 1812, deeming Turku too close to Sweden for safety. The "Guards of Finland" helped crush the Polish rebellion and fought in the Russo-Turkish conflict. This, along with the French and English attacks on Finnish harbours during the Crimean War, accentuated the bond between the two countries. Many Finns came to regard the tsar as their own monarch.

There was, however, an increasingly active **Finnish-language movement**. A student leader, the future statesman **Johan Vilhelm Snellman**, had met the tsar and demanded that Finnish replace Swedish as the country's official language. Snellman's slogan "Swedes we are no longer, Russians we cannot become, we must be Finns" became the rallying cry of the **Fennomen**. The Swedish-speaking ruling class, feeling threatened, had Snellman removed from his university post and he retreated to Kuopio to publish newspapers espousing his beliefs. His opponents cited Finnish as the language of peasants, unfit for cultured use – a claim undermined by the efforts of a playwright, **Aleksis Kivi**, whose works marked the beginning of Finnish-language theatre. In 1835, the collection of Karelian folk tales published in Finnish by **Elias Lönnrot** as the **Kalevala** became the first written record of Finnish folklore, a solidifying force for standardization of the language and a focal point for Finnish nationalism.

The liberal tsar Alexander II appointed Snellman to Turku University, from where he went on to become minister of finance. In 1858 Finnish was declared the official language of local government in areas where the majority of the population were Finnish speaking, and the **Finnish Diet**, convened in 1863 for the first time since the Russian takeover, finally gave native-tongued Finns equal status with Swedish speakers. The only opposition was from the so-called **Svecomen**, who sought not only the maintenance of the Swedish language but unification with Finland's westerly neighbour.

The increasingly powerful Pan-Slavist contingent in Russia was horrified by the growth of the Finnish timber industry and the rise of trade with the west. They were also unhappy with the special status of the Grand Duchy, considering the Finns an alien race who would contaminate the eastern empire by their links with the west. Tsar Alexander III was not swayed by these opinions but, after his assassination in 1894, Nicholas I came to power and instigated a **Russification process**. Russian was declared the official language, Finnish money was abolished and plans were laid to merge the Finnish army into the Russian army. To pass these measures the tsar drew up the unconstitutional **February Manifesto**.

Opposition came in varying forms. In 1899, a young composer called **Jean Sibelius** wrote his majestic and dynamic *Finlandia*. The Russians banned all performances of it "under any name that indicates its patriotic character", causing Sibelius to publish it as Opus 26 No. 7. The painter **Akseli Gallen-Kallela** ignored international art trends and depicted scenes from the *Kalevala*, as did the poet **Eino Leino**. Students skied to farms all over the country and collected half a million signatures against the manifesto, and over a thousand of Europe's foremost intellectuals signed a document called "Pro-Finlandia".

But these efforts had no effect, and in 1901 the **Conscription Law** was introduced, forcing Finns to serve directly under the tsar in the Russian army. A programme of civil disobedience began, the leaders of which were soon obliged to go underground in Helsinki, where they titled themselves the **Kagel** – borrowing a name used by persecuted Russian Jews. The Finnish population became divided between the "compliants" (acquiescent to the Manifesto) and the "constitutionalists" (against the Manifesto), causing the rival sides to do their shopping in different stores and even splitting families.

The stand against conscription was enough to make the Russians drop the scheme, but their grip was tightened in other ways. A peaceful demonstration in Helsinki was broken up by cossacks on horseback, and in April 1903 the tsar installed the tough **Nicolai Bobrikov** as governor-general, giving him new and sweeping powers. The culmination of sporadic acts of violence came on June 16, 1904, when the Finnish civil servant **Eugen Schauman** climbed the Senate staircase and shot Bobrikov three times before turning the gun on himself. After staggering to his usual Senate seat, Bobrikov collapsed and died – and his assassin became a national hero.

In 1905 the Russians suffered defeat in their war with Japan, and the general strike that broke out in their country spread to Finland, the Finnish labour movement being represented by the Social Democratic Party. The revolutionary spirit that was moving through Russia encouraged the conservative Finnish Senate to reach a compromise with the demands of the Social Democrats, and the result was a gigantic upheaval in the Finnish parliamentary system. In 1906, the country adopted a single-chamber parliament (the **Eduskunta**) elected by national suffrage – Finnish women being the first in Europe to get the vote. In the first election under the new system the Social Democrats won eighty seats out of the total of two hundred, making it the most left-wing legislature seen so far in Europe.

Any laws passed in Finland, however, still needed the ratification of the tsar, who now viewed Finland as a dangerous forum for leftist debate (the exiled Lenin met Stalin for the first time in Tampere). In 1910 Nicholas II removed the new parliament's powers and reinstated the Russification programme. Two years later the **Parity Act** gave Russians in Finland status equal to Finns, enabling them to hold seats in the Senate and posts in the civil service. The outspoken anti-tsarist parliamentary speaker **P.E. Svinhufvud** was exiled to Siberia for a second time.

As World War I commenced, Finland was obviously allied with Russia and endured a commercial blockade, food shortages and restrictions on civil liberties, but did not actually fight on the tsar's behalf. Germany promised Finland total autonomy in the event of victory for the Kaiser and provided clandestine military training to about two thousand Finnish students – the Jäger movement who reached Germany through Sweden and later fought against the Russians as a light infantry battalion on the Baltic front.

Towards independence

When the tsar was overthrown in 1917, the Russian provisional government under Kerensky declared the measures taken against Finland null and void and restored the previous level of autonomy, so making Finland an **independent** and **nation-state**. Within Finland there was uncertainty over the country's constitutional bonds with Russia. The conservative view was that prerogative powers should be passed from the deposed ruler to the provisional government, while socialists held that the provisional government had no right to exercise power in Finland and that supreme authority should be passed to the Eduskunta.

Under the **Power Act**, the Eduskunta vested in itself supreme authority within Finland, leaving only control of foreign and military matters residing with the

Russians. Kerensky refused to recognize the Power Act and dissolved the Finnish parliament, forcing a fresh election. This time a bigger poll returned a conservative majority.

The loss of their parliamentary majority and the bitterness felt towards the bourgeois-dominated Senate, who happily complied with Kerensky's demands, made the Social Democrats adopt a more militant line. Around the country there had been widespread labour disputes and violent confrontations between strikers and strike-breaking mobs hired by landowners. The Social Democrats sanctioned the formation of an armed workers' guard, soon to be called the **Red Guard**, in response to the growing **White Guard**, a right-wing private army operating in the virtual absence of a regular police force. A general strike was called on November 13, which forced the Eduskunta into reforms after just a few days. The strike was called off, but a group of dissident Red Guards threatened to break from the Social Democrats and continue the action.

After the Bolsheviks took power in Russia, the conservative Finnish government became fearful of Soviet involvement in Finnish affairs and a de facto **statement of independence** was made. The socialists, by now totally excluded from government, declared their support for independence but insisted that it should be reached through negotiation with the Soviet Union. Instead, on December 6, a draft of an independent constitution drawn up by **K.J. Ståhlberg** was approved by the Eduskunta. After a delay of three weeks it was formally recognized by the Soviet leader, Lenin.

The civil war

In asserting its new authority, the government repeatedly clashed with the labour movement. The Red Guard, who had reached an uneasy truce with the Social Democratic leadership, were involved in gun-running between

Viipuri and Petrograd, and efforts by the White Guard to halt it led to full-scale fighting. A vote passed by the Eduskunta on January 12, 1918, empowered the government to create a police force to restore law and order. On January 25 the White Guard was legitimized as the Civil Guard.

In Helsinki, a special committee of the Social Democrats took the decision to resist the Civil Guard and seize power, effectively pledging themselves to **civil war**. On January 27 and 28, a series of occupations enabled leftist committees to take control of the capital and the major towns of the south. Three government ministers who evaded capture fled to Vaasa and formed a rump administration. Meanwhile, a Finnish-born aristocrat, **C.G.E. Mannerheim**, who had served as a cavalry officer in the Russian army, arrived at the request of the government in Ostrobothnia, a region dominated by right-wing farmers, to train a force to fight the Reds.

Mannerheim, who had secured a 15 million markkaa loan from a Helsinki bank to finance his army, drew on the German-trained Jäger for officers, while the Ostrobothnian farmers – seeking to protect their landowning privileges – along with a small number of Swedish volunteers, made up the front-line troops. Their initial task was to mop up the Russian battalions remaining in western Finland, which had been posted there by the tsar to prevent German advancement in world war I, and which by now were politicized into Soviets. Mannerheim had achieved this by the beginning of February, and his attention then turned to the Reds.

The Whites were in control of Ostrobothnia, northern Finland and parts of Karelia, and were connected by a railway from Vaasa to Käkisalmi on Lake Ladoga. Although the Reds were numerically superior they were poorly equipped and poorly trained, and failed to break the enemy's line of communication. Tampere fell to the Whites in March. At the same time, a German force landed on the south coast, their assistance requested by White Finns in Berlin (although Mannerheim opposed their involvement). Surrounded, the leftists' resistance collapsed in April.

Throughout the conflict, the Social Democratic Party maintained a high level of unity. While containing revolutionary elements, it was led mainly by socialists seeking to retain parliamentary democracy, and believing their fight was against a bourgeois force seeking to impose right-wing values on the newly independent state. Their arms, however, were supplied by the Soviet Union, causing the White taunt that the Reds were "aided by foreign bayonets". Many of the revolutionary socialists within the party fled to Russia after the civil war, where they formed the Finnish Communist Party. The harsh treatment of the Reds who were captured – 8000 were executed and 80,000 were imprisoned in camps where more than 9000 died from hunger or disease – fired a resentment that would last for generations. The Whites regarded the war as one of liberation, ridding the country of Russians and the Bolshevik influence, and setting the course for an anti-Russian Finnish nationalism. Mannerheim and the strongly pro-German Jäger contingent were keen to continue east, to gain the whole of Karelia from the Russians, but the possibility of direct Finnish assistance to the Russian White Army – who were seeking to overthrow the Bolshevik government – came to nothing thanks to the Russian Whites' refusal to guarantee recognition of Finland's independent status.

Later that year, a **provisional government of independent Karelia** was set up in Uhtua. Its formation was masterminded by Red Finns, who ensured that its claims to make Karelia a totally independent region did not accord with the desires of the Finnish government. The provisional government's congress, held the following year, also confirmed a wish for separation from the Soviet Union and requested the removal of the Soviet troops; this was agreed, with a proviso that Soviet troops retained a right to be based in eastern Karelia. The eventual collapse of the talks caused the provisional government and its supporters to flee to Finland as a Finnish battalion of the Soviet Red Army moved in and occupied the area. Subsequently the Karelian Workers' Commune, motivated by the Finnish Communists and backed by Soviet decree, was formed.

A few days later, the state of war which existed between Finland and Russia was formally ended by the **Treaty of Tartu**. The existence of the Karelian Workers' Commune gave the Soviet negotiators a pretext for refusing Finnish demands for Karelian self-determination, claiming the new set-up to be an expression of the Karelian people's wishes. The treaty was signed in an air of animosity. A bald settlement of border issues, it gave Finland the Petsamo area, a strategic shoulder of land extending to the Arctic coast, an ice-free harbour on the Arctic coast, providing valuable access to a northern waterway.

The republic

The White success in the civil war led to a right-wing government with a pro-German majority, which wanted to establish Finland as a monarchy rather than the republic allowed for under the 1917 declaration of independence. Although twice defeated in the Eduskunta, Prime Minister **J.K. Paasikivi** evoked a clause in the Swedish Form of Government from 1772, making legal the election of a king. As a result, the Finnish crown was offered to a German, Friedrich Karl, Prince of Hessen. Immediately prior to German defeat in world war I, the prince declined the invitation. The victorious Allies insisted on a new Finnish government and a fresh general election if they were to recognize the nation's independent status. Since the country was now compelled to look to the Allies for future assistance, the request was complied with, sealing Finland's

future as a republic. The first president was the liberal **Ståhlberg**.

The termination of the monarchists' aims upset the unity of the right and paved the way for a succession of centrist governments. These were dominated by two parties, the **National Progressives** and the **Agrarians**. Through a period of rapidly increasing prosperity, numerous reforms were enacted. Farmers who rented land were given the opportunity to buy it with state aid, compulsory schooling was introduced, laws regarding religious freedom were passed and the provision of social services strengthened. As more farmers became independent producers, the Agrarians, claiming to represent the rural interests, drew away much of the Social Democrats' traditional support.

Finnish economic development halted abruptly following the world slump of the late 1920s. A series of strikes culminated in a dock workers' dispute which began in May 1928 and continued for almost a year. It was settled by the intervention of the Minister for Social Affairs on terms perceived as a defeat for the strikers. The dispute was seen by the right as a Communist-inspired attempt to ruin the Finnish export trade at a time when the Soviet Union had re-entered the world timber trade. It was also a symbolic ideological clash – a harbinger of events to come.

Moves to outlaw Communist activity had been deemed an infringement of civil rights, but in 1929 the Suomen Lukko was formed to legally combat Communism. It was swiftly succeeded by the more extreme and violent **Lapua Movement** (the name coming from the Ostrobothnian town, where a parade of Communist youth had been brought to a bloody end by "White" farmers). The Lapuans rounded up suspected Communists and Communist sympathizers, and drove them to the Russian border, insisting that they walk across. Even the former president, Ståhlberg, was kidnapped and dumped at the eastern town of Joensuu. The Lapuans' actions were only half-heartedly condemned by the non-socialist parties, and in private they were supported. But when the Lapuans began advocating a complete overthrow of the political system, much of this tacit approval dried up.

The government obtained a two-thirds majority in the elections of October 1930 and amended the constitution to make Communist activity illegal. This was expected to placate the Lapuans but instead they issued even more extreme demands, including the abolition of the Social Democrats. In 1932, a coup d'état was attempted by a Lapuan group who prevented a socialist member of parliament from addressing a meeting in Mäntsälä, 50km north of Helsinki. They refused to disperse, despite shots being fired by police, and sent for backup assistance from Lapuan bases around the country. The Lapuan leadership took up the cause and broadcast demands for a new government. They were unsuccessful due to the loyalty of the troops who surrounded the town on the orders of the then prime minister, Svinhufvud. Following this, the Lapuans were outlawed, although their leaders received only minor punishments for their deeds. Several of them regrouped as the Nazi-style Patriotic People's Movement. But unlike the parallel movements in Europe, there was little in Finland on which Nazism could focus mass hatred and, despite winning a few parliamentary seats, the movement quickly dwindled into insignificance.

The Finnish **economy** recovered swiftly, and much international goodwill was generated when the country became the only nation to fully pay its war reparations to the USA after World War I. Finland joined the League of Nations hoping for a guarantee of its eastern border, but by 1935 the League's weakness was apparent and the Finns looked to traditionally neutral **Scandinavia** for protection as Europe moved towards war.

World War II

The Nazi–Soviet Non-Aggression Pact of August 1939 put Finland firmly into the Soviet sphere. Stalin had compelled Estonia, Latvia and Lithuania to allow Russian bases on their land, and by October was demanding a chunk of the Karelian isthmus from Finland to protect Leningrad, as well as a leasing of the Hanko peninsula on the Finnish Baltic coast. Russian troops were heading towards the Finnish border from Murmansk, and on November 30 the Karelian isthmus was attacked – an act that triggered the **Winter War**.

Stalin had had the tsarist military commanders executed, and his troops were led by young Communists well versed in ideology but ignorant of war strategy. Informed that the Finnish people would welcome them as liberators, the Soviet soldiers anticipated little resistance to their invasion. They expected to reach the Finnish west coast within ten days and therefore carried no overcoats, had little food, and camped each night in open fields. The Finns, although vastly outnumbered, were defending their homes and farms as well as their hard-won independence. Familiarity with the terrain enabled them to conceal themselves in the forests and attack through stealth – and they were prepared for the winter -temperatures, which plunged to -30°C (-18°F). The Russians were slowly picked off and their camps frequently surrounded and destroyed.

While Finland gained the world's admiration, no practical help was forthcoming and it became simply a matter of time before Stalin launched a better-supplied, unstoppable advance. It came during February 1940, and the Finnish government was forced to ask for peace. This was granted under the **Treaty of Moscow**, signed in March by President **Kyösti Kallio**, who cursed "let the hand wither that signs such a paper" as his hand put pen to paper. The treaty ceded 11 percent of Finnish territory to the Soviet Union – there was a mass exodus from these areas, with nearly half a million people travelling west to the new boundaries of Finland. Kyösti Kallio was later stricken by paralysis on his right side.

The period immediately following the Winter War left Finland in a difficult position. Before the war, Finland had produced all its own food but was dependent on imported fertilizers. Supplies of grain, which had been coming from Russia, were halted as part of Soviet pressure for increased transit rights and access to the important nickel-producing mines in Petsamo. Finland became reliant on grain from Germany and British shipments to the Petsamo coast, which were Interrupted when Germany invaded Norway. In return for providing arms, Germany was given transit rights through Finland. Legally, this required the troops to be constantly moving, but a permanent force became stationed at Rovaniemi.

The Finnish leadership knew that Germany was secretly preparing to attack the Soviet Union, and a broadcast from Berlin had spoken of a "united front" from Norway to Poland at a time when Finland was officially outside the Nazi sphere. Within Finland there was little support for the Nazis, but there was a fear of Soviet occupation. While Finland clung to its neutrality, refusing to fight unless attacked, it was drawn closer and closer to Germany. Soviet air raids on several Finnish towns in June 1941 finally led Finland into the war on the side of the Nazis. The ensuing conflict with the Russians, fought with the primary purpose of regaining territory lost in the Winter War, became known as the **Continuation War**. The bulk of the land ceded under the Treaty of Moscow was recovered by the end of August. After this, Mannerheim, who commanded the Finnish troops, ignored Nazi encouragement to assist in their attack on Leningrad. A request from the British prime minister, Winston Churchill, that the Finns cease their advance, was also refused, although Mannerheim didn't cut the Murmansk railway which was moving Allied supplies. Even so, Britain was forced to acknowledge the predicament of its ally, the Soviet Union, and declared war on Finland in December 1941.

In 1943, the German defeat at Stalingrad, which made Allied victory almost inevitable, had a profound impact in Finland. Mannerheim called a meeting of inner-cabinet ministers and decided to seek a truce with the Soviet Union. The USA stepped forward as mediators but announced that the peace terms set by Moscow were too severe to be worthy of negotiation. Germany, meanwhile, had learned of the Finnish initiative and demanded an undertaking that Finland would not seek peace with Russia, threatening to withdraw supplies if it was not given. (The Germans were also unhappy with Finnish sympathy for Jews – several hundred who had escaped from central Europe were saved from the concentration camps by being granted Finnish citizenship.) Simultaneously, a Russian advance into Karelia made Finland dependent on German arms to launch a counterattack. An agreement with the Germans was signed by President **Risto Ryti** in June 1944 without the consent of the Eduskunta, thereby making the deed invalid when he ceased to be president.

Ryti resigned the presidency at the beginning of August and Mannerheim informed Germany that the agreement was no longer binding. A peace treaty with the Soviet Union was signed in Moscow two weeks later. Under its terms, Finland was forced to give up the Pestamo region and the border was restored to its 1940 position. The Hanko peninsula was returned but instead the Porkkala peninsula, nearer to Helsinki, was to be leased to the Soviet Union for fifty years. There were stinging reparations, and the Finns had to drive the remaining Germans out of the country within two weeks. This was easily done in the south, but the bitter fighting that took place in Lapland caused the total destruction of many towns. It was further agreed that organizations disseminating anti-Soviet views within Finland would be dissolved, and that Finland would accept an Allied Control Commission to oversee war trials.

The postwar period

After the war, the Communist Party was legalized and, along with militant socialists expelled from the Social Democratic Party, formed a broad leftist umbrella organization – the **Finnish People's Democratic League**. Their efforts to absorb the Social Democrats were resisted by that party's moderate leadership, who regarded Communism as "poison to the Finnish people". In the first peace-time poll, the Democratic League went to the electorate with a populist rather than revolutionary manifesto – something that was to characterize future Finnish Communism. Both they and the Social Democrats attained approximately a quarter of the vote. Bolstered by two Social Democratic defections, the Democratic League narrowly became the largest party in the Eduskunta. The two of them, along with the Agrarian Party, formed an alliance ("The Big Three Agreement") that held the balance of power in a coalition government under the premiership of Paasikivi.

Strikes instigated by Communist-controlled trade unions allowed the Social Democrats to accuse the Democratic League of seeking to undermine the production of machinery and other goods destined for the Soviet Union under the terms of the war reparation agreement, thereby creating a scenario for Soviet invasion. Charges of Communist vote-rigging in trade union ballots helped the Social Democrats to gain control of the unions. The Democratic League won only 38 seats in the general election of 1948, and rejected the token offer of four posts in the new government, opting instead to stay in opposition. Their electoral campaign wasn't helped by the rumour – almost certainly groundless – that they were planning a Soviet-backed coup.

To ensure that the terms of the peace agreement were adhered to, the Soviet-dominated Allied Control Commission stayed in Finland until 1947. Its presence engendered a tense atmosphere both on the streets of Helsinki – there were several incidents of violence against Soviet officers – and in the numerous clashes with the Finnish government over the war trials. Unlike the eastern European countries under full Soviet occupation, Finland was able to carry out its own trials, but had to satisfy the Commission that they were conducted properly. Delicate manoeuvring by the Chief of Justice, **Urho Kekkonen**, resulted in comparatively short prison sentences for the accused, the longest being ten years for Risto Ryti.

The uncertain relationship between Finland and the Soviet Union was resolved, to some extent, by the signing of the **Treaty of Friendship, Cooperation and Mutual Assistance** (FCMA) in 1948. It affirmed Finnish responsibility for its own defence and pledged the country not to join any alliance hostile to the Soviet Union. In the suspicious atmosphere of the Cold War, the treaty was perceived by the western powers to place Finland firmly under Soviet influence. The Soviet insistence that the treaty was a guarantee of neutrality was viewed as hypocritical given that they were still leasing the Porkkala peninsula. When it became clear that Finland was not becoming a Soviet satellite and had full control over its internal affairs, the USA reinstated credit facilities – carefully structured to avoid financing anything that would be of help to the Soviets – and Finland was admitted to western financial institutions such as the IMF and World Bank.

The postwar **economy** was dominated by the reparations demand. Much of the bill was paid off in ships and machinery, which established engineering as a major industry. The escalating world demand for timber products boosted exports, but inflation soared and led to frequent wage disputes. In 1949 an attempt to enforce a piece-work rate in a pulp factory in Kemi culminated in two workers being shot by police, a state of emergency being declared in the town, and the arrest of Communist leaders. Economic conflicts reached a climax in 1956 after right-wingers in the Eduskunta had blocked an annual extension of government controls on wages and prices. This caused a sharp rise in the cost of living and the trade unions demanded appropriate pay increases. A general strike followed, lasting for three weeks until the strikers' demands were met. Any benefit, however, was quickly nullified by further price rises.

In 1957 a split occurred in the Social Democrats between urban and rural factions, the former seeking increased industrialization and the streamlining of unprofitable farms, the latter pursuing high agricultural subsidies. By 1959 a group of breakaway ruralists had set up the Small Farmers' Social Democratic Union, causing a rift within the country's internal politics that was to have important repercussions in Finland's dealings with the Soviet Union. Although the government had no intention of changing its foreign policy, the Social Democrat's chairman, **Väinö Tanner**, had a well-known antipathy to the Soviet Union. Coupled with a growing number of anti-Soviet newspaper editorials, this precipitated the "**night frost**" of 1958. The Soviet leader, Khruschev, suspended imports and deliveries of machinery, causing a rise in Finnish unemployment. **Kekkonen**, elected president in 1956, personally intervened in the crisis by meeting with Khruschev, so angering the Social Democrats, who accused Kekkonen of behaving undemocratically; meanwhile, the Agrarians were lambasted for failing to stand up to Soviet pressure.

In 1960 Tanner was re-elected as chairman and the Social Democrats continued to attack Kekkonen; the Agrarians refused to enter government with the Social Democrats unless they changed their policies. As global relations worsened during 1961, the Soviet Union sent a note to Kekkonen requesting a meeting to discuss the section of the 1948 treaty dealing with defence of the Finnish–Soviet border. This was the precursor to the "**note crisis**". The original note went unanswered, but the Finnish foreign secretary went to Moscow for exploratory talks with his opposite number. Assurances of Soviet confidence in Finnish foreign policy were given, but fears were expressed about the anti-Kekkonen alliance of conservatives and Social Democrats formed to contest the 1962 presidential election. Kekkonen again tried to defuse the crisis himself: using his constitutional powers he dissolved parliament early, forcing the election forward by several months; in so doing, he weakened the alliance. Kekkonen was re-elected and foreign policy remained unchanged. This was widely regarded as a personal victory for Kekkonen and a major turning point in relations with the Soviet Union. Through all subsequent administrations, the maintenance of the **Paasikivi-Kekkonen line** on foreign policy became a symbol of national unity.

Following Tanner's retirement from politics in 1963, the Social Democrats ended their stand against the established form of foreign policy, making possible their re-entry to government.

Throughout the early 1960s there was mounting dissatisfaction within the People's Democratic League towards the old pro-Moscow leadership. In 1965, a moderate non-Communist was elected as the League's general secretary, and two years later he became chairman; a similar change took place in the Communist leadership of the trade unions. The new-look Communists pledged their desire for a share in government. The election of May 1966 resulted in a "popular front" government dominated by the Social Democrats and the People's Democratic League, under the prime ministership of **Rafael Paasio**.

This brought to an end a twenty-year spell of centre-right governments in which the crucial pivot had been the Agrarian Party. In 1965, the Agrarians changed their name to the Centre Party, aiming to modernize their image and become more attractive to the urban electorate. A challenge to this new direction was mounted by the **Finnish Rural Party**, founded by a breakaway group of Agrarians in the late 1950s, who mounted an increasingly influential campaign on behalf of "the forgotten people" – farmers and smallholders in declining rural areas. In the election of 1970 they gained ten percent of the vote, but in subsequent years lost support through internal divisions.

The Communists retained governmental posts until 1971, when they too were split – between the young "reformists" who advocated continued participation in government, and the older, hard-line "purists" who were frustrated by the failure to implement socialist economic policies, and preferred to stay in opposition.

Modern Finland

Throughout the postwar years Finland promoted itself vigorously as a **neutral country**. It joined the United Nations in 1955 and Finnish soldiers became an integral part of the UN Peace-Keeping Force. In 1969 preparations were started for the European Security Conference in Helsinki, and in 1972 the city was the venue for the **Strategic Arms Limitation Talks** (SALT), underlining a Finnish role in mediation between the superpowers. But an attempt to have a clause stating Finland's neutrality inserted into the 1970 extension-signing of the FCMA Treaty was opposed by the Soviet Union, whose foreign secretary, Andrei Gromyko, had a year earlier defined Finland not as neutral but as a "peace-loving neighbour of the Soviet Union".

In 1971 the revelations of a Czech defector, General Sejna, suggesting that the Soviet army was equipped to take over Finland within 24 hours should Soviet defences be compromised, brought a fresh wave of uncertainty to relations with its eastern neighbour; as did the sudden withdrawal of the Soviet ambassador, allegedly for illicit scheming with the People's Democratic League.

The stature of Kekkonen as a world leader guaranteed continued support for his presidency. But his commitment to the Paasikivi-Kekkonen line ensured that nothing potentially upsetting to the Soviet Union was allowed to surface in Finnish politics, giving – as some thought – the Soviet Union a covert influence on Finland's internal affairs. Opposition to Kekkonen was simply perceived as an attempt to undermine the Paasikivi-Kekkonen line. Equally, the unchallengeable nature of Kekkonen's presidency was considered to be beyond his proper constitutional powers. A move in 1974 by an alliance of right-wingers and Social Democrats within the Eduskunta to transfer some of the presidential powers to parliament received a very hostile reaction, emphasizing the almost inviolate position that Kekkonen enjoyed. Kekkonen was re-elected in 1978, although forced to stand down due to illness in 1981.

Because Finland is heavily dependent on foreign trade, its well-being has closely mirrored world trends. The international financial boom of the 1960s enabled a range of social legislation to be passed and created a comparatively high standard of living for most Finns – albeit not on the same scale as the rest of Scandinavia. The global **recession** of the 1970s and early 1980s was most dramatically felt when a fall in the world market for wood pulp coincided with a steep increase in the price of oil. Although the country tackled the immediate problems of the recession, industry remained heavily concentrated in the south, causing rural areas further north to experience high rates of unemployment and few prospects for economic growth – save through rising levels of tourism.

The election of 1987 saw a break with the pattern of previous decades. Non-socialist parties made large gains, mainly at the expense of the Rural Party and Communists. The new government of **Harri Holkeri**, however, appeared inept – particularly in its hesitant reaction to events in the Soviet Union and continued deference to Moscow, whether real or apparent.

Public disillusionment resulted in large gains for the Centre Party in the election of March 1991. The Centre Party chairman, 47-year-old **Esko Aho**, subsequently became prime minister, leading a new coalition in which many of the members reflected the comparative youth and fresh ideas of its leader.

In 1992 celebrations to mark 75 years of Finnish independence were muted by the realization that the country was entering a highly critical period, facing more problems (few of its own making) than it had for many decades. The end of the Cold War had diminished the value of Finland's hard-won neutrality, the economic and ethnic difficulties in Russia were being watched with trepidation, while another global **recession** hit Finland just as the nation lost its major trading partner – the Soviet Union – of the last fifty years.

Throughout the early 1990s Finland's economic depression was among the worst in the industrial west. Its banking system was in crisis and unemployment figures were almost the highest in Europe, while the country's growing number of asylum seekers became a scapegoat for the resultant social problems, culminating in a spate of anti-immigrant violence during the mid-1990s. Such economic and societal strife forced Finland to pin its hopes on closer links with western Europe. On January 1, 1995, Finland became a full member of the **European Union** and, in the same year, the Social Democratic Party's **Martti Ahtisaari** was elected as president, with the general election resulting in a coalition win for the Social Democrats, their Chairman Paavo Lipponen forming a majority government that included conservatives, socialists, the Swedish Folk Party and the Green Party.

By the millennium, as Russia descended into farce, Finland had become more firmly linked to the EU and its economy had recovered sufficiently for it to be accepted into the first wave of countries to join European Monetary Union. In 1999, for the first time, Finland assumed the presidency of the European Union, while President Ahtisaari established himself as an important international statesman through his interventions in the war in Kosovo. When Ahtisaari decided not to seek re-election in 2000, long-standing member of parliament and then Foreign Minister **Tarja Halonen** ran a victorious campaign and became Finland's first female president. The independent-minded Halonen has since taken an active role in leading the country, while maintaining a 95 percent approval rating in opinion polls; in 2004, she was nominated one of ten *suuret Suomalaiset* "greatest Finns" – the only living person on the list.

The 2006 presidential campaign sparked a nationwide discussion over limiting the president's powers – an issue which brought to light Finnish concern over the degree of "democratic" decision-making effected by current heads of government – as well as talk over the age-old issue of NATO membership and its link to threats of terrorism; most Finns are concerned that joining NATO would increase Finland's risk of terrorist attacks – by all accounts relatively low compared to its more politically vocal continental neighbours. On January 29, 2006, Halonen was re-elected by tiny margin for a second six-year presidential term. The future of Finland's long-standing neutrality in Europe was the campaign's focal issue, and Halonen's second win suggests that Finland will remain outside NATO until at least 2012.

Economically, Finland's highly educated populace and technological expertise has made it a powerful player in the world IT market, and it consistently ranks among the top three countries in the world for **technological innovation**. Finland's other industrialized sectors have helped it to maintain a per-capita output on par with that of the UK and Germany, and while the country boasts the highest prices in the EU – a whopping 23 percent above the average for EU member states – Finns have been earning money at an unprecedented rate since the turn of the millennium. The adoption of the **euro** as Finland's currency in 2002 brought a new pride to the Finnish nation after years of living in the shadow of the Soviet Union; political and economic freedom had finally – and, most importantly, tangibly – been won. And with neighbouring Estonia now a full member of the EU, a former foe has emerged from behind the Iron Curtain to establish itself as a trade and tourism ally on equitable, if not entirely equal, footing.

But while EU membership has provided a new sense of security and confidence, the contemporary picture is not entirely rosy: the age-old issue of alcoholism and the chaos of Russia's gangster economy on the doorstep provide major worries, as do continuing debates around the role of the welfare state. The hot potato of Karelia has also crept steadily into public debate as Halonen has endeavoured to strengthen cultural and economic ties with Putin's Russia. Other pressing issues include the need to diversify an economy that is over-reliant on the Nokia phone company, and the means by which to continue development in rural areas without the support of big government subsidies. Thankfully, **unemployment** is finally on the decline, with the 2005 rate of 7.2 percent close to half what it was a decade earlier. But as the baby-boomers of the early postwar period

near retirement age, the labour force will need to be further empowered if Finland hopes to continue to provide adequate levels of care for its elderly and poor.

How these issues are addressed remains Finland's major concern in the first decade of the new millennium. However, it's the role of the **environment** that's likely to grab the headlines in the coming years. Construction of Finland's fifth nuclear power station is slated to finish in 2009, at which point nuclear energy will provide well over thirty percent of the country's total energy needs; all this at a time when the rest of Europe – and neighbouring Sweden – is scaling down nuclear power because of excessive cost, increasing fears of pollution and the possibility of terrorist attacks. While Finland does currently spend close to €1 billion annually on environmental protection, and is considered the most successful of all EU members in its efforts to achieve sustainable development, questions are being raised about the security and efficacy of the government's energy projects, not least by the vocal Green Party, which fled the government coalition in 2002 when approval for construction of the new plant was approved. A heated public debate on these very sensitive issues now looks set to take the established practice of Finnish consensus politics to new extremes.

Books

D ue to Finland's relative obscurity in terms of English-language audiences, there's a real dearth of decent publications about anything Finnish. As for traditional literature itself, many Finnish authors have found a wider audience in French, German, Italian and Swedish readers than amongst English-speaking ones, so coming to grips with who's who in the contemporary Finnish literary scene might prove problematic without a knowledge of one of these languages. Although most of the books listed below are easily found in bookstores or on the Internet, those that are out of print (designated "o/p") should still be available in larger public libraries. It's a testament to the superiority of technology in Finland that you will always find much more written information about Finland on the Internet than in any reasonably priced book. Titles marked with a 🛪 represent essential reads.

History and Society

Eloise Engel and Lauri Paananen *The Winter War: The Soviet Attack on Finland 1939–1940.* An excellent and popular account of the Finns' resistance and final defeat by overwhelming numbers of Soviet troops during the Winter War.

D.G. Kirby *Finland in the Twentieth Century – A History and Interpretation.* By far the best insight into contemporary Finland and the reshaping of the nation after independence.

Veli-Pekka Lehtola *The Sámi People: Traditions in Transition.* A well-written, fully-illustrated contemporary history of the Sámi across Scandinavia, which details the social changes experienced by these once fully-nomadic reindeer herders and explains how they are currently forging for themselves a delicate path between the traditional and the modern.

Kenneth D. McRae *Conflict and Compromise in Multilingual Societies: Finland.* Although academic in tone, this is an excellent account of the unique problems faced by Finland's Swedish-speaking minority, explaining how the language of Finland's former colonial masters fell into minority use.

Nikki Rajala *Some Like It Hot: The Sauna, Its Lore and Stories.* History of the most famous social institution in Finland, plus lots of interesting factoids about the ritual and its role in the nation's development over the years.

Fred Singleton *A Short History of Finland.* A very readable and informative account of Finland's past. It lacks the detail of most academic accounts, but is an excellent starting point for general readers.

Literature

Tove Jansson *The Moomin books.* Enduring children's tales, with evocative descriptions of Finnish nature.

Matti Joensuu *Harjunpää and the Stone Murders* (o/p). The only one of the Harjunpää series, involving the Helsinki detective, Timo Harjunpää, to have been translated into English. It's set in contemporary Helsinki during a bout of teenage gang warfare.

Christer Kihlman *The Rise and Fall of Gerdt Bladh* (o/p). Supremely evocative study of personal anguish set against a background of Finland's ascent from rural backwater to prosperous modern nation.

Väinö Linna *The Unknown Soldier* (o/p). Based on his experiences fighting in the Winter War, and for the first time depicting Finnish soldiers not as "heroes in white" but as drunks and womanizers, Linna's novel triggered immense controversy. Less well known but equally as poignant, *The North Star*, his first tome in the trilogy, describes a late nineteenth-century rural Finnish community, highlighting the seminal historical events which helped to mould the Finnish national character.

Elias Lönnrot *Kalevala.* The classic tome of Finnish literature, this collection of folk tales was transcribed over twenty years by Lönnrot, a rural doctor. Set in an unspecified point in the past, the plot centres on a state of war between the mythical region of Kalevala (probably northern Karelia) and Pohjola (possibly Lapland) over possession of a talisman called the Sampo. The story is regarded as quintessentially Finnish, but it's not an easy read, due mainly to its length (some 22,750 lines), and the non-linear course of the plot. Its influence on Finnish literature is huge, though, and it was a linchpin of the Finnish nationalist and language movements.

Arto Paasilinna *The Year of the Hare.* Finland's most well-known author, Paasilinna's forty-odd books have been translated into dozens of languages. He has a keen eye for the Finnish character and sense of humour, and this 1977 novel, his best known, is inventive, satirical and mythical, offering profound insight into late twentieth-century Western society. The story concerns a Finnish journalist who, after running over a rabbit and then nursing it back to health, pursues his own rebellion against social mores, politics and relationships.

Oscar Parland *The Year of the Bull.* Absorbing look at the civil war-torn Finland of 1918 through the eyes of a young boy.

Runar Schildt *The Meat-Grinder and Other Stories.* Intriguing tales, set mostly in Helsinki before and during the Finnish civil war. Schildt (1888–1925) is probably Finland's finest short story writer.

Kirsti Simonsuuri (ed) *Enchanting Beasts.* A slender but captivating tome, and one of the few English translations of Finland's best modern poets.

Johanna Sinisalao *Troll: A Love Story.* Sodankylä native Sinisalao wrote her debut novel to critical acclaim in Finland and abroad, capturing the prestigious Finlandia prize. In this account, a young gay photographer is viscerally influenced by a curious find from his courtyard: a small troll which comes to awaken dark desires within him. Merging folklore with psychology, the book fuses an engaging mythological love story with subtly astute insight into modern human relationships.

Miscellaneous

Beatrice Ojakangas *Finnish Cookbook.* Originally published in 1964,

these timeless, all-round recipes shed light on one of Scandinavia's least known cuisines – everything from fish stew to prune tarts, as well as short stories about the Finnish way of life.

Micha Ramakers *Dirty Pictures: Tom of Finland, Masculinity, and Homosexuality.* An excellent account of the social and cultural issues touched upon by the work of gay-themed comic strip artist Touko Laaksonen (aka Tom of Finland), who once memorably stated "If I don't have an erection when I'm doing a drawing, I know it's no good." Offers ample examples of the often graphically sexual penmanship of Finland's most well-known pictorial artist, alongside enlightening prose.

Linus Torvalds & David Diamond *Just for Fun: The Story of an Accidental Revolutionary.* The autobiography of the twentysomething Finn who revolutionized modern computer technology with his Linux operating system, all the while remaining true to his deeply religious belief in open-source computing. Reads a little choppily, with irreverent banter and off-the-cuff, email-like entries, but an enjoyable read all the same.

Richard Weston *Alvar Aalto.* Excellent overview of Aalto's life and work, with beautiful photographs and unpretentious language. Not a historical monograph, but a solid introduction to one of Finland's most beloved artistic geniuses.

A brief guide to Finnish

I t has been a year now since my arrival and I still have difficulty making myself understood in this most difficult Karelian language. There are fifteen different cases of nouns and twenty seven different words for snow. I find, however, that the following are sufficient for almost all situations: "Moi", "Moi Moi" and "Hei Toveri! Kupissani ei ole votkaa [Hey mate! There's no more vodka in my cup]."

Sir Hillman Ledbelly, 1884

Finnish is going to pose a problem to anyone whose mother tongue is an Indo-European language such as English. There's very little common ground between Finnish and any other mainstream western European language, and this can frustrate basic understanding and communication – simple tasks like deciphering a menu are often fraught with overwhelming difficulty.

Finnish also has nothing in common with the other Scandinavian languages – something that has led to considerable misunderstanding of the Finns, particularly in neighbouring Sweden. Part of the Finno-Ugric group of languages, Finnish is closely related to Estonian, Sámi and much more distantly to Hungarian, and its grammatical structure is complex: with fifteen cases alone to grapple with, it's initially a tricky language to learn, although once a basic vocabulary is attained things become less impenetrable. Unlike Indo-European German, for example, which uses prepositions to determine the case of a noun, Finnish employs a set of complex suffixes, which, although straightforward to learn, are further complicated by a slew of vowel and consonant elision rules and, to a lesser extent, a process of obligatory vowel harmony. For instance, autossa means "in the car", autolla "at the car"; whereas autosta is "out of the car". Thankfully, in the large cities and main towns, English is spoken by the younger generation with amazing fluency – many have spent a school year abroad in an English-speaking country – but second-language ability drops significantly once you head to smaller, more remote areas and start conversing with older Finns. Swedish is a common second language, although many Finns are reluctant to use the language of their former colonial masters; though it is, of course, the mother tongue of the Finland-Swedes, who live mainly in the western parts of the country, and the only language spoken on Åland. If the idea of learning Finnish makes you weak at the knees, at least memorize the longest palindrome in the world, Finnish saippuakivikauppias – the extremely useful "soapstone salesman".

If you're really turned on by the notion of attempting to crack Finnish, Fred Karlsson's Finnish: An Essential Grammar is the most accessible and comprehensive reference. Of the few available phrasebooks, Finnish For Travellers (Berlitz) is the most useful for practical purposes, sold with an accompanying audio CD; the best Finnish–English dictionary is The Finnish Standard Dictionary (Continuum International Publishing Group).

Pronunciation

In Finnish, words are pronounced exactly as they are written, with the stress always on the first syllable: in a compound word the stress is on the first syllable of each part of the word. Each letter is pronounced individually, and doubling a letter lengthens the sound: double "kk"s are pronounced with two "k" sounds and the double "aa" pronounced as long as the English "a" in "car". The letters b, c, f, q, w, x, z and å are only found in words derived from foreign languages, and are pronounced as in the language of origin.

a as in father but shorter
d as in riding but sometimes so soft as to be barely heard
e like the a in late.
g (only after "n") as in singer

h as in hot
i as in pin
j like the y in yellow
np like the m in mother
o like the aw in law
r is rolled
s as in said, but with the tongue a little
   further back from the teeth
u like the oo in cool
y like the French u in "sur"
ä like the a in hat
ö like the u in fur.

Basics

Puhutteko englantia?	Do you speak English?
Minä en puhu suomea.	I don't speak Finnish
kyllä/joo	Yes
ei	No
En ymmärrä	I don't understand
Ymmärrän	I understand
Olkaa hyvä/ole hyvä	Please
Kiitos	Thank you
Anteeksi	Excuse me
Terve/Moi	Hello
Hyvää huomenta	Good morning
Hyvää päivää	Good afternoon
Hyvää iltaa	Good evening
Hyvää päivää (usually shortened to päivä)	Good day
Hyvää yötä	Goodnight
Näkemiin/hei hei	Goodbye
Eilen	Yesterday
Tänään	Today
Huomenna	Tomorrow
Ylihuomenna	Day after tomorrow
Aamulla/ Aamupäivällä	In the morning
Iltapäivällä	In the afternoon
Illalla	In the evening
Yöllä	At night

Some signs

Sisään	Entrance
Ulos	Exit
Miehille/Miehet/ Herrat	Gentlemen
Naisille/Naiset/ Rouvat	Ladies
Kuuma	Hot
Kylmä	Cold
Avoinna	Open
Suljettu	Closed
Työnnä	Push
Vedä	Pull
Saapuvat	Arrival
Lähtevät	Departure
Poliisi	Police
Sairaala	Hospital
Tupakointi kielletty	No smoking
Pääsy kielletty	No entry
Läpikulku kielletty	No trespassing
Leiriytyminen kielletty	No camping

Questions and directions

Missä on … ?	Where's … ?
Koska/milloin?	When?
Mikä/mitä?	What?
Miksi?	Why?
Miten sanotaan … suomeksi?	How do you say … in Finnish?
Kuinka pitkä matka on … n?	How far is it to …?
Missä on rautatieasema?	Where is the railway station?
Juna/bussi (or) linja auto/vene/laiva	Train/bus/boat/ship
Missä on retkeilymaja?	Where is the youth hostel?
Voimmeko leiriytyä tähän?	Can we camp here?
Tiedätkö ketään joka voisi maijoitaa meidät yöksi?	Do you know anyone who could put us up for a night?
Onko teillä mitään parempaa/ isompaa/ halvempaa?	Do you have anything better/bigger/ cheaper?
Se on liian kallis	It's too expensive
Kuinka paljon?	How much?
Paljonko se maksaa?	How much is that?
Haluaisin	I'd like
Halpa	Cheap
Kallis	Expensive
Hyvä	Good
Paha/Huono	Bad
Täällä	Here
Siellä	There
Vasemmalla	Left
Oikealla	Right
Ajakaa suoraan eteenpäin	Go straight ahead
Onko se lähellä/ kaukana?	Is it near/far?

Lipputoimisto	Ticket/ticket office
Rautatieasema/	Train/bus station/
linjaautoasema/	bus stop
bussipysäkki	

Numbers

nolla	0
yksi	1
kaksi	2
kolme	3
neljä	4
viisi	5
kuusi	6
seitsemän	7
kahdeksan	8
yhdeksän	9
kymmenen	10
yksitoista	11
kaksitoista	12
kolmetoista	13
neljätoista	14
viisitoista	15
kuusitoista	16
seitsemäntoista	17
kahdeksantoista	18
yhdeksäntoista	19
kaksikymmentä	20
kaksikymmentäyksi	21
kolmekymmentä	30
neljäkymmentä	40
viisikymmentä	50
kuusikymmentä	60
seitsemänkymmentä	70
kahdeksankymmentä	80
yhdeksänkymmentä	90
sata	100
satayksi	101
sataviisikymmentäyksi	151
kaksisataa	200
tuhat	1000
kaksi tuhatta	2000

Days and months

maanantai	Monday
tiistai	Tuesday
keskiviikko	Wednesday
torstai	Thursday
perjantai	Friday
lauantai	Saturday
sunnuntai	Sunday
tammikuu	January
helmikuu	February
maalisku	March
huhtikuu	April
toukokuu	May
kesäkuu	June
heinäkuu	July
elokuu	August
syyskuu	September
lokakuu	October
marraskuu	November
joulukuu	December

(Days and months are never capitalized)

Glossary of Finnish terms and phrases

Järvi	Lake
Joki	River
Katu	Street
Kauppahalli	Market hall
Kauppatori	Market square
Kaupungintalo	Town hall
Keskusta	Town centre
Kirkko	Church
Kylä	Village
Linja-autoasema	Bus station
Linna	Castle
Lipputoimisto	Ticket office
Matkailutoimisto	Tourist office
Mäki	Hill
Museo	Museum
Mökki	Cabin
Neuvonta	Information
Pankki	Bank
Poro	Reindeer
Posti	Post office
Puisto	Park
Rautatieasema	Train station
Saari	Island
Sairaala	Hospital
Taidemuseo	Art museum
Tie	Road
Tori	Square
Torni	Tower
Tiekirkko	Roadside church
Tunturi	Lappish mountain
Tuomiokirkko	Cathedral
Yliopisto	University
Vastannotto	Hotel/guesthouse reception

4.1

Helsinki and the south

The southern coast of Finland is the most populated, industrialized and the richest part of the country, centred around the capital, **Helsinki**, a city of half a million people with the friendliness of a peasant village on market day. Helsinki's innovative architecture and batch of fine museums and galleries collectively expose the roots of the national character, while at night the pubs and clubs strip it bare. It may seem the perfect prelude to exploring the rest of Finland, and in the practical sense it is, being the hub of the country's road, rail and air traffic routes. However, if you can, try to arrive in Helsinki *after* seeing the rest of the country, as only with some prior knowledge of Finland does the significance of the city as a symbol of Finnish self-determination become clear.

A couple of towns **around Helsinki** further evince the change from ruralism to modernism. **Porvoo** sits placidly locked in the nineteenth century, while the suburban area of **Espoo** forms a showpiece of twentieth-century design. Further away, in the country's southeastern extremity, the only community of significant size and importance between Helsinki and the Russian border is the shipping port of **Kotka** – not wildly appealing in itself, but at the heart of a historically intriguing coastal region.

Helsinki only became the capital in 1812, after Finland had been made a Russian Grand Duchy and Tsar Alexander I had deemed the previous capital, **Turku**, too close to Sweden for comfort. Today Turku, facing Stockholm across the Gulf of Bothnia, handles its demotion well. Both historically and visually it's one of Finland's most enticing cities; indeed, the snootier elements of its Swedish-speaking contingent still consider Åbo (its Swedish name) the real capital, and Helsinki just an uncouth upstart.

Between Helsinki and Turku, along the entire southern coast, only small villages and a few slightly larger towns break the continuity of the forests. Beyond Turku,

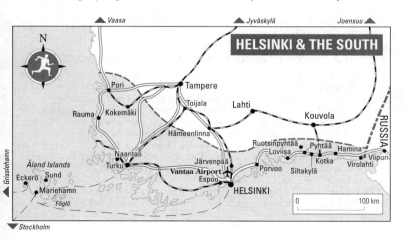

though, things are more interesting, with the two most southerly of the Finland-Swedish communities: **Rauma**, with its unique dialect and well-preserved town centre; and the likeably downbeat **Pori**, famous for its summer jazz festival.

Where this corner of Finland meets the sea it splinters into an enormous archipelago, which includes the curious **Åland Islands** – a grouping of thousands of fragments of land, only about half a dozen of which are inhabited, connected by small roadways skirting the sea. There's a tiny self-governing population here, Swedish-speaking but with a history that's distinct from both Sweden and Finland.

Much of the region is most easily reached from Helsinki, from where there are frequent bus and rail services to Turku. Rauma and Pori are best reached by bus from Turku, and from Pori there are easy rail connections to Tampere and the Lake Region (covered in the following chapter). Daily ferries also connect Turku to the Åland Islands.

Helsinki and around

HELSINKI has a character quite different from the other Scandinavian capitals, and in many ways is closer in mood (and certainly in looks) to the major cities of eastern Europe. For years an outpost of the Russian empire, its very shape and style was originally modelled on its powerful neighbour's former capital, St Petersburg. Yet throughout the twentieth century the city was also a showcase for independent Finland, much of its impressive **architecture** drawing inspiration from the dawning of Finnish nationalism and the rise of the republic. Equally the **museums**, especially the National Museum and the Art Museum of the Atheneum, reveal the country's growing awareness of its own folklore and culture.

Much of central Helsinki is a succession of compact granite blocks, interspersed with more characterful buildings, alongside waterways, green spaces and the glass-fronted office blocks and shopping centres you'll find in any European capital. The city is hemmed in on three sides by water, and all the things you might want to see are within walking distance of one another – and certainly no more than a few minutes apart by tram or bus. The streets have a youthful buzz, and the short summer is acknowledged by crowds strolling the boulevards, cruising the shopping arcades and mingling in the outdoor cafés and restaurants; everywhere there's prolific **street entertainment**. At night the pace picks up, with a great selection of pubs and clubs, free rock concerts in the numerous parks, and an impressive quota of fringe events. It's a pleasure just to be around, merging with the multitude and witnessing the activity.

Arrival, information and city transport

However you arrive you'll be deposited somewhere close to the heart of town. Helsinki's **airport**, Vantaa, 20km to the north, is served by frequent airport buses (30min; €5.20 or €3.40 with a tourist ticket, see p.688). These stop at the Finnair terminal behind the *Scandic Hotel Continental*, halfway between the city centre and the Olympic Stadium, before continuing to the train station; they leave from lane 30, adjacent to the east entrance to the train station, just across from the post office. A cheaper, if slightly slower, airport connection is city bus #615; this costs €3.40 and runs roughly every fifteen minutes from the airport to the city bus terminal beside the train station, though if you ask the driver you can get off beforehand at any number of fixed stops.

The Viking and Silja **ferry** lines have their terminals on opposite sides of the South Harbour (at docks known respectively as Katajanokka and Olympia), and disembarking passengers from either have a walk of less than 1km to the centre.

△ Central train station facade

Central train station, equipped with luggage lockers, is right in the heart of the city on Kaivokatu, next door to the **city bus terminal**. All trams stop immediately outside or around the corner along Mannerheimintie, across which, on Simonkatu, is the ultra-modern Kamppi shopping centre, which houses the new **long-distance bus terminal**.

Information

The **City Tourist Office**, at Pohjoisesplanadi 19 (May–Sept Mon–Fri 9am–8pm, Sat & Sun 9am–5pm; Oct–April Mon–Fri 9am–5pm, Sat & Sun 10am–4pm; ☎09/169 3757, ⊛www.hel.fi/tourism), supplies free street and transport maps, along with the useful free tourist magazine *Helsinki This Week*, which contains masses of listings for forthcoming events in the capital as well as a couple of decent maps on the back pages. While here, try to get hold of another worthy free brochure, *See Helsinki On Foot*, which uses both Finnish and Swedish street names on its maps; since Finland is officially bilingual you will find this dual-naming

HELSINKI

Viking

▲ Vantaa Airport

▲ B

▲ Seurasaari, ① & ②

Museum of Workers' Housing

SÖRNÄINEN

HÄMEENTIE

③
④

KALLIO
Kallion kirkko

FLEMINGINKATU

KIRSTINKATU

BRAHENKATU

HAKANIEMI

Kaupahalli

Military Museum

Burgher's House

KRUUNUN-HAKA

Tuomiokirkko

Linnanmäki Amusement Park

VAUHTITIE

Eläintarhanlahti

Botanical Gardens

KLUUVI

Kaisaniemenlahti

UNIONINKATU

FABIANINKATU

VUORIKATU

City Bus Terminal

Töölönlahti

Finlandia Hall

Hakasalmi Villa ⑩

Train Station

Post Office

Lasipalatsi

Opera House ⑥

National Museum

Parliament Building ⑪

MANNERHEIMINTIE

Olympic Stadium A

MAAVO NURMENTIE

TAKA-TÖÖLÖ

⑤

⑥
⑦
⑧
⑨

Temppeliaukio kirkko

ETU-TÖÖLÖ

RUNEBERGINKATU

MECHELININKATU

Sibelius Park

Sibelius Monument

MECHELININKATU

Taivallahti

Hietaranta Beach

Line Katajanokka Terminal, ▲ ❶ & ❷   ▲ Suomenlinna

Lapinlahti

Uspenski Cathedral

LUOTSIKATU

KAPTEENINKATU

SENATE SQUARE
ALEKSANTERINKATU

City Hall

City Tourist Office ℹ

POHJOISESPLANADI

Boats to Suomenlinna

Kauppahalli

Kauppatori

South Harbour
(Eteläsatama)

Sightseeing boat tours

Valkosaari

Klippan

Olympia Terminal (Silja Line ferries)

Mannerheim Museum

Cygnaeus Gallery

Kaivopuisto Park

Harakka

Merisatama

Uunisaari

Sirpalesaari

⑰

N

500m
0

❹
4.1 | FINLAND

KLUUVIKATU

ETELÄESPLANADI

KASARMIKATU

Finland Tourist Board ℹ

KAARTIN-
KAUPUNKI

KORKEAVUORENKATU

ETELÄRANTA

LAIVASILLANKATU

⑭

ULLANLINNA

⑮

NEITSYTPOLKU

KAPTEENINKATU

TEHTAANKATU

HUVILAKATU

LAIVURINKATU

EIRA

Merisatama Harbour

MIKONKATU
KESKUSKATU

EROTTAJANKATU

YRJÖNKATU

Vanha kirkko

Forum Shopping Centre

Johanneksen kirkko

Mikael Agricola kirkko

⑯

Pihlajasaari

& Postal Museum

ANNANKATU

FREDRIKINKATU

ALBERTINKATU

PUNAVUORI

Sinebrychoff Art Museum

Kamppi Centre & Long-distance Bus Terminal

KAMPPI

MALMINKATU

ABRAHAMINKATU

LAPINLAHDENKATU

RUNEBERGINKATU

MECHELININKATU

TELAKKATU

⑬

HYLKEENPYYTIKA

Hietalahti

see 'Central Helsinki' map for more detail of this area

Hietaniemi Cemetery

SELKÄMERENKATU

KELLOSAARENKATU

TAMMERENKATU

PORKKALANKATU

RUOHOLAHTI

Ruoholahti

LÄNSISATAMA

Kaapelitehdas

687

ACCOMMODATION

Euro Hostel   D
Rastila Campsite   B
Scandic Continental   C
Stadion   A

CAFÉS, RESTAURANTS & BARS

Abin Baari   4
Ani   16
Caramelli   10
Elite   9
Hariton   14
Katajanokan Kasino   12
Kola   3
Kuu   6
Mamma Rosa   7
Merimakasiini   13
Sea Horse   15
St Urho's Pub   11
Tamminiemtie   2
Tin Tin Tango   8
Tombeton Kahvila   1
Ursula   17
William K   5

practice in use throughout the city. If you're staying for a while and plan to see as much of the capital and its museums as possible, consider purchasing a **Helsinki Card** (available from the city tourist office), which gives unlimited travel on public transport, including the ferry to Suomenlinna, and entry to around fifty museums. The three-day card (€45) is the best value, although there are also two-day (€35) and one-day (€25) versions.

For information on the rest of the country, visit the **Finland Tourist Board**, one block south of the City office at Eteläesplanadi 4 (May–Sept Mon–Fri 9am–5pm, Sat & Sun 11am–3pm; Oct–April Mon–Fri 9am–5pm; ☎09/4176 9300, ⊛www .mek.fi).

City transport

Much of Helsinki is quite easily covered on foot, and, between June and August, you can avail yourself of one of the lime-green **bicycles** parked at 26 spots around the city centre, and available for use for free – you pay an €2 deposit, which is refunded when you return the bike. Otherwise, the central area and its immediate surrounds are covered by an integrated transport network of buses, trams and a small metro system. A **single-journey ticket** costs €2, while a group ticket, valid for two adults and up to four children is €8; both are valid for unlimited transfers allowed within one hour. A **tram** ticket entitling you to one single journey without changing costs €1.80 if bought from the driver, or €1.50 if bought in advance. You can also buy a **tourist ticket** covering the city and surrounding areas such as Espoo and Vantaa for one (€7.50), three (€15) or five days (€22.50), which permits travel on buses and trams displaying double arrows (effectively all of them); obviously, this is only a cost-cutter if used frequently. If you don't intend to leave the city proper, you're better off with a **Helsinki-only tourist ticket**, again available in one- (€5.60), three- (€10.80) and five-day (€16.20) versions. All these tickets can be bought from drivers or conductors, R-kiosk stands, the long-distance bus station at Kamppi or the City Tourist Office.

On **buses** you enter at the front, where you must either buy or show your ticket. On **trams**, get on at the front or back, and stamp your ticket in the machine. **Metro** tickets can be bought from the machines in the stations. If you're tempted to fare-dodge in Helsinki, note that there's a €60 on-the-spot fine plus the cost of a single ticket. **Taxis** can either be hailed in the street (a vehicle is free if the yellow "taxi" sign is illuminated) or pre-booked: call the *Taxi Centre* on ☎0100/0700 for immediate travel, or ☎0100/0600 for trips more than an hour or so away. There's a basic charge of €4.30, with a further €1.10 per kilometre, plus an €1.70 surcharge between 8pm and 6am weekdays and from 4pm Saturday to 6am Monday.

Tram **#3T** follows a figure-of-eight route around the city, and if you're pushed for time will take you past the most obvious attractions. For a more leisurely exploration, join one of the two-hour guided **walking tours** (€20) run by Helsinki Expert, Lönrotinkatu 7B (☎09/2288 1200, ⊛www.helsinkiexpert.fi); you'll finish up knowing more about the city than most of its residents do. For details, phone the above number or visit them at the City Tourist Office. There are also numerous **boat sightseeing tours** from the south harbour, Eteläsatama, costing around €14 for an hour and a half. These run daily from around 11am to 7pm, and brochures are available at the tourist office, or from touts at the harbour itself.

Accommodation

There's plenty of **accommodation** in Helsinki, although the bulk of it is in mid-range chain hotels. Various discounts (see p.655) can reduce costs in these places, or alternatively there are a couple of cheaper summer hotels, several tourist hotels and a few hostels. If you arrive without a reservation, the very helpful **Hotel Booking Centre** in the train station, to the left of the platforms near the left-luggage office (June–Aug Mon–Sat 9am–7pm, Sun 10am–6pm; Sept–May Mon–Fri 9am–5pm;

$\textcircled{\tiny T}$09/2288 1400, $\textcircled{\tiny W}$www.helsinkiexpert.fi), will book you a hotel or hostel room for a fee of €5, though there is no charge if you phone them. If you're planning on staying in town for more than just a few days, it might be worth considering a short-term **apartment rental**; try either Domin, Uudenmaankatu 4–6 ($\textcircled{\tiny T}$09/687 7940, $\textcircled{\tiny W}$www.dominrental.com) or Citykoti, Telakkakatu 1C ($\textcircled{\tiny T}$050/555 0058, $\textcircled{\tiny W}$www.citykoti.com).

Hotels and tourist hotels

Although the cost of a room in one of Helsinki's top-flight **hotels** can be high, the better places aren't necessarily completely out of reach: many drop their rates dramatically in the summer tourist season, while nearly everywhere offers reductions at weekends. To take advantage of any bargains, it's essential to book as early as possible – either online, by phoning the hotel directly or by making a reservation through a travel agent or the Booking Centre (see above). However much you pay, it's unlikely that you'll leave any Helsinki hotel feeling ripped off: service and amenities – such as the inclusive help-yourself breakfast which is generally included in the price of the room – are usually excellent. And unlike many other Finnish cities, most of Helsinki's main chain hotels retain unique characteristics and some degree of charm. The city does have a few moderately-priced hotels, and while they lack some luxuries they can be a good-value alternative, especially for three or four people sharing. All provide basic accommodation in private rooms, most have en-suite bathrooms and offer inexpensive meals as well. Of Helsinki's **campsites**, only one makes a reasonable base if you're planning to spend time in the city. This is *Rastila* ($\textcircled{\tiny T}$09/321 6551, $\textcircled{\tiny F}$344 1578), 13km to the east in Itäkeskus, conveniently on the metro line (Itäkeskus station) and also served by buses #90, #90A, #965 and #98 from Mannerheimintie. Open year-round with an array of cottages (❶–❺) as well as a beach, restaurant, saunas, Internet access and bicycle and kayak rentals, it's one of the most popular camping spots in all of Finland.

Note that unless otherwise stated, the places below are marked on the central Helsinki map (pp.692–693).

Moderate and inexpensive

Finn Kalevankatu 3B $\textcircled{\tiny T}$09/684 4360, $\textcircled{\tiny W}$www .hotellifinn.fi. Compact and rather down-at-heel hotel, though the slightly-cramped rooms (the cheapest have shared bathrooms) are still good value considering the city-centre location. ❸

🏃 **Matkakoti Margarita** Itäinen Teatterikuja 3 $\textcircled{\tiny T}$09/622 4261, $\textcircled{\tiny W}$www.matkakoti -margarita.com. Fairly basic guesthouse in a quiet street close to the train and bus stations, and quite adequate for a night's rest. It also rents rooms cheaply by the day for those arriving in the city early and leaving later the same day. ❷

Omapohja Gasthaus Itäinen Teatterikuja 3 $\textcircled{\tiny T}$09/666 211, $\textcircled{\tiny F}$09/6228 0053. Downstairs from *Matkakoti Margarita*, this tourist hotel has en-suite rooms with colour TVs and other mod cons. ❸

Expensive

Anna Annankatu 1 $\textcircled{\tiny T}$09/616 621, $\textcircled{\tiny W}$www .hotelanna.com. Small, central place with plain rooms but a cosy atmosphere, set in a former Christian mission. ❺/❻

Arthur Vuorikatu 19 $\textcircled{\tiny T}$09/173 441, $\textcircled{\tiny W}$www .hotelarthur.fi. You can save money in this

good-quality hotel by getting a room with a shared bathroom – but book ahead as there's only a couple. ❺/❻

Cumulus Kaisaniemi Kaisaniemenkatu 7 $\textcircled{\tiny T}$09/172 881, $\textcircled{\tiny W}$www.cumulus.fi. Adequate, clean rooms that are good value at weekends, though the chain-hotel feel is very much in evidence. ❺/❻

Cumulus Seurahuone Kaivokatu 12 $\textcircled{\tiny T}$09/69 141, $\textcircled{\tiny W}$www.cumulus.fi. A stylish, classic hotel opposite the train station, with the historic *Café Bellman* attached. Big, splendid rooms with original features. ❻

Helka Pohjoinen Rautatiekatu 23 $\textcircled{\tiny T}$09/613 580, $\textcircled{\tiny W}$www.helka.fi. Rather plain-looking exterior but very welcoming on the inside, and within easy reach of everything. Some weekend reductions. ❺/❻

Kämp Pohjoisesplanadi 29 $\textcircled{\tiny T}$09/675 111, $\textcircled{\tiny W}$www .hotelkamp.fi. Opened in 1887, this belle époque affair is Helsinki's most luxurious hotel – it played host to the secret meetings of the underground Kagel movement in the early 1900s, and Sibelius and Gallen-Kallela were regular guests. Today, marble bathrooms, polished stonework and lavish rooms make for decadent glamour. ❻

Palace Eteläranta 10 ☎09/1345 6656, ⓦwww
.palacehotel.fi. Sleek, luxurious property next to
the *kauppahalli* overlooking the Olympic Harbour.
Boxy rooms and baths are functional enough,
but you're really paying for the spectacular
sea views. A quiet day in summer can bring
substantial reductions, although it's difficult to
get discounts on panorama rooms unless you're
really pushy. Also has a fancy restaurant with
splendid views. ⑥

Radisson SAS Royal Runeberginkatu 2 ☎09/69
580, ⓦwww.radisson.com. White-tiled and
glamorous, resembling buildings like the Opera
House and Finlandia Hall, this is not surprisingly
expensive; visit in summer, when rates are cut by
half. ④/⑥

Scandic Continental Mannerheimintie 46 (see
Helsinki map, pp.686–687) ☎09/40 551, ⓦwww
.scandic-hotels.com. Close to the parliament
building, this is very good value at weekends and
in summer. Excellent service. ⑤/⑥

Scandic Grand Marina Katajanokanlaituri 7
☎09/16 661, ⓦwww.scandic-hotels.com. The
vast former harbour customs house from the
1930s, now transformed into an elegant, very
Scandinavian-looking hotel just a few strides from
the arrival point of Viking Line boats from Sweden.
⑤/⑥

Scandic Hotel Marski Mannerheimintie 10
☎09/68 061, ⓦwww.scandic-hotels.com. Opposite the Stockmann department store and named
after Marski (Marshal) Mannerheim, this is one of
the best hotels in the city, though less atmospheric
than the *Palace*, above. ⑤/⑥

Scandic Simonkenttä Simonkatu 9
☎09/68 380, ⓦwww.scandic-hotels.com.
Pine, steel and glass overtake the senses in one
of the city's newest and most spectacular hotels,
offering hundreds of rooms, some with French
balconies, others with terrace and sauna, all
meticulously constructed. Advance booking recommended for the cheapest rates. ⑤/⑥

Sokos Helsinki Kluuvikatu 8 ☎09/43 320,
ⓦwww.sokoshotels.fi. The best aspect of this
place is its location, a stone's throw from Senate
Square in one of Helsinki's prime central streets,
though its modern rooms are characterless and
typical of the homogenized chain-hotel feel. ④/⑥

Sokos Torni Yrjönkatu 26 ☎09/43 360,
ⓦwww.sokoshotels.fi. Across from the
classic sauna and pools on Yrjönkatu, this sophisticated hotel saw a 2005 renovation in Jugend
Art Nouveau-styled grandeur. On a clear day, the
thirteenth-floor bar with a patio gives views, so the
locals claim, all the way to Estonia, but the drinks
are pricey, as are the rooms – though weekend
rates can drop dramatically, especially last-minute.
⑤/⑥

Sokos Vaakuna Asema-Aukio 2 ☎09/43
370, ⓦwww.sokoshotels.fi. In the heart
of the city facing the train station, built for the
1952 Olympic Games, this smart hotel still
contains many of its original, quintessentially
Finnish architectural features. The lobby is a grand
semi-circular sitting room reminiscent of a Soviet
legislation chamber, while the restaurant on the
top floor – where breakfast is served – has lovely
grand views ⑤/⑥

Hostels

There are a number of **hostels** about the city, all with excellent facilities and all but
one with no evening curfew. All are open all year unless otherwise stated.

Academica Hietaniemenkatu 14 ☎09/1311 4334,
ⓦwww.hostelacademica.fi. Well-placed summer
hostel with morning sauna and pool. Many of the
doubles (❸) were renovated in 2004, while the
dorms (€18) are spic-and-span clean and have
their own cooking facilities. Open June–Sept.

Erottajanpuisto Uudenmaankatu 9
☎09/642 169, ⓦwww.erottajanpuisto.com.
Small and homely place set on a quiet, central
street near some great bars, offering simply
furnished dorms (€22.50) and some doubles (❸),
as well as friendly staff and a large salon with
worn leather couches, often abuzz with travellers
trading war stories.

Euro Linnankatu 9 (see Helsinki map,
pp.686–687) ☎09/622 0470, ⓦwww.eurohostel.
fi. Comfortable place in a clean modern building

with free morning sauna and a restaurant. It's in
the quiet Katajanokka area, close to the Viking Line
arrival point; take tram #4. Dorm beds (€22.90)
are set in double rooms, and there are private
doubles (❷) as well.

Hostel Suomenlinna Suomenlinna ☎09/684
7471, ⓦwww.leirikoulut.com. While hardly central,
this year-round hostel with dorms (€20) and doubles (❶) does have an idyllic location on the island
of Suomenlinna, fifteen minutes by ferry from the
market square. It gets very quiet here, even in the
summer, and you can be fairly certain that if you
arrive in the winter, you'll have the whole place to
yourself. Last ferry is at 2am, first one at 6am.

Mekka Vuorikatu 8B ☎09/630 265, ⓦwww
.hostelmekka.com. Simple hostel located two
blocks from the Senate Square; rooms have

shared toilet and shower, and there are laundry facilities. There are private doubles (❸) as well as dorms (€25).

Stadion Olympic Stadium (see Helsinki map, pp.686–687) ☎09/477 8480, ⊛www.stadion hostel.com. A two-kilometre hike from the city centre up Mannerheimintie; the hostel entrance is on the far side of the stadium complex. A great

setup, with dormitories sleeping up to twelve (beds €15), large and well-equipped shower rooms and private doubles (❶). You'll be asked to vacate the premises from 10am to 4pm and there is a 3am curfew. Trams #3T, #4, #7A and #10 from Mannerheimintie stop outside, as does the Finnair bus from the airport (ask for "Opera").

The City

Following a devastating fire in 1808, and the city's elevation to capital in 1812, Helsinki was totally rebuilt in a style commensurate with its status: a grid of wide streets and Neoclassical, Empire-style brick buildings, modelled on the then Russian capital, St Petersburg. This grid forms the basis of the modern city, and it's a tribute to the vision of planner Johan Ehrenström and architect Carl Engel that in and around **Senate Square** the grandeur has endured, often quite dramatically. The square itself, overlooked by the gleaming Lutheran cathedral, is still the city's single most eye-catching feature, while just a few blocks away, past the South Harbour and the waterside market, the twin thoroughfares of Pohjoisesplanadi and Eteläesplanadi, known collectively as **Esplanadi**, are a handsome tree-lined avenue with a narrow strip of greenery along the centre. Meeting the western end of Esplanadi, the great artery of **Mannerheimintie** – the main route into the centre from the suburbs – carries traffic and trams past Finlandia Hall and the Olympic Stadium on one side, and the National Museum and the streets leading to Sibelius Park and the vast Hietaniemi Cemetery on the other. The bulge of land that extends **south of Esplanadi** has long been one of the most affluent sections of town. Dotted by palatial embassies and wealthy dwellings, it rises into the rocky **Kaivopuisto** park, where the peace is disturbed only by the rumble of the trams and the summer rock concerts.

West of Kaivopuisto are the narrow streets of the equally exclusive **Eira** quarter, while to the north of the city centre and divided by the waters of Kaisaniemenlahti, the districts of **Kruununhaka** and **Hakaniemi** contain what little is left of pre-seventeenth-century Helsinki, in the small area up the hill behind the cathedral, compressed between the botanical gardens and the bay; over the bridge is a large marketplace and the hill leading past the formidable **Kallion kirkko** towards the modern housing districts further north. Helsinki also has innumerable offshore islands, the biggest of which are **Suomenlinna** and **Seurasaari**. Both of these, despite their location close to the city centre, offer untrammelled nature and a rewarding crop of museums.

Senate Square and Esplanadi

The heart of Helsinki lies in and around **Senate Square**, a compact area of broad bustling streets, grand buildings, famous (to Finns) shops, and, in Esplanadi, the most popular promenading spot in the entire country. Most of the streets leading into Senate Square are fairly narrow and unremarkable, however, a fact that serves to increase the impact as the square comes into view and you're struck by the sudden burst of space, the graceful symmetry of the buildings, and most of all by the exquisite form of the **Tuomiokirkko**, or Lutheran Cathedral (June–Aug daily 9am–midnight; Sept–May Mon–Sat 9am–6pm, Sun noon–6pm), raised on granite steps that support it like a pedestal. Designed, like most of the other buildings on the square, by Engel, its construction was overseen by him until his death in 1840, before being finally completed, with a few variations, in 1852. Among the post-Engel additions are the statues of the twelve apostles that line the roof, which may seem familiar if you've visited Copenhagen: they're copies of Thorvaldsen's sculptures for Vor Frue Kirke. After the Neoclassical extravagances of the exterior, the

CENTRAL HELSINKI

spartan Lutheran interior comes as a disappointment; better is the gloomily atmospheric **crypt**, which is now used as a café (June–Aug daily 10am–4pm; entrance on Kirkkokatu). On the eastern side of the cathedral's pedestal at Snellmaninkatu 2 is the entrance to the **Museum of the Bank of Finland** (Tues–Fri noon–6pm, Sat & Sun 11am–4pm; free; ⊛www.rahamuseo.fi), which features examples of the pre-euro Finnish currency, the *markkaa*, as well as an interesting exhibition on shortlisted designs for euro notes.

The buildings around the square contribute to the pervading sense of harmony, and although none is open to the public, some are of great historical significance. The **Government Palace** (*Valtioneuvosto*), known as the Senate House until independence and seating the Senate from 1822, consumes the entire eastern side. It was here that an angry Finnish civil servant, Eugen Schauman, became a national hero by assassinating the much-hated Russian governor-general Bobrikov in 1904. Opposite are the Ionic columns of **Helsinki University** (*Helsingin Yliopisto*), next door to which is the **University Library** (*Yliopiston Kirjasto*), considered by many to be Engel's finest single building, although only students and bona fide researchers are allowed in.

Just north of the square between Kirkkokatu and Rauhankatu is **The House of Scientific Estates** (*Säätytalo*), the seat of the Diet that governed the country until 1906, when it was abolished in favour of a single-chamber parliament elected by universal suffrage (at the time, Europe's most radical parliamentary reform). In the small park behind the Government Palace is the **House of**

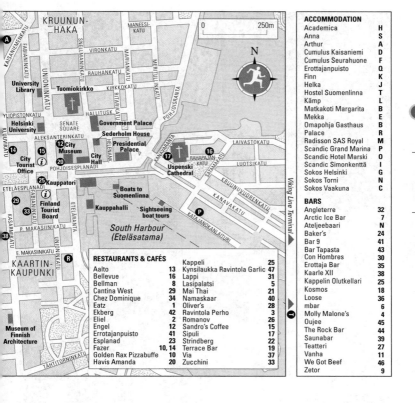

Nobility (*Ritarihuone*), where the upper crust of Helsinki society rubbed shoulders a hundred years ago.

Directly opposite the cathedral at Aleksanterinkatu 18 is Helsinki's oldest stone building, **Sederholm House** (June–Aug daily 11am–5pm; Sept–May Mon–Thurs & Sun 11am–4pm; €3), dating from 1757. It now houses a small museum concentrating on aspects of eighteenth-century life in the city, with particular reference to industrialist Johan Sederholm. There are exhibitions on trade, education and construction, but what makes it perhaps most enjoyable is the eighteenth-century music collection – you can ask to hear a range of classical CDs while you wander around. A more high-tech record of Helsinki life can be found one block south from Sederholm House at the **City Museum**, Sofiankatu 4 (Mon–Fri 9am–5pm, Sat & Sun 11am–5pm; €3; ⓦwww.helsinkicitymuseum .fi), where a permanent exhibition entitled "Time" gives glimpses of Helsinki from its origins as a country village right up to the present day. It's an impressive show, beautifully lit with fibre optics and halogen lamps, though the chronology jumps around disconcertingly.

The square at the eastern end of Aleksanterinkatu is overlooked by the red-and-green onion-shaped domes of the Russian Orthodox **Uspenski Cathedral** (Mon–Fri 9.30am–4pm, Sat 9.30am–2pm, Sun noon–3pm, closed Mon Oct–April; ⓦwww.ort.fi; tram #4) on Katajanokka, a wedge of land extending out to sea between the North and South harbours and currently the scene of a dockland development programme, converting the area's old warehouses into pricey new

△ Helsinki Tuomiokirkko

restaurants and apartments. In contrast to its Lutheran counterpart, the cathedral is drab outside, but as the largest orthodox church in western Europe, it houses a rich display of icons and other sumptuous adornments, including an impressive array of chandeliers dangling from the vaulted ceiling.

Esplanadi and around

Walking from the Uspenski Cathedral towards the South Harbour along Ale-ksanterinkatu takes you past the **Presidential Palace**, noticeable only for its conspicuous uniformed guard, and the equally bland **City Hall**, used solely for administrative purposes. There's more colour and liveliness along the waterfront among the stalls of the **kauppatori**, or market square (Mon–Thurs 8am–5.30pm, Fri 8am–6pm, Sat 8am–3pm), laden with fresh fruit and vegetables; you can buy fresh fish directly from the boats moored around the edge of the harbour and, if your principles allow it, the market is also the best place to buy fur – mink and fox hats and coats are cheaper here than in the city's many fur salons. A bit further along, the **kauppahalli** or market hall (Mon–Fri 8am–5pm, Sat 8am–2pm), with its interior of original carved mahogany and carved pediments, is a good place for snacks such as reindeer kebab and Russian caviar.

Across a mishmash of tram lines from here lie the twin thoroughfares of Poh-joisesplanadi and Eteläesplanadi, together known as **Esplanadi**. At the height of the Swedish/Finnish language conflict that divided the nation during the mid-nineteenth century, this neat boulevard was where opposing factions demonstrated their allegiance – the Finns walking on the south side and the Swedes on the north. Nowadays it's dominated at lunchtime by office workers, later in the afternoon by buskers, and at night by strolling couples. Musical accompaniment is provided free on summer evenings from the hut in the middle of the walk – expect anything from a Salvation Army band to rock groups. Entertainment of a more costly type lies at the far end of Esplanadi in the dreary off-white horseshoe of the **Swedish Theatre** building – its main entrance is on Mannerheimintie.

Around the Stockmann Department Store

If you think Esplanadi is crowded, wait until you step inside the brick Constructivist **Stockmann Department Store**, at the junction of Mannerheimintie and Aleksanterinkatu. Europe's largest department store, this is the place to buy everything from bubble gum to a Persian rug. Also part of Stockmann's (though it has its own entrance on Aleksanterinkatu), the **Academic Bookstore** (complete with Internet café) allegedly holds more titles than any other bookstore in Europe, including many English-language paperbacks and a sizeable stock of foreign newspapers and magazines. Directly across Mannerheimintie is the massive **Forum shopping mall**, which has been cutting into the Stockmann profits in recent years.

Opposite Stockmann's main entrance is the eye-catching *Three Smiths* statue by Felix Nylund; a trio of naked men swinging hammers in unison around a centrally positioned anvil, it commemorates the workers of Finland who raised money to erect a building for the country's students. This building is the **Vanha Ylioppistalo** – the old Students' House – its main doors facing the statue. The Finnish Students' Union is based here, owning what is now some of the most expensive square metres of land in Finland and renting them out at considerable profit. In the Vanha, as it's usually known, is the **Vanhan Galleria** (during exhibitions usually 10am–6pm; free), a small gallery with frequent displays of modern art. It's worth becoming acquainted with the building's layout, as it contains a couple of lively bars which are worthy of an evening visit. Taking a few strides further along Mannerheimintie brings you to the Bio cinema; beside it, steps lead down into a little modern court-yard framed by burger joints and pizzerias, off which runs the entrance to **Tunneli**, an underground complex containing shops, the central metro station and a pedestrian subway to one of the city's most striking structures – the train station.

The train station and National Theatre

Erected in 1914, **Central train station** ranks among architect Eliel Saarinen's greatest achievements. In response to criticism of his initial design, Saarinen jettisoned the original National Romantic features and opted for a style more akin to late Art Nouveau. Standing in front of the huge doors (so sturdy they always give the impression of being locked), it's hard to deny the sense of strength and solidity the building exudes. Yet this power is tempered by gentleness, a feeling symbolized by four muscular figures on the facade, each clasping a spherical glass lamp above the heads of passers-by. The interior details can be admired at leisure from either one of the station's two restaurants. Later, Saarinen was to emigrate to America; his son in turn became one of the best-known postwar American architects, whose most famous creation is the TWA terminal building in New York.

Just northeast of the station is the imposing granite form of the **National Theatre**, home of Finnish drama since 1872. Under the country's then governing Swedish-speaking elite, "Finnish culture" was considered simply a contradiction in terms, while later under the tsars it was felt (quite rightly) to pose a nationalist, anti-Russian threat – Finnish theatre during the Russification process became so politically charged that it had to be staged away from the capital in the southwest coastal town of Pori. At the forefront of Finnish drama during its early years was Aleksis Kivi, who died insane and impoverished before being acknowledged as Finland's greatest playwright. He's remembered here by Wäinö Aaltonen's bronze sculpture. Interestingly, nobody knows for sure what Kivi actually looked like, and this imagined likeness, finished in 1939, has come to be regarded as a true one.

Just across from the train station inside the city's main post office is the surprisingly enjoyable **Postal Museum** (*Posti Museo*; Mon–Fri 9am–6pm, Sat & Sun 11am–4pm; €4; ⓦwww.posti.fi/english/postmuseum), a remarkably innovative collection displaying the unlikely-looking implements connected with more than 350 years of Finnish postal history, along with interactive computer games, multi-screen displays and a special crayoning area for toddlers.

The Atheneum Art Museum

Just southeast of the train station is the **Atheneum Art Museum** (Tues & Fri 9am–6pm, Wed & Thurs 9am–8pm, Sat & Sun 11am–5pm; €5.50, €7.50 for special exhibitions). Chief among the large collection of Finnish paintings here is the stirring selection of works from the late nineteenth century, the so-called Golden Age of Finnish painting, when the spirit of nationalism was surging through the country and the movement towards independence gaining strength; indeed, the art of the period was a contributing factor in the growing awareness of Finnish culture, both inside and outside the country. Among the prime names of this era were **Akseli Gallen-Kallela** and **Albert Edelfelt**, particularly the former, who translated many of the mythic scenes of the *Kalevala* onto canvas – about a half-dozen of them are on display here, the rest spread around at museums all over Finland and abroad. Slightly later came **Juho Rissanen** with his moody and evocative studies of peasant life, and **Hugo Simberg**, responsible for the eerie *Death and the Peasant* and the powerful triptych *Boy Carrying a Garland*. Cast an eye, too, over the works of **Helene Schjerfbeck**, for a long time one of the country's most underrated artists but now enjoying an upsurge in popularity – and collectability. Among the best examples of pure Finnish landscape are the works of **Pekka Halonen**: *Pioneers in Karelia* is typical, with soft curves expressively denoting natural scenes.

The first floor holds a series of installations by innovative contemporary local artists, but best of the Finnish art is assembled on the floors above: the second floor contains the bulk of the museum's Golden Age works, while the third floor houses the provocative expressionism of **Tyko Sallinen** and the November Group, most active around 1917, as well as some token **foreign** masters – a couple of large Munchs, a Van Gogh, a Chagall and a few Cézannes. Before you leave, check out the excellent art bookshop on the ground floor.

North along Mannerheimintie

The logical route for exploring north of the city centre, the wide thoroughfare of **Mannerheimintie** is named after the military commander and statesman C.G.E. Mannerheim, who wielded considerable influence on Finnish affairs in the first half of the twentieth century. He's commemorated by a statue near the busy junction with Arkadiankatu, a structure on which the city's bird population has left its mark.

The Lasipalatsi

Opposite the Postal Museum is the recently renovated **Lasipalatsi** (@www.lasipalatsi
.fi), built for the 1940 Olympics as the main transit and entertainment building.
Reopened in 1998, the functional two-storey building is typical of late 1930s
Finnish Art Nouveau design, and contains some 25 shops, galleries, exhibition sites
and cafés, as well as a media centre embodying the Finns' faith in publicly accessible new technology – enough to feed mind and body for a few hours at least.
On the glass-fronted lower level check out the **mbar** (Mon–Fri 8.30am–1am, Sat
10am–1am, Sun 11.30am–9pm), with Internet terminals inset into glass-topped
tables, and the glass-fronted studio of **MTV3**, one of the main Finnish TV companies – it overlooks the street and is periodically surrounded by hordes of teenagers
anxious to catch a glimpse of the stars at work inside. Also on the ground floor is
Bio Rex (☎09/611 300, @www.biorex.fi), a cinema that specializes in screening
independent films that you probably won't find anywhere else in the city. Upstairs,
the **Cable Book Library** (Mon–Thurs 10am–midnight, Sat & Sun noon–6pm)
has magazines and a couple of dozen more free Internet terminals and wi-fi access.

Behind the Lasipalatsi stands the sleek, aluminum-and-glass framed **Kammpi**
shopping and apartment complex; completed in 2005, it also houses the long-
distance bus terminal .

Museum of Contemporary Art: Kiasma

Just beyond the Lasipalatsi at Mannerheiminaukio 2 is the **Kiasma Museum of
Contemporary Art** (Tues 9am–5pm, Wed–Sun 10am–8.30pm; €5.50, free Fri
evenings; @www.kiasma.fi), a slightly forbidding, steel-clad and tube-like structure
that looks from the side like a mix of the Sydney Opera House and the Guggen-
heim in Bilbao – a rather pretentious building for the usually functionalist Finns.
Inside the catacomb-like interior are sweeping curves and well-lit hallways; on the
ground floor natural light pours in from a variety of angles onto a brilliant-white
interior that looks like it gets a new coat of paint on a weekly basis. Entry to this
floor is free, and there's a decent café, Internet access, one of the best art bookshops
in Finland and an interactive children's playroom.

The Kiasma draws its **exhibition** material from an archive of four thousand pieces
of contemporary art, as well as works by visiting artists. Nothing is permanently on
display, although as you explore you begin to feel that it's the building itself – with
its play on space, light and technology – that is the principal exhibit. Some rooms
are blacked out completely; others have high overhanging arches through which
the light spills into the display area, giving the place an almost religious feel. Various
touchscreen terminals built into the walls at strategic points tell you all you need to
know about the works on display, and there's also a room in which about ten state-
of-the-art computers are set up with numerous CD-ROMs on art and culture; one
about the Kiasma itself is projected continuously onto the wall. Exhibitions change
every two to three months – check the museum's website for details, and keep an
eye out, too for performances, lectures and film screenings staged at the museum's
small **theatre** (☎09/1733 6502.

The Parliament Building and National Museum

The section of Mannerheimintie north from the Kiasma passes a number of outstanding buildings, the first of which is the **Parliament Building** on the left
(guided tours July & Aug Mon–Fri 1pm, Sat 11am & noon, Sun noon & 1pm;
Sept–June Sat & Sun only, same times; when in session, access is to the public
galleries only; free; @www.eduskunta.fi). The work of J.S. Sirén, the porridge-
coloured building, with its fourteen pompous Corinthian columns and choking
air of solemnity, was completed in 1931. Intended to celebrate the new republic, its
style was drawn from the revolutionary Neoclassicism that dominated public buildings from Fascist Italy to Nazi Germany, and its authoritarian features can appear
wildly out of place in Helsinki, though it's worth a look nonetheless.

North of here things improve with the **National Museum** (Tues & Wed 11am–8pm, Thurs–Sun 11am–6pm; €5.50; ⑳www.nba.fi), whose design was the result of an early twentieth-century competition won by the three Young Turks of Finnish architecture – Armas Lindgren, Herman Gesellius and Eliel Saarinen. With National Romanticism at its zenith, they steeped their plan in Finnish history, drawing on the country's legacy of medieval churches and granite castles (even though many of these were built under Swedish domination), culminating in a weighty but slender tower that gives the place a cathedral-like profile. The entrance is guarded by Emil Wikström's sculptured bear and the interior ceilings are decorated by Gallen-Kallela with scenes from the *Kalevala*.

The museum may seem the obvious place to discover what Finland is all about but, especially if you've spent hours exploring the copiously stocked national museums of Denmark and Sweden, you might well find the **collections** disappointing. Being dominated by other nations for many centuries, Finland had little more than the prerequisites of peasant life to call its own up until the mid-1800s (when moves towards Finnish nationalism got off the ground), and the rows of farming and hunting tools alongside endless displays of bowls and spoons from the early times do little to fire the imagination. The most interesting sections are those relating to the rise of Finnish self-determination and the early years of the republic. Large photographs show the enormous crowds that massed in Helsinki's streets to sing the Finnish anthem in defiance of their (then) Russian rulers, and cabinets packed with small but intriguing objects outline the left–right struggles that marked the early decades of independence and the immediate postwar years – periods when Finland's political future teetered precariously in the balance, a long way from the stability and prosperity enjoyed in more recent times.

Finlandia Hall to the Olympic Stadium

Stylistically a far cry from the National Museum building but equally affecting, **Finlandia Hall** (guided tours when not in use; ring ☎09/40 241 or check at the City Tourist Office) stands directly across Mannerheimintie, partially hidden by the roadside foliage. Designed by the country's premier architect, **Alvar Aalto**, a few years before his death in 1976, Finlandia Hall was conceived as part of a grand plan to rearrange the entire centre of Helsinki. Previously, Eliel Saarinen had planned a traffic route from the northern suburbs into a new square in the city centre, to be called Vapaudenkatu ("Freedom Street") in celebration of Finnish independence. Aalto plotted a continuation of this scheme, envisaging the removal of the rail-freight yards, which would enable arrivals to be greeted with a fan-like terrace of new buildings reflected in the waters of Töölönlahti. Finlandia was to be the first of these, and only by looking across from the other side of Töölönlahti do you perceive the building's soft sensuality and the potential beauty of the greater concept. Inside the hall, Aalto's characteristic wave pattern (the architect's surname, as it happens, means "wave" in Finnish) and asymmetry are in evidence. From the walls and ceilings through to the lamps and vases, the place has a quiet and graceful air – but the view from the foyer is still of the rail-freight yards, and the great plan for a future Helsinki remains under discussion.

Next door is **Hakasalmi Villa** (Sun–Thurs 11am–4pm, closed mid-June to mid-July; €3), one of four satellite museums belonging to the new City Art Museum (see p.703). An Italian-style Neoclassical villa built in the 1840s by a councillor and patron of the arts whose collection inspired the founding of the museum, it houses long-term temporary exhibitions, often strikingly designed and worth a peek. Finland's **Opera House** (Mon–Fri 9am–6pm, Sat 3–6pm, Sun open 2hr before performances; ⑳www.operafin.fi), a little way beyond Finlandia, is, like so many contemporary Finnish buildings, a Lego-like expanse of white-tiled facade. Its light-flooded interior is enlivened by displays of colourful costumes though, and its grounds and entrance spiked with minimalist black-granite sculptures.

From this point on, the decisive outline of the **Olympic Stadium** becomes visible. Originally intended for the 1940 Olympic Games, the stadium eventually staged the second postwar games in 1952. From the **Stadium Tower** (Mon–Fri 9am–8pm, Sat & Sun 9am–6pm; €2) there's an unsurpassed view over the city and a chunk of the southern coast. If you're a stopwatch-and-spikes freak, ask at the tower's ticket office for directions to the **Sports Museum** (Mon–Fri 11am–5pm, Sat & Sun noon–4pm; €3.50; ✺www.urheilumuseo.org), whose mind-numbing collection of track officials' shoes and swimming caps overshadows a worthy attempt to present sport as an integral part of Finnish culture. The nation's heroes, among them Keke Rosberg and Lasse Virén, are lauded to the skies. Outside, Wäinö Aaltonen's sculpture of Paavo Nurmi captures the champion runner of the 1920s in full stride, and fully naked – this atypically Finnish expression of public nudity caused quite a stir when the sculpture was unveiled in 1952.

West of Mannerheimintie

As there's little of note north of the stadium, it's best to cross Mannerheimintie and follow the streets off it leading to **Sibelius Park** and Eila Hiltunen's monument to the composer, made from 24 tons of steel tubes, like a big silver surrealist organ; next to it, there's an irrefutably horrid sculpture of Sibelius's dismembered head. The shady and pleasant park is rudely cut by a main road, Mechelininkatu; following this back towards the city centre brings you first to the small Islamic and Jewish cemeteries, and then to the expanse of tombs comprising **Hietaniemi Cemetery** (usually open until 10pm). A prowl among these is like a stroll through a "Who was Who" of Finland's last 150 years: Mannerheim, Engel and a host of former presidents are buried here, while just inside the main entrance lies Alvar Aalto, his witty little tombstone consisting partly of a chopped Neoclassical column; behind it is the larger marker of Gallen-Kallela, his initials woven around a painter's palette. Local schoolkids head to the cemetery when skipping off lessons during warm weather, not for a smoke behind the gravestones but to reach the **beaches** that line the bay just beyond its western walls. From these you can enjoy the best sunset view in the city.

On the way back towards Mannerheimintie, at Lutherinkatu 3, just off Runeberginkatu, is the breathtaking **Temppeliaukio kirkko** (Mon, Tues, Thurs & Fri 10am–8pm, Wed 10am–6.30pm, Sat 10am–6pm, Sun noon–1.45pm & 3.30–6pm; closed Tues 1–3.30pm in winter and during services). Brilliantly conceived by Timo and Tuomo Suomalainen and finished in 1969, the underground church is built inside a massive block of natural granite in the middle of an otherwise ordinary residential square. Whilst here, try and see it from above if you can (even if you have to shin up a drainpipe), when the copper dome that pokes through the rock makes the thing look like a ditched flying saucer. The odd combination of man-made and natural materials has made it a fixture on the tourist circuit, but even when crowded it's a thrill to be inside. Classical concerts frequently take place here, the raw rock walls making for excellent acoustics – check the noticeboard at the entrance for details.

South of Esplanadi: Kaivopuisto, Eira and Pihlajasaari island

From the South Harbour it's a straightforward walk past the Silja terminal to Kaivopuisto, but it's more interesting to leave Esplanadi along Kasarmikatu and take in some small, offbeat museums along the way. First of these is the **Museum of Finnish Architecture** (Tues & Thurs–Sun 10am–4pm, Wed until 8pm; €3.50–5, depending upon exhibitions; ✺www.mfa.fi) at no. 24, which is aimed at the serious fan: architectural tours of less accessible buildings both in Helsinki and around the country can be arranged here. Combined with an extensive archive, it's a useful resource for a nation with an important architectural heritage.

A block from Kasarmikatu is Korkeavuorenkatu, with the excellent **Design Museum** at no. 23 (June–Aug daily 11am–6pm; Sept–May Tues–Sun 11am–6pm,

Wed until 8pm; ⓦwww.designmuseum.fi; €7), which traces the relationship between art and industry in Finnish history. There are full explanatory texts and period exhibits, from Karelianism – the representations of nature and peasant life from the Karelia region in eastern Finland that dominated Finnish art and design in the years just before and after independence – to the modern movements, along with the postwar shift towards the more familiar, and less interesting, pan-Scandi-navian styles.

Kaivopuisto park

Kasarmikatu ends close to the base of a hill, from where footpaths lead up to the Engel-designed **Astronomical Observatory**. Down on the other side and a few streets on is the large and rocky **Kaivopuisto** park. In the 1830s this was developed as a health resort, with a spa house that drew Russian nobility from St Petersburg to sample its waters. The building, another of Engel's works (although greatly modified), can be found in the middle of the park's central avenue, today pulling in the crowds as a restaurant.

Off a smaller avenue, Itäinen Puistotie, runs the circular Kallionlinnantie, which contains the house where Gustaf Mannerheim spent the later years of his life, now maintained as the **Mannerheim Museum** (Fri–Sun 11am–4pm, other times by appointment, call ☏09/635 443; €7 including guided tour; ⓦwww.mannerheim -museo.fi). A Finnish-born, Russian-trained military commander, Mannerheim was pro-Finnish but had a middle-class suspicion of the working classes: he led the right-wing Whites during the Civil War of 1918 and two decades later the Finnish campaigns in the Winter and Continuation wars (for more on which, see the "Mili-tary Museum", opposite). His influence in the political sphere was also considerable, and included a brief spell as president. While acknowledging his importance, the regard that Finns have for him these days, naturally enough, depends on their own political viewpoint.

Ideology aside, the house is intriguing. The interior is left much as it was when the man died in 1951, and the clutter is astounding. During his travels Mannerheim raided flea markets at every opportunity, collecting a remarkable array of plunder – assorted furniture, antiques, ornaments and books from all over the globe. Upstairs is the camp-bed which Mannerheim found too comfortable ever to change, and in the wall is the vent inserted to keep the bedroom as airy as a field-tent.

If he had lived a few decades earlier, one of Mannerheim's Kallionlinnantie neighbours would have been Frederik Cygnaeus, art patron and Professor of Aesthetics at Helsinki University. In 1860 Cygnaeus built a summer house at no. 8, a lovely yellow-turreted affair, and filled it with an outstanding collection of art. Later he donated the lot to the nation and today it's displayed as the **Cygnaeus Gallery** (Wed 11am–7pm, Thurs–Sun 11am–4pm; €3; ⓦwww.nba.fi). Everything is beautifully laid out in the tiny rooms of the house, with whole walls of work by the most influential of his contemporaries. The von Wright brothers (Ferdinand, Magnus and Wilhelm) are responsible for the most touching pieces – the bird and nature studies. Look out, too, for a strange portrait of Cygnaeus by Ekman, showing the man sprouting sinister wings from under his chin.

The edge of Kaivopuisto looks out across a sprinkling of little islands and the Suomenlinna fortress. You can follow one of the pathways down into **Merikatu**, along which lie several of the Art Nouveau villas lived in by the big cheeses of Finnish industry during the early part of the twentieth century. Easily the most extreme is no. 25, the Enso-Gutzeit villa, now portioned off into offices and with a lingering air of decay hanging over its decorative facade.

Eira

Inland from Merikatu, the curving alleys and tall, elegant buildings of the **Eira** district are landmarked by the needle-like spire rising from the roof of **Mikael Agricola kirkko**, named after the translator of the first Finnish Bible but making no demands on your time. A few blocks northeast, the twin-towered Johanessen kirkko is again not worth a call in itself but functions as a handy navigation aid. Following Yrjönkatu northwards from here takes you past the partly pedestrianized Iso Roobertinkatu, before reaching Bulevardi and the square containing **Vanha kirkko**, or Old Church. A humble wooden structure, and another example of Engel's work, this was the first Lutheran church to be erected after Helsinki became the Finnish capital, predating that in Senate Square by some years but occupying a far less glamorous plot – a plague victim's burial ground dating from 1710.

Heading left along Bulevardi for a couple of hundred metres brings you to the Sinebrychoff brewery which, besides bestowing a distinctive aroma of hops to the locality, also finances the **Sinebrychoff Foreign Art Museum** at no. 40 (Tues & Fri 10am–6pm, Wed–Thurs 10am–8pm, Sat & Sun 11am–5pm; €4, higher for special exhibitions; ☻www.fng.fi). This rather precious museum houses mostly seventeenth-century Flemish and Dutch paintings, along with some excellent miniatures, delicately illustrated porcelain and refined period furniture. Continuing east along Bulevardi to the waterfront brings you to the wide **Hietalahdentori**, a concrete square that perks up with a daily morning flea market and, in summer, an evening market (3.30–8pm).

Pihlajasaari island

One of Helsinki's most enjoyable islands, ideal for a day-trip from the capital, **Pihlajasaari island** is barely a fifteen-minute boat ride from the Merisatama small-boat harbour on Merisatamanranta, opposite the junction of Merikatu and Laivurinkatu. Creaking thirty-year-old wooden pleasure boats leave once or twice hourly from here (mid-May to Aug; €4.50 return) for the short trip across to the island, which also goes by its Swedish name of Rönnskär. Actually two small islands linked by a narrow isthmus and footbridge, Pihlajasaari is a summer haven of wild flowers, long grasses and swaying pine and rowan trees vying for space between the outcrops of smooth bare rock that are perfect for catching a few rays. In fact, on the smaller of the two islands, reached by turning left from the boat jetty and crossing the small footbridge, is Helsinki's best **nudist beach** – follow the signs for the *naturistiranta* and note that the outer limits of the area are obsessively marked by signposts so as not to offend the Finns' very un-Scandinavian unease with public nudity. Back on the main island, itself no more than one or two kilometres in length, a network of walking paths leads through the forest to a series of rocky beaches and a **café** near the southwestern tip, a pleasant place to sit and watch the enormous superferries glide towards their destinations in Helsinki en route from Sweden.

Kruununhaka and Hakaniemi

North of Senate Square is the little district of **Kruununhaka**. Away from the city hubbub, its closely built blocks shield the narrow streets from the sunlight, evoking a forlorn and forgotten mood. At Kristianinkatu 12, the single-storey wooden **Burgher's House** (June–Aug & Dec Sun–Thurs 11am–4pm; €3; ☻ www.hel.fi/kaumuseo) stands in vivid contrast to the tall granite dwellings around it – and gives an indication of how Helsinki looked when wood was still the predominant building material. The interior has been kitted out with mid-nineteenth-century furnishings, the period when a city burgher did indeed reside here.

Kristianinkatu meets at right-angles with Maurinkatu, a short way along which is the **Military Museum** (Mon–Thurs & Sun 11am–4pm; €3.50), a rather formless selection of weapons, medals and glorifications of armed-forces life, but with some excellent documentary photos of the Winter and Continuation wars of 1939–44. Finland was drawn into World War II through necessity rather than choice. When Soviet troops invaded eastern Finnish territories in November 1939, under the guise of protecting Leningrad, they were repelled by technically inferior but far more committed Finns. The legends of the "heroes in white" were born then, alluding to the Finnish soldiers and the camouflage used in the winter snows. Soon after, however, faced with possible starvation and a fresh Soviet advance, Finland joined the war on the Nazi side, mainly in order to continue resisting the threat from the east. For this reason, it's rare to find World War II spoken of as such in Finland: much more commonly it's divided into these separate conflicts.

Hakaniemi

The western edge of Kruununhaka is defined by the busy Unioninkatu (if it's a sunny day, take a stroll around the neat **botanical gardens**, just off Unioninkatu), which continues northwards across a slender body of water into **Hakaniemi**, a district chiefly visited for its **kauppahalli**, or indoor market (Mon–Fri 8am–5pm, Sat 8am–2pm) in the Hakaniementori square, where you'll find an excellent array of fresh fruit, vegetables, meats and fish. Although the square is surrounded by drab storefronts and office blocks, the *kauppahalli* here is about the liveliest in the city – mainly due to its position near a major junction for city buses and trams, as well as a metro station. From the square you can see right up the hill to the impressive Art Deco brickwork of the **Kallion kirkko**, beyond which is the busy Sturenkatu and the open green area partly consumed by **Linnanmäki amusement park**. After crossing Sturenkatu, head for the nearby **Museum of Workers' Housing** at Kirstinkuja 4 (June–Aug Mon–Thurs & Sun 11am–4pm; €3; @ www.hel.fi /kaumuseo), for some fascinating social history. The series of wooden buildings that now hold the museum were constructed during the early 1900s to provide housing for the impoverished country folk who moved to the growing, increasingly indus- trialized city to work as street cleaners and refuse collectors. Six of the one-room homes where the new arrivals settled have been re-created with period furnishings, and a biography on the door describes each flat's occupants – woeful tales of over- crowding, overwork, and sons who left for America and never returned.

Suomenlinna

Located in the southeast of the Kaivopuisto district and built by the Swedes in 1748 to protect Helsinki from seaborne attack, the fortress of **Suomenlinna** stands on five interconnected islands, reached by half-hourly ferry from the South Harbour, which make a rewarding break from the city centre – even if you only want to laze around on the dunes. (These were created by the Russians with sand shipped in from Estonia to strengthen the new capital's defences after they'd wrested control of Finland.) For information, head just west of the ferry terminal to the **Inventory Chambers Visitors Centre** (March, April & Oct Mon–Fri 11am–4pm, Sat & Sun 11am–5pm; May–Aug daily 10am–6pm; Sept daily 11am–5pm, Sat & Sun 10am–5pm; Nov–Feb Tues–Sun 11am–4pm), housed in a former naval stores. Here you'll also find the **Suomenlinna Museum and Experience** (Jan–April Tues–Sun 11am–4pm; May–Aug daily 10am–6pm; Sept daily 11am–4pm; Oct–Dec Tues–Sun 11am–4pm; €5; @ www.suomenlinna.fi), which charts the history of the fortress. Suomenlinna has a few museums, none particularly riveting, although the **Ehrensvärd Museum** (Jan–April 11am–4pm; May–Aug daily 10am–5pm; Sept daily 11am–4pm; €3) is worth a look, occupying the residence used by the first commander of the fortress, Augustin Ehrensvärd. He oversaw the building of Suomenlinna and now lies in the elaborate tomb in the grounds; his personal effects remain inside the house alongside displays on the fort's construction. Finally, the **Coastal Artillery Museum** (mid-May to Aug daily 10am–6pm; €2) records Suomenlinna's defensive actions and – for an extra €3.50 – allows you the opportunity to clamber around the darkly claustrophobic World War II submarine *Vesikko*.

Seurasaari and around

A fifteen-minute tram (#4) or bus (#24) ride northwest of the city centre (get off one stop after the big hospital on the left, from where it's a one-kilometre walk) lies **Seurasaari**, a small wooded island delightfully set in a sheltered bay. The three contrasting museums on or close by Seurasaari make for a well-spent day. Access to the island proper is by a bridge at the southern end of Tamminiementie, conveniently close to the **Helsinki City Art Museum** (Tues–Sun 11am–6.30pm; €6; ⊛www.taidemuseo.fi). Though one of the best collections of modern Finnish art, with some eerily striking work, the museum is hardly a triumph of layout, with great clumps of stuff of differing styles scattered about the walls. But the good pieces shine through. Be warned, though, that during temporary exhibitions the permanent stock is locked away.

A few minutes' walk from the art museum, towards the Seurasaari bridge, is the long driveway leading to the **Urho Kekkonen Museum** (mid-May to mid-Aug daily 11am–5pm; mid-Aug to mid-May Wed–Sun 11am–5pm; €4, includes guided tour; ⊛www.nba.fi) at Tamminiemi, the villa where the esteemed president lived until his death in 1986. Whether they love him or loathe him, few Finns would deny the vital role Kekkonen played in Finnish history, most significantly by continuing the work of his predecessor, Paasikivi, in the establishment of Finnish neutrality. He accomplished this largely through delicate negotiations with Soviet leaders – whose favour he would gain, so legend has it, by taking them to his sauna (open for viewing in summer only) – narrowly averting major crises and seeing off the threat of a Soviet invasion on two separate occasions. Kekkonen often conducted official business here rather than at the Presidential Palace in the city, yet the feel of the place is far from institutional, with a light and very Finnish character, filled with birchwood furniture, its large windows giving peaceful views of surrounding trees, water and wildlife.

Close by, in another calm setting across the bridge on Seurasaari itself, is the **Open-Air Museum** (June–Aug daily 11am–5pm; early Sept & late May Mon–Fri 9am–3pm, Sat & Sun 11am–5pm; mid-Sept to mid-Nov Sat & Sun 11am–5pm; €5), a collection of vernacular buildings assembled from all over Finland, connected by the various pathways that extend around the island. There are better examples of traditional Finnish life elsewhere in the country, but if you're only visiting Helsinki this will give a good insight into how the country folk lived until surprisingly recently. The old-style church is a popular spot for city couples' weddings.

Aside from the museums and the scenery, people also come to Seurasaari to strip off. Sex-segregated **nudist beaches** line part of the western edge – also a popular offshore stop for the city's weekend yachtsmen, armed with binoculars; however, Pihlajasaari island (see p.701) is an altogether more pleasing location for nude sunbathing.

Outlying museums

Helsinki has a few other **museums** outside the centre that don't fit into any walking tour. All are within fairly easy reach with public transport, and sometimes a little legwork. A few kilometres northwest of the centre on the Tarvaspää peninsula, the **Gallen-Kallela Museum**, Gallen-Kallelantie 27 (mid-May to Aug daily 10am–6pm; Sept to mid-May Tues–Sat 10am–4pm, Sun 10am–5pm; €8; ⊛www .gallen-kallela.fi), is housed inside the Art Nouveau studio of the influential painter Akseli Gallen-Kallela (1865–1931), who lived and worked here from 1913. Sadly, it's a bit of an anticlimax, lacking either atmosphere or a decent display of the artist's work. There are a few old paints and brushes under dirty glass coverings in the studio, while in an upstairs room are the pickled remains of reptiles and frog-like animals collected by Gallen-Kallela's family. Inscribed into the floor is a declaration by Gallen-Kallela: "I Shall Return". Unless you're a huge fan, it's probably not worth the bother. To get there, take tram #4 from the city centre to the end of its route (on Saunalahdentie), then walk 2km along Munkkiniemi on the bay's edge to a footbridge which leads over the water and towards the poorly signposted museum. Alternatively, bus #33 runs from the tram stop to the footbridge about every twenty minutes.

To the west of the city centre, the former cable factory at Tallberginkatu 1F is now a cultural centre, the **Kaapelitehdas** (⍟www.kaapelitehdas.fi) home to dance and theatre companies and a clutch of museums, accessible on tram #8. The **Hotel and Restaurant Museum** (Tues–Sun noon–7pm; €2; ⍟www.hotellijaravintolamuseo .fi) is specifically designed for aficionados of the catering trade, although the photos on the walls of its two rooms reveal a fascinating social history of Helsinki, showing hotel and restaurant life from both sides of the table, alongside a staggering selection of matchboxes, beer mats emblazoned with the emblems of their establishments, and menus signed by the rich and infamous.

Despite its grand title, the **Finnish Museum of Photography** (Tues–Sun noon–7pm; €6; ⍟www.fmp.fi) comprises a shabby herd of old cameras that suggest Finnish photography never really progressed beyond the watch-the-birdie stage. Amends are made by the innovative temporary collections of photos that regularly adorn the walls. The third museum in the complex is the city's **Theatre Museum** (Tues–Sun noon–7pm; €5.50; ⍟www.teatterimuseo.fi), displaying a permanent collection of costumes, stage sets and lights. Frequent temporary exhibitions focus on different aspects behind the scenes in Finnish theatre.

Eating

As in the rest of the country, **eating** in Helsinki isn't cheap, but there is plenty of choice and, with careful planning, plenty of ways to stretch out funds. Other than all-you-can-eat **breakfast** tables in hotels (hostel breakfasts in the city tend to be rationed), it's best to hold out until **lunch**, when many restaurants offer a reduced fixed-price menu or a help-yourself table, while in almost every pizzeria you'll get a pizza, coffee and all you can manage from the bread and salad bar for under €10. **Picnic food**, too, is a viable option; visit the markets and market halls at the South Harbour or Hakaniementori for fresh vegetables, meat and fish. Several supermarkets in Tunneli, by the train station, stay open until 10pm. The popular **Forum** shopping centre (see p.709), directly opposite the Stockmann, has a number of popular, inexpensive eateries on two floors, while the **precinct** opposite the train station contains a range of mid-standard, filling eateries open till late.

Throughout the day, up until 5pm or 6pm, you can also get a coffee and pastry or a fuller snack for around €5 at one of the numerous local **cafés**. The best cafés are stylish, atmospheric affairs dating from the beginning of the twentieth century; alternatives include myriad multinational hamburger joints and the slightly more unusual *grilli* roadside stands, which sell hot dogs and the like – if you're tempted, experts claim the *Jaskan Grilli*, in Töölönkatu behind the National Museum, to be the best of its kind. If you're hungry and impoverished (and are, in theory at least, a student), you can get a full meal for €5 from one of the **student mensas**, the largest of which are centrally located in the main university buildings at Fabianinkatu 33, and at Kaivopiha, the triangular, cobbled plaza to the side of the Vanha Yliop-pilastalo. Both are open during the summer, and a dozen more are open during term time. The *mensas* can be cheaper still in the late afternoon, from 4pm to 6pm, and are also usually open on Saturdays from 9am to 1pm.

Unless otherwise stated, the cafés and restaurants listed here appear on the central Helsinki map, pp.692–693.

Cafés

Aalto Academic Bookstore, Pohjoisesplanadi 39. Designed by the world-famous Finnish architect whose name it bears, and well worth a visit after a morning's book-browsing. Sandwiches are pricey at €8.50, but you can always soak up the atmosphere over a coffee.

Bellman Kaivokatu 12. Big, cosmopolitan and very beautiful – though also very expensive.

Caramelli Near Hakasalmi Villa, Karamzininkatu 2 (see Helsinki map, pp.686–687). Small, intimate and serving gorgeous gooey cakes.

Ekberg Bulevardi 9 ⍟www.cafeekberg.fi. Opened in 1852, this landmark café retains nineteenth-century fixtures and a *fin de siècle* atmosphere, with starched waitresses bringing the most delicate of open sandwiches and pastries to green-marble tables.

Eliel Central train station. On the station's ground floor, this has an airy, vaulted Art Nouveau interior, good-value self-service breakfasts (Mon–Sat 7–10am, Sun 8–10am) – and a roulette table.

Engel Aleksanterinkatu 26 ⊛ www.cafeengel.fi. Named after the Berlin-born designer of all the buildings you can see from its window, this is a haven of gourmet coffee, pastries, cakes and intellectual chitchat, just across from Senate Square. Try the smoked-fish salad, or the French breakfast for €8.40.

Esplanad Pohjoisesplanadi 37. This classic establishment may have a bit of the walnut-grain Starbucks feel, but it's still the best place in town for inexpensive eating. Filled baguettes, a choice of fresh soups daily and always a queue. Outdoor seating catches the morning sun.

Fazer Kluuvikatu 3 ⊛ www.fazercafe.fi. Helsinki's best-known bakery, justly celebrated for its lighter-than-air pastries; there's another branch in the Forum Shopping Centre. At either, try the speciality, "Bebe", a praline cream-filled pastry for €2.50.

🏃 **Kappeli** Esplanad Park, Esplanadi. An elegant, classic-meets-modernist glasshouse with massive wrought-iron decorated windows overlooking Esplanadi and the harbour, with lots of live entertainment outside and in during the summer.

🏃 **Sandro's Coffee** Unioninkatu 28. Don't be fooled by the Starbucks look-alike logo out front – the aesthetic sensibilities at this new café are all original, with lavish velour divans and ornate wooden chairs occupying a meticulously Egyptian-themed sitting room with coffee-table books for browsing. Great cheesecake, though the coffee is a bit more expensive than in other cafés.

Strindberg Pohjoisesplanadi 33. Stylish outdoor coffee sipping – though it's expensive if you want to eat, with a large menu from the restaurant upstairs listing such items as smoked reindeer with Lapland cheese followed by slow-fried grayling and arctic cloudberry. More familiar items like roast beef sandwiches (€8.50) are sizable.

Tamminiementie Kahvila Tamminiementie 8 (see Helsinki map, pp.686–687). A good stop-off when visiting the nearby City Art Museum or Seurasaari Island, for high-quality tea or coffee served in elegant surroundings, with Chopin playing in the background.

🏃 **Tin Tin Tango** Töölöntorinkatu 7 (see Helsinki map, pp.686–687) ☎ 09/2709 0972. As the name suggests, the stereo here plays classic Argentine tango and the walls are adorned with original and derivative Tin Tin art. Cool boho feel, with breakfasts, sandwiches and Beamish bitter on tap, though many come for the sauna (€28 per hour) and on-site self-service laundry €3.50); both require reservations.

Tomtebon Kahvila Tamminiemi, opposite the Kekkonen Museum at Seurasaari (see Helsinki map, pp.686–687). Coffee served with home-made cookies and cakes in a lovely old wooden villa set in a lush garden.

Ursula Ehrenströmintie 3 (see Helsinki map, pp.686–687) ⊛ www.ursula.fi. On the beach at the edge of the Kaivopuisto park, with a wonderful sea view from the outdoor terrace. Decent cakes, sandwiches and light lunches (around €10). All profits from here go to charity.

Restaurants

Foreign restaurants are reasonably plentiful in Helsinki, and in a typical **pizzeria** you can expect to pay €12–24 per person for dinner, provided you don't drink anything stronger than mineral water. There are also a few **vegetarian** restaurants, which charge about the same. **Finnish** restaurants, on the other hand, and those serving **Russian** specialities, can be terrifyingly expensive; expect to spend around €30 per person for a night of upmarket overindulgence. Restaurants are usually open daily until around 1am, though the kitchens close at about 11pm.

Note that we've given phone numbers only for restaurants where you need to book.

Finnish and Russian

🏃 **Bellevue** Rahapajankatu 3, behind the Uspenski Cathedral ☎ 09/179 560, ⊛ www .restaurantbellevue.com. A superb Russian restaurant opened, ironically, in 1917, the year Finland won independence from Russia. Polished samovars create a period ambience for the expensive, gourmet Russian food that is considered some of Europe's best: try Marshal Mannerheim's favourite of minced lamb flavoured with herring for €25; for the more adventurous, there's also bear steak (€65). Closed Sat & Sun lunchtime.

Chez Dominique Ludviginkatu 3 ☎ 09/623 7393, ⊛ www.chezdominique.fi. The only restaurant in Finland with two Michelin stars, this white-hued, minimalist place serves Scandinavian cuisine with a distinctive French touch. The menu changes weekly, but perennial mains (€40 and up) include pigeon filled with duck foie gras, roasted pike perch and boiled lobster. Closed Sat lunch, and Sun & Mon.

Hariton Kasarmikatu 4 (see Helsinki map,pp.686–687) ⌖09/622 1717, ⓦwww.hariton.fi. One of Finland's most respected Russian restaurants, and better-priced than the city's other high-brow Russian places. The menu, following the Orthodox calendar, changes several times a year, but the expensive blinis – vendace or whitefish roe – always make an appearance, as do any number of wild mushroom dishes.

Havis Amanda Unioninkatu 23. The oldest and best seafood restaurant in the city, albeit pricey and somewhat staid. Superb service, and most mains around €25.

Katajanokan Kasino Laivastokatu 1 (see Helsinki map, pp.686–687). Just east of the Uspenski Cathedral, this theme restaurant offers the chance to feast on à la carte gourmet dishes such as elk or reindeer in anything from a mock wartime bunker to the "Cabinet Room", decorated with markers to Finnish independence. A great place if someone else is paying – mains are around €25. The terrace onto the sea makes this one of the city's most romantic spots for dinner.

Kuu Töölönkatu 27 (see Helsinki map, pp.686–687) ⓦwww.ravintolakuu.info. Between the Opera House and Sibelius Park, this is an unpretentious place to consume filling, down-to-earth Finnish food. Mains from €15.

Lappi Annankatu 22 ⌖09/645 550, ⓦwww .lappires.com. If your wallet can handle the prices, this is a must while in Helsinki, specializing in real Finnish foods like pea soup and oven pancakes, as well as Sámi specialities of smoked reindeer and warm cloudberries. Count on at least €40 for a three-course meal not including drinks.

Lasipalatsi The upscale Finnish dishes – most around €22 – are tasty enough, though the casual atmosphere and views up and down Mannerhe-imintie are what draw the crowds.

Kynsilaukka Ravintola Garlic Fredrikinkatu 22 ⌖09/651 939 ⓦwww.kynsilaukka.com. Pricey, but the ultimate pleasure if you like garlic, as its name suggests; the snails in garlic sauce are a huge hit.

Ravintola Perho Mechelininkatu 7 (near corner of Hietaniemenkatu) ⓦwww.perho.fi/ravintola. The restaurant of the Finnish Culinary College and an excellent choice for lunch, which is normally a three-course buffet for around €20. Prices are much lower than you'd expect and service impeccable.

Romanov Yrjönkatu 15. Old-style Russian restaurant with a deliciously over-the-top spirit-of-the-tsars atmosphere: red velvet carpeting and lavish chairs accentuated by portraits of Russian military victors and noblemen. Lunchtime is popular among office workers, while evenings see more of a tourist crowd. Try the sumptuous grilled spiced steak Romanov (€22). Closed Sat lunch and Sun.

Sea Horse Kapteeninkatu 11 (see Helsinki map, pp.686–687) ⓦwww.seahorse.fi. This cavernous and smoky restaurant has been around for nearly a century and remains a favourite with locals, making it an excellent place for people-watching. Serves a range of fairly inexpensive Finnish dishes, though it's especially renowned for its various fish plates, which start at €12.50.

Sipuli Kanavaranta 7. Set in an old brick warehouse just west of the Uspenski Cathedral, and offering a tastebud-thrilling, formal and glamorous – though financially ruinous – choice of Franco–Finnish gourmet dishes, several based on traditional Sámi fare. Closed weekends.

Terrace Bar Stockmann Department Store. Situated on the top floor – bright and relaxed, with Lloyd loom-style seating. Specialities are salads, soups and grills such as potato and anchovy bake or grilled chicken; reckon on €8 for a main dish.

Tori Punavuorenkatu 2 ⓦwww.fredantori .com. Inexpensive Nordic dishes served up by lively waiters to trendy twentysomethings chatting away amidst lounge music. The terrace faces Frederikintori square and is a great spot to enjoy your breakfast eggs (€3) or a glass of wine in the evening.

Ethnic and vegetarian

Ani Telakkakatu 2 (see Helsinki map, pp.686–687) ⓦwww.ani.fi. Turkish food at its best; go for the €7.90 buffet table laid out at lunchtime, though dinner is quite reasonable too.

Cantina West Kasarmikatu 23 ⓦwww .cantinawest.net. Fiery, reasonably priced Tex-Mex food in a large and lively, western-themed restaurant. Gets loud late at night.

Oliver's Annankatu 21. Simple, filling dishes like steak, sushi, salad and curry noodles, starting at €8 and served until the wee hours at weekends. For a starter, try the tasty and creamy goats' cheese spring rolls (€3).

Eatz Mikonkatu 15 ⌖09/6877 2450, ⓦwww .eatz.fi. Massive gilded restaurant with food from all over the world, including Indian, Japanese and Brazilian cuisine. Also has a sauna (€80 and up per hour) and at night it turns into a popular bar and club. Enter at Kaisaniemenkatu 2.

Golden Rax Pizzabuffet Mannerheimintie 18, second floor of the Forum Shopping Centre. Bargain-basement unlimited pizza and pasta buffet for €8.

Mai Thai Annankatu 32. The least expensive and quite possibly the best of the city's crop of Thai restaurants. Mains from €11, lunches for €7.

Mamma Rosa Runeberginkatu 55 (see Helsinki map, pp.686–687) ⓦwww.mammarosa.fi. One of the best mid-priced restaurants in the city; unsurprisingly, it's generally full. You're best off with the amply-sized pizzas, though there's fish, steaks and pasta, too. Mains from €9.

Namaskaar Bulevardi 6 ⓦwww.namaskaar.fi. Helsinki's first Indian restaurant – the Bulevardi branch

is the best of the six dotted around the city. The dinner menu, while extensive, offers rather pricey mains, so it's best to come here at lunchtime when you can get dishes like the creamy *murgh chettinand* (chicken in coconut sauce) for around €8.

🏃 **Via** Ludviginkatu 8 ☏09/681 1370, ⓦwww.viaravintola.com. Large, reasonably-priced restaurant and wine bar with lots of light and a fairly well-heeled crowd. The menu features both Italian and pan-Asian dishes (around €13) such as spicy skewered king prawn.

Zucchini Fabianinkatu 4. A friendly and stylish lunch-only vegetarian restaurant big on aubergines, courgettes and salads – a filling meal here will cost around €9. Closed weekends.

Drinking

Although never cheap, alcohol is not a dirty word in Finland, and **drinking**, especially beer, can be enjoyed in the city's many café-like pubs, which are where most Helsinki folk go to socialize. You'll find one on virtually every corner, but the pick of the bunch are listed below. The neighbourhood of Punavuori, southwest of the train station, has the highest concentration of places – have a wander along Uudenmaankatu or Iso Roobertinkatu to get a sense for what's on – while some students opt for the cheaper, decadent dives in the Kallio district. Only the really swanky places have a dress code, and they are usually too elitist – and expensive – to be worth bothering with anyway. Most bars are open from the afternoon until 2am, though a few of the more popular ones will keep the juices flowing until 3am or 4am, especially on the weekends. On the whole, Sundays to Thursdays are normally quiet, though Wednesday, known to many locals as *pikkulauantai* ("little Saturday"), can be a popular clubbing night; on Fridays and Saturdays on the other hand, it's best to arrive as early as possible to get a seat without having to queue. Most drinking dives also serve food, although the grub is seldom at its best in the evening (where it's good earlier in the day, we've included it under "Restaurants").

If you really want to find out the trendiest, of-the-moment nightspots, try contacting Rent-a-Party-Mate, Mannerheimintie 33A (☏50/438 8091, ⓦwww .bizarreone.fi), a group of in-the-know locals who will take you out for a queue-free night at Helsinki's most fashionable bars and clubs, though bar-hopping this hip doesn't come cheap. If you want a drink but are feeling antisocial, or just very hard-up, the cheapest method, as ever, is to buy from the appropriately named ALKO shop: there are self-service ones at Fabiankatu 7 and Vuorikatu 7.

Unless otherwise stated, the places listed below appear on the Central Helsinki map, pp.692–693.

Abin Baari Fleminginkatu 13 (see Helsinki map, pp.686–687). Denizens of working-class Kallio muse over world affairs from the stools of this crowded bar, full of local character. The first – and for many the only – stop of a long night. Metro: Sörnäinen.

Angleterre Fredrikinkatu 47. Utterly Finnish despite the flock wallpaper and Dickensian fixtures – good for a laugh and cultural disorientation.

Arctic Ice Bar Yliopistonkatu 5 ⓦwww.uniq.fi. This tiny bar seating just twelve is a novel place for a drink, with walls made from two-metre-thick blocks of ice and a constant temperature of a cool

5°C. The cover charge (€10) includes a drink and the loan of a thermal cape and gloves. Closed Mon & Tues.

Ateljeebaari *Sokos Torni* hotel, Yrjönkatu 26. On the thirteenth floor of a plush hotel: great views, great posing and pricey drinks – be warned that the women's toilet has bizarre ceiling-to-floor windows.

Baker's Mannerheimintie 12 ⓦwww.ravintolabakers .com. A good place to initiate yourself into drinking Helsinki-style, though it has a reputation as a last-chance pick-up spot.

Bar 9 Uudenmaankatu 9 ⓦ www.bar9.net.
This sleek and unpretentious neighbourhood bar has been a standby for local personalities
and bohos for a few years, and doesn't show any
signs of losing its edge. Good food, too, including
massive grilled cheese sandwiches.

Bar Tapasta Uudenmaankatu 13 ⓦ www
.marcante.fi. Small and intimate, with strikingly
striped walls, this Parisian-style café-bar is often
full and is a regular stop for nightowls, with cheap
tapas and sangria served until late.

Elite Etläinen Hesperiankatu 22 (see Helsinki map,
pp.686–687). Northwest of the National Museum,
this Art Deco bar-restaurant was once the haunt of
the city's artists, many of whom would settle the
bill not with money but with paintings – a selection
of which line the walls. Especially good in summer,
when you can drink on the terrace.

Erottaja Bar Erotajankatu 15–17. Central,
aqua-blue bar just up from the Swedish
theatre with a bit of an underground feel to it.
Popular with students from Helsinki's art and
design school.

Kaarle XII Kasarmikatu 40. Fine Art Nouveau
features hewn into the red-granite walls make
this the most traditional-looking of the city's bars
– not that the customers allow the surroundings to
inhibit their merrymaking.

Kappelin Olutkellari Esplanadi Park, Esplanadi.
Multipurpose building of glass and fancy ironwork
(see also *Kappeli*, p.705), where the bar draws a
garrulous and gloriously eclectic clientele.

Kola Helsinginkatu 13 (see Helsinki map, pp.686–
687). Manhattan's East Village transplanted to
Kallio. Young and hip loungesters sprawl out in
this carpeted 1960s-style bar reading design
magazines and sipping €3.50 pints or espressos.
Metro: Sörnäinen.

Kosmos Kalevankatu 3. This is where the big
media cats – TV producers, PR people, the glitzier
authors – hang out and engage in loud arguments
as the night wears on. The wonderful interior is
unchanged since the 1920s, but you'll only see it if
you get past the officious doorman.

Loose Fredrikinkatu 34 ⓦ www.barloose.com.
Downhome rock 'n' roll pub done up with Stones
photos and paisley wallpaper, and offering pints of
beer for €4.

mbar Lasipalatsi, Mannerheimintie 22–24 ⓦ www
.mbar.fi. Cigarette-drawing ladies and their
bespectacled boyfriends groove in a designer-ish
setting to electronica DJs and the occasional live
band. The terrace is popular in summers and there
are Internet terminals.

Merimakasiini Hietalahdenranta 4 (see Helsinki
map, pp.686–687). Slightly out-of-the-way, on

a street running off Hietalahdentori towards the
waterfront, but worth sampling on a Friday or
Saturday night when the customers spill onto the
terrace to drink while gazing at the cranes of the
city's cargo harbour.

Molly Malone's Kaisaniemenkatu 1C ⓦ www
.mollymalones.fi. Helsinki's best Irish bar, just a
few steps from the train station and with live Irish
music most nights.

Oujee Uudenmaankatu 28. Dimly-lit, red-walled
bar that stands out for its hip, unpretentious feel.
DJs play drum 'n' bass and hip-hop. Next door *Åbo*
has a similarly buzzing scene.

The Rock Bar Bulevardi 28. True grunge ambience with Anthrax and Megadeth on the tubes, but
not so loud that you can't hear yourself ordering
the €3.20 pints of Karhu.

Saunabar Eerikinkatu 27 09/586 5550, ⓦ www
.saunabar.fi. A popular hangout, but separate
saunas (make advance reservations Tues–Sat) for
men and women mean this may not be the pick-
up point you'd hoped for.

St Urho's Pub Museokatu 10 (see Helsinki map,
pp.686–687) ⓦ www.botta.fi. Close to the National
Museum, this is one of the most popular student
pubs – which accounts for the lengthy queue that
forms from about 9pm on Fri and Sat.

Teatteri Pohjoisesplanadi 2. Spend a few hours in
this sometimes rowdy complex and you'll encounter a cross-section of Helsinki characters – some
coming, some going, others falling over.

Vanha Mannerheimintie 3. A self-service and
hence comparatively cheap bar. It fills quickly, so
try to arrive early for a seat on the balcony overlooking the bustle of the streets below. Downstairs
has a more underground feel, with bench seating
and a cosy – if smoky – atmosphere.

We Got Beef Iso Roobertinkatu 21. Modish bar
that resembles a dimly-lit diner, popular with
students, artsy types, schmoozers and their arm-
candy. DJs spin slamming beats in a back room,
and there's stand-up comedy on the first Sunday
of each month, though the humour may be lost on
non-Finnish speakers (or non-Finns).

William K Mannerheimintie 72 (see Helsinki map,
pp.686–687). A cosy locals' pub with old Indian
carpets for tablecloths and every beer you could
want, though the imported ones are expensive.

Zetor Kaivopiha (Mannerheimintie 3)
ⓦ www.zetor.net.. A loud, country-themed
bar designed by the people behind the irreverent
Leningrad Cowboys rock group, with a rusty
tractor in the middle. An older crowd gets down
to hard rock and 1980s tunes, and after midnight
the kitchen serves a limited menu of basic grub
– think meatballs and potatoes – until 3.30am.

Nightlife and entertainment

Helsinki probably has a greater number of ways to spend the evening than any other Scandinavian city; there is, for example, a steady diet of **live music**. Finnish rock bands, not helped by the awkward metre of their native language, often sound absurd on first hearing, but at least seeing them is relatively cheap at €9–15 – around half the price of seeing a British or American band – and sometimes even free. The best gigs tend to be during term-time, but in summer there are dozens of free events in the city parks, the biggest of which take place almost every Sunday in Kaivopuisto. Many bands also play on selected nights in one of the growing number of surprisingly hip **clubs and discos**, in which you can gyrate, pose or just drink into the small hours – admission is usually around €5.

For up-to-the-minute details of **what's on**, read the entertainment page of *Helsingin Sanomat* or the free fortnightly paper *City* (found in record shops, bookshops and department stores), which has listings in English covering rock and classical music, clubs, cinema, theatre and opera. The Lasipalatsi (see p.712) has a youth service centre with information on festivals, concerts and events, or else simply watch out for posters on the streets. **Tickets** for most events can be bought at the venue or, for a small commission, at Tiketti, Yrjönkatu 29c on the third floor of Forum shopping centre, Mannerheimintie 18 (Mon–Fri 10am–7pm, Sat 10am–4pm; ☎0600/11 616, ⊛www.tiketti.fi).

In terms of **cinema**, both the latest blockbusters and a good selection of fringe **films** are normally showing somewhere in Helsinki. A seat is usually €8–10, although some places offer a €6.50 matinee show. Check the listings in *City* (see p.650) or pick up a copy of *Elokuva-Viikko*, a free weekly leaflet that lists the cinemas and their programmes; it's available at the cinemas themselves. English-language films are shown with Finnish subtitles – there's no overdubbing. The Finnish Film Archive's theatre *Orion*, Eerikinkatu 15 (☎09/6154 0201, ⊛www.sea.fi/esitykset) screens art-house films thrice daily, while for Hollywood blockbusters and Finnish films, the megaplexes to head for are Tennispalatsi (☎0600/007 007, ⊛www.finnkino.fi/teatterit), Salomonkatu 15; and Kinopalatsi (☎0600/94 444, ⊛www.kinopalatsi.fi), just east of the train station at Kaisaniemenkatu 2.

Clubs and music venues

Clubs in Helsinki change ownership, style and format with baffling rapidity, and the listings below are only a pointer to what may be on offer. For up-to-the-moment information, check out the city's listings magazines, or head for the club-heavy streets Iso Roobertinkatu and Frederikinkatu in Punavuori. Most clubs operate Wednesday to Saturday from10pm until 4am, though some occasionally will open a bit earlier; when there is a cover charge, it won't usually be much more than €5. Another venue to check out is the Kaapelitehdas (see p.704), which organizes mammoth, deafening raves. If you're lucky enough to be in town to catch it, Unity (⊛www.clubunity.org) is a dance extravaganza put on several times a summer on the nearby island of Uunisaari, offering spectacular DJs, gorgeous people and non-stop dancing till dawn. Tickets sell out almost before they go on sale, so plan well ahead.

Botta Museokatu 10. Joined to *St Urho's Pub* (see opposite), this was the birthplace of Helsinki house and techno, and today features vibrant dance music of various hues.

Fever Annankatu 3. Popular new nightclub with a rather small dancefloor that can make for much more intimate grinding than you might have bargained for.

Helmi Eerikinkatu 14 ⊛www.helmi.net. The only non-gay venue on this block – very crowded and loud, with zebra-striped seats and a well-stocked bar. A favourite among investment bankers, ad execs and lawyers.

Helsinki Club Yliopistonkatu 8 ⊛www.helsinki club.com. This legendary nightclub is still going strong, every day of the week. Minimum age 24.

Kaivohuone Kaivopuisto Park. Just renovated, one of the city's longest established late-night party spots; come here to dance, drink and join the very long taxi queues for home.

KY-Exit Pohjoinen Rautatiekatu 21. Sometimes has visiting foreign bands, more often lively disco nights for clubbers in their early twenties.

Manala Dagmarinkatu 2. Just below *Botta*, with two floors and long queues for anything from ballroom dancing to grinding to MTV's latest offerings.

Rose Garden Iso Roobertinkatu 10 ⓦwww .clubrosegarden.com. Large, labyrinthine lounge bar-cum-club with several DJs – many of them well-known international names – playing in a various themed rooms. It can get pretty hot in here when it packs in the weekend crowds after midnight; enter below the neon "Swengi" sign and head towards the silver door in the back.

🏃 **Storyville** Museokatu 8 ⓦwww.storyville .fi. Buzzing jazz joint, with live Dixieland, swing or bebop on stage every night. In the summer, there's music outside on the idyllic garden terrace until 9pm. Cover is always under

€10, and you can eat a pricey and filling Finnish dinner at your table.

Studio 51 Frederikinkatu 51–53 ⓦwww.studio51 .fi. Built in the image of New York's Studio 54 and with a deliberately decadent 1970s decor of sequined walls, red mood lighting and large disco balls. If your clubbing desires still remain unconsummated, *Highlight* just across the street is a bit more low-key.

Tavastia Urho Kekkosenkatu 4–6 ⓦwww.tavastia klubi.fi. The country's premier rock club, and a major showcase for Finnish and Swedish bands. Downstairs holds the stage and self-service bar; the balcony is waitress service. Next door, *Semifinal* is much smaller but similar in clientele.

Vanha Ylioppilastalo Mannerheimintie 3 ⓦwww .vanha.fi. The main venue for leading indie bands from around the world, just next to Stockmann's department store.

Gay Helsinki

Always the slowest of the Scandinavian countries to reform sexuality laws, Finland finally decriminalized homosexuality in 1971 and passed partnership laws in 2002. These days, public displays of affection are accepted, while the **gay scene** in Helsinki has flourished in recent years: today there's a gay choir, a biannual pride parade and an impressive number of exclusively gay and gay-friendly establishments, the latter clustered around **Eerikinkatu** and the southern end of **Mannerheimintie**. For the latest details, pick up a copy of the monthly *Z* **magazine** – in Finnish only but with a useful listings section (ⓦwww.z-lehti.fi); it's widely available in larger newsagents, or from the state-supported gay and lesbian organization SETA, Mannerheimintie 170 A4 (☎09/681 2580, ⓦwww.seta.fi).

Bars, clubs and saunas

Birdie Annankatu 10 ⓦwww.birdie.fi. Helsinki's newest gay bar is trendy, very straight-friendly and plastered with wall-size photos of Hollywood celebs. Laid-back disco and soul music is played upstairs, while downstairs you can dance and go deaf to blaring house and techno DJs. Arrive on the early side to avoid the velvet rope. Wed–Sun 10pm–4am.

Con Hombres Eerikinkatu 14 ⓦwww.conhombres .fi. The most popular gay bar in Helsinki and one of the oldest in the country. If it's quiet elsewhere, the chances are there'll be people here. Very cruisey at weekends and on the whole an older (35+) crowd. Open daily from 2pm–2am.

DTM (Don't Tell Mamma) Iso Roobertinkatu 28 ⓦwww.dtm.fi. Known to regulars as *mama* or *mummola*, this legendary gay and lesbian nightclub is the largest in northern Europe. It's still *the* place to go, with occasional drag shows and great house music most nights; on Saturdays, the upstairs dancefloor is women-only. During the day, the downstairs café offers pastries, snacks and coffee.

Hercules Lönnrotinkatu 4b ⓦwww.herculesgay club.com. Not quite as trendy as *DTM*, this club is quite popular with young, leather-clad men and plays a variety of music, including some of Finland's best home-grown offerings.

Lost and Found & Hideaway Annankatu 6 ⓦwww.lostandfound.fi. Two very popular bars on two floors, with a small dance floor downstairs, though weekends may feel more like a gay-friendly straight club than the inverse.

Mann's Street Mannerheimintie 12 (upstairs) ⓦwww.mannsstreet.com. If you're looking for karaoke, Finnish music and older gay men, you'll find generous helpings here.

Room Erottajankatu 5–7. Next to *Lost and Found* and one of Helsinki's better neighbourhood bars; a laid-back place that attracts the young, beautiful and leather-clad.

Vogue Sturenkatu 27A ⓦwww.conhombres .fi/vogue.html. Set just north of the centre in Kallio, Finland's only (officially) gay sauna has three saunas, a steam bath, jacuzzi, pool and massage facilities.

Ferries from Helsinki to Estonia

Following Estonia's regaining of its independence and membership in the EU, a growing number of passenger vessels are plying the 85-kilometre route across the Baltic between Helsinki and the Estonian capital, Tallinn. EU citizens as well as Americans, Canadians, Australians and New Zealanders no longer need a visa but other nationalities should check the latest situation at the tourist office in Helsinki.

Estonia and Finland have similar languages, a common ancestry, and histories which had largely run parallel up until the Soviet Union's annexation of Estonia in 1940. Despite the decades of Soviet occupation, **Tallinn**, within its medieval walls, is a beautifully maintained Hanseatic city with many museums and some fine old churches, all just a few minutes' walk from the harbour – its entire old town is a Unesco world heritage site. If you have time, take a look, too, at the enormous Song Festival Grounds just outside the old centre, scene of the much-publicized pro-independence rallies of the late 1980s.

While independence and EU citizenship has brought Estonia's culturally rich population many new freedoms and opportunities, it hasn't yet brought them any money. The introduction of the kroon (rhymes with "prawn", not "prune"), a new version of the pre-Soviet currency, ultimately did rather little to ease the uphill struggle faced by the country's economy and although development was slow after independence, many believe that EU membership will solidify Estonia's role as a northern European transport hub.

Crossings (1hr 30min–3hr 15min) are offered by Tallink (tickets from South Harbour booking office; ☎09/228 311, ⊛www.tallink.fi); Linda Line, Makasiini Terminal (☎09/668 9700, ⊛www.lindaline.fi); Nordic Jet Line, Kanavaterminaali, Katajanokan-laituri (☎09/681 770, ⊛www.njl.fi) and Silja Line, Olympiaterminaali (☎09/180 4422, ⊛www.silja.fi). Expect to pay €25–65 for a one-way ticket; cars cost €80–100. Buying in advance gets you the cheapest tickets, but look out for last-minute bargains in travel agency windows and on the front page of *Helsingin Sanomat*. If you're really pressed for time, Copterline (☎0200/18 181, ⊛www.copterline.com) offers helicopter shuttles between the two cities for around €100 each way.

Listings

Airlines British Airways, Aleksanterinkatu 21A ☎09/650 677; Finnair, Töölönkatu 21 ☎09/818 800; SAS, Keskuskatu 7A ☎09/228 021.

Airport Enquiries ☎09/8277 3103 or 0200/14636.

American Express Kanavaranta 9 (Mon–Fri 9am–4pm; ☎09/6132 0400). After-hours and for lost cards call ☎0800/114 646.

Banks and exchange As well as the banks dotted all around the city, the bank at the airport opens long hours (daily 6.30am–11pm), and there's an exchange counter at Katajanokka harbour, where Viking and Finnjet ferries dock (daily 9–11.30am & 3.45–6pm). The Forex desk in the central train station (daily 8am–9pm) doesn't accept Visa; Otto, opposite the station (Mon–Fri 8am–8pm, Sat 10am–6pm), handles cash advances on all major cards.

Bike Rental GreenBike Mannerheimintie 13, just under the bridge opposite the parliament building (daily 10am–6pm, sometimes later; €10 per day; ☎09/8502 2850).

Bookstore Akateeminen Kirjakauppa, Pohjois-esplanadi 39 (⊛www.akateeminen.com), has the city's largest selection of books (many in English), magazines and newspapers. Suomalainen Kirja-kauppa, Aleksanterinkatu 23, sells fewer titles but offers regular discounts, especially on phrasebooks and dictionaries (⊛www.suomalainen.com).

Bus enquiries Long-distance buses ☎9/682 701 or 0200/4000; city buses ☎09/4721 or 0100/111.

Car rental Avis, Pohjoinen Rautatiekatu ☎09/441 155; Budget, Malminkatu 24 ☎09/686 6500; Europcar, Mannerheimintie 50 ☎09/4780 2220.

Dentist Dentarium (24hr), Mikonkatu 7A, 6th floor ☎09/622 1533. Expect to pay €60 for a consultation.

Doctor ☎10023.

Embassies Canada, Pohjoisesplanadi 25B ☎09/228 530; UK, Itäinen Puistotie 17 ☎09/2286

5100; USA, Itäinen Puistotie 14A ☏09/171 931. Citizens of Australia and New Zealand should contact the Australian Embassy in Stockholm (see p.490).

Emergencies Ambulance ☏112; Police ☏10022.

Ferries Reservations and information: Silja Line ☏09/18 041, @www.silja.fi; Tallink ☏09/228 211, @www.tallink.fi; Viking Line ☏09/123 577, @www.vikingline.fi.

Hospital Marian Hospital, Lapinlahdenkatu 16 ☏4711 or 09/4716 3339.

Internet cafés *Café Aalto*, 2nd floor Akateeminen kirjapauppa, Keskuskatu 1; Telecenter, Vuorikatu 8; Netcup, Aleksanterinkatu 52. In the Lasipalatsi, Mannerheimintie 22–24, there's mbar or the main post office (no charge).

Late shopping The shops in Tunneli, the underground complex by the train station, are open Mon–Sat 10am–10pm, Sun noon–10pm.

Laundry Punavuorenkatu 3 (Mon–Thurs 8m–8pm, Fri 8am–6pm, Sat 10am–3pm, Sun noon–4pm); *Café Tin Tin Tango*, Töölöntorinkatu 7 (Mon–Thurs 7am–midnight, Sat 9am–2am, Sun 10am–midnight; ring ☏09/2709 0972 to reserve).

Left luggage There are lockers (around €2) in the long-distance bus station (Mon–Thurs & Sat 9am–6pm, Fri 8am–6pm), or in the train station (Mon–Fri 7am–10pm).

Libraries (*kirjasto*) Central branches at Topeliuksenkatu 6 in Töölö, at Rikhardinkatu 3 near

Esplanadi, and at Viides linja 11, close to Kallio kirkko (all Mon–Fri 9.30am–8pm, Sat 9.30am–3pm).

Lost property (*löytötavaratoimisto*) 3rd floor, Päijänteentie 12A (Mon–Fri 8am–4.15pm; ☏09/189 3180).

Maps KarttaPiste, Vuorikatu 14 (Mon–Fri 9am–6pm, Sat 10am–4pm; @www.karttapiste.fi).

Newspapers Almost every central Helsinki newsstand stocks some UK or US papers. Try at the train station, the airport, or inside Stockmann Department Store.

Pharmacy Yliopiston Apteekki, Mannerheimintie 96 (☏09/4178 0300 or 0203/20 200), is open 24hr; its branch at Mannerheimintie 5 is open daily 7am–midnight.

Police Pieni Roobertinkatu 1–3 ☏1891.

Post office The main office is at Elielinaukio1A (Mon–Fri 7am–9pm, Sat & Sun 10am–6pm); poste restante at the rear door (Mon–Fri 9am–6pm). Stamps are available from post offices or the yellow machines in shops.

Train enquiries ☏0307/10.

Travel agents Kilroy Travels, Kaivokatu 10D (☏09/680 7811, @www.kilroytravels.fi), is the Scandinavian youth travel agent, specializing in discounted tickets for students and young people. Suomen Matkatoimisto (SMT), the Finland Travel Bureau, Kaivokatu 10A (☏09/18 261, @www.smt.fi), organizes trips to Russia and the necessary visas.

Around Helsinki

To be honest, there's little in Helsinki's outlying area that's worth venturing out for. But three places, all an easy day-trip from the city, merit a visit: the visionary suburbs of **Espoo**; the home of the composer Sibelius at **Järvenpää**; and the evocative old town of **Porvoo**, which also serves as an obvious access point to the underrated southeastern corner of the country.

The Espoo area

Lying west of Helsinki, the suburban area of **Espoo** (Esbo in Swedish) comprises several separate districts. The one nearest to Helsinki, directly across the bay, is the "garden city" of **TAPIOLA**. In the 1950s Finnish urban planners attempted to blend new housing schemes with the surrounding forests and hills, frequently only to be left with a compromise that turned ugly as expansion occurred. Tapiola was the exception to this rule, built as a self-contained living area rather than a dormitory town, with alternating high and low buildings, abundant open areas, parks, fountains and swimming pools. Much praised on its completion by the architectural world, it's still refreshing to wander through and admire the idea and its execution. The **tourist office** at Pohjantie 3 (daily: Sept–May 8.30am–4pm, June–Aug 9am–5pm; ☏09/8164 7230, @www.espootravel.com) handles enquiries about the whole Espoo area.

About 3km north of Tapiola, the traffic-filled Hagalundintie brings you to the little peninsula of **Otaniemi** and a couple more notable architectural sites. One of these is the Alvar Aalto-designed campus of Helsinki University's technology faculty; the other – far more dramatic – is the Dipoli student union building on the same campus. Ever keen to harmonize the artificial with the natural, architects

Reimi and Raili Pietilä here created a building which seems fused with the rocky crags above, the front of the structure daringly edging forward from the cliff face.

Though the town of Espoo itself has little to delay you, just beyond lies the hugely absorbing **Hvitträsk** (daily: June–Aug 10am–6pm; Sept–May 11am–6pm; €4), the studio-home built and shared by architects Eliel Saarinen, Armas Lindgren and Herman Gesellius until 1904, when their partnership dissolved amid the acrimony caused by Saarinen's independent (and winning) design for Helsinki's train station. Externally, this is an extended and romanticized version of the traditional Finnish log cabin, the leafy branches that creep around making the structure look like a mutant growth emerging from the forest. Inside are frescoes by Gallen-Kallela and changing exhibitions of Finnish art and handicrafts. Saarinen and his wife are buried in the grounds.

Frequent buses run throughout the day from Helsinki's long-distance bus station **to Tapiola**, but you usually need to request them to stop there; check details and times at the bus station or the City Tourist Office. To get from central Helsinki **to Hvitträsk**, take the local (line L) train to Louma (37min) and follow the signs for 3km, or take bus #166 from Helsinki (55min). To get to **Otaniemi** from central Helsinki, take bus #102 or #103 (20min); from Tapiola, take bus #2, #4 or #195 (5min).

Järvenpää: Ainola

Around 40km north of Helsinki in **JÄRVENPÄÄ**, easily reached by either bus or train, is **Ainola** (May–Sept Tues–Sun 10am–5pm; €5) – the house where Jean Sibelius lived from 1904 with his wife, Aino (sister of the artist Eero Järnefelt), after whom the place is named.

Though now regarded as one of the twentieth century's greatest composers, **Jean Sibelius**, born in Hämeenlinna in 1865, had no musical background, and by the age of nineteen was enrolled on a law course at Helsinki University. He had, however, developed a youthful passion for the violin and took a class at the capital's Institute of Music. Law was soon forgotten as Sibelius's real talents were recognized, and his musical studies took him to the cultural hotbeds of the day, Berlin and Vienna. Returning to Finland to teach at the Institute, Sibelius soon gained a government grant, which enabled him to begin composing full time, the first concert of his works taking place in 1892. His early pieces were inspired by the Finnish folk epic, the *Kalevala*, and by the nationalist movement of the times; in 1899 the country's Russian rulers banned performances of Sibelius's rousing *Finlandia* under any name that suggested its patriotic sentiment – it was instead published simply as "Opus 26 No. 7".

While the overtly nationalistic elements in Sibelius's work mellowed in later years, his music continued to reflect a very Finnish obsession with nature: "Other composers offer their public a cocktail," he said, "I offer mine pure spring water." He is still revered in his own land, although he was also notorious for his bouts of heavy drinking, and a destructive quest for perfection which fuelled suspicion that he had completed, and destroyed, two symphonies during his final thirty years. This was an angst-ridden period when no new work appeared, which became known as "the silence from Järvenpää". Sibelius died in 1957, his best-known symphonies setting a standard younger Finnish composers have only just begun to approach.

The house is just the kind of home you'd expect for a man who included representations of flapping swans' wings in his music: a tranquil place, close to lakes and forests. The wood-filled grounds are as atmospheric as the building, which is a place of pilgrimage for devotees, although books, furnishings and a few paintings are all there is to see. His grave is in the grounds, marked by a marble stone inscribed simply with his name. For more tangible Sibelius memories, and more of his music, visit the Sibelius Museum in Turku (see p.722).

While in Järvenpää, it would be a pity to miss out on a visit to the **Halosenniemi Museum** (Tues–Sun: May–Aug 11am–7pm; Sept–April 11am–5pm; €5). On the

Tuusula Lakeside road, just a few minutes' walk from Ainola, this is the rustic home of Pekka Halonen, one of Finland's most renowned artists. A beautifully serene place, its National Romantic decor has been painstakingly restored and now houses some of Halonen's pictures and painting materials in their original setting.

Porvoo

Some 50km northeast of Helsinki, **PORVOO** (Borgå in Swedish) is one of the oldest towns on the south coast. Lined by small wooden buildings, its narrow cobbled streets give a sense of the Finnish life that predated the capital's bold squares and Neoclassical geometry. This, coupled with its elegant riverside setting and unhurried mood, means you're unlikely to be alone – word of Porvoo's peaceful time-locked qualities has spread.

First stop should be the **tourist office** at Rihkamakatu 4 (July & Aug Mon–Fri 9am–6pm, Sat & Sun 10am–4pm; Sept–June Mon–Fri 9.30am–4.30pm, Sat 10am–2pm; ☏019/520 2316, ☜www.porvoo.fi), for a free map of the town. For something more historic, look in at the preserved **Johan Ludwig Runeberg House**, Aleksanterinkatu 3 (May–Aug daily 10am–4pm, Sun 11am–5pm; Sept–April Wed–Sat 10am–4pm, Sun 11am–5pm; €5), where the man regarded as Finland's national poet lived from 1852 while a teacher at the town school. Despite writing in Swedish, Runeberg greatly aided the nation's sense of self-esteem, especially with *Tales of Vänrikki Ståhl*, which told of the people's struggles with Russia in the 1808–09 conflict. The first poem in his collection *Our Land* later provided the lyrics for the national anthem. Across the road, the **Walter Runeberg Gallery** (same hours Runeberg House; ticket valid for both) displays a collection of works by Runeberg's third son, one of Finland's more celebrated sculptors. Among many acclaimed pieces, he's responsible for the statue of his father that stands in the centre of Helsinki's Esplanadi.

The old town (follow the signs for "Vanha Porvoo") is built around the hill on the other side of Mannerheimkatu. Near the top, its outline partially obscured by vegetation, is the fifteenth-century **Tuomiokirkko** (May–Sept Mon–Fri 10am–6pm, Sat 10am–2pm, Sun 2–5pm; Oct–April Tues–Sat 10am–2pm, Sun 2–4pm). It was here in 1809 that Alexander I proclaimed Finland a Russian Grand Duchy, himself Grand Duke, and convened the first Finnish Diet. This, and other aspects of the town's past, can be explored in the **Porvoo Museum** (May–Aug Mon–Sat 10am–4pm, Sun 11am–4pm; Sept–April Wed–Sun noon–4pm; €5) at the foot of

△ Porvoo riverside

the hill in the old town's main square. There are no singularly outstanding exhibits here, just a diverting selection of furnishings, musical instruments and general oddities, largely dating from the years of Russian rule.

Practicalities

Buses run all day from Helsinki to Porvoo from the long-distance bus station; a one-way trip costs around €8–12, depending on type of bus and time of departure. Idling around the town is especially pleasant late in the day as the evening stillness descends; the last bus back to the city conveniently departs around midnight. There are also a couple of **boats** from Helsinki in summer: the *J.L. Runeberg* (May, June & Aug Wed, Sat & Sun; July daily; €3 return) departs at 10am, arrives at 1.20pm, and returns to Helsinki at 4pm; and the quicker *M.S. King* (late June to mid-Aug daily 10.20am; €22 single), which arrives at 1pm and leaves Porvoo at 3pm. Tickets for both boats can be bought from their respective ticket offices in the *kauppatori* in Helsinki.

If you've exhausted Helsinki, **spending a night** in Porvoo leaves you well placed to continue into Finland's southeastern corner. If possible, try to arrange accommodation while in Helsinki, particularly if you're after hotel bargains – rates in Porvoo can be rather steep. There is, however, a **youth hostel**, open all year, at Linnankoskenkatu 1 (℡019/523 0012, ⓦwww.porvoohostel.cjb.net; dorms €15); while *Onni*, Kirkkotori 3, is a central, family-run guesthouse with designer rooms (℡050/525 6446, ⓦwww.hotelonni.fi; ⑥). There's a summer **campsite** (℡019/581 967; June–Aug) 2km from the town centre. For **eating**, *Sevilla*, Mannerheiminkatu 9, has good Spanish food, and there's decent café fare at the charming *Helmi*, Välikatu 7. Across the road at Välikatu 8, *Timbali* is famous for being one of the only places to get snails in Finland; wash them down with a drink at the friendly *Glory Days*, on Raukanhatu by the market square.

The Southeast

As it's some way from the major centres, foreign tourists tend to neglect the extreme **southeastern corner** of Finland; Finns, however, rate it highly, flocking here to make boat trips around the islands and to explore the many small communities, which combine a genuine rustic flavour with sufficient places of minor interest to keep boredom at bay. For Finns, the region also stirs memories: its position on the Soviet border means it saw many battles during the Winter and Continuation wars, and throughout medieval times it was variously under the control of Sweden and Russia. It's an intriguing area, worth two or three days of travel – most of it will be by bus, since rail lines are almost nonexistent.

East toward Kotka

If Porvoo seems too tourist-infested, make the 40km journey east to **LOVIISA**, an eighteenth-century fishing village pleasantly free from Helsinki day-trippers. The village, whose 7500-strong population divides into equal numbers of Finnish- and Swedish-speakers, is overlooked by the two old **fortresses** of Rosen and Ungern, both worth exploring. The **tourist office** (Mon–Fri 8.30am–4pm; ℡019/555 234, ⓦwww.loviisa.fi), at Tullisilta 5, can supply details of how to get to them; off the square, a row of prettily preserved houses points the way to the **Municipal Museum** (June–Aug Tues–Sun 11am–4pm; Sept–May Sun noon–4pm; €2), containing, besides the usual local hotchpotch of bits and pieces, a fine stock of romantic postcards. Later on, if you have the cash, spend it on a slap-up meal at *Degerby Gille*, Sepänkuja 4 (℡019/50 561, ⓦwww.degerby.com; ④/⑤), a restaurant set in a seventeenth-century house that's one of the town's most important historical sights; the menu has amazingly tasty American-style dishes like Cajun pork fillet and barbeque salmon for around €15. If you don't eat here, poke your head around the door anyway to marvel at the wonderfully maintained interior; the hotel rooms, though well-apportioned, are in an uninspiring annexe round the corner.

In the bay off Loviisa, some 13km distant, there's a less welcome modern sight – the oldest of the country's **nuclear power plants**. Finland's Cold War balancing act between East and West led to the country buying its nuclear hardware from both power blocs; this one spent the last few decades producing plutonium for (allegedly) Soviet nuclear weapons, and its run-off nuclear waste was exported to Russia for disposal – though this practice has now been made illegal. The other, Western-backed, plants are housed at Olkiluoti (near Rauma), but at the centre of the power debate these days is the construction of a fifth nuclear reactor – to be the world's most powerful – approved in 2002 by parliament to help Finland meet its greenhouse gas emission targets. The Finnish public is divided over the merits of nuclear power in general: the country takes thirty percent of its energy from nuclear sources, but the growing anti-nuclear movement is calling for a switch to hydroelectric power. Whatever the outcome of the debate, mindful of the design flaws in Soviet-built reactors, the view from Louviisa is an unnerving one.

If you have the time, a couple of smaller settlements between Loviisa and Kotka can comfortably consume half a day. In 1809 the Swedish–Russian border was drawn up in this area, splitting the region of Pyhtää in two. Some 20km from Loviisa is **RUOTSINPYHTÄÄ** (**Strömfors** in Swedish), whose local **tourist office** (June–Aug daily 8am–4pm; Sept–May Mon–Fri 8am–4pm; ☎019/618 474, ⦿www .ruotsinpyhtaa.fi) is diplomatically positioned within a café on the bridge over the inlet that once divided the two feuding empires; in the winter, the office moves to the Krouvimäki hostel (see below). Historical quirks aside, the main attraction here is the seventeenth-century **ironworks**, now turned into craft studios, with demonstrations of carpet-weaving, jewellery-making and painting – all quite enjoyable to stroll around on a sunny day. You might also want to visit the oddly octagonal-shaped **wooden church** (mid-June to mid-Aug daily 11am–6pm; Oct–May, book with tourist office) to admire Helene Schjerfbeck's beautiful altarpiece. It was here, incidentally, that a Finnish TV company filmed a very popular soap opera, *Vihreän Kullanmaa* ("The Land of the Green Gold"), making good use of the contrast between the spacious mill-owners' houses and the cramped workers' cottages. There is also a simple, inexpensive **hostel** here, the *Krouvimäki Hostel* (book with tourist office), with rooms for €26 in summer, slightly cheaper in winter.

The village of **PYHTÄÄ** is a twenty-minute bus ride further east. There's a **stone church** here (June to mid-Aug daily 10am–6pm; mid-Aug to May Sun 10–noon); dated at around 1300, it's one of the oldest in the country. The interior frescoes are primitive and strangely moving, and were discovered only recently when the Reformation-era whitewash was removed. From the quay on the other side of the village's sole street there's a ferry service to the nearby islands, including Kaunissaari ("Beautiful Island"), where you can connect with an evening motorboat straight on to Kotka (see opposite).

The land route to Kotka takes you through **SILTAKYLÄ**, a small town significant only for the hills around it and its **tourist information** counter (Mon–Fri 8am–3.45pm; ☎05/758 3202, ⦿www.pyhtaa.fi) at the town hall, beside the main road, which has information on walks in the district. The hills afford great views over a dramatic legacy of the Ice Age: spooky Tolkienesque forests and many miles of a red-granite stone known as *rapakivi* that's unique to southeast Finland, covered by a white moss. A number of waymarked hiking trails lead through the landscape, which is strewn with giant boulders – some are as big as four-storey buildings and support their own little ecosystems of plant and tree life. After a day's trek, you can reward yourself with food and drink – or even a swim – at the reasonably-priced *Mantyniemen Lomakeskus* (☎05/353 3084, ⦿www.mantyniemenlomakeskus.com; ❸), 15km east on Munapirtti island, with simple balconied doubles and a sauna.

Kotka to the Russian border

After the scattering of little communities east of Porvoo, **KOTKA**, a few kilometres on from Siltakylä, seems immense. Built on an island in the Gulf of Finland, Kotka's past reflects its proximity to the sea. Numerous battles have been fought off its shores, among them the Sweden–Russia confrontation of 1790, the largest battle ever seen in Nordic waters: almost 10,000 people lost their lives. Sixty-odd years later during the Crimean War, the British fleet reduced Kotka virtually to rubble. In modern times, though, the sea has been the basis of the town's prosperity: sitting at the end of the Kymi River and boasting a deep-water harbour, the town makes a perfect cargo transit point – causing most locals to live in fear of a major accident occurring in the industrial section, or in the freight yards. Only two roads link Kotka to the mainland and a speedy evacuation of its inhabitants would be almost impossible.

The town itself doesn't have a huge amount to offer to visitors, though there a few ways while away an afternoon. The new **Maretarium**, located at the passenger harbour at Sapokankatu 2 (daily mid-May to mid-Aug 10am–8pm, mid-Aug to mid-May 10am–5pm; closed second half of Jan; €9.50; @ www.maretarium.fi) has an impressive display of fish species native to Finland. If the life aquatic isn't your thing, spend some time touring the eighteenth-century Orthodox **St Nicolai kirkko** (June–Aug Tues–Fri noon–3pm, Sat & Sun noon–6pm), a sizeable structure which has been kept in pristine condition after surviving the British bombardment, and houses a number of well-preserved icons, including the exquisite St Nicholas on Kotka Island, gilded and brooding in the afternoon *ruska* light. Another option is a visit to the **Langinkoski Imperial Fishing Lodge** (May–Aug daily 10am–7pm; Sept & Oct Sat & Sun 10am–7pm; €4), off the main island, about 5km north of the town centre (bus #12). It was here that Tsar Alexander III would relax in transit between Helsinki and St Petersburg; the wooden building, a gift to him from the Finnish government, is most striking for its simplicity and the attractive setting in the

Trips to Russia

Overland from Helsinki

Two trains – one Finnish and one Russian – leave Helsinki every morning (Finnish train; 7.42am) and afternoon (Russian train; 3.42pm) for the six-hour trip to St Petersburg; there's also an overnight 14hr Russian train to Moscow, which stops briefly in St Petersburg and which departs Helsinki at 5.42pm. All border formalities are carried out on the train, but you must have a Russian visa before you leave – the tourist office has a list of travel agencies that can arrange these, though be warned that they take a week to process. A one-way second-class ticket to St Petersburg on both the Finnish and Russian trains costs €50.80 including seat reservation; a sleeping compartment to Moscow costs €85.

Day cruises

If sailing to St Petersburg for a short visit sounds more attractive, you could book a place on a Silja Line cruise, though these depart only once or twice monthly. There are both one- and two-day cruises, all leaving Helsinki's Olympia Terminal, off Laivasillankatu, at 6pm, arriving in St Petersburg at 8.30am the following morning and returning at 7pm the next day, arriving Helsinki 10am; all-inclusive packages with cabin start at €190. If you're a Scandinavian or EU citizen, you can get a Russian group visa through Silja for €20, but you must apply fourteen days in advance and must stay with the tour group at all times – this means paying a bit extra for some mandatory excursions. Travellers holding other passports need to arrange their own visas, though Silja can provide the requisite invitation letter for €15. Irregular overnight cruises also leave from Lappeenranta for the Russian city of Vyborg, allowing several hours ashore before returning to Finland (see p.748).

woods near the fast-flowing Kymi River. Opportunities for salmon and sea trout fly fishing abound here, and the lodge can organize permits and equipment rental.

Practicalities

Rail and road connections bring you right into the compact centre, where the **tourist office** at Kirkkokatu 3 (June to mid-Aug daily 9am–7pm; rest of the year Mon–Fri 9am–5pm; ☎05/234 4424, ⓦwww.kotka.fi) will fill you in on local bus details – essential for continuing around the southeast.

Grumbling stomachs can be quietened in *Canttiini*, Kaivokatu 15, an excellent Tex Mex **restaurant** that also serves up Finnish dishes, pastas and steaks. Alternatively, try *Fenix*, Kapteeninkatu 14, which has a very similar menu and equally reasonable prices. Although Kotka is no longer popular with eastern European sailors due to shorter onshore times, there is still a lively bar scene – the best pub in town is *Jack Up* at Kirkkokatu 10, although the Irish bar *Karoliina*, at Puutarhakatu 1, puts up strong competition. A good-value **hotel** is the pleasant *Merikotka*, Satamakatu 9 (☎05/215 222, ⓦwww.hotellimerikotka.fi; ❹), offering bright, well-decorated rooms; or there's the more upmarket *Seurahuone*, Keskuskatu 21 (☎05/35 035, ⓦwww.sokoshotels.fi; ❹/❺). The nearest guesthouse, *Kärkisaari*, is 6km north of Kotka in Mussalo (bus #13 and #27), overlooking a spectacular bay (☎05/260 4804, ⓦwww.villakarkisaari .com; mid-May to mid-Sept; ❹), where there's also a beachside holiday village (☎05/260 5055, ⓦwww.santalahti.fi) with **camping** spaces and cabins (❸).

Hamina and east to the Russian border

Twenty-six kilometres east of Kotka is **HAMINA**, founded in 1653 and sporting a magnificently bizarre town plan, the main streets branching out of and forming concentric circles around the central plaza. It was built this way to allow the incumbent Swedish forces to withstand attack – the town being the site of many Swedish–Russian battles. You can still amble around the base of the original defending wall, preserved and restored in various parts; follow the signs to the "bastoni" from the centre. Besides this, however, there's not an awful lot to amuse, although you can pick up suggestions and local information from the **tourist office** at Raatihuonetori 16 (Mon–Fri 9am–4pm; ☎05/749 2641, ⓦwww.hamina .fi), which can assist with accommodation.

The tourist office can also give you the latest schedule of the bus that runs to the densely-wooded environs of **VIROLAHTI** (ⓦwww.virolahti.fi), 31km east, and within a few kilometres of the **Salpalinjan Bunkkerit** (daily June–Aug 10am–6pm; €4), or Salpa Line Bunkers – massive hunks of granite stretching from here to Lapland, which acted as fortifications and were intended to protect Finland from Soviet attack during the run-up to the Winter War of 1939. These days Finnish war veterans are eager to show off the bunker's details and lead visitors to the seats (and controls) of ageing anti-tank guns. Buses from Helsinki to Viipuri, the formerly Finnish town now on the Russian side of the border (see p.745), pass through Hamina; again, details are best checked at the tourist office. If you have a burning desire for a sojourn here, you'd do well to stay in Virolahti in the creaky but familial cabins at *Hurpun Tila* (☎05/357 3125, ⓦwww.hurpuntila.com; ❶), where you can rent rowing boats for a comradely paddle out to Russo–Finnish No Man's Land.

The Southwest

The area between Helsinki and Finland's **southwestern** extremity is probably the blandest section of the whole country. By road or rail the view is much the same, endless forests interrupted only by modest-sized patches of water and virtually identical villages and small towns. Once at the southwestern corner, however, things change considerably, with islands and inlets around a jagged shoreline, distinctive Finnish–Swedish coastal communities and a spectacular archipelago stretching halfway to Sweden.

Turku and around

There is very little in Åbo which has entertained me in the survey, or can amuse you by the description. It is a wretched capital of a barbarous province. The houses are almost all of wood; and the archiepiscopal palace, which has not even a single storey, but may be called a sort of barrack, is composed of no better materials, except that it is painted red. I inquired if there was not any object in the university, meriting attention; but they assured me that it would be regarded as a piece of ridicule, to visit it on such an errand, there being nothing within its walls except a very small library, and a few philosophical instruments.

A Tour Round The Baltic, Sir N.W. Wraxall, 1775.

TURKU (or **Åbo** as it's known in Swedish) was the principal town in Finland when the country was a province of Sweden, losing its status in 1812, along with most of its buildings in a ferocious fire soon after – occurrences that clearly improved the place, if the above quotation is to be believed. These days Turku is small and highly sociable – and thanks to the boom years under Swedish rule and the students from its two universities, it's bristling with history and culture, with a sparkling nightlife to boot.

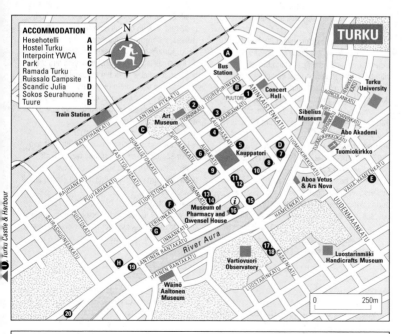

ACCOMMODATION	
Hesehotelli	A
Hostel Turku	H
Interpoint YWCA	E
Park	C
Ramada Turku	G
Ruissalo Campsite	I
Scandic Julia	D
Sokos Seurahuone	F
Tuure	B

CAFÉS, RESTAURANTS, BARS & CLUBS

Baan Thai	3	Cow	11	Herman	20	Uusi Apteekki	17
Blanko	15	Dynamo	8	Koulu	13	Vaakahuone	19
Börs Night Club	5	El Gringo	10	Päiväkoti	18	Vessa	1
Bossa	4	Enkeliravintola	2	Pizzeria Dennis	14	Via	7
Café Qwensel	16	Foija	9	Prima	6	Viikinkiravintola Harald	12

Arrival and information

The River Aura splits the city, its tree-lined banks forming a natural promenade as well as a useful landmark. The cathedral and castle stand at opposite ends of the river, while the main museums are found along its edge. There are gleaming department stores, banks and offices on the northern side of the river in Turku's central grid, where you'll also find the **tourist office** at Aurakatu 4 (Mon–Fri 8.30am–6pm, Sat & Sun 9am–4pm; ☏02/262 7444, ⊛ www.turkutouring.fi), which has plenty of maps and leaflet, and also rents bicycles (€10 per day) and scooters (€40 per day). Outside banking hours you can **change money** at Forex, Eerikinkatu 12 (Mon–Fri 8am–7pm, Sat 8am–5pm). Both the **train station** and **bus station** are within easy walking distance of the river, just north of the centre.

Accommodation

Finding **accommodation** in Turku is rarely a problem – even in the height of summer. In addition to two solid hostel choices and an inexpensive bed and breakfast, the city has a good array of comfortable hotels, though they tend towards the pricier side of things.

Hesehotelli Läntinen Pitkäkatu 1 ☏045/634 3443, ⊛www.hesburger.fi/hesehotelli. Close to the bus station, this new hotel is run by the Heseburger fast-food chain and features modern rooms with satellite TV and free Internet access. Annoyingly, "reception" is the tills at the burger joint downstairs, but the rates are better than most places in town. ❸

Hostel Turku Linnankatu 39 ☏02/262 7680, ⊛www.turku.fi/hostelturku. This excellent year-round official youth hostel is situated between the harbour and city centre. In addition to well-sized doubles (❶), it offers dorms (€13.50), plus ample cooking and laundry facilities, and bicycle hire. To get there, take bus #30 from the train station or #1 from the airport and bus station.

Interpoint YWCA Vähä-Hämeenkatu 12a ☏02/231 4011, ☎02/231 2584. Set across the river a few blocks south of the cathedral, this bare-bones hostel is the destination of choice for those on a tight budget, offering the cheapest dorm beds in town (€8.50) plus a few basic doubles (❶). Open mid-July to mid-August.

Park Rauhankatu 1 ☏02/273 2555, ⊛www.parkhotelturku.fi. A five-minute walk from the train station, this hotel was built in 1902 and oozes turn-of-the-century Art Nouveau charm. It's the best choice in Turku though the stylish rooms don't come cheap. ❻/❺

Ramada Turku Eerikinkatu 28 ☏02/338 211, ⊛www.restel.fi. Chain hotel which does its best to shake off the *Ramada* feel, but doesn't quite succeed. Comfortable rooms and an excellent buffet breakfast, though overall nothing special. ❹/❺

Ruissalo Camping Ruissalo Island ☏02/262 5100. Turku's most accessible campsite is located on the small island of Ruissalo overlooking the harbour, reachable from the city centre by bus #8 (15min). The campsite offers basic rooms (❶), and the island's sandy beaches, lush botanical garden and superb archipelago panoramas are just paces away. Open June–Aug.

Scandic Julia Eerikinkatu 4 ☏02/336 000, ⊛www.scandic-hotels.com. Smart, elegant and full of Scandinavian design features such as tasteful glassware and lighting. Summer and weekend bargains make this a good choice out of season. ❹/❻

Tuure Tuureporinkatu 17C ☏02/233 0230, ⊛www.tuure.fi. Near to the bus and train stations, this bed and breakfast sports teeny double rooms with a bit more character than those in the local hostels. ❷

The City

Arriving in Turku by train, you'll quickly make the pleasing discovery that the major places of interest unintentionally arrange themselves into a very logical pattern. By beginning at the Art Museum, a few strides from the station, and from there moving south through the city centre and heading westwards along the river's edge, you'll be able to take in everything worth seeing in a day – although allowing two days might be more sensible if you want to have energy left for the Turku nightlife. During the 1970s and 1980s parts of Turku were subjected to some thoughtless redevelopment, resulting in a number of really hideous buildings, and a new national byword, the "Turku Disease". However, streets of intricately carved wooden houses still survive around the Port Arthur area, a lovely part of the city for simply strolling around.

The Art Museum

Though it's not much of a taster for the actual city, the newly renovated **Turku Art Museum** (Tues–Fri 11am–7pm, Fri–Sun 10am–5pm; €6, or €7 for special exhibitions; ⊛ www.turuntaidemuseo.fi), housed in a purpose-built Art Nouveau granite structure close to the train station on Torninkatu, is one of the better collections of Finnish art, with works by all the great names of the country's Golden Age – Gallen-Kallela, Edelfelt, Pekka Halonen, Simberg and others – plus a commendable stock of moderns. Not least among these are the wood sculptures of Kain Tapper and Mauno Hartman, which stirred up heated debate on the merits of carefully shaped bits of wood being presented as art when they were first shown during the 1970s.

△ Flower market, Turku

4

The Cathedral and around

To get to grips with Turku itself, and its pivotal place in Finnish history, cut through the centre to the river, and the tree-framed space that, before the great fire of 1879, was the bustling heart of the community, and which is still overlooked by the **Tuomiokirkko** (daily: mid-April to mid-Sept 9am–8pm; rest of the year until 7pm). The cathedral, erected in the thirteenth century on the "Knoll of Sheep", a pre-Christian place of worship, was at the centre of the Christianization process inflicted by the crusading Swedes on the pagan Finns, and grew larger over the centuries as the new religion became stronger and Swedish involvement in Finland escalated. The building, still the heart and soul of the Finnish Church, has been repeatedly ravaged by fire, although the thickness of the walls enabled many of its medieval features to survive. Of these, it's the tombs that catch the eye: Torsten Stålhandske, commander of the Finnish cavalry during the seventeenth-century Thirty Years' War, in which Sweden sought to protect its domination of the Baltic and the Finns confirmed their reputation as wild and fearless fighters, lies in a deliriously ornate coffin (to the right as you enter) opposite Samuel Cockburn and Patrick Ogilvie, a couple of Scots who fought alongside him. Entombed on the left-hand side is Catharine Månsdotter, commoner wife of the Swedish king Erik XIV, with whom, in the mid-sixteenth century, she was imprisoned in Turku Castle. As the only queen Finland every produced, Catharine is as popular in death as she reputedly was in life, judging by the numbers who file past her simple black-marble sarcophagus. The window behind it carries her stained-glass image – and if you crane your neck to the left, you can see a wall plaque bearing the only known true likeness of her. You can also visit the **cathedral museum** upstairs (same times as cathedral; €2), which gives a stronger insight into the cathedral's past. There's an assortment of ancient jugs, goblets, plates and spoons, though more absorbing are the collections of church textiles.

Immediately outside the cathedral is a statue to **Per Brahe**, governor-general of Finland from 1637 and the first Swedish officer to devote much attention to the welfare of the Finns, encouraging a literacy programme and founding the country's first university. The site of this is within the nearby yellow Empire-style buildings, although the actual seat of learning was moved to Helsinki during the era of Russian rule. Next to these are the oldest portions of the **Åbo Akademi** – one of only two Swedish-language universities in Finland – while the modern, Finnish-language **Turku University** is at the other end of Henrikinkatu: these days both are more notable as places for eating, at their student *mensas* (see p.738), rather than sightseeing.

Turku's newest and most splendid museum is the combined **Aboa Vetus** and **Ars Nova** (April to mid-Sept daily 11am–7pm; rest of the year closed Mon; €8 for either museum, €9.50 combined; @www.aboavetusarsnova.fi) on the bank of the Aurajoki River just a few steps from the university. With a name that translates in Latin as "Old Turku, New Art", the place was intended to be simply a modern art gallery, but when the building's foundations were dug a warren of medieval lanes and cellars came to light, an unmissable opportunity to present the history and archeology of the city, and glass flooring allows a near-perfect view of the remains. The New Art part comprises a striking collection of 350 works, alongside frequent temporary exhibitions. There's a great café, too: prepare yourself here by browsing through the museum's English-language brochure, since the guided tours are in Finnish only.

Back past the cathedral and across Piispankatu is the sleek low form of the **Sibelius Museum** (Tues–Sun 11am–4pm, Wed also 6–8pm; €3; @www.sibelius museum.abo.fi). Although Sibelius had no direct connection with Turku, this museum is a fitting tribute to him and his contribution to the emergence of an independent Finland. Chances are that the recorded strains of *Finlandia* will greet you as you enter: when not the venue for live concerts (which usually take place during the winter), the small but acoustically perfect concert area pumps out recorded requests from the great man's oeuvre; take your place beside dewy-eyed Finns for a lunch hour of Scandinavia's finest composer. Elsewhere, the Sibelius collection gathers family photo albums and original manuscripts along with the great man's hat, walking stick and even a final half-smoked cigar. Other exhibits cover the musical history of the country, from intricate musical boxes and the frail wooden *kantele* – the instrument strummed by peasants in the *Kalevala* – to the weighty keyboard instruments downstairs.

The Luostarinmäki, Aaltonen and pharmacy museums

On the other side of the cathedral from the Sibelius museum, you'll see the small Vartiovuori hill, topped by the wooden dome of the **Observatory**, designed – rather poorly – by Carl Engel, who had arrived in Turku seeking work in the days before his great plan for Helsinki made him famous. Originally the building was intended to serve the first Turku University as an observatory, but disputes between Engel and his assistants and a misunderstanding of scientific requirements rendered the place useless for its intended purpose. To make things worse, the university moved to Helsinki, and the building was then turned into a navigational school. From the observatory, head directly down the side of the hill to the far more engrossing **Luostarinmäki Handicrafts Museum** on Luostarinkatu (mid-April to mid-Sept daily 10am–6pm; mid-Sept to mid–April Tues–Sun 10am–3pm; €3.40), one of the best – and certainly the most authentic – open-air museums in Finland. Following a severe fire in 1775, rigorous restrictions were imposed on the city's new buildings, but due to a legal technicality they didn't apply in this district. The wooden houses here were built by local working people in traditional style and evolved naturally into a museum as descendants of the original owners died and bequeathed their inherited homes to the municipality. Unpaved streets run between tiny wooden houses, which once had goats tethered to their chimneys to keep the turfed roofs cropped. The chief inhabitants now are the museum volunteers who dress up in period attire and demonstrate the old handicrafts.

A short walk from the handicrafts museum, on the southern bank of the river, is another worthwhile indoor collection: the **Wäinö Aaltonen Museum** (daily 11am–7pm, closed Mon in winter; entry fee varies according to exhibition; ⓦwww.wam.fi). Unquestionably the best-known modern Finnish sculptor, Wäinö Aaltonen was born in 1894, grew up close to Turku and studied for a time at the local art school. His first public show, in 1916, marked a turning point in the development of Finnish sculpture, introducing a freer, more individual style to a genre struggling to break from the restraints of the Neoclassical tradition and French realism. Aaltonen went on to dominate his field throughout the 1920s and 1930s and his influence is still felt today; the man's work turns up in every major town throughout the country, and even the parliament building in Helsinki was designed with special niches to hold some of his pieces. Much of his output celebrates the individuals who contributed to the growth of the Finnish republic, typically remembering them with enormous heads, or as immense statues that resemble massive social-realist chunks. But Aaltonen, who died in 1966, really was an original, imaginative and sensitive sculptor, as the exhibits here demonstrate. There's also a roomful of his paintings, some of which show perhaps why he concentrated on sculpture.

Across the river from the Aaltonen museum, there's a sign in the grass which spells out TURKU:ÅBO; immediately behind this is a wooden staircase running up to the front door of the **Museum of Pharmacy and Qwensel House** (mid-April to mid-Sept daily 10am–6pm; mid-Sept to mid-April Tues–Sun 10am–3pm; €3.40). Qwensel was a court judge who moved to the house in 1694, and it later became the home of Professor Josef Gustaf Pipping – the "father of Finnish medicine" – in 1785. Period furnishings remain, proving just how wealthy and stylish the life of the eighteenth-century bourgeoisie actually was. Many chemists' implements from around the country are on show, among them some memorable devices for drawing blood.

Turku Castle

The city's museums, and its cathedral and universities, are all symbols of Turku's elevated position in Finnish life, though by far the major marker to its many years of importance stands at the western end of Linnankatu. Follow the signs for "Turun Linna", or take bus #1 from the harbour, and you'll eventually see, oddly set among the present-day ferry terminals, the relatively featureless, piebald exterior of **Turku Castle** (mid-April to mid-Sept daily 10am–6pm; mid-Sept to mid-April Tues–Sun 10am–3pm; €6.50; ⓦwww.nba.fi/en/turku_castle). Fight any dismay, though, since the compact cobbled courtyards, maze-like corridors and darkened staircases of the interior provide a good place to wander – and to dwell on the fact that this was the seat of the government of the country for centuries, as well as that much of Finland's (and a significant portion of Sweden's) medieval history took shape within these walls. Unless you're an expert on the period, you'll get a migraine trying to figure out the importance of everything that's here, and it's a sensible idea to buy one of the guide leaflets on sale at the entrance – you can safely give the guided tour a miss.

The castle probably went up sometime around 1280, when the first bishop arrived from Sweden; gradual expansion through the following years accounts for the patchwork effect of its architecture – and the bewildering array of finds, rooms and displays. The majority of the fortification took place during the turbulent sixteenth century, instigated by Swedish ruler Gustavus Vasa for the protection of his son, whom he made Duke Johan, the first Duke of Finland. Johan pursued a lavish court life but exceeded his powers in attacking Livonia and was sentenced to death by the Stockholm Diet. Swedish efforts to seize Johan were successful only after a three-week siege, and he was removed to Stockholm. The subsequent decision by the unbalanced Erik XIV to release Johan resulted not only in Johan becoming king himself, but also in poor Erik being imprisoned here – albeit with a full quota of servants and the best food and wine. The bare cell he occupied for a few weeks contrasts strongly with the splendour from Johan's time, offering a cool reminder of shifting fortunes. There's a gloomy nineteenth-century painting here, by Erik Johan Löfgren, of Erik with his head on the lap of his queen (Catharine Månsdotter), while the lady's eyes look askance to heaven.

Momminworld

Some 16km northwest of Turku, **Naantali** is famous as the home of **Moominworld** (mid-June to mid-Aug daily 10am–6pm; adults and children from €16; ⓦwww.muumimaailma.fi), a theme park set on an island and based on Tove Jansson's famous creations. It's a must-see if you have kids in tow, and many tour operators run buses to the park from Turku. Naantali itself is pleasant enough, with its wooden buildings and slight passageways, but hardly worth hanging around for more than a few hours, and with regular buses there's no need to stay, though there's a tourist office at Kaivotori 2 should you need further information (early June to mid-Aug Mon–Fri 9am–6pm, Sat & Sun 10am–3pm; mid-Aug to early June 9am–4.30pm; ☎02/435 9800, ⓦwww.naantalinmatkailu.fi). For a quick, tasty bite, *Merisali*, Nunnakatu 1, has a fresh fish, affordable salads and a good *smorgasbord* for around €10.

Eating, drinking and nightlife

You'd need to be very fussy not to find somewhere to **eat** in Turku that's to your liking. Walking around checking the lunchtime offers can turn up many bargains, plus there's the usual selection of economical pizzerias and a few inexpensive ethnic eateries. Floating restaurants are popular among tourists, if not with too many locals, and the boats change each summer, though the names *Papa Joe*, *Svarte Rudolf* and *Samppalinna* reappear year after year: all have decent enough restaurants, and often put on live music.

Cafés and restaurants

Baan Thai Kauppiaskatu 15. Right in the heart of town, and offering an excellent range of tasty Thai dishes from €6.80, cheaper during lunch. No-frills interior but always popular.

Bossa Kauppiaskatu 12 ⊛ www.restaurantebossa .fi. Animated Brazilian place with weekly live music. Most of the rich meat and fish main dishes – give the *picanha* beef a try – are under €20.

Café Qwensel Läntinen Rantakatu 13. Fabulous cakes in the atmospheric eighteenth-century surroundings of a courtyard behind the Museum of Pharmacy.

Enkeliravintola Kauppiaskatu 16 ⊛ www .enkeliravintola.fi. A stylishly old-fashioned café serving up wonderful cakes and coffee, although a little out of the centre up a steep hill.

Foija Aurakatu 10 ⊛ www.foija.fi. Busy cellar restaurant with great service opposite the *kauppatori*, with good-value and delicious pizzas from €8.20. They've been around for over 150 years and are still popular with the city's younger set.

Gadolinia Henrikenkatu. This student *mensa* is part of Åbo Akademi – look in the courtyard near the junction of Piispankatu and Porthaninkatu. Easily the cheapest option in town, but closed during the summer.

Herman Läntinen Rantakatu 37 ☎ 02/230 3333, ⊛ www.ravintolaherman.com. Set in a bright and airy storehouse dating from 1849, and right on the riverside in an area that was renovated when Turku hosted the Tall Ships Race in 1996 – ask to reserve the table for two overlooking the river. Fantastic food that comes at a price, with main courses at €16.50 and up. Lunch is tremendous value at €7.

Pizzeria Dennis Linnankatu 17. Although this place looks a bit tatty on the outside, don't be put off. It's renowned for its range of decent, well-priced pizzas, priced from €8.

Vessa Puutori ⊛ www.puutorinvessa.fi. Bizarre restaurant housed in a former public toilet. The excellent Finnish home cooking is reasonably priced – reckon on €10–20 per main dish – and there are regular showings of local artists.

Via Linnankatu 3 ⊛ www.viaravintola.com. The menu at this popular restaurant on the banks of the Aura features both Italian and pan-Asian mains from €13 including pastas, pizzas, curries, noodle dishes and salads, as well as a number of tapas appetizers.

Viikinkiravintola Harald Aurakatu 3 ⊛ www.ravintolaharald.com. Capitalizing fully on the Viking mythology, with chiselled wooden furnishings and reindeer busts adorning the walls. The €7.40 buffet lunch is a good bargain, but for a hearty meal, try the West Gothic's Red Deer Sword, huge cuts of venison marinated in garlic sauce and skewered on a sword (€21.70); the tar ice cream for dessert is sweet and smoky.

Bars and entertainment

Thanks to a thriving cultural scene, a lively student population and a good number of tourists and visitors, nights out in Turku have something for everyone. A **drink** at one of the many boats moored along Itäinen Rantakatu is a popular summer tradition, and if you want to fill your nights with something more energetic than boozing, there are several **discos**. During August, the **Turku Music Festival** (☎02/251 1162, ⊛www.turkumusicfestival.fi) packs thousands into a number of venues for performances in a wide range of musical genres. If your tastes are for classical music, try and get a ticket for a performance one of the oldest symphony orchestras in Europe, the **Turku Philharmonic**, founded in 1790 and currently based in the Concert Hall at Aninkaistenkatu 9. The box office telephone line (☎02/262 0800) opens in mid-August, one month before concerts begin. Alternatively, check with the tourist office for a rundown of the week's films: Turku has a number of **cinemas**, the largest of which, Kinopalatsi, Kauppiaskatu 11, has nine screens. Diana, Humalistonkatu 3 and Thalia, Aurakatu 10, both screen smaller European Art-House productions.

Bars and clubs

Blanko Aurakatu 1. Voted trendiest bar in Scandinavia for 2004, the down-to-earth bartenders at this chilled-out lounge will still serve you even if you don't look like Paris Hilton. Funky interior with pillowed couches in the back, DJs spinning the newest electronica at weekends and tasty, well-priced fusion food.

Börs Night Club *Hotel Hamburger Börs*, Kauppiaskatu 6. One of Turku's better-known nightclubs, these days frequented by a professional, tucked-in-shirt crowd.

Cow Aurakatu 3 ⊛ www.thecow.fi. Funky, bovine-themed bar where thirty-somethings come to sink a few inexpensive cocktails.

Dynamo Linnankatu 7 ⊛ www.dynamoklubi.com.

Moving on from Turku

Continuing from Turku **north along the coast**, there are direct bus services to the nearest main towns, Rauma and Pori. It's also possible to reach Pori by train, although this takes virtually a whole day and involves going via Tampere and changing at least once, possibly three times. From **Turku harbour** ferries sail through the vast archipelago to the Åland Islands, and on to Sweden. The harbour is 3km from the city centre and bus #1 covers the route frequently.

A raw kind of place that doesn't really get going until after midnight, and draws an irreverent, alternative crowd who come for a drink and a dance to soul and disco tunes.

El Gringo Kauppiaskatu 6. Though the decor is Spanish in theme, the music at this dive of a bar runs the gamut from reggae to gangsta rap and R&B. Draught pints of Lapin Kulta for €2.50.

Koulu Eerikinkatu 18 ⊛www.panimoravintola koulu.fi. Set in a grand old late-1880s school building, this is the largest restaurant brewery in Finland, with a large selection of beers and wines. Bar food favourites like a bratwurst and sauerkraut platter go for around €10.

Päiväkoti Kaskenkatu 3 ⊛www.paivakoti.biz. Home of the underground in Turku, this gritty hard-rock bar is set in a dingy building plastered with graffiti near the river. Regularly features bands playing everything from indie-pop to 1970s soul, and it's the venue of choice for Turku's grunge

bands. Happy hour gets you €3 pints until 11pm daily and all day Sun and Tues. Closed Mon.

Prima Aurankatu 14 ⊛www.prima.fi. A wine bar on the ground floor, and the most popular nightclub in town upstairs , frequented by young jetsetter types.

Uusi Apteekki Kaskenkatu 1 ⊛www.uusiapteekki .fi. Allegedly predating Damien Hirst's famous *Pharmacy* London bar-restaurant, this smoky, laid-back drinking hole is housed in an old chemist's shop, with drug and pill bottles scattered about the place. Popular with bikers, cigar aficionados and multiply-pierced locals.

🏃 **Vaakahuone** Linnankatu 38 ⊛www .ukkopekka.fi/vaakahuone. A very lively place, buzzing with Finns of all ages. An established house band plays Dixieland and bebop jazz every night during the summer, and there are reasonably priced salads, soups and pizzas on offer, too.

Rauma

RAUMA, 90km north of Turku, is one of the few places in Finland where you can't help but stop at every street corner to admire the elegance and understated charm of a town whose appearance has barely changed since the Middle Ages. Although Finns know Rauma as the most complete and best preserved wooden town in Scandinavia, with its historic importance reflected by its designation as a UNESCO World Heritage Site, relatively few foreigners have yet realized that a couple of days spent exploring the cobbled eighteenth- and nineteenth-century streets are likely to be some of the most enjoyable spent in Finland. True, Rauma is becoming increasingly touristy, but the town still retains plenty of quiet lanes and alleyways where you can explore undisturbed.

Until the early 1900s, **Old Rauma** was entirely contained within a narrow triangle of land (bordered on two sides by the small Raumanjoki River), which had been established as a toll-free zone three hundred years before. Although modern Rauma gracelessly encircles this medieval core completely today, it's this undisturbed medieval centre that makes the town so appealing – the layout of the narrow winding streets, alleys and curiously shaped gardens and allotments has barely changed since the last great fire in 1682, a remarkable achievement for a wooden town. Rauma's architectural delights are best explored by simply strolling along the two main streets, **Kauppakatu** and **Kuninkaankatu**, and heading off down whichever lane takes your fancy. Although most houses are now clad in the decorative neo-Renaissance style and painted in a riot of pastel shades, you can still see a few dressed with the vertical boarding of the 1700s, or the wider empire cladding of the 1820s. The town's rich past is expertly documented via the **Rauma Museum**, in the eighteenth-century town hall at Kauppakatu 13 (mid-May to Aug daily 10am–5pm; Sept to mid-May Tues–Fri & Sun 10am–5pm, Sat 11am–2pm; summer €4, winter €2), where you'll find a couple of scale models of the sailing ships that once brought such wealth into the town. Further evidence is on show at **Marela**, Kauppakatu 24 (same times as Rauma Museum; €4), a house preserved in the style of a rich shipowner's residence from the beginning of the twentieth century. Combined entry to Marela and the History Museum costs €4 (€2 Sept to mid-May) with a day pass available from either museum. If you want to plunge even further into local history, the **Old Rauma Renovation Centre** at Vähäkirk-kokatu 8 (June–Aug Mon–Sat 10am–6pm, Sun noon–6pm; free) runs evening classes (unfortunately, all in Finnish) covering activities such as Rauma-style community sing-ing, lessons in how to tie seafarers' knots and instruction in the local dialect – strangely for the west coast, this is a mainly Finnish-speaking community, although with an archaic dialect that many other Finns find hard to understand. The **Rauma Maritime Museum**, Kalliokatu 34 (Tues–Sun noon–4pm; €7), offers extensive displays on local maritime history, but the real draw is the navigation simulator, a fascinating contraption that allows would-be mariners the chance to man their own open-sea voyage. The system offers a choice of over 100 sailing routes, including New York harbour and the English Channel, and the computer-generated visuals are projected onto a huge screen in front of the ship's bridge, allowing you to plot a course, navigate obstacles and bring your ship safely into port.

Practicalities

Unfortunately there are no longer train services to Rauma, and coming from Turku, the easiest solution is to take one of the frequent buses (#372 or #810) which run along the west coast. From the bus station it's a two-minute walk to the **tourist office** at Valtakatu 2 (June–Aug Mon–Fri 8am–6pm, Sat 10am–3pm, Sun 11am–2pm; Sept–May Mon–Fri 8am–4pm; ℡02/8378 7730, ✆www.rauma .fi), where you can pick up leaflets on local history and walking tours. Free Internet access is available at Rauma public library, Ankkurikatu 1 (Mon–Fri 10am–7pm, Sat 10am–2pm). If you want to stay, it's just 1km along Poroholmantie from the old town centre to *Poroholma*, the combined **youth hostel** and **campsite** (℡02/8388 2500, ✆poroholma@kalliohovi.fi; mid-May to Aug), with dorms (June–Aug; ❸), which offers basic double rooms, and allows free use of its sauna. In terms of **hotels,** try the *Cumulus*, Aittakarinkatu 9 (℡02/837 821, ✆www.cumulus.fi; ❹/❻), which boasts two saunas, a pool and summer terrace.

Rauma doesn't throw up a multitude of **eating** options, but filling lunches (around €10) are served at *Villa Tallbo*, in a shipowner's restored *fin-de-siècle* summer villa near the sea at Petäjäksentie 178 (℡02/8220 733); *Wähä Tallbo*, Vanhankirkonkatu 3, is a similar option in the town itself. Best option for dinner is *La Bamba*, at Kappakatu 16 in the Old Town, with an extensive choice of pizzas and pasta dishes from around €7. *Wanhan Rauman Kellari*, Anundilankatu 8, has quality, well-priced Finnish food.

Pori

Due to its yearly jazz **festival** – increasingly rock- and pop-oriented in recent years – **PORI** has become one of the best-known towns in Finland. For one week each July, its streets are full of music and the 150,000 people who come to hear it – for more on the event, see p.729. Throughout the rest of the year Pori reverts to normalcy as a small, quiet industrial town with a worthy regional museum and a handful of architectural and historical oddities. The central section, despite its spa-cious grid-style streets, can be crossed on foot in about fifteen minutes.

In the centre of Pori at Hallituskatu 14, just across the road from the tourist office, stands the recently renovated **Pori Theatre** (Mon–Fri 11am–6pm; free), the tem-porary home of Finnish-language theatre during the period of Russification when Finnish drama was considered too provocative to appear in a larger centre like Turku or Helsinki. Built in 1884, it has a striking Renaissance facade, and the tiny interior – seating just 300 – is heavy with opulent frescoes and sculptured chandeliers. To see inside, ask at the tourist office. A few steps away, at Hallituskatu 11, the **Satakunta Museum** (Tues–Sun 11am–5pm; €4) has three well-stocked floors which trace the life of both Pori and the surrounding Satakunta region through medieval findings, late nineteenth-century photos and shop signs, and typical house interiors, alongside interesting memorabilia from the powerful labour movement of the 1930s.

Pori's strangest sight, however, is in the big **Käppärä cemetery**, a twenty-minute walk along Maantiekatu. In the cemetery's centre is the Gothic-arched **Juselius Mausoleum** (May–Aug daily noon–3pm; Sept–April Sun noon–2pm; free), erected in 1898 by local businessman F.A. Juselius as a memorial to his daughter, Sigrid, who died aged 11. The leading Finnish church architect of the time, Josef Steinbäck, was called on to design the thing, while Gallen-Kallela decorated the interior with some of his best large-scale paintings. The artwork was adversely affected by both fire and the local sea air, but has been restored by Gallen-Kallela's son from the original sketches, enabling the structure to fulfil its purpose as powerfully, and as solemnly, as ever.

Practicalities

It's a short walk from either the **bus station** – into Isolinnankatu and straight on – or the **train station** – follow Rautatienpuistokatu – into the centre of town, where the **tourist office** sits in the Promenadi Centre shopping mall, Yrjönkatu 17 (Mon–Fri 9am–5pm, plus June–Sept Sat 10am–3pm; ☎02/621 1273, ⊛www .pori.fi). There's free Internet access both here and at the library, Gallen-Kalle-lankatu 12 (Mon–Fri 10–7pm, Sat 10am–3pm). The city's **campsite**, *Isomäki* (☎02/641 0620), is 2km from the centre in the Isomäki Sports Centre, next to the outdoor swimming pool, but it's only open during the jazz festival; buses #7 and #8 run from the centre to the hospital (*sairaala*) close by. During the festival the Porin Linjojen Jazzliikenne bus links the main festival sites, the town square and campsite (10–4am, every 20min). At other times of year, the nearest campsite is *Yyteri*, amid sandy beaches 20km distant (☎02/634 5700, ⊛www.pori .fi/vav/yyteri), though it does have a shop, café, sauna and many cabins (❷/❸); the #32 bus stops just by the campsite. Among the **hotels**, you could try the *Cumulus*, Itsenäisyydenkatu 37 (☎02/550 900, ⊛www.cumulus.fi; ❹), one of the larger places and with its own restaurant. A smarter option is the *Vaakuna*, Gallen-Kallelankatu 7 (☎02/528 100, ⊛www.sokoshotels.fi; ❺), a business-oriented place with good weekend discounts. Around the corner from the *kauppatori* at Itäpuisto 13, *Buisto* (☎02/633 0646, ⊛www.hostelbuisto.net; ❷) has tidy, colourful rooms.

In the **evening** most people gravitate to the town centre and watch a procession of highly polished cars heading aimlessly up and down the main streets. Cafés and bars fall in and out of favour quite rapidly, although one of the most consistently popular is *Café Anton* at Antinkatu 11, where a €2 cup of coffee comes with a cloudberry liqueur chocolate. *Café Anton* also offers a decent lunch, though in the evening it's primarily a place to drink beer. Otherwise, for **eating** there are numerous fast-food outlets – particularly *grillis*, which tend to serve a local speciality called the *porilainen*, a large, thick slice of grilled onion sausage served hamburger style in a roll with pickles, ketchup and chopped onion. Of Pori's pizza places, the best are *Mestarit Pizza*, Länsipuisto 16, where pizzas and pasta dishes go for around €12; and the ubiquitous *Rax Pizza Buffet* at Itäpuisto 3, where €8 gets you all the pizza you want. If you fancy something more substantial, try the excellent *Raatihuoneen Kellari* in the cellar of the Promenadi Centre, Yrjönkatu 17, where lunchtime spreads of various Finnish-style meat and fish dishes cost €16–23, and there's an all-you-can-eat lunch buffet at €12. Check out also the all-year spin-off from the jazz festival, the *Jazz-Café*, at Eteläranta 6 on the banks of the Kokemäenjoki; just a few doors down, there's Finnish food at the excellent, reasonably priced *Suomalainen Klubbi* at no. 10. Pori has a good selection of smaller **bars**, as well: *Kino*, set in an old cinema, attracts students and young professionals, while *Punainen Kukko*, just across, sees a more mature crowd.

If you're planning to come here for the **jazz festival**, it's best to have accommodation fixed up at least six months in advance – hotels, hostel and campsite fill very quickly, although the tourist office endeavours to house as much of the overspill as possible in private homes (€22 per person in a double room, €31 single) or on mattresses in local schools (€10–20 per person). It's easiest to purchase festival **tickets** online at ⓦ www.porijazz.com, the main festival website; alternatively, contact the Pori tourist office. A third of the festival's 150-odd concerts are free, in any case. If you plan to stay the whole week it's best to buy a pass (costing up to €140; on sale from mid-April). Individual tickets range from €30 to €50 for the bigger acts (in the past these have included Lauryn Hill, Stevie Wonder, Paul Simon, Elvis Costello and Herbie Hancock). During the festival there's a Festival Centre at Pohjoisranta 11, in an old cotton mill on the left-hand side just after you cross the main Pori bridge heading away from the town centre. Here you can buy any tickets that haven't already been sold and pick up festival programmes and information.

The Åland Islands

The flat and thickly forested **Åland Islands**, all 6000-plus of them, lie scattered between Finland's southwest coast and Sweden. Politically Finnish but culturally Swedish, the islands cling to a weird form of independence, with their own parliament and flag (a red and yellow cross on a blue background). The currency is the euro but the language is Swedish – which explains why the main and only sizeable town is more commonly known by its Swedish name of **MARIEHAMN** than by the Finnish **Maarianhamina** – and as Swedish is mercifully closer to English, a visit here can make a welcome break from the perpetual battle with the Finnish language. Although Mariehamn – known locally as the "town of a thousand linden trees" after the elegant specimens that line virtually every street – is a peacefully uneventful seaside resort and a pleasant place to rest up for a couple of days, the real appeal here is sea, sun and beckoning terrain in unlimited quantities. There are plenty of secluded spots perfect for nude bathing, and you can hire a boat and sail out to your very own island.

The Åland islands (**Ahvenanmaa** in Finnish) were in Swedish hands through the Middle Ages, but, coveted by the Russians on account of their strategic location on the Baltic, they became part of the Russian Grand Duchy of Finland in 1807. When Finland gained independence, the future of the Ålands was referred to the League of Nations (though not before several Åland leaders had been imprisoned in Helsinki on a charge of high treason). As a result, Finnish sovereignty was established, in return for autonomy and complete demilitarization: the Ålanders now regard themselves as a shining example of Nordic cooperation, and living proof that a small state can run its own affairs while being part of a larger one.

The islands' ancient history is as interesting as the modern: many Roman coins have been found and there are scores of Viking burial mounds, plus the remains of some of the oldest Finnish churches. The excellent **Ålands Museum** (June–Aug daily 10am–4pm, open until 7pm on Tues and throughout July; Sept–May Tues–Sun 10am–4pm, Wed until 8pm; €2) in Mariehamn's Stadshusparken tells the full story, spicing it up with exhibits on modern Swedish and Finnish artists and designers. It's complemented by the ship-shaped **Åland Maritime Museum** on Hamngatan (daily: May, June & Aug 9am–5pm; July 9am–7pm; Sept–April 10am–4pm; €3.50–7 depending on season; ⓦ www.sjofartsmuseum.aland.fi), 1km away at the other end of Storagatan, which celebrates the fact that, despite their insignificant size, the Åland islands once had the world's largest fleet of wooden sailing ships.

Smaller local history museums in the Ålands' other communities reflect the surprisingly strong regional differences among the islands; it seems the only thing that's shared are the ubiquitous Åland maypoles – which stand most of the year round – and the fact that specific sights generally take a back seat to the various forms of nature. There are, however, several things worth making for. Toward the northeast of Mariehamn, in Tosarby Sund, are the remains of **Kastelholm**, a fourteenth-century fortress built to consolidate Swedish domination of the Baltic. Strutted through by numerous Swedish monarchs, it was mostly destroyed by fire in the mid-nineteenth century and is now being restored. In summer guided tours (€5) run several times a day from the gate to the nearby open-air **Jan Karlsgärden Museum** (May daily 10am–4pm; June–Aug daily 10am–5pm; early to mid-Sept Mon–Fri 10am–4pm; late Sept daily 10am–5pm; free). The Russians also set about building a fortress, **Bomarsund**, but before it could be completed the Crimean War broke out and an Anglo-French force stormed the infant castle, reducing it to rubble; just the scattered ramparts remain. Both would-be castles are on the same bus route from Mariehamn.

Elsewhere, you can trace the route of the old **post road**, the only mail link from Stockholm to what was then tsarist St Petersburg. To their long-lasting chagrin, the Åland people were charged with seeing the safe passage of the mail, including taking it across the frozen winter sea – and quite a few died in the process. The major remnant of these times is the nineteenth-century Carl Engel-designed **Post House** in **ECKERÖ**, at the islands' western extremity. Standing on the coast facing Sweden, the building was intended to instil fresh arrivals with awe at their first sight of the mighty Russian empire. Despite retaining its grandeur, it now looks highly incongruous amid the tiny local community.

Practicalities

Ferries from Finland and Sweden (see "Travel details", opposite) stop in Mariehamn's West Harbour, and there's a **tourist office** fifteen minutes' walk away at Storagatan 8 (March to mid-June & mid-Aug to Oct Mon–Fri 9am–4pm, Sat 10am–3pm; mid-June to mid-Aug daily 9am–6pm; rest of the year Mon–Fri 9am–4pm, ☎018/24 0000, ⊛www.mariehamn.aland.fi), which can provide the latest details regarding travel and accommodation. The library at Strandgatan 29 has several **Internet** terminals for use free of charge, though you may have to book a slot if you need to do more than check your mail.

You're going to have a hard time finding **accommodation** if you turn up in summer on spec and without a tent: there are no official youth hostels on the islands and, although there are a number of cheapish guesthouses, some of which offer hostel-type facilities, these fill quickly. If you're at a loose end in Mariehamn, try *Kronan* at Neptunigatan 52 (☎018/12 617; ❷/❸), or *Kvarnberget*, Parkgatan 28 (same phone number; ❷). For more luxury, there's the *Scandic Savoy* at Nygatan 12 (☎018/15 400, ⊛www.scandic-hotels.com; ❺/❻) with well-appointed rooms, though a little on the small size. Other villages around Åland offer more rustic options: in Eckerö, *Villa Kuckeliku*, Sandmovägen 80 (☎018/38 659, ⊛www .villakuckeliku.tk; ❷) has several rooms in a charming cottage with spectacular sea views, while in Degerby on Föglö, the *Föglö Wärdshus* (☎018/50 002, ⊛www .wardshus.com; ❹) is a cosy, idyllic inn with home cooking, sauna and Internet access. The wisest option, though, is to **camp**: there are plentiful sites (in isolated areas you should be able to camp rough with no problems).

There's a fairly thorough **bus service** covering the main islands, but **cycling** is a sound alternative, offering not only more freedom but also slightly cheaper rental rates than on the mainland; reckon on €9 per day for a bike with gears. In Mariehamn, RO NO is the best bet, with outlets at Hamngatan (☎018/12821) right opposite the ferry terminal, and on the waterside at Österhamn (☎018/12820) in the town proper; both open 9am to 6pm daily from June to mid-August. They also rent out Vespa **scooters** (€23 for five hours) and **boats** with outboard motors (€70 for five hours), and will provide advice and tips on some of the best islands to visit in the archipelago, just outside Mariehamn harbour.

Eating in the Ålands is not cheap, and many restaurants hike up their prices during the summer months to make a killing from the Swedish tourist traffic, but there are a few places in Mariehamn where you can try some fresh local seafood. *Sollan's Café*, Havsgatan 29 at the west harbour, is a small terrace café with coffee, cakes and loaves of tasty local *svårtbröd*, a dark and chewy syrup-based bread. 🍴 *Restaurang Nautical*, a regally outfitted place above the Maritime Museum with views to the water, serves the Brändö Archipelago Board, an excellent introduction to local cuisine with lightly-salted herring, roe and other seafood, plus *svårtbröd*; there's also a €14 set lunch menu. More casual is *Indigo*, Nygatan 1, offering standard Scandinavian dishes for around €20, and bottles of Stallhagen, Åland's own slightly-bitter microbrew. Alternatively, there's the less evocative *Cha Shao Tropical* at Torggatan 10, serving up pizzas and traditional Finnish food at reasonable prices. However, the best and most atmospheric place to eat is on board the ♣ *F.P. von Knorring*, moored in the Österhamn near RO NO, with fish and steak dishes starting at €20 and sandwiches for half that. In the summer, eat on the aft deck, where there's a cheaper selection of good-quality bar meals such as burgers, kebabs and salads; the seats here catch the evening sun, and after a day's hard cycling or archipelago exploration, they're the ideal place to sip a beer and watch the sun sink (very) slowly towards the horizon. For **nightlife**, the upstairs bar at *Indigo* is Åland's trendiest bar, replete with mood lighting, white leather couches and can't-be-bothered bar staff. *Dino's*, just next door, is a small, tidy bar with some good live music. Weekends are busy at both these places, and most locals usually make them a requisite stop before heading to dance the night away at either *Arken*, in the *Hotel Archipelago*, Strandgaten 31; or *Alvas*, Ålandsvägen 42, which attracts more of a younger crowd.

Travel details

Trains

Helsinki to: Espoo (half-hourly; 30min); Järvenpää (half-hourly; 30min); Jyväskylä (9 daily; 3hr 10min); Kajaani (4 daily; 7hr 30min); Kuopio (7 daily; 5hr); Lahti (hourly; 1hr 20min); Mikkeli (5 daily; 3hr 30min); Oulu (8–10 daily; 6hr 45min); Rovaniemi (4 daily; 10hr); Tampere (hourly; 1hr 40min); Turku (hourly; 2hr).
Pori to: Tampere (4–6 daily; 1hr 30min).
Turku to: Helsinki (hourly; 2hr); Tampere (7–9 daily; 1hr 50min).

Buses

Helsinki to: Joensuu (Mon–Fri 5 daily, Sat & Sun 1–2 daily; 6hr 55min–9hr 5min); Jyväskylä (hourly; 4hr–6hr); Kotka (Mon–Fri hourly, Sat & Sun 7–11 daily; 2hr 10min–3hr 10min); Mikkeli (Mon–Fri hourly, Sat & Sun 11–12 daily; 3hr 30min–4hr 35min); Porvoo (every 20min; 1hr); Tampere (hourly; 2hr 15min–3hr); Turku (every 30min; 2hr 10min–2hr 50min).
Kotka to: Hamina (hourly; 45min); Kouvola (5–8 daily; 1hr 10min).
Mariehamn to: Bomarsund (5 daily; 30min); Eckerö (5 daily; 45min); Kastelholm (5 daily; 30min).
Pori to: Rauma (hourly; 1hr 5min); Turku (13 daily; 2hr 10min).
Porvoo to: Helsinki (every 20min; 1hr); Kotka (hourly; 1hr 30min); Loviisa (hourly; 40min); Pyhtää (Mon–Fri hourly, Sat & Sun 4–8 daily; 1hr).

Rauma to: Pori (hourly; 45min); Turku (Mon–Fri 14 daily, Sat 7–8 daily; 1hr 30min).
Turku to: Helsinki (every 30min; 2hr 30min); Pori (every two hours; 2hr 15min); Rauma (hourly; 1hr 30min).

Ferries

Helsinki to: Mariehamn (2 daily; 10hr–11hr).
Mariehamn to: Helsinki (2 daily; 10hr–11hr); Turku (4 daily; 5hr 20min).
Turku to: Mariehamn (4 daily; 5hr 30min).

International trains

Helsinki to: Moscow (1 daily; 13hr 40min); St Petersburg (2 daily; 6hr 40min).

International buses

Helsinki to: St Petersburg (3 daily; 8hr 10min–9hr 30min); Viipuri/Vyborg (3 daily; 5hr 25min–6hr 10min).

International ferries

Eckerö to Grisslehamn: (2–5 daily; 2hr).
Helsinki to: Lübeck–Travemünde (1 daily; 36hr); Stockholm (2 daily; 16hr); St Petersburg (1–3 weekly; 14hr 30min); Tallinn (every two hours; 1hr 30min–3hr 30min).
Mariehamn to: Kappelskär (2–3 daily; 3hr); Stockholm (6 daily; 6hr).
Turku to: Stockholm (3 daily; 10–11hr).

4.2

The Lake Region

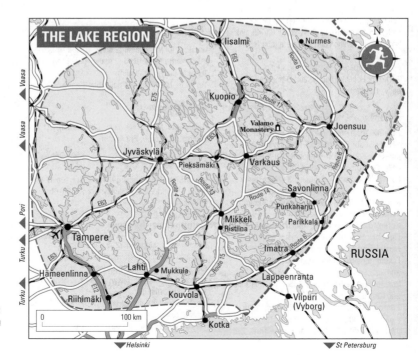

Known unofficially as *tuhansien järvien maa*, which loosely translates as "the land of a thousand lakes", Finland boasts more than 40,000 waterways and lake chains, the majority of them – chiefly the Päijanne and Saimaa systems – located in the **Lake Region**. Unique in Finland, and indeed in Scandinavia and Western Europe, a third of the area here is taken up by water. Each of the lake chains features countless bays, inlets and islands interspersed with dense forests, while the settlements have grown up around paper mills which used natural waterways and purpose-built canals to transport timber to pulping factories powered by gushing rapids.

Wherever you go in the Lake Region, water is never far away, further pacifying an already tranquil and verdant landscape. Even **Tampere**, Finland's major industrial city, is likeable as much for its lakeside setting as for its cosmopolitan cultural delights. It's also the most accessible of the region's centres, being on the railway line between Helsinki and the north. Also reachable by train from Helsinki, **Lahti** comes into its own as a winter sports resort; during summer the town is

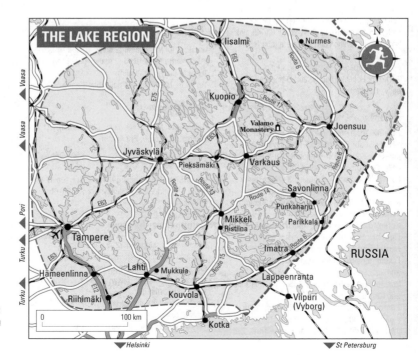

THE LAKE REGION

Iisalmi
Nurmes
Kuopio
Route 17
Valamo Monastery
Joensuu
Jyväskylä
Pieksämäki
Varkaus
Savonlinna
Punkaharju
Mikkeli
Parikkala
Ristiina
Tampere
Imatra
Hämeenlinna
Lahti
Mukkula
Lappeenranta
Riihimäki
Kouvola
Viipuri (Vyborg)
Kotka

RUSSIA

0   100 km

Helsinki   St Petersburg

comparatively lifeless. Diminutive **Mikkeli** has more character, and makes a good stopover en route to the atmospheric eastern part of the Lake Region, where slender ridges furred with conifers link the few sizeable areas of land. Its regional centre, **Savonlinna**, stretches delectably across several islands, and boasts a superbly preserved medieval castle. Just east of here, a stone's throw from the Russian border, the forests and bays around **Parikkala** offer plenty of outdoors enjoyment in the form of canoeing, hiking and horse riding. To get a sense of Karelian culture (for more on which, see p.663) visit **Joensuu**, **Lappeenranta** or the city of **Kuopio**, three towns where many displaced Karelians settled after World War II. In the heart of the region lies **Jyväskylä**, whose wealth of buildings by Alvar Aalto draws modern architecture buffs to what is otherwise a sleepy, quaint student town. Down-to-earth **Iisalmi** is effectively a bridge between the Lake Region and the rougher, less watery terrain further north.

Unless you want total solitude (which is easily attained), it's best to spend a few days in the larger towns and make shorter forays into the more thinly populated areas. Although the western Lake Region is mostly well served by **trains**, rail connections to – and within – the eastern part are awkward and infrequent. With daily services between the main towns and less frequent ones to the villages, **buses** are generally handier for getting around. Slow, expensive **ferries** (including a few offering day-trips to Russia) also link the main lakeside towns, while practically every community runs short pleasure cruises, but to really explore the countryside, you'll need to rent a **car** or **bicycle**.

Tampere and around

"Here it was as natural to approve of the factories as in Mecca one would the mosques," wrote John Sykes of **TAMPERE** in the 1960s – and you soon see what he meant. But although Tampere has long been Finland's biggest manufacturing centre and is currently Scandinavia's largest inland city, it's a highly scenic place, with leafy cobbled avenues, sculpture-filled parks and two sizeable lakes. The factories that line the Tammerkoski rapids in the heart of the city actually accentuate its appeal, their chimneys standing as bold monuments to Tampere's past – it's no coincidence that the town is known colloquially as the Manchester of Finland's north. Its rapid growth began just over a century ago, when Tsar Alexander I abolished taxes on local trade, encouraging the Scotsman James Finlayson to open a textile factory here, drawing labour from rural areas where traditional crafts were in decline. Metalwork and clothing factories soon followed (mobile phone giant Nokia was founded here in 1865 as a wood-pulp manufacturer), their owners paternalistically supplying culture to the workforce by promoting a vigorous local arts scene. Free outdoor rock and jazz concerts, lavish theatrical productions and one of the best modern art collections in Finland maintain such traditions to this day.

Arrival, information and accommodation

Tampere's **airport**, Pirkkala, lies 15km south of the city centre. Buses (35min; €6) meet the flights and drop passengers at the central train station; the return ride leaves from the train station approximately two hours before scheduled airline departures. Almost everything of consequence is within the central section of the city, bordered on two sides by the lakes Näsijärvi and Pyhäjärvi. The main streets run off either side of Hämeenkatu, which leads directly from the **train station** across Hämeensilta, the bridge over Tammerkoski River, notable for its weighty bronze sculptures by Wäino Aaltonen which represent four characters from local folklore. Although there's little call to use local **buses**, most routes begin from the terminal on Hämeenkatu. Tampere's friendly and helpful **tourist office**, Verkate-htaankatu 2 (June–Aug Mon–Fri 9am–8pm, Sat & Sun 10am–5pm, Sept–Oct 9am–5pm, Sat & Sun 9am–7pm; Oct–May Mon–Fri 9am–4pm, Sat & Sun 10am–5pm; ☎020/716 6800, ✆www.tampere.fi), hands out maps, hiking itineraries and

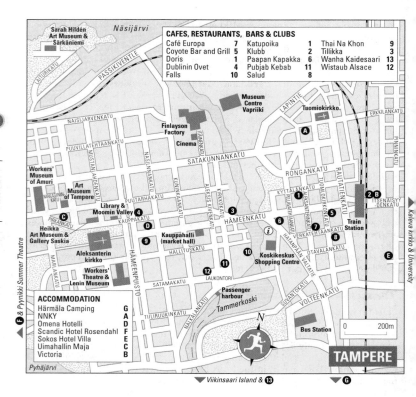

CAFES, RESTAURANTS, BARS & CLUBS

Café Europa	7	Katupoika	1	Thai Na Khon	9
Coyote Bar and Grill	5	Klubb	2	Tillikka	3
Doris	1	Paapan Kapakka	6	Wanha Kaidesaari	13
Dublinin Ovet	4	Pubjab Kebab	11	Wistaub Alsace	12
Falls	10	Salud	8		

ACCOMMODATION

Härmälä Camping	G
NNKY	A
Omena Hotelli	D
Scandic Hotel Rosendahl	F
Sokos Hotel Villa	E
Uimahallin Maja	C
Victoria	B

TAMPERE

Viikinsaari Island & 13

copies of the excellent free *Tampere* guide; free **Internet** access is also available. Be sure to ask staff about the new Tampere Card, which offers discounts on many city museums and attractions. From June to August the office also organizes two-hour sightseeing tours of the town (daily at 2pm; €12).

Accommodation

Being one of Finland's most popular destinations, Tampere has plenty of central accommodation options for all types of budget, especially in the summer when both the main **youth hostels** are open. Still, many of these get booked up early so you'll want to book ahead if possible, lest you be left foraging for the more expensive leftovers. If you're **camping**, there are lakeside facilities at Härmälä (☎03/265 1355 or ☎09/6138 3210, ⊛www.lomaliitto.fi/harmala), 5km south, which also rents out cabins for three people (€35) and up to five (€56); take bus #1.

NNKY Tuomiokirkonkatu 12A ☎03/254 4020, ⊛www.tnnky.fi/hostel.html. The dorm rooms at this Finnish YWCA (all sexes welcome) are institutional and simple but represent the cheapest beds in town (€15), though the doubles (❷) are also a comparatively good bargain. Open June to late August.

Omena Hotelli Hämeenkatu 28 ☎200/39 000, ⊛www.omena.com. Tampere's newest and best bargain hotel, this central, post-modern concept establishment eschews human interaction. There is no receptionist and bookings must be made in advance via the Internet or at the kiosk in the downstairs "lobby" (note that booking by phone will incur an extra €6 charge); an electronic code then grants you access to the sleek, very modern rooms. ❸

Scandic Hotel Rosendahl Pyynikintie 13 ☎03/244 1111, ⊛www.scandic-hotels.com.

Lakeside luxury a couple of kilometres west of the city centre, right inside Pyynikki park and next to the observation tower. The hundred or so newly renovated rooms are comfortable and many have views to the lake, as well as access to the pool and several saunas. Bus #21. ⑥

Sokos Hotel Villa Sumeliuksenkatu 14 ☏03/262 6267, ⓦ www.sokoshotels.fi. Central but pricey for the bland, predictable rooms you get. ④/⑥

🏃 **Uimahallin Maja** Pirkankatu 10–12 ☏03/222 9460, ⓦ www.hosteltampere.com.

Centrally located about a kilometre from the train station and just next to the Aleksanterin kirkko, this superb and clean hostel is in the same building as the city's municipal swimming pool. There are dormitories (€20) as well as rooms (②) sleeping one to six people. Open June to August.

Victoria Itsenäisyydenkatu 1 ☏03/242 5111, ⓦ www.hotellivictoria.fi. Directly opposite the train station, the *Victoria*'s recently renovated rooms are simple but spacious and well appointed. ④/⑥

The City

Short, broad streets make central Tampere very easy to explore. From the train station, Hämeenkatu runs across the Tammerkoski into the heart of the city, and almost everything of interest lies within a few minutes' walk of this busy thoroughfare. You'll need to cross back over the river (most easily done by following Satakunnankatu) to reach Tampere's historic cathedral, as well as a couple of worthwhile museums, the cinema and several upmarket restaurants – and to get the best view of the superbly maintained Finlayson factory, on which the city's fortunes were founded; it's now home to the editorial offices of the region's main newspaper.

Hämeenkatu and around

Walking the length of Hämeenkatu from the train station leaves you in front of the upwardly thrusting neo-Gothic **Aleksanterin kirkko** (daily: May–Aug 10am–5pm; Sept–April 11am–3pm). With a riot of knobbly ceiling decorations, the effect inside is something like an ecclesiastical train station, with an unusually unpleasant artexed altar. To the left, following the line of greenery south down Hämeenpuisto, is the Tampere Workers' Theatre and, in the same building, the excellent **Lenin Museum** (Mon–Fri 9am–6pm, Sat & Sun 11am–4pm; €4; ⓦ www.lenin.fi), which, oddly, is the only permanent museum dedicated to Lenin anywhere in the world. After the abortive 1905 revolution in Russia, Lenin lived in Finland for two years and attended the Tampere conferences, held in what is now the museum. It was here that he first encountered Stalin, although this is barely mentioned in the displays, one of which concentrates on Lenin himself, the other

△ Tampere riverside

on his relationship with Finland and on his visits to numerous Finnish cities. For a detailed explanation, borrow the English-language brochure from reception. If you want more Lenin, head to Kyttälänkatu, one block north of the railway station off Rautatienkatu, where a plaque marks the otherwise undistinguished house (no. 11) where he lived during his stint in Tampere. Several blocks north of Hämeenkatu, the Amuri district was built during the 1880s to house Finlayson's workers. Some thirty homes have been preserved as the **Amuri Museum of Workers' Housing** at Makasiininkatu 12 (*Amurin Työläismuseokortteli*; mid-May to mid-Sept Tues–Sun 10am–6pm; €4; during the rest of the year only the museum shop is open, same times; ⓦwww.tampere.fi/amuri), a simple but affecting place that records the family life of working people over a hundred-year period. In each home is a description of the inhabitants and their jobs, and authentic articles from the relevant periods – from beds and tables to family photos, newspapers and biscuit packets.

Just around the corner at Puutarhakatu 34 is the **Art Museum of Tampere** (Tues–Sun 10am–6pm; €5; guided tours by arrangement on ⓣ03/3146 6580; ⓦwww.tampere.fi/tamu), whose first floor holds powerful if staid temporary exhibitions featuring Finnish and international artists; the large basement galleries are filled with contemporary local work. If you're looking for older Finnish art, head instead for the far superior **Heikka Art Museum**, a few minutes' walk away at Pirkankatu 6 (Tues–Thurs 3–6pm, Sun noon–3pm; other times by arrangement ⓣ03/212 3973; €4; ⓦwww.heikantaidemuseo.fi). Kustaa Heikka was a gold- and silversmith whose professional skills and business acumen made him a local bigshot around 1900. The art collection he bequeathed to Tampere reflects his interest in traditional lifestyles; borrow a catalogue from reception, since most pieces are identified only by numbers. Amongst the most notable work (including sketches by Gallen-Kallela and Helene Schjerfbeck) are two of Heikka's own creations: a delicately wrought brooch marking the completion of his apprenticeship, and a finely detailed bracelet with which he celebrated becoming a master craftsman. Well worth the diversion, and free too, is the next-door **Gallery Saskia** (daily noon–6pm free; ⓦwww.tampereensaskiat.com), showing intriguing and unusual new work.

Nearby, at Pirkankatu 2, stands the **Tampere Library** (June–Aug Mon–Sat 9.30am–7pm; Sept–May Mon–Fri 9.30am–8pm, Sat 9.30am–3pm), an astounding feat of user-friendly modern architecture. The work of Reimi and Raili Pietilä (who also designed the epic Kaleva kirkko – see p.738), and finished in 1986, the library's curving walls give it a warm, cosy feel; believe it or not, the building's shape was inspired by a certain type of grouse (a stuffed specimen of which sits in the reception area). Strolling around is the best way to take in the many small, intriguing features, and will eventually lead you up to the top-floor café, which gives a good view of the cupola, deliberately set eleven degrees off the vertical to match the off-centre pivot of the earth. In the basement of the library, with its own entrance at Hämeenpuisto 20, **Moomin Valley** (June–Aug Mon–Fri 9am–5pm, Sat & Sun 10am–6pm; Sept–April Tues–Fri 9am–5pm, Sat & Sun 10am–6pm; €4; ⓦwww.tampere.fi/muumi) uses dolls and 3-D displays to re-create scenes from the incredibly popular children's books by Tove Jansson.

A few blocks south of Hämeenkatu, the passenger harbour is the departure point for summer **lake cruises**. The guided trip (Mon 12.30pm & Wed 5.30pm; 90min; €10) to the town of **Nokia** – a small hamlet which predated the mega-company that made Nokia a household name – provides an informed tour of the Pyhäjärvi lake and the Tampere suburbs, but more enjoyable is the quick trip over to nearby **Viikinsaari** (hourly Tues–Sun; 20min; €6). First known as Jomasaari ("Island of God"), this small wooded island served as a popular weekend destination for nineteenth-century Finnish nobility, but fell into some disrepute after local ne'er-do-wells claimed it as their private watering hole. Today, it houses a small chapel and a nature reserve, making it popular with many locals looking for some fresh air. At midsummer, Viikinsaari hosts evening fêtes, tango dancing and a traditional *kakko*, a large bonfire lit right on the banks of lake Pyhäjärvi. The island also holds the *Wanha Kaidesaari* restaurant (see p.739).

The Näsijärvi lakeside

Just north of Tampere's central grid-plan streets, the tremendous **Sara Hildén Art Museum** (daily 11am–6pm, closed Mon Sept–May; €4–7 depending on exhibitions; ⊛www.tampere.fi/hilden), built on the shores of Näsijärvi, displays Tampere's premier modern art collection by means of changing exhibitions. The museum is on the other side of the northern arterial road, Paasikiventie, from Amuri (take bus #16, or the summer-only #4 bus from the town centre or train station).

Occupying the same waterside strip as the Hildén collection is **Särkänniemi** (⊛www.sarkanniemi.fi; €5), Tampere's most popular tourist destination. A sizable complex incorporating an adventure park, dolphinarium, aquarium, planetarium and an observation tower with rotating restaurant, the site is open year-round (daily 11am–7pm, closes later during summer), though the zoo and theme park rides operate between May and August only. Seen from the **tower** (April–Sept daily 11am–11.30pm; Oct–March Tues–Sat 10am–11.30pm, Sun & Mon 10am–9.30pm; €5), itself an unmistakeable element of Tampere's skyline, the city seems insignificant compared to the trees and lakes that stretch to the horizon. The rapids that cut through them can be identified from afar by the factory chimneys alongside. The tower's admission charge is waived if you're eating at its restaurant; the other diversions cost €5 apiece and are usually crowded with families. To make a day of it, buy the €29 Särkänniemi Key, valid for all parts of the complex except parasailing. Särkänniemi's café serves half-decent, inexpensive pizza, quiche and the like.

The Tuomiokirkko and around

Cross to the eastern side of the Tammerkoski River along Satakunnankatu and you'll not only see – foaming below the bridge – the rapids that powered the **Finlayson Factory**, but also the factory building itself, still standing to the north and well worth a wander for its crafts shops. Also within the Finlayson complex is an absorbing addition to Tampere's museums, the **Spy Museum** (*Vakoilumuseo*; Mon–Fri noon–6pm, Sat & Sun 10am–4pm, opens daily in summer; €7). The range of gadgets, clothing, machines and documents – including a collection of now-declassified KGB maps – attest to the rampant espionage on both sides of the Finnish and Russian border during the last century; English-language information panels help you get the most from the displays.

Immediately ahead of the Finlayson complex in a grassy square, the **Tuomiokirkko** (daily: May–Aug 9am–6pm; Sept–April 11am–3pm) is a picturesque cathedral in the National Romantic style, designed by Lars Sonck and finished in 1907. It's most remarkable for the gorily symbolic frescoes by Hugo Simberg – particularly the *Garden of Death*, where skeletons happily water plants, and *The Wounded Angel*, showing two boys carrying a bleeding angel through a Tampere landscape – which caused an ecclesiastical outcry when unveiled. So did the viper (a totem of evil) which Sonck placed amongst the angel wings on the ceiling; Simberg retorted that evil could lurk anywhere – including a church.

Out from the centre

To learn more about Tampere's origins, visit the **Museum Centre Vapriikki** (Tues & Thurs–Sun 10am–6pm, Wed 11am–8pm; €5; ⊛www.tampere.fi/vapriikki), housed in a former mill just across the river from the Finlayson factory. Though the museum covers everything from archeology to handicrafts, its most interesting section deals with the impact of the early twentieth century – a turbulent time for both Tampere and Finland. As an industrial town with militant workers, Tampere instigated a general strike against the Russification of Finland, filling the streets with demonstrators and painting over the Cyrillic names on trilingual street signs. After independence the city became a Social Democratic stronghold, and one ruthlessly dealt with by the right-wing government following the civil war of 1918 – yet the municipal administration remains amongst the most left-leaning in Finland. Vapriiki also contains the **Finnish Ice Hockey Museum** (same times and entrance fee), which accords due honour to local teams Ilves and Tappora, which have won more national championships than all of Finland's other teams combined.

Away to the east of the centre, Itsenäisyydenkatu runs uphill behind the train station to meet the vast concrete folds of the **Kaleva kirkko** (daily: May–Aug 9am–6pm; Sept–April 11am–3pm). Built in 1966, it was a belated addition to the neighbouring **Kaleva estate**, which was heralded in the 1950s as an outstanding example of high-density housing. Though initially stunning, the church's interior lacks the subtlety of the city library, despite being designed by the same team of Reimi and Raili Pietilä, who this time based their plan on a fish.

Eating

Tampere boasts an eclectic range of **restaurants** and **cafés** to suit all pockets. Several places in the *Koskikeskus* shopping mall, Hatanpään valtatie 1, offer cheap lunchtime specials, but, as usual, the cheapest places to eat are the student **mensas** – in the university at the end of Yliopistonkatu, just over the railway line from the city centre – where full meals can cost as little as €5.

There are numerous **supermarkets** at which to stock up on provisions. Two central options are the big Sokos store at Hämeenkatu 21, or Anttila, Puutarhakatu 10. Slightly further out, and cheaper, are City Market, Sotilaankatu 11, and Prisma at Sammonkatu 73. There's also a large **kauppahalli** (market hall) at Hämeenkatu 19 (Mon–Fri 8am–6pm, Sat 8am–4pm), and open-air markets at Laukontori (Mon–Fri 6am–2pm, Sat 6am–1pm), Keskustori (first Mon of month 6am–6pm) and Tammelantori (Mon–Fri 6am–2pm, Sat 6am–1pm).

Katupoika Aleksanterinkatu 20 ⓦwww
.aleksinravintolat.fi. Popular with the city's youthful set, this inexpensive local eatery is known for its tasty vegetarian dishes – but it's also a great place to try the local speciality *mustamakkara*, a rich blood sausage (€8).
Pubjab Kebab Kirkkokatu 10. One block from the passenger harbour, serving the city's favourite kebabs (€5–6).
Salud Tuomiokirkonkatu 19 ⓦwww.salud.fi. A lively Spanish restaurant serving mixed tapas plates (€8.40), and sizable Iberian meat dishes such as *costillas de cerdo* (pork ribs; €16.70).
Thai Na Khon Hämeenkatu 29. Enormous portions of excellent Thai food at very reasonable prices. Ask for extra helpings of the spicy chilli oil, if you dare.

Tillikka Hämeenkatu 14. Very classy place dressed up in early twentieth-century flair and with terraces overlooking the Tammerkoski rapids. The continental fare includes dishes like entrecote (€16.90) or porcini stew (€14.90).
Wanha Kaidesaari Viikinsaari island ⓦwww
.ravintolawanhakaidesaari.fi. This grand old place has been in operation since 1900 and is a wonderful venue for upscale dinners at downtown prices. Most of the traditional Finnish dishes, like tender medallion of salmon or hearty pork escalope, cost well under €15.
Wistaub Alsace Laukontori 6B ⓦwww
.wistaubalsace.com. Right at the harbour, this newish place serves great southeastern French food, with mains for around €15.

Drinking and entertainment

Tampere is very much alive and buzzing after dark, with numerous late-night bars, cafés and clubs. One of the most popular **pubs** is the Irish *Dublinin Ovet* ("Doors of Dublin") at Kauppakatu 16; another summertime favourite is *Falls*, down by the rapids. Despite its name, *Café Europa*, Aleksanterinkatu 29, is more of a bar and restaurant than café, and a good place to meet some of Tampere's trendy young things, while the newest addition to the city's nightlife scene is the colourful *Coyote Bar and Grill*, Hämeenkatu 3, a full-on retro affair with loads of young locals smoking and drinking against murals of Castro. One of Finland's few **gay bars** outside Helsinki, the friendly and laid-back *Mixei* (closed Mon), Itsenäisyydenkatu 7–9, is worth seeking out for some insight into the gay social scene in the Finnish provinces – sadly, not an immediately appealing prospect, which perhaps explains the lack of other gay establishments outside the capital.

For live **music**, try the laid-back *Klubbi*, a nightclub set in an old customs house behind the train station on Itsenäisyydenkatu or, almost opposite the tourist office, *Paapan Kapakka*, a swing-style jazz club with up-and-coming bands. On the same street, the extremely popular rock disco *Doris*, in the basement of *Restaurant Katupoika*, Aleksanterinkatu 20, is the place where boho locals go to drink and dance till morning.

On warm nights the crowds head out to the Pyynikki area, a natural ridge on the edge of Tampere, beside Pyhäjärvi. Tickets for the **Pyynikki Summer Theatre** (☎03/216 0300, ⓦwww.pyynikinkesateatteri.com) cost €26, but it's worth trekking out just to look at the revolving auditorium which slowly rotates the audience around during performances, blending the surrounding woods, rocks and water into the show's scenery – though remember that all performances here are in Finnish only.

Plevna, Itäinenkatu 4 (☎03/313 831), is the city's largest **cinema**, with ten screens and frequent runs of English-language pictures.

Around Tampere

Half an hour from Tampere on the busy rail line to Helsinki, **HÄMEENLINNA** (Tavastehus in Swedish) is revered both as the birthplace of Sibelius and as Finland's oldest inland town. The major attraction is **Häme Castle** (daily May to mid-Aug 10am–6pm; mid-Aug to April 10am–4pm; €5), the sturdy thirteenth-century fortress from which the town takes its name; free guided tours are available in English by appointment – call ☎03/675 6820. Next comes the **Sibelius Childhood Home** (daily: May–Aug 10am–4pm; Sept–April noon–4pm; €3) at Hallituskatu 11, where the great composer was born and now reverentially restored to how it was during the first years of his life. A few blocks away at Viipuriintie 2, the **Art Museum** (Tues–Sun noon–6pm, Thurs until 8pm; €5) musters a mundane collection of minor works by major Finnish names, among them Järnefelt, Gallen-Kalella and Halonen.

Seeing all this won't take long, and any spare hours are better spent in the outlying town of **Hattula**, roughly 5km from the centre of Hämeenlinna. The local **Hattulan kirkko** (daily mid-May to mid-Aug 11am–5pm; other times by appointment on ☎03/631 1540) is probably the finest medieval church in Finland – outwardly plain, with an interior totally covered by 180 sixteenth-century frescoes of biblical scenes. En route to the church, a combined **youth hostel** (☎03/682 8560; May to mid-Aug; dorms €14, doubles ❹) and **campsite** (same number; June–Aug) face Hämeenlinna across the river, 4km from the town centre.

Moving on from Tampere

Tampere has excellent **train links** to the rest of Finland. To reach the rest of the Lake Region, however, there are two main choices. Aiming for Jyväskylä also puts you within comparatively easy reach of Varkaus, Joensuu and Kuopio. Alternatively, heading for Lahti (change at Riihimäki) makes more sense if you want to press on to Mikkeli or Lappeenranta, or see more of the eastern Lake Region. For Savonlinna, there are two alternative routes: either take a train to Pieksämäki, from where there are direct buses (which accept train passes and tickets) to the town, or head east through Riihimäki and Lappeenranta to Parikkala for the branch line to Savonlinna.

Jyväskylä

JYVÄSKYLÄ (pronounced "EWE-vah-skoo-lah") is the most low-key and provincial of the main Lake Region towns, despite an industrial section that takes up one end and a big university which consumes the other – though the latter does provide something of a youthful feel. The town also has more than its fair share of buildings by **Alvar Aalto**. The legendary architect grew up here and opened his first office in the town in 1923, and his handiwork – a collection of buildings spanning his entire career – litters the place.

After some minor projects, Aalto left Jyväskylä in 1927 for fame, fortune and Helsinki, but returned in the 1950s to work on the teacher-training college. By the 1970s this had grown into the **Jyväskylä University**, whose large campus halts traffic where the main road gives way to a series of public footpaths, leading to a park and sports ground. Although Aalto died before his ambitious plan for an Administration and Cultural Centre was complete, the scheme is still under construction along Vapaudenkatu. Across the road from the (perhaps intentionally) uninspiring police station – unveiled in 1970 – stands a **City Theatre** resembling a scaled-down version of Helsinki's Finlandia.

Two of the town's most important **museums** are situated close together on the hill running down from the university towards the edge of the lake, Jyväsjärvi. At the request of the town authorities rather than through vanity, Aalto built the **Alvar Aalto Museum** at Alvar Aallon Katu 7 (Tues–Sun 11am–6pm; €6, free on Fri; ⓦwww.alvaraalto.fi). The architect's best works are obviously out on the streets, making this collection of plans, photos and models seem rather superfluous, but the Aalto-designed furniture makes partial amends. The first floor hosts temporary art exhibitions and the ground floor has a pleasant if unexciting café. Aalto also contributed to the exterior of the nearby **Museum of Central Finland** (*Keski-Suomen Museo*; Tues–Sun 11am–6pm; €4, free on Fri; ⓦwww.jkl.fi/ksmuseo), which contains two separate exhibitions: one devoted to Middle Finland – well designed but with no English translations – and the other representing each decade of the twentieth century through the car number-plates, music and kitchen gadgetry of the day. The collection of room interiors is worth the visit alone.

Jyväskylä also holds an impressive **Art Museum** (Tues–Sun 11am–6pm; €5, free on Fri; ⓦwww.jyvaskyla.fi/taidemuseo) at Kauppakatu 25, which is split into two exhibition sites. The main site houses the permanent collection of the Ester and Jalo Sihtola Fine Arts Foundation, plus that of the Association of Finnish Printmakers. The site next door houses temporary exhibitions reflecting the latest trends in modern art from Finland and the rest of the world. Also at Kauppakatu 25, the **Finnish Craft Museum**, with displays ranging from bell-making to spectrolite jewellery, and the **National Costume Centre** (both Tues–Sun 11am–6pm; €5,

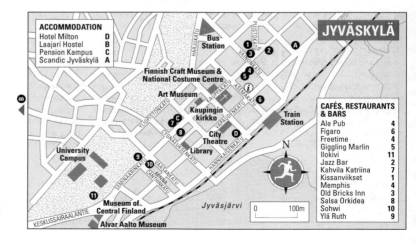

free on Fri;) which holds a definitive collection of Finnish and Karelian smocks, bodices and headdresses. Don't leave Jyväskylä without seeing the nineteenth-century **Kaupungin kirkko** (June–Aug Mon–Fri 11am–6pm, Sat & Sun 11am–2pm; Sept–May Wed–Fri 11am–2pm), in the small park one block west of the tourist office. The church was the centrepiece of town life a century ago, but declined in importance as Jyväskylä gained new suburbs and other churches. Despite recent restoration – when the interior was repainted in its original pale yellow and green – the church looks authentically dingy.

Practicalities

From the train and bus stations, right in the centre, it's a short walk to the **tourist office**, in a beautiful wooden building at Asemakatu 6 (mid-June to Aug Mon–Fri 9am–6pm, Sat & Sun 10am–3pm; Sept to mid-June Mon–Fri 9am–5pm, Sat 10am–3pm; ☎014/624 903, ⓦwww.jyvaskylanseutu.fi), which can supply a useful free leaflet on the local buildings designed by Aalto and has **Internet** access. There's also free Net access in the public library at Vapaudenkatu 39–41 (June to mid-Aug Mon–Fri 11am–7pm, Sat 11am–3pm; rest of the year Mon–Fri 11am–8pm, Sat 11am–3pm), though you'll need to book in advance – call ☎14/624 464.

For **accommodation**, both *Pension Kampus*, Kauppakatu 11A (☎014/338 1400, ⓦwww.kolumbus.fi/pensionkampus; ❸), and the central, family-run *Hotel Milton*, Hannikaisenkatu 27–29 (☎014/337 7900, ⓦwww.hotellimilton.com; ❹), right by the train station, are good choices. For a bit more luxury, try the *Scandic Jyväskylä* at Vapaudenkatu 73 (☎014/330 3000, ⓦwww.scandic-hotels.com; ❹/❻) – some rooms have their own private saunas. The local **youth hostel**, *Laajari* (☎014/624 885, ⓦwww.laajavuori.com), is a state-of-the-art affair, 4km from the centre at Laajavuorentie 15 – take bus #25 from Vapaudenkatu. The local **campsite** is closed indefinitely and the nearest option is roughly 30km away; check with the tourist office for the latest details on pitching tents or parking campers in the area.

Eating

Jyväskylä's **eating** options range from the quotidian pizza establishments along the main streets to a few worthy upscale places. For real budget lunches during the school year, try the student *mensa* at Ilokivi, Keskussairaalantie 2; if you get tired of Finnish cuisine, you may want to explore the town's fetish for Tex-Mex restaurants – or, rather "Mix-Tex" as one of them advertises.

Cafés and restaurants

Figaro Asemakatu 14 ☎014 212 255, ⓦwww.figarorestaurant.com. This central, comfy family-style restaurant matches fair-priced salads, pastas, steaks and fish dishes with a well-endowed wine list and is justifiably busy. A three-course meal won't run over €30. Reservations recommended on weekends.
Kahvila Katriina Kauppakatu 11. A modern café serving deliciously calorific cakes and some excellent vegetarian dishes.

Kissanviikset Puistokatu 3. "The Cat's Whiskers" serves sizeable Finnish fish and meat dishes (most under €20) in elegant ambience.
Salsa Orkidea Kauppakatu 10. One of the towns better Tex-Mex restaurants, with tacos, tortillas, quesadillas, burritos and chimichangas, all for under €10.
Sohwi Vaasankatu 21. A popular, light and airy place serving inexpensive burgers, ribs, steaks and a number of tapas dishes. Evenings frequently feature live music, and the bar stays hopping until well after midnight.

Drinking and entertainment

Jyväskylä's student population ensures a good crop of bars, though things are somewhat sedate in the summer out of term-time. The neighbourhood around the university is the focal point for the town's **nightlife**, and as the university hosts events in and out of term-time, it's always worth looking out for posters advertising parties and live music events. There is quite a strong **gay** scene in town; for information on local gay events, call in at SETA, Kilpisinkatu 8 (℡045/638 9540), which organizes regular parties at *Ilokivi* and other venues.

Bars and clubs

Freetime Kauppakatu 26. A relaxed bar playing 1980s rock to twentysomething Finns.
Giggling Marlin Kauppakatu 32. The local branch of the ubiquitous Finnish chain disco is currently *the* place to be for local ravers.
Ilokivi Keskussairaalantie 2 ⊛ www.jyy.fi/ilokivi. Located in the university grounds, this lively cultural space is a hot student destination on account of its live bands, art exhibitions, theatre and stand-up "comedy" performances.
Jazz Bar Kauppakatu. Live music (mostly jazz) several days a week, and open jam sessions on Tuesday nights.

Memphis Kauppakatu 30. This central restaurant-cum-bar has massive front windows and attracts younger Finns, especially on Thursday nights, when live rock bands take the stage. Less expensive beer is on offer downstairs at the *Ale Pub*.
Old Bricks Inn Kauppakatu 41. On sunny evenings, the outdoor seating at this popular pub really pulls the crowds. There's a good selection of imported beers, great coffee and several scrumptious dinner dishes to boot.
Ylä Ruth Seminaarinkatu 19. Often smoky and filled with lively characters, generally members of the university's philosophy and politics departments here for a game of chess and/or some hard drinking.

Lahti

LAHTI doesn't know if it's a Lake Region town or a Helsinki suburb, and it's perhaps this confusion that conspires to make the place so dull. Its entire growth took place in the twentieth century (mostly since Alvar Aalto opened several furniture factories, which kept him going between architectural commissions), and although it's now the major transport junction between the Lake Region and the south, it lacks any lake-area atmosphere, while local cultural life is diminished by the relative proximity of Helsinki. Lahti's one compensation is its status as a **winter sports** centre of international renown: three enormous ski jumps hang over the town, and there's a feeling of biding time when summer grass, rather than winter snow, covers their slopes.

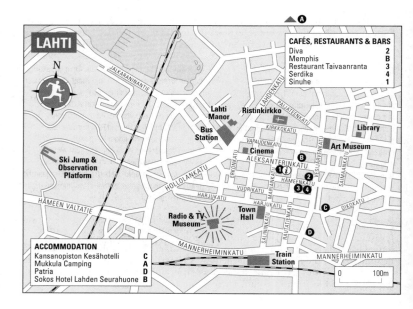

Unless you're here to ski, Lahti isn't a place you'll need or want to linger in – the town can easily be covered in half a day. Head first for the **observation platform** on the highest ski jump (June–Aug daily 10am–5pm; Sept–May Sat & Sun 11am–3pm; €4 including the chairlift to the top), whose location is unmistakeable. From such a dizzying altitude the lakes and forests around Lahti stretch dreamily into the distance, and the large swimming pool below the jump resembles a puddle (when frozen in winter it's used as a landing zone).

The only structures matching the ski jumps for height are the twin radio masts atop Radiomäki hill, between the train station (a fifteen minute walk away) and the town centre. Steep pathways wind uphill towards the **Radio and Television Museum** (*Radio Ja TV Museo*; Mon–Fri 10am–5pm, Sat & Sun 11am–5pm; €4.30), inside the original transmitting station at the base of one of the masts. Here, two big rooms are packed with bulky Marconi valves, crystal sets, antiquated sound-effect discs, room-sized amplifiers and intriguing curios. Look out for the Pikku Hitler – the German-made "little Hitler", a wartime portable radio that forms an uncanny facsimile of the dictator's face.

At Radiomäki's foot, the distinctive red brickwork of Eliel Saarinen's **town hall** injects some style into the concrete blocks that make central Lahti so dull and uniform. Built in 1912, many of its Art Nouveau features were considered immensely daring at the time, and although most of the originals were destroyed in World War II, careful refurbishment has re-created much of Saarinen's design. Viewable during office hours, the modish interior is definitely worth seeing. Lahti's other notable building is at the far end of Mariankatu, which cuts through the town centre from the town hall: the **Ristinkirkko** (daily 10am–6pm), whose white roof slopes down from the bell tower in imaginative imitation of the local ski jumps. Interestingly, this was the last church to be designed by Alvar Aalto: he died during its construction and the final work was overseen by his wife. Outside, Wäinö Aaltonen's discreetly emotive sculpture marks the war graves in the cemetery.

By now you've more or less exhausted Lahti, although Hämeenkatu, running parallel to the far more hectic Aleksanterinkatu, contains a number of little galleries owned by local artists, and a few secondhand bookshops. The **Art Museum** (Mon–Fri 10am–5pm, Sat & Sun 11am–5pm; €4.30), just around the corner at Vesijärvenkatu 11, exhibits nineteenth- and twentieth-century works, most notably by Gallen-Kallela and Edelfelt.

Finally, near a hazardous web-like junction by the bus station and hidden behind a line of trees, is the wooden nineteenth-century **Lahti Manor**. Now a historical museum (Mon–Fri 10am–5pm, Sat & Sun 11am–5pm; €4.30), it contains regional paraphernalia, numerous Finnish medals and coins, plus an unexpected hoard of French and Italian paintings and furniture.

Practicalities

The **tourist office** is at Aleksanterinkatu 13 (Mon–Thurs 9am–5pm, Fri 9am–4pm; ☎03/877 677, ⊛www.lahtitravel.fi). Both the tourist office and the library at Kirkkokatu 31 (Mon–Fri 10am–6pm, Sat 10am–3pm) provide free Internet access. There are some good budget **accommodation** options in Lahti. A decent choice is the *Patria* hostel at Vesijärvenkatu 3 (☎03/782 3783, ☏782 3793), near the train station, which has double rooms (②) only. In summer, try the excellent *Kansanopiston Kesähotelli* (☎03/878 1181, ☏878 1234; June to mid-Aug) also with doubles (②) and dorms (€21) in a very central position in the town's vocational school at Harjukatu 46. For more luxury the *Sokos Hotel Lahden Seurahuone*, Aleksanterinkatu 14, boasts a sauna and pool, and TV and video in all rooms (☎03/851 11, ⊛www.sokoshotels. fi; ④/⑤). About 4km to the north of Lahti at **Mukkula**, reached directly by bus #30 from the bus station at the end of Aleksanterinkatu, is a lakeside **campsite** (☎03/874 1442, ⊛www.mukkulacamping.fi; June–Aug) with cottages (②).

Low-priced **eating** options include *Serdika* at Hämeenkatu 21, which not only claims to be the cheapest steakhouse in Lahti but also serves up some tasty and otherwise hard-to-find Bulgarian food, while the best place for cakes and pastries is the central *Sinuhe*, Mariankatu 21. You'll find the larger **supermarkets** clustered along Savonkatu. Though hardly remarkable for its nightlife, Lahti can hold its own compared to smaller towns in the Lake Region. For an evening **drink**, the best place is undoubtedly *Restaurant Taivaanranta*, Rautatienkatu 13, which makes its own beer, blueberry cider and whisky. Otherwise try the lively *Memphis* in the *Sokos Hotel Lahden Seurahuone* (see above), or *Diva*, at Hämeenkatu 16.

Lying so close to Helsinki, **train and bus connections** onwards from Lahti are good. Mikkeli, to the north, is the sensible target if you're ultimately making for Kuopio, while Lappeenranta is a better destination if you're keen to discover the small towns and glorious scenery of the eastern Lake Region, and makes an enjoyable stop en route to Savonlinna.

Mikkeli

In 1986 a Helsinki bank robber chose the market square in **MIKKELI** as the place in which to blow up himself, his car and his hostage. This, the most violent event seen in Finland for decades, was perhaps an echo of Mikkeli's blood-spattered past. In prehistoric times the surrounding plains were battlegrounds for feuding tribes from east and west, and the Finnish Infantry has a long association with the town, and it was from Mikkeli that General Mannerheim conducted the campaign against the Soviet Union in the Winter War.

Military matters are a strong local feature, but you don't need to be a bloodthirsty warmonger to find interest in the town's military collections – the insights they provide into Finland's recent history can be fascinating. More generally, Mikkeli lacks the heavy industry you'll find in some Lake Region communities, functioning instead as a district market town (the daily crowds and activity within its market hall – *kauppahalli* – seem out of all proportion to its size), while sporting a handsome cathedral and a noteworthy art collection.

The military museums

Older Finns visiting Mikkeli tend to make a beeline for Ristimäenkatu, where the office used by Mannerheim is preserved as the **Headquarters Museum** (May–Aug daily 10am–5pm; rest of the year Fri–Sun 10am–5pm; €4). It's not so much the exhibits that give the museum its significance – the centrepiece is Mannerheim's desk, holding his spectacles and favourite cigars – but the fact that

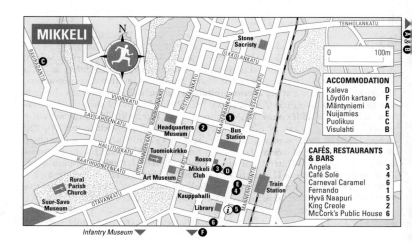

the Winter War, which effectively prevented a Soviet invasion of Finland in 1939 (see p.671), was waged and won from this very room. An adjoining room on the ground floor has photo displays and a not-to-be-missed English-language video which offers a first-class account of the predicament Finland found itself in during the Winter War. For more Mannerheim, peek through the windows of his **saloon car** at the railway station, which clocked up an impressive 78,000km during the war years when the General used it to travel around Finland – sadly, the carriage interior is only open for viewing on Mannerheim's birthday (June 4).

When not travelling, Mannerheim spent much of his time at the **Mikkeli Club**, a cross between a speakeasy and a Masonic lodge, which still exists, occupying what is now part of the Sokos department store on Hallituskatu, facing the *kauppahalli*. The club's walls are lined with photos of Mannerheim and his staff, although less prominence is given to the snaps of the Marshal riding with Hitler during the Führer's birthday visit (these are in an unmarked folder usually lying on a side table). The club is not strictly open to the public, but *Sokos Hotel Vaakuna* (see p.757) can arrange for interested individuals to be shown around.

A few minutes' walk south from the town centre is the **Infantry Museum**, Jääkärinkatu 6–8 (*Jalkaväkimuseo*; May–Aug daily 10am–5pm; Sept–Dec Fri–Sun noon–4pm; €4), which records the key armed struggles that marked Finland's formative years as an independent nation. Assorted rifles, artillery pieces and maps of troops' movements provide the factual context, but it's the scores of frontline photos and display cases of troops' letters and lucky charms that reveal the human story. A second, substantially less interesting section of the museum concentrates chiefly on the Finnish role in the United Nations Peace-Keeping Force.

The rest of the town

Raised in 1897, Mikkeli's Gothic Revival **Tuomiokirkko** (daily: June–Aug 10am–6pm; Sept–May 10–11am) sits primly on a small hill in the middle of Hallituskatu. Inside, Pekka Halonen's 1899 altarpiece attracts the eye, a radiant Christ against a dark, brooding background. Take a close look, too, at Antii Salmenlinna's stained-glass windows and you'll spot depictions of three Finnish towns (Viipuri, Sortavala and Käkisalmi) ceded to Russia after World War II.

Opposite the cathedral, the excellent **Art Museum**, at Ristimäenkatu 5A (Tues–Sun 10am–5pm, Sat 10am–1pm; €3), stages some engaging temporary exhibitions of the latest Finnish art, and has two permanent displays of artworks bequeathed to the town. The Martti Airio Collection is a forceful selection of early twentieth-century Finnish impressionism and expressionism – Tyko Saalinen's *Young American Woman* and *On the Visit* are particularly striking. The museum's other benefactor was the Mikkeli-born sculptor Johannes Haapasalo, who bequeathed nearly three hundred finished works and over a thousand sketches. One of Haapasalo's better works can be seen beside the cathedral: called *Despair*, it marks the graves of Mikkeli's Civil War dead.

If you've ever wondered how vergers in eighteenth-century Finland kept their church congregations awake, the answer (a big stick) can be seen at the tiny **Stone Sacristy**, to the north at Porrassalmenkatu 32A (July daily 11am–5pm; other times by appointment on ☎015/194 2424; free); the church which the sacristy served was demolished in 1776. Several other historic items from the Mikkeli diocese sit in the room, a wooden pulpit, a "shame bench" (for women deemed unvirtuous) and a wood-framed bible among them.

A fifteen-minute walk from the town centre along Otavankatu (easily combined with a visit to the Infantry Museum) leads to the **Rural Parish Church** (mid-June to mid-Aug daily 11am–5pm), believably claimed to be one of the largest wooden churches in Finland. Size aside, the church is a modest sight, but is a more satisfying time-filler than the small stone building in its grounds which houses the **Suur-Savo Museum** (May–Aug Tues–Fri 10am–5pm, Sat 2–5pm; Sept–April Wed 10am–5pm, Sat 2–5pm; €2), a hotchpotch of broken clocks, cracked crockery, and even a bent-wheeled penny-farthing bicycle, which purports to be a record of regional life.

Practicalities

The **train and bus stations** are each a block away from the *kauppatori*, the southern corner of which is opposite the **tourist office**, at Porrassalmenkatu 15 (June to mid-Aug Mon–Fri 9am–5.30pm, Sat 9am–2pm; mid-Aug to May Mon 9am–5pm, Tues–Fri 9am–4.30pm; ☎0203/700 71, ⊛www.travel.mikkeli.fi). Free **Internet** access is available at the library (Mon–Fri 10am–8pm, Sat 9am–2pm), opposite the tourist office at Raatihuoneenkatu 6.

Of Mikkeli's **hotels**, the best deal is the newly-rebuilt *Puolikuu* residence hall, 1km west of the centre at Raviradantie 8 (☎2041 441; ❶; look for the sign "Aikuiskoulutuskeskus asuntola") – rooms must be booked ahead, as the hall is not staffed and the key is left with the *Kahvila Pauliina* café at the corner of Savilahdenkatu and Raviradantie. Two good middle-range choices are the plainish, functional accommodations at *Kaleva* (☎015/206 1500, ☏015/206 1415; ❸), on the north face of the *kauppatori*, and the cheery and spacious rooms at *Nuijamies* (☎015/321 150, ⊛www.hotellinuijamies.com; ❹/❻), Porrassalmenkatu 21, some of which look onto the square. The nearest official **youth hostel**, one of the most beautiful in the country, *Löydön kartano* (☎015/664 101, ⊛personal.inet.fi/yritys/kartano) lies 20km to the south, at Kartanontie 151 just outside **Ristiina** (5 or 6 Kouvola-bound buses a day stop there). This family-run hostel occupies a large, atmospheric pink-painted wooden house, for two hundred years home to an aristocratic Russian general and his descendants, who bought it in 1752. Beds are €14.50 and a generous breakfast costs €5. Mikkeli also has a couple of nearby **campsites** outfitted with cabins and bungalows: *Visulahti* (☎015/18 281, ⊛www.visulahti.com; mid-May to mid-Aug), 5km from the centre (a convoluted bus ride – get details of services at the bus station or tourist office); and *Mäntyniemi*, Ihastjärventie 40B (☎015/174 220, ⊛www.gasthausmantyniemi.fi), 7km north of the centre (no public transport).

When it comes to **eating**, a tasty range of pizzas, fish and pasta dishes are served up by the mid-priced *Hyvä Naapuri*, Raatihuoneenkatu 4, and *Café Sole* on Porrassalmenkatu, opposite the *kauppatori*, serves filling, cheap lunches. If you want excellent pizza (€8) try *Angela*, a Turkish-run place between the bus station and the *kauppatori*. Excellent Mexican food (tacos €10.20, fajitas €15.90) can be found at *Fernando*, Maaherrankatu 17. Of an evening, locals gravitate towards *King Creole* at Vuorikatu 11, a spacious bar which also serves simple burger meals for €4. On the other end of town at Porrassalmenkatu 10, Mikkeli's youth dance the night away at *Carneval Caramel*, while next door the sedate *McCork's Public House* pours €5 draughts of Hoegaarden and Beamish. The main square hosts a particularly good daily market selling fresh breads, fish, fruit and snacks.

Lappeenranta and around

Likeable **LAPPEENRANTA** (Villmanstrand in Swedish) provides an excellent first taste of the eastern Lake Region, conveniently sited on the main rail line between Helsinki and Joensuu and along all the eastern bus routes. It's a small, slow-paced town where summer evenings find most of the population strolling around the linden tree-lined harbour. Once holding a key position on the Russian border, Lappeenranta boasts historical features that its neighbouring towns don't share, and provides an eye-opening introduction to political conflicts that not only affected medieval Finland but also had an impact on recent generations.

It's a twenty-minute walk from the train station, and ten minutes from the bus station, through the town centre to the harbour, where the main activity is strolling and snacking from the numerous stands selling the local specialities – spicy meat pastries called *vetyjä* and *atomeja*. If you're feeling more energetic, climb the steep path on the harbour's western side, which brings you to the top of the town's old

△ Lappeenranta fortress

earthen ramparts and into the Russian-built fortress area, where Lappeenranta's past soon becomes apparent. Its origins as a trading centre reach back to the mid-seventeenth century, but it was with the westward shift of the Russian border in 1721 that the town found itself at the frontline of Russian–Swedish conflicts. After the Peace of Turku in 1743, the border was again moved, this time leaving Lappeenranta inside Russian territory. Subsequently, a garrison of the Tsar's army arrived and, by 1775, had erected most of the stone buildings of the **fortress**, which sits on the short headland that forms the western wall of the harbour. You can buy a joint ticket for both the South Karelian museums (€6; see below) inside the fortress.

Several of these structures still line the cobblestoned Kristiinankatu, which leads across the headland before descending to the shores of the lake, three of them housing museums. Unless you've a particular interest in the military role of horses and the uniforms worn by their riders, however, the collections of the **Cavalry Museum** (June–Aug Mon–Fri 10am–6pm, Sat & Sun 11am–5pm; rest of the year by appointment on ☎05/616 2257; €2.50) can safely be ignored. A better quick stop is the **Orthodox Church** (June to mid-Aug Tues–Sun 10am–6pm; rest of the year by appointment on ☎05/451 5511), just opposite, where the glow of beeswax candles helps illuminate the icons of what is Finland's oldest Orthodox church, founded in 1785.

Step back across Kristiinankatu and you're outside the **South Karelian Art Museum** (June–Aug Mon–Fri 10am–6pm, Sat & Sun 11am–5pm; Sept–May Tues–Sun 11am–5pm; €5), which rotates its permanent stock of paintings with south Karelian connections – mostly a mundane bunch of landscapes and portraits, although some important Finnish artists are represented – and stages exhibitions of emerging regional artists in an adjoining building. Much more rewarding, however, is the **South Karelian Museum** (same hours; €5) towards the end of Kristiinankatu. Surprisingly, it isn't collections from Lappeenranta that form the main displays here, but ceramics, souvenirs and sporting trophies from Viipuri, the major Finnish town 60km from Lappeenranta that was ceded to the Soviet Union after World War II (see the box on p.748). Many of those who left Viipuri to stay on the Finnish side of the border began their new lives in Lappeenranta, and it's mostly they who shed a tear when looking at these reminders (including a large-scale model of their home town). Elsewhere in the museum are numerous Karelian costumes, subtle differences in which revealed the wearer's religion and (for women) marital status, and worthy displays on hunting, farming and traditional handicrafts.

Practicalities

The **tourist office**, looking out over the *kauppatori*, is at Kievarinkatu 1 (℡05/667 788, ℻www.lappeenranta.fi; June–Aug Mon–Fri 8am–5pm, Sept–May Mon–Fri 10am–4.30pm). There's also a small tourist booth open by the harbour in summer (℡05/411 8853, daily June to mid-Aug 9am–8/9pm). There's free Internet access at the town library, Valtakatu 47 (June to mid-Aug Mon–Fri 10am–6pm; rest of the year Mon–Fri 10am–8pm).

Lappeenranta is easily covered in a day, though you may need to stay overnight between transport links. The pick of several high-standard **hotels** is *Sokos Lappee*, Brahenkatu 1 (℡05/678 61, ℻www.sokoshotels.fi; ❹/❻), and the *Cumulus*, Valtakatu 31 (℡05/677 811, ℻www.cumulus.fi; ❹/❻). There are also some cheaper **guest-houses**, such as the summer *Citi Motel Lappee*, Kauppakatu 52 (℡05/415 0800, ℻415 0804; ❷). The town's two **youth hostels** are 2km west of the centre: *Karelia Park*, Korpraalinkuja 1 (℡05/453 0405, ℻452 8454; June–Aug; dorms €14), and *Huhtiniemi*, Kuusimäenkatu 18 (℡05/453 1888, ℻www.huhtiniemi.com; June–Aug; dorms €20), which is also where you'll find the local **campsite** (same phone number). Both hostels also have double rooms (❶/❷); those at Huhtiniemi are available year-round.

Reward yourself after a tour of the fortress area with coffee and a home-baked pie or cake at the colourfully-decorated ⚜ *Café Majurska*, close to the Orthodox

---

Viipuri

Before it was ceded to the Soviet Union in 1944, **VIIPURI** (Vyborg in Russian and Swedish) was one of Finland's most prosperous and cosmopolitan towns. Once a major port, being the Saimaa waterway's main link to the Baltic Sea, with a mixed population of Finns, Swedes, Russians and Germans, the town's fortunes declined under Soviet administration. Lack of investment (Viipuri was never allowed to challenge Leningrad's place as the USSR's major western seaport) resulted in a dearth of new construction, and allowed many of the town's once elegant structures to reach advanced states of dilapidation.

Viipuri today has a strange, time-locked quality – a crumbling reminder both of the conflicts that have enveloped the region and of the fading power of the Soviet Union. There's still a host of medieval buildings, the magnificent Alvar Aalto public library, and an enthralling covered market, while Lenin's statue continues to stand in the town's Red Square. But the depths to which the great Russian Bear has fallen are self-evident, with the town's entire infrastructure seemingly in danger of imminent collapse and aggressive-looking moneychangers clutching wads of hard currency on street corners.

From Lappeenranta, there's a **daily bus** to Viipuri (€24 return), which continues to St Petersburg (€62 return). Russian visas, which can take up to ten days to acquire, are needed for this journey. An alternative is a **visa-free day-trip by boat** (€46) from Lappeenranta, though Americans, Canadians and other non-EU or non-Scandinavian citizens must apply for a separate visa at least a week beforehand (€70). There is usually one daily sailing between mid-May and mid-September, and it's best to reserve as far in advance as possible (at least one week) as these trips get booked up early; if you do call with the hope of a last-minute booking, try asking if there have been any cancellations, but remember all bookings must be finalized the night before the cruise. Boats depart the main harbour at 8am. Contact Saimaa Matkaverkko (℡05/541 0100, ℻www.saimaatravel.fi) for tickets and more details.

Church on Linnoitus. Sour rye bread and the softer *rieska* bread are easily found in Lappeenranta's marketplace or by the harbour, where you'll also find stuffed waffles as well as *atomeja* and *vetyjä* pastries. For more substantial **eating**, try the fair-priced pizzas at *Suzan Kebab Pizzeria*, Kirkkokatu 8, or the tasty fish dishes at *Serra*, Satamatie 4, facing the harbour. A good choice for affordable pizzas, meat, fish and vegetarian dishes is *Huviretki* at the *Cumulus* hotel, Valtakatu 31; or there's excellent Finnish food on offer at around €10 per dish at *Grammari*, Kauppakatu 41. For **drinking**, you might venture to the eclectic wild-west atmosphere at *Totem*, Raatimiehenkatu 17, but the best chance of finding a full pub is the Irish-style *Old Park*, Valtakatu 36. During long summer evenings, locals head instead to the harbour where you can catch the last rays and enjoy a beer on the deck of the *Prinsessa Armaada*.

Around Lappeenranta

Northeast of Lappeenranta, the forests grow denser whilst the road straddles the tranquil Saimaa lake to the west and the increasingly more proximate Russian border to the east. If you're looking for outdoor adventure, there won't be much for you in the moderately sized industrial town of **IMATRA**, which offers little more of interest than the summer Rapids Shows (mid-June to mid-Aug Wed–Sun 7pm), sound-and-light affairs in the evenings above the fierce, gushing Vuoksi river. Instead, push on through for another 57 kilometres to the small town of **PARIKKALA**. Heavily wooded with oak and maple trees, the surrounding forested area offers ample opportunities for hiking, boating and goggling at the numerous species of birds – over 280 at last count – that call this part of Finland home. Solo exploration is possible, though you might be better off with a local who knows the area; try contacting the knowledgeable birder Hanna Aalto (℡050 524 6597, ℠www.ornio.net) or ask at either of the accommodations options listed below. Arriving without a car can be problematic, as the town centre, wherein lie the train and bus stations, is several kilometres from any decent places to stay. Tourist information is a ten-minute walk from the station at Harjukuja 6 (℡05/686 11; ℠www.parinet.fi). Your best choices for **accommodation** are two small places just outside of town: *Laatokan Portti* (℡05/449 282, ℠www.laatokanportti.com), six kilometres south of the centre, offers double rooms (❸) as well as smaller *aitta* ("granary") rooms (❷). Run by a Finnish-born American, it's a wonderfully idyllic setting, with a large wooden deck at the lakes edge; you can also rent boats and fishing gear for around €12 per day. There are slightly more comfortable rooms, as well as a lakeside sauna and indoor swimming pool, a few kilometres north from *Laatokan Portti* at the rustic *Karjalan Lomahovi* (℡040/518 8220). The friendly staff here can also arrange year-round **horse-and-carriage** trips (2hrs; €25) along the Russian border from the nearby thoroughbred farm in Kolmekanta, as well as **snowmobiling** tours (1hr; €40). Both of these guesthouses offer hearty, well-portioned meals to both guests and non-guests. In terms of other **eating** options in the area, you're pretty much limited to €12 lunchtime dishes like lasagna and potato gratin at *Kaakonranta*, Parikkalantie 19, also a **bar** hangout for local old-timers winning big on the electronic poker machines.

Mother nature aside, there's little else in Parikkala to hold your interest – the town's church is mostly modernised inside and holds little of real interest – though you might fancy a **lake tour** (℡050-528-3864; 1hr 40min; €12) aboard the m/s *Princess of Saimaa*. The old passenger junk plies lake Simpele at 11am, 1pm and 3pm daily between June and August, departing from the tiny dock behind the *Kaakonranta* restaurant.

Savonlinna and around

Draped across a series of tightly connected islands, **SAVONLINNA** is one of the most relaxed towns in Finland. Formerly sustained by its woodworking industries

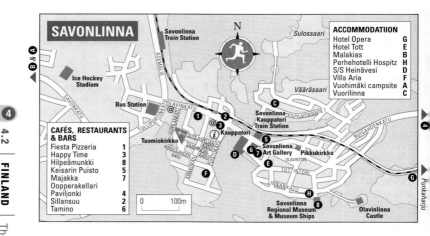

and position at a major junction on the Saimaa route, the town nowadays prospers on the income generated from tourism, and the cultural kudos derived from its annual international opera festival. It's packed throughout July (when the opera festival takes place) and early August, but on either side of the peak season the town's streets and numerous small beaches are uncluttered. The easy-going mood, enhanced by the slow glide of pleasure craft in and out of the harbour, makes Savonlinna a superb base for a two- or three-day stay, giving ample time to soak up the mellow atmosphere, discover the local sights and curiosities – such as a remarkable modern art centre and a huge nineteenth-century church – that lie within the town's idyllic surrounds.

The Town

Savonlinna's centrally placed passenger harbour and *kauppatori* are pleasant spots to mingle with the crowds and enjoy a snack from one of the numerous **food stalls** – ask for a *lörtsy*, a local pie which comes in two varieties: savoury with meat and rice, or sweet with apple jam and sugar. Within a few strides, you might poke your head inside the **Savonlinna Art Gallery**, Olavinkatu 40 (Tues–Sun 11am–5pm, July also Mon same hours; €2), which provides a spacious home for temporary shows usually mounted in tandem with those at the Savonlinna Regional Museum (see p.751); or the smartly restored **Pikkukirkko** (June to mid-Aug daily 11am–5pm), a Lutheran church which began life serving the Greek Orthodox faithful.

Fine as these places may be, however, none of them holds a candle to Savonlinna's greatest possession: the engrossing **Olavinlinna Castle** (daily: June to mid-Aug 10am–5pm; mid-Aug to May 10am–3pm; €5), a fifteen-minute walk from the harbour at the end of Linnankatu. Perched on a small island and looking like some great grey sea monster surfacing from the deep, the castle was founded in 1475 to guard this important lake-transport junction at the eastern extremity of what was then the Swedish empire – a region being eyed by an expansionistic Russia. The Swedes built walls five metres thick to resist attack on the eastern side, but the castle was to switch hands fairly frequently in later years; the last change saw the Russians moving in after the westward shift of the border that followed the 1743 Peace of Turku. They added the incongruous Adjutant's Apartment which, with its bright yellow walls and curved windows, resembles a large piece of Emmenthal cheese. With military importance lost when Finland became a Russian Grand Duchy in 1809, the castle ended its pre-restoration days rather ignominiously as the town jail.

The castle can only be visited on guided **tours** (in English), included in the admission fee and offered hourly during the summer, less frequently in other months. The guides' commentary is a vital aid to comprehending the complex historical twists and turns that the castle endured, and for pointing out the numerous oddities, such as the sole original indoor toilet in the maiden's chamber, through which there's a sheer drop to the lake below.

Occupying an 1852 granary a stone's throw from the castle, the **Savonlinna Regional Museum** (July to early Aug daily 11am–5pm; rest of the year Tues–Sun 11am–5pm; €5, ticket also covers the art gallery – see opposite) presents one of the Lake Region's better accounts of the evolution of local life, beginning with an intriguing display on the prehistoric rock paintings found near Savonlinna. The bulk of the museum's collection charts hunting and farming techniques, and the birth of the area's tar and logging industries, although the upper level holds temporary art exhibitions, often culled from the country's most interesting private collections.

Outside, docked at the end of a jetty, are three c.1900 steamers known as the **Museum Ships** (June–Aug only, same times as regional museum; admission with same ticket), which earned their keep plying the Saimaa waterways, sometimes travelling as far as St Petersburg and Lübeck.

Practicalities

While there are very few trains to Savonlinna, there is a choice of **train stations**: Savonlinna-Kauppatori is by far the most central, although if you're making straight for the *Malakias* youth hostel (see below), get off at Savonlinna, 1km to the west. The **bus station**, served by six buses a day from Mikkeli and Helsinki, is also a short distance west of the centre, just off Olavinkatu. The **tourist office**, Puistokatu 1 (June & Aug daily 9am–5pm; July daily 8am–8pm; rest of the year Mon–Fri 9am–5pm; ☎015/517 510, ⍟www.savonlinnatravel.com), faces the passenger harbour. Staff can point you in the right direction to rent bicycles and also supply useful route maps for cycling in the area. Unusually for a provincial Finnish town, Savonlinna has two **Internet cafés**: *Knut Posse*, Olavinkatu 44, and *Kastelli*, Olavinkatu 53.

Savonlinna has several budget accommodation possibilities and some good **hotels**, but don't expect the big discounts you might find elsewhere, as there's no shortage of summer business, and prices shoot up for the Opera Festival in July. The listings below give the standard rate followed by the higher, festival-time price, where applicable. There's a marked absence of **campsites** in Savonlinna: the nearest is *Vuohimäki* (☎09/613 832 10; June to late Aug), 7km west of the centre and served by bus #3.

When it comes to **eating**, the usual pizza joints line Olavinkatu – *Fiesta Pizzeria* in the courtyard at no. 46 has huge pizzas for just €5. With a bit more to spend you might try the filling Chinese dishes at *Keisarin Puisto*, Olavinkatu 33 (dinner mains around €10, lunch €6). For **Finnish food**, sample the extensive menu at *Majakka*, Satamakatu 11, though mains here start at around €12. The most adventurous place to dine, however, is *Paviljonki*, Rajalahendenkatu 4, where Finland's top trainee chefs serve up their latest creations. The service is excellent, and the food imaginative and well prepared; lunch here costs around €10. *Hilpeämunkki*, 100m or so to the left as you exit the castle, serves very good dishes (€12 and up) in the whittled environs of cow pelts, antler horns and other assorted medieval accoutrements. If you're in town for an opera performance, top the night off with a meal at the cream-of-the-crop, *Oopperakellari*, Kalmarinkatu 10 (☎020 744 3445). Pre- and post-performance set menus of excellent Finnish cuisine are €50, but the excitement really begins when the waiters – many of them local opera students – start bellowing out arias as they prance about the restaurant.

For **drinking** during the festival, all you need do is follow the crowds to see what's on. Outside of opera season, though, nightlife in diminutive Savonlinna is amazingly tranquil, though sooner or later you'll probably end up at *Sillansuu*, Verkkosaarenkatu 1, close to the *kauppatori* and railway station, known for its wide selection of beers. *Happy Time*, nearby at Olavinkatu 36, is the most popular place to imbibe. At the *kauppatori*, the hotel *Seurahuone* contains *Tamino*, about as rocking a nightclub as you're going to find here.

Accommodation

Hotel Opera Kyrönniemenkuja 9 ☎015/521 116; advance bookings when closed on ☎015/476 7515, ☎476 7540. Decent option, just past the castle near the road to Punkaharju. **④**

Hotel Tott Satamakatu 1 ☎015/573 673, ⊛www .savonhotellit.fi. This bland summer-only hotel is a sound if uninspiring choice, offering both rooms and apartments with or without a sauna. **⑤/⑥**

Malakias Pihlajavedenkatu 6 ☎015/533 283, ☎533 283. A summer hotel 2km west of the centre, offering dorms (€22.50) as well as doubles. **③/④**

Perhehotelli Hospitz Linnankatu 20 ☎015/515 661, ☎515 120. Good-value rooms, but you'll need to book ahead as they're very popular. **③/⑤**

S/S Heinävesi Savonlinna Harbour. For an atmospheric summertime option, it's hard to beat the crew quarters of a working steamboat, moored in the harbour overnight once it returns from its day-trips to Punkaharju (see below). The shared-bath cabins are a bit cramped, but loaded with character, and evenings here during the festival are known for being some of the liveliest in town. **①**

Villa Aria Puistokatu 15 ☎020/744 3447. A score of very nice rooms in a renovated wooden building on the lake, just down the street from the tourist office. Summer only. **⑥**

Vuorilinna Kylpylaitoksentie 7, Vääräsaari ☎015/739 5430, ☎272 524. Set on the island linked by a short bridge to the *kauppatori*, the private rooms at this four-star hotel include free use of the sauna and pool. **③/④**

East of Savonlinna: Punkaharju Ridge and beyond

According to local belief, the **Punkaharju Ridge** is the healthiest place to breathe in the world, thanks to an abundance of conifers that super-oxygenate the air. This narrow, seven-kilometre-long thread of land between lakes Puruvesi and Pihlalavesi begins 27km east of Savonlinna, and three roads and a railway line are squeezed onto it. With the water never more than a few metres away on either side, this is the Lake Region at its most beautiful, and is easily reached on any train heading this way from Savonlinna. However, it's also the most hyped destination in Finland, and, although you should make an effort to see the ridge, don't rule out other places further north.

Along the ridge, at the centre of things, you'll find **Lusto**, the national forest museum (May & Sept daily 10am–5pm, June–Aug daily 10am–7pm; Oct–April Tues–Sun 10am–5pm; €7; ⊛www.lusto.fi). Designed, predictably, from wood, its permanent exhibits examine how forests function and survive; there's also a shop stocked with wooden items, though perhaps the best part is the restaurant-café, where you can fill up on sautéed reindeer, fillet of elk and *kuusenkerkkä*, a gloriously rich cake of *smetana*, pine kernels and Lappish berries. For exploring the area further, you can rent bikes here for €5 a day.

It's a better idea to spend the night in Savonlinna than to be stuck out on the ridge, dependent on skeletal public transport to continue your journey. Should you want to stay, the most atmospheric **hotel** is *Punkaharjun Valtionhotelli*, Punkaharju 2 (☎015/739 611, ⊛www.lomaliitto.fi/punkaharju; July **④/⑥**, rest of the year **⑤**), an ornate wooden house on the ridge that still summons up the tsarist era, despite an insipid restoration. Only a little cheaper in season but decidedly ugly is *Gasthaus Punkaharju*, Palomäentie 18 (☎015/473 123, ⊛www.naaranlahti.com; ❸).

Retretti Arts Centre

About 25km southeast from Savonlinna, just before reaching the village of Punkaharju, the main road passes the extraordinary **Retretti Arts Centre** (daily: June & Aug 10am–6pm; July 10am–7pm; €15; ⊛www.retretti.fi), a place devoted to the visual and performing arts. The unique element is the setting – man-made caves gouged into three-billion-year-old rock by the same machines which dug the Helsinki metro – it cost so much to build that the project bankrupted the original owner. Outside, in the large sculpture park, fibreglass human figures by Finnish artist Olavi Lanu entwine cunningly with the forms of nature; tree branches suddenly become human limbs, and plain-looking boulders slowly mutate under your gaze into a pile of male and female torsos. Inside the caves, the exhibitions are changed every year, with artists developing site-specific projects to complement the dramatic setting. The interior also features underground streams, whose gushings and bubblings underpin the music piped into the air. There are also several aboveground sites that show work from well-known European masters – the last few years have seen major displays by Cézanne, Monet, Repin and Munch.

The few daily **trains** between Savonlinna and Parikkala call at Retretti train station; their timings can be very inconvenient, however, and buses provide a more reliable alternative. Another option, though an expensive one (€25 return), is to travel by **boat** from Savonlinna's passenger harbour via the *S/S Heinävesi*, which departs at 11am, and returning from Punkaharju at 3.30pm (mid-June to mid-Aug only). All these transport details should be checked at the tourist office as they can occasionally fluctuate. One way to enjoy the art without keeping an eye on your watch is to stay virtually next door at *Punkaharjun Lomakeskus* (☎015/739 611, ℻441 784; ❻), an extensive camping area with simple cabins (❷) and fully equipped cottages (❻) as well.

Kerimäki kirkko

Though, like Retretti, it lies to the east of Savonlinna (23km distant), the village of **Kerimäki** is nearly impossible to reach by public transport without first returning to Savonlinna, from where there are several daily buses (check the latest details at the tourist office). The reason to come to this otherwise unremarkable village on the shores of Lake Puruvesi is to see the **Kerimäki kirkko** (May 10am–4pm; June 10am–6pm, July 10am–7pm, early Aug 10am–6pm, mid-Aug to late Aug 10am–4pm), an immense wooden construction built in 1848 to hold 3000 people, and claimed to be the largest wooden church in the world. Complete with double-tiered balconies, and a yellow- and white-painted exterior beaming through the surrounding greenery, it's a truly astonishing sight. Kerimäki can be a pleasant place to spend a quiet couple of days: there's a nice little place to swim and a decent guesthouse, the *Kerihovi* (☎015/541 225; ❸), which has a traditional bar/restaurant that offers home-cooking and alcoholic beverages.

Varkaus, Valamo Monastery and Joensuu

Due to the preponderance of water in the vicinity, **train connections** around Savonlinna are extremely limited, only running east to Parikkala to link with Helsinki and Joensuu-bound express trains. However, **buses** (accepting train tickets and passes) operate from Savonlinna to **Pieksämäki**, the major rail junction in central Finland from where there are good connections north to Kuopio, Kajaani and Oulu, west to Jyväskylä, Vaasa, Tampere and Turku and east to the industrial town of **Varkaus**, which lies on the Turku–Joensuu line. In all cases, the latest timetables should be carefully checked before making plans. **Valamo Monastery,** situated off the railway line between Varkaus and Joensuu, makes for an intriguing stop, but one fraught with difficulties unless you have your own transport.

Varkaus

The sawmills and engineering factories that dominate diminutive but commercially important **VARKAUS** sit amid gentle hills and dense forests. On a good day, the billowing chimneys and steel pipes are attractively mirrored in the placid waters of the town's lakes; on a bad day, unwelcome smells fill the air and there can be few Finnish towns where nature seems so obviously to be losing the battle against heavy industry. Even if you hate Varkaus on arrival, stick around long enough to see the canal and mechanical music museums: both, in their very different ways, are unique.

The Town

In such a place, it seems appropriate that the **Varkaus kirkko**, about a kilometre east of town on Savontie 3 (early June to late Aug daily 9am–7pm; rest of the year by appointment only on ☎017/578 5205), should be designed in a severe functional style. Inside, the church is notable less for its architecture than for an immense altar fresco. Measuring almost 300 square metres, it was painted – with the aid of several helpers and a large amount of scaffolding – by revered Finnish artist Lennart Stegerstråle.

A short walk from the church at Savontie 7, a group of yellow wooden buildings from 1916 hold the **Museum of Working Class Housing Conditions** (*Työväenasuntomuseo*; early June to late Aug Tues, Thurs & Sun 11am–4pm, Wed 2–7pm; other times by appointment only on ☎017/579 4440; €3), comprising a briefly interesting succession of single rooms furnished to show typical living conditions from the 1920s (when Varkaus factory labourers kept pigs and cows to remind them of their country origins) to the 1960s. The **Museum of Esa Pakarinen**, in the same complex (same times as above; same ticket valid), remembers a tremendously popular Finnish comic actor of the postwar years who was a Varkaus resident. Pakarinen's forte was playing the fool (he rejoiced in the on-screen nickname "wood head") and singing with his false teeth removed. Besides assorted mementos of his glittering career, a TV runs videos of Pakarinen's finest films – though the subtleties are well and truly lost on non-Finnish speakers.

A fifteen-minute walk from Savontie along factory-dominated Ahlströminkatu brings you to the **Varkaus Museum**, Wredenkatu 5A (Tues & Thurs 10am–4pm, Wed noon–7pm, Sun 11am–5pm; €2), which provides some proof – with displays on the beginnings of local settlements and early agricultural life – that Varkaus did exist before the discovery of iron ore in local river beds set the town on course to becoming an engineering powerhouse. Much of the museum, however, charts the rise and rise of the local firm founded in 1909 by Walter Ahlström (after whom most things in the town appear to be named); by the 1950s, the company was – and continues to be – among the world's leading innovators in industrial machinery.

The canal and mechanical music museums

Leaving the town centre on Taipaleentie takes you over the rapids that made lake transport around Varkaus difficult until 1835, when a rough canal was built a kilometre east of the ferocious waters (look for the tower above the locks of the modern-day Taipale Canal). Following successive poor harvests, emergency labour was used to build a second, wider canal in 1867. Before this task was completed, 227 labourers had died from hunger or disease and been buried in mass graves; their final resting places can still be seen at the end of a rough track on Varkausmäki hill, some 7km from Varkaus. Rather than make the long and morbid trek to the grave sites, however, a visit to the **National Central Canal Museum**, inside a former warehouse beside the modern canal (June–Aug daily 10am–6pm; Sept–May by appointment on ☎017/579 4440; €2), provides all the background you'll need on the building of the Varkaus canals and the growth of canals generally in Finland. It's less drab than you might expect: the early canals not only opened up important new transport routes in the pre-motorized days, but had strategic importance in the border disputes between Finland and Russia.

Close to the canal museum, the bizarre and superb **Museum of Mechanical Music**, Pelimanninkatu 8 (June & July daily 11am–6pm; Aug to mid-Dec & March–May Tues–Sat 11am–6pm, Sun 11am–5pm; €10; @www.mekaanisenmusiik inmuseo.fi), is really more of a personal show than a museum, with the eccentric German curator and his family singing along with the extraordinary collection of 250 music-making devices – from an ancient pianola to a prototype stereo gramophone – gathered from all over Europe and restored to working order.

Practicalities

From the **bus and train terminals** on Relanderinkatu, it's a walk of just a few minutes to Kauppakatu, Varkaus's main street. To reach the **tourist office** at Kauppatori 6 (Mon–Fri 9am–4.30pm; ☎017/579 4944, @www.varkaus.fi/matkailu), however, you'll need to walk for a further ten minutes along Taipaleentie across the bridge. The well-stocked library (Mon–Thurs 10am–7pm, Fri 10am–6pm) on Osmajoentie has free **Internet** access.

There's little incentive to spend longer than you have to in Varkaus, but if you do need to **stay overnight**, try the adequate but old-fashioned (and receptionless) *Keskus-Hotelli*, Ahlströminkatu 18 (④/③), which has a wonderful mirrored entrance hall. If you want to get in touch with the *Keskus* then you need to contact the more modern *Oscar*, around the corner at Kauppatori 4 (☎017/579 011, ⓕ579 0500; ⑥/⑤), which handles reservations for both hotels. A more basic alternative is *Joutsenkulma*, Käämeniementie 20 (☎017/366 9797, ⓕ366 9798; ③). The recently renovated **youth hostel**, *Varkauden Retkeilymaja* (☎017/579 5700, ⓔretkeilymaja@varkaus.fi), Kuparisepänkatu 5, offers clean dorm beds for €14.30. More budget accommodation can be found at the *Taipale* **campsite** (☎017/552 6644, @www.campingtaipale.com; June–Aug), 3km west of town on Leiritie, which has cabins (②) as well as pitches.

Varkaus isn't the nation's culinary hot spot, but you can find snacks and good coffee at *NekkAmo Kafé*, Kauppakatu 41, or a filling €5 takeaway meal at the *Dahong* Chinese restaurant, Ahlströminkatu 10. For something nicer, the colourful restaurant inside the *Oscar* hotel (see above) offers a tasty rosemary reindeer filet for €27.50.

Valamo Monastery

The original **Valamo Monastery**, on an island in Lake Ladoga, was the spiritual headquarters of Orthodox Karelia from the thirteenth century onwards. In 1940, however, with Soviet attack imminent, the place was abandoned and rebuilt well inside the Finnish border, roughly halfway between Varkaus and Joensuu. One of only two Eastern Orthodox cloisters in Finland, today's Valamon Monastery (☎017/570 1504, @www.valamo.fi) is located halfway between Joensuu and Varkaus, and is one of the most popular destinations in this part of the country. Volunteer workers arrive each summer to assist the monks in their daily tasks, and shorter-term visitors are welcome to imbibe the spiritual atmosphere and enjoy the tranquillity of the setting, though the somewhat austere regime won't suit everyone. Daily English-language guided tours (€3.50) are given on request during the summer, and take in the grounds as well as several churches and chapels housing original accoutrements from the earlier monastery, and provide some informed perspective on the complex. Without transport of your own, however, **getting to the monastery** is not easy. Two daily buses leave from Varkaus for the hour-long journey, one at 1.45pm and another at 7pm (the evening bus does not operate on Saturdays). The return journey departs the monastery daily at 12.15pm, weekdays at 8.30am and weekends at 5.25pm. Both these services operate from Helsinki to

△ Valamo Monastery

Joensuu, calling at Lahti, Mikkeli, Varkaus and the monastery. To get there from other destinations, try contacting the monastery directly. There are both dormitories (€25) and private rooms (**①**) if you want to **stay** overnight.

Joensuu

The capital of what remained of Finnish Karelia after the eastern half was ceded to the Soviet Union in 1944, **JOENSUU** was central to the immigration debate in the 1990s following a spate of racist violence against Somali refugees. The closure of several large industrial plants had plunged the local economy into depression, and as unemployment soared, the sizeable neo-fascist skinhead movement that grew up in Joensuu made the immigrant community a scapegoat for the social problems that accompanied the decline. While the city's economy isn't exactly booming these days, anti-immigrant violence is a thing of the past and Joensuu – with a fairly cosmopolitan population and a large student presence – appears to be making a considered effort to welcome all visitors.

Whether you arrive by bus or train (the terminals are adjacent to one another), the kilometre-long walk into the centre of Joensuu is one of the most enjoyable introductions to any Lake Region town: the route crosses the broad Pielisjoki River and bridges Ilosaari island and the narrow Joensuu Canal before reaching Eliel Saarinen's epic Art Nouveau town hall and the wide *kauppatori*. Pleasing first impressions apart, compact and modestly sized Joensuu doesn't have too much beyond the usual round of local museums and churches to fill your time – you can cover it in a day with ease.

The culture and tourist centre, **Carelicum** (Mon–Fri 10am–5pm, Sat & Sun 11am–4pm), in the centre of town at Koskikatu 5, houses the **tourist office** (Mon–Fri 9am–5pm, Sat 11am–4pm; ☎013/267 5319, ⓦwww.jns.fi); staff hand out maps and useful city guides. There's also free Internet access, a **box office** (☎013/267 5222) selling tickets for all the town's theatrical and musical performances, and a decent café and gift shop. Also housed in the centre is the well-organized **North Karelian Museum** (same hours as Carelicum; €4); displays upstairs (many of which have interpretive information in English) trace Karelia's historical position in the middle of an East–West power struggle, with plenty of space given to the ever-changing borders between Russia and Finland. There's also a detailed scale model of early Sortavala (see p.758), now a decaying Russian town but once of great import on account of its seminary and teachers' college, which served as early training grounds for Karelian intellectuals; and diverting ethnographic pieces include a seventh-century Sámi wooden ski and a number of original Karelian women's costumes. Downstairs holds a space for rotating exhibitions about the region, as well as a permanent display on the lives of Finnish artists like Sibelius and Järnefelt who came to Karelia in search of romantic inspiration.

Considering the devastation caused by World War II, Joensuu has a surprising number of intact nineteenth-century buildings. These include the wood-framed structure that used to house the tourist office at Koskikatu, and the red-brick former schoolhouse at Kirkkokatu 23 which holds the **Art Museum** (Wed 11am–8pm; Tues & Thurs–Sun 11am–4pm; €4). The museum's minor pieces and an unexpected crop of Far Eastern and Greek antiquities fail to divert attention from Edelfelt's finely realized portrait, *The Parisienne* – worth the admission fee alone. Some of Finland's more radical new artists get a showing just next door at **Ahjo** (Tues–Fri noon–6pm, Sat & Sun noon–3pm; free). Leaving the art museum and glancing either way along the aptly named Kirkkokatu, you'll spot Joensuu's major churches standing at opposite ends. To the right, the neo-Gothic **Lutheran Church** (June to mid-Aug Mon 11am–4pm; other times by arrangement through the tourist office) can seat a thousand worshippers but, aside from Antti Salmenlinna's impressive stained-glass windows, it's not wildly different from its counterparts in other towns. At the northern end of Kirkkokatu, the **Orthodox Church of Saint Nikolaos** (mid-June to mid-Aug Mon–Fri 10am–4pm; other times by arrangement on ☎013/266 000 or 050/587 5066) is a few years older and much more deserving of a swift peek, with some excellent examples of gilded relief iconography.

If you find yourself with time to spare, take a trip through the cactus-filled greenhouses of Joensuu University's **Botanical Gardens**, Heinäpurontie 70 (April–Aug Mon & Wed–Fri 10am–5pm, Sat & Sun 11am–4pm; Sept–March Mon & Wed–Fri 10am–4pm, Sat & Sun 11am–4pm; €4). In summer the greenhouses are also home to flocks of tropical butterflies which are flown in weekly from Malaysia. Afterwards, you could explore the gardens themselves, which are claimed to hold a specimen of every plant native to northern Karelia – there are many more of these than you might expect. You might also want to cross the bridge from the town centre to Ilosaari, the island which sits between the train station and town centre. The sandy **beach** here is fairly tranquil during the week, but is busy on summer weekends with locals soaking up some much-needed sun.

Practicalities

For an overnight stay, you'll find some very good summer rates at the central and comfortable *Sokos Hotel Vaakuna*, Torikatu 20 (☎013/277 511, ⊛www .sokoshotels.fi; ❹/❺). Cheaper is the central summer hotel *Elli*, Länsikatu 18 (☎013/225 927, ⊛www.summerhotelelli.fi) or, for rock-bottom prices, the scouts-run **hostel**, *Partiotalo* (☎013/123 381, ⊛www.youthhostel-joensuu. net; June–Aug; dorms €15; ❷), located 1km north of the town centre at Vanamokatu 25; the town **campsite** is beside the Pyhäselkä lake at Linnunlahdentie 1 (☎013/126 272, ⊛www.linnunlahticamping.fi; June–Aug) and also has small **cottages** from €35.

Besides the tasty morsels which can be picked up for a few euro inside the *kauppahalli* (beside the *kauppatori*), Joensuu's bargain **eating** options include the usual pizza joints – *Rosso*, Siltakatu 8, is the most dependable. For something more extravagant, try the French and Finnish cuisine and subdued atmosphere provided by an old-fashioned live orchestra at the *Hotel Kimmel* restaurant, Itäranta 1, or the central *Teatteri*, in the city theatre building just east of the market square, which serves hearty continental meat dishes such as *coq au vin* (from €16). For good Hungarian food, head for the *Astoria*, overlooking the river at Rantakatu 32, where

Crossing the Russian border: Sortavala

If you've visited the Carelicum in Joensuu, you'll have seen a scale model of **Sortavala**, one of the many Finnish towns to come under Soviet control following the postwar realignment of the border. Since the collapse of the Soviet Union, it's been possible for Finns (and indeed any other Westerners equipped with Russian visas) to visit the town with comparative ease. Despite occupying a scenic position on the shores of Lake Ladoga, Sortavala itself has no intrinsic appeal whatsoever, and has become even less appealing of late since it developed into a summer sex-tourism hub for Finns on the chase. The **journey from Joensuu to Sortavala** takes nearly four hours and several local tour companies go there in the summer for around €100 including visa, transportation and hotel; get the latest details from the Joensuu tourist office.

you can eat outside in warm weather; this is the most enjoyable restaurant in town by a long chalk.

Two major festivals enliven Joensuu's entertainment calendar. The last weekend of July sees the **Gospel Festival** (@www.suomigospel.net), when thousands of singers turn up from all around Europe. Even bigger, however, is the annual **Ilosaari Rock Festival** (middle weekend of July; @www.ilosaarirock.fi), attracting top Finnish and international acts along with upwards of 20,000 of thrill-seeking Finnish youths. If you're in any doubt as to the sheer scale of these events, take a look at the huge **Song Bowl**, which sits beside the Pyhäselkä lake, just southwest of Joensuu's centre. Tickets to both festivals can be booked via the box office in the Carelicum.

North from Joensuu: Nurmes

Should Joensuu be as rural as you want to get, swing inland (change trains at Pieksämäki) to the more metropolitan Kuopio (see below). Otherwise, continue north from Joensuu into some of the eastern Lake Region's least populated but most scenically spectacular sections, with hilltop views stretching out above the tips of fir trees across watery expanses that stretch far into Russia. The small town of **NURMES**, 120km from Joensuu and linked to it by twice-daily train, is the obvious base for exploration, though you'll need private transport – or a lot of careful juggling with bus local timetables – to find the best of the forested and lake-studded landscape. Superbly quiet and with an appealing location between forest and saturated marshland, Nurmes offers pleasant relief from the comparative bustle of Karelian cities as well as a being well-placed point of departure for destinations further north. There's a useful **tourist office**, though it's several kilometres west of town in the ABC petrol station at Välitie 2–4. (June–July daily 8am–10pm; rest of the year Mon–Fri 8am–5pm; ☏013/248 5613, @www.nurmes.fi); staff can book tickets for local events. Budget **accommodation** in Nurmes can be found at the *Hyvärilä* (☏013/687 2500, @www.hyvarila .com; dorms €15, doubles ❹), Lomatie 12, which is also the location of the town's summer-only **campsite**. There's traditional-style accommodation at the *Bomba House* (☏013/687 2501; @www.bomba.fi; ❸), Suojärvenkatu 1, whose stout lodge building was rebuilt in the image of an 1855 construction. There's also an exceedingly ordinary, central **hotel**, *Nurmeshovi*, Kirkkokatu 21 (☏013/480 750, @www.nurmeshovi.com; ❸). **Moving on** from Nurmes is surprisingly easy for such a relatively remote location – **buses** (accepting train tickets and passes) run to **Kajaani** or Kontiomäki (one stop further north), both of which are on the Kuopio–Oulu train line.

Kuopio

Located on a major inland north–south rail route and the hub of local long-distance bus services, **KUOPIO** has the feel – and, by day, much of the hustle and bustle – of a large city, although it is in fact only marginally bigger than most of the

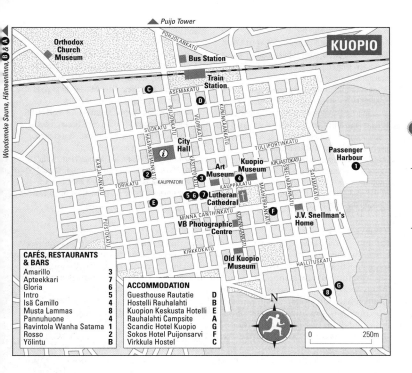

KUOPIO

Puijo Tower

Orthodox
Church
Museum

Bus Station

Train
Station

City
Hall

Art
Museum

Kuopio
Museum

Passenger
Harbour

Lutheran
Cathedral

VB Photographic
Centre

J.V. Snellman's
Home

Old Kuopio
Museum

CAFÉS, RESTAURANTS & BARS	
Amarillo	3
Apteekkari	7
Gloria	6
Intro	5
Isä Camillo	4
Musta Lammas	8
Pannuhuone	4
Ravintola Wanha Satama	1
Rosso	2
Yölintu	B

ACCOMMODATION	
Guesthouse Rautatie	D
Hostelli Rauhalahti	B
Kuopion Keskusta Hotelli	E
Rauhalahti Campsite	A
Scandic Hotel Kuopio	G
Sokos Hotel Puijonsarvi	F
Virkkula Hostel	C

0   250m

other Lake Region communities. Nonetheless, it's an important Finnish town and, especially if you're speeding north to Lapland, provides both a break in the journey and an enjoyable taste of the region. One of the best times to visit is mid June, when the Kuopio Tanssi ja Soi **dance festival** (ⓦ www.kuopiodancefestival.fi) inundates the streets with a week of performances, workshops, classes and the like, turning Kuopio into a veritable mecca of artistic activity. Early July also sees the slightly more bacchanalian **wine festival** (ⓦwww.kuopiowinefestival.com), where a world wine region is selected and fêted in restaurants, bars and other venues all over the city.

Arrival, information and accommodation

Adjacent to one another at the northern end of Puijonkatu, Kuopio's **train and long-distance bus stations** are an easy walk from the town centre. There are good bus and train connections north from Kuopio to Iisalmi (see p.763) and on to Kajaani and Oulu (see the following chapter), as well as with Helsinki and all the main southern towns. The **tourist office** faces the *kauppatori* at Haapaniemenkatu 17 (June to Aug Mon–Fri 9.30am–5pm, plus Sat 10am–3pm in July; Sept–May Mon–Fri 9.30am–4.30pm; ☎017/182 584, ⓦ www.kuopioinfo.fi). If you're in town for more than a day, you'd be well advised to pick up a Kuopio Card from the tourist office (€11), which gets you discounts of up to fifty percent on local museums and attractions, as well as a cruise on Kallavesi lake.

Though Kuopio has no official HI youth hostel, there are a couple of rock-bottom budget accommodation options around the train station, while most of the pricier places are closer to the town centre. The **campsite**, *Rauhalahti* (☎017/312 244; May–Aug), is 500m further south from *Hostelli Rauhalahti*; to get there take bus #7.

Accommodation

Guesthouse Rautatie Vuorikatu 35 ☏017/580 0569. Decent place with no-frills double rooms (and a few singles); reception is at the railway station restaurant. ❸

Hostelli Rauhalahti Katiskaniementie 8 ☏030/608 30, ⦿www.rauhalahti.com. Within a spa complex 4km south of the town centre, the doubles here are quite spacious – if you want real luxury, though, plump for a room in the adjacent spa hotel, which have access to numerous pools, jacuzzis and saunas. Take bus #7 from the *kauppatori*. ❸, spa rooms ❻

Kuopion Keskusta Hotelli Haapaniemenkatu 20 017/261 8800. Set inside the H&M complex opposite the market square, this is a clean

and professional hotel with decent-sized rooms. ❹

Retkeilymaja Virkkula Asemakatu 3 ☏017/263 1839, ⦿www.kuopionsteiner koulu.fi/retkeilymaja_virkkula. Perfectly located a block from the train station, with 26 dorm beds at €15 per night. Summer only.

Scandic Hotel Kuopio Satamakatu 1 ☏017/195 111, ⦿www.scandic-hotels.com. Unsurpassed views of the Kallavesi lake as well as a superb ground-floor sauna and pool. ❺

Sokos Hotel Puijonsarvi Minna Canthinkatu 16 ☏017/170 111, ⦿www.sokoshotels.fi. Stellar, luxurious rooms with lake views and private saunas make this the most luxurious place to stay in town. ❺/❹

The Town

Kuopio's broad *kauppatori*, overlooked by the nineteenth-century city hall, is very much the heart of the town, with live jazz and rock music issuing from its large stage in summer. Walk the kilometre eastwards from here along Kauppakatu, towards the busy passenger harbour on the Kallavesi lake, and you'll pass most things worth seeing in town, with the exception of the extraordinary Orthodox Church Museum (see p.761). Summer lake **cruises** are a great way to take in Kuopio's environs. Leaving from the passenger harbour, the m/s *Osmo* makes daily trips from mid-June to early August (noon, 2pm, 4pm & 6pm; €10–12).

At Kauppakatu 35, the **Kuopio Art Museum** (Tues–Fri 10am–5pm, Wed until 7pm, Sat & Sun 11am–4pm; €2.50; for guided tours call ☏017/182 633) fills a sturdy granite building with an enterprising assortment of contemporary exhibitions and, on the upper floor, keeps a less stimulating stock of twentieth-century Finnish painting with local connections. Further along the same street at no. 23, first glances might suggest that the **Kuopio Museum** (May–Aug Mon–Sat 9am–4pm, Wed until 8pm, Sun 10am–5pm; Sept–April closed Sat; €4), with its turreted

△ Kuopio harbour

battlements, aged stucco exterior and red-hatted towers originally functioned as a neo-medieval castle; in fact, it was purpose-built as a museum in 1807. The collection charts the evolution of local settlements, from motley Stone Age findings to the thousand-and-one uses that tree bark was put to in pre-industrial Finland. The switch from rural to urban life caused great changes in Finnish society, but one thing that remained constant was a dependency on that Nordic speciality, coffee. Using the original fittings, the museum re-creates the Kuopio institution of *Alli Karvonen's* coffee shop, which dispensed the beverage from 1933 to 1969 in cups etched with Finnish landscapes. Unless stuffed reindeer munching plastic lichen and a bleak collection of painted wooden insects set your pulse racing, the rest of the museum can be ignored, though keep an eye out for Juho Rissanen's *The Builders* on the staircase, a massive study of eleven naked Nordic men that still turns many a conservative head. Also within the Kuopio Museum, and included in the entrance fee, the **Museum of Natural History** houses a spectacular, full-size reconstruction of a woolly mammoth, one of only four in the world. Musk oxen hides have been used to simulate the beast's shaggy appearance, based on a real mammoth found in Siberia two hundred years ago. Satisfy yourself instead, however, with the knowledge that there once were mammoths in this part of Finland and that an upper molar of one was discovered near Kuopio in 1873 – hence all the museum excitement.

Turn right out of the museum and cross the road to the **Lutheran Cathedral** (Mon–Thurs 10am–3pm, Fri 10am–midnight), a handsome creation erected in 1815 using local stone. Although spacious, the cathedral's interior could hardly be described as opulent, but years ago it did contrast dramatically with the cramped living quarters of most Kuopio folk. South of here, at Kuninkaankatu 14, the **VB Photographic Centre** (June–Aug Mon–Fri 10am–7pm, Sat & Sun 11am–4pm; Sept–May Tues–Fri 11am–5pm, Wed until 7pm, Sat & Sun 11am–3pm; €5 summer, €3 winter) is a small museum of local and international photography, some of it quite inspiring; a recent show featured Linda McCartney's work. A few buildings further south on Kunniankatu is the more explicitly ethnographic **Old Kuopio Museum** (mid-May to mid-Sept daily 10am–5pm, Wed until 7pm; mid-Sept to mid-May Tues–Fri 10am–3pm, Sat & Sun 10am–4pm; €2.50; ⊛korttelimuseo .kuopio.fi), an open-air museum where the stock of mostly wooden dwellings reveals the nineteenth century domestic conditions that prevailed for both Kuopio's poor as well as the region's nobler-than-thou.

Another old house, interesting for a quite different reason, stands at Snellmaninkatu 19, preserved as **J.V. Snellman's Home** (mid-May to Aug daily 10am–5pm, Wed until 7pm; rest of the year by appointment on ☎017/182 624, in winter ☎017/182 625; €1.50). From 1844, when the 39-year-old Snellman (for more on whom, see p.666) married his 17-year-old bride, the couple spent several years in this large but far from grand home. At the time, Snellman was earning a living as head of Kuopio's elementary school after the country's Swedish-speaking ruling class had booted him out of his university post, angry at his efforts to have Finnish made an official language. Aided by a few original furnishings in perfect condition and a pastel colour scheme devised by Snellman, the house is an excellent testament to the modest, pre-modernist style of Scandinavian design that informed later minimalist artistic and architectural styles in Finland, Sweden and beyond.

Set on the brow of the hill at Kuopio's northwest corner, the enormously impressive **Orthodox Church Museum**, Karjalankatu 1 (May–Aug Tues–Sun 10am–4pm; Sept–April Mon–Fri noon–3pm, Sat & Sun noon–5pm; €5), draws the Orthodox faithful from many parts of the world. Even if the workings of the Orthodox religion are a complete mystery to you, there's much to be enjoyed, from elaborate Russian-made icons to gold-embossed bibles, gowns and prayer books. The placing of the museum in Kuopio is no accident. This part of Finland has a large Orthodox congregation, many of them (or their parents) from the parts of eastern Finland that became Soviet territory after World War II. Many objects from the original Valamo Monastery (see p.753), likewise caught on the wrong side of the border, are also on display here.

One of Kuopio's highlights is an evening at the world's biggest **woodsmoke sauna** (€10), an enormous unisex affair out at the *Rauhalahti* hostel (see p.760) which can hold well over a hundred people. Its size is such that it takes 24 hours just to heat up – consequently, it's only open on Thursdays (summer only) and Tuesdays (year-round). For €27 you can avail yourself of an inclusive deal combining sauna and a traditional Finnish feast – these amazingly tame evenings also feature "lumberjack shows," replete with accordions, flannel shirts and hordes of tangoing and waltzing Finns. Visit the tourist office or call the hostel for more details.

Situated about 2km behind the train station on a ridge is the 75-metre-high **Puijo Tower** (May–Sept daily 9am–10pm, July until 11pm; Oct–April Mon–Sat 11am–10pm, Sun noon–5pm; €3), with fantastic views over the surrounding countryside, a somewhat upscale revolving restaurant (closed during winter) and access to some of the good ski trails that wend through the pines.

Eating, drinking and nightlife

While you're in Kuopio, look out for *kalakukko* – a kind of bread pie, baked with fish and pork inside it. While it's found all around the country, Kuopio is *kalakukko*'s traditional home and the town's bakeries generally sell it warm and wrapped in silver foil; a fist-sized piece costs about €2.50. You can also buy *kalakukko* hot from the oven at the *Hanna Partanen*, in a backyard at Kasarmikatu 15 (daily 5am–9pm); it's reckoned to be the best place in town, if not the whole of Finland, to sample it. A kilo loaf costs about €12.

In addition to Kuopio's expertise in pies, the city offers a number of solid options for more substantial eating, while several of the pubs offer good-value lunches, too. Kuopio's options for evening **drinks** are central and mostly located on the same block of Kauppakatu just east of the *kauppatori*. *Gloria* at no. 16 makes the most out of its real estate to offer bar, garden café, restaurant and disco all in one complex, though the disco here only gets hopping weekends after midnight. For midweek drinking and dancing you're probably better off next door at *Intro* (🅦www .ravintolaintro.net), a large bar done up in red leather, with DJs playing a mixed bag of Latin, soul and disco music. The basement *Pannuhuone*, three blocks down at no. 25–27, claims to offer over 200 varieties of whiskey, though most of its youthful clientele go for the draught pints of Lapin Kulta. Kuopio has a reputation for being the stamping ground of some of Finland's best rock musicians, and the town has a number of pubs where you can hear live music, several of which are packed together on Kauppakatu; *Apteekkari*, at no. 18, sees jam sessions and a number of live bands. Away from central Kuopio (but close to the campsite), the *Yölintu* bar at the *Rauhalahti* hostel stages some wild bashes on Friday nights. Find out what's happening there by asking at the tourist office, or try phoning the hotel itself on 🅣017/473 473.

Cafés and restaurants

Amarillo Kirjastokatu 10. Sizeable and tasty Mexican-style lunches for under €8.

Isä Camillo Kauppakatu 25–27 🅣017/581 0450. Set in a lovely terraced ex-depository, this popular, casual restaurant serves a range of Mediterranean dishes starting at €10.

🏃 **Musta Lammas** Satamakatu 4 🅣017/581 0458. This cellar restaurant has been in business since 1862 and is still Kuopio's finest. Try the mutton sautéed in dark balsamic vinegar sauce (€19.80). Book ahead during the summer.

Ravintola Wanha Satama At the harbour. Set in a former customs house, this modern Finnish restaurant is very popular on sunny summer evenings. The standard local-style mains are good, but the sandwich meals are less expensive and just as filling: try the *kalaleipä ja perunoita*, a tasty grilled chicken and cheddar sandwich topped with horseradish sauce and served with chips and a basil salad (€9.50)

Rosso Haapaniemenkatu 24–26. Just at the *kauppatori*, this is the best bet for inexpensive if predictable pizza dishes.

Iisalmi and around

The farmland around **IISALMI**, an hour north of Kuopio by bus, makes a welcome break from pine forests and marks the centre of northern Savolax, a district that, in public opinion polls, is regularly voted the least desirable place to live in Finland. The reason for this is slightly mysterious – the modestly sized town looks nice enough – but might be due to the locals' reputation for geniality mixed with a dash of laziness. Whether this is innate, or a defensive reaction by country folk who've been pitchforked into urban life, is debatable.

Whatever the stereotype, Iisalmi's two museums give a very good insight into local life. The **District Museum** (June to mid-Aug Mon–Fri 9am–6pm; rest of the year Mon–Fri 9am–5pm; free), at Kivirannantie 5 on the shores of the Paloisvirta river – cross the river from the centre of town and turn right – reveals the down-at-heel life of the peasantry via a number of wooden farmhouses once occupied by local farmers and fishermen; while the **Juhani Aho Museum** (May–Aug daily 10am–6pm; €2) in Mansikkaniemi, 5km along the main road, Pohjolankatu, by local bus, shows how the other half lived. Juhani Aho was a major influence on Finnish literature as it emerged around the beginning of the twentieth century, and the simple buildings filled with the author's possessions manage to convey the commitment of the artists who came together in the last years of Russian rule. However, it's the **Brewery Museum**, Luuniemenkatu 4 (Mon–Fri 10am–5pm; free) which is Iisalmi's greatest draw – from the tourist office, head west one block on Satamakatu before turning left into Riistakatu and walking another block; Luuniemenkatu begins at the junction with Veikonkatu. Finns flock here to see the brewing process that has created one of the nation's favourite tipples, *Olvi*, and although there's no tasting as part of the tour, there is a beer hall, *Holvi Oluthalli*, attached to the site, where it's possible to lay your hands – against hard cash – on some of the hard stuff. Don't think of coming here in the evening for a drink – it's closed.

Practicalities

Aside from the vaguely church-like *Artos* **hotel** at Kyllikinkatu 8 (℡017/812 244, ⌚www.hotelliartos.fi; ④), and the restaurant-outfitted *Iisalmi Seurahuone*, Savonkatu 2 (℡017/838 31, ⌚www.iisalmenseurahuone.fi; ④), budget accommodation in the town is limited. The **tourist office** (June to mid-Aug Mon–Fri 9am–6pm; Sept–May Mon–Fri 9am–5pm; ℡017/8303 391, ⌚www.iisalmiregion.info), at Kauppakatu 22 on the corner with the main street, Pohjolankatu, can point you towards summertime budget options on the outskirts, and to **campsites** with cabins (③), such as *Koljonvirta Camping*, Ylemmäisentie (℡017/825 252, ⌚www.campingkoljonvirta.fi; May–Sept). **Eating and drinking** in Iisalmi won't set your heart racing, though there is one unique option: Aside from the predictable *Rosso* at Savonkatu 18 and the stodgy Finnish dishes at *Olutmestari* down at the harbour (May–Aug only), you can wine and dine intimately at the harbourside *Kuappi* (℡017/192 6430), which claims to be the smallest restaurant in the world, with seating for just two; book ahead. Afterwards, for an evening drink, head for the slightly larger *Nelly's*, Savonkatu 20.

Around Iisalmi: Sonkajärvi

The reputation that the village of **Sonkajärvi** (⌚www.sonkajarvi.fi), 20km east of Iisalmi, has gained over recent years is quite out of proportion with its tiny size. Throughout Finland, and increasingly abroad, too, this otherwise undistinguished forest village is becoming known for that quintessentially northern Finnish event: the **world championships in wife carrying**. During the first Saturday in July (occasionally the second; check with the tourist office in Iisalmi for the latest details) hundreds of people from across the world crowd into Sonkajärvi to gawp at dozens of burly men negotiating obstacles as they stagger round the 250m course bearing a wife in their arms or on their backs. Confusingly, the borne female need not be the man's wife; however, she must be over seventeen years of age, weigh at least 49kg and must not touch the ground during the race (otherwise penalty seconds are incurred). The winner, clearly, is the first man to cross the finishing line. Although cheesy in the extreme, it's actually quite a fun time to be in this part of Finland, and once the event is over the entire village degenerates into one mass drunken party. About your only option for accommodation in Sonkajärvi are the **cabins** or **camping site** at Lohiranta (☎017/712 125, ◍www.saunalahti.fi/~ieva1; ❶), from where you can also rent out canoes and pedal boats. Getting to Sonkajärvi isn't too much of a hassle, as a daily **bus** makes the journey out here from the bus station in Iisalmi. Other than a few snack bars on the day of the event, there are no **eating** opportunities in the village either.

Travel details

Trains

Iisalmi to: Kajaani (8 daily; 1hr); Oulu (4 daily; 3hr 30min).

Joensuu to: Helsinki (5–7 daily; 5hr 15min–8hr 45min).

Jyväskylä to: Tampere (9–10 daily; 1hr 35min).

Kuopio to: Iisalmi (7–9 daily; 1hr–1hr 30min); Jyväskylä (6 daily; 2hr); Kajaani (5 daily; 2hr); Mikkeli (6 daily; 1hr 45min), Tampere (4–5 daily; 3hr 30min).

Lahti to: Helsinki (hourly; 1hr 30min); Mikkeli (6 daily; 2hr).

Lappeenranta to: Helsinki (6–7 daily; 2hr 40min–3hr 30min); Lahti (6–7 daily; 1hr 15min); Parikkala (5 daily; 1hr 10min).

Mikkeli to: Kuopio (6 daily; 1hr 45min); Lahti (6 daily; 2hr).

Savonlinna to: Parikkala (4–6 daily; 50min).

Tampere to: Hämeenlinna (hourly; 40min–1hr); Helsinki (hourly; 1hr 50 min–2hr 25min); Jyväskylä (9–10 daily; 1hr 35min); Kuopio (4–5 daily; 3hr 30min); Oulu (8 daily; 5hr); Pori (6 daily; 1hr 25min); Turku (9 daily; 2hr).

Varkaus to: Joensuu (4 daily; 1hr 35min).

Buses

Joensuu to: Kuopio (10–11 daily; 1hr 50min–2hr 30min); Valamo monastery (1–2 daily; 55min–1hr 25min).

Kuopio to: Jyväskylä (4–8 daily; 2hr 15min–3hr 40min).

Lahti to: Mikkeli (11 daily; 2hr); Savonlinna (3–4 daily; 3hr 15min).

Lappeenranta to: Helsinki (4–7 daily; 4hr); Parikkala (1–5 daily; 1hr 45min–2hr 5min).

Mikkeli to: Savonlinna (4–9 daily; 1hr 15min–2hr 10min).

Savonlinna to: Kuopio (5–6 daily; 2hr 50min–3hr 40min); Parikkala (1–2 daily; 1hr 20min); Punka-harju (1–2 daily; 50min); Varkaus (2–5 daily; 1hr 30min–2hr 20min).

Tampere to: Helsinki (hourly; 2hr 15min–2hr 45min); Pori (4–5 daily; 1hr 40min); Turku (fre-quent; 2hr 10min–4hr 5min).

Varkaus to: Joensuu (2 daily; 2hr); Kuopio (8 daily; 1hr 15min).

International buses

Joensuu to: Sortavala (1 daily in summer; 3hr 45min).

Lappeenranta to: St Petersburg (1 daily; 5hr); Viipuri (1 daily; 1hr 30min).

4.3

Ostrobothnia, Kainuu and Lapland

B etween them, these three regions take up nearly two-thirds of Finland, but unlike the populous south or the more industrialized sections of the Lake Region, they're predominantly rural, with small and widely separated communities. Despite this – or perhaps because of it – each region has a very individual flavour. Living along the coast of **Ostrobothnia** are most of the country's Swedish-speaking Finland-Swedes, a small subsection of the national population whose culture differs from that of both Swedes and Finns. Towns hereabouts are known as often by their Swedish names as by their Finnish, while their distance from the ravages of World War II enabled them to retain some of their old wooden architecture. Much of the region's affluence stems from its flat and fertile farmlands, although the coastal area's fortunes are changing as the once-numerous ferry connections from Sweden – the "booze cruises" – have all but gone now that European law has done away with duty-free alcohol, the main reason for the ferries' existence; today, **Vaasa** is the area's only maritime entry point. Overall, though, given the lack of exciting scenery – save for a few fishing settlements scattered along the jagged shoreline – and the region's social insularity, you'd be generous to devote more than a couple of days to it. Even busy and expanding **Oulu**, the major city, has a surprisingly anodyne quality, although you could always join the Swedes drinking their way into oblivion slightly further north at the border town of **Tornio**.

Kainuu is the thickly forested, thinly populated heart of Finland. It's traditionally peasant land – something perhaps felt more strongly here than anywhere else in the country – and over recent decades has suffered a severe economic decline as wealth has become concentrated in the south. There's still a surprising level of poverty in some parts, although tourism is beginning to help alleviate this. The only sizeable town, **Kajaani** is a good base for wider explorations by foot, bike or canoe, and, since no railways serve the area, it's also the hub of a bus network which connects the region's far-flung settlements. **Kuhmo**, east of Kajaani, is at the centre of a notable web of nature trails and hiking routes, while heading north past **Kuusamo**, the landscapes become wilder, with great gorges, river rapids and fells on which reindeer are as common as people. Hikers here are well catered for by a number of marked tracks, and there are also totally uninhabited regions traversable only with map, compass and self-confidence. The villages have little to offer beyond accommodation and transport to and from the end-points of the hikes, so stay away if you're not the rambling type.

Much the same applies to **Lapland**, one of the most thrilling places to hike in the world. **Rovaniemi**, the main stopover en route, is useful mainly for its transport connections and information on the area beyond. Beyond Rovaniemi, two roads lead into the **Arctic North**. Here you'll find wide open spaces that are great for guided and solo treks through gold-panning country and along the edges of mountain chains which continue far into Sweden and Norway. Elsewhere you can be totally isolated, gazing from barren fell-tops into Russia.

765

But while the Arctic settlements are small, and few and far between, the whole region is home to several thousand **Sámi** (for more on whom, see p.780), who've lived in harmony with this special, often harsh environment for millennia. Discovering their culture and way of life can be as exciting as experiencing the Arctic North itself.

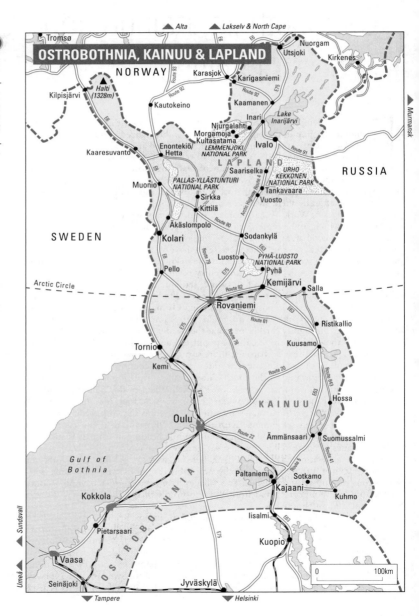

The curious and little encountered Latin word, **Ostrobothnia**, is allied to the Swedish name *Österbotten*, meaning "east of the Gulf of Bothnia", and confusingly refers to the western Finnish coast. To understand this apparent contradiction, it's necessary to go back to the centuries of Swedish rule when this Finnish province, on the east of the Gulf as seen from Sweden, was administered from Stockholm. *Österbotten* looked out across the sea towards the Swedish province of *Västerbotten*, "west of the Gulf of Bothnia", two Swedish provinces separated by a physical divide. Today the name *Österbotten* is still in use by the many Swedish-speaking communities in this part of Finland and stretches roughly from Vaasa to Oulu. Thankfully in Finnish there is no such confusion, since *Pohjanmaa*, the Finnish name for Ostrobothnia, simply means "northern land".

Vaasa and around

There's little reason to visit **VAASA**, although it's a useful stopover if you're travelling along the coast and has good travel connections with Oulu to the north and Pori to the south; there's also a little-advertised but very useful cross-country rail line connecting Vaasa directly with Jyväskylä. The lifeblood of the town is its harbour, through which the produce of southern Ostrobothnia's wheat fields is exported and the lucrative tourist traffic from Sweden arrives. Years of steady income have given the town a staid, commercial countenance, and its wide avenues (the old centre was obliterated by fire a century ago) are lined with shipping offices, consulates and a plethora of boozing venues aimed at Swedes from Umeå, who come here to get smashed.

Eighty-odd years ago, Vaasa was briefly the seat of the provisional government after the Reds (an alliance of Communists and Social Democrats who had taken up arms against Finland's repressive Civil Guard) had taken control of Helsinki and much of the south at the start of the Civil War in 1918; it was among Ostrobothnia's right-wing farmers that the bourgeois-dominated government drew most of its support. This barely endearing fact is recalled by the reliefs of the then president Svinhufvud, and Mannerheim, who commanded the Civil Guard, on the front of the town hall and by the monument outside it.

Since then, it seems, little besides drunkenness has broken the peace. The pinnacle of local cultural activity is represented by the **Ostrobothnia Museum** (daily 10am–5pm, Wed until 8pm; €2) at Museokatu 3, which recounts the history of the town and boasts an enjoyable collection of sixteenth- and seventeenth-century Dutch, Italian and Flemish art.

Practicalities

The **bus** and **train** stations are at the northern end of the town centre, within walking distance of the **tourist office**, which is located in part of the town hall at Raastuvankatu (June–Aug Mon–Fri 9am–6pm, Sat & Sun 10am–6pm; Sept–May Mon–Fri 10am–4pm; ☎06/325 1145, ❂www.vaasa.fi). There's free **Internet** access close by at the town library, Kirjastonkatu 13 (Mon–Thurs 11am–8pm, Fri 10am–6pm, Sat 10am–3pm).

If you have to stay overnight before moving on, there are a few central **hotels**, and rates are quite reasonable, but oddly for such a comparatively large place, **eating** and drinking establishments are thin on the ground in Vaasa. The best deals are to be found at the *Golden Rax Pizzabuffet*, at the top end of the main square at Kauppapuistikko 13, where the all-you-can-eat buffet is just €8. For more pleasant surrounds, head for *Fondis*, Hovioikeudenpuistikko 15, which specializes in Mediterranean food – the beef casserole with garlic, and red pepper stuffed with vegetable couscous are especially good value. A night's **drinking** in a multi-lingual town like Vaasa (one in four people here speak Swedish as their mother tongue), is divided on linguistic lines: Finnish speakers tend to be found at *Hullu Pullo*, Kauppapuitikko 15 or *Birra* at no. 16, whereas the Finland-Swedes prefer *Oliver's Inn* at no. 8. For dancing, *Royal*, Hovioikeudenpuistikko 18 inside the *Radisson SAS Hotel*, is one of the more popular discos in town, regardless of mother tongue.

Accommodation

Astor Asemakatu 4 ☎06/326 9111, ⊛www .astorvaasa.com. Small, pleasant and central hotel with classy and charming doubles and suites. For €20 extra, you can get a room with private sauna. ④/⑤

Best Western Hotel Silveria Ruutikellarintie 4 ☎06/326 7611, ⊛www.hotelsilveria.com. The most enticing of the city's hotels, with use of the pool, morning sauna and breakfast included in the room rate. ④/⑤

EFÖ Rantakatu 21–22 ☎06/317 4913, ⊛www .efo.fi. Located within a vocational school, this affordable summer hotel is simply furnished and agonizingly decorated in pale wood furnishings against white and off-white walls. Open mid-June to mid-Aug. ②

Kenraali Wasa Hostel Korsholmanpuistikko 6–8 ☎040/066 8521, ⊛www.kenraaliwasahostel.com. Situated in an old army barracks, this is the best option amongst Vaasa's budget accommodation,

with a dozen homey and warm doubles with shared bathroom. ②

Omena Hotelli Hoivokeudenpuistikko 23 ☎020/428 2119, ⊛www.omenahotelli.fi. The newest hotel in town, with tidy, modern rooms but no reception – you must book via the phone Internet or kiosk downstairs; note that booking over the phone incurs an extra €6 fee. ③

Tekla Palosaarentie 58 ☎06/327 6411, ⊛www .hoteltekla.net. Some 3km from the town centre via bus #3A, this simple hotel has chintzy furnishings that make it feel more like a youth hostel, though the rooms do have private bathrooms. The downstairs restaurant serves very affordable Finnish meals. ③

Top Camping Vaasa ☎06/211 1255, ⊛www .wasalandia.fi. Adequate camping facilities are 2km from the town centre right on a waterfront near the ferry harbour; take bus #5. Open late-May to mid-Aug. ②

Onward from Vaasa

Ferries currently run from Vaasa to **Umeå** and **Sundsvall** in Sweden (RG Line; ☎06/320 0300, ⊛www.rgline.com; €50), generally once-daily in June and July, less during the rest of the year; remember that Umeå is Uumaja in Finnish. In June and August, the same company also runs daily ferries to Sundsvall in Sweden (€60).

Heading **south from Vaasa** usually involves changing trains at Seinäjoki, from where there are direct services to Tampere, Turku and Helsinki. There's also a direct rail service **east** to Jyväskylä where connections can be made for Kuopio and Joensuu, as well as numerous buses running to Pori and Turku. About 70km south of Vaasa, these pass through Kaskinen (in Swedish, Kaskö) and neighbouring Kristiinankaupunki (Kristinestad), notable for its surviving seventeenth-century layout.

Travelling **north from Vaasa** by bus to the major coastal city of Oulu involves a mildly scenic journey passing fishing hamlets along the archipelago, and the small and still largely wooden towns of Uusikaarlepyy (Nykarleby) and Pietarsaari (Jakobstad). Northbound **trains** (once again changing in Seinäjoki) swing inland before meeting up with the coastal road north in the uninspiring port of **KOKKOLA**. If you feel like hanging around, the **tourist office** on Kauppatori (June–Aug Mon–Fri 8am–4pm; ☎06/831 1902, ⊛www.kokkola.fi) can help sort out accommodation and point you towards the only remotely interesting local sight: the **English Park**, at one end of Isokatu, which contains a boat captured when the British fleet tried to land here during the Crimean campaign in 1854. A much more welcome sight, though, is the **train station** at Isokatu's other end. **Travelling on** from Kokkola is straightforward since the town is on the main rail line between Oulu and Helsinki.

Oulu

Despite **OULU**'s role as national leader in the computing and microchip industries, the city still has sufficient remnants from the past to remind visitors of its
nineteenth-century status as a world centre for tar. The black stuff was brought by
river from the forests of Kainuu, and the international demand for its use in ship-
and road-building helped line the pockets of Oulu's merchants. Their affluence and
quest for cultural refinement made the town a vibrant centre, not only for business,
but also for education and the arts. Today, a handsome series of islands, a couple of
highly conspicuous old buildings, and a nightlife fuelled by the university's fun-
hungry students bring colour into an otherwise pallid city. Though it has its share
of faceless office blocks, there's an ancient feel to Oulu, too, as seen in tumbledown
wooden shacks around the intricately carved *kauppahalli*.

Arrival and accommodation

Oulu is handy for **trains** in various directions, most usefully the direct services to
and from Helsinki, Kajaani in the east (see p.774) and Rovaniemi in the north (see

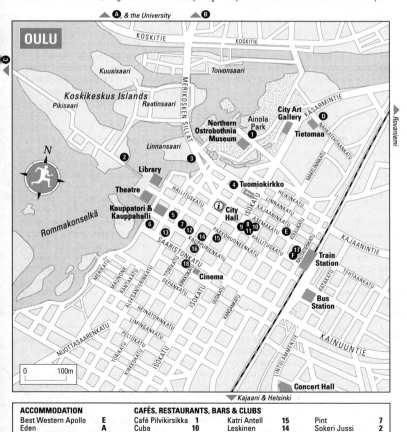

ACCOMMODATION		CAFÉS, RESTAURANTS, BARS & CLUBS					
Best Western Apollo	E	Café Pilvikirsikka	1	Katri Antell	15	Pint	7
Eden	A	Cuba	10	Leskinen	14	Sokeri Jussi	2
Kesähotelli Oppimestari	D	45 Special	18	Matala	5	St Michael's	9
Nallikari Camping	C	Franzén	4	Never Grow Old	11	Tahtitorninkahvila	3
Toppilanpukseri	B	Hoan	12	Oskarin Kellari	17	Uleåborg 1881	6
Turisti	F	Kaarlenholvi	13	Pannu	16	Zakuska	8

p.778). Arriving here, you'll find the platforms of the **train station** feed conveniently into an underground walkway with two exits: one runs to the nearby **bus station** (with regular services to and from Kuusamo), while the other leads towards the compact city centre, where the **tourist office** (mid-June to mid-Aug Mon–Fri 9am–6pm, Sat 10am–3pm; rest of the year Mon–Fri 9am–4pm; ☎08/5584 1330, ◍www.oulutourism.fi) is close to the City Hall at Torikatu 10.

Low-cost **accommodation** is, unfortunately, limited, as Oulu's youth hostel has closed down, though there are a number of respectable mid-range places.

Accommodation

Best Western Apollo Asemakatu 31–33 ☎08/374 344, ◍www.bestwestern.fi. This chain hotel fortunately doesn't feel too much like one, with spectacular rooms and 1970s-meets-21st century decor. ❹/❺

Eden Nallikari island ☎08/884 2000, ◍www.holidayclub.fi. If you're after luxury, this paradise won't disappoint – it's got a superb pool and offers spa treatments and steam rooms, and there's a fine restaurant. Take bus #5. ❻

Kesähotelli Oppimestari Nahkatehtaankatu 3 ☎08/884 8527, ◍www.merikoski.fi. The less-than-exciting rooms at this summer hotel are north of the city centre, just across from the lush Ainola park. Open mid-June to early Aug. ❸

Nallikari Camping Hietasaari Island ☎08/5586 1350, ◍www.nallikaricamping.fi. Set on an island 4km from town and near to the sliver of sand that locals call a beach, with well-appointed cabins (❶/❸) as well as pitches.

Toppilanpukseri Satamatie 13 ☎ & ☎08/554 3335. A small and friendly Russian-run guest-house, with a few simple beds in an old house a few kilometres north of the centre; take bus #1 or #30. ❶

Turisti Rautatienkatu 9 ☎08/563 6100, ◍www.hotellituristi.fi. Set above a convenience store, this very central hotel has the cheapest year-round rooms, done out in florals and pastels and sporting delightful wood flooring and crisp modern furnishings. ❸/❹

The City

Leaving either the bus or train station, it's just a few minutes' walk straight ahead to the **harbour** and the neighbouring **kauppatori** and **kauppahalli** (Mon–Thurs 8am–4pm, Fri 8am–5pm, Sat 8am–3pm), an appealing and ornate place, good for cheap eats. Nearby, the sleekly modern **library** and **theatre** rise on stilts from the water. The library frequently stages art and craft exhibitions, which are usually worth a look.

Built as a luxury hotel symbolizing the affluent and cosmopolitan tar-rich town, the **City Hall**, a few minutes away on Kirkkokatu, retains some of its late nineteenth-century grandeur. A local newspaper called it "a model for the whole world. A Russian is building the floor, an Austrian is doing the painting, a German is making the bricks, an Englishman is preparing the electric lighting, the Swede is doing the masonry, the Norwegian is carving the relief and the Finn is doing all the drudgery." Nowadays, the drudgery is performed by local government officials, who've become accustomed to visitors stepping in to gawp at the wall paintings and enclosed gardens that remain from the old days. While inside, venture up to the second floor, where the Great Hall still has its intricate Viennese ceiling paintings and voluminous chandeliers.

Further along Kirkkokatu, the copper-domed, yellow-stuccoed **Tuomiokirkko** (summer daily 11am–8pm; winter Mon–Fri noon–1pm; free) was built in the 1770s following a great fire that more or less destroyed the city, and underwent a full and successful restoration in 1996. Within the cathedral is a portrait of Swedish historian Johannes Messinius, supposedly painted by **Cornelius Arenditz** in 1612. Restored and slightly faded, it's believed to be the oldest surviving oil painting in Finland, despite the efforts of the Russian Cossacks, who lacerated the canvas with their sabres in 1714.

Cross the small canal just north of the cathedral to reach **Ainola Park**, a pleasantly wooded space which makes a nice spot for a picnic or a late evening stroll. In the park, the **Northern Ostrobothnia Museum** (Tues 10am–6pm, Wed 10am–7pm, Thurs & Fri 10am–6pm, Sat & Sun 11am–6pm; €3, free on Fri) has numerous tar-stained remnants from Oulu's past and an interesting Sámi section. There's no English labelling, but the displays are mostly self-explanatory.

If the future does more to excite your imagination than the past, or if you've got kids in tow, head for **Tietomaa**, the Science Museum, a few minutes' walk away at Nahkatehtaankatu 6 (May, June & Aug daily 10am–6pm; July daily 10am–8pm; Sept–April Mon–Fri 10am–4pm, Sat & Sun 10am–6pm; €12; ⍟www.tietomaa .fi). Housed in an old power station, this is a great place to explore the bounds of technological possibility, with several floors of gadgets to test mental and physical abilities as well as video games, holograms, a ski jump simulator, a giant-screen IMAX cinema and a glass elevator that takes you to the top of a tower from which you can get unparalleled views of Oulu.

Just around the corner, the **City Art Gallery** (Tues–Thurs 11am–5pm, Fri 10am–6pm, Sat & Sun 10am–5pm; €3; free on Fri; ⍟www.ouka.fi/taidemuseo /english), Kasarmintie 7, is located in a renovated glue factory. One of the largest galleries in Finland, it houses permanent and visiting international and Finnish contemporary art collections, plus a pleasant café – a good place to kill a few hours on a cold day.

Koskikeskus, the University and Botanical Gardens

A pleasant way to pass an afternoon is to set off for the four small islands across the mouth of Rommakonselkä, collectively known as **Koskikeskus**. The first island, Linnansaari, has the inconsequential remains of Oulu's sixteenth-century castle, most of which was destroyed in an eighteenth-century thunderstorm when lightening struck its cellar gunpowder stores. Next comes Raatinsaari, followed by Toivonsaari, beyond which lie the rapids that drive a power station designed by Alvar Aalto, with twelve fountains added by the architect to prettify the plant. Pikisaari, the fourth island, is much the best to visit, reached by a short road bridge from Raatinsaari. A number of tiny seventeenth-century wooden houses here have survived Oulu's many fires, and Pikisaari has become the stamping ground of local artists and trendies, with several **art galleries** and **craft shops**.

The islands can also be glimpsed through the windows of buses #4, 6, 7 and 19, which pass them during the twenty-minute ride to the **University**, itself not a bad destination for a visit if you're at a loose end, if only for the opportunity to gorge in the student *mensa*. To work up an appetite, try finding the **Geological Museum** (Mon–Fri & Sun 11am–3pm; free) or the **Zoological Museum** (Mon–Fri 8.30am–3.45pm, Sun 11am–3pm; free), both secreted within the university's miles of corridors. The former is much as you'd expect, with a large collection of rare gems; the latter's best feature is the painstakingly hand-painted habitats created for each of the numerous specimens of stuffed Finnish wildlife.

Once you've ventured onto the campus you may as well take a look at the tropical and Mediterranean flora inside the two glass pyramidal structures that make up the **Botanical Gardens** (Tues–Fri 8am–3pm, Sun noon–3pm; €2).

Eating, drinking and nightlife

Oulu and its outlying islands boast some delightful **cafés** for lunch or a snack, and you shouldn't have a problem finding a good place for a sit-down meal, as the city's **restaurants** run the full gamut from basic to upscale. We've given phone numbers only for places where you need to book a table.

With an active Finnish and international student population, Oulu's lively nightlife revolves around its numerous **pubs** and **bars**, most within a block or two of the centre; after hours, several **clubs** provide all-night entertainment.

Cafés and restaurants

Café Pilvikirsikka Ainola park. A cosy place set in an old greenhouse, serving coffee, cakes and other snacks.

Concert Hall Lintulammentie 1–3. Sip a coffee in classy surroundings – though snacks don't come cheap, this is a great vantage point from which to admire the concert hall's gleaming Italian marble interior.

Franzén Kirkkokatu 2 ☎08/311 3224. In a charismatic old building diagonally opposite the Tuomiokirkko, the ultra-swish street-level restaurant serves nouveau dishes such as duck fricassee (€19), while the cellar bar serves German beers and sausages.

Hoan Kauppurienkatu 5. Don't let the yellowing photos of the dishes turn you off from the best Chinese food in town. Open until 4am weekdays and 5am weekends.

Katri Antell Kirkkokatu 17, entrance on Rotuaari. This small patisserie on the pedestrian walkway smack in the centre of town makes the best cakes in Oulu.

Matala Rantakatu 6 ☎08/333 013, ☜www .matala.fi. Just across from the market square, this truly classy upper-end place is Oulu's finest restaurant. The designer dishes include reindeer in juniper sauce (€24.50) and tarragon monkfish (€26), and there's an array of cognacs and boxes of cigars for sale.

NUKU Hallituskatu 7. Cultural centre for the town's youth, with a laid-back courtyard café that's a great place to lounge about on a Sunday. Movies are shown every evening at the Oulu Film Centre in the same building.

Oskarin Kellari Rautatienkatu 9. Opposite the train station, and in the same block as the *Hotel Turisti*, this is a good choice for a reasonably priced Finnish meal, and is usually busy with locals.

Pannu Kauppurienkatu 12 ☜www.ravintolapannu .com. Oulu's most popular pizzeria, with a family restaurant feel. The menu serves standard Finnish dishes like fillet of wild boar (€19.50) but the deep-pan pizzas (€10–15) are the best in town. Usually full, even at lunchtime, but they don't take reservations.

Sokeri Jussi Kasarmintie 13, Pikisaari island. Set in an old salt warehouse just over the bridge from the mainland, and great for a traditional Finnish lunch or just a drink outside on the huge terrace.

Tähtitornin kahvila Linnansaari island. Set high up in a century-old observation tower just across the Linnansaari bridge, this is one of Oulu's most picturesque options for a coffee or tea.

🏃 **Uleåborg 1881** Aittatori 4–5☎08/881 1188, ☜www.ulea.org. Rivals *Matala*

as the pick of Oulu's restaurants. Set at the waterside in an nineteenth-century granary, and offering mains such as fried scampi (€12.60), herring in sherry (€9) and grilled veal liver (€24); it also has a sizeable wine menu. The terrace waterfront out back makes for excellent sunset/moonlight meals.

🏃 **Zakuska** Hallituskatu 20, This authentic mid-priced Russian restaurant is Oulu's first "ethnic" restaurant, and it's very popular for its spot-on period eighteenth-century tsarist decor. The extensive menu features scrumptious selections like the "Vladimir in Sheep's Clothing", tasty chops of garlic pork with creamy, gratin potatoes and beetroot (€17). Closed Sun.

Bars and clubs

Cuba Uusikatu 22. This downstairs club, done out in black with lots of mirrors, is known for three things: high-schoolers, drunken fights outside and €1 pints of Karjala all night long. If this doesn't appeal to you, consider dropping in between 4pm and 10pm, where older Finns waltz and tango together.

45 Special Saarisonkatu 12 ☜www.45special .com. A legendary rock club whose three floors each has a different atmosphere and clientele. Frequent live bands, and the Sunday jams are very popular.

Jumppru Pub Kauppurienkatu 6. Popular bar and nightclub chock full of early-twentieth century charm, sporting opulent leather armchairs, dark wood detailing and heavy velvet drapery; pub food is available.

Leskinen Isokatu 30. With a wide selection of European beers, this is Oulu's bar of choice for international students and expat workers.

Never Grow Old Hallituskatu 13–17. Oulu's boho, dreadlocked crowd has finally found its home. Swinging wicker bungalow chairs, a painted Caribbean beachscape and reggae music all night long bring in Finns by the camperload. Gets smoky at night.

Pint Kauppurienkatu 5. Popular after-work spot with bench seating, a terrace out front and two Internet terminals – free if you're drinking.

St Michael's Uusikatu 23. Oulu's best Irish pub, with 240 types of whiskeys, plus Guinness, Murphy's Stout and Kilkenny on draught.

Towards Tornio: Kemi icebreaker tours

If you want to cross overland into Sweden, the place to make for is Tornio, 130km northwest of Oulu – reached by bus from **KEMI**, a small town on the Oulu–Rovaniemi train route around 110km northwest of Oulu. Although undistinguished during the summer months, bar the stench of wood pulp issuing from

△ *Sampo* icebreaker cruise

the nearby sawmills, it's during the dark winter months that Kemi really comes to life. From mid-December to late April, hundreds of people pour through this small town to experience one of Finland's most alluring winter attractions: a tour on the only private **icebreaker** in the world. The *Sampo* departs once daily for a four-hour "cruise" through the icefields at the very top of the Gulf of Bothnia, breaking ice several metres thick (the ice is at its thickest in February and March). During the tour there's also an unmissable opportunity to don a bright orange rubber survival suit and float in the icy waters off the ship's stern – all this costs a pricey €196, but is undoubtedly worth the expense. The icing on the cake, however, is to depart by snowmobile from the centre of Kemi, travelling out over the ice to join the ship at its parking position out in the icefield – this 7hr tour doesn't come cheap at €326 per person but, if you can afford it, is a once-in-a-lifetime experience; for more information, contact Sampo Tours at Torikatu 2 in Kemi (☏016/256 548, ☻www.sampotours.com). Prices come down if these tours are booked via a travel agent (see p.29). If you want to **stay** in Kemi, there's the *Snow Castle* (☏016/259 502, ☻www.snowcastle.net; open late Dec to March; ◉) at the harbour, a hotel and restaurant carved entirely out of snow and ice – guests are guaranteed warmth inside sub-thermal sleeping bags. For more a traditional night's stay, *Merihovi*, Keskuspuistokatu 6–8 (☏016/458 0999, ☻www.merihovi .fi; ◓/◉), has smart rooms with plush and stylish furniture, and a good downstairs **restaurant**. Down at the harbour, the massive villa of *Hullun Mylly*, Urheilukatu 1, was once the town hall and is now a lovely restaurant serving a wide range of well-priced Finnish dishes. Later on in the evening, it becomes a lively **bar** and **dance club**, though you may prefer the more sedate bar scene at *Corner Inn*, back in town at Kauppakatu 10.

Tornio

Situated on the extreme northern tip of the Gulf of Bothnia and on the border with Sweden, **TORNIO** once made its living by selling booze to fugitives from Sweden's once-harsh alcohol laws. Today, Finnish alcohol prices only slightly cheaper than those in Sweden, and the border customs house that formerly fought cross-border spirits smuggling is long gone. Nonetheless, the bulk of Tornio's nightlife remains on the Finnish side of the border rather than in Swedish Haparanda, and Tornio also sees a good number of Finnish visitors, who come here to enjoy the fishing, shoot the Tornionjoki Rapids or take to the golf course, which has holes in both Sweden and Finland.

Tornio today is as low-key as any other town in the region, but this may change following construction of a colossal new Ikea complex right at Swedish border, which began in 2005 and may, by all accounts, bring some life to these two otherwise flatlining settlements. In the meantime, the loose border controls between Finland and Sweden mean liver-damaged Swedes still cross the border for a bit of boozing, and if you find the drink-fuelled atmosphere unappealing, try visiting the seventeenth-century **Tornionkirkko** (late May to mid-Aug Mon–Fri 9am–5pm; mid-June to early Aug Mon–Fri 9am–7pm, Sat & Sun 11.30am–5pm) on the edge of the town park, or taking the rickety lift up the **observation tower** (June to mid-Aug daily 11am–8pm; €1) for impressive views all around. There's also the **Tornio River Valley Historical Museum** (Mon–Fri noon–5pm, Sun noon–3pm; July to mid-Aug also Sat noon–3pm; €2), near the corner of Torikatu and Keskikatu, a small but well organized collection of information on the region's past, with an interesting section on the role played by western Finnish Lapland World War II. Elsewhere, the **Aine Art Museum** (Tues–Thurs 11am–7pm, Fri–Sun 11am–3pm; €2), Torikatu 2, has a few small exhibitions on Finnish and international artists of mild renown. The **Lapin Kulta brewery**, Finland's largest, runs interesting free one-hour tours of its premises at Lapinkullankatu 1, which includes sample tastings of the brew (☎020/717 151; June–Aug Tues & Thurs 2pm). After exhausting Tornio's few attractions, you might do well to hop across the border to Haparanda, which has several interesting sights (see p.612).

Practicalities

If you're **arriving by bus**, the journey will terminate in Suensaari. The friendly **tourist office** is located in the Green Line Centre at the Swedish border (mid-June to mid-Aug Mon–Fri 8am–7pm, Sat & Sun 11am–6pm; mid-Aug to May Mon–Fri 9am–5pm; ☎016/432 733, ⓦwww.tornio.fi/tourism).

The best **accommodation** remains just across the border in Haparanda (see p.612), but if you really can't bear to part with Finland, your best option is the *Kaupunginhotelli*, Itäranta 4 (☎016/433 11, ⓦwww.tornionkaupunginhotelli.fi; ❹/❺), boasting a trio of restaurants, a nightclub and five saunas. Much cheaper is the *Ammatti-Insititutti*, Kauppakatu 35A (☎016/451 207; June & July only; ❶), a vocational school which has sparkling doubles with private bath; you must ring ahead during the week to reserve. The **campsite** on Matkailijantie (☎016/445 945, ⓦwww.campingtornio.com) has two-bed cottages (❷).

Tornio's dominant features are its **restaurants** and **bars**. For coffee and fresh bread and cakes, it's hard to beat *Karkiaisen Leipomo*, Länsiranta 9. *Tiramisu*, Kauppakatu 12, is a popular stop for cakes, wraps and salads, while *Umpitunneli* (ⓦwww.umpitunneli.fi), by the second road bridge over the Tornionjoki River, is a large restaurant-cum-disco serving dependable bar food like fried chicken or arctic char (€14), while for excellent Chinese food, *Golden Flower*, Eliaksenkatu 8, cooks up great seafood dishes – try the spicy and filling curried jumbo shrimp (€12.75). Alternatively, you can buy a bag of salted and smoked whitefish along the banks of the rapids (roughly €2 for a meal's worth). For drinks, *Wanha Mestari*, Hallituskatu 5, and *Café Nina*, Laivurinkatu 5, get quite crowded in the evenings, while at Satamakatu 3, *Wiini Huone* is a friendly wine bar and, next door, *Jetset* is a small rock bar, attracting the few jetsetters who haven't yet boarded the fast boat out of town.

Into Kainuu: Kajaani and around

KAJAANI, 178km southeast of Oulu by bus, could hardly be more of a contrast to the communities of the Bothnian coast. Though small and pastoral, the town is by far the biggest settlement that the Kainuu province, a very rural part of Finland, has to offer; trains and buses are rare here and the pleasures of nature take precedence over everything else. Obviously there's little bustle or nightlife, but Kajaani offers some insight into Finnish life in one of the country's less prosperous regions. Fittingly, it was here that Elias Lönnrot completed his version of the *Kalevala*, the nineteenth-century collection of Finnish folk tales that extolled the virtues of traditional peasant life. During the first week of July Kajaani also hosts Finland's biggest annual **poetry festival** (ⓦwww.kainuunkuvia.com/demot/runoviikko), during which the main street, Kauppakatu, turns into a bustling market; in late May, meanwhile, the Kainuun Jazzkevät (ⓦwww.jazzkevat.fi) sees performances from a number of big-name **jazz** groups.

From the gloriously Art Nouveau **train station**, Kauppakatu leads directly into Kajaani's minuscule centre, but first turn left into Asemakatu and you'll spot the decorative exterior of the **Kainuun Museum** at no. 4 (Mon–Fri noon–4pm, Wed until 8pm, Sun noon–5pm; €2). Inside, the engrossingly ramshackle collection of local art and history says a lot about the down-to-earth qualities of the area. Pressing for the centre along Pohjolankatu, you'll pass the dramatic **Kajaani kirkko** (summer daily 10am–6pm; winter Mon–Sat 5–7pm), whose wooden frame, weird turrets and angular arches were heralded as the epitome of the neo-Gothic style when completed in 1896. Resembling a leftover from a *Munsters* set, its spectral qualities are most intense by moonlight. At the far end of Kauppakatu, at the junction with Linnankatu, is the **Old Town Hall**, designed by Carl Engel.

More historically significant, perhaps, but far less thrilling is the ruined **Kajaani Castle**. Built in the seventeenth century to forestall a Russian attack, it later served as a prison where, among others, Johannes Messenius, the troublesome Swede, was incarcerated. Although there's constant talk of schemes to rebuild it, the castle was ruined so long ago that nobody's sure what it actually looked like, and the present heap of stones is only worth seeing if you're already idling along the riverside beside it.

Given the lack of other evening activities, idling is what you're likely to be doing if you stay here overnight. The problem of complete boredom is no less severe for the local youth, who've taken to lining the pavements of Kauppakatu in their

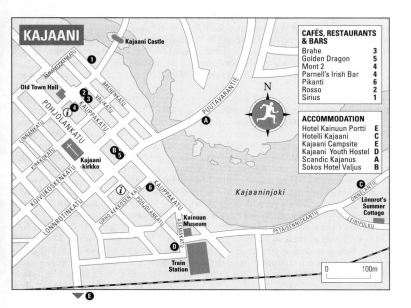

KAJAANI

Kajaani Castle

Old Town Hall

Kajaani kirkko

Kainuun Museum

Train Station

Kajaaninjoki

Lönnrot's Summer Cottage

CAFÉS, RESTAURANTS & BARS	
Brahe	3
Golden Dragon	5
Mont 2	4
Parnell's Irish Bar	4
Pikanti	6
Rosso	2
Sirius	1

ACCOMMODATION	
Hotel Kainuun Portti	E
Hotelli Kajaani	C
Kajaani Campsite	E
Kajaani Youth Hostel	D
Scandic Kajanus	A
Sokos Hotel Valjus	B

0   100m

hundreds, waiting for something to happen. About the only other way to pass the sunset hours is to take a quiet walk along the riverside footpath, from the corner of Ämmäkoskenkatu and Brehenkatu. Heading west, the path passes the **open-air theatre**, and also provides a chance to gaze at logs sliding blissfully towards destruction at the pulp mill ahead. Following the river eastwards leads to **Lönnrot's summer cottage**. Built by Elias Lönnrot, of *Kalevala* fame, for his wife, the small wooden structure now stands totally empty, isolated and seemingly insignificant; the only acknowledgement of its existence is in the name of the neighbouring *Elias Restaurant* inside the neighbouring *Hotelli Kajaani* – an odd neglect for a man whose life's work was so influential, and revered.

Practicalities

The least expensive place to stay is currently *Huone ja Aamiainen Hostel*, near the railway station at Pohjolankatu 4 (☎ & ☎08/622 25440; ②), but there is talk of it shutting down – check with the **tourist office** at Pohjolankatu 16 (June–Aug Mon–Fri 9am–4.30pm, Sat 9am–noon; Sept–May Mon–Fri 8.30am–2.30pm; ☎08/615 5555, ◍www.kajaani.fi). Another inexpensive option is *Kainuun Portti*, 4km south of town on Route 5 (☎08/613 3000, ☎613 3010; ②) with regular singles and doubles, as well as rooms for five with kitchen; to get there, take bus #7 from the bus station – Kajaani's tent-only **campsite** is also located here (same contact details; open May–Aug). Closer to town is the quiet *Hotelli Kajaani* (☎08/615 31, ◍www.solaris-lomat.fi/kajaani; ③), in a handsome setting on the river. For a bit more money, the town centre holds several adequate choices, and rates drop during the summer and at weekends. Of these, *Sokos Hotel Valjus*, Kauppakatu 20 (☎08/615 0200, ◍www.sokoshotels.fi; ④/⑤) is one of the better options, though if you can afford it, the best is the *Scandic Kajanus* (☎08/616 41, ◍www.scandic -hotels.com; ⑤/⑥) across the main bridge in pleasant riverside surroundings at Koskikatu 3 (entrance on Puutavarantie).

There's not a huge number of decent places to **eat** in Kajaani, the most reliable option being the *Golden Dragon* at Kauppakatu 18. Other options lined up along Kauppakatu include the *Pikanti*, at no. 10–12, where an all-you-can-eat lunch costs €8.90; and the ubiquitous *Rosso* at no. 21. The most atmospheric place to dine is *Sirius*, just off the main drag by the river at Brahenkatu 5, in a building originally constructed as a residence for the Kajaani paper company and later used to accommodate visiting dignitaries including Soviet and Finnish Presidents Leonid Brezhnev and Urho Kekkonen. The Finnish food here is not cheap but is certainly tasty. *Parnell's Irish Bar* at Kauppakatu 30 and *Brahe*, immediately opposite at no. 21, are the only decent places to **drink**, while *Mont 2*, above Parnell's, is one of the town's better clubs.

Around Kajaani: Paltaniemi

The hourly #4 bus from Kajaani winds its way to the well-preserved village of **PALTANIEMI**, 9km away on the shores of Oulujärvi – an attractive place but, since the closure of its campsite, one without anywhere to stay. In contrast to down-at-heel Kajaani, eighteenth-century Paltaniemi was home to Swedish-speaking aesthetes lured here by the importance of Kajaani Castle during the halcyon days of the Swedish empire. Their transformation of Paltaniemi into something of a cultural hotbed seems incredible given the place's tiny size and placid setting, but evidence of a refined pedigree isn't hard to find. Most obviously there's the **Paltaniemi kirkko** (summer daily 10am–6pm; winter guided tours only, bookable in the tourist office in Kajaani), built in 1726, a large church whose interior is deliberately chilled in order to preserve **frescoes** painted by Emmanuel Granberg between 1778 and 1781, which include a steamy vision of hell in a gruesome *Last Judgement*.

It's also fun to ferret around behind the pews, trying to decipher centuries-old graffiti. Even Tsar Alexander I paid a visit to Paltaniemi after Finland had become a Russian Grand Duchy, and his impromptu meal in a stable is reverentially commemorated in the **Tsar's Stable** by the church. **Hövelö**, the reconstructed cottage across the road, was the birthplace of **Eino Leino**, whose poems captured the increasingly assertive mood of Finland at the beginning of the twentieth century: his life and the history of Kajaani Castle form the subject of an eminently missable exhibition within (June–Aug Sun–Fri 10am–8pm; €6).

Moving on from Kajaani

Buses provide the easiest way of **moving on** from Kajaani. The only rail links are west to Oulu (5–6 daily), plus the six daily connections for Iisalmi, Kuopio and beyond, including a useful sleeper service direct to both Helsinki and Turku. The best direction to head for more rural delights is east towards Kuhmo, where the scenery becomes increasingly spectacular, especially around the town of Sotkamo (39km from Kajaani) and the acclaimed beauty spot of **Vuokatti** – a high, pine-clad ridge commanding views all the way to Russia. The rolling hills make this Finland's premier ski-training area.

Kuhmo

With belts of forests, hills and lakes, and numerous nature walks and hikes within easy reach, **KUHMO** makes a fine base for exploring the countryside. The terrain is in some ways less dramatic than that further north, but then again it's also far less crowded.

You can get details of hiking routes, maps and other practical information from the **tourist office**, Kainuuntie 126 (Mon–Fri 8am–6pm, Sat 10am–4pm; ☎08/655 6382, ⓦwww.kuhmo.fi/matkailu). The tourist office can also explain how best to reach the **Kalevala Village** on the outskirts of the town. This re-creation of a wooded Karelian village provides an illuminating account of traditional building methods, plus it's a good excuse to indulge in some pricey souvenirs – and interesting handicrafts – which are sold to the many genuine Karelians who visit. It's also the only thing close to Kuhmo of appeal to non-hikers.

Budget **accommodation** options in Kuhmo include several boarding houses, the most well-established of which is the *Matkustaja Koti Uljakka*, Koulukatu 38 (☎08/655 0545; ❸). Just near the tourist office, *Hotelli Kainuu* (☎08/655 1711, ⓦwww.hotellikainuu.com; ❸), Kainuutie 84, is the only hotel option in town, but *Hotel Kalevala*, 3km from the centre (☎08/655 4100, ⓦwww.hotellikalevala.fi; ❺), is a better bet, with clean, modern room set on a lake with great views; it also rents out **canoes** and **bikes**. The town **campsite** (☎08/655 6388, ☏655 6384; June–Aug) is 4km from the centre along Koulukatu.

Continuing northwards from Kuhmo leads only to more hiking lands, and if you need urbanity, nightlife and easy living, now's the time to own up and duck out. If not, and your feet are itching to be tested over hundreds of kilometres of untamed land, simply clamber on the bus for Kuusamo.

Hiking routes around Kuhmo

The local section of the several hundred kilometres of track that make up the **UKK hiking route** starts from the Kuhmo Sports Centre and winds 70km through forests and the Hiidenportti canyon. Several other hikes begin further out from Kuhmo and can be reached by bus from the town. **Elimyssalo**, to the east, is a fifteen-kilometre track through a conservation area, and also to the east is **Kilpelän-kankaan**, where a cycle path runs 3.5km across heathland, passing a number of Winter War memorials. To the north, **Sininenpolku** is a hike of more than 20km over a ridge, past small lakes and rivers. In the northwest, **Iso-Palosenpolku** has two paths through a thickly forested area, where there are overnight shelters. Additionally, several **canoeing routes** trace the course of the old tar-shipping routes between Kuhmo and Oulu.

Kuusamo and around

KUUSAMO, 211km northeast of Oulu, is reached by daily express buses from Oulu, plus regular services from Rovaniemi. For full details of local hiking and accommodation, and the many summer events that bring some life to the town, call in at the **Karhuntassu Tourist & Nature Centre**, Torangintaival 2 (early May to mid-June daily 9am–5pm; mid-June to early Aug daily 9am–8pm; early Aug to mid-Sept 9am–5pm; mid-Sept to early May Mon–Fri 9am–5pm; ☎08/850 2910, ◍www.kuusamo.fi) and pick up the excellent *Green Adventure* guide. For accommodation, try the well-kept, independently run **youth hostel**, across the street from the bus station at Kitkantie 35 (☎08/852 2132, ◍edu.kuusamo.fi /kansanopisto; doubles ❷, dorms €11), though you must book in advance between Monday and Friday and arrive between 8am and 3.45pm, as there's no reception at other times. Alternatively, the soulless *Sokos Hotel Kuusamo* (☎08/859 20, ◍www .sokoshotels.fi; ❺/❻), Kirkkotie 23, is a ten-minute walk from the centre of town at the junction with Ouluntie; it overlooks the Toranki lake, and has an exceptionally large indoor swimming pool. Before setting out hiking, the best places in town to **eat and drink** is *Martina's* and the adjoining *Parnell's Irish Bar* at Ouluntie 3 – fried chicken, chips, salad and a beer will cost around €15.

Kuusamo is the starting point for the **Karhunkierros Trail** (also known as the Kuusamo Bear Circuit); one of the most popular hiking routes in Finland, it's a seventy-kilometre trek weaving over the summit of Rukatunturi, dipping into canyons and across slender log suspension bridges over thrashing rapids. Herds of hikers are a far more common sight than bears, but the hike is still a good one and there are several interesting shorter routes off the main track. From Kuusamo, take the bus to **Ristikallio** for the start of the hike. Wilderness huts are placed roughly at ten-kilometre intervals along the route, though during peak months these are certain to be full. Fortunately there's no shortage of places to pitch your own tent, and about halfway along the route are three **campsites**, *Juuma* (☎08/863 212; late May to Sept), *Jyrävä* (☎050/361 4631; June–Aug) and *Retki-Etappi* (☎08/863 218; June–Sept).

Heading north again, the tougher and little known **Six Fells Hiking Route** (more commonly known by its tongue-twisting Finnish name *kuudentunturinkevelyreitti*) starts at **Salla** (◍www.salla.fi). Buses run here from Kuusamo several times a day, pulling up at *Hotel Revontuli* (☎016/879 711, ◉revontuli@salli.fi; ❺); nearby, there are also some **cabins** (☎016/837 766, ◍www.tunturimokit.com; ❷), for which showers cost extra. The 35-kilometre hike, actually part of the UKK trail, begins a couple of kilometres north of Salla at the *Sallan Maja* roadside café, and includes some stiff climbs up the sides of spruce-covered fells, with spectacular views from their bare summits. **Niemelä**, close to the road between Kuusamo and Salla, marks the other end of the trail. From Salla you can continue by bus into the Arctic North (see p.782), or to Kemijärvi to meet the train for Rovaniemi and all points south.

Rovaniemi and around

Easily accessible by train or bus, **ROVANIEMI** is touted as the capital of Lapland. Just south of the Arctic Circle it may be, but anyone arriving with an expectation of sleighs and tents will be disappointed by a place whose administrative buildings, busy shopping streets and *McDonald's* (the most northerly in the world) make it a far cry from the surrounding rural hinterland. Like many places in Finnish Lapland, the elegant wooden houses of old Rovaniemi were razed to the ground by departing Germans at the close of World War II, and the town was completely rebuilt during the late 1940s. Alvar Aalto's bold but impractical design has the roads forming the shape of reindeer antlers, though the centre of town is based on a familiar grid pattern. Although Rovaniemi can be quite dismal in summer, with its uniform greyish-white buildings and an unnerving newness to everything

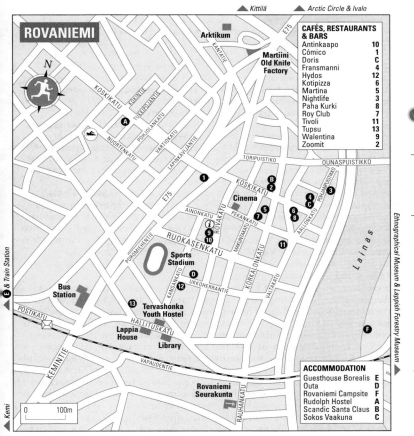

ROVANIEMI

N

Arktikum

Martiini
Old Knife
Factory

**CAFÉS, RESTAURANTS
& BARS**

Antinkaapo	10
Cómico	1
Doris	C
Fransmanni	4
Hydos	12
Kotipizza	6
Martina	5
Nightlife	3
Paha Kurki	8
Roy Club	7
Tivoli	11
Tupsu	13
Walentina	9
Zoomit	2

KOSKIKATU

KOKINTIE

TUKKIPOJANTIE

POHJOLANKATU

VARTIOKATU

NUORTENKATU

LAPINKÄVIJÄNTIE

E75

TORIPUISTIKKO

OUNASPUISTIKKO

KOSKIKATU

Cinema

AINONKATU

POHJANPUISTIKKO

AARTOLONKATU

PEKANKATU

ROVAKATU

MAKIJANKANTU

RUOKASENKATU

PÖROMIEHENTIE

**Sports
Stadium**

KANSANKATU

KORKALONKATU

VALTAKATU

UKKOHERRANTIE

**Bus
Station**

L a i n a s

**Tervashonka
Youth Hostel**

HALLITUSKATU

**Lappia
House**

Library

POSTIKATU

VAPAUDENTIE

KEMINTIE

**Rovaniemi
Seurakunta**

RAUHANKATU

0   100m

E & Train Station

Kemi

ACCOMMODATION

Guesthouse Borealis	E
Outa	D
Rovaniemi Campsite	F
Rudolph Hostel	A
Scandic Santa Claus	B
Sokos Vaakuna	C

– even the smattering of antique shops contains nothing older than 1970s junk – during the **winter** the city really comes into its own, with the neutral colour of the buildings working in perfect harmony with the snow and ice that covers the streets for almost six months of the year. During the cold months, the town plays host to busloads of nervous southern Europeans swathed from head to toe in the latest cold-weather gear, heading out on snowmobile safaris (see p.782) or simply stumbling around the icy streets as proof that they have endured an Arctic winter. The best idea is to use Rovaniemi only as a short-term stopover, or as a base for studies in Sámi culture, before heading off to one of the north's smaller villages for a more genuine taste of Finnish Lapland.

Arrival, information and accommodation

Rovaniemi's bus and train stations are just a couple of minutes' walk from each other, located on the western edge of the city centre. From either terminus, the best route into town is to take the subway under Valtatie (the E4 highway) and to walk down Hallituskatu, turning left into Rovakatu, where the friendly **tourist office** is at no. 21 (June–Aug Mon–Fri 8am–6pm, Sat & Sun 10am–6pm; rest of the year Mon–Fri 8am–4pm; ☏016/346 270, ☻www.rovaniemi.fi).

Budget **accommodation** in Rovaniemi is not hard to find as the city has several good guesthouses – but booking ahead, especially around midsummer and Christmas, is recommended.

Accommodation

Clarion Santa Claus Korkalonkatu 49 ☎016/321 321, ✺www.hotelsantaclaus.fi. If you can get over the name, this place is a top-notch place to stay, with well appointed rooms and great deals in the summer. ❹/❻

Guesthouse Borealis Asemieskatu 1 ☎016/342 0130, ✺guesthouseborealis. com. Good-value, family-run guesthouse with en-suite rooms; close to the train station and very popular with InterRailers. The price includes breakfast and the staff is very knowledgeable about local goings-on. ❷

Ounaskoski Camping Jäämerentie 1 ☎016/345 304. The city's only camping facility, located on the far bank of the Kemijoki River; facilities include a kiosk, café and sauna. Open late May to Aug.

Outa Ukkoherrantie 16 ☎016/312 474 or 492 6991, ✉outa@elisanet.fi. An eccentric guesthouse on a very quiet street a block from the tourist office. ❷

Rudolph Koskikatu 41. The rooms at Rovaniemi's all-year youth hostel are spacious, spotless and devoid of any soul, but you're nearly always guaranteed one to yourself. There is no reception here so you book via the *Clarion Santa Claus* hotel (see below). Dorms beds are €21.

Sokos Vaakuna Koskikatu 4 ☎016/332 211, ✺www.sokoshotels.fi. Fully gutted and renovated in 2003, the modernist rooms here are saturated with designer throughout, and overall this is possibly the swankiest hotel in town. Sits close to the Ounaskoski River. ❹/❻

The City

If you have any interest in Sámi culture, make a beeline for the fascinating **Arktikum**, in the northern part of town at Kantatie 74 (mid-June to Aug daily 10am–6pm; Sept–April same hours, closed Mon; €11; ✺www.arktikum.fi). Its great arched atrium emerges from the ground like a U-boat, with almost all the exhibition areas submerged beneath banks of stone. The complex contains both the **Provincial Museum of Lapland** and the **Arctic Centre**, which together provide a varied insight into the history and present-day lives of the peoples of the Arctic North. Taking an intelligent, unsentimental approach, the museum superbly evokes the remarkable Sámi culture and is well worth a couple of hours. Displays range from raincoats made of seal intestine and trousers fashioned from polar bear hides to superb photographic displays on reindeer husbandry – modern technology has made its mark, with cellular phones, snowmobiles and four-wheel-drive buggies now the norm. There are also pictures of the horrific devastation caused by German soldiers in 1944, when they were forced to retreat, burning every building in sight – look out for the two scale models showing the city before and after the retreat, and be sure to take in the poignant video footage that compares the heady life in Rovaniemi before the war, when loggers and lumberjacks would pour into the city's hotels and bars at weekends, with the sharply contrasting scenes of total devastation just a couple of years later – the people of Lapland have clearly still not forgiven the Germans for what happened. Adjacent to the Arktikum is the **Marttiini Old Knife Factory** (Mon–Fri 10am–6pm, Sat 10am–1pm; ✺www .marttiini.fi), Vartiokatu 32. In the kingdom of the sharp edge, the Marttiini multipurpose knife reigns supreme, and the prices in the factory shop are the cheapest you'll find – plus you can have your name inscribed on the blade. Prices range from a few euro up to €100 for the latest model.

Back in the town centre, **Lappia House**, an Aalto-designed building a short distance from the bus and train stations at Hallituskatu 11, contains a theatre and concert hall, plus an excellent **library** (Mon–Thurs 11am–8pm, Fri 11am–5pm, Sat 11am–4pm) with several free Internet terminals. There's also a **Lapland Department** (turn immediately left as you enter the building), housing a staggering hoard of books, magazines and newspaper articles in many languages covering every conceivable Sámi-related subject. This constantly growing collection is already the largest of its kind in the world, and probably the best place anywhere for undertaking Lapland-related research.

Other points of interest in Rovaniemi are few. At Rauhankatu 70, **Rovaniemi Seurakunta** (daily 9am–4pm), the parish church, repays a peek on account of its jumbo-sized altar fresco, *Fountain of Life* by Lennart Segerstråle, an odd work that pitches the struggle between good and evil into a Lapland setting. If you're here in winter, ask about the concerts that are staged here.

If you have more time to kill and the weather isn't too cold (Rovaniemi is prone to chilly snaps even in summer), visit one of the two outdoor museums that lie near each other just outside town, accessible by bus #6. The **Ethnographical Museum** in Pöykkölä, 3km southeast of town (June–Aug Tues–Sun noon–4pm; €2), is a collection of farm buildings that belonged to the Pöykkölä family between 1640 and 1910, and forms part of a potpourri of objects pertaining to reindeer husbandry, salmon fishing and rural life in general. About 500m up the road is the **Lappish Forestry Museum** (June–Aug Tues–Sun noon–6pm; €2), where the reality of unglamorous forestry life is remembered by a reconstructed lumber camp. Rovaniemi also boasts a decent public **sauna** and **swimming pool**, Vesihiisi, at Nuortenkatu 11, a fifteen-minute walk from the town centre west along Koskikatu and then left into Kokintie.

Around Rovaniemi: the Arctic Circle and Santa Claus Village

Most people are lured to Rovaniemi solely for the dubious thrill of crossing the **Arctic Circle**. While the "circle" itself doesn't remain constant (it's defined as the area where the midnight sun can be seen, which shifts a few hundred metres every year), its man-made markers do – 8km north of town along Route 4 – generally heralded by a crowd of visitors taking photographs of each other with one foot either side of the line. Bus #8 goes to the circle from the train station around every hour (€5.20 return; more frequent in summer), and also calls at several stops in town.

Near the circle and served by the same bus is the **Santa Claus Village** (daily: June–Aug 9am–7pm; rest of the year 10am–5pm; free). Considering its tourist pitch, the place – inside a very large log cabin – is quite within the bounds of decency: you can meet Father Christmas all year round, contemplate the reindeer grazing in the adjoining farm and leave your name for a Christmas letter from Santa (€6). Within the village is the ticket office for **Santa Park** (mid-June to mid-Aug Tues–Sat 10am–4pm; late Nov to early Jan Tues–Sun 10am–6pm; €20; ⊛www .santapark.fi) from which a train connects to the park itself. A collection of themed fairground rides within a cavern inside a granite hill, Santa Park is predominantly aimed at those who believe the big guy with the white beard is real. For those without children, it's most definitely worth missing, unless you want to pretend you're four again.

Eating, drinking and entertainment

While Rovaniemi has a few pleasant **cafés**, its opportunities for fine or exotic dining leave a lot to be desired – though dishes featuring reindeer are very easy to find. Most numerous are the standard kebab and pizza joints around Koskikatu, nearly all of which offer late-night snacks to bar-hoppers.

Cafés and restaurants

Antinkaapo Rovakatu 13 ⊛www.antinkaapo.fi. Rovaniemi's best café, serving a lavish range of delicious pastries. Closed Sun.

Cómico Koskikatu 25 ⊛www.comicobar.fi. Jumping on Finland's Tex-Mex bandwagon, this place is a big hit with younger locals, and the burritos (€10) and fajitas (€15) are not bad. In the evenings it turns into a popular drinks place, with student bands occasionally taking to the stage.

Fransmanni *Sokos Vaakuna* hotel, Koskikatu 4. If you haven't yet tried reindeer or any other Lappish specialities, this is a great place to take the plunge. Prices and a tad high but the food is excellent, and you're likely to find everything from reindeer heart to cloudberry liqueur on the menu.

Hydos Kansankatu 10 ⒲www.hydos .com. The interior to this Turkish fusion restaurant is done up in 1980s Ottoman chintz, making it one of the more eccentric local finds. The €7 lunch specials are popular with local workers and dinners are well-priced, too. Don't mistake the entrance with that of the erotic showbar next door.
Kotipizza Koskikatu 5 ☎310 303. Tasty takeaway

pizzas, starting at €4.50, and busiest when the surrounding bars close.
Martina/Rax Koskikatu 11. Pizza and pasta dishes are €9 and steaks around €17 at this predictable chain-restaurant, though the decor here is a bit warmer than most places in town. Just upstairs, *Rax* has an all-you-can-eat pizza buffet for €8.
Walentina Rovakatu 21. Just next to the tourist office, with very good coffee and great sticky buns.

Bars and clubs

With a sizeable university population during term-time and thousands of tourists visiting throughout the year, Rovaniemi offers a lively **nightlife** for every school of libation. The most popular places for a drink are just off the pedestrian walkway of Koskikatu, and there are several places for a dance, some set within the hotels. Though winter offers the most excitement, the town does wake up a bit in the summer when ROPS, the Rovaniemi football team – one of the best in the country – are playing at home. You'll hear the cheering all over town, and can even see the game for free through gaps in the fencing of the stadium, on Pohjolankatu; after the matches, the partying continues all over town, when Rovaniemi's bars are ablaze with first-rate displays of Finnish drunkenness.

Bars and clubs

Doris *Sokos Vaakuna*, Koskikatu 4. Set in the hotel basement, this is the most popular club in town and gets away with charging an €5–10 cover. The young and beautiful of Lapland come to dance, drink and play the €1 minimum casino tables at the back.
Nightlife *Hotel Pohjanhovi*, Pohjanpuistikko 2. Three bar in one, aimed at a mature crowd. Upstairs is a meat-and-potatoes Finnish bar that at times has the vague sense of a fortysomething pick-up joint; at the back, there's a relaxed tango and *humppa* dance floor, and downstairs an ever-popular karaoke bar.
Paha Kurki Koskikatu 5. Dark and dingy rock club that fills up with hardcore- and boho-types from all over the Arctic.

Roy Club Makuntakatu 24 ⒲www.royclub.fi. A somewhat relaxed atmosphere pervades upstairs, while downstairs the floor is beer-sticky and the DJs have a thing for the dry-ice button. Usually less drunken than most other places.
Tivoli Valtakatu 19 ⒲www.cafetivoli.fi. Great, unpretentious bar popular with students and other locals not into the disco scene. Closed Mon & Tues.
Tupsu Hallituskatu 24. This favourite local hangout is as authentic a Finnish bar as you'll probably find. Because it's a bit out of the way near the bus station, the atmosphere is somewhat tranquil
Zoomit Koskikatu 10, at the corner of Korkolankatu. Popular chrome- and glass-fronted, place often stuffed with trendy young things from the Lapland University.

Listings

Airport ☎016/363 6710.
Bus information ☎0200/4060; national enquiries ☎0200/4000.
Car hire Avis, Valtakatu 26 ☎016/310 524; Budget, Koskikatu 9 ☎016/312 266; Hertz, Pohjanpuistikko 2 ☎016/332 332; Europcar, Koskikatu 6 ☎016/315 645.
Cinema Maxim, inside the Sampokeskus shopping centre on Pekankatu.

Hospital Lapin Keskussairaala, Ounasrinteentie 22 ☎016/328 2100.
Railway station ☎0307/47 643.
Safari companies Arctic Safaris, Koskikatu 6 ☎016/340 0400, ⒲www.arcticsafaris.com; Lapland Safaris, Koskikatu 1 ☎016/362 811, ⒲www.laplandsafaris.com.
Train information VR ☎030/710.

The Arctic North

Squeezed inland by the northern tip of Norway, Finland's **Arctic North** mixes undulating forests, lakes and rivers with tracts of desolate upland that rise high

Moving on from Rovaniemi – cross-border bus routes in northern Scandinavia

With the exception of the train from Rovaniemi to Kemijärvi, all public transport north of the Arctic Circle is by **bus**. From Rovaniemi services follow two main routes: north-east to Sodankylä, Ivalo, Inari and Utsjoki or northwest to Kittilä, Muonio, Karesuvanto and Kilpisjärvi – it's not possible to travel between these two routes without first back-tracking to Rovaniemi. However, from the far north, cross-border services operate into Norway. Throughout the year, a daily bus leaves Rovaniemi around 11.45am for the North Cape via Inari (5pm), crossing into Norway at **Karasjok** – a total journey of eleven hours. The bus waits at the North Cape for two and a half hours before return-ing overnight via the same route to Rovaniemi. Connections can be made in Karasjok east towards Kirkenes and west ultimately for Tromsø. During the rest of the year this service terminates in Karasjok.

It's also possible to reach Norway and the Nord-Norgeekpressen services from **Utsjoki**: from June to September there is a direct bus from Rovaniemi departing at 5pm via Inari and Utsjoki to Vadsø (June to late Sept daily; Oct–May Wed–Fri & Sun). Alternatively, you can reach Norway by simply walking across the bridge in Utsjoki yourself (remember the hour's time difference between Finland and Norway); Norwe-gian buses do not drive over the bridge into Finland.

From June to mid-September a daily service leaves Rovaniemi at 11.30am for **Tromsø** (where it arrives at 7.30pm Norwegian time) via Muonio, Kaaresuvanto (walk on foot over the bridge here to connect with Swedish bus services in Karesuando for Kiruna) and Kilpisjärvi. Be sure to check timetables carefully and plan several days ahead: either visit ⊛www.matkahuolto.fi or get the *Pikavuorot*, available at the bigger bus stations and at most tourist offices, where they should be able to help decipher the Finnish key.

above the treeline. In these uncompromising latitudes, a fair number of the indig-enous Sámi population still herd their reindeer and maintain their traditions despite serious threats from a number of sources, including modernization, tourism and – most dramatically – the fallout from Chernobyl. With the exception of attrac-tions like reindeer farms and appearances at a few annual festivals, the Sámi tend to remain far from the prying eyes of visitors, though their angular *lávvus*, *kotas* and *tipis* (tents), wreathed in reindeer antlers, skins, and all sorts of Arctic ornaments, are to be found along the region's main roads during the summer, in what can seem a rather crass and commercially inspired conformity. This racial stereotyping is intended to appeal to the wallets of the thousands of motorists who use the **Arctic Highway**, the E75/4, the fastest approach to the Nordkapp (see p.419). But don't let this put you off: the Arctic wilderness is a ready escape, its stark and often haunt-ing landscapes easily accessible.

Two main roads lead north from Rovaniemi: the Arctic Highway, which services the **northeast**, linking the communities of Sodankylä, Ivalo, Inari and Utsjoki; and Route 79/E8, which crosses the **northwest**, connecting Muonio and Kilpisjärvi. Inari and Sodankylä are the only settlements worth a second look, but the landscape which surrounds the Arctic North's minuscule communities will hold your gaze for much longer – provided you take the trouble to do at least some **hiking**. There's also plenty of outdoor adventure here for those who seek it – **dog-sledding**, **skiing** and **snowmobiling** are the most popular diversions – though none of it comes cheap. If you're planning to travel north from Rovaniemi on one route then back on the other, be warned that there are no roads in between, only rough tracks – with no facilities – traversing some desolate landscape. For safety, you need either to retrace your steps to Rovaniemi before taking the other route, or travel in an arc into Norway and over the other side, a journey by car of around four hours.

The best way to experience the Arctic North is to get off the bus and explore slowly, which means on foot. The rewards for making the physical effort are manifold. There's a tremendous feeling of space here, and the wild and inhospitable terrain acquires a near-magical quality when illuminated by the constant daylight of the summer months (the only time of year when hiking is feasible).

Many graded **hiking routes** cover the more interesting areas; most of the more exhilarating are distributed among the region's four national parks: **Pyhä-Luosto**, southeast of Sodankylä; **Urho Kekkonen** and **Lemmenjoki**, further north off the Arctic Highway; and **Pallas-Yllästunturi**, near Muonio in the northwest. There are challenges aplenty for experienced hikers, though novices need have nothing to fear provided basic common sense is employed. The more popular hikes can become very busy and many people find this an intrusion into their contemplation of the natural spectacle – others enjoy the camaraderie. If you're seeking solitude you'll find it, but you'll need at least the company of a reliable compass, a good-quality tent, and emergency supplies.

We've included broad introductions to the major hikes throughout this chapter, and described the type of terrain that you'll find on them. Bear in mind that, though, that these aren't definitive accounts as conditions and details often change at short notice; always gather the latest information from the nearest tourist centre or park information office. Most tourist offices hand out free trail descriptions in English and also sell excellent 1:10000 hiking maps. For copious information on hiking in Finland, visit the Finnish Forest Service's excellent English-language web site, ⊛ www.outdoors.fi.

Hiking rules and tips

Obviously you should observe the **basic rules** of hiking, and be aware of the delicate ecology of the region: never leave litter, don't start fires in any old place (most hikes have marked spots for this), and don't pitch your tent out of specified areas on marked routes. You should always check that you have maps and adequate supplies before setting out, and never aim to cover more ground than is comfortable. Bathe your feet daily to prevent blisters, and carry some form of mosquito repellent – the pesky creatures infest the region and will descend en masse anytime after noon.

Hiking accommodation

To be on the safe side, you shouldn't go anywhere without a good-quality **tent**, although the majority of marked hikes have some form of basic shelter, and most have a **youth hostel** and **campsite** (and at times even comfy hotels) at some point on the trail. These fill quickly, however, and few things are worse than having nowhere to relax after a long day's trek – so make advance reservations whenever possible.

Bus connections up in these parts are few and far between so if you're without your own vehicle, try to plan ahead to avoid finding yourself stuck in the middle of nowhere.

The northeast: Sodankylä and the national parks

North of Rovaniemi, it's an uneventful 130-kilometre drive along the Arctic Highway to **SODANKYLÄ**, a modest, comfortable town whose modern appearance belies its ancient foundation. From the late seventeenth century, Finnish settlers and Christian Sámi gathered here on high days and holidays to trade and to celebrate religious festivals. Unusually, their wooden **church** (summer daily 10am–6pm) of 1689 has survived intact, its rough-hewn timbers crowding in upon the narrowest of naves and with the pulpit pressing intrusively into the pews. The old church nestles beside the Kitinen River, in the shadow of its uninspiring nineteenth-century replacement and a stone's throw from the **Alariesto Art Gallery** (June to mid-Sept Mon–Sat 10am–5pm, Sun noon–6pm; rest of year Mon–Fri 10am–5pm, Sat 10am–4pm, Sun noon–4pm; €5), which features the work of Andreas Alariesto, a twentieth-century Sámi artist of some renown. Each canvas is an invigorating representation of traditional native life and custom, notably a crystalline *View from the Arctic Ocean* embellished with chaotic boulders, predatory fish jaws and busy Sámi. A useful catalogue available at reception explains the background to the exhibits. Other nearby activities include the **horseback rides** at Laphorse, Mantovaarantie 17 (☎040/068 3417, ⓦwww.laphorse.com; €25) and outdoor activities like **parasailing** with Nature X-Ventures (☎040/867 1786, ⓦwww.naturex-ventures .fi; €100).

Sodankylä is little more than an elongated main street: Jäämerentie. The bus station, post office and petrol stations are within a few metres of each other, while the **tourist office** (Sept–May Mon–Fri 9am–5pm; June–Aug Mon–Fri 9am–5pm,

△ Hikers, Arctic North

Sat 9am–5pm; ☎016/618 168, ⊛www.sodankyla.fi) is in the centre of the village, a ten-minute walk from the bus station. In winter it's a good idea to book accommodation in advance, since Sodankylä is used by test drivers from *Peugeot* who come here for several months to test new models in Arctic conditions. There are just two **hotels** in the village, the bear-themed *Karku* (☎016/613 801, ⊛www .hotel-bearinn.com; ❸), a five-minute walk from the bus station at Sodankyläntie 10, and offering rooms with either sauna or hydromassage shower; and the less inspiring *Sodankylä*, Lapintie 21 (☎016/617 121, ⨍613 545; ❹/❺); both are open year-round. The *Kolme Veljestä* guesthouse, north of the bus station at Ivalontie 1 (☎016/611 216, ⊛www.majatalokolmeveljesta.fi; ❸), has comfortable rooms – breakfast and use of the kitchen and sauna are included. There's also a **campsite** right on the river (☎016/612 181, ⓔantti.rintala@naturex-ventures.fi; early June to mid-Aug; cabins ❷), which rents cheap canoes and an expensive jetskis. As for **meals**, the pizzas served up at *Pizza Paikka à la Riesto*, Jäämerentie 25, are the best in town, while for a wider choice of local meat and fish dishes for under €10, try *Ravintola Revontuli*, Jäämerentie 9, which is also a popular place for a drink. Just up the road at Jäämerentie 20, *Seita-baari* serves up the best local food, earning its reputation for its excellent reindeer stew, but the orange plastic chairs and tacky feel are off-putting. *Disco Paradise*, in the same building as *Revontuli*, is the choice of places to dance the night away.

Around Sodankylä: Pyhä-Luosto National Park

Off the Arctic Highway some 65km southeast of Sodankylä lies **Pyhä-Luosto National Park**, and the steep slopes and deep ravines of the most southerly Finnish fells. Here, the 45-kilometre **Pyhätunturi hiking trail** rises from marshlands and pine woods and rounds five fell summits, connecting the holiday resorts of Pyhä and Luosto. Five kilometres from the start is the impressive waterfall of the Uhrikuru gorge, after which the track circles back for a short stretch, eventually continuing to Karhunjuomalampi ("The Bear's Pool"). There's a *päivätupa* (cabin) here, but the only other hut on the route is by the pool at Pyhälampi.

Near the hike's starting point at Pyhä are a **nature centre** (June–Sept daily 9am–6pm; Oct–May Tues–Fri 9am–4pm, Sat 9am–2pm; ☎016/882 773, ⨍882 824), a **campsite** (☎016/852 103, ⨍852 140), and two reasonably priced **hotels**: the *Pyhätunturi* (☎016/856 111, ⨍882 740; ❸) and *Pyhän Asteli* (☎016/852 141, ⨍852 149; ❸). The hike ends at Luostotunturi, where accommodation includes the *Scandic Hotel Luosto* (☎016/624 400, ⊛www.scandic-hotels.com; ❹/❺), and the more basic *Luostonhovi* (☎016/624 420, ⨍624 297; ❷). The daily **bus** between Sodankylä and Kemijärvi (on the rail line from Rovaniemi) stops close to both ends of the trail.

Continuing north: Urho Kekkonen National Park

Travel north by car from Sodankylä on the Arctic Highway for 110km and just after the village of **Vuotso** you'll arrive at **Koilliskaira Visitor Centre** (June–Sept daily 9am–5/6pm; Oct–May Mon–Fri 10am–6pm; ☎020/564 7251, ⊛www .tankavaara.fi), where you can reserve cabin beds, get information on dozens of hikes and watch a film about the local terrain. Just 100m from the centre lurks a gaggle of tourist establishments: the **Tankavaara Gold Museum and Panning**

Centre (same hours; €5), the *Nugget* restaurant, serving Lapland specialities for around €15, and a guesthouse, the *Korundi* (☎016/626 158, ℻626 261; ❸), with **cabins** (❷). Over the first weekend in August the town puts on the **Goldpanning Finnish Open**, where burly lumberjack types from all over the world compete to slosh out the most gold bits from piles of dirt and rock.

Twenty kilometres further north (130km from Sodankylä), at the hamlet of Kakslauttanen, is the turning for **Fell Centre Kiilopää** (daily 8am–10pm, closed May & Oct; ☎016/670 0700, ℻667 121), a popular and well-equipped fell-walking centre on the edge of the **Urho Kekkonen National Park**. The park is one of the country's largest, incorporating the uninhabited wilderness that extends to the Russian border – pine moors and innumerable fells scored by gleaming streams and rivers. With regular bus connections to north and south, the Fell Centre (also known by its Finnish name, Tunturikeskus) is easily the most convenient base for exploring the park. It's at the head of several walking trails, from the simplest of excursions to exhausting expeditions using the park's chain of wilderness cabins. As well as providing park information, selling detailed trail maps, renting mountain bikes and organizing guided walks, staff can arrange accommodation in the adjoining year-round **youth hostel** (same phone number; dorms €22); the Centre also has some en-suite rooms (❹/❺), a good restaurant and a smoke sauna.

Ivalo, Inari and around

Try not to get stuck in **IVALO**, a town of singular, wearisome ugliness on the Arctic Highway 40km north of the Fell Centre Kiilopää. If you do have to stay, however, the riverside *Hotelli Ivalo* (☎016/661 901, ℗www.hotelivalo.fi; ❹), is the most palatable option, with breakfast and sauna included in the price, though the much cheaper *Näverniemen Lomakylä* (☎016/677 601), just south of town, has **camping** spots and a few simple summer **cabins** (❶). As the staff at Ivalo's ersatz **tourist office**, Yhdystie 2, speak no English and have little to hand out, you're best off at the more helpful one in Inari (see below). **Eating** options amount to the hotel restaurants, *Anjan Pizza* on the main road near the *Shell* filling station, and the *Lauran Grilli*, opposite, which has pizzas and kebabs. Whilst Ivalo lacks any obvious charm, it does offer a rare direct **bus to Russia**: a once-daily (Mon, Wed & Fri) service leaves the village at 3.30pm for the 300-kilometre trip to **Murmansk** via the border at Raja-Jooseppi – however, you'll need advance planning if you want to use the service, as you'll need to be equipped with a Russian visa to get on, which can be obtained in Helsinki (and, for several hundred euro more, in Kirkenes). For more information and help with visas, contact the tourist office in Inari, which also organizes trips across the border.

The road heading north to Inari winds around numerous lakes dotted with islands – it's a spectacular route if you can time your trip with the glorious Lapland **Ruska**, a season that takes in late summer and autumn, when the trees take on brilliant citrus colours that reflect in the still waters. **INARI** itself, 40km away, is quite a bit more amenable than Ivalo, straggling along the bony banks of the Juutuanjoki River as it tumbles into the freezing-cold, islet-studded waters of Lake Inarijärvi. There's nothing remarkable about the village itself, but it's a pretty little place with several appealing diversions and buzzes in the summer season with transitory visitors taking a break from the Rovaniemi-Nordkapp beaten path. The bus stops outside the **tourist office** (daily June–Aug 9am–7pm; Sept–May Mon–Fri 9am–5pm; ☎016/661 666, ℗www.inarilapland.org) on the one and only main road, where helpful staff can advise on accommodation, trips to Russia and organize a fishing licence (from €20). Across the road is the Sámi handicraft store, *Sámi Duodji* (daily: July to early Sept 9am–8pm; rest of the year 10am–5pm), whose exhibits are of markedly higher quality than the tourist souvenirs that pop up everywhere else in Lapland. Close by lies the Sámi museum and nature centre, **Siida** (June–Sept daily 10am–6pm; Oct–May Tues–Sun 10am–5pm; €8), one of the best museums in Lapland if not all of Finland. An excellent outdoor section features a re-sited nineteenth-century village and various reconstructions illustrating aspects of Sámi life – principally handicrafts and hunting or fishing techniques – while the indoor section has a well-laid-out and easy-to-understand exhibition on all aspects of life in the Arctic, including a timeline tracing the Sámi from pre-history to the present day, detailing all the social, cultural and political changes which have affected them. Beginning about 2.5km from the museum, the four-kilometre **Pielpajärvi Wilderness Church hiking trail** leads to the isolated remains of a 1752 church – this trail, though, can be very slippery when wet. If you don't fancy expending any energy to see some scenery, head for the bridge over the Juutuanjoki, from where, in summer, you can take a two-hour **lake cruise** (June to mid-Sept 1–2 daily; ☎016/663 562 or 040/029 5731; €13), as well as fishing trips (all year); for the latter, a twelve-seat boat and a guide for two and a half hours costs €40–60 per person, depending on the group number. In the winter, popular snowmobile trips (see below) set out over the frozen lake, while cross-country skiing is the transport of choice for most locals.

Many travellers pass through Inari during the summer, so it's best to reserve **accommodation** during this period. One of the most enjoyable places is to stay is with ⚓ *Nativa* (☎040/748 0984, ☻www.nativa.fi; ❹), run by a sociable Finnish-Sámi couple who rent out a few charming apartments opposite the tourist office, as well as a nearby cottage on a secluded peninsula; they also organize fishing, hiking and snowmobile excursions starting at €115 per person per day. Elsewhere in the village, the *Inarin Kultahovi* **hotel** (☎016/671 221, ☻www.saariselka.fi/kultahovi; ❹), Saariskoskentie 2, offers comfortable rooms with river views and an excellent, reasonably-priced restaurant; the *Lomakylä Inari* (☎016/671 108, ☻www.saariselka .fi/lomakylainari), Inarintie 26, has good-quality cabins (❹); the **campsite**, *Uruniemi Camping* (☎016/671 331; June–Sept), 3km away on the southern outskirts of the town, has smaller cottages (❶). The ⚓ *Siida Ravintola* **restaurant** at the Siida museum (see p.787) is also very good – go for the fresh hollandaise Lake Inari trout with potatoes (€16). If money's tight, stick to the popular *Ranta-Mari* restaurant and café, beside the bus stop, though be prepared to share the place with drunken locals at weekends.

Around Inari: Lemmenjoki National Park

A vast tract of birch and pinewood forest interrupted by austere, craggy fells, marshland and a handful of bubbling rivers, **Lemmenjoki National Park**, about 40km southwest of Inari, witnessed a short-lived gold rush in the 1940s. A few panners remain, eking out a meagre living.

The park's most breathtaking scenery is to be found on its southeastern side along the Lemmenjoki river valley. To get there, take the daily bus from Inari to **Njurgalahti**, a tiny settlement on the edge of the park about 12km off Route E75 to Kittilä (the district's main road), which is where the 55-kilometre, two-day hike down the river valley begins; taking the twice-daily boat (June–Aug; €14 one way) from Njurgalahti to Kultasatama cuts 20km off the hike's full distance.

At **Härkäkoski**, hikers cross the river by a small boat, pulled by rope from bank to bank; the track then ascends through a pine forest to **Morgamoja Kultala**, the old gold-panning centre, where there's a big unlocked hut. There are a couple of other huts set aside for those walking the trail, but the nearest **campsite** (☎ & ☎016/673 001), with cottages, is back on the main road at **Menesjärvi**. For organized goldpanning and camping trips, plump for those offered by Kaija and Heikki Paltto (☎016/673 542, ☻www.lemmenjoki.org), a friendly Sámi family in the hamlet of **Lemmenjoki**, who also rent out several comfortable **cabins** with free use of a rowing boat and sauna. Just across the river, *Ahkun Tupa* (☎ & ☎016/673 435, ☻akhuntupa@hotmail.com; ❷), has similar-priced accommodation in smaller cottages. For more information on the park, ask at the Lemmenjoki nature hut (June–Sept varying hours, ☎020/564 7793) at the park entrance, which is well signposted from Inari.

North from Inari: crossing into Norway

Travelling north from Inari is rather pointless unless you're aiming for Norway. The Finnish section of the Arctic Highway continues to dreary **KAAMANEN**, though on the way, 2km past the *Kaamasen Kievari* campsite, is a bold, stark and deeply evocative memorial in rusty red metal to World War II in Finland. In simple words, it states "the battles of these light infantrymen in the wilds of Lapland were brought to an end in Kaamanen, Inari towards the end of October 1944. 774 killed, 262 missing, 2904 wounded". In Kaamanen there's an all-year **campsite** with cottages (⊕016/672 713; ❶). The route then swings westwards on its way to the Nordkapp, exiting Finland at **KARIGASNIEMI**, an unprepossessing hamlet that has a restaurant, *Soarve Stohpu*, which serves a yummy smoked reindeer-and-cheese soup for €10, and pleasant rooms in the small and basic *Kalastajan Majatalo* hotel next door (⊕ & ⊕016/676 171; ❷). You might also be tempted by the excellent **youth hostel** facilities at the *Engholm Husky Vandrerhjem*, 18km further on in Karasjok, Norway (see p.413). Karigasniemi does have two **campsites**: *Lomakylä* (⊕016/676 160; June–Sept), and the *Tenorinne* (⊕016/676 113; early June to mid-Sept), both with simple cabins (❷), though the latter is better situated on a small beach with picnic tables looking right onto the river dividing Finland and Norway. Incidentally, **petrol** is generally quite a bit cheaper here than across the border, so you'd be wise to fill up before venturing on.

From Kaamanen, a minor road branches due north to **UTSJOKI**, a small border village beside the Tenojoki River. The nearest **campsite** (⊕016/678 803; mid-June to Aug) is a few kilometres away, by the river's edge in Vetsikko. The road on from Utsjoki runs parallel to the Norwegian border, then crosses it just beyond the hamlet of **Nuorgam**, where there's a guesthouse, the *Nuorgamin Lomakeskus* (⊕016/678 312, ⊛www.nuorgaminlomakeskus.fi; ❷) and a year-round **campsite** (⊕016/678 312). Once across the border, it's a 160-kilometre journey to Kirkenes (see p.421).

The northwest

Heading northwest from Rovaniemi, Route 79 sticks close to the banks of the Ounasjoki River before it reaches the straggling settlement of **KITTILÄ**, a distance of 150km. There's little to detain you here – the departing German army burnt the place to the ground in 1944, and the rebuilding has been uninspired – though both the **youth hostel**, Valtatie 5 (⊕016/648 508; ❷), and neighbouring **campsite** are conveniently located beside the main road, while the *Hotel Kittilä*, Valtatie 49 (⊕016/643 201, ⓔhotelli.kittila@levi.fi; ❸/❹) has standard rooms, a pool and an inexpensive restaurant.

It's a further 20km to the town of **SIRKKA**, where the posh ski resort of **Levi** attracts thousands of wintering Finns with its numerous downhill trails, several dozen lifts and gondola and ample après-ski attractions. Outside of winter, there is relatively little going on here, though the surrounding hills boast seven hiking (or, in winter, cross-country skiing) routes, including the enjoyable river and fell walking of the eighteen-kilometre Levi Fell trail. All the routes begin in or near the centre of Sirkka, where you should find a whole range of places to stay – during summer expect to pay around €60 for a room, double that in winter – ask at the tourist board for information. For more information on outdoor activities around Sirkka, visit the **tourist office** (Mon–Fri 9am–7pm, Sat & Sun 11am–5.30pm; ⊕016/639 3300, ⊛www.levi.fi) in the centre of town, which can also assist with finding accommodation.

Muonio and around

Sleepy **MUONIO** lies 60km northwest of Sirkka beside the murky river that separates Finland from Sweden. What passes for the town centre falls beside the junction of the E8, the main north–south highway, and Route 79 from Kittilä; the ESSO filling station at the crossroads here functions as the bus station. The **tourist** office (mid-Dec to mid-April, June & mid-Aug to mid-Sept daily 10am–6pm; July to mid-Aug daily 10am–8pm; rest of the year Mon–Fri 11am–5pm; ☎016/532 280, ⊛www.muonio.fi) lies beside this junction inside the *Kiela Naturum* nature centre (same hours), whose star attraction is its **northern lights planetarium** (€7), a worthy film show which explains how the phenomenon occurs. Incidentally, if you're in Muonio during the winter months there's a 55 percent chance of seeing the northern lights; however, it must be a clear night. For accommodation, head for the superbly located year-round **hostel** 🏠 *Lomamaja Pekonen* (☎016/532 237, ⊛www.lomamajapekonen.fi; ❶), on a small hilly site overlooking a lake at Lahenrannantie 10. There are also well equipped **cabins** here (❷); the ones at the top of the hill have their own saunas (❸). **Canoes** can also be hired here for €21 per day. For **snacks**, the woodsy *Naapuro*, Kosotuskeino 1, has fresh cakes and coffee, while solid meals can be found next door at 🏠 *Uncle Laban*, run by a friendly Palestinian family who dish up pizza and reindeer dishes for around €8.

South of Muonio: the Harriniva Holiday Centre

Some 3km south of Muonio along the road to Kolari lies the well organized and well equipped *Harriniva Holiday Centre* (☎016/530 0300, ⊛www.harriniva .fi), where you can pitch a tent, hook up your camper van or stay in a range of accommodation that runs from basic cabins (❷) to fully equipped apartments (❹). However, what makes this place special is the range of summer and winter **activities** on offer. A haven for dog lovers, Harriniva has around 400 huskies – making it the biggest husky centre in Finland – and if you're here in winter and thinking of a **husky safari**, this is *the* place to do it. Although safaris are quite pricey – a week-long round-trip safari from Muonio up towards Enontekiö, covering a daily distance of around 40km, costs upwards of €1150 – you may be able to cut costs slightly by booking via a travel agent such as Norvista rather than at the centre itself. The final price will include all food, your huskies and sledge plus overnight accommodation in log cabins – and, of course, the experience of riding across frozen lakes, winding through Lapland's silent snow-covered forests and ending the day with a roll in the snow after a genuine smoke sauna. The centre's other winter activities include a week-long **snowmobile safari** (€1625), a four-hour **reindeer safari** (€156), and a **dog-sled day-trip** (€198). In summer, the centre offers such things as **whitewater rafting** (€155), **salmon fishing** and **reindeer farm** tours (€60), and **canoe trips** (€60). There are several other adventure groups in town – ask for a list at the Muonio tourist office – though you may be gambling on level of professionalism, quality of equipment and knowledge of English.

Pallas-Yllästunturi National Park

From Muonio, buses leave for Kilpisjärvi (see p.792) and (once-daily) to Enontekiö/Hetta, skirting the **Pallas-Yllästunturi National Park**, a rectangular slab of mountain plateau whose bare peaks and coniferous forests begin about 30km northeast of Muonio. A bus leaves Muonio at 9.30am Monday to Friday for the National Park, stopping outside the **visitor centre**, Pallastunturi (mid-June to Sept daily 9am–5pm; rest of the year Mon–Fri 9am–4pm; ☎020/564 7930). Pallastunturi marks the start of the **Pallas-Hetta hiking route**, an arduous 55-kilometre trail that crosses a line of fell summits, with several *autiotupa* and *varaustupa* (locked and unlocked huts) and camping areas en route, as well as a sauna about halfway along in the hut at **Hannukuru**. The highest point is the summit of Taivaskero, near the start. The track ends at Lake Ounasjärvi, which you'll need to cross by **ferry** (daily 7am–11pm); if the boat isn't there, raise the flag to indicate that you want to cross.

On the other side of the lake is the unremarkable village of **HETTA** (known administratively as **ENONTEKIÖ**). Outside of the Christmas rush, when daily charter flights flood the town with thousands of Santa-seeking Brits, there isn't a whole lot going on, but it's a good jumping-off point for exploring the Finnish (and Norwegian) outdoors, and if you're here in early March, the festive celebrations

Hikes in the Pallas-Yllästunturi park: the Pallas-Olos-Ylläs trail

The Pallas-Yllästunturi National Park was created in 2005 when the Pallas-Ounasturi park was merged with the Ylläs-Aakenustunturi nature reserve, adding around 500 square kilometres and making the park Finland's third largest. Although the Pallas-Hetta trail is the park's most impressive walk, and the one with the best transport links, there are several other options. Of these, the most notable is the 87-kilometre **Pallas-Olos-Ylläs trail**, which also begins from Pallastunturi visitor centre. With several unlocked huts en route, this track twists south past fells and lakes until it leaves the park and reaches the Muonio–Sirkka road close to the swanky *Hotel Olostunturi* (☎016/536 111, ✆www.pallas-hotel.com; ⑥). The hotel is primarily geared towards skiers, and is open only between September and April, but the hills that surround it are crisscrossed by a number of shorter walking trails that make for very pleasant hikes in the summer months.

From the hotel, the Pallas-Olos-Ylläs trail continues south, soon reaching the dam on the Särkijoki River before proceeding down to Lake Äkäsjärvi, where there's a café in a former grain mill. From here, the track heads onto the eastern slopes of Äkäskero, passing the remarkably good-value *Äkäskero Wilderness Lodge* (☎016/533 077, ✆www.akaskero.com; ❸) and continuing for 4km to the tiny settlement of **ÄKÄS-LOMPOLO**, on the upper slopes of Yllästunturi.

The **bus service** on from Äkäslompolo is dreadful: there's a twice-weekly summer service to Kolari at 1.30pm (Sat) and 3.20pm (Sun), eventually reaching Tornio, Kemi and Oulu. Buses north to Muonio depart Äkäslompolo on Sundays year-round at 1.45pm.

---

of **Marianpäivä** are well-attended by people from all over the region and make a great introduction to the traditions and pastimes of the Sámi. The services on offer in town are also quite good, including Enontekiö Flights (☎016/521 230), whose air taxis can take you quickly (and expensively) into the depths of Lapland. There's also the **Fell Lapland Nature Centre** (mid-June to Sept daily 9am–5pm; rest of the year Mon–Fri 9am–4pm; ☎020/564 7959, ✆www.enontekio.fi), where you can buy maps and get help with reservations for a host of cottages in the Pallas-Yllästunturi National Park. For accommodation in Enontekiö, try the well-appointed **cabins** at the *Hetan Lomakylä* (☎016/521 521, ✆521 293; June–Sept; ❶/❸) or the slightly less-posh *Ounasloma* (all year, but call ahead on ☎016/521 055, ✆521 004; ❸), both of which also have **camping** facilities. Among the settlement's **hotels**, a good choice is the *Hetan Majatalo* (☎016/554 0400, ✉hetan-majatalo@co.inet. fi; ❸), which offers excellent, rustic-style en-suite rooms as well as cheaper and more basic options. In winter they organize a host of activities, from ice-fishing, reindeer safaris and dog-sleigh tours to summer fishing trips, as well as offering boat and bike rental, the latter year-round, while the hotel restaurant cooks up highly recommended traditional Lappish dinners. The *Hotelli Hetta* (☎016/521 361, ✆www.hetta-hotel.com; ❸/❹) offers a plush alternative, with several rooms overlooking the lake.

If you're driving north through Hetta towards Norway, 6km before you get to the border on the Alta road is **PALOJÄRVI**, where the log cabins of *Galdotieva* (☎016/528 630; ❷), some with their own sauna, offer a reasonable, if somewhat isolated, overnight spot.

North from Muonio: Kilpisjärvi and around

The thumb-shaped chunk of Finland that sticks out above the northern edge of Sweden is almost entirely uninhabited, a hostile arctic wilderness whose tiny settlements are strung along the only road, the E8. For the most part this seems a gloomy route of desolate landscapes and untidy villages, comparing poorly with the splendour of the parallel road to the south that connects Sweden's Kiruna and Norway's Narvik. However, the E8 does have its moments as it approaches the Norwegian frontier, with the bumpy uplands left behind for dramatic snow-covered peaks.

From the E8, you might cross into Sweden via **KAARESUVANTO**, a dreary village 95km north of Muonio, to reach the Kiruna–Narvik road. Otherwise there's little reason to cross the border here or stay longer than you need to in Kaaresuvanto – if you do, use the all-year **campsite** (☎016/522 079), which has some smart cabins (❶). Otherwise, try the *Hotelli Davvi* (☎016/522 101, ⊛www .davvihotel.com; ❸), which has fully equipped cabins (❷) as well as regular rooms, and a good restaurant.

There's more to be said for continuing for 110km on the E8 to the hamlet of **KILPISJÄRVI**, on the Norwegian frontier. On the way, about 25km south of Kilpisjärvi, you'll pass the welcoming *Peeran Retkeilykeskus* **youth hostel** (☎016/532 659, ⊛www.peera.fi; dorms €16), which also serves good food. At Kilpisjärvi itself, perched beside the coldest of lakes in the shadow of a string of stark tundra summits, the *Hotelli Kilpis* (☎016/537 761, ⊛www.pallas-hotel.com; ❸) has a gorgeous location which means it gets booked up months ahead for the March to mid-June period; however, 5km further down the road, the *Kilpisjärven Retkeilykeskus* hotel (☎016/537 771, ⊛www.kilpisretkeilykeskus.fi; ❷) offers rooms and cottages in just as fine a setting. The **Kilpisjärvi Visitor Centre** (mid-March to Sept Mon–Fri 9am–8pm, Sat & Sun 9am–5pm; closed first two weeks in June; ☎020/564 7990) sells maps and offers helpful information on the Käsivarsi region, and on a number of **local hikes**, the most popular of which are the brace of ten-kilometre trails running to the top of the neighbouring Saanatunturi, 1029m high. The main way up (and down) is the track on the steep north side, although another route runs behind the fell to the northern shore of Saanijärvi, where there's a *päivätupa* (cabin). For more expensive adventure, Heliflite (☎016/532 100, ⊛www .heliflite.fi), at the *Lapland Hotel Kilpis* on Käsivarrentie, offers helicopter tours of the region – though at €245 for a twelve-minute flight, you might be more content with an aerial-view postcard from the visitor centre.

Another hiking option is the 24-kilometre loop trail, beginning and ending at Kilpisjärvi, that runs north through the **Malla Nature Reserve** to the **Three Countries Frontier** where Finland, Norway and Sweden meet. The track crosses the rapids of Siilajärvi by footbridge, after which a secondary track ascends to the summit of Pikku Malla. The main route continues to Iso Malla. There's a steep and stony section immediately before the waterfalls of Kihtsekordsi, and then a reindeer fence marking the way down to an *autiotupa* cabin beside the Kuokimajärvi lake. From the tourist office, a stone path leads to the cairn marking the three national borders. There's a **campsite** at the tourist centre (June–Sept) and, nearby, a **guest-house**, *Saananmajat* (☎016/537 746; ❷).

Travel details

Trains

Kemi to: Kilpisjärvi (1 daily; 6hr 40min); Muonio (1–2 daily; 5hr).
Kolari to: Kilpisjärvi (1 daily; 3hr 40min).
Oulu to: Helsinki (3 daily; 9hr); Kajaani (6 daily; 2hr 20min); Kemi (7 daily; 1hr 20min); Rovaniemi (7 daily; 3hr).
Rovaniemi to: Helsinki (4 daily; 10hr 50min); Kemi (7 daily; 1hr 30min); Kemijärvi (2–4 daily; 1hr 15min–1hr 30min); Oulu (6 daily; 3hr).

Vaasa to: Helsinki (7 daily via Seinäjöki; 4hr 30min); Oulu (5–7 daily; 4hr 30min–6hr 30min); Tampere (9–10 daily; 2hr 30min).

Buses

Inari to: Ivalo (4–6 daily; 40min); Kaamanen (6 daily; 1hr 45min); Kargasneimi (2 daily; 1hr 45min); Utsjoki (2 daily; 3hr 45min); Rovaniemi (5–6 daily; 5hr 10min).
Ivalo to: Murmansk (3 weekly; 7hr 30min).

Kajaani to: Ämmänsaari (1 daily; 2hr 30min direct, longer by slower, indirect routes); Kuhmo (Mon–Fri 8 daily, Sat 5 daily; 1hr 40min); Kuusamo (3–5 daily, 3hr 35min–4hr 15min).

Kemi to: Tornio (Mon–Fri 11 daily, Sat & Sun 3–6 daily; 40min).

Kolari to: Äkäslompolo (1 weekly; 50min).

Kuhmo to: Kajaani (Mon–Fri 8 daily, Sat 5 daily; 1hr 40min)

Kuusamo to: Kajaani (3–5 daily, 3hr 35min–4hr 15min); Ristikallio (Mon–Fri 2–3 daily, Sat 1 daily; 1hr 15min); Salla (1–2 daily; 3hr).

Muonio to: Kilpisjärvi (2 daily; 2hr 55min–4hr 15min).

Oulu to: Kuusamo (6 daily; 4hr); Rovaniemi (3–5 daily; 3hr 15min).

Pallastunturi to: Enontekiö (1 daily; 2hr 30min); Muonio (1 daily; 40min).

Pietarsaari to: Kokkola (Mon–Fri 7 daily, Sat & Sun 3–5 daily; 40min).

Rovaniemi to: Enontekiö/Hetta (2 daily; 5hr 15min); Inari (3–4 daily; 4hr 45min–6hr); Ivalo (4–7 daily; 3hr 55min–4hr 50min); Kiilopää (1–2 daily; 3hr 45min); Kilpisjärvi (2 daily; 6hr 15min–8hr); Kittilä (4 daily; 2hr–2hr 20min); Muonio (3 daily; 4hr); Pallastunturi (1 daily; 4hr 45min); Sodankylä (6–10 daily; 1hr 50min).

Sodankylä to: Kemijärvi (Mon–Fri 2 daily, Sat 1 daily; 2hr).

Tornio to: Äkäslompolo (1 weekly; 3hr 45min).

Utsjoki to: Nuorgam (2 daily; 55min).

Vaasa to: Pori (6–7 daily; 2hr 45min); Turku (5–7 daily; 5hr).

International ferries

Vaasa to: Sundsvall (June & July 1 daily; Aug–May 1 weekly; 9hr); Umeå (1 daily; 4hr).

4

4.3 | FINLAND | Travel details

Small print and

Index

A Rough Guide to Rough Guides

Published in 1982, the first Rough Guide – to Greece – was a student scheme that became a publishing phenomenon. Mark Ellingham, a recent graduate in English from Bristol University, had been travelling in Greece the previous summer and couldn't find the right guidebook. With a small group of friends he wrote his own guide, combining a highly contemporary, journalistic style with a thoroughly practical approach to travellers' needs.

The immediate success of the book spawned a series that rapidly covered dozens of destinations. And, in addition to impecunious backpackers, Rough Guides soon acquired a much broader and older readership that relished the guides' wit and inquisitiveness as much as their enthusiastic, critical approach and value-for-money ethos.

SMALL PRINT

These days, Rough Guides include recommendations from shoestring to luxury and cover more than 200 destinations around the globe, including almost every country in the Americas and Europe, more than half of Africa and most of Asia and Australasia. Our ever-growing team of authors and photographers is spread all over the world, particularly in Europe, the USA and Australia.

In the early 1990s, Rough Guides branched out of travel, with the publication of Rough Guides to World Music, Classical Music and the Internet. All three have become benchmark titles in their fields, spearheading the publication of a wide range of books under the Rough Guide name.

Including the travel series, Rough Guides now number more than 350 titles, covering: phrasebooks, waterproof maps, music guides from Opera to Heavy Metal, reference works as diverse as Conspiracy Theories and Shakespeare, and popular culture books from iPods to Poker. Rough Guides also produce a series of more than 120 World Music CDs in partnership with World Music Network.

Visit www.roughguides.com to see our latest publications.

Rough Guide travel images are available for commercial licensing at www.roughguidespictures.com

Rough Guide credits

Text editors: Polly Thomas, Keith Drew
Layout: Amit Verma
Cartography: Maxine Repath and the Map Studio
Picture editor: Jj Luck
Production: Katherine Owers
Cover design: Diana Jarvis
Editorial: London Kate Berens, Claire Saunders,
Geoff Howard, Ruth Blackmore, Richard Lim,
Clifton Wilkinson, Alison Murchie, Karoline
Densley, Andy Turner, Keith Drew, Edward Aves,
Nikki Birrell, Helen Marsden, Alice Park, Sarah
Eno, Joe Staines, Duncan Clark, Peter Buckley,
Matthew Milton, Tracy Hopkins, David Paul,
Lucy White, Ruth Tidball; **New York** Andrew
Rosenberg, Richard Koss, Steven Horak,
AnneLise Sorensen, Amy Hegarty, Hunter Slaton,
April Isaacs, Sean Mahoney
Design & Pictures: London Simon Bracken, Dan
May, Mark Thomas, Harriet Mills, Chloë Roberts;
Delhi Madhulita Mohapatra, Umesh Aggarwal,
Ajay Verma, Jessica Subramanian, Ankur Guha,
Pradeep Thapliyal

Production: Sophie Hewat, Aimee Hampson
Cartography: London Katie Lloyd-Jones,
Ed Wright; **Delhi** Manish Chandra, Rajesh
Chhibber, Jai Prakash Mishra, Ashutosh Bharti,
Rajesh Mishra, Animesh Pathak, Jasbir Sandhu,
Karobi Gogoi, Amod Singh
Online: New York Jennifer Gold, Suzanne Welles,
Kristin Mingrone; **Delhi** Manik Chauhan, Narender
Kumar, Shekhar Jha, Lalit K. Sharma, Rakesh
Kumar, Chhandita Chakravarty
Marketing & Publicity: London Richard Trillo,
Niki Hanmer, David Wearn, Demelza Dallow,
Louise Maher; **New York** Geoff Colquitt, Megan
Kennedy, Katy Ball; **Delhi** Reem Khokhar
Custom publishing and foreign rights: Philippa
Hopkins
Manager India: Punita Singh
Series editor: Mark Ellingham
Reference Director: Andrew Lockett
PA to Managing and Publishing Directors:
Megan McIntyre
Publishing Director: Martin Dunford
Managing Director: Kevin Fitzgerald

Publishing information

This seventh edition published April 2006 by
Rough Guides Ltd,
80 Strand, London WC2R 0RL
345 Hudson St, 4th Floor,
New York, NY 10014, USA
14 Local Shopping Centre, Panchsheel Park,
New Delhi 110017, India
Distributed by the Penguin Group
Penguin Books Ltd,
80 Strand, London WC2R 0RL
Penguin Putnam, Inc.
375 Hudson Street, NY 10014, USA
Penguin Group (Australia)
250 Camberwell Road, Camberwell,
Victoria 3124, Australia
Penguin Books Canada Ltd,
10 Alcorn Avenue, Toronto, Ontario,
Canada M4V 1E4
Penguin Group (New Zealand)
Cnr Rosedale and Airborne Roads
Albany, Auckland, New Zealand
Cover design by Peter Dyer.

Typeset in Bembo and Helvetica to an original
design by Henry Iles.

Printed and bound in Italy by Legoprint S.p.A.

© Rough Guides 2006

No part of this book may be reproduced in any
form without permission from the publisher except
for the quotation of brief passages in reviews.

808pp includes index

A catalogue record for this book is available from
the British Library

ISBN-10: 1-84353-605-6
ISBN-13: 978-1-84353-605-5

The publishers and authors have done their best
to ensure the accuracy and currency of all the
information in **The Rough Guide to Scandinavia**,
however, they can accept no responsibility for
any loss, injury, or inconvenience sustained by
any traveller as a result of information or advice
contained in the guide.

1   3   5   7   9   8   6   4   2

Help us update

We've gone to a lot of trouble to ensure that
this seventh edition of the **Rough Guide
to Scandinavia** is accurate and up to
date. However, things change – places get
"discovered", opening hours are notoriously
fickle, restaurants and rooms raise prices or lower
standards. If you feel we've got it wrong or left
something out, we'd like to know, and if you can
remember the address, the price, the time and
the phone number, so much the better.

We'll credit any contributions, and send a copy
of the next edition (or any other Rough Guide if you

prefer) for the best letters. Everyone who writes
to us and isn't already a subscriber will receive
a copy of our full-colour thrice-yearly newsletter.
Please mark letters "**Rough Guide to Scandinavia
Update**" and send to: Rough Guides, 80 Strand,
London WC2R 0RL, or Rough Guides, 4th Floor,
345 Hudson St, New York, NY 10014. Or send an
email to **mail@roughguides.com**

Have your questions answered and tell others
about your trip at **www.roughguides.atinfopop
.com**

Readers' letters

Thanks to all those readers of the sixth edition who took the time to write in with amendments and additions. Apologies for any misspellings or omissions.

Jon Alcock; Tom Andrews; Henning Arp; Geir Benden; Philip Borg-Wheeler; Graeme Brock; Ross Brown; Dora Caldwell; Peggy Chen; Heidi Dahl; K. Everett; Silje Figenschou; Kim Fitzpatrick; Melanie Francis; Adrian Enok Friis; Sarah Fuller; Heather and Martin Gill; Lewis Graham; Christine Griffin; Annlinn Grossman; Isebaert Gustaaf; Joe Gumino; Lars Gustavsen; Julie Hansen; Øyvind Heen; Lousewies and Dennis Hesseling; A.E.W. Hudson; Kari Jorgensen; John Joyner; Juha Kiviniemi; Brent Knoll; Per Krogsrud; Ahn Le; Elizabeth Lerner; Verena Maehr; Jeffrey Mahn; Charlotte Marceau; Marie Massa; Richard McDonough; Sharon Messenger; Core Minnema; Andre Moreira; Lupe Moreno; Colin Nachenius; Luke Nikolaides; David and Win Normington; Marie Oerstedholm; Jessica Osborn; Trine Pedersen; Piergiorgio Pescali; Helge Dahl Pettersen; Michael Plunkett; Joseph Prichard; Jane Rackley; Tarmo Rajasaari; Robert A. Reese; Yizhar Regev; Paul Richards; Edward H. Rowan; Harry Saltzman; H. Sefi; Elly Shepherd; Jan Skotheim; Blaine Stothard; A. Sorensen; Laura Stone; Nick Williamson; Derek Wilde; Tom Wolfenden; Gemma Woodhouse; Jasmin Wyler; Peter Zombori.

Acknowledgements

Phil Lee would like to thank his editor, Polly Thomas, for her thorough and diligent work on this new edition of Scandinavia – all done with style and humour. He would also like to thank his stepdaughter, the delightful Emma Rose Rees, for her help on this new edition.
Jeroen van Marle would like to thank Marta Karwat; Pia Albinsson of the Swedish Travel and Tourism Council; Tina Brännstrom of the Stockholm Visitors Board; Martina Tengvall, Amanda and Timo Glave; the receptionists of the *Norrköping Scandic* hotel; and staff at the local tourist offices, who were without exception friendly and professional.

Lone Mouritsen would like to thank Henrik Thierlein of Wonderful Copenhagen for his usual invaluable help and support; the Svarstads for housing me and Pepé during research in Copenhagen; Helle and Paul Mulder for continual help in Jutland; Jan and

Mads Egelund in Århus for sharing their in-depth knowledge on fast food and nightlife; and Marianne, Charlotte and Kaare Eriksen for standing in when nightlife gaps needed filling. Finally, a big thank you to the many tourist offices throughout the country, whose devotion to duty made my job a lot easier.
Roger Norum wishes to thank Riita Balza at the Finnish Tourist Board, London; Finnish State Railways; *Sokos Hotel Vaakuna*, Helsinki; Anu Huusko and Anne Harju at Inari Event Lapland; Mari Lihr at the Helsinki City and Tourist Convention Bureau; Kuopio Tanssii ja Soi; Tampere City Tourist Office; Ira Virtanen and Katja Tammela at the Savonlinna Opera Festival; Scott Yoder and Mike Garant in Tampere. Finally, Jenni Kouri for sauna chats, Petra Vartia for early inspiration; and Patrick Alexander, Chad Robertson, Nicole Silverman and Ania Szatkowska.

Photo credits

Title page
Farm fields, near Motala, Sweden © Photolibrary

Full page
Frozen Lake Mälaren, Stockholm © Frank Chmura/Alamy

Introduction
Roadsign, Norway © Index Stock Imagery/Photolibrary
Briksdalsbreen glacier © Mikael Utterström/Alamy
Helsinki café © Jon Arnold Images/Alamy
Sauna, Arctic Circle © Stephanie Maze/Corbis
Traditional Swedish houses © Frank Chmura/Alamy
Bergen, Norway © Jan Stromme/Alamy
ABBA © Swedish Tourist Board

Reindeer © James Proctor
Midnight sun © Cephas Picture Library/Alamy

Things not to miss
01 Svalbard © Kevin Schafer/Alamy
02 Vigeland © Robert Harding Picture Library Ltd/Alamy
03 Aurora borealis © Danita Delimont/Alamy
04 Courtesy of Louisiana Museum of Modern Art
05 Jotunheimen National Park © Leslie Garland Picture Library/Alamy
06 Nyhavn, Denmark © Stockfolio/Alamy
07 Courtesy of The Inlandsbanan Railway
08 Vikingskipshuset © Hideo Kurihara/Alamy
09 Gamla Stan © Frank Chmura/Alamy
10 Flåmsbana railway © R. Belbin/Trip
11 Husky safari © Finnish Tourist Board

12 Courtesy of Vox Hall, Århus, Denmark
13 *Icehotel*, Sweden © Robin Whalley/Alamy
14 Church carving © Werner Forman/Corbis
15 Danish pastries © foodfolio/Alamy
16 Edvard Munch, *The Avenue in Snow* © Munch Museum/Munch-Ellingsen Group/BONO 2005 photo: © Munch Museum (Andersen/de Jong)
17 Olavinlinna Castle © Lebrecht Music & Arts Photo Library/Alamy
18 Sauna © Chad Ehlers/Alamy
19 Tivoli Gardens © Neil Egerton/Travel Ink
20 Skåne, Sweden © Neil Roland
21 Whale-watching © Favio Pagani/Sygma/Corbis
22 Alta rock carvings © Phil Lee
23 Århus © Chris Lisle/Corbis
24 Grenen, Denmark © Danish Tourist Board
25 Kalmar castle, Sweden © James Proctor
26 Lofoten Islands © Royalty-Free/Corbis
27 Marinated herring © ABPL /Martin Brigdale
28 Santa Claus © Bryan & Cherry Alexander Photography/Alamy
29 Fürstenburg Galleries © Gotesborgs Konstmuseum
30 Skagen, Denmark © Bob Krist/Corbis

Great Outdoors colour insert
Geirangerfjord © Jon Arnold Images/Alamy
Cross-country skiers © Travel Ink/Alamy
Göta Kanal © Mikael Utterström/Alamy
Beach, Ærø © Robert Harding Picture Library Ltd/Alamy
Arctic fox © Che Garman/Alamy
Aurora borealis © Robert Harding Picture Library Ltd/Alamy

Scandinavian Style colour insert
Finlandia Hall © Adam Woolfitt/Corbis
Gamla Stan, Stockholm © Nicholas Pitt/Alamy
Arne Jacobsen's Swan chair © Martine Hamilton Knight
IKEA flags © Peter Titmuss/Alamy
Helsinki station © Clive Tully/Alamy
Øresunds Link © Lucky Look/Alamy
Stockholm T-Bana © Bob Krist/Corbis

Black and whites
p.60 Ny Carlsberg Glypotec © Helena Smith
p.101 Copenhagen bikes © Neil Setchfield/Alamy
p.116 Arne Jacobsen's Egg Chair © Elizabeth Whiting & Associates/Alamy
p.120 Copenhagen kiosk © Lone Mouritsen
p.136 Roskilde Cathedral © E. Simanor/Axiom
p.145 Fishhouse, Bornholm © Robert Harding Picture Library Ltd/Alamy
p.153 Hans Christian Andersen paper cut © Det Kongelige Bibliotek 2002
p.158 Wind turbines, Denmark © Adam Woolfitt/Corbis
p.168 *Man Meets the Sea* © Tim Caswell/Alamy
p.184 Århus Town Hall © Carlos Dominguez/Corbis

p.191 Ebeltoft, Jutland © Tom Nebbia/Corbis
p.208 Puffin © Leslie Garland Picture Library/Alamy
p.248 Oslo tram © Leslie Garland Picture Library/Alamy
p.260 Karl Johans gate, Oslo © DK Images
p.270 Vikingskipshuset, Oslo © DK Images
p.280 Konserthus, Oslo © DK Images
p.290 Rondane National Park © Hubert Stadler/Corbis
p.297 Borgund stave church © Peter Szekely/Alamy
p.308 Stavanger harbour © Robert Harding Picture Library Ltd/Alamy
p.314 Preikestolen © Gordon Hulmes/Alamy
p.323 Bergen fish market © Johan Furusjö/Alamy
p.335 Hardangervidda © Yann Arthus-Bertrand/Corbis
p.351 Geirangerfjord © JLImages/Alamy
p.367 Trondheim cathedral © DK Images
p.390 Whale-watching © Jan Baks/Alamy
p.398 Hamnoy © Chad Ehlers/Alamy
p.405 Hurtigrute © Tor Eigeland/Alamy
p.422 Polar bear © Elvele Images/Alamy
p.426 Visby, Gotland © Westend61/Alamy
p.473 Gamla Stan © PCL/Alamy
p.492 Stockholm archipelago © Chad Ehlers/Alamy
p.498 Rune stone © Robert Harding Picture Library Ltd/Alamy
p.509 Gothenburg © Leslie Garland Picture Library/Alamy
p.520 Fishing cottages © Mikael Utterström/Alamy
p.526 Varberg Kallbadhuset © Lucky Look/Alamy
p.536 Ferry, Helsingborg © Travel Ink/Alamy
p.554 Ales Stennar © Westend61/Alamy
p.566 Öland windmills © Jon Arnold Images/Alamy
p.575 Vadstena castle © Bo Zaunders/Corbis
p.591 Limestone stacks © Frank Chmura/Alamy
p.602 Höga Kusten © Lucky Look/Alamy
p.611 Gammelstad © Juliet Ferguson/Alamy
p.620 Brown bear © Staffan Widstrand/Corbis
p.629 Skiing, Kiruna © John Noble/Corbis
p.639 *Icehotel* © Patrick Harrison/Alamy
p.644 Åland Islands © Nik Wheeler/Corbis
p.685 Helsinki Station © allOver photography/Alamy
p.694 Helsinki cathedral © ImageState/Alamy
p.714 Porvoo © Kari Niemeläinen/Alamy
p.721 Turku market © Stephen Saks Photography/Alamy
p.735 Tampere © imagebroker/Alamy
p.747 Lappeenranta © Kari Niemeläinen/Alamy
p.756 Valamo Monastery © Roger Norum
p.760 Kuopio harbour © f1 online/Alamy
p.773 Courtesy Sampo Icebeaker Tours © Roger Norum
p.785 Oulanka National Park © Jon Sparks/Alamy

ROUGH GUIDES

SMALL PRINT

Index

Map entries are in colour.

R

S

T

INDEX

Map symbols

maps are listed in the full index using coloured text

– – –	Chapter division boundary	⊙	Statue/memorial
▬▬▪▬	International boundary	⊠—⊠	Gate
▬ ▪▪ ▬	Provincial/regional boundary	✈	Airport
▬▬▬	Motorway	🛪	Lighthouse
═══	Major road	🎿	Ski trails
───	Minor road	] [	Tunnel/bridge
▭▭▭	Pedestrianized street	⬛	Fuel station
⊞⊞⊞⊞	Steps	(i)	Tourist office
- - - - -	Path	⊠	Post office
▬●▬●▬	Railway	(C)	Telephone
▪▪▪▪	Wall	@	Internet access
— —	Ferry route	P	Parking
───	Waterway	🏊	Swimming pool
┴┴┴┴	Canal	★	Bus stop
♦	General point of interest	⊞	Hospital
🦋	Waterfall	⚠	Campsite
▲	Mountain peak	⦿	Accommodation
⬇	Viewpoint	▣	Restaurant/café/bar
∴	Ruin	▬	Building
♜	Castle	⊞	Church (town maps)
▮	Tower	⊞	Cemetery
🏛	Stately home	▨	Park/National Park
♟	Museum	▨	Forest
‡	Church (regional maps)	▨	Sand/beach
♙	Monastery/convent	▨	Glacier
✡	Synagogue		

We are wherever you are.

- ● Scandic
- ● Hilton

The Hilton hotel network
includes 2400 hotels in
65 countries.
For booking and information,
please visit:
www.scandic-hotels.com
www.hilton.com